CIVILIZATIONS OF THE WEST

The Human Adventure

Brief Edition

CIVILIZATIONS OF THE WEST

The Human Adventure

Brief Edition

Richard L. Greaves
Florida State University

Robert Zaller
Drexel University

Jennifer Tolbert Roberts
Southern Methodist University
and
City College of the City University of New York

HarperCollins*CollegePublishers*

Executive Editor: Bruce Borland
Director of Development: Betty Slack
Cover Design: York Production Services
Production Coordination: York Production Services
Production Administrator: Jeffrey Taub
Printer and Binder: R. R. Donnelley & Sons
Cover Printer: The Lehigh Press, Inc.

Cover Painting: Anonymous, *View of Genoa in 1481,* Naval Museum Pegli, Genoa, Italy. Photograph: Art Resource.

For permission to use copyrighted material, grateful acknowledgment is made to the copyright holders whose work appears on page 493. From C. Day Lewis, *Collected Poems of Wilfred Owen.* Reprinted by permission of New Directions and Chatto & Windus. Copyright © Chatto & Windus, Ltd., 1946, 1963, and The Owen Estate.

Civilizations of the West: The Human Adventure, Brief Edition

Library of Congress Cataloging-in-Publication Data

Greaves, Richard L.
   Civilizations of the West : the human adventure / Richard L. Greaves, Robert Zaller, Jennifer Tolbert Roberts. —Brief ed.
     p.   cm.
   Includes bibliographical references and index.
   Contents: v. 1. From antiquity to 1715 — v. 2. From 1660 to the present.
   ISBN 0-06-501260-7 (v. 1). — ISBN 0-06-501261-5 (v. 2). — ISBN 0-06-501259-3 (1 v. combined ed.)
   1. Civilization, Western—History. I. Zaller, Robert. II. Roberts, Jennifer Tolbert, 1947– . III. Title.
CB245.G69   1994
909–dc20
                                          93-21582
                                           CIP

94 95 96 97 9 8 7 6 5 4 3 2

CONTENTS IN BRIEF

CONTENTS

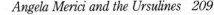

MAPS

PREFACE

Our ability to shape our future intelligently and to comprehend other cultures and peoples requires that we understand the diverse sources of our own civilization. Without this knowledge there can be no responsible citizenship, no informed judgment, and no effective commitment to seek peace and dignity for all peoples. Our ability to understand and respect one another is founded on an awareness of our historical roots.

Civilizations of the West underscores the fact that the West has never been wholly isolated from its non-Western neighbors, who helped to shape the Western heritage and with whom it now shares membership in a global community. Six illustrated essays trace the West's evolving perception of the non-Western world. In turn, the main narrative frequently shows how non-Western traditions and societies have influenced the culture of the West. We believe that this approach will enrich the students' understanding of Western civilization by adding a perspective that is often missing in other Western civilization books.

In writing this text we have employed innovative ways to meet today's educational needs. At the same time we have maintained the coverage of themes and events that is standard for the Western civilization course.

TOPICAL COVERAGE

Social, Cultural, and Intellectual Themes

Recent scholarship has placed considerable emphasis on social and cultural history. That scholarship is reflected throughout this text, particularly in two chapters that are unique among survey texts. Chapter 14, "Early Modern European Society," provides a systematic overview of such key elements of early modern Western society as marriage, the family, sexual customs, education, poverty, crime, diet, and medical care. Chapter 25, "Culture and Crisis," presents an intriguing examination of the landmark scientific advances in the late nineteenth and early twentieth centuries in relation to parallel developments in religion, philosophy, the arts, and psychology.

The Role of Women in Western Civilization

This text is particularly sensitive to the place of women in Western civilization. The contribution of women to Western societies—whether as rulers, artists and writers, social activists, workers, or wives and mothers—is systematically considered. The biographical portraits of women such as the pharaoh Hatshepsut, the abbess St. Clare of Assisi, the pioneer African-American entertainer Josephine Baker, and the British prime minister Margaret Thatcher are focal points of the discussion of women, but the role of women in Western societies is interwoven throughout the text's narrative.

The Jewish Tradition

As one of the founding cultures of Western civilization and a significant force throughout its history, the Jews are treated more comprehensively in this text than in any comparable work. We follow them from their settlement in ancient Palestine to their persecution and exile under the Romans and from their medieval migrations to their modern experience, including the founding of modern Israel. By recounting the history of the Jews we hope to make students aware of their special contribution to the West.

FEATURES AND PEDAGOGY

Biographical Portraits

Histories of civilization often fail to give students a sense of personal engagement with the subject. Migratory movements, famines and plagues, trading patterns, social and cultural upheavals, and the challenges of war and empire are the stuff of history, but individual experience is its basis and its ultimate reference point. To emphasize the role of individual men and women in history, we have included biographical portraits in most chapters. Our subjects are not necessarily history's most famous personalities, although each made a significant contribution to Western society. Among them are cultural figures, such as the Italian poet Vittoria Colonna and the German writer Goethe. Others are religious leaders, including Pope Leo the Great; St. Clare, founder of the Roman Catholic order of Poor Sisters; and the Quaker Margaret Fell. Some were prominent in the political world: the Byzantine empress Theodora; Jean Baptiste Colbert, Louis XIV's finance minister; and David Ben-Gurion, a founding father of Israel. Others, such as England's Mary Wollstonecraft and Germany's Rosa Luxemburg, devoted their lives to revolutionary social change. We include portraits of adventurers, such as Alcibiades and Cecil Rhodes, and of scientists and philosophers, including Eratosthenes, Spinoza, and Nietzsche. The lives of these people offer special insights into the cultures of which they were a part and enrich the student's perception of the relationship between the individual and social change.

Urban Portraits

Civilization began with the city, and modern society is increasingly urban. We have accordingly concentrated on the development of urban life in the West and have made individual urban portraits an integral part of the historical narrative. Some of the featured cities—Italy's Pompeii and ancient Tarquinia, for example—are now in ruins, while others—London, Madrid, and Moscow—are thriving. Some of them—Florence and Barcelona—were especially renowned as cultural centers, while others were hubs of commerce and industry, such as Antwerp, Liverpool, and Manchester. Athens was distinctive as the birthplace of democratic government, Venice as a trading empire, Geneva as the center of an international religious movement, and New Delhi as an imperial capital. Jerusalem, Paris, and Rome are revisited at different periods to give a sense of their changing development. Like the biographical features, the urban portraits provide instructors with excellent topics for discussion, essay questions, and unusual lecture themes, while students will find them intriguing subjects for term papers.

The West and the World Essays

One of the unique features of *Civilizations of the West* is a series of six essays that explore the changing perceptions of Westerners toward the rest of the world. Beginning with antiquity, we chart these responses as they develop in the Middle Ages, the Renaissance, the Enlightenment, the Age of Empire, and the modern era. Commerce, travel, military contacts, religious and cultural interaction, and imperial conquest provide a common thread of experience, but perceptions changed as Westerners slowly relinquished their often fanciful views of non-Western peoples. For several millennia, visions of the outside world were often exotic and mysterious, though in more recent times, Westerners have begun to see themselves as part of a global community, however diverse its traditions and outlook.

Historiographic Issues

To emphasize the sense of history as a living discipline, we have provided surveys of the conflicting historiographic interpretations of selected critical issues, including the decline of the Roman Empire in the West, the Renaissance, the French Revolution, and imperialism. These surveys are ideal starting points for class discussion and term papers.

Reading Lists

Historical study demands analysis, synthesis, and a critical sense of the worth of each source. It thus teaches skills that are important to every citizen. As a guide to students who wish to hone their historical understanding and their analytical skills and to pursue further interest or research in the major themes and topics of the text, a brief reading list is provided at the end of each chapter. The Instructor's Manual provides further bibliographic suggestions for special lecture themes.

The task of writing a history of Western civilization is both challenging and humbling. This book is the result of not only our own research but also that of many others, all of whom share our belief in the importance of historical study. To the extent that we have succeeded in introducing students to the rich and varied heritage of the past, we owe thanks in a very special way to our fellow historians, whose labors are the foundation of ours. In the spirit of our common enterprise we dedicate this volume to our students and our colleagues.

Richard L. Greaves
Robert Zaller
Jennifer Tolbert Roberts

SUPPLEMENTS

The following supplements are available for use in conjunction with this book.

FOR THE STUDENT

- *Student Study Guide* in two volumes, Volume 1 (chapters 1–15) and Volume II (chapters 15–30). Prepared by the authors of the text, each chapter contains a chapter overview; map exercises; study questions; a chronology; and identification, completion and short answer exercises, along with a list of term paper topics.
- *Mapping Western Civilization: Student Activities.* A free student map workbook by Gerald Danzer, University of Illinois, Chicago. Features numerous map skill exercises to enhance students' basic geographical literacy. The exercises provide ample opportunities for interpreting maps and analyzing cartographic materials as historical documents. The instructor in entitled to one free copy of *Mapping Western Civilization: Student Activities* for each copy of the text purchased from HarperCollins.
- *SuperShell II Computerized Tutorial,* an interactive program for computer-assisted learning prepared by Edward D. Wynot of Florida State University and David Mock of Tallahassee Community College. This tutorial features multiple-choice, true-false, and completion quizzes; comprehensive chapter outlines; "Flash Cards" for key terms and concepts; and diagnostic feedback capabilities. Available for IBM computers.
- *TimeLink Computer Atlas of Western Civilization* by William Hamblin, Brigham Young University. A highly graphic HyperCard-based atlas and historical geography tutorial for the Macintosh.

- *Sources of the West* by Mark Kishlansky, a collection of primary source documents available in two volumes, features a well-balanced selection of constitutional documents, political theory, intellectual history, philosophy, literature, and social description. Review questions follow each selection. Each volume includes the introductory essay, "How to Read a Document," which leads students step by step through the experience of using historical documents.

FOR THE INSTRUCTOR

- *Instructor's Resource Manual* by Richard L. Greaves and Robert Zaller. Prepared by the authors of this text, this Instructor's Resource Manual includes lecture themes, special lecture topics, bibliography, topics for class discussions and essays, a media resource directory, and lists of identification and map items. Each chapter concludes with a list of suggested term paper topics.
- *Test Bank* by Edward D. Wynot, Florida State University. This test bank contains a total of over 1500 questions, including 50 multiple-choice and 5 essay questions per chapter, with questions to pages in the text.
- *TestMaster Computerized Testing System.* This flexible, easy-to-master test bank includes all the test items in the printed *Test Bank* and allows users to add, delete, edit, and print test items and tests. Available free to adopters for the IBM or Macintosh.
- *Discovering Western Civilization Through Maps and Views,* by Gerald Danzer, University of Illinois at

Chicago, winner of the AHA's 1990 James Harvey Robinson Prize for his work in the development of map transparencies. This set of 100 four-color transparencies from selected sources is bound in a three-ring binder and available free to adopters. It also contains an introduction on teaching history through maps and a detailed commentary on each transparency. The collection includes cartographic and pictorial maps, views and photos, urban plans, building diagrams, classic maps, and works of art.

- *Map Transparencies.* A set of 30 transparencies of maps from the full edition of *Civilizations of the West: The Human Adventure.*
- *Grades,* a grade-keeping and classroom management software program that maintains data for up to 200 students.

ACKNOWLEDGMENTS

This book could not have been completed without the invaluable assistance of Judith Dieker Greaves, editorial assistant to the authors. The authors wish additionally to thank the following persons for their assistance and support: Lili Bita Zaller, Philip Rethis, Kimon Rethis, Robert B. Radin, Julia Southard, Robert S. Browning, Sherry E. Greaves, Stephany L. Greaves, and Professors Eric D. Brose, Stephen Carter, Roger Hackett, Sean Hawkins, Robert Lejeune, Victor Lieberman, Winston Lo, Christopher Roberts, Donald F. Stevens, Thomas Trautmann, and Edward D. Wynot, Jr.

The following scholars read the manuscript in whole or in part and offered numerous helpful suggestions:

Glenn J. Ames
University of Toledo

Edward M. Anson
University of Arkansas at Little Rock

William S. Arnett
West Virginia University

Gail Bossenga
University of Kansas

Ronald J. Caldwell
Jacksonville State University

Helen Callahan
Augusta College

William J. Connell
Rutgers University

Gary Cross
Pennsylvania State University

Kenneth E. Cutler
Indiana University—Purdue University at Indianapolis

Gerald H. Davis
Georgia State University

Dennis S. Devlin
Grand Valley State University

Ron Doviak
Borough of Manhattan Community College

Frank Garosi
California State University, Sacramento

Johnpeter Horst Grill
Mississippi State University

David Hood
California State University, Long Beach

Kenneth Glenn Madison
Iowa State University

William Jerome Miller
Saint Louis University

David B. Mock
Tallahassee Community College

Gordon R. Mork
Purdue University

Marian Purrier Nelson
University of Nebraska at Omaha

Carl Strikwerda
University of Kansas

Jan Karl Tanenbaum
Florida State University

Franklin C. West
Portland State University

ABOUT THE AUTHORS

Richard L. Greaves. Born in Glendale, California, Richard L. Greaves, a specialist in Reformation and British social and religious history, earned his Ph.D. degree at the University of London in 1964. After teaching at Michigan State University, he moved in 1972 to Florida State University, where he is now Robert O. Lawton Distinguished Professor of History, Courtesy Professor of Religion, and Chairman of the Department of History. A Fellow of the Royal Historical Society, Greaves has received fellowships from the National Endowment for the Humanities, the American Council of Learned Societies, the Andrew Mellon Foundation, the Huntington Library, and the American Philosophical Society. The 22 books he has written or edited include *John Bunyan* (1969), *Theology and Revolution in the Scottish Reformation: Studies in the Thought of John Knox* (1980), *Saints and Rebels: Seven Nonconformists in Stuart England* (1985), *Deliver Us from Evil: The Radical Underground in Britain, 1660–1663* (1986), *Enemies Under His Feet: Radicals and Nonconformists in Britain, 1664–1677* (1990), *Secrets of the Kingdom: British Radicals from the Popish Plot to the Revolution of 1688–1689* (1992), and *John Bunyan and English Nonconformity* (1992). The Conference on British Studies awarded Greaves the Walter D. Love Memorial Prize for *The Puritan Revolution and Educational Thought: Background for Reform* (1969), and his *Society and Religion in Elizabethan England* (1981) was a finalist for the Robert Livingston Schuyler Prize of the American Historical Association. He was president of the American Society of Church History in 1991.

Robert Zaller. Robert Zaller was born in New York City and received a Ph.D. degree from Washington University in 1968. An authority on British political history and constitutional thought, he has also written extensively on modern literature, film, and art. He has taught at Queens College, City University of New York; the University of California, Santa Barbara; and the University of Miami. He is currently Professor of History and former head of the Department of History and Politics at Drexel University. He has been a Guggenheim Fellow and is a member of the advisory board of the Yale Center for Parliamentary History and a Fellow of the Royal Historical Society. His book *The Parliament of 1621: A Study in Constitutional Conflict* (1971) received the Phi Alpha Theta prize for the best first book by a member of the society, and he was made a fellow of Tor House in recognition of *The Cliffs of Solitude: A Reading of Robinson Jeffers* (1983), the inaugural volume of the Cambridge Studies in American Literature and Culture series. His other books include *Lives of the Poet* (1974) and *Europe in Transition, 1660–1815* (1984). He has edited *A Casebook on Anaïs Nin* (1974) and *Centennial Essays for Robinson Jeffers* (1991) and has coedited, with Richard L. Greaves, the *Biographical Dictionary of British Radicals in the Seventeenth Century* (3 volumes, 1982–1984). His recent publications include studies of Samuel Beckett, Philip Guston, Bernardo Bertolucci, and the English civil war.

Jennifer Tolbert Roberts. Born in New York City and educated at Yale University, Jennifer Roberts is Professor of History at Southern Methodist University in Dallas, Texas, and Associate Professor of Classical Languages and History at the City College of New York and the City University of New York Graduate Center. She previously taught at Wheaton College in Massachusetts, where she served as Chair of the Department of Classics. A former president of the Friends of Ancient History, the Metroplex Classical Association, and the Texas Classical Association, she is President of the New York Classical Club and serves on the Board of Directors of the American Philological Association. In 1982 she was awarded the Southwestern Historical Association's Walter R. Craddock Prize in European-Asian History. She has held fellowships from the National Endowment for the Humanities and the American Council of Learned Societies and was a member of the Institute for Advanced Study at Princeton in 1985. With Walter Blanco she edited the Norton Critical Edition of Herodotus' *Histories,* and her translation of Erasmus' *De Vidua*

Christiana appeared in the *Collected Works of Erasmus* published by the University of Toronto Press. She has published scholarly articles in a variety of journals and is the author of two books on Athens, *Accountability in Athenian Government* (University of Wisconsin Press, 1982) and *Athens on Trial: History, Politics, and the Antidemocratic Tradition* (Princeton University Press, 1994).

HISTORY AND HUMAN BEGINNINGS

The human genus has existed for several million years and human cultures for tens of thousands, perhaps hundreds of thousands, of years. Only within the past 10,000, however, have these cultures exhibited the form that we call civilization, a word derived from *civilis,* a Latin term meaning "relating to a citizen or a state." A civilization is a culture characterized by the building of cities, the development of a complex social and political structure through stratification, and the evolution of a formal economic structure through the division of labor. Civilization implies the willingness of familial groups to embrace outsiders, although clan and kinship patterns may remain important even in the most highly developed civilizations.

Civilization also came to entail the keeping of records and, for this purpose, the development of a system of writing. The first records were kept to levy taxes, take inventories, and chronicle business transactions. They were also used later for compiling royal genealogies, preserving sacred texts and accounts of military expeditions, and recording laws, poems, and stories that had hitherto been transmitted orally. From such functions evolved the idea of keeping chronologies of major events and, in time, the notion of binding these together as a narrative. Such narratives of past events came to be called histories by the early Greeks. History as a human activity thus grew out of the basic processes of civilization itself and, in its most developed form, is not only the record of civilization but also civilization's way of reflecting upon itself.

HISTORY AND THE HISTORIAN

Historical study is a living process that involves the systematic discussion and interpretation of issues, not simply the chronicling of past events. The historian is not the mere conservator of the past but its active shaper. To study the past is to help mold the future by providing the basis for informed judgments. The historical consciousness of modern society is inseparable from the attempt to consider options and to make decisions. Not surprisingly, historians often differ in the philosophical approaches they bring to their material. Writing history entails making critical judgments and selecting events. Most historians strive for objectivity and cite the evidence on which their conclusions are based; others reflect a predetermined ideological position. All historians necessarily reflect their time and culture.

In seeking to make sense of the past, historians have focused on key themes. Religion has often been a major factor in interpreting the past. The Christian and Islamic historians of the Middle Ages and the early modern era viewed the past through the lenses of their faiths, but the eighteenth-century British author Edward Gibbon, who adopted a secular, rationalistic outlook, assessed Christianity's historical role in largely negative terms. Other historians, such as the classical Greek Thucydides and the sixteenth-century Florentine Niccolò Machiavelli, sought to explain earlier societies on the basis of theories of human behavior. Some, from Thucydides in classical times to the twentieth-century historian Arnold Toynbee, have searched for patterns and cycles of repetition in past events. In contrast to this has been the conviction that the study of history reveals a steady improvement in human life. Marxist historians have seen progress as a series of class conflicts that will ultimately lead to an egalitarian society. Few historians would now deny the importance of social and economic elements in the historical process, just as few would seek to explain the past primarily in terms of the actions of great men and women. We should expect history neither to determine our future nor to impose neat patterns on the past. Historians try to establish as clear an understanding as possible of past events and cultures and of the place of our own society in the historical context. All of these attempts are colored by the prejudices and cultural backgrounds of the respective scholars.

Fields of History

Much modern historical writing has concentrated on political institutions and practices, diplomatic relations, and warfare—subjects that have formed the traditional core of historical study. Beginning especially in the period after World War II, historians have looked increasingly to wider fields, often with the aid of new research techniques, many of them borrowed from the social sciences. Social historians are concerned with social organization and behavior in the past. Interaction between the sexes, the role of women, attitudes toward death, the rearing of children, class and kinship structure, patterns of mobility, the rules of inheritance and property, and the formation of elites are major concerns of the social historian. A special aspect of social organization is the study of urban life, one of the key distinguishing marks of civilization.

Economic, demographic, and environmental history is crucial to an understanding of the past. The movement of people, the flow of trade, the development of technology and its diffusion, the fluctuations in population, and the changing patterns of climate all contribute to our perception of human dealings with the world, with each other, and with survival.

The history of ideas, including religious beliefs and political ideologies, casts light on the principles and assumptions of society, the transmission of elite norms, the interplay and conflict between cultural values, and the common threads that unite religion, art, science, and law. Cultural historians concentrate on such subjects as art, architecture, music, and literature. Indeed, virtually every product of human endeavor sheds light on the period from which it comes.

Sources and Their Interpretation

Historians draw on a wide range of materials. These sources fall into two categories: *primary sources,* which consist of materials produced in the period under examination, and *secondary sources,* which comprise accounts by writers of a later age. Primary sources include letters, diaries, tax rolls, treaties, statutes, birth and death registers, census returns, sermons, and court records. Historians work largely from primary sources, even as they keep abreast of findings by other scholars and incorporate those results in their own studies.

In preliterate societies, all knowledge of the past was transmitted orally from generation to generation. This was true, for example, of myths, which constitute a special category of evidence. Myths are tales that incorporate religious or supernatural notions to explain natural phenomena and social events or to express cultural values. The earliest civilizations used myths to account for floods and drought, birth and death, and gender differences. In a prescientific era, myths functioned in lieu of scientific explanations. Among the most famous myths are those that sought to explain the creation of the universe and the origins of life. Most modern scholars regard the biblical accounts of creation in the book of Genesis as part of the corpus of ancient myth; Jewish and Christian theologians who accept this conclusion believe that the myths nevertheless point to the underlying truth of divinely ordered creation. Myths provide invaluable clues to the perpetual human effort to understand the world and our place in it.

Primary sources include much more than written records. Tools, clothing, religious artifacts, and eating and cooking utensils, for instance, tell us much about the aesthetic preferences, the social structure, and the values of earlier societies. Fecal remains as well as foodstuffs preserved in graves and tombs can teach us about prehistoric and ancient diets.

Such objects can often be dated with reasonable accuracy by measuring organic deposits of carbon-14, a radioactive form of carbon that disintegrates over time. This form of dating has been usable only for objects less than 50,000 years old, although current research should increase this period to 100,000 years. The accuracy of radiocarbon dating has been enhanced by coupling it with dendrochronology, the study of annual growth rings in trees (particularly the bristle-cone pines in California's White Mountains, which date back to the seventh millennium B.C.). By subjecting ring samples to radiocarbon analysis, the latter can be accurately calibrated. Items can also be dated by their position in the successive strata of objects that have accumulated over centuries at a specific location. At the Koster site, near St. Louis, Missouri, for example, archaeologists have identified 15 distinctive strata covering a period from approximately 6000 B.C. to A.D. 1200.

Dramatic scientific advances have resulted in other systems of dating that are especially useful in working with cores of sediment from ocean bottoms and with loess (wind-borne soil) and microfauna deposited between glacial cycles. Measuring potassium and argon enabled scientists to determine that human fossils found at the Olduvai Gorge in Tanzania were 1.786 million years old. Some objects can be dated by measuring the decay of uranium, changes in the earth's magnetic field, or thermoluminescence (for such things as burned artifacts, teeth, and rocks heated by a campfire). Approximate dates for human and animal remains can also be determined by measuring the proportion of "left-handed" to "right-handed" amino acid molecules; at the time of death the number of molecules oriented in a leftward direction begins to increase through the action of aspartic acid in a process known as amino acid racemization.

The fine arts reveal much about the civilizations of previous eras. Paintings, sculpture, music, and architecture reflect the values of those who produced them as well as the audience for whom they were intended and the patrons who made their creation possible.

The historian of more recent times has a wide range of additional material in the form of films, recordings, and other products of the era of mass communication. Newspapers (which originated in the seventeenth century), magazines, film, photography, popular literature, and folk songs are valuable historical evidence. For recent events, oral accounts can provide significant information; a special subfield now exists called *oral history,* the practitioners of which interview people who participated in or witnessed historical events, thereby preserving their accounts as data for future scholars.

Interpreting the evidence demands appropriate analytical skills. Most historians are trained in the methodology of at least one additional field. Social historians must be familiar with the techniques of sociology and demography; economic historians with statistics and economists' models; church historians with theology and philosophy; intellectual historians with philosophy and textual criticism; historians of science with scientific theory and methodology. Legal historians are often trained in the law. The field of psychohistory, which attempts to apply psychological theories and models to explain the behavior of historical personalities, requires training in psychology. Historians of the ancient world work closely with archaeologists, who analyze such remains as pottery, inscriptions, and ruins. Anthropological studies of tribal behavior in modern times are used to formulate hypotheses about prehistoric society. In sum, historians work closely with specialists in virtually all fields to explain the past and its relationship to the present.

THE ORIGINS OF HUMANITY

Although the earth is approximately 4.5 to 5 billion years old, the earliest humanlike ancestors appeared several million years ago. They were hominids: primates similar to the modern human, although with considerably smaller brain capacities. Hominids walked on two feet, used tools, and ate meat. About 1.4 to 1.6 million years ago, hominids evolved into *Homo erectus,* probably in temperate regions of Africa first, after which some migrated into western and southern Asia and Europe. Many anthropologists believe that *H. erectus,* with its enlarged brain (about two-thirds the size of a modern person's), evolved independently in Java, the Philippines, and China.

Because *H. erectus* used stone tools, the earliest period in the human saga is known as the Paleolithic, or Old Stone Age. During this long period, which probably began 600,000 or more years ago, tools, which were originally only primitive chips of stone, gradually became more sophisticated. *H. erectus* developed the hand axe, which could be used to chop, cut, scrape, and punch holes. Tools for scraping could also be fashioned out of flint.

Paleolithic people fed themselves with grain, fruits, vegetables, roots, and nuts and with game hunted with spears. Hunting large animals required organization and communication, thus encouraging the development of speech and rudimentary social groups. These people organized themselves into bands, typically numbering several dozen people, for the purposes of protection, the provision of food, and probably simple religious rituals. The basic social unit of this hunter-gatherer society was the family. Because of their role as gatherers and their bearing and raising of children, women were presumably the social equals of men. Nevertheless, the gradual division of labor along sexual lines contributed to the distinction of occupational roles that has lasted into the twentieth century.

In geological terms the Paleolithic Age was roughly coterminous with the Pleistocene Epoch, which extended from 2 million years ago to approximately 10,000 years ago. During this epoch, glaciers advanced and retreated at least four and possibly as many as six or seven times, causing substantial climatic and topographical changes that required humans to adapt. They were forced to think and thus to develop their critical capacities. Evolution therefore continued, leading to the appearance of

Homo sapiens neanderthalensis between about 100,000 and 55,000 years ago; "Neanderthal man" was so named because the first remains of these people were discovered in the Neander River valley in modern Germany.

Neanderthal people lived in both caves and open-air sites, hunted mammals, and warmed themselves by large stone fireplaces. More striking was their preparation of elaborate funeral rites to deal with the needs of those who had died and presumably lived in some afterlife. Bodies were interred in graves filled with shells and ornaments made of ivory and bone, while the skin or bones of the deceased were colored with red ocher, apparently to commemorate life. The corpses were buried in a fetal position, possibly to facilitate rebirth or to restrict the movements of the dead and prevent them from returning to haunt the living.

About 40,000 years ago, modern humans, known as *Homo sapiens sapiens,* first appeared. Many anthropologists group these people with the Neanderthals, who coexisted with the new people for 5,000 or 10,000 years; both were part of one larger category, *Homo sapiens* ("wise man"). The earliest record of *H. sapiens sapiens* were found at Cro-Magnon, a cave in southwestern France. Like the Neanderthals, Cro-Magnon people were hunter-gatherers. The Cro-Magnon period was marked by changes in tools, some of which were constructed of bone, ivory, and antler for the first time. Needles made of antler or bone were used to sew clothing fashioned from animal skins, and flint was useful to make microliths, such as arrow tips and barbs.

The earliest surviving paintings come from this period and were found in southwestern France, particularly at Lascaux. Most of the drawings depict animals, such as bulls and deer. Because the drawings were located in the inner recesses of caves rather than in the inhabited areas or near the mouths where natural illumination was available, they were probably associated with religious rites. Rarely do humans appear in these paintings.

Sculptures of humans from the same period typically depict women with enlarged breasts, thighs, and stomachs, emphasizing reproduction. The artists thus reflected women's crucial role as the source of life. Rarely do the statues show facial features, and some omit the head altogether; the emphasis was on fertility rather than the lifelike reproduction of physical features. Some scholars believe that these female figures reflect a primitive belief in a mother-goddess.

Recent research suggests that some of the people of this age, although hunter-gatherers, were the first to settle in permanent communities, with facilities for the storage of food, patterns of trade that extended over long distances, and social and political hierarchies. The existence of such hierarchies is suggested by standardized beads and pendants made by western European foragers as long as 32,000 years ago. These people also knew how to fire clay to make ceramics. In central Russia, archaeologists have found the remains of elaborate settlements constructed of mammoth bones; the people who lived here some 20,000 years ago traded for materials from the Black Sea region, 500 miles away. Presumably, they stored their food because their population was expanding, although this practice limited their mobility. As they settled into permanent communities, internal conflicts must have occurred, leading to the development of social and political organization to maintain order. Probably because of climatic changes characterized by severe weather, this society came to an end some 12,000 years ago, when the Europeans broke up into small bands and returned to a nomadic life.

By the end of the Paleolithic Age, some 10,000 years ago, the more advanced people customarily lived in shelters made of wood, hides, sod, or bones; dressed in clothing sewn from skins; used dogs to control, insofar as possible, herds of wild animals; traded with other regions; painted and sculpted; participated in primitive rituals; and buried their dead.

Bone harpoons from western France, about 14,000 years old. [Reproduced by Courtesy of the Trustees of the British Museum]

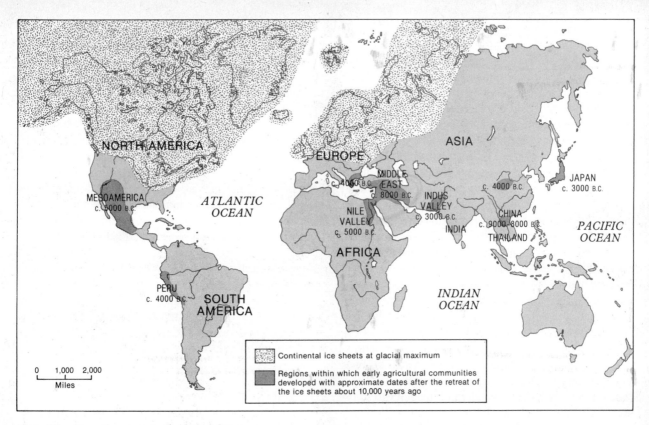

P.1 The Development of Agriculture

AGRICULTURAL AND SOCIAL DEVELOPMENTS IN THE NEOLITHIC AGE

As long as there was an ample supply of animals to hunt and population remained small, incentives to raise crops and domesticate animals were few. However, as the glaciers retreated and temperatures gradually warmed, large herbivores such as mammoth and bison began to disappear in many regions of human habitation. At the same time, the human population continued to increase rapidly. Specialists estimate that the population grew from 125,000 hominids 1 million years ago to 5.32 million humans at the end of the Paleolithic Age and from that figure to 133 million about 2,000 years ago. The demands this increasing population placed on the food supply were met by the introduction of herding and agriculture; this development marked the end of the

Paleolithic and the beginning of the Neolithic (New Stone) Age.

Agriculture probably originated in the hill country and then was adapted to the valleys of the Tigris and Euphrates rivers in southwestern Asia and in eastern Asia Minor. Other peoples in the world, including those in Mesoamerica, southeastern Asia, China, western Africa, and the Andes, developed agricultural techniques independently. The earliest farmers in western Asia grew wheat, barley, oats, and rye and grazed herds of sheep, goats, pigs, and cattle. People who lived near rivers or lakes could supplement their diet with fish. In time, Neolithic people discovered how to brew beer from fermented grain and, in the Mediterranean region, to make wine from grapes.

Farming, in the view of some specialists, spread very slowly throughout Europe from its western Asian origins. These experts, using carbon-14 dating, calculate that it took 1,500 years for agricultural techniques to expand from central Asia Minor to central Italy and another 1,500 years to reach the central Iberian peninsula. In effect, each generation, they believe, extended the agricultural frontier an average of 11 miles, until farming populations existed throughout Europe by approximately 3800 B.C. Some scholars have challenged this view on the basis of evidence that points to the development of European agriculture by indigenous peoples, not colonizers from western Asia.

The change from a nomadic to a settled life made possible by agriculture had both advantages and disadvantages. A greater incentive now existed to build permanent homes, with improved shelter from the elements and with room to store manufactured products. Once the crops were in the ground, many Neolithic people had time to hone skills for making tools, cooking utensils, and clothing, thus inaugurating a technological revolution. They learned to make better tools by grinding and polishing stone rather than by chipping, and they discovered how to make pottery, fire it in kilns, and glaze it to improve its capacity to hold liquids. The domestication of sheep provided supplies of wool and thus encouraged the invention of weaving. In time, Neolithic people invented the plow and the wheel, improving both agricultural yield and the ability to transport their crops. Dependence on agriculture, however, rendered these people much more susceptible to climatic fluctuations such as drought, floods, or unseasonable freezes. Settlements also increased the likelihood of illness through greater exposure to contaminated water, excrement, spoiled food, and decaying animal entrails.

Specialists have learned much about Neolithic trading patterns through chemical and physical analyses of raw materials, such as obsidian and flint. Obsidian, a volcanic glass used for grinding and flaking, spread throughout the Mediterranean and western Asia from various regional centers. Neolithic communities were probably less self-sufficient than was once assumed, just as their trading patterns were more sophisticated than was once thought. Raw materials and manufactured items were presumably exchanged for food and perhaps hides.

Like the Paleolithic hunter-gatherers who had established communities in central Russia, Neolithic settlers developed rudimentary forms of social and political organization. As in the Paleolithic Age, the family continued to be of prime importance. Some scholars have argued that the basic unit was the extended family, embracing perhaps three generations or siblings and their spouses and children. The extended family could provide the labor necessary for such agricultural tasks as clearing land or harvesting and could ensure that the work was performed even if one or more people became incapacitated. Against this assumption, however, is evidence that late Neolithic houses were normally too small to shelter more than the nuclear family (parents and children).

Scholars generally agree that within the community, little emphasis was placed on the individual. Instead, the people of the village worked together, essentially as equals, to build houses, clear forests, and plant crops. Each family had access to the community's resources as need required. The emphasis was on mutual welfare, not, as in modern Western society, productivity for the sake of social differentiation and material accumulation. Archeological excavation in Neolithic cemeteries tends to confirm this view of a largely egalitarian society, for there is usually little differentiation in goods from one grave to the next. We do not know, however, whether all the deceased were interred in these cemeteries or whether Neolithic people buried only the elite.

Women played a key role in Neolithic society and may have enjoyed a higher status than men. Some scholars believe that women were largely responsible for the agricultural revolution in the Neolithic period. Mythology suggests confirmation of this: women are associated with raising crops, men with herding animals. The Neolithic village, however, could support a larger population than the hunter-gatherer tribe, intensifying the burden on women as bearers and raisers of children in addition to their expanded agricultural duties. Women's contribution to the agricultural revolution may have unwittingly sown the seeds for their later subjugation by men. As mythology suggests, that repression may have begun with the introduction of the animal-drawn plow, which was widely used in western Asia by 3000 B.C.; early myths associated female deities with the hoe and their male counterparts with the plow. Yet competition between the sexes, so common to much of recorded history, may not have existed, or at least may have been less pronounced, in the prehistoric era.

Archaeological discoveries have made it possible to reconstruct the outlines of Neolithic religious beliefs. Numerous figurines have been unearthed throughout eastern Europe. Most of these depict females, although others portray males and animals; many probably represented deities, especially an earth mother, responsible for both human and animal fertility and agricultural yields. Neolithic Europeans worshiped both the Great

Goddess, who transformed death into life and was linked with moon crescents, and the Goddess of Vegetation, her intimate companion. Religious practice was thus concerned with nature and the cycle of the seasons and occurred in both private houses and shrines or temples. Worshipers sacrificed humans, animals, and assorted objects on altars, some of which were found in temples, others in open-air sanctuaries or caves. The widespread acceptance of ritual practices reflected a growing sense of community.

THE COMING OF CIVILIZATION

The Neolithic Age, with its development of cereal cultivation and animal husbandry, permanent settlements, expanded trading patterns, and social groups, provided the roots from which civilization grew. Most Neolithic settlements were small, ranging from homesteads with fewer than ten people to villages with several hundred inhabitants. Around 8000 B.C. the transition from village to city life began at Jericho in what was later called Palestine; 2,000 to 3,000 people lived at Jericho in multi-roomed houses. The large fortifications that protected the city suggest that warfare must have been commonplace, as it apparently was in prehistoric Europe. The people of Jericho raised grain, probably with the aid of an irrigation system that utilized spring waters, and traded sulfur and salt for precious stones from the Sinai and obsidian from Anatolia. Their artists created portrait busts by modeling plaster over human skulls.

Comparable cities developed at such places as Jarmo, in what is now Iraq, around 7000 B.C. and at Çatal Hüyük in Anatolia. The latter, founded in approximately 6700 B.C., was considerably larger than Jericho. Its inhabitants raised grains, nuts, peas, apples, grapes, and oil-producing seeds; grazed sheep; and hunted deer and wild boar. Residents made pottery, baskets, and wooden vessels; crafted fine weapons from flint; wove cloth; fashioned necklaces and bracelets; and applied cosmetics as they looked into polished obsidian mirrors. Like the people of Jericho, the Çatal Hüyükans traded widely for items that included shells from the Mediterranean and stones from southern Anatolia. The walls of their religious shrines were decorated with paintings of dancers, wild animals, vultures,

and funeral rituals. Their chief deity, a female, was attended by both males and females.

The development of metallurgy was also important for the rise of civilization. In both western Asia and the Balkans, late Neolithic people acquired the ability to smelt, hammer, and cast copper ores in the fifth millennium B.C. The earliest items fashioned of copper included personal ornaments, axes, daggers, and hooks. Copper is a relatively soft metal, and it was not until about 3000 B.C. that metalworkers learned the technique of alloying it with tin to produce the more durable bronze. In the beginning, copper, like gold and silver, was rather scarce, and objects made of it would have been prized. People who were fortunate enough to possess items made from gold, silver, copper, or precious stones distinguished themselves from others on the basis of their wealth. Social differentiations undoubtedly were encouraged as some people mastered

A Neolithic carving of a man holding a sickle and wearing bracelets on his arms, c. 5.000 B.C. Sickles like this were made of copper. [Courtesy of Professor Marija Gimbutas]

metallurgical technology and more sophisticated techniques of pottery making and decorating. Essentially classless societies faded in the face of emerging distinctions based on wealth and technical skills.

A skill of a different kind involved the ability to write. Scholars may someday find that writing first appeared in southern and central Europe if the engravings on the Neolithic figurines found there prove to be more than simple markings. For now, however, the earliest known writing system was devised by the people of Uruk (now Tal al-Warka), one of the principal city-states in ancient Sumer (modern Iraq). In the late Neolithic period, records were kept by using small tokens, some of which were marked with incisions.

Late in the fourth millennium B.C., as cities and large-scale trade developed, the use of tokens to maintain records became too cumbersome. The people of Mesopotamia substituted written images known as ideographs for the tokens. During the third millennium B.C. these ideographs evolved into a series of wedge-shaped marks that could be impressed on a clay tablet quickly and easily with a split reed. The system of wedge-shaped marks on clay is known as *cuneiform,* after the Latin word *cuneus,* which means "wedge." Cuneiform combined the use of pictographic signs (representing objects) and phonetic signs (representing sounds) with a total of some 350 characters. This method of writing was useful to record financial transactions, religious beliefs, political and military achievements, and laws.

About the time the people of Sumeria in Mesopotamia evolved their system of writing, a transportation revolution was underway that provided additional impetus to the emergence of civilization. The invention of the wheel enabled farmers and others to haul large quantities of goods on animal-drawn, two- and four-wheeled carts. Bulky goods in particular could be moved more efficiently on the rivers, thanks to the invention of the sail in the fourth millennium B.C. The new means of transportation were crucial in handling the increasing amounts of agricultural produce made possible by the development of better plows (antlers replaced sticks beginning in the fourth millennium) and the larger quantities of pottery produced after the introduction of the potter's wheel. The first peoples to combine all these developments lived in the river valleys of Mesopotamia, Egypt, and India. Civilizations developed somewhat later in China and Southeast Asia.

Suggestions for Further Reading

Barker, G. *Prehistoric Farming in Europe.* Cambridge: Cambridge University Press, 1982.

Briffault, R. *The Mothers.* New York: Atheneum, 1977.

Champion, T., Gamble, C., Shennan, S., and Whittle, A. *Prehistoric Europe.* London: Academic Press, 1984.

Cohen, M. N. *The Food Crisis in Prehistory.* New Haven, Conn.: Yale University Press, 1977.

Gimbutas, M. *The Goddesses and Gods of Old Europe, 6500–3500 B.C.: Myths and Cult Images,* 2nd ed. Berkeley: University of California Press, 1982.

Gowlett, J. *Ascent to Civilization: The Archaeology of Early Man.* New York: Knopf, 1984.

Johnson, D., and Edey, M. *Lucy: The Beginnings of Humankind.* New York: Warner Books, 1981.

Keightly, D. N., ed. *The Origins of Chinese Civilization.* Berkeley: University of California Press, 1983.

Leakey, R. E., and Lewin, R. *Origins.* New York: Dutton, 1977.

Lerner, G. *The Creation of Patriarchy.* New York: Oxford University Press, 1986.

Phillips, P. *The Prehistory of Europe.* Bloomington: Indiana University Press, 1980.

Sieveking, A. *The Cave Artists.* London: Thames & Hudson, 1979.

WESTERN ASIA AND EGYPT

The story of civilization is intertwined with the growth of cities. The world's first cities, though humble by today's standards, nonetheless had much in common with the modern metropolis. In ancient cities as in modern ones, people followed specialized occupations, erected monumental buildings for common use, came together for worship, established a formal state structure, and kept elaborate written records. The first cities developed toward the beginning of the Bronze Age (c. 3500–c. 1100 B.C.) in western Asia, the part of the world known today as the Middle East. Perhaps originally designed as centers for manufacture and commercial exchange, cities were also indispensable for intellectual development.

With cities came greater opportunities for human interaction. Working together, people were able to profit from one another's skills to make life richer and more varied. More intense human contact yielded not only a broader range of sophisticated artifacts but also a wider spectrum of new ideas. At the same time, city life brought with it greater inequalities among individuals and groups. More complex economies widened the gap between rich and poor, and though increased specialization improved the quality of many products, it also created a hierarchy of occupations. As people had more to protect and to gain, cities resorted more readily to warfare against each other.

Warfare meant captives, and so every city came to be divided into two groups, the free and the unfree. Slavery was universal in the towns of western Asia, both as a consequence of frequent warfare and because the very poor were often compelled to become the slaves of those to whom they were in debt. In addition, the changed condition of urban life increased the difference in status between the sexes; throughout the Bronze Age and the Iron Age that followed it (around 1100 B.C.) the evolution of cultures shows an almost universal increase in the gap between the dignity and authority of males and that of females. With increasing population, moreover, came overcrowding in cities and food shortages. Urban life thus generated problems as well as opportunities.

THE BEGINNINGS OF CITY LIFE IN MESOPOTAMIA

Where there is no water, there can be no life. Not surprisingly, the civilization we call "Western" traces its roots to an area bounded by two rivers, the Tigris and the Euphrates. The land between them was known to the ancient Greeks as Mesopotamia ("middle river"), and it was the cradle of four civilizations: Sumer, Akkad, Babylon, and Assyria.

The Sumerians were a farming people who settled in southern Mesopotamia around 3500 B.C., where they created a rich urban culture that became the model for later Mesopotamian civilization. The Akkadians from

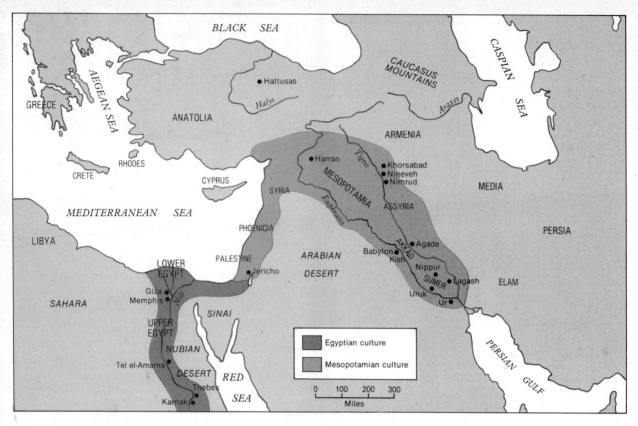

1.1 Western Asia and Egypt

the north conquered the Sumerians militarily but adopted their culture. Like the Hebrews and many of the Ethiopians, the Akkadians belonged to the group of peoples known as Semites. The Semites were semipastoral nomads who in their early days were organized into patriarchal families and tribal units rather than into tightly organized territorial states, and the various Semitic peoples spoke similar languages. Ultimately, the Akkadians' power fell to the Amorites, another Semitic people who had migrated from Arabia. Based in the strategically placed city of Babylon, the Amorites, who became known as the Babylonians, absorbed Mesopotamia's culture while modifying its political system and religious beliefs. Under their great king Hammurabi (c. 1792–1750 B.C.) the Babylonians spread this enriched culture north to Asia Minor and west to Syria and Palestine. Yet another Semitic people, the Assyrians, conquered the Babylonians in the eighth century B.C. and went on to establish an empire that eventually reached as far as Egypt.

Mesopotamia was a dry, forbidding region whose geography and climate profoundly shaped the culture and politics of the people who lived there. Between the rivers lay swamp and desert; consequently, the cities long remained isolated from each other, and it took millennia to unify the region politically. The evolution of a complex irrigation system during the fourth millennium B.C. produced an area of more than 10,000 square miles of extremely fertile soil. Within this area it was possible for families to produce the food surplus necessary for the specialization, trade, and leisure that were the building blocks of city life. But if the rivers made life possible, they could also take it away. Both the Tigris and the Euphrates flooded often and unpredictably, wiping out whole cities. The biblical story of the flood was probably inspired by a similar Babylonian tale, and these frequent riverine catastrophes helped to imbue Mesopotamian religion with a deep pessimism.

During the middle of the fourth millennium it was also discovered that a combination of copper and tin in a proportion of about 9 to 1 formed an alloy, bronze, that was substantially harder than either metal used separately. The consequences of this discovery were manifold. The search for additional sources of ore contributed to the exploration of new lands, the expansion of trade, the construction of better ships, and the mastery of foreign languages. The invention of a complex system of notation transformed Mesopotamian society still further. Writing facilitated day-to-day activity, making possible the precise measurements necessary for constructing elaborate temples and sophisticated canal systems as well as taking inventories, transacting business, collecting taxes, and preserving sacred texts. Such records are precious to the historian, but they must be used with care, for we cannot be sure that they reflect what was important to most of the people who lived in the ancient world. Much of the writing that survives from antiquity was the work of elites or clerks in the service of authority, and very little of it was produced by women.

Sumerian Religion and Society

Ancient writing began in Sumer. From shortly after 3000 B.C. to about 2370 B.C., Sumer consisted of a collection of communities known as city-states, the largest of which probably contained approximately 35,000 people. The city-state, usually an urban center surrounded by countryside whose nonslave residents also enjoyed citizenship, was a common unit in the ancient world, similar to a city in size but operating as a sovereign nation in foreign policy. Religion pervaded all aspects of life in Sumer. Sumerians imagined their deities to be very much like themselves. The gods' actions were seen as menacing and capricious, their character as jealous and possessive. The Sumerians consequently viewed life on earth as mirroring contention among the gods. The rivalries of the city-states of early Mesopotamia reflected the belief that each Sumerian city was the private property of a particular god. The town of Nippur, for example, was possessed by Enlil, the storm god, and Uruk by Inanna, the fertility goddess. Any attempt to encroach on a city's territory was thus conceived as a direct attack on the local divinity.

The belief that the gods were temperamental was in part a product of the inhospitable climate of the Tigris-Euphrates valley, where floods, quakes, and storms represented a constant threat to the stability of daily life. In Egypt, where the Nile rose and fell predictably and life was more secure, the gods were perceived as far gentler and more amiable. The notion that the universe was managed by moody gods who needed to be placated constantly was encouraged by an ambitious priesthood, which persuaded the farmers and artisans that regular donations on their part were necessary for the people to maintain divine favor. Sumerian myth told how the deities had created humans to work for them; although this tale probably reflected the relationship between laborers and the temple elite, it could also be used to sanction it. Enforced labor built the massive *ziggurats* that adorned Sumerian cities. These immense layered brick platforms decked out with terraces were designed to serve as artificial mountains by which the gods might be approached more closely than from the ground.

The temple elite owned much land, and the temple served as a redistribution center for the substantial quantities of food and craft products that were brought to it. In time, however, priests were forced to yield political power to secular leaders. The encouragement the priesthood gave to economic development promoted not only trade but also warfare, which in turn revealed the need for effective and continuous secular leadership. The prominence of the assembly of the gods in Sumerian mythology suggests that at some point in their early history, decisions in the city-states were made by gatherings of the people.

Many slaves also lived in Sumer. Most were owned by the temple and were set to work in farming or manufacture, but some were attached to individual households. As elsewhere, slavery in Sumer arose sometimes from capture and sometimes as a consequence of heavy debts that resulted in the debtor's becoming the property of the creditor. Sumerian slaves had a number of rights; they could contract marriages with free people and, through hard work, earn the money to purchase their freedom. On the whole, most work in Sumer seems to have been done by free labor, and many projects were probably accomplished by free and slave laborers working side by side.

The most remarkable and enduring achievement of the Sumerians was the development of writing. As we have seen, primitive symbols had long been used for record keeping—various tokens for counting and pictograms and ideograms to convey first objects and then actions. The limited possibilities of this kind of notation were expanded with the development of phonograms that denoted sounds rather than images. The Sumerians were the first people to develop a concrete set of signs to denote individual syllables. They impressed these signs on clay with a wedge-shaped stylus. This practical form of writing known as *cuneiform* came to be used not only by the Sumerians but by a variety of other peoples as well.

This portrait of an Akkadian king could well be of Sargon himself. [Hirmer Fotoarchiv, Munich]

Sargon and His Successors

Sumer was conquered around 2370 B.C. by the Akkadian ruler Sargon. The empire Sargon forged by uniting the Akkadians and Sumerians played a major role in fostering commercial and cultural exchange throughout large parts of western Asia. Lands that had previously been thought distant from one another, such as Elam, Syria, and Cyprus, now exchanged their products. Sargon used religion to help graft Akkadian culture onto the existing Sumerian civilization by identifying Akkadian and Sumerian gods with one another and by appointing his daughter Enheduanna as a high priestess in the prominent cities of Ur and Uruk. Enheduanna also played an important role in fusing the Akkadian Ishtar with the Sumerian Inanna, goddess of love, to whom she wrote hymns that were frequently cited in later Sumerian literature. Sargon's grandson Naram-Sin (c. 2250 B.C.) also appointed his daughter to be high priestess of Ur.

Naram-Sin's empire eventually fell after an invasion by the warlike, nomadic Guti from the east. A period of chaos followed. Sumerian historians later asked, "Who was king? Who was not king?" The prosperous city of Lagash, however, remained an important trading center in the Guti era. Under its ruler Gudea (c. 2100 B.C.), a dedicated patron of the arts, Lagash recovered some of its earlier power and prestige. Toward the end of the third millennium, Ur replaced Lagash as the leading city of Mesopotamia. Around the beginning of the second millennium the power of Ur was broken by the Semitic Amorites from Arabia.

The Babylonians

The Amorites settled in the previously insignificant town of Babylon, which gave its name to the complex civilization that subsequently arose in Mesopotamia. Babylonian culture was carried by way of Syria to Europe; key elements of Etruscan and Roman culture, such as the use of the arch and the forecasting of events from omens, were of Sumerian origin. The influence of Babylonian religion is evident in the Hebrew Bible, particularly in the myths of creation and the story of a huge flood, and it was from the Babylonians that the Greeks derived their calendar and their system of weights. The tradition of counting a day in two sets of 12 hours also derives from Babylon, as did the 12 signs of the zodiac. In these ways the culture of the Babylonians survived the destruction of their kingdom around 1600 B.C. by the Hittites from Asia Minor (modern Turkey) and by the Kassites, whose origins are disputed.

The Babylonians were the first to use writing to record the Sumerian *Epic of Gilgamesh,* a moving tale of a courageous Sumerian king. If Gilgamesh really lived, he probably ruled around 2600 B.C. The poem deals with Gilgamesh's adventures and the painful questions about death the hero must confront when his closest friend, Enkidu, is killed by the gods. In addition to demonstrating the Mesopotamians' concern about death, the *Epic of Gilgamesh* reveals the qualities they prized in their heroes. Gilgamesh is brave, powerful, assertive, adventurous, and reflective. Several of the important themes in the *Epic of Gilgamesh* were echoed in the later Greek epics associated with the poet Homer. Gilgamesh's travels are echoed in Homer's *Odyssey,* and the painful recognition of human mortality that follows the death of a companion is similar to the suffering of Achilles in Homer's *Iliad.*

The Code of Hammurabi

Although Mesopotamia was ruled successively by a variety of peoples, the codification of law remained a consistent preoccupation. The earliest elaborate law code that survives from the ancient world is that of the Babylonian king Hammurabi, which was inscribed on a slab of black stone some 8 feet high. The nearly 4,000 lines of the code, which embraced both civil and criminal law, regulated practically every aspect of the lives of Hammurabi's subjects. Although Hammurabi sought to protect the weak from the strong, he did not eliminate social distinctions. The rights of disadvantaged groups such as women and slaves were defined and defended, but no thought was given to abolishing slavery or according equal status to the sexes. Men could seek divorce at will, but a woman who petitioned for divorce had to demonstrate that she had lived a blameless life; if in the course of the proceedings her neighbors denounced her, she was to be thrown in the river.

Hammurabi's code divided individuals into three groups, and punishments varied considerably depending on the social status of both the perpetrator and the victim, each of whom might be an aristocrat, an ordinary citizen, or a slave. Thus if the pregnant daughter of a gentleman was struck and miscarried, the punishment was a fine of 10 shekels, whereas it was only 5 shekels if the woman was the daughter of an ordinary citizen. If the latter woman died, the perpetrator had to pay a fine, but his own daughter faced execution if an ordinary citizen killed a gentleman's daughter.

The Status of Women

The Code of Hammurabi carefully spelled out the rights of women, who were entitled to own property and make legal contracts. Important inequalities prevailed, however. It was assumed that the male head of household had sexual access not only to his wife and as many concubines as he wished but also to all female slaves under his roof. He was also free to hire his women slaves out as prostitutes or to sell his wife and children into slavery. In Mesopotamia, as elsewhere, most economic power and nearly all political authority were in male hands. Women seem to have exercised significant influence in religion, for wives and daughters of kings were often appointed to high priesthoods by their husbands and fathers. When Urukagina of Lagash placed the administration of a temple in the hands of his wife, Queen Shagshag, he was following in the footsteps of his predecessor, Lugulanda, whose wife Baranamtarra had served as a religious administrator. Shagshag administered a staff consisting of more than 1,000 people. Just as Sargon's daughter had owed her priesthood to her father, however, these women were indebted for their positions to their husbands.

EARLY EGYPTIAN CIVILIZATION

Civilization began in Egypt at about the same time as in Mesopotamia. Throughout the centuries, ancient Egypt has cast a powerful spell over the human imagination, and the longevity of Egyptian society and culture gives it pride of place among the civilizations that formed the West. The art of writing developed early in Egypt, and meticulous record keeping was ingrained in the Egyptian mentality. In addition, the archaeological remains of Egypt have been exceptionally well preserved because of the dryness of the climate and the abundance of stone for building. For these reasons a great deal is known about Egyptian culture, especially since the decipherment of hieroglyphics by the Frenchman Jean François Champollion at the beginning of the nineteenth century.

Nowhere has geography contributed more to the shape of civilization than in Egypt. The Nile rises in the lakes and highlands of Ethiopia and central Africa and, after falling over several formidable cataracts, flows north for some 650 miles without interruption until it branches out into several mouths in the delta, traveling in various streams the additional 100 miles or so to the sea. Egypt is considered to begin at the first cataract (the northernmost one), where the Aswan Dam stands today. The Nile made communication almost effortless along the whole length of its valley, virtually ensuring Egypt's eventual political unification. While Mesopotamia's rivers flooded violently and unpredictably, the Nile rose with remarkable regularity every summer, gently covering its broad valley. As it retreated during the following two months, it left behind a layer of mud that fertilized the soil, making farming easy and highly productive.

Geography also minimized the danger of foreign invasion, for impassable deserts lay to the west and the east of the fertile Nile valley. Sheltered in their relatively easy existence, the Egyptians developed a serene and comforting religion, very unlike the grim Mesopotamian outlook. They could also afford an insular world view. Egypt seemed the best of all possible lands. Indeed, in the Egyptian mind, other lands scarcely existed; the word for "human being" was the same as the word for "Egyptian."

During the fourth millennium B.C., Egyptians were organized into small principalities known as *nomes*. By around 3100 B.C. the nomes of Lower Egypt (the area of the Nile delta and the land just south of it) and those of Upper Egypt (the narrow valley of the Nile farther south) had been organized into two kingdoms. Around 3100 B.C. the two kingdoms were united, and it is from this point that historians date the dynasties of Egypt. These have been numbered at 31, stretching from the unification of the two lands to their conquest in 332 B.C. by Alexander the Great, a chronology devised by the third-century B.C. Egyptian priest Manetho.

Egyptian Religion

Some of the most deeply rooted elements in the Egyptian world view evolved during the first centuries after the unification of the two realms. Perhaps the most important of these was the belief in the divinity of the *pharaoh,* as the Egyptian ruler was called. This concept seems to have explained, or at least rationalized, the marriage of pharaohs to their sisters, since ancient Egyptians as a rule avoided brother-sister marriage just as most other people traditionally have. Probably during this period the Egyptians also evolved the concept of *maat.* Maat contained elements of truth, justice, and order, embodying the underlying harmony and stability of the universe. It both reflected and consolidated the rule of the pharaoh, who was committed to govern in accordance with its principles.

Belief in a harmonious universe also characterized Egyptian religion. No doubt the hospitable climate provided by the predictable behavior of the Nile and the easily visible rising and setting of the desert sun contributed to the happy oneness with nature that marked elite Egyptian culture; such Egyptians saw in the world a gracious continuum that linked human, plant, and animal life just as it joined sky, land, and water. The bewildering variety of Egyptian deities might manifest themselves in the form of men or women, but they might just as well appear as jackals or dogs, crocodiles or hippopotamuses.

The Egyptians' religion also revealed much about their attitudes to women and the family. The god Horus, for example, was sometimes viewed as the son of Osiris, king of the dead. Osiris' wife, the supportive and resourceful Isis, had gathered up the assorted parts of her husband's dismembered body and reassembled him after he had been killed by his wicked brother, Seth. Both clever and loving, Isis was a far cry from the volatile temptress Inanna, who persecuted Gilgamesh for rejecting her, and from other female figures such as Eve and the Greek Pandora, who were regarded as the source of folly and evil.

Alive, the pharaoh was the incarnation of Horus. Once dead, he was united with Osiris, although he could also be joined with Osiris' father, the sun god Re. As time went on, humbler Egyptians came to believe that they too could achieve union with the lord of the dead, who could assess the good and evil that had been done in each person's life and then determine whether he or she deserved punishment or admittance into the realm of bliss. The texts placed in Egyptian graves, collected in the *Book of the Dead,* suggest the standards of ethical and social behavior to which Egyptians were supposed to aspire:

> I have not done evil to mankind. I have not oppressed the members of my family, I have not wrought evil in the place of right and truth. . . . I have not brought forward my name for exaltation to honors. I have not ill-treated servants. . . . I have not defrauded the oppressed one of his property. . . . I have made no man to suffer hunger. . . . I have done no murder. . . . I have not committed fornication. . . . I am pure.[1]

The Age of the Pyramids: The Old Kingdom

Conveniently located near the boundary between Upper and Lower Egypt, Memphis served as the capital for several centuries after their union, a period known as the

Old Kingdom (c. 2575–2130 B.C.) Outside Memphis, Imhotep, vizier to the pharaoh Zoser, erected an edifice that was probably at that time the largest stone monument on earth. Rising to a height of over 200 feet at the edge of the desert, the enormous step-pyramid consisted of a series of benchlike structures of decreasing size and must have resembled a huge stone wedding cake.

It was not long before the pharaohs of the Fourth Dynasty had a smooth facing added to create the pyramids for which the Old Kingdom is famous. The lively Egyptian interest in the afterlife, combined with strikingly materialistic criteria for happiness, made lavish tombs for the pharaohs seem particularly important. Elaborate goods were buried along with the pharaoh to assure him a gracious life in the world beyond, and each pyramid was linked by a processional causeway to a temple constructed for the worship of the pharaoh; adjacent to the pyramid was a building to house the special cedar boat that would carry him on his voyage to the land of the dead. The pyramid served as the core of an entire necropolis, or city of the dead, which included small pyramids for the wives and daughters of the pharaoh and benchlike monuments known today as *mastabas* for the nobility. The largest of the tombs, known as the Great Pyramid, was that of Khufu. Built around 2530 B.C., it stood nearly 500 feet high and covered 13 acres. It contained more than 2 million limestone blocks weighing as much as 30,000 pounds each, adding up to a grand total of nearly 6 million tons of stone.

The early pharaohs probably used the construction of the pyramids as unifying projects that would give their subjects a major investment in their power and divinity; nobody who had labored for years building a pyramid for the pharaoh was likely to be open to the suggestion that the king was an ordinary bureaucrat. Slave labor apparently aided in building the pyramids, but the bulk of the work seems to have been done by nominally free Egyptians pressed into service but paid for their labor, many of them farmers who worked on the pyramids during flood season. When the Nile was flooding, the same high waters that made it impossible to till the soil facilitated the transportation of building materials.

The First Intermediate Period and the Middle and New Kingdoms

By 2180 B.C. the central authority of the earliest dynasties had broken down, for members of the nobility had begun to claim privileges that had formerly belonged only to the pharaoh. The Old Kingdom came to an end, and during the era known as the First Intermediate Period (c. 2130–1938 B.C.) many nomes were ruled not by the pharaoh but by local administrators known as *nomarchs*. This era of anxiety and strife ended with the institution of the Middle Kingdom (1938–c. 1630 B.C.), during which pharaohs ruled from the new capital city of Thebes and advocated the worship of its god Amon-Re, a conflation of Amon, the Theban god, with the sun god Re. The Middle Kingdom was marked by a new sophistication in the visual arts and the development of an intricate bureaucracy.

Around 1630 B.C. the Middle Kingdom collapsed, perhaps because of rivalries within the royal family, giving way to the Second Intermediate Period (c. 1630–c. 1540 B.C.). This era differed from the earlier age of disintegration, for it involved a prolonged foreign occupation. The Hyksos, who seized the government of Egypt in the late eighteenth century, apparently came from western Asia, bringing with them horse-drawn war chariots, new types of weapons, and the composite bow. It is possible that they originally came as peaceful settlers and took power only after the Middle Kingdom disintegrated. They ruled from the delta region for approximately a century until they were driven out. Ahmose I, founder of the New Kingdom (c. 1540–1075 B.C.), pursued the Hyksos into Palestine, an invasion that ushered in the first era of Egyptian imperialism.

The conquests of Ahmose were designed to restore the Egyptians' self-esteem, which had suffered from the experience of foreign domination. Although the Egyptians during the New Kingdom expanded south to Nubia and east to Punt (probably Somalia), the principal thrust was into Palestine and Syria. The empire was a fragile creation. Because the Egyptians forged no imperial structure, their conquests depended fundamentally on the acquiescence of the subject peoples. When rebellion broke out in Syria during the fourteenth century B.C., the empire began to disintegrate. Imperialism also led to difficulties within Egypt itself arising from the introduction of large numbers of slaves who were brought captive to Egypt from foreign lands. This phenomenon led to unemployment and urban growth as people moved to the cities seeking work, and Egyptian cities experienced many social problems.

Two of the most creative rulers of the New Kingdom ignored imperial adventures to focus on domestic concerns. Hatshepsut, who ruled in her own right from approximately 1503 B.C. to 1482 B.C., devoted her energy to elaborate building projects; Akhenaton (1353–1336

B.C.) sought to overturn the country's polytheistic traditions and replace them with the worship of one god.

HATSHEPSUT, MATRIARCH AND BUILDER

Daughter of the renowned conqueror Thutmose I (c. 1525–c. 1512 B.C.) and wife of Thutmose II, her half-brother, Hatshepsut seized the reins of government on her husband's death and maintained her position as ruler of Egypt for 21 years despite bitter opposition from supporters of her stepson, the future Thutmose III. Hatshepsut's memorable projects included the obelisks she erected at the temple of Amon at Karnak and the peaceful, graceful temple she built at her tomb in Deir

This painted limestone head of Hatshepsut shows her wearing the crown of Egypt and a stylized beard symbolizing royalty. [The Metropolitan Museum of Art, Rogers Fund, 1911 (31.3.157)]

el-Bahri. The temple at Deir el-Bahri, nestled against an immense semicircular bay of cliffs, consisted of colonnaded courtyards of decreasing size that blended slowly into the steep banks. The temple walls portray trading expeditions to Punt. The usual boastfulness of Egyptian pharaohs reappears in the temple's inscriptions, which tell how impressed the people of Punt were by the skill and daring the Egyptians had demonstrated in reaching their distant land. The detailed drawings of the inhabitants of Punt and their homes constitute the oldest extant visual images of African tribal life.

Hatshepsut had hoped to be succeeded by her daughter Neferure, but she predeceased Hatshepsut. The queen herself may have died of natural causes, although contemporaries suspected that Thutmose and his supporters had her murdered. After her death, Thutmose had her statues at Deir el-Bahri thrown into a quarry, and his artisans dismantled the shrine she had built for the statue of Amon-Re at Karnak. The new pharaoh immediately resumed the imperialism of his famous grandfather, and in the 30 years of his reign he led more than 15 expeditions to Palestine and Syria.

Akhenaton and the Idea of One God

By 1353 B.C., when Amenhotep IV succeeded to the throne, the power of the pharaoh had come to be threatened by that of the wealthy and prestigious priesthood of Amon. Because Thebes was heavily invested in the worship of Amon, Amenhotep moved his capital to a new city he called Akhetaton (modern Amarna) and decreed the worship of one god alone, the solar deity Aton; he also changed his name to Akhenaton ("[he in whom] Aton is satisfied").

An innovative thinker in a conservative society, Akhenaton has fascinated the modern world. Information about his reforms, however, is scanty. Genuine religious belief may have played a part in his decision to overhaul Egypt's traditional eclectic system of worship, but he was also motivated by a determination to break the power of the priesthood of Amon, which had gathered into its hands a good deal of the land and wealth of Egypt.

Aton was symbolized by a disk with rays extending downward and turning eventually into hands. The new religion seems to have focused on thanksgiving to god for his goodness to humanity and an insistence on truth as the supreme virtue. Aton was probably imagined as a universal god rather than an exclusively Egyptian deity. In the words of the "Hymn to Aton":

O sole god, like whom there is no other!
Thou didst create the world according to thy desire,
Whilst thou were alone.[2]

It is not clear whether the worship of Aton constituted monotheism (belief in one god) or henotheism (the worship of one god while acknowledging the existence of others), but it certainly represented a dramatic departure from the religious diversity the Egyptians had always cultivated.

Other obstacles besides the opposition of the traditional priesthoods and the powerful pluralistic religious traditions of Egypt stood in the way of the new religion's success. While Akhenaton planned to worship Aton, he cautioned his subjects that they could not approach this god directly. Their relations with the deity had to be conducted through an intermediary, the pharaoh himself (who was also divine). It would be sufficient for the pharaoh and his family to worship Aton; official art showed Akhenaton and his wife Nefertiti adoring the sun disk. Everyone else was to revere the pharaoh. Because of the determination of the traditional priesthoods and the bewildered indignation of many other people, Akhenaton's reform did not endure past his death, and the derivation of the name of his son-in-law and successor Tutankhamen (c. 1332–c. 1322 B.C.) from the god Amon pointedly underscored the restoration of Amon to his original primacy. Akhetaton was abandoned, and the pharaohs returned to Thebes.

Egyptian Woman

Family life in Egypt differed in many respects from that in other ancient societies, for Egyptian women had significantly more independence than females in most parts of western Asia. Though females were normally excluded from government, Hatshepsut and the Macedonian Cleopatra were not the only women to rule Egypt. Mer-neith of the First Dynasty may have been pharaoh in her own right, and Nitocris ruled at the end of the Old Kingdom; Sebeknefu was pharaoh at the end of the Middle Kingdom. Women from ordinary families also enjoyed what were, for their times, extraordinary rights. They could own property, retain it during marriage, and bequeath it as they wished. Women might own slaves, witness documents, buy land, and lend money; they were also compelled to pay taxes. Census lists show individuals identified with the names of both fathers and mothers and occasionally mothers alone.

As in other ancient societies, there were limits to a woman's rights. Although Egyptian women served in the work force in a variety of capacities and may even have received equal pay for equal work, they were excluded from many jobs; women were merchants, bakers, and waitresses, but they were not bureaucrats, though an occasional daughter of a scribe may have been allowed into her father's profession. For every woman who served as pharaoh, dozens of men did.

The Art of the Egyptians

The art and architecture of the Egyptians, beautifully preserved in the dry sands of North Africa, are testimony to the affirmation of a view of life and society that remained fundamentally intact for nearly 2,000 years. The focus for most Egyptian art was a religion that sought to provide assurance of a happy afterlife. The Egyptians' determination to assert the fundamental goodness and permanence of life gave their art two of its most memorable characteristics—fundamental continuity over many centuries and an air of serenity and repose.

The vitality of Egyptian art can be traced to its ability to reconcile opposites. Devoted largely to the adornment of tombs for the dead, it conveyed an unabashed delight in life. Hedged in by conventions, it was marked nonetheless by a freshness that depicted nature convincingly. The Greek philosopher Plato admired Egyptian art for what he perceived as its "rationality," and others have cherished its naturalism and spontaneity.

Whereas ordinary artisans and laborers were depicted in paintings, busily assembling the items deceased aristocrats would need for a gracious afterlife, portrayal in the large, imposing sculptures for which Egypt is famous was reserved for the elite. Egyptian statuary draws its power from its monumentality, for it was basically high-relief, not free-standing sculpture. There are no holes in Egyptian statues; they seem to grow naturally out of a solid block, massive and overpowering, from which they never fully free themselves. Painting and sculpture thus show two distinctly different aspects of the Egyptian character, the one playful and spontaneous, the other stately and sober.

Egypt in Decline

Some of the most impressive Egyptian architecture dates from the reign of Rameses II (c. 1290–1224 B.C.), who built on a magnificent scale. The temple he expanded at Karnak, with columns up to 70 feet high and more than

20 feet in diameter, is one of the largest buildings on earth. This edifice bespoke a desperate determination to assure the Egyptians and the world that all was still well in Egypt, but in fact centuries of foreign invasions, dynastic disputes, and religious conflicts had taken a heavy toll on the power and prestige of the pharaohs. During the twelfth century B.C., bands of marauders known as the Sea Peoples came from the north and raided the Mediterranean kingdoms so relentlessly that by 1100 B.C., Egyptian power had been drastically eroded, and the once mighty kingdom of the Hittites in Asia Minor had disappeared from history. Egypt came to be ruled by a series of foreign dynasties. After two centuries in the Persian Empire, it was conquered in 332 B.C. by Alexander the Great. Following his death in 323 B.C., power over Egypt passed into the hands of the Macedonian family of the Ptolemies, who ruled in power until the last of them, Cleopatra VII, was conquered by the Roman Octavian (Augustus) in 31 B.C. For centuries afterward, Egypt remained a territory of the Roman Empire.

THE HITTITES

The same reshuffling of peoples that led to the collapse of Egyptian power also ended the power of the Hittites in Asia Minor. Unlike the Hebrews and other Semitic peoples, the Hittites belonged to the large Indo-European language family whose various members spoke such related tongues as Greek, Persian, Sanskrit, and, later, Latin. The Hittites adopted the Mesopotamian cuneiform script, and much of what we know about them comes from their own careful records. A uniquely Hittite development was the compilation of detailed, dramatic royal annals. Their authors explained the past in secular terms, attributing successes to human efforts and failure to human inadequacies. The Hittites also developed a law code that stressed reparation rather than retribution and that paralleled the code of Hammurabi in the distinctions it made based on the social rank of the parties concerned:

> If anyone breaks a freeman's arm or leg, he pays him twenty shekels of silver and he [the plaintiff] lets him go home.
> If anyone breaks the arm or leg of a male or female slave, he pays ten shekels of silver and he [the plaintiff] lets him go home. . . .
> If a freeman kills a serpent and speaks the name of another [a form

of sorcery], he shall give one pound of silver; if a slave does it, he shall die.[3]

The Hittites may have introduced the horse into western Asia. Facilitating both trade and warfare, the horse significantly increased contact among the various civilizations of the Bronze Age. The Hittites fought frequently with the Egyptians and other peoples, and the Hittite empire was at its height in the fourteenth century B.C. under its ambitious king Suppiluliumas (c. 1375–1335 B.C.), who seized northern Syria from Egypt during the reign of the pharaoh Akhenaton. By 1200 B.C., however, the general migration of peoples that marked the end of the Bronze Age brought invaders to Asia Minor, and the Hittite kingdom collapsed along with other great Bronze Age states.

Little is known for certain about the invaders who raided the Bronze Age kingdoms around the thirteenth century B.C. Identified in Egyptian texts as the Sea Peoples, some of them seem nonetheless to have come by land. Who they were is uncertain. Invaders from the north may have turned some of these peoples into refugees, besieging others in their turn. Greek legends such as that of the Trojan War tell of wanderings and invasions during the late Bronze Age. By 1200 B.C., powerful kingdoms had collapsed throughout the lands around the Mediterranean. Not only the Hittite empire but also the strong monarchy of Egypt and the wealthy Greek kingdoms of Crete and mainland Greece disintegrated. Invasions may only tell part of the story. A serious drought may have caused widespread famine, and natural disasters may have played a part. The island of Santorini (Thera) was the site of several strong volcanic eruptions during this period.

Although the Hittite empire did not survive the transition from the Bronze Age to the Iron Age, it served as a vital cultural transmitter to the West. The Greeks, for example, acquired key elements of their mythology from Hittite sources. The Kumarbi epic shows striking similarities to the Greek account of the origin of the gods as set down in poetry by Hesiod around 700 B.C.. The three generations of the Greek gods—Ouranos, Kronos, and Zeus—correspond perfectly to the three generations of deities in the Hittite cycle, Anu (heaven), Kumarbi (father of the gods), and Teshub (the weather god). Kronos' mutilation of his father Ouranos similarly parallels the emasculation of Anu by his son Kumarbi, and in both cases other deities sprang from this act of treacherous sexual violence.

With the collapse of their capital at Hattusas (modern Bogazköy) around 1190 B.C., the Hittite population scattered. Traces of a Hittite culture can be found in a few cities in the extreme south, in what is now Syria, but these sites were soon taken over by the Assyrians. The heirs of the Hittites in Asia Minor were the Phrygians, whose worship of Cybele, "the Great Mother," became widespread in the Roman world, and the Lydians, who were the probable inventors of coinage.

THE HEBREWS

South of Asia Minor to the west of the Aegean Sea, a variety of cultures sprang up after the fall of the Egyptian and Hittite kingdoms. One of these was the civilization of the seafaring Phoenicians, who traded widely and invented the alphabet that was eventually adapted by the Greeks and subsequently by the Romans. Since the Roman alphabet is the common alphabet of Europe and the Americas, it can be said that the Phoenicians first developed the alphabet in which this book is written. The wares of Phoenician artisans were much admired early in the first millennium B.C., and Phoenician cities such as Byblos and Tyre flourished on the coast of the Mediterranean. To the south of Phoenicia lay the more famous land of Palestine, where the Hebrews built their civilization. The Hebrews never exercised a political or military force comparable to that of the Egyptians or the various powers in the ancient world that conquered Palestine. Because of their enduring religious legacy, however, their influence on world history exceeds that of their conquerors. The doctrine of ethical monotheism that they developed has given a prominent place in history to the numerically small, geographically marginal people of western Asia known successively as Hebrews, Israelites, and Jews.

Hebrew History

Most of our knowledge of the Hebrews comes from their Scriptures, composed over a period extending from around 1250 B.C. to A.D. 100. Combined with archaeological discoveries, these Scriptures—the Christians' Old Testament—are useful in reconstructing their early history.

Sometime between 2000 B.C. and 1700 B.C., northwest-ern Semites settled in Palestine, and the migration from Mesopotamia of Abraham, the traditional founder of the Semitic tribe known as the Hebrews, may have occurred in that period. Tradition also records how the Hebrew tribe of Levi, oppressed by famine, settled in Egypt and was eventually enslaved there. Egyptian records neither confirm nor deny this tradition. It is possible that the Hebrews settled in Egypt during the era of Hyksos domination in the seventeenth century B.C. and were enslaved when the Hyksos were expelled by Ahmose around the middle of the sixteenth century B.C. According to this chronology they might have lived in bondage until the flight from Egypt across the Red Sea known as the Exodus, probably shortly before 1200 B.C., and Rameses II may have been the pharaoh mentioned in the Hebrew tradition.

The Hebrews settled among the Canaanites in Palestine, where their worship of the god they called Yahweh came into conflict with the cults of local fertility deities, the *baalim*. At first the authority of individual "judges" seemed an adequate substitute for formal political organization, but attacks by their neighbors the Philistines prompted the Hebrews to establish a central authority. Around the middle of the eleventh century B.C. they united under Saul, a dynamic military leader. Although Saul was ultimately killed, his son-in-law and successor, David (c. 1000–970 B.C.), decisively defeated the Philistines and made Jerusalem into an impressive capital.

The glories of the tenth century B.C. were substantial. David's son Solomon ruled in an elegant city. This splendor, however, was purchased at a high price. Solomon's temple to Yahweh took 7 years to build, and his palace 13 years. Dividing Israel into districts for the collection of taxes and the imposition of forced labor for the building projects, Solomon destroyed much regional independence. Massive disaffection resulted, and when Solomon died, his kingdom split in two. In the north, Israel set up its capital at Samaria; Jerusalem remained the capital of Judah in the south.

The divided kingdoms had little capacity to resist attack. Sargon II of Assyria destroyed Samaria in 722 B.C. and deported the leaders of the kingdom of Israel, and the Mesopotamian monarch Nebuchadnezzar overran the kingdom of Judah in 597 B.C. and destroyed the temple at Jerusalem in 586 B.C. The leaders of Judah were carried off to exile in Babylon. Only when the Persian Cyrus the Great conquered Mesopotamia nearly 50 years later were the exiles from Judah permitted to return home and the so-called "Babylonian captivity" ended. Palestine then became a subject state in the Persian Empire.

The Torah and the Prophets

The Hebrews' religion formed part of an imposing framework that was not only spiritual but also intellectual. No straightforward ancient account details the evolution of this system. The Hebrew Bible represents a compilation of poetry, history, prayer, folk wisdom, and theology amassed over a millennium and recorded by many different hands. Hebrew religious belief developed slowly from the earliest days, when Yahweh was perceived as self-interested and capricious, to the era of the prophets, who asserted Yahweh's commitment to righteousness and truth. The early Yahweh, god of the desert nomads, was worshiped with animal sacrifice. In the first stages of the Hebrews' religious development, Yahweh competed for attention with a variety of foreign deities whose existence was freely admitted and on whom the Hebrews made war when they attacked the worshipers of these gods. The Hebrews, in other words, developed their distinctive creed in a long tradition that led from the veneration of many gods (polytheism) through the worship of a single deity (monolatry or henotheism) to the belief that only one god existed (monotheism).

The Hebrew Bible recounts the evolution of the relationship between Yahweh and his chosen people. Yahweh had signaled his choice first by the covenant (pact) he made with Abraham because of Abraham's willingness to sacrifice his only son, Isaac. This compelling tale is emblematic of the commitment Yahweh demanded of his worshipers. Abraham, it was written in the Book of Genesis, consented to sacrifice his son because God had commanded it. But when Abraham had picked up the knife to kill Isaac, then God was convinced of his piety and provided a ram to be slaughtered in Isaac's place, proclaiming,

> because you have done this, and have not withheld your son, your only son, I will indeed bless you, and I will multiply your descendants as the stars of heaven and as the sand which is on the seashore. And your descendants shall possess the gate of their enemies, and by your descendants shall all the nations of the earth bless themselves, because you have obeyed my voice.[4]

God later renewed this covenant with Moses. Because of their profound sense of covenant, history for the Hebrews was the story of their relationship with Yahweh as it unfolded through the centuries, and they construed the varying course of their fortunes as a series of tests, punishments, and rewards devised by their god.

The Hebrews' belief in the omnipotence of Yahweh led them to perceive their experiences as products of Yahweh's response to their behavior. The right to interpret the mind of Yahweh was not confined to a priestly elite; individuals were encouraged to make their own determinations of Yahweh's will. Judaism was therefore not an easy faith, and while it offered hope of the protection and nurture of a personal God, it also demanded a great deal—faithfulness to ritual prescriptions, ethical behavior, and vigilance in ascertaining the will of Yahweh. The uniqueness of this community that identified itself as God's chosen people, moreover, had to be preserved by the careful observance of religious traditions and dietary restrictions that in later centuries, when the Jews were scattered around the world, frequently had the effect of distancing them from their neighbors.

The first five books of the Hebrew Bible, known as the Torah, set forth the religious and moral requirements of Judaism. Although the Hebrews regarded themselves as the chosen people, they insisted on a uniform moral standard in dealing with Jews and non-Jews alike. The Torah was committed to the elimination of class distinctions and hence contrasts sharply with the legislation of Hammurabi, which enshrined social inequalities in the Babylonian world view. As in other civilizations of the same time, however, important distinctions remained between the two sexes among the Hebrews, and some people were slaves. The Torah included detailed instructions for the preparation and consumption of food and drink. These dietary restrictions continue to be observed by many Jews throughout the world.

Because the Hebrews were surrounded by other peoples who worshiped differently, the purity of their observances was constantly challenged. The prophets arose to meet this challenge. Passionate, eloquent, volatile, and generally male, they alternately threatened death and destruction if Yahweh's will was not followed and promised God's aid and comfort if it was. They decried the evils around them, from political corruption to social decadence and ritual laxity. One of the first prophets was the shepherd Amos, who denounced all who "turn justice to wormwood, and cast down righteousness to the earth" (Amos 5:7). Jeremiah inveighed relentlessly against the emptiness and hypocrisy of the religious observance he saw around him and the Hebrews' "idolatry"—literally, the worship of idols, the "graven images" whose making is prohibited in the second of the ten commandments Moses announced from Mount Sinai. The fall of Israel to Assyria appeared to offer confirmation that Yahweh was displeased with his people, and the prophets continued their efforts during the Babylonian captivity.

The Hebrews had no doubt that Yahweh was male. He had no consort, however, and had not created the universe through sexual interaction. Rather, he was perceived as a transcendent god—above and beyond the natural universe rather than an element of it. The scriptural injunction against graven images, moreover, discouraged speculation about his physical appearance (although a survival of early thinking appears in a number of references in the Hebrew scriptures to the bodily attributes of God, such as the famous description in Daniel 7:9 of an aged man with white hair). In this transcendence lay much of the Hebrews' unique contribution to religious thought and their important legacy to Christianity and Islam.

Women in Hebrew Society

Before Yahweh became the sole god of the Hebrews, they had cultivated a variety of divinities of both sexes, worshiping them in some instances in a highly emotional and even sensual style. The cult of the fertility couple Baal and Asherah was associated with impassioned female devotees. By forbidding diversity of ritual and religion, the cult of Yahweh effectively excluded women from the priesthood.

The role of frequent warfare and increasingly strong central government in lowering the status of women is evident in Hebrew society. In the early nomadic period, Hebrew men and women were on a more equal footing than was the case when the Hebrew tribes became a formal and monarchic state. The Book of Judges tells how Deborah, a prophet and judge, inspired Barak to rally his troops and resist the Canaanites and prophesied that Sisera, the Canaanite leader, would be delivered into the hands of a woman; in the event, he was killed by the bravery and cleverness of another Hebrew woman, Jael. Other women prophets are also mentioned in these early centuries, and women apparently played an active role in religious observances.

The construction of the temple and the palace in the tenth century B.C. seems to have differentiated roles for males and females in Hebrew society to the detriment of women. The inner temple was restricted to male priests, and women were precluded from entering, as were children, foreigners, the insane, and slaves. When the social and religious centers known as synagogues developed after the Babylonian exile, women, though technically allowed to participate in their activities, were frequently barred from doing so. Women were not allowed to carry their babies outside the home on the Sabbath and were considered too impure to enter the synagogue on numerous days of the year because of periods of ritual uncleanliness connected with menstruation and childbirth.

The account of the creation of the two sexes in the biblical book of Genesis offered a basis for patriarchal rule. Genesis 1:27–29 states that God created male and female at the same time, but the version in Genesis 2:18–25 tells of God's fashioning Eve out of Adam's rib, as an afterthought to improve his life. Later, when Eve had succumbed to the lure of the serpent and Adam to the temptation of Eve, Yahweh proclaimed that henceforth wives would be subordinate to their husbands. Thus Genesis traces the rule of male over female to the first generation of humans, portraying it as a necessary punishment for Eve's disobedience to Yahweh.

JERUSALEM: THE HOLY CITY

Perched dramatically on the hills north of the Negev desert, Jerusalem has been regarded for centuries as sacred by the practitioners of Judaism, Christianity, and Islam. Originally sacred to the Semitic god Shalem, from whom it got its name, it was captured from the Jebusites, a local tribe, around the year 1000 B.C. by David. David made the city not only his capital but also a national shrine and set up in it the Ark of the Covenant, the sacred wooden chest overlaid with gold that the Hebrews cherished as the symbol of their relationship with God. David's successor, Solomon, enlarged the city and constructed a lavish palace for himself as well as an enormous temple to house the Ark of the Covenant. Solomon's building projects reflected not only his political power but also his economic resources. Vast amounts of money and materials from many nations went into the palace and temple, and innumerable artisans were imported for the projects.

A massive rectangular building of squared stones and cedar beams, the temple was 48 feet wide, 110 feet long, and over 50 feet high. In the sanctuary stood the ark, a large cube paneled with richly carved cedar. The ark was surmounted by two cherubim, fantastic composite creatures having human heads, the bodies of lions, and the wings of birds; each was 15 feet high, constructed of olive wood overlaid with gold. The delicate and ornate appointments of the temple reflected Assyrian, Egyptian, Palestinian, and Syrian influences.

Reconstruction of the temple in Jerusalem as it appeared in Herod's day (A.D. **41–44**). [Drawing from *In the Shadow of the Temple* by Meir Ben-Dov, translation by Ina Friedman. Copyright © 1982 by Keter Publishing House Jerusalem, Ltd.; English translation © 1985 by Keter Publishing Jerusalem, Ltd. Reprinted by permission of HarperCollins Publishers.]

The cosmopolitanism of Solomon's building projects was evident not only in their art and architecture but also in the scale on which the enterprises were undertaken. Solomon's palace, for example, had to be large enough to accommodate the many wives and concubines he acquired through political alliances. Although the figure given in 1 Kings of 700 wives and 300 concubines is doubtless an exaggeration, Solomon certainly bolstered his stature with numerous foreign consorts, including the daughter of an Egyptian pharaoh.

Jerusalem functioned as an important market, where farmers brought their surpluses to exchange for the many artifacts produced in the city (although local artisans were sometimes unable to compete successfully with the highly skilled labor imported by the kings). The gates to the city became focal points of both economic and social life, and names such as the Pottery Gate, the Fish Gate, and the Sheep Gate reveal the kind of exchange that went on at each. Some of Jerusalem's affluent citizens profited from both city and country life in a more direct way, holding important jobs in the court bureaucracy while serving as absentee landlords of country estates.

The Jewish exiles pined for Jerusalem and its temple during the Babylonian captivity. From the Babylon of Nebuchadnezzar to the death camps of Adolf Hitler, the religion that evolved among the Hebrews during the first millennium before Christ sustained its practitioners through centuries of dispersion and persecution. Judaism also formed the basis for two other enormously influential world religions, Christianity and Islam.

THE ASSYRIANS

The Hebrews were not alone among ancient peoples in fearing the warlike Assyrians. A Semitic people related to the Amorites, the Assyrians experienced their most glorious period in history in the eighth and seventh centuries B.C. Their iron weapons were put to particularly good advantage by their ruler Tiglath-pileser III (c. 745–727 B.C.), who developed a disciplined army made up of both militia and professional soldiers and was able to cross even the most challenging terrain with speed, conquering the Syrian stronghold of Damascus and absorbing Babylon into the Assyrian empire. After the defeat of Israel, the northern kingdom became a vassal state of the Assyrians. In time the Assyrians replaced the vassal system of dependent kingdoms with imperial provinces whose governors were charged with the collection of taxes. This Assyrian innovation anticipated the later administration of the Persian empire, as did the construction of roads that linked Assyria and its subject territories.

After Tiglath-pileser's death the Assyrians continued their march down the Mediterranean coast, capturing Tyre and Sidon. Even Egypt fell to them, though it rebelled in the reign of Ashurbanipal (669–630 B.C.) Ashurbanipal was a learned man who had studied mathematics and astronomy and boasted of his ability to write ancient Sumerian. However, he faced major revolts. The Babylonians had been restive for some time, and with the conquest of Egypt the Assyrians had expanded their frontiers beyond the point at which they could effectively be defended. Finally, in 612 B.C. the new kingdoms of the Medes and the Chaldeans joined with the Scythians to bring the Assyrian empire to a violent end.

The Assyrians struck terror in their enemies—so much so that several Hebrew prophets regarded them as the instrument of God for punishing his wayward people. Evidence from Assyria confirms that the Assyrians were a cruel people. Annals inscribed on palace walls report the dismemberment, boiling, impaling, and flaying of their enemies while still alive, and Assyrian law codes reveal that women who had displeased their husbands could be punished by having their noses, ears, or breasts torn off.

Assyrian Culture

The culture, history, and ideology of the Assyrian ruling class can perhaps best be understood through the expensive capital cities erected by successive kings. The many slaves won on the battlefield were used in the construction of these cities. For 12 years some 10,000 captives worked to raise the platform for the great buildings of Nineveh, whose double walls and moats encircled the city for a distance of 8 miles. The guests at the ten-day party Ashurnasirpal held to celebrate the completion of his palace at Calah (modern Nimrud) in 879 B.C. included 50,000 workers who had been transported from conquered territories to help assemble it. Assyrian palaces contained thousands of documents, many of them dealing with history and administration. Copies of older Babylonian records account for a good number of tablets as well. Ashurbanipal's scribes at Nineveh copied the religious and literary texts of Sumer and Babylon, compiled dictionaries, and made translations into Assyrian. The preservation of numerous Akkadian and Sumerian texts is due to Ashurbanipal's reverence for literary tradition.

Much of the artwork that adorned Assyrian palaces remains in fairly good condition. Assyrian art was probably the work of artisans imported from subject territories. Assyrian palaces were noteworthy chiefly for their glazed tiles and for a style of relief sculpture that told a chilling story of Assyrian conquest. Although these reliefs served the propagandistic purpose of glorifying the exploits of Assyrian warriors, they were also remarkably naturalistic, particularly in their portrayal of animals. Dying lions, sometimes tearing at the arrows in their flesh, are particularly prominent in hunting scenes.

The stately Assyrian capitals reveal much about the civilization that gave them birth. Characterized by vigor and determination, Assyrian civilization mobilized the skills of its subject peoples and combined a sensitivity to nature with extraordinary brutality.

Historians have often compared Assyria to Rome. Like the Romans, the Assyrians of early times developed the military skills necessary to hold their own against the incursion of hill tribes and eventually used those abilities to forge an irresistible military machine. The Assyrian absorption and preservation of Babylonian culture in many ways foreshadowed the Roman assimilation of Greece, whose culture the Romans were largely responsible for transmitting to future civilizations.

THE PERSIANS

The collapse of the Assyrian empire in 612 B.C. was in part the work of peoples who inhabited ancient Per-

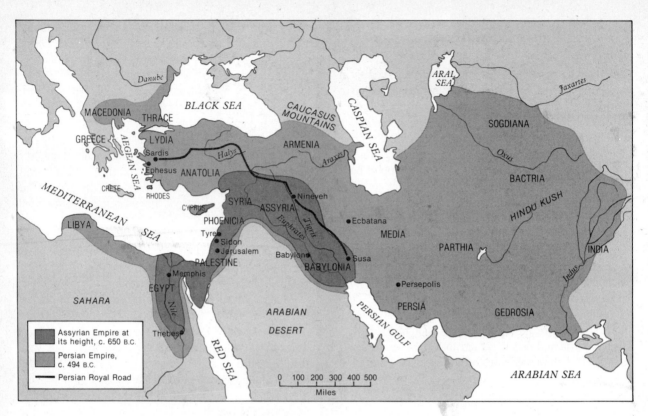

1.2 The Empires of Assyria and Persia

sia (modern Iran). Toward the beginning of the Iron Age, Persia was invaded by Indo-European nomadic tribes who brought with them horses, which enabled them to overrun the horseless inhabitants. These tribes included the Medes and the Persians, both of whom were related to the Aryans who had invaded India some centuries before. Joining forces with the Chaldeans and with the Scythians, who had been driven from their homeland in eastern Asia, the Medes helped to bring about the end of Assyrian power and the rise of the Chaldean or New Babylonian empire, whose most famous ruler, Nebuchadnezzar (604–562 B.C.), figures prominently in the Hebrew Bible. Two revolts in Jerusalem finally led to Nebuchadnezzar's destruction of the Hebrew temple in 586 B.C., when he carried off many of the remaining inhabitants to Babylon. Determined to evoke the memories of a magnificent and romantic past, Nebuchadnezzar decked out the city of Babylon with imposing temples and hanging (roof) gardens planted on terraces.

Cyrus the Great

During the first half of the sixth century B.C., the Medes forged an immense empire that stretched from central Asia Minor to the Indian frontier. Around 550 B.C., however, one of the early organizers of the Achaemenid dynasty of Persia, Cyrus the Great, conquered Media, the first step in the foundation of a sizable empire for the Persians. Media became the first of many satrapies (provinces) of the Persian Empire. Cyrus went on to annex the wealthy kingdom of Lydia in western Asia Minor after defeating its king Croesus in 546 B.C., and within a few years he had also conquered the Greek cities on the coast of Asia Minor, giving him possession of many bustling ports. In 539 B.C., Babylon also fell before his army.

A talented diplomat as well as a skillful general, Cyrus made a point of not only tolerating but in fact encouraging religious and cultural diversity in his empire. He respected the worship of Marduk in Babylon and urged the Hebrews in Babylon to return to their homes and rebuild their temple. When Babylon finally fell into Cyrus' hands, a huge Indo-European state was created. The era of the powerful Semitic monarchies was over. The Persian Empire under the Achaemenids would extend at one time from northern Greece to Afghanistan and from the Caucasus to the Sudan. It endured until its conquest by Alexander the Great more than 200 years later.

A difficult period for the Persians followed Cyrus' death. His son and successor, Cambyses, had to contend with considerable unrest, and a period of anarchy followed Cambyses' death until the accession of the next king, Darius. The first Persian king to engage in warfare with the mainland Greeks, Darius came to the throne around 522 B.C. He was a capable and energetic administrator, and under his leadership the Persians adopted standardized weights and measures, gold and silver coins, a calendar derived from that of the Egyptians, a postal service, and a law code based on Mesopotamian principles.

Zoroastrianism and Mithraism

Darius also gave his support to Zoroastrianism, the most celebrated of the Persian religions. The belief system established by the prophet Zoroaster was dualistic, that is, it perceived life in terms of the conflict between two antagonistic principles. Zoroastrianism represents an early attempt to address one of the most vexing questions that trouble a religion based on a just god, namely, the origins of evil. Considerable mystery surrounds the life of Zoroaster (*Zarathustra* in Persian). Some traditions place him as early as the end of the second millennium, others as late as the fifth century B.C. He apparently lived in the eastern reaches of Persia, not far from India, and his belief in the need to wage war on evil spirits owes much to Indian thought.

Zoroaster believed that Ahura Mazda, the founder of the universe, communicated directly with him through angels, and the various poetic sayings of Zoroaster were cast as angelic utterings. He heartened his followers by preaching of a god who cared intensely for each individual and encouraged all people to believe that they had a task to fulfill in the world. Zoroaster characterized the universe as an ongoing struggle between good, represented by Ahura Mazda, and evil, embodied by Ahriman, Ahura Mazda's antagonist in the realm of darkness. The evil spirits known as Daevas who aided Ahriman probably represented Zoroaster's view of the traditional polytheistic gods, although Zoroaster also imagined some of the old gods, such as Mithras, fighting on the side of Ahura Mazda.

Zoroaster viewed everything on earth—human, plant, and animal life and even minerals—as manifestations of the continuing struggle between Ahura Mazda and Ahriman. A champion of the settled ways that were replacing predatory nomadism, Zoroaster cast farmers and cattle on the side of Ahura Mazda and robbers who disturbed their peace as Ahriman's agents. Even some poisonous plants were viewed as abettors of Ahriman. In keeping with this dualistic vision, Zoroastrianism preached a judgment after death that took place in two stages. First, the souls of good individuals would cross the bridge that led to paradise as they died, while those of the wicked would find the bridge shrinking beneath them and tumble into the abyss of hell. A second judgment would take place when a huge fire produced a massive purification wherein the good would rise to immortality and the wicked sizzle in the flames. Zoroaster encouraged each person to seek righteousness and salvation by studying his sayings and performing good works. The notion that the righteous would be rewarded and the wicked punished offered hope to those whose daily life compelled them to suffer while observing the prosperity of people they perceived as unworthy.

The religion Zoroaster preached was universal, open to all people who chose Ahura Mazda over Ahriman. Although Zoroastrianism did not spread beyond Persia, Mithras, whom Zoroaster viewed as an ally of Ahura Mazda, had followers in the later Roman Empire, where he was particularly popular with soldiers. Identified with the sun, Mithras became something of a patron deity of the Roman army. Mithraism and Christianity were parallel in several ways. Their beliefs involved a miraculous birth attended by shepherds, and Mithraism celebrated the birthday of the sun on December 25. Both religions used holy water and espoused the concepts of heaven and hell and of atonement, and both preached the conflict between good and evil and the need for righteous conduct. Christianity, however, was ethically pacifist in the beginning, whereas Mithraism was militant and excluded women.

Although Zoroaster's religion did not spread outside Persia, it nonetheless represents one of the most important Persian contributions to Western thought. Zoroaster's notion of a fiery judgment day appears in late Hebrew thought and in both Christian and Muslim teachings. The concept of angels and the idea of Satan also owe much to his doctrine. Above all, the dualism that Zoroastrianism preached and the ethical basis on which it was founded played important roles in shaping Western religious thought.

Life and Government in the Empire

The Persian Empire at its height was both wealthy and cosmopolitan. Foreign artisans worked with materials that came from Greece, Lebanon, and India to decorate the royal palaces at Susa and Persepolis. The Persians traded widely, using their gold coin, the daric. Many of the people under their control did not speak their language, and the monuments on the impressive Royal Road were accompanied by inscriptions in Babylonian and Elamite as well as Persian. Some 1,600 miles long, the Royal Road extended from Susa in western Persia to Sardis, near the Aegean port of Ephesus. It took caravans three months to travel this road, although royal couriers, using fresh horses provided at the 111 post stations along the route, could make the trip in a week.

For all the power of their ruler, the "King of Kings," the Persian view of their monarchy differed from that of the Assyrians. The king was not an instrument of fear but rather a righteous leader, elected by all the gods. The empire was in general ruled with efficiency, justice, and tolerance. It was so large that it had to be divided into satrapies, each of which was administered by a governor (or satrap), aided by a military force under a separate commander. The governors, who were Median or Persian nobles, were prevented from exercising inordinate power by the presence of both military officials and royal agents and spies. From the satraps the king was primarily interested in receiving appropriate tribute and recruits for the military. If those demands were fulfilled, the governors enjoyed a good deal of autonomy.

Darius' successors maintained the Persian Empire until it was conquered by Alexander the Great between 334 and 326 B.C. The arrival of Alexander and his troops thrust Europe and Asia into the long period of mutual influence that has lasted, despite interruptions, to our own times.

SUMMARY

The inhabitants of the world's first cities grappled with many of the same problems that confront us today. In western Asia and Egypt, people first began to explore the most efficient structures for mutual cooperation and sustenance, to ask questions about the meaning of life, and to suggest possible answers. From the pyramids rising out of the Egyptian desert to the poignant *Epic of Gilgamesh* to the struggle of the Hebrews to maintain their identity by the waters of Babylon, the peoples of the ancient Middle East demonstrated great resourcefulness in responding to challenge. Much of their energies also went into the subjugation of others. The invention of writing enables us to know a great deal about their societies. When this invention was transmitted from the Phoenicians to the Greeks around the eighth century B.C., it transformed the world yet again and ushered in the classical civilizations of Greece and later Rome.

Notes

1. E. A. Wallis Budge, trans., *The Book of the Dead According to the Theban Recension,* in *Egyptian Literature,* ed. E. Wilson (London: Colonial Press, 1901), passim.
2. In J. B. Pritchard, ed. *Ancient Near Eastern Texts Relating to the Old Testament,* trans. J. Wilson (Princeton: Princeton University Press, 1969), p. 370.
3. O. R. Gurney, *The Hittites* (Harmondsworth, England: Penguin Books, 1954), p. 96.
4. From the Book of Genesis, 22: 15–18 (Revised Standard Version).

Suggestions for Further Reading

Baron, S. W., ed. *A Social and Religious History of the Jews,* 2nd ed., 18 vols. New York: Columbia University Press, 1952–1983.

The Book of J, trans. D. Rosenberg; interpreted by H. Bloom. New York: Grove Weidenfeld, 1990.

Cameron, A., and Kuhrt, A., eds. *Images of Women in Antiquity.* Detroit: Wayne State University Press, 1983.

Cook, J. M. *The Persian Empire.* New York: Schocken Books, 1983.

Frankfort, H. *The Art and Architecture of the Ancient Orient.* Harmondsworth, England: Penguin Books, 1970.

———, et al. *The Intellectual Adventure of Ancient Man: An Essay on Speculative Thought in the Ancient Near East.* Chicago: University of Chicago Press, 1977.

Gardiner, A. H. *Egypt of the Pharaohs: An Introduction.* London: Oxford University Press, 1978.

Knapp, A. B. *The History and Culture of Ancient Western Asia and Egypt.* Chicago: Dorsey Press, 1988.

Lerner, G. *The Creation of Patriarchy.* New York: Oxford University Press, 1986.

Nagle, D. B. *The Ancient World: A Social and Cultural History.* Englewood Cliffs, N.J.: Prentice-Hall, 1979.

Negev, A., ed. *The Archaeological Encyclopedia of the Holy Land,* rev. ed. Nashville, Tenn.: Nelson, 1986.

Neugebauer, O. *The Exact Sciences in Antiquity,* 2nd ed. New York: Harper, 1962.

Oppenheim, A. L. *Ancient Mesopotamia: Portrait of a Dead Civilization.* Chicago: University of Chicago Press, 1977.

Silver, M. *Prophets and Markets: The Political Economy of Ancient Israel.* Boston: Kluwer-Nijhoff, 1983.

Zaehner, R. C. *The Dawn and Twilight of Zoroastrianism.* New York: Putnam, 1961.

THE MAKINGS OF GREEK CIVILIZATION

As elsewhere in the ancient world, geography played an important role in shaping the course history would take in Greece for the prevalence of mountain ranges and the vast expanse of the Aegean Sea discouraged the development of a unified Greek nation. Rather, ancient Greece for most of its history consisted of a very large number of independent city-states. Although a great deal of attention has always been focused on the city-state of Athens, the achievements of other city-states were also considerable. Athens did not come into prominence until the fifth century B.C., and many distinguished Greek thinkers and artists came from elsewhere. The little town of Abdera in northern Greece, for example, produced the philosopher Protagoras, who was famous for proclaiming that "each person is the measure of all things." Protagoras angered his contemporaries by questioning the existence of the gods, but his daring assertion about the centrality of human judgment reflected something fundamental about the Greek mentality. A profoundly religious people, the Greeks nonetheless gave full play to their fascination with the human psyche and the natural world.

The Greeks built the magnificent temples that still ring the Mediterranean and devised the secular state that served as a prototype for modern government. The origins of the universe, the difficulty of obtaining certain knowledge, the ideal proportion in all things, the relationship between the human and the divine, the best kind of political community—all this the Greeks explored in each generation. The questions they posed have influenced the intellectual and political agenda for Western civilization down to our own time.

MINOANS AND MYCENAEANS

Historians are divided about what to make of the engaging stories later Greeks told about their early history. Few written records have survived from Bronze Age Greece, but the desire to ground myth in history prompted important archaeological expeditions in the nineteenth and early twentieth centuries that laid the groundwork for reconstructing the Bronze Age civilization that began in Greece around 2000 B.C.

In 1863 the German businessman Heinrich Schliemann (1822–1890) began excavating in northwestern Turkey in the hopes of finding the Troy about which he had heard since childhood. Legend told how King Agamemnon of Mycenae in mainland Greece had mounted a large expedition against the Trojans to recover his sister-in-law Helen, who had been carried off by Paris, the son of the Trojans' king Priam. Although Schliemann was unable positively to identify Priam's city, he found many interesting layers of habitation at a site he confidently claimed to be Troy. He also discovered impressive remains at Mycenae on the Greek mainland that revealed a wealthy and warlike civilization that has

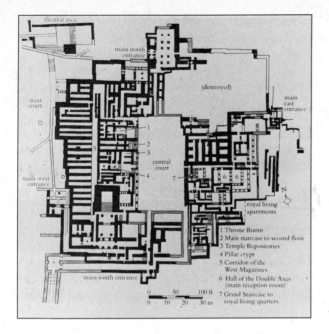

Plan of the palace at Knossos, c. 1600–1400 B.C. The building surrounded a central courtyard, with the public and religious rooms to the west and royal living quarters to the east. [After S. Marinatos, *Kreta und das Mykenische Hellas*, Hirmer Verlag, Munich. 1959, fig. 4]

come to be known as Mycenaean. Schliemann's enthusiasm inspired many subsequent researchers, including British archaeologist Sir Arthur Evans (1851–1941). Evans uncovered an elaborate palace at Knossos on Crete that he identified with the legend of King Minos, who the Greeks believed had built a labyrinth to house the Minotaur, a creature his wife had produced by a union with a bull. Evans also found a script he labeled Linear B that was deciphered in 1952 by Michael Ventris and identified as an early form of Greek, leading historians to conclude that at least in the later period of their history the inhabitants of Knossos were ruled by Greeks.

The combination of written and archaeological remains makes plain that the Minoans, as we call the inhabitants of Bronze Age Crete, farmed and raised cattle, and they must have traded widely. The Linear B tablets show that the government played a major role in the economy of Bronze Age Greece, and large numbers of both men and women served in the labor force. The Minoans had a highly developed culture and a flair for style, exhibited, for example, in the long flounced skirts, high heels, scanty vests, and stylized ringlets that

marked women's fashions. Their exuberant frescoes demonstrate a marked Egyptian influence, and they show as well a comfortable interaction between the two sexes and a participation of females in public life that contrasts with most later Greek society.

Probably during the fifteenth century B.C., Knossos was captured by mainland Greeks. The economy of mainland Greek society was similar to that of Crete. In both places, labor was highly specialized, though Mycenaean artifacts generally lack the artistry of Minoan products. As the Iron Age began around 1100 B.C., monarchy, the dominant form of government in Bronze

In contrast to some of the rigid and grandiose Mesopotamian and Egyptian statues, those of the Minoans were small and animated. This priestess holds snakes, possibly reflecting Minoan religious rituals. [Hirmer Fotoarchiv, Munich]

Age Greece, was replaced by oligarchy (government by an aristocratic body, literally "the rule of the few"). The predominance of kings and aristocrats is confirmed by the aristocratic character of Mycenaean warfare, which relied heavily on chariots.

THE HOMERIC AGE

Invasions, famines, floods, volcanic eruptions, and tidal waves have all been put forward by historians as possible explanations for the collapse of Bronze Age civilization throughout the eastern Mediterranean around 1150 B.C. About the same time as the collapse of the Hittite and Egyptian empires, the Iron Age began in Greece with a period known as the Greek Dark Age (c. 1100–800 B.C.) Some evidence about life in early Greece survives in the epic poems attributed to Homer. Though the stories they tell of the Trojan War and the wanderings of Odysseus during the years that followed may not reflect actual historical events, the *Iliad* and the *Odyssey* are rich in evidence about the customs and values of the late Bronze Age and the early Iron Age. Composed in more or less final form around 700 B.C., these poems represented the culmination of a long oral tradition. The name Homer has been given to the guiding intelligence that shaped the poems into the form in which they now survive, but there is no way to know how many people made up the personage we call Homer. Nor is it always possible to be certain when the poet is describing life in the Bronze Age—as he maintained—and when he is depicting a world closer to his own day.

Like Gilgamesh, the Achilles of Homer's *Iliad* is a hero who, having led a rewarding life, is forced by misfortune to confront the central questions of human existence. His faith in appearances is undermined when his commander-in-chief, Agamemnon, insults him and takes away his war prize—a female captive—in front of the entire community. When his closest friend, Patroclus, is killed in battle while wearing Achilles' armor, Achilles is able to put Agememnon's insult to him in perspective, but only because he is overcome with grief at the loss of his soul mate. Achilles' mourning for Patroclus is reminiscent of the mourning of Gilgamesh for Enkidu. Achilles seeks to purge his agony by killing his friend's slayer—Hector, the crown prince of Troy. Achilles does this knowing that he is fated to die soon after Hector, and

so the funeral of Hector, with which the poem closes, also presages the death of Achilles. A tireless hero who has done and learned much, Achilles too is mortal.

The *Odyssey* was probably composed about half a century after the *Iliad*. A tale of wanderings in unsettled times, the poem is also one of self-discovery. Odysseus, the hero, turns the seeming misfortune of losing his way on the journey home from Troy into an occasion to develop himself by responding to the crises that challenge his resourcefulness. At the same time the *Odyssey* reflects the political disintegration of the late Bronze Age as the kingship of Odysseus' native island of Ithaca hangs in the balance during his absence. After enjoying relationships with an assortment of mortal and divine females—the witch Circe, the sea nymph Calypso, the princess Nausicaa—Odysseus returns to Ithaca with the help of the goddess Athena. There he defeats the unmannerly suitors whom he finds encamped in his palace courting his wife.

The *Odyssey* is less aristocratic in its ethos than the *Iliad*. The one common person who figures in the *Iliad* is Thersites, a soldier who has dared to insult Agamemnon. Thersites is described as comically ugly, and when Odysseus beats him, the army laughs at his tears. In the *Odyssey* another common Greek, Eumaeus, plays an important role in helping Odysseus regain his rightful place on the throne of Ithaca. Faithful throughout the years of Odysseus' absence, Eumaeus is portrayed as noble in character despite his humble birth. The differences in Homer's treatment of these two figures suggests the increasing importance of nonaristocratic classes in late-eighth-century Greek society.

The Homeric poems give us our first glimpse of the Greeks' view of divinity. Vain, vengeful, and volatile, Greek deities were essentially self-indulgent aristocrats who enjoyed the privilege of immortality. Their society was patriarchal, and the marriage of the chief god, Zeus, to Hera may reflect the absorption of an early people who worshiped an earth goddess by invaders who venerated a sky god. Male gods were identified in terms of different spheres of interest. Poseidon engineered sea storms and earthquakes, Ares incited war, and Hermes was a messenger. Female deities, by contrast, were defined largely in terms of their sexuality. Hera was a nagging wife, the intellectual (and warlike) Athena and the athletic Artemis were virgins, Aphrodite was associated with love and sex, Demeter devoted herself to fertility and motherhood, and Hestia was an asexual homebody attached to the family hearth.

Inevitably, deities of this sort were better at inspiring

awe than at offering comfort, but some of the Olympians were conceived as nurturing; devotees of the cult of Demeter were initiated into a religion that offered myths of rebirth, and in time Dionysus (Bacchus) was admitted to the Olympian pantheon, bringing with him a religion whose practitioners reportedly enjoyed ecstatic frenzies. Some foreign cults, moreover, such as that of the loving Isis, later acquired large followings in Greece, and by the third century B.C. many Greeks had come to think of religion primarily in terms of solace.

THE DEVELOPMENT OF THE GREEK POLIS

The Greek Dark Age (c. 1100–800 B.C.) was a time of material and cultural poverty during which the art of writing was apparently lost. Monarchy gave way to oligarchy, but with the revival of the economy during the eighth century B.C., people began to question the merit of entrusting power to a handful of men from established families. Assemblies of free men dated from a very early time in Greece, and involvement of the populace in questions of justice is probably reflected in a passage in Homer's *Iliad* written around this time. In describing the city that the blacksmith god Hephaestus portrayed on Achilles' shield, Homer tells how

> The people were assembled in the market place, where a quarrel had arisen, and two men were disputing over the blood price for a man who had been killed. One man promised full restitution in a public statement, but the other refused and would accept nothing.
> Both then made for an arbitrator, to have a decision; and people were speaking up on either side, to help both men.
> But the heralds kept the people in hand, as meanwhile the elders were in session on benches of polished stone. . . .[1]

Population began to increase at this time, and the resulting land shortage led some people into commerce. Trade in turn was facilitated by improvements in navigational instruments and by the adoption of coinage. Inevitably, the more successful merchants challenged the monopoly on political power exercised by the landed aristocracy.

Both land hunger and class conflict played a role in the decisions of many Greek states to establish colonies throughout the Mediterranean world. Between 750 B.C.

and 550 B.C., thousands of colonists were sent eastward to the northern Aegean and the Black Sea and westward to Sicily, southern Italy, France, Spain, and North Africa. The challenge of forming stable, prosperous states in unfamiliar surroundings led the colonists to experiment with new forms of government in the colonies.

New developments in military technology also undermined the position of the hereditary aristocracy. The prominence first of chariot warfare and then of cavalry warfare had reinforced the notion that wealthier people were of greater value to the state, and political power remained concentrated in the hands of those who could afford a horse. Shortly after 700 B.C., however, the hoplite, a heavily armed infantry soldier, replaced the horseman as the principal unit of the Greek military. Organized into a tightly disciplined formation known as the phalanx, hoplites carried shields, spears, and short daggers. The political consequences of this military innovation were enormous, since it opened warfare to a vastly larger number of people. The poor, however, remained excluded, since only men who could afford a spear and a shield could participate, and these were costly.

The outgrowth of these developments was the distinctively Greek sociopolitical institution known as the *polis,* a city-state usually composed of well under 100,000 inhabitants. The polis differed from the city-states of Mesopotamia and the nomes of early Egypt in the energy many citizens put into politics and in the very concept of a citizen—a member of a carefully defined community with rights and responsibilities in both government and society. Women did not enjoy as many rights as men and were completely excluded from government, but they played important parts in the religious life of the community, and their citizenship set them off from slaves and resident aliens in that men were frequently required to trace citizenship through both parents. Each polis was an independent political unit consisting of a town or village and the surrounding territory. Geographic conditions in Greece played a crucial role in shaping these small political units, for the mountainous terrain encouraged communities to develop in comparative isolation. As in early Mesopotamia, however, disunion went hand in hand with warfare, and Greek city-states fought one another constantly.

The polis provided the basis for social, political, religious, and cultural life. The loyalty of its citizens toward their city was far more powerful than any sense of fellowship with other Greeks. The resulting competitive spirit eventually produced fierce rivalries. The polis was thus both the highest achievement of Greek civilization and its most destructive element, responsible for nurturing not only unrivaled intellectual and cultural achievement but also a tendency toward intercommunal conflict.

Although it might in the worst of times be governed by a narrow and myopic aristocracy, and in a crisis a strong man might take over for a while, a polis was rarely ruled by a king, with the exception of Sparta, which by tradition had two monarchs reigning concurrently (though they shared power with a number of other bodies). The typical polis offered its citizens daily participation in a close-knit civic and religious community united by a powerful sense of belonging. The fourth-century B.C. philosopher Aristotle is often credited with the observation that man is a political animal, but what he really said was that man is a creature whose nature it is to live in a polis. Before the conquests of Alexander, the polis represented the limit beyond which Greek political thought was unable to go. In speculating about the best human community, Socrates, Plato, and Aristotle took the polis as the norm.

The Greeks in the Mediterranean

The colonists sent out during the two centuries from 750 B.C. to 550 B.C. dramatically expanded the Greek-speaking world. Plato aptly compared the Greeks around the Mediterranean to frogs around a pond. Already before the eighth century B.C. many powerful Greek cities had been in existence far from the Greek mainland—in the Aegean islands or on the coast of Asia Minor. Consequently, many mainland Greek *poleis* (plural of polis) that were interested in founding colonies turned their attention westward. So many colonies were established in southern Italy and Sicily that the region came to be known to the Romans as Magna Graecia, "Greater Greece."

The Bay of Naples was the site of several colonies

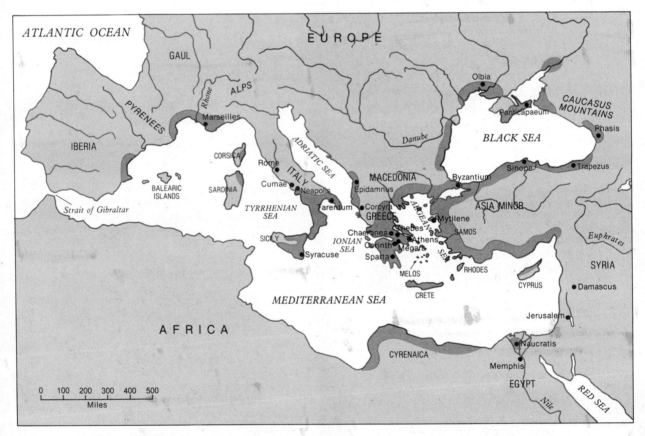

2.1 The Classical Greek World, c. 550 B.C.

founded by the polis of Chalcis. Its settlement at Cumae in turn established its own colony, Neapolis ("New City"), known today as Naples. It was not unusual for colonies themselves to found new settlements. Unlike the British, Dutch, and Spanish colonies of later times, the Greek colonies were autonomous from the start and were bound to the mother city (*metropolis*) only by sentimental and religious ties. Some colonies opted to remain close to their mother cities; the Corinthian settlement of Potidaea in northern Greece, for example, took its annual magistrates from Corinth. Others, however, chose differently; relations were so hostile between Corinth and its colony Corcyra (modern Corfu) that they fought each other at sea.

Tyrants and Reformers

A number of memorable figures stand out in the Greek transition from the narrow aristocracies of the early Iron Age to the more broadly based governments of the classical period. During this era of growth and ferment, strong men known as *tyrants* frequently seized power from the landed aristocracy with support from the middle or lower classes. Though tyrants often passed their power to their sons, tyrannies in mainland Greece did not generally outlive the third generation. The word *tyrannos* did not at first imply a harsh or autocratic ruler, but with the growth of political consciousness in Greece, all unaccountable rule came to be seen as repugnant, and the word *tyrant* acquired its modern connotation.

In the seventh and sixth centuries B.C., tyranny became commonplace in mainland Greece, where tensions between the rising merchant class and the landed aristocracy had risen dramatically. Although common patterns are discernible, every Greek tyranny was different. In Athens' neighbor Megara, a dynasty that owed its wealth to the weaving industry seized power. In Corinth the narrow aristocracy of the Bacchiad family was overthrown by a fringe member of the clan, Cypselus, who further developed the thriving pottery trade to which Corinth was ideally suited by its location.

The Athenian tyrant Pisistratus (560–527 B.C.) and his sons fortified their position by their lavish patronage of culture and the economy. Many public buildings were erected under their rule, and religious festivals became a more integral part of civic life. Pisistratus sponsored a definitive edition of the Homeric epics and instituted the festival of the City Dionysia in honor of the god Dionysus. The first Greek tragedies were produced there,

and the presentation of tragedies at the Dionysia became a regular feature of Athenian civic life.

The Evolution of Athenian Democracy

The era of the Pisistratids, which lasted until 510 B.C., played an important part in the evolution of Athenian democracy. Located on the peninsula of Attica, northeast of the Peloponnesus, Athens had been inhabited since the Bronze Age. Early in its history the Attic peninsula was unified under Athenian leadership, and all citizens of Attic towns automatically became citizens of Athens. Not long afterward the original system of monarchy was replaced with an oligarchy, and in time the executive power came to be shared by nine magistrates, called *archons,* chosen from among the elite.

During the seventh century B.C., Athens experienced severe political tensions. Around 620 B.C. the Athenians appointed Draco to formulate new laws in hopes of achieving stability. Draco's code helped redress the balance between the nobility and the poor by establishing specific penalties that inhibited aristocratic judges from imposing arbitrary sentences. It was extraordinarily harsh, however, imposing the death penalty for a wide variety of minor offenses, and it did not succeed in ending class strife.

The widespread social discontent was rooted primarily in tension between the aristocracy and small farmers. Because the farmers apparently planted wheat almost exclusively, they faced decreasing yields as they depleted the soil's fertility. Increasingly, they were forced to borrow from the aristocrats, pledging one-sixth of future crops as surety until the loan was repaid. As those who could not repay their debts faced enslavement, demands predictably mounted for the cancellation of debts and the redistribution of land.

About 594 B.C. the Athenians appointed a mediator, Solon, to overhaul their political system and redress social tensions. Solon's chief accomplishment was to replace birth with income as the qualification for office, thus providing for middle-class representation. He divided Athenians into four classes based on income. Magistrates were to be selected from the two highest classes, but the third class was apparently able to serve in the new Council of 400, made up of 100 members from each of the four Athenian tribes. The Council would prepare business for meetings of the *ekklesia,* the assembly of all male citizens. Poor laborers, who comprised the last class, were able to participate only in the *ekklesia,* but more important was their inclusion in a new institution created by Solon, the popular courts, on which all male citizens over the age of 30 were entitled to serve. Placing justice in these hands represented a dramatic change from the system of arbitration described by Homer, which had enabled ordinary citizens to speak up on behalf of litigants but not to determine verdicts directly. Solon also abolished debt slavery and canceled some existing debts.

The Athenians were disappointed in their hope that Solon's reforms would avert tyranny, but his work was not in vain. Although Pisistratus seized power in 560 B.C., he was careful not to disturb the machinery of democracy that Solon had established. The courts and the assembly continued to function, and the people received valuable practice in the bureaucratic labors of government. When the last of the Pisistratids was expelled in 510 B.C., the Athenians had a workable government in place.

One more step, however, was needed to give Athenian democracy definitive form. Shortly before 500 B.C., Cleisthenes, a reformer from a prominent family, reorganized Athens into ten new tribes according to a novel system. Dividing each of Attica's main regions—the hills, the coast, and the plain—into ten sections, he combined three sections from each of the different regions to form the new tribal units. This innovative redistricting was intended to break the power of the aristocracy in the four traditional tribes. Each of Cleisthenes' tribes elected one man to serve on a Board of Ten Generals. In addition the old Council of 400 was replaced by a new Council of 500 consisting of 50 members chosen by lot from each tribe. This Council was to handle some minor business and to prepare the agenda for the assembly.

Cleisthenes' reforms moved Athens significantly toward a democracy in which free adult males of all social classes could participate in politics. Because members of the council were selected by lot and no one could serve more than twice in a lifetime, a large portion of the Athenian male citizenry acquired some experience in government.

The Spartan Way of Life

Many of the people who had invaded from the north toward the end of the Bronze Age settled in Sparta, which was located on the large peninsula of the Peloponnesus in southwest Greece. There they reduced the previous inhabitants to the status of serfs, known as *helots*. Conflict with Messenia, a strong state to the west, prompted the Spartans to adopt a rigidly military social order under the governance of two kings. All Spartan males became part of a permanent standing army, and women were trained and educated to become hardy breeders of soldiers. A code of rigid equality was designed to eliminate economic distinctions among Spartan citizens (though in reality class differentiation was not obliterated), while state-owned helots worked the plots assigned to each soldier and the colonized population of the surrounding area, known as *perioikoi,* produced the necessary artifacts. The perioikoi could be conscripted into the Spartan army, but they were permitted self-government in their villages and were often more prosperous than the Spartans themselves. Thus a three-tiered society evolved, with a soldierly elite, an artisan class, and a servile agricultural population.

The rigidity of this system was unique to Sparta. All Greek states had slaves, but outside Sparta a good deal of farming and artisanal labor was in the hands of citizens, and war was conducted by a militia of citizens who also had to make a living. Spartan men, however, spent the bulk of their lives in barracks. Stealth and cunning were encouraged as a preparation for military life: tradition records that Spartan children deliberately received insufficient food so that they would become resourceful in stealing more. The army met in an assembly and voted, but debate was kept to a minimum, and common soldiers were not encouraged to voice their opinions. Instead, speaking in the assembly was limited to the two kings, the other 28 members of the *gerousia* (council of elders), and the five *ephors,* magistrates who were elected to keep the kings in check.

The Spartan system was fraught with irony. The most powerful land force in Greece, the Spartans were nonetheless reluctant to campaign for fear of rebellion on the part of the helots, who outnumbered citizens about ten to one. Sparta was held up in antiquity and well into the nineteenth century A.D. as a model of *mixed government,* that is, one that combined features of monarchy, oligarchy, and democracy (popular government). In reality, however, Sparta was in many respects a brutal oligarchy more exclusive and elitist than any other in Greece. The narrowness of the Spartans' focus led some to mock their lack of imagination and intellect, yet many Greeks, including the philosopher Plato, saw in the Spartans an inspiration for others. This enthusiasm was partly due to the stability of the Spartan state. In an age of constant unrest and civil conflict, the unchanging

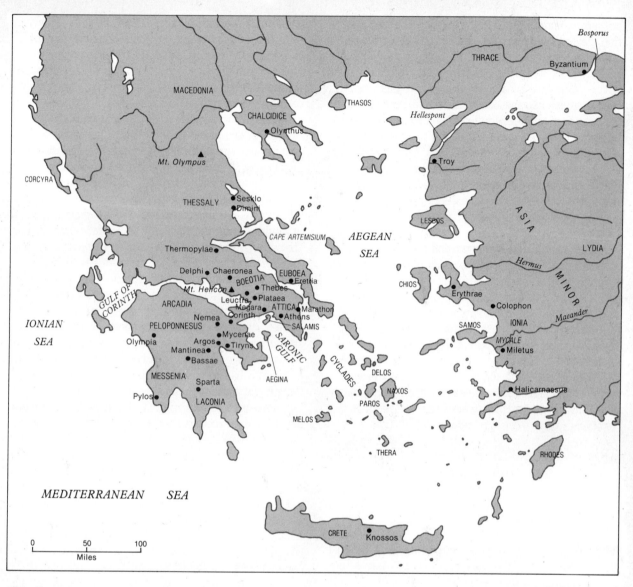

2.2 Greece

nature of the Spartan constitution was a source of admiration. Sparta's military strength also contributed to its reputation. In part, however, the adulation the Spartans inspired in so many of their neighbors may be traced to the keen sense of belonging that the Spartan system had inculcated in its citizens, male and female. In a universe in which a person's identity was so closely bound up with his or her city-state, the common bond that joined all Spartans in a shared effort was inevitably a source of envy.

The Poleis of Mainland Greece

By 500 B.C., Sparta was regarded as the most powerful state in Greece. The Spartans had brought most of the poleis in the Peloponnesus, as well as some states outside it, into a loose confederation subsequently known as the Peloponnesian League. Sparta's most crucial ally was Corinth, and the Corinthians, who possessed the strongest navy in the league, exerted great influence over Spartan policy. Their enviable location on the narrow isthmus that connected the Peloponnesus with the rest of Greece gave them two key ports, and commerce developed early in Corinth, reportedly the only polis in which the artisan was esteemed more highly than the soldier. The citadel of Acrocorinth, fortified from early times, towered so high above the city that someone standing atop the hill on a clear day could catch a glimpse of the corresponding citadel of Athens, the Acropolis.

Proceeding eastward out of the Peloponnesus into central Greece, a traveler passed through Megara, a small polis whose rocky soil had prompted the inhabitants to manufacture woolens for a living. Turning northward at Attica, one would come to Boeotia, where the most powerful city, Thebes, belonged to the Peloponnesian League and struggled constantly to maintain its hegemony over the other Boeotian cities. The Boeotians were primarily an agricultural people, and the earliest farming manual in Greece was written by the Boeotian poet Hesiod, probably early in the seventh century B.C. Hesiod is also regarded as the principal author of another long poem, the *Theogony,* which treats the genealogy of the gods. The Athenians, who considered the Boeotians slow and muddle-headed, enjoyed making jokes at their expense, but under Theban leadership the Boeotians were a force to be reckoned with.

THE PERSIAN WARS

As the Persians marched westward in the sixth century B.C., the Greeks in the coastal region of Asia Minor known as Ionia came under their rule. In 499 B.C. the Ionian cities rebelled unsuccessfully. King Darius of Persia (522–486 B.C.) had long been interested in extending his power to the Greek mainland, and the support the Ionian rebels had received from Athens and from the small city of Eretria to the north of Attica served as a pretext for the invasion. In 490 B.C., after sacking Eretria, the Persians were defeated by an outnumbered force of Athenians under their general Miltiades on the Attic plain of Marathon, some 20 miles north of Athens. The Persians retreated from mainland Greece, which enjoyed a decade of reprieve.

The decade of the 480s B.C. was a pivotal one at Athens. Elated by their success against the Persians and convinced that the democratic assembly was capable of responsible leadership, the Athenians were also persuaded of the importance of the position of general. Consequently, they opened the traditional aristocratic office of archon to selection by lot. In this way the prestige of the archonship was lowered in relation to that of the more democratic Board of Ten Generals, who continued to be elected.

Athens also began building a navy at the instigation of the ambitious politician Themistocles. After the death of Miltiades in 489 B.C., Themistocles' principal rival for the leadership of Athens was Aristides, a man with a reputation for straightforwardness and incorruptibility. When a rich vein of silver was discovered in Attica, Aristides recommended that it be divided evenly among the citizens. Themistocles, who warned of the continuing Persian threat, wanted the Athenians to use the money to construct a navy, and his arguments won the day. The competition between the two politicians was resolved by the use of an unusual practice known as *ostracism.*

Ostracisms began in Athens shortly after the battle of Marathon. The procedure called for a vote in the assembly with a quorum of 6,000. The man who received the most votes was compelled to go into exile for ten years; no pretext was necessary to ostracize someone. Although ostracism was originally designed to prevent any one man from acquiring excessive power, it later helped to resolve major conflicts without civil war. During the fifth century B.C., approximately ten Athenians were ostracized before the practice was abandoned.

In 482 B.C. the Athenians ostracized Aristides, leaving Themistocles free to build the navy he advocated. By this time, Persian preparations for a new invasion under Darius' son Xerxes were already far advanced. Under Themistocles' leadership the Athenians took a prominent role in repelling the new Persian assault. When Xerxes' huge army crossed northern Greece in 480 B.C., many states panicked and submitted to the Persians without a struggle. The Greeks who decided to fight tried to hold the line that stretched from the pass of Thermopylae to the sea. To defend this position, the Spartan king Leonidas and a largely Spartan Greek force made a heroic stand at Thermopylae in August of 480 B.C., reportedly defending it to the last man against hopeless odds. A statue of Leonidas stands at the site today, commemorating the defeat that was Sparta's finest hour. The epitaph written for the Spartans stresses their unquestioning obedience to orders:

Go tell the Spartans, stranger passing by,
That here, obeying their commands, we lie.

After their success at Thermopylae, the Persians moved south, where Themistocles tricked Xerxes into pursuing the Greek fleet into the narrow channel that divided Attica from the island of Salamis to the west. Trapped there, the Persians were decisively defeated.

Xerxes then returned home, leaving his brother-in-law Mardonius behind with a portion of the army. Mardonius was defeated in 479 B.C. at Plataea, and at about the same time—perhaps on the same day—the Greek fleet was victorious over the Persians at Mycale off the coast of Asia Minor. The Persians withdrew, never to return in force. In one of the most decisive engagements in history, Greece was spared conquest at the moment of its finest cultural flowering.

THE GROWTH OF THE ATHENIAN EMPIRE

At the time of the Persian invasions, Sparta had been the most powerful state in Greece, but the role of Athens in repelling both Darius and Xerxes sparked a shift in the balance of power. The Greek states nearest Persia, understandably nervous about the prospect of further attacks, formed a defensive alliance, and when plans for the Spartans to lead it collapsed, the hegemony fell to Athens. The respected Aristides, who had been recalled during the war with Xerxes, was given the task of determining how much each ally should pay into the league treasury. The treasury was to be housed on the island of Delos to allay fears of Athenian dominance. Many Greek states close to the mainland also joined the league to ensure protection from the Persians. To fortify their own position, the Athenians built long walls to link their city with its port, Piraeus, a few miles away.

Headed by Cimon, the son of Miltiades and a military hero in his own right, the naval operations of the league went so well that after a few years, Athens' allies began to feel sufficiently safe from the Persians that they questioned the need for the league to continue. When Athens met attempts at secession with armed force, the allies suspected that the Athenians were converting the league into an empire. Their suspicions were confirmed when in 454 B.C. the Athenians moved the league treasury to Athens, ostensibly to protect it from pirates. Even in Athens some questioned the propriety of continuing the league when the Persian threat had receded

and of using league funds to beautify the Athenian acropolis.

The development of an empire abroad went hand in hand with the advance of democracy at home in the city of Athens, where there was tension between the advocates of popular government and those who preferred a more conventional system that left power in the hands of the well-to-do. This conflict would continue in one form or another throughout Athens' history. Shortly before 460 B.C. the rising democratic party, led by Ephialtes, enacted important reforms. Although the details of this legislation are uncertain, the majority of trials that still remained within the purview of the aristocratic Council of the Areopagus were transferred to juries of the people. This dealt a powerful blow to Athens' rich families, for it was they who formed the core of this venerable Council, which received its name from the hill of the god Ares and had exercised important judicial functions for as long as anyone could remember. When Ephialtes was assassinated shortly after the enactment of these reforms, probably by disaffected aristocrats, leadership of the democratic party fell to his ally Pericles (c. 495–429 B.C.). Pericles and his associates realized that the income from the empire could foster the growth of democracy, for with league funds the Athenian government could remunerate its citizens for jury duty and other political activities, thus expanding the size of the group that could afford to take time off from work to assume civic responsibilities. In addition, the splendid temples and other public buildings financed by imperial tribute heightened the popularity of the democratic regime both by their majestic beauty and by the numerous jobs their construction provided.

THE PELOPONNESIAN WAR

The polis system underwent a crisis in the late fifth century B.C. because of a great war that drained dozens of states, left Greece vulnerable again to outside intervention, and threatened the Athenian experiment in democracy. The war arose out of tensions between Athens and Sparta that might have been resolved had it not been for the anxieties of Sparta's powerful naval ally, Corinth, which had a long-standing commercial rivalry with Athens.

Athens and Sparta:
The Struggle for Hegemony

In the decades after the defeat of Xerxes' army in 479 B.C., relations between the Athenians and the Spartans oscillated between guarded coexistence and overt hostility. In both Athens and Sparta, citizens were divided over the degree to which the other state's ambitions posed a threat. Although the dramatic rise in Athenian power and prestige after the Persian Wars made many Spartans nervous, others saw no harm in allowing the Athenians to dominate their own sphere of influence as long as the Spartans remained supreme in mainland Greece. In Athens, tensions ran high between the democratic party, which tended also to be imperialistic, and the more conservative politicians of oligarchic leanings, who advocated peace with Sparta and limited democracy at home. Throughout Athenian history, democrats suspected oligarchs of treacherous pro-Spartan leanings. Frequently, they were correct. Athens' final defeat in the Peloponnesian War was partly the result of a betrayal to the Spartans by antidemocratic Athenians. The philosopher Plato was only the most famous of many Athenian aristocrats who combined contempt for democracy with Spartan sympathies.

In 432 B.C., Sparta declared war on Athens, partly because of pressure from its valued ally Corinth. At first sight, Pericles' strategy for winning the war with Sparta appeared promising. Pericles persuaded the inhabitants of Attica to seek refuge behind the walls that linked Athens to Piraeus rather than face the Spartans in pitched battle. Starvation by siege was not a danger, since supplies could be brought in through Piraeus from other parts of the empire. After disappointing the Spartans in their attempt to force a battle and harassing Peloponnesian ports with the Athenian navy, Pericles expected that the Spartans would sue for peace within two years.

Disease in the city wrought havoc with this clever plan. The crowding of Attica's residents into Athens strained sanitation, and this, combined with a plague that erupted in the city shortly after the outbreak of the war, proved devastating. Thousands died. The victims included Pericles himself, and after his death in 429 B.C. no other statesman of his stature was forthcoming. Pericles had been elected general 30 times at Athens. His eloquence and vision had earned him as much respect as any leader could command. The oration for the war dead that he delivered at the end of the first year of fighting

This Roman copy of Cresilas' marble bust of Pericles is an idealized image rather than a realistic portrait. The sculpture depicts Pericles wearing a helmet, symbolic of his office as general. [Alinari/Art Resource, New York]

remains a magnificent defense of democratic society. The Athenian system of government, he said,

> is called a democracy because power is in the hands not of a minority but of the whole people. When it is a question of settling private disputes, everyone is equal before the law; when it is a question of putting one person before another in positions of public responsibility, what counts is not membership of a particular class, but the actual ability which the man possesses. . . . And, just as our political life is free and open, so is our day-to-day life in our relations with each other. We do not get into a state with our next door neighbor if he enjoys himself in his own way, nor do we give him the kind of black looks which, though they do no real harm, still do hurt people's feelings. We are free and tolerant in our private

lives; but in public affairs we keep to the law. This is because it commands our deep respect.[2]

The best-known among Pericles' immediate successors was Cleon. Lacking Pericles' aristocratic pedigree Cleon was portrayed in contemporary literature as crass and self-interested. Ironically, in his determination to hold out against the Spartans and his recognition of the naked force on which the Athenian empire rested, Cleon was in many respects the heir to Pericles' policies, but his abrasive and tactless manner alienated many. After Pericles' death the Athenians met the Spartans in several land battles. Their success was mixed, and one unsuccessful campaign led to the exile of the Athenian general and historian Thucydides, who wrote a history of the war that is still much admired. In 422 B.C. both Cleon and Brasidas, Sparta's most charismatic general, were killed. Soon after their deaths the Athenians and Spartans signed the so-called Peace of Nicias, named after the conservative Athenian statesman who negotiated it. The peace, however, was short-lived. In part its failure must be traced to the machinations of the ambitious and unprincipled Alcibiades, one of the most fascinating figures of late-fifth-century Greece.

ALCIBIADES AND ATHENS

Born around 450 B.C. and brought up in the household of his relative and guardian Pericles, Alcibiades had traveled in the inner circles of power at Athens since his childhood. Handsome and athletic, he was courted by lovers of both sexes, and his vanity seems to have grown together with his popularity. He was one of Socrates' most cherished pupils, and his defection to the Spartans in 415 B.C. contributed to the Athenians' displeasure with his teacher, for it was known that Socrates poked fun at the Athenian democracy and encouraged his students to question its merits.

Shortly after the Peace of Nicias, Alcibiades agitated for renewed hostilities with Sparta, and he persuaded his fellow Athenians to send a massive naval force to Sicily, an expedition that was bound to anger the Corinthians. Just as the expedition was about to set sail, the Athenians discovered that unknown vandals had mutilated many of the images of the god Hermes that customarily stood outside people's homes. This defacement was suspected to presage a political coup. It was also reported that scandalous parodies of the sacred mystery religions practiced just outside the city at Eleusis had been performed. Alcibiades' enemies insisted that he had been involved in these acts. When the Athenians called him back from the Sicilian voyage to stand trial, the wily adventurer jumped ship and defected to the Spartans.

Predictably, Alcibiades soon wore out his welcome in Sparta. (Among other things, he was believed to have impregnated the wife of one of the kings.) After some years of maneuvering he finally persuaded the Athenians to recall him. Shortly afterward, however, he was blamed for a defeat suffered by a subordinate whom he had unwisely left in charge in his absence, and his enemies impeached him. He took refuge in the Persian Empire, where he was later murdered. Much is revealed about the character of the Athenians by their tempestuous love affair with this impudent aristocrat who told the Spartans that no one in Athens took democracy seriously. Looks, charm, and aristocratic lineage made it possible for Alcibiades to remain the darling of the people despite abundant evidence that his behavior was determined solely by self-interest. It is significant that Socrates, an elderly man from an ordinary family who used reason to undermine the premises of democracy, was put to death, while the youthful and well-born Alcibiades, who betrayed his country to its deadliest enemy, retained his popularity.

The Sicilian Expedition and the Athenian Defeat

The Sicilian expedition ended in disaster. Thucydides says that the Athenian army was so exhausted and demoralized when it reached a cool river in its retreat that the soldiers stopped to drink even though this meant certain death at the hands of the enemy. Some 50,000 men died in Sicily, and the Athenians lost their naval superiority. The war, however, continued. The Spartans, who had justified their original declaration of war by proclaiming their intention to liberate Greek states from external domination, now began bargaining with the Persians, offering to trade the coastal states of Asia Minor for Persian assistance in the war. As the fighting continued with no end in sight, tempers at Athens grew increasingly short. In 406 B.C. the Athenians executed six generals for failing to retrieve survivors—or, according to another account, dead bodies for burial—from the stormy waters of the Hellespont after a major naval victory. Finally, in 405 B.C. the Spartans captured the Athenian fleet at Aegospotami in Ionia, in part through the complicity of Athens' pro-Spartan oligarchs, and the war was over.

It was night when word reached Athens of the defeat. Xenophon, whose narrative of the war began where that of Thucydides had broken off unfinished, vividly conveys the terror that seized the Athenians. They had long administered a savage justice to their enemies, and they had every reason to imagine that the same fate would befall them. Some doubtless believed that they deserved it. That night, Xenophon reports, nobody slept.

As it turned out, the Spartans decided not to destroy Athens and kill its inhabitants. Instead, they installed a savage puppet government known to history as the Thirty Tyrants. The Thirty were so bloodthirsty that they alienated even the Spartan king, Pausanias, and it was with his assistance that they were overthrown in 403 B.C. and the democracy was restored. The bitter civil war that led to the restoration of democracy in Athens was ended by the first recorded amnesty in history. According to its terms, no one could be prosecuted for crimes committed prior to 403 B.C. except the Thirty Tyrants and other specified officials. Despite this agreement, however, some vengeance was unavoidable, as the case of the philosopher and teacher Socrates demonstrates. A trenchant critic of Athenian democracy, he was an obvious target for those wishing to settle scores with the oligarchs. He was accused of impiety toward the Olympian gods, of introducing new deities, and of corrupting the youth of the city through his teaching. The speech known as Socrates' *Apology* (an explanation of his mission, not an apology in the modern sense) was composed by Plato after Socrates' death and purports to be the words spoken by Socrates at his trial in 399 B.C. If it accurately represents what Socrates said, he was a man of extraordinary courage and vision.

Instead of trying to placate his accusers or appeal for their mercy, Socrates used his trial as an opportunity to extend his teachings and provoke his fellow citizens into examining their own motivations and conduct. When imprisoned and awaiting execution, he refused the opportunity to flee into exile, saying that a citizen was bound to submit to lawful penalties even though they might be unjust. His execution made him the first martyr of intellectual freedom in the Western tradition, and his defense of free inquiry continues to inspire men and women to this day.

LIFE IN DEMOCRATIC ATHENS

The democracy practiced in Athens represented a bold departure from traditional ideas of government, which had divided people into rulers and ruled. As we have seen, it developed gradually. After Attica's unification the kingship was abolished and the office of archon was created. The reforms of Solon provided for social mobility and created the first popular courts, and experience in the daily business of democracy was gained in the succeeding half century. The reforms of Cleisthenes broke down aristocratic tribal loyalties and established the Council of Five Hundred and the Board of Ten Generals, while those of Ephialtes transferred power from the aristocratic Council of the Areopagus to the people's courts; finally, under Pericles, pay was instituted for state service. Each polis had its own constitution (*politeia*), and for the classical Greeks a politeia was more than a blueprint for government; it was also a way of looking at the world. Democracy to Athenians did not simply mean that no affluent minority could dictate to the poor majority; it meant regular, active participation in government on the part of tens of thousands of citizens. Hundreds of minor positions had to be filled every year in addition to the 500 places on the council. Over a lifetime, every male citizen could expect to hold some public office at least once. Generals, however, were chosen not by lot but by election, and such a contest required education and money. Family connections might help as well. Despite its democratic underpinnings, in other words, Athenian government remained principally in the hands of men who, if not rich, were at least not poor.

Ordinary people, however, might enjoy the splendid temples that adorned the city, and even Athens' less affluent citizens (certainly men, and perhaps women as well) attended the magnificent dramatic performances that accompanied religious festivals, delighting in the boisterous comedies and returning from the sober tragedies to debate with one another the important questions about the human condition that Greek drama regularly engaged. A shared cultural treasure like the 40-foot high statue of Athena in the Parthenon (now recreated in the United States in Centennial Park in Nashville, Tennessee) could be appreciated by Athenians of all social classes. The home of democracy was also an affluent imperial city, and life within it had much to offer both residents and visitors.

THE INHABITANTS OF ATTICA

Despite the important role played by the Greeks in the development of democratic thinking, nearly all classical Greeks believed that some people had more rights than others, and Athenians were no exception. Their willingness to accord theoretical equality to rich and poor citizens alike did not arise from a commitment to the equality of humanity as a whole. In many respects, the opposite was true: because the privileges of participating in government and being paid for doing so were cherished, the Athenians confined the citizenship to a minority of even the male population. Not only was it close to impossible for immigrants to gain citizenship after long periods of residence in Attica, but it was also unlikely that their children, grandchildren, or great-grandchildren would ever become citizens. In addition to resident aliens, known as *metics,* there was a large population of slaves. Women, moreover, could possess citizenship only in a latent form; they could pass on many rights to their male children but had few privileges themselves. Modern social critics have pointed out that the Athenian state was not so much a democracy as a "men's club."

Athenian Women

The position of women in classical Athens presents a paradox. In Greek tragedies they appear as central actors in the human drama. Aeschylus' Clytemnestra took charge of the government when her husband Agamemnon was off at war and murdered him to avenge his decision to sacrifice their daughter Iphigenia. Sophocles' Antigone chose death over dishonor when she insisted on burying her dead brother even though her uncle the king forbade it on the grounds that he had been a traitor to his city. Medea punished her faithless husband by killing their children. Yet what we know about the social life of the Athenian democrats suggests that most of Athens' politicians and intellectuals discounted women. Pericles lived with one of the most celebrated women of his day, the cultivated metic

Aspasia, yet he was famous for saying that the greatest glory of a woman was never to be spoken of either for good or for evil. Aristotle seems to reflect the prevailing view when he describes women as the natural inferiors of men, the products of undeveloped embryos who would under better circumstances have turned into males; he even denied them a full share in procreation, arguing that the male seed alone contained the full germ of the child, with the womb serving only as its receptacle. In some ways the status of women was closer to that of slaves than to that of male citizens. Women had no independent legal standing and could have legal rights exercised for them only through male guardians. Unlike wives, husbands could obtain divorce whenever they liked and could even dispose of their wives in their wills; the orator Demosthenes describes the case of a widow ordered to marry her husband's former slave in his will. Adultery, tolerated for men, was regarded as automatic grounds for divorce in the case of women.

Poor women might leave their homes to work, but women of the upper and middle classes were largely confined to the house. There a woman was responsible for duties such as spinning, weaving, and the supervision of slaves. Even within the house, the sexes were socially segregated, women being consigned to their own part of the house while men entertained their visitors as they wished in gatherings that might include prostitutes and concubines. A litigant speaking in an Athenian courtroom around 400 B.C. boasted that his sister and nieces had been "brought up so well that they were embarrassed to be in the presence even of their male relatives."

Though there were doubtless many happy marriages, as a rule Greek men viewed procreation rather than romantic love as the purpose of the marital relationship. The sexual energies of Athenian men were often directed at noncitizen women, the famous *hetairai,* or courtesans, who in addition to their sexual availability were also frequently educated in a way that citizen women were not. Because hetairai were generally of metic status, Athenian men desiring to beget sons who would enjoy citizenship were limited in their choice of wives to the comparatively uneducated women of the citizen class. Predictably, they also established liaisons with the more sophisticated and stimulating hetairai. The division of women at Athens into a cultivated, sexually liberated courtesan class and an uneducated citizen class suitable for providing heirs created considerable tension. It is the hetairai who are largely represented in the vase paintings, often performing acts that were frowned upon in the marriage bed. In addition to forming connections with hetairai, Athenian husbands of the upper classes were often attracted to other males, and relationships between an older, established man and a good-looking adolescent boy were fairly common. Though Athenians who had no such inclinations often made homosexual liaisons the object of jokes, the intense anxiety with which many cultures have regarded homosexuality and bisexuality was lacking in Athens.

For a woman to work outside the home was a sign of considerable poverty. Women of the lower classes hired out as weavers, spinners, and wet nurses; many worked as vendors in the public market. Though these women probably envied their wealthier sisters, in truth their less sequestered lives may have been more interesting than those of the more privileged women who were compelled to spend their days indoors and who may have had very little human contact beyond a narrow circle of other females.

Slaves and Metics

Metic women generally moved around the city with considerably more freedom than the confined daughters and sisters of well-to-do citizens. Some even owned businesses; so did many metic men. Though metics could not vote or own property, they were free to rent pleasant homes and conduct commerce, and it was trade that brought most of them to Athens. A person walking through the city's streets and coming upon a prosperous shield or leather factory would have no way of knowing whether its owner was a citizen or a metic. Metics thus mingled easily with citizens, though they lacked political rights. At the time of the outbreak of the Peloponnesian War, when the total adult population of Attica was probably around 340,000, this figure included some 25,000 or 30,000 metics.

For every metic in Athens there were perhaps four slaves. As in western Asia, slaves in Greece were frequently won in war and then bred to produce more slaves. Some Greeks were plainly uncomfortable about enslaving fellow Greeks, but they were not sufficiently distressed to abandon the practice. The nature of slaves' lives varied radically depending on both gender and talent. On the whole, female slaves were kept in the home to wait on the mistress of the house, care for the children, and help with the weaving. Male slaves were also used in private homes, but slave owners might well turn a profit

by renting their male slaves to work in factories alongside free laborers. Particularly bright slaves might hold important jobs as estate stewards or bank managers. Some slaves were owned by the state, and the Athenian police force was composed of slaves from Scythia. Though many state slaves lived comfortably, the majority of them worked in the silver mines at Laurium near the southern tip of Attica and had short, wretched lives.

The Athenian Achievement

The population of Athens included only about 45,000 adult male citizens, and the principles of democracy operated only within this small minority. Despite this narrow exclusivity, the Athenians set the pattern for the ideal of a secular state dedicated to the principle that all citizens were equal before the law regardless of economic circumstances or social background. To the Athenians, democracy entailed the active, enthusiastic participation of thousands of citizens in the business of the state—business that included not only legislation but also a wide variety of festivals in which citizens might enjoy the beautiful public buildings of Athens and the majestic tragedies that were presented every spring at the festival of Dionysus. Free Athenian males lived energetic and engaged lives, and their experiment laid the groundwork that made it possible for the privileges they cherished to be enjoyed in later times by a far more diverse group than anyone of their day could have envisioned.

SUMMARY

The political consciousness that flowered in the Hellenic world bequeathed an enduring legacy to humankind. Nowhere else in the West had people thought quite so reflectively and analytically about the just and equitable ordering of the human community. At the same time, the denigration of non-Greeks, the constraints of the polis system, and the exclusion of large numbers of slaves and women from the body politic pointed up the limitations of Greek thought. The Peloponnesian War, moreover, did grave damage to the concept of the polis as a dominant force that could inspire and fulfill its citizens.

When the fourth-century B.C. campaigns of Alexander the Great of Macedonia produced a new fusion of the civilization of Egypt and Western Asia with that of Greece, a vigorous culture would flower. Though slavery and the second-class status of women remained crucial elements in the structure of ancient society, the world forged by Alexander's conquests would combine many of the most vibrant of the older traditions with the most thoughtful and promising of the new.

Notes

1. From *The Iliad of Homer,* trans. R. Lattimore (Chicago: University of Chicago Press, 1951), p. 388.
2. From Thucydides' *History of the Peloponnesian War,* trans. R. Warner (Harmondsworth, England: Penguin Books, 1954), p. 117.

Suggestions for Further Reading

Andrewes, A. *The Greek Tyrants.* London: Hutchinson's University Press, 1956.

Austin, M., and Vidal-Naquet, P. *The Economic and Social History of Ancient Greece.* Berkeley: University of California Press, 1977.

Finley, M. I. *Slavery in Classical Antiquity: Views and Controversies.* Cambridge, Mass.: Harvard University Press, 1983.

Frost, F. *Greek Society.* Lexington, Mass.: Heath, 1987.

Hanson, V. D. *The Western Way of War: Infantry Battle in Classical Greece.* New York: Knopf, 1989.

Hooker, J. T. *Mycenaean Greece.* London: Routledge & Kegan Paul, 1976.

Joint Association of Classical Teachers. *The World of Athens: An Introduction to Classical Athenian Culture.* Cambridge, England: Cambridge University Press, 1984.

Just, R. *Women in Athenian Law and Life.* London: Routledge, 1990.

Michell, H. *Sparta.* Cambridge, England: Cambridge University Press, 1964.

Poliakoff, M. B. *Combat Sports in the Ancient World.* New Haven, Conn.: Yale University Press, 1987.

Pomeroy, S. *Goddesses, Whores, Wives, and Slaves: Women in Classical Antiquity.* New York: Schocken Books, 1976.

Sealey, R. *A History of the Greek City-States, 700–338 B.C.* Berkeley: University of California Press, 1977.

Sinclair, T. *A History of Greek Political Thought.* London: Routledge & Kegan Paul, 1951.

Snodgrass, A. *Archaic Greece: The Age of Experiment.* Berkeley: University of California Press, 1980.

Williams, B. *Shame and Necessity.* Berkeley: University of California Press, 1993.

3

GREEK CULTURE AND
THE HELLENISTIC WORLD

The astonishing fertility of Greek culture between the sixth and third centuries B.C. laid the foundations for the Western tradition in science, medicine, mathematics, philosophy, and the arts. The Greeks sought harmony not by renouncing but by balancing opposing tensions and impulses. The ideas by which they construed the world— matter and spirit, individual and community, attraction and repulsion—set the terms by which Western thought still conceives the natural and social universe. The questions that engaged the Greeks are ones that people continue to ponder today: What is the nature of the cosmos (a Greek word) and how do people fit into it? What is the good life? What does it mean to be a citizen? The standards of beauty and proportion that the Greeks bequeathed to us remain ideals against which we measure our own aesthetic imagination.

Greek thought and art developed against a background of rapid and intense social change. The Persian and Peloponnesian wars, the flourishing of the autonomous polis, the conquests of Alexander, and the diffusion of Greek culture throughout western Asia and the Mediterranean provided both practical challenges and creative stimulus to the Greek spirit. The Greek achievement was above all a response to the complex demands of a world in flux.

GREEK RELIGION

For most Greeks of the classical age, religion entailed more ritual than belief. The priesthood was a part-time job, and there were no seminaries to train people for the profession. Although occasional thinkers such as Socrates provoked religious objections, conservative attacks on them were largely political, and in general there was no creed or orthodoxy from which divergence was considered threatening. What mattered was the conscientious performance of sacrifices and other rites.

Many Greeks believed that life was shaped by the unpredictable Olympian gods and took care to worship each of them, though an individual devotee might have a special attachment to one god. Individual Olympians were often identified with particular poleis. Although at times the gods were portrayed as living on Mount Olympus, a misty peak in northern Greece, they were sometimes perceived as residing in the cities they favored—Athena in Athens, Hera on Samos off the coast of Asia Minor. Some Panhellenic shrines existed, such as that of Zeus at Olympia in the Peloponnesus, where the Olympic games were held, but during the classical period the traditional deities were not conceived as extending to non-Greeks.

Not always satisfied with worshiping the tempestuous Olympians, many people were attracted to "mystery" cults that offered a kind of salvation through secret rites, such as those attached to the mythical poet Orpheus. Orphism, as the doctrine associated with his name was called, taught the inherent sinfulness of humankind and claimed that humanity had descended from the evil Titans, who had dismembered and eaten Dionysus. Because of these associations, humans were believed to possess elements of both the divinity of Dionysus and the wickedness of the Titans; worshipers therefore sought to live pure lives and abstain from eating meat. The pious would be rewarded by a happy afterlife, an unusually comforting belief, since most Greeks expected to spend eternity in a dank, joyless underground. Even some of the Olympians were associated with secret ecstatic rites, such as Demeter, who was worshiped outside Athens at Eleusis, and Dionysus (also known as Bacchus), who also figured in the Orphic cult.

LITERATURE DURING THE ARCHAIC AND CLASSICAL PERIODS

Many Greek authors, following the lead of Homer and Hesiod, expressed their ideas in verses that could be sung, chanted, and easily committed to memory, a useful tool in a largely nonliterate age. This was particularly true in the Archaic Period, roughly the seventh and sixth centuries B.C. Even some scientists, such as the Sicilian Empedocles, wrote in verse, and poetry served as the medium for Solon's political views. Of those who composed in meter, the most famous were the lyric poets; the era between the Homeric period and the Classical Age of the fifth and fourth centuries B.C. is sometimes also known as the Lyric Age.

The Lyric Poets

Lyric verse was named for the stringed instrument known as the lyre to the accompaniment of which it was chanted; it is from this practice that we get our English word *lyrics*. This new verse form reflected a growing sensitivity to an interior sphere of experience separate from wars and the quarrels of rival monarchs. A similar approach characterized elegiac poetry, performed to the accompaniment of the flute. Departing from the six-beat hexameters in which the epic writers had treated their grand themes, the lyric poets cast their more delicate creations in a wide assortment of meters.

The poets of the Lyric Age frequently proclaim their intention of breaking with the grand epic genre of the Homeric past and its values. The seventh-century poet Archilochus of Paros is famous for the inflammatory

challenge he presented to the heroic ethic in a merry poem on the loss of his shield:

> Well, some barbarian's glad to have the shield
> I had to leave behind—a really nice one too—
> Thrown underneath a bush. But I'm alive!
> I got away—the hell with that old shield!
> I'll get another some day just as good.

The sixth-century poet Anacreon from the island of Teos produced several poems about his decision to write about love in preference to heroic themes. In one he tells how he tried to sing about the heroes of ancient legend, but instead his lyre would sound only the chords of love:

> Lately I changed the strings
> And all the lyre;
> And I began to sing the labors
> Of Hercules; but my lyre
> Resounded loves.
> Farewell, henceforth, for me,
> Heroes! for my lyre
> Sings only loves.[1]

The literary controversy about values reflected the mood of thoughtful inquiry and constructive ferment that characterized the Lyric Age; it also reveals something of the competitive spirit of the early Greek writers. Tyrtaeus of Sparta, who lived in the seventh century B.C., proclaimed in his verses that no one could surpass the excellence of the brave fighter, and others awarded the highest place to victors in the Olympic games. The sixth-century poet Xenophanes, however, claimed that nobody could compare to the philosopher, and Sappho (born c. 612 B.C.), whose poetry celebrated the private world of the emotions, advocated love as the supreme value. Sappho ran a finishing school on the island of Lesbos where young ladies could study music and literature. In the ancient world her pupils became the prototypes for liberated women: educated, assertive, and capable of finding fulfillment in their lives without depending on men. The close association of the women of Lesbos with homosexuality did not come until centuries later, but the warmth of the poetry Sappho addressed to other women certainly suggests sexual love. Some people, she acknowledged, will maintain that the loveliest sight in the world is a troop of cavalry or a navy, but "I say the woman one loves best is the most beautiful." As challenging as the sentiment itself is the daring "I say" by which she reveals a striking confidence in the importance of her own feelings and beliefs.

Interpreting the Past: Herodotus and Thucydides

Prose developed more slowly, and the first remarkable works of Greek prose date from the Classical Age, the era between the Persian Wars at the beginning of the fifth century B.C. and the conquest of Greece by Macedonia at the end of the fourth century B.C. These memorable creations are the histories of Herodotus and Thucydides. Sometimes called the "father of history," Herodotus manifests a lively curiosity about the non-Greek world in his *History* of the Persian Wars. Although he attributed the Greeks' victory over Persia to the superiority of their political institutions, he admired the Persians' courage and was fascinated by the cultural diversity of the wider world. He traveled extensively, not only bringing home to the Greeks much information about other lands but also pointing out to his compatriots how much their culture had been influenced by those of their neighbors, particularly Egypt.

Herodotus, like the great tragic dramatists who were his contemporaries, emphasized the role of fate and the actions of the gods in shaping human events. In the end, however, he considered human character itself—the arrogance of Xerxes, the cunning of Themistocles—to be the prime determinant of history. Thucydides (c. 460–c. 400 B.C.), in his *History of the Peloponnesian War*, attributed events solely to human character and causality. For Thucydides the inborn human craving for power explained the outbreak of war between the Athenians and the Spartans, and human psychology determined not only how people behaved under the strains of that war but how they would behave in similar circumstances in the future. Thucydides' tight, analytical style provided a model of historical narrative that is still admired today. Above all, Thucydides insisted on the duty of the historian to provide not only a factual description of events but also an explanation of their causes.

Tragedy and Comedy

Deeply rooted in civic and religious life, Athenian drama emerged gradually from rituals and choral chants performed at the annual festivals of Dionysus. By the mid-fifth century B.C., tragedies were performed in the framework of contests at festivals, the winners receiving prizes. Unfortunately, only a tiny fraction of the plays survive—seven each by Aeschylus (525–456 B.C.) and Sophocles (c. 496–406 B.C.) and nineteen by Euripides (c. 485–406 B.C.).

Tragedies were performed in groups of three, but only one trilogy survives intact, Aeschylus' *Oresteia*, first produced in 458 B.C. Like other Greek tragedies, the plays that made up the *Oresteia* dealt with the limitations placed on human happiness by the impossibility of certain knowledge, the inevitability of death, the pervasiveness of conflict, strains in family and gender relations, and the ambiguity inherent in dealings between gods and mortals. In the *Oresteia*, Aeschylus uses the myth of the curse on the house of Atreus, Agamemnon's father, to illustrate the replacement of the old order, in which religion and the family held the highest importance, with the new, in which the highest position was accorded to the state. In the old universe, powerful, emotional female forces prevailed, whereas the new world was governed by orderly, rational institutions planned and staffed by men. The new order is proclaimed when Orestes, having killed his mother Clytemnestra to avenge the death of Agamemnon, his father, is acquitted by an Athenian jury on the grounds that it is the father and not the mother who is the true parent and thus has the greater claims on the child's loyalty. Law is thus exalted as the modern solution to social problems over the blood vengeance that the snake-haired Furies, goddesses of the earth, had sought to exact from Orestes for Clytemnestra's murder.

Other tragedies also drew on popular myths, with an emphasis on murderous family discord. The most famous Greek tragedy, Sophocles' *Oedipus the King* (c. 428 B.C.), uses the painful tale of a man who inadvertently kills his father and marries his mother to analyze the nature of destiny and the problem of responsibility. Despite his stress on the suffering that life can entail, Sophocles conveys enormous excitement at human potential, an excitement that is particularly evident in the passage in *Antigone* sometimes called the "Ode to Man":

Many the wonders but nothing walks stranger than man.
This thing crosses the sea in the winter's storm,
making his path through the roaring waves....

Language, and thought like the wind
and the feelings that make the town,
he has taught himself, and shelter against the cold,
refuge from rain. He can always help himself.
He faces no future helpless. There's only death
that he cannot find an escape from.
He has contrived refuge from illnesses once beyond all cure.

Clever beyond all dreams
the inventive craft that he has
which may drive him at one time or another to well or ill.[2]

Although they were portrayed only by male actors, female characters were prominent in Greek tragedy and often played leading roles like that of Sophocles' Antigone. The angry, vengeful women in Euripides' *Medea* (431 B.C.; discussed later in this chapter) and *Hippolytus* (428 B.C.) show compassionate understanding for the violence to which women could be driven by social constraints. Euripides' *Trojan Women* was produced in 415 B.C., just after the Athenians had massacred the men of the island of Melos and enslaved the women and children because the Melians had resisted involvement in the Peloponnesian War. In this play, Euripides depicted the horrors of war by portraying the destruction of Troy through the eyes of its women—raped, enslaved, and forced to endure their children's murder.

Social commentary also played a large role in the comedies of Aristophanes (c. 450–c. 385 B.C.). In *Lysistrata,* produced in 411 B.C., the women of Greece take an oath to withhold sex from their husbands until the men agree to end the Peloponnesian War. *The Clouds* (423 B.C.), which ridiculed Socrates and depicted him sweeping across the skies in a crane thinking about lofty questions, contributed to his ill repute among Athenians. Although the later execution of Socrates demonstrated the limits of free speech in Athens, the liberty with which Aristophanes challenged public policy and social convention suggests a very open society.

VISUAL ARTS AND THE HUMAN IDEAL

The Greeks' principal contribution in the visual arts lay in their development of the human ideal through vase painting and sculpture. The Greeks used differently shaped vases to hold olive oil, wine, perfume, and funeral ashes. Early Greek vessels were adorned with stylized stick drawings, but toward the eighth century B.C., painters began to make use of more naturalistic designs, including real and imaginary animal figures. As time passed, the human form was more realistically rendered. By 600 B.C., Athens and Corinth led the market in black-figure ware, a style in which dark forms were painted over the original reddish-brown color of the vase. Around the end of the sixth century B.C., Athenian artists pioneered a new, more versatile style—red-figure ware, in which the subjects were left in the original wash

color of the pot while the rest of the surface was covered with a deep brown slip that turned black when fired. The new style enabled painters to impose details on the red figures by adding brown lines.

Greek vases provide one of the historian's most valuable sources for details of daily life. Scenes depict women weaving, farmers plowing, housewives supervising servants, men wrestling, and children playing with toys. Greek vase painters made skillful use of the space at their disposal to create dramatic scenes, depicting episodes from mythology. One of the best examples is Exekias' portrayal of the death of Ajax. Myth related that Ajax killed himself when he was passed over in the competition to receive the armor of the dead Achilles. Rather than depicting Ajax falling on his sword, Exekias shows him bent with sorrow, implanting his weapon in the ground point up. Any Greek viewer would have known what followed.

Sculpture was a less delicate medium. Images of manly heroism played a dominant role in Greek sculpture, and male figures outnumbered females. In sculpture as in painting, the heroic male was regularly portrayed nude, and because the Greeks in many ways viewed gods as outsize mortals, it is not always possible to know which male statues portray gods and which depict humans. Citizen women, by contrast, were always shown wrapped in robes, perhaps symbolizing seclusion as well as chastity.

Early Greek statues reveal a marked influence from Egypt and western Asia, portraying weighty figures of mass and dignity advancing slowly with one foot in front of the other. The characteristic statues of this so-called archaic period (c. 630–c. 480 B.C.) were the *kouros,* the nude standing male, and the *kore,* the clothed standing female; both were depicted with wide eyes and haunting smiles. In contrast to the stillness of archaic statues, the sculpture of the classical period vividly portrayed muscularity and movement. Like Exekias' Ajax vase, the classical *Discobolos* (discus thrower) by Myron (c. 450 B.C.) captures a dramatic moment by depicting the instant of equilibrium when the athlete, his strength pent up and his concentration intense, is about to hurl the discus. As in archaic sculpture, this statue shows little emotion, but the body is naturally taut and poised in an anticipation the viewer shares.

A number of magnificent fifth-century B.C. female statues survive, at least in fragments. Classical females were often wrapped in swirling garments that achieved an effect of sensuality and motion, highlighting the breasts and legs outlined beneath.

Myron's *Discobolos* (discus thrower) survives in this Roman copy. [Copyright © 1989 Loyola University of Chicago, R.V. Schoder, S.J., Photographer]

Temples and the Greek Ideal

Some of the most striking female statues were the caryatids that graced the porch of the temple on the Athenian acropolis known as the Erechtheum, after Athens' mythical king Erechtheus. The Erechtheum shared the Acropolis with what is perhaps the most famous building in Western history, the temple to Athena the Virgin (Athena Parthenos), known as the Parthenon. Of the three standard orders of Greek architecture, each defined by the capitals (tops) of the columns it employed, the Athenians chose the stark Doric for the Parthenon, whereas the Erechtheum was designed in the gracious scrolled Ionic style. Corinthian columns, with

their elaborate capitals in the shape of the acanthus plant, were more popular in later centuries.

Begun in 447 B.C. under Pericles and designed by Callicrates and Ictinus, the Parthenon had an inner chamber that housed a 40-foot gold and ivory statue of Athena, who also served as the focus of the sculptural program. The east pediment—the triangular space supporting the roof—pictured her birth and the west pediment her contest with Poseidon for the territory of Athens. The Parthenon was severely damaged by war in the seventeenth century A.D., and the statue of Athena has long since disappeared. In its basic style the Parthenon was typical of temples throughout the Greek world. Many of the best preserved of these, such as Hera's temple at Paestum in southern Italy, are found outside Greece.

A comparison of the temples and Attic tragedy reveals much about the Greek view of life as it had developed through the earliest times to the classical period. Both the drama and the temple were intensely bound up with civic life and the worship of the gods. Both sought to express epic themes within a highly contained and disciplined art form. Although a tragedy might treat the misery of an ill-fated family for generations, convention allowed the playwright to represent the action of only a 24-hour period. Violence, while it formed an important element of tragedy, was always enacted offstage, and facial expressions were stylized by the use of masks. Architecture, too, found challenge in constraint. The portion of the temple in which the tension between human aspiration and the limits of space was most evident is the pediment; developing a sculptural scene for the gentle slope below the roof required considerable ingenuity. The efforts of Greek artists to express themselves in this confining space are symbolic of the human struggle to achieve greatness despite the shortness of life and the inevitability of death. The essential elements of the Greek view of life—restraint, dignity, and proportion as well as violence, passion, and competitiveness—are all present in classical Greek art.

GREEK SCIENCE AND PHILOSOPHY

Science and philosophy developed together in sixth-century B.C. Greece. Since early Greek science or *physis*

The Acropolis, Athens, from the south. [Alison Frantz]

(from which our word *physics* is derived) relied on speculation and casual observation rather than systematic experiment or careful observation, it shaded off easily into the more general thought about the nature of the world and the human place in it that we call philosophy. The Greeks had the benefit of existing knowledge, notably Babylonian astronomy. From the beginning, however, Greek science differed from earlier traditions in that it attempted to provide an essentially material description of the world without assuming the intervention of divine forces. This was a radical departure from previous thought, and more than any other factor it laid the basis for Western science to the present day.

Classical mythology had attempted to account for the development of the natural universe by the actions of the gods, but several early Greek thinkers sought to explain it by material processes alone. Thales, Anaximander, and Anaximenes, all residents of the city of Miletus in Ionia, posed an extraordinary question: What is the world made of? Thales suggested that the fundamental

substance was water. Anaximander boldly guessed that life had first arisen in the warm mud or slime, producing first reptiles, than land animals, and ultimately the human race. He thus hit on the first theory of evolution, which he defended by pointing to fossilized seashells he had discovered in the mountains and by the parallel between infant helplessness and that of certain fish species. A third thinker, Anaximenes, attempted to explain the existence of spirit or intelligence by positing not water but air as the primary substance. In its most perfect and rarefied forms, he argued, air was spirit, a part of which, trapped in the body, formed the soul. This idea of the soul as confined by the body, to be released only upon death, had a profound influence on the thought of Plato and, through him, on Christianity as well. The importance of the soul and its proper care also formed part of the thinking of Pythagoras (sixth century B.C.), whose followers in the Italian city of Croton in which he settled included both men and women. Pythagoras believed that souls migrated after death into new bodies, and for this reason he encouraged his followers to perform purification rites and observe strict dietary rules so that they would be reincarnated in a higher rather than a lower animal. Eating meat was forbidden, as any creature might contain a human soul. Pythagoras ascribed the workings of the universe to mathematical principles, and his interest in numeric relationships led him to discover their role in musical harmony; our modern eight-note scale derives from his research.

Greek thinkers of the fifth century B.C. were dissatisfied with the theories of their predecessors. Heraclitus (flourished c. 500 B.C.) of Ephesus rejected the idea of any moment of creation or process of evolution, contending that the world was always in a similar state of flux and creation. This notion gave rise to his famous statement that it is impossible to step into the same river twice. Parmenides of Elea (c. 515–c. 450 B.C.) argued that, on the contrary, motion was impossible, since the idea of an unoccupied space through which matter could pass was logically out of the question. When it was pointed out that things did appear to move (for example, the lips of Parmenides denying that motion existed), the philosopher replied loftily that this was merely an illusion.

A somewhat younger contemporary, Empedocles of Akragas in Sicily (c. 493–433 B.C.), propounded an ambitious cosmogony based on the idea of four primary elements—earth, air, fire, and water—which produced variety in physical substances depending on the proportions in which they were combined. Because chance alone determined such combinations, monstrous forms had probably been created at an earlier period, but these, failing to adapt, had perished. Empedocles thus propounded an early form of Darwinian natural selection. His theory of the four basic elements was accepted down to the seventeenth century A.D., although two later figures, Leucippus and Democritus of Abdera (c. 460–c. 370 B.C.), put forth a rival theory that posited that all physical entities were composed of tiny, undifferentiated pellets of matter, which they called *atoms* (literally, "without parts," "indivisible.")

These daring thinkers, often called the Pre-Socratics, propounded many of the basic questions that Western science would later pursue. Another group, the Sophists, were largely indifferent to speculation about the physical world and devoted most of their energy to the arts of persuasion. Their professed aim was not to discover the nature of the world but rather to learn how to get along in it, and for a fee they offered lessons in argumentation and eloquence to aspiring politicians. The Athenian upper class rejected the notion that wisdom could be bought for money and derided the education the Sophists offered social climbers as empty rhetoric, but the teachings of one famous sophist, Protagoras (c. 481–411 B.C.), make clear that many Sophists engaged in substantive philosophical speculation. Protagoras' belief that humankind was the measure of all things reflected a serious concern with the relationship between perception and reality.

Parmenides, Protagoras, and many other figures of the middle and late fifth century B.C. would be brought to life in the dialogues of Plato, whose chief character was his own teacher, Socrates (469–399 B.C.) Unlike the Sophists, Socrates took no payment for his teaching. He delighted in leading young men in the direction of greater understanding by a method of question and answer. But his intellectual playfulness and his refusal to subscribe to popular opinion, as well as the association of several of his students with the unpopular oligarchy that ruled Athens at the end of the Peloponnesian War, made him a natural target for those searching to find a scapegoat for the city's military defeat. Arraigned on charges of impiety and corrupting the young, he was condemned to death by an Athenian jury.

Plato

Socrates' pupil Plato (c. 427–c. 347 B.C.) was deeply affected by his teacher's death. In a unique tribute he couched most of his writings in the form of dialogues in which Socrates has the chief role and which recreate the atmosphere of his lively philosophical discussions.

The basis of Plato's philosophy is his theory of forms. All human ideas, he asserts, whether of material entities such as chairs and tables or of conceptual ones such as beauty or justice, are intuitions of immaterial forms that are at the same time the basis for all physical and mental reality. We first perceive a physical object (such as a table) or intellectual category (such as beauty) that embodies an ideal form and then proceed to recognize the permanent form it represents.

In the hierarchy of forms, goodness is the ultimate value, and later Christian philosophers, deeply influenced by Plato, would declare goodness to be the primary quality of God. If goodness is the final object of philosophy, however, the object of civil society is justice, a quest Plato pursued in his best-known dialogue, *The Republic,* composed about 374 B.C. As in other dialogues, his characters weigh various definitions of justice. Ultimately, Plato settles on the idea that justice is the harmony that arises when each person is able to pursue his or her best talent—the artisan to build, the musician to play, and the ruler to govern.

To ensure that each talent is found and properly employed, Plato constructs a three-tiered society that resembles an idealized version of Sparta. At the top are the *guardians,* who live communally and enjoy neither family nor possessions and whose function is wisdom and government. Surprisingly, considering Plato's Athenian birth, guardians were to be both male and female. The guardians are assisted by *auxiliaries,* or soldiers, chosen especially for their strength and courage. The majority, meanwhile, are trained and assigned to perform the other functions of society. Plato is famous for saying that a truly successful state would come about only when kings were philosophers and philosophers were kings, and the education he proposed for the guardian elite was consequently protracted and difficult. Only men and women who have demonstrated both the necessary philosophical aptitude to grasp and internalize the nature of the forms and the practical ability to apply them to affairs may be entrusted with the responsibility of the state.

Aristotle

Plato offered a real-life education similar to the one he recommended for the guardians of the *Republic.* Plato's school came to be known as the Academy, after the district outside Athens where it was founded, the groves sacred to the hero Academus. His chief pupil, Aristotle (384–322 B.C.), in time broke away and founded his own school in Athens, the Lyceum. Aristotle was born in Stagira in northern Greece and so, unlike Socrates and Plato, was not a native Athenian. Aristotle rejected Plato's conception of ideal forms that lacked any direct connection with material substance. Form and matter, which had long been distinct in Greek philosophy and which Plato had completely separated, were reunited in Aristotle's conception of substance. The world was neither static nor chaotic but a dynamic process; change was neither illusory nor random but orderly and patterned.

This conception had significant implications for the study of both the material world and human society. In rejecting the material world as illusory, Plato rejected science for philosophy, the truths of observation for the truths of contemplation. Aristotle restored science by asserting the final and indivisible reality of material substance, and by conceiving the world in terms of

orderly process he gave empirical knowledge a new and far more sophisticated basis.

Aristotle's own quest for knowledge was tireless. One ancient commentator numbered his works at 400, another at 1,000. He wrote on a wide variety of subjects— metaphysics, natural science, ethics, politics, history, literature, and rhetoric. In addition his pupils undertook a complete history of the sciences at his direction. It was no wonder that the Middle Ages called him the "Master of Those Who Know," and when the poet Dante referred to Aristotle as simply "the philosopher," readers understood at once who was meant.

The prejudices Aristotle shared with other Greeks of his day sometimes got in the way of his research. Disagreeing with Plato about women's intellectual potential, he offered scientific rationales for the unequivocal inferiority of women to men, and he defended slavery, claiming that "the slave completely lacks the capacity for deliberation; the female has it but in an underdeveloped form; and the child has it but incompletely." In his tendency to speak of slaves and women in the same breath with children, Aristotle was following a common Greek tradition.

Pragmatic rather than heroic, Aristotle praised the "golden mean" in both private and political conduct and counseled against excess in any form. Between them, Aristotle and Plato set the terms for much of subsequent Western thought. The British philosopher Alfred North Whitehead remarked that Western philosophy was a mere series of footnotes to Plato, and Christianity owed much to him. As for Aristotle, it is no exaggeration to say that he created the Western intellectual curriculum, stamping and defining its various disciplines and branches of knowledge.

Health and Medicine

Early Greek notions of health and medicine were often more religious than scientific, and prayer was for centuries the most common means of warding off illness and restoring health. At the same time, however, the Greeks of Asia Minor began to learn about anatomy from the observations Mesopotamians had made on entrails used in divination. Egyptians accustomed to dismantling corpses before mummification taught the Greeks something about the human body and were also familiar with various drugs. Greek medicine developed in Ionia concurrently with other scientific speculation. By the end of the sixth century B.C., medical schools were established on the island of Cos off the coast of Asia Minor and on the nearby peninsula of Cnidos. Cos was home to the most famous physician of the ancient world, Hippocrates (c. 460–c. 377 B.C.), whose name attached itself to a considerable body of writings (some written probably by Hippocrates himself, others by fellow doctors) that included the famous Hippocratic Oath still taken by physicians today. The oath is reminiscent of a second-millennium B.C. Egyptian papyrus and may have been of Egyptian origin. Stressing the bond between doctors and their teachers, it also commits physicians to transmit their skills to others, to act in the best interest of patients, and to preserve doctor-patient confidentiality.

The principal contribution of Hippocrates and his colleagues lay in their unshakable insistence on the rational explanation of natural phenomena. One of the most famous of the Hippocratic treatises, *On the Sacred Disease,* is devoted to refuting supernatural explanations of illness, particularly epilepsy. Epilepsy had been regarded as sacred, the author complained, because its physiological cause had not been discovered, and embarrassed physicians sought to conceal their ignorance with religious explanations. "It appears to me," the author wrote,

> that those who first attached a sacred nature to this disease were similar to the characters we now call magicians, purifiers, charlatans, and imposters: people who pretend to be extremely pious and to know something more than others. . . . They prescribed [cures] pretending that they possessed some superior knowledge and using other excuses so that if the patient's health was restored their reputation for cleverness would be enhanced; if the patient died, however, they would have safe explanations to offer, for they could claim that they themselves were not at all responsible for the patient's death, but the gods!"[3]

According to the Hippocratics, the only thing sacred about illness was the holy bond that tied doctors to each other and to their patients.

PHILIP AND ALEXANDER OF MACEDON

The nature of Greek civilization would be dramatically transformed by the rise of Macedonia. The first half of the fourth century B.C. was an era of shifting alliances, as the Athenians, Spartans, and Thebans vied to be the leading state in Greece. Skilled in innovative military tactics, the Theban leader Epaminondas (died 362 B.C.)

bequeathed an ominous legacy to posterity in the young Macedonian hostage whom he had instructed in the art of warfare. This brilliant youth, Philip, was to use what he had learned from Epaminondas to bring Greece under his domination; he would also sire a prince, Alexander, who would change the face of Greece, Egypt, and western Asia for centuries to come.

Closely related to the Greeks, the Macedonians spoke a Greek dialect but enjoyed a distinctly different culture. The idea of the polis had never taken root in Macedonia, a wild land dependent on agriculture and without major cities. Macedonia became a power to contend with only under Philip II (359–336 B.C.), who employed a devious combination of warfare and diplomacy to extend his country's influence. After modernizing the Macedonian army along Theban lines, Philip seized the Thracian gold mines and conquered many cities in northern Greece.

Although the Athenians were alarmed by Philip's conquests, many of which involved the destruction of their own allies, Athens hesitated to oppose Macedon. In part, this reluctance was due to the presence of Macedonian partisans in the city. Some were in Philip's pay, while others sincerely believed that the intercity rivalries of the Greek poleis were counterproductive and that Greek interests would be better served by a coordinated campaign against the Persians led by Philip. In part as well the Athenians appear to have tired of the sacrifices that war demanded. Effective resistance to Philip meant raising taxes, which the Athenians were unwilling to do. They showed bad judgment. Whatever the cost, resistance was essential if the polis was to survive either in Athens or elsewhere in Greece.

Philip and his supporters were staunchly opposed by the Athenian orator and politician Demosthenes (c. 385–322 B.C.). A man of tremendous energy and resolve, Demosthenes had overcome a speech defect and an unhappy childhood to become one of the foremost rhetoricians in Athens. His eloquent speeches alerted the Athenians to the danger that Philip posed to their independence. By the time the Athenians finally recognized how great the Macedonian threat really was, the time to act was past. Backed by the Thebans, the Athenians took their final stand at Chaeronea in Boeotia in 338 B.C. The Macedonians, aided by crack cavalry commanded by Philip's 18-year-old son Alexander (356–323 B.C.), defeated the Greek coalition, and the freedom of the Greek city-states was no more.

Philip's plans to lead the combined forces of Macedonia and Greece against Persia were cut short two years later when he was murdered, possibly at the wishes of his

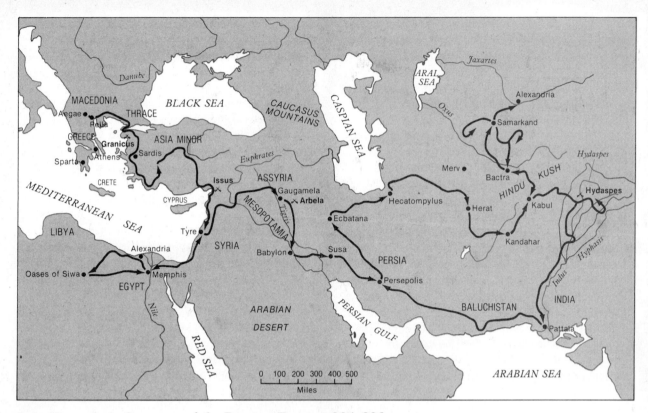

3.1 Alexander's Conquest of the Persian Empire, 334–323 B.C.

estranged wife, Olympias (or conceivably of Alexander himself, though this seems unlikely). Alexander carried out Philip's projected war, but on a scale his father could never have dreamed of and with permanent consequences for the civilizations of both East and West.

When Alexander was 13, his father engaged Aristotle to tutor him. Alexander may have owed to his teacher some of the great curiosity he later exhibited about the natural world, but he cast aside Aristotle's deep-seated belief in the superiority of Hellenic over non-Greek culture. Conquering Egypt and large parts of western Asia, Alexander forged a cosmopolitan empire unlike any political unit previously known in Greece. His incorporation of non-Greeks into his command structure and the mass marriages he celebrated between his soldiers and Persian women, combined with the ethnic diversity of the regions he conquered, laid the foundations for a world in which many traditional distinctions were blurred.

Alexander was an exceptionally skillful general who inspired extraordinary loyalty in his men and never lost

a battle. Although his career included episodes such as his ill-received request that Macedonian officers prostrate themselves before him in the Persian style, Alexander generally worked hard to project a favorable image. Before invading Persia, for example, he stopped to make offerings at Aulis, where Agamemnon was said to have made a sacrifice en route to Troy, and on his campaigns he carried a copy of the *Iliad* annotated by Aristotle. Combined with his military genius, Alexander's remarkable personality explains how legends about him lived on in Europe, Persia, India, and Arabia for more than 1,000 years after his death.

In 334 B.C., Alexander set out for Persia with an army of more than 30,000 foot soldiers and 5,000 cavalry. Proclaiming himself the liberator of the Greeks, he freed the Ionian poleis and replaced their Persian-imposed oligarchies with democracies. Proceeding southward, Alexander defeated the forces of the Persian monarch Darius III and proceeded to capture Palestine. In 332 B.C. he invaded Egypt, where the anti-Persian priesthood of Memphis hailed him as pharaoh. At the northern end of the Nile delta he founded Alexandria, which eventually became the leading city of the eastern Mediterranean. From North Africa, Alexander marched over 1,000 miles east to defeat Darius once more on the field of Gaugamela (331 B.C.). The following year the Persian king was assassinated by one of his own guards, and Alexander assumed the throne.

On becoming the king of Persia, Alexander surrounded himself with the pomp that normally attended Eastern potentates, thereby irritating his Macedonian and Greek troops. The eastward march continued, but after Alexander had crossed the Hindu Kush and defeated Porus, the king of Punjab, his troops refused to go farther. Grudgingly, Alexander agreed to return to Susa; the march proved so horrendous that much of his army perished. In 323 B.C., Alexander went to Babylon to supervise the building of a temple and to plan the exploration of the Caspian Sea. There he died of a fever at the age of 32.

Alexander's plans for the empire will never be known. He may have planned to augment its extent by a major expedition to the west. In 327 B.C. he married Roxane, a Bactrian princess, and in 324 B.C. some 80 of his officers were married to Persian women at a mass wedding. Alexander himself took Darius' daughter Barsine as an additional wife and hosted a banquet not only for the newlyweds but also for the nearly 10,000 Macedonian-Persian couples who had married in previous years. As king of Persia, Alexander adopted Persian dress and appointed a number of Persians to important positions in his army and government. Although his fusion of the Macedonians and the Persians did not necessarily betoken any wider conception of the unity of humankind, it contrasted with the Greeks' traditional belief in their racial superiority and the distinctiveness of their culture. The many cities Alexander founded would become important centers of cultural diffusion and would afford fertile ground for the growth of a far more cosmopolitan society than was customary in the poleis of classical Greece.

THE HELLENISTIC KINGDOMS

Because Alexander had made no plans for an orderly succession, his generals fought bitterly over the disposition of his conquests. Ptolemy, who became satrap of Egypt after Alexander's death, struggled for nearly 20 years to establish himself as the undisputed ruler of Alexandria. His family ruled Egypt for three centuries until the last Ptolemaic sovereign, Cleopatra, committed suicide in 30 B.C. after her defeat at the hands of Rome. Another general, Seleucus, defeated his competitors for what was essentially the old Persian Empire in 312 B.C., but his family had less success than the Ptolemies in holding their territory. By 303 B.C., Seleucus had lost his easternmost provinces to Chandragupta Maurya, founder of the Mauryan dynasty in India.

The Parthians, who inhabited northeastern Persia, gradually made themselves masters of the rest of Persia and Bactria, and the city of Pergamum in Asia Minor became the center of an independent kingdom. By the end of the second century B.C. the Seleucid kingdom did not extend much beyond Syria. Following Alexander's death, the former governor of Phrygia in Asia Minor, Antigonus "the One-Eyed," supported by his son Demetrius "the Besieger," contested the rule of the east with Seleucus, but after their defeat in 301 B.C. the Antigonids had to content themselves with ruling Macedonia, where their family reigned until they were defeated by the Romans in 167 B.C..

Within about a generation of Alexander's death a balance of power had been established around the Mediterranean, and thousands of Greeks emigrated to the newly founded cities in the regions Alexander had conquered. The degree to which Hellenistic cities enjoyed a practical day-to-day independence from their Macedonian overlords varied. No cities had freedom to make their own foreign policy, but many enjoyed domestic self-government. Nonetheless, the ultimate lack of autonomy made it impossible for men to derive the same fulfillment from participation in politics that had characterized the Classical Age. One consequence of this development was a relaxation in the tensions between men and women within Greek states, particularly Athens, for the exclusion of most men from the centers of power put males and females more on a par. In aristocratic circles, women played important roles as dynasts and as wives, mothers, and sisters of dynasts.

The expansion of the Hellenic world led the Greeks to think in a new way about their place in it. The Homeric poems had not presented them as racially or culturally superior to other peoples, but the Persian Wars engendered a chauvinistic Hellenic consciousness that presupposed the inferiority of "barbarians." During the later fifth century B.C., however, Herodotus had noted the wealth of cultural diversity in the Mediterranean world and had questioned the facile dismissal of all non-Hellenic peoples. Euripides' tragedy *Medea,* which portrayed the abandonment of the barbarian princess Medea by her husband, the Greek hero Jason, likewise challenged the cult of Hellenic superiority. In the world forged by Alexander's conquests, new philosophies arose that stressed the universality of the human condition and, severing the close bond that had united the individual and the community in the classical polis, emphasized the need for individuals to find a personal serenity divorced from the governments under which they lived.

COSMOPOLITANISM AND FEDERALISM

The loss of autonomy among the city-states of the classical period combined with the cosmopolitan outlook of the Hellenistic Age to produce new political structures in mainland Greece. During the late fourth and early third centuries B.C., several Greek cities banded together in loose organizations, the Aetolian League in north-central and western Greece and the Achaean League in the Peloponnesus. Each was governed by a federal body of elected representatives. The Aetolian league established a council composed of delegates from member cities, and all citizens were welcome to attend the biennial assembly of the league. Both leagues sought to protect Greek freedoms against Macedonia. The Achaean League at one time embraced 60 cities. Its assembly met less regularly than its Aetolian counterpart, but both confederations collected taxes and determined foreign policy. The Hellenistic leagues were often cited by America's founders as precedents for their own bold venture.

ECONOMIC DEVELOPMENT

The Peloponnesian War had drained the economies of many of the Greek poleis, and the recovery of the fourth century B.C. was only partial. Alexander's conquests ultimately aggravated the economic decline of the mainland. At first, the expansion had created new markets for Greek exports. Yet as time passed, the influx of artisans into the Hellenistic kingdoms of Egypt and western Asia enabled them to produce a wide variety of local wares. Sidon became famous for its glassware, Tarsus for its linen, and Antioch for its gold and silver. Alexandria came to serve not only as the port of transit for produce from Africa and the harbors of the Red Sea but also as a manufacturing center for linen, jewelry, cosmetics, papyrus, and glass. Delos and Rhodes, lying on the routes connecting Greece and Italy with the east, rivaled each other as centers of international exchange. The northern coast of the Black Sea retained its primacy as a major source of slaves, fish, fur, wheat, and timber. To the south, the great caravan routes connecting the Mediterranean with Arabia, India, and central Asia passed through Phoenician and Syrian ports, and Egypt prospered as a result of the grain trade.

The growth of the city at the expense of the countryside taxed the food resources of the ancient world. The swelling of urban centers with itinerant mercenaries and sailors also combined with the increasing use of slave labor in both city and country to create widespread unemployment. Although the initial expansion of the Greek world had benefited local economies by creating new jobs in the building industry, this growth was short-lived.

Throughout the Hellenic world a Greek bureaucracy formed the core of a prosperous upper class. The thriving international business conducted by this class fostered the spread of *koine,* a simplified Greek dialect. The aristocracy was set off from the lower orders not only by its Hellenic heritage but also by its affluence. Beneath it sprawled a large population plagued by unemployment and hunger.

ALEXANDRIA, COSMOPOLITAN CAPITAL

Founded by Alexander immediately after his conquest of Egypt, Alexandria became the Egyptian capital under Ptolemy I, and the immense wealth of the Ptolemies helped make it one of the most renowned cities of antiquity. Its planner was Deinocrates of Rhodes. He laid it out on a grand scale, with a main street lined with shops and bazaars said to be 100 feet wide.

The principal building complex was the royal palace, which served both as the residence of the Ptolemies and as the seat of government. Surrounded by gardens and fountains, it was occupied mainly by the Greek-speaking bureaucrats who administered Ptolemaic Egypt. The famous Pharos, a lighthouse that stood more than 400 feet tall, was visible at a distance of some 20 miles. Long colonnades, lit at night by torches, lined the capital's broad streets, and the city was renowned for its gardens, parks, and zoo. With a dense population of Greeks, Jews, and other ethnic groups in addition to native Egyptians, Alexandria developed a truly cosmopolitan outlook. At first the Greek community tried to keep out the native Egyptians, but as intermarriage became more common, Alexander's plan of fusing cultures was partly fulfilled.

In Alexandria the Ptolemies established an important research institute called the Museum because it was dedicated to the Muses, the nine goddesses traditionally believed to inspire art and wisdom. Perhaps the earliest "think tank" in history, it supported approximately 100 scholars at state expense. Alexandria became an important center for the study of anatomy and astronomy. Several schools of Hellenistic poetry originated in Alexandria, and the most famous Hellenistic poet, Theocritus, lived there shortly after 300 B.C. The library at Alexandria became the largest of its day, housing the scrolls that were the ancient form of books; over 500,000 manuscript rolls could be found there. Not all Alexandrians spent their time conducting research or writing poetry; residents of Alexandria were notorious for being rowdy, pleasure-loving, noisy, opinionated, and condescending to foreigners.

Ptlomey I had encouraged the establishment of a Jewish community, and by the time of Ptolemy III (246–221 B.C.) there were three synagogues in the city. The Jews were housed in one particular quarter, where they were supervised by their own magistrate. The Jews of Alexandria were allowed to own land and were often employed as tax collectors but were rarely involved in trade or moneylending. On several occasions, Jewish generals led Egyptian forces, and many Jewish soldiers served as mercenaries. In time the Jews came to speak Greek, and the Hebrew Bible was translated into Greek, a version known as the Septuagint. Services at the synagogues were conducted in Greek, and many Jews took Greek names. Jewish scholars in Alexandria developed a school of Greco-Jewish thought; the most memorable of these was Philo (c. 30 B.C.–A.D. 45), who combined Greek philosophical ideas with a belief in a personal, moral Yahweh.

Alexandria retained its importance in Roman times and did not begin to decline until the Arab conquest of the seventh century A.D. There are, however, few traces of Ptolemaic Alexandria today. A change in sea level left most of the ancient city under water, and the Pharos was destroyed by an earthquake in the fourteenth century A.D.

HELLENISTIC WOMEN

As we have seen, the social life of women in classical Greek society was largely restricted to the household. By the end of the fifth century B.C., however, a number of artists had begun to show a marked interest in female subjects and several intellectuals questioned the traditional role of women in Greek society. One of the earliest examples of this can be found in Euripides' play *Medea,* first performed in 431 B.C. It describes the vengeance of Medea upon her husband Jason, who had abandoned her for a new, aristocratic bride. In the eyes of an Athenian audience, Medea labors under two crushing disadvantages: she is both a woman and a foreigner. As such she is denied basic rights; although she is married to a Greek, Jason, and has two children by him, Athenian law did not recognize children by foreign wives as citizens. Thus Jason has no responsibility when he abandons her for a Greek wife who can provide legitimate children. The deserted Medea leaves the confines of her home to go outdoors and express her rage, frustration, hopelessness, and loneliness to anyone who will listen, claiming that

> *We women are the most unfortunate creatures. . . .*
> *A man, when he's tired of the company in his home,*
> *Goes out of the house and puts an end to his boredom*
> *And turns to a friend or companion of his own age.*
> *But we are forced to keep our eyes on one alone.*
> *What they say of us is that we have a peaceful time*
> *Living at home, while they do the fighting in war.*
> *How wrong they are! I would very much rather stand*
> *Three times in the front of battle than bear one child.[4]*

In the end, Medea kills both her own children and Jason's intended bride in what has remained the most famous act of vengeance in literature.

In the fine arts, sculptors had begun by the fourth century B.C. to turn to the naked female form to express concepts of ideal beauty that in the previous century had been expressed through male subjects. The most famous example was Praxiteles' much imitated Aphrodite of

Cnidos. The statue combines the dignity of a goddess with a clearly erotic message. Aphrodite is depicted in the act of bathing; surprised by an intruder, she covers herself modestly with one hand—thus drawing the viewer's attention to the very area she seeks to conceal. Throughout the Hellenistic period the female nude remained one of the most popular of artistic subjects.

Women's lives also interested Hellenistic writers. In a poem set in Alexandria, Theocritus (c. 310–250 B.C.) depicts two women from Syracuse who have moved to the big city and become suburban housewives. Theocritus describes their walk around town on a festival day and records their gossip and their comments on the various sights. It is hard to imagine so witty, realistic, and familiar a note having been sounded in the fifth century B.C., whose writers showed little or no interest in women's daily lives.

Improvement in the status of women was thus slow but perceptible. Where their legal and economic rights were concerned, the old barriers remained, but the Hellenistic kingdoms made it possible for some women of extraordinary character to achieve power. The generalship of Arsinoë II, the wife of Ptolemy II, seems to have led the Egyptian forces to victory in the wars between Egypt and the Seleucids (276–272 B.C.), and she was deified. Arsinoë and other Hellenistic queens and princesses began to play an increasing cultural role as well. Berenice II, wife of Ptolemy III, corresponded with the leading poet of the day, Callimachus, and Stratonice, wife of the Seleucid monarch Antiochus I (ruled 280–261 B.C.), helped to build the art collection at Delos. Following such aristocratic examples, other women began to write and publish and even to appear in public. Aristodama of Smyrna traveled through Greece in the mid-third century B.C. giving recitals of her poetry; her brother went along as business manager. The city of Lamia was so impressed by her compositions that the voters there passed a decree honoring her not only with citizenship, something very unusual for a person from a different city-state to achieve, but also with the position of *proxenos* of the city, a sort of informal diplomatic representative, declaring

Whereas Aristodama, daughter of Amyntas of Smyrna in Ionia, an epic poetess, came to the city and gave several readings of her own poems in which she made appropriate mention of the Aetolian nation and the ancestors of the people . . . , showing zeal in her declamation, that she be a *proxenos* of the city and a benefactor, and that citizenship, the right to acquire land and property, grazing rights, exemption from reprisals, and safety by land and sea in peace or in war be granted to her and her children and her property for all time together with all the grants made to other *proxenoi* and benefactors.[5]

Not surprisingly, two new schools of Hellenistic philosophy actively encouraged the participation of women at their meetings and made no distinction between the sexes: Stoicism and Epicureanism.

HELLENISTIC THOUGHT

Plato and Aristotle were citizens of the polis and saw in it the norm and limit of human community. The Hellenistic world of empire called for a different approach to philosophy, one that expressed both the inward turn of Greek thought and the changed relationship between the individual and the state.

The earliest of the Hellenistic philosophies was Cynicism. The Cynics believed that people should imitate the naturalness of animals, shunning artificiality and convention. Self-sufficiency was their goal, and they believed that it was most easily attained by rejecting the trappings of civilization—not only material possessions but also the arts, which were deemed unnatural. The principal thinker of the Cynic movement was Diogenes of Sinope (c. 412–c. 323 B.C.). He taught by his own example the virtues of an ascetic life, complete freedom of speech, and shamelessness of action; this last won him his nickname of the Cynic ("the dog"). Cynicism had little intellectual content, for its very point was to demonstrate that life can be lived at a minimum level of material, emotional, and spiritual needs.

Epicurus (c. 342–270 B.C.), a contemporary of the Cynics, was also concerned to promote self-sufficiency, but the route he recommended was quite different. Epicurus recombined natural science with philosophy to form the first clearly articulated humanist philosophy of the West. Building on the atomic theory of Leucippus and Democritus, Epicurus developed a materialistic philosophy based on the belief that all change and growth resulted from the rearrangement of these primary particles. He maintained that atoms falling from the sky periodically swerved, colliding at various angles to produce the multiplicity of substances in the universe. Ascribing such phenomena as thunder and lightning to the movement of these atoms, Epicureans denied that people needed to maintain the favor of the gods to avoid suffering. The gods, they argued, existed, but they lived serene, untroubled lives and were indifferent to human affairs.

In the absence of eternal rewards and punishments, Epicurus saw earthly happiness as the goal of human life. Epicureans defined happiness as the attainment of *ataraxia,* an untroubled state neither agitated by excessive pleasure nor subject to avoidable discomfort and pain. To achieve ataraxia, Epicurus advocated withdrawal from activities such as moneymaking, politics, and romantic love, since participation in such things made people vulnerable to failure, disappointment, and suffering. In modern usage the word *epicurean* has come to be synonymous with *pleasure-loving,* but Epicurus counseled moderation in food and drink, since the consequences of overindulgence were likely to be unpleasant.

Around the same time, Zeno (335–263 B.C.) was holding forth by the so-called Painted Porch of Athens, the Stoa Poikile, advocating a different path to serenity. Zeno and his fellow Stoics ("Porchers") also believed in the importance of distancing oneself from daily life and aspired to a detachment that would offer protection against excessive pleasure and pain. The Stoics, however, did not advocate withdrawal from public life; on the contrary, they believed that serenity was impossible without the confidence that one had fulfilled one's duties to others, and they preached a high ethical standard of humanitarianism, including general pacifism.

Unlike the Epicureans, the Stoics believed that a divine order governed the universe. This belief discouraged them from widening their ethical commitments to embrace social reform. While they preached the essential equality of slaves and free people, the Stoics made no effort to abolish slavery. They were less tolerant of absolutist government, which they viewed as a violation of natural order. The comfort people drew from believing that the suffering in their lives was part of an orderly divine plan seems to have been great, and among the elite in Roman times, Stoicism was the most popular of the Greek philosophies in Italy. It also influenced Christianity, particularly in its discouragement of sexual passion separate from procreation.

Skepticism, associated with the name of its chief proponent, Carneades, enjoyed some popularity around 200 B.C.. The Skeptics stressed the impossibility of certain knowledge and urged people to withdraw from the world around them, abandoning the hopeless quest for power and truth. In their nihilism the Skeptics were the Cynics' heirs, and in their disillusionment with public life they echoed the Epicureans. Only Stoicism among the major philosophical schools of the Hellenistic Age counseled engagement in the world, and even the Stoics no longer looked to fulfillment in a particular community but rather saw themselves as citizens of the world.

Changing Religious Views

The Hellenistic world forced the Greeks to widen the scope of the Olympian gods. No longer could it be the mission of Athena, Apollo, and Poseidon to defend the interests of the Greeks against those of "barbarians." Elegant temples to the Olympian gods were constructed throughout the Hellenistic empires. Some attempts were also made at syncretism, the fusion of deities. In Egypt, worshipers were encouraged to combine Zeus and Amon-Re, while Syrians could unite the fertility goddess Atargatis with Aphrodite. Greeks in Egypt and western Asia frequently attached themselves to the cults of non-Greek gods. The fertility cult of Cybele was popular, particularly among women, and the bull-god Mithras was worshiped by many men. Judaism too attracted many admirers. In Egypt the Ptolemies patronized the cult of Sarapis, a Macedonian-inspired fusion of the venerable Egyptian fertility god Osiris with the divine bull Apis. The religion never caught on among the Egyptians, who saw no need to improve on Osiris in his original form, but it was popular among the Macedonian aristocracy both in Egypt and subsequently throughout the Mediterranean area.

Like Mithras, Sarapis was portrayed as a universal god, gentle and caring, but unlike Mithras, he welcomed worshipers of both sexes. His popularity reflected the desire for a religion that transcended the civic cults of earlier days, one that had never discriminated between Greeks and non-Greeks and was not tied to the state as Olympian religion had often been. The limitations of Olympian worship were reflected in the duties of priests, who devoted themselves to ritual and the care of sacred precincts rather than to theological pursuits. Pastoral counseling was apparently unknown. Thus the Olympian religion had little meaning for hungry souls seeking contact with the divine. The sharpening of this hunger in an era when civic commitments no longer offered fulfillment would eventually open the door to a new religion, Christianity.

SCIENCE IN THE HELLENISTIC AGE

Science probably made greater strides in the Hellenistic Age than in any other period of history before the seventeenth century A.D. Advances in the life sciences were due in part to the tremendous energy and output of

Aristotle, and many discoveries were made by his successors at the Lyceum.

Already during the middle of the fourth century B.C., Heraclides of Pontus (c. 390–310 B.C.) had discovered that the earth revolved daily on its axis, and during the third century B.C., Eratosthenes (c. 275–194 B.C.) calculated the circumference of the earth. Aristarchus of Samos (c. 310–230 B.C.) concluded that the earth rotated around the sun, although his theories were discarded in favor of the geocentric system of Hipparchus of Nicaea (c. 190–c. 126 B.C.), a talented astronomer who measured the lunar month and the solar year with surprising accuracy and discovered the equinoxes. In the field of mathematics, Euclid (flourished c. 300 B.C.) systematized geometric knowledge in his *Elements,* one of the most influential textbooks ever written. Archimedes of Syracuse (c. 287–212 B.C.) wrote the first works on hydrostatics and electrical discharge in the atmosphere and calculated the ratio of a circle's circumference to its diameter (*pi*).

The Hellenistic age witnessed tremendous advances in medicine, particularly at Alexandria, where the anato-

mist Herophilus, working in the early third century B.C., discovered that the brain was the center of the nervous system and that the arteries carried blood. The first person to measure the pulse, Herophilus was apparently also the first to practice public dissection of human corpses. Vivisection may also have been performed on criminals. It was probably no coincidence that the Egyptians, accustomed to removing organs from corpses before mummification, were less likely than others to regard the dissection of human bodies as sacrilegious. Herophilus' procedures enabled him to discover the ovaries and possibly also the Fallopian tubes.

ERATOSTHENES, GLOBAL GEOGRAPHER

Chief librarian at Alexandria, Eratosthenes was born at Cyrene in North Africa around 275 B.C. He studied both

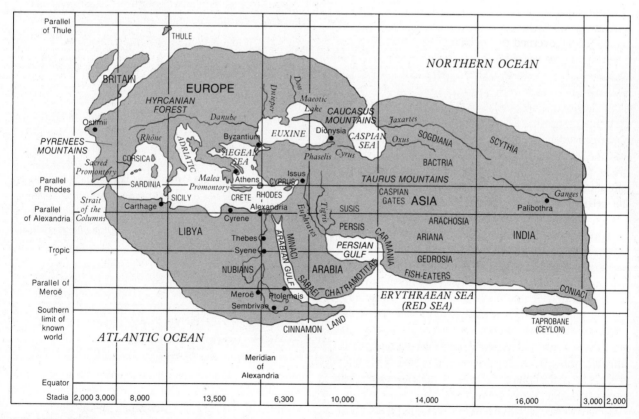

3.2 *The World According to Eratosthenes*

in Alexandria and in Athens, and he acquired more from his wide travels than from book learning. The geographer Strabo (c. 63 B.C.–c. A.D. 21) credited him with the observation that people should be classified not as Greek or barbarian but as good or bad.

Although nothing remains of Eratosthenes' writings beyond fragments, much is known about his work. His literary output included an important treatise *On Ancient Comedy,* which dealt not only with the texts of the comic poets of the fifth and fourth centuries B.C. but also with stagecraft. In addition to a history of philosophy, he prepared a study of chronology that sought to date the important events of history beginning with the fall of Troy, and he compiled a list of victors at the Olympian games.

The first to use lines to represent latitude and longitude, Eratosthenes made a more detailed map of the known world than had previously been drawn. Convinced that all oceans were really one, he was the first to suggest that sailors proceeding west would eventually reach India. Most educated Greeks of his day agreed that the earth was round, but it was Eratosthenes who determined the size of the sphere, using geometry to compute the circumference of the earth with an error of less than 10 percent. Eratosthenes' calculation was far more accurate than the one used by Columbus when he sailed to the New World in 1492.

The Winged Victory of Samothrace was sculpted around 200 B.C.; it stood 96 inches tall. [Scala/Art Resource, New York]

HELLENISTIC ART

The visual arts of the Hellenistic period, like other aspects of the culture, reflect the ideals and interests of the Greek aristocracy in the cities of western Asia and Egypt. Nonetheless, the expansion of the Greek world led to some widening of scope as artists began to portray non-Greek characters with curiosity and empathy and chose a greater variety of subject matter for their work. The depiction of females increased, as did the representation of individuals who were neither young nor beautiful nor Greek. Hellenistic sculpture might portray Nubians from Africa, dying Gauls, poor elderly people, or dwarfs. The faces of Hellenistic subjects were also more likely than those of earlier periods to show distinctive expression, and portraiture was one of the most popular genres of the age.

Not all the characteristics of Hellenistic art, however, were traceable to the expansion of the Greek world, for important changes in artistic convention were already visible in the early fourth century B.C. Praxiteles' statue of Hermes holding the baby Dionysus shows a shift from the pronounced muscularity of the previous century. Although Hermes is youthful and athletic, there is a pensive softness about him as he holds the squirming infant.

Many Hellenistic statues are striking and innovative. Among them is the Winged Victory of Samothrace. Dating from the middle of the third century B.C., it captures in its swirling marble an extraordinary sense of incipient motion. In a remarkable blending of human aspiration and divine grandeur, huge birdlike wings grow naturally out of the human torso in place of arms. Innovation is also evident in the sensuality of a lifelike Eros (Cupid) and the pathos of an anguished Gallic chieftain determined to kill himself and his wife rather than endure the savagery of their captors. Combining the

This life-size portrayal of the sleeping Eros is typical of Hellenistic sculpture. [The Metropolitan Museum of Art, Rogers Fund, 1943 (43.11.4)]

traditional with the unusual, the stately with the bizarre, Hellenistic sculpture was widely copied in classical Rome, in the Renaissance, and in the baroque and rococo styles of later centuries.

Hellenistic culture also opened up new avenues of architecture. In the past, Greek architecture had been deliberately austere. Public buildings and private homes had generally been kept to a modest scale. During the Hellenistic period, great inequalities between rich and poor, the desire to establish new cities with a flourish, and the influence of the palace traditions of western Asia encouraged monumental architecture. The art of city planning developed, and splendid public avenues were laid out with impressive structures arranged around them.

The most outstanding example of Hellenistic monu-mental architecture is the huge Altar of Zeus at Pergamum, which has been restored in the State Museum in Berlin. A monumental flight of stairs leads up the enormous altar; atop the stairs is an Ionic colonnade, and around the base of the altar runs a frieze 400 feet long and nearly 8 feet tall. The battle between the gods and the giants depicted on the vivid frieze symbolizes the victories of Attalus I, whose son erected the monument. In this way the Attalids identified themselves with divinity. It was probably this bold structure that prompted the writer of the Apocalypse in the New Testament to refer to Pergamum as "Satan's Seat" (Revelations 2:13). The blending of the divine monarchy of western Asia with Greek images of human aspiration in the Altar of Zeus illustrates the typically hybrid culture of the Hellenistic Age.

SUMMARY

The artistic and intellectual achievements of the Greeks within a relatively brief period were remarkable. Greek sculpture established aesthetic standards that guided subsequent artists for centuries, and the influence of Hellenic architecture is still powerful in the West today. The tragedies of fifth-century B.C. Athens and the myths with which they dealt have formed the basis of a long and continuing literary tradition. The influence of Plato and Aristotle on Western thought has been incalculable. The Hellenistic Age witnessed the culmination of centuries of scientific speculation in which Greeks drew on the accumulated wisdom of Egypt and western Asia. Western political thought also owes much to the Greeks in general and to the articulation of democratic ideals in Athens in particular. The Greeks' difficulty in envisioning a state larger than the polis, however, undermined the endurance of their civilization. Intensely self-conscious about their cultural inferiority to their Greek predecessors, the Romans, with their wider political vision, would nonetheless draw on both their own resources and those of the Greek world to build a complex empire that bequeathed much of the Greek achievement to the modern world.

Notes

1. Translated by Henry David Thoreau in *The Writings of Henry D. Thoreau* (Princeton: Princeton University Press, 1986).
2. Translated by E. Wyckoff in D. Grene and R. Lattimore, eds., *Sophocles I: Three Tragedies* (Chicago: University of Chicago Press, 1954), pp. 170–171.
3. S. Spyridakis and B. Nystrom, eds., *Ancient Greece: Documentary Perspectives* (Dubuque, Iowa: Kendall/Hunt, 1985), p. 258.
4. In *Euripides I,* trans. R. Warner (Chicago: University of Chicago Press, 1955), p. 67.
5. F. W. Walbank, *The Hellenistic World* (Cambridge, Mass.: Harvard University Press, 1982), p. 74.

Suggestions for Further Reading

Borza, E. N. *In the Shadow of Olympus: The Emergence of Macedon.* Princeton: Princeton University Press, 1990.

Burkert, W. *Greek Religion.* Cambridge, Mass.: Harvard University Press, 1985.

Dover, K. J. *Greek Popular Morality in the Age of Plato and Aristotle.* Oxford: Blackwell, 1974.

Finley, M. I. *The Ancient Economy.* Berkeley: University of California Press, 1973.

Gouldner, A. *Enter Plato: Classical Greece and the Origins of Social Theory, Part II.* New York: Harper & Row, 1971.

Grant, F. *Hellenistic Religions: The Age of Syncretism.* New York: Liberal Press, 1953.

Green, P. *Alexander to Actium: The Historical Evolution of the Hellenistic Age.* Berkeley: University of California Press, 1990.

Guthrie, W. K. C. *The Sophists.* Cambridge: Cambridge University Press, 1971.

Hamilton, J. R. *Alexander the Great.* Pittsburgh: University of Pittsburgh Press, 1974.

Jaeger, W. *Paideia: The Ideals of Greek Culture.* Oxford: Oxford University Press, 1986.

Knox, B. *The Oldest Dead White European Males and Other Reflections on the Classics.* New York: W. W. Norton, 1993.

Lesky, A. *A History of Greek Literature.* London: Methuen, 1966.

Long, A. A. *Hellenistic Philosophy,* 2nd ed. London: Duckworth, 1986.

Pollitt, J. J. *Art and Experience in Classical Greece.* Cambridge: Cambridge University Press, 1972.

Pomeroy, S. *Women in Hellenistic Egypt: From Alexander to Cleopatra.* New York: Schocken Books, 1984.

THE ROMAN REPUBLIC

While the Greek cities were quarreling among themselves in the fifth and fourth centuries B.C., a state of very different character was taking shape not far away. Rome, originally a small town near the western coast of central Italy, was to grow into a power that would absorb the Hellenistic monarchies along with the rest of the Mediterranean world in an empire greater than any previously known. As Greece had defined the culture of the West, so Rome gave it the stamp of its laws, its institutions, and finally its religion.

The Romans attributed the cohesiveness and durability of their state to the virtue of its citizens, whereas Greek historians such as Polybius (c. 203–c. 120 B.C.) ascribed it to the perfection of its mixed constitution. The Romans' enduring genius was for organization. Aware that they were unlikely to match the Greeks in philosophy or the arts, they strove instead to master and expand their environment. Ultimately, their determination to endure no threats from neighbors led them to conquer first the Italian peninsula and then the entire Mediterranean basin. In time they would command an empire that stretched across much of continental Europe, northern Africa, and western Asia.

By its absorption of Greece, Rome became the transmitter of Hellenic culture to modern Europe and America. The Greco-Roman civilization of the Roman Empire is still the basis of much political and philosophical thought as well as art and literature. Many of the languages spoken in western Europe derive directly from Latin, and the domes, arches, and columns of American architecture proclaim the continuing vigor of the classical tradition in the New World. Latin is the only language no longer spoken as a vernacular tongue that is routinely taught in public schools in the United States.

EARLY ROME

Iron Age Italy was inhabited by a wide variety of peoples with whom the Romans alternately fought and commingled. Early in the Bronze Age the first Indo-European invaders of Italy had displaced the oldest inhabitants of the peninsula, who were related to the native populations of Spain and Gaul, and built their houses on platforms resting on poles. They had probably acquired these building habits in their original homes in central Europe. Toward the end of the Bronze Age, various groups who spoke Italic dialects arrived—the Umbrians, the Latins, and the Samnites. Prominent among the peoples of early Italy were the Etruscans. Among others they dominated were the inhabitants of Rome, a village built on the hills surrounding the river Tiber and founded according to legend in 753 B.C., although archaeological evidence suggests that the site was inhabited as early as 1400 B.C.

"Ice Man" 5100 years old

The Etruscans

As is clear from the ornate funerary objects found in their tombs, the Etruscans were a rich and technologically sophisticated people. Their engineers drained the marshes around the city of Rome and constructed temples, shrines, and roads. The Etruscans influenced the Romans in a variety of ways. The Romans took not only Etruscan ideas about the gods but also the art of divination, that is, the forecasting of events from omens. Early Roman officials subsequently had the right to interpret the will of the gods by the analysis of such omens as the flight of birds, the position of heavenly bodies, and the entrails of animals. The status of Etruscan women may have contributed to the greater freedom women enjoyed in Rome compared to classical Greece, and the respect that Romans accorded to wives and mothers probably owes much to Etruscan origins. From the Etruscans the Romans also adopted chariot racing, engineering techniques, the folding white costume known as the toga, and the alphabet (which the Etruscans had borrowed from the Greeks.)

TARQUINIA, JEWEL OF ETRURIA

Founded in the eighth century B.C. when local villages merged, Tarquinia, perhaps the most significant of the Etruscan cities, was situated 5 miles from the sea and some 40 miles north of the Tiber River. Its population may have reached 25,000 at its peak. The secret to its prosperity was control of the region around Mount Tolfa, approximately 10 miles away, where iron, tin, and copper were mined. Although the city was located inland, it controlled 15 miles of coastline that included no fewer than three ports. From Tarquinia, roads fanned out to other Etruscan towns.

Lid of an Etruscan funerary urn depicting the couple whose ashes it contains. Note the characteristic Etruscan concern for vividness of facial expression and lack of interest in proportions. [Alinari/Art Resource, New York]

Although virtually all of the ancient city was destroyed long ago, archaeologists have determined that it had a circumference of 5 miles, clearly demarcated streets, and a temple that housed the famous sculpted winged horses now on display in the local museum. Tarquinia was a center of manufacturing and commerce. Among the items produced in the city were metalwares, pottery, and linen. As early as the eighth century B.C. the Tarquinians engaged in commerce with Greek colonies in southern Italy. At first some of the colonists were allowed to live in Tarquinia, though by 600 B.C. they were encouraged to settle in their own quarter in one of the city's ports. The Tarquinians traded by sea not only with the island of Sardinia to the southwest and Campania to the south but also with places as far away as the Aegean basin and North Africa. To defend themselves, they built a navy.

Most of what we know about life in Tarquinia comes from the thousands of tombs found in the area hewn out of the subterranean rocks. The walls of these tombs were plastered and often painted, and the dead were laid on benches or interred in sarcophagi, typically with effigies of the deceased reclining on the lids. The tomb paintings, like the illustrations on pots and vases, reveal substantial Greek influence, both in style and in content, and their subjects reveal much about Tarquinian pastimes, including music, dancing, hunting, wrestling, juggling, and feasting.

Tradition maintained that the Etruscan dynasty that ruled Rome commencing in the late seventh century B.C. came from Tarquinia. The city began to decline, however, after neighboring Cerveteri seized control of the mines at Mount Tolfa. Commerce suffered after 480 B.C., when relations between the Greeks and the Etruscans deteriorated. The end came for Tarquinia after its defeat at the hands of the expanding Romans between 324 and 311 B.C.

The Romans' View of Their Origins

Romans from powerful families tended to dwell on their glorious history, and many legends attached to the founding of the city and its early development. One suggested that Rome was established after the fall of Troy by Aeneas, son of the goddess Venus (the Roman equivalent of the Greek Aphrodite) and a Trojan mortal, Anchises. Another attributed the founding to Romulus and Remus, twins supposedly raised by a wolf. In time the legends were combined, and it was believed that Aeneas' son Ascanius had established a city at nearby Alba Longa from which Rome was founded by Romulus and Remus 12 generations later. In a story evocative of the biblical tale of Cain and Abel, Romulus soon killed Remus, became the first of Rome's traditional seven kings, and made the city an asylum for runaway slaves and debtors.

The era of the kings was said to have lasted 244 years, during the last century of which the Etruscans were dominant. In 509 B.C., according to Roman tradition, the son of King Tarquin the Proud raped a Roman matron, provoking the Roman aristocracy to expel the Etruscans and end the monarchy. Thus was born the Roman republic. In reality, Tarquin was probably ousted by another Etruscan, Lars Porsenna, the ruler of nearby Clusium, but the Romans preferred to attribute Tarquin's deposition to their own action.

These stories had special meaning for the Romans. They took pride in the courage and persistence of Aeneas, who endured shipwreck and warfare to fulfill his destiny of settling Italy, and they made heroes of the patriots who had supposedly expelled the Etruscan kings. The Romans cherished the qualities that they believed their ancestors had embodied: *dignitas* (dignity), *gravitas* (seriousness), *pietas* (piety), and *virtus* (courage or virtue). *Dignitas* was generally achieved through recognition for state service; *gravitas* was reflected in the sobriety of one's bearing; *pietas* entailed reverence for gods and parents; and a person of *virtus* would demonstrate fortitude in battle if a man, chastity if a woman. These and similar qualities were grouped among the *mores maiorum,* the customs of the ancestors, which the Roman aristocracy developed into a coherent value system that gave them, in their own eyes, the right to rule.

The Growth of the Roman Constitution

In the new republic the chief magistracy was the consulship, shared simultaneously by two men. They were elected annually by all male citizens in an assembly, although for the first century and a half of the republic they were chosen exclusively from among the elite class known as patricians. The origins of the patriciate are obscure, but the patricians apparently derived from the old aristocracy of land and birth that formed the mounted guard of the kings in earliest times. During the monarchic era these kings had ruled with the guidance of popular assemblies and a Senate. The Senate, consisting of several hundred men, continued to function throughout the republic and the empire that followed it, supervising legislation, controlling finances, and serving as the bulwark of the aristocracy. Determining just who belonged in the Senate was one of the important roles of the two officials known as *censors,* who were chosen every five years to examine the Senate roster, compile lists of citizens for tax and draft purposes, and let out contracts for the maintenance of temples and roads. The censors stayed in office for 18 months.

Like the consulship and the censorship, most other Roman offices were held collegially, that is, jointly by more than one person, for terms of one year. Together, the offices of quaestor (a financial official), praetor (a justice), and consul made up the so-called *cursus honorum*—the "career of offices." Because Roman officials were not salaried, the *cursus honorum* was open in practice only to men of means, and the close supervision exercised by senior officials over junior ones created a system of patronage that helped the closed circle of patrician families retain an effective monopoly of power. The principle of collegiality also underscored the conservative spirit of the Roman nobility. When either consul disapproved of the other's plan, he could pronounce the word *veto* ("I forbid") to block it. Among the few offices occupied by one man was that of *pontifex maximus,* or high priest, which was held for life. Because the Roman gods such as Jupiter (a version of Zeus) and Minerva (parallel to Athena) were viewed as gods of the state who needed to be worshiped with proper rites and sacrifices, the pontifex maximus was in fact an official of the government. So were the augurs, whose job it was to determine the will of the gods by divination. Decisions not made by the Senate or by individual magistrates might be the work of assemblies, though until the last century of the republic it was rare for Roman citizens meeting in an assembly to challenge the authority of the aristocracy. Roman men gathered to vote in a variety of assemblies, many of them consisting of the same people organized according to different principles. The Curiate Assembly was the oldest of the popular assemblies, but in time its jurisdiction was severely circumscribed, and laws came to be made in the Centuriate Assembly, which arranged voters according to military divisions. The Centuriate Assembly elected major magistrates, ratified treaties, and could declare war. Legislation could also be enacted in the Tribal Assembly, in which Romans were grouped in a fluctuating number of tribes, each of which had one vote. Magistrates cleverly tended to organize the poor into

only four tribes to minimize their power. In addition to legislating, the Tribal Assembly elected quaestors. A third popular body, the Plebeian Assembly, consisted only of plebeians. These assemblies met infrequently, however, and despite their operation, Roman government remained oligarchic. The principal result of the plebeian challenge to the patrician monopoly on offices was to transform the original patrician oligarchy of birth into a patrician-plebeian oligarchy of wealth that sought to defend its interests against plebeians of the middle and lower classes.

The Struggle of the Orders

As far back as Romans could recall, they had been divided into two distinct groups or orders. Political power, as we have seen, rested with the small group of wealthy patricians who probably accounted for no more than 10 percent of the citizenry, while the bulk of the populace, the plebeians, were excluded from the Senate and the magistracies. Plebeians might enjoy the protection of patricians in exchange for their political support, but they were barred from holding public office. Such clientage relationships played a crucial role in the Roman power structure. Patrons offered jobs, protection, and legal representation, a cherished service during the early republic when justice was generally administered by the wealthy in their own interest. Originally, most clients may have been poor tenant farmers who tilled their patrons' land, but in time many plebeians acquired clients of their own; it was not unusual for a moderately successful farmer or small businessperson to be the client of one man and the patron of others. Commanders often recruited soldiers from among their clients, and the patron-client bond between recruits and their generals became an important factor in Roman politics.

Through agitation that continued over more than two centuries, the plebeians gradually gained direct access to political power. Two major factors accounted for this: the increasing affluence of many plebeians and the patricians' need for plebeian support in the continual wars that racked the Italian peninsula. The first step in the struggle of the orders was probably the creation of the office of "tribune of the people." The tribunes were designated to protect the plebeians and their interests. The person of a tribune was sacrosanct; that is, assaulting him was deemed both a political and a religious offense. The tribunes were granted veto power over measures that seemed to them to violate plebeian interests. The tribunician veto remained a powerful instrument throughout the republic, but it was not unusual for powerful oligarchs to manipulate at least one of the ten tribunes and thereby undermine tribunal effectiveness.

Around 450 B.C. the tribunes persuaded the Senate to codify the laws, and as time passed, the patricians lost their monopoly on public offices. In 367 B.C. the Licinian-Sextian laws stipulated that one consul should be a plebeian, and a law passed in 300 B.C. opened important priesthoods to the plebeians. Finally, the Hortensian law of 287 B.C. determined that all decrees of the plebeian assembly would be binding on the entire state.

THE EXPANSION OF ROME

While these republican institutions were evolving, the Romans extended their sway throughout the Italian peninsula, and in the late third century B.C. they found themselves engaged for the first time in warfare beyond Italy. This conflict continued with minor interruptions for the rest of Rome's history. The consequences for domestic politics were profound. With many members of the assemblies away on campaign and anxiety mounting for the government's stability, considerable authority reverted to the Senate.

The Unification of the Italian Peninsula

Rome's wars outside Italy stemmed from its conquest of the Italian peninsula. During the first two and a half centuries of the republic's history the Romans brought the entire Italian peninsula under their power, fighting the Etruscans, the Samnites (a ferocious hill people skilled in guerilla warfare), and their own former allies, the cities that belonged to the alliance known as the Latin League. By 290 B.C. the Romans controlled the entire portion of Italy that protruded into the Mediterranean with the exception of the Greek-speaking areas to the south. The conquest of "Magna Graecia," as southern Italy was known, soon followed.

While the Romans were battling their enemies in the north, the Greek cities in the southern part of the peninsula were feuding among themselves. In 282 B.C. the Romans answered an appeal for aid from the city of Thurii, and when rival Tarentum brought in a Greek

general, Pyrrhus, the Romans again found themselves at war. Pyrrhus won two battles, but his casualties were so heavy that they are evoked to this day in the expression "Pyrrhic victory." By 275 B.C. the exhausted Greek states of southern Italy had submitted to Rome.

Rome's treatment of conquered peoples was radically different from that of the Greeks. The Romans recognized quite early that their interest lay in extending various degrees of citizenship to their Italian neighbors. By doing so, they created a loose but stable confederacy that lasted for centuries. Some towns were granted full citizenship, and residents of the colonies that the Romans founded in conquered territory had full citizenship but were free from military obligations, since their communities served as garrisons. Other towns enjoyed self-government and in some cases possessed the rights associated with Roman citizenship.

Rome's Overseas Wars

The unification of the Italian peninsula brought the Roman sphere of influence close to Sicily, which had been colonized by Greeks and Carthaginians. Rome and Carthage had generally enjoyed peaceful relations, and Carthage resembled Rome in certain respects. Ostensibly a broadly based republic, in fact it was an oligarchy of wealth. Like the Romans, the Carthaginians had two chief magistrates, elected annually, but the government was run by the heads of prominent households, who made up the Senate and the Council. Carthaginians had little previous reason to see the land-based Romans as rivals. Now, however, Sicily appeared as the next object of Roman expansion. For both states the island was the key to control of the central Mediterranean. In 264 B.C. they went to war over it.

The seafaring Carthaginians possessed the advantage of a powerful navy. The Romans responded to the challenge by constructing a fleet of their own. In 241 B.C., after a stunning Roman victory at sea, Carthage sued for peace. Several influential Carthaginians, however, continued to harbor hostility to Rome, and in 218 B.C. the two states went to war a second time. A major role in the outbreak of the Second Punic War was played by the Carthaginians' charismatic general Hannibal (247–c. 183 B.C.). From Spain, Hannibal crossed the Alps with his entire train, including war elephants. At Cannae in 216 B.C. he annihilated a Roman army in a battle long remembered by Romans as the greatest catastrophe in their military history. The Romans continued to en-

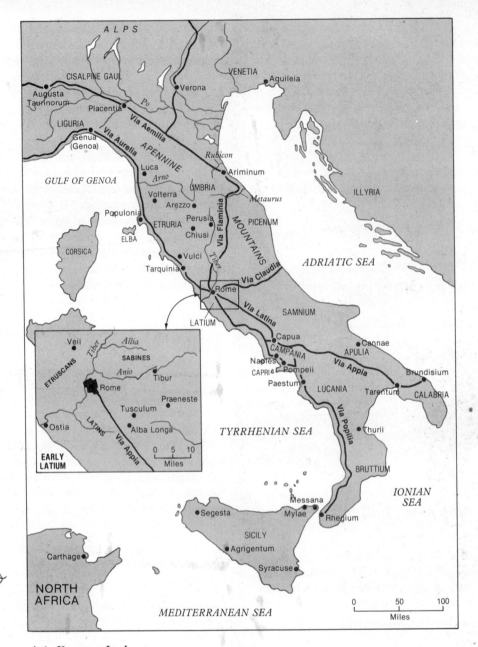

4.1 Roman Italy

"Fabia," a general of Rome, sent Hannibal back to Africa

dure Hannibal's presence in Italy for 15 years. In time the Carthaginian government, which was divided about the war, recalled Hannibal to Africa, where the Roman Publius Cornelius Scipio defeated him at Zama in 202 B.C..

The war years were terrible ones in the Italian peninsula, and tradition tells that the Romans resorted to human sacrifice to capture the favor of the gods—a routine practice at Carthage, where small children were offered up to the Phoenician god Moloch. The Romans finally hounded Hannibal to death in Asia Minor, where he committed suicide about 183 B.C. His courage and determination earned him the admiration of Roman historians, and he continued for generations to be an

Gold coins minted at Carthage. [Ronald Sheridan/ Ancient Art & Architecture Collection]

Greek hostages back to Italy to ensure that the mainland Greeks would behave in accord with Rome's interests. Among the captives was the historian Polybius, to whose work we owe much of our knowledge of the third and second centuries B.C. In time the Romans conquered Greece as well as Macedonia. In 146 B.C. they destroyed the city of Corinth and laid waste to Carthage. It is no coincidence that both Corinth and Carthage had been heavily involved in trade and that neither posed a serious military threat to Rome. Plainly, the Romans had come to value the economic possibilities of a world empire.

The annexation of Greece, much of Spain, and North Africa into the Roman empire transformed the lives of the farmers and townsfolk of Italy. Successful generals and their staffs returned from the wars greatly enriched, and the massive influx into Italy of Greek slaves and artifacts encouraged the development of a sophisticated Greco-Roman culture that undermined traditional values. However, tens of thousands of soldiers returned to find their farms fallen into ruin during their long absence, and Italian farmers found it hard to compete with the cheap foreign grain that poured into Italy from overseas markets. Many veterans sold their land and sought employment in the cities, usually without success. Once they had changed their lives in this way, they were no longer able to find employment in the army; only landowners, the Romans believed, had sufficient incentive to fight for their state. When those whom war had enriched began to exploit the helplessness of those whom war had impoverished, grave social and economic problems developed that in the course of a century would destroy the republic and replace it with a semihereditary imperial system.

THE REPUBLIC IN CRISIS

Political power in Rome was still limited to men from a small number of prominent families, both patrician and plebeian. Winning elections could be costly. Of the 108 men who served as consul between 200 and 146 B.C., 90 belonged to families that could boast a previous consul, and over half belonged to only eight families. The popular assemblies too were largely under the control of the upper classes.

The values of the Roman elite had been designed for

object of horror and fascination in the Roman mind. Scipio, for his part, earned the name Africanus because of his victory, was honored with a splendid triumphal procession, and became one of the most influential politicians in Rome.

Rome acquired three overseas provinces in the wars with Carthage—Sicily, Sardinia, and Spain. Around the same time, two wars in Illyria on the eastern shore of the Adriatic gained the Romans a sphere of influence in the east as well. Rome was establishing itself as a powerful force in Mediterranean politics. The Romans soon became involved in a series of conflicts in Greece known as the Macedonian wars. In the years following their success at the Battle of Pydna in 168 B.C. during the Third Macedonian War, the Romans looted Greece for slaves, books, and works of art. They also took a number of

a landed aristocracy ambitious only to preserve a lei-
sured and dignified way of life. In the early centuries,
public service had provided a satisfying arena for
achievement. Glory was easily won on the battlefield; the
Roman aristocracy agreed on which wars needed to be
fought; and the poor, despite their periodic political
agitation, were generally deferential to their social
superiors. The backbone of the Roman army was a
hardy peasantry that made good soldiers and caused
little trouble.

Overseas wars changed all this. The peasantry languished under the strain of long campaigns, while
soldiers who had served in the highest ranks acquired
wealth that had previously been inconceivable. An ambitious business class also developed in response to the
commercial possibilities opened up by the acquisition of
provinces. Since the era of the kings, Romans who had
enough annual income to maintain a horse had belonged
to an order known as the *equites,* or equestrians. In
income and prestige this class stood between the senatorial aristocracy and the ordinary citizens. By the third
century B.C. the equites had developed strong commercial interests; they prospered because of the wars. More
senators also developed commercial aspirations than
had been the case in earlier centuries. Thus the traditional Roman values of civic virtue and rustic simplicity
came into conflict with the commercialism and cosmopolitanism of the cities.

Inadequate planning for provincial administration
also enabled greedy Romans of the middle and upper
classes to enrich themselves at the expense of the less
fortunate. Because provincial administrators were unsal-
aried and far from home, they had both motive and
opportunity to extort as much wealth as possible from
the defenseless inhabitants of their provinces, and the
corruption of provincial government became notorious.
Moreover, the government let out tax collection to private companies, which, eager to maximize profits, often
behaved in the same unprincipled manner as officials of
the state.

Rome's problems were soluble. Corruption in the
provinces could have been controlled had officials in
Rome not winked at the abuses of their friends and
relations. Italy afforded enough land for everyone if it
was properly distributed, and commerce had the power
to enrich people's lives. A government dominated by
wealthy landowners apprehensive about change, however, was ill-equipped to address these problems, and
agitation for reform provoked bloodshed.

The Gracchi and the Failure of Reform

The regeneration of the peasantry was the chief problem
facing Rome. The large estates known as *latifundia* were
mostly worked by the slaves whom Roman conquests
had brought into Italy, not by veterans, many of whom
had been forced off their land. Some former soldiers
became tenants; others flocked to the cities, swelling the
ranks of the unemployed.

Tiberius Gracchus (163–133 B.C.) resolved to make his
name by alleviating these strains. The son of Scipio
Africanus' daughter Cornelia, Tiberius belonged to the
powerful Scipio family, but a less influential branch.
Spurned by the inner circles of the senatorial aristocracy,
he and his younger brother, Gaius, sought distinction as
champions of the people.

As tribune for 133 B.C., Tiberius proposed a bill in the
Senate calling for the government to reclaim state land
that had been illegally occupied by wealthy landowners
and to distribute the repossessed holdings to the needy.
When the Senate rejected his proposal, he took his
program to the Plebeian Assembly. Once the land bill
had passed, Tiberius ran for a second term as a tribune.
The Senate panicked at this unusual strategy, and on
election day, Senate-backed mobs murdered Tiberius
and about 300 of his followers. A similar fate overtook
his younger brother Gaius in 121 B.C. Resolved to carry
on Tiberius' policies, Gaius proposed to have the government distribute grain regularly to needy citizens at cost
and to found colonies in North Africa. To gain support
for his program, he cultivated the equestrians as a
counterweight to the Senate, placing them in charge of
tax collection in the provinces, a lucrative concession,
since tax-farming companies were permitted to make
large profits. When violence again erupted, the Senate
passed a decree of martial law in 121 B.C. proscribing
Gaius and his followers; a massacre of thousands resulted, and Gaius himself was killed.

CORNELIA AND THE WORLD
OF THE GRACCHI

Few Roman women were more controversial than Cornelia, mother of Tiberius and Gaius Gracchus. Born in
the late 190s B.C., she was the younger daughter of Scipio

Africanus, victor over the Carthaginians at Zama, and Aemilia, whose brother was killed as he led the Romans against Hannibal in 216 B.C. Probably in the late 170s B.C., Cornelia married Tiberius Sempronius Gracchus. Politically, the marriage seems to have marked the temporary alliance between two families that were normally rivals, the patrician Aemilii Paulli and the plebeian Gracchi. The elder Tiberius was a prominent political leader in his own right, twice serving as consul and once as censor.

Of Cornelia's 12 children, only three survived—the future tribunes Tiberius and Gaius and their older sister, Sempronia. Widowed around 154 B.C., Cornelia was extraordinarily diligent in raising her children. Probably with a view toward maintaining the family ties with their Hellenistic clients, she procured a Greek tutor for her sons. Cicero was among those impressed by her reputation, writing that the elegance of her letters suggested that her sons were reared more on their mother's discourse than on their mother's milk. Substantial controversy surrounds Cornelia's role in her sons' political careers. Some contemporaries charged her with urging Tiberius to take up the agrarian problem and supporting him when he appealed to the assembly. Others asserted that she and Sempronia were at least partly to blame for the murder in 129 B.C. of the latter's husband, Scipio Aemilianus, who had opposed the work of the land commissioners responsible for implementing Tiberius' reforms. She was also accused of aiding Gaius' political activities, even to the point of hiring men to disguise themselves as harvesters and agitate for her son.

Although her life was scarred by tragedies, not the least of which were the brutal deaths of Tiberius and Gaius, Cornelia remained undaunted in spirit. Even after the killing of her sons, she continued to move in prominent political circles in Rome. At one point she rejected a marriage proposal from Egypt's King Ptolemy VII, who was anxious for the support of her eastern connections in his own dynastic quarrels. Toward the end of her life she lived at Misenum on the Bay of Naples, presiding over a celebrated literary salon. Whether any of her writings have survived is unclear; plainly, Cicero was familiar with some of her letters, although historians have questioned the authenticity of the fragments that remain. But her combination of ambition, fidelity, virtue, and personal modesty made her the prototypical Roman matron and one of the few figures of either sex in the later republic to win the general admiration of posterity.

Marius, Sulla, and the Rise of Pompey

The conflicts of the 130s and 120s B.C. polarized Rome into two classes, each vying for the support of the equestrians. The party that would be known as the *Optimates* (literally, the "best men") comprised the senatorial aristocracy. The opposing party, the *Populares,* was more diverse, consisting of both representatives of the less affluent classes and aristocrats who were ambitious to lead them.

Restored for a time to its former primacy, the Senate soon embarrassed itself by accepting bribes from a powerful North African prince, the unscrupulous Jugurtha. Having murdered some of his rivals for the throne of Numidia (modern Algeria) and provoked others to war, Jugurtha boasted that Rome was for sale to the highest bidder. In time the Senate was pressured into declaring war against Jugurtha by the equestrian class, whose business activities in North Africa he seriously hampered. The Romans made little headway in the war until Marius, an ambitious equestrian, was elected consul for 107 B.C. and with his quaestor, the patrician Sulla, took command of an army that defeated Jugurtha.

Elected repeatedly to the consulship, Marius made dramatic changes in the structure of the Roman army, equipping soldiers with a better spear, reorganizing the legions, and, most important, accepting landless men for service. Such men became career soldiers dependent on the patronage of their generals. Marius thus replaced military loyalty to the state with a personal bond between soldiers and their commanders, who in turn engaged in political machinations to obtain land for their veterans. This bond was especially important because clear distinctions between military and civilian authority did not exist in Rome, and time would show that the commander with the most soldiers could control the Roman state.

Bloody civil strife erupted in Italy from 90 to 88 B.C. when Rome's Italian allies revolted, demanding a fuller share of citizenship. There was great loss of life in this Social War (fought with Rome's allies, or *socii*) as some Italians continued to fight even after the Romans had yielded to their demands.

In 88 B.C., Rome also found itself at war with King Mithridates of Pontus in Asia Minor. The Senate ordered Marius' former ally Sulla to conduct the war, but Marius' backers managed to have the command transferred to him. In the ensuing struggle, tens of thousands perished on both sides. Even after Marius died in 86 B.C., his partisans fought on against Sulla. Four years later, Sulla, who had gone east to fight with Mithridates and had finally made peace with him in order to return to Italy, marched on Rome. After another civil war, he became master of the capital, posting daily proscription lists in the Forum offering rewards for the execution of his political enemies. This judicial murder enabled him to settle 150,000 of his veterans on the land of the slain. The bloody Sulla served as dictator in 82 and 81 B.C. His primary agenda, besides shoring up his own position, was the exaltation of the Senate over the equestrians and the assemblies.

Rome soon confronted a new rebellion from an unexpected quarter. A charismatic slave, Spartacus, organized a revolt in 73 B.C. in Italy itself, striking terror into Rome. After defeating Spartacus' forces, Roman commanders crucified some 6,000 of the rebels. The praetor Crassus (115–53 B.C.), a wealthy and ambitious politician, got most of the credit for suppressing the rebellion, though some went to Sulla's young protege Pompey (106–48 B.C.).

Enslaving prisoners had been a Roman practice since 396 B.C., when the citizens of the captured city of Veii were taken to Rome. Throughout the second century B.C., thousands of prisoners were shipped to Italy and put to work on the great estates. Slave uprisings such as the one led by Spartacus were a continuous threat in Italy and made travel through remote rural areas unsafe.

In general, the Romans were liberal in granting freedom to domestic slaves, if not in their treatment of them during the years of servitude. Because slaves were permitted to hire out their services when their owners did not need them, they were often able to earn the money to purchase their freedom. The freed slaves, known as *liberti,* were subject to certain legal restrictions, but their children became full citizens.

The Rise of Caesar and the First Triumvirate

Shortly after suppressing Spartacus' rebellion, Pompey and Crassus joined forces to ensure their election as consuls for 70 B.C. While in office, they effectively repealed the oligarchic constitution of Sulla. Troubles abroad in the 60s B.C. prompted the Senate to confer extraordinary commands on Pompey, who became the dominant figure in Roman politics.

While Pompey was away on campaigns, other politicians rose to prominence. One was Julius Caesar (c. 102–44 B.C.), a patrician who nonetheless had political ties with the Populares. Marcus Tullius Cicero (106–43 B.C.) distinguished himself as a lawyer and an orator and made a place for himself in Roman politics that was remarkable in view of his equestrian background and lack of military experience. Other politicians active at Rome in the 60s B.C. included Cato the Younger, a Stoic philosopher who espoused traditional republican values, and Catiline, a ruined patrician whose unsuccessful attempt at a coup in 63 B.C. gave Cicero the opportunity to write the famous *Orations Against Catiline,* which still stand as monuments of classical rhetoric.

Cicero hoped to save Rome from the rivalries of ambitious generals by establishing a united front of senators and equestrians that would stave off a military dictatorship. But Rome soon fell into the hands of the so-called First Triumvirate, an unofficial alliance of Pompey, Caesar, and Crassus. The three men pooled their political assets to procure Caesar's election as consul in 59 B.C. After his term, Caesar set about establishing his own military reputation. He obtained the governorship of Gaul, where he enhanced his prestige by subjugating the Gallic tribes and extended Latin civilization into the heart of Europe. He recounted these triumphs in his *Commentaries on the Gallic Wars,* a brilliant achievement as both propaganda and literature that is still used today as a primer of Latin style.

Tensions between Pompey and Caesar, along with the death of Crassus, contributed to the collapse of the alliance. Cato, moreover, threatened to prosecute Caesar for illegal actions in Gaul, where the latter had frequently acted without senatorial authority. In 49 B.C. the Senate declared Caesar a public enemy and ordered Pompey to defend the Roman state against him. Caesar's forces defeated Pompey's at Pharsalus in Greece in 48 B.C. When Caesar subsequently pursued Pompey to Egypt, he found that Pompey had been executed by local officials. After punishing Pompey's murderers and making the young queen, Cleopatra, his mistress, Caesar returned to Rome. Cato committed suicide, and Cicero, bowing to the inevitable, made peace with Rome's new master.

The Final Crisis

Caesar ruled Rome from his arrival there in July 46 B.C. to his assassination in March 44 B.C. His position rested ultimately on the support of his clients and veterans. He also held the office of consul and enjoyed some of the privileges of a tribune. His reforms were many. He replaced the chaotic lunar calendar with the calendar known as "Julian," after him. The Julian calendar that Caesar adapted from the Egyptian model remained the sole system in much of Europe until it was corrected by Pope Gregory XIII in 1582. Caesar also settled approximately 80,000 poor Romans in provincial colonies and was liberal in conferring Roman citizenship on some of his supporters in the provinces. His reform of local government throughout Italy eased the burden on Roman magistrates by placing more authority in the hands of municipal governments.

Such reforms show Caesar to have been a creative and enlightened statesman with a vision of Rome far more generous than that of its previous dictator, Sulla. He was ambitious, self-seeking, and despotic, however, and it was inevitable that many aristocrats would oppose his ascendancy. In the winter of 44 B.C. a conspiracy was formed involving some 60 senators, chief among them the praetor Gaius Cassius and Marcus Brutus, the husband of Cato's daughter. Brutus was not Caesar's personal enemy but his friend. His leadership demonstrates that genuine republican sentiment played an important role in the conspiracy. The conspirators assassinated Caesar in the Senate on March 15, 44 B.C.

The civil war that ensued pitted the conspirators, the Senate, and Caesar's former political ally Mark Antony (83–30 B.C.) in a three-cornered struggle. In addition, a new figure of importance appeared in Rome after Caesar's death in the person of his grandnephew Octavian (63 B.C.–A.D. 14), whom Caesar had adopted as his son. In 43 B.C. the Senate ratified a Second Triumvirate consisting of Octavian, Antony, and the consul Lepidus. Octavian and Antony defeated Brutus and Cassius in battle, whereupon the conspirators committed suicide. Lepidus was soon pushed into the background, though he continued to serve as pontifex maximus, and Octavian and Antony divided the empire into two spheres of influence: Octavian remained in Rome to oversee the west, while Antony lived in Alexandria and supervised the east.

Antony's marriage to Cleopatra, ruler of Egypt, afforded Octavian the opportunity to charge that the couple planned to remove the capital of the empire to Egypt and to bequeath it to Cleopatra's children by Antony and her son by Caesar. Octavian cleverly cast his attack on Antony in the guise of a foreign war designed to defend Roman power against Egyptian aggression and Roman virtue against eastern decadence. Antony and Cleopatra were defeated at a naval battle of Actium off the coast of Greece in 31 B.C., and both committed suicide, leaving Rome exhausted from a century of civil wars and Octavian the undisputed master of the Roman world. The death of the capable and ambitious Cleopatra ended the Ptolemaic line in Egypt; henceforth, it was governed as a Roman province.

THE AUGUSTAN SETTLEMENT

After the defeat of Antony and Cleopatra, Octavian faced the task of reestablishing the Roman state and consolidating his own position. His solutions to the many problems confronting him were masterful. Instead of establishing a formal monarchy or restoring the republic to one of its earlier forms, he implemented a new and deceptively fluid system that blended traditional elements with essentially dictatorial control. In this way he enjoyed near-absolute power over Rome and its armies while simultaneously persuading many Romans that the republic had been restored.

Octavian's first challenge was to establish his personal authority. Step by step, he gathered into his hands the various powers once held by such officials as proconsuls, tribunes, and censors without directly proclaiming himself an autocrat. He also enjoyed the unrestricted power to make war or peace, the right to convene the Senate, and the honorary paraphernalia that had customarily attended consuls. Carefully avoiding the unpopular title *rex* (king), Octavian chose the appellation *Augustus,* an unusual term derived from a root meaning "exalted." He also began styling himself *princeps,* "first citizen," and adopted the title *imperator* ("successful commander"), which had been granted as an honor to victorious generals during the republic. Henceforth the ruler of Rome was known as the imperator, which has come into English as *emperor.* The military nomenclature was appropriate, for in the last analysis the emperor's power rested on military force.

Under Augustus and his successors, the Senate met and Roman aristocrats continued to be elected to the consulship, but all decisions of importance ultimately originated with the princeps. Throughout the centuries that followed, the tone of the imperial government established by Augustus varied depending on the degree to which each emperor chose to share power with the Senate. The Senate had no redress against autocracy, and its authority rested entirely on the emperor's good-

This statue of Augustus reflects the influence of classical Athens, whose culture and power Augustus wanted Rome to emulate. [Scala/Art Resource, New York]

will. Augustus himself was outwardly deferential to the Senate, though he never allowed it to thwart his will except in trivial matters, and in reality his regime was a thinly disguised military dictatorship: there was no way to remove him from power short of assassination. Recognizing the need to maintain republican appearances, he

held regular elections for most of the traditional magistracies, and senators played key parts in provincial administration.

To Augustus' political power was added religious authority. Casting himself as the champion of the traditional Roman religion, he assumed the office of pontifex maximus when Lepidus died, revived a number of old priesthoods, rebuilt more than 80 temples, and encouraged the worship of Venus, to whom Julius Caesar had traced his lineage. Although Augustus stopped short of accepting divine honors, he encouraged the erection of temples, monuments, and statues throughout the empire dedicated to himself and his wife, Livia.

One of Augustus' chief priorities was to stabilize the empire's military and administrative structures. He took care to establish a police force and fire brigade in Rome, installing the beginnings of an imperial bureaucracy to replace the old family corporations that had helped to fortify the power of the aristocracy under the republic. He also fixed the permanent size of the army at 25 legions (300,000 men), all directly responsible to himself, and regularized pay, pensions, and length of service to make the military an attractive career. The 9,000-man Praetorian Guard, administered by the praetorian prefect, provided personal protection to Augustus. Although the emperor spent three years in the east (22–19 B.C.) achieving a diplomatic settlement with the hostile Parthians in Persia, he campaigned very little. The operations he ordered in Germany, which were designed to establish a secure frontier on the Danube, the Rhine, and, if possible, the Elbe, met with mixed success. His stepsons, Tiberius and Drusus, organized the area they had conquered into provinces, but a humiliating defeat in A.D. 9 damaged Roman prestige in Germany.

Pax Romana – Roman Peace

Economic Development

The economy of the empire clearly needed attention. One of the chief problems was the system of taxation that had developed during the last two centuries of the republic. The principal sources of revenue were the provinces, and Augustus introduced new censuses to assess population, assets, and resources. Population shifts, agricultural conditions, and commercial enterprises could thus be regularly evaluated and the tax burden shifted accordingly.

Within Italy the principal occupation was still farming. Owners of latifundia were encouraged to diversify their crops to guard against poor years or changes in the market. Augustus encouraged agriculture not only for its practical benefits but also as a symbol of the bounty guaranteed by political stability. Italian industry flourished under Augustus, partly for obvious economic reasons and partly because the emperor seems to have favored businessmen and manufacturers rather than the ingrown, snobbish aristocracy. A style of pottery called Arretine was developed in the ceramics factories of Arretium (modern Arezzo); Arretine vessels were exported throughout the empire, from Britain to India. Such demand required new, more efficient methods of production. One factory at Arezzo could mix 10,000 gallons of clay at a time, and similar mass production techniques were used for the extraction and working of metals. Furthermore, Augustus' building program throughout Italy stimulated demand for bricks, tiles, and other construction materials.

Augustan legislation stimulated industry and commerce in the provinces. Egypt, with its fine sand, became a center for glass manufacture, and Alexandria retained its importance as an international port for the buying and selling of raw materials. With a return to prosperity the demand for luxury goods such as silk, rare fruits, and fine wines rose sharply, and Roman traders found themselves exploring ever more distant markets. In the late first century B.C., Roman sailors discovered that monsoon winds greatly aided the sea journey from Egypt to India. The trip there took some 40 days, and the speed with which commercial links grew is demonstrated by the large quantities of Arretine pottery discovered at ports on India's east coast. The Indian connection also gave the Roman world better access to China, with its production of high-quality silk, than the dangerous overland route that passed through the territory of the Parthians in northeastern Persia.

Social Legislation

Not content with fostering a revival of traditional religion, Augustus also dedicated himself to the purification of Roman morals and the reconstruction of family life, establishing rewards for the production of heirs and penalties for bacherlorhood and childlessness. Much of Augustus' social reform was intended to correct the general moral laxity many people believed had developed during the last decades of the republic. In part the legislation reflected Augustus' attempt to promote the family as a social unit and his concern with the falling population of native Roman citizens.

Augustus himself lived simply and unostentatiously, at least in public, and placed great emphasis on duty to the state as well as traditional values and morality. He even exiled his daughter Julia for what he considered wanton behavior. High society must have found the new austerity difficult to adapt to, and Augustus' successors had little success in maintaining his high moral tone—nor, in most cases, had they much inclination to do so.

ROMAN LAW AND THE IDEAL OF JUSTICE

Among Rome's major contributions to civilization was its legal system, the principles of which still undergird the jurisprudence of most European countries, Latin America, Quebec, and Louisiana. The effectiveness and relative fairness of Roman law derived from two principles: that the judicial decisions of magistrates must be based primarily on equity rather than on rigid legality and that all persons of the same status should enjoy identical legal rights. Yet all persons were not equal, for Roman law distinguished, for example, between slave and free, male and female, citizen and alien.

Roman magistrates frequently sought the advice of a specialist "learned in the law" (*jurisprudens*), who, with the judge, not only determined its meaning, but also applied it to the case at hand to reach an equitable resolution. Thus judges and jurists (*jurisprudentes*) actually made law, though always under the watchful eyes of citizens, since the legal process was conducted in public. Popular surveillance thus provided a practical check on magistrates, who were sensitive to the people's concern that fair verdicts be rendered. Frequently, magistrates issued edicts at the outset of their annual terms in which they enunciated the principles by which they intended to interpret legislation. This practice had the benefit of making law flexible and responsive to changing circumstances. The legal system was more efficient than the cumbersome process of amending existing laws through new legislation.

Like other ancient societies, the Romans at first applied the *jus civile*, or civil law, only to themselves, leaving visiting foreigners without rights in the absence of a treaty between their state and Rome. Strictly applied, this system would have discouraged foreigners from transacting business within the Roman domain, thus impeding commercial development. In practice, therefore, magistrates began building up a body of law—the *jus gentium,* or law of nations—applicable to all persons, whether citizens or aliens. This body of law was also applied to residents of Rome's provinces who were not citizens. As the empire developed, magistrates and jurists tended to blend elements of the *jus civile* and the *jus gentium,* creating a common imperial law that embodied basic principles of equity.

WOMEN AND THE ROMAN FAMILY

In both law and practice, Roman civilization was patriarchal; the primacy of the male head of household, the *pater familias,* was unquestioned. Roman fathers had power of life and death over their wives and children. A man could, for instance, execute his spouse for drunkenness or prevent his grown male children from owning property. These prerogatives were rarely exercised, however, and Roman families were often warm and loving. Wives were revered, and the intellect and character of women were often admired; both sons and daughters were cherished, and girls were sent to school alongside their brothers.

Adult males were emancipated at the father's death, but women were subject, at least in theory, to the guardianship of a male relative until marriage. Although originally all females had to be in the custody of a man, a woman whose guardian interfered with her liberty in such activities as making a will, signing contracts, or freeing slaves could have a magistrate appoint another man in his place. Beginning in the reign of Augustus, women who gave birth to three children were rewarded by being emancipated from guardianship altogether. In the families of Rome's elite, wives, sisters, and daughters played important roles as the educators and nurturers of future rulers.

Married Roman women often retained strong ties with their families of origin, and a bride's father could, as in Greece, initiate divorce. Among the upper classes, divorce was surprisingly casual in the late republican and imperial periods. No reason was legally required for it, and no particular stigma attached to it unless scandal was involved. Despite the official exhortations to increased childbearing, infanticide and abortion were commonly practiced to limit the size of families. Not until the third century A.D. was the latter made to some degree a legal offense. Among the many advertised techniques for contraception was the suggestion that a woman hold her breath at the moment of male ejaculation.

Before the conquest of Greece during the second century B.C. the education of Roman boys and girls was largely of a moral and patriotic nature. Both at home and at school, Roman children learned about brave men and women from the past whose actions they were encouraged to emulate. With the conquest of Greece, Roman education became more complex, and upper-class boys began to get the advantage over girls by studying with expensive tutors at the age when girls were marrying. Determined women, however, often continued their studies on their own, and Roman women of letters were not unusual. The dignity accorded to Roman matrons was great, and having an educated parent such as Cornelia, the mother of the Gracchi, was considered an advantage.

With the growth of the empire and of contact with the Hellenized east, the position of upper-class women became freer. Wealthy and aristocratic women were able to preside over literary salons and to dabble in politics. Some women won fame as orators, and political demonstrations by women were not unknown. In 42 B.C., when women were taxed to pay the expenses of the civil war, a group of them burst into the Forum, where their spokeswoman, Hortensia, made an impassioned speech:

> Why should we pay taxes when we do not share in the offices, honors, military commands, nor, in short, the government, for which you fight between yourselves with such harmful results? . . . Let war with the Celts or Parthians come, we will not be inferior to our mothers when it is a question of common safety. But for civil wars, may we never contribute nor aid you against each other.[1]

Hortensia's speech made her famous and was quoted with approval by later male commentators. Frequently, though, men were scandalized by women's involvement in politics and were alienated by excessive cultivation in females. Julius Caesar's contemporary, the historian Sallust (86–c. 34 B.C.), claimed that several women became involved in the conspiracy of Catiline in 63 B.C. because of financial straits brought on by their own excessive spending. His account of the conspiracy included a portrait of a certain Sempronia, who often committed crimes with "masculine daring." Favored by fortune with respect to both family and beauty, she was nevertheless, in Sallust's view, more cultivated than a modest woman should have been, well read in the literature of Greece and Rome, able to play the lyre and dance more skillfully than an honest women need, and having many other accomplishments which minister to voluptuousness. . . . [H]er desires were so ardent that she sought men more often than she was sought by them. Even before the time of the conspiracy she had often broken her word, repudiated her debts, [and] been privy to murder; poverty and extravagance combined had driven her headlong.[2]

Proper Roman matrons were expected to develop such traditional domestic skills as spinning and weaving. With little restriction on their movements they were able to visit, shop, and attend public functions. In this and other respects they enjoyed greater freedom than their Greek counterparts. The differences between what was expected of Romans of each sex is exemplified in two epitaphs of the second century B.C. The epitaph of Lucius Cornelius Scipio reports that the deceased was

> the very best of all Rome's good men. A son of Long-beard, he held the offices of aedile, consul and censor; he also captured Corsica, and Aleria too, a city. He gave deservedly a temple to the goddesses of weather.

The epitaph of an otherwise unknown Roman woman, Claudia, stresses fertility and domesticity:

> Stranger, my message is short. Stop and read it through. Here is the unlovely tomb of a lovely woman. Her parents named her Claudia. She loved her husband with her whole heart. She bore two sons, one of whom she leaves on earth; beneath the earth she has placed the other. She was charming in conversation, yet she behaved decently. She kept house. She made wool. That's all; now go.

Outside Rome's elite, women fell into three broad categories: slaves, freedwomen, and the freeborn poor. The female slaves of well-to-do families were perhaps the best off economically; they were permitted to accumulate property and even to buy other slaves. Their duties were varied, including cooking, cleaning, clothesmaking, and the care and nursing of children. More specialized slaves might serve as secretaries, ladies' maids, masseuses, entertainers, and midwives. Some acquired considerable education. Because there was always more demand for male slaves, however, slave daughters were often left to die of exposure or sold. As elsewhere in the ancient world, all female slaves, whatever their function, were at the sexual disposal of their masters. Freedwomen comprised a large part of the Roman working class, serving as laundresses, shopkeepers, waitresses, and prostitutes or working at artisanal trades or as domestics. Some attained prosperity, though many continued to work for their former owners.

ROMAN LITERATURE AND ART

The Romans' intellectual and artistic contribution to the Western heritage is significant. In many ways, Roman culture was imitative rather than original. Early Roman writing was heavily dependent on Greek models and remained so throughout Rome's history. The Romans were no less awed by the brilliance of Greek visual art, and many of their own chief monuments are marked by a reliance on classical models. Nonetheless, Roman forms of art gradually developed their own distinctive features.

Rome's first poets included two comic playwrights. Plautus (c. 251–184 B.C.) and Terence (c. 195–159 B.C.) took their inspiration not from the bawdy Old Comedy of Aristophanes but rather from the Hellenistic New Comedy of Menander (c. 342–291 B.C.), whose elegant and lighthearted plots involved domestic humor and the merry mix-ups that arise from twins switched at birth or fathers presumed dead who turn up at inconvenient moments. Nervous about offending serious-minded Romans by portraying them as frivolous, Plautus and Terence were careful to bill their mischievous characters as Greeks and to set their plays far from Italy. Despite their preoccupation with *dignitas* and *gravitas,* Romans knew how to have fun. Plautus and Terence drew enthusiastic audiences, and the few native Italian genres included mime, farce, and satire.

The little early Latin prose that remains makes clear that the vastly smaller vocabulary of Latin as compared with Greek made it a less sophisticated mode of communication. Latin prose was shaped into a supple tool for expression primarily by Cicero. A prolific writer, he has provided scholars with most of the materials with which the history of the late republic has been reconstructed. His many letters make possible a day-by-day account of the political issues of his time. His philosophical treatises, mostly written late in life as he mourned the death of his daughter Tullia, show the strain that practical-minded Romans experienced in seeking to digest Greek thought. Though unoriginal, Cicero's philosophical writings transmitted classical Greek thought to the Latin-speaking scholars of the Middle Ages and the Renaissance.

Two of Rome's most impassioned poets wrote during the first century B.C. Lucretius (c. 99–55 B.C.) composed an epic poem titled *De rerum natura*—literally, "On the Nature of Things," or more colloquially, "The Way Things Are." Lucretius' poem is the most remarkable humanist document of antiquity. Combining anthropology, history, physics, and Epicurean philosophy, Lucretius set forth a world view aimed at demythologizing the cosmos and reassuring a tortured generation that suffering did not await them in a punitive afterlife. Lucretius depicted a universe in which all things had material causes and the gods were indifferent to human concerns, doling out neither punishments nor rewards. Imagination alone, he said, created the terrors of hell, but reason could dispel such phantoms.

Lucretius' poetry was impelled by a powerful sense of mission, but in the end it persuaded few Romans to exchange their frenetic lifestyles for a simpler existence. The economic opportunities brought by overseas conquests had added financial ambition to the preoccupation with warfare and politics that had always characterized the literate classes of Rome, and no amount of poetic argument would convert Romans into Epicureans.

More typically Roman in his thinking was Catullus (c. 84–54 B.C.), whose short poems show the fervor of youth. His love poems recount a tempestuous affair with a cultivated but fickle Roman matron, whom he calls Lesbia. He is equally renowned for his violent and often profane political barbs. Even today his verse has lost none of its power to shock, and his love poetry is rivaled in ancient literature only by that of Sappho, whose memory he deliberately invoked in the unusual name he gave his mistress. One of his more famous poems calls upon Lesbia to join him in thumbing their noses at stuffy Romans who might disapprove of love affairs:

Why don't we just live and love, Lesbia,
And consider all the gossip of censorious old men
Put together to be worth . . . oh, about a nickel.
The sun can set and then come back,
But you and I, once our brief light has gone out,
Are just going to sleep one night that never ends.
So give me a thousand kisses, then a hundred,
Then another thousand, and a second hundred,
And finally, when we've kissed thousands and thousands of
*   times,*
We'll mix up all the kisses. That way we won't know
How many times we've kissed—and no malicious person
Can count them all up and put the evil eye on us, either.[3]

The Augustan Age

Augustus, a masterful propagandist, made full use of the arts to reinforce the impression of peace and prosperity. Much of the art produced at Rome during his reign was official, commissioned by the state to serve government purposes. Through his cultural minister, Maecenas, he offered patronage to artists who were interested in casting the newly constituted state in a favorable light. Yet if he can justly be accused of cultural manipulation, it must be admitted that the literature and art of his age are of the highest quality.

Under Maecenas' sponsorship the poet Virgil (70–19 B.C.) blossomed into the greatest figure in Latin literature. His first commission, the *Georgics,* took for its underlying theme the regeneration of Italian agriculture and the satisfaction of hard work. Strong Epicurean underpinnings marked Virgil's stress on the rewards of the simple rustic life:

Though the farmer has
No mansion with proud portals which spits out
A monster wave of morning visitors
From every room, nor do his callers gasp
At inlaid columns, bright with tortoiseshell,
Or gold-embroidered clothes . . . .
He has untroubled sleep and honest life.
Rich in all sorts of riches, with a vast
Estate, he has the leisure to enjoy
A cave, a natural pond. . . .
*   young people grow up strong,*
Hardworking, satisfied with poverty.[4]

Virgil also composed the premier work of Latin literature, the *Aeneid.* Written both in homage to the Homeric epics and in competition with them, the *Aeneid* reenacts Rome's beginnings in the career of its mythical founder, Aeneas of Troy. Although a poem glorifying Augustus had been requested, Virgil saw that the political events of his own day were too sensitive to treat. Consequently, he chose to celebrate the regeneration of Rome indirectly in themes woven through an epic celebrating the city's beginnings.

Virgil's variations on the Homeric epics helped him to define what was uniquely Roman. His hero, Aeneas, was a valiant soldier like Achilles and the leader of a wandering band like Odysseus, but Aeneas' dedication to public service contrasted markedly with the independence and self-involvement of the Greek heroes. Achilles had been known as the swift-footed one, and Odysseus as the wily one, whereas Aeneas' epithet was *pious*. Piety for the Romans entailed respect for gods, parents, and the state, and Aeneas displayed all three, bringing both his household gods and his aged father on his journey to found Rome.

Virgil never lost sight of the cost at which Rome's identity was established. His poem provokes considerable sympathy for Dido, Aeneas' abandoned lover, and Turnus, whom the hero kills in war. The *Aeneid* is imbued with Virgil's conviction that Rome had a place to fill in the world. At the core of the work is Aeneas' visit to the underworld. His trip is rich in history and prophecy as the ghost of his father, Anchises, enumerates the heroes who will help Rome fulfill its destiny. Other states, he says, will excel in the arts and the sciences, but Rome will hold sway over the world. "These," he declares, "will be your arts: to instruct those you conquer in the ways of peace, to spare the defeated and wear down the proud in war."[5]

A lighter tone was struck in the poems of Virgil's friend Horace. Combining elements of Stoicism and Epicureanism, Horace advocated a patriotism that was tempered with a relaxed detachment from politics and focused most of his poetry on love, human nature, and the countryside. His *Satires* mocked familiar social types, and his *Odes* used the lyric meters of Sappho and other Greek poets to celebrate the beauties of the Italian soil and the tribulations of romance.

The principal prose author of the Augustan revival was the historian Livy (59 B.C.–A.D. 17). Like Virgil, Livy turned away from the sensitive material of his own day and began with the foundation of the city. His energy was focused on glorifying Rome rather than uncovering the truth about the past, and Rome's falling off from the glorious days of its ancestors formed his constant theme. He exhorted his reader to contemplate the steady process of decline leading to "the dark dawning of our modern day when we can neither endure our vices nor face the remedies needed to cure them." In their history, he wrote, his fellow Romans could find for themselves and their country "both examples and warnings; fine things to take as models, base things, rotten through and through, to avoid."[6] His patriotism, moralistic outlook, and polished style tend to obscure important differences between political factions and time periods; all his courageous aristocrats sound much the same. Nonetheless, his writings convey a vivid sense of what Romans thought was important, and because he made use of sources no longer available, his work is of great value.

Not all of Virgil's contemporaries worked under Augustus' patronage. Ovid (43 B.C.–A.D. 17), no supporter of Augustus' severe program of moral regeneration, spent his last years in exile. In the *Metamorphoses* his witty accounts of the creation and the many myths that were part of the Greco-Roman heritage gave little offense, but the sexual material in *The Art of Love* outraged a government determined to discourage adultery and promote family values.

The visual as well as the literary arts flourished in the Augustan Age, particularly sculpture and architecture. Roman portraiture of the late republic departed from classical Greek models as sculptors shaped highly naturalistic heads that contrasted sharply with the idealized renditions of classical Greece and owed more to Hellenistic styles.

Determined to evoke the glories of the Athenian empire, Augustus encouraged a revival of the classical style. A gracious sense of proportion marked the relief sculpture he commissioned for his monumental Ara Pacis, the Altar of Peace, completed in 9 B.C. The combination of historical and mythological motifs on the altar reflects the same blending of myth and history revealed in the writings of Virgil and Livy. On one panel, Tellus (Mother Earth) appears, flanked by the winds, offering her bounty to the Romans; on another the imperial family marches in procession, the solemnity of the occasion relieved by the restlessness of the imperial children in their tiny togas.

Augustus boasted that he found Rome a city of brick and left it a city of marble. Many of the best specimens of the architecture of his age, however, are found in the provinces. In southern Gaul, for example, the Romans made good use of their characteristic building blocks— the arch, the vault, and concrete—to construct the Greek-inspired temple at Nimes called the Maison Carrée ("Square House") and the Trophy of the Alps, a monument placed at the highest point on the road from Rome to Spain.

Such structures demonstrate Rome's considerable achievements in the field of engineering, perhaps none more impressive than the large barrel vault (in simple terms, a deep arch), the cross-barrel vault (two intersecting vaults), and the dome. Such devices, which in part reflect Etruscan influence, enabled Roman architects of the imperial period to enclose great interior spaces. Engineering skills were also reflected in the massive aqueducts such as the Pont du Gard in southern Gaul, the largest arches of which span 82 feet and are constructed of uncemented blocks weighing as much as 4,000 pounds apiece. From 312 B.C., commencing with the construction of the Appian Way, a road leading southeast from Rome, to the second century A.D., Roman engineers built thousands of miles of roads throughout southern Europe, England, the eastern Mediterranean, and North Africa. This highway network contributed significantly to the prosperity of the Augustan Age and facilitated communications throughout the empire.

SUMMARY

The Romans had mixed success in meeting the challenges that confronted them. Displaying a broad political vision, they succeeded where the Greeks had a failed in creating an enduring republican government and a cohesive federation. The empire that developed during the last centuries of the republic would extend the life of Rome for hundreds of years. The Romans served Western civilization as the transmitters of Greek culture, and they showed ingenuity not only in the engineering for which they are rightly renowned but in literature and the arts as well. More than any other people of the ancient world, they made contributions in law and jurisprudence that have shaped Western civilization.

The unification of the Mediterranean basin manifested wisdom and temperance as well as persistence and daring. At home, however, the Romans failed to resolve the underlying conflict between rich and poor, aristocrat and commoner. The reluctance of the Roman elite to confront grave economic inequities continued even after the plebeians attained nominal political equality with the patricians. Rather then vanishing, lines of demarcation simply shifted as the plebeian aristocracy allied with the patricians in their indifference to the plight of soldiers, farmers, workers, and slaves. In the end the flexibility of the republican constitution was not adequate to surmount the rivalries of ambitious aristocrats or resolve the class struggle. Political freedom came to an end, and Roman citizens, rich and poor, were slowly converted into the subjects of a semihereditary and increasingly authoritarian monarchy.

Notes

1. Appian, *Civil Wars,* 4:33.
2. Sallust, *The War with Catiline,* trans. J. C. Rolfe, in *Sallust* (Cambridge, Mass.: Harvard University Press, 1931), p. 45.
3. Catullus 5.
4. Virgil, *The Georgics,* in *Roman Poetry from the Republic to the Silver Age,* trans. D. Wender (Carbondale, Ill.: Southern Illinois University Press, 1980), pp. 59–60.
5. *The Aeneid of Virgil,* trans. A. Mandelbaum (New York: Bantam Books, 1971), pp. 160–161.
6. Livy, *History of Rome,* trans. A. de Selincourt (Harmondsworth, England: Penguin Books, 1971), p. 34.

Suggestions for Further Reading

Alföldy, G. *The Social History of Rome,* rev. ed. Baltimore: Johns Hopkins University Press, 1988.

Badian, E. *Roman Imperialism in the Late Republic.* Ithaca, N.Y.: Cornell University Press, 1971.

Bloch, R. *The Origins of Rome.* London: Thames & Hudson, 1960.

Bradley, K., *Discovering the Roman Family.* New York: Oxford University Press, 1990.

Brunt, P. A. *Social Conflicts in the Roman Republic.* New York: Norton, 1974.

Earl, D. C. *The Moral and Political Tradition of Rome.* Ithaca, N.Y.: Cornell University Press, 1984.

Gardner, J. F. *Women in Roman Law and Society.* Bloomington: Indiana University Press, 1986.

Gruen, E. *The Hellenistic World and the Coming of Rome.* Berkeley: University of California Press, 1984.

Harris, W. F. *War and Imperialism in Republican Rome.* Oxford, England: Oxford University Press, 1979.

Hopkins, K. *Conquerors and Slaves.* Cambridge, England: Cambridge University Press, 1981.

Pallottino, M. *The Etruscans,* rev. ed. Bloomington: Indiana University Press, 1975.

Scullard, H. H. *From the Gracchi to Nero,* 5th ed. London: Methuen, 1982.

Taylor, L. R. *Party Politics in the Age of Caesar.* Berkeley: University of California Press, 1949.

Thompson, L. *Romans and Blacks.* Norman: University of Oklahoma Press, 1989.

Wiedemann, T. *Greek and Roman Slavery.* London: Routledge, 1989.

CHAPTER

5

THE ROMAN EMPIRE AND THE RISE OF CHRISTIANITY

The Roman Empire was a remarkable creation. It was often won and held by terrible slaughter. Nonetheless, on the whole, Roman administration brought peace and prosperity and provided amenities such as roads, baths, theaters, and a ready water supply without destroying local customs and traditions. Cultural and religious plurality prevailed for the most part. Latin was spoken alongside Celtic, Punic, Aramaic, and Greek; and before the triumph of Christianity, religions generally competed amicably for worshippers. Life in the capital city was lively and invigorating, and the administration of the empire was increasingly shared among senators, equestrians, and freedmen from both Italy and the provinces.

Signs of decay, however, could already be discerned during this period. The economy was stagnating, and attacks on the frontiers had begun to demand frequent warfare and increased taxation. By the third century, economic decline and political anarchy had set in. The following century saw a vigorous recovery, but traditional systems at Rome were weakening; and as paganism was supplanted by Christianity and economic mobility diminished, new structures arose to replace the old.

THE JULIO-CLAUDIANS AND FLAVIANS

From the accession of Augustus in 31 B.C. to the death of Nero in A.D. 68, Rome was ruled by the Julio-Claudian dynasty, the descendants of Augustus and of Livia. A thrifty and conscientious ruler, Augustus' stepson and successor Tiberius lacked Augustus' graces and never equaled him in popularity. Tiberius was succeeded by his grandnephew Gaius, called Caligula (Little Boots), his childhood nickname. Shortly after Caligula's accession, a serious illness may have affected his mind. Subsequently convinced that he was a god, Caligula treated the consuls with contempt and spent the money Tiberius had saved on extravagant building projects, including an ivory stall and a furnished house complete with slaves for his favorite horse. Not surprisingly, the Praetorian Guard assassinated Caligula in A.D. 41 after a reign of only four years.

Before the Senate could formulate a plan for the succession, the Praetorian Guard proclaimed Caligula's uncle Claudius (A.D. 41–54) as their new emperor. Claudius treated the Senate with respect. He also granted citizenship to many provincials and admitted several Gallic chieftains to the Roman Senate. He was largely responsible for initiating the civil service composed of talented former slaves (freedmen). The empire owed a good deal of its endurance to his civil service, which carried out the routine business of running the government during periods of violence and turmoil. Under Claudius' rule, the island of Britain, a target of Roman expansion for a century, was subdued and colonized. His fourth wife, Agrippina, apparently poisoned him to facilitate the accession of her son, Nero (A.D. 54–68). When a fire destroyed large parts of Rome in A.D. 64, suspicion fell on Nero. He responded with a bloody purge that included artists and intellectuals, republican opponents, and many Christians, possibly including the apostles Peter and Paul. By A.D. 68, with the empire in revolt, Nero committed suicide after the senate condemned him to death.

Because propaganda precluded official recognition that the republic was dead, no machinery could be devised for a smooth and legal means of imperial succession. Nero's death brought a struggle for the succession among various military commanders, but by the end of A.D. 69, Vespasian, the general in Judaea, had disposed of his rivals and firmly established himself in the capital. Vespasian had been occupied in suppressing a major revolt by the Jews when the succession struggle erupted. Shortly after Rome annexed Judaea in A.D. 6, violence had broken out between Jews and Roman census officials, and tension between Jews and non-Jews compounded the conflict. Although Augustus had generally allowed the Jews to retain their religion and customs and had permitted considerable secular as well as religious jurisdiction by the High Priest and his council, the Sanhedrin, the Jews resented even nominal Roman control. Violence flared when Caligula and Nero reversed Augustus' policy and demanded to be worshipped by Jews as well as pagans. In A.D. 66, fighting broke out between Jews and non-Jews in the coastal town of Caesarea. When he became emperor in A.D. 69, Vespasian put his son Titus in charge of continuing efforts to suppress the bloody uprising. Titus succeeded in restoring order, largely destroying Jerusalem in the process. The temple was burned, and the Romans decreed that it would never be rebuilt.

Although Vespasian was not related to the Julio-

Following the Jewish revolt against Roman rule in A.D. 66, Roman troops looted Jerusalem, taking such religious objects as the menorah, or seven-branched candlestick, and the sacred trumpets from the temple. The scene is depicted here on the arch of Titus in Rome. [Alinari/Art Resource, New York]

Claudians, he took the name Caesar as part of his title, setting a precedent for his successors. The dynasty he founded was called Flavian, after his own middle name, Flavius. Like Claudius, Vespasian extended citizenship to a number of Roman colonies and admitted provincials to the Senate on a large scale. By making Titus his co-ruler, Vespasian ensured a smooth succession at his death in A.D. 79, though Titus died of the plague two years later.

The purges and proscriptions engaged in by Titus' younger brother and successor Domitian provoked the Senate to assassinate him in A.D. 96 and to appoint as the next emperor the elderly Nerva, one of its own. Nerva instituted public assistance programs, including food relief for poor children. He also designated a respected general, Trajan, as his heir. The five reigns from A.D. 96 to 180 are often called the Age of the Good Emperors. During this period a series of able and conscientious administrators, none but the last of whom had a natural born son, arranged a smooth succession by the timely adoption of the next emperor. The empire flourished and, apart from border wars and the occasional rebellion of a client state or province, enjoyed a general peace, the *pax Romana* (Roman peace).

ROME UNDER THE ADOPTIVE EMPERORS

Under Trajan (98–117) the empire achieved its largest geographical extent. Trajan conquered Dacia (modern Romania), a region rich in minerals, as well as Armenia, Assyria, and Mesopotamia, thus pushing the empire deep into western Asia. His successor Hadrian (117–138) consolidated the frontier, which he considered too extensive to defend, and built a wall across Britain between the Tyne River and the Solway Firth to repel marauding tribes from Scotland. An intellectual with a lively curiosity, Hadrian traveled throughout the empire, acquiring works of art from many provinces with which he adorned his Greek-style villa outside Rome at Tivoli.

A widespread Jewish rebellion erupted under Trajan in Cyrenaica and spread to Cyprus, Egypt, and Mesopotamia. Trajan suppressed it with great bloodshed, but a bitter three-year struggle (132–135) broke out when Hadrian prohibited circumcision as inhumane and proposed to establish a Roman colony at Jerusalem with an altar to Jupiter on the site of the temple. Led by Simon Bar-Kochba, the revolt ended in the Roman extermination of most of the Jewish population of Judaea.

SOCIAL AND ECONOMIC LIFE DURING THE EMPIRE

Economic life in the early empire followed the patterns laid down during the later republic. The demise of the republic, however, increased social mobility, for the emperors, apprehensive about the loyalty of the Senate, encouraged the growth of two classes whose members owed their good fortune to the executive himself. Beginning with Augustus, emperors promoted their equestrian supporters to important bureaucratic posts, particularly positions of financial responsibility. The emperors also horrified the senatorial elite by making increasing use of freed slaves in the imperial civil service.

The provinces prospered during the first two centuries of empire. The economy was at its height during the first century A.D., when uniform coinage prevailed, sophisticated systems of banking and credit were in operation, and general peace and security were the norm. As the provinces became industrially self-sufficient, Italy lost its economic primacy. Pottery production, once the specialty of Greece and later of Italy, was extended first to Spain and southern Gaul and subsequently to northern Gaul and the Rhine valley. Italy's once dominant position in the west in metalwork and glassblowing was also lost to Gaul, and Italy faced increasing competition from Spain, Gaul, and North Africa in the production of olive oil and wine. Meanwhile, the eastern part of the empire became increasingly important, not least because of its proximity to Asian markets. Roman merchants traveled as far as India, Ceylon, and China. From the East, traders imported spices, pepper, muslin, and jewels, usually in exchange for precious metals, pottery, and glass. Chinese silk was imported over trade routes that extended through central Asia, while a caravan route across the Sahara brought African gold and such exotic items as ostrich eggs.

By the second century A.D., however, signs of stagnation were noticeable. Like the people of the Hellenistic world, the Romans had little interest in developing new technology. Vespasian reportedly prohibited technologi-

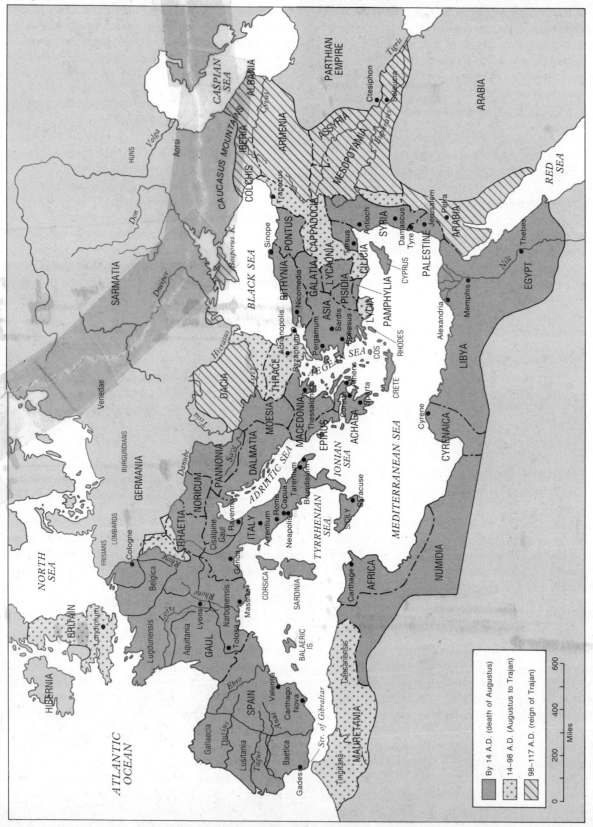

5.1 The Expansion of the Roman Empire

cal innovations on the grounds that they would reduce employment.[4] When Rome's frontiers ceased to expand, the economy began to contract, underscoring the fact that its strength had lain in the acquisition of new resources rather than in the improved use of existing ones. The lack of new conquests also gradually dried up the slave market. By the third century the economy was in marked decline.

ROME: LIFE IN THE CAPITAL

Rome – the eternal city   "All Roads led to Rome"

As the empire became more cosmopolitan, throngs of Egyptians, Syrians, and Jews crowded the streets of the capital along with the more Romanized Gauls and Spaniards. Practitioners of every profession lived in Rome, from doctors and undertakers to contractors,

prostitutes, and astrologers. The first-century satirist Juvenal accused the Roman populace of having no interests beyond "bread and circuses," and emperors were indeed careful to provide free public spectacles along with grain. Under Augustus, 77 days a year were devoted to festivals; under Tiberius, 87; and under Marcus Aurelius, 135.

The public spectacles included theater performances as well as races. The largest arena, the Circus Maximus, had a seating capacity of over 250,000. Gladiatorial combats and staged hunts took place in the Colosseum, *45–50,000* which was also equipped for large-scale flooding to reenact naval battles. Theater performances catered to the taste for sex and violence; light-hearted revues predominated, and between main acts the intermission diversions often featured the execution of criminals.

By the reign of Hadrian, Rome's center had become filled with the temples, monuments, and public buildings that still dot the city today and give it much of its grandeur and romance. Hadrian himself designed the great domed Pantheon, constructed about A.D. 126. Its

Part of a large plastic scale model of Rome in A.D. 350, showing the Circus Maximus in the center with the Domus Augustana behind it. Note the arches of the aqueduct. [Alinari/Art Resource, New York]

imposing portico with its 16 monolithic granite columns leads into a central rotunda, the roof of which consists of a huge concrete dome. The building is lit only by a central *oculus,* or eye, in the top of the dome. As the sun moves across the sky, its rays travel around the inside of the Pantheon, whose form thus became symbolic of the world itself. The Forum, where the political life of the republic had been concentrated, remained at the heart of the city's activities. During the empire, however, effective political control passed to the emperor and his staff, who lived on the Palatine (from which our word "palace" is derived), the hill overlooking the ancient assembly place of the people.

Rome was plentifully provided with fresh water.[3] A huge system of aqueducts carried pipes through which millions of gallons of water flowed each day. For all the ingenuity of its public works, however, imperial Rome was overcrowded, and life must often have been uncomfortable. Most Romans lived in one of the approximately 45,000 apartment blocks. These buildings sometimes collapsed, and fire was a continual hazard. The streets were crowded and noisy, and it is little wonder that on weekends and in the summer, affluent Romans escaped to their rural villas.

Life in the Provinces

The provinces combined Roman laws and institutions with local folkways. Provincial cities had their own charters and senates, chosen by the emperor, and the local senators (*curiales*) constituted a regional elite. Throughout the empire an educated Greco-Roman aristocracy had developed—more Roman in the west, more Greek in the east—whose members often had more in common with Italian aristocrats than with the ordinary citizens of their own provinces. By the time of Hadrian, nearly half the Roman Senate consisted of provincials.

At its height in the mid-second century A.D. the Roman Empire extended for about 3.5 million square miles and embraced a population of some 75 million. More than 85 percent of its inhabitants were probably engaged in agriculture; of its approximately 1,000 cities,

Theater at Leptis Magna (Libya) built in A.D. 1–2. [Art Resource, New York]

few contained more than 15,000 inhabitants. Some larger cities such as Pergamum may have contained as many as 100,000 people, while Alexandria in Egypt and Antioch in Syria were several times that size, and Rome itself probably had a population of 1 million. Only a fraction of the inhabitants of the empire held Roman citizenship, a privilege that was awarded by the emperor, sometimes to individuals and families of local aristocrats, sometimes to entire communities.

Connected by an extensive road network and provided with a ready supply of water by aqueducts, provincial cities boasted theaters, forums, courts, markets, elegant colonnaded streets, underground sewage systems, and baths where men and sometimes women could congregate, conduct business, and converse. Some of the larger cities had public libraries. During the first two centuries of the empire the imperial administration saw no profit in standardizing custom or culture. Except for Judaism and Christianity, the Romans tolerated the many diverse religions of their empire. Deities such as Isis, Mithras, and Cybele were worshiped side by side with the traditional Greek divinities the Romans had taken over and renamed, such as Jupiter, Juno, and Minerva; and tension with Jews and Christians was by no means universal.

The Romanization of the provinces was accelerated by the erection of Roman-style public buildings and by the constant presence of the army. The military also spread the knowledge of Latin, especially in the western provinces; in the east, many provincials who saw their own culture as older than the Roman and superior to it disdained Latin and used Greek as a common tongue.

POMPEII

Roman architects planned their cities carefully. Extensive urban remains still stand both in Italy and in the provinces; one of the most splendid is that of Leptis Magna in North Africa, home to the family of the emperor Septimius Severus (193–211). We owe several remarkable sites within Italy itself to the eruption on August 24, A.D. 79, of the volcano Vesuvius, which buried a number of small towns near Naples, the best known of which is Pompeii. The finds excavated there in the past 250 years have provided detailed evidence about life in a town of the period—from the shrines of the religious cults and the

houses and gardens to the meals Pompeiians had prepared at the time of the eruption. The spacious streets, elegant forum, stone amphitheater, temples to the gods, delicate statuary, and brightly colored mosaics of Pompeii were all typical of Italian towns.

Lying approximately 150 miles south of Rome, Pompeii was a prosperous town of some 20,000 people that served both as a commercial center for the Bay of Naples region and as a retreat for Romans of modest means who sought to escape the heat of summer. Houses were spacious, comfortable, and sometimes decorated with murals. Hellenistic influence is evident in the vibrant wall paintings, whose sense of perspective created an illusion of depth and windows. Much of the art, which appears erotic to a modern eye, was designed to bring good luck and fertility to the inhabitants of the homes in which it was placed. Many homes had private gardens, sheltered from the noise of the streets, which served both to cool the house and to provide a quiet family hideaway. The furniture, bronzeware, tableware, and other household goods were often elaborately designed and reveal a high level of craftsmanship.

Pompeii's layout followed the Greek system of town planning, adapted to the irregularities of its hillside. Long, narrow residential blocks were separated by access roads running at right angles to the main avenues. As in all town plans of this kind, there were two principal arteries, one running north-south and the other east-west. Ruts in the paved streets are still visible, revealing the repeated passage of wagons transporting merchants' and farmers' wares. The town offered a concert hall, a theater, an amphitheater capable of accommodating all the citizens, three public baths, and houses of prostitution; a famous sign in the form of an erect phallus pointed to the red-light district.

In addition to serving the needs of tourists, Pompeii and neighboring towns such as Herculaneum had their own commercial life. The largest building in Pompeii's forum, for example, was neither religious nor political, but a large hall for the clothmakers and dyers. It combined storage and sales facilities with a meeting place for fabric manufacturers. Nearby was a large open market at which farmers sold their produce. At its center, where fishmongers had their stands, was a pool in which they cleaned their fish; archaeologists found scales in it. Other shops sold utensils, wine and olive oil, and bread, including flat loaves that look like modern pizza bases. In addition to the usual artisans, Herculaneum boasted a colony of artists.

THE ART AND LITERATURE OF THE EMPIRE

Impressive building continued in both Italy and the provinces throughout the first two centuries of the empire. Roman engineering skills were especially evident in the enormous Baths of Caracalla in Rome, built around A.D. 215, the vaults of which soar to a height of 140 feet. The hot and cold alabaster pools and steam baths could accommodate 1,600 bathers.

Roman visual arts continued to proclaim the theme of imperial glory. Relief sculpture illustrated the achievements of the emperors and their victories over Rome's enemies. The arch of Titus was followed by the commemorative columns of Trajan and Marcus Aurelius. Each column was adorned with a long frieze wound around it, illustrating the triumphs of the emperors. Portrait sculpture continued to develop as well, its frank and unadorned naturalism in striking contrast to the classical Greek statuary of the fifth and fourth centuries B.C. that continued to be reproduced in large numbers.

Like Roman art and architecture, Roman literature owed much of its character to Greek models, but it boasted one new form, the satire. Roman satires were playful and sometimes sexually explicit. In his mock epic the *Satyricon,* Petronius (died A.D. 66) poked fun at the mores of his day, from the stuffy declamations of self-important rhetoricians to the conspicuous consumption of the newly rich. While exaggerated, his portrait of an ostentatious banquet on the estate of the wealthy freedman Trimalchio gives some sense of what life was like among affluent Romans as well as the degree of social mobility accorded to emancipated slaves. Petronius caricatures Trimalchio's affluence through the description given of his lifestyle by a guest at the banquet:

> Buy things? Not him. No sir, he raises everything right on his own estate. Wool, citron, pepper, you name it. By god, you'd find hen's milk if you looked around. Now take his wool. The home-grown strain wasn't good enough. So you know what he did? Imported rams from Tarentum, bred them into the herd. Attic honey he raises at home. Ordered the bees special from Athens.... And, you know, just the other day he sent off to India for some wild mushroom spawn.... And you see those pillows there? Every last one is stuffed with purple or scarlet wool. That boy's loaded![1]

Petronius, like his colleague, the poet Lucan, paid for his biting tongue; both lost their lives in Nero's purges.

Another satirist, Martial (A.D. c. 40–c. 104), wrote piercing epigrams that attacked pretensions of every kind, and Juvenal aimed his barbs at traditional targets such as social climbing and the vices of women. The greater liberty of women under the empire is reflected in Juvenal's complaints about the freedom with which females of his era entered traditionally male realms such as athletics and intellectual life. Women of his day must have been fairly well educated to provoke his complaints of dinner parties spoiled by female erudition:

> Worse still is the well-read menace, who's hardly settled for dinner
> Before she starts praising Virgil, making a moral case
> For Dido (death justifies all), comparing, evaluating
> Rival poets, Virgil and Homer suspended
> In opposite scales, weighed up one against the other....
>   ... Such matters are men's concern.[2]

During the second century A.D. the memorable literature of the empire came increasingly to be written in Greek, the language not only of the *Meditations* of the emperor Marcus Aurelius (161–180) but also of the satires of Lucian of Samosata (c. 120–c. 190), whose dialogues treated such fanciful subjects as life on the moon. Historians of the empire wrote sometimes in Greek, sometimes in Latin, Among these, pride of place must be given to Tacitus, who used a taut Latin prose to lay bare what he considered the hypocrisy and autocracy of the imperial class. Plutarch (c. 46–c. 120), a Greek from Chaeronea, composed *Parallel Lives,* paired biographies of illustrious Greeks and Romans. The tenor of these sketches has had a profound effect on the history of biography, which until the twentieth century focused largely on the adulation of successful politicians.

CRISIS AND RECOVERY

The problems that had surfaced in the age of the adoptive emperors rapidly intensified in the ensuing decades. Following the disastrous reign of Marcus Aurelius' profligate son Commodus, a protracted civil war brought an African senator, Septimius Severus (193–211), to the throne in 193 with the support of his troops. The Severan dynasty lasted only until 235, when a period of chaos set in that imposed varying degrees of misery on the empire's inhabitants. Between 235 and 284, 26 emperors ruled Rome, only one of whom died a natural death. But Rome was able to recover and avoid final disintegration for another two centuries.

The Severi

Ambitious and cunning, Septimius Severus was determined to establish a hereditary monarchy grounded in military power. To this end, he awarded important privileges to the army, such as the right to marry while stationed in the provinces, and raised the pay of the legionaries. Septimius curtailed the power of the Senate at every turn, making the army and the civil service the principal avenues to imperial preferment. He also encouraged the codification of Roman law, and under the jurist Papinian the humanitarian aims of Hadrian, Antoninus Pius, and Marcus Aurelius were carried forward. Septimius gave important new judicial functions to the praetorian prefect, his own appointee, to whom he granted jurisdiction over a number of cases previously tried in magisterial courts.

When Septimius died campaigning in Britain in 211, he was succeeded by a series of chiefly adolescent emperors, none of comparable ability or longevity. Fortunately, his energetic and capable widow, Julia Domna, a highly educated Syrian who presided over the most celebrated literary salon of her day, maintained continuity with the assistance of her female relatives. Despite watching her older son Caracalla (ruled 211–217) murder his brother in her arms, she continued to play an active role in political life.

Caracalla's most important act was the citizenship decree of 212, whereby the emperor declared virtually all free inhabitants of the empire to be Roman citizens. His action was traceable in part to the desire of jurists to foster a sense of community in Roman territory and in part to his recognition of the immense tax advantages to the crown from conferring general citizenship. In 235 the army assassinated the young Alexander Severus (ruled 222–235) and placed one of their generals on the throne. This act ended the Severan dynasty, remarkable chiefly for the codification of law, the active role of imperial women in government, and the elevation of the army over the Senate as the bulwark of empire.

The Third Century and the Establishment of the Tetrarchy

From the third century on, the emperors demanded to be called *Dominus* (Lord) instead of *Princeps*. With the increase in the judicial powers of the prefects at the expense of traditional magisterial courts, in time nearly all jurisdiction in Italy was exercised by the emperor and his appointees. The growing centralization of government failed, however, to stem the tide of decay, not least because the state lacked the funds to support the expanding army and the bureaucracy, and increased taxation imposed considerable hardship on the populace. At the same time, tensions on Rome's extensive frontiers provoked more costly wars.

The economy languished throughout this era of constant civil strife, and there was a shortage of labor in almost all spheres. The absence of offensive wars meant a sharp drop in the availability of slaves. A serious plague further sapped the population. Increasingly throughout the third and fourth centuries, imperial legislation sought to deal with the labor shortage by tying people to their hereditary occupations and locales. The third century also gave birth to the institution known as the *colonate*, which opened the door to a system of indentured farm labor. Whereas the growth of the latifundia during the second century B.C. had driven impoverished peasants to seek jobs in the city, the decline of the free peasantry in the third century A.D. prompted poor farmers to become the tenants (*coloni*) of rich landlords. In time they became a class of tenant laborers and lost their mobility.

The Reforms of Diocletian

The empire's vulnerable frontiers had made one-man rule at Rome untenable. Under Diocletian (284–305), an Illyrian soldier who at last stabilized the empire, the old system of a single ruler was replaced by a body of four emperors known as *tetrarchs*. According to Diocletian's plan, two senior rulers, called Augusti, and two junior rulers, or Caesars, would live in different cities and share responsibility for the empire. The tetrarchy ("rule of four") was also designed to solve the problem of succession. When an Augustus died, he was to be replaced by his Caesar, who in turn would appoint a new junior associate, sometimes by marrying the prospective heir to his daughter.

Despite sharing power, Diocletian remained the dominant figure in the empire. Convinced that only uniformity and centralization could stem its decline, he formulated an elaborate plan to monitor and control social and economic life. Previously, emperors had declined to regulate the economy in detail; now an edict on maximum prices fixed costs for goods and services and threatened death to anyone who refused to comply. Nor could diversity of religious belief be permitted. Diocletian destroyed Christian churches and demanded that everyone worship the traditional Roman gods on pain of execution.

Both the authoritarianism and the hostility to individuality that characterized Diocletian's rule are evident in the sculpture of his age, as the thoughtful imperial portraits of an earlier era gave way to a massive imperial style. In Venice stands a block of black porphyry carved into four figures representing the tetrarchs, each indistinguishable from the others. The way in which it conveys the majesty of the imperial office without addressing the individuality of the public servant who holds it is the sign of a new way of looking at the world.

When Diocletian retired in 305 because of poor health, he had difficulty persuading his fellow Augustus Maximian to join him, and in time civil war broke out. Soon Rome had three Augusti, an irregularity typical of the fourth century. In 312 the Augustus Maximian's son Maxentius fought against the Caesar Constantine at the Milvian Bridge in Rome to determine who would rule the empire as senior Augustus. The outcome was fateful in more ways than one, for Constantine attributed his victory to the assistance of the Christian God, whose followers he elevated from a persecuted minority to privileged sharers in imperial power.

THE RISE OF CHRISTIANITY

Constantine's accession marked the beginning of Christianity's emergence as the dominant religion in the empire. From the time of its adoption by Constantine, the history of Christianity has been inextricably linked with that of Western culture. During the centuries of its diffusion and transmission throughout virtually the entire world, it has taken on a variety of different forms.

Jesus and Paul: The Founders

Christianity grew out of the late Jewish belief that a messiah would appear among the Jews to usher in the millennium. By the time Jesus was crucified in Jerusalem around A.D. 29, many of his followers had come to believe that he was the long-awaited messiah. Like Socrates,

Jesus left no written legacy. What we know of his teachings derives from the writings of men who lived in the two or three generations after Jesus' death—the texts collected in the New Testament.

Shortly before Jesus' ministry began, around A.D. 26, another popular Jewish teacher, John the Baptist, had begun to preach the importance of righteousness rather than ritual as the means of serving God. John used the rite of baptism to symbolize the cleansing of sins and the turning of the soul to God. When Herod Antipas, the ruler of Galilee, had John executed, Jesus took up John's mantle. Jesus decried the hypocrisy of his day and denounced those who ostentatiously paraded their piety. Although he could be harsh in condemning evil, he preached a message of love and humility. It is easy, he argued, to love those who love you in return; the real challenge is to love your enemies.

These ideas were not new. Though they were hardly the dominant element in Hebrew thinking, they could be found in the biblical book of Exodus, in which Jews were commanded to do good even to their enemies; in Leviticus, which enjoined Jews to love strangers as themselves; and in the words of the prophets, who had exhorted their listeners to an uncompromising righteousness. But Jesus had a profound appeal that convinced his followers that he spoke with the voice of Yahweh and that adherence to his teachings would prepare them to enter the kingdom of God. Jesus' penetrating criticism of contemporary society and his proclamation of the imminent kingdom of God troubled both Jews and Romans. His execution resulted from the fears of Jewish leaders as well as Roman concern about the apparent subversive potential of his movement, especially after his followers proclaimed him king of the Jews. Three days after Jesus was crucified, several of his followers found his tomb empty and concluded that he had risen from the dead. Belief in Jesus' resurrection and his teachings about the importance of faith for salvation united his followers into a sect that slowly began to separate itself from Judaism.

The universality of Jesus' message, combined with the hostility of the Jewish community, prompted many of his followers to seek converts among the Gentiles. Thinkers such as Peter and Paul eventually persuaded many of their fellows that Gentiles should be permitted to bypass circumcision and become Christians as long as they abstained from the meat of animals sacrificed in pagan rites and from fornication. A Pharisee from Tarsus in Asia Minor, Paul has often been regarded as the second founder of Christianity. He had been educated in an eclectic environment of Greek, Roman, and Hebrew culture. A devout student of the Torah, he was summoned to Damascus to aid Jewish authorities in ferreting out Christians. On his way to Syria he underwent a dramatic conversion experience, and he later became a powerful apostle for his new faith. After more than a decade of missionary activity in the eastern Mediterranean, Paul returned to Jerusalem, where many Jews were angry about his activities among the Gentiles. When he was arrested in Jerusalem, he demanded to be heard at Rome, since he was a Roman citizen. What happened to Paul in Italy is unclear; according to one tradition, after some years of preaching he was executed in Nero's purge, possibly in the same year as Peter, the leader of the Roman church.

Paul was chiefly responsible for the early development of Christian theology. Stressing the universal sinfulness of humankind, Paul articulated the connection between Adam's transgression and the life of Jesus, who, he argued, had died to lay the groundwork for redemption. This argument answered the complaints of many of Christianity's critics that Christ could have escaped death had he truly been divine; in Pauline thought, Jesus willingly embraced death to provide salvation for believers.

Paul's letters to the congregations he visited form a large part of the New Testament and show him to have been a man of visionary intensity. His famous words to the Corinthians about love, which had been so crucial to Jesus' message, underline the commitment that he saw as the basis of the Christian faith:

> Though I speak with the tongues of men and of angels, and have not charity [love], I am become as sounding brass, or a tinkling cymbal. And though I have the gift of prophecy, and understand all mysteries, and all knowledge; and though I have all faith, so that I could remove mountains, and have not charity, I am nothing. And though I bestow all my goods to feed the poor and though I give my body to be burned, and have not charity, it profiteth me nothing.
>
> Charity . . . beareth all things, believeth all things, hopeth all things, endureth all things. . . .
>
> . . . And now abideth faith, hope, charity, these three; but the greatest of these is charity.[3]

Paul's views on women and marriage have been immensely influential in shaping Western culture. In theological terms he espoused a doctrine of strict spiritual equality: in Christ "there is neither male nor female; for you are all one in Christ Jesus." Yet he also regarded the celibate life as superior to the state of marriage, a teaching that provided the principal foundation for the later development of monastic communities in the church. Paul counseled wives to be subordinate to their husbands and admonished women to be silent in church. Throughout most of the church's history, therefore, women were barred from the professional ministry. Yet Paul made it clear that women labored side by side with male apostles in spreading the Christian message, and women in fact served as deaconesses, aiding the needy, and as widows who received church support in return for their special ministry of prayer. Historically, women's role in the establishment of Christianity has seldom been given due credit.

The Church and the Roman Empire

Christianity clearly offered something that was judged superior to the teachings of paganism and the beliefs associated with such deities as Mithras, Isis, Sarapis, and Cybele. Its triumph in supplanting these cults was due in part to the egalitarianism of its teachings. Although Christianity did not seek to abolish political and social distinctions, the church taught the dignity and worth of all persons and the spiritual oneness of believers. This inclusiveness set it apart from Mithraism, which accepted only male devotees. Christianity also owed its popularity to the zeal of its missionaries, its superior organization, and the demanding nature of its monotheistic faith. The exclusive commitment required by Christianity as well as its assurance of salvation to believers were undoubtedly keys to its success.

Christianity was especially popular among disadvantaged groups such as poor people and and women. The promise of a rewarding afterlife held particular attraction for those whose days on earth were unfulfilling, and Jesus' egalitarian professions and exaltation of the virtue of meekness also had great appeal. So did his advocacy of poverty as a road to holiness. Jesus' elevation of gentleness and humility to primary virtues contrasted sharply with classical values of self-assertion and competition. No traditional citizen of the Roman Empire would have been likely to compose the passage in the Book of Matthew known as the "Sermon on the Mount," in which Jesus said to his disciples, "Blessed are the meek, for they will inherit the earth."

Christian organizers also helped to spread their religion by establishing a network of congregations throughout the cities of the empire. Perhaps the alienation often entailed in urban living explains why Christianity flourished originally in cities; no doubt, popula-

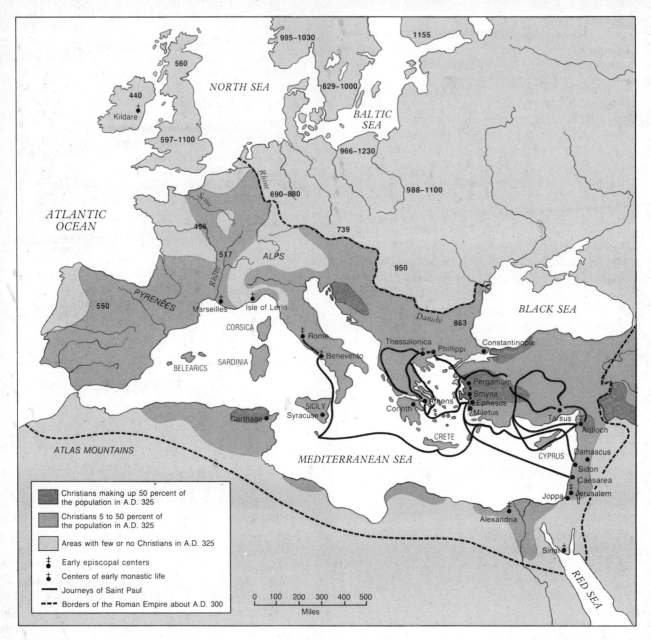

5.2 The Spread of Christianity

tion density in urban areas also caused ideas to spread faster. Each congregation was supervised by deacons ("those who serve") and presbyters ("elders"), who in turn were responsible to an *episkopos* ("overseer"), a term that came into English as "bishop." By A.D. 100, bishops were in regular touch with each other throughout the empire, and shortly after 200 the bishop of the principal city in a province (the *metropolis*) began to convene regular synods of local bishops at which arrangements were made for mutual financial support and disputed doctrines were discussed. Bishops administered the property of the church as well as performing the ceremony of the Eucharist, the partaking of the wine and bread that represented the blood and body of Christ and commemorated the Last Supper of Jesus. Originally an evening ceremony celebrated after the community meal known as the *agapé* (a Greek word meaning "love"), the Eucharist was in time observed in the morning, accompanied by hymns, prayers, and Bible readings.

Many contemporaries were quick to suspect the early church of assorted offenses. Because the feast of the agapé culminated in the exchange of kisses among the congregation, it figured prominently in slanders leveled at believers by pagan critics, some of whom believed that sexual orgies accompanied Christian rites. Moreover, some critics imagined that the consumption of the wine and bread—regarded as the blood and body of Christ—was a cloak for cannibalism. (Early followers of Christianity held a wide variety of beliefs about sex and morality, and it is possible that some Christian sects actually did engage in practices considered scandalous by most people.) Because Christians disdained worldly goods and occasionally held property in common, some pagans worried that they intended to abolish private property. Many pagans also believed that Christians had withdrawn from civic responsibilities. Refusal to worship the emperor was provocative, and some Christians avoided holding public office because of the attendant pagan rites. Some opposed war on principle and refused to serve in the army. The authorities were understandably suspicious of a group that proclaimed the ultimate return of a universal king and the end of earthly empires.

Most pagans, however, saw Christians as socially responsible people who looked after the infirm and the indigent and provided financial and emotional support to each other. For these reasons, persecution of Christians in the Roman Empire was sporadic. Nero's purge after the great fire was largely the product of his own political difficulties. But persecution only reinforced Christian commitment. Believers interpreted the growing incidence of plagues and barbarian invasions as well as the economic decline as divine punishment for a decadent empire, whereas some pagans attributed these catastrophes to the Christians' refusal to worship traditional deities.

After a decade of persecution inaugurated by Decius in 250, Christians had some respite between 260 and 303. Many entered government service and even, under Diocletian, became provincial governors. In Diocletian's last years, however, the policy of persecution was revived, and although some provincial governors were lax in enforcing the anti-Christian decrees, thousands perished. In Phrygia, soldiers burned an entire town of Christians to the ground; elsewhere, Christians were mutilated,

Head of the colossal statue of Constantine from the Basilica of Constantine, Rome. [Werner Forman Archive, London]

beaten, drowned, branded, decapitated, hanged, or tossed to wild beasts in amphitheaters.

Persecution ended in 313, when Constantine, believing he had defeated his rival Maxentius with the aid of Christ, persuaded his colleague Licinius to join with him in issuing the Edict of Milan, which granted toleration to Christians. Throughout his reign, Constantine favored the growth of Christianity over paganism. His nephew Julian's attempt to return the empire to paganism between 361 and 363 was a resounding failure.

At the end of the fourth century, Theodosius (379–395), the last emperor of the united east and west, made Christianity the state religion. The central role of Christianity in the absolutism of Theodosius looked ahead to the Christian monarchies of the Middle Ages. Identifying paganism with treason, Theodosius proclaimed that anyone performing pagan rites should suffer the penalties appropriate to traitors. All who did not accept the sacred Trinity of Father, Son, and Holy Spirit, to be worshiped in equal majesty, were declared heretics.

Orthodoxy and Heresy: Defining Boundaries

No sooner had the Edict of Milan been promulgated than the energies that had previously been devoted to keeping the church alive were diverted into passionate doctrinal quarrels. More important than the specific questions at issue was the response of secular and ecclesiastical authorities to these disputes. When the minority sects of the fourth century had been branded as heresies and suppressed by the decrees of state-sponsored episcopal councils, a single Christian orthodoxy was confirmed, and the involvement of the emperor established a precedent for the interference of the temporal government in religious debates.

The most serious heresies developed during the fourth century in Africa, where a sect known as Donatists had denied that a priest in a state of sin could effectually administer the sacraments. The matter was resolved at a synod of bishops that Constantine summoned at Arles in Southern Gaul in 314, which declared the sacraments valid irrespective of the virtue of those who administered them. North Africa was also the source of a bitter conflict regarding the nature of the Holy Trinity. Arius (died c. 335), an Alexandrian priest, maintained that since fathers beget their sons, there must have been a time when God the Father existed but Jesus the Son did not. God, therefore, was antecedent to Jesus, who did not fully share his divinity. Arius' principal opponent, Athanasius, considered the analogy with biological fatherhood unsound and argued that the Son had always existed, albeit not in the incarnate form in which humans had beheld him during his life on earth. In 325, Constantine summoned a council of bishops to meet at Nicaea in Asia Minor to end the debate. After three months the debate was resolved in favor of Athanasius. The council drew up the Nicene Creed, setting forth the orthodox interpretation of the person of Christ, according to which he was fully human and fully divine, "the only-begotten of his Father, of the substance of the Father, . . . very God of very God, begotten not made." A later and enlarged version of this creed is still recited in many Christian churches today.

Christianity and Classical Culture

Early Christians were uncertain how to treat pagan traditions. What sorts of values were inculcated by reading about the triumphs of Achilles, the romantic adventures of Odysseus, or Aeneas' preoccupation with the glory of Rome? What, the second-century theologian Tertullian asked, had the values of Athens to do with Jerusalem?

Some Christian intellectuals decried the entire heritage of pagan culture. Lactantius (c. 250–c. 317) rejected classical philosophy on the grounds that it offered no insight into divine truth, failed as an instrument for reforming morality, and had exhausted itself in a misguided search for a purely human justice. Jerome (c. 347–c. 420) feared that on judgment day he would be accused of greater devotion to Cicero than to Christ, and Augustine (354–430) repented the misdirected enthusiasm for classical poetry that had occupied his youth. In the end, however, the church fathers attempted to assimilate classical culture to Christianity rather than to eradicate it.

The groundwork for the process had been laid in Alexandria by thinkers such as the Jewish philosopher Philo (c. 30 B.C.–A.D. 45), who had labored to demonstrate the compatibility of the Hebrew Bible with Platonic thought. While the Jews who had migrated to Mesopotamia evolved the legal code of the Talmud to set themselves apart from contemporary society, Alexandrian Jews became Hellenized and assimilated classical culture.

What Philo accomplished for Judaism and the classics, Clement of Alexandria (c. 150–c. 215) and his pupil Origen (c. 185–c. 254) did for Christianity. Clement insisted that a classical education was not only helpful but necessary for understanding Judaism and Christianity. Many of the 800 works that Jerome ascribed to Clement's pupil Origen were devoted to interpreting Christianity in Platonic terms. Although Origen was posthumously accused of heresy, in part because of his use of Greek concepts, his work was read throughout the Middle Ages, and his influence was substantial.

Despite Jerome's misgivings, his translation of the Bible into Latin, a version known as the Vulgate, was heavily dependent on his classical training, and he eventually decided that classical learning was a powerful tool in spreading Christianity. Augustine, too, incorporated much of the Platonic tradition in his works. He was not alone in his admiration for Plato, whom many Christians saw as a forerunner of Christianity. Plato's notion that material objects were degenerate copies of pure forms corresponds in certain respects to the Christian distinction between the earthly and the heavenly—a contrast that would be spelled out in detail in Augustine's *The City of God* (discussed in a later section of this chapter). During the third century a Platonic mysticism known as Neoplatonism flourished, largely associated with the Greek philosopher Plotinus (c. 205–270). Plotinus saw the divine element, known as the One, as the ultimate constituent of the world of mind and of spirit. Clearly, this view owed much to Plato's belief in a descending hierarchy from pure being. Like Plato, Plotinus considered physical life a handicap to spiritual development. One of his most famous sayings was that he was embarrassed to have a body.

The Neoplatonic view of physicality was shared by many of the church fathers. Although Hebrews, Greeks, and Romans alike had condemned the sexual activity of unmarried women and had been equally harsh toward married women who committed adultery, men had been under few constraints. The church fathers, however, held sexual desire to be intrinsically sinful in both males and females.

Though women were often viewed as embodiments of temptation, in reality Christianity improved the situation of women in many ways. Like humility, pacifism, and obedience, chastity helped to exalt the traditionally "feminine" values over the "masculine" ones of militarism and political ambition that had characterized the pagan world. The virtues traditionally associated with women were thus prescribed for all people. In this way early Christianity promoted a more balanced relationship between men and women than had been characteristic of classical civilization.

In many respects, however, the promise of genuine equality was not fulfilled. Like Yahweh, the Christian God was perceived as male, and like the Hebrew Scriptures (the Christian Old Testament), the New Testament apparently was written exclusively by men. Women could not become priests, and Paul's writings served as the basis on which many subsequent Christian theologians espoused female subordination. As in the pagan world, the literate intellectuals among early Christians were male; one exception may have been the author of the nonbiblical Gospel of Mary, written by a member of a heretical group known as Gnostics. Early church writers generally associated sexual desire and its attendant perils with the temptation offered by females and tended therefore to regard women more harshly than had their pagan counterparts.

The Growth of Monasticism

Monasticism derived from the practice of individual holy men who had fled the temptations of city life into forests and deserts. The word *monk* comes from the Greek "monos," meaning "alone," and the first monks were in fact hermits who withdrew from society to seek communion with God by fasting and self-denial. The hermits attracted passionate admirers, and their unshakable devotion probably won some converts to the church. On the whole, however, the clergy were alarmed by their practices. Priests rejected the notion that union with God could come through self-denial alone, with no help from clergy or sacraments, the rites through which the grace of God was principally channeled. The competitive asceticism of the hermits, moreover, seemed to contain within it an element of pride. Although asceticism remained an essential component of monastic life throughout the Middle Ages, the shapers of medieval monasticism, Basil and Benedict, wanted to replace self-abasement with a more balanced and healthier regimen and to substitute cenobitic (communal) monasticism for eremitic (solitary) living.

Pachomius, the first monastic founder, had lived for a time as a hermit, but around 320 he established a small community of monks near Thebes in Egypt. He demanded of his monks poverty, asceticism, and unconditional obedience to the head monk, the abbot. The father of monasticism in Asia Minor was Basil (c. 330–c. 379) of Caesarea. Trained in Greek philosophy, Basil advocated the study of both classical and Christian literature in monasteries and insisted that monks channel their energies into communal labor.

Christian hermits had been less common in western Europe, where the cold, damp climate and the unsettled living conditions in the time of the Germanic invasions made life arduous. Cenobitic monasticism, however, was popular. A rejection of the extreme asceticism of the solitary monks is evident in the manual drawn up about 540 by Benedict of Nursia (c. 480–c. 547). Originally designed for his own monastery at Monte Cassino south of Rome, the Rule of Saint Benedict became the standard handbook of monasteries throughout western Europe. Benedict prescribed regular meals and sufficient sleep for monks. In addition to allotting several hours a day for prayer, he recommended that monks devote part of each day to manual labor. His emphasis on the importance of physical toil contrasts strikingly with the philosophy of classical Greek thinkers such as Aristotle, who were convinced that such labor inhibited the life of contemplation.

THE SUCCESSORS OF CONSTANTINE AND THE GERMANIC INVASIONS

In addition to granting official toleration to Christianity, Constantine recognized the importance of the eastern half of his empire, both as a military frontier and as the core of the empire's population and wealth. In 330 he founded a new imperial capital, Constantinople, on the site of the Greek city of Byzantium overlooking the straits that separate the Mediterranean from the Black Sea. For more than a thousand years, Constantinople served as both imperial capital and the center of eastern Christendom. In many respects, Byzantine civilization (discussed in Chapter 6) was a new departure, though it was Roman in its foundation, and in a wider sense it represented the continuation of the Hellenized culture of the eastern Mediterranean and western Asia.

Invading Germanic Tribes

In the late fourth century the empire was pressured anew by Germanic tribes who wished to settle within it. The Ostrogoths (East Goths), who had been living more or less peaceably along the middle and upper Danube, were being pushed from their homes by the Visigoths (West Goths); these in turn had been driven from the Ukraine by the Huns. Central Asian nomads who seem first to have settled on the steppes north of the Caspian Sea, the Huns terrified the Romans by their unusual appearance and ferocity. The Visigoths also posed a serious threat, and after an unsuccessful attempt at peaceful negotiation the Romans met them in a bloody engagement at Adrianople in Thrace (378), in the course of which the emperor Valens (364–378) was killed and two-thirds of his army was lost. In 410, under the command of their leader Alaric, the Visigoths sacked the city of Rome itself, an event that shocked the Roman world. For 800 years no enemy army had entered the city. Even Christians who had lived in expectation of judgment day were horrified; in the sack of Rome, Jerome lamented, the whole world had perished.

Simultaneously, the Vandals, another Germanic tribe, invaded Gaul and Spain and established a powerful seafaring kingdom in North Africa, from which they disrupted the supply of grain to Rome and inhibited communications between the eastern and western empires. In the 420s two Germanic tribes, the Angles and Saxons, settled in Britain, the first province abandoned by the empire, while the Alemanni and the Franks moved into Gaul. In 455 the Vandals invaded Italy by sea and sacked the capital once more. Finally, in 476 a coalition of Germanic tribes deposed the young emperor of the west, Romulus Augustulus, and replaced him with one of their own, Odoacer. By 500 the Angles and Saxons held Britain; northern Gaul was in the hands of the Frankish king Clovis; the Visigoths ruled Spain and southern Gaul; and the Vandals occupied Rome's domains in northwest Africa. The face of the world had changed dramatically.

Ambrose, Augustine, and the Christian Response

Enduring where the secular Roman Empire had collapsed, the Christian church formed the basis for the growth of a new culture. The church's capacity to provide leadership in chaotic times was due in large part to several men of determination and talent. Ambrose, bishop of Milan (c. 339–397), set a powerful precedent for church-state relations when he disciplined the emperor Theodosius after a massacre of civilians in Thessalonica, refusing to celebrate mass in the emperor's presence until Theodosius had done public penance for the slaughter and personally barring his entry to the cathedral.

Ambrose deeply impressed his most famous pupil, Augustine. An African from the province of Numidia, Augustine was the son of a Christian mother, Monica, and a pagan father. Trained in rhetoric at Carthage, he was deeply impressed by the religion of the Manichaeans. Named after its founder Mani, a Persian of the third century A.D., Manichaeanism was an offshoot of Zoroastrianism that saw existence as a continuing war between good and evil in which redemption could be won only by living ascetically. Augustine spent nearly ten years living among the Manichaeans and teaching rhetoric, first in North Africa and later in Italy. Finally, influenced by Ambrose in Milan, he decided at the age of 32 to embrace Christianity. In 396, Augustine became bishop of the African see of Hippo, and it was probably shortly after this that he composed his *Confessions,* a moving account of his spiritual growth.

Central to Augustine's theology, which owed much to Pauline teachings, was his belief in the depravity of human nature, the omnipotence of God, and predestination. Since Adam's transgression, he argued, all humans inherited his guilt and deserved eternal damnation; this was the doctrine of original sin. Because of that sinfulness, no one could attain righteousness by his or her own efforts. Although God could justly have damned the entire human race, mercy moved him to spare some, whom Augustine called the elect. They were, he said, chosen by God before the creation of the world, and only they will receive the grace that enables them to believe.

Of Augustine's nearly 100 works, the most influential was his Christian interpretation of history, *The City of God,* written in response to the sack of Rome in 410. Was this disaster, people wondered, the result of Rome's abandonment of the traditional gods? Augustine responded by setting forth his thesis of two "cities," the heavenly and the earthly. The essence of the former was love of God; of the latter, love of self. Although Christians live bodily in the latter, their ultimate loyalty is to the former, especially in its spiritual sense as the body of Christ.

The City of God constituted a frontal assault on the traditional Roman view of history. For the Romans, history was either cyclical, with alternating cycles of growth and decay, or degenerative, as moral decline progressively weakened the fiber of the community. In contrast, Augustine viewed history as a linear process involving the unfolding drama of the two cities. He stressed, however, that during their sojourn on earth, members of the heavenly city were law-abiding, so long as those laws did not impede Christian worship:

> The heavenly city, therefore, while in its state of pilgrimage, avails itself of the peace of earth, and, so far as it can without injuring faith and godliness, desires and maintains a common agreement among men regarding the acquisition of the necessaries of life, and makes this earthly peace bear upon the peace of heaven.[4]

Implicit in Augustine's phrase "so far as it can" is the recognition that Christians reserve the right to disobey temporal authorities who attempt to suppress Christianity. In the centuries that lay ahead, this right was invoked on many occasions.

LEO THE GREAT AND PAPAL AUTHORITY

A key element in future controversies between church and state was the concept of papal primacy, or the headship of the church by the bishop of Rome, identified as the direct apostolic successor of Peter. The term *pope,* or *papa* (father), was originally applied to all bishops, but since the ninth century it has been restricted in the west to the bishop of Rome. One of the people most responsible for the development of the doctrine of papal primacy was Pope Leo I (440–461), a former Roman aristocrat. Before his election to the papacy he had been intensely engaged in doctrinal conflicts, and his efforts culminated when, as pope, he persuaded the Council of Chalcedon to endorse his orthodox interpretation of the Trinity in 451. Leo was a dedicated educator who stressed the importance of a learned clergy and labored to improve the liturgy and promote the development of canon (church) law. His most important work, however, was his articulation of the doctrine of the Petrine succession.

According to the Gospel of Matthew, Jesus told his disciple Peter that as the name *Petros* meant "rock," then "on this rock I will build my church." Leo took this to mean that Christ intended the leadership of the church to be in the hands of Peter and of those who succeeded him in his capacity as bishop of Rome. The eastern bishops never recognized Leo's claim, but it was gradually accepted in the west, and the supremacy of the bishop of Rome as pope of what would come to be known as the Catholic church continued to evolve over several centuries. Leo further buttressed his authority by assuming the title Pontifex Maximus, long associated with the Roman emperors, and by claiming to possess a plenitude, or fullness, of power.

Leo's pontificate enhanced the prestige of the papacy. He followed the precedent of Innocent I, the Roman bishop who had arranged the withdrawal of Alaric from Rome, by leaving the city to negotiate with the Huns (452) and the Vandals (455). His resolve contrasted markedly with the paralysis of the eastern emperor, Marcian. Hastening north when he learned that Attila's long siege of Aquileia had brought the city to its knees, Leo met the Hun leader by the Po River and dissuaded him from attacking Rome. His success with Gaiseric the

Vandal was less dramatic, but his entreaties mitigated the bloodshed and plunder visited on Rome in 455 by the Vandals, who refrained from the customary murder and arson. These interventions established the pope as a force in temporal affairs.

The Transformation of the Roman World

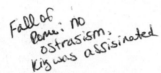
Fall of Rome: no ostracism, King was assisinated

No question in history has been more widely debated than the reasons for the decline of Rome's western empire. Some have sought to isolate a single factor as the underlying cause; others see a number of developments combining to produce an ultimate disintegration of authority.

In his monumental *History of the Decline and Fall of the Roman Empire,* the first volume of which appeared in 1776, Edward Gibbon offered two explanations of Rome's fall. One was philosophical: having grown too heavy, the fabric of Roman culture collapsed of its own weight. Another was more concrete: Christianity, Gibbon asserted, had diverted vital energy and attention from pressing civil problems.

More recent historians have focused on social, economic, political, and demographic factors. Some have pointed to the absence of any means of reforming the government short of violent revolution; others have pointed to the low level of technology as the weak link in the economy and connected it to slavery, which deprived Greeks and Romans of the incentive to develop more efficient means of production. The decline has sometimes been ascribed to a labor shortage, and some historians have suggested that the invasions of the Germans and the Huns were too much for an empire whose economy was exhausted.

The structural weaknesses of Roman society should also be borne in mind. The Romans never resolved the tensions that had destroyed the republic. The aristocracy clung fiercely to its privileges, prompting commoners to assert their interests in violent ways. Augustus reconstituted the state on the basis of an equilibrium founded on social exhaustion. No regular method of succession, moreover, was ever devised. Revolution and assassination all too often filled the place of legislation and election.

Beginning in the reign of Marcus Aurelius, pressures on the frontiers mounted, and the basic weakness of the economy was aggravated. This weakness had its origin in a fundamentally aristocratic ethos that refused to deal seriously with economic problems and preferred to address them by philanthropy. The use of slave labor lowered the incentive for technological improvement. The same economic stagnation that had set in during the Hellenistic era sapped the resources of Rome as soon as its borders stopped expanding. Gibbon's view that Rome collapsed because it had become too large has been shared by many, but the truth may be rather that Rome declined when it ceased to expand.

The survival of the eastern empire must be contrasted with the collapse of Roman power in the west. The empire in Constantinople endured until it was overthrown by the Turks in 1453. To some degree the east and west had shared in the common problems of the third and fourth centuries. In both regions, imperial decrees sought in vain to freeze the empire's inhabitants in hereditary vocations. It was hard to find sufficient numbers of people to do anything—to farm, to work at crafts, even to serve in the army. Nonetheless, the east never experienced the sweeping demoralization that overwhelmed the west. The ability of the eastern empire to endure while the west collapsed was due in large part to the greater economic health of its cities. Ancient civilization had been based on a productive relationship between the city and the country. Although at least 85 percent of the population was engaged in farming, trade with the cities for goods and services stimulated commerce and agriculture. Perhaps because the cities of the east were centuries older than those of the west, they proved more stable in the crises of the third and fourth centuries. In contrast, the wealthiest western aristocrats withdrew to their country estates, where they converted many of their slaves and free neighbors into coloni, thus paving the way for the feudal system of the Middle Ages.

But the question of Rome's decline has perhaps been wrongly posed by historians. What is remarkable is not that Rome at last succumbed but that it survived so long, encompassing the cultures of three continents within a single system of law and government. The dissolution of Rome was in reality a process rather than an event. If the empire's political center of gravity was the city of Rome, its economic and cultural base had always been in the eastern Mediterranean, a fact that Constantine recognized when he built his new capital on the shore of Asia. In a sense, then, the stronger, more viable half of the empire survived there, its history and culture continuous down to the Turkish conquest of 1453.

SUMMARY

The erosion of central authority in the west entailed the replacement of one kind of loyalty by others. Where Roman citizens had once been preoccupied with the border that divided their huge empire from the alien and dangerous world outside, now a new religion made it possible to see people as united by a bond more profound than Roman citizenship. It also become easier for local cultures to develop freely, untrammeled by the uniformity that the later empire had imposed throughout the realm. In time, different regions of the empire would develop not only their own governments but also their own languages, several of which, including French, Spanish, Portuguese, Italian, and Romanian, derived originally from Latin.

The civilization that rose from the ruins of classical culture had much in common with it but was also very different. The dogmatic orientation of the Christian church marked a dramatic departure from the religious and philosophical pluralism of Greece and Rome. Although the modern notion of an inherent freedom of speech and belief would have been puzzling to Greeks and Romans, diversity of thought was a fundamental characteristic of classical society, which had room for many systems of belief. In addition, the association of chastity with morality and the denigration of sexuality even in the context of marriage represented a departure from most views found both in the classical world and in western Asia.

Although Christian ideas differed from classical thinking in all these respects, the church absorbed a great deal from the civilization of Rome. The characteristic Roman sense of order and discipline passed over into the church, whose efficient organization helped it to attain primacy in the empire and maintain some degree of stability in people's lives when the state was crumbling. The fundamentally patriarchal nature of classical society was carried over into medieval civilization as women were excluded 'from the clergy and generally discouraged from intellectual, political, business, and military pursuits. The hierarchical class system Rome had shared with other ancient states translated itself first into the church hierarchy and in time into the feudal order of the Middle Ages.

Notes

1. Petronius, *The Satyricon,* trans. W. Arrowsmith (New York: New American Library, 1959), p. 46.
2. Juvenal, *Satire* 6, in *The Sixteen Satires,* trans. P. Green (Harmondsworth, England: Penguin, 1967), p. 144.
3. 1 Corinthians 13 (Authorized Version).
4. *Basic Writings of St. Augustine,* trans. M. Dods, ed. W. J. Oates (New York: Random House, 1948), p. 494.

Suggestions for Further Reading

Bowersock, G. *Julian.* Cambridge, Mass.: Harvard University Press, 1978.

Brown, P. *The World of Late Antiquity.* New York: Norton, 1989.

Crook, J. A. *Law and Life of Rome, 90 B.C.–A.D. 212.* Ithaca, N.Y.: Cornell University Press, 1967.

Fox, R. L. *Pagans and Christians.* New York: Knopf, 1986.

Grant, M. *The Jews in the Roman World.* New York: Scribner, 1973.

Hopkins, K. *Conquerors and Slaves.* New York: Cambridge University Press, 1977.

Jolowicz, H. *Historical Introduction to the Study of Roman Law.* Cambridge: Cambridge University Press, 1952.

Kagan, D., ed. *The End of the Roman Empire: Decline or Transformation?,* 2nd ed. Lexington, Mass.: Heath, 1978.

MacMullen, R. *Corruption and the Decline of Rome.* New Haven, Conn.: Yale University Press, 1988.

McNamara, J. *A New Song: Celibate Women in the First Three Christian Centuries.* New York: Haworth, 1983.

Pagels, E. *Adam, Eve, and the Serpent.* New York: Vintage, 1988.

Renko, S. *Pagan Rome and the Early Christians.* Bloomington: Indiana University Press, 1986.

Shelton, J. *As the Romans Did: A Sourcebook in Roman Social History.* Oxford: Oxford University Press, 1988.

Salmon, E. T. *A History of the Roman World from 30 B.C. to A.D. 138,* 6th ed. New York: Harper and Row, 1968.

Wheeler, M. *The Art of Rome.* New York: Praeger, 1964.

The West and the World

Antiquity

Modern authors sometimes refer to "spaceship Earth" or "the global village" to signify the extent to which the peoples of our planet have become increasingly intertwined in their daily lives. State-of-the-art communications enable millions of people to watch major events as they occur in other parts of the world. For most of the past, however, people in the West had little direct knowledge of the diverse cultures and societies beyond their own lands. Over time, explorers and traders, mariners and soldiers, and missionaries and travelers brought back bits of information about non-Western civilizations. The great voyages of exploration that commenced in the fifteenth century greatly intensified contacts between Europe and the rest of the world, setting the stage for the West's dramatic outward thrust in the modern era. In the six essays titled "The West and the World" we will explore the changing views of westerners toward non-Western civilizations, noting in particular the sense of the exotic and the mysterious that has often been the hallmark of such perceptions.

"The extreme regions of the earth, which surround and shut up within themselves all other countries, produce the things which are rarest, and which people reckon the most beautiful."[1] For the fifth-century B.C. Greek historian Herodotus, as for people of learning and curiosity throughout subsequent centuries, the world beyond their borders was of continuing interest, its lands alternately believed to be blessed or cursed, its inhabitants practitioners of strange customs, many of which existed only in the minds of the imaginers. Herodotus, for instance, reported that in India, a land he had never visited, the people risked their lives to steal gold from the ants that had mined it, notwithstanding the fact that the ants that guarded the gold were reputedly the size of foxes. However fantastic, such tales helped to pique interest in faraway places. So too did the accounts of traders, travelers, soldiers, and sailors, whose information contributed over time to a more accurate and useful understanding of the outside world.

For most people of antiquity, especially before the great empires of Alexander the Great

A map of the world as Herodotus understood it: note the central location of Greece and Asia Minor.

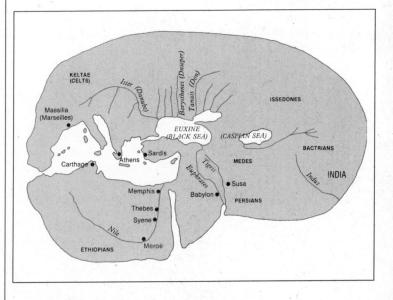

101

and the Romans, virtually all lands beyond their own were regarded as alien. Most Greeks, for instance, regarded all who could not speak the Greek language as barbarians. For Herodotus, foreign peoples were different from, but not necessarily inferior to, the Greeks. Those whom he met on his travels he found intriguing, comparing their ideas and customs with those of the Greeks and seeking connections between their intellectual world and his own. He argued, for example, that the Greeks had borrowed their deities from the Egyptians: "Almost all the names of the gods came into Greece from Egypt."[2] Although he clearly respected the Egyptians, Herodotus erroneously concluded that their customs and laws were contrary to those of other people. He reported that the men stayed home to weave while the women engaged in commerce; that Egyptians kneaded dough with their feet and clay with their hands; that women carried burdens on their shoulders, whereas men bore them on their heads; that Egyptians urinated in their houses but ate in the street and picked up dung with their hands; and that unlike other peoples, they believed it was inappropriate to live on wheat and barley. Herodotus, we must remember, knew Egypt at first hand, and observations such as these underscore the profound extent to which he was impressed by social and cultural differences as well as by similarities in religious belief.

Both Herodotus and his contemporary, the playwright Aeschylus, showed a somewhat surprising respect for the Persians, who in the fifth century had become the main enemy of most Greeks. Herodotus' circle of friends included Persians, who provided him with information about their empire. Persian manners, the lengthy and seemingly magnificent Persian names, and the courage of Persian warriors impressed him. So too did the Persians' ability to administer their vast empire and the laws they enacted. But Herodotus was perceptive enough to recognize that not all Persians—nor all Greeks—were admirable; he denounced the Persian king Cambyses, for instance, as a madman who mocked religion and custom when he conquered Egypt. In the end, Herodotus' respect for foreigners did not sway him from the widespread Greek conviction that Hellenic culture was better: "The Greeks have been from very ancient times distinguished from the barbarians by superior sagacity and freedom from foolish simpleness."[3]

Aeschylus' tragedy *The Persians* is of great interest not least because the author himself participated in the crucial naval battle of Salamis (480 B.C.), the recounting of which is a key part of the play. The story of this great confrontation is told not from the vantage point of the victorious Greeks but from that of the Persians. By the end of the play, the Greek audience is led not to exult in their victory but to have compassion for the profound losses of their foes:

> *Persians at the peak of life,*
> *   best in soul, brightest in lineage,*
> *   first always to give the King loyalty—*
> *they're dead without glory,*
> *   and shamed by that fate.[4]*

Greeks were thus taught by Aeschylus not to despise but to respect and to have compassion for the Asians whom they had defeated.

Alexander's conquest of the Persian Empire enormously widened the exposure of many westerners to the peoples and customs of Egypt and Asia. The Hellenization of the eastern Mediterranean was already underway when Alexander began his campaigns. One of the by-products of previous wars had been the growing reputation of Greek soldiers, who were increasingly sought by many Asian rulers. Money and employment had also lured many Greeks to the east, as did their curiosity about these lands. Alexander himself did much to enhance Western awareness of Asian customs and values, not least by founding more than 70 cities that became cultural melting pots. Alexander generally retained the administrative structure of the Persian Empire and employed former Persian governors. He wore Persian dress, bestowed Persian brides on his troops, and required his soldiers to render obeisance before him in the style of a Persian monarch. Such behavior bothered some of his troops, who clearly signaled their disapproval of such Asian ways. Callisthenes, Aristotle's nephew and Alexanders' chief scientific observer and court philosopher, admonished the great general not to forget Greece "because we are few and in a strange land." For some, exposure to the wider world had only reinforced their devotion to Hellenic culture; others found the broader horizons much to their liking, remained in the conquered territories well beyond Alexander's death, and continued the process of Hellenization.

Alexander marched eastward to the Indus valley. The earliest information the Greeks had about India had apparently come from the physician Ctesias, who had traveled to the east in the late fifth century B.C. His account, like that of Herodotus, was a mixture of fact and fiction; his fantasies included reports of Aryans who lived as long as 200 years and griffins that guarded gold. A century later, Megasthenes, an ambassador from the Seleucid king, provided valuable accounts from the court of Chandragupta Maurya, founder of the first Indian empire. In addition to describing the workings of Mauryan government and the social (caste) system, Megasthenes wrote with admiration about the morality of the people, the absence of slavery, the relative freedom of women, and the infrequency with which citizens sought redress in the courts. Like Herodotus, he was intrigued by Indian religious and philosophical beliefs; he noted, for instance, similarities between the teachings of the Buddhists and those of Pythagoras and Plato. Apart perhaps from the opportunities for trade, what seemed to intrigue the Greeks the most about the Asian world were its religious beliefs, political institutions, social customs, and animal life.

Greeks were regularly in contact with India in the centuries after Alexander. From India, Greek ships transported cotton textiles, brasswork, spices, incense, precious stones, and a variety of animals and birds to the Mediterranean. By approximately A.D. 80, information concerning the source and cost of such goods as well as sailing routes and more general observations about Indian culture could be found in a Greek handbook known as the *Periplus of the Erythrean Sea* (the Indian Ocean, Persian Gulf, and Red Sea). As early as the third century B.C. the Greeks encountered Chinese silk, which was vastly superior to that produced from the wild silkworms of Asia Minor. By about 150 B.C. the Chinese were dispatching silk-laden caravans to the Mediterranean, although the Greeks themselves apparently had little or no direct contact with the Chinese, dealing instead with Indian, Syrian, and Arab middlemen. In the end such trade outlived both the presence of Greeks in India and the impact of Hellenic culture on the Indians.

Western contact with India and China increased after Roman armies conquered the Hellenistic kingdoms in the second century B.C. About the time of Jesus, oceangoing ships from the west called at Indian ports, and agents of Greco-Roman trading companies lived in their own quarters in Indian cities. Increasingly, Chinese silk and other goods were transported to the West by sea, coming from China to India in Indian or Malayan ships and thence to the Mediterranean in Western vessels. By the late second century A.D., Western ships had sailed to Indonesia, searching for the source of silk and finding cloves and other spices. Roman interest in the eastern lands was largely economic; from the Asians they sought such items as silk, camphor, cinnamon, jade, and eventually porcelain and lacquer goods, although the Chinese seem to have wanted little or nothing from the West other than gold. The Malayans, however, were interested in Roman pottery, and Roman glass reached Korea in small amounts.

Direct contact between Westerners and the Chinese was relatively slight; we know of only two instances. The first was in A.D. 97, when a Chinese envoy reached Mesopotamia, only to be discouraged from further travel by tales that the voyage across the Mediterranean required two years and that many travelers died of homesickness; local merchants clearly wanted to preserve their role as middlemen in the trade between Asia and the West. In A.D. 166, Roman merchants, posing as official ambassadors from the imperial court, reached Annam (modern Vietnam), where they offered ivory, rhinoceros horns, and tortoise shells in the hope of establishing direct contact with Chinese silk manufacturers; their effort failed. However, there must have been other occasions, though unrecorded, when westerners were in direct contact with East Asians during the course of their commercial activities.

Romans who knew enough to have an opinion about the Chinese thought them very virtuous, probably because of the human tendency to attribute extremes of behavior to people about whom we know little. Apparently, the Romans knew nothing of Chinese inventions. Such devices as cranks, treadles, and wheelbarrows did not appear in the West until the Middle Ages; rotating fans, printing presses, power-driven bellows for forges, blast furnaces, and chain-mounted suspension bridges were not manufactured by Westerners until modern times. As interested as the Romans were in engineering and construction techniques, they surely would have applied Chinese technology had they known about it.

A Chinese statue of a Persian or Arabic merchant-middleman in the trade between China and the West. [Collection of Dr. Dorothy Needham; reproduced in Joseph Needham, *Science and Civilization in China*, vol. 1. Cambridge: Cambridge University Press, 1954.]

The Romans typically viewed many of the peoples beyond their frontiers as barbarians to be conquered. The carving on this marble sarcophagus from the third century A.D. depicts such a conquest. [Alinari/Art Resource, New York]

Obviously, therefore, such knowledge was not transmitted during the course of the minimal contact that occurred in seagoing commerce and the caravan trade.

The Romans knew more about East Asia than the other lands beyond their borders. The geographer Claudius Ptolemy (c. 90–c. 168) peopled Russia with Amazons and a tribe of Lice-Eaters and thought that Scandinavia was an island. Some Romans believed that the land where Zeus had exiled his father, Cronos, was a mere five days by sea west of Britain. As in the days of Herodotus, unknown lands inspired flights of fantasy. Nevertheless, Roman armies, like those of the Greeks before them, expanded western frontiers, making it possible for merchants and travelers to push beyond them in search of commercial profit and knowledge. The Roman historian Tacitus (c. 55–c. 117) wrote vivid accounts of the peoples and customs of Germany (in *Germania*) and Britain (in *Agricola*), both of which provided Roman readers with fascinating glimpses of the tribes whom their armies had conquered. In an almost detached manner, Tacitus recorded their virtues as well as their vices, paying tribute to noble adversaries.

As Christianity grew, its missionaries penetrated into southern Asia and into Ethiopia in northeastern Africa. According to tradition, the apostle Thomas founded the first Christian communities in India, although they probably did not exist before the second century. By the fifth century, Christian outposts had been established in central Asia as well. Important missions were also undertaken to the Goths by Ulfilas and to the Gauls by Martin of Tours, both in the fourth century, and to the Irish by Patrick in the fifth. Such work attests to the Christian perception of the wider world as a source of converts and to the Christian belief, popularized especially by Augustine, in a "City of God" whose members—the godly elect— were drawn from all nations. A similar belief had previously been espoused in a nonreligious context by the Stoics, who believed both in a universal society in which all men were citizens and in a republic in which only the good could be citizens. Both the Stoic and Christian conceptions of a society unlimited by political borders reflected the multiethnic empire established by the Romans.

Like the Hellenistic kingdoms, the Roman Empire eventually disintegrated, but the interest in Christian missions and the desire to trade with foreign lands remained. Although weakened by the collapse of the empire in the west, both concerns revived in the Middle Ages and provided a powerful impetus to increased contacts with the non-Western world.

1. Herodotus, *The Persian Wars,* trans. G. Raw-linson (New York: Modern Library, 1942), p. 267.
2. Ibid., p. 142.
3. Ibid., p. 31.
4. Aeschylus, *Persians,* trans. J. Lembke and C. J. Herington (New York: Oxford University Press, 1981), ll. 717–721.

BYZANTIUM AND ISLAM

east continued to prosper & grow while west declined

While western Europe was being transformed by nomadic invaders after the collapse of Roman rule, the eastern half of the empire, despite initial setbacks at the hands of the Goths and the Huns, laid the foundation in the sixth century for a period of imperial brilliance. The Byzantine Empire, or Byzantium, derived its name from the former Greek colony of Byzantium, which Constantine had transformed into the site of his new capital, Constantinople, in 330. Strategically located on the Bosporus, part of the great water route between the Black and Aegean seas, the city, surrounded on three sides by water, was easily defended. It was also a natural site for a commercial center, since it was the crossroads for the great east-west trading routes that extended from Asia to Europe, as well as the north-south routes that reached from southern Russia to the Mediterranean. Byzantine culture, a distinctive fusion of Greco-Roman and Christian traditions, made a lasting impact on many of the peoples of eastern Europe.

After a thousand-year history, Byzantium fell in 1453 to the Ottoman Turks, who conquered it on behalf of Islam, the youngest of the world's major religions. Islam began in Arabia in the early seventh century. From there it spread throughout the Middle East and beyond, into Iran, North Africa, the Iberian peninsula, and the Balkans. Virtually from the beginning, Islamic expansion brought the Arabs into conflict with their Byzantine neighbors, and as early as 674, Muslim armies made their first, albeit unsuccessful, attempt to conquer Constantinople. During the ensuing eight centuries, relations between the Muslims and the Byzantines were often characterized by hostility and periodic warfare, but the peoples of the two civilizations also traded with each other and synthesized classical culture.

BYZANTIUM

The Byzantine Empire was a remarkable achievement. The last of its emperors, Constantine XI, could trace the imperial succession back to the Roman emperor Augustus in the late first century B.C., although many of the institutions familiar to Augustus had long since ceased to exist. There was, nevertheless, continuity of culture and tradition that helped to make the Byzantine Empire the most durable political entity in medieval Europe. It not only preserved and enhanced classical culture but also made important contributions in law, religion, commerce, and the arts. Moreover, the empire provided a crucial buffer between waves of invaders from Asia and the peoples of western Europe as they constructed new states in the aftermath of the Roman decline and the Germanic, Viking, and Magyar invasions.

The Historical Background

Despite its administrative separation in the late fourth century, the Roman Empire was still regarded as a single

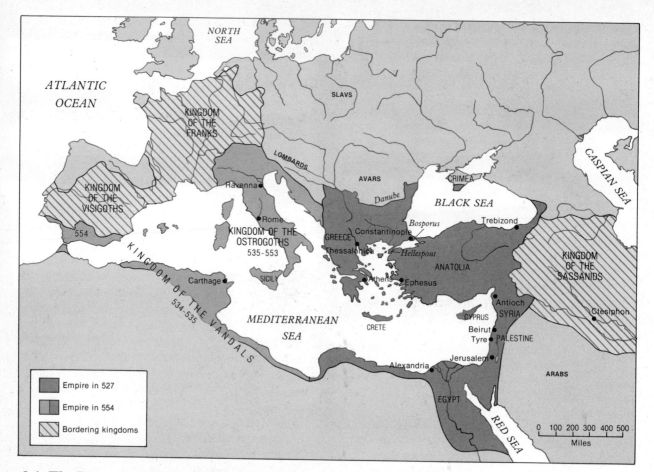

6.1 The Byzantine Empire Under Justinian

state. Yet the roots of the future division were already present. The western part of the empire, which traditionally enjoyed political supremacy, had always been inferior to the east in terms of natural resources, population, urban centers, commerce, and industry. When, in the fifth century, it became increasingly apparent that the west could not defend itself against outside invaders, rulers in the east concentrated on protecting their own domains. Suspicion, conflict of interest, and jealousy were stronger than feelings of unity and responsibility, especially as the two halves of the empire evolved into separate states, each with its own set of laws and coinage. Even religion played a modest role in dividing the empire, as the Latin Christians found themselves at odds with the Monophysites, who emphasized Christ's divinity at the expense of his humanity and who had

substantial support in Egypt, Syria, Palestine, and Constantinople.

3Although the eastern half of the empire survived, it did not escape the blows of nomadic invaders. As early as 378 a Visigoth army defeated the Emperor Valens and the Roman army of the Danube at Adrianople. The empire saved itself by allowing the Visigoths to settle in the Balkans in return for serving in the Byzantine army. Faced with the threat of an invasion by the Huns in the mid-fifth century, the government at Constantinople paid the tribute demanded by Attila (died 453), the Huns' leader. When the Ostrogoths threatened the eastern empire in the late fifth century, their chieftain, Theodoric (died 526), was persuaded to invade Italy instead. Thus by the early sixth century, when the western empire had for all practical purposes ceased to exist, the Byzantine domains still embraced the Balkan peninsula, Armenia, Syria, Palestine, Egypt, and Asia Minor.

The Age of Justinian

An empire that stretched from the Nile to the Black Sea was not enough to satisfy Justinian (527–565), a strong-willed, pious emperor determined to recover conquered Roman lands. He first ended a war with the Persians, thus freeing troops to reclaim much of North Africa from the Vandals. Belisarius, the most prominent of his generals, accomplished this task in 533 and 534. The following year, Belisarius overran Sicily; in the ensuing years he reconquered the Italian peninsula from the Goths. In 550, Justinian sent an expedition against the Visigoths in Spain, which soon brought the southern part of the Iberian peninsula under his rule. The boundaries of the ancient Roman Empire were still a long way from being restored, and Justinian's campaigns had exacted a heavy toll. Overtaxed, the empire was on the verge of fiscal collapse; the defenses in the east had been undermined; and trade with India and China had been disrupted by renewed fighting with Persia.

Justinian ruled as an agent of God, enjoying supreme authority over both church and state. Just as there was only one God, so there could be only one Christian empire governed by one emperor, himself subject to divine law alone. The emperors became the focal point of an elaborate, partly Persian, partly Roman court ritual designed to enhance their power and image. Later, beginning in the seventh century, the emperor styled himself *basileus,* or "ruler of all the world," a title analogous to the Persian notion of "king of kings," in addition to the title *autocrat,* or "sole ruler," to underscore his absolute power.

Keeping the church in order was part of Justinian's imperial responsibility as well as a means of preserving unity. Generally, he preferred to convert dissidents to this point of view rather than impose harsh punishment. Yet he burned to death a number of heretics, known as Manichaeans, when they refused to retract their belief in a dualistic universe that identified goodness with the spirit and evil with matter. Thanks primarily to the patronage of his wife, the empress Theodora, the Monophysites, who refused to distinguish between the divine and human natures in Christ, fared much better. Justinian issued an imperial edict seeking a compromise between orthodox Christians and Monophysites, but he also used his authority to close pagan schools in Athens.

Justinian enjoyed considerable success in his reform of the law, which he deemed, like religion, a source of social and political cohesion. A royal commission imposed order on the mass of surviving Roman imperial edicts, issuing a code in which repetitions had been deleted and contradictions resolved. It also compiled a digest of Roman judicial opinion gleaned from 2,000 volumes. In addition, to train law students in this material, the commissioners prepared a handbook called the *Institutes,* which remained in use in Europe into the twentieth century. All three of these documents were in Latin, still the official language of the empire, but a volume of new laws, called *Novels,* was issued in Greek, the language of most citizens in the east. Later, these compilations were collectively known as the *Corpus Juris Civilis,* or "Body of Civil Law."

Although Justinian's legal reform was intended to be a work of conservation, it offered some significant improvements, including simpler ways to convey property and the replacement of the extended family in law with a nuclear core of parents and children. The influence of the code was profound. In the twelfth century it spread to western Europe, where the principle of mutual interest—enshrined in the phrase "that which touches all concerns all"—provided much of the basis for Western medieval law, both religious and secular. This concept contributed to the development of representative institutions in the West during the fourteenth century and eventually to modern parliamentary government, although Byzantium itself remained autocratic. Justinian's *Code, Digest,* and *Institutes* constituted the most significant single body of legal documents in Western history and the primary means by which the Roman legal heritage was preserved and transmitted.

THEODORA: FROM ACTRESS TO EMPRESS

"Whether or not a woman should give an example of courage to men, is neither here nor there. . . . Flight, even if it brings us to safety, is not in our interest."[1] With those words the Empress Theodora persuaded Justinian not to flee from his capital in the midst of the greatest crisis of his reign, the Nika riot of 532. The Greens and the Blues, the principal rival organizations that provided charioteers and acrobats as well as avid supporters for the games in Constantinople's stadium, the Hippodrome, made common cause against the government. In support of two of their number, whom the government had unsuccessfully tried to hang, they set fire to the city and besieged the imperial palace. Shamed into action by Theodora, Belisarius ordered the imperial army to suppress the rioters. Before the troops were called off, some 30,000 people had been killed, but Justinian's throne was secured.

Justinian had married Theodora, daughter of a bearkeeper, seven years earlier, when he was in his early forties and she in her late twenties. Before she became Justinian's mistress and eventually his wife, she had followed her sister onto the stage, an occupation associated with promiscuity. What little we know about these years in Theodora's life comes from the historian Procopius, her bitter enemy. The portrait he draws is one of a courtesan and strip-tease artist who had frequent abortions and indulged in sexual orgies. In pursuit of a better life she became the mistress of a bureaucrat, who took her to North Africa before tiring of her. In Alexandria she met and was probably converted by prominent Monophysite clergymen. Justinian met her after she had returned to Constantinople and taken up the trade of spinning wool. Under Roman law a man of Justinian's rank could not marry an actress, but this barrier was removed on Justinian's behalf in a special edict issued by Justinian's predecessor, his uncle Justin I. Two years after their marriage in 525, the patriarch of Constantinople crowned Justinian and Theodora.

As empress, Theodora generally acquitted herself well. She took a special interest in the prostitutes of the capital, at one point purchasing their freedom from their keepers and returning each to her parents with a gold coin. She extended monetary assistance to the churches and villages of Asia Minor. In addition to her work on behalf of the Monophysites, she attempted, without success, to obtain the election of a pope who would look more tolerantly on them. Her experience in government prepared her to run it when Justinian was ill with the bubonic plague in 542. The empress died of cancer six years later.

Theodora's life is paralleled by Evita

BYZANTINE ECONOMY AND SOCIETY

An important part of the empire's lengthy existence and relative stability can be attributed to its economic and social structure. As long as its aristocracy was service-based, its free farmers were prosperous, and its trade was in Byzantine hands, the empire was quite strong. But the rise of a military aristocracy, the decline of free, independent farmers, and the domination of trade by Italians fatally weakened the Byzantine state.

Economic Patterns

Much of the wealth of the Byzantine Empire came from agriculture, especially commencing in the seventh century when manufacturing and commerce began to decline as a result of continuing warfare and a decreasing population. During the fourth and fifth centuries the basic agricultural unit was a large estate worked by hundreds of sharecroppers tied to the land as *coloni,* or serfs, that is, peasants who were legally bound to those estates. Coloni who fled their estates were hunted down and enslaved. During the sixth and seventh centuries the Persian, Slavic, and Arab invasions increased the need for higher taxes and military recruits, thus encouraging the development of a free peasantry who could provide the necessary labor and shoulder the increased financial burden. By the eighth century, coloni and slaves had virtually disappeared. In the tenth century the large lay and ecclesiastical estates began expanding again, especially when members of the landed aristocracy acquired control of the throne in the eleventh century. Many peasants were forced into a nearly servile status, particularly in the face of staggering taxes that left them heavily in debt or bankrupt.

Nevertheless, agriculture continued to develop in the eleventh and twelfth centuries, as reflected in efforts to reclaim abandoned land and in exports of grain, wine, and meat to the west. Western European visitors in this period were impressed by the abundance of grain, olive oil, wine, and cheese. During the last centuries of the empire this prosperity was destroyed when peasants were valued more as sources of military manpower than as farmers. In this period the great landowners held their estates virtually tax free in return for providing the imperial army with troops. The gross abuse of the peasantry and the consequent decline of agriculture significantly weakened the empire, whose greatest strength had been its independent farmers.

Commerce, although less important in the Byzantine economy than agriculture, played a significant role. Constantinople was the primary center of trade between the Middle East and Asia on the one hand and Europe on the other. Byzantine merchants traveled as far as East Asia and Spain in the early centuries of the empire. From Asia came Chinese silk, prized by the wealthy as an alternative to abrasive, heavy wool; spices to season and sugar to sweeten food; and jewels, pearls, and ivory, imported to adorn the rich and to beautify churches. Africa provided slaves as well as ivory, and the Black Sea region was a source of wheat, furs, hides, slaves, salt, and wine. From France and Italy came textiles and weapons.

In addition to these items, many of which passed through the empire en route to more distant locations, the Byzantines exported commodities of their own, including cotton, glassware, and enamels from Syria and timber, flax, and honey from the Balkans. The greatest Byzantine export was silk, whose manufacture the Byzantines first learned in the mid-sixth century, thanks to two monks who smuggled silkworm eggs out of China. To prevent a small number of wealthy people from monopolizing the new industry, the various stages of production were assigned to separate guilds, each of which operated under government regulation. Until the eleventh century, manufacturing and sales were limited to Constantinople, but in the eleventh and twelfth centuries, silk production spread to Greece and Sicily. The Byzantine emperors also enjoyed a monopoly in the production of gold embroidery and purple dye.

By the tenth century most of the carrying trade had been taken over by foreign merchants, particularly Italians. These merchants were increasingly exempted from the 10 percent customs tax in return for providing naval assistance to the Byzantine government. In the later centuries of the empire the Italians received much of the profit of the extensive trade network that centered on Constantinople. This too was a factor that contributed to the empire's decline.

Merchants, Artisans, and the Aristocracy

Although Constantinople was the center of Byzantium's major industries as well as the hub of its international trade routes, the provincial towns were the home of artisans and merchants who plied their wares at rural fairs. The greatest of these fairs was held at Thessalonica, which became second in importance only to Constantinople in the last centuries of the empire. Probably larger than its famous counterpart at Champagne in France, the Thessalonica fair attracted traders from as far afield as Spain and France, although most merchants were native Greeks.

Merchants and artisans alike were subject to government regulation, as were bankers, lawyers, and notaries. In general, government control was designed to protect the trade guilds in the capital from nonguild artisans and peddlers and from control by powerful landowners. State inspectors monitored the quality of manufacturers, workers' wages, shop size, and the prices of goods, all for the purpose of ensuring a stable supply at regulated prices. In other words, guilds existed to serve the state. Government control of the guilds declined in the twelfth century, and during the later period of the empire they became more like their counterparts in western Europe, concerned primarily with their own welfare.

The notion of service to the state was also at the root of the Byzantine conception of nobility. Aristocrats enjoyed superior social status because of their service as courtiers and government officials. Vertical mobility was a characteristic of Byzantine society, unlike the feudal societies of contemporary western Europe. Not until the tenth century did a landed, hereditary nobility emerge as the result of military needs.

Defensive requirements prompted the emperors to organize their territories into military districts, called *themes,* each of which was governed by a general in charge of civil and military affairs. Troops were recruited locally and allotted grants of land in return for military service. These grants could not be sold, but passed to the soldiers' sons, who assumed responsibility for military duty. The theme system had an adverse impact on the traditional, service-based aristocracy but gave rise to a new military nobility, which in general was less educated and culturally refined than the old aristocracy.

A civil aristocracy continued to exist side by side with the new military one; members of the former continued to function as tax collectors, judges, and heads of government offices. By the eleventh century the Byzantine aristocracy included foreigners who served as officers in the military. Vertical mobility may have peaked in the middle of that century when efforts were made to draw large numbers of merchants and foreigners living in Constantinople into state government.

Shortly thereafter, Byzantine society underwent a major transformation when the elite families in the military aristocracy banded together through intermarriage, forming a powerful "clan" linked to the Comnenian dynasty. Those who were not part of this clan were forced out of the military aristocracy; some found their way into the civil aristocracy, which henceforth was deemed inferior. In the late twelfth century the latter briefly regained supremacy, but the last centuries of the empire were in general characterized less by the rule of a civil bureaucracy than by that of semifeudal warlords whose power was based on family networks. In general terms, the history of Byzantium entailed its evolution from a highly centralized state into a virtually feudal society ruled by a military aristocracy. In contrast, western Europe evolved in the opposite direction.

Women in the Byzantine Empire

The social role of most Byzantine women was defined within the confines of the family. From the sixth to the late eleventh century the nuclear family, not the clan, was at the heart of the social structure. As a result the social position of women generally was less than it had been in the late Roman era. There were exceptions, such as the Empresses Theodora and Irene (797–802), on the one hand, and, on the other, the women who defied traditional standards of propriety by becoming actresses, public dancers, or courtesans. Issues of public import, such as a controversy over the use of religious images, were debated by women as well as men. Women served in emergencies, as when a governor in Asia Minor ordered young women to dress in men's clothing and help defend the city's walls when an Arab fleet attacked about 825. For the most part, however, women generally spent their lives in a tightly knit patriarchal family.

An examination of Byzantine laws offers insight into the status of women. Except in matters pertaining exclusively to women, they could not act as witnesses in the signing of contracts because such a practice supposedly made them too bold. Yet an eighth-century law treated husband and wife virtually as equals with respect to property and stipulated that a widow with children control all of the property in her capacity as the new head of the family. A fourth-century law pertaining to coloni who had escaped or been abducted provided for the return of males within a period of 30 years but established a lower limit of 20 years for women, presumably reflecting a lack of worth once their childbearing years were past. By law a free woman could be punished if she had sexual intercourse with a slave, but such activity by a free man was not similarly prohibited.

Beginning in the late eleventh century the nuclear core broadened into an extended family, perhaps because of the changing outlook of the ruling Comnenian dynasty, which found its primary political support in a kinship network. Educated, politically intelligent women became more active in court and aristocratic circles. The Emperor Alexius I Comnenus (1081–1118) officially shared imperial power with his mother, Anna Dalassena. A number of prominent women, including Alexius' daughter, Anna Comnena, who had a special interest in Aristotle, patronized scholarship. In the late twelfth century the Empress Euphrosyne governed the empire for her husband.

The greater prominence of women was accomplished by a growing disregard for traditional standards of morality in court circles, as reflected in the open practice of adultery and incest. Among the masses, however, the traditional role of the ideal spouse as submissive and generally confined to the home undoubtedly continued. Anna Comnena, a major public figure, observed that the common women of her society still wore veils when they left the privacy of their homes. In Byzantium at least, the social mores of the elite apparently were slow to influence commoners.

CONSTANTINOPLE, JEWEL OF THE BOSPORUS

Constantinople is located on the boundary between Europe and Asia, on a hilly peninsula between the Sea of Marmora and the Golden Horn. With a 7-mile long inlet and a natural harbor, it had a population of perhaps 1 million in the time of Justinian. Others lived in the suburbs, which comprised outlying commercial centers, residential villages, and, along the shores of the Bosporus, resorts for the wealthy. The city was home to many peoples, including Greeks, Italians, Jews, North Africans, Syrians, Armenians, and Goths. Greek was the normal language of daily discourse, although the imperial government and the law courts used Latin. Beginning in the early fifth century, the city was protected by mammoth walls 15 feet thick and 40 feet high, stretching the length of the city.

Constantine had originally planned the capital in imitation of Rome, to the point of including seven hills within the original walls. At the heart of the city was the Augusteum, a great open square, like the Roman Forum, around which were grouped the Church of Hagia Sophia (Holy Wisdom), the public baths, the Senate House, and the entrances to the Hippodrome (a large oval arena) and the royal palace. The latter consisted of assorted buildings, courtyards, and gardens commissioned by various emperors and built on terraces that extended down toward the sea. A broad avenue stretched westward from the Augusteum to the Golden Gate, and a second avenue branched off to the city's other principal entry, the Gate of Charisius, in the northwest. The rest of the city was a web of narrow lanes lined with houses, shops, monasteries, and hundreds of churches. The greatest of these was Hagia Sophia, where emperors were crowned, and the Church of the Holy Apostles, where they were buried. In this truly cosmopolitan city the marketplaces featured wares from around the world.

The houses of the wealthy were multistoried structures built around circular courtyards, many of which had fountains. More modest houses might have simple patios. The houses of the poor, constructed of wood, were constantly threatened by fire. The destitute, often victims of chronic unemployment, slept in the streets unless they were fortunate enough to find temporary shelter in the hostels, hospitals, and orphanages run by the churches or under arcades and other public structures kept open by the government during the winter. The impoverished could usually find food in church kitchens, although beggars were common. All registered householders in the city could obtain bread free or at a nominal cost, and price controls were placed on other basic foods with the exception of fish, which was immune from hoarding. Distribution of free bread ended in 618 when the Persians conquered Egypt, a major grain supplier. The government's interest in maintaining stable food prices stemmed from the need to prevent riots, not humanitarian concerns.

The old Church of Hagia Sophia was destroyed by the rioting Greens and Blues in 532, but its replacement,

The church of Hagia Sophia, completed in A.D. **535; the minarets were added a thousand years later by the Turks. [Photo by Wim Swaan]**

Added on 9/13 commissioned by Justinian, became the city's greatest monument. The church's distinctive feature is a soaring dome resting on four arches, a feat made possible by the use of pendentives—spherical triangles that distribute the dome's weight to the arches. The dome of the Roman Pantheon, in contrast, rested on round walls. Though the exterior of Hagia Sophia was plain, the interior was adorned with sumptuous mosaics as well as gold, silver, and variegated marble. Lighting was provided through numerous windows, including a ring of 40 at the base of the dome, as well as 1,000 lamps. Hagia Sophia was an architectural jewel and an appropriate focal point for the Byzantine Empire. After the city was conquered by the Ottoman Turks in 1453, the church's appearance was permanently altered to meet the needs of Islam.

BYZANTINE CHRISTIANITY AND CULTURE

In contrast to the largely secular culture of the modern West, Byzantine society was framed in religious terms. Conflict between church and state in the modern sense was impossible because one Christian emperor ruled, in theory, both civilian and ecclesiastical government in a single Christian commonwealth. This form of government is usually referred to as *Caesaropapism,* a term that underscores the unity of civil and ecclesiastical power, of emperor and patriarch, in imitation of God's rule over a universal heavenly kingdom. The Byzantine ideal might be summed up as one church, one creed, one sovereign.

Caesaropapism did not give the emperor absolute power in religious affairs. He did not possess either a priestly title or priestly functions, such as the ability to administer the sacraments. Emperors were periodically challenged by ecclesiastical figures, particularly patriarchs, and religious dissidents such as the Monophysites. No emperor was powerful enough to alter doctrine or liturgy arbitrarily, although the imperial position entitled him to mediate religious disputes.

Byzantine Christianity was very conservative, with an emphasis on tradition, liturgy, and pomp. All aspects of worship, from the ritual to the design and decoration of churches, were intended to promote a sense of mystery and otherworldliness. Aids to worship, such as images and relics, were accorded special importance; supposed pieces of the cross, thorns from Jesus' crown,

and Mary's robe and shroud were especially valued. Not only was there a trade in relics, but devout Christians sometimes stole them for their churches. In light of the emphasis on otherworldly values, ascetic living was highly regarded, and monks were typically held in great esteem.

Religious Controversy

Given the importance of religion in Byzantine society, theological disputes were virtually unavoidable. Perhaps the most serious controversy erupted around 726 when the emperor Leo III (717–741) banned the use of religious images, such as pictures or statues of Christ and the saints, as graven images. This was the view already held by Jews and Muslims, but long before the eighth century, religious images had become commonplace in both western and eastern Christendom, largely for devotional reasons but also as political symbols and commercial objects.

Leo's ban incited a furious debate, known as the Iconoclastic Controversy, that lasted until 787 and then was renewed between 813 and 843. The monks in particular opposed the prohibition even in the face of persecution; some were executed, exiled, or maimed. A church council upheld the iconoclastic position in 754, but 33 years later, under the influence of the Empress Irene, another council accepted icons as a channel of divine grace on the condition that they be revered but not worshiped. It was another empress, Theodora, widow of Theophilus, who settled the issue in 843 in yet another council that reaffirmed the use of religious images.

The popes' opposition to Byzantium's attempt to abolish images strained relations between the empire and the papacy. Other factors contributed to a deteriorating relationship, including an imperial decision during the Iconoclastic Controversy to transfer ecclesiastical jurisdiction over the Balkans, southern Italy, and Sicily from the pope to the patriarch of Constantinople. The feuding culminated in 1054 when each side excommunicated the other, causing a schism between the Roman Catholic and Eastern Orthodox churches that has never been fully healed. The fundamental cause of the breach was conflicting views over the respective roles of emperor and pope in the church.

Religion and Culture

Byzantine culture was shaped largely by religious convictions and reverence for classical antiquity. The importance of the classical tradition encouraged many writers to imitate its literary forms, such as history, satire, and orations. Byzantine writers did not, however, produce secular, lyrical poetry, nor were they very interested in classical drama; classical tragedies were read but not performed, perhaps because of church opposition. Generally, Byzantine authors were imitative rather than creative. This conservative tone was evident in their interest in grammars, encyclopedias, and commentaries. Some literary forms, such as sermons and the lives of saints, were intended as religious pedagogy and composed for common people; those who were illiterate could have such works read to them. One of the finest forms of Byzantine literature was liturgical poetry, which set religious verse to music.

The most characteristic Byzantine art form was the mosaic, which blended classical and Christian influences. Mosaics adorned the surfaces of domes, semi-domes, and apses and were placed to take maximum advantage of the limited light in churches. Artists tilted the glass, ceramic, marble, or shell cubes that made up their pictures to create a shimmering effect. The mosaicists illustrated both sacred and secular themes, although the advocates of iconoclasm wanted religious art restricted to abstract symbols, animals, and plants, much as in contemporary Islamic art.

Byzantine artists were fond of painting icons, or devotional panels. These images, rendered according to strict formal rules, reflect the spiritual devotion of Orthodox Christians. The figures in the icons are traditionally painted frontally, to create the impression that the subjects are communicating with the viewer about the mysteries of the Christian faith.

The prevailing conservatism in the empire is reflected in art forms, which show only modest changes from the age of Justinian to the fall of the Byzantine Empire in the fifteenth century at the hands of a rival religion, Islam.

ISLAM AND THE ARABS

By 750, thanks in large measure to the appeal of its vision of society and the religious commitment of its adherents, Islam had spread from its homeland in Arabia into Iran and through the Middle East and North Africa as far as the Iberian peninsula. The Arabs who spread the Islamic message were Semites from the Arabian peninsula. Economically, the lives of its inhabitants depended on the camel, which facilitated trade between the Mediterranean and India. Camel caravans had played a significant role in the spice trade during the Hellenistic and Roman eras and were still important in the sixth century, when Muhammad was born.

Mecca, Muhammad's native city, was strategically located at the crossroads of the caravan routes from Palestine and Syria to Yemen, at the southern end of the peninsula, and from Mesopotamia to Ethiopia. There was little manufacturing or agriculture in the area, but Mecca was a pilgrimage center, where visitors came to worship assorted deities. Because pilgrims contributed to the local economy, commerce and religion were closely entwined.

Muhammad and Islam

Born about 570, Muhammad was orphaned as a small boy and raised by an uncle. He worked for a while as a shepherd, lived with the nomadic Bedouins, and traveled with caravans on the Syria-Yemen route. This experience served him in good stead when the wealthy widow Khadija employed him to manage her caravan business. When Muhammad was about 25, he married her; they subsequently had several children and an apparently happy relationship.

A devout disciple of traditional Arabic religion, Muhammad regularly went into the hills near Mecca to pray, and there, in 610, he heard a voice proclaim that he was the messenger of God. According to Muslim tradition, the voice was that of the archangel Gabriel. Khadija became Muhammad's first convert. Others followed, including younger sons of prominent Mecca families. Most, however, were young people of modest background who were sympathetic to the traditional ideals of family solidarity, honor, and generosity, as distinct from the profit-oriented values of the wealthy merchants.

The religion that Muhammad founded is known as Islam ("submission"). A Muslim is one who submits to the will of Allah (God) and fulfills the five duties known as the Pillars of Islam. The first of these is the sincere profession of the *Shahada,* a simple credal statement: "I bear witness that there is no god but God; I bear witness that Muhammad is the messenger of God." In time, Muhammad professed a strict monotheism, although at the outset of his ministry he accepted three traditional Arabic deities as lesser beings who could intercede with God on behalf of believers; he later renounced this view, the expression of which became known as "the satanic verses." As Allah's servant, Muhammad was the last and greatest of the prophets, whose number included Adam, Abraham, Moses, and Jesus. Four prophets were transmitters of divine revelation: Moses in the Torah, David in the Psalms, Jesus in the Gospels, and Muhammad in the Koran.

The second of the Pillars is *Salat,* formal prayer at five specified times each day. Following ritual purification, worshipers face Mecca and together move through a cycle of standing, bowing, prostration, and sitting. *Salat* often occurs in a mosque, an Arabic word meaning "place of prostration." Each mosque has a niche indicating the direction of Mecca, a raised pulpit from which sermons are preached, and, normally, a minaret from which the call to prayer is made.

Almsgiving, in the form of a mandatory tax called the *Zakat,* or "purification", is the third Pillar. It renders the rest of the believer's property religiously acceptable and symbolizes the strong sense of community among Muslims. In effect, it is viewed as a loan to God, who will repay it many times over. The fourth Pillar consists of fasting during the lunar month of Ramadan, during which time no food, drink, medicine, or sensual pleasure can be taken during daylight hours.

The final Pillar is the *Hajj,* a pilgrimage to Mecca, if circumstances allow, to visit the *Kaaba,* a temple that Muslims believe was built by Abraham and his son Ishmael. Some Muslims regard *Jihad* (literally, "exertion" in God's service) as a sixth Pillar. It can take two forms: the greater jihad involves an internal spiritual struggle, and the lesser jihad entails physical conflict against the enemies of Islam.

Muslims believe that the Koran, the sacred text of Islam, contains the word of God as revealed to Muhammad. The text in its present form was established about 650 by Muhammad's companions. Proper recitation of the Koran, according to Muslims, results in a special sense of divine presence. Within its pages are found social as well as religious maxims, including instructions about inheritance, dowries, and marriage. Men are generally treated as superior to women, and slavery is allowed, subject to restrictions on how slaves can be treated and when they should be freed. Further guidance was expressed in the *Hadith,* sayings based on recollections of Muhammad's words and acts; thousands of these have been collected. As a guide to godly living, Muslims created the *Shari'a,* or "way" of the believer, including laws governing behavior and belief.

Sunnis, Shi'ites, and Sufis

Muhammad's teachings incited opposition at Mecca, and in 622 he moved some 200 miles north, to Yathrib, later called Medina. This event became known as the *Hejira,* or migration, the date of which became the first year of the Muslim era. There he remained, gathering followers and launching expeditions against Meccan caravans, until he was powerful enough to return to Mecca in 630. He died in Medina from a fever in June 632.

Upon news of Muhammad's death his key advisers agreed that his closest friend, Abu Bakr (c. 573–634), should be the new leader, or caliph ("deputy") of the prophet. Abu Bakr and the caliphs who succeeded him had no status as prophets but functioned as the head of the Arab state, commander of the army, supreme judge, and leader of public worship. By 656 the armies of Abu Bakr and his two successors had carried Islam throughout western Asia, across North Africa to Tunisia, and northward into Armenia and Afghanistan. Muslim fleets defeated the powerful Byzantine navy and captured Cyprus.

The modern division of Islam into two main branches, the Shi'ites and the Sunni, had its origins in the claim of Ali (656–661), Muhammad's son-in-law and cousin, that he had been designated Muhammad's successor before the prophet died. Ali's party, or *shi'ah,* supported this claim, but much of the Islamic world backed Muawiya, governor of Syria and a member of the powerful Umayyad clan. When Muawiya died in 680, Ali's son, Husayn, led the Shi'ites in a rebellion, only to be massacred with his family by Umayyad troops the same year.

The core of the Shi'ite movement is the conviction that Ali was the true successor of Muhammad and thus the first *imam,* or caliph. Some Shi'ites expand the *Shahada* ("creed") by adding the phrase, "and Ali is his comrade." Shi'ites accept only those laws and beliefs found in the Koran or set forth by a true imam, who is the beneficiary of divine revelation. In contrast, most Muslims, known as Sunni, follow the tradition (*sunnah*) established by Muhammad and the Koran; they regard the latter as complete and do not attribute special religious knowledge to their leaders.

As in the case of early Christianity, some devout Muslims were attracted to an ascetic life, characterized by meditation, fasting, prayer, lengthy vigils, and poverty. Some of the devout were content to wear simple woolen frocks and soon became known as *Sufis,* after the

A page from the Koran, written in Kufic script. [Courtesy of the Freer Gallery of Art, Smithsonian Institution, Washington, D.C. (30.60)]

Arabic word *suf* ("wool"). The Sufis were mystics whose ultimate goal was union with God through love and the purification of the soul. An important means to this end is the special remembrance of God by repeating his 99 "most beautiful names," whether in a rhythmic chant, in silence accompanied by special breathing exercises, or in a dance that culminates in a swoon. In the tenth century the Sufis began organizing brotherhoods, each of which was led by a master who taught disciples and inducted them into the order. As in the case of Christian monasticism, most orders had affiliated lay members who periodically participated in the order's religious worship.

The Umayyads at Damascus

Between 661 and 750 the Umayyad family provided the caliphs who ruled the Islamic world from their capital at Damascus. This period was marked by further Arab conquests. Between 674 and 678, Arab troops besieged Constantinople, but the fortifications proved too formidable. The Arabs returned again in 717–718, only to be foiled by new defenses, a harsh winter, disease, and "Greek fire," a fearsome substance (possibly made with quicklime or distilled petroleum) that ignited on contact with water. By the early eighth century all of North Africa was in Muslim hands; the first raids into Iberia came in 710 and 711. Because the peninsula was already in a state of political chaos, it fell into Muslim hands before the end of the decade. With their allies, the Berber tribesmen of North Africa, the Arabs crossed the Pyrenees into the Frankish kingdom in 718. Islamic penetration north of the Pyrenees might have been more extensive had it not been for the bitter fighting that erupted between the Arabs and the Berbers in Spain and North Africa between 734 and 742 and the factional struggles among the Arabs themselves. These factors were more important than the military skills of the Franks in halting Muslim expansion in Europe near Tours in 732.

In the meantime, Arab armies resumed their push

into Asia, reaching as far as the Indus River. In the early eighth century they established themselves in the north-western corner of India (now Pakistan), which to this day remains Muslim. Not until the eleventh century, however, did Turks from central Asia establish Islam as a major force in much of the Indian subcontinent.

The Umayyads organized their empire into five states, each of which was governed by a viceroy appointed by the caliph in Damascus. The speed of the Arab conquest was such that the conquerors had to rely on native bureaucrats to administer the subject areas; in Spain the Jews were particularly useful in this regard. Administrative effectiveness was undermined in the later years of Umayyad rule by viceroys who tried to govern from Damascus as well as by viceroys and provincial governors who siphoned tax revenues into their personal coffers. The tax structure itself became a major source of trouble. All free non-Muslims paid a poll (head) tax, and those with land paid a tax on it as well, whereas Arabs outside of Arabia did not. Converts to

Islam were freed from the poll tax but not the land tax, a situation that caused them to resent Arab landowners.

Umayyad power was undermined by a variety of factors, including the problematic tax structure. No less important was the disaffection caused by the specter of an opulent court in Damascus. The Abbasids, who claimed to be the heirs of Ali and who traced their ancestry to Muhammad's uncle, revolted in 747, conquered Iraq in 749, and took Damascus the following year. Shortly thereafter, the Abbasids built a new capital at Baghdad.

The Abbasids

The years of the Abbasid caliphate (750–1258) were marked by factional intrigue, violence, and the decentralization of power. Abu al-Abbas (750–754), the founder of the Abbasid caliphate, referred to himself as "the Blood-letter," an apt sobriquet in view of his slaughter of many

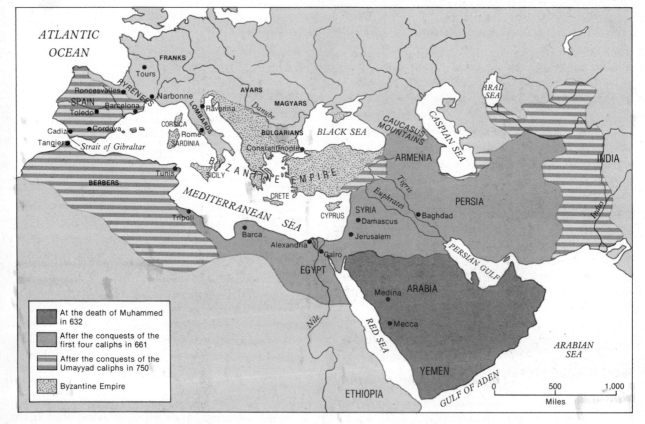

6.2 The Expansion of Islam

deposed Umayyads. Many of his successors were no less vicious in executing Shi'ites who challenged their authority. Imperial ministers and generals openly intrigued to manipulate the succession, while the caliphs enjoyed court living as avidly as had the Umayyads. With tens of thousands of staff members and servants, the palace complexes in Baghdad were centers of waste, inefficiency, and decadence, their cultural splendor notwithstanding.

The Abbasid period was characterized by the decentralization of power and the breakup of the empire. Spain had gone its own way when the Umayyad prince Abd al-Rahman (756–788) established an independent caliphate at Córdoba. Like its counterpart in Baghdad, it became a brilliant cultural center, but it succumbed to turbulent palace guards in the mid-tenth century. The caliphate of Córdoba then fragmented into smaller Muslim states, making it easier for the Christians to begin their reconquest of the peninsula. Morocco broke away in 788. Tunisia became independent in 800 and, in the ensuing century, conquered Malta, Sicily, and Sardinia in addition to plundering the coasts of France and the Italian peninsula. Egypt pursued its own course beginning in the mid-ninth century and in 969 fell under the dominion of the Shi'ite Fatimid family of Tunisia, who ruled from the new capital of Cairo. By 1000 their empire embraced North Africa, Syria, and much of the Arabian peninsula, but in the eleventh century it too was undermined by inept caliphs and rebellious slave armies, making possible the modest gains of Christian crusaders in the late 1090s.

The story was much the same in the east as Abbasid power decayed. In 1055 the Seljuk Turks found it useful to maintain the Abbasids as figureheads, but the caliphate was extinguished in 1258 when Mongols overran Baghdad and murdered the last caliph. From Baghdad the Turkish sultans ruled Iraq, Syria, and Iran, but not until the sixteenth century would another group of Turks, the Ottomans, extend their sway throughout most of North Africa. The Abbasid period marks the end of Arab dominance in the Muslim world and the emergence of Islam as an international religion.

ISLAMIC CIVILIZATION

The driving force in Islamic civilization was the teaching of Muhammad, but wherever Islam spread, it assimi-lated native cultures. The result was the creation of a distinctive civilization, with major cultural centers in Damascus, Baghdad, Cairo, Córdoba, and, later, Delhi and Constantinople. The economy and the culture of the Islamic world had a substantial impact on the peoples of Europe and Asia.

Economic Life

As a merchant, Muhammad gave Islam a keen appreciation of commerce and, indeed, of all forms of productive activity, provided that they were carried out in an honest, charitable spirit. Sayings attributed to him in the Hadith describe merchants as "the couriers of the horizons and God's trusted servants on earth," who, if honest, "will stand with the martyrs on the Day of Judgment." Tilling and sheepherding were occupations also created and blessed by God, but "the best of gain is from honorable trade and from a man's work with his own hands." Muhammad condemned moneychangers, prostitutes, hoarders, greedy merchants, and those who charged interest on loans.[2] Similiar ethical maxims are found in contemporary Christian teaching and underscore the common attempt to curtail acquisitiveness and dishonesty on the one hand while instilling thrift and humaneness on the other. However, contemporary Christianity did not place a comparable positive emphasis on commerce per se.

Muslim trade routes eventually extended from the Pyrenees to the Indus. Muslim traders also traveled well beyond the boundaries of Islamic states, ranging as far as Southeast Asia and China. Others crossed the Sahara into western and central Africa or sailed down Africa's east coast. They traded as well with the peoples of Byzantium, western Europe, and Russia, although much of this commerce was in the hands of Jewish and Christian merchants. Commercial growth was enhanced by the fact that non-Muslim merchants could live and work in Islamic states. The absence of internal tariff barriers in the Muslim world between the eighth and twelfth centuries also helped to foster commercial expansion. So too did the development of bills of exchange (checks) and joint-stock companies, which enabled many people to invest in business activities, thus sharing both profits and risks.

Manufacturing in the Islamic world was extensive and varied. Linen, cotton, wool, and silk were produced, as were glass, ceramics, metals, soaps, dyes, and perfume. Some areas were renowned for their products: Córdoba for its leather, Egypt for glass and linens,

A detail from one of the eighth-century mosaics that line the walls of the Great Mosque at Damascus. [Ronald Sheridan/Ancient Art & Architecture Collection]

Toledo and Damascus for steel, Baghdad for porcelain, and Bukhara (in Central Asia) for carpets. The Muslims learned how to make paper from the Chinese in the eighth century and later founded their own mills. The widespread availability of paper stimulated scholarship and encouraged publishing.

Islamic Society

"The noblest among you in the eyes of God is the most pious," said Muhammad, "for God is omniscient and well-informed." This principle could serve as a new basis for social valuation, in contrast to the traditional Arab recognition of an aristocracy based on birth and family ties. A similar position is expressed in the New Testament, but as Islam and Christianity evolved, each accommodated notions of a social hierarchy.

During the Umayyad period, Muslims recognized four social classes, the first of which comprised Arab Muslims, the de facto aristocracy. The government in Damascus recorded their names in a special registry and gave each Arab Muslim a regular payment from the imperial treasury. Arab women were discouraged from marrying non-Arabs.

Non-Arab Muslims made up the second class. Because they typically affiliated themselves with an Arab clan or family, they were known as *mawali,* or clients. By the early eighth century they not only were more numerous than the Arabs but also resented their inferior status, especially since some of them were more educated than their Arab counterparts. Some mawali reacted by embracing Shi'ite views, while others claimed to have become Arabs through clientage. In time the Arabs of the conquered lands tended to intermarry with the mawali, giving rise to a broader definition of an Arab as one who spoke Arabic and embraced Islam.

The third class in Islamic society was comprised of free non-Muslims, who were primarily Jews, Christians, and Zoroastrians. Such people, known as *dhimmis,* or covenanted people, received personal security and substantial local autonomy in return for accepting Muslim rule and paying additional taxes. Dhimmis were free to worship according to their own rites, engage in business activities, own property, and for the most part govern themselves through their own laws and in their own courts. They could not bear arms, testify in court against Muslims, dress in Muslim fashions, or use saddles on their horses. For the most part the dhimmis were treated with more tolerance and respect than medieval European Christians accorded Jews. There was periodic repression, however, either when the dhimmis' commercial success threatened the Muslims, when they were suspected of collaborating with the crusaders or the Mongols, or when they ignored the terms of their covenant.

Slaves were the lowest class in Islamic society. Although Muhammad had reservations about slavery, he accepted its legality. Muslims could not be enslaved, but conversion did not automatically bring manumission. Nor could masters and slaves marry, though the former could take slaves as concubines. The children of such a union were free, and their mother enjoyed a special status, could not be sold, and was liberated when her master died. Children of slave parents, however, were born slaves.

The Islamic economy was not heavily dependent on slaves, as were those of the Roman Empire and the southern United States before the American civil war, but large numbers of slaves were traded and used primarily in the military or as servants. Some caliphs were the sons of slave mothers. The wealthiest Muslims possessed thousands of slaves. Captured prisoners were enslaved, but many slaves were purchased in slave markets. There were slaves of nearly all races and from a wide variety of places, including Spain, Greece, sub-Saharan Africa, India, and Central Asia. Despite the popularity of slavery, Islamic teaching recommended manumission and urged that slaves be allowed to purchase their freedom.

Muslim Women

Women in traditional Arabic society, although important in the home, were subordinate to men. They could neither inherit nor claim a share of spoils won on the battlefield, and their husbands enjoyed an absolute right of divorce. In some instances, baby girls were regarded with such disdain that they were buried alive at birth or killed at the age of five or six.

Muhammad sought to improve the treatment of women, according them spiritual if not social equality. They were to be obedient to men, into whose hands the management of affairs was entrusted. The proper relationship between husbands and wives, according to Muhammad, entailed love, and marriage itself was conceived contractually, each party having both rights and responsibilities. According to the Koran, however, men were allowed to have up to four wives, but no woman was entitled to more than one husband. Behind this practice was the conviction that procreation was a fundamental purpose of marriage.

The Koran exhorted women to dress circumspectly, taking special care to cover their breasts and to draw their veils around them when they left the home. Such admonitions led some Muslim women to veil their faces in public and to seclude themselves within their own part of the home (harem). The harem system did not originate with Islam but had roots in ancient Mesopotamia. Nevertheless, it became a characteristic part of Islamic society by the late eighth century. The seclusion of women in harems or behind veils, the practice of polygamy, and a willingness to beat disobedient wives underscore the fact that Islam, though making important advances over traditional Arab society, was a long way from establishing the social equality of the sexes. This is also apparent with respect to the inheritance of property; in pre-Islamic Arabic society, women could not inherit at all. The Koran lifted this absolute prohibition but still limited women's rights in specified circumstances.

In practice, the role of women in medieval Islam varied substantially. Some played an active part in politics, including the scheming that became a regular part of determining succession to the caliphate. The wife of the Umayyad caliph al-Walid I (705–715) engaged in political activities to promote justice and encouraged her husband to enlarge mosques. One of the greatest of the Abbasid caliphs, Harun al-Rashid (786–809), apparently owed his position to his fabulously wealthy mother, Khayzuran, a former slave, who may have had a rival son assassinated. Harun's wife, Zubaydah, contributed money to build an aqueduct in Mecca and took an interest in urban development, much as aristocratic Turkish women patronized hospitals and schools. Women were de facto rulers of Egypt in the 1020s, late 1040s, and 1250s.

Muslim women participated in a wide range of cultural and intellectual pursuits. During the Umayyad caliphate they provided salons in which scholars, poets, and other educated people could gather. As in pre-Islamic society, some women wrote poetry, and female professionals sang elegies at funerals. Throughout the Umayyad period, women studied law and theology, while in the caliphate of Córdoba, women as well as men taught in schools. Female scholars were prominent in the towns of Muslim Spain, and some lectured at the universities of Córdoba and Valencia. Women were also active in the Sufi movement. The Abbasids employed women to spy against the Byzantines in the guise of merchants, physicians, and travelers, which suggests that they undertook such activities in their own society.

There were, of course, instances, of repression. During the Abbasid caliphate, women's public appearances and clothing were increasingly regulated by government decree. About 1030, women were banned from public ceremonies. In twelfth-century Seville, "decent women" were prohibited from holding their own parties, even with their husbands' permission. Some of these regulations were intended to stress female modesty. In Seville, women could not run hostels because of the possibility of sexual improprieties, and they could not enter Christian churches because the priests had reputations as fornicators and sodomites. For the most part, such regulations, though patronizing, suggest concern for the role of women in Islamic society.

The Muslim Synthesis in Medicine, Science, and Philosophy

The Muslims assimilated and advanced the medical and scientific knowledge of classical antiquity. Because Muhammad himself had reportedly praised the study of medicine, the subject received considerable attention by medieval Muslim scholars, especially after the works of Galen, Hippocrates, and other classical writers were translated into Arabic. The great age of medical advance occurred in the Abbasid period, when schools of medicine were founded and hospitals were introduced. The contributions of two men are especially noteworthy in this field: the Iranian physician al-Razi (Rhazes; died c. 925), head of the Baghdad hospital, wrote approximately 120 medical books, including a pioneering study of smallpox and measles; and the Iranian scholar Ibn Sina (Avicenna; died 1037) wrote *The Canon of Medicine,* which synthesized classical and Islamic medical knowledge, was translated into Latin in the twelfth century, and served as the leading medical text in Europe as late as the seventeenth century. One of the keys to Ibn Sina's success was his willingness to learn from his medical practice.

The importance of experimentation was appreciated in other sciences as well. Although alchemy—the attempt to transform common metals into gold and other valuable substances—was a pseudoscience, its practitioners acquired invaluable chemical knowledge and developed the world's first laboratories. In the field of optics, Ibn al-Haytham (Alhazen; died 1039) of Cairo rejected the classical theory that the eye emits visual rays, arguing instead that it sees by receiving rays of light.

The Muslim ability to synthesize is perhaps best illustrated in the field of mathematics. Islamic scholars adopted "Arabic" numerals from India, including the placement of numbers in series to denote units, tens, hundreds, and so forth, and geometry and simple trigonometry from the Greeks. One of the leading scholars in this field was Muhammad ibn Musa al-Khwarizmi, whose ninth-century treatises on arithmetic and algebra (*al-jabr* means "integration") were subsequently influential in Europe. Later mathematical work involved quadratic and cubic equations and led to the development of analytical geometry and spherical trigonometry.

Beginning primarily in the twelfth century, Muslim advances in mathematics and science spread to Europe through Sicily and Spain, where the Jews played a crucial role as cultural intermediaries. In the sixteenth century those achievements provided much of the foundation for the Scientific Revolution.

Islamic philosophy was heavily indebted to the works of Plato, Aristotle, and the Neoplatonists. No question was more basic to Muslim philosophers than the proper relationship of reason to revelation. The celebrated Ibn Rushd (Averroës, 1126–1198) of Córdoba, a judge and court physician, defended Aristotelian and Neoplatonic philosophy against those who emphasized belief over reason. Like Ibn Sina, he was convinced that the truths of reason and revelation were compatible. The same truth, he argued, could be expressed either philosophically or symbolically; when the Koran seemed to advocate an irrational belief, he resolved the apparent contradiction by interpreting the sacred texts allegorically. Through his commentaries on Aristotle, which were translated into Latin in the thirteenth century, Ibn Rushd had a major impact on the development of scholastic thought in medieval universities. His views were equally influential in shaping late medieval Jewish philosophy, as reflected especially in the teaching of Gersonides (1288–c. 1344), a French rationalist noted for his commentaries on Aristotle. The Western religious and philosophical heritage was greatly indebted to Islam, not least for introducing European thinkers to much of Aristotle's work.

Islamic Literature

Medieval Muslims were extraordinarily fond of verse. Indeed, the Koran itself was written in quasi-verse form. Verse was the medium used by Firdawsi (c. 935–c. 1020) to compose what became the Iranian national epic, the *Shah-Nameh* (Book of Kings), which recounted Persian history from legendary times to A.D. 641. Nearly 60,000 verses long, it was instrumental in establishing the definitive form of the Persian language, much as the King James Bible and the works of Shakespeare did for English. Another Iranian poet, Shams ud-din Hafiz (c. 1325–c. 1389), composed some 500 short lyric poems using simple language and proverbial expressions. Hafiz' works reveal sympathy for common people, a dislike of hypocrisy, and a preoccupation with love.

Apart from the Koran, the best known Islamic literary work was *The Thousand and One Nights,* a collection of stories from the Middle East and Asia that were originally transmitted orally, much like the ancient Homeric epics. In their extant form, most are set against the background of Baghdad during the caliphate of Harun al-Rashid or Cairo under the Fatimids. A fragment of the work existed by the ninth century, although it was another 600 years or so before a final version existed.

Final mention must be made of history as a literary form. The greatest medieval Muslim historian was the Tunisian Ibn Khaldun (1332–1406), a pioneer of sociological methodology in explaining the past. To write history, he insisted, required a knowledge of geography, climate, economics, religion, and culture. He called attention to the necessity of evaluating documents preparatory to writing history, since all records are likely to contain inaccuracies. A sense of group consciousness was basic to Ibn Khaldun's philosophy of history; a strong communal identity enabled a people to triumph, but their civilization decayed as that spirit weakened.

SUMMARY

The Byzantine and Islamic civilizations, thrown together by geography, lived in troubled proximity, sometimes engaging fruitfully in a commerce of goods, ideas, and values but periodically erupting into conflict and attempted conquest. Both civilizations made incalculable contributions to Western civilization by preserving and transmitting classical culture, the Byzantines primarily in literature and the arts, the Muslims especially in science and mathematics. Religion permeated both societies, providing their foundations and shaping their outlook. The Byzantine religious tradition was largely inherited from previous centuries, while the Arabs founded a new religion, borrowing parts of the Judeo-Christian heritage. They also differed with respect to the religious issues that most deeply divided them: Byzantines fought over religious images, whereas Muslims debated the succession to the caliphate and the relationship of faith and reason. Both cultures revered the law, the Byzantines through Justinian's epic code and the Muslims through the Shari'a. Although neither society accorded women social equality, women enjoyed certain legal rights with respect to property and were occasionally active at the highest levels of politics and in cultural pursuits.

Economically, the Byzantine Empire was based primarily on agriculture, while the Muslim states were oriented toward trade. Although the two civilizations shared certain manufacturing interests, Muslim trade and production were in general more sophisticated than those of Byzantium. Indeed, a major source of Byzantine weakness in the later centuries of the empire was that it relinquished commerce to the Italians. Nor were Byzantine rulers successful in preserving the welfare of the free peasantry on whom the empire's strength rested; the rise of a military aristocracy undermined the strength and stability of the empire. The Islamic states, in turn, were sapped by the periodic rebellion of slave armies. Both Byzantine and Muslim governments were weakened by violence, intrigue, bloated bureaucracies, and inadequate tax structures. Their conflicting imperial ambitions further undercut their strength, eventually leaving both prey to the Turks (see Chapter 9). The legacy of both civilizations continues to shape the lives of millions of people, particularly in southeastern Europe, the Middle East, and North Africa.

Notes

1. R. Browning, *Justinian and Theodora* (London: Thames & Hudson, 1971), p. 72.
2. B. Lewis, trans. and ed., *Islam from the Prophet Muhammad to the Capture of Constantinople* (New York: Walker, 1974), vol. 2, pp. 125–129.

Suggestions for Further Reading

Crone, P. *Meccan Trade and the Rise of Islam.* Princeton, N.J.: Princeton University Press, 1987.

Daniel, N. *The Arabs and Medieval Europe,* 2nd ed. London: Longman, 1978.

Donner, F. M. *The Early Islamic Conquests.* Princeton, N.J.: Princeton University Press, 1981.

Endress, G. *Islam: A Historical Introduction,* trans. C. Hillenbrand. New York: Columbia University Press, 1987.

Haldon, S. F. *Byzantium in the Seventh Century: The Transformation of a Culture.* Cambridge, England: Cambridge University Press, 1991.

Hussey, J. M. *The Byzantine World.* Westport, Conn.: Greenwood, 1982.

————. *The Orthodox Church in the Byzantine Empire.* Oxford, England: Clarendon Press, 1986.

Kitzinger, E. *Byzantine Art in the Making.* Cambridge, Mass.: Harvard University Press, 1977.

Lapidus, I. M. *A History of Islamic Societies.* Cambridge, England: Cambridge University Press, 1988.

Lewis, B. *Islam: From the Prophet Muhammad to the Capture of Constantinople.* 2 vols. New York: Oxford University Press, 1987.

Loverance, R. *Byzantium.* Cambridge, Mass.: Harvard University Press, 1988.

Maclagan, M. *The City of Constantinople.* New York: Praeger, 1968.

Mottahedeh, R. P. *The Mantle of the Prophet.* New York: Simon & Schuster, 1985.

Runciman, S. *The Byzantine Theocracy.* Cambridge, England: Cambridge University Press, 1977.

Watt, W. M. *Muhammad: Prophet and Statesman.* New York: Oxford University Press, 1974.

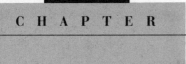

CHAPTER 7

THE RISE OF EUROPE

400-800 - Early Middle Ages
800-1050 - Middle Ages Period
1050-1300 - High Middle Ages

Magyars or Hungarians

The development of a distinctively European civilization occurred during the period that extended from the Germanic invasions of the Roman Empire to the establishment of the first European empire by Charlemagne in the early ninth century. The need to defend against further Muslim attacks, as well as Magyar and Viking incursions, caused major social and political changes. After surviving the challenges of the early Middle Ages, Europeans embarked in the eleventh century on an era of vigorous growth, the basis of which was economic expansion, urban development, political unification, and religious renewal. But the High Middle Ages (c. 1050–c. 1300) were also a time of bitter conflict—between popes and sovereigns, monarchs and feudal lords, Muslims and Christians, and Christians and Jews. The clashes of cultures, religions, and political ideals profoundly changed the Western world.

MIGRATION AND TRANSFORMATION

Generally, the invasions that transformed Europe between the fifth and ninth centuries pitted nomads against the inhabitants of settled communities and were thus a clash of distinctive lifestyles and cultures. Nomads threatened much of Europe and Asia; only remote southern China and southern India eluded their grasp. The impact of the incursions was greatest in the West, partly because the nomads tended to migrate westward, where the land was more fertile and water was more plentiful, and partly because the more advanced cultures of China and India resisted transformation.

The eastern Roman Empire, with its well-defended capital at Constantinople, its thriving economy, and its strong navy, survived the invasions, but by the end of the fifth century its western counterpart was gone, its lands fallen into the hands of Germanic rulers: the Visigoths in southern Gaul and Spain; the Ostrogoths in Italy; the Franks in northern Gaul; the Angles, Saxons, and Jutes in England; the Burgundians in the Rhône Valley; and the Vandals in North Africa and the western Mediterranean.

Unlike the Romans whom they conquered, the Germans were at first organized in social units, as tribes based on kinship rather than a state founded on political rights and obligations. German laws, unlike those of the Romans, were unwritten and grounded in custom. German families were responsible for the conduct of members of their household and thus played a crucial role in upholding the laws. The Germans elected their kings or tribal leaders as well as the chiefs who led the warriors into battle. In return for serving those chiefs, the warriors received weapons, subsistence, and a share of any spoils.

When the Germans were nomads, their livelihood revolved around cattle raising, but as they settled on their new lands, they began raising grain and vegetables. Over time the Germans assimilated some aspects of classical culture, including Roman language, law, and principles of government, thus creating a distinctively European society. The fusion of Germanic and classical elements was eased by the fact that the Visigoths, Ostrogoths, and Vandals had been introduced to Christianity before they migrated into western Europe. They were disciples of Arian Christianity, however, and it was not until about 500 that the Nicene Christianity of the Latin church began to make headway among the Germans following the conversion of Clovis, king of the Franks (481–511). With the support of the Gallo-Roman population, which was loyal to Nicene Christianity, Clovis expanded the Frankish kingdom until it extended from the Pyrenees to the Rhine and beyond.

THE FRANKS

The dynasty that Clovis founded, called the Merovingian in honor of a legendary ancestor, was undermined by the physical weakness of his successors. With kings too young to rule, authority was exercised by aristocratic mayors of the palace. Civil war plagued the kingdom for much of the sixth and seventh centuries. Unity had been restored by the early eighth century, when new invaders, the Islamic Moors from North Africa, threatened western Europe. By 711 the Iberian peninsula was theirs. Turning next to Gaul, the Moors were finally rebuffed by the Frankish mayor of the palace, Charles Martel ("the Hammer"), near Tours in 732. The battle was less significant for the Muslims, who in crossing the Pyrenees had overextended themselves, than for the Franks, whose military prowess attracted papal attention.

In 751, Charles' son and successor, Pepin the Short (died 768), deposed the Merovingian monarch and claimed the Frankish throne as his own. After the fact, he obtained papal approval for his action to make his usurpation seem legitimate. He repaid the debt in 754–755 by defending Rome from Lombard aggression and in addition granted certain Italian lands to the papacy. By this "donation," Pepin laid the foundation for a papal state in central Italy.

Charlemagne

The dynasty founded by Pepin became known as the Carolingian (from *Carolus,* Latin for "Charles"). Its greatest ruler was Pepin's son Charlemagne ("Charles the Great," 768–814), who established an empire larger than any in Europe between that of Rome in the third century and that of Napoleon in the nineteenth. Charlemagne crushed the Lombards and claimed their crown for himself when they tried to regain the land Pepin had given to the papacy. Against the Moors his gains were modest but strategic, consisting of a *march,* or frontier district, on the southern slopes of the Pyrenees. Campaigns against the Saxons gave him control of much of what is now northern Germany, and in the southeast he overran Bavaria and pushed back the nomadic Avars. The Abbasid caliph in Baghdad sent him gifts that included spices, monkeys, and an elephant.

Because Charlemagne had no capital to rival Baghdad or Constantinople, he determined to create a "second Rome" at Aachen (Aix-la-Chapelle), in the heart of his kingdom. Its layout and principal buildings were inspired by Rome, and its royal chapel by the Byzantine church of San Vitale in Ravenna. The new capital became the center of a cultural renaissance that Charlemagne sponsored to enhance the reputation of his realm and to improve the quality of the clergy. To direct his palace school, Charlemagne recruited one of the foremost scholars of the age, Alcuin (c. 735–804), from Anglo-Saxon England. Alcuin employed a curriculum inspired by classical Rome and refined by European writers that became the model for education throughout medieval Europe. The seven liberal arts were divided into the *trivium,* comprising grammar, rhetoric, and logic, and the *quadrivium,* consisting of arithmetic, geometry, music, and astronomy. Charlemagne acquired legal and religious manuscripts for his scribes to copy and distribute to the monasteries of the realm. His scholars issued new editions of learned works and developed a new, more readable script, called the Carolingian minuscule, from which modern scripts are derived. Much of what we know about Charlemagne comes from a biography by Einhard (c. 770–840), one of the leading palace scholars. The manuscripts produced by Carolingian writers influenced fifteenth-century scholars and thus that later, more famous renaissance.

Charlemagne's apparent interest in being the equal of the Byzantine emperor culminated in 800. In 799, Pope Leo III (795–816) had been kidnapped by his enemies; after he escaped, he sought Charlemagne's help to re-

7.1 The Empire of Charlemagne

store his control in Rome. Thus it was that the Frankish sovereign was in Rome on December 25, 800, when, following Mass, Leo crowned him emperor of the Romans. The coronation strained relations with Constantinople, which claimed the imperial title solely for its own ruler. Not until 813 did both parties agree that Charles would be recognized as emperor of the Franks and the Byzantine sovereign as emperor of the Romans. For the West the significance of the Christmas coronation was the revival of the imperial tradition in the West and the question of ultimate authority raised by the way in which the crown was bestowed—from the pope to the emperor.

DISINTEGRATION AND INVASION

Hoping to preserve most of the empire intact, Louis I (814–840), Charlemagne's successor, designated his eldest son heir to the imperial title and, following the Frankish custom, promised his other two sons royal titles and the territories of Aquitaine and Bavaria. Unsatisfied, the younger sons revolted against their father. By the time peace was made in the Treaty of Verdun in 843, Louis was dead and the empire was

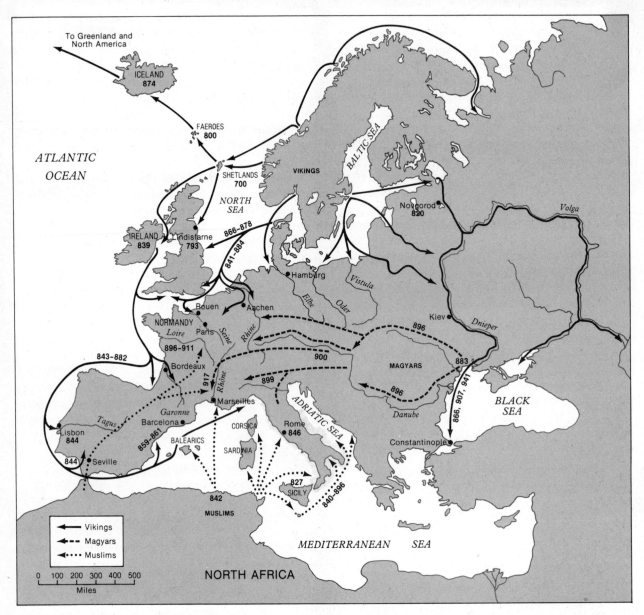

7.2 Viking, Magyar, and Muslim Invasions

irrevocably fragmented. Between the western and eastern kingdoms, out of which eventually emerged France and Germany, was a middle kingdom that retained the imperial title and extended from the modern Netherlands into Italy. The Carolingian dynasty continued until 987, a pale reflection of its grandeur under Charlemagne.

As the Frankish states struggled to survive, new waves of invaders struck Europe. From North Africa, Arab raiders attacked the islands of the Mediterranean, southern France, and Italy. Before the ninth century was over, the Mediterranean was virtually a Muslim lake. A second group, the Magyars, a nomadic people from central Asia, invaded Germany, France, and Italy. Although the German king, Otto I, defeated them in 955, they retained control of the Hungarian plain. There they established their own kingdom and converted to Christianity.

entertain the vassal for 30 days

A third group of invaders, the Norsemen or Vikings, came from Scandinavia in swift, mobile ships. Beginning in the late eighth century, the Vikings sacked the coastal regions of Europe and sailed up rivers to reach such cities as Paris and Hamburg. They even plundered Seville in Spain and various Italian towns reached by ships that sailed into the Mediterranean. Vikings also sailed the Atlantic to Iceland and Greenland, both of which they settled, and North America. The reasons for this activity varied: some Vikings sought land for new settlements, but others apparently regarded the raids as a prelude to a settled life or as a means to establish new trade routes. Norsemen from Sweden used the rivers of Russia to contact the Byzantines and the Persians.

The Vikings established settlements at Kiev in Russia, on the coast of Ireland, in northeastern England, and in northwestern France, a region later called Normandy. In the eleventh century, descendants from that area seized control of southern Italy and Sicily, and in 1066, William, duke of Normandy, conquered England. As the Normans settled, they embraced Christianity and European culture.

800 – Charlemagne

FEUDAL SOCIETY

The breakup of the Carolingian empire and the impact of the invasions caused changes in European lifestyles and governments. As royal authority ebbed, landowners turned elsewhere for protection, thereby providing the nobility and other powerful men with an opportunity to increase their power. The nobles ruled their districts with miniature governments of their own, dispensing justice, collecting fees, raising troops, and sometimes minting money. The heart of this way of governing was the personal bond: whereas in modern society we owe allegiance to a state, in the early medieval world allegiance was rendered to a person, and that person was in turn bound to fulfill his or her part of the contractual arrangement.

Lords and Vassals: The Feudal Aristocracy

Free landowners sought protection by offering their lands to powerful men whom they agreed to serve. These landholders were known as *vassals*. In return for their service they lived in the lord's household or received money or the use of land, called *fiefs*. Normally, the most important service was military, for together the vassals comprised the lord's private army, which protected its collective members. Vassals were expected to perform other duties, such as serving on the lord's court or providing him with hospitality. As these feudal arrangements developed, various safeguards were added. In eleventh-century France, for example, the normal amount of military service required of a vassal each year was 40 days. A vassal could receive fiefs from several lords, thereby raising the question of which lord had first claim on his obedience. This was resolved by designating a *liege lord* as the one to whom primary obedience was due. Vassals with substantial landholdings could have vassals of their own. The feudal order was not a neat hierarchical arrangement but a complex web of loyalties and obligations, the effect of which was to decentralize power.

Because fiefs were normally inherited, they could be acquired by women. Yet a woman could not perform the required military service, so she had to have a husband. Younger sons, who normally had no fief to inherit, often married such heiresses as a means of acquiring a place in the feudal order. Women exercised an important role in feudal society, managing the family estates while their husbands were away and sometimes even defending their castles or fortified manor houses if they were attacked. Legally, however, a woman could not buy or sell property or even appear in court in her own right. Yet as the wife of a noble or a knight, she enjoyed considerable status in the community and could normally expect the deference of her social inferiors, male or female.

The impact of the feudal order on monarchs was considerable. Although kings were normally the most substantial landowners, with vassals who owed them military and other forms of service, in some states the nobles were more powerful than their monarchical lords. In such places a king was only as dominant as his great vassals allowed him to be: if they collectively refused his bidding, he had no other army to enforce his will. In Germany the substantial size of the Magyar armies meant that the nobles could not marshal adequate defenses on their own; hence the kings, who were able to field larger armies, actually increased their influence, as exemplified by Otto I's revival of the imperial tradition. In western continental Europe, by contrast, the smallness and swiftness of the Viking raiding parties enhanced the power of local lords, who could respond more quickly to the threat than the kings could.

The Early Medieval Economy

manorial system - Europe each Manor - 200 acres - village 130-140 people

Beyond their impact on government, the invasions altered the economy of Europe. Muslim domination of the Mediterranean did not eliminate Europe's trade with the East, but it substantially reduced shipping and profits. This in turn adversely affected European towns, particularly in coastal areas. The population of early medieval Europe became overwhelmingly rural, with peasants comprising up to 90 percent of the population.

Seeking protection and a livelihood from the large landowners, many free peasants gradually lost their lands and became dependent. Many peasants worked on large estates or manors, which became the basic social and economic unit at the local level. These manors were essentially descended from the Roman latifundia. In return for labor services for the owner, peasant families received the right to till tracts on the manor for their own sustenance and profit. Such arrangements allowed them considerable security—housing, land, and food—but bound them to the land; serfs could not leave the manor without permission from their lord. In addition to the agricultural labor and other services that peasants owed, they had to pay fines (often in produce or livestock) to the lord of the manor for the opportunity to marry someone from another manor, for a son to inherit the right to his father's lands on the manor, or for the use of the lord's mill to grind grain.

The conditions of peasant life varied greatly. Many peasants retained their freehold farms and their freedom and were quite prosperous, while numerous others possessed few rights and endured abject poverty. The peasant diet was simple, with black bread the primary staple. There was normally little meat, though poaching wild game was fairly common, and the more fortunate peasants ate pork. Fish was available fresh to those who lived near water or otherwise in salted form. The basic vegetables were beans, cabbage, peas, and onions; fruit, apart from berries and nuts, was scarce. Peasants who were lucky enough to have sheep, goats, or cows could make cheese, and those with chickens could eat eggs.

Peasant women not only had to perform the typical childrearing and household duties but also worked in the fields with the men and cared for the animals. They endured a life of hard toil with little amusement other than drinking, perhaps watching cockfights, and amusing themselves on the numerous holy days that dotted the church calendar. Their lives, like those of their families, must in some cases have begun to improve, however marginally, as the result of better economic conditions in the High Middle Ages.

provincialism - people never moved more than 3 to 4 miles from their birthplace or never moved.

NEW FOUNDATIONS: ECONOMIC EXPANSION

The dramatic achievements of the High Middle Ages—urban growth, the organization of guilds and universities, the construction of majestic cathedrals and guildhalls, and the revival of monarchical authority—were possible only because of the large-scale economic expansion that grew out of an agricultural revival that began in the tenth century. That revival was largely spurred by population growth probably resulting from a decline in the prevalence of fatal disease. The development of the three-field system and crop rotation; the use of horses, properly harnessed and shoe-clad, and fertilizer; the recovery of new land by deforestation and drainage; and the increased use of heavy wheeled plows, metal tools, and windmills permitted Europeans to produce more food with less human labor. This opened up possibilities for some people to specialize in manufacturing or commerce and for some landowners to plant crops, such as flax and hemp, that were not needed for basic sustenance. Others converted their land from tillage to pasturage, specializing in sheep, cattle, or horses, sometimes even cross-breeding to improve their stock.

Agricultural and pastoral developments spurred both a rise in population and the growth of manufacturing and commerce. In the year 1000 the population of Europe, including Russia, was approximately 38 million; by the early fourteenth century the population had doubled. During this period, agricultural and commercial advances and the economic boom fostered by the crusades made it possible for towns to develop rapidly. Europeans again began to participate extensively in the trade routes that extended from England and Scandinavia to India and China, especially the commerce that had developed in the Mediterranean in the tenth and eleventh centuries. Byzantine, Muslim, and Jewish merchants remained active throughout much of Europe, but they were soon surpassed by western Europeans.

Much of the commerce of the High Middle Ages was conducted at fairs. Local markets handled weekly retail sales; the international fairs involved primarily wholesale transactions and were carefully regulated. The most influential of these met under the aegis of the counts of Champagne six times a year. Merchants found these fairs attractive because of their strategic location at the crossroads of the European trade routes and the protection offered by the counts. Transactions at the fairs required the development of more sophisticated business practices, including the use of standard weights and measures, and the evolution of an international mercantile law.

Because the fairs were international in scope, money-changers were needed. Customarily seated on benches (*bancs*), these exchange specialists became known as bankers. They accepted deposits and were instrumental in instigating the use of paper credit, which facilitated the distribution of goods over long distances and encouraged commercial transactions when bullion and coins were in short supply. Eventually, governments found it advantageous to finance some of their activities by credit. These developments collectively led to the emergence of capitalism.

Commercial expansion stimulated the development of new organizations to meet the demand for products and to facilitate international trade. Partnerships became commonplace, despite one serious limitation: the responsibility of each partner for the total indebtedness of the firm in the event of default. Because of this drawback, partnerships were usually formed only by family members, perhaps with a few close associates. An alternative was the *commenda,* an association in which an investor provided capital to a merchant in return for a share of the profits but which limited the investor's potential loss to the funds invested. Merchants and artisans also organized in guilds. On a much larger scale, beginning in the twelfth century, various cities joined forces in commercial leagues designed to promote their interests. The best known was the Hanseatic League of North German cities.

The increase in trade stimulated industrial production, particularly cloth manufacturing. English and Frisian cloth was sold throughout Europe by the ninth century and in Russia by the eleventh. The major textile centers of the High Middle Ages were in Flanders and northern Italy. Metal industries, which produced weapons, tools, and cutlery, expanded, thanks especially to renewed interest in mining. Mining was pursued primarily in the eastern Alps, Bohemia, England, and northern Spain. In addition to gold and silver—crucial for the expansion of coinage—the mines produced tin, copper, mercury, iron, and coal. The adoption of such technology as pulleys, cranks, and pumps and the har-

nessing of waterpower to crush the ore improved productivity.

Artisans manufactured such items as leather goods, paper (primarily in Italy and Spain), plate and blown glass (especially in Venice), and stained glass (France). Maritime states had shipbuilding industries, and some coastal cities produced salt by evaporating seawater. Throughout Europe the food industry developed as people specialized in salting fish, curing meat, brewing, making wine, and milling grain. The building industry flourished, particularly beginning in the eleventh century, when it became fashionable north of the Alps to use stone instead of wood and plaster for major construction.

The manufacture of textiles and metals as well as the construction of large buildings required capital, reliable transportation, adequate supplies of raw materials, and a skilled labor force. All of this was possible only in a climate that could offer reasonable security and legal protection; hence industrial expansion and the reappearance of reasonably stable governments went hand in hand. Trade and industry provided the revenues without which effective governments could not exist, and the authorities, in turn, had to maintain conditions conducive to the further development of commerce and manufacturing. The High Middle Ages achieved dramatic progress because of the fortunate combination of agricultural expansion, technological and commercial development, and increasing political stability.

URBAN DEVELOPMENT AND TOWN LIFE

The High Middle Ages witnessed extraordinary urban growth in western and central Europe prompted largely by the expansion of trade and manufacturing to meet the needs of a rising population. No single factor accounts for the sites on which medieval cities developed. Some, such as Rome and Marseilles, were rebuilt on the decayed foundations of old Roman cities and administrative centers. Ports such as Pisa and Genoa recovered in the aftermath of Lombard and Arab domination. Many were located at the sites of natural harbors, such as Barcelona; on major rivers, such as London (on the Thames) and Cologne (on the Rhine); or at strategic locations astride major trade routes, such as Milan and Vienna. Some cities, such as Bruges, emerged where key bridges crossed rivers. Many towns developed where people congregated for protection in fortified settlements, a trend commemorated in names ending in *fort, furt, burg(h),* or *borough:* Frankfurt and Edinburgh are examples. An ecclesiastical center could serve as the nucleus of an emerging town; Paris and Rouen were seats of bishops and sites of important monasteries.

The largest medieval cities—Paris, Venice, Florence, Naples, Milan, and Genoa—probably never had more than 100,000 inhabitants in the High Middle Ages, and the Flemish cities of Bruges, Ghent, and Ypres, as well as London and Cologne, were roughly half their size. Apart from Cologne, the largest German towns, such as Hamburg and Augsburg, had fewer than 30,000 people. In contrast, Cairo's population reached 500,000 by 1300, and the largest Muslim cities of late medieval Spain were nearly as big.

The traditional description of medieval European cities as overcrowded is often an exaggeration, though space within the city walls came to be at a premium. Beyond the walls there was open space where residents could farm or build houses. Some cities erected new walls, but wall construction and maintenance were expensive. Vertical expansion was also possible, and medieval builders often made each successive story wider than the one below, with the result that many streets received little sunlight. Pollution was common, as refuse of all types, including human excrement, was routinely dumped in the streets. Horses, dogs, and oxen added their own dung. The popularity of ale was no doubt partly due to the prevalence of contaminated water. Fires were a severe hazard wherever buildings were made of wood. In the absence of urban planning, medieval cities were like mazes, their winding streets and narrow alleys a mixture of fortified houses, shops, and the ramshackle shanties of the poor.

The towns were the achievement of a new social order, the burghers or bourgeoisie—the urban merchants who took their place beside the aristocracy, the clergy, and the peasants. In some circles the newcomers were not welcome: a fourteenth-century English preacher thundered that "God made the clergy, knights, and laborers, but the devil made townsmen and usurers." The traditional social orders had little understanding of the merchants' role in the economy. Although merchants and artisans originally came from humble backgrounds, in time some of them acquired substantial wealth and eventually rivaled the aristocracy. Wedded to the land and steeped in tradition, most nobles treated the merchants with disdain.

The lure of the towns was due in no small measure to the privileges set forth in their charters. These were usually granted by nobles or monarchs who were interested in tax revenues or income from the sale of charters. In cities such as Cologne and Liège, however, the townspeople had to rebel to secure their charters. The heart of the typical charter was the assurance of personal freedom for anyone who lived in the town for a year and a day. Charters usually guaranteed the people the right to hold markets and often to govern themselves, even to the point of making and enforcing their own laws to regulate commerce. Towns normally had to pay a stipulated sum to their overlords each year, but usually the citizens determined the taxes they would levy on themselves.

Although townspeople were personally free, urban governments were not democratic. Power customarily rested with the prosperous merchants and master artisans. Control was exercised not only through town councils but also through *guilds,* groups of people pursuing the same economic activity that were organized first by merchants in the eleventh century and thereafter by artisans. As the craft guilds developed, they insisted on at least sharing city government with the merchant guilds. Because guilds were so well organized, they dominated government affairs, particularly since they could vote as a bloc and thereby elect their own leaders to city offices.

The guilds protected the interests of their members by restricting membership, limiting competition, and setting prices. In effect, a guild enjoyed a monopoly over a particular craft or trade and controlled prices; consumers benefited too in that the guild regulated quality. Guilds trained apprentices to become journeymen and possibly master artisans and guild members, and some guilds educated members' children. The guilds also aided needy members or their families, providing health care and financial assistance, particularly for victims of fire and flood as well as for widows and orphans. Some guilds, especially those involved with textiles or brewing, included women. Religion often played an important part in guild life, whether in activities honoring their favorite saints, in donations to churches, or in the construction and maintenance of their own chapels.

The guilds could not absorb all those who wished to enter. Hence, as peasants kept flocking to the towns, many could find employment only as unskilled laborers. Poorly paid, devoid of political rights, and often barely able to survive, they constituted the proletariat. Although these people were nominally free, few had any chance of improving their social status.

THE GROWTH OF MONARCHY: ENGLAND AND FRANCE

No sovereigns made more effective use of the improved economic conditions to enhance their power than the rulers of England and France, particularly through their efforts to establish internal security and their interest in legal reform. In both countries the dominant political theme of the High Middle Ages was the struggle of the crown to establish a position of authority reasonably secure from the claims of the church on the one hand and the feudal aristocracy on the other. Simultaneously, the seeds were also sown for the bitter conflict between the two countries that lasted for centuries.

From the Norman Conquest to the Angevin Empire

One of the most significant dates in English history is 1066, the year William, duke of Normandy, defeated the last Anglo-Saxon monarch, Harold, at the battle of Hastings to seize the English crown. The Norman Conquest brought fundamental changes to England, principally the imposition of a Norman-French feudal aristocracy that owed military allegiance directly to the new king and was thus more centralized than its French counterpart. The Anglo-Saxon nobility disappeared, and England was henceforth governed by Normans. Nevertheless, William retained most Anglo-Saxon laws and institutions, including some of the traditional courts and the sheriffs, who as royal officials exercised administrative and military command in the shires. The royal council, the Witenagemot, however, was replaced by the Great Council, an advisory body and court of feudal law, and its nucleus, the Small Council, composed of the king's principal advisers and officials. One of William's major accomplishments was a detailed survey of landed property in England—the *Domesday Book*—probably undertaken to aid tax collection. William also extended royal control over the church, gradually replacing Anglo-Saxon bishops and abbots with Normans.

During the reign of William's great-grandson, Henry II (1154–1189), the territory in France under English control increased dramatically. In addition to Normandy, Henry inherited Maine, Touraine, and Anjou from his father, the count of Anjou, and added Aquitaine and Poitou by marrying Eleanor, duchess of Aquitaine. The Angevin empire, as all this was called, stretched from the Scottish border to the Pyrenees and included more than half of France. In feudal terms, Henry held his French lands as a vassal of the French king.

ELEANOR OF AQUITAINE: COURT POLITICS AND COURTLY LOVE

In her life, Eleanor of Aquitaine linked several of the major themes of the High Middle Ages—the political struggles of France and England, the crusades, and the courtly love tradition.* Born in 1122, Eleanor, the daughter and heiress of William X, duke of Aquitaine, inherited the ducal title at the age of 15. Her guardian, King Louis VI, arranged her marriage to his son, who succeeded to the French throne as Louis VII in 1137. When Louis set out on the Second Crusade in 1147, Eleanor too "took the cross" of the crusaders as her grandfather, William IX, had done in the First Crusade. At Antioch, Eleanor shocked Louis by announcing that their relationship was illegitimate because of their blood ties. Whether Eleanor was now sexually unfaithful, as the king's friends charged, is impossible to prove, but Louis forced her to remain with him, and she undoubtedly was with the crusaders when they reached Jerusalem.

Papal intervention kept the royal couple together until 1152, when their marriage was annulled. Happy to be rid of Louis, who was "more monk than king," Eleanor married Henry Plantagenet two months later. When Henry succeeded to the English throne in 1154, she was crowned queen of England. She bore Henry eight children, among them two future kings of England, Richard I and John. A political force to be reckoned with during her first decade in England, Eleanor served as regent when Henry was out of the country. Beginning in 1163, however, she was largely reduced to ceremonial functions, and in 1168, Henry dispatched her to Aquitaine to govern her duchy. Eleven years her junior, Henry was left free to pursue an affair with his mistress. Eleanor schemed to use her children to get revenge on Henry. Unwittingly, he played into her hands in 1169 by dividing his continental lands among his sons, giving them a base from which to oppose him. An exasperated

---

*The crusades are discussed later in this chapter, and the courtly love tradition is explained in Chapter 8.

Henry finally placed Eleanor in captivity in 1174, thus keeping her from actively supporting her sons when they rebelled against him in 1183. She appeared in court on rare occasions in the mid-1180s, but her official release came only when Henry died in July 1189.

At Poitiers in the 1160s, Eleanor presided over the beginnings of the courtly love tradition, with its exaltation of women. Although experts debate the extent of her role as a patron of literature and art, the roots of courtly love were undoubtedly in her court. The tradition flourished for the first time at the court of her eldest daughter, Marie of Champagne. The emphasis on love, music, and poetry was something of a family tradition that dated back to Eleanor's grandfather, William IX, reputedly the first troubadour. The troubadours who gathered at her court to sing her praises eventually spread their passionate lyrics throughout much of France, England, Spain, and Sicily.

Eleanor virtually governed England until Richard I (1189–1199), who had been estranged from his father, arrived in the country. Close to Richard, she exercised considerable power throughout his reign, especially after he was captured while returning from the Third Crusade. In addition to raising funds for his ransom, she called on the pope to help free Richard. Four months after Richard's return, she retired to Fontevrault Abbey in France in June 1194. She was buried there ten years later in a nun's habit.

Law and Monarchy in Norman and Angevin England

Henry I and Henry II undertook significant reforms in law and administration. The former shifted administrative authority from barons to men of lesser rank who operated under the direction of a new official called the *justiciar.* The justiciar's court, known as the *Exchequer,* served as the royal treasury and the accounting arm of the government. The two kings were instrumental in the emergence of common law, a body of legal principles based on custom and judicial precedents, uniformly applicable throughout England and administered by royal judges. In contrast, the civil law that increasingly prevailed throughout much of the European continent was derived from Roman law, especially Justinian's *Corpus Juris Civilis.* English royal justice was not only legally superior to that dispensed in the local courts but more popular as well, and people were willing to purchase *writs* (legal orders) to have their cases decided by panels of jurors over which the crown's judges presided. In addition to operating a court at Westminster, the kings dispatched justices on regular circuits throughout the country, thus furthering the notion of a common law. Henry II required residents to appear before these justices to report alleged criminals, a practice that later evolved into the modern grand jury. Henry II also instituted the *grand assize,* which gave persons whose land titles were challenged the opportunity to have their cases judged by a jury in a royal court rather than by compurgation (the oaths of neighbors) or trial by combat.

Henry II's efforts to impose legal reforms on the church provoked a major confrontation. He was troubled that the clergy had the right to be tried and sentenced in church courts, where the penalties were less severe than those imposed in secular courts. The Constitutions of Clarendon, which he issued in 1164, prohibited legal appeals to Rome without the king's permission, required that clergy convicted of a secular crime be sentenced in a royal court, and provided basic rights to laity tried in ecclesiastical courts. Thomas à Becket (1118–1170), whom Henry had appointed archbishop of Canterbury, rejected any notion of clerics being subject to a secular court. Becket incurred Henry's wrath when he excommunicated bishops loyal to the king. When Henry, in a fit of anger, asked whether no one would rid him of "this troublesome priest," four knights murdered Becket in Canterbury Cathedral. In the storm of outrage that ensued, Henry was forced to yield on two crucial points: clergy would be tried and sentenced in church courts, and appeals could still be made to the papal court.

The church and the barons each won a major victory during the reign of King John (1199–1216), who quarreled with Pope Innocent III (1198–1216) over a disputed election to the archbishopric of Canterbury. Innocent finally excommunicated John and placed England under an interdict, severely restricting religious services to the people. Faced with widespread unrest and the threat of a French invasion, John capitulated and made England a papal fief, thereby winning the pope's support.

With the church controversy settled, John determined to invade France to regain territory seized by Philip II. Although John had the support of the Holy Roman Empire and Flanders, his French vassals refused to fight against Philip, their supreme lord, and Philip crushed the imperial and Flemish forces at Bouvines in 1214. The financial demands of the war had forced John to use extreme measures to raise money, thereby violating the feudal rights of his barons. In June 1215 the barons compelled John to accept the Magna Carta. Far from being a charter of rights in the modern sense, the Magna Carta served as an affirmation of feudal principles, though some of its provisions touched the clergy, the peasants, and the townsfolk. Among other things, the charter limited feudal payments, promised the church freedom from royal interference, restricted fines on peasants, and confirmed the special privileges of London and other boroughs. The significance of the Magna Carta was its embodiment of the principle that monarchs are subject to the law and can be constrained if they violate it. Beginning in the seventeenth century, creative interpreters argued that the Magna Carta contained such principles as due process of law and the right of representation for people being taxed.

Another important legal precedent was established in 1295 when Edward I (1272–1307) broadened the Great Council of nobles and prelates by summoning knights and representatives from the towns. The purpose of this *Parliament,* as it came to be called, was to approve taxes to fund a war against France. Edward justified his decision to consult this wider group on the basis of a principle used by the church in convening a general council: "What touches all should be approved by all." This principle also influenced the development of representative bodies in France and elsewhere.

Capetian France

When Hugh Capet was elected king of France in 987, France was a patchwork of fiefs that were largely independent of royal authority. Hugh's own territory, the Île de France around Paris, was considerably smaller than that of the two vassals who flanked him, the duke of Normandy and the count of Champagne. Hugh, however, had two advantages over his vassals: his lordship over them in feudal theory and his consecration by the church in the coronation ceremony. The Île de France, moreover, was centrally located and the site of Paris. The early Capetian monarchs improved their political fortunes by cultivating support from the church and by having their heirs crowned and given some governmental responsibility before assuming the throne. The Capetians were fortunate in that they produced male heirs, most of whom reigned for relatively long periods. Beginning in the twelfth century, the kings also began to rely less on the greater nobles for their officials, preferring lesser nobles, clerics, and burghers whose loyalty to the throne was stronger.

By the time Philip II (1180–1223)—Philip Augustus, as he was called—became king, the gravest threat to the monarchy was posed by the English because of their extensive holdings in western France. Philip devoted much of his attention to reducing English influence, an endeavor made easier by King John's domestic problems. French troops forced John to surrender everything but Aquitaine and Gascony, more than trebling the territory under Philip's control.

Philip's domestic policies contributed significantly to the growth of monarchical power. Earlier kings had conferred land on local officials in return for their service, thus making many of their offices hereditary. Philip restored greater royal control over local affairs by appointing new officers who worked for a salary and could be replaced as necessary; they reported directly to the king. To fund his enlarged government, Philip insisted on the full payment of feudal dues by his vassals. By the end of his reign, his increase of royal revenues was no less impressive than his enlargement of the royal domain. He further enhanced his authority by issuing 78 town charters, thereby forging strong links between the townsfolk and the crown.

Philip's grandson, the saintly Louis IX (1226–1270), was distinguished by his devotion to Christian principles, symbolically represented by his washing of lepers' feet during Holy Week and his bestowal of alms to the poor. Few rulers have been as dedicated to justice, both in the workings of the royal courts and in his personal capacity as the source of French justice. One of the endearing images of medieval Europe is that of Louis sitting under an oak tree dispensing justice to all comers. More formally, Louis encouraged appeals from lower courts to the Parlement of Paris, which the king recognized as the highest tribunal in France. A concern for justice and good government also prompted Louis to appoint special commissioners to monitor the work of the bailiffs and seneschals. When conflict between wealthy merchants and artisans erupted in the towns, the king intervened to preserve order, an action that resulted in a decrease in the number of privileges the towns enjoyed. Louis made effective use of *ordonnances,* or royal decrees, to prohibit private warfare and dueling and to require the acceptance of royal money throughout France. But for all his accomplishments, Louis failed to continue Philip II's policy of reducing English influence in France.

Louis' cunning grandson, Philip IV (1285–1314), "the Fair," sought to expand royal authority, in part by using itinerant members of Parlement to extend royal justice throughout the realm at the expense of feudal courts. He also resumed hostilities against England, prohibiting Flemish towns from importing English wool. This endeavor failed when Philip's army proved unable to defeat the rebellious Flemish cities. As military expenses mounted, Philip imposed forced loans, debased the coinage, and taxed the clergy. He also expelled Jews and Italian moneylenders as a pretext to confiscate their property.

Still short of funds, Philip summoned urban representatives to meet with his council of nobles and clergymen in 1302, thus marking the beginnings of a more representative assembly that later became known as the Estates General. In contrast to the English Parliament, the Estates General never became powerful enough to establish permanent control over the levying of taxes and thus to serve as an effective check on monarchical power. By the early fourteenth century, then, the French monarchy had substantially centralized authority at the expense of the feudal nobility, and in England, despite the success of the nobles in checking the growth of royal power in the 1200s, legal reform had done much to lay the foundation of a unified state.

THE HOLY ROMAN EMPIRE AND THE CHURCH

Unlike their French and English counterparts, the German emperors of the High Middle Ages failed to lay the foundations of a unified Germany. In part this was due to the strength of the feudal nobility and the emperors' quest to dominate Italy, but perhaps the most crucial factor was a furious struggle with the papacy that culminated in the disintegration of the Holy Roman Empire. The church's victory was made possible by reforms in the tenth and eleventh centuries that gave it new vigor and a stronger claim to moral leadership (see Chapter 8).

Germany and the Imperial Revival

When the Carolingian empire declined in the ninth century, essentially independent duchies were established in the eastern Frankish lands. Out of this territory the Saxon duke Henry the Fowler founded the medieval German monarchy, which he governed as Henry I (919–

936). His success in controlling the dukes was due partly to the freedom he allowed them in their duchies and partly to his ambitious foreign policy. He annexed Lorraine, strengthened Saxon defenses against the Magyars and Vikings by encouraging the building of fortified towns, and urged Saxon expansion in the Slavic lands beyond the Elbe River.

The policies of Henry's son, Otto I (936–973), were basically an extension of his father's, but on a grander scale. His efforts to centralize royal power incited no fewer than four rebellions, all of which he repressed. When the Magyars took advantage of the civil strife to invade Germany, Otto crushed them at Lechfeld, near Augsburg, in 955. Like his father, he appointed churchmen to offices of state, knowing that they could not undermine royal authority by passing their positions to their sons. The clergy, moreover, was better educated. The church welcomed the alliance with the state, which brought greater influence and grants of land. The churchmen who held those estates were responsible for providing Otto with many of his soldiers and much of his revenue.

When political turmoil in Italy offered Otto an excuse to intervene in 951, he claimed the Lombard throne as his own. Renewed conflict brought a call for his assistance from Pope John XII (955–964), who rewarded him with the imperial crown in 962. That crown had several advantages, including the legal title to the Carolingian middle kingdom and reinforcement of Otto's supremacy over the German dukes, but it also thrust his successors into an untenable relationship with the head of a church that they had to dominate to maintain their power. The imperial policy of relying on ecclesiastical officials as the primary servants of the crown was effective as long as the papacy did not insist on appointing only those who had its approval.

Beginning in the late eleventh century, the papacy attempted to assert the church's independence from secular control. In 1059 a church council took a major step in freeing the papacy itself from imperial control by establishing the right of the College of Cardinals to elect future popes. In 1075, Pope Gregory VII (1073–1085) attempted to restore the election of bishops and abbots to the church by ending lay investiture—the bestowal of the insignia of a church office by a layperson. Practically speaking, lay investiture entailed the right of the laity, such as emperors or kings, to select bishops and abbots, though this violated church law and tradition. A reformed church could hardly be established if its key officials were selected with a view to political, monetary, and family considerations rather than spiritual qualifications and if the loyalty of such officials was ultimately to the sovereign who had appointed them rather than to the pope.

The immediate target of Gregory's decree was the emperor Henry IV (1056–1106), who enjoyed the support of his bishops but not of the German territorial princes. The latter stood to gain by any reduction of imperial power. Recognizing the implications of the decree, Henry had his prelates declare Gregory deposed. The pope responded by excommunicating Henry, absolving his subjects from their duty to obey him, and depriving the imperial bishops of their offices. Unprepared to cope with a rebellion, the emperor intercepted Gregory at Canossa in Italy to seek absolution. As a priest, Gregory had to forgive the penitent Henry, thereby giving the emperor the upper hand in the civil war that ensued in Germany.

The investiture struggle dragged on until 1122, when the emperor Henry V (1106–1125) and Pope Calixtus II (1119–1124) agreed in the Concordat of Worms that the

The German emperor Henry IV is shown kneeling at Canossa to ask Countess Matilda of Tuscany and Abbot Hugh of Cluny to intercede on his behalf with Pope Gregory VII. As a priest, Gregory had no recourse but to pardon him. [Biblioteca Apostolica Vaticana]

church would henceforth give prelates their offices and spiritual authority but that the emperor could be present when German bishops were elected and invest them with fiefs. In theory, the clergy were now more independent of secular control, though in practice their selection and work were still very political. The winners in the investiture struggle were the territorial princes, who consolidated their hold over their own lands while imperial attention focused on Rome, and the emerging urban communes of northern Italy, which seized this opportunity to achieve a semi-independent status. In the end the biggest losers were not only the emperors but the German people, who were increasingly subjected to feudal conflict.

Papal Triumph and the Imperial Challenge

The papacy reached the zenith of its political power in the thirteenth century but only after a renewal of its struggle with the empire. The first prominent emperor from the Hohenstaufen dynasty, Frederick I (1152–1190), called "Barbarossa" because of his red beard, made domination of northern Italy (Lombardy) a cornerstone of his policy. Together with Burgundy, which he acquired by marriage, and his native Swabia, Lombardy would give him a solid territorial base from which to dominate Germany and Italy. Recognizing this, the pope joined with the cities of the Lombard League and the Normans in Sicily to thwart Frederick's ambitions, an end they achieved in the Peace of Constance (1183), which forced Frederick to relinquish virtually all meaningful power in the Lombard cities. The imperial cause in Italy received new life when Barbarossa's son, Henry VI (1190–1197), married Constance, heiress of Sicily and southern Italy. The papacy was now caught in the imperial vise, but rather than solidifying his Italian holdings, Henry prepared to attack the Byzantine Empire.

Innocent III took advantage of the chaos that followed Henry's untimely death to undermine the link between Germany and Sicily. Germany was thrust into civil war when the leading Hohenstaufen candidate for the imperial throne, Philip of Swabia, Henry VI's brother, was challenged by Otto of Brunswick. Although Innocent crowned Otto in 1198, the latter's attempt to control Sicily prompted the pope to excommunicate him. Innocent recognized the claim of Henry's son, Frederick II, as king of the Romans (and hence emperor-elect) in 1212.

Philip's victory over Otto at Bouvines in 1214 decided the struggle in Frederick's favor.

Innocent III enhanced papal authority in decrees that spelled out the pope's powers in clear legal terms. The "plenitude of power" that he asserted (as had Pope Leo the Great) did not claim temporal world power but supreme spiritual sovereignty, including the right to intervene in secular affairs when the faith or morals of the church were affected. As we have seen, he acted on these principles when he humbled England's King John. In a quarrel that lasted two decades he also forced Philip Augustus to take back his wife. Innocent strengthened the church in numerous other ways, including approval for new religious orders (see Chapter 8).

After Frederick's death in 1250 the papacy encouraged civil strife in Germany so successfully that between 1254 and 1273 there was no generally recognized emperor. Moreover, the Hohenstaufen line itself died out in 1268. The Great Interregnum, as the period without a recognized emperor was called, marked the triumph of the papacy over the empire.

Boniface VIII and the End of Papal Hegemony

The century between the pontificates of Innocent III and Boniface VIII (1294–1303) witnessed a dramatic change in the political fortunes of the major European states, with France and England now the dominant powers. Boniface seriously blundered when, in 1296, he rejected the right of monarchs to tax the clergy without papal authorization. Neither Philip IV of France nor Edward I of England would tolerate such a challenge. Edward denied legal protection to clerics who refused to pay, and Philip prohibited the export of funds from France to Rome, crippling papal finances. Boniface retreated, allowing Philip the right to tax the clergy in an emergency and canonizing Louis IX for good measure.

Emboldened by the jubilee in 1300, when tens of thousands of pilgrims flocked to Rome, Boniface was ready when a new crisis erupted in 1301. When Philip had a French bishop tried in a royal court on charges of heresy and treason, Boniface protested that this violated the clergy's privilege to be judged in a church court and warned Philip to submit to his authority as the vicar of Christ. Philip countered by summoning the first Estates General (1302), which protested to Rome. The pope responded with the papal bull (or edict) *Unam sanctam* (1302), in which he argued that God had given the church

two swords; the spiritual sword, which was superior, was retained by the church, but the temporal sword was bestowed by the church on secular authorities to be wielded on behalf of the church and at its direction. The bull also asserted that "submission on the part of every man to the bishop of Rome is altogether necessary for his salvation."

Whether *Unam sanctam* was a desperate ploy or the logical culmination of medieval papal claims is debatable, but Philip was undaunted. He dispatched agents to Italy to arrest the pope, whom Philip hoped to try on fabricated charges ranging from heresy to sodomy and sorcery. Boniface was rescued by Italian loyalists, but not before he had been physically abused and the prestige of the papacy badly tarnished. In a matter of weeks, Boniface was dead, and with him perished the heady days of papal supremacy. A French pope, Clement V (1305–1314), formally praised Philip's devotion, heralding the beginning of a long period in which the papacy found itself in the shadow of the French monarchy.

THE WANING OF THE BYZANTINE EMPIRE

While western Europe was achieving remarkable political progress in the High Middle Ages, the Byzantine Empire was plagued by internal decay and external assault. In many respects the eleventh century was pivotal in its decline. The emperor Basil II (976–1025) had secured the frontiers and brought the Balkans under Byzantine domination by defeating the Bulgars. From 1028 to 1056, however, the empire was ineffectually governed by Basil's nieces, Zoë and Theodora, who supported large landowners in their acquisition of smaller holdings. The result was the growth of a body of powerful magnates capable of fielding their own armies and posing a threat to imperial control. In effect, the empire was being feudalized. Much of the internal instability of the eleventh century was also attributable to a fierce power struggle between the bureaucratic elite and the aristocracy, the effects of which weakened the army and undermined the government's financial stability. The lavish expenses of the imperial court and the increasing exemption of the aristocracy from taxation forced the government to devalue its coins in the mid-eleventh century.

The internal crises made it difficult for the Byzantines to cope with the pressure on their frontiers. The Seljuk Turks destroyed a Byzantine army at Manzikert in 1071, resulting in the loss of eastern Anatolia and Armenia. In the same year the Normans of Sicily drove the Byzantines out of southern Italy and attacked Greece. Alexius I Comnenus (1081–1118) regained some of the lost territory by allying with the Venetians against the Normans and by successful military campaigns against the Turks. His military needs were so great, however, that he appealed to the papacy for volunteers to fight the Turks, thus setting the stage for the crusades.

The Clash of Faiths:
Muslims Against Crusaders

The Turks had moved from the Asian steppes into the Islamic empire to serve in its armies. By 1055 one group of Turks, the Seljuks, had established themselves as the real rulers of the Abbasid caliphate. In the two centuries that followed their victory at Manzikert they extended their control over most of Asia Minor, changing it from a Christian to an Islamic civilization. Turkish domination extended into Palestine as well. In 1095, against a background of alleged hostilities against Christian pilgrims, Alexius Comnenus urged Pope Urban II (1088–1099) to dispatch military aid. At the Council of Clermont (1095) the pope proclaimed a crusade to liberate the holy places from a "pagan race," free the persecuted Christians of the East, and acquire wealth and power in a land of "milk and honey."

The motives of the church and the crusaders varied. For the papacy the crusades offered the possibility of leadership in Europe and the opportunity to heal the breach between the eastern and western churches that had been formalized in 1054. While some crusaders were moved by spiritual considerations, including the promise of a plenary indulgence (a complete discharge of punishment for sin), others were motivated by stories of atrocities purportedly inflicted on pilgrims by the Muslims, the hope of material gain, the lure of adventure, or the desire to participate in an activity that quickly became fashionable.

The Byzantine emperor Alexius I Comnenus is best known for his appeal to the West for help in fighting the Turks, thus inaugurating the crusades. [Biblioteca Apostolica Vaticana]

Children's Crusade ~~5th~~ between 5th & 6th ended in failure

Alexius wanted western knights trained and equipped to fight, but instead the first crusaders, some 15,000 to 20,000 strong, were largely commoners, including women and children, devoid of military experience or suitable weapons. Inspired by faith and led by Peter the Hermit, most of the unruly force was annihilated or enslaved by the Muslims. Fired by hopes of founding the New Jerusalem, the Peasants' Crusade ended in disaster, not only for the crusaders but also for the thousands of Hungarians and Jews they killed en route and the Byzantines they robbed or whose homes they burned.

Later in the same year, 1096, some of Europe's most illustrious princes, including Godfrey of Bouillon, duke of Lower Lorraine, launched the Crusade of the Princes, traditionally called the First Crusade. In all, there were 5,000 to 10,000 knights, more than 25,000 soldiers, and at least that many noncombatants, both male and female, including servants, pilgrims, and prostitutes. The crusaders captured the Syrian cities of Edessa and Antioch, and then, in July 1099, Jerusalem itself fell. The victors massacred the inhabitants, whether Muslims or Jews, sparing neither women nor children.

The crusaders offered the crown of Jerusalem to Godfrey of Bouillon, who agreed only to serve as protector in deference to the kingship of Christ. Following Godfrey's death in 1100, his brother Baldwin became king of Jerusalem and nominal overlord of the three other crusader states, Edessa, Antioch, and Tripoli, which together formed a 500-mile strip along the coast of the eastern Mediterranean. Feudal knights were used to defend this outpost of European civilization but at the cost of developing a strong central government. Imposing castles were built, and the crusaders founded military orders in which the knights took the monastic vows of poverty, chastity, and obedience while dedicating their lives to the defense of the Holy Land. The Knights Hospitalers and the Knights Templars wore distinctive dress, defended castles, and generally distinguished themselves as warriors. German crusaders established a third order, the Teutonic Knights, in 1198, though most of its efforts were devoted to campaigns in Hungary and the Baltic region.

The conquests of the first crusaders were possible largely because the Muslims had been disunited. In the early twelfth century the Muslims regrouped. Their capture of Edessa in 1144 sparked the call for the ineffectual Second Crusade (1147–1149). After Saladin (1138–1193) established himself as the master of much of the Muslim Middle East, he launched a holy war of his own to recover Palestine, taking Jerusalem in 1187.

3rd Crusade

The loss of Jerusalem roused Europe to launch a formidable crusade led by Frederick Barbarossa, Philip II of France, and Richard I of England. Frederick drowned in Asia Minor, and Philip soon returned home, leaving Richard "the Lion-Hearted" to negotiate an agreement with Saladin permitting Christian pilgrims to visit Jerusalem. This was not enough for Pope Innocent III, who called for the Fourth Crusade (1202–1204). In return for food and transport, the crusaders helped Venice to conquer the Dalmatian port of Zara, an act that resulted in their excommunication because Zara was a Catholic city. The crusaders then embroiled themselves in a disputed succession to the Byzantine throne that ended with their sack of Constantinople and the establishment of a Latin kingdom there that lasted until 1261. Among the later crusades, only the sixth (1228–1229), led by Frederick II, enjoyed any success, and in 1291 the last of the crusader possessions was lost.

In terms of their stated objective—the conquest of the Holy Land—the crusades were a failure. The heavy expenditure in lives and resources as well as the undercutting of spiritual motives by worldly considerations cast a pall over the movement. One of the most significant long-term legacies was the incitement of deep-seated religious hostility between Christians and Muslims and of Christians toward Jews. Nor did the crusades heal the breach between eastern and western Christendom. In the short term the papacy probably enhanced its prestige as the spiritual leader of the West, but in the end its use of crusades to eradicate heresy in France and its deepening involvement in secular affairs began to erode its influence. The monarchs of Europe improved their position by gaining the right to levy direct taxes to obtain crusading funds, and Europe was perhaps subjected to less fighting because so many lords and knights directed their militancy against the Muslims.

The crusades had economic and cultural benefits. The heightened contact between Europe and the Middle East stimulated commerce, especially in such commodities as fine textiles, spices, and perfumes. Expanded commerce encouraged improvements in shipbuilding and banking, including greater use of letters of credit and bills of exchange. Although Islamic culture was already spreading to the West through the Iberian peninsula and Sicily, the crusades facilitated the exchange of ideas and the increase of geographic knowledge. The notion of "crusading" for a worthy cause lived on well past the last crusade and is still a frequent concept, usually in secular guise; the Islamic notion of the *jihad* is similar. The crusades were also significant as a chapter in the history of Western expansion and the backdrop for the great voyages of exploration that began in the fifteenth century, in part as a means of renewing the crusading movement.

Byzantium After the Crusades

While the Europeans ruled Constantinople as a Latin kingdom, Greek refugees established a rival government at Nicaea in Asia Minor. In 1261 the Nicaean regime regained Constantinople, but the restored Byzantine Empire was territorially smaller and economically weaker than it had been in 1200. It survived for two more centuries, during which its economy eroded and its strength was sapped by bitter social divisions. External threats were a recurring problem. The Byzantines were unable to repel the periodic incursions of the Serbs in the west and the Turks in the east. Their diminished territories meant decreased resources and workers, and the government at Constantinople was further weakened by civil wars in the 1300s. Perhaps the greatest cause of the Byzantines' decline was their inability to recover their once phenomenal prosperity, in no small measure because much of their commerce had fallen into the hands of Italian merchants.

THE IBERIAN PENINSULA AND THE RECONQUISTA

Although the crusaders failed to regain the Holy Land, a much longer campaign against the Muslims in the Iberian peninsula was slowly being won. The *reconquista* ("reconquest") had begun in the ninth century, but by the dawn of the High Middle Ages, only a thin band across the north of the peninsula was in Christian hands. Three centuries later, the Muslims held only Granada at the peninsula's southern tip. Christian gains were due largely to the collapse in 1031 of the caliphate of Córdoba, which had been torn by internal dissension among Arabs, Jews, Berbers, and native Spaniards. As the caliphate, once the most prosperous state in Europe, disintegrated into petty principalities, the Christians' task was greatly simplified.

During the reign of Sancho the Great of Navarre (1005–1035), Christian Spain was largely united, but Sancho, viewing his state in personal terms, divided it among his four sons. Out of their inheritances eventually emerged the kingdoms of Navarre, Castile, and Aragon. The kingdom of Portugal was the result of a decision by Alfonso VI of Castile (1065–1109) to reward a Burgundian count for his services against the Muslims. In 1143, Alfonso VII and the papacy officially recognized the count's son as a king, and Portugal henceforth pursued its own historical path.

The reconquista, which officially became a holy crusade in 1063, helped to shape the ideals and institutions of the Iberian kingdoms. Iberian culture, especially in the Spanish states, combined Arabic influence with a fanatical religious zeal born in northern Spain of the crusading spirit. The need for troops and the funds to support them during the long campaign against the Muslims resulted in the appearance of representative institutions, or Cortes, in the states of León (1188), Castile (1250), and Portugal (1254) well before the development of similar institutions in France and England, although they never acquired the power of the English Parliament. In Castile, which supplied the bulk of the men for the reconquista, the need for urban support also brought charters for the towns. Above all, the reconquista paved the way for the establishment in the fifteenth century of a unified Spain, which concluded the reconquest with the acquisition of Granada in 1492.

GRANADA, THE "GARDENS OF PARADISE"

Situated on the slopes of the Sierra Nevada and the banks of the Genil River, the Islamic city of Granada developed rapidly after the disintegration of the caliphate of Córdoba in 1031. As late as the ninth century, Granada had been little more than a fortified village distinguished by its large Jewish population. Blessed with fertile soil and a Mediterranean climate, the population of the city grew from 20,000 in the tenth century to 26,000 in the eleventh century, about one-third the size of neighboring Seville. As the reconquista picked up speed, Muslim refugees fled south to Granada, enriching the city with an influx of artisans and merchants. When the monarchs of Castile and Aragon expelled thousands of Muslim agricultural workers in the 1260s, many moved to the kingdom of Granada. By the fifteenth century the population of the state had probably reached 350,000, of whom at least 50,000 resided in the capital, by then the wealthiest city in Spain.

As the city expanded, the role of the Jews declined. Their influence had peaked in the early eleventh century, when many Jews held fiscal and administrative offices and were prominent in the merchant community. In 1066 a violent reaction to Jews in government office resulted in the massacre of as many as 4,000 Jews. Yet unlike Mozarabs (Christians who had adopted Arabic culture), Jews were still to be tolerated in Granada, though their numbers were small by the fifteenth century.

Throughout the medieval period, Granada retained the appearance of a crowded Middle Eastern city. It was devoid of planned open spaces, and most of its maze of streets were no more than 3 to 4 feet wide. The narrow, crooked streets at least offered some protection from the intense sunlight, as did an abundance of shady gardens and courts. Artisans, who were grouped according to their craft in distinct quarters, produced linen and silk, much of it for export. Fruit, sugarcane, and almonds were also exported to pay for the grain that had to be imported to supplement inadequate domestic crops.

The city reached the peak of its glory during the rule of the Nasrid dynasty (1231–1492), which conquered Granada in 1238. For two and a half centuries, Granada was the sole Islamic state in Iberia, but it survived as such only by becoming a vassal of Castile. The latter exacted a heavy tribute and required Granada to provide military assistance, even in the work of the reconquista. The Nasrids patronized education and the arts, and their court attracted numerous learned Muslims. A university and a hospital for the sick and insane were

The Court of the Lions in the Alhambra is not only an exceptionally exquisite walled garden but a symbol of paradise. The four waterways that converge at the fountain represent the four rivers of paradise, while the twelve lions on the fountain symbolize the signs of the zodiac. [Arxiu Mas, Barcelona]

founded in the mid-1300s, and the city had three important libraries.

The grandest monuments of Granada's golden age are the Alhambra and the Generalife. The Alhambra, constructed mostly between 1238 and 1358, was a palatial fortress replete with barracks, mosques, and gardens. Built on a hilly terrace overlooking the city, the palace is richly decorated in an ornate Arabesque style with colored tiles and marble, geometric figures, and floral motifs. Its horseshoe arches, delicate columns, and graceful arcades are the culmination of Islamic architecture in Iberia. The nearby Generalife beautifully illustrates the description of paradise in the Koran as "a garden flowing with streams." Intended for summer use, the Generalife, with its pools, fountains, and trees, perfectly blends building and landscape architecture. A fourteenth-century observer justifiably described Granada in glowing terms: "No city can be compared to it as to its exterior or interior, and no country is like it with respect to the extent of its buildings, and the excellence of its position."[1]

RUSSIA AND THE MONGOL CONQUEST

While Christians were launching their crusades against the Muslims in Iberia and Palestine, the Mongols invaded Russia, which they ruled for two centuries. Just as the initial success of the crusaders in Palestine and the advances of the Christians in Iberia were facilitated by the internal weaknesses of their Muslim enemies, so the Mongol advance was made easier by Russian disunity.

The last of the great Kievan princes, Yaroslav the Wise (1019–1054), had been an effective ruler, extending the territory of his state, issuing the first written codification of East Slavic law, building numerous churches including the Kiev Cathedral, and supporting the translation of religious literature from Greek into Slavic. He had also strengthened ties between Russia and western Europe, in part by marrying his daughter Anne to the French King Henry I. But Yaroslav made a fatal mistake by implementing the rota system to determine succession to the throne. According to this system, the crown passed to the senior member of the ruling family rather than to the eldest son of a deceased ruler; in other words, brothers normally had preference over sons. Moreover,

each prince was assigned to a town suitable to his place in the line of succession. When the grand prince died, each prince was supposed to move up one step to the next highest town. Instead of providing for the peaceful succession of experienced rulers, the rota system fostered dissension. Rather than evolving into a centralized state, Russia disintegrated into a confederation of essentially independent principalities.

Long before the Mongols struck, Kiev was crippled by the assaults of the militant Cumans, a nomadic people who lived on the steppes. Their attacks, which began in the 1060s, eventually severed Kiev's access by the Dnieper River to the Black Sea and trade with Byzantium. This had the effect of directing Russian expansion to the forests of the north and west, away from the steppes and from ties with the Byzantine Empire. By 1200 the Russians were experiencing less and less contact with the rest of Christian Europe.

Commonly called Tartars or Tatars, the Mongols who invaded Russia in the early thirteenth century were militant nomads from Mongolia who had been united into a powerful confederation by Chinghis Khan (1155–1227). They had already launched assaults on China and Korea, while other military units pushed westward into Russia. At the death of Chinghis Khan the Mongols withdrew to their homeland to participate in the selection of his successor, but in 1237 they returned and within three years had overrun Russia. From there they invaded Poland, Silesia, Bohemia, Moravia, and Hungary, only to pull back to Russia when another khan died in 1241. In the late thirteenth century, under the leadership of Kubilai Khan, Chinghis' grandson, the Mongol Empire included Russia, Iran, China, and part of Southeast Asia—the largest empire known to this time. Within its borders, new possibilities existed for peoples of different cultures to communicate with and learn from each other.

Henceforth, medieval Russia was essentially divided into four regions. The Mongols dominated the southern steppes but exercised only moderate control over Great Russia, the region between the Volga and Oka rivers, which included the principality of Moscow. Western Russia, including the Ukraine, freed itself of Mongol control in the late medieval period, only to fall under the sway of Lithuania. The Mongols had the least influence over the vast principality of Novgorod in northern Russia. Novgorod enjoyed the advantage of a strategic commercial site on the Volkov River, but most of its territory was thinly populated because of its poor soil. Immigrants who left southern Russia to escape the Mongols gravitated mostly to the northeast, where the

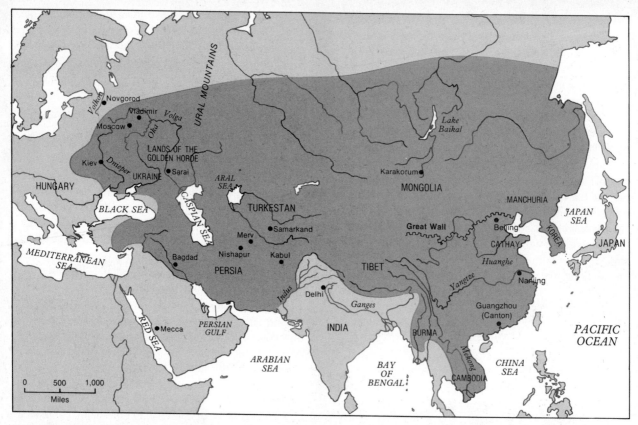

7.3 The Mongol Empire, c. 1300

soil was better and the rivers were more conducive to commercial development. This region provided the nucleus of the modern Russian state in the late medieval period. By that time the Mongols had left their impact on the Russians in such areas as military tactics, labor levies, and the development of new trade routes. Eastern influence remained strong well into the eighteenth century, when Russian rulers made a conscious effort to westernize their country.

SUMMARY

In political terms the Middle Ages witnessed the transition of England and France from decentralized feudal states to emerging national monarchies, but the course of

German and Italian history was strikingly different because of the imperial ambitions of the German rulers and the determination of the papacy to rejuvenate the church by controlling episcopal appointments. Although the popes won the struggle, destroying the Hohenstaufens in the process, they in turn succumbed to growing secular concerns and the forceful resistance of the French and English monarchs.

The century between the pontificates of Innocent III and Boniface VIII saw the beginnings of a process that eroded papal prestige and power over secular rulers. The change in papal fortunes was mirrored in the history of the crusading movement over which they tried in vain to preside. The early successes were more than offset by later failures as well as the increasingly materialistic motives of the participants. In the end, only the Iberian crusades achieved their objectives. The accomplishments of the High Middle Ages were nevertheless significant, not only with respect to the political achievements in France and England and the reforms in the church but also in terms of commerce and urban development, the founding of universities, scholastic and scientific thought, and the construction of majestic cathedrals.

Notes

1. A. G. Chejne, *Muslim Spain: Its History and Culture* (Minneapolis: University of Minnesota Press, 1974), p. 156.

Suggestions for Further Reading

Baldwin, J. W. *The Government of Philip Augustus: Foundations of French Royal Power in the Middle Ages.* Berkeley: University of California Press, 1986.

Barraclough, G. *The Origins of Modern Germany.* New York: Norton, 1984.

Chazan, R. *European Jewry and the First Crusade.* Berkeley: University of California Press, 1987.

Ennen, E. *The Medieval Town,* trans. N. Fryde. New York: Elsevier North-Holland, 1979.

Frame, R. *The Political Development of the British Isles, 1110–1400.* New York: Oxford University Press, 1990.

Hanawalt, B. A. *The Ties That Bound: Peasant Families in Medieval England.* New York: Oxford University Press, 1986.

Haverkamp, A. *Medieval Germany, 1056–1273,* trans. H. Braun and R. Mortimer. New York: Oxford University Press, 1988.

Hohenberg, P. M., and Lees, L. H. *The Making of Urban Europe, 1000–1950.* Cambridge, Mass.: Harvard University Press, 1985.

Imamuddin, S. M. *Muslim Spain, 711–1492 A.D.* Leiden: Brill, 1981.

James, E. *The Franks.* Oxford: Blackwell, 1988.

Lopez, R. S. *The Commercial Revolution of the Middle Ages, 950–1350.* Cambridge: Cambridge University Press, 1976.

Mayer, H. E. *The Crusades,* trans. J. Gillingham. London: Oxford University Press, 1972.

Obolensky, D. *The Byzantine Commonwealth: Eastern Europe, 500–1453.* New York: Praeger, 1971.

Petit-Dutaillis, C. *The Feudal Monarchy in France and England, from the Tenth to the Thirteenth Century,* trans. E. D. Hunt. New York: Barnes & Noble Books, 1964, 1980.

Postan, M. M., and Miller, E. *The Cambridge Economic History of Europe,* vol. 2: *Trade and Industry in the Middle Ages,* 2d ed. Cambridge: Cambridge University Press, 1987.

8

LIFE AND CULTURE IN MEDIEVAL EUROPE

The culture of Europe was forged primarily from Judeo-Christian values, classical concepts, and Germanic traditions. As it developed, it also owed much to the Islamic world. By the High Middle Ages (1050–1300), European culture was vigorously creative. Commercial developments were instrumental in shaping the new outlook, as the burgeoning cities became the setting for the cathedral schools and the first universities as well as Romanesque and Gothic cathedrals. Troubadours, professors, students, affluent merchants, and crusaders took their place in a Europe hitherto largely confined to feudal aristocrats, peasants, and parish clergy. This was an age of spiritual renewal, as reflected in the growth of papal power, the founding of new religious orders, and the brilliance of scholastic thought. But it was no less an age whose darker side boded ill for Jews as anti-Semitism mushroomed. Nor did the status of women improve despite their contribution to the accomplishments of the age.

THE MEDIEVAL CHURCH

Although Christianity was the dominant religion in medieval Europe, its adherents struggled to overcome a widespread belief in primitive natural forces and magic. Early medieval priests were missionaries in their own parishes, though in the course of time they won at least nominal adherence to Christianity. With its warnings of eternal damnation and its message of salvation through the sacraments, the church gradually shaped a code of conduct and a basic system of belief that was a unifying force.

In their efforts to win the hearts of the people, church leaders periodically clashed with their secular counterparts. Yet they were commonly allies in maintaining control over their subjects. Most rulers governed with the church's blessing, while secular authorities protected the church and assisted it in carrying out its policies. When conflicts did erupt, church leaders could seek support from their secular allies or employ two spiritual weapons, excommunication and the interdict. Excommunication technically prohibited an offender from participating in church rites or maintaining contact with other Christians, and if the sentence was not lifted prior to one's death, the offender was eternally damned. An interdict, imposed on a particular area, could bar all church services with the exception of baptism and extreme unction (last rites). To be effective, these penalties required popular support and could not be overused.

Monastic Communities

A characteristic feature of medieval Christianity was the founding of religious communities in which men and women lived in relative isolation from the rest of society. Such communities were initially established in Egypt and then spread throughout the Roman Empire. The first monastic communities in the West appeared in the late fourth and fifth centuries, but it was a monastery founded in Italy in 529 by Benedict of Nursia (480–547) that eventually had the greatest impact on European monasticism.

As a guide for the monks who joined him at Monte Cassino, south of Rome, Benedict wrote a rule designed to provide for an orderly existence conducive to the dedication of one's life to God. Unlike some of the other early monastic leaders, Benedict did not call for extreme forms of self-denial but insisted on moderation in a life of prayer, contemplation, study, communal worship, and labor. Monks vowed to follow a life of poverty, to be chaste, to obey their superiors, and not to leave the monastery without permission. An abbot, elected for life by the monks and consecrated by a bishop but accountable only to the Rule and to God, directed the monastery. Each monastery was intended to be self-sufficient; hence its members had to perform a variety of tasks that ranged from farming to making clothes. To educate novices and provide service books, Bibles, and other religious literature, the monks also had to teach and copy manuscripts. By the seventh century there were communities for Benedictine nuns, who regarded Benedict's sister Scholastica as their patron. Like the monasteries of the men, their convents spread throughout Europe in the ensuing centuries.

Apostolic Renewal: The New Religious Orders

Although the imperial revival under Otto I in the mid-tenth century threatened the independence of the papacy, a contemporary reform movement helped to restore its vigor and spiritual leadership. In 910, Duke William "the Good" of Aquitaine founded a monastery at Cluny in Burgundy, with a charter guaranteeing independence from secular control. By this time, control over other monasteries had fallen into the hands of feudal lords, who stripped their revenues and sold the monastic offices. To prevent this from happening at Cluny, William placed the monastery under papal protection; henceforth, its abbots owed their allegiance only to Rome. They insisted on major reforms in the church, including renewed emphasis on the Rule of Benedict and the monastic liturgy, an end to the sale of church offices, and the enforcement of clerical celibacy, which, though widely disregarded, had been church policy since the fourth century. The call to reform received a stunning

response: new foundations and converted Benedictine houses swelled the total of institutions based on the Cluniac model to more than 300, all of which were administered by priors who were subordinate to the abbot of Cluny.

The Cluniacs were the first wave of a series of reform-oriented monastic movements that swept the Latin church in the High Middle Ages. The Cistercians, founded in the twelfth century, were a Benedictine reform movement that emphasized individual devotion rather than public worship and agricultural labor rather than other forms of work. With austerity as their ideal, the Cistercians followed a rigorous vegetarian diet. They earned a well-deserved reputation for their skills in making marginal lands productive. Like other monastic orders, the Cistercians were less than enthusiastic about the thousands of women who wanted to become Cistercian nuns, though in the end the church resolved the issue by placing the convents under monastic supervision as a subordinate branch of the male order.

The richness of medieval Christian religious life is illustrated in the variety of orders that were founded. The Carthusians were far more rigorous than the Benedictines, insisting that each monk live in a separate cell, fast every Friday, and eat with his fellow monks only on Sundays and the major holy days. In sharp contrast to this solitary life, *canons regular* combined the monastic concept of living according to a rule with the duties of secular priests. Unlike the Benedictines and Cluniacs, they refused to amass large endowments, preferring instead to follow a humble lifestyle and aid the needy.

A third form of religious vocation originated in the thirteenth century with the founding of *mendicant* (begging) orders, so called because their friars depended on alms for their living. Like the monks and canons regular, they took vows of poverty, chastity, and obedience, and they lived in communities; unlike the monks, they devoted their lives to ministering to the laity. One of the principal mendicant orders was founded by the Spaniard Dominic (1170–1221) to fight the spread of heresy in southern France. The Dominicans, formally constituted in 1216, combated heresy by preaching, education, and holy living.

The other major mendicant order, the Franciscans, was established by Francis of Assisi (1182–1226), the son of an Italian cloth merchant. Francis and his followers, whose ideal was absolute poverty and humility, obtained papal approval for their order in 1209. The friars devoted themselves to the spiritual and material

needs of the lowly, particularly in the towns. At first the Franciscans shunned learning in preference to apostolic simplicity, but their growing competition with the Dominicans gradually persuaded them to engage in scholarly endeavors. Both mendicant orders became prominent in the universities and engaged in missionary work among the Muslims and the Mongols.

ST. CLARE AND THE POOR SISTERS

The life of Clare of Assisi illustrates the problems experienced by women attracted to the new religious movements. For most, including Clare, the lure was spiritual, though some may have been drawn to the religious life because they had little prospect of marriage, shunned the dangers of childbirth, or sought spiritual status to compensate for their inferior role in medieval society. But churchmen were generally troubled by the prospect of separate female orders. How could they support themselves? Because women were excluded from the priesthood, who would provide cloistered convents with pastoral care? Women, moreover, were thought to be unusually susceptible to heresy.

Born into a pious aristocratic family at Assisi in 1194, Clare was influenced by a mother known for her charitable deeds and pilgrimages. While her parents were arranging her marriage, Francis of Assisi secretly met with Clare to persuade her to pursue a more rigorous spiritual life. One night in 1212, at the age of 18, she fled to a nearby chapel, where Francis received her vows to lead a life of poverty and to imitate Christ and Mary. The "Poor Clares" or "Poor Sisters" date their origins from that event. The sisters were housed in the convent of San Damiano, near Assisi, where Clare acquired the title of abbess in 1216, a position she retained until her death.

The problem of procuring a rule for her order, already difficult because of antifemale sentiment, was compounded by the decision of the Fourth Lateran Council in 1215 not to allow any new orders. Francis had given Clare only verbal advice and a brief "way of life," but

Clare of Assisi, disciple of Francis and founder of the Poor Clares, as portrayed by the fourteenth-century Italian artist Simone Martini. [Scala/Art Resource, New York]

this had not been officially recognized. In 1219, therefore, Cardinal Ugolino, the future Pope Gregory IX, provided a rule based on Benedictine and Cistercian principles: an austere life, strict seclusion from the world, and the right of the community as a whole to own property. Having already taken a vow of absolute poverty, Clare opposed the property provision, an issue that remained a sore point until the last days of her life. Ugolino's intent was to place all the female groups under papal protection, with a single uniform rule and with pastoral care provided by the Franciscans. Francis, however, refused to be associated with any female community apart from that of Clare at San Damiano: "God has taken away our wives, and now the devil gives us sisters," he fumed, afraid that Ugolino's scheme would ruin his order.

Despite Francis' reluctance to accept pastoral responsibility for convents, he maintained close relations with Clare, who seems to have been his confidant. On one occasion she nursed him back to health at San Damiano, during which period he wrote his famous *Canticle of the Sun,* reflecting his remarkable sense of oneness with and love of nature. Her own writings reveal a strong commitment to poverty, which was especially striking because Clare and most of her followers came from aristocratic backgrounds. As she lay dying in 1253, she was visited by Pope Innocent IV, who at last approved the rule she had sought for more than three decades. It embraced a concept of poverty that allowed neither personal nor communal possessions apart from enough land on which to grow food. The continuation of the Poor Clares to the present day is largely due to the persistence and devotion of Clare, who was canonized in 1255.

Dissidents and Heretics

The spirit of reform that swept the church increased lay interest in religion, but one unintended result of this was the rapid growth of beliefs that the church considered heretical (unorthodox). In the 1170s the French merchant Peter Waldo of Lyons attracted disciples by emphasizing poverty and simplicity as well as attacking the moral corruption of the clergy. The Waldensians insisted on the right of laymen to preach, rejected some of the sacraments, and accepted the Scripture alone as authoritative in religion. Moreover, they wanted translations of the Bible in the language of the people. Although they were excommunicated in 1184, the Waldensians remained popular in southern France and northern Italy.

A more serious threat to the church was posed by the Albigensians in southern France. Their teaching viewed the universe in terms of a struggle between the forces of good and evil. The Cathari ("pure ones") were supposed to abstain from most material things, including marriage, worldly possessions, and meat, in their quest to attain a state of perfection. Some rejected the mass, infant baptism, and even the church itself. Voluntarily starving oneself to death was highly praised. Not only were the Albigensians condemned by the church, but Innocent III called for a crusade to exterminate them. Knights from northern France rallied to the call, interested more in the possibility of seizing land than in uprooting heresy. The harshest fighting lasted 20 years (1209–1229) and ultimately eradicated many of the heretics.

Another weapon to combat heresy was the Inquisition, instituted by Pope Gregory IX in 1231. The inquisitors' task was to convert the heretics if possible but in any case to prevent the deadly "disease" of heresy from spreading. The Inquisition embraced the principles of Roman law, including the use of torture. Suspects had no right to counsel, no opportunity to question witnesses, nor even the right to know the charges against them. Those who refused to relinquish their heretical beliefs or were convicted a second time were subject to imprisonment, loss of property, or burning at the stake. Because the inquisitors were not allowed to shed blood, executions were carried out by the state, but the church nevertheless left itself open to condemnation by relying on force rather than moral suasion to maintain its spiritual supremacy.

THE WORLD OF LEARNING

School Church Castles

The need to staff expanding governments with educated officials and the growth of towns, with their increasingly sophisticated businesses, their law courts, and their collection of taxes and fees, led to a greater demand for literate people. This was a major cause of the educational revolution of the late eleventh and twelfth centuries, as was the Gregorian stress on the importance of a better-educated clergy. Previously, most schooling in Europe had been provided by the monasteries and a few cathedral and secular schools. These early schools were insufficient, both in number and in curriculum, to meet the needs of the towns, the expanding royal courts, and the growing ecclesiastical bureaucracy.

The better cathedral schools, such as those at Chartres and Paris, included a music school, a school for the seven liberal arts (grammar, rhetoric, logic, arithmetic, geometry, astronomy, and music), and an advanced school for theological studies. Some ecclesiastical schools provided education in law, medicine, philosophy, and the natural sciences. At a humbler level, some parish priests taught reading, writing, mathematics, and the other liberal arts. The church's growing interest in education was evident in the late twelfth century, when it became mandatory for every cathedral to have a school and for each to be provided with funds sufficient to educate the children of the poor without charge.

In Italy, Germany, and the Netherlands, merchants took the lead in establishing municipal schools. Young people could also be trained as apprentices by surgeons, barbers, dentists, lawyers, notaries, architects, and artists.

The educational revolution of the High Middle Ages also involved curricular changes. Before the eleventh century the curriculum was heavily oriented toward biblical studies, but thereafter the emphasis shifted to logic. As more Latin translations of Arabic and Greek works on philosophy and natural science became available, these subjects too were the object of greater attention. The educational revolution increased lay literacy, though only a small minority could read and even fewer could write.

Scholarly Guilds: The Medieval University

As growing numbers of students traveled to Paris, Bologna, and Salerno in search of the best teachers, formal organization became necessary to secure the rights and privileges of students and teachers. There was also a need for some form of academic recognition— a "degree"—that would enable qualified individuals to teach in other cities. In a society accustomed to craft and merchant guilds, the natural solution was an academic guild, a universitas or corporation, that could protect the interests of faculty and students as well as issue licenses to teach. Organization was essential to ensure academic standards, provide protection from townspeople inclined to overcharge students for board and room, and obtain the right of faculty and students to be tried in church rather than local courts. In southern Europe, universities were initially guilds of students; in northern Europe they were guilds of teachers.

The earliest universities emerged at Bologna and Paris in the mid-twelfth century, and Salerno had a medical school. The University of Bologna, which became the leading center of legal studies, was chartered by the emperor Frederick Barbarossa in 1158. Students established regulations to govern the number, length, and content of lectures and fined or boycotted teachers who failed to cover the specified material or missed classes. The faculty controlled the granting of degrees, however, and, because of their permanence, gradually increased their authority in the university.

At Paris, teachers formed a guild to control the granting of licenses to teach, at least in part because the chancellor of the archdiocese of Paris had been selling them to unqualified individuals. After a "town-gown" conflict in which several students were killed, King Philip II gave the university its charter in 1200. Paris was famous for its teachers of logic, philosophy, and theology.

The growing demand for educated people in church and state, national and urban rivalries, and the search for more hospitable environments led to the founding of more universities—over 20 by 1300, more than 75 by 1500. A number of these were royal or papal foundations; others were the result of migrating students. In 1167, for instance, worsening relations between England and France forced King Henry II to order English students to return from Paris. They settled at Oxford, which had its own chancellor by 1214.

Most universities were organized into four faculties: the arts, which comprised the trivium (grammar, rhetoric, and logic) and the quadrivium (arithmetic, geometry, astronomy, and music), theology, medicine, and civil and canon law. The standard form of instruction was the lecture, which consisted of reading and expounding on a Latin text. A typical student listened to lectures for about seven hours a day. Formal debates were also standard, but because of the expense there were few books and small libraries. Students were not examined at the conclusion of a series of lectures but at the end of a program of study, when examinations were oral and usually public. A bachelor of arts degree typically took three to six years of study and qualified one to instruct others under a master's supervision. A license to teach required several more years of study. To lecture as part of the arts faculty, one had to become a master of arts, which required the preparation and defense of a thesis. Substantial additional study was required for a doctorate in law (up to 7 years) or theology (up to 15 years).

At first, universities had no permanent campuses or

buildings but made do with rented rooms. To assist needy students, residence halls or "colleges" were endowed, and these eventually acquired their own instructional staff. Among the best known are the Sorbonne, founded at Paris in 1257 or 1258, and Merton College, established at Oxford around 1263. Such colleges provided the nucleus of a permanent campus.

PARIS: MONKS, MERCHANTS, AND STUDENTS IN THE ROYAL CITY

By the time the University of Paris received its charter in 1200, the city was in the midst of a period of dramatic growth. At the beginning of the eleventh century its outskirts were still in ruins as the result of ninth-century Viking raids, but by 1300 the city's population had reached 100,000 and gloried in a majestic new cathedral, imposing new walls, and a flourishing commerce in addition to its university. The growth reflected in part the increasing power of the French monarchy, in part the city's strategic location at the crossroads of the trade routes between southern Europe and Flanders and, by way of the River Seine, between eastern France and the English Channel. Because the Capetian monarchs made Paris their capital, the city attracted both the nobility and ecclesiastical and educational institutions, thereby increasing the demand for luxury items and other goods. Parisian artisans produced a wide range of jewelry, swords, saddles, and linens. Merchants traded these goods at the Champagne fairs for Flemish and Italian woolens, Asian spices and sugar, Byzantine silks, Spanish leathers, and English tin.

The heart of Paris was the Île de la Cité, an island in the Seine whose western half was dominated by the royal palace. The eastern portion became the site of the magnificent Gothic cathedral of Notre Dame ("Our Lady"), begun in 1163. The city's commercial center, site of its guilds and principal markets, was on the right bank of the Seine. The Left Bank, or Latin Quarter, was the home of the university and of several religious orders. The Roman walls enclosed only some 25 acres and were therefore inadequate for the burgeoning city. Philip II ordered the construction of new ramparts on both banks. The resulting walls, which enclosed approximately 625 acres, were up to 20 feet high and 10 feet

thick. Just beyond the wall, where the rampart met the river, stood the Louvre, a fortified palace that also functioned as a treasury, an armory, and a prison. Philip's ambitious building program also included three new hospitals to care for the needy and three aqueducts to supply the city with fresh water.

Paris was a colorful amalgam of the secular and the sacred, the royal and the common. Law enforcement was the responsibility of the provost of Paris, who was appointed by the crown, but in general, city affairs were handled by a municipal council. Despite the presence of the crown and major religious orders, Paris was far from a puritanical city. Prostitutes were so abundant that two streets were named after them. The churchmen of Paris themselves sometimes behaved bawdily, and in 1212 a council convened in the city tried to curtail their more outlandish behavior, including the keeping of mistresses, the Feast of the Drunken Deacons on December 26, and the Feast of Fools on January 1, when they parodied the liturgy, burned old shoes instead of incense, and marched through the streets in grotesque costumes. All in all, Paris was one of the most exciting European cities of its day.

The Scholastics

Well before the evolution of the first universities, the schoolmen, or scholastics, of western Europe were engaged in heated debates. The scholastics, who used Aristotelian methodology and adopted the Aristotelian world view, were concerned with three fundamental and intimately related problems: the proper study of theological knowledge, the nature of ultimate reality, and the relationship of faith and reason.

Although the roots of Christian theology go back to the first century, only in the 1100s did the discipline of systematic theology emerge through the application of logic to fundamental religious questions. The leaders in this endeavor were Peter Abelard (1079–1142), a master in the cathedral school at Paris, and his disciple Peter Lombard (c. 1095–1160). Their technique, known as the *dialectical method,* juxtaposed seemingly contradictory statements to encourage students to seek a logical resolution. Abelard applied this technique to theology in his book *Sic et Non* ("Yes and No"), a compilation of contradictory statements by early church fathers on a variety of religious issues. Students were encouraged to resolve the conflicts by taking into account the way in which words change meaning over time, the possibility of inaccurate texts, historical context, and the need to weigh the credibility of different authorities. Peter Lombard used the same method in his *Four Books of Sentences,* which served as the standard theological text in the universities until the sixteenth century. Traditionalists condemned the logical approach to theology on the grounds that divine mysteries could not be probed by human reason.

The debate over the nature of reality reflected the indebtedness of the scholastics to classical Greek philosophy. In the eleventh century the French scholar Roscellin rejected the Platonic notion that universal concepts are real and instead insisted that reality consists only of individual things. Individual men and women are real; humanity is simply the name (*nomen*) for a mental category or concept. Roscellin and his followers thus came to be called Nominalists. Because they attached primary significance to the experience of individual things through the senses, the nominalists radically altered traditional theology, which had relied heavily on philosophical concepts. Nominalists asserted most religious beliefs solely on the basis of faith and biblical teaching, not rational demonstration.

In contrast to the Nominalists, Realists such as the Italian monk Anselm (1033–1109) asserted that individual things are knowable only because they reflect universal ideas, which are accessible by reason. Realists agreed that initially an act of faith is required for things beyond the reach of the senses. "I believe," said Anselm, "so that I may know." Once beyond this, reason could demonstrate the existence of universal ideas and even of God. It is impossible, Anselm argued, to conceive of a being greater than God; a being who exists is greater than a being who does not exist; therefore, the idea of God must include the existence of God.

A middle ground in the debate over universals was advocated by Moderate Realists. Influenced by Aristotle, they accepted the reality of both individual things and the general ideas upon which they were patterned. The idea of humanity was thus as real as the experience of individuals. The leading Moderate Realist, Thomas Aquinas (c. 1225–1274), taught that each particular thing has the universal within it, as that which gives it its essence; by studying individual things, one can rationally discover their essence and thus formulate valid general concepts.

At the heart of the debate over universals and the dialectical method was the question of the relationship between faith (or revelation) and reason. The scholastics generally agreed that theology and philosophy are intimately related, but Franciscan and Dominican thinkers disagreed over the nature of that relationship. The great Franciscan theologians Alexander of Hales (died 1245) and his pupil Bonaventure (1221–1274), both of whom taught at the University of Paris, stressed the primacy of revelation. To them, faith was an act of the will by which one accepts revealed truth; reason is useful only to explain the truth gleaned from revelation. The leading Dominican theologians, Aquinas and his teacher Albertus Magnus (died 1280), who also taught at Paris, accorded reason a greater role than did the Franciscans in the discovery of knowledge but stopped short of making revelation subordinate to reason. Aquinas believed that because faith and reason are complementary paths, by rational processes an unbeliever can be led to the point of making a commitment of faith.

Alexander of Hales and Aquinas wrote lengthy *summae* (summations) in which major theological issues were rationally analyzed through a process that included the meticulous refutation of opposing viewpoints. The blending of theology and philosophy is evident in Aquinas' *Summa Theologica,* particularly in the sections devoted to rational proofs for the existence of God, such as the argument from an orderly universe to the existence of a Great Designer. Aquinas' work represents the culmination of the attempt to synthesize the revealed tenets of Christianity with the rational principles of classical philosophy. Christian scholastics such as Aquinas, Jewish theologians such as Maimonides, and Muslim philosophers such as Averroës reflect the basic human quest to order existence and reaffirm basic ideals through the use of reason. Aristotle vs. Christianity

Law and Political Thought

Other scholars revived the study of Roman law in the late eleventh and early twelfth centuries. The revival began in southern France and northern Italy as teachers and attorneys turned to the *Corpus juris civilis* of Justinian for guidance. At Bologna, Irnerius and his successors lectured on the *Corpus* using the dialectical method popularized in theology by Abelard. Their work was largely confined to glosses or comments on the *Corpus,* but legal scholars soon began exploring the general principles on which the laws were based and adapting the laws to the conditions of their own time and locale. There was thus a gradual blending of Roman and customary law. Roman influence was especially evident in the work of codifying and systematizing the law, but it also resulted in the reintroduction of judicial torture. The impact of Roman law was greatest on the Italian and Iberian peninsulas.

Roman principles and procedures heavily influenced the development of church or canon law, which was codified in the twelfth century by Gratian, a monk who taught at Bologna. His text, the *Decretum* (c. 1140), used the dialectical method to organize and reconcile approximately 3,900 laws. Canon law in this period involved not only such religious matters as sacraments and church property but also slander, morals, tithes, wills, and oaths. Gratian's codification was the prelude to an increasingly judicial relationship between the church and its members.

Interest in political theory grew in large measure because of issues raised in the investiture controversy. Theorists who were sympathetic to the papacy claimed ever broader papal powers until at last they asserted the pope's right to intervene in secular matters as part of his responsibility to supervise temporal sovereigns. This was unacceptable to secular rulers, whose theorists extended the claim of royal authority until it included the duty to intervene in ecclesiastical affairs should the papacy prove incapable of reforming the church. Whereas papal writers contended that temporal sovereigns received their right to govern through the church as a divine agency, monarchical theorists insisted that God directly bestowed such power on the rulers.

Monarchical government was made to seem natural by the depiction of society in organic terms. The English scholar John of Salisbury (c. 1115–1180) developed the notion of the body politic, in which the sovereign is the head; the judges and governors are the ears, eyes, and tongue; the magistrates and soldiers are the hands; and the peasants are the feet. As an apologist for papal supremacy, John was then able to argue that the church is the soul of the body. John accepted the right of people to overthrow a tyrannical ruler on the grounds that tyranny was an abuse of the power God had bestowed on a ruler. Despite the democratic implications of this theory, John refused to consider rulers as being responsible to their subjects; if tyrants were overthrown, people acted only as divine agents, not in their own right. In general, medieval thinkers preferred monarchical government but expected sovereigns to rule justly in accord with divine law. The tendency was to see society and government in positive, natural terms: the state, said Aquinas, was a natural institution, not a necessary evil as Augustine had taught in the fifth century.

Science and Medicine

Although medieval thinkers failed to free science from its subservience to theology, they pointed the way to a more accurate understanding of the physical universe. The increased availability of Greek and Arabic treatises on science in Latin translation gave strong impetus to scientific study in Europe. One of the earliest interpreters of Arabic science was the twelfth-century English scholar Adelard of Bath, whose translation of Euclid's *Elements* from Arabic became the principal textbook for the study of geometry in the West. His own *Natural Questions* gave European students an insight into Arabic knowledge in such fields as astronomy, botany, zoology, and meteorology.

One of the most important contributions of medieval science was a growing awareness of the significance of observation and experiment as the best means to acquire knowledge of the physical world. Among the early advocates of this methodology were Albertus Magnus of Paris and Robert Grosseteste (c. 1175–1253) of Oxford, both of whom were influenced by Aristotle. Grosseteste's pupil, the English Franciscan Roger Bacon (c. 1220–1292), is noted more for his advocacy of experimental study than for specific contributions to scientific knowledge. Grosseteste and Bacon also made a significant contribution by advocating the importance of mathematics as a key to understanding the natural world.

Medical knowledge, too, was dependent on translations of Greek and Arabic works, among them the treatises of the Jewish physician Maimonides (1135–1204) and Avicenna, whose *Canon of Medicine* went through numerous editions. Arabic doctors had made major advances in the use of drugs, and this knowledge passed to Europeans, especially through the medical school at Salerno. Until it was surpassed by Montpellier in France about 1200, Salerno was the leading center of medical education in Europe, thanks largely to the presence of Greek and Arabic physicians. Among those who taught at Salerno were a number of women, including Trotula, author of the treatise *On Feminine Disorders*. Students at Salerno learned surgical techniques, though medieval operations were generally crude affairs in which modified butchers' instruments were used and amputation was common. Although anesthetics were coming into use, many patients suffered through operations, their pain deadened only by alcohol or opium. Death from shock or infection was common. The advance of medicine was reflected in the growth of hospitals; England had 18 in 1123 but 428 by 1300. Because of interest in optics, eyeglasses became fairly common in Italy in the thirteenth century, and there were even operations for cataracts. Much medieval practice was still grounded in superstition, such as the belief that sexual intercourse with a virgin would cure a man of various illnesses. Medicine remained primitive, not least because of its reliance on the Hippocratic theory of disease. The best treatment was often that administered by folk doctors who used herbal remedies and common-sense practices.

THE MEDIEVAL VISION

Between the eleventh and the fifteenth centuries, European artists developed new styles that reflected not only their Christian faith but also the outlook first of the monastic and feudal orders and then of the expanding cities. The Vikings, Normans, and Magyars had destroyed many wooden churches; hence the eleventh and twelfth centuries had ample incentive to rebuild—in stone wherever possible. Perhaps even greater motivation to build stemmed from the expanding economy, the need to provide churches for pilgrims on their way to holy places, and the pious spirit engendered by the religious reforms.

The Age of the Romanesque

The artistic style of the eleventh and twelfth centuries was largely shaped by the monastic revival and the militant ideals of the feudal order. The great abbey churches that epitomize the Romanesque style reflect the monastic values of order, simplicity, and otherworldliness. The religious revival also led to a substantial increase in the number of people who undertook pilgrimages to the shrines of the saints. The churches along the pilgrimage routes had to be larger than the traditional basilicas to accommodate the throngs of pilgrims. In the aftermath of the Viking and Magyar invasions there was also a desire to make the churches stronger, with stone instead of wooden ceilings and with facades that sometimes were reminiscent of feudal castles. Some Romanesque churches, such as that of Notre-Dame-la-Grande in Poitiers, look almost like fortresses because of their towers and thick walls.

Romanesque churches were constructed throughout

The nave and choir of the pilgrimage church of St. Sernin in Toulouse, France (c. 1080–1120) were built using a barrel, or tunnel, vault. The interior lighting is dim and indirect. [Marburg/Art Resource, New York]

Europe, the greatest number being in France. There were regional differences as the form developed, but the Romanesque (Roman-style) buildings shared fundamental characteristics, including a floor plan in the shape of a cross, the use of round arches and barrel (tunnel) vaults, and heavy buttresses to support the legs of the arches. The weight of the stone ceiling made it virtually impossible to cut windows into the sides of the barrel vault; hence the interior of early Romanesque churches was dark. Later Romanesque architects revived the Roman principle of the groined vault, by which intersecting arches distribute the weight of the ceiling to specific points along the wall. These points must be heavily buttressed, but windows can then be cut in the intervening spaces to illumine the interior of the church.

To adorn the churches, Romanesque artists revived the technique of stone sculpture, which had largely been forgotten during the eighth and ninth centuries. The figures they sculpted were intended to teach as well as to adorn, a function that was especially significant in an age when the overwhelming majority of the population was illiterate. Rich in symbols easily remembered by the faithful, Romanesque sculpture was a visual reminder of

Amiens Cathedral. Note the series of tiny chapels that radiate around the exterior of the choir in the lower part of the building. [Marburg/Art Resource, New York]

the fundamental teachings of the church. One of the most common locations for Romanesque sculpture was the semicircular space, called a *tympanum,* above the door of a church, which was often used to show Christ at the Last Judgment.

The monastic spirit of the Romanesque was also reflected in the paintings of the period, the most important of which were either murals in abbey churches rendered in a Byzantine style or miniatures that "illuminated" (illustrated) manuscripts. The latter were often painted by monks and nuns already devoted to copying manuscripts. Some miniaturists depicted religious scenes; others created intricate capital letters. The miniatures served as models for murals and later for the stained glass windows that decorated Gothic churches.

The Gothic Achievement

The world of the Gothic artist was not primarily that of the monastic and the pilgrim but of the city and the scholastic theologian. Gothic cathedrals were triumphs of the urban spirit, a testimony to the civic pride that

manifested itself in rivalries between the cities. The Gothic achievement was equally a testimony in stone to the synthesis of theology and philosophy that the scholastics were forging. Just as reason became the servant of faith to bridge the gap between heaven and earth, so the soaring spires and lofty vaults of the Gothic cathedral carried the vision of the worshiper logically and compellingly heavenward. The principles of scholastic theology and Gothic architecture share the conviction that reason and nature are not stumbling blocks but pathways to spiritual truth.

The principles of the Gothic style were initially worked out in the abbey church at St. Denis, near Paris, in the 1130s and 1140s. The goal was to construct a skeletal framework strong enough to support the stone roof yet airy enough to permit the extensive use of stained glass. By using pointed instead of round arches, the architects could achieve greater height and enclose rectangular as well as square spaces. At Beauvais the groined vaulting with its supporting ribs soared to the incredible height of 157 feet, only to collapse and have to be rebuilt. The Gothic architect also introduced the flying buttress, a support that carried the horizontal thrust of the arch to heavy piers outside the church. The purpose was twofold: placing the massive piers outside the church created a more spacious interior, and the flying buttress, like the pointed arch, guided the eye of the beholder heavenward.

The abundant stained glass windows, some of which may have been done by women, give the interior of a Gothic cathedral an ethereal quality. Like sculpture, the windows had a pedagogical as well as an aesthetic function, and to the degree that they encouraged worship, they had a liturgical role as well. The windows took the place of the mosaics and murals that had decorated earlier churches.

As in the Romanesque period, sculpture adorned the cathedrals, but more lavishly. The cathedral at Chartres, for instance, has more than 2,000 carved figures. In keeping with the attempt to unite the physical and the spiritual, Gothic statuary became more naturalistic in its representation of people and in its rendering of plants and animals. Unlike their Romanesque predecessors, Gothic artists, some of whom were women, began to use human models for their statues so that their work captured elements of individual personality. Simultaneously, convention required the continued use of traditional iconographic symbols, which restricted artistic freedom but ensured that viewers would be able to interpret the art's religious meaning. The range of subject matter was more extensive than that of the Romanesque era, so much so that Gothic cathedrals, with their myriad statues and stained glass, may be likened to visual encyclopedias.

VERNACULAR CULTURE AND THE AGE OF CHIVALRY

Apart from the Anglo-Saxon tradition, the literature of the early medieval period was nearly all in Latin, though a rich oral tradition created and preserved stories and poems in the *vernacular,* the language of the people. The most important vernacular work from the early medieval period is *Beowulf,* a poem about a Swedish hero who saved the Danes from a monster and its mother. Written in England by a monk around the eighth century, *Beowulf* reflects the values of the period: loyalty, valor, and aristocratic worth. About the same time, Bede (c. 673–735), a Benedictine monk commonly called "the Venerable" because of his piety and learning, wrote the

Ecclesiastical History of the English Nation, the primary source of our knowledge about English history from the time Christianity was introduced in 597 until 731. His classic, written in Latin, was translated into Anglo-Saxon by King Alfred the Great (871–899) and the scholars at his palace school.

During the High Middle Ages much of the material that had only been transmitted orally was written down, still in the vernacular; to this body of material were added new works, both secular and religious. The richness of this body of vernacular literature is reflected in the fact that it appeared in no fewer than eight major literary forms: heroic epics, minstrel songs, courtly romances, allegorical romances, mystery and miracle plays, pious writings, historical works, and popular stories. Latin was the language of the learned—of lawyers, ecclesiastics, and scholastics—but beginning in the eleventh century, the vernacular tongues increasingly became the language of literary entertainment. Although literacy rates remained low, these works undoubtedly reached wide audiences as the literate read them aloud to others.

The earliest heroic epics were the *chansons de geste* ("songs of heroic deeds"), composed in the northern French vernacular. In oral form, they go back to the ninth and tenth centuries, when they were used to entertain pilgrims traveling to the shrines of southern France and northern Spain. The most popular is the *Song of Roland,* the legendary account of a Muslim attack on Charlemagne's rear guard as it retreated across the Pyrenees. The poem exalts feudal virtues: personal loyalty, Christian faith, and individual honor. The conflict with Islam is also the setting for the famous Spanish *chanson* of the twelfth century, the *Poem of My Cid,* the fictionalized account of a chivalric lord who conquered Valencia. The great German epic, the *Nibelungenlied* (c. 1200), recounts the mythical quest for a hoard of Rhine gold in an atmosphere of love, treachery, and violence. Although the written version has a Christian veneer, at root it reflects pagan Germanic mythology. In spirit it is akin to the twelfth- and thirteenth-century Scandinavian *Eddas,* which recount the stories of pagan gods and heroes. Such works represent a simple historic interest in a largely mythical past dominated by valiant heroes and heroines.

French poets took the lead in composing minstrel songs, particularly in the south, where troubadours sang their lyrical lines in the Provençal dialect. These *chansons d'amour* ("songs of love") were popular in the twelfth and thirteenth centuries throughout western

Europe. Whereas the *chansons de geste* helped establish the code of knightly conduct called chivalry, the *chansons d'amour* popularized the concept of courtly love. The key to this concept is the exaltation of women and love, sometimes in a platonic rather than a physical sense. The minstrels encouraged the adoration of the wife of someone of a higher social degree, expecting in return at least simple kindness and inner joy if not physical pleasure. The Germans had their counterpart to the troubadours in the *Minnesingers* ("love singers"), whose lyrics were more spiritual than those of the French *chansons.* Women wrote romantic lyrics, though they did not exalt men as the male poets did women in the literature of courtly love.

The courtly love of the minstrels was united with the *chansons de geste* to create the courtly romance, the most famous of which are the late-twelfth-century works of Chrétien de Troyes about King Arthur. In these stories the adventurous knight sought his identity in the dangerous world beyond the royal court. Cistercian influence in the thirteenth century led to the addition of the theme of the Holy Grail, purportedly the chalice used by Christ at the Last Supper and later taken to Britain. In the 1200s, two French authors, William de Lorris and Jean de Meun, combined allegory and satire with the romance to create the popular *Romance of the Rose.* William's portion treats traditional troubadour themes of love in an allegorical mode, but Jean satirizes everything from women to clerical celibacy.

Although most religious literature was still written in Latin, vernacular works began to win a wider audience. Mystery plays—religious dramas about biblical subjects, especially Christ's life—were often in Latin and in fact originated as part of the Latin liturgy. As fictitious matter was added, the plays acquired a separate identity, opening the way for vernacular versions. Beginning in the fourteenth century, these plays were no longer the province of the clergy but community productions typically performed, by women as well as men, during church festivals. A variation of the mystery play, the miracle play, took as its theme the life of a saint; one such was the twelfth-century English drama about St. Catherine, which must have been particularly interesting to women. The miracle and mystery plays gave rise to morality plays, such as *Everyman,* which personified vices and virtues in the context of a struggle for the soul.

The variety of vernacular literature provides a healthy corrective to the common notion that medieval people were inordinately concerned with religious issues. Instead, they demonstrated a pronounced interest

in such themes as chivalry, courtly love, and the mythical and mysterious past and in bawdy stories and tales of violence and romance.

MEDIEVAL JEWRY

usury—
charge intrest on
borrowed money

No discussion of medieval life and culture can fail to acknowledge the significant contribution of the Jews. During the period of the Roman Empire they migrated throughout Europe, as far afield as Spain, France, and the Crimea. Small Jewish communities also established themselves to the east, from Arabia and Persia to India and China. Many of the earliest Jewish settlers in the West were farmers, an occupation in which they continued for centuries in southern Europe, but most of the Jews who settled farther north engaged in commerce as town life developed. Charlemagne welcomed Jewish immigrants by granting them charters that guaranteed protection and privileges. The Capetian kings of France continued this policy, making France a center of medieval Jewry. The German Jewish communities were founded by immigrants from France and southern Europe beginning in the ninth century. Few Jews emigrated to Scandinavia, and England was the last major European country where they settled. The extensive Jewish settlements in Europe and their contributions to Jewish culture ensured that in the future the Jews would be fundamentally European in outlook.

As Europeans turned increasingly to commercial activities in the High Middle Ages, Jewish merchants were slowly squeezed out of commerce and into money-lending. Because the Christian church prohibited usury—lending money at unjust rates of interest—many people had to obtain their loans from Jewish businessmen. When the Lombards introduced systematic banking, many Jewish moneylenders were forced to become pawnbrokers.

The crusades had a devastating impact on European Jews as various church leaders incited hatred against non-Christians in general. The Jews were a tempting target, particularly to Christians inflamed by charges that Jews had murdered Christ and were sacrificing Christian children at the Passover feast. The first persecution occurred at Metz in Lorraine and then spread from the Rhineland into France and England. Christian bigotry reached as far as Palestine, where the crusaders burned a synagogue full of Jews in 1097. Some

Jews preferred to die with swords in their hands, but many committed suicide rather than be killed by Christians. The pattern of persecution was reinforced in the 1300s, when Jews became scapegoats for the Black Death, for which they continued to be blamed well into the sixteenth century. ~~forced to live in ghetoes~~

The Third and Fourth Lateran Councils furthered the climate of hostility against the Jews. Despite the fact that the Councils' decrees were not thoroughly implemented, Gentiles were not supposed to be servants of Jews, nor were they allowed to live in the same districts, a regulation that encouraged the development of separate Jewish quarters. Jews had to wear identifying badges and attend Christian sermons designed to convert them. Christian officials censored or confiscated Jewish books. The Holy Roman Empire asserted proprietary rights over its Jews, making them virtually the property of the crown, and other states followed suit. Many Jews fled to Poland and Lithuania, only to become the legal property of the nobility. In practice, proprietary rights had little effect on Jewish life or freedom of movement, but they provided the justification for special taxes and finally for the expulsion of the Jews from much of Europe. The expulsions forced the Jews eastward, particularly to Poland—where King Boleslav the Pious granted them a charter in 1264 to guarantee their liberties—and to the Ottoman Empire. ~~August of 1492 - 20 ships full of Jews going to N. Africa because of exile~~

Between Two Cultures: The Jews in Spain

One of the principal centers of Jewish culture in the medieval era was Spain, where the pre-Islamic community was strengthened by Jewish colonists and traders who followed in the wake of the Arab conquests. Jews enjoyed considerable freedom in Islamic Spain, mostly because of their key role in commerce and their intellectual attainments. One of the important patrons of Jewish learning was Hasdai ibn-Shaprut (c. 915–970), himself a Jew and the confidant of two caliphs. Trained in medicine and skilled in Latin as well as Arabic, Hasdai supported Jewish poets and Hebrew scholars, initiating a brilliant era of Jewish culture. The poetic revival culminated in the hymns to Zion by the physician Judah ha-Levi (1086–1141). Jewish scholars translated Greek classics into Arabic and then from Arabic into Latin, paving the way for advancements in mathematics, medicine, astronomy, and cartography. The more enlightened Christian rulers, such as the emperor Frederick II and Alfonso the Wise, king of Castile, recognized the significance of these contributions and extended their patronage to Jewish scholars. Thus one of the principal avenues for the revival of classical learning in Europe came by way of the Arabs and the Jews.

The greatest medieval Jewish scholar was Moses ben Maimon (1135–1204), popularly known as Maimonides. A native of Spain, he spent most of his life in Cairo, where he served as court physician. As a philosopher he made contributions to Judaism comparable to those of Thomas Aquinas in Catholic theology. His major work, the *Mishneh Torah* ("Repetition of the Law"), was a *summa* of Judaism—a systematic presentation of rabbinic teachings that earned him the reputation of being a second Moses. Maimonides' approach to religion was highly rational, reflecting the views of Aristotle and Avicenna. His *Guide to the Perplexed* includes rational arguments for the existence of God, among them the thesis that there must be an Unmoved Mover. Although his views influenced Christian scholastics, the Dominicans were finally persuaded by conservative rabbis that Maimonides' works endangered the Christian faith, and they were banned in 1234.

Medieval Judaism also had a mystical tradition. In the twelfth and thirteenth centuries, Jewish mystics known as *Hasidim* ("Pietists") were active in the Rhineland. Probably influenced by Christian monks, they combined a penitent's life with the conviction that God can be found through humility rather than visions. Much of the opposition to Maimonides came from mystics in Provence and Spain known as Cabalists ("Traditionalists"), who believed that every letter of the Law has a mystical meaning that can be revealed only to the initiated. Jewish and Christian mystics were one in their conviction that the deepest meaning of religion is profoundly spiritual and cannot be attained by rational processes. Christianity and Judaism were thus strikingly similar in their search for a rational synthesis and the subsequent reaction of those who favored a mystical approach to God.

WOMEN AND MEDIEVAL SOCIETY

Although medieval women were rarely subjected to the kind of persecution experienced by the Jews, their social position began to erode around the late eleventh century. In the early medieval period, wives of clergymen and warriors often enjoyed social prominence and economic responsibility because they managed their households or estates while their husbands were away. Women often owned land, particularly in southern France and Spain, where there were no legal restrictions on a woman's right to administer family property. Within the feudal order, the chivalric ideal reinforced the role of women as managers of domestic and estate affairs by stressing the male's role as a warrior and a vassal. This was truer in France and Germany, where chivalry had the greatest impact, than in Italy, where chivalric ideas were slow to win acceptance.

Throughout the medieval era, women tended to enjoy greater power and prominence in periods of heavy military activity or vigorous expansion into new regions. The military campaigns of Charlemagne, the crusades, and the reconquista took men from their homes for lengthy periods and exposed them to the hazards of war and disease. During such periods, substantial amounts of property were left in the care of wives and sisters as well as the church. Against the background of the crusades, western Europeans developed the cult of courtly love, and troubadours exalted aristocratic ladies.

Simultaneously, however, developments in the religious and political sphere began to undermine the position of clerical wives and women of the feudal order. In religion the decline was sparked by the Gregorian reforms of the late eleventh century, which had an adverse effect on women by insisting on clerical celibacy, thereby weakening the role of women in parish activities, and by seeking to curtail the ability of laymen and women to nominate candidates for church offices. These reforms were not fully effective until well beyond the medieval period, but the attempts to enforce them boded ill for women. So too did the growing importance of the bishops in the High Middle Ages, a development related to the growth of urban life. Bishops had no female counterparts, whereas during the period when the church had been dominated by monasteries, women had achieved positions of leadership as prioresses and abbesses. Monastic life continued, but power gradually shifted into the hands of the bishops. The trend toward more exclusively male leadership was encouraged by the growth of cathedral schools and universities, neither of which were open to females. Unless they had private tutors, girls could hope for education only in the convents, but from the twelfth century on, these establishments were interested primarily in religious rather than academic pursuits.

The church's repressive attitude toward women became especially apparent in the thirteenth century, by which time thousands of women had organized themselves into religious communities. The male orders reluctantly agreed to provide some form of discipline, but female orders remained subservient branches of their male counterparts. In general this was because women were thought to be undisciplined, prone to heretical ideas, and less than serious in their commitment to the religious life. The Franciscans, Dominicans, and Cistercians resisted the attachment of subordinate convents but were overruled by the papacy. Faced with a church hierarchy determined to relegate them to subordination in all things spiritual, some women joined heretical groups such as the Waldensians, in which they could preach and administer the sacraments.

The influence of Christianity on medieval women was in other respects positive, as in the attention given to the Virgin Mary, whose influence extended throughout the High and late Middle Ages. The faithful credited her with performing miracles and commemorated her life with special festivals. Revered as the queen of heaven, Mary symbolized the dignity to which women could aspire. Pilgrims flocked to her shrines, many churches were dedicated to her, and numerous other churches had lady chapels in her honor. Expressions of love to the Virgin paralleled those to aristocratic women in the literature of courtly love; the practical effect of both movements was a tendency to idealize women.

In the secular realm the development of stronger governments blocked women from many areas of political involvement. As long as state governments were ineffectual and real power resided in the great aristocratic families, women had an opportunity to assert themselves in political affairs. But as state governments revived, they required the services of lawyers and clerks to staff their treasuries and courts, and women had no access to the training that prepared people for such positions.

Changing inheritance laws also adversely affected women. A woman in the feudal order was generally allowed to inherit a fief, subject to her ability to meet the feudal obligations. In practice this meant the lord's right to arrange her marriage to a suitable vassal. Because a fief typically involved military responsibilities, her husband usually assumed control of the estate. But aristocratic families were increasingly determined to preserve their power by excluding females and younger sons from any substantive inheritance in order to keep their estates intact. This was accomplished by the principles of primogeniture and the indivisibility of *patrimony,* by which an estate had to pass to the eldest son. Daughters received dowries and dowers, the latter being the assurance of an income during widowhood, but they were excluded from inheriting a portion of the family estate. If she had no brothers, the eldest daughter could usually inherit the estate.

For women of humbler status, economic needs often mandated a relative equality between men and women, particularly those in rural areas who worked beside their husbands in the fields or who devoted some of their time in the home to brewing ale or making cloth to sell. In the countryside, women regularly hired themselves out to bailiffs on the greater estates, where they performed virtually every form of labor except heavy plowing. Much of the sheepshearing was done by women, as were the dairy and poultry chores. In the towns, women were found in virtually all crafts. Masters' wives were active in many guilds, often training female apprentices. Widows regularly carried on their husbands' crafts, and those who had been married to merchants sometimes took over their husbands' business dealings. Many women were employed in domestic service; others managed their own shops. Some women worked in the mines, although their pay was less than that of the men. The female labor force was crucial to the medieval economy.

SUMMARY

The High Middle Ages was a period of intellectual and cultural achievement. The growth of cathedral schools and the rise of universities invigorated European life and made possible the training of better-educated clergy and government officials. Scholastics made a daring attempt to synthesize all knowledge, a development that focused attention on natural science. The growth of medical schools set the stage for improved health care. Virtually all of these accomplishments occurred in the context of an urban revival sparked by an expanding economy. The cities provided the setting for brilliant artistic achievements, particularly the age of the Gothic, which owed so much to the Romanesque era. The Gothic cathedrals, resplendent with their towering spires, soaring vaults, flying buttresses, and stained glass, were the perfect visual symbol of the age of faith.

But for two groups—women and Jews—the High Middle Ages brought a relative deterioration in their position. Excluded from the cathedral schools and the universities, women increasingly found themselves shunted aside in politics as well. Law and theology were forbidden areas, and women were banned from the parsonages in which they had once lived as priests' wives. The exalted status women received in the courtly love tradition was scant compensation. The Jews, whose intellectual accomplishments influenced and were the equal of scholastic thought, were thrust into a nightmarish world of expulsion, exile, and massacre.

Suggestions for Further Reading

Artz, F. B. *The Mind of the Middle Ages, A.D. 200–1500,* 3d ed. Chicago: University of Chicago Press, 1980.

Ben-Sasson, H. H., ed. *A History of the Jewish People.* Cambridge, Mass.: Harvard University Press, 1976.

Berman, H. *Law and Revolution: The Formation of the Western Legal Tradition.* Cambridge, Mass.: Harvard University Press, 1983.

Bony, J. *French Gothic Architecture of the Twelfth and Thirteenth Centuries.* Berkeley: University of California Press, 1983.

Brooke, C. N. L. *The Twelfth Century Renaissance.* New York: Harcourt Brace & World, 1969.

Cobban, A. B. *The Medieval Universities: Their Development and Organization.* London: Methuen, 1975.

Herlihy, D. *Medieval Households.* Cambridge, Mass.: Harvard University Press, 1985.

Jackson, W. T. H. *Medieval Literature: A History and a Guide.* New York: Collier, 1966.

Keen, M. *Chivalry.* New Haven, Conn.: Yale University Press, 1984.

Lawrence, C. H. *Medieval Monasticism: Forms of Religious Life in Western Europe in the Middle Ages.* White Plains, N.Y.: Longman, 1984.

McInerny, R. *Romanesque.* New York: Harper & Row, 1978.

Moore, R. I. *The Formation of a Persecuting Society: Power and Deviance in Western Europe, 950–1250.* New York: Blackwell, 1987.

Russell, J. B. *A History of Medieval Christianity: Prophesy and Order.* New York: Crowell, 1968.

Shahar, S. *The Fourth Estate: A History of Women in the Middle Ages,* trans. C. Galai. New York: Methuen, 1983.

Talbot, C. H. *Medicine in Medieval England.* London: Oldbourne, 1967.

9

CRISIS AND RECOVERY IN EUROPE

F amine, pestilence, war, and death—the four horse-men·of the Apocalypse—ravaged Europe in the fourteenth century. The devastation inflicted by the bubonic and pneumonic plagues, recurring famine, and the Hundred Years' War contributed to serious economic decline and a change in people's outlook. The prestige of the papacy suffered too when its headquarters shifted to Avignon, which proved to be the prelude to the most scandalous schism in the history of the western church. About 1450, Europe began to experience a dramatic revival as population growth resumed, commerce and manufacturing expanded, and the states of western Europe and Russia attained greater unity and built strong central governments. In Italy, Germany, Hungary, and Poland, however, territorial princes and cities prevented the growth of centralized states. Europe in the fourteenth and fifteenth centuries moved from an age of adversity to one of recovery and, in doing so, laid the foundations for the early modern era.

FAMINE AND THE BLACK DEATH

From the late tenth through the thirteenth centuries the population of Europe grew as farmers expanded the amount of land under cultivation and increased the supply of food. But neither the population nor the food supply increased uniformly, and marginal settlements, where the possibility of extreme hunger was always high, arose throughout Europe. Even in the more prosperous agricultural regions, poor distribution facilities often resulted in pockets of famine. By 1300 the population had expanded so rapidly that most Europeans faced grave peril should the fragile agricultural economy be disrupted by unfavorable changes in the weather patterns. The warming trend that characterized the mid-eighth to the mid-twelfth centuries was reversed as Europe entered the first Little Ice Age, which lasted approximately two centuries.* In the late thirteenth century, heavy rains and unexpected freezes began to wreak havoc on the food supply. The threat of famine culminated between 1315 and 1317 in the greatest crop failures of the Middle Ages. Soaring grain prices placed food beyond the reach of many, especially in urban areas, where sometimes as many as one person in ten died from starvation or malnutrition. As famines recurred throughout the fourteenth century, the most serious consequence was the debilitating effect of chronic and severe malnutrition on much of the population. Physically weakened, most Europeans were highly vulnerable to disease, especially tuberculosis.

The most dreadful disease in the late Middle Ages, the bubonic plague, is caused by bacteria that live in an

---

*Another occurred in the late seventeenth century.

The fourth horseman of the Apocalypse: "And I saw, and behold, a pale horse, and its rider's name was Death, and Hades followed him; and they were given power over a fourth of the earth, to kill with sword and with famine and with pestilence and by wild beasts of the earth" (Revelation 6:8). To the people of the fourteenth and fifteenth centuries this prophecy seemed to be coming true in their own age. [Giraudon/Art Resource, New York]

fatal, especially if the pus was thoroughly drained from the boil; up to half its victims survived. A more virulent form of the plague—the pneumonic variety—was transmitted by coughing and was nearly always fatal. Both forms devastated Europe.

The bacterial strains responsible for the plague came from the Gobi Desert of Mongolia. By 1339 the plague had begun its westward march, carried by migrating central Asian rodents and by traders along the caravan routes and shipping lanes. In the ensuing decade it spread throughout the Muslim world, killing a third of the people and possibly as many as half of those who lived in towns.

The Black Death was brought to Sicily in October 1347 by a Genoese ship carrying infected rats. Within months the plague struck Venice and Genoa, then spread throughout the rest of Italy. By 1349 the infected areas stretched from Ireland and Norway to Vienna, finally reaching western Russia in 1351. Severe outbreaks again struck Europe in 1362 and 1375. Until the end of the fifteenth century, no decade passed without at least one outbreak, and the plague continued to pose a serious threat to Europeans for two centuries after that. The Black Death of the late 1340s probably claimed 25 million lives, perhaps a third of Europe's population. No war in history has destroyed so large a percentage of the people.

Europeans had no knowledge of the cause of the plague, though many attributed it to something mysterious in the atmosphere; many Christians were convinced that it was divine punishment for their sins. Some people fled from the towns to the countryside, where the pestilence was less frequent. Convinced of imminent death, some people pursued sensual pleasures. Others turned to ascetic extremes; itinerant flagellants, for example, whipped themselves, wore penitential dress, and bore crucifixes. Others turned to black magic and witchcraft, while some blamed the Jews, many of whom were massacred. Many physicians fled, whereas the clergy often ministered to the sick and thus suffered extensively themselves.

Hundreds of villages were severely depopulated or disappeared altogether, reducing the value of land and driving up wages as the labor supply plummeted. Peasants who survived found their services in greater demand and could obtain better terms from their landlords or find more accommodating ones elsewhere, while others moved into the towns as artisans. Falling rents and rising wages prompted landowners to seek legisla-

animal's blood or a flea's stomach and is thus easily transmitted, particularly by fleas on rats. The first symptom in a human is a small pustule at the point of the flea bite, followed by the swelling of the lymph nodes in the neck, armpit, or groin. Then come dark spots (buboes, for which the plague is named) on the skin caused by internal bleeding. In the final stage the victim, convulsed by coughing spells, spits blood, exudes a foul body odor, and experiences severe neurological and psychological disorders. Bubonic plague was not always

tion fixing wages at low levels and restricting access to urban occupations.

Catastrophe and Rebellion

In Europe the dislocation caused by the plague coupled with the restrictive measures against the peasants and the artisans contributed to explosive unrest in the late fourteenth century. In 1358 many peasants in northern France joined in uprisings known as the Jacquerie (*jacques* was a name nobles used to address a peasant). Already embittered by efforts to limit their wages, the peasants were angered by heavy financial exactions to support French forces in the Hundred Years' War and by marauding bands of mercenaries from whom the nobles offered them no protection. The peasants killed, raped, burned, and even destroyed a number of castles. They had, however, neither strong leaders nor a program of reform. Priests, artisans, and lesser merchants joined them before the nobles ruthlessly suppressed the rebellion. In the end, some 20,000 people died.

Social revolt erupted in England in 1381, fueled by the peasants' resentment of efforts to restrict their economic advances, bitterness over aristocratic cruelty toward them, and governmental efforts to impose a poll (head) tax to pay for the war against France. Peasants in the south, where the rebellion broke out, were also upset by French raids on their lands. Led by the priest John Ball and the journeyman Wat Tyler, the revolt soon spread throughout much of the country as urban workers joined the peasants. The nobles regrouped and carried out a campaign of retribution. Radical rebel demands—the equality of all men before the law, the granting of most church property to the people, and the end of mandatory peasant labor on the lords' personal lands—were not met, though the government ceased collecting the poll tax.

The Jacquerie and the Wat Tyler rebellion are but the most famous examples of the revolts that swept parts of Europe in the century after the Black Death first appeared. The peasants of Languedoc rose up in 1382 and 1383, Catalonian peasants were frequently in arms, and peasants and miners rebelled in Sweden in 1434. Much of the unrest erupted in the cities, where artisans demanded more political power and where the working poor were chained in poverty by repressive guilds. The greatest urban revolt was that of the *ciompi* (cloth workers) in Florence in 1378. No other period in the Middle Ages experienced as much social unrest as the century 1350–1450.

THE HUNDRED YEARS' WAR

Between 1337 and 1453 the English and French engaged in the Hundred Years' War, though they spent less than half of this period in actual fighting. Each side went to war because it felt that the other threatened its security and blocked its rightful ambitions. The war began when Edward III of England (1327–1377) claimed the French throne as his own. The last three Capetian monarchs, the sons and heirs of Philip IV, had died without leaving a male heir. Although Edward III, Philip's maternal grandson, was the closest male heir, the French nobles supported the claim of Philip of Valois, a nephew of Philip IV's sons. English involvement in France stood squarely in the way of the ambition of the French sovereigns to extend their authority throughout the country. No less important as a cause of the war was Anglo-French rivalry over Flanders. Its count was Philip's vassal, but Flemish towns depended on English wool for their textile industry. English support for the Flemings when they rebelled against their count threatened French domination in the region, whereas French control jeopardized English trade. Another grievance was France's support for the Scots, which prevented the English from exercising lordship over their northern neighbors.

As the two sides embarked on war, France was seemingly the stronger, with greater wealth and a population three times the size of England's. The French had the advantage of fighting on terrain they knew, but this subjected their peasants to the ravages of war. The French kings, moreover, had to cope with the fact that some of their own subjects, such as the Burgundians, allied with the English at various times during the war. For most of its duration the French monarchs were unable to provide either strong military leadership or sound fiscal policies to finance the fighting. The English, despite the popular support marshaled by Edward III and a string of military victories, were unable to inflict a total defeat on France because they had neither the troops nor the funds to dominate such a vast land. In the end the English were largely reduced to a policy of intimidation, which failed in the face of renewed French resolve.

England's early victories were the result of the military superiority of its longbowmen, who could lay down a barrage of arrows powerful enough to pierce French armor at a distance of up to 200 yards. The effectiveness of the English archers was demonstrated at Crécy in 1346, at Poitiers a decade later, and at Agincourt in 1415. The turning point of the war came in 1429 as the English besieged Orléans. Charles, the dauphin (crown prince), his plight desperate, gambled on an illiterate peasant girl who claimed to have been sent by heavenly messengers. Accompanied by fresh troops, Joan of Arc, though only 17, inspired the French with a vision of victory. When the Burgundians captured Joan a year later, the English hoped to discredit her by having her tried and executed as a heretic, but instead they created a martyr; in 1920 she was canonized as a saint. In the years that followed her death in 1431, the French, with the Burgundians at their side after 1435, drove the English out of France, leaving them in 1453 with only Calais.

The French victory was facilitated by the growth of national feeling and the effective use of gunpowder and heavy artillery. In the end the war was beneficial to the French monarchy, for during its course the kings acquired both a monopoly on the sale of salt, the *gabelle* (tax), which became a major source of royal income, and the right to impose other taxes, including a direct tax called the *taille,* without the approval of the Estates General. These funds were necessary to support the standing army introduced in the war. In contrast, the English monarchs repeatedly had to seek parliamentary approval for taxation, thereby making Parliament an indispensable part of the government. By the war's end the principle was established that neither taxes nor other forms of legislation could be implemented without parliamentary approval. England and France thus began to follow different paths of monarchical government, the former eventually culminating in constitutional monarchy, the latter in absolute rule.

The social consequences of the war were profound. In both countries the rural economy was hit hard by the loss of men in the fighting. The English, moreover, murdered thousands of French civilians. The war brought higher taxes and disrupted trade. The change in the manner of fighting had significant long-term effects. Both the longbow and the use of guns enhanced the value of commoners on the battlefield and thus encouraged the development of larger armies. Those armies in turn required greater financial support from the state in contrast to the smaller feudal forces. The use of cannons meant major changes in the construction of city walls, which had to be much thicker. At the same time, siege trains capable of attacking towns were generally beyond the means of all but sovereigns and the greater princes; the military changes thus contributed to the evolution of more unified states. Economically, the demand for cannons, guns, and ammunition sparked the growth of the armaments industry and the mining companies that provided it with raw materials.

THE SPIRITUAL CRISIS OF THE LATE MEDIEVAL CHURCH

Against a backdrop of misery caused by famine, pestilence, and war, the church was rocked by scandal and division. The French king, Philip IV, emboldened by his earlier victory over Pope Boniface VIII, pressured Pope Clement V (1305–1314) to move the seat of the papacy from Rome to Avignon in 1309. Although an imperial city under papal control, Avignon was on the French border and was French in language and culture. The papacy remained at Avignon until 1377, a period usually referred to as the Babylonian Captivity, an allusion to the period in which the ancient Hebrews were held captive in Babylon. Avignon had the advantage of freeing the popes from the turmoil then disrupting Rome and the Papal States, but it also placed the papacy under a greater degree of French influence. The English, the Germans, and many Italians were displeased at the specter of a papacy in the shadow of French power, and Rome was particularly hard hit because its economy had rested so heavily on papal revenues. But perhaps most of the resentment against the Avignon popes stemmed from their efforts to create new sources of income to offset decreased revenue from the Papal States. These fees created the impression that the popes were concerned more with material than spiritual matters.

Disillusion with the papacy became even more pronounced as a result of the great schism that scandalized the church from 1378 to 1417. In 1377, Pope Gregory XI (1370–1378), persuaded by Catherine of Siena and Bridget of Sweden, moved the papal court back to Rome. When he died a year later, Roman mobs intimidated the cardinals to elect an Italian pope who would keep the papacy in Rome. The cardinals obliged with Urban VI (1378–1389), but five months later a group of mostly

French cardinals declared Urban's election void and elected a rival pope, Clement VII. Europeans had witnessed schisms before, but nothing like the spectacle that now divided Christendom. Clement, ruling from Avignon, had the support of France and its allies, whereas Urban was backed by England and its friends. As each pope claimed to be the true vicar of Christ and condemned the other, the schism raised serious questions about the authority of priests and the sacraments they administered. In addition to casting disrepute on church leaders, the schism encouraged the spread of heresy and mysticism, which stressed the inner life of the spirit.

Reformers called for a church council to end the scandal, contending that such a body exercised authority superior to that of a pope. Conciliar theory drew on a controversial intellectual tradition. In 1324, Marsiglio of Padua, rector of the University of Paris, had argued in his *Defender of the Peace* that because the people are the ultimate source of authority in church and state, a church council is above the pope. Marsiglio insisted that the church's power was restricted to spiritual matters; hence the pope had no claim to temporal authority. Although the church condemned Marsiglio's theories in 1327, his ideas provided a useful arsenal for those intent on disputing papal primacy.

With the support of most monarchs, a group of cardinals representing Rome and Avignon summoned a council to meet at Pisa in 1409. It deposed both popes and chose a new one, but because neither pope accepted the council's action, there were now three claimants to Peter's chair. The embarrassing schism was resolved only when a new council met in the German city of Constance beginning in 1414. It took three years and the support of the Holy Roman Emperor Sigismund to restore unity through the election of an Italian cardinal as Pope Martin V (1417–1431).

The Challenge of Heresy: Wyclif and Hus

Symptomatic of the church's problems was the enthusiastic reception in England and Bohemia of ideas that challenged the very core of orthodox teaching. The Oxford professor John Wyclif (c. 1330–1384) not only denied papal claims to temporal power, as Marsiglio had done, but also demanded that cardinals and bishops relinquish their political offices and that the church divest itself of its property. Wyclif believed that authority rested in the Bible alone, which should be in the language of the people, and he therefore began preparing an English version of Scripture. He also called for the abolition of many traditions, including pilgrimages, the sale of indulgences, and the doctrine of transubstantiation—the belief that the substance of the bread and the wine miraculously becomes the body and blood of Christ in the Eucharist. Convinced that the true church is composed only of people divinely predestined to believe in God, Wyclif asserted that salvation was independent of the sacraments. He enjoyed powerful support among aristocrats in England, who saw in his teachings the possibility of acquiring the church's wealth. Many of his ideas were condemned, and he was expelled from Oxford, but followers, known as Lollards, kept his ideas alive well into the sixteenth century.

Wyclif's views were carried to Bohemia by Czech students studying at Oxford and by members of the household of Anne of Bohemia, wife of England's King Richard II. The leader of the Bohemian reformers, John Hus (1369–1415), rector of the University of Prague, embraced some of Wyclif's teachings, especially his concept of the true church as a body of saints and the need for sweeping reforms. Hus' views struck a responsive chord among Czech nationalists resentful of the domination of foreign ecclesiastics. The Council of Constance, which had previously condemned Wyclif's tenets, accused Hus of heresy. He was tried and convicted, turned over to imperial officials, and burned at the stake in 1415. His followers, inspired in part by Czech patriotism, mounted a fierce rebellion that lasted from 1421 to 1436. In the end the Bohemians were left with considerable authority over their own church, an example that was not lost on Martin Luther a century later as he pondered the need for reform in the German church.

THE LATE MEDIEVAL OUTLOOK

The crises of the fourteenth and early fifteenth centuries had a striking effect on people's outlook: famine, plague, and war influenced the cult of death and decay; the Hundred Years' War affected the cult of chivalry and the growth of national literature; and the Babylonian Captivity and the papal schism promoted social criticism and the views of nominalists and mystics.

The Cult of Death

The preoccupation with death induced by the massive fatalities resulting from famine and plague manifested itself in various ways. In the minds of the pious, greater attention was given to the Last Judgment, a popular motif in art and literature. Others found solace in the Pietà, a depiction of Mary holding the dead Christ in her arms—a poignant symbol for grieving parents who shared her sense of personal loss and the hope of resurrection. Painters commonly drew figures of death, and sculptors placed skeletal figures instead of traditional effigies on tombs. Nothing more graphically reveals the fascination with death than the *danse macabre,* the dance of death that was portrayed in art, acted out in drama, and celebrated in poetry. The *danse macabre* may be related to the psychological and neurological disorders that accompanied the plague. A recurring theme in these representations is the equality of all persons in death, a sharp counterpoint to a society preoccupied with social hierarchy.

The Chivalric Ideal

Juxtaposed with this cult of death and decay was another cult, more positive in outlook and restricted in its social appeal—the cult of chivalry. Here was a code for knights and nobles, the last gasp of a way of life and warfare that was being pushed into the shadows by new methods of fighting, the rising mercantile order, and a gradual shift in importance from ancestry to talent as the key to a successful political career. The cult of chivalry, with its idealized knights and ladies, was the swan song of the old order. The chivalric code exalted war, but there was nothing particularly glorious when England's peasant archers cut down the cream of French knighthood at Crécy, Poitiers, and Agincourt. Efficiency, technology, and discipline replaced bravado, loyalty, and dignity on the battlefield, a change that ultimately revolutionized and depersonalized warfare by shifting the burden from the landed elite to the masses. As if to protest the passing of the old order, the aristocracy put greater emphasis on the trappings of chivalry: pageants and tournaments. Extravagance was indicative of the fact that chivalry, once primarily a military code of conduct, had been transformed into an elegant charade, a form of escapism.

National Literatures

The late Middle Ages witnessed the further development of national vernacular literature. The contributions of Dante, Chaucer, and Villon were critical in shaping national languages out of regional dialects. All three writers sharply criticized late medieval society and the church. *The Divine Comedy,* the epic poem of the Florentine Dante Alighieri (1265–1321), was so named because it progresses from a fearsome vision of hell in the first part, the Inferno, to a happy ending as the reader is guided through Purgatory to Paradise. Dante uses the scenes from hell, peopled with everyone from actual popes and priests to politicians and queens, to condemn such evils as church corruption, political treachery, and immorality. On other levels the journey is an allegory of the Christian life and a pictorial *summa* of medieval ethical and religious teachings.

Disenchantment with the defects in contemporary society, especially the church, is also reflected in Geoffrey Chaucer's *Canterbury Tales.* It was probably on a mission to Florence as a royal official that Chaucer (c. 1340–1400) learned of Dante's work, which influenced his own writings. In the characters, anecdotes, and moral fables of *The Canterbury Tales,* Chaucer probed English society, making incisive and satirical comments about the foibles and hypocrisy of ecclesiastics.

The poetry of the Frenchman François Villon (1431–c. 1463) is the voice of the downtrodden and criminal element in a society thrown into turmoil by the Hundred Years' War. A convicted murderer and thief, Villon ranged in·his ballads from the ways of the Parisian underworld to meditations on the beauty of life. The specter of death stalks much of his work, reflecting the popularity of this theme in the fifteenth century.

Nominalists and Mystics

While the great vernacular writers criticized their social and religious world, William of Ockham (c. 1290–1349), an English Franciscan theologian, challenged prevailing scholastic views. A Nominalist, he argued that the principal Christian doctrines, such as the existence of God and the immortality of the soul, were incapable of rational proof and had to be affirmed on the basis of faith alone. By removing the rational basis for Christian belief, Ockham opened the way to Scepticism, a path followed by some of his disciples.

The rational and institutional approach to Christianity

was also challenged by mystics, who urged the importance of seeking God within oneself. One of the most influential mystics was the Dominican friar Meister Eckhart (c. 1260–1328), a German, who taught that the union of the human and the divine could be achieved in the soul through God's grace. Because the views of Eckhart and Ockham challenged traditional teaching, they had to defend themselves against charges of heresy before the papal court at Avignon, and Eckhart had to recant.

The strength of late medieval mysticism was among the laity, particularly in Germany and the Netherlands. There the Dutchman Gerhard Groote (1340–1384) founded a movement known as the *devotio moderna* ("modern devotion"), which combined a strong sense of morality with an emphasis on the inner life of the soul rather than liturgy and penitent acts such as fasting and pilgrimages. After his death his followers established the Brethren and the Sisters of the Common Life—lay believers who lived in strictly regulated religious houses and devoted themselves primarily to the education of young boys. Some of the most influential religious leaders of the late fifteenth and sixteenth centuries, including Erasmus, studied in these schools. The literary classic of this movement, Thomas à Kempis' *Imitation of Christ,* was a devotional handbook that emphasized personal piety and ethical conduct.

ECONOMIC RECOVERY

Europe recovered from the calamities of the fourteenth and early fifteenth centuries in large measure because of renewed population growth, economic diversification, and technological inventions spurred by the labor shortages resulting from the Black Death. As the population began to return to its former levels in the late fifteenth and sixteenth centuries, there was once again an abundant labor supply as well as improved productivity and greater economic diversification. Merchants increasingly branched out into fields as varied as banking, textile and weapons manufacturing, and mining. The Germans modernized the mines by harnessing horsepower and waterpower to crush ore, operate their rolling mills, and pump water from mine shafts. Blast furnaces were constructed to make cast iron. Dutch fishermen learned to salt, dry, and store their fish while at sea, thus enabling them to stay out longer and increase their catch. The Hundred Years' War stimulated

the armaments industry, and the introduction of movable metal type led to the printing industry and encouraged paper manufacturing.

The textile industry grew in this period. The production of woolens in Flanders and the cities of northern Italy, however, declined in the fifteenth century, primarily because the English monarchs built up their native woolen industry by imposing low export duties on cloth and high ones on raw wool. Woolen manufacturing also expanded in France, Germany, and Holland, and new textile industries such as silk and cotton began to develop.

The growth in manufacturing went hand in hand with a dramatic increase in commerce and the rise of great merchants and their organizations. The latter included the seven major guilds in Florence, the six merchant corporations known as the *Corps de Marchands* in Paris, and the twelve Livery Companies in London. Firms in Europe's leading commercial centers established branch offices in other cities, and exchanges were opened to facilitate financial transactions. Banking houses developed rapidly, especially in northern Italy. The demand for credit grew, undermining the medieval church's hostility to most interest charges. The Genoese pioneered the development of insurance, especially for merchants engaged in seaborne trade.

Ships in the Mediterranean trade called at the Italian ports of Pisa and Genoa as well as at Marseilles and Narbonne in France and Barcelona in Aragon, but the heart of this commerce was Venice. Its 3,300 ships plied the waters from the North Sea and Spain to North Africa, Syria, and the Black Sea. Cloth from Europe was traded in the East for spices, dyes, sugar, silks, and cotton. Shipping in northern Europe was mostly the province of the Hanseatic League, whose ships ranged from Scandinavia and Russia to northern Italy. From the states of the Baltic and the North Sea they obtained fish, timber, naval stores, grain, and furs in exchange for wine, spices, and cloth. Much of the commerce moved through the ports of the Low Countries.

POLITICAL RENEWAL: THE QUEST FOR UNITY AND AUTHORITY

Economic revival was accompanied in western Europe and Russia by the development of relatively strong centralized states. The political crises had increased the need for state governments to raise substantial tax revenues. Such income made it feasible to think in terms of a professional army rather than a feudal levy, but this in turn increased the costs of government. So too did the growth of bureaucracies, which were essential to raise revenue and administer the realms. Greater unity was in general beneficial to the business community; hence the monarchs typically found important allies in the towns. Urban support was translated into tax revenues (though many French towns enjoyed exemptions), an enlarged pool from which government officials could be selected, and political backing in the drive for sovereignty.

The decline of *particularism*—the dominance of local and regional authorities rather than a central government—was in most respects a blow to the landed aristocracy, but the aristocrats were appeased by exemptions from most taxes and appointments to political office. Members of the landed elite were prominent in the national assemblies, where they enjoyed power and prestige greater than those of urban delegates. The achievement of national sovereignty was possible in large measure because the power of the landed aristocracy was not so much crushed as altered: in the new system, many aristocrats became staunch supporters of the crown.

The Rise of Muscovy

In the fourteenth century the princes of Moscow began to "gather the Russian land" by expanding their borders through marital alliances, inheritance, purchases, and conquest. Three factors aided them: the strategic location of Moscow near tributaries of the Volga and Oka rivers; Mongol reliance on the Muscovites to collect tribute from other Russians; and the support of the Russian Orthodox church, whose metropolitan (archbishop) made Moscow the religious capital of the Russians in the fourteenth century. As Mongol power declined late in that century, the Muscovite princes ceased to be agents for the Mongols and took up the mantle of patriotic resistance. The war of liberation continued well into the fifteenth century.

The foundation of a strong Russian state was laid by Ivan III, known as "the Great" (1462–1505). To counterbalance the power of the hereditary boyars (nobles), Ivan created a class of serving gentry by offering them lifetime grants of land in return for their service. Ivan enhanced his status by his marriage to Zoë, niece of the last Byzantine emperor. Henceforth, Ivan began to refer to himself as the successor of the Byzantine emperors, adopting the Byzantine double eagle as the symbol of Russia, introducing Byzantine ceremonies at court, and calling himself Autocrat and Tsar ("Caesar"). Russian scholars contributed to the new image by asserting that Moscow was the third Rome (after Rome and Byzantium, each of which had fallen) and thus the true center of Christianity. Ivan expanded the boundaries of his state by conquering the republic of Novgorod and invading Lithuania. Above all, he advanced his claim to be ruler "of all the Russians," in part by issuing a new code of laws in 1497.

The Spain of Isabella and Ferdinand

The unification of Spain was made possible by the marriage in 1469 of Isabella, the future queen of Castile (1474–1504), and Ferdinand, the future king of Aragon (1479–1516). Of the two kingdoms, Castile was the more populous and wealthy. It was, moreover, an expanding state as it continued the campaign to reconquer Granada from the Muslims, a goal achieved in 1492. The marriage of Isabella and Ferdinand did not effectively unite the two countries, each of which spoke a different language and retained its own laws, taxes, monetary system, military, and customs. The two sovereigns permitted Aragon to keep its provincial assemblies, the Cortes, although royal supervision was exercised through viceroys appointed by the crown. The monarchs concentrated on Castile, whose Cortes supported their quest for order and whose new council was the principal agency for the implementation of royal policy. In the work of centralization the sovereigns had the support of the towns, which were liberally represented in the Cortes, and of the *hidalgos*—knights who did not enjoy the tax-exempt status of the nobles and therefore sought employment from the crown. Hidalgos administered local districts, performed judicial functions, and supervised urban affairs. Although the role of the nobles in the government was somewhat reduced, they still exercised considerable influence through the powerful military brotherhoods established in the twelfth century. To bring them under greater royal authority, Ferdinand became the head of each brotherhood.

The devout Isabella and the pragmatic Ferdinand made the Catholic church a key instrument in their centralizing work. Isabella's chief minister, Cardinal Francisco Ximenes (c. 1436–1517), restored ecclesiastical

The marriage of Ferdinand of Aragon and Isabella of Castile made the unification of Spain possible. [Arxiu Mas, Barcelona]

discipline, thus reinforcing central authority. In 1482, Pope Sixtus IV granted the sovereigns the *Real Patronato* ("Royal Patronage"), giving them the right to make the major church appointments in Granada; this was later extended to Spanish America and then to Spain as a whole. Royal authority in religion was increased by Isabella and Ferdinand's campaign to enforce religious orthodoxy. Although the Inquisition had been introduced into Spain by a papal bull in 1478, it soon became an instrument controlled by the crown. In 1492 the Jews were given the choice of being baptized as Christians or losing their property and going into exile; approximately 150,000 Jews left. Ten years later, Ximenes persuaded Isabella to expel professing Muslims. Jews and Muslims who converted—*conversos* and *Moriscos,* respectively—were subject to the terrors of the Inquisition if their sincerity was doubted. Spain achieved religious unity at the cost of expelling or alienating productive minorities, curtailing intellectual freedom, and destroying toleration.

England: The Struggle for the Throne

By the end of the Hundred Years' War in 1453, English royal authority had been undermined by bastard feudalism. By this practice, a small group of powerful nobles who controlled much of the country's landed property used their wealth to employ private armies. The retainers in their hire, most of them veterans, served primarily for pay rather than for the use of land as in the traditional feudal arrangement. The magnates who hired them exerted enormous influence on the monarchs through the royal Council and commanded support from their followers in Parliament. These circumstances made it possible for Henry of Bolingbroke, a nephew of Edward III, to force the abdication of Richard II in 1399. Parliament dutifully confirmed Bolingbroke's assumption of the crown as Henry IV (1399–1413), the first ruler of the house of Lancaster.

During the reign of Henry VI (1422–1461), civil war broke out between the feuding factions, the houses of Lancaster and York. In the sixteenth century this came to be known as the Wars of the Roses when William Shakespeare, in *Henry VI,* assigned the symbol of the Tudor dynasty, a red rose, to the Lancastrians; the Yorkist symbol was a white rose. The fighting ended with the triumph of the Yorkist king Edward IV (1461–1483). He improved his position by shepherding his finances, establishing firm control over the Council, and expanding royal authority in Wales and northern England.

At Edward's death in 1483 his brother Richard, regent for the young Edward V, imprisoned the new king and his brother. They died mysteriously, possibly at the instigation of their uncle, who assumed the throne as Richard III (1483–1485). In 1485, Henry Tudor, who was remotely related to the house of Lancaster, invaded England with French backing and defeated Richard. Once again, Parliament recognized the victor's claim to the throne.

Henry VII (1485–1509) resumed the task of strengthening royal authority that Edward IV had begun, notably by making the crown financially secure and building up a modest surplus in the treasury. He relied heavily on income from crown lands, judicial fees and fines, and feudal dues such as wardship rights, and he avoided costly foreign adventures. Henry made good use of unpaid justices of the peace drawn from the ranks of the gentry to maintain order in the counties. He also used his Council, which could sit as a court (called the Star Chamber), to maintain order and impose swift justice; people cited before this court had no right to legal counsel and could be compelled to testify against themselves. Henry negotiated two strategic alliances, one of which involved the marriage of his daughter Margaret to James IV of Scotland. From that line came the Stuart dynasty, which would govern both countries in the seventeenth century. The second alliance led to the marriage of Henry VII's son, Prince Henry, to Catherine of Aragon, daughter of Ferdinand and Isabella. When Henry (now Henry VIII) tired of Catherine in the late 1520s, he set in motion the events that led to England's break with the Catholic church.

Valois France

Charles VII (1422–1461) laid the foundation for the recovery of the French monarchy, not least by his victory over the English in the Hundred Years' War. Despite the large size of the kingdom, the continuation of feudal traditions and local privileges, and the existence of a representative assembly, the Estates General, the French kings, aided by a spirit of national feeling, were at last in a position to unify the country. During the war, Charles had organized the first French standing army, which he financed with the *taille,* a direct tax for which he did not have to seek the approval of the Estates General after 1439. In fact, meetings of the Estates were rare between 1441 and 1614, after which there were no sessions until 1789. In 1438, Charles brought the French church under royal control in the Pragmatic Sanction of Bourges, which set forth such "Gallican liberties" as the right of the French church to choose its own bishops.

Once England was defeated, the greatest threat to the French monarchy was the duchy of Burgundy, whose dukes entertained thoughts of making their state a powerful middle kingdom between France and the Holy Roman Empire. Louis XI (1461–1483) responded to this threat by subsidizing the armies of the Swiss Confederation, which defeated the Burgundians in 1477, enabling him to annex Burgundy. The royal domains were increased again in 1480 and 1481 when Louis inherited the Angevin lands of Anjou, Maine, and Provence. Only Brittany remained beyond the pale of his authority, but that was remedied in 1491 when his son and heir, Charles VIII (1483–1498), married the duchess of Brittany.

Charles VIII involved France in a disastrous attempt to dominate Italy. The stage had been set when Louis succeeded not only to the Angevin lands in France but also to the Angevin claim to the throne of Naples, now occupied by the Aragonese. Louis had done nothing about the claim, but Charles was determined to assert it. In 1494 he invaded Italy, precipitating a power struggle for control of the peninsula that lasted 65 years. Although Charles failed to take Naples, his successor, Louis XII (1498–1515), was determined to seize Milan, which he claimed as his own because his mother had been a member of the Visconti family, rulers of the duchy until 1447. Pope Julius II (1503–1513) enlisted Spain, Venice, the Swiss Confederation, and the Holy Roman Empire in a Holy League to drive France out of Italy, an end they accomplished in 1513. Under Francis I (1515–1547) the French returned in 1515, sparking a series of wars with the Habsburgs that financially drained France. Nevertheless, as in the case of the Hundred Years' War, military needs and financial demands led to the continued expansion and centralization of the royal administration, thus strengthening the king's hold on the realm.

ITALY: PAPAL STATES AND CITY-STATES

While Russia and the western European states were developing stronger, more centralized governments in the fifteenth century, in Italy, Germany, Hungary, and Poland regional states and princes consolidated their power, effectively blocking the emergence of national states. The struggle in the High Middle Ages between the papacy and the Hohenstaufen emperors left the Italians without a government capable of extending its control throughout the peninsula. Nor did any state possess a theoretical claim to serve as the nucleus for a unified nation. From Rome the popes governed the Papal States, a band extending across central Italy, but their claims to authority were international in scope. The papacy's temporal authority in Italy was severely reduced during the Avignon period and further damaged during the great schism. Beginning with Martin V, the fifteenth- and early sixteenth-century popes were preoccupied with reestablishing their temporal power. Popes such as Alexander VI and Julius II were less spiritual leaders than temporal princes willing to use any means to extend their rule.

In the fourteenth and fifteenth centuries the communal governments of northern Italy experienced substantial internal tensions resulting from economic and social change. Rapid urban growth, the development of textile industries, and the rise of a sizable proletariat that was excluded from the hope of prosperity by privilege-conscious guilds created such strife that Milan and Florence turned to virtual despots to preserve order. So too did some of the smaller cities. Often these men were *condottieri,* mercenary generals whose hired armies provided them with the force necessary to keep order.

In the south the kingdom of Naples and Sicily had problems of a different nature because of foreign domination. In 1282 the Sicilians revolted against their French Angevin rulers and turned for assistance to Aragon. Throughout the fourteenth century the Angevins and Aragonese contested for southern Italy until, in 1435, the Aragonese drove the Angevins out of Naples. As we have seen, Charles VIII's reassertion of the Angevin claim led to the French invasion of Italy in 1494.

The Duchy of Milan

From its strategic position in the heart of the Po valley and at the base of the trade routes leading across the Alps into northern Europe, Milan developed rapidly as an industrial center specializing in textiles and arms. The medieval commune suffered however, from social tensions and a struggle for power between Guelph (propapal) and Ghibelline (proimperial) factions. Under the leadership of the Visconti family the Ghibellines triumphed in 1277, effectively ending communal government and establishing despotic rule. The Visconti—dukes of Milan beginning in 1395—employed condottieri to extend their control in the Po valley.

When the last of the Visconti dukes died in 1447 without a male heir, the Milanese revived republican government, but it was ineffective. Therefore in 1450 the condottiere Francesco Sforza reestablished ducal rule. Francesco attempted to maintain a balance of power in Italy among the five principal states: Milan, Venice, Florence, Naples, and the Papal States. To this end he was an architect of the Italian League (1455), which was designed in part to prevent French aggression. However, Francesco's son Ludovico connived with Charles VIII to intervene in Italian affairs, thereby contributing not only to the devastating wars that ensued but to the demise of the Sforza dynasty as well. After the French were ousted, the family's rule was briefly restored between 1512 and 1535, at which time the Holy Roman Empire acquired Milan.

CATERINA SFORZA, THE DESPOT OF FORLÌ

The talented and beautiful Caterina Sforza (c. 1463–1509) was the daughter of Francesco Sforza's grandson. For political reasons her father arranged her marriage to Pope Sixtus IV's nephew, Girolamo Riario. The pope subsequently gave them control of the towns of Forlì and Imola, northeast of Florence, but Caterina's husband was

Caterina Sforza, countess of Forlì [Marburg/Art Resource, New York]

which she wrote to the reformer Girolamo Savonarola, who urged her to seek redemption through pious works and just rule.

Caterina's final period of political crisis began in 1498 when the Venetians raided her lands, but she was saved by military aid from Milan and the outbreak of fighting between Venice and Florence. While Caterina was occupied with Venice, Pope Alexander VI and his son, Cesare Borgia, plotted to increase their control over the Papal States, particularly the region that included Caterina's lands. Her main ally, Milan, was preoccupied with the threat of a new French invasion. The pope, calling Caterina a "daughter of iniquity," claimed her territory. Negotiations with Niccolò Machiavelli, the Florentine envoy, failed to achieve an effective alliance, nor were the assassins she dispatched to kill Alexander VI successful. Cesare's army struck in the autumn, forcing Caterina to send her children and treasures to Florence for safety. She destroyed all buildings in the area that might shelter the enemy, cut down the trees, and flooded the marshes. Italy watched as the papal army relentlessly attacked until Caterina was finally captured—and raped by Cesare—in January 1500. For a year she was imprisoned in a Roman dungeon. Without support from any major Italian state, her efforts to regain her territories failed, forcing her to seek refuge in Florence. Her last years were spent attending to her garden, her horses, and her soul. Contemporaries called her the "Amazon of Forlì," a tribute to her ability to hold her own in a political world governed by the ethics of power.

Florence and the Medici

Bitter social conflict disrupted Florence throughout the fourteenth and early fifteenth centuries. Thanks to its banking houses and textile industry the city was usually prosperous in this period, though it suffered severely when England's Edward III repudiated his debts and caused major banking houses to fail and again when 55,000 of its 95,000 inhabitants died in the plague. The periodic crises intensified existing social tensions. In part an unusual degree of social mobility in Florentine society caused the turmoil. The older nobles had been effectively excluded from power in 1293 by the newly rich capitalists who dominated the seven greater guilds. In 1343 the capitalists in turn were successfully challenged by the artisans of the lesser guilds and their allies, the shopkeepers and small businessmen. The

assassinated by political rivals in 1488. She retained power by ruling in her son's name, thanks to assistance from the armies of Milan and Bologna, and avenged Girolamo's murder by staging a spectacle of brutality in which the dismembered bodies of some of the conspirators were scattered in the piazza of Forlì. That done, she sought to restore unity to her possessions by launching an extensive program of public building.

Although a campaign to extend her territory to the northeast failed because of opposition from Venice, her importance was such that she was courted as an ally by all the major Italian states. When the French invaded Italy in 1494, Caterina, fearful of Venice, refused to join the Holy League against France. The brutal assassination of her lover in 1495 prompted her to instigate another bloody vendetta, but it also opened the way for her secret marriage a year of two later to Lorenzo the Magnificent's second cousin, Giovanni de' Medici. About this time she underwent a period of spiritual searching in *ciompi* had their turn in 1378, when they revolted and won the right to organize their own guilds and have a say in political affairs. Feuding between the lesser guilds and the ciompi enabled a group of wealthy merchants to regain control in the early 1380s, but they were ousted by the Medici family in 1434.

Cosimo de' Medici (1389–1464) and his successors, who dominated Florentine politics except for brief intervals until 1737, governed as despots by manipulating republican institutions, often from behind the scenes. In addition to working with Francesco Sforza to create a balance of power in Italy and prevent French aggression, Cosimo introduced a graduated income tax and curried favor among the lesser guilds and workers. His grandson, Lorenzo the Magnificent (1449–1492), was the object of an assassination plot by the Pazzi family that killed his brother while the two were worshiping in the cathedral at Florence. The plot had the support of Pope Sixtus IV, who resented the Medici's alliance with Venice and Milan, the intent of which was to block the extension of his authority in the northern Papal States. Like his grandfather, Lorenzo diligently sought a balance of power in Italy and opposed French aggression. The Florentines ousted Lorenzo's son Piero when he made territorial concessions to the French in 1494. Republican government was restored, and for four years a spirit of religious frenzy prevailed under the sway of the fiery Dominican Girolamo Savonarola (see Chapter 10). The republic's alliance with France isolated Florence from other Italian states, but in 1512, Julius II persuaded the Florentines to join the Holy League against Louis XII and to allow the Medici to return.

VENICE: THE REPUBLIC OF ST. MARK

Unlike the Florentines and Milanese, the Venetians enjoyed social and political stability. The merchant oligarchy that governed the republic was a closed group limited to families listed in the Golden Book, a register of more than 200 names that included only families represented in the Great Council prior to 1297. Venice had neither a landed nobility nor a large industrial proletariat to challenge the dominance of its wealthy merchants, and the republic, because of its relative isolation, had not become embroiled in the Guelph-Ghibelline feud that left cities such as Florence with a tradition of bitter fac-

tionalism. There was never a successful revolution in Venice.

The Venetian government was tightly knit. The approximately 240 merchant oligarchs who sat in the Great Council elected the Senate, the principal legislative body, as well as the ceremonial head of state, called a *doge,* and other government officials. The most powerful body in the state was the annually elected Council of Ten, which met in secret, focused on security, and in an emergency could assume the powers of all other government officials. To the Venetians' credit, the merchant oligarchy disdained despotic rule, thereby maintaining the support of those excluded from the political process.

In the fourteenth and fifteenth centuries the Venetians 3300 ships became a commercial empire. This involved a bitter contest with Genoa for control of trade in the eastern Mediterranean, a struggle that ended with Genoa's defeat in 1380. In the meantime the Venetians attempted to acquire territory in northern Italy in order to ensure an adequate food supply and access to the Alpine trade routes. This brought the Venetians face to face with Milan and the Papal States, both of which were also expanding, as well as with the Habsburgs and the Hungarians, who were unsettled by Venetian expansion around the head of the Adriatic. The struggle on the mainland diverted crucial resources from the eastern Mediterranean, where Turkish expansion threatened Venetian interests. More dangerous than the lengthy war with the Turks (1463–1479) was the threat posed to Venice by the League of Cambrai, formed in 1508 and 1509 by Julius II to strip Venice of its territorial acquisitions. Members of the league included the emperor Maximilian, Louis XII, and Ferdinand of Aragon. Although the league seized some of Venice's Italian lands, a reprieve came when the pope, increasingly fearful of French ambitions, negotiated peace. Venice was still an important state, but Turkish expansion coupled with the discovery of new trade routes to Asia eroded its role as a Mediterranean power.

At the peak of its influence in the fifteenth and early sixteenth centuries, Venice was a city of striking contrasts. The fabulous wealth of the merchant oligarchy was reflected in the palatial houses that lined the Grand Canal. Living space in the city was at a premium; hence not even the wealthiest patricians could acquire spacious lots. Away from the Grand Canal there was no special residential district for the merchant oligarchy, whose homes were scattered throughout the city. Venice had its poor, but generally there was employment for them, particularly in the shipbuilding, textile, and fishing industries. Food prices were regulated, and grain was periodically distributed without charge to the needy. The Venetians traded in slaves, some of whom were kept in Venice as household servants, though the slave trade declined as the Turks pushed the Venetians out of the Mediterranean. The Venetians were mostly tolerant of the foreign minorities who settled in the city, but that attitude did not fully extend to the Jews. In the late fourteenth century the Jews of Venice were required to wear yellow badges, and beginning in 1423 they could not own real estate. Finally, in 1516 the Jews were forced to live in a special district known as the *ghetto*. It was, however, unthinkable to expel them from the republic, as they had been from Spain, for the community required their medical expertise and their ability to provide substantial loans, particularly in time of war. Venice was more tolerant of the Jews than were other Italian states.

THE HOLY ROMAN EMPIRE

The destruction of imperial power in the thirteenth century during the struggle between the Holy Roman Empire and the papacy left Germany badly divided. When the princes ended the Great Interregnum (1254–1273) by placing Rudolf of Habsburg (1273–1291) on the imperial throne, they were not interested in creating a strong centralized government. Although the Habsburgs dreamed of ruling a powerful dynastic state, their own dominions were limited to Austria, giving them little control over the princes and towns in other regions. The virtual independence of the more powerful princes was confirmed in 1356 when the emperor Charles IV (of the house of Luxembourg) issued the Golden Bull, a charter affirming that the empire was an elective monarchy. Henceforth new emperors were chosen by four hereditary princes, each of whom was virtually sovereign, and three ecclesiastical princes. In the century and a half that followed, lesser princes emulated the seven electors by establishing a strong degree of authority within their own states, a process that involved them in a struggle with the knights and administrative officials who wanted virtual independence for their fiefs. In Germany the territorial princes triumphed over both the emperor and the knights. Their power was reflected in the Imperial Diet, a representative assembly whose three estates comprised the electoral princes, the lesser princes, and the imperial free cities. Meanwhile, the Swiss took advantage of weak imperial authority to organize a confederation of essentially independent cantons or districts.

Maximilian negotiated a series of strategic marriage alliances that vastly increased Habsburg power. His own marriage to Mary of Burgundy had led to the acquisition of the Low Countries, and the marriage of his son Philip to Ferdinand and Isabella's daughter Joanna made it possible for Maximilian's grandson Charles to inherit Spain and its possessions. The emperor Charles V (1519–1556) thus ruled the Habsburg lands in Germany, Austria, the Low Countries, Spain, Spanish territories in the New World, and the Aragonese kingdom of Naples and Sicily. No larger dominion had existed in Europe since the time of Charlemagne.

Spanish possessions in Italy brought Charles V into a bitter confrontation with the French king, Francis I, who was no less determined to press his own Italian claims. In 1525, Charles crushed the French at Pavia, near Milan. Francis then allied with the Turks, who defeated the Hungarian army at Mohács in 1526. When the major Italian states (except Naples) allied with France in the League of Cognac, the imperial armies again invaded, this time sacking Rome in 1527, an event that was widely regarded as the major atrocity of the sixteenth century. Although Francis renewed the war against Charles twice more, not even an alliance with the Turks and German Protestant princes was sufficient to achieve a decisive military victory. When the Habsburg-Valois wars finally ended in 1559, Milan and Naples remained under Habsburg control. The Habsburgs, however, had failed to establish a unified state in Germany.

EASTERN EUROPE

Although the Hungarians had developed a reasonably strong state in the 1200s, during the following century they were weakened by dynastic struggles. There were further problems due to the frequent absences of King Sigismund (1387–1437) from the country, partly because of his campaigns against the Turks and partly because of his responsibilities as Holy Roman Emperor (1433–1437). Matthias Corvinus (1458–1490) increased royal authority through administrative and judicial reforms,

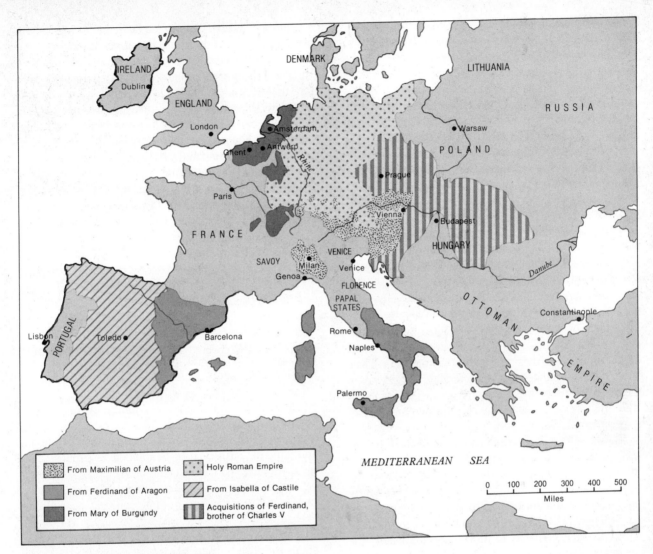

9.1 The Empire of Charles V

Legend:

From Maximilian of Austria

From Ferdinand of Aragon

From Mary of Burgundy

Holy Roman Empire

From Isabella of Castile

Acquisitions of Ferdinand, brother of Charles V

higher taxes, and the creation of a standing army. Abroad, he used Hungary's new power to conquer Bohemia, Moravia, and Austria. Following his death, a disputed succession enabled Maximilian to regain Austria and to bring Hungary into the imperial orbit by dynastic marriages involving his grandchildren. The nobles later took advantage of weak rulers to disband the standing army. As in Germany, the real struggle in Hungary then occurred between the magnates and the lesser nobility. Although the latter won their claim to equality in the eyes of the law, in practice the magnates were dominant.

Poland was an immense state—the largest in Europe after its union with Lithuania in the late 1300s—but it too failed to establish a strong central government. The position of the nobles was enhanced when King John Albert (1492–1501), in need of funds, allowed a national diet composed only of nobles to impose taxes on the towns and peasants. His successor accepted a statute requiring the diet's approval of all new legislation, further eroding royal authority. Although Sigismund II (1548–1572) allied with the lesser nobles to curtail the power of the magnates, his death without an heir enabled the nobles to assert their right to elect a successor.

Henceforth Poland was in fact as well as in theory an elective monarchy in which real power rested in the hands of the nobility.

THE OTTOMAN EMPIRE

While Europe suffered through the famine, war, and plague of the fourteenth century, a new dynasty of Turkish sultans, the Ottomans, established itself in Asia Minor. For nearly three centuries the Ottomans expanded their conquests, until in 1683 they ranged from Hungary to the Persian Gulf and from the Crimea to North Africa. The followers of the Ottoman founder, Osman (1299–1326), were mostly Islamic warriors who saw their sacred duty in extending the faith by attacking unbelievers. Motivated by religion and a thirst for booty, disciplined by a code of honor, and aided by the weakness of their enemies, the Ottomans were successful out of all proportion to their relatively small numbers. Their success was also aided by their tolerance of other faiths after their first conquests and by the disgust of many Byzantine subjects with the corrupt and oppressive imperial government.

Taking advantage of political chaos in the Balkans, the Ottomans defeated the Serbs, Bulgars, and Macedonians in the late 1300s, opening up the Balkans to Turkish immigrants. Europeans were now sufficiently alarmed to send a crusading army. The Ottomans took only three hours to defeat the Europeans at Nicopolis in 1396. As they prepared to attack Constantinople, the Ottomans themselves became the victims of a Turco-Mongol invasion led by Tamerlane, who defeated them in 1402. After Tamerlane withdrew, the Ottomans renewed their conquests, defeating the Greeks and finally taking Constantinople in 1453. Under Mehmet II (1451–1481) the city, renamed Istanbul, was rebuilt and repopulated with new immigrants, including Jews and Christians as well as Muslims. Mehmet hoped to make his new capital the center of a world empire far greater than that to which Alexander the Great and Julius Caesar had aspired. In the decades after the fall of Constantinople the Ottoman armies completed the conquest of the Balkans and established a foothold in the Crimea; by the late 1400s the Black Sea was virtually a Turkish lake.

In the following century, two of the greatest sultans, Selim I (1512–1520) and Suleiman I, known as "the Magnificent" (1520–1566), made further advances. Selim overran Syria, Palestine, and Egypt, and Suleiman captured Belgrade, gateway to central Europe, and much of Hungary. He besieged Vienna, but his forces lacked both the supplies and the resolve to take the city, and he was forced to retreat in 1529. Elsewhere, his armies were victorious in North Africa as far west as Algeria and in the Middle East, where they captured Baghdad. In the course of these campaigns, Suleiman became an ally of France against the Habsburgs. As a consequence, France gained special trade privileges in the Ottoman Empire and later acted as protector of Catholic subjects in the empire and of the Christian holy places in Palestine.

SUMMARY

Politically, the fifteenth and early sixteenth centuries were a major watershed in European history as well as the period of dramatic Ottoman expansion, including the conquest of Constantinople. The failure of the Italians, Germans, Hungarians, and Poles to establish strong centralized states left them vulnerable to their neighbors and a perpetual source of temptation to expansionist-minded states. In contrast, the newly unified states of western Europe found themselves in an excellent position to take advantage of the economic possibilities opened up by the great voyages of discovery. It took the combined economic and military resources of these states to prosper in the expanding global trade. As the Black Death waned, Europe's population began growing again, prompting the expansion of commerce and manufacturing. Although the Italian states failed to unify, their impressive economic growth, historical tradition, and sense of civic independence enabled them to provide intellectual and cultural leadership for Europe in the Renaissance.

Suggestions for Further Reading

Contamine, P. *War in the Middle Ages,* trans. M. Jones. New York: Blackwell, 1984.

Goodman, A. *A History of England from Edward II to James I.* New York: Longman, 1977.

Gottfried, R. S. *The Black Death: Natural and Human Disaster in Medieval Europe.* New York: Free Press, 1983.

Guenee, B. *States and Rulers in Later Medieval Europe,* trans. J. Vale. Oxford and New York: Blackwell, 1985.

Hale, J. R. *Florence and the Medici: The Pattern of Control.* London: Thames & Hudson, 1977.

Holmes, G. *Europe: Hierarchy and Revolt, 1320–1450.* New York: Harper & Row, 1975.

Huizinga, J. *The Waning of the Middle Ages.* New York: Doubleday, 1954.

Kenny, A. J. P. *Wyclif.* New York: Oxford University Press, 1985.

Lane, F. C. *Venice: A Maritime Republic.* Baltimore: Johns Hopkins University Press, 1973.

Larner, J. *Italy in the Age of Dante and Petrarch, 1216–1380.* London and New York: Longman, 1980.

Leff, G. *The Dissolution of the Medieval Outlook: An Essay on Intellectual and Spiritual Change in the Fifteenth Century.* New York: New York University Press, 1976.

Mollat, M., and Wolff, P. *The Popular Revolutions of the Late Middle Ages,* trans. A. L. Lytton-Sells. London: Allen & Unwin, 1973.

Renouard, Y. *The Avignon Papacy, 1305–1403,* trans. D. Bethell. London: Faber & Faber, 1970.

Seward, D. *The Hundred Years' War: The English in France, 1337–1453.* London: Constable, 1978.

Tierney, B. *Foundations of the Conciliar Theory.* Cambridge: Cambridge University Press, 1955.

The West and the World

The Middle Ages

Direct Western contact with south and East Asia was effectively terminated when the Arabs and later the Turks established dominance over the land and maritime routes between East and West. Spices and other luxury items could still be obtained through Arab and Jewish middlemen, though at higher prices, but the lack of direct contact deprived Westerners of meaningful information about East Asia. Although the Arabs wrote a great deal about Asian geography, such information apparently did not circulate in the West for centuries. The absence of direct contact was one reason why the people of early medieval Europe perpetuated traditional visions of Asia as a region populated by strange peoples and mythical animals.

Christianity also contributed to the popularity of such views in the West. Augustine, the most influential theologian of the early medieval church, suggested that God had probably created monstrous beings in alien lands. Building on old geographical misconceptions, medieval cartographers made India an extension of Africa and identified one of the four biblical rivers in the book of Genesis with the Nile and the Oxus, and a second with the Indus and the Ganges. This made it possible to identify Asia and its inhabitants with scriptural places and people. Gog and Magog, from which the Devil would, according to the book of Revelation (20:7–8), eventually be liberated to destroy Jerusalem, was located north of the Caucasus Mountains in what is now Russia. Simultaneously, however, Westerners imagined the spread of Christianity into Asian lands on a scale wholly unwarranted by the facts. The story of the wise men who worshipped the infant Jesus in the gospel of Matthew was embellished to make them kings, setting the stage for the assumption that Christian states existed in Asia. By the ninth century this legend had merged with the story of the apostle Thomas' trip to India, so the apostle was believed to have visited the lands of the wise men, baptized them, and co-opted them for his missionary campaign.

The continued popularity of the largely fictitious view of Asia was also reinforced by the circulation of semifictional accounts of Alexander's exploits in India. In the second and first centuries B.C. such tales had been recounted in such imaginary correspondence as the *Letter of Alexander to Aristotle,* which depicted India as a magical land populated by wild creatures and strange peoples. Beginning in the fourth century A.D. such material was incorporated into Alexandrian romances, which circulated for centuries in Latin as well as vernacular languages and provided material for wandering minstrels. Kept alive by the Alexandrian romances and the Christian tradition, the fabled creatures captured the imagination of medieval sculptors, who depicted many of them on the exteriors of Gothic cathedrals.

The legend of Prester (Elder) John emerged from an amalgamation of these romantic and Christian perceptions of a largely mythical Asia. In 1145 a Syrian bishop informed the pope that a powerful Asiatic priest-king, reputedly descended from the biblical wise men, had

A medieval depiction of the Blemmyae, or Headless Ones, who were believed to inhabit India. [Bibliothèque Nationale, Paris]

defeated Muslim armies and was prepared to come to the aid of the Western crusaders. Twenty years later a letter purportedly from Prester John addressed to the Byzantine emperor stated the former's claim to rule most of Asia and Ethiopia, a land, he said, that extended from the biblical Tower of Babel to the place where the sun rises. The description of this mythical empire incorporated all of the strange peoples and animals in the popular imagination. Accepting the document as genuine, Pope Alexander III dispatched an envoy to Prester John, but the hapless ambassador apparently became lost in the deserts of Palestine or Arabia and was never heard from again. As late as the early fifteenth century the Portuguese were still hoping to forge an alliance with Prester John against the Muslims, a goal that helped to motivate their efforts to explore the western coast of Africa.

In the meantime the expansion of Islam, a religion that looked with favor on commerce, contributed to the development of trading networks that ultimately extended from the Pacific to the Atlantic and from central Africa to Russia and Scandinavia. Contacts with the Islamic world brought Europeans not only expanded economic opportunities but also the benefits of Muslim culture in such fields as science, medicine, and philosophy. As the history of the crusades makes abundantly clear, however, the Muslim world was an object of intense hatred for most westerners. In his call for crusaders in 1095, Pope Urban II described the Muslims as an "accursed" and "wicked race." The influential preacher of the Second

Gothic cathedrals typically contained sculptures depicting the imagined beasts of the East. These examples are from the Cathedral of Notre Dame, Paris. [Marburg/Art Resource, New York]

Crusade, Bernard of Clairvaux, followed papal bidding in 1147 by also seeking recruits for a crusade against the non-Christian Slavs of eastern Germany, whom he depicted as an "evil seed, wicked pagan sons," and people with "poisoned heads"; the crusaders, he admonished, should seek no truce with them but push on until "they shall be either converted or wiped out."[1] Thus in the minds of many western Europeans their immediate neighbors in the outside world, whether Muslims or Slavs (the Indo-European inhabitants of eastern Europe and parts of northern Asia), were wicked enemies to be converted or destroyed at God's behest.

While the crusading movement was still under way, the Mongols invaded Russia in the early thirteenth century. There was substantial confusion about the Mongols' identity. The Russians themselves were puzzled, for the author of the *Novgorodian Chronicle* reported that only God knew the place from which he had launched them. Some Westerners, including Pope Honorius III and King Andreas II of Hungary (1202–1235), had identified the Mongol chieftain, Chinghis Khan, with Prester John or another mythical priest-monarch, King David, often associated with Prester John or described as his son. As reports of Mongol ferocity reached Europe, however, some westerners doubted that this was a Christian army. In 1237 a Dominican friar learned from two Mongol envoys that the real aim of these people, as he understood it, was world domination, with Rome itself the target for their next invasion. The friar borrowed the name Tatars, by which the Mongols were typically known, but altered it to Tartars, a term evocative of *tartarus*, Latin for "Hades" or "hell." Henceforth, Europeans viewed the Tartars as evil creatures from Hades' depths, although many simultaneously saw them as instruments of divine providence sent to punish Christendom—the "hammer of God." To others they were the newly unleashed inhabitants of Gog and Magog whose invasion heralded the coming of the Antichrist and the imminent Last Judgment.

Realizing that Europeans needed to know who the Tartars really were and what their intentions were toward the West, Pope Innocent IV (1243–1245) dispatched Franciscan and Dominican friars on special missions to Asia. Ostensibly, the friars' goal was to establish diplomatic relations with the Mongols, although their fundamental purpose was to learn more about Tartar armies and aims. Only one of the envoys, Friar John of Pian de Carpini, a Franciscan, was directed to meet personally with the great khan (emperor). He reported what he and a colleague learned in their 2½-year journey (1245–1247) in his *History of the Mongols,* an account that ranks in importance with Marco Polo's later record. The two friars had an audience with the great khan, whose response to the papacy was a command to acknowledge Tartar supremacy and an invitation to the pope and monarchs of Europe to submit themselves at the Mongol court. A later mission, undertaken by the Franciscan friar William of Rubruck in 1253–1255, was intended primarily to seek religious converts among the Tartars. William's account, the *Itinerary,* notes that he found no evidence of the strange peoples and monsters that many westerners thought inhabited Asia. William spent six months with the entourage of the great khan, who was tolerant of Christianity and whose court included a number of Nestorian Christians. William's efforts to persuade those Christians to adopt Roman Catholic Christianity failed, and the khan himself was displeased when William threatened him with eternal damnation if he refused to convert. Upon his return to the West, William urged Europeans to unite for the purpose of conquering the lands in Asia Minor that had fallen into Tartar hands. The great khan was obviously not the priest-king Prester John.

Six years after William returned from his sojourn at the court of the great khan, the Venetian merchants Niccolò and Matteo Polo took a business trip to a Venetian outpost in the Crimea and then traveled to Sarai on the Volga River, where they spent a year with friendly Tartars. Hostilities in the area forced them to seek an alternative route. During the search they stayed in Bukhara in central Asia for three years. While at Bukhara, the Polo brothers were invited by Tartar envoys to visit the court of Kubilai Khan at Beijing (Peking), where they remained for several years. Returning at last to Venice in 1269, they carried letters from Kubilai to the pope asking that missionaries be sent to Asia. Although two Dominicans were eventually dispatched, they turned back before reaching China.

Accompanied by Niccolò's son Marco, the Polo brothers launched a second expedition to China in 1271, reaching Kubilai's summer

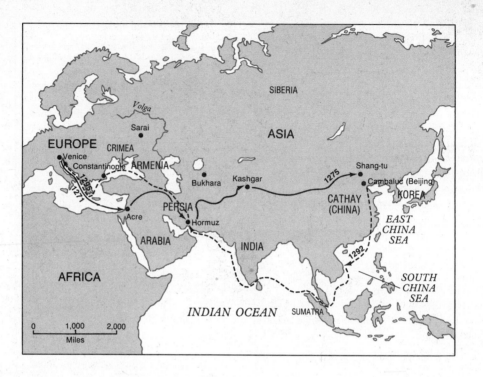

Marco Polo's voyage.

palace at Shang-tu in 1275. Marco studied Mongolian, represented the khan on assorted missions throughout the empire, and reported what he saw to Kubilai. The three Polos left Kubilai's court in 1292, carrying messages to the pope and the monarchs of Europe; they reached Venice in 1295, a quarter-century after their long journey had begun.

Marco Polo's primary interest was the customs of the Asian peoples whom he visited or learned of through conversations. His observations, reported after the expedition to a professional writer in Italy, cover a world that extended from Armenia to Korea and from Siberia to the tropical regions of India and Africa. Systematically, he considered these peoples' religion, government, history, and customs, focusing primarily on the unusual and the folkloric. Like the Mongols for whom he worked, he developed an unfortunate contempt for subject populations and therefore said little about the religious traditions of China, Persia, or, outside the empire, Muslim India. Linguistic barriers severely handicapped his comprehension of Chinese civilization and of Persian culture. His urban upbringing in Venice, however, gave him a keen appreciation of the "noble" cities of Asia and their architecture,

though, curiously, he displayed almost no interest in Asian painting or music.

In keeping with the widespread European fascination with exotic Asian animals, whether real or imaginary, Marco Polo devoted considerable attention to descriptions of Asian fauna. His skills were honed through association with the nomadic Tartars and observations in the huge parks that Mongol rulers had filled with exotic animals and birds. Marco tried to make sense of the imaginary animals so beloved in the West by finding a plausible Asian source; he thought that the Sumatran rhinoceros, for instance, was the inspiration for the unicorn and that Sumatran apes prompted the Western belief that Asia was filled with men that had tails. However, Marco's observations on Asian birds and animals provided more reliable information than any other work available in the thirteenth century.

Marco Polo's book had virtually no impact on the Western view of the world during the author's lifetime. The preconceived ideas of his contemporaries and the popularity of the traditional fables about Asia were too deeply ingrained for most people to take Marco's work seriously. Indeed, it was widely regarded as a work of romance rather than a factual description. A 1392 manuscript of the work closes with the transcriber's observation that "I copied it for my pleasure [as it consists of] matters not to be believed or credited."[2] Among the first to appreciate the value of Marco's book were the makers of *portolani,* or atlases for sailors; a map of 1375 followed Marco in its rendition of eastern Asia, the Deccan peninsula (much of modern India), and the Indian Ocean. By the end of the fourteenth century, cartographers appreciated and used Marco's work, and in 1426 or 1428, Marco's book and possibly a copy of a map he made during his Asian adventures were presented to Prince Pedro, elder brother of Prince Henry the Navigator. Henry was the patron of the Portuguese geographers, navigators, and sailors who launched the voyages along the coast of western Africa that were the precursors of the ones that led to the discovery of the New World. Marco Polo thus merits a place in the transition from the fable-dominated medieval view of the world to the more realistic one that emerged in the fifteenth and sixteenth centuries during the great age of exploration.

1. J. A Brundage, *The Crusades: A Documentary Survey* (Milwaukee: Marquette University Press, 1962), pp. 94–95.
2. H. H. Hart, *Marco Polo: Venetian Adventurer* (Norman: University of Oklahoma Press, 1967), p. 259.

10

NEW HORIZONS: THE EUROPEAN RENAISSANCE

The social, political, and economic developments of the fourteenth and fifteenth centuries wrought major changes on the culture of the Middle Ages: a fresh approach to the heritage of "pagan" antiquity and an attempt to blend its values with those of Christianity; the rise of court- and city-sponsored scholars known as humanists, whose espousal of ancient values was linked to the secularization of political power; and a new style in the arts that reflected these changes. At the heart of the cultural renaissance was a shift in the way in which people viewed themselves, based on a fresh evaluation of the legacy of classical antiquity.

THE URBAN SETTING OF THE RENAISSANCE

The Renaissance originated in fourteenth- and fifteenth-century Italy. In Italian towns, where wealth was crucial in establishing social status, the emergent capitalists patronized people of intellectual and aesthetic talent to demonstrate piety, cultural refinement, and civic pride. When this development combined in Florence with a special sense of civic and historical awareness, particularly of the value of humanistic ideals as a unifying element in the face of dangers from rival city-states, the stage was set for the Renaissance. It is easy to understand why the Renaissance, inspired by the classical world, should have begun in Italy,

with its abundance of classical monuments, but it is somewhat more difficult to explain why it first developed in Florence. Unlike Rome, Florence had few classical remains, nor did it possess the advantages of a port and a maritime economy like Genoa and Venice, which might bring it into contact with new currents of thought from the Byzantine and Islamic worlds.

Florence's principal advantage was its location astride the trade route between Rome and Naples to the south and Milan and the north. Because of its location, Florence was coveted by Milan, and the Florentines' efforts to preserve the independence of their city fostered civic pride and a stronger awareness of their historical heritage. In turn, their interest in Greek and Roman politics reinforced their fascination with classical ethics, literature, and education. Like some of their medieval predecessors, writers and artists tested themselves against Roman models, hoping to find in a glorious past the inspiration to meet the challenges of the present.

FLORENCE: A PANORAMA

The thirteenth century had been one of economic growth for Florence, especially in the fields of finance and textiles. Florentines established themselves as the preeminent bankers of Europe as well as tax collectors for the papacy. Using wool imported from England and Spain, they manufactured high-quality cloth for the markets of western Europe and the eastern Mediterranean. Florence's economy was organized around 21 guilds, of which the most important were the wool manufacturers, the wool finishers, the silk manufacturers, and the bankers.

The political, social, and economic life of the city was dominated by the patricians, whose wealth enabled them to purchase land and contract marriages with the landed aristocracy, thus expanding the city's sway over the countryside. When the patricians feuded among themselves in the 1430s, a faction led by Cosimo de' Medici triumphed, leaving the Medici family in control of Florence for the rest of the Renaissance era, except for the brief republican periods in 1494–1512 and 1527–1530.

Florence underwent striking changes during the Renaissance period. Located on the banks of the Arno River, the city was surrounded by fertile fields and picturesque hills. The last of its three walls was erected between 1284 and 1328; nearly 40 feet high and 6 feet thick, the outer wall had 73 towers and was surrounded by a moat. By the mid-1200s there were over 275 other towers and tall buildings within the city, partly because of the need for space but mostly because towers were symbols of aristocratic power as well as refuges during the vendettas that plagued Italian society. Some towers were as high as 230 feet, roughly the equivalent of a modern 20-story building. On the eve of the Renaissance the towers were reduced in size when the patricians, who dominated the urban economy, triumphed over their landed aristocratic rivals. From the late thirteenth century the more substantial homes were built for merchants with different needs and tastes from those of the landed aristocracy. The great fire of 1304, the result of feuding between rival Guelph (propapal) factions, destroyed some 1,700 houses and resulted in a major rebuilding effort. After the bubonic plague, recovery was slow, and by 1500, Florence had grown only to between 50,000 and 70,000 inhabitants, roughly half the size of Venice and Milan.

Well into the Renaissance period, Florence's main buildings made it visually a Gothic city. The great cathedral, begun in 1296, was Tuscan Gothic, apart from the innovative dome added in the fifteenth century, which heralded the beginning of Renaissance architecture. The cathedral manifested civic pride and reflected Florence's rivalry with Pisa and Siena, each of which was also building a cathedral. Two of Florence's most beautiful churches, Santa Croce and Santa Maria No-

vella, were rebuilt in the Gothic style in the 1200s. The two major palaces, the Palazzo del Popolo and the Palazzo della Signoria, are also Gothic and fortresslike in appearance. Erected in 1255, the former (now called the Bargello) was the residence of the captain of the people, who commanded armed societies representing the people's interests during periods when they exercised political dominance over the nobility. The Palazzo del Popolo was also a meeting place for the city's councils. The Palazzo della Signoria (commonly known as the Palazzo Vecchio, or "old palace") was begun in 1299 to house the guild representatives who governed the city. The palaces and chapels constructed during the Renaissance contrast sharply with the Gothic structures, symbolizing a new outlook and a changing set of values.

The Patronage of Arts and Letters

Support for humanists and artists in the Renaissance came principally from secular and religious guilds, the state, and wealthy families and oligarchs. People with newly acquired wealth patronized artists and scholars as a means of demonstrating their status and enhancing their reputation. This meant commissions for painters to depict religious themes that incorporated portraits of the donors, for architects to design funeral chapels, and for sculptors to create impressive tombs.

As guild and civic patronage declined in the early fifteenth century owing to an economic recession, families and individuals increasingly supported artists, writers, and scholars, thus increasing the scope for innovative themes and styles, particularly ones that reflected the patrons' values and interests. All of this helped to improve the artists' social and economic status. In the medieval period they had been commonly regarded as mere artisans, but by the early sixteenth century the best-known artists were much in demand. A sophisticated appreciation of their individual styles and talents developed, thus inaugurating the modern Western cult of the artist. Giorgio Vasari recorded anecdotes about artists and facts about their careers in his book of biographical sketches, *The Lives of the Painters.*

Florence, with its status-conscious patricians, its deep-rooted civic pride, its historical interest in classical Rome, and its willingness to embrace new concepts and styles, became the first setting for the Renaissance. Before long, Rome and Milan also became important centers of patronage. The economy of Rome, which relied heavily on the papacy, had declined when the popes resided at Avignon, but prosperity returned with the papal administration. Papal patronage brought Renaissance painters such as Fra Angelico (1387–1455) to Rome, sponsored the philologist Lorenzo Valla (1405–1457), and established a major library of classical authors. With Pope Sixtus IV (1471–1484) and his nephew, Pope Julius II (1503–1513), providing patronage to the greatest artists of their age, Rome supplanted Florence as the heart of the Renaissance in the early 1500s.

The Renaissance spread to Venice under different circumstances. The Venetian merchant oligarchy, primarily concerned with affairs of the republic and foreign trade, was still heavily influenced by Byzantine taste in the fourteenth and early fifteenth centuries. Because merchants returning from the Middle East brought art objects for St. Mark's Cathedral, the styles of the eastern Mediterranean were familiar. Byzantine mosaics adorned the interior of St. Mark's as well as the churches of neighboring Ravenna. Nevertheless, Renaissance ideals began to make headway as Florentine artists worked in nearby Padua and as humanists established a printing press. Two technical developments—the introduction of oil-based paints from the Flemings about 1475 and the use of canvas—were important to the development of Venetian painting. The new canvases were more adaptable to the humid Venetian climate than the traditional wood or plaster and thus could readily be used to decorate religious and civic buildings. The Renaissance adapted to the merchant oligarchy's luxurious tastes and fondness for pageantry, thereby setting a rather different course from the Renaissance in Florence and Rome.

THE HUMANISTS

The bond that knit humanists together was a commitment to study classical literary texts for their own sake rather than as handmaidens to theology. The goal of such study was the revitalization of political, social, and religious institutions through the infusion of classical values. An awareness of the thought and art of classical antiquity had never been completely lost in the medieval period and in fact had grown substantially since the late eleventh century. The reorientation in the approach to the classics that began in the 1300s entailed a shift in emphasis from the study of theology and metaphysics to the study of grammar, rhetoric, poetry, ethics, and history.

The humanists generally espoused two basic ideals: reverence for the full scope of "pagan" as well as Christian antiquity and belief in the distinctiveness of the individual, though the civic humanists of the early fifteenth century tended to subordinate the individual to the city-state. In contrast to the medieval tendency to seek virtue through the monastic life and spiritual solitude the humanists sought virtue in the public sphere. Although Italian humanists focused almost exclusively on secular things, and some even assumed a personal attitude of religious skepticism, most remained orthodox Catholics. In time their interest in pagan literature gave way to a concern for early biblical and patristic literature, especially north of the Alps, where they were determined to blend humanistic and Christian concerns. Many Italian humanists stressed the performance of civic duties, the fulfillment of which brought a civic renown that pushed the medieval quest for spiritual immortality into the shadows.

The Age of Petrarch

The earliest humanists addressed the needs of the social groups that triumphed in the political struggles within the Italian city-states in the fourteenth century. As these groups consolidated their hold on power, the humanists provided the flattering self-image the patricians sought by praising the worth of the individual, the dignity of political affairs, secular accomplishments, and the pursuit of personal glory. The humanists' success was directly related to the existence of a responsive audience of the social and political elite, an audience receptive to the humanist use of eloquence to validate the lifestyle and public role of the patriciate, the urban merchants of substance.

The most prominent of the early Renaissance humanists, Petrarch (Francesco Petrarca, 1304–1374), devoted himself to a public literary career. Fascinated by classical antiquity, he wrote biographies of famous Romans and composed *Africa,* a Latin epic in the style of the *Aeneid* to honor the Roman general Scipio Africanus. His best-known work is a collection of love sonnets to Laura, a married woman in Avignon. For more than 20 years he idealized her beauty, always from a distance. Although much of Petrarch's work was secular, he made some efforts to harmonize classical and Christian teachings. Cicero's Stoic concepts, he thought, were compatible with the Gospel. Contemptuous of both scholastics and the uneducated, committed to the critical study of manuscripts, and concerned about his reputation with posterity, Petrarch was a model for later humanists.

Petrarch's divergence from an essentially medieval outlook is evident when he is compared with the greatest figure of the previous generation, Dante Alighieri (1265–1321). Dante foreshadowed one aspect of the Renaissance by using vernacular Italian for *The Divine Comedy,* but it more closely reflects the spirit of Thomas Aquinas' *Summa Theologica* than the ideals of the humanists. Its three-line stanzas symbolizing the Trinity, its treatment of the present life as a preparation for eternity, and its traditional interpretation of sins and virtues are evocations of the medieval world. The subordinate role of classical knowledge in Dante's scheme is apparent when Virgil, after guiding Dante through hell and purgatory, is replaced for the journey through paradise by Beatrice, a symbol of revelation. Beatrice also figures prominently in Dante's *Vita nuova* ("New Life"), his spiritual autobiography. Unlike Petrarch's love for Laura, which is intensely personal and secular, Dante's passion for Beatrice is symbolic of Christ's love for his church. The two types of love reflect the difference between the medieval and Renaissance outlooks.

Petrarch's friend and student, Giovanni Boccaccio (1313–1375), is remembered for his *Decameron,* a collection of 100 short stories related by young people who fled the plague that ravaged Florence in 1348. The racy tales were mostly borrowed from classical, medieval, and Eastern sources. Unlike Chaucer, who used some of the same material in *The Canterbury Tales,* Boccaccio gave his work a more secular flavor by omitting the usual moral commentary.

Civic Humanists

The second stage of humanism, which lasted from approximately 1375 to 1460, was committed to the proposition that humanistic scholarship must be brought to bear on public affairs. Civic humanists held community service in high regard as a justification for the privileges of the patriciate. Learning thus became a tool to benefit society as well as a means to assert political influence. Taking note of their predecessors' interest in rhetoric, the civic humanists extolled it as the basis for a new standard of nobility to which patricians should aspire. Rhetoric, which entailed both eloquence and the application of knowledge to specific problems,

could reputedly mold good citizens by making law and morality effective.

The civic humanists espoused a belief in political liberty for a broadly defined elite and in civic patriotism, which in Florence involved the preservation of the city from Milanese aggression. In the late fourteenth and early fifteenth centuries, Florence had three chancellors who were civic humanists: Coluccio Salutati, Leonardo Bruni, and Poggio Bracciolini. During his 31-year chancellorship, Salutati, a disciple of Petrarch, boasted that Florence was the "mother of freedom," a theme echoed by Bruni and Poggio. Bruni's *History of Florence* was written in the conviction that history involves the use of examples to teach philosophy and that "the careful study of the past enlarges our foresight in contemporary affairs." The political liberty extolled by the civic humanists was never fully realized in Renaissance Florence, and such liberty as did exist was sharply reduced after Cosimo de' Medici began to dominate city politics in 1434. Faced with the realities of the Medici oligarchy, which undermined constitutional government, the humanists accepted Medici patronage and generally retreated from the political arena to their scholarship and contemplation.

The Florentine Academy and the Neoplatonists

The decline of the civic humanists and the flowering of Neoplatonism in late fifteenth-century Florence marked the beginning of humanism's third stage. Instead of a primary concern with the duties of civic life and a preoccupation with such works as Aristotle's *Ethics,* interest shifted to Plato and the contemplative life. The seeds of this transformation had been planted in the 1390s when the Greek scholar Manuel Chrysoloras taught Greek in the city; among his pupils was the civic humanist Bruni, who later translated Plato. Greek studies received a further impetus in 1439 when Greeks came to Ferrara and Florence to attend an ecumenical council. At the urging of one of them, Cosimo de' Medici eventually endowed an academy near Florence in 1462. The academy provided the setting for philosophical discussions presided over by Marsilio Ficino (1433–1499). The atmosphere was semireligious: the disciples sang hymns praising Plato, burned a lamp before his bust, and adopted as their motto "Salvation in Plato." Ficino himself prepared editions of the works of Plato and Plotinus.

Renaissance Neoplatonism blended ideas from classical thought, Christian dogma, and astrology. Ficino and his followers stressed the uniqueness of humankind, including personal worth and dignity as well as the power to transform oneself spiritually by choosing the good. Those who opted to pursue the higher things of life aspired to the release of their souls from the perishable world of matter. The Neoplatonic ideal was otherworldly, and the Neoplatonic experience emotional. Its moving force was love, and its direction was the rational life. To know God was the ultimate goal, attainable only by separating from the material world. The Neoplatonists were sensitive to beauty, which they associated with truth and goodness, all of which were earthly manifestations of Platonic Forms. The Neoplatonic love of symbolic allegory, Christian mysticism, and beauty made the philosophy attractive to such artists as Botticelli, Raphael, and Michelangelo.

The Florentine Neoplatonists moved beyond the range of traditional humanists. The latter's shift of emphasis from metaphysics to ethics was reversed by the Neoplatonists but without returning to the views of the medieval scholastics. The Neoplatonists also broke with the civic humanists by turning their backs on public affairs and the campaign for political freedom—perhaps a prudent choice in the treacherous political atmosphere of Medici Florence. Nevertheless, something of the original humanist ideal remained in their respect for human dignity and the freedom to choose one's destiny. This ideal was eloquently expressed in the *Oration on the Dignity of Man* by Ficino's disciple, Pico della Mirandola (1463–1494). Pico accorded humans a special rank in the universal chain of being where they could ponder the plan of the universe and marvel at its beauty. Although Renaissance Neoplatonism avoided political activism, it was radical in its rejection of church hierarchy in favor of an emphasis on individual enlightenment.

Education and Scholarship

The central goal of a humanist education was to develop the virtuous individual, one who would live a moral, disciplined life both for personal enrichment and for the benefit of society. This education was intended for the socially elite, not commoners. A number of humanists urged major changes in the educational curriculum, particularly at the secondary level, to accomplish this end. An education focusing on the humanities was deemed to have the greatest practical relevance for daily

living because it addressed the whole person. For the humanists, virtue entailed both the fundamental principles of morality and an ethical ideal that encompassed self-determination and an awareness of personal worth.

The ideas of the humanist educators are reflected in the Renaissance's most influential handbook of manners, *The Book of the Courtier* by Baldassare Castiglione (1478–1529). Intended as a guide for aristocrats in the service of their prince, the book depicts the ideal courtier as someone knowledgeable in Greek, Latin, and the vernacular and accomplished in music, poetry, dancing, and sports. Castiglione's courtier is a well-mannered and versatile gentleman, as much at home in the salon and the concert chamber as in the halls of power. The courtier, moreover, must be an educator—not of young people but of the prince, who must be taught the ways of virtue, especially temperance. Many of the same qualities are to be found in the aristocratic lady who, said Castiglione, should be adorned with "admirable accomplishments." She was to shun "manly" sports such as riding and tennis as well as musical instruments that required ungainly physical effort, such as trumpets and drums. While Castiglione idealized women as objects of courtly love, in practice he expected them to be subservient to men.

Another fundamental concern of the humanists was the search for accurate classical texts in archives. To produce good texts, they had to develop critical tools, especially philology (the study of the origins of language), paleography (the study of ancient manuscripts), and textual criticism. Lorenzo Valla used textual criticism to demonstrate that the eighth-century Donation of Constantine was a forgery. Some experts already suspected that this document, by which Constantine (died 337) had allegedly endowed the papacy with vast lands, was fraudulent, but Valla laid any doubt to rest by demonstrating that it contained language and references that were unknown in Constantine's day. Valla also used his command of classical languages to prove that there were errors in the official version of the Bible, the Latin Vulgate. Valla's application of philological and historical techniques to the Donation and the Vulgate provided the foundation for major advances in textual criticism in the sixteenth century, particularly in the field of biblical scholarship.

Humanists Outside Italy

The ideals of the Italian humanists were carried beyond the Alps in the late fifteenth century by students, scholars, and merchants. The rapid development of the printing industry also facilitated the spread of humanist scholarship. The pioneers were the German poet Peter Luder (c. 1415–1474) and the Dutchman Rudolf Agricola (c. 1443–1485), both of whom helped to make the University of Heidelberg a leading center of humanist thought. In England, too, the humanists carried their message to the universities. William Grocyn (c. 1466–1519), who lectured at Oxford, had studied in Florence. Among his friends were three of the greatest humanists of the sixteenth century, his pupil Thomas More, John Colet, and Erasmus (all discussed in Chapter 11). The English were also acquainted with humanist ideals through the presence of Italian scholars at the royal court. Other Italian humanists took their views to the courts of Spain, Hungary, and Poland.

French humanists made notable contributions. Guillaume Budé (1468–1540) persuaded Francis I to found a library at Fontainebleau, the origin of the Bibliothèque Nationale in Paris. Marguerite d'Angoulême (1492–1549), sister of Francis I and a prolific writer, was primarily noted for her *Heptaméron,* a collection of 70 short, racy stories akin to Boccaccio's *Decameron. Gargantua* and *Pantagruel,* tales about giants enamored of life and drinking by Françdois Rabelais (c. 1495–1553), offer a satirical portrait of sixteenth-century society peppered with humanist insights about the human condition.

Women and Renaissance Culture

Although most Renaissance humanists were men, more than 30 women humanists have been identified. Few wrote major works, probably because of social barriers rather than lack of creative talent. Women almost never attended a university and thus had virtually no opportunity to enter the learned professions. Women humanists typically acquired their education from their fathers or private tutors, which effectively eliminated all women but those of princely, aristocratic, or patrician status. During the early Renaissance, women's intellectual careers were confined to their late teens and early twenties if they opted to marry, for marital obligations and spousal pressure made intellectual commitments extremely difficult. The advent of printing, however, provided literate women with the opportunity to pursue such studies as medicine, religion, and the classics. The usual alternative to marriage—entry into the religious life—was tantamount to rejecting the world in favor of a book-lined cell. For intellectually gifted young women the choice was difficult, more so because men typically regarded learned women as intellectual oddities, male minds in female bodies.

Although male humanists praised women in general, they usually preferred that learned women remain safely unwed and likened them to Amazon queens and armed warriors. In the courtly love tradition of the Middle Ages, men were supposed to please the ladies, whereas in the Renaissance, women were molded to satisfy the gentlemen. As the Renaissance ideal of learning spread, girls and young women of the upper estates received better educations than their medieval counterparts, but the classical material they studied reinforced notions of male superiority. Women's education was not to enable them to enter the learned professions but to act as ladies of the court, patronesses of the arts, and decorative presences who added gracefulness to their households.

The contributions of learned Renaissance women were varied. Many wrote Latin letters, orations, treatises, and poems. Alessandra Scala of Florence had a command of Greek equaled by few Western scholars. The ranks of humanist poets embraced such women as Christine de Pisan (c. 1364–c. 1431), a French writer of Italian descent whose works included a biography of the French King Charles V, an autobiography, and a study of heroic and virtuous women from around the world entitled *The Book of the City of Ladies.* As the Renaissance extended north of the Alps, more young women received a humanist education and took up their pens to write literary, religious, and historical works. The range of topics available to women was restricted by social custom, since most secular subjects were thought to be the province of men. Even in the religious realm, women were expected to confine themselves to hymns and poems, devotional works, and translations. Thus humanist education tantalized bright young women even as society thwarted their ambitions by hedging in their possibilities for intellectual expression.

VITTORIA COLONNA, POET AND PHILOSOPHER

One of the most gifted Renaissance women, Vittoria Colonna belonged to a powerful Roman family with vast holdings in the Papal States and southern Italy. Among her relatives were a pope and 30 cardinals. Born in 1492, she was the daughter of the grand constable of the kingdom of Naples. Although her marriage at the age of 19 to the marchese of Pescara, a Spaniard, had been arranged for political reasons 15 years earlier, she nevertheless fell in love with him. Often absent on military service, the marchese died in 1525, leaving her childless. In his memory, Vittoria wrote sonnets idealizing him as a saint despite the fact that he had been faithless to her, contemptuous of Italians, and treasonous in his political dealings. Imbued with Neoplatonic concepts, Vittoria envisioned a reunion with him in a better, spiritual life. Her love sonnets, written in the tradition of Petrarch, won her acclaim in humanist circles, particularly from Castiglione, who gave her a manuscript of his *Courtier* to critique.

Vittoria's religious sonnets reflect both her ascetic piety and her Neoplatonism, which together sought to liberate the spirit by subduing the flesh. In Neoplatonic imagery she expressed her hope to "mount with wings" to reach true light and love. Hers was an intensely personal experience: "I write," she said, "only to free myself from my inner pain." Her sonnets manifest a keen interest in church reform, a concern she shared with a number of her friends, including Cardinal Contarini, a chief architect of the Catholic Reformation. Although one of her closest friends, Bernardino Ochino, ultimately defected to the Protestants, she remained loyal to the Catholic church.

Vittoria found a kindred spirit in Michelangelo, whom she met shortly after he had begun painting the Sistine Chapel ceiling in 1508. He was Vittoria's "most singular friend" and she his "love," capable of causing "a withered tree to burgeon and to bloom." Their intimacy, in which Michelangelo found spiritual solace and artistic inspiration, was platonic. They corresponded extensively and exchanged sonnets, the tone of which is reminiscent of Petrarch's sonnets to Laura but in an unmistakably Christian context. Michelangelo wrote madrigals and painted at least three works for Vittoria and probably a portrait as well. He must have been sympathetic to her ascetic convictions, which were pronounced after her husband's death. She fasted and wore hair shirts until Cardinal Reginald Pole, a key figure in the Catholic Reformation, persuaded her to adopt a more moderate course. She spent much of the period between 1541 and her death in 1547 in monasteries, a reminder that many Renaissance humanists saw their religious and humanist principles as fully compatible.

MACHIAVELLI AND THE CULTURE OF POWER

The evolution of the humanist movement is nowhere more apparent than in its attitude toward history. Initially, the humanists were preoccupied with the recovery of classical texts that could be used as a standard against which to measure their own society. They then broadened their horizon to the study of classical history with a view to using its lessons as a guide to human affairs and the improvement of political and social institutions. Finally, in the sixteenth century, disillusioned by their inability to reshape the present by the application of historical ideals, humanist historians relinquished their belief in the ability of virtue to triumph over external forces. Instead of examining the past with a view to improving the present, most historians used the historical record to justify their religious beliefs or the political ambitions of their respective states.

The disillusionment of sixteenth-century humanist historians was a product of earlier conditions, particularly in northern and central Italy. The failure of republican government in Florence and the French invasion of 1494 virtually demolished the hopes of the earlier humanists. Power replaced virtue as the cardinal principle in the conduct of human affairs, particularly in the thought of Niccolò Machiavelli (1469–1527). He was in his twenties when the Florentines ousted Piero de' Medici, revived their republican government, and rallied to the reforming message of the Dominican friar Girolamo Savonarola (1452–1498). For four years the Florentines were caught up in a frenzy of revivalism. The "bonfires of vanities" claimed everything from sumptuous clothing and stylish wigs to books and works of art. By 1498 the zeal had ebbed, and Savonarola, having infuriated the immoral Pope Alexander VI by his criticism, was burned as a heretic on trumped-up charges. The Council of Ten, which assumed the direction of Florentine affairs, made Machiavelli its secretary and one of its diplomats, dispatching him throughout Italy on behalf of the republic. His career was abruptly terminated in 1512 when the Medici returned to Florence and ousted the republican government. Machiavelli was tortured and sent into exile.

As an exile he reflected on the political problems of Italy and its history in his principal works, *The Prince* and the *Discourses on Livy*. A master of Italian prose *[handwritten note at top of page:]* Scriptorium— where monks wrote scriptures each scripture was chained to a desk so no one could walk off w/ it.

style, he also wrote *Mandragola,* a satirical comedy attacking human foibles and immorality. Machiavelli brought to his writing not only a knowledge of Roman history and the works of such humanist historians as Bruni and Poggio but also firsthand experience of politics and diplomacy. *The Prince* (1513), dedicated to Lorenzo de' Medici, grandson of Lorenzo the Magnificent, has sometimes been interpreted as a satire on the politics of despotism. On the contrary, it reflects the sober realism of a middle-aged diplomat and a theoretical brilliance that has earned Machiavelli a reputation as the founder of modern political science. *The Prince*'s primary theme discusses the "new prince"—the political innovator who has just seized power—and his dealings with his subjects.

The Medici now dominated both Florence and Rome, where Leo X (1513–1521), Lorenzo the Magnificent's son, was pope. Machiavelli intended to prod the Medici into embracing an ethic of power shorn of religious or ethical limitations as the only effective means to achieve a stable, secure Italy free of "barbarian" intervention. His was a creed of action, not reflection, of pragmatism rather than idealism. He praised Roman republicanism because it had been a successful tool of power and praised republican government in general if it embodied *virtù,* or inner strength.

Machiavelli believed that history was shaped by a recurring cycle of events; instead of evolution and progress, there was mere repetition. As it was for Bruni, history is a storehouse of examples and should be studied to ascertain the causes and cures of current problems. Because history repeats itself, present ills can be treated by imitating solutions that were successful in the past. Everything in the present and the future has a counterpart in antiquity, the happiest time in history. Machiavelli's concept of the imitation of antiquity is an extreme application of the humanist tendency to venerate the classical world. In formulating his principles of statecraft, Machiavelli ransacked classical history to find material for his argument and also drew on his political experience. Between them he found justification for the principles that make *The Prince* famous: Be deceitful and cunning in dealing with rivals; do as people actually do rather than as they ought to do; regard the state—the prince—as supreme, recognizing that the end justifies the means; place military security first; avoid neutrality, especially in dealing with other states; instill fear in one's subjects as the best means to compel obedience; undertake great enterprises to divert atten-

tion from internal problems. Such was the culture of power, and in espousing it, Machiavelli broke with the traditional model of the good ruler, whether Aristotelian or Judeo-Christian.

THE PRINTING REVOLUTION

Machiavelli's *Prince* was too scandalous to be published during his lifetime, but other works of Renaissance scholarship were printed despite some humanist opposition to putting learned works in the hands of commoners. Movable metal type, developed in Germany in the fifteenth century, was vastly superior to the technique of block printing. The Chinese and Koreans had already invented movable type, but it had little appeal to them because their scripts consisted of thousands of different characters. Metal type was more durable as well as more flexible than wooden blocks because individual letters could be reused in new combinations. By 1300, linen paper, which had been introduced from East Asia through the Islamic world, was in common use, thus setting the stage for the new presses. Johann Gutenberg of Mainz, one of the pioneers of the new technology, published his first known work, a papal proclamation, in 1454. The first of his magnificent Bibles appeared two years later. The new press spread rapidly throughout western and central Europe.

The changes brought about by the printing press reached virtually every aspect of life. As the price of books fell and their number increased, there was a greater incentive to acquire and improve reading skills. The expansion of the literate population offered new opportunities to writers. Religious topics, legal studies, works on astrology, and popular tales were prominent on the early book lists, as were editions of the Bible, especially once vernacular versions became common in the sixteenth century. The press proved a boon to scholarship by making more accurate editions possible, by standardizing maps and images as well as texts, and by encouraging cross-cultural interchange. Ideas spread with greater rapidity, and there was more inducement to develop new theories. Printing also increased the likelihood of a document's preservation. Through printing, collections of laws and ordinances became available to a wider public, with beneficial effects for the practice of law as well as for public discourse about political affairs. By the sixteenth century, however, both church and state found it necessary to step up their censorship. The advent of printing made propaganda possible, and in the seventeenth century, newspapers began replacing the pulpit as the primary source of news in urban areas. Printing also increased the reputation—or infamy—of authors and eventually made it possible for some writers to earn a living by their pens alone. Gutenberg and his colleagues thus set in motion one of the most sweeping revolutions in history.

THE FINE ARTS

The Renaissance ushered in significant changes in artistic style and taste, reflecting the absorption of humanist ideals. The most prominent hallmarks of Renaissance painting and sculpture—fascination with classical themes, expressions of individualism, a more self-confident embracing of secular themes—reflected humanist concerns. Technical advances in painting were also possible after oil-based paints were brought to Italy from Flanders in the late fifteenth century. Painters had previously worked in fresco, which involved the application of pigment to wet plaster, and tempera, which entailed mixing pigments with a sizing, such as eggs. Oils enabled the painter to achieve detail, clarity, and permanence of color that were not possible with fresco or tempera. Renaissance artists also acquired the ability to give the illusion of dimensionality (perspective) by using gradations between light and dark to model their figures and by applying mathematical principles to create the visual illusion of objects receding into space.

Early Renaissance Painting

In the Middle Ages, painting was the least developed of the principal fine arts. Giotto (c. 1266–1337), a Florentine, revitalized it and provided the bridge between the medieval era and the early Renaissance. In a series of frescoes in a chapel in Padua depicting the life of Christ, Giotto's narrative power, evocation of human emotion, and use of spatial depth turned the walls into a stage on which the central events of the Christian faith were acted out. His work was seen as the harbinger of a new era. Although none of Giotto's immediate disciples equaled their master, his frescoes on the walls of Florentine churches became textbooks for later generations of Renaissance painters, including Masaccio and Michelangelo.

Masaccio, *The Holy Trinity,* 1428. God the Father holds the cross while the Holy Spirit descends in the form of a dove. Mary is to the left of the cross, St. John to the right, and below them are the kneeling donors. Masaccio's use of linear perspective gives the fresco a striking sense of depth. [Alinari/Art Resource, New York]

The frescoes of the Florentine artist Masaccio (1401–1428) revolutionized painting. His treatment of the nude figures of Adam and Eve being expelled from the Garden of Eden displays a naturalism and psychological penetration that made his work very different in spirit from Giotto's paintings. Masaccio links the Christian and the classical by setting his scene against a Roman arch. His work demonstrates a dramatic advance in the ability to render a sense of depth, and the expulsion scene in particular is notable for its use of shading, a technique known as *chiaroscuro,* which enhanced the pictorial effect by conveying the reflection of light from three-dimensional surfaces. Masaccio's discoveries encouraged his contemporaries and successors to continue experimenting, and Michelangelo himself was among those who sketched Masaccio's work in order to learn his techniques.

The impact of Neoplatonism on Renaissance painting is manifest in the works of the Florentine Sandro Botticelli (1444–1510). Through his Medici patrons he came into contact with Marsilio Ficino and the Academy. His paintings of Venus—emerging from the sea on a giant shell, celebrating the arrival of spring in the company of Mercury and Cupid, or reclining with Mars as mythological lovers—reflect the Neoplatonic notion of Venus as the source of divine love.

Later Renaissance Painting: A New Phase

The early Renaissance achievements in rendering the human figure, three-dimensionality, chiaroscuro, and individualized portraiture became the foundation of the mature period of Renaissance painting that began in the late 1400s and lasted approximately a century. The later Renaissance is distinguished as an era in which the great artists combined creative talents with intense individuality to produce a highly personal style. At the end of the fifteenth century there was a noticeable rise in the status of leading artists, the result of which was greater freedom from the dictates of patrons. Information about the artists was disseminated more widely, and the great ones were increasingly thought of in terms of genius and referred to as "divine." Interest in and respect for the artist's personality grew, and two artists—the sculptor Benvenuto Cellini and the painter Albrecht Dürer—wrote autobiographies, expressing the Renaissance fascination with the individual. It became increasingly common too for artists to paint their own portraits.

Leonardo da Vinci

Although no single painting marked a sharp cleavage between the early and late Renaissance, Leonardo da Vinci's depiction of the *Virgin of the Rocks,* done in the early 1480s, might be considered the first late Renaissance painting. By this point in his career, Leonardo (1452–1519) had already developed a keen interest in

Leonardo da Vinci's *Virgin of the Rocks* combines the artist's intense interest in natural phenomena and human anatomy with traditional religious devotion. [Cliché des Musées Nationaux, Paris]

nature. In the *Virgin of the Rocks* he chose a semidark grotto with an abundance of plant life and a pool for his setting. Although the natural details are faithfully rendered, the total effect is one of mystery and poetic vision—of a psychological world. The *Virgin of the Rocks* is an intensely personal statement by the artist, as is his portrait of the Mona Lisa with its dreamlike background expressive of the personality of the subject.

About the time he was working on the *Virgin of the Rocks,* Leonardo left Florence for Milan, where he acquired the duke's patronage. There he painted his masterpiece, *The Last Supper,* on the wall of a church refectory, unfortunately using an experimental paint that has decayed over the years. Gestures and body posture reveal the inner drama as the disciples react to

A portion of the Sistine Chapel ceiling, by Michelangelo, depicting the expulsion of Adam and Eve from the Garden of Eden. [Alinari/Art Resource, New York]

Christ's statement that one of them will betray him. Space is mathematically ordered through the use of recurring rectangles and the placement of the disciples in groups of three, united by their gestures. Christ, his arms outstretched and his head framed against a window of symbolic light, is in the shape of a pyramid, Leonardo's favorite organizing device, while Judas, his profile rendered in symbolic darkness, has not been separated from the rest of the disciples as had been usual in earlier paintings of the same subjects. The innovation is deliberate, the psychological insight unsurpassed.

Leonardo's genius as a painter was only one of his many interests. He is the supreme example of the Renaissance ideal—a virtuoso whose intellectual curiosity led him into a host of fields. His notebooks contain sketches for military inventions, many of which were not realized for centuries, including submarines and prototypes of a tank and a helicopter. His studies of human anatomy were based on the dissection of more than 30 corpses. Town planning, architecture, geology, botany, music, and optics were among his wide-ranging interests.

Raphael, Michelangelo, and the Roman Renaissance

After Julius II became pope in 1503, he used his patronage to make the city the cultural capital of the West. Raphael Sanzio (1483–1520), a native of Umbria in central Italy, studied various works of Leonardo and Michelangelo in Florence before going to Rome. Commissioned by Julius to paint frescoes in the Vatican, Raphael reflected the synthesis of the classical and the Christian in the Renaissance by juxtaposing two magnificent scenes, one linking the earthly and heavenly churches by the sacrifice of the mass, the other an assembly of classical philosophers and scientists grouped around Plato and Aristotle. Raphael is also renowned for a series of gentle Madonnas that blend naturalism with idealized beauty.

Michelangelo Buonarroti (1475–1564), another native of Tuscany, was in Rome to paint the ceiling of the Sistine Chapel when Raphael arrived in 1508. Deeply influenced by Neoplatonism, the temperamental Michelangelo created a massive work (128 by 44 feet) fusing Hebrew and classical themes. Christianity is only implicitly present in the sense that the pagan sibyls and the Hebrew prophets were thought to point to the advent of the Messiah. The work abounds in symbolism: the Neoplatonic contrast between light and darkness, spirit and matter; the recurring triads, basic to the numerical symbolism of Neoplatonism; the relationship of earthly knowledge (pagan sibyls) and divine revelation (Hebrew prophets). Michelangelo's painting *The Last Judgment* on the east wall of the chapel was added much later, between 1532 and 1541, and reveals both the somber, deeply religious mood that characterized the final period of the artist's life and his fascination with Dante.

Titian and the Venetian Renaissance

In their basic conviction that art must transcend nature, Michelangelo and Titian (c. 1487–1576) were in full accord, yet their paintings are strikingly different. In contrast to Michelangelo's preoccupation with statuesque figures and Neoplatonic symbolism, Titian epitomizes Venice's fascination with light and color, reflecting the play of light on its waterways and palatial buildings. His themes range from Christian subjects to sensuous reclining nudes, from classical mythology to contemporary portraits. His is an elegant art, befitting the clients for whom he painted. Only in his late paintings does he forsake vibrant colors and rich textures in favor of subdued tones and gloomy light. Like Michelangelo, Titian spent his last years engaged in deep religious introspection.

[handwritten marginal note: painted one painting each month / age 99 died at]

Sculpture: From Virtuosity to Introspection

In sculpture as in painting, Renaissance artists strove to achieve greater naturalism, individualization, and, in sculptural reliefs, a keen sense of depth. Sculptors such as Lorenzo Ghiberti (1378–1455) and Donatello (1386–1466) influenced contemporary painters as they pioneered these developments. Ghiberti's crowning achievement, the bronze doors of the baptistery in Florence, were intended to imitate nature in the classical Greek style. He used only scenes from the Old Testament in his ten panels, flanked with portrait busts of pagan sibyls and Hebrew prophets as the heralds of Christ's coming.

Ghiberti's pupil, the Florentine Donatello, exhibited a bold style that is evident in his bronze statue of David, the first freestanding nude sculpture since antiquity. Wearing only a shepherd's hat and military leggings, David, with his idealized face and physique, is the antithesis of Donatello's melancholy, emaciated figure of Mary Magdalene. In his portrayal of her as a time-ravaged penitent, there is no hint of the usual Renaissance preoccupation with beauty, for Donatello's outlook has become more introspective, his concern with matters of the spirit more predominant. In the works of Donatello, Leonardo, and Michelangelo a steady progression can be seen from an early concern with innovation and virtuosity to a later preoccupation with inward states and spiritual experience.

Michelangelo's first love was sculpting, an art he approached through his Neoplatonic convictions in the belief that his task was to liberate the living figure encased in a block of marble. In his early years, Michelangelo produced statues of sublime beauty, as if he were

Michelangelo's Pietà of 1498–1499. [Alinari/Art Resource, New York]

perfecting rather than duplicating nature. Instead of pursuing mathematically ordered perfection in the manner of Leonardo, he relied on inspiration to determine ideal proportions. His success is apparent in two majestic works completed in his twenties: the Pietà, in which Mary's youthful face is as supremely beautiful as Raphael's Madonnas, and a towering statue of David, his heroic physique an idealized rendition of male anatomy. Michelangelo's last works stand in vivid contrast to these idealized, confident statues. The Pietàs of his final years are unfinished, two of them partially smashed by his own hand. The late Pietàs were a plea for his own redemption, the culmination of the Renaissance quest for individual fulfillment at the deepest, most personal level.

Women Artists

Some women artists in this period achieved fame. Michelangelo took a special interest in the painter Sofonisba Anguissola (c. 1535–1625) of Cremona. For nearly two decades, Anguissola, who specialized in individual and group portraits, painted at the court of Philip II of Spain. The English monarch Henry VIII patronized a number of women painters, paying one of them—Levina Teerling (c. 1515–1576), a manuscript illuminator—more than the famous portraitist Hans Holbein for her work. Royal patronage was also bestowed on Catharina van Hemessen (1528–c. 1587) of the Netherlands, who enjoyed the support of Queen Mary of Hungary and painted intriguingly introspective portraits. The leading woman sculptor was probably Properzia Rossi (c. 1490–1530) of Bologna, whose work is reminiscent of the sculptural reliefs of Ghiberti. That women artists were active and relatively prosperous during the Renaissance is unmistakable, although it is difficult to reconstruct their contributions because so many of their works have been lost or destroyed.

Architecture and Classical Inspiration

Inspired by the architectural principles and motifs of classical antiquity, Renaissance architects rejected the Gothic style in favor of one that recalled the arches, columns, capitals, and ordered simplicity of Greco-Roman buildings. The artist who pioneered Renaissance architecture, the Florentine Filippo Brunelleschi (1377–1446), solved the greatest architectural puzzle of the fifteenth century—the design and construction of a suitable dome for the cathedral in Florence—by studying ancient Roman buildings, particularly the Pantheon. His solution was to build an inner dome to support the massive outer dome, thus avoiding the supports that had become unsightly to the tastes of his time, to use a drum below the dome to contain its outward thrust, and to place a lantern atop the dome to stabilize the entire structure. The result was technologically innovative and aesthetically pleasing. Brunelleschi's other designs, including a chapel for the Pazzi family in Florence, are even more distinctly Renaissance in spirit with their concern with classical order.

When Michelangelo set about designing the dome for St. Peter's Basilica in Rome, he studied Brunelleschi's dome. Other architects had already worked on St. Pe-

St. Peter's, Rome, as Michelangelo intended it to appear. [Alinari/Art Resource, New York]

ter's, and Michelangelo's main contribution was the soaring dome. It was intended to crown a church in the shape of a Greek cross, with four equal arms, but in the early seventeenth century the western arm was extended into a long, traditional nave, upsetting the careful balance that Michelangelo had envisioned.

Like Brunelleschi, Andrea Palladio (c. 1518–1580), the leading architect of the Venetian Renaissance, studied classical buildings in Rome. Convinced that the numerical ratios basic to musical harmony were found throughout the universe and were thus derived from God, Palladio designed his buildings to embody mathematical symmetry. His specialty was the rural villa, of which his best known example is the Villa Rotunda near Venice. The building, mathematically perfect, is cubical, with an interior cylinder, a saucer-shaped dome, and four matching Ionic porches reminiscent of Greek temple facades.

Northern Art

North of the Alps, the transition from Gothic to Renaissance came in the fifteenth century. Flemish artists took advantage of oil paints to capture realism by depicting intricate details; surface appearances mattered more than form, anatomy, and motion. The fascination with detail is evident in the work of Jan van Eyck (c. 1390–1441). In his portrait of the Medici banker Giovanni Arnolfini and his bride, van Eyck's ties to the medieval world are still apparent in the painting's traditional symbolism: the dog represents fidelity, the single burning candle the all-seeing Christ; the statue on the bedpost is St. Margaret, patron saint of childbirth, and the shoes have been removed to symbolize the holy ground of the sacrament of matrimony. Although the work is suffused with religious meaning, in the last resort the painting is about the union of two individuals and the status they enjoy—concerns common to Italian Renaissance painters.

Renaissance art culminated in the Netherlands in the work of Pieter Brueghel the elder (c. 1525–1569). Although he visited Italy, he was never very impressed by classical art but was intrigued by peasant life. His peasant scenes celebrate folk customs such as dances and wedding feasts, often with a touch of humor. There was a serious side to Brueghel, who used his works to

Pieter Brueghel, *The Wedding Dance.* Brueghel depicts rustic scene full of robust peasants. His paintings do not manifest the usual Flemish concern with sharp detail. [© The Detroit Institute of Arts, City of Detroit Purchase]

condemn religious bigotry and Spanish barbarity in the Netherlands. His almost total lack of interest in classical models and his continued use of traditional symbolism and moralizing underscore the fact that northern Renaissance artists retained far more of the medieval heritage than did their counterparts in Italy.

PERSPECTIVES ON THE RENAISSANCE

"Out of the thick Gothic night our eyes are opened to the glorious torch of the sun," wrote the French writer François Rabelais, reflecting the Renaissance belief in the birth of a new age of cultural brilliance following a millennium of darkness and ignorance. Thus was born the unfortunate notion of the Dark Ages. It was a natural step to describe the new epoch as a *rinascita*—a rebirth or renaissance, a term adopted by Giorgio Vasari to describe the renaissance of the arts. The notion of the Renaissance was expanded by later historians to include developments in such areas as philosophy, literature, and statecraft.

A tendency to exalt the Renaissance developed in the eighteenth century, as reflected in the French philosopher Voltaire's depiction of Italy as the successor to the glories of classical Greece. The corollary of this was the denigration of the Middle Ages, which appeared to Voltaire as a dark age of irrationality. The romantics who followed, however, evaluated the Middle Ages more positively, taking their inspiration from its religious culture and finding their historical roots in medieval states rather than the classical heritage. But the Renaissance was once again thrust to the fore by the Swiss historian Jacob Burckhardt (1818–1897) in *The Civilization of the Renaissance in Italy* (1860). He regarded the Renaissance as an age dominated by the revival of classical antiquity, the development of a pronounced individualism (the awareness and expression of personality), and a fresh discovery of the world of nature and humankind. This was possible, he argued, because of the genius of the Italians, "the first modern people of Europe who gave themselves boldly to speculations of freedom and necessity." According to Burckhardt, the Renaissance as a distinctive epoch in the history of civilization was born in the political turbulence that engulfed Italy in the fourteenth and fifteenth centuries.

The sharp break drawn by Burckhardt between the Middle Ages and the Renaissance was challenged by medieval specialists, whose research demolished the stereotype of the Middle Ages as a time of ignorance and "semibarbarism." Claiming to find the roots of the Renaissance in the twelfth century, some medievalists asserted that it should be considered the last phase of the Middle Ages, not the beginning of the modern world. In 1927 the American historian Charles Homer Haskins published *The Renaissance of the Twelfth Century*. Pointing to such phenomena as the revival of the Latin classics and Roman law, the recovery of Greek science and philosophy, and the beginnings of the European universities—a revival of learning in the fullest sense—Haskins argued that the more famous Italian Renaissance was in reality the culmination of a movement that had begun in the late eleventh century and continued without a major break into the early modern period. Haskins' attack on the Burckhardt school did not deprecate the achievements of the Renaissance. Some medievalists did, however, pointing out that in many respects, such as its emphasis on magic and the occult, the Renaissance was less "rational" than the Middle Ages, and its science less advanced than that in the thirteenth and fourteenth centuries.

After World War II, Wallace Ferguson asserted a compromise interpretation according to which the Renaissance was an age of transition between the medieval and modern eras. Basic to this argument is the conviction that the changes that occurred in the Renaissance were profound, encompassing a transformation of institutions, outlook, culture, and economies. Taken together, the changes produced a distinctive cultural period that is neither medieval nor modern, though elements of both can be found in it.

The debate continues today. Much of the discussion has concentrated on the nature of Renaissance humanism, which has been variously defined as an educational system focusing on Greek and Roman classics, a cult of rhetoric and oratory, a method of rational inquiry, a philosophy of human dignity and individualism, or scholarly endeavor devoted to establishing new criteria of political liberty and civic responsibility. The simplest definition of humanism treats it as the study of grammar, rhetoric, poetry, history, and ethics in classical texts as distinct from the scholastic emphasis on logic and metaphysics. By this interpretation, humanism is an academic movement rather than a philosophy or, as Federico Chabod has argued, a pattern of life based on the quest to imitate classical antiquity. Chabod recognizes the medieval interest in the classics but distinguishes the scholastics' selective approach—picking and choosing things that supported the Christian world view—from the humanist attempt to use all of antiquity as a means of challenging medieval assumptions and reconciling the full legacy of Western culture with its religion.

Other historians trace the origins of humanism to the political conditions in Italy and the need to develop a predominantly secular interpretation of government in order to throw off the bondage of the church. Some suggest that the leaders of the city-states encouraged the emphasis on the glories of classical antiquity to assert their own political identity and to unite the people behind their rule. Humanistic ideals in this view were welcomed because they healed rifts between competing social groups and unified the community in the face of threats from other city-states. Historians have come to realize that humanists were a diverse group of individuals whose concerns were far from identical.

SUMMARY

Although the intellectual and artistic developments in the Renaissance were initially the province of the socially elite, in the long run many commoners enjoyed them as well. Statues and paintings were displayed in churches, civic buildings, and town squares, and such architectural gems as the Florence Cathedral and St. Peter's Basilica were open to the public. Michelangelo's statue of David was placed in the Palazzo della Signoria, while statues of Donatello were publicly displayed in Florence and Padua. As printing spread, books became less expensive, making it possible for the literary achievements of the Renaissance to reach a wider audience than anyone could have anticipated in 1400. Because husbands or wives could read to families and masters to apprentices, the high levels of illiteracy were less of a barrier to the dissemination of literature than might be imagined. As humanist ideas entered the curriculum and new schools were founded, Renaissance teachings reached a wider and wider audience. Despite the unwillingness of many humanists to support a liberal education for the masses, the Renaissance was the first step in an educational revolution that swept Europe beginning in the sixteenth century. The Renaissance concern with accurate texts, the keen interest in the classical world (the birthplace of Christianity), and the spread of the printed word also contributed to the Protestant Reformation in the same century. So did the humanist interest in reviving Christianity and integrating it with the culture of antiquity.

Suggestions for Further Reading

Baron, H. *The Crisis of the Early Italian Renaissance: Civic Humanism and Republican Liberty in the Age of Classicism and Tyranny,* rev. ed. Princeton, N.J.: Princeton University Press, 1966.

Brucker, G. A. *Renaissance Florence,* rev. ed. Berkeley: University of California Press, 1983.

Eisenstein, E. L. *The Printing Press as an Agent of Change: Communications and Cultural Transformations in Early Modern Europe,* 2 vols. Cambridge: Cambridge University Press, 1979.

Gilbert, F. *Machiavelli and Guicciardini: Politics and History in Sixteenth-Century Florence.* Princeton, N.J.: Princeton University Press, 1965.

Hale, J. R. *Renaissance Europe: Individual and Society, 1480–1520.* Berkeley: University of California Press, 1978.

Holmes, G. *Florence, Rome, and the Origins of the Renaissance.* New York: Oxford University Press, 1987.

King, M. L. *Venetian Humanism in an Age of Patrician Dominance.* Princeton, N.J.: Princeton University Press, 1986.

Klapisch-Zuber, C. *Women, Family, and Ritual in Renaissance Italy.* Chicago: University of Chicago Press, 1985.

Kristeller, P. O. *Renaissance Thought and Its Sources.* New York: Columbia University Press, 1979.

Maclean, I. *The Renaissance Notion of Woman.* Cambridge: Cambridge University Press, 1980.

Martines, L. *Power and Imagination: City-States in Renaissance Italy.* New York: Knopf, 1979.

Murray, P., and Murray, L. *The Art of the Renaissance.* London: Thames & Hudson, 1978.

Stinger, C. S. *The Renaissance in Rome.* Bloomington: Indiana University Press, 1985.

Ullmann, W. *Medieval Foundations of Renaissance Humanism.* London: Elek, 1977.

Weinstein, D. *Savonarola and Florence: Prophecy and Patriotism in the Renaissance.* Princeton, N.J.: Princeton University Press, 1970.

THE REFORMATION

The forces unleashed in the Reformation struck at the roots of Western values and shattered the fragile unity of medieval Christendom. Sparked by Protestant and Catholic reformers who raised profound questions concerning conscience and authority, the new movements succeeded because of favorable political and social conditions that supported alternative Christian views. The crisis of conscience that marked the dismantling of medieval Christendom was a poignant one for reformers on all sides of the struggle. In a society in which belief and conduct had always been regulated by authority from above, the rival claims of Christian leaders initiated a period of militant zeal and frightening upheaval. Since neither camp proved able to impose its views on its opponents, the West was henceforth divided by competing ecclesiastical institutions, creeds, and claims to religious authority. Fear, doubt, and hostility led to persecutions and witch-hunting, but the Reformation was also an age in which the goals of religious renewal were embodied in high ideals.

THE LATE
MEDIEVAL CHURCH

The medieval church derived strength from its ability to renew itself from within. The Gregorian reform of the eleventh century, subsequent monastic reforms, and the founding of the mendicant orders in the thirteenth century vitalized the church. In the early fifteenth century, reformers ended the Papal Schism, but further reform attempts generally failed. The major reason was lack of effective papal leadership. Fifteenth-century popes were occupied not only with their roles as Italian princes and patrons of the arts but also with the challenge to their power posed by the reformers. The latter were intent on preserving the unity or spiritual supremacy of the church, not on destroying it; theology was not an issue, except in the cases of heretical groups such as the Hussites and the Lollards.

Popular piety remained strong, particularly in German-speaking lands. The development of the printing press dramatically increased the circulation of religious material, including sermons and devotional manuals, though Bibles were still fairly expensive on the eve of the Reformation. Religious organizations for laypeople grew at a striking pace in the fourteenth and fifteenth centuries. Typical of these was the Brethren of the Common Life, established in the Netherlands. Some brotherhoods, such as the Common Life, were involved in education, but most were associations to foster piety through common praying and singing. In large measure, the Reformation was possible because the heightened sense of religious awareness among the people was not matched by reform of chronic problems.

Two of the church's most critical problems involved the quality and training of the clergy and ecclesiastical finances. Although the moral standards and educational preparation of the ministry did not decline substantially in the fifteenth century, many people, particularly north of the Alps, were growing impatient with priests who were sometimes flagrantly immoral or semiliterate, particularly as the educational level of many laypeople began to rise. The problem was compounded by the moral laxity of many church leaders, including Pope Alexander VI (1492–1503). Sensitivity to spiritual needs was often lacking among the higher clergy, who were normally younger sons from aristocratic families pursuing ecclesiastical careers for wealth and political power. At the level of the parish priesthood, minimal incomes made it difficult to recruit educated men. As a result, most parish priests came from the lowest ranks of society. In the absence of seminaries they received on-the-job training from colleagues and were ill prepared to instruct parishioners in the church's complex teaching.

Although the church was a wealthy institution with vast landholdings, its riches were unequally distributed. In contrast to the opulent lifestyles of the archbishops and bishops, most parish priests barely eked out a living. Some administrators in the church improved their positions by holding multiple benefices (church livings), a practice that normally detracted from religious duties. Others hired poorly paid vicars to perform their duties. Beneficed priests were also in the awkward position of obtaining income from their parishioners by collecting tithes and fees (for baptisms, marriages, and burials). Tithes, being mandatory, often caused disputes and resentment.

CHRISTIAN HUMANISTS AND THE QUEST FOR REFORM

The need for institutional reform in the church was a dominant theme of the Christian humanists of northern Europe. To the principles of the Italian humanists they fused the teachings of primitive Christianity in the hope of returning to the purity of the early church. Many northern humanists emphasized the study of biblical languages and the publication of accurate scriptural texts. The humanist attack on corruption and meaningless ceremony in the church prepared the way for Protestant demands for reform and a justification for the break with Rome. The older generation of northern humanists generally remained loyal to Catholicism, whereas many in the younger generation, such as John

Calvin and William Tyndale, found their humanist principles compatible with Protestantism.

Reuchlin and Erasmus

One of the leading biblical scholars among the Christian humanists was Johann Reuchlin (1455–1522), a German authority on Hebrew language and thought. He ran afoul of a converted Jew named Johann Pfefferkorn, who attempted to suppress all Jewish literature because of its hostility to Christianity. Reuchlin objected because Jewish texts had religious and cultural value. Pfefferkorn had the backing of several leading theological faculties, but Reuchlin was defended by various German humanists, notably Ulrich von Hutten and Crotus Rubeanus. These two men wrote the satirical *Letters of Obscure Men* (1515), which purportedly came from the pens of Pfefferkorn's friends and made them appear ridiculous.

The greatest Greek scholar among the northern humanists was Desiderius Erasmus of Rotterdam (c. 1466–1536). One of the triumphs of Renaissance scholarship was his edition of the New Testament in Greek, first published in 1516. In its preface he made an eloquent plea for Bibles in the vernacular, thus anticipating one of the primary accomplishments of the Protestant Reformation: bringing the Bible to the common people.

Erasmus' religious beliefs are summarized in his idea of a "philosophy of Christ," by which he meant a disciplined life of love and service to God and others. In contrast to the complexities of the scholastics, Erasmus stressed the simple teachings of Jesus; the heart of religion was faith and love in action, not ritualistic observance. In the *Praise of Folly* he satirized such Catholic practices as pilgrimages, the veneration of relics, and the sale of indulgences. Erasmus condemned war as a denial of Christian love and insisted that peace was essential for the spread of education and scholarship. Nowhere is his repudiation of the philosophy of might more evident than in his *Education of a Christian Prince* (1516), written for the future emperor Charles V. Erasmus' ideal ruler—devoted to peace, guided by honesty and right religion, concerned for the welfare of his people—was diametrically opposite to Machiavelli's prince.

The Humanists in England

John Colet and Sir Thomas More, both friends of Erasmus, were the leading Christian humanists in England. Colet (c. 1466–1519) founded St. Paul's School for boys in

London, with a curriculum devoted to the critical study of Latin and Greek as well as religion. Colet's scriptural expositions were noted for their attention to historical context and literal meaning, and his sermons denounced corruption in the church.

More (1478–1535) depicted the model society of a Renaissance humanist in *Utopia* (1516). His book envisioned a communal society in which "life and work [are] common to all," education is universal and compulsory, and crime is largely nonexistent because there would be no extremes of wealth and poverty. Utopia (a word meaning "nowhere" in Greek) was a tolerant society in which one enjoyed the freedom to believe as one wished, as long as one did not coerce others or use religion to promote sedition. There is tragic irony in the fact that More, who was beheaded for refusing to accept Henry VIII's headship over the English church, dreamed of a day when a ruler would recognize that it was foolish to enforce conformity by threats or violence. Yet More himself had supported the persecution of heretics in his capacity as Henry's chancellor.

LUTHER AND THE GERMAN REFORMATION

The event that triggered the Protestant Reformation—or Revolt, as Catholics often call it—was associated with the church's financial policy as well as popular piety. Late in 1514, Pope Leo X revived a campaign to rebuild St. Peter's Basilica in Rome, the money for which was to be raised partly through the sale of indulgences. An indulgence canceled or reduced the temporal punishment for sin. Catholic theology taught that few people could pay the necessary penalties for their sins through good works in this life. Most Christians therefore had to be purified in purgatory after they died before they could enter heaven. Beginning in 1476, the papacy, building on earlier views, claimed the power to reduce the time that souls spent in purgatory by transferring to them the surplus good deeds of Christ and his saints. This it would do for anyone who purchased indulgences.

In the spring of 1517 the papacy completed preparations for the sale of indulgences in northern Germany. However, Martin Luther (1483–1546) raised serious questions about indulgences and soon challenged the authority of the papacy itself. No issue was more central to the Reformation than this question of authority.

Luther: The Early Years and the Attack on Indulgences

As Luther prepared to study law, he was deeply troubled by religious doubts. In search of spiritual peace he became an Augustinian friar, but monastic life brought no relief from his deep-seated fears of divine wrath. A trip to Rome in 1510 confirmed his feeling that the church needed reform. As he prepared lectures on the Bible at the University of Wittenberg, to whose faculty he had been assigned, he became convinced that human effort could not save a person from God's judgment; salvation (or justification) could come only through the divine gifts of grace and faith. Luther vividly likened the human condition to that of a worm trapped in excrement, unable to escape unless God plucked the soul from the filth. Luther's unusual sensitivity to human unworthiness and the need for divinely bestowed faith made him rebel at the commercialism of the indulgence hawkers.

Intended at first only for academic debate, the 95 theses that he issued on October 31, 1517, challenged belief in papal authority to release souls from purgatory. Finding no scriptural authority for indulgences, Luther insisted that believers received full forgiveness for their sins through faith and repentance, not letters of indulgence. Within weeks the theses were translated from Latin into German, printed, and distributed throughout Germany, creating a sensation. Summoned to Rome for examination on charges of heresy, Luther instead received a hearing in Augsburg, thanks to the intervention of his prince, Frederick of Saxony. For political reasons, no effective action was taken to suppress Luther.

Toward a New Theology

In 1519, Luther moved closer to an open break with the church by rejecting the authority of the pope and the infallibility of church councils and by referring with approval to John Hus, the Bohemian heretic. Luther wrote three reform manifestos in 1520. The first of the treatises was the *Address to the Christian Nobility of the German Nation,* an appeal to the emperor, the German princes and knights, and the imperial cities to cast off papal bondage. With pronounced nationalistic overtones, Luther repudiated three fundamental papal claims: superior jurisdiction over temporal powers, the sole authority to interpret Scripture, and the exclusive right to summon a general council of the church.

In his second treatise, *On the Babylonian Captivity of the Church,* Luther rejected four of the sacraments for which he found no biblical basis, retaining only baptism, the Lord's supper, and penance (which he later dropped). Here too he set forth his concept of the priesthood of all believers, repudiating the traditional Catholic distinction between the clergy and the laity. He conceded that to preach required the church's approval, thereby preserving a sense of order. Finally, in *The Liberty of the Christian Man,* Luther explained his doctrine of salvation by faith alone, insisting that good deeds were necessary fruits of this faith. On these principles, Protestantism was founded.

Before the last two of these treatises appeared, Pope Leo issued a bull, *Exsurge Domine,* commanding Luther to retract his assertions or be excommunicated. Luther and his supporters responded to this challenge by burning copies of the bull and the canon law. Luther finally received a formal hearing in April 1521, three months after his excommunication, when he appeared before the imperial Diet at Worms. There he refused to recant his views. The break with Rome was now complete, for Luther had rejected the fundamental Catholic doctrine of the combined authority of Scripture and tradition. Neither pope nor church councils could be the final court of appeal, as authority resided in the Bible and the conscience of the believer, enlightened by the Holy Spirit through Scripture.

After Luther's appearance at Worms, Frederick hid him in his castle at Wartburg, where Luther translated Erasmus' Greek New Testament into German. Excommunicated by the church and outlawed by the empire, Luther could not return to Wittenberg for nearly a year. He remained there until his death in 1546, secure only because of political and religious rivalries within the empire and Charles' preoccupation with military campaigns against the French and the Turks.

Religion and Social Reform

Luther's program of reform had major religious and social consequences. He set out to establish a church that conformed to his view of the New Testament. He and his supporters rejected prayers to the saints, the veneration of relics, indulgences, and pilgrimages as superstitious and unscriptural. The monasteries in Lutheran territories were dissolved, resulting in a major redistribution of wealth that ultimately improved the social position of the wealthier urban citizens as well as the princes and the aristocracy. Luther opposed mandatory celibacy for the clergy. Regarded by Catholics as a superior state, celibacy now had no more importance than marriage, which gained a new dignity. Luther himself married a

former nun, Katherine von Bora. The effects of these changes on women were mixed, for although wives were no longer regarded as inferior to celibate women, the closing of nunneries deprived women of a vocational option. Fathers, however, could no longer place their daughters in convents to avoid providing dowries for them.

In most respects, Luther's view of women was traditional, predicated on their subordination to men and a belief in the inferiority of their abilities. They should, he said, "remain at home, sit still, keep house, and bear and bring up children." But even though he regarded wives as subject to their husbands, he viewed them as partners in marriage. Because Luther made the family the focal point of society and church, wives had a new dignity. Luther accepted women's spiritual equality with men, but he refused to allow them a formal role in the preaching or teaching ministry of the church or in politics. Nevertheless, some women helped to spread Lutheranism. Argula von Grumbach, who came from an aristocratic Bavarian family and had a humanist education, distributed Lutheran books and conducted religious services in her home. Elizabeth of Braunschweig won converts to Lutheranism and furthered its cause in letters to political leaders. Argula's and Elizabeth's roles in the Lutheran movement owed more to their aristocratic status than to Luther's encouragement of female activity.

In Lutheran churches the sermon had a prominent place, services were conducted in the vernacular, and congregational participation increased, especially through the singing of hymns. The more active role of the laity and the significance attached to the sermon led to greater attention to education. Luther wanted a primary school in every parish and a secondary school in every sizable town, with provision for the education of girls as well as boys. Because of the importance of the Bible, which Luther insisted must be in the vernacular, Protestantism became a major incentive to the growth of literacy.

Luther and his colleagues successfully pressed civic officials and territorial princes to establish new schools and universities. The Lutherans had several outstanding educational reformers, including Johannes Bugenhagen, who organized school systems in Germany and Denmark that included separate institutions for girls. The most influential Lutheran educator was Johannes Sturm, whose secondary school (called a "gymnasium") at Strasbourg became the pattern for similar schools throughout Europe. Divided into ten grades, the curriculum included Latin, Greek, religion, and logic.

The Growth of the Lutheran Movement

Luther's views spread rapidly, aided by the printing press, the zeal of numerous German merchants, especially in the Hanseatic towns, and the prospects for material gain by people who coveted Catholic lands and wealth. Various German princes as well as cities such as Hamburg and Magdeburg requested that Luther's friends and pupils fill their pulpits and lecterns. The work of reform went forward by winning the support of established leaders, not by revolution. For this reason, Luther strenuously opposed any attempt to alter the political order.

In the German cities the reform typically followed a threefold course, beginning with the preaching of Protestant tenets, followed by the growth of popular support, and concluding with the backing of the magistrates. The magistrates were cautious, not wanting to introduce religious change until they were assured that it would not destroy traditional social ties. The magistrates were also pressured by Charles V to remain Catholic. Those who supported Protestantism did so with deliberation, often stretching out the work of reform over a period of many years. Wary of creating new popes, the magistrates were frequently unwilling to grant the preachers all the changes they sought. Because of their concentration, urban populations were especially open to the influence of popular preaching and the Protestant works that flowed from the press.

Luther corresponded with Hussite leaders in Bohemia, and his doctrines were preached as far afield as Hungary, Prussia, and the Netherlands. Beyond the German states, however, only the Scandinavian lands adopted Lutheranism, which suited the political needs of the kings of Denmark and Sweden as they unified their countries. Adopting Lutheranism made it possible for them to confiscate ecclesiastical lands and assert greater authority over the clergy. As a province of Denmark, Norway too became Lutheran, and Protestant teachings spread into Finland.

Within Germany, Luther's views provoked bitter divisions that led to social upheaval and civil war. Initially, the peasants regarded Luther as a leader who would help them to attain social as well as religious reform. The success of Luther's movement was tied, however, to the support of princes, nobles, and wealthy burghers, without whose backing he would have been subjected to the power of the empire and the church. Despite his sympathy for many peasant demands—including lower rents and the abolition of serfdom—he urged patience when peasants rebelled in southern and central Germany in 1524. He refused to support their call for the termination of serfdom on the grounds that such action not only violated biblical respect for property but "would make all men equal, and turn the spiritual kingdom of Christ into a worldly external kingdom." As the Peasants' Revolt became increasingly violent the following year, Luther reacted against the killing, arson, desecration of churches, and destruction of property. In his pamphlet *Against the Rapacious and Murdering Peasants* he urged the nobility in God's name to "cut, stab, and strangle" the rebels. The peasants were crushed with dreadful severity; altogether the revolt claimed between 70,000 and 100,000 lives.

Charles V was prevented from suppressing the Protestants by hostilities with the French as well as the advancing Turkish forces, which reached the gates of Vienna before retreating. Political and military pressures forced him to allow the German princes a degree of religious toleration in 1526, but he revoked this freedom three years later. Civil war eventually erupted, but in 1555 both sides agreed in the Peace of Augsburg that each prince had the right to determine whether the people of his territory would be Catholic or Lutheran. Only in some of the German cities where toleration was already practiced did the people themselves retain the right to choose their faith. Northern Germany became mostly Lutheran, as did most of the cities of the south, though much of southern Germany remained loyal to Catholicism.

THE REFORMED TRADITION

A different variety of Protestantism emerged in Switzerland under the leadership of Ulrich Zwingli in Zurich and later John Calvin in Geneva. The Reformed tradition distinguished itself from Lutheranism by simpler forms of worship, emphasis on the weekly sermon rather than the celebration of the Lord's supper, greater stress on moral discipline, and a denial of Christ's physical presence in the Lord's supper. In Switzerland, a loose confederation of 13 independent states (cantons) and allied areas, there was widespread disenchantment with conditions in the church, stemming mostly from the impact of the Christian humanists and the reforming spirit kindled by the Councils of Constance (1414–1418) and Basel (1431–1449).

Ulrich Zwingli and the Swiss Reformation

The son of a peasant and village magistrate, Ulrich Zwingli (1484–1531), the founder of the Reformed tradition, was educated by humanists. As a priest in the Great Minster at Zurich, he condemned indulgences and fasting during Lent as unscriptural and reformed the liturgy. Finding no biblical evidence for clerical celibacy, he denounced it and married a poor widow. He also called for a return of the church to its original simplicity and for the removal of all images, relics, and altars. For Zwingli, nothing was acceptable in religion unless it was approved in Scripture. From Zurich the reform movement spread to Bern and Basel as well as to the German cities of Strasbourg and Constance.

In 1529, Zwingli met with Luther at Marburg to forge a Protestant union, but the two leaders disagreed on the nature of the Lord's supper. Zwingli, believing that Christ was present only spiritually in the sacrament, rejected Luther's insistence on a "real" (physical and spiritual) presence. The failure at Marburg was followed by civil war in Switzerland when, despite Zwingli's protests, the Protestant cantons blockaded the Catholic districts in 1531. Captured in the fighting, Zwingli was quartered and burned as a heretic. Following the war, each canton acquired the right to choose its religion.

John Calvin

The Reformed tradition founded by Zwingli became an international force under the guidance of John Calvin (1509–1564), the son of a French attorney. After a broad

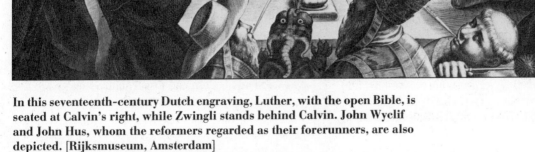

In this seventeenth-century Dutch engraving, Luther, with the open Bible, is seated at Calvin's right, while Zwingli stands behind Calvin. John Wyclif and John Hus, whom the reformers regarded as their forerunners, are also depicted. [Rijksmuseum, Amsterdam]

education in theology, law, classical languages, and humanistic studies, Calvin became a Protestant around 1533. Shortly thereafter, he fled to Basel when the French government stepped up the persecution of Protestants. There he wrote the classic of Reformation Protestantism, the *Institutes of the Christian Religion* (1536). Later that year, he visited Geneva, which had just begun to adopt Protestantism under the leadership of Guillaume Farel. Together the two men imposed a public confession of faith on citizens and punished immorality. These measures, coupled with changes in worship and the abolition of holy days, provoked such strong resentment that Geneva exiled the two men in 1538.

Settling in Strasbourg, Calvin became the pastor of a congregation of French exiles and revised his *Institutes*. Influenced by the teachings of Paul and Augustine, he proclaimed that because human nature was totally corrupt, belief in God was impossible without the irresistible gift of faith. Only those chosen by God before creation—the elect—received this gift; all others—the reprobate—were left to their sins and condemned to eternal damnation. In Calvin's mind the doctrine of predestination revealed not only God's justice but also his mercy in providing salvation for the elect despite their unworthiness. Like Luther and Zwingli, Calvin accepted the authority of Scripture alone; only those enlightened by the Holy Spirit could properly understand the Bible. With other Protestants, Calvin recognized only two sacraments, baptism and the Lord's supper; his concept of the latter was closer to Zwingli's idea of a spiritual presence than to Luther's view. Influenced by the Strasbourg reformer Martin Bucer, Calvin developed a "democratic" plan for church government that called for the election of ministers by the congregation and the joint participation of ministers and popularly elected lay elders in running the church.

One of the most important themes in Calvin's thought was his treatment of vocation as a Christian duty, a concept he shared with other Protestants. He gave all legitimate professions a sense of Christian purpose, so one's job became a principal means of serving God. This outlook brought new dignity to occupations as diverse as business, the crafts, and agriculture.

Calvin's view of wealth was equally significant for economic development. In his judgment, God intended that money be used to better the human condition, and therefore, within limits, usury (interest) had a positive function. Like Luther, Calvin was conscious of the plight of debtors, but if charging interest was consistent with the good of the community, usury was acceptable. Interest rates, however, could never be excessive. Luther,

by contrast, prohibited all usury as unscriptural with the exception of loans by which the borrower prospered. For Calvin the governing economic principle was the mutual responsibility of citizens for the common welfare. Although he never approved the unlimited acquisition of wealth or equated riches with godliness, his emphasis on work and discipline in the context of Christian vocation and his limited acceptance of usury were compatible with the growth of a capitalistic economy.

GENEVA IN THE AGE OF CALVIN

After the election of men favorable to his cause, Calvin returned to Geneva in 1541. The city was the largest in its region, with a population of approximately 10,000. Under Calvin, Geneva became the international center of Reformed Protestantism and attracted religious refugees from France, Italy, England, and Scotland, many of whom were artisans and merchants who contributed to the city's prosperity. Among the newcomers were many booksellers and printers, who helped to make Geneva one of Europe's foremost publication centers. Throughout much of the 1500s, books were the city's primary export and were supplanted only late in the century by the export of silk, an industry introduced by Italians. For the most part, Geneva's economy was based on commerce.

The heart of Genevan government was its three councils: a 25-member Little Council served as an executive body, a Council of 200 determined municipal policy, and a Council of 60 conducted foreign relations. Under Calvin's leadership these institutions protected the Protestant church, safeguarded property, and imposed moral standards on private behavior. Although Calvin never held political office, the councils often sought his advice. They approved his ecclesiastical ordinances, establishing four offices in the church: pastors, teachers, elders, and deacons (who were responsible for poor relief and assisting the sick). Each of the 12 elders was assigned a district in Geneva and required to oversee its families. Through the Consistory, composed of the ministers and elders, Calvin imposed strict discipline on the people for such offenses as absence from church, immorality, drunkenness, and card playing. The city government handled more serious offenses.

Despite the importance he accorded to individual conscience, Calvin, like Luther, grew intolerant of opposition and demanded that his critics be punished. The intolerance of the two leaders, like that of most of their fellow reformers, grew out of their belief in the need for a unified Christendom and was the practical result of having to define the churches they had created. In 1552, Calvin persuaded the city councils to declare that his *Institutes* contained the "pure doctrine" and should not be questioned. The extent to which Calvin's supporters would go in defending his theology became apparent the next year when the Spanish physician Michael Servetus (1511–1553) visited Geneva. The author of works attacking the doctrine of the Trinity, the baptism of infants, and original sin, he was already a man whom the Catholics regarded as a heretic. After a trial in which he clashed with Calvin, Servetus was burned at the stake, a fate praised by Catholic and Protestant leaders alike.

Geneva made a determined effort to deal with the needy. Before Calvin's arrival the small medieval hospitals were reorganized into the Hospital of the Holy Spirit, which cared for the elderly, the sick, the indigent, and widows and orphans. Outside the city walls was a smaller hospital for victims of the plague. Responsibility for the main hospital rested with the deacons, who obtained funding from the city government as well as from private charity. In addition to the provision of free care for the needy in the hospital, every medical doctor was required, beginning in 1569, to treat the poor without charge.

Calvin supervised a sweeping reform of the school system that replaced the old secondary schools with a gymnasium patterned after Johannes Sturm's in Strasbourg. A new academy, established to train superior students for leadership in church and state, developed into the modern University of Geneva. Beginning in 1536, all children had to attend primary school, but girls were barred from the secondary level.

Like Luther, Calvin accepted the traditional notion of female inferiority and the subject position of women in marriage. He too recognized women's spiritual equality but refused to allow women a ministerial role in the church. In the secular sphere, when a woman inherited a crown, Calvin interpreted the event as a divine reproach to men. Apart from their responsibilities in the home, women had to educate the young. In practice, however, Calvinist women of aristocratic background were prominent in the movement and often influenced their husbands to convert. Jeanne d'Albret, mother of King Henry IV of France, was a leader of the Huguenots (as the French Calvinists were called), while Madeleine Mailly, Comtesse de Roye, worked on behalf of the Huguenot cause with both the French government and German Protestant princes. In Geneva, Calvin neither allowed women to serve as deaconesses nor favored their participation in city government, although his own wife was virtually his partner in the work of religious reform.

Under Calvin, Geneva was the focal point of an expanding network of reformers who carried his message to France, the Netherlands, England, Scotland, and Hungary. With its strict morality and religious fervor, Geneva was the nerve center of a militant, determined Protestantism.

THE RADICAL REFORMATION

Although both the Lutheran and Reformed traditions appealed to Scripture as their authority and worked to restore the church to its original simplicity, as early as the mid-1520s radical critics expressed dissatisfaction with the extent and pace of reform. In their judgment, Luther and Zwingli had compromised their priiples to win the support of the powerful. Most of the radical critics became known as Anabaptists ("Rebaptizers").

The Anabaptists

In 1523, Conrad Grebel (1498–1526), a follower of Zwingli and a member of a prominent patrician family in Zurich, became impatient with the slowness of reform. The following year he attacked Zwingli's view of baptism, insisting that the rite must be confined to believing adults as a mark of their spiritual rebirth. The Zurich town council supported Zwingli, but Grebel and his followers—the Swiss Brethren—refused to conform. For their defiance they faced banishment or execution by drowning, a cruel parody of their baptismal practices. The Brethren rejected the traditional concept of a state church in favor of congregations composed of believers alone. Accepting the Lord's supper as a simple meal to commemorate Christ's death, they celebrated it in private homes. Of more concern to the landed classes, the Brethren insisted that pastors must be chosen by individual congregations and supported by voluntary gifts, not tithes. Because so many tithes were now paid directly to the laity rather than the clergy, the Anabaptist call for voluntary tithing was viewed as an attack on property rights. Equally radical was the Brethren's refusal to participate in civil government or military service, both of which involved the taking of life. They also declined to pay taxes for military purposes and rejected oaths, which traditionalists regarded as basic to the maintenance of law and order. In the eyes of the authorities the Anabaptists were dangerous social revolutionaries.

Initially, the Anabaptists were not identified with any social group, but in the aftermath of the Peasants' Revolt they attracted large numbers of peasants and artisans. In 1534 the Anabaptists seized control of the German city of Münster, where they expelled or persecuted all who disagreed with them. Under the leadership of a charismatic Dutch tailor, John of Leiden, they founded a theocratic kingdom based on the laws of the Old Testament. Polygamy was practiced, and property was held in common. Within the city walls there was wild anticipation that King John would soon rule the world in preparation for the second coming of Christ, but the rest of Europe was appalled. Acting together, Protestant and Catholic armies recaptured the city in 1535 and executed the Anabaptist leaders. The Münster fiasco intensified the persecution of Anabaptists throughout the Holy Roman Empire, which had made rebaptism a capital offense. By the early 1600s, several thousand Anabaptists had been executed.

Persecution encouraged the migration of Anabaptists to other areas, particularly the Netherlands, Poland, Bohemia, and Moravia. Shunning the excesses of Münster, these groups distinguished themselves by their quiet piety and strict morality. The most prominent of these sects was that of the Mennonites, founded by Menno Simons (1496–1561), whose followers eventually spread as far as Russia and North America.

Spiritualists and Rationalists

A handful of radicals claimed to be prophets bearing special revelations from God. One of the most prominent was Thomas Müntzer (died 1525), who accepted only the authority of the Holy Spirit and endorsed the use of violence to advance the Gospel. He preached social revolution in southern Germany and helped to incite the Peasants' Revolt, during which he was executed. In contrast to such men, Sebastian Franck (c. 1499–c. 1542) rejected Lutherans and Anabaptists alike for their dogmatism. Repudiating the authority of the Bible, he argued for a religion based entirely on the inner life of the Spirit and free from all dogma and sacraments.

Whereas the Spiritualists were essentially mystics,

another group of Protestant radicals advocated a religion that was predominantly rational and ethical. Distinguishing themselves by their rejection of the Trinity, they criticized predestination and original sin and favored religious toleration. In addition to Servetus, the leading rationalists included Lelio Sozzini (1525–1562) and his nephew Faustus (1539–1604), whose followers, the Socinians, lived primarily in Poland and England. There they helped to prepare the foundation for seventeenth-century Deism, the ancestor of modern Unitarianism. One of the greatest literary works of the radical Reformation was Sebastian Castellio's *Concerning Heretics and Whether They Should Be Punished by the Sword of the Magistrate.* Castellio (1515–1563) offered a ringing defense of religious toleration. To burn a heretic, he asserted, "is not to defend a doctrine, but to kill a man." The legacy of the religious radicals was the concept of religious freedom, an idea slow to win acceptance because of the conviction that religious diversity led to the breakdown of the social and political order.

THE ENGLISH REFORMATION

In contrast to the reform movements instigated by Luther, Zwingli, and Calvin the Reformation in England was fundamentally an act of state rather than the work of a religious leader. The relative ease with which the break with Rome was accomplished owed much to widespread dissatisfaction with the Catholic church and to the work of early reform movements. Many Lollards, an underground group whose radical views were inherited from John Wyclif, embraced Lutheran ideas in the 1520s. Lutherans formed cells at Oxford and Cambridge, and from them Protestant theology began to influence the clergy. In London a covert group of merchants known as the Christian Brethren spread the Protestant message, which they had learned as traders on the Continent. With their support, William Tyndale (c. 1492–1536) translated the New Testament and the Pentateuch into English, with marginal notes attacking the papacy and the Catholic priesthood. Many early Protestant leaders in England had been educated as humanists and were deeply influenced by Erasmus. Well before the Reformation, English humanists such as John Colet had made strong pleas for reform, helping—unwittingly—to prepare the way for the break with Rome.

11.1 The Division of Christendom, c. 1550

The King's "Great Matter" and the Break with Rome

The state's decision to reject papal authority was not made primarily for religious reasons. Henry VIII (1509–1547), the second of the Tudor rulers, was married to Catherine of Aragon, by whom he had one surviving child, Princess Mary. The prospect of leaving the new dynasty in a woman's hands raised fears of another struggle like the fifteenth-century Wars of the Roses. The fact that Henry had become infatuated with Anne Boleyn, a lady of the court, contributed to his decision to seek a new wife and produce a male heir. But to marry Anne required a church-approved annulment of his marriage to Catherine, whose position was strengthened by the fact that Pope Clement VII did not want to antagonize her nephew, Charles V.

When Henry learned in January 1533 that Anne was pregnant, he secretly married her without waiting to resolve the status of his marriage to Catherine. In March, Parliament passed the Act in Restraint of Appeals, drafted largely by Thomas Cromwell (1485–1540), Henry's key adviser; the act prohibited legal appeals to Rome without royal permission. Two months later, the new archbishop of Canterbury, the Protestant Thomas Cranmer (1489–1556), moved the Convocation of the Clergy to declare Henry's marriage to Catherine null and void, and on June 1, Anne Boleyn was crowned queen of England. Three months later she gave birth to Princess Elizabeth.

Most of the religious changes during Henry's reign involved the seizure of papal authority by the crown rather than theological issues as on the Continent. Church funds that had previously been paid to Rome now went to the English government. The king received the right to make appointments to all major church offices, as well as the final authority for all ecclesiastical legislation. In the 1534 Act of Supremacy, Parliament recognized the king as "the only supreme head in earth of the Church of England." To deny him this title was treason. An act of succession recognized the children of Henry and Anne as heirs to the throne. For refusing to accept the succession and the royal supremacy in the church, Sir Thomas More and Bishop John Fisher, Catherine's outspoken supporters, were executed in 1535. Catherine remained loyal to the Catholic faith until her death in 1536. Four months later, Anne was executed on trumped-up charges of adultery and incest. In reality, Henry could forgive neither her arrogance nor her failure to bear him a son.

Although Henry generally remained loyal to Catholic dogma, an official translation of the Bible in English was published in 1535, and the following year Cromwell ordered that every church have a copy of the Bible in English and Latin. Between 1536 and 1540 the crown dissolved the monasteries and confiscated their properties. Some of the land was sold, enabling the lesser aristocracy (the gentry) in particular to expand their holdings. Because the monasteries had been centers of education and hospitality, the social effects of their dissolution were profound. The religious position of the Church of England in this period is best described as Henrician Catholicism, or Catholicism without monastic institutions or obedience to Rome.

The Edwardian Reformation

After Henry's death in 1547 the Church of England became increasingly Protestant. Henry was succeeded by his nine-year-old son, Edward VI (1547–1553), whose mother, Jane Seymour, Henry's third queen, had died after childbirth. Real power rested at first in the hands of the king's uncle, Edward Seymour, duke of Somerset. In 1549, Parliament passed an act of uniformity requiring all ministers to use the *Book of Common Prayer,* an English liturgy prepared by Archbishop Cranmer. When Somerset failed to suppress rioting peasants in 1549, John Dudley, soon to be duke of Northumberland, overthrew him. Under Northumberland's leadership the English church became more firmly Protestant. A second act of uniformity required clergy and laity alike to use the revised *Book of Common Prayer,* which simplified the worship service and required ministers to wear only a plain black robe and a white vestment. Communion tables replaced altars, and confession was made by the congregation as a whole rather than individually to priests. Edward approved the Forty-Two Articles, a Protestant confession of faith.

The Edwardian Reformation was secure only as long as the king lived, for the heir apparent, Princess Mary, was a determined Catholic. As Edward lay dying of tuberculosis in 1553, Northumberland tried to save himself by preventing Mary from becoming queen. He persuaded Edward to name as his heir Lady Jane Grey, Northumberland's daughter-in-law and a great-granddaughter of Henry VII. But when Edward died in July, the English people supported Mary as the rightful ruler. Northumberland died on the scaffold as the new queen prepared to restore Catholicism.

THE CATHOLIC REVIVAL: A CHURCH MILITANT

The spirit of reform prevailed within the Catholic church as well as outside it, stimulated partly by the shock of the Protestant secession, partly by a determination to maintain the ideals of the medieval church. Conciliarism, the major source for reform in the late Middle Ages, had lost much of its force by the early 1500s. Efforts to improve the church, however, were underway in various states. In Spain, for example, Queen Isabella's confessor, Francisco Cardinal Ximenes (c. 1436–1517), improved education for the clergy, placed tighter controls on priests and monks, and encouraged humanist learning at the new University of Alcala.

A characteristic feature of the Catholic revival was the founding of new organizations, beginning with the Oratory of Divine Love, established in Italy in 1494. Composed of clergy and laity, its members emphasized piety and charitable work for the poor and the sick. The Capuchins (1528), inspired by Francis of Assisi's ideal of poverty, devoted themselves to helping the common people. Other new orders, such as the Barnabites (1530) and the Somaschi (1532), focused on the problems of poverty and disease. The Somaschi, who founded hospitals and orphanages, also took an interest in the plight of prostitutes. The role of women in the Catholic revival is reflected in the Congregation of the Holy Angels (an auxiliary of the Barnabites), the Capucines (the female counterpart of the Capuchins), and the Ursulines, who specialized in educating young women.

ANGELA MERICI AND THE URSULINES

The new sense of spiritual dedication that was reviving the Catholic church is exemplified in the life of Angela Merici, the daughter of a minor country gentleman. Born in 1474 in the republic of Venice, she was orphaned at age 10. As a young woman she was deeply influenced by the piety of nuns and recluses as well as by the Oratory of Divine Love. She took part as a layperson in the work of the Franciscans but did not take formal vows. Merici devoted herself to charitable work, helping the sick and the poor as well as teaching girls. While praying in the fields in 1506, she had a vision in which she was promised that "before your death, you will found a society of virgins." Ten years later, she established a school for girls, primarily to teach the catechism.

At Brescia in 1531, Merici, now partially blind, recruited a dozen young women as teachers, and in 1535, when the group had grown to 28, she founded the Company of St. Ursula (Ursulines). Like the Franciscans, she rejected a cloistered order in favor of social activism, insisting that her religious sisters live and work among

the people. Because of the novelty of this idea, the pope did not approve her order until 1565, after her death. Although no formal vows were required, Merici's rule demanded poverty, chastity, and obedience. Each sister was allowed to live in her own home and work with her family and neighbors. Until her death in 1540, Merici served as superior general of the Ursulines. Her *Testament and Souvenirs* expresses her ideals, especially gentleness and concern for others. Her movement had more than doubled in size by 1536 and became the greatest teaching order for women.

Ignatius of Loyola and the Society of Jesus

The most influential of the new orders, the Society of Jesus, was founded by Ignatius of Loyola (1491–1556), the son of a Basque nobleman. A French cannonball shattered his right leg as he fought in Charles V's army in 1521. Influenced during his recovery by biographies of Francis and Dominic, he dedicated his life to the Virgin Mary. After a period of meditation in monasteries and study at the Universities of Alcala and Paris, Ignatius, with a small band of disciples, vowed to go to the Holy Land to convert Muslims. Finding the way to Palestine blocked by fighting between the Venetians and the Turks, they preached instead to the Italians. Ignatius' constitution for a new order, which reflected the trend toward centralized government in this period, was approved by Pope Paul III in 1540. Governed by a superior general directly responsible to the pope, the order was highly structured in order to supervise its active, mobile apostles. Although the traditional monastic vows were required, Jesuits were exempt from the typical duties of monks, such as reciting the church offices. The society's purpose was to advance and defend the Catholic faith.

The Jesuits concentrated on four activities. To persuade secular rulers to suppress Protestantism, they served as confessors and propagandists in Catholic courts. To keep the masses loyal to the Catholic faith, the Jesuits stressed confession, achieving some popularity because of their principle that there is "no sin without specific intent" to commit it. The society's third major activity was improving education, especially at the secondary level, where strict discipline and obedience to the church were emphasized. The Jesuits launched a program to build new schools (or "colleges"). By 1640 there were approximately 520 of these secondary schools in Europe, teaching some 150,000 boys. Up to half of the students were the children of peasants and artisans, who paid no tuition. The curriculum combined the best of humanist teaching with traditional Catholic beliefs, and instilled in students a strong sense of obedience to the church. Jesuit schools were highly successful in providing church and state with educated officials and slowing the expansion of Protestantism.

The Jesuits' fourth principal activity was the dispatching of missions to Asia, Africa, and North and South America as well as to such European states as England and Poland. Their leading missionary, Francis Xavier (1506–1552), who preached in India, Ceylon, the Moluccas, and Japan, died half frozen and starved as he prepared to enter China. By 1557 the Jesuits had missions in the Congo, Morocco, and Ethiopia, and they also worked in Florida (1566) and Virginia (1570) as well as Brazil, Peru, and Mexico. Late in the century, the Jesuit Matteo Ricci established the nucleus of a Christian church in China (see Chapter 12). The Jesuits' willingness to tolerate non-Western cultures coupled with their knowledge of Western science and technology helped to make them effective missionaries.

The religious experience of Ignatius provided the basis for his *Spiritual Exercises,* a handbook to develop self-mastery and spiritual discipline. The *Exercises* call for a period of intense self-examination and meditation, at the culmination of which the disciple experiences a sense of unity with God through the surrender of the mind and will. In contrast to Protestantism, which stressed the importance of the individual conscience, Ignatius emphasized the church's authority: "To be right in everything, we ought always to hold that the white which I see, is black, if the Hierarchical Church so decides it." This unqualified devotion and obedience to the church was at the heart of the Catholic revival.

The Council of Trent and the Inquisition

Catholic reformers urged the papacy to convene a general council to deal with the Protestant challenge and make needed changes, but the popes, fearing a loss of their power and preoccupied with political concerns, were slow to act. Pope Paul III finally yielded to pressure from the emperor Charles V and summoned a council. Convened in 1545 at Trent in northern Italy, it met intermittently until 1563 and was dominated by conservative Italians loyal to the papacy.

In matters of theology the council reasserted all the doctrines challenged by the Protestants. On the crucial issue of authority it reaffirmed the importance of both Scripture and tradition, "with an equal pious devotion and reverence" to each. It recognized the Latin Vulgate as the official version of the Bible, with the church having the sole right to determine its "true sense and interpretation." The doctrine of salvation by faith and good works was reasserted, as were all seven sacraments. The council also reaffirmed the doctrine of transubstantiation—the belief that the substance of the bread and wine miraculously becomes the body and blood of Christ in the Eucharist. Trent insisted on celibacy for the clergy, reaffirmed the invocation of saints and the veneration of relics, and refused to abolish indulgences and the doctrine of purgatory.

The council also reformed church discipline. Henceforth, every bishop, unless he had a papal dispensation, was required to live in his diocese and supervise his clergy. To improve the education of priests, a seminary was to be established in every diocese. Selling ecclesiastical offices and appointing relatives to church positions were condemned. Such reforms brought a new spirit of determination to the church in its struggle with Protestantism.

The church launched the Roman Inquisition in 1542 at the urging of Loyola and Giampietro Cardinal Caraffa (1476–1559). As head of the Inquisition, Caraffa directed a commission empowered under Roman law to use torture, accept hearsay evidence, and keep the accused ignorant of the charges against them. The Inquisition stamped out Protestantism in Italy, but it also stifled intellectual life. One of the Inquisition's most notable victims was the Dominican monk Giordano Bruno, who was burned at the stake in Rome in 1600 for unorthodox views about God and for teaching that the universe is infinite and contains innumerable suns and planets like our own (see Chapter 16). The Sacred Congregation of the Holy Office, which oversaw the Inquisition, also imposed an *Index of Prohibited Books.* Among the works it banned were Erasmus' writings, vernacular translations of the Bible, Boccaccio's *Decameron,* and Machiavelli's *The Prince.*

The Counter-Reformation in England

Mary Tudor's accession to the English throne in 1553 provided the Catholics with an opportunity to recover an entire state that had been lost to Protestantism. She began by having Parliament repeal the religious legislation of Edward VI's reign. This action, coupled with the

[handwritten annotation: + Causation - no heir from Mary, Elizabeth took thrown]
[handwritten annotation: Teleological - religion & God (& His will)]

announcement of her impending marriage to Charles V's son, Philip of Spain, provoked a Protestant rebellion led by Sir Thomas Wyatt. After the revolt was crushed, Parliament repealed the antipapal legislation of Henry VIII, and in November 1554, England was officially reconciled to the Catholic church. Most of the lands previously confiscated from the church were not, however, returned. Prodded by Mary, Parliament revived a fifteenth-century law allowing the church to condemn and the state to burn heretics. Nearly 300 Protestants, including Cranmer, died in the flames. Accounts of the martyrs hardened Protestant commitments.

Faced with persecution, some 800 Protestants fled to the Continent, where most settled in such Reformed cities as Geneva, Zurich, and Frankfurt. In exile, John Foxe collected material for his *Acts and Monuments,* a popular history of Christian martyrs from the early church to his own day. Other exiles prepared a new edition of the Bible in English—the Geneva version (1560)—complete with marginal notes attacking Catholicism and advocating Calvinism. Until it was finally supplanted by the Authorized (King James) version in the next century, the Geneva Bible was probably the most influential book in England. Three other exiles—

John Ponet, John Knox, and Christopher Goodman—made lasting contributions to political theory by advocating that common people have the right to overthrow tyrannical and idolatrous rulers, a theory also espoused by the Jesuits against Protestant sovereigns.

The Counter-Reformation failed in England largely because of the intense revulsion the burnings caused and also because Mary had no Catholic heir. The unpopularity of Mary's marriage to Philip, a symbol of Catholic orthodoxy and Spanish imperialism, also contributed to the failure. If Mary had been able to give birth to the heir she desperately wanted, Catholicism might have regained its dominance in England, but the accession in 1558 of Elizabeth I, Mary's half sister and the daughter of Anne Boleyn, destroyed the English Counter-Reformation. The foundation of the Elizabethan religious settlement was an act of supremacy that made Elizabeth supreme governor of the church and an act of uniformity that required the use of the *Book of Common Prayer*. In 1563 the queen issued the Thirty-Nine Articles, a revised version of Edward VI's doctrinal statement. England thus moved firmly into the Protestant orbit, as did Scotland under the leadership of John Knox in 1560.

Archbishop Thomas Cranmer was burned at the stake in Oxford on March 21, 1556, after reaffirming his Protestant faith. [Ronald Sheridan/Ancient Art & Architecture Collection]

THE REFORMATION
AND THE JEWS

The repressive side of the Catholic Reformation had an immediate and negative impact on European Jews. They were less affected by the Protestant Reformation, in part because they had been evicted from Geneva in 1490, well before Calvin's era, as many had been from German cities. In the earliest stages of the Reformation, Luther expected the Jews to convert to his movement, but when they failed to do so, he became increasingly hostile toward them. Finally, he insisted that the German princes deport the Jews to Palestine or at least force them to return to agricultural occupations and prohibit them from practicing usury. Luther even demanded that Jewish books be confiscated and synagogues burned. In the course of the Catholic Reformation the plight of the Jews similarly worsened as the papacy reversed its hitherto tolerant position. Beginning in 1553, the Talmud was publicly burned in Italy, and two years later, Caraffa, now Pope Paul IV, ordered the Jews to be segregated in their own quarter (the *ghetto*), which was to be enclosed with high walls and, at night, locked gates. Jews were banned from the professions, prohibited from employing Christian servants, refused the right to own real estate, and forced to wear yellow hats as a badge. Although the Jews were not expelled from the Papal States, they could live only in cities such as Rome and Avignon under close supervision. The ghetto concept gradually spread until it became a hallmark of European Jewish life.

As the persecution of the Jews intensified, substantial numbers of them migrated to Poland, which tolerated minorities. In some of the bigger towns, such as Cracow and Lublin, large ghettos developed. Polish Jews generally enjoyed far greater choice of occupation than Jews in western Europe, and they were permitted substantial self-government in matters involving Jewish law.

THE WITCH-HUNT

In striking contrast to the idealism that characterized much of the Protestant movement and the Catholic revival, the Reformation also contributed to a terrifying wave of cruelty. The age of spiritual renewal paradoxically coincided in part with the most extensive period of witchcraft persecutions in Western history, sparked in large measure by the breakdown of religious unity, social tension, changes in criminal procedure (especially the use of torture), and a growing belief in pacts between witches and the Devil. Belief in witches originated in ancient times, and the medieval church had organized those ideas into a systematic demonology. Witchcraft persecutions were most severe in the period 1435–1500 and again from 1580 to 1650.

Reformers and Witches

At the heart of the witch-hunt was acceptance of the reality of the Devil and the pervasive effects of his influence in the world. The reformers intensified this belief by linking Catholicism and especially the pope with Satan. Luther attacked monks on the grounds that they had made a pact with Satan to obtain supernatural powers. For this reason, Luther believed that witches too must be burned. In Geneva, Calvin appealed to the Bible (Exodus 22:18) as a divine sanction for the execution of witches.

Catholic persecution of witches had, of course, begun before the Reformation. Protestant attempts to associate the papacy with Satan were countered by Catholic charges that Luther and his colleagues were tools of the Devil. Catholics also drew on late medieval demonology to justify their accusations of witchcraft. The persecution of witches increased as the intensity of religious hostility provoked by Catholics and Protestants grew. Persecution was especially vicious in areas such as the Rhineland and Bavaria that were reconquered from the Protestants. Witch-burnings also followed in the wake of the Catholic recapture of Poland and Flanders, but in areas where Catholic uniformity was not effectively challenged, such as Italy and Spain, witchcraft was relatively rare. Burning witches—like burning heretics—became a means of purging society of evil, of purifying the community while the reformers cleansed the church.

Choosing the Victims

Most victims were female, probably because of the medieval notion that as the "weaker sex" they were more susceptible to the Devil's enticements. In England, women apparently were accused more often than men because they were more likely to resist economic and social change. Although many of the victims were older widows or spinsters, younger women often suffered on the Continent, as did some men and children. To extract confessions, torture was often used (except in England), which led to more accusations and executions. Between 1450 and 1750, more than 100,000 Europeans were prosecuted for witchcraft. Only as religious passions waned, social upheaval receded, and a new spirit of rationalism took hold in the mid-1600s did the hunt die down.

Although the witchcraft trials were in part due to the breakdown of religious unity, religion alone cannot account for the full force of the persecutions. The social and economic changes that occurred in the West beginning in the fifteenth century created enormous tension, adding to the uncertainties and hostility resulting from the religious upheavals. A growing population, increasing poverty, crop failures, and rising crime made many people insecure. They continued to find scapegoats for their problems in social nonconformists—witches, Jews, and homosexuals, all of whom were persecuted. The link between them was sometimes explicit: Jews, for instance, were often accused of witchcraft.

THE CULTURAL IMPACT OF THE REFORMATION

Protestantism had a significant impact on the arts in the areas it dominated, whereas the effects of the Catholic revival on culture were not generally visible until the late sixteenth century. Because Protestantism opposed the use of images and the veneration of saints, artists in Protestant regions found virtually no demand for religious statues and little interest in paintings for churches. They adapted by catering to the growing secular market for paintings and providing artwork for publishers. Similarly, although architects initially were not needed by Protestant leaders, who took over their churches from the Catholics, they found an outlet for their talents by designing palatial residences for princes and nobles. The Protestant rejection of the mass and the simplification of the church service created a demand for suitable music, particularly hymns and psalm settings. The artistic impact of the Reformation on the Catholic church was more delayed, but its influence was felt in the revival of the church after the Council of Trent and in the seventeenth-century movement known as the Baroque (see Chapter 16).

Grünewald, Dürer, and Holbein

The dilemma that the Reformation posed for the artist is illustrated by the career of Matthias Grünewald (c. 1460–1528), a German who became court painter for the archbishop of Mainz. He completed his major work, an altarpiece for the church at Isenheim in Alsace, on the eve of the Reformation. The massive altarpiece, with its flanking panels closed, depicts the anguish of Christ on the cross, his body discolored, his feet blackened, and his flesh lacerated. With the panels opened, the inner pane reveals the triumphant resurrected Christ bathed in the glow of an eerie red light. After Grünewald became a Lutheran, he participated in the Peasants' Revolt. The archbishop of Mainz dismissed him for his beliefs in 1526.

Albrecht Dürer (1471–1528) became the greatest artist of the German Renaissance. Twice he went to Italy,

Albrecht Dürer's engraving *Knight, Death, and the Devil* (1513) reflects the confidence of humanists in the ability of the Christian faith to triumph over the enemies of humankind. [Harvey D. Parker Fund, Courtesy Museum of Fine Arts, Boston]

bringing back to Germany an understanding of Renaissance ideals and techniques. He was one of the first non-Italian artists to acquire an international reputation and the first northern artist to provide a rich account of his life through self-portraits, personal correspondence, and a diary. In addition to his paintings, he produced superb woodcuts and engravings. A Christian humanist in the early 1500s, Dürer captured the spirit of his friend Erasmus' *Handbook of a Christian Knight* in his engraving *Knight, Death, and the Devil.* After his conversion to Lutheranism his style became more austere. His engraving of the Last Supper reveals the simple style of his Protestant years. Like Grünewald, Dürer continued to accept commissions from Catholic patrons after his conversion, although he hoped to establish a distinctively Protestant tradition of monumental art.

The son of an Augsburg painter, Hans Holbein the Younger (1497–1543) achieved prominence as the greatest portrait painter of the sixteenth century. Like Dürer, he was a friend of Erasmus (whose portrait is one of Holbein's masterpieces) as well as a book illustrator. Holbein settled in Basel, but when the Protestant reform created a hostile atmosphere for artists there, Erasmus recommended him to Sir Thomas More. Henry VIII commissioned some of Holbein's most famous portraits, including several of the king himself. Among Holbein's most fascinating works are 41 woodcuts depicting the late medieval "dance of death" and a series of drawings satirizing abuses in the Catholic church. His influence on English portraiture continued for decades.

Music and the Reformation

Although Protestant reformers repudiated the ornate polyphonic masses of the late medieval period, they retained music in the worship service. To Luther, music was "an endowment and a gift of God" that made people cheerful and chased away the Devil. Luther composed at least eight hymns, including "A Mighty Fortress Is Our God," and wrote sacred texts for German folk tunes. Although Zwingli's radical liturgical reform led to the destruction of church organs in Zurich, the year after his death a new organ was built in the cathedral, and congregational singing was introduced. In Geneva, Calvin approved of psalm singing, and the practice quickly spread throughout the Reformed churches. A main objection to traditional religious music was the difficulty of understanding the words, which prompted English reformers in the 1560s to condemn most choral music.

The Catholics too were concerned that elaborate musical compositions were obscuring the sacred texts. The Council of Trent enacted regulations designed to encourage simplicity as well as to ban the use of secular themes in religious works. Polyphony was acceptable, as long as the words of the mass could be clearly understood. After the council the Roman Curia urged an end to the use of all instruments except the organ in religious services, but compliance was never complete. The challenge to blend simplicity with musical beauty was brilliantly met in the masses and motets (sacred compositions) of the Italian composer Giovanni Palestrina (c. 1525–1594), whose works manifest a sense of monumental grandeur and remained the model for Catholic devotional writers down to the nineteenth century.

SUMMARY

The changes in art and music that occurred in the first half of the sixteenth century reflect the effects of the religious convulsions that shook Europe. Henceforth the West was permanently divided in its religious beliefs and institutions. Yet out of that diversity eventually came the demands for freedom of religion and thought that are now fundamental to the concept of liberty. In other ways, too, the Reformation made significant contributions to the quality of Western life. Better education and improved care for the needy and the helpless were direct fruits of Protestant and Catholic idealism. But there was a dark side to the Reformation era, manifested in the religious wars to which the bellicose attitudes of Protestants and Catholics alike led. For more than a century the hostilities rooted in rival religious convictions parodied the love that was at the core of Christian teaching. This aspect of the Reformation was also reflected in brutal religious persecutions and in witchcraft trials and executions. The Reformation era dramatically pitted the authority of religious institutions against the claims of individual conscience. Unresolved in the sixteenth century, this clash remained a source of tension well into modern times. The fervency of the religious debate had global implications as well, particularly as Catholic missionaries carried their message to Asia, Africa, and the Americas.

Suggestions for Further Reading

Bainton, R. H. *Erasmus of Christendom*. New York: Scribner, 1969.

————. *Women of the Reformation in Germany and Italy*. Minneapolis: Augsburg, 1971.

Benesch, O. *The Art of the Renaissance in Northern Europe: Its Relation to the Contemporary Spiritual and Intellectual Movements*, rev. ed. London: Phaidon, 1965.

Bouwsma, W. J. *John Calvin: A Sixteenth-Century Portrait*. New York: Oxford University Press, 1987.

Caraman, P. *Ignatius Loyola: A Biography of the Founder of the Jesuits*. San Francisco: Harper, 1990.

Dickens, A. G. *The English Reformation*. London: Batsford, 1964.

Jensen, D. *Reformation Europe: Age of Reform and Revolution*, 2nd ed. Lexington, Mass.: D. C. Heath, 1992.

Levack, B. P. *The Witch-Hunt in Early Modern Europe*. New York: Longman, 1987.

Monter, E. W. *Calvin's Geneva*. New York: Wiley, 1967.

Oberman, H. A. *Luther: Man Between God and the Devil,* trans. E. Walliser-Schwarzbart. New Haven, Conn.: Yale University Press, 1989.

O'Connell, M. R. *The Counter-Reformation, 1559–1610*. New York: Harper & Row, 1974.

Ozment, S. E. *The Age of Reform (1250–1550): An Intellectual and Religious History of Late Medieval and Reformation Europe*. New Haven, Conn.: Yale University Press, 1980.

————. *The Reformation in the Cities: The Appeal of Protestantism to Sixteenth-Century Germany and Switzerland*. New Haven, Conn.: Yale University Press, 1975.

Potter, G. R. *Zwingli*. Cambridge: Cambridge University Press, 1976.

Williams, G. H. *The Radical Reformation*. Philadelphia: Westminster Press, 1962.

12

THE AGE OF EUROPEAN DISCOVERY

The period from 1450 to 1600 was an extraordinary time in Western history. The religious convulsions that shattered Christian unity and helped to spur a global missionary effort occurred in the context of daring voyages of exploration and the beginnings of extensive trade that laid the foundation for a world economy. By 1450 the West, which had long lagged behind the more culturally and technologically sophisticated Indians and East Asians, developed the technological innovations, commercial organizations, and spiritual and materialistic ideals that enabled it to dominate much of the world by the nineteenth century. Mastery of the high seas was the key to global expansion, and the financial support and incentives for this endeavor were made possible by the development of merchant capitalism and the increasing centralization of European states.

EUROPE ON THE EVE OF EXPLORATION

By the mid-fifteenth century, Europe was on the road to recovery after the demographic catastrophe caused by the Black Death. One of the most crucial elements in the revival was a rapid growth in population. Between 1460 and 1620 the population of Europe nearly doubled, to approximately 100 million people. In some places, particularly the cities of western Europe, the rise was even

sharper. Antwerp grew from 20,000 in 1440 to 100,000 in 1560. This growth increased the pressure on land and food as demand outstripped supply, thus spurring inflation while preventing many Europeans from rising above subsistence level. Demographic recovery, which increased the supply of labor, also meant the end of the period of improved conditions for the peasantry brought on by the Black Death in the mid-1300s. The rising population provided both an abundant labor supply and economic incentives for agricultural improvements, commercial expansion, and overseas exploration and settlement.

Land Tenures and Agricultural Development

The decimation of the population by the Black Death and, in France, the Hundred Years' War (1337–1453) resulted in a shortage of peasant labor and a decrease in the amount of land under cultivation. For many peasants in western Europe the resulting demand for their services made it possible to escape the bonds of serfdom, trading the security of the old system for freedom and its attendant risks. Those who rented lands might profit by their industry, but they were also subject to potentially ruinous increases in rent. Whether the landlord or the tenant prospered was normally determined by the terms on which the land was held, as well as by tax obligations. Long-term leases, which some English peasants enjoyed, were usually beneficial to the holders. Tenants in parts

enclosure movement
farm land = 50 acres
6 bushels per acre

of France and western Germany whose tenure could be inherited might likewise prosper, for they were free to farm the land and sell the produce as they saw fit in return for a fixed payment to their landlords. In parts of Italy and France, short-term leases, which required the peasants to pay a fixed share of their crops to landlords, were common and helped the latter keep pace with rising food costs. Peasants without secure tenure faced a troubled future in which the value of their services was as uncertain as their ability to continue working the land. Such tenants were at the mercy of landlords, who had to choose between opportunities for economic advancement and traditional obligations for their tenants' welfare.

Landed aristocrats whose tenants could inherit tenure or had long-term leases suffered a loss in real income as prices rose faster than rents. The lesser aristocracy often reacted by supporting wars and overseas conquest because of the prospect of new lands and financial gain. When the reconquest of the Iberian peninsula from the Moors was completed in 1492, the interest of the Spanish hidalgos (lesser nobles) shifted to the Americas. Other aristocrats shored up their finances by forming strategic alliances—typically by marriage—with rising merchant families, who shared their wealth in return for social prestige. Although some of the old nobility resented this infusion of new blood into their ranks, those who formed such alliances brought the landed elite into a closer relationship with the emerging world of overseas exploration and capitalistic investment.

Landlords whose tenants did not enjoy secure tenure had a wider range of options. This was especially the case in Spain, Portugal, southern Italy, parts of England, eastern Germany, and Poland. Some lords were content to raise rents at will, but the more enterprising embarked on new economic ventures. In some instances this meant enclosing their lands, evicting their tenants, and converting from tillage to the pasturing of sheep. More often it meant an end to the old open-field system of farming, in which land was divided into strips and production was largely for the local market, in favor of larger, more productive farms that produced commercially for the wider marketplace. These new farms required the employment of agricultural hands, usually for subsistence wages, in place of peasants with a degree of personal attachment in the land. In many places, agriculture thus became a commercial endeavor. This pattern occurred often in England but rarely in Spain, where most hidalgos thought that anything pertaining to business was beneath their dignity as warriors. In eastern Germany, Poland, and Russia, landlords took advantage of western

Europe's inability to feed itself by enclosing their lands in order to produce large quantities of grain for export. Unlike English lords who enclosed their lands, they did not evict their peasants but forced them into gradual serfdom.

The changes in the period from 1450 to 1600 caused substantial agrarian unrest in the English Midlands and eastern Europe, where large-scale commercial agriculture became commonplace, and throughout western Europe, where most peasants worked small plots and often worried about the security of their holdings. Commercial farming was essential, however, if the expanding population was to be fed.

Commercial Innovation and Expansion

The economic depression that gripped Europe in the fourteenth and early fifteenth centuries had been beneficial to the towns in certain respects. Despite urban riots, declining production caused by the drop in population, and war, the price of manufactured goods and wages for skilled workers generally rose while the cost of grain declined, thus increasing urban prosperity.

Merchants adapted to the new conditions by developing stronger organizations, diversifying their activities, and improving business procedures. Temporary partnerships, neither efficient nor conducive to expansion, were replaced by permanent companies. These firms were vulnerable during recessions when borrowers defaulted on their loans. Businessmen learned to break up their firms into several independent partnerships. The importance of diversification was also recognized, as merchants engaged in a combination of commerce, banking, manufacturing, and sometimes overseas trade. Diversification encouraged the development of new industries. Economic growth was enhanced by more widespread use of double-entry bookkeeping, which uses parallel columns to balance credits and debits, and bills of exchange, which facilitate the transfer of large sums of money without risking the shipment of currency or bullion. These developments helped to provide the capital accumulation that made exploration and the growth of overseas trade possible.

Spices were crucial for the preparation of meat in an age that lacked refrigeration and for the enhancement of foods that were otherwise dull or tainted. Fresh meat was commonly available only in the fall; during the rest of the year most people who had beef ate the salted variety, which spices made more palatable. Spices were

also used for medicines, perfumes, and incense in religious ceremonies. As population increased, the demand for spices, most of which came from southern and eastern Asia, intensified. In addition to spices, there was commerce in cotton cloth from India; silk and porcelain from China; and precious stones from India, Tibet, and Ceylon. Despite the enormous expense of conducting this trade, the profits were substantial. There was, then, ample incentive to discover new routes to the East, particularly since so much of the spice trade had fallen into the hands of the Muslims and was monopolized in the Mediterranean by the Venetians.

THE SEARCH FOR NEW TRADE ROUTES

Crusading zeal against the Muslims and the quest for profit impelled the voyages of exploration that began in the late fifteenth century. However, they would not have been possible without technological developments that were no less significant than the later inventions that led to the Industrial Revolution. Europeans already possessed some knowledge of Asia, thanks largely to the thirteenth-century travels of Franciscan missionaries and merchant-explorers such as Marco Polo. But only the sea afforded an opportunity to establish direct commercial links with the sources of spices and other goods. Direct sea contact required improvements in ships, weapons, and navigational tools.

Technology and Seafaring

Oars powered the galleys that plied the Mediterranean, giving them independence from the wind but requiring too much human labor to make overseas voyages feasible. Venetian and Genoese galleys also lacked the cargo space to make long voyages practicable. By 1400 the maritime states of Europe had developed large ships powered primarily by square-rigged sails. Because such

The greatest of the merchant-capitalists was Jakob Fugger of Augsburg, shown here with his chief accountant in 1519. The signs on the wall indicate Fugger branches in such cities as Lisbon, Cracow, Rome, and Innsbruck. [Herzog Anton Ulrich—Museum, Braunschweig. Photo by E. P. Keiser.]

ponderous vessels generally had to sail with the wind, their maneuverability was severely restricted. By studying Arab ships that sailed the Indian Ocean and by borrowing multiple masts and sternpost rudders from the Chinese, the Portuguese developed a new vessel, a two- or three-masted caravel that could make long voyages profitable and, with triangular sails, travel at an angle to the wind instead of only with it.

The ability of the new vessels to sail the high seas created navigational problems, but these were surmountable with instruments that were already at hand. The compass, originally Chinese but in use in the West by the thirteenth century, enabled a navigator to steer a course; the astrolabe facilitated the determination of latitude by measuring the approximate height of the sun and stars. However, the accuracy of the astrolabe and its successor, the quadrant, was adversely affected by the rolling of the ship. Portuguese navigators commonly hugged the coasts of Africa, landing every few days to use their instruments on shore. The increased sophistication of maritime charts known as *portolani,* prepared primarily from firsthand observations of sailors, also aided navigation. The portolani mapped coastlines, rivers, and harbors.

Europeans acquired naval mastery by employing artillery on their vessels and by improving naval gunnery and the ability to maneuver their ships for maximum military effectiveness. This gave them a considerable advantage over Arab galleys, which relied on the traditional tactics of ramming or sailing alongside and boarding, and the often larger Chinese junks. Cannons, invented in twelfth-century China, were first used in the West by the Venetians in the fourteenth century. The Portuguese were the first Westerners to recognize the value of directing fire against an enemy's ships rather than the soldiers they carried.

Voyages of Exploration

The Portuguese originally viewed expansion in terms of a new crusade against the Muslims. Their second goal was to bypass Islamic middlemen by going directly to West Africa for gold and pepper. Initially, then, the voyages did not stem from a desire to discover new lands or a search for a direct route to Asian spices and wealth.

After 1415, Prince Henry the Navigator (1394–1460), the younger son of King John I of Portugal, dispatched expeditions to explore the western coast of Africa. As a result of these voyages, in the 1460s and 1470s Portugal established relations with the rulers of West Africa and constructed forts and trading stations. By 1500 the Portuguese had replaced the Muslims as the dominant commercial power in this region. In the fifteenth century the Portuguese also developed plantations on their islands in the eastern Atlantic, where they forced black slaves to grow sugarcane for export to Europe. Portuguese traders sent thousands of slaves to Lisbon in the late 1400s, and by 1530 the traffic in slavery was more valuable than the shipments of gold.

In 1487 the voyages of exploration along the West African coast culminated when Bartholomeu Dias sailed around the African cape, which was soon named "Good Hope." Another decade passed before Vasco da Gama arrived at Calicut on the Malabar coast in 1498 after a voyage of $10^{1}/_{2}$ months from Lisbon. Neither the Hindu rulers nor the Arab merchants were pleased to see the Portuguese, who represented a threat to their domination of the spice trade. Portuguese fleets, spurred on by the 3,000 percent profit realized by da Gama's voyage, sailed again in 1500 and 1502. The 1500 voyage was notable because Pedro Cabral, blown off course in a storm, sailed far enough westward to reach Brazil.

The Portuguese missed the opportunity to sponsor the voyages that led to the European arrival in the Americas. As early as 1484 the Genoese sailor Christopher Columbus (1451–1506) tried unsuccessfully to persuade Portugal's King John II (1481–1495) to support a westward expedition whose goal was to find a sea route to the Indies. Not until 1492 did Columbus find backing when the Spanish rulers Ferdinand and Isabella gave him their support. With a fleet of three ships, Columbus reached what were probably the Bahamas in October 1492 but mistakenly identified them as part of the Japanese archipelago. He also visited Cuba and Hispaniola, whose natives he called "Indians." He made three subsequent voyages, convinced that he had discovered a sea route to eastern Asia. He carried some 1,500 settlers on his second voyage, but not until his third trip (1498) did the first Spanish women migrate to the New World. For his exploits, Columbus wanted to be honored as "the Admiral of the Ocean Sea," yet in his later years he also thought of himself as one who was divinely ordained to help Spain liberate the Holy Land. Reflecting the late medieval belief that the end of the world was imminent, he was convinced that God had made him "the messenger of the new heaven and the new earth" described in the book of Revelation.

When the Portuguese learned of Columbus' initial voyage, John II, unwilling to believe that Columbus had landed in eastern Asia, laid claim to the territory on the

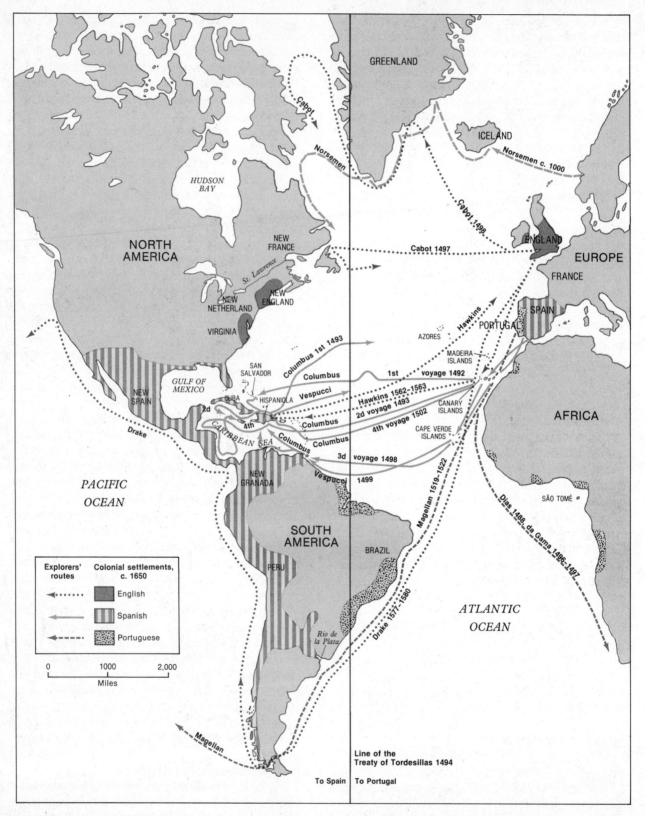

12.1 Voyages of Exploration to the Americas

GREENLAND

ICELAND

Norsemen c. 1000

Cabot

Norsemen

Cabot 1498

HUDSON
BAY

NORTH
AMERICA

NEW
FRANCE

Cabot 1497

ENGLAND

EUROPE

FRANCE

St. Lawrence

NEW
NETHERLAND

NEW
ENGLAND

SPAIN

PORTUGAL

Hawkins

VIRGINIA

AZORES

MADEIRA
ISLANDS

Columbus 1st 1493

Columbus

1st   voyage 1492

NEW
SPAIN

GULF OF
MEXICO

SAN
SALVADOR

Vespucci

Hawkins 1562–1563

CANARY
ISLANDS

CUBA

HISPANIOLA

2d voyage 1493

2d

4th

Columbus

4th voyage 1502

CAPE VERDE
ISLANDS

AFRICA

Drake

CARIBBEAN SEA

Columbus   Columbus

3d   voyage 1498

SÃO TOMÉ

PACIFIC
OCEAN

NEW
GRANADA

Vespucci   1499

Magellan 1519–1522

Dias 1488 da Gama 1496–1497

SOUTH
AMERICA

BRAZIL

PERU

ATLANTIC
OCEAN

Drake 1577–1580

**Explorers'
routes**

**Colonial settlements,
c. 1650**

English

Spanish

Portuguese

Rio de
la Plata

0   1000   2,000

Miles

Magellan

Line of the
Treaty of Tordesillas 1494

To Spain   To Portugal

grounds of its proximity to the Azores. Ferdinand and Isabella thereupon appealed to the pope, the Spaniard Alexander VI, who awarded the lands to Spain. The pope also drew a line of demarcation approximately 300 miles west of the Azores, giving Spain the rights of exploration to territory west of the line. In the Treaty of Tordesillas (1494), John II persuaded the Spanish to move the line some 800 miles farther west. Although no one apparently realized it at the time, Brazil fell into the Portuguese sphere of influence because of the change.

The significance of Columbus' voyage became apparent only as other explorers made new findings. Sailing for England in 1497 and 1498, the Venetian John Cabot reached the region of Cape Breton and Labrador, where he found an abundance of fish but no spices. Undeterred, Cabot was convinced that he had almost reached Japan. It was not Cabot or Columbus who persuaded Europeans to accept the existence of another continent but the Florentine Amerigo Vespucci (1454–1512), a geographer who participated in Spanish and Portuguese voyages. His published letters popularized the idea of the New World, which came to be called America in his honor.

Accepting the presence of a new continent did not dissuade Europeans from their belief in the viability of a western sea route to Asia by which the Portuguese monopoly of the spice trade could be broken. The key, they reasoned was the discovery of a western passage. The Spaniard Vasco Núñez de Balboa's sighting of the Pacific Ocean in 1513 as he was searching for gold on the Isthmus of Panama stimulated interest. Ultimately, the Portuguese mariner Ferdinand Magellan (1480–1521) found a westward route in 1519 by taking a small Spanish fleet through the dangerous straits near the southern tip of South America that now bear his name. From there he sailed across the Pacific to the Philippines, where he and 40 of his men were killed. Magellan's navigator, Juan Sebastián del Cano, returned to Spain by way of the Indian Ocean and the Cape of Good Hope, thus accomplishing the first circumnavigation of the globe. It took three years to complete.

EUROPEANS IN AFRICA AND ASIA

The Portuguese were the first Europeans to establish an overseas colonial empire, though they confronted people of technological and cultural sophistication. From the time that Vasco da Gama reached Calicut in 1498, if not before, the primary focus of Portugal's attention overseas was Asia, although the Portuguese had demonstrated economic and religious interest in Africa as well. By 1500 they had acquired some 150,000 African slaves as well as gold in exchange for such commodities as wheat, textiles, brass utensils, and glass beads. The discovery of an all-water route to the Indian Ocean required that provisioning bases for the lengthy voyage be acquired along the African coastline.

The Portuguese in Africa and Asia

In the aftermath of da Gama's epic voyage, Portuguese interest in Africa centered primarily on the southeast owing to sailing conditions on the *carreira da India,* the voyage to South Asia. Each leg of the arduous journey took six to eight months; altogether a round trip covered some 23,000 miles, a distance nearly equal to the earth's circumference. In sailing around most of the African perimeter, the only significant way stations were in the southeast. In addition to its strategic location on the path of the *carreira,* southeast Africa was appealing because of its wealth and a tempting target because its towns were weakly defended. Although the Portuguese had relatively little difficulty in establishing supremacy along the coast, attempts to gain control of the gold mines in the interior were sporadic and generally unsuccessful. Portuguese domination of coastal southeast Africa impoverished the once thriving city-states.

The huge sweep of the Portuguese commercial empire was based on strategically located naval bases and trading centers and control of the major sea lanes. Much of the credit for creating this empire belongs to Affonso de Albuquerque (1453–1515), viceroy of the Indies, who established Goa in western India as his headquarters. Its seizure in 1510 impressed Indian rulers and established Portugal as an imperial power in Asia. "Golden Goa," as it became known, served as the hub of a major trade network. In 1511, Albuquerque seized Malacca, the principal center of distribution for the Indonesian spice trade, and in 1515 he captured Hormuz, which controlled entry to the Persian Gulf. Two years earlier, however, he had failed to seize Aden, thereby losing an opportunity to take over the Muslim spice route through the Red Sea. Nevertheless, the rest of the spice trade in the Indian Ocean was now in Portuguese hands.

The Portuguese established additional trading posts and forts until by the mid-sixteenth century their commercial empire in Asia stretched from Hormuz to Macao in

Situated on the Tagus River, Lisbon became one of Europe's busiest ports in the sixteenth century because of Portugal's trade with Africa and Asia. During the course of the century, however, much of this trade shifted to Antwerp. [The Granger Collection, New York]

China. The Chinese authorities allowed the Portuguese local autonomy at Macao but walled off the tiny isthmus on which the settlement was located. Unlike most Portuguese settlements, which the nobility dominated, businessmen founded and governed Macao. They made it an entrepôt for much intra-Asian trade, shipping pepper, cloves, and sandalwood from Indonesia to China; carrying Chinese silk to Japan in return for silver; and later engaging in illicit trade with the Spanish Philippines. The Portuguese virtually monopolized Japanese foreign trade in the late sixteenth and early seventeenth centuries.

The Portuguese succeeded in Asia in large measure because the crown itself provided the necessary capital. Without such financing, no private corporation or individual could have provided the backing necessary to send ships to the Indian Ocean and beyond and, once there, to intrude successfully into established Asian trade patterns. The Spanish government, by contrast, merely licensed the exploratory voyages to America, funding for which came from private parties. The Portuguese crown operated like a merchant corporation in Africa and Asia, although private capital funded its interests in the Atlantic islands and Brazil. In general, the government took a direct role in governing its African and Asian empire, while in the Atlantic and Brazil it entrusted management—and a greater share of the profits—to private parties. The economic base of the two regions of the Portuguese empire differed as well: interests in Asia and Africa were largely commercial; those in the Atlantic and Brazil were predominantly agricultural.

The government in Lisbon administered its Asian and African interests in part through permanent representatives, called "factors," who resided in Portuguese settlements. A factor served as an ambassador to foreign governments, handled the crown's business interests, collected taxes, and governed the local community. The community was known as a "factory," that is, a trading post in a foreign country. A second important instrument of imperial crown capitalism was the *Casa da India* ("House of India"), which handled the receipt and sales of Asian and African goods, prepared fleets for departure, licensed personnel, and handled correspondence.

The crown's chief administrative officer was the viceroy, who typically served a term of three years and had little or no previous experience in Africa and Asia. In practice, viceroys exercised a good deal of independence, not least because of the length of time it took to communicate with Lisbon. Only during the first year or so of his tenure could the viceroy expect to send an inquiry and receive a response before his successor arrived. He was assisted by an advisory council, judges, financial officers, and inspectors; as the empire grew, so did the bureaucracy.

Of the goods shipped by the Portuguese to Lisbon, the most important was pepper. By the mid-sixteenth century, Portuguese traders could normally procure pepper in southern Asia only in return for bullion. South Asia also supplied cinnamon, ginger, and cardamom, but the more exotic spices—cloves, nutmeg, and mace—were obtained in Indonesia, thousands of miles to the east, and were therefore costly. The Portuguese also exported items such as camphor and musk to Europe for medicinal purposes, but demand for them, and therefore profits, were lower than those for spices. They also shipped cotton textiles from India and silk and porcelain from China.

Portugal had neither the population nor the material wealth to establish a truly colonial empire. With a population of approximately 1.5 million the country could hardly afford the 2,400 or so people who left each year to live in the empire. In contrast, the much larger country of Spain lost to the Spanish empire fewer than 1,000 people a year out of its population of perhaps 8 million. The Portuguese communities in Asia, including servants and people of mixed birth, probably numbered no more than 14,000.

Christianity in Asia

Portuguese expansion into Africa and Asia was intended to win converts as well as to amass profits. Christianity was, of course, not new to Africa; the Gospel had been preached in North Africa during the Roman Empire, and Ethiopia was still a Christian land. Christians lived along the Malabar coast in India as well. The interest in making inroads against the Muslims, which had been a motivating factor in the Portuguese exploration of Africa in the fifteenth century, was no less important in the Portuguese drive into Asia.

Although they enjoyed some early success in the Congo, Portuguese missionaries, mostly Franciscans and Dominicans, made little headway in southeastern Africa and Asia before the arrival of the Jesuits in 1542. The only mass conversions before this date occurred among Hindus of low caste who lived at the southern tip of India. Most Indians had no interest in conversion because those who refused to observe the Hindu rites were deemed untouchables. Fiercely opposed to Christianity, the Muslims were even less likely to convert. The relatively few Asians who did embrace Christianity before 1542 tended to be affiliated with the Portuguese as merchants, concubines, servants, or slaves. As in Muslim lands, there were enticements, such as improved commercial opportunities, for those who converted. Force too was used, as when the Portuguese prohibited the public exercise of Hinduism, Buddhism, and Islam in their territories.

Francis Xavier launched the Jesuit campaign in Asia shortly after he arrived in Goa in 1542. In 1545 he preached to the Malayans, and the following year he took his message to the Moluccas. Between 1549 and 1551 he worked in Japan, apparently the first Christian missionary to that country. The economic benefits resulting from Portuguese trade with Nagasaki helped the work of conversion, and in 1582, one Jesuit estimated that there were 150,000 Japanese Christians. The Portuguese destroyed Buddhist and Shinto temples and shrines wherever they could, a factor that may in part have motivated a government edict that expelled the missionaries in 1587.

A council in Goa formulated the missionary policy for Portugal's Asian empire in 1567. It condemned all faiths except Catholicism as defined by the Council of Trent and endorsed the use of secular power to spread the Catholic message. Although the council prohibited forcible conversion, the viceroy ordered the destruction of all pagan temples and non-Christian religious literature, prohibited Muslims from using Muhammad's name in their prayer calls, expelled all non-Christian priests and other religious leaders, and banned ritual bathing by Hindus. Polygamy was forbidden, and every man with more than one wife was allowed to keep only his first. Christians could not associate with people of other faiths except for business purposes, and non-Christians could not continue their religious processions.

These and similar regulations were not uniformly enforced, particularly the bans on social intercourse and the keeping of harems. Some Portuguese men found harems attractive, while others had recourse to Hindu temple-prostitutes. In Indonesia especially, Portuguese authorities relied on Asians to staff various administrative posts. Clearly, a difference in outlook existed between the missionaries, who normally approached their work with zeal, and many of the Portuguese merchants, soldiers, and bureaucrats, who often found Asians and their customs attractive.

MATTEO RICCI AND THE "CHINA MISSION"

During his sojourn in Japan, Xavier had opened doors by presenting gifts that reflected advanced European technology, including a clock. Thirty-five years later, another Jesuit, the Italian-born Matteo Ricci (1552–1610), used the same tactic to win admission to the court of the Ming emperor, Wan-li, in Beijing (Peking).

A native of central Italy, Ricci studied law before joining the Society of Jesus in 1571. After further studies in geography and mathematics he left in 1577 for Goa, where he completed his theological education and taught in the Catholic college. Ordered to Macao in 1582, he joined Michele Ruggieri, a Jesuit from Naples, who was preparing for a mission to China. Although their first efforts to enter the country were repulsed, Ricci and Ruggieri settled near Canton in September 1583. Sensitive to Chinese customs, they proceeded circumspectly, continuing their study of the Chinese language and seeking converts by leading exemplary lives. Ricci impressed the Chinese with his knowledge of mathematics and geography, his nearly photographic memory, and his gifts of maps, clocks, and paintings. He dressed in the garb of a Confucian scholar, thereby identifying himself with respected men of learning.

In January 1601 the emperor Wan-li, enticed by gifts that included clocks, a crucifix, and a clavichord (a precursor of the piano), finally permitted Ricci to settle in Beijing. Interest in the clavichord was so keen that Ricci composed songs with lyrics that dealt with ethical themes and included quotations from Christian authors. The ethical focus was at the heart of Ricci's message, for he found the Chinese, with their grounding in the moral teachings of Confucius, more interested in Christian morality than theology. He wrote some two dozen pamphlets dealing with moral issues, friendship, and science and revised a Jesuit compendium of Christian doctrine, basing arguments for Christianity on reason rather than the Bible, hoping thereby to appeal to more Chinese readers. The compendium even included quotations from Chinese authors.

By 1605, 17 missionaries were working in China under Ricci's direction. The number of converts they won was never large, but he and his colleagues played an important role in disseminating western scientific, mathematical, and technological knowledge in China. The Chinese were more interested in Ricci as a scholar than as a missionary, and during his Beijing years he received numerous Chinese visitors and corresponded with people throughout the country. On his deathbed in 1610 he told his fellow Jesuit missionaries, "I am leaving you on the threshold of an open door, that leads to a great reward, but only after labors endured and dangers encountered."

The Spanish in the Philippines

The approximately 7,100 islands that make up the Philippines had been visited by Indian, Chinese, and Arab traders and settlers long before Magellan reached them in 1521. Other Spanish expeditions followed, but not until the spring of 1565 did the Spaniards, under the leadership of Miguel López de Legazpi, found a permanent settlement. Legazpi established his headquarters at Manila in 1571, which subsequently became the commercial and missionary center for the islands. Most of the islands were in Spanish hands by 1600, despite fierce resistance from Muslims in the south. The Moros, as the Spanish called them, remained unsubdued until the early nineteenth century, during which time they periodically raided Spanish settlements.

Each year the Spaniards dispatched a galleon laden with silver from Acapulco to Manila; it returned with Chinese silk, porcelain, and other Asian goods. However, Spanish traders from the Philippines had little success in competing with the Portuguese for control of trade with Japan. Merchants and bureaucrats nevertheless prospered in Manila, where they competed commercially with the Chinese community and sometimes persecuted its members as well. To encourage settlers, the government offered Spaniards land grants, known as *encomiendas,* that entitled them to forced labor and tribute from the Filipinos. Unlike Christian efforts in China, the missionary campaign in the Philippines was highly successful, and the islands remain largely Roman Catholic today.

From Moscow to the Pacific: The Russians in Asia

While the western European powers used the sea routes to extend their influence in Asia, the Russians conquered the vast expanses of sparsely populated Siberia. Russians had traded in this region since the twelfth century, mostly for furs, but the first conquests were made only in the early 1580s. The Russian advance was primarily the work of half-Russian, half-Mongol people of the frontier known as Cossacks, many of whom had fled to the steppes to escape serfdom. The Cossacks pushed across the Urals, attacking the Siberian Tatars, and by 1647 had reached the Pacific Ocean, a distance of some 5,000 miles from the Russian heartland.

In less than 70 years the Cossacks had conquered more than a quarter of the Asian continent, a feat made possible not only by the scattered population but also by the terrain, most of which consisted of flat plains crossed by a belt of forests. The Cossacks were no strangers to the cold, dry climate, and to facilitate transportation, they took advantage of the Siberian rivers, one of which, the Amur, flows into the Pacific. They also had a monopoly on firearms. The Cossacks founded strategically located towns, from which they controlled the surrounding territory. From the Russian heartland came merchants, administrators, and missionaries to help settle the region.

THE EUROPEAN CONQUEST OF THE AMERICAS

While the Portuguese fashioned a commercial empire in the East, the Spanish imposed a colonial empire throughout much of Mexico, South and Central America, and Florida. Faced with uncertain economic prospects at home, the hidalgos who led the assault on the Aztecs and the Inca came in search of gold, but they were also influenced by a crusading ideal. They confronted civilized peoples who vastly outnumbered them. The keys to

their success were technological superiority and the fact that both the Aztecs and the Inca were the overlords of a vast Amerindian population, some of whom fought on the side of the Spaniards. The Aztecs and Inca were also at a disadvantage because their empires, unlike those in Africa, were highly centralized and thus ill-suited to keep up resistance once their rulers had fallen.

Conquistadors, Aztecs, and Inca

The conquests of the Spanish conquistadors began in 1519. Under the command of Hernando Cortés (1485–1547) a force of some 600 men, 16 horses, and a few cannon landed in Mexico near Veracruz, which Cortés founded. Although the Amerindians initially resisted him, Cortés gradually won them over, aided by his Amerindian mistress and translator, Doña Marina. Fortuitous assistance reputedly came too from phenomena such as a comet visible in the daytime and lightning unaccompanied by thunder that demolished two temples; the Aztecs interpreted such signs to mean the

The Aztec capital at Tenochtitlán was dominated by a great temple where humans were sacrificed. It was from this temple that Cortés and his party surveyed the city. [Neg. No. 326597. Photo by Rota. Courtesy Department of Library Services, American Museum of Natural History.]

possible return of Topiltzin-Quetzalcóatl, a priest-king exiled 500 years earlier. With the aid of 1,000 Tlaxcalas, the long-standing enemies of the Aztecs, Cortés advanced on the capital at Tenochtitlán, whose population of approximately 90,000 was nearly the equal of those of Europe's largest cities. Dominated by an enormous temple, pyramids, and the royal palace, the city was impressive for its orderly streets and canals and its bustling commerce. Montezuma ruled Tenochtitlán from 1502 to 1520. In a society dominated by war, all able-bodied Aztec men received military training. So many warriors died in battle that the Aztecs had to practice polygamy. Bearing children was therefore highly regarded, and a woman who died in childbirth received the same ceremonial rites as a warrior who perished on the battlefield. The main motive for the warfare was the need to acquire victims with whom to appease the sun god, who fed on blood obtained by ripping out the hearts of living people. Women were rarely among the sacrificial victims. Human sacrifice functioned as a means to terrorize subject peoples, which helps to explain their unwillingness to defend the Aztecs against Cortés.

The Aztecs allowed Cortés to enter the capital peacefully, but in a matter of days he used the pretext of an attack on his garrison at Veracruz to imprison Montezuma. An Aztec uprising in which Montezuma was killed forced Cortés to flee in 1520, though a year later he regained Tenochtitlán with the help of the Tlaxcalas. The fighting destroyed most of the city, but amid its ruins the Spaniards built Mexico City.

Francisco Pizarro (c. 1474–1541) led the attack on the Inca, whose South American empire included much of what is now Peru and Chile. With a force of only 180 men and 27 horses he set out in 1531 to conquer an empire ruled by Atahualpa with his army of 30,000. Atahualpa underestimated Pizarro, who took him prisoner, extracted an enormous ransom, and then executed him. In 1533, Pizarro captured the Inca capital at Cuzco in the Andes, after which the remaining Inca maintained a tiny but independent state high in the mountains at Machu Picchu. To have better communications with other Spanish authorities, Pizarro founded Lima on the Peruvian coast in 1535. Conquest of the Inca was facilitated by the dissatisfaction of subordinate peoples with Inca domination, as well as by internal dissension among the Inca themselves.

Spanish Rule in the Americas

The Spanish confronted difficult legal questions concerning the status of the Amerindians. Religious consid-erations compounded the problem, for the papal decision in 1493 that recognized Spain's claim to most of the Western Hemisphere also made the Spaniards responsible for the conversion of its inhabitants. As Spanish subjects and, in time, Christians, what legal rights did they possess? The conquerors, vastly outnumbered by their subject population, sought an essentially feudal form of government, with considerable local autonomy for their own colonists, and the right to treat the Amerindians as forced laborers. However, the Dominican friar Bartolomé de las Casas contended that as fellow Christians and subjects of the Spanish crown, the Amerindians were entitled to full legal rights and protection. Although the Spanish government was unwilling to provide the colonists much autonomy, it gave certain Spaniards the right to collect tribute from specified villages and to impose forced labor. Those who exercised this power—the *encomenderos* (protectors)—had to render military service and pay the salaries of the clergy. Because of abuses, in the mid-sixteenth century the authority to compel labor was transferred to colonial officials, and forced workers earned a fixed rate. Legally, the Amerindians could not be enslaved, but in practice their situation was little different from slavery.

Administration of the Spanish empire in America was directed by two viceroys who received their instructions from the Council of the Indies in Spain. The viceroyalty of New Spain, with headquarters in Mexico City, embraced Spanish territories in North America, the West Indies, Venezuela, and the Philippines, whereas the viceroyalty of Peru, governed from Lima, included the rest of Spanish South America. Under the viceroys were provincial governors. The viceroys and the governors shared authority with conciliar courts known as *audiencias,* which gave them advice and had the power to overturn their decisions. This system of checks and balances safeguarded royal prerogatives, but it also deprived colonial government of administrative efficiency.

Nothing was more important in determining the pattern of Spanish settlement than the sites of gold and silver deposits and the availability of native labor to mine them. On his first voyage, Columbus had found gold in Hispaniola, and more was soon discovered in Cuba and Puerto Rico. At first, workers mined the gold from shallow diggings or extracted it from stream beds. Such mining was labor-intensive, and as the Amerindian population declined, it became more profitable to graze cattle or raise sugarcane. The conquest of the Aztecs and Inca led to the discovery of rich silver deposits in the 1540s, especially at Potosí in the Andes. Silver became the most important export, amounting to 97 percent of the bullion shipped to Spain by 1570. As the output of European mines declined in the late sixteenth century, the flow of silver from the New World continued to increase. Altogether, the Spanish treasure fleets transported 180 tons of gold and 16,000 tons of silver to Seville between 1500 and 1650. Much of the wealth, 20 percent of which went to the crown as the "royal fifth," helped to pay for imports, service the royal debt, and finance war.

No less significant was the introduction of large estates. Some, the *haciendas,* reared animals or raised cereal crops, but in tropical regions, sugar and tobacco plantations were established, patterned after the sugar plantations of Atlantic islands such as the Azores. Unlike the haciendas, which used Amerindian workers, the primary laborers on the plantations were African slaves. Although both the plantation system and the trade in African slaves predated the Spanish conquests in the Americas, the success of the conquistadors opened up vast new markets for the sale of blacks. Africans were accustomed to working in tropical climates, possessed some immunity from the diseases that decimated the Amerindians, and had lower mortality rates in the New World than the Europeans.

In Spain the economic effects of its new colonial empire were a mixed blessing. Seville, which enjoyed a monopoly of trade with the colonies, prospered for several centuries. Ultimately, its prosperity was undermined by the heavy hand of the Spanish government, which overregulated everything, and by the reluctance of the Spaniards to seize the commercial opportunities that their empire made possible. Some new manufacturing developed in Spain, but in general, Spaniards continued to rely on France and the Netherlands for their goods. Nor did large numbers of Spaniards emigrate to America, the total number amounting to some 100,000 in the sixteenth century. The influx of bullion into Spain was so badly mismanaged that for many Spaniards the most direct result was a spiraling cost of living.

The most dramatic effect of Spanish domination in the New World was the catastrophic decline in the Amerindian population, one of the greatest demographic disasters in history. By 1510, nearly 90 percent of the Amerindians of Hispaniola were dead, while in Mexico the Amerindian population, which had numbered 11 million, fell by more than 75 percent. Famine and ruthless exploitation accounted for some of the deaths, but the biggest killer was disease, especially smallpox. The fact that Europeans introduced universities and printing to the New World and that Spanish law and Christianity ended the Aztec practices of human sacrifice

and polygamy was small comfort in the face of such suffering. Although Aztecs and Inca suppressed other Amerindians, the Spanish exploitation of the native inhabitants and the introduction of slave plantations were hardly an improvement, though the Amerindians were treated better than the blacks. Because of the shortage of Spanish women in the New World, intermarriage with Amerindians was so frequent that the descendants of mixed marriages—the *mestizos*—eventually outnumbered both the Spaniards and the Amerindians.

The Portuguese in Brazil

Portugal paid relatively little attention to Brazil in the early 1500s, particularly since no gold or silver was found there. The region did produce brazilwood, used in making red dye. The threat of Spanish and French incursions forced Portugal to act in 1533. It organized Brazil into 15 hereditary fiefs whose holders—the *donatários*—enjoyed sweeping powers, including the right to levy internal taxes. When most of the *donatários* proved ineffectual, the Portuguese king imposed a centralized administration under the direction of a governor-general in 1549. After Spain's conquest of Portugal in 1580, Spanish-style colonial administration, headed by a viceroy, was introduced in Brazil.

As in the Spanish colonies, controversy erupted over the treatment of the Amerindians. Jesuit missionaries worked tirelessly to convert and settle them in Christian villages. Their efforts ran counter to the needs of settlers who established sugar plantations in northern Brazil in the late 1500s. Brazil, in fact, became the world's leading producer of sugar in the early seventeenth century. In 1574 the Portuguese government resolved the dispute between the Jesuits and the plantation owners by allowing the former to protect residents of their Christian villages while giving settlers the right to enslave Amerindians captured in war. Unable to procure sufficient labor in this manner, the colonists increasingly relied on African slaves.

The North Atlantic States and the Americas

The Portuguese were the first to profit from John Cabot's discovery of the cod fisheries off Newfoundland. For the masses, salted fish was a vital item in the diet, particularly during the winter and on the frequent fast days throughout the year. A ready market thus existed for cod to feed the growing population. Although Portugal claimed Newfoundland, French and English fishermen were soon hauling in catches from its waters. In addition to providing food the development of new fisheries led to the beginning of the fur trade with the Amerindians and to an increase in the number of ships and mariners capable of sailing the Atlantic.

As their naval expertise improved, the English were determined to participate in the spice trade. Unwilling to challenge Portugal's control of the route around the Cape of Good Hope, the English searched for a northeast or northwest passage to Asia. Richard Chancellor set out in 1553 to find a northeast passage. After sailing through the White Sea to Archangel he traveled overland to the court of Ivan the Terrible in Moscow. His trip resulted in the founding of the Muscovy Company (1555), which pursued direct trade between England and Russia. Later attempts by the English and the Dutch to find a northeastern passage were unsuccessful, as were English efforts to find a northwestern route. The latter, however, led Europeans to Hudson Strait and Hudson Bay.

As the search for a northern passage progressed, the English turned their attention to the possibility of trade with Spain's American colonies, notwithstanding the fact that the Spaniards considered unauthorized trade illegal. In 1562, John Hawkins launched the English slave trade with the backing of a private syndicate. In Hispaniola he traded the 300 or 400 slaves he had acquired in Sierra Leone for hides and sugar. Impressed by the potential of this trade, Elizabeth I quietly helped to finance two later voyages. As relations with Spain worsened, the English restricted their activity in the New World primarily to privateering—government-approved piracy—for the rest of the century. During his circumnavigation of the globe in 1577–1580, Francis Drake challenged the Spanish sphere of dominion by claiming California for England. In the 1580s, Sir Walter Raleigh's attempt to found an English colony near Roanoke Island (now part of North Carolina) resulted in dismal failure. The French, whose activities in the New World in the sixteenth century consisted largely of plundering Spanish shipping, were equally unsuccessful in attempting to establish a colony in Florida in the early 1560s.

Economic and political events of the late sixteenth century largely determined the ability of the English, French, and Dutch to make inroads into Spanish America. England's successful war with Spain (1585–1604) severely crippled the latter and provided substantial freedom of action to the Dutch. France, disrupted by a long and bitter civil war, began to build the strong monarchy and economy necessary for colonial expansion only in the 1590s. In all three states, a key to future success in colonial expansion and the emerging global economy was the development of aggressive capitalism.

THE ECONOMY IN THE AGE OF EXPLORATION

In the fifteenth and sixteenth centuries the European economy underwent dramatic changes. The most important involved not only the founding of commercial and colonial empires but also the rapid growth of capitalism and a price revolution.

Merchant Capitalism

Capitalism involves three elements: (1) the acquisition and investment of capital to obtain profit, (2) private ownership of the principal means of production and distribution, and (3) a division in the productive and distributive process between the owners of the capital (the employers) and the laborers. Capitalism cannot exist without the capacity and the willingness to invest and to take risks, which in turn presupposes the possibility of significant profits. The medieval concepts of the just price and the wrongfulness of usury were thus impediments to capitalistic development. Medieval theologians had generally recognized the right of a lender to additional compensation beyond the principal if he incurred a loss by forgoing the use of his money. The acceptability of reasonable interest was gradually extended until, in the sixteenth century, bankers regularly paid interest on deposits and merchants routinely operated on credit. The expansion of capitalistic activities was also furthered by the increased use of bills of exchange, improved facilities for interregional trade, stable coinage, and an adequate and affordable labor supply. Finally, the rise in prices stimulated capitalistic investment as merchants and others with surplus wealth sought profits through investment rather than spending their money on consumables.

As the European states centralized in this period, they exercised a threefold influence on capitalism. First, their demands for weapons, supplies, and luxury items created an expanding market for merchant capitalists. Second, the encouragement of overseas commercial and colonial activity by the governments of the maritime states was a major incentive to invest in such ventures. Finally, these governments introduced economic policies intended to strengthen their respective states. Collectively, these policies constitute mercantile capitalism.

At the heart of mercantile policy was the principle of state regulation, which was designed primarily to benefit the state itself. Free enterprise—the right of merchants and manufacturers to respond to market conditions as they deem best—was not part of mercantile capitalism. Both rulers and merchants who profited from business dealings with the state accepted economic controls as necessary. However, some of these controls, particularly those creating monopolies, became increasingly unpopular in the late sixteenth and seventeenth centuries among the people, who blamed them for high prices. Governments used controls to ensure the availability of strategic items, to provide order in the economy, and to regulate commerce with other states. Economic regulation was an important facet of the campaign to impose greater order on the early modern state. The most common controls were tariffs on imported goods, subsidies (grants) to strategic industries, and monopolies, which conveyed the exclusive right to manufacture, sell, or trade in a specific commodity. Some governments also attempted to regulate the export of raw materials, such as wool.

Some proponents of mercantile capitalism were convinced that the strength of the state depended on the amassing of bullion. To accomplish this, they favored strict controls on foreign commerce to produce a favorable balance of trade, whereby the value of exports exceeded the value of imports. The Dutch, who dominated the carrying trade, recognized the sterility of this concept and instead pursued a policy geared to maximize the volume and value of trade. Profit, they recognized, was obtained by increasing trade, not hoarding bullion. The English converted to this view for a time in the 1600s but then reverted to a protectionist policy. The Spanish, who wanted to amass bullion, had to use it instead to finance their wars and the conspicuous consumption of their elite and to import goods that they were unwilling to manufacture. Supporters of the bullionist theory tried to reduce the export of bullion by encouraging the immigration of skilled artisans, thereby reducing the need of the host country for imports and perhaps even creating new export commodities from the goods the immigrants manufactured.

Government intervention in the economy was not always beneficial, as in the case of most monopolies. Nevertheless, mercantile policies helped France to build a stronger economy in the 1600s by expanding trade and assisting farmers. Government intervention also had positive results as companies received charters to trade with Asia, Africa, and America; as internal barriers to trade gradually ended (though France was a major exception); and as new industries obtained subsidies.

The Price Revolution

Europeans in the sixteenth century were unprepared for the price rises that occurred throughout Europe. By today's standards the inflation rate was low, often hovering around 2 percent per year, though in some years the rate was much higher. Prices varied greatly from region to region, especially over the short run. In Spain, prices quadrupled in the sixteenth century, and the increase was nearly as great in England. Inflation began later in Italy, where prices doubled by 1600. The largest increases came between the 1540s and 1570s, when bad weather and crop failures added additional pressures to the inflationary spiral and the impact of American bullion began to be felt. The main cause of inflation was a rise in population and thus in a demand for goods without a corresponding increase in production, thereby creating shortages of goods and services. The shortages put pressure on prices, as did the expansion of the money supply because of the large quantities of imported bullion. War destruction, crop failures, and the requirements of expanding governments also contributed to a demand that outstripped production.

Food prices rose approximately twice as much as those of other goods. Rising food prices caused severe hardship for the poor and acted as a brake on population growth by the mid-seventeenth century, but they also spurred the development of the Atlantic fisheries and commercial agriculture. Prices, however, rose faster than agricultural yield. Economic conditions encouraged the Dutch not only to continue reclaiming land from the sea but also to develop the techniques of crop rotation. Traditionally, a third of the land had been left fallow each year on a rotating basis to restore fertility, but the Dutch discovered that the same end could be achieved by periodically planting beans or peas (to return nitrogen to the soil) and grazing animals, whose manure acted as fertilizer. The adoption of crop rotation by the English and the French in the late seventeenth and eighteenth centuries was crucial to the growth in agricultural productivity that would make the Industrial Revolution possible.

Industrial and Commercial Development

The spread of merchant capitalism led to a major reorganization of the means of producing textiles, the demand for which increased as the population grew. In the cities of the Netherlands and northern and central Italy, merchant capitalists distributed raw wool from

England or raw silk from Asia and western Europe to master artisans. These craftsmen, who still belonged to their own guilds, typically owned their shops, though not the materials on which they worked. Beginning in the late sixteenth century, English capitalists altered the system by distributing raw wool directly to village workers for spinning, dyeing, and weaving. From the merchants' standpoint this system of "putting out" the work to villagers had the advantage of bypassing the traditional guilds with their controls over working conditions, wages, and prices. Because the labor was undertaken in the workers' cottages rather than in shops, the merchants' overhead was lower. In contrast to the guild system the workers had no hope of improving their condition by completing an apprenticeship, and the division between employer and worker gradually became permanent. The price revolution provided additional incentive for the expansion of this system as the cost of goods outpaced the rise in wages. The introduction of the domestic system of textile production could bring substantial profits to the merchant capitalists but sharpened the division between the haves and have-nots as workers were exploited. The domestic system, which involved entire families working together in the home, gradually spread throughout western Europe until it was phased out by the introduction of factories in the Industrial Revolution. By that time, rural workers were manufacturing not only textiles but buttons, gloves, and household goods as well.

Merchant capitalists were also responsible for new forms of business organization that were intended primarily to take advantage of the trade opportunities with Asia, Africa, and America. The partnerships and family firms of the medieval period were not in a position to raise sufficient capital to fund these voyages. With government approval, merchants began banding together as "regulated" companies with a monopoly on a particular item or trade within a given area. Even so, the amount of capital was limited to what the merchants themselves could raise. The solution was the formation of the joint-stock company, an organization of investors rather than an association of traders. Funds came not only from the business community but also from the aristocracy and government officials, and management was in the hands of directors experienced in commercial affairs. The firms normally had monopolies. The English (1600), Dutch (1602), French (1664), and others had East India companies organized on a joint-stock basis by private businessmen with government encouragement. Other companies were formed for such endeavors as colonizing Virginia and Massachusetts and trading furs in North America.

ANTWERP'S GOLDEN AGE

No city more clearly reflected the opportunities and the glory of the age of exploration than Antwerp. In the late fifteenth and sixteenth centuries it stood at the crossroads of Europe, the hub of trade between England and the Continent, the Baltic and the Mediterranean. In terms of international commerce, Antwerp enjoyed the position formerly held by Venice. Antwerp's dominant position among a host of secondary towns moved the Belgian historian Henri Pirenne to refer to the Netherlands—which in the sixteenth century included what is now Belgium as well as Holland—as Antwerp's "suburb." Antwerp was a major cultural center as well. Albrecht Dürer was impressed by the city and the art on view there. The great Flemish painters Pieter Brueghel the Elder (c. 1525–1569) and Peter Paul Rubens (1577–1640) lived in Antwerp.

Antwerp's rise to commercial greatness was facilitated by its geographic advantages. In the late 1400s the preeminence of Bruges as a trading center was undercut when the Zwyn River silted up. Antwerp, situated on the Scheldt River, thereupon became the leading port and commercial center in the Netherlands. Antwerp's rise was also aided by Bruges' insistence on maintaining outmoded commercial regulations; by its hostility to the Burgundian dukes, who turned their attention to Antwerp; and by Habsburg favoritism toward Antwerp in the collection of customs duties. Many of the city's major buildings were constructed in the period of prosperity that ensued, including the great Gothic cathedral of the Holy Virgin (begun in the 1300s), the castle, the Renaissance town hall, and the Bourse, the center of foreign exchange. So great was the expansion that in 1542 a third set of costly city walls had to be constructed. With a population of 100,000 in the mid-sixteenth century, Antwerp was one of the largest cities in Europe.

Commencing in the late 1400s, the shift in the center of European commerce from Venice and the cities of the Hanseatic League brought more than 1,000 foreign businesses to Antwerp. It became the hub of the Portuguese spice trade and the center for the import of English cloth. Its bustling harbor handled as many as 500 ships a day, and more than 1,000 freight wagons arrived in the city each week carrying the overland trade. Recognizing the amount of capital necessary to participate in the spice trade, as early as 1505 the king of Portugal allowed the merchants of Antwerp to purchase a sizable cargo in the Indies and transport it directly to Antwerp in Portuguese ships. Antwerp also imported large quantities of raw materials for use in its own industries, especially cloth manufacturing and finishing. Antwerp artisans pioneered in the production of "new draperies," a lighter and less expensive material than traditional woolen broadcloth, and they also manufactured silk, velvet, and similar luxury goods. Antwerp designers determined European fashions. Like Geneva, Antwerp was a center of the printing industry, boasting approximately 50 print shops in the mid-1500s. The English Bible translators William Tyndale and Miles Coverdale worked for a time in Antwerp, and by the late sixteenth century its printers were among the leading publishers of Counter-Reformation literature.

Antwerp, facing growing commercial competition from the English, became a casualty of the religious wars that plagued much of Europe in the late sixteenth century. In 1576, as the Netherlands struggled against Spanish domination, Spanish troops plundered Antwerp and slaughtered 6,000 of its citizens. The people rallied, expelled the Spaniards, and were governed by Calvinists until 1585, when the Spanish regained control and exiled the Protestants. Antwerp's troubles enabled Amsterdam to replace it as the leading commercial center of Europe in the seventeenth century.

SUMMARY

By the time Antwerp began to decline, the beginnings of a global economy had been established. Antwerp was the first city in the world to serve as the hub of such a commercial network. Compared to the tempo of economic change in preceding centuries, the speed with which a global economy developed in this period was striking. Europeans experienced a social and economic revolution in the late fifteenth and sixteenth centuries. The emergence of merchant capitalism provided substantial opportunities for the acquisition of wealth and power. In England, progressive aristocrats recognized this and profited by their association with the business community, whereas in Spain the hidalgos' resistance to commercial activity contributed to that nation's declining economy. As European rulers centralized their states, they adapted to the economic changes by formulating policies designed to control or expand trade. The governments of France, England,

and the Netherlands were especially successful, and the resulting wealth was the basis of their growing power in the late 1500s and 1600s. Indeed, one of the effects of the commercial revolution was the increased ability of states to field large, better-equipped armies.

The lives of countless ordinary people changed. The domestic system of manufacturing eventually created significant numbers of workers who had no reasonable prospect of improving their position. Many continued to live at the subsistence level despite shifting from agriculture to manufacturing. To feed the expanding population, commercial agriculture blossomed, aided by the introduction of crop rotation and the further enclosing of land. For many the general living standard declined in the face of bad harvests, higher taxes, the adverse effects of war on the economy, and capitalistic developments, especially on the farms. Colonial expansion, however, brought Europeans new foods—tomatoes, lima beans, maize, squash, potatoes, and chocolate—in turn the people of the New World came into contact with horses, cattle, and the Eurasian diseases that largely decimated them. The development of global trade patterns also gave Europeans readier access to such items as tea, coffee, and sugar. As sugarcane cultivation spread from the eastern Mediterranean to the eastern Atlantic and then to the New World, so did the slave trade through the agency of the Portuguese and the Spanish. The slave trade was not a European invention; it was already thriving among the Africans. Nevertheless, for the enslaved Africans and the decimated Amerindians, European expansion often had cruel results. In Europe the discovery of new continents and the increased contact with Africa and Asia forced a rethinking of traditional views. As travelers and explorers documented their observations, a more accurate understanding of the physical world began to replace myth and superstition. The developments of this period also marked the first steps toward a Western hegemony in the world that has lasted into the twentieth century.

Suggestions for Further Reading

Andrews, K. R. *Trade, Plunder and Settlement: Maritime Enterprise and the Genesis of the British Empire, 1480–1630.* Cambridge: Cambridge University Press, 1984.

Ball, J. N. *Merchants and Merchandise: The Expansion of Trade in Europe, 1500–1630.* London: Croom Helm, 1977.

Braudel, F. *Civilization and Capitalism,* trans. S. Reynolds. 3 vols. New York: Harper & Row, 1981–1984.

Cipolla, C. M. *Before the Industrial Revolution: European Society and Economy, 1000–1700,* 2d ed. New York: Norton, 1980.

————. *Guns and Sails in the Early Phase of European Expansion, 1400–1700.* London: Collins, 1965.

Cole, J. A. *The Potosí Mita, 1573–1700: Compulsory Indian Labor in the Andes.* Stanford, Calif.: Stanford University Press, 1985.

Curtin, P. D. *Cross-Cultural Trade in World History.* Cambridge: Cambridge University Press, 1984.

Diffie, B. W., and Winius, G. D. *Foundations of the Portuguese Empire, 1415–1580.* Minneapolis: University of Minnesota Press, 1977.

Hemming, J. *The Conquest of the Incas.* New York: Harcourt Brace Jovanovich, 1970.

Israel, J. I. *Dutch Primacy in World Trade, 1585–1740.* New York: Oxford University Press, 1989.

Kriedte, P. *Peasants, Landlords and Merchant Capitalists: Europe and the World Economy, 1500–1800.* Leamington, England: Berg Press, 1983.

McAlister, L. N. *Spain and Portugal in the New World, 1492–1700.* Minneapolis: University of Minnesota Press, 1984.

Mintz, S. W. *Sweetness and Power: The Place of Sugar in Modern History.* New York: Viking, 1985.

Morison, S. E. *The European Discovery of America: The Northern Voyages,* A.D. *500–1600.* New York: Oxford University Press, 1971.

————. *The European Discovery of America: The Southern Voyages,* A.D. *1492–1616.* New York: Oxford University Press, 1974.

Murray, J. J. *Antwerp in the Age of Plantin and Brueghel.* Norman: University of Oklahoma Press, 1970.

The West and the World

The Renaissance

Between 1400 and 1600, European explorers and colonizers discovered and conquered most of the Western hemisphere, sailed around Africa for the first time, settled traders and missionaries in Asia, and circumnavigated the globe. Ironically, the frontiers of Europe itself were severely contracted during this period by the fall of the Byzantine Empire and the conquest of the Balkans and the lower Danube valley by the Ottoman Turks. The campaign that led Suleiman the Magnificent to the gates of Vienna in 1529 coincided with the onset of the Reformation and the outbreak of war between Catholics and Protestants across the continent. Europe was thus divided at the very moment when it faced its greatest threat from militant Islam in 800 years.

The crisis represented by the Reformation and the Ottoman invasion was exacerbated by the discovery of the New World. Before Columbus, the world was believed to consist of only three continents—Europe, Africa, and Asia—and the map Columbus himself carried on his first voyage estimated the distance westward to Asia to be little more than that from Portugal to the Azores islands. Not until 1507 did the German cartographer Martin Waldseemüller produce a map suggesting that "America," as he called the landmass Columbus believed to be part of the Indies, was actually a continent in its own right, separated from Asia by an unknown and unnamed ocean. Six years later, Vasco Núñez de Balboa made the first sighting of the western Pacific, and six years after that, Ferdinand Magellan undertook the circumnavigation of the globe that enabled

Columbus coming ashore in the New World, from a Swiss edition of his letter of 1493. Some of the natives flee in terror, while others bear gifts. [Rare Books and Manuscripts Division, The New York Public Library; Astor, Lenox and Tilden Foundations]

Europeans to gauge the approximate size and shape of the globe accurately for the first time.

The effect of these discoveries was stunning. Older maps had placed Jerusalem in the center of the world and hence of the cosmos. The revelation that half the world had been as hidden from view as the dark side of the moon compelled Europeans to abandon the medieval belief that planetary geography had been shaped to reflect the passion of Jesus and the truth of the Christian faith. When Copernicus displaced the earth itself from the center of the universe, he dealt another blow to traditional cosmology, and by the end of the sixteenth century there was speculation that other worlds, perhaps even an infinite number of them, were as yet undiscovered in the heavens. The impact of the New World thus compelled Europeans to reassess not only the centrality of their own position on the globe but also that of humanity itself in the cosmos.

The discovery of the New World's inhabitants was no less unsettling. The world as conceived by Europeans was made up of two classes of people, those who accepted the truth of Christianity, the faithful, and those who rejected it, the heathen. The existence of hitherto unsuspected cultures whose populations were wholly ignorant of Christianity posed painful and difficult questions. Saint Paul had written that the Gospel had been heard "unto the end of the world" (Romans 10:18), and some clerics argued that the existence of a New World was theologically impossible. Where could the peoples described by the first explorers have originated? Why had they been excluded from the Christian revelation for so many centuries?

A further complication lay in the fact that the peoples of the New World were highly diverse in their cultural attainment. The first people encountered by Columbus were the Caribs, who went naked and practiced polygyny (the keeping of many wives) and cannibalism. These attributes naturally impressed the early explorers; Amerigo Vespucci spoke to a man who claimed to have eaten 300 men and saw human flesh hanging from the beams of houses "as we hang pork." Yet the explorers also reported the Amerindians to be friendly and docile despite the apparent absence of any form of government, worship, or even a marketplace. Confronting the contrast between the natives' appalling customs and their gentle disposition, European observers oscillated in their beliefs that the peoples of the New World were either unspoiled descendants of Adam and Eve or depraved children of the Devil.

The problem was complicated by the discovery of the advanced civilizations of the Aztecs in Mexico and the Inca in Peru. Upon entering the marketplace of the Aztec capital, Tenochtitlán, the Spaniards "were astounded at the number of people and the quantity of merchandise that it contained, and at the good order and control that was maintained, for we had never seen such a thing before."[1] They were appalled as well by the sacrifices performed by Aztec priests, who cut out the hearts of living battle captives. But neither the Aztec nor the Incan empire long survived the arrival of the Spaniards. The capitals were reduced to ruins, their temples and pyramids were abandoned, and their culture was suppressed. The extraordinary speed and thoroughness of the Spaniards' triumph convinced them that God favored their work, and this in turn reinforced the proselytizing fervor of their church. Columbus had embarked on his Atlantic voyage to find profitable trade routes, but within 30 years his successors had established a different goal: to rule a vast army of souls newly converted to Christ.

The Spaniards built their new colonial capital on the ruins of Tenochtitlán. By 1550, Mexico City had a population of 100,000, more than any city in Spain itself. The encounter with Aztec and Incan civilizations had been too brief, and their destruction too sudden and complete, to make any lasting impression on the European consciousness. They faded away into the limbo of fabulous imaginary kingdoms, like that of Prester John.

The image of the Amerindian that finally prevailed in Europe was a hybrid—the "noble savage." The noble savage was a creature both more and less human than the European. On the one hand, the nudity, docility, and absence of government that Columbus had observed among the Caribs seemed to evoke the innocence of humanity before the Fall; on the other hand, those same attributes also connoted brutishness, shamelessness, and perhaps stupidity. The artists who illustrated the wildly popular accounts of the New World that circulated in Europe drew on their own imaginations as well as the stock imagery of their own culture. One of the most influential was Johann Froschauer, who depicted Amerindians as noble Romans in feathered headdresses and skirts, arrayed in tender family scenes beneath rude huts while feasting on human limbs.

Such stereotypical images remained current well into the seventeenth century. Jean de Léry (1534–1611), a French missionary and ethnographer who traveled among the Brazilian Indians, noted the difficulty that even firsthand observers had in accurately depicting the inhabitants of the New World:

Because their gestures and countenances are so different from ours, I confess it is difficult to represent them properly in words or even in

painting. In order to see them as they are, one must visit them in their own country.[2]

In fact, very few illustrators did so, the most notable exception being the Englishman John White, whose depiction of the Virginia Indians in the 1580s is the most valuable visual record of the early New World.

Pope Alexander VI (1492–1503) was the first European authority to pronounce the natives of the New World human—and therefore capable of conversion to Christianity. This position was reiterated in 1537 by Pope Paul III, who declared that the Amerindians were not to be treated as "dumb brutes created for our service" but "as truly men . . . capable of understanding the Catholic faith." But many Europeans both within and without the church remained unconvinced. The savagery of New World customs seemed to mark its inhabitants as subhuman or depraved. "The God of Hispaniola is the Devil," wrote the Spaniard Francisco López de Gomara, who had never set foot there. Another Spanish commentator remarked: "How can we doubt that these people—so uncivilized, so barbaric, contaminated with so many impieties and obscenities—have been justly conquered by such an excellent, pious, and most just king, and by a nation so humane and so excelling in every kind of virtue?" To enslave such creatures to a Christian nation was an ennoblement, and the eradication of their customs was a duty.

Gradually, the peoples of the New World became part of the folklore and pageantry of the Old. In this process, stereotypes and exaggerations tended to prevail, and none proved more persistent than the legend of the Patagonian giant sighted by Antonio Pigafetta, the chronicler of Magellan's voyage:

One day . . . we saw a giant, who was on the shore of the sea, quite naked, and was dancing and leaping, and singing, and whilst singing he put the sand and dust on his head. . . . He was so tall that the tallest of us only came up to his waist. . . . He had a large face, painted red all around, and he had two hearts painted on his cheeks; he had but little hair on his head, and it was painted white. . . . The captain caused food and drink to be given to this giant, then they showed him some things, amongst others, a steel mirror. When the giant saw his likeness in it, he was greatly terrified, leaping backwards, and made three or four of our men fall down.[3]

The Patagonian giant was perhaps the most frequently depicted image of the New World, and the incident of the mirror became a symbol of the encounter between primitive innocence and the vanity of civilization.

The assimilation of the New World would have been enough work for the consciousness of any age, but Europe also faced its first systematic contacts with sub-Saharan and east Africa, India, and the Far East. In 1497 and 1498, Vasco da Gama sailed around the southern tip of Africa to Calicut on the west coast of India, a voyage as epochal as Columbus' and an even greater feat of seafaring. For a

AMACAO.

Macao, c. 1600. [Rare Books and Manuscripts Division, The New York Public Library; Astor, Lenox and Tilden Foundations]

century thereafter, the Portuguese anchored a seaborne empire in Goa and Macao, respectively 10,000 and 14,000 miles from Lisbon.

The principal objectives of the Portuguese were trade and missionary work. Goa had its own archbishop and proudly called itself the Rome of *Asia Christiana*—Christian Asia. Da Gama, lured by the legend of Prester John, had hoped to find Christian communities in India; he and his successors proved intolerant of the local Hindu sects, and their temples were ordered burnt in 1540. Elsewhere, however, the Portuguese traded at the sufferance of local rulers. At Macao the Portuguese colony of 10,000 was sealed off from the Chinese hinterland by a huge gate on which was written, "Dread our Greatness and Respect our Virtue." In Japan, which the Portuguese reached in 1543, traders were at first confined to an artificial island that could be cut off from the mainland at will.

Despite the intolerance of the Portuguese in religious matters, they were far more adaptive in responding to native cultures than the Spanish, the Dutch, or the English. They exhibited relatively little race prejudice and intermarried freely. It was the Portuguese, however, who pioneered the European slave trade, as a source not only of labor and commerce but also of fashion; by 1550 there

were 9,500 domestic slaves in Lisbon among a total population of 100,000.

The most remarkable European visitors to Asia, Africa, and the Americas were the Jesuits. Their goal was the conversion of heathens to Christianity, a task they supplemented with shrewd commercial dealings. Jesuit priests in the New World offered a haven from slavery, particularly in the communities they founded in Paraguay, but the price of freedom from physical bondage was the surrender of the Amerindians' cultural heritage. In Asia the Jesuits adopted a more flexible position, often winking at the blending of local traditions with Christian ritual. Their most spectacular success was in Japan, where they had won 150,000 converts before a backlash drove them from the country. Perhaps the most extraordinary of their number was Matteo Ricci (1552–1610), an Italian who made Christianity palatable by stressing its resemblance to Confucian ethics and omitting such potentially disturbing elements as the crucifixion, the virgin birth, and the equality of all persons. The papacy rejected this adulteration of doctrine, and the Jesuits, too, were ultimately expelled from China (see Chapter 12). Their presence was deeply significant, however, not only in laying the ground for future East-West relations but also in providing Europeans with their first detailed knowledge of Chinese civilization.

Not even the splendors of the Ming court could compare, however, with the impact of the Americas on the Western imagination. An Italian commentator noted in 1539 that the chief events of his age had been the invention of printing and the discovery of the New World. The Spanish chronicler Gomara, going even further, wrote that "the greatest event since the creation of the world (excluding the incarnation and death of Him who created it) is the discovery of the Indies."

1. B. Díaz de Castillo, *The True History of the Conquest of New Spain,* trans. A. P. Maudslay, ed. G. Garcia (London: Hakluyt Society, 1910), vol. 2, p. 70.
2. O. P. Dickason, *The Myth of the Savage and the Beginnings of French Colonialism in the Americas* (Edmonton: University of Alberta Press, 1984), p. 15.
3. A. Pigafetta, *Magellan's First Voyage Round the World,* trans. Lord Stanley of Alderney (London: Hakluyt Society, 1874), p. 49.

13

STATE-BUILDING AND REVOLUTION

Emboldened by the wealth of its empire, Spain made a bid in the late sixteenth century to establish domination in Western Europe. This was largely the outgrowth of the determination of Charles V and Philip II to rule their inherited territories and of the equally strong resolve of the English and French to prevent the expansion of Habsburg power. The Netherlands, Portugal, England, Italy, and France were all threatened by a militant Spanish imperialism imbued with the spirit of the Counter-Reformation. By the end of the century, Philip II had largely failed in his quest, although fighting continued in the Netherlands, and Portugal remained under Spanish rule until 1640. Two decades after Philip's death in 1598, the Thirty Years' War erupted. Most of Europe was involved in what proved to be one of the bloodiest wars in the continent's history. The wars, internal tensions and rebellions stemming from the increasing burdens of government centralization and taxation, and competing religious ideologies contributed to a series of crises in the mid-1600s that threw almost every major European state into turmoil.

PHILIP II AND THE QUEST FOR SPANISH HEGEMONY

Spain's bid for supremacy in the late 1500s was a natural outgrowth of earlier Habsburg policy, the development of political absolutism, the zeal of the Counter-

Reformation, and the wealth and power created by its colonial empire. It was also made possible by the division of the unwieldly Habsburg domain between two crowns. When Charles V abdicated in 1556, his brother, Ferdinand I (1556–1564), received the imperial crown and the Austrian Habsburg territories. The Spanish throne, together with the Netherlands, Milan, Naples, and Spanish America, went to Philip II (1556–1598), whose wife ruled England in her own right as Mary I (1553–1558).

Spanish power in Philip's reign grew in part at the expense of France. Charles V's troubles with the Lutherans and the Turks had prevented him from attaining a permanent victory over his archenemy, Francis I of France (1515–1547). For most of their reigns the two monarchs quarreled, particularly over northern Italy. Both rulers had died by the time the Treaty of Cateau-Cambrésis, which confirmed Spanish possession of Milan and Naples, ended 65 years of fighting in northern Italy in 1559. Philip II's prospects for the extension of Spanish Habsburg hegemony were good, not least because France was ruled by a succession of weak kings in the late 1500s and was immersed in civil war. Spain was without peer in Europe.

Although the work of centralizing had been underway in the major western European states since the late 1400s, the Spain that Philip inherited was still far from unified. Unlike England, where a single Parliament served as a unifying bond, Spain had a separate assembly called a Cortes for Castile, for each of the three regions of Aragon, and for Navarre. France and the

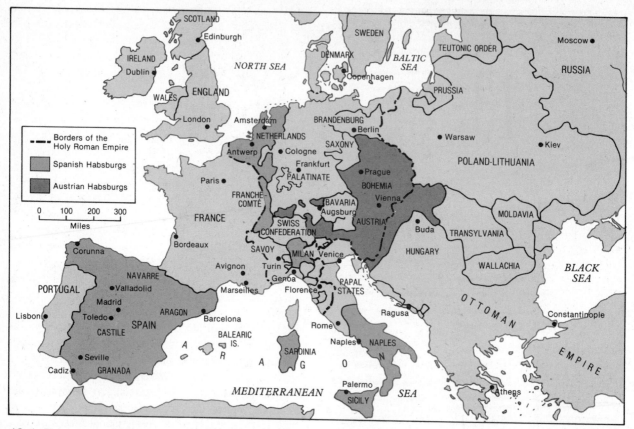

13.1 Europe, c. 1560

Netherlands similarly had regional assemblies, but in both cases an Estates General, albeit weak, represented the country as a whole. Philip made no attempt to create such a body in Spain but instead governed each of the three states—Aragon, Castile, and Navarre—independently with the help of local agents whom he appointed.

The distinctive feature of Spanish government was the system of higher councils Philip used to supervise his empire. He had a major council for each region of the empire: Castile, Aragon, the Netherlands, Italy (Milan and Naples), and Spanish America. Viceroys carried out the instructions of these councils. Specialized councils handled such matters as state affairs, finance, war, and the Inquisition. Distrustful of his officials and jealous of his power, he played his officers against each other and set up a system of checks and balances that made Spanish administration inefficient.

Although Philip apparently hoped to wield absolute power based on the idea that his subjects owed him unquestioning obedience as a right and a Christian duty, in practice the top-heavy administrative system and limited revenues circumscribed his authority. The nobles paid only sales taxes, and though Philip taxed merchants and professionals, there were fewer of them proportionately in Spain than in other western European countries. An unreasonable tax burden therefore fell on those least able to pay, the peasants. The result was insufficient revenue, forcing Philip to declare bankruptcy three times during his reign. Because the government protected the ships that transported American bullion to Spain, it received a royalty of 20 percent, but smuggling decreased the potential value of this revenue, and the king mortgaged much of what he did receive to finance military campaigns. Like the English monarchs in the early 1600s, he sold offices and titles and received income from crown lands and the sale of papal dispensations. None of this, however, compensated for the loss of funds that would have been obtained by properly taxing the nobility.

A pious, brooding, bookish man, Philip II of Spain was described by an English admirer as "the most potent monarch of Christendom," [National Portrait Gallery, London]

THE SPANISH CITADEL: MADRID AND THE ESCORIAL

The development of royal authority and the bureaucracy to administer it made a permanent capital necessary. Unlike Charles V, who frequently moved around his empire, Philip favored a sedentary life, though when he established the capital at Madrid in 1561 he had no apparent intention of making it permanent. Located on a plateau at an altitude of more than 2,000 feet, Madrid had as its major advantages its healthy climate and its centrality. The city had a population of only 25,000 in 1561, but by the early 1600s it had quadrupled in size. Madrid's rise adversely affected Valladolid and Toledo; the latter's population of more than 50,000 decreased by two-thirds during Philip's reign. By the mid-1600s, Madrid was the only Spanish city whose population was substantially larger than it had been in the 1500s.

Madrid's growth was not the result of new industry but of bureaucratic expansion and the capital's attraction to younger sons of the nobility, declining hidalgos, and impoverished workers in search of a living. In a futile attempt to curb the growth of the city, the crown ordered the nobles to return to their estates in 1611, hoping the hangers-on would follow. Gypsies were also attracted to the city despite repeated attempts to expel them. Urban growth in Madrid was relatively easy because of ample space. The city was enclosed only with a mud wall to denote its boundaries, and as late as the nineteenth century there was still open space inside the walls. The city's importance as a financial center grew in the 1600s. Although Madrid had neither a university nor a bishop, it became a leading cultural center in the early seventeenth century.

The site selected for Philip's massive new palace, the Escorial, was in the hills some 30 miles northwest of Madrid. The building had been planned because of a provision in Charles V's will that his son construct a "dynastic pantheon" to house the bodies of Spanish sovereigns. In the octagonal Pantheon of the Kings the gray marble coffins now rest four high along the walls. Philip, a deeply religious man, took a direct interest in the design, at one point admonishing one of the architects to remember the basic ideals of "simplicity of form, severity in the whole, nobility without arrogance, majesty without ostentation." The Escorial took two decades to build (1563–1584). Laid out in the shape of a gridiron, which probably reflected the influence of Italian Renaissance palace architecture, the gray stone building housed a monastery, a mausoleum where Charles V was interred, a domed church inspired by Michelangelo's plan for St. Peter's in Rome, a library, and the royal palace and apartments. From a window in the apartments, Philip could look out on the high altar in the chapel.

The Culture of the Spanish Counter-Reformation

The spirit of religious austerity revealed in the Escorial reflected the severer side of the Catholic Reformation.

Philip II's palace, the Escorial, as it appeared in the seventeenth century. According to a popular legend, the ground plan symbolized the gridiron on which St. Lawrence, whom Philip admired, was martyred. Philip tried to locate the martyr's head to keep as a relic at the palace. [Cliché des Musées Nationaux, Paris]

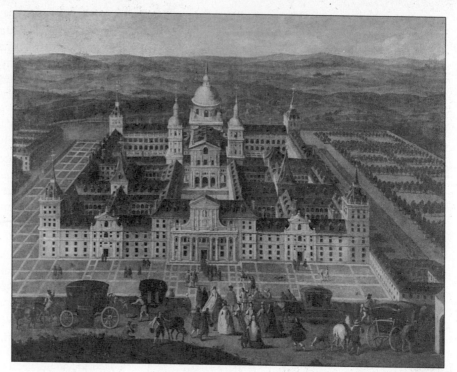

The Spanish Inquisition, founded in 1478, persecuted Protestants and other suspected heretics. The extent of its power was demonstrated when it jailed the archbishop of Toledo and primate of Spain (the highest-ranking ecclesiastical official) for 17 years on falsified charges of heresy. Obsessed with the need to keep the Spanish church pure, Philip supported the Inquisition, which averaged 1,000 cases a year during his reign. The Inquisition also supervised the *Conversos* (converted Jews) who remained in Spain.

When Philip struck at the *Moriscos*—the Christianized Moors of Granada—by banning their language, customs, and distinctive dress, he incited a rebellion. Later efforts to assimilate the Moriscos were largely unsuccessful, and in the early 1600s they were deported by the tens of thousands. Altogether, the number of Jews and Moors expelled from Spain between 1492, when they were given the choice of becoming Christians or going into exile, and 1609 probably exceeded half a million. Philip also exiled the Jews from northern Italy much as his father had expelled them from Naples in 1544. Some 300,000 Conversos survived the threat of the Spanish Inquisition and remained active in professional and commercial activities, though most lived in their own districts.

Despite the brutal repression that characterized Span-ish religious policy and was an important facet of absolutism, there was a positive side to Spanish piety in this period. This is beautifully manifested in the work of the mystics Teresa of Avila (1515–1582) and John of the Cross (1542–1591), both of whom were of Converso ancestry. Teresa, the daughter of a hidalgo, was a nun. Much of her work was devoted to the Carmelite Reform, an order dedicated to recapturing the original spirit of Carmelite austerity. She shared her religious experience in an autobiography, and in writings such as *The Way of Perfection* she described the progress of the Christian soul toward its goal of unity with the divine. John of the Cross, a Carmelite who assisted Teresa, expressed his mystical experiences in poetry and in a meticulous analysis of mysticism. Together they inspired Spaniards to maintain their devotion to the Catholic church.

Philip's favorite painter was Titian, the late Renaissance Venetian master, who was famous for his sumptuous colors. For more than a quarter of a century, Titian supplied Charles V and Philip with paintings. A number of these depicted mythological themes, often including sensuous female nudes. Like most of his contemporaries, Titian saw no contradiction between the veneration of the Virgin Mary and the appreciation of physical beauty in the Venus figures.

Directly as well as through Tintoretto (1518–1594),

his brilliant successor at Venice, Titian influenced the painter whose work best captures the spirit of the Spanish Counter-Reformation, Domenico Theotokopoulos (1541–1614), known as El Greco ("the Greek"). Born in Crete, El Greco studied in Venice before moving to Spain in the 1570s. Most of his paintings convey the tension between the spiritual and material realms through spiral composition—swirling motion that drives the eye upward—and elongated figures. By accentuating color rather than form, he heightened the spiritual sense and created an art that was more emotional than intellectual or naturalistic. The canvases of El Greco reflect the spiritual ecstasy expressed in the writings of Teresa and John of the Cross.

Although religion dominated much of the culture of Counter-Reformation Spain, other themes were popular as well, especially in literature and drama. The great masterpiece of Spanish literature, *Don Quixote,* was the work of Miguel de Cervantes (1547–1616). A satire of chivalric romances, the book entertained readers by humorously juxtaposing the idealist Don Quixote with the realist Sancho Panza. Despite Sancho's warnings, Don Quixote pursued his "righteous warfare" to rid the world of "accursed" giants, which in fact were windmills and sheep.

The prolific Lope de Vega (1562–1635) wrote 1,500 plays by his own count. His works fall into two categories: heroic plays dealing with Spanish history and legend and comedies of manners and intrigue. Several of his plays break down the stereotyped image of the secluded Spanish lady. Some of Lope's women reject love and marriage, pursue careers, and even become outlaws. One of his most important themes deals with the king as the fount of justice and protector of the poor. Reflecting the spirit of his age, his plays demonstrate respect for the crown and the church.

Spain and the Mediterranean

Two spheres of military activity occupied Philip. He focused on the Muslims in the Mediterranean during the first part of his reign and later on the Protestants in the North Atlantic. With the Ottoman Turks already in control of three-quarters of the Mediterranean coastline, their seizure of Cyprus from Venice in 1571 alarmed Europe. Spain, Venice, and the papacy responded by forming the Holy League to attack the Turks. The league's fleet engaged the Turks near Lepanto in Greece, winning a decisive victory—the first major one in centuries over a Muslim fleet. The significance of Lepanto lay primarily in its impact on European morale and its check on Islamic expansion. Though the Turks refused to be driven from the western Mediterranean, henceforth they concentrated on North Africa.

Philip's second major foreign policy triumph came in 1580 when he annexed Portugal and its empire. The death of the Portuguese king without a direct heir gave Philip, the son of a Portuguese princess, his opportunity. After bribes and promises had won the support of the nobility and higher clergy for his own succession, the Spanish army completed the conquest. The Spanish failed to exploit their victory by coordinating the economic policies of the two countries and their empires. Spain's failure to unify the Iberian peninsula by anything more than a common crown made it possible for Portugal to recover its independence in the next century. The annexation gave Philip additional ships and Atlantic ports, which he sorely needed for his campaigns in the Netherlands and France and for the armadas that he sent against the English.

Rebellion in the Netherlands

The revolt of the Netherlands was the first significant setback to Philip II's dream of Habsburg hegemony in western Europe and the Americas. The Low Countries were the wealthiest region in Europe and the center of the developing global economy, and its people were accustomed to considerable local autonomy and religious diversity. The roots of the rebellion against Spanish authority were bound up in Philip's attempt to impose a more centralized and absolute government. The first crucial step occurred when he reorganized the Catholic church in the Netherlands and ordered that the decrees of the Council of Trent be enforced. Leading members of the council of state, which helped Philip's regent, Margaret of Parma, govern the Netherlands, protested in vain.

Violence erupted in 1566 when Calvinists ransacked Catholic churches. Unable to keep order, Margaret was replaced by the duke of Alva, who professed a willingness to destroy the country rather than see it fall into the hands of heretics. Backed by an army of 10,000, he attempted to enforce absolute rule through a tribunal called the Council of Troubles. Because it executed thousands of heretics, confiscated their property, and imposed heavy new taxes, Netherlanders called it the "Council of Blood." Thousands fled.

The heavy-handed Spanish tactics were enormously expensive. Alva and his successors mobilized more than 65,000 men for their campaigns, but insufficient funds meant chronically unpaid troops who were prone to rebel against their own officers. Instead of cowing the Nether-landers, Alva's cruelty prompted them to rally around William the Silent, prince of Orange (1533–1584). As *stadholder* (governor) of the northern provinces of Holland, Utrecht, and Zeeland, where Calvinism was strong, he had a natural base of support. He also had the allegiance of a group of pirate-patriots who preyed on Spanish shipping and captured Brill and other ports, providing a haven for Calvinists.

The high point of rebel fortunes came in 1576 after unpaid Spanish troops sacked Antwerp. The "Spanish Fury" left more than 7,000 dead and persuaded the largely Catholic provinces in the south to ally with the primarily Protestant areas of the north. But the Spanish refused to quit, and by 1579, Philip's new commander, the duke of Parma (Margaret's son), had regained a large degree of control by combining military victories in the south with an appeal to Catholic Netherlanders to stand firm with Spain. The ten southern provinces made their peace with Philip, but under William's leadership the seven northern provinces declared their independence in 1581.

The Dutch cause was jeopardized when a Catholic partisan assassinated William in 1584 with the pope's blessing. Unwilling to see the Protestant cause in the Netherlands crushed, the English and French provided military assistance. Whatever chance Philip had of destroying the Dutch rebels was lost when he became directly embroiled in war against England. By 1593 the Spaniards had been driven out of the northern provinces, though fighting continued until 1609. War resumed in 1621, and not until 1648 did the Spanish formally recognize the independence of the Dutch Republic.

The English Challenge

Relations with Spain had been deteriorating well before Elizabeth I's decision to send an army to the Netherlands. On the queen's part the reasons for the hostility were less religious than political and economic. The English wanted to trade with Spain's American colonies, a point made by John Hawkins' three voyages in the 1560s. Spanish rule in the Netherlands, a major market for English cloth, was also a source of friction. Although Elizabeth was reluctant to support rebels and was not committed to Dutch independence, she was unwilling to accept either a massive Spanish military presence in the Netherlands or Dutch reliance on the French, which could result in French domination of the entire Channel coast.

Relations between Elizabeth and Philip were further complicated by the problem of Mary Stuart, queen of Scotland (1542–1567) and a member of the powerful French Catholic family of Guise. As the great-granddaughter of the first Tudor king, Henry VII, Mary claimed the English throne, insisting that Elizabeth, as Anne Boleyn's daughter, was illegitimate. Mary, however, had fallen on hard times in Scotland because of a scandalous marriage. Irate Protestants forced her to abdicate in 1567. After her escape to England a year later, she remained under arrest for 19 years in remote castles. Although Elizabeth tried to negotiate Mary's return to the Scottish throne, Mary supported plots for Elizabeth's overthrow. Following a trial, Elizabeth reluctantly authorized Mary's execution in February 1587. Philip had determined to invade England well before Mary's death, but her execution gave him an excuse to claim the English throne as his own.

Philip's plan called for a fleet to control the English Channel while Parma's veterans invaded England from the Netherlands. Preparation of the armada was delayed by Sir Francis Drake's daring attack on Cadiz in 1587. Shortly thereafter, Spain's experienced admiral, the marquess of Santa Cruz, died, leaving the inexperienced duke of Medina Sidonia in command. When the two fleets met in July 1588, they were roughly equal in size, though the English vessels had greater maneuverability and superior long-range guns. The English scattered the Spanish fleet by launching burning ships against it. The Spaniards fled north through the Channel, suffering major losses when they rounded northern Scotland and were struck by Atlantic gales. In the ensuing years, two more armadas were readied to attack England, but storms prevented either from reaching its target. Until peace was officially concluded in 1604, both sides concentrated on helping their allies in the French civil war.

The French Civil War

The struggle in France had begun in 1562 when soldiers of the duke of Guise slaughtered a congregation of Huguenots, or Reformed Protestants. The Guise family—patrons of a militant Catholicism—were political rivals of the Bourbon and Montmorency-Chatillon families, both of whom supported the Huguenots. Because the crown of France was in the hands of a minor, Charles IX (1560–1574), his mother, Catherine de' Medici, exercised authority. To preserve her power, she played a shrewd game of shifting alliances, working with first one and then the other of the factions. Although this helped to prevent either side from dominating the other, it also kept France in a state of political and religious instability. The "wars of religion" in France were at root a struggle for political dominance in which religion, itself a potent and divisive factor, was used to justify the fighting and to attract adherents.

The worst atrocity of the war—the St. Bartholomew's Day massacre in August 1572—grew out of Catherine's fear that the Huguenots were becoming too powerful, in part because of the marriage of the king's sister, Marguerite of Valois, to a prominent Huguenot, Henry of Navarre. On August 24, leading Huguenots were assassinated with Catherine's blessing. Spurred on by this example, militant Catholics slaughtered Protestants, butchering at least 3,000 in Paris and perhaps 20,000 in all of France. As the Huguenots plotted revenge, Henry of Guise in 1576 organized the Catholic League, which soon received financial support from Philip II. By the mid-1580s the league controlled Paris, forcing King Henry III (1574–1589) to adopt desperate means to save his crumbling authority: the assassination of Henry of Guise and his brother, a cardinal in the Catholic church. Although the king allied with Henry of Navarre in an effort to crush the Catholic League, he was assassinated in August 1589.

With Henry of Navarre now claiming the throne as Henry IV (1589–1610), the civil war entered its final stage. Unprepared to see France governed by Protestants, Philip II ordered his army to invade France. Elizabeth I, determined to prevent France from falling under Spanish hegemony, sent her troops to Henry's aid. To achieve peace, Henry converted to Catholicism in 1593, but five years later he provided some solace to his Huguenot allies by issuing the Edict of Nantes, giving Protestants liberty of conscience, full civil and political rights, and control of 100 fortified towns. Catholicism was recognized as the official religion of France, however, and Protestant worship was prohibited in the Paris area.

From Philip's standpoint the 1590s was a decade of military disaster. Spain had no power in France, the Dutch Netherlands were virtually irretrievable, and the English had checked Spain on the seas. By the time of Philip's death in 1598 the Spanish quest for hegemony had been blunted.

The Age of the Queens

The second half of the sixteenth century is notable as an age of unusual political prominence for women in west-

ern Europe. Mary I (1553–1558) and Elizabeth I (1558–1603) in England and Mary Stuart in Scotland (whose effective rule was from 1561 to 1567) governed as queens, while other women exercised power as regents: Mary of Guise in Scotland (1554–1560), Margaret of Parma in the Netherlands (1559–1567), and Catherine de' Medici in France beginning in 1560. Women had governed before, of course, sometimes very successfully, as in the case of Queen Isabella of Castile (1474–1504), cofounder of a unified Spain. Although some Renaissance writers had recognized women's ability to govern, men were still reluctant to accept their authority. The classic statement of this view was a treatise by John Knox titled *The First Blast of the Trumpet Against the Monstrous Regiment of Women* (1558), which argued that female rule was contrary to divine and natural law, though God occasionally made an exception. The queens had their defenders, but even supporters of women's right to rule were unwilling to admit women to governing bodies or deliberative assemblies. No woman sat in the English or Scottish royal councils or Parliaments during the reign of these queens; government remained an essentially male preserve throughout Europe.

Elizabeth I exerted an enormous impact on England, not only by thwarting Spanish ambitions and supporting Protestanism but also by creating an atmosphere conducive to brilliant cultural achievements. The glorious image of her rule, which she carefully cultivated, is reflected in the literary masterpieces of William Shakespeare (1564–1616) and Edmund Spenser (c. 1552–1599), whose allegorical poem *The Faerie Queene* exalted "the most excellent and glorious person of our sovereign the queen, and her kingdom in Fairy Land." In no small measure, England's achievements were attributable to its queen. During the early 1600s the image of Elizabeth—more exalted in death than in life—proved to be more than her successors, James I and Charles I, could emulate.

EUROPE IN CRISIS

As Spanish ascendancy waned, Europe became preoccupied with the Thirty Years' War and the general crisis of authority that followed it in the mid-1600s. The two problems were directly related, for the unparalleled destruction inflicted in the Thirty Years' War, much of it by undisciplined troops, underscored the need to bring armies and warfare under strict control. Ultimately, monarchs and nobles found it advantageous to work together to determine policy and implement discipline. By 1660 there was also a consensus that even religious convictions had to be subordinated to the maintenance of order. The period 1600–1660 was thus a major watershed in European history.

The Thirty Years' War   1618-1648

The Peace of Augsburg (1555) that had ended the first round of religious warfare in the German states had given no rights to Calvinists, whose growing strength alarmed the Lutherans. Considerable tension existed too between Protestants and Catholics because of changes in religious allegiance. When the Catholic rulers of ecclesiastical principalities became Protestant, Catholics demanded that they surrender both their religious office and their lands, but Lutherans refused. After the Protestants organized the Evangelical Union in 1609 and their opponents responded with a Catholic League, Germany was divided into two armed camps.

The event that sparked the fighting occurred when the Habsburg Ferdinand of Styria, king of Bohemia, curtailed religious toleration for Protestants and Hussites. In 1618, Bohemian nobles protested, and a year later the rebels deposed Ferdinand as their king and gave the crown to a Calvinist prince, Frederick V of the Palatinate, son-in-law of James I of England. Had the rebels succeeded in placing a Protestant on the Bohemian throne, Protestants would have had a majority of the seven votes needed to elect future emperors. Ferdinand, a staunch Catholic who had been educated by the Jesuits, became emperor in August 1619 and had little choice but to reassert his control over Bohemia.

At first the war went well for Ferdinand, whose troops defeated Frederick in 1620. After the Danes entered the war in 1625, Ferdinand's general, Albrecht von Wallenstein, invaded Denmark, leaving destruction in his wake. With Ferdinand on the verge of establishing total control over his empire, the Swedish king, Gustavus Adolphus, invaded Germany. He was supported militarily by Brandenburg and Saxony and financially by the Dutch and the French, both of whom were threatened by Habsburg expansion. The fighting was carried into Catholic regions, especially Bavaria, whose residents were brutalized. In November 1632 the Swedish king was killed, but neither side was strong enough to defeat its enemies in the ensuing years.

The final and most destructive period of the war (1635–1648) reverted to a dynastic struggle that pitted the Habsburg powers, Austria and Spain, against the French and the Swedes. The real victims were the German people. As peasants fled before the marauding armies, the destruction of crops triggered famine. The loss of population was catastrophic: 40 percent in rural areas, 33 percent in the cities. The overall population of the empire decreased by as much as 8 million during the war.

Most of the fighting ended in 1648 with the Peace of Westphalia, which recognized the sovereignty of each German state; altogether there were now some 300 entities with sovereign rights and nearly 1,500 minor lordships. Each prince, whether Catholic, Lutheran, or Calvinist, could determine the religious beliefs of his subjects. The treaty also recognized the independence of the Swiss Confederacy and the Dutch Republic, but it did not end hostilities between France and Spain, which lasted until the Treaty of the Pyrenees in 1659. The bid of the Austrian Habsburgs to dominate central Europe perished in the Thirty Years' War. Not until 1871 would the Germans achieve political unity. The war also had disruptive effects on the domestic politics of the major European states, thereby contributing to the midcentury crises.

Rebuilding France: Foundations of Bourbon Rule

France's ability to act decisively in the Thirty Years' War and to impose peace terms on Spain in 1659 was made possible by the rebuilding of its institutions in the aftermath of the Huguenot wars. The first Bourbon monarchs pursued a course of absolutism in politics and mercantilism in economics. In the Bourbon view, stability mandated a centralized state capable of maintaining order at home and fielding large armies. Centralization could be accomplished only at the expense of local and special interests, which were sometimes strained severely by the burden of financing a war. The attempt to impose royal absolutism coincided with the costly struggle to prevent the establishment of Spanish or Austrian hegemony. By the 1640s, grinding taxation, aristocratic discontent, and resistance to centralized control had built to the crisis point and erupted in a new civil war, the Fronde.

Although no monarch came close to achieving total power in this period, interest in the concept of absolute rule grew, particularly in its national, monarchical form. The political theorist Jean Bodin (c. 1529–1596) had

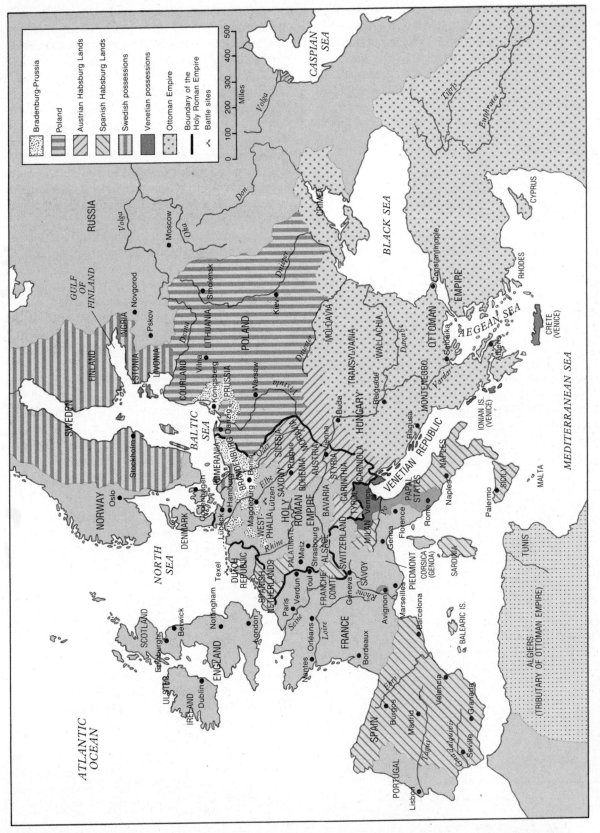

13.2 Europe in 1648

Legend:
- Bradenburg-Prussia
- Poland
- Austrian Habsburg Lands
- Spanish Habsburg Lands
- Swedish possessions
- Venetian possessions
- Ottoman Empire
- Boundary of the Holy Roman Empire
- Battle sites

Miles 0 100 200 300 400 500

ATLANTIC OCEAN

NORWAY
Oslo

SWEDEN
Stockholm

FINLAND

GULF OF FINLAND

RUSSIA
Moscow
Novgorod
Pskov
Smolensk

INGRIA
ESTONIA
LIVONIA
COURLAND
LITHUANIA
Vilna
Kiev

Volga
Oka
Don
Dvina
Dnieper
Dniester

POLAND
Warsaw

PRUSSIA
Königsberg
Danzig

BALTIC SEA

DENMARK
Copenhagen
Rügen
Lübeck
Hamburg

NORTH SEA

SCOTLAND
Edinburgh
Berwick

ENGLAND
London
Nottingham

IRELAND
ULSTER
Dublin

Texel
DUTCH REPUBLIC
SPANISH NETHERLANDS

BRANDENBURG
POMERANIA
Berlin
Magdeburg
Elbe
Oder
WEST-PHALIA
Lützen
Rhine

HOLY ROMAN EMPIRE
SAXONY
SILESIA
BOHEMIA
Prague
MORAVIA
AUSTRIA
Vienna
STYRIA
BAVARIA
CARINTHIA
CARNIOLA
TYROL
MILAN
Venice

PALATINATE
Metz
Strasbourg
ALSACE
Verdun
Toul
FRANCHE COMTÉ
SWITZERLAND
Geneva
SAVOY
Avignon
Marseilles

FRANCE
Paris
Seine
Orleans
Loire
Nantes
Bordeaux
Rhône

SPAIN
Burgos
Madrid
Tagus
Seville
Granada
Guadalquivir
Valencia
Ebro
Barcelona

PORTUGAL
Lisbon

CORSICA (GENOA)
SARDINIA
BALEARIC IS.

PIEDMONT
Genoa
Florence
PAPAL STATES
Rome
Naples
NAPLES
Palermo
SICILY
MALTA

MEDITERRANEAN SEA

MOLDAVIA
TRANSYLVANIA
WALLACHIA
HUNGARY
Buda
Belgrade
MONTENEGRO
Ragusa
VENETIAN REPUBLIC

CRIMEA

BLACK SEA

OTTOMAN EMPIRE
Constantinople
Salonika
Athens
AEGEAN SEA
RHODES
CRETE (VENICE)
CYPRUS

IONIAN IS. (VENICE)

Danube
Vardar

CASPIAN SEA
Tigris
Euphrates

TUNIS
ALGIERS (TRIBUTARY OF OTTOMAN EMPIRE)

stressed the importance of a sovereign power whose authority was beyond challenge, though he also insisted that monarchs were responsible to God for their actions. Building on this traditional notion, various seventeenth-century thinkers asserted that kings and queens derived their right to govern directly from God and were therefore above human law. The concept that sovereignty was divinely bestowed suited the needs of rulers intent on centralizing their control, for they were in a position to claim the unquestioning obedience of their subjects as both a right and a Christian duty.

Henry IV revived the goals of the Renaissance sovereigns Francis I and Henry II, who had aimed at centralizing royal authority and expanding French territory. Although he opted not to summon the Estates General after 1593, he secured the support of the more powerful aristocrats—the nobility of the sword—especially by strategic bribes. Offices were traditionally sold in France, but Henry took the practice one step further by allowing his principal bureaucrats, the nobility of the robe, to pay a voluntary annual fee called the *paulette* that made the offices hereditary. These men, most of them members of the bourgeoisie (the upper merchant and professional class), were thus closely linked to the government.

Henry faced daunting economic problems. He was nearly 300 million livres in debt, with annual revenues amounting to only half that amount. His finance minister, the duke of Sully, repudiated part of the debt, renegotiated a lower rate of interest on the balance, and sought new sources of revenue, such as the paulette. As a proponent of mercantile policies, Sully established monopolies on salt, gunpowder, and mining. France was already a food-exporting nation, and Sully strengthened agriculture by building more bridges, roads, and canals. To reduce the export of bullion, new laws restricted the use of gold and silver, and royal factories were constructed to produce luxury goods. By 1601 the budget was balanced.

When a fanatic assassinated Henry in 1610, the throne passed to his 9-year-old son, Louis XIII (1610–1643). The regency was in the hands of Louis' mother, Marie de' Medici. For ten years, France lacked an energetic government, but Marie maintained a semblance of peace by lavishing pensions and bribes on the nobles and allowing them a greater role in provincial affairs.

The appointment of Cardinal Richelieu (1585–1642) as the king's chief adviser in 1624 once more meant a strong hand at the controls of government. Nobles who defied royal edicts were imprisoned and some even executed, and their castles were destroyed. Responsibility for local administration was transferred from the nobles to *intendants,* commissioners appointed by the crown who held their posts at the king's pleasure. Their responsibilities included tax collection, the administration of justice, and local defense. To deal with rebellious Huguenots, Richelieu ended the political and military rights given to them in the Edict of Nantes, although they retained religious freedom. He enhanced French power by building effective Atlantic and Mediterranean fleets, but his policies were expensive and required deficit financing. Occupied with his centralizing schemes and the Thirty Years' War, Richelieu failed to undertake desperately needed tax reform.

The death of Richelieu in 1642 and Louis XIII a year later left the 5-year-old Louis XIV on the throne and power in the hands of Richelieu's protégé, Cardinal Jules Mazarin (1602–1661). Discontent was pronounced because of the effects of centralization on local authority and Mazarin's inability to pay interest on war loans. The situation was made worse by famine, especially in the late 1640s, when many peasants lost their holdings to bourgeois creditors.

Against this backdrop of economic dislocation and political unrest the Parlement of Paris, France's main law court and a stronghold of the nobility of the robe, called for reform, including the abolition of the office of intendant, a habeas corpus law, and the right to approve taxes. Mazarin arrested its leaders, inciting an uprising. Unwilling to sanction popular rebellion, the Parlement of Paris came to terms with Mazarin in the spring of 1649, but the revolt spread nevertheless. The end of the Thirty Years' War enabled prominent nobles of the sword to march their forces against Mazarin, and urban and agrarian uprisings erupted. Ultimately, the Fronde collapsed because the *frondeurs* were too fragmented in their goals. The prospect of a France divided into feudal principalities was unpalatable to the nobility of the robe, while neither they nor the nobility of the sword were interested in the plight of the peasants and the urban workers.

Spain: Disillusionment, War, and Revolt

As in France, Spain during the reigns of Philip III (1598–1621) and Philip IV (1621–1665) experienced mounting reaction against centralization, economic hardship, and the impact of foreign war, all of which finally triggered open rebellion. The economic problems stemmed from several factors. Seventeenth-century Spain experienced a severe decline in population: that of Castile and Aragon dropped from 10 million to 6 million, a percentage decrease greater than that in any other European country. The reasons for the fall include plague, crop failures, mismanaged financial resources, and a decline in the wealth coming from Spain's overseas empire, due mostly to the decimation of the Amerindian population and the loss of its forced labor. The Spaniards failed to compensate for this drop in income by developing new industries. When Spain renewed the war against the Dutch in 1621 and later became embroiled in the Thirty Years' War, the government squeezed funds from an already overburdened people. The price of elusive glory abroad was grinding poverty at home.

Philip IV's chief minister, the count of Olivares (1587–1645), attempted to increase revenues and rationalize the administration. He increased the church's tax burden and reduced the number of officeholders, but in Castile the Cortes blocked his attempt to introduce new direct taxes. Administratively, he wanted to impose uniform laws on the semiautonomous Spanish kingdoms and make each provide its fair share of taxes and troops. His reduction of regional autonomy and redistribution of some of Castile's burden to other provinces touched off revolts. The first rebellion erupted in the northern province of Catalonia in 1640, triggered by the billeting of soldiers sent north to repel a French invasion. Rebellious peasants, overtaxed clergy hostile to Castilian domination, and rioting urban mobs joined forces. Barcelona revolted, but the Catalans had no effective rebel leaders. They tried to establish an independent republic, but dependence on French funds forced them to acknowledge Louis XIII as king. Disillusioned with foreign rule, the insurgents lost heart, and the revolt collapsed in 1652.

Revolts against Spanish rule also occurred in Portugal, Naples, and Sicily. Resentment against Castilian rule and financial support for Spanish wars triggered a national war of liberation in Portugal in December 1640. The nobles restored the Portuguese monarchy, the Lisbon masses rose in support, and a French fleet provided naval protection. Funded by the profits of the Brazilian sugar fleet, the Portuguese continued defiantly until Spain recognized their independence in 1668. In contrast, the government suppressed the 1647 revolts in Sicily and Naples in a matter of months. The Sicilians wanted their local privileges restored and the new taxes abolished, but they were leaderless. The rebellion in Naples began with attacks on anything Spanish and quickly developed into a class war of peasants against landlords. When not even the French were willing to lend support, a Spanish fleet restored order.

The crises of the 1640s made it apparent that Spain could no longer afford the foreign policy of a great power. The Treaty of the Pyrenees in 1659, though it involved only modest territorial losses to France on the frontiers and in the Spanish Netherlands, was nevertheless humiliating. The nobles came to dominate the monarchy, particularly after the inept Charles II became king in 1665. Spanish institutions, however, were sufficiently strong to enable the country to survive Charles' reign and the subsequent accession of a Bourbon dynasty, and in the eighteenth century Spain once again became a major power.

The Dutch Republic and the House of Orange

Although the Dutch had to renew their war for independence between 1621 and 1648, they were unusual in their ability to keep the state solvent. Severe political tensions existed, but with rare exceptions they were resolved without recourse to violence. The principal source of friction was the role of the House of Orange in Dutch politics. Because each of the seven Dutch provinces normally chose the prince of Orange as its stadholder, he was not only the symbol of national unity but often the most powerful man in the country. The Dutch had an Estates General to which each province elected representatives. Delegates traditionally split, some supporting the House of Orange and a militant foreign policy, others favoring a greater degree of provincial autonomy and peaceful relations with foreign countries in order to improve trade. In the early 1600s, Jan van Oldenbarneveldt, founder of the Dutch East India Company, challenged Maurice of Nassau, from 1618 the prince of Orange, on the issue of resuming the war with Spain when the truce expired in 1621. Maurice used the army to purge Oldenbarneveldt's supporters from the town governments in the province of Holland, and in 1619 the state executed Oldenbarneveldt for treason.

The conflict between Holland and the House of Orange erupted again after William II became stadholder in 1647. When William died unexpectedly in 1650, the Hollanders and their allies took over the government, maintaining their supremacy until a French invasion in 1672 necessitated the return of a strong military leader from the House of Orange.

Although the restoration of the republic in 1650 was a quasi-revolutionary event, the Dutch avoided a civil war and enjoyed continued prosperity. When Antwerp declined in the late 1570s, Amsterdam established itself as the center of European commerce. By the mid-seventeenth century the Dutch operated more than half of the world's commercial vessels. In addition to trading and shipbuilding, the economy of Amsterdam was based on banking, insurance (including the first life insurance policies), printing, and manufacturing. Other towns became famous for particular products, such as Delft for ceramics and Schiedam for gin. The Haarlem area achieved fame by cultivating tulips, which were first imported from the Ottoman Empire. Jews, who benefited greatly from the normally tolerant religious atmosphere in the Netherlands, played a prominent role in the Dutch business community. The Dutch were economically the most progressive Europeans in the seventeenth century, and the people of Amsterdam enjoyed the highest per capita income in Europe. Although there were a substantial number of poor people, whose ranks were swollen by immigrants and refugees, the Dutch provided enough relief to stave off the misery that attended political crises in other European states in the mid-1600s.

Early Stuart England: From Consensus to Conflict

Alone among the European states, England experienced not only a severe crisis but a revolution in the 1640s and 1650s as well. Under Elizabeth I (1558–1603) and James I (1603–1625), who also governed Scotland as James VI (1567–1625), England attained religious stability and a reasonably effective working relationship between crown and Parliament. Elizabeth's Protestant settlement withstood the challenge of Catholics, nearly 200 of whom she executed for treason, and of a handful of radical Protestants who repudiated the state church. James, raised as a Calvinist, disappointed English Puritans who wanted further reforms in the established church, including a better-educated clergy, stricter sabbath observance, and an end to such "unscriptural" customs as the wedding ring. He did, however, agree to a Puritan request for a new translation of the Bible into English, the so-called King James version of 1611.

The work of centralization was carried forward, particularly through the appointment of lords lieutenant and their deputies in the counties. Because England had no standing army, local defense was in the hands of these men, but as long as the crown appointed local magnates, the system worked well. The use of conciliar courts, especially the Star Chamber and the Court of High Commission, which enforced the laws and doctrine of the Church of England, also enhanced central authority. Both courts functioned without juries and could compel accused individuals to incriminate themselves.

Although the war against Spain (1585–1604) was popular, its cost forced Elizabeth to adopt measures that reduced future income, such as the sale of various crown lands. Finances were increasingly a problem for James, especially with respect to foreign policy. Dreaming of the glory of the 1580s, his Parliaments were willing to support a naval war against Spain but had little desire to become embroiled directly on the Continent in the Thirty Years' War on behalf of his son-in-law, Frederick V. Nor did they understand the king's desire to establish an alliance with their traditional enemy, Spain, by means of a marriage involving Prince Charles and a Spanish princess. The proposed match was crucial to James' dream of a partnership between Catholic Spain and Protestant England that could serve as the vehicle to maintain peace in Europe.

James, conscious of his role as a divinely ordained monarch, heightened concern by actions that seemed to challenge traditional constitutional procedures. Chronically short of funds, he sought additional revenue by levying a special import duty without parliamentary approval. He also provoked controversy by dismissing one of his chief justices, Sir Edward Coke, for attempting to assert judicial independence. Yet when James died in 1625, he left a country whose tensions were still largely contained beneath the surface.

The consensus that Elizabeth had achieved was rapidly undermined by the policies of James' son, Charles I (1625–1649). Angered by his inability to conclude an agreement to marry a Spanish princess, he was determined to go to war against Spain, though a distrustful Parliament refused to give him sufficient funds. Charles blundered further by going to war against France while still fighting Spain. With his finances depleted, he tried to raise money by forced "loans," billeting his troops in private homes to compel payment. Critics in the House of Commons responded in 1628 with the Petition of Right, which demanded that no taxes be levied without parliamentary consent, no person be imprisoned without knowing the charge, no troops be billeted in private homes without the owners' consent, and martial law not be imposed in peacetime. The king accepted the document in principle in return for further taxes. In 1629 a bitter attack on newly appointed Arminian bishops who supported Charles led to Parliament's dismissal. The

Charles I, by his ineptitude, and Henrietta Maria, by her Catholicism, contributed to the outbreak of civil war in England. In the cultural atmosphere of the royal court the leading painter was Rubens' disciple Anthony Van Dyck (1599–1641), whose twin portrait of the king and queen was the basis for this engraving by G. Vertue. [Alinari/Art Resource, New York]

Arminian position that Puritans and others found so offensive rejected the Calvinist doctrine of predestination, insisted that Christ died for all people rather than for the elect alone, and affirmed the freedom of each person to accept or reject divine grace.

For 11 years, Charles ruled without a Parliament, raising revenue by unpopular expedients that stretched his legal powers. One of these was ship money, a tax traditionally levied on coastal areas for naval expenses but now extended to the entire kingdom. Religious grievances continued to mount, much of the hostility being directed at Charles' French Catholic queen, Henrietta Maria, and his Arminian archbishop of Canterbury, William Laud. Committed to the principle that a unified state required unity in religion, Laud vigorously persecuted his Puritan critics. When Charles and Laud attempted to force the English liturgy on the Presbyterian Scots, the latter rebelled, forcing Charles to summon Parliament.

The English Revolution

Some historians contend that the English revolution was only a civil war, while others perceive a full-scale revolution that altered the structure of government, religion, the economy, educational thought, and society. Lawrence Stone has gone back to the early sixteenth century to find such preconditions of revolution as the crown's failure to establish a standing army and a paid local bureaucracy; criticism by Puritans in the state church; the growing wealth and power of the gentry and the decline of many of the greater nobility; and a crisis of confidence in high government officials. Against this background, he argues, the crown precipitated a revolution by encouraging Laud's campaign against the Puritans, curtailing the political role of the gentry, and enforcing tighter economic controls. Military defeat at the hands of the Scots and financial bankruptcy triggered the outbreak of civil war.

Regicide - hanging of King

Analysts who hold to the more limited notion of a civil war place the origins much later, either in 1637 and 1638, when the Scots rebelled against the English liturgy, or even in early 1642, when the king and Parliament failed to agree on control of the militia. According to this interpretation, the civil war was largely an accident that neither side intended. Marxist historians concentrate on economic factors as the primary cause of the revolution, observing that Parliament drew most of its support from the economically advanced south and east of England, while the king's strength was greatest in the more backward regions of the west and north. Marxists have also tried to demonstrate that most of the aristocracy supported the king, whereas the "middling sort" of artisans, merchants, and yeoman farmers allied with Parliament. By any interpretation the revolutionary period was the gravest and most sustained political and military crisis in English history.

After the Scots invaded England in 1640, Charles had to call Parliament into session. It abolished the Star Chamber and the High Commission and outlawed ship money and other questionable forms of revenue that lacked parliamentary sanction. By circumscribing royal authority this legislation prevented the establishment of absolute government. Parliament also imprisoned and tried the king's principal advisers, the earl of Strafford and Archbishop Laud; both were eventually executed for high treason. Troops had to be raised to suppress a Catholic rebellion that erupted in Ireland in 1641, but neither side trusted the other with command. The distrust finally persuaded both sides to take up arms, and the civil war began in August 1642.

The Cavaliers supported Charles, while the Roundheads (so called for their short hairstyles) fought for Parliament. The latter established military supremacy through an alliance with the Scots, more effective military organization, and greater wealth made possible by the support of London and the commercial southeast. Charles finally surrendered in 1646. The price of the Scottish alliance was a promise to make the Church of England Presbyterian, thereby reducing royal control and ending government by bishops. This was unacceptable to the army, which favored religious toleration for Protestants. In 1648, civil war broke out again, this time with the Scots on Charles' side. Led by Oliver Cromwell (1599–1658), the parliamentarian army crushed its enemies. After Parliament was purged of moderates, the remnant—derisively called the Rump Parliament by its critics—appointed a special tribunal to try the king on charges of treason. Found guilty, he was beheaded in January 1649.

The Rump made England a republic—the Commonwealth—and allowed a good deal of religious toleration. It used the army to crush the rebellion in Ireland and then to suppress the Scots when they rallied on behalf of Charles I's son. It also dispatched the navy to fight an inconclusive trade war against Europe's other major republic, the Dutch Netherlands, in 1652. When Cromwell's patience with the Rump finally ran out in 1653, he forcibly dismissed it.

Army officers drew up a constitution called the Instrument of Government that made Cromwell Lord Protector, enabling him to govern in conjunction with Parliament and a council of state. Cromwell fared no better with his Parliaments than had the early Stuart kings. Dissension raged over the structure of the government, religious toleration, the enormous cost of a standing army, and the appointment of major generals to maintain order throughout the country. With the political and economic crisis unresolved at Cromwell's death in 1658, his son Richard proved unable to govern. In 1660 the propertied classes, fed up with military rule, accepted the return of monarchy in order to achieve stability and security, and Charles II returned from exile.

Although the monarchy was restored, its position was seriously altered. Absolutism such as existed in France had been rendered impossible. The despotic royal courts of the Star Chamber and the High Commission did not return, and the principle of parliamentary approval for taxes was firmly established. Religious toleration ended in the early 1660s, but the dissenters were now strong enough to survive the sporadic persecution that ensued. The Jews, who had been welcomed to England in the 1650s in the expectation that their return signaled the coming of a millennial age and because of their expertise and contacts in international trade, were not expelled. Moreover, the shakeup in the universities left proponents of the new science firmly established and set the stage for the foundation of the Royal Society in 1660. New directions in political thought had also been initiated by the work of the Levellers, who advocated a moderate form of democracy; by Thomas Hobbes, who developed a theory of secular absolutism; and by Gerrard Winstanley (1609–c. 1676), who advocated a commonwealth based on the abolition of property. Most important, the revolution established the principle in England that there must be a government of laws, not of men.

MARGARET FELL: A WOMAN IN THE ENGLISH REVOLUTION

The collapse of censorship, of the authority of bishops, and ultimately of the monarchy in revolutionary England enabled women who belonged to such Protestant sects as the Congregationalists, Baptists, and Quakers to preach and publish their views in a manner that had hitherto been impossible. Of these groups, however, only the Quakers, with their rejection of a professional ministry and the sacraments, were relatively comfortable with active female participation in ministerial activities. Quaker women crisscrossed England carrying their message of the Inner Light, and the more daring extended their work as far afield as Ireland, Portugal, Malta, the West Indies, and the American colonies, including Massachusetts, which expelled or hanged them. Two Quaker women even went to Adrianople in a futile attempt to convert the Turkish sultan.

The most influential woman as well as one of the key figures in the Society of Friends, as the Quakers called themselves, was Margaret Fell (1614–1702), daughter of a Lancashire gentleman. The Quaker founder George Fox (1624–1691) persuaded her to adopt his views in 1652, after which she held Quaker meetings in her home. The mother of eight children, she was at first unable to become a traveling minister, but she provided the Friends with an even more important contribution by her extensive correspondence with Quakers of both sexes who sought her advice on religious questions. Enormously influential in shaping the Quaker movement and its ideals, she frequently argued the Friends' case in assertive letters to non-Quaker clergymen and judges.

Margaret Fell's wide-ranging activities included the authorship of numerous pamphlets, several of which were translated into Dutch, Hebrew, and Latin. She pleaded with Cromwell and Charles II for religious toleration, petitioned the Rump Parliament with 7,000 other women for an end to mandatory tithing, and worked for the release of imprisoned Quakers. She was jailed several times, once for four years, because of her religious beliefs. Among her concerns was the conversion of the Jews to Christianity, a cause for which she wrote five pamphlets. Her best-known work, *Women's Speaking Justified,* which argued for the right of women to preach and prophesy, helped to lay the foundation for the establishment of Quaker women's meetings.

Soon after her first husband died in 1658, Fell began traveling throughout England of behalf of the Society. In 1669 she married George Fox, partly to end unfounded rumors of an illicit relationship between them but also to symbolize the union of male and female Quakers. Until her death in 1702 she remained active in the Society's work, particularly its women's meetings. The example that she and other sectarian women set made it difficult to force women back into their traditional places in the home, the shop, and the field. Nevertheless, after 1660, with the revolutionary crisis in England essentially concluded, only the Quakers allowed women to preach. In the 1680s and 1690s a flurry of protofeminist works appeared in England by writers such as Mary Astell, but so successful was the restoration of traditional male authority in the 1660s that the new writers were content to plead only for their spiritual equality with men. Viewed in this context, the work and careers of Margaret Fell and her colleagues were an extraordinary product of the midcentury crisis.

CENTRAL AND EASTERN EUROPE

Although the institutions of the Holy Roman Empire survived the Thirty Years' War and the Peace of Westphalia, the more powerful German princes went their own way, leaving the emperors to govern the small German states and their own patrimony in Austria, Bohemia, and Hungary. Increasingly, they ruled through ancestral institutions, especially the Austrian Chancellery—where Habsburg policy was formulated—rather than imperial institutions. The result was the gradual establishment of a Danubian state governed from Vienna and mostly Catholic in religion. Because the emperors shared power with the landed aristocracy, the peasant rebellions of the 1640s and 1650s were doomed, and the empire avoided a serious crisis.

The gradual enserfment of the peasants sparked much of the unrest in central and eastern Europe. The process of enserfing, carried out by the landed aristocracy with the acquiescence of the monarchs, was intended both to increase agricultural production, particularly for the market in western Europe that resulted from the increase in population, and to end the mobility of peasants by binding them to the land. Whereas peasants in western Europe might suffer from heavy debts and eviction from their lands, their counterparts in eastern Europe not only lost their freedom of movement but also were saddled with increasingly heavy burdens, including personal labor on landlords' estates and financial exactions that covered virtually every aspect of their lives. Widespread misery engendered social upheaval.

Unrest in Poland and Russia

In common with most of the major states in western Europe, Poland and Russia experienced crises in the mid-1600s. In Poland the centralization of royal authority was not a factor, for the country was fragmented. Power lay in the hands of the nobles, who secured the principle of elective monarchy in 1572. Their assembly, the Sejm, met at least every two years to determine policy. Poland was also split between Catholics, Greek Orthodox, Jews, and adherents of the Uniate church, who recognized the pope but worshipped according to Greek rites. Under Sigismund III (1587–1632), Catholics tried to destroy Polish Protestantism, causing a civil war in which the Orthodox Cossacks allied with the Protestants. The Jews were cruelly victimized, as many as 100,000 being murdered in the pogroms (organized massacres) of the decade 1648–1658.

The Cossacks, who were free herdsmen and peasants, were a major cause of unrest in Poland and Russia. In 1648 the Cossack leader Bogdan Khmelnitsky ignited a major revolt against the Polish government, partly in defense of the Orthodox faith and partly because of economic grievances. In 1654 he and his supporters in the Ukraine offered their allegiance to the tsar and were incorporated into the Russian state. Refusing to accept the loss of the Ukraine, Poland went to war twice until peace was finally achieved in 1667 by partitioning the Ukraine between Russia and Poland.

The roots of Russia's troubles in the seventeenth century stemmed primarily from the imposition of serfdom and the centralizing work of Ivan IV, "the Terrible" (1533–1584). He ruled by divine right in a land dominated by an Orthodox faith that stressed the subservience of the church to the state. At first he governed well, consulting with the great nobles, or *boyars,* formulating a new law code, instituting direct trade with western Europe, and convening Russia's first consultative assembly, the *zemski sobor.* In the late 1550s, however, Ivan became increasingly paranoid and vindictive. Setting aside a portion of Russia exclusively for himself, he used its troops to brutalize his opponents. He summarily imprisoned and executed boyars who resisted him and confiscated their estates. Ivan tortured priests, burned towns, and forcibly resettled large numbers of people on the frontiers.

Ivan's son and successor, Fëdor I, died in 1598 without an heir, plunging Russia into a period of turmoil known as the "Time of Troubles." While the boyars struggled to regain their power, peasants rioted, and the Poles and the Swedes intervened militarily. Dismayed at the civil war and foreign intervention, the zemski sobor awarded the crown in 1613 to Ivan's grandnephew, Mikhail Romanov. The new dynasty would rule Russia until its overthrow in the 1917 revolution. Rather than risk their estates in more civil war, the boyars cooperated with the first Romanovs, enabling them to finish the work of centralization. In return the tsars allowed the boyars to complete the process of enserfing the peasants, who bore the overwhelming burden of taxation.

The greatest peasant uprising in seventeenth-century Europe erupted in 1667. Incited by the Cossack Stenka Razin, runaway serfs and Cossacks proclaimed a message of freedom, equality, and land for all. Razin led his followers up the Volga River, replacing local governments with Cossack rule. His ships attacked Muslim villages on the Caspian Sea and even defeated a Persian fleet. The tsar's army finally crushed his forces in 1670, a year before Razin was beheaded. The resulting repression that ended the last of the midcentury crises entailed the death of as many as 100,000 peasants.

OLD WORLD RIVALRIES IN A GLOBAL SETTING

The political struggles that enveloped Europe in the century from 1560 to 1660 had profound consequences for the entire world. By 1660 the two countries that had dominated European expansion in the preceding two centuries—Portugal and Spain—had largely been supplanted by the Dutch, the English, and the French. Spain retained control of most of South and Central America, and Brazil remained in Portuguese hands. North America increasingly became the province of the northwestern European powers, which would eventually extend their sway over much of the globe.

The Dutch and English in Asia

After the Spanish annexed Portugal in 1580, they excluded the Dutch from their accustomed role of transporting Asian products from Lisbon to northern Europe. At first the Dutch responded by seeking a northeastern water route to East Asia, but when it proved impassable, they challenged the Portuguese by sailing around the Cape of Good Hope. The first such voyage, which occurred between 1595 and 1597, resulted in a trade agreement with an Indonesian sultan. Dutch merchants seized the new opportunity, dispatching between 60 and 70 ships to India and Indonesia in the next five years. The Dutch ships outnumbered their Portuguese rivals, were larger and more powerful, and were financed by a stronger merchant economy. Asians were more receptive to the Dutch, who displayed no interest in missionary activities, than the Portuguese, whose efforts to repress Hinduism and Islam had made numerous enemies. In the meantime, Portugal's new masters, the Spanish, were too preoccupied with their own empire as well as a war with England and a rebellion in the Netherlands to provide adequate defense for the Portuguese empire.

The Estates General in the Netherlands chartered the Dutch East India Company in 1602, giving it authority to import Asian goods free of customs duties, establish colonies, make war and peace, maintain military forces, coin money, and conclude treaties. The Company drove the Portuguese out of Malacca in 1641 and Ceylon by 1658. Six years earlier, it had started a colony on the Cape of Good Hope, the foundation of the European presence in South Africa. In addition to transporting Asian goods to Europe, the Company participated in the carrying trade within Asia itself.

The Company's determination to monopolize commerce between Europe and the East Indies propelled it into conflict with the English, who had established their own East India Company in 1600. The English company subsequently founded trading posts in Java and at several places in India. For two decades, beginning in 1613, the Dutch and the English engaged in a bitter rivalry for the East Indian trade. The ultimate success of the Dutch forced the English to concentrate elsewhere, particularly in India, although they traded with Iran and with the Chinese at Canton.

At first, England's primary base in India was at Surat, where Arab and Indian merchants traded in textiles and gold. But the English quickly realized that the finest cotton and silk were produced in Bengal, in eastern India, which was also a rich source of sugar and of saltpeter, a vital component of gunpowder. The Indians had little interest in English goods, so silver had to be traded for textiles and other items. The first English trading post was established in the Bengal region in 1633, and others followed in the 1640s, by which time the

English had also founded Madras. In 1641 the latter became the Asian headquarters of the East India Company. In their settlements the English made a deliberate effort to attract Indian spinners, weavers, dyers, and other skilled workers by offering protection and employment. English trade with Asia prospered, especially in the late seventeenth century, when annual dividends occasionally soared to 50 percent. On the whole, however, the English could not match the average Dutch dividend of 18 percent, nor did they have as many ships engaged in the trade as did their Dutch competitors. Like the Dutch, the English became adept in the carrying trade, and both, with the French, challenged Spanish dominance in the Americas.

Colonial Conflict in the Americas

The Spanish annexation of Portugal in 1580, which was so important for Asia, had less impact on the Americas, where the Portuguese held only Brazil. Because Portuguese settlers went to Brazil in growing numbers in the seventeenth century, the colonists were strong enough to repulse Dutch and French attempts to establish permanent footholds. The Dutch began colonizing Guiana, to the north of Brazil, in the 1610s. The Dutch West India Company, founded in 1621, supplied the settlers with slaves for their sugar plantations. The demand for sugar was also a major factor in the colonial efforts of the English and the French in Guiana, the only area in South America where these countries established settlements.

A stronger challenge to Spanish domination was mounted in the West Indies, which were strategically important as bases for fleets sailing to and from Mexico and Central America and valuable as well for the raising of tobacco and sugar. The islands attracted so many privateers and smugglers in the late sixteenth century that the Spaniards had to build heavy fortifications and organize their shipping in convoys. Beginning with the voyages of John Hawkins in the 1560s, the English intruded themselves into the West Indies trade. By the mid-1600s the English, Dutch, and French all had colonies in the West Indies. The development of sugar plantations meant a growing demand for African slaves, who soon outnumbered Europeans.

Apart from Mexico and Florida, where St. Augustine was founded in 1565 to check French incursion, the Spaniards were unable to settle North America. Not until 1607 did the English establish a permanent colony at Jamestown in Virginia, soon to become famous for its tobacco. Puritan dissatisfaction with the Church of England provided crucial motivation for the founding of colonies at Plymouth (1620) and Massachusetts Bay (1629) in New England, whereas the settlement of Maryland in 1634 was largely made by Catholics. By 1670, English colonies stretched from Maine to South Carolina, the development of which angered Spaniards in Florida.

England's main competitors in North America—the Dutch and the French—could not keep pace. Rebuffed by the Spanish in Florida, the French concentrated their efforts in the north, establishing settlements at Port Royal, Acadia, in 1605, and at Quebec three years later. In the short term the English faced a graver threat from the Dutch, who established New Amsterdam at the mouth of the Hudson River in 1624 and ended Sweden's bid for a colonial stake on the Delaware River in 1655. Fortunately for the English, the Dutch were preoccupied with their Asian trade and their African colony on the Cape of Good Hope. The commercial and colonial rivalry between the Dutch and the English, which now extended from Asia to the Americas, culminated in a series of three wars, the first of which was launched by the Rump Parliament in 1652. The Second Dutch War (1665–1667) brought New Jersey and New Amsterdam—henceforth known as New York—to the English and removed the Dutch from North America as a colonial power, though Dutch settlers remained in New York and thousands more made homes in Pennsylvania later in the century. Thereafter, the contest for North America was among the English, the French, and the Spanish, who were exploring northward from Mexico into California.

SUMMARY

The century that began in 1560 witnessed the failure of Spanish and Austrian attempts to impose hegemony, the former on western and the latter on central Europe. The frequent wars of the period, normally funded by deficit financing and the imposition of onerous taxes on the peasantry, were a major cause of domestic instability. By the mid-1600s, every major state in Europe except the Dutch Netherlands underwent a severe crisis: the vicious destruction of the Thirty Years' War in Germany, the Catalan and Portuguese revolts against the government in Madrid, the Fronde in France, the English revolution, and the Cossack uprisings in Poland and Russia. Although the specific conditions differed in each country,

certain common themes stand out: reaction against centralized government, the financial burden of war, and, in most areas, religious conflict. Order was restored when monarchs and nobles discovered a common self-interest, though this realization did not lead to political uniformity. Poland retained its feudal monarchy, England brought its sovereign under the rule of law, and France and Russia, their nobles pacified, were governed by absolute monarchs. Of the major European states, only the Dutch Netherlands was a republic, though even there the House of Orange was very influential. In the end, except for Poland, the costly quest for centralization was successful. With order restored, Europe in the late seventeenth century was threatened by new visions of hegemony, this time in France, but at the same time European expansion around the world offered dramatic new opportunities for commercial and industrial development.

Suggestions for Further Reading

Aylmer, G. E. *Rebellion or Revolution? England, 1640–1660.* New York: Oxford University Press, 1986.

Braudel, F. *The Mediterranean and the Mediterranean World in the Age of Philip II,* trans. S. Reynolds. 2 vols. New York: Harper & Row, 1972–1973.

Buisseret, D. *Henry IV.* London: Allen & Unwin, 1984.

Elliott, J. H. *Richelieu and Olivares.* Cambridge: Cambridge University Press, 1984.

Fennell, J. L. I. *Ivan the Great of Moscow.* New York: St. Martin's Press, 1961.

Geyl, P. *The Revolt of the Netherlands, 1555–1609,* 2d ed. London: Benn, 1966.

Haley, K. H. D. *The Dutch in the Seventeenth Century.* New York: Harcourt Brace Jovanovich, 1972.

Hill, C. *The World Turned Upside Down: Radical Ideas During the English Revolution.* New York: Viking, 1972.

Hirst, D. *Authority and Conflict: England, 1603–1658.* Cambridge, Mass.: Harvard University Press, 1986.

MacCaffrey, W. T. *Queen Elizabeth and the Making of Policy, 1572–1588.* Princeton, N.J.: Princeton University Press, 1981.

Parker, G. *Europe in Crisis, 1598–1648.* Brighton, England: Harvester Press, 1980.

——. *Philip II.* London: Hutchinson, 1978.

——. *The Thirty Years' War.* London: Methuen, 1985.

Stradling, R. A. *Europe and the Decline of Spain: A Study of the Spanish System, 1580–1720.* London: Allen & Unwin, 1981.

Wilson, C. *The Transformation of Europe, 1558–1648.* Berkeley: University of California Press, 1976.

14

EARLY MODERN EUROPEAN SOCIETY

In 1400, Europeans were beginning to recover from the worst effects of the Black Death, but France and England were still in the throes of the Hundred Years' War, no one in Europe yet knew of the Americas, and the West, apart from its Jewish communities, still embraced one religion. Four centuries later, new colonies thrived in the Americas, European trading routes extended around the globe, Guttenberg's press had revolutionized communications, Christian unity had been shattered, and dramatic discoveries had broadened the vistas of knowledge. Europe had moved from the peasant revolts of Wat Tyler and the Jacquerie to the English, American, and French revolutions, in each of which urban groups played an increasingly prominent role.

In many ways these were centuries of dramatic change—the bridge between the medieval and the modern worlds. Social structures, behavioral patterns, and value systems underwent fundamental changes. The nature of the family evolved among the aristocracy, Protestant states embraced more liberal notions of divorce, and the printing revolution helped to provide the necessary impetus for dramatic educational growth. The age of women's rights lay in the future, but women made significant contributions to their societies, sometimes in terms of political power at the highest levels of government. But the economic changes of the period threatened to engulf the lower orders in abject poverty despite efforts by state and local governments to control vagrancy and aid the destitute. Criminal activity burgeoned, forcing governments to find new ways to control it. The growing gulf between the rich and the poor was evident in their diets, although paradoxically the wealthy, with their unwise choice of foods, were perhaps no healthier than many peasants, whose diet, if meager, was more balanced. Medical care improved in these centuries, thanks especially to scientific discoveries and better education.

SOCIAL HIERARCHY

Europeans valued a hierarchical society, which they believed was ordained by both divine and natural law. Civic and religious leaders insisted that the duty of each person was to accept his or her place in the social order, an ideal that was intended to promote social stability and domestic tranquility. The hierarchical societies of early modern Europe were not, however, structured according to a class system in which groups were defined by similar levels of income and lifestyles, as in the modern West. In the early modern period the common basis of aristocratic power—landed wealth and the control of labor—was modified by the source of one's wealth, the antiquity of one's title, and the number of armed and paid retainers at one's disposal. A noble, though possibly not as rich as an urban businessman, outranked the latter in prestige—so much so that business families often tried to marry their daughters to landed aristocrats as a means of enhancing their social status.

The dress and many of the pursuits of the aristocracy—such as hunting, lawn bowling, and formal afternoon promenades—set them apart from the other social estates. This is a detail from *Le Rendez-vous pour Marly* by Moreau le Jeune. [The Metropolitan Museum of Art, Harris Brisbane Dick Fund, 1933 (33.6.11)]

The European system was divided into *estates,* or social groups defined by status, that is, by the dignity and respect with which each group was regarded by society in general. The aristocratic estate was generally expected to possess significant wealth in order to fulfill its social function as leader, exemplar, local ruler, maintainer of order, and reliever of the poor. The duty of the lower orders, both religious and political, was to accept the rule of the upper, although in reality there was often resentment and occasionally rebellion. Good behavior demanded deference to superiors, courtesy to equals, and kindness to inferiors. More was expected of, but also tolerated from, the higher orders, in which gentility was supposed to entail a combination of birth, breeding, and virtue.

Status entailed responsibility. Europeans used the analogy of paternal authority to justify monarchical power, especially in the 1600s. With the general exception of the Dutch, Europeans tried to reinforce the social hierarchy by reserving distinctive styles of dress for the aristocracy, although such efforts were largely unsuccessful. Social distinctions were reflected in numerous other ways, such as the number of a noble's retainers or clients or the number of coaches in his procession. Funerals too were distinctive pageants designed to reflect the social status of the deceased and their families.

Before the mid-sixteenth century the aristocracy generally improved its social position and became more involved in public affairs at the local or state level. Most nobles strove to acquire additional land, usually by strategic marriages, or greater status, normally by obtaining more elevated titles of nobility. To meet the demand for status, monarchs created additional noble titles and founded new chivalric orders, such as Knights of the Garter in England. New nobles were usually recruited from the landed gentry (the lesser aristocracy) rather than the bourgeoisie (the upper merchant and professional class), especially in France and England.

Conditions among the gentry varied widely. Whereas the more successful among them could be as wealthy and powerful as some nobles, others, especially on the Continent, sometimes turned to banditry to improve their sagging fortunes. Disaffected knights often supported reform movements, including Lutheranism in Germany and Calvinism in France, hoping to better their position. On the Continent an administrative aristocracy developed. In France and Milan, for example, officials acquired aristocratic privileges and became known as the nobility of the robe, after their gown of office.

Beginning in the mid-sixteenth century, the aristocracy entered a period of difficulty. Incomes did not keep pace with the money squandered on elaborate dress, excessive food, fine jewelry, lavish hospitality, and luxurious buildings. Some governments, especially the ministries of Richelieu in France and Olivares in Spain, pressed the nobility for cash to repay war debts. Raising funds by the sale of lands only reduced the income from rents. Nor did income keep pace with the rising cost of living owing to inflation, rents fixed by custom, and in some areas the existence of long-term tenant leases. The position of the aristocracy was further undermined by the growing reliance of governments on talent rather than rank. The prestige of the older aristocracy was hurt when sovereigns in France, Spain, and England sold titles to raise funds and accommodate the demand for status among the wealthy elites.

The upper aristocracy normally suffered less from these problems than did the lower; in England, however, much of the gentry improved its position in this period through careful land management, advantageous marriages, and the purchase of lands from the monasteries dissolved during the Reformation. The lesser provincial aristocracy also fared well in Poland and Russia, thanks in the latter case to Ivan IV's success in crushing the rebellious boyars and magnates in the mid-seventeenth century. By way of contrast, the country gentry of France were plagued with debt.

Urban Society

The social eminence of urban merchants, or patricians, stemmed from their involvement with long-distance trade, their ownership of city property, and their control of town government. Patricians intermarried to preserve the exclusiveness of their privileges, though some married their daughters to aristocrats in order to acquire the prestige that went with ownership of the land; similarly, some nobles sought marital alliances with wealthy merchants to augment their fortunes. Many members of the bourgeoisie invested in land or broadened their business interests to include finance in order to enhance their economic well-being and diversify their investments. The French bourgeois in particular purchased offices and land to improve their status, and Spanish merchants used much of the profit obtained from their trade with America to purchase estates. Townsfolk treated the urban patriciate as a noble class, particularly in republican Venice, where the absence of a monarch or a landed aristocracy elevated the patricians' status. In the Netherlands and the German states, too, the wealthy patricians were virtually a noble class, although their supremacy was disputed by the landed nobility. The growth of an autonomous bourgeoisie was retarded in Russia, however, because of the feudal structure of society.

In contrast to the patricians, the guildsmen continued, as in the medieval era, to concern themselves primarily with local production and services. In most towns they had considerably less influence than the patricians but were better off than the artisans and unskilled workers, who were poorly organized and had little voice in town government. Only by joining with the guildsmen could the artisans and laborers bring about change. Another urban group, the lawyers, found their services in increased demand as commerce expanded, land transactions became more complex, and landowners sought ways to evade the fiscal payments that were still part of feudal land tenure. Together these middling and upper urban groups began insisting upon a greater share of political power, particularly in France and England, where their demands contributed to the outbreak of civil war in both countries in the 1640s.

The Peasants

For centuries, peasant virtues—hard work, thrift, obedience, patience, and piety—shaped the fundamental values of western society. Numerous writers extolled the peasants for their productivity and honesty. The peasantry, whose ranks comprised most early modern Europeans, toiled hard, ate simply and sometimes inadequately, owned little, enjoyed few amusements, and were rarely educated. Yet they provided the foundation upon which the rest of the social and economic structure rested. The condition of the peasantry was a barometer by which to gauge the general health of society. When the peasants suffered, as in the 1550s, the 1590s, and the 1640s, the governments and societies of Europe plunged into instability.

The conditions of the peasantry varied throughout Europe, those in the west generally enjoying a better life than their eastern counterparts. Most western European peasants were personally free, although relatively few owned their own lands. Many still had to perform various services for their lords in return for the use of land, but even these peasants were fortunate in comparison to those who subsisted as mere day laborers with no access to land on which to raise crops or animals for themselves. Only in England were virtually all peasants free of labor services by the sixteenth century, yet many still suffered as numerous lords enclosed their lands, some to convert from tillage to pasturage, others to consolidate and modernize their production. Other peasants became victims of insecure land tenures that forced them to become day laborers. Throughout western Europe the peasantry became increasingly polarized; a small number of independent farmers with their own land prospered and became a rural bourgeoisie, while most of their fellow peasants became a landless rural proletariat.

In central and eastern Europe, where the population was sparse and the value of labor high, the nobility favored serfdom to assure themselves of an adequate labor force. Unlike the west, where hired labor was common, in eastern Europe aristocrats demanded manorial services, normally including three days of unpaid labor per week on their estates. Mounting taxes and labor services so impoverished Russian peasants that the government officially reduced their status to that of serfs in 1649. By the late eighteenth century, Russian serfs toiled in their masters' fields six days a week. Sometimes, as in Saxony and Bavaria, the state opposed serfdom, although not for humanitarian reasons; because most aristocrats were exempt from taxation, it was in the government's interest to keep at least some land in peasant hands as a source of taxation. Ultimately, the revival of serfdom in central and eastern Europe occurred because of two key factors: the consolidation of power in the hands of the landed aristocracy and the church and the determination to use the land primarily for the commercial production of grain, especially for the export market.

THE FAMILY AND MARRIAGE

Before 1700 the extended three-generational family may have been relatively common in Europe among the aristocracy, where patterns of ownership, inheritance, and status were complex. Below this level, the conjugal or nuclear family was a more or less self-contained unit. Except in eastern Europe, most couples married late, in their mid-twenties, by which time they were usually in a position to establish their own households. A widowed parent might subsequently take up residence with a married child. The prevalence of the nuclear family at the lower social levels was disadvantageous in the sense that mistreated spouses received less kin support and smaller family units were more vulnerable to economic hardship if a spouse became unemployed. The large family network that was common among the aristocracy provided an important support system, but smaller family units among the commoners presumably made it easier for many couples to make the personal adjustments necessary for a successful marriage without the intervention of relatives and in-laws.

The importance of preserving the family's status and property was responsible for the centuries-old practice of arranged marriage. Often a young person had no choice in the determination of a partner, for matrimony was a collective decision of the family and kin in which the key issues were property and power. Protestant reformers generally favored arranged marriage as a means to discourage young people from selecting spouses because of sexual attraction. Some parents allowed their children a veto over the proposed spouse, and occasionally headstrong young people defied the system by eloping, but at the risk of losing their inheritance. Young men's acceptance of arranged marriages was aided by the knowledge that once an heir was born, mistresses could be enjoyed, although obviously not with the church's approval. A double standard existed, for wives were denied such freedom.

Daughters were often an economic liability among the propertied classes, since a dowry had to be provided for marriage. In return, the groom's father guaranteed the bride an annuity if her husband died before she did. As heirs and potential fathers of future heirs, older sons usually married earlier than other young men. In sixteenth-century England, men normally wed at about age 28, but aristocratic heirs typically married at 22 to facilitate property settlements and enhance the prospects of providing a male heir in the next generation.

Primogeiture - inherit all land to eldest son.

Because a younger son had considerably less property and wealth than his elder brother, who benefited in England and parts of western Europe from the practice of primogeniture (bequeathing all of a landed estate to the eldest son), he faced a decline in social position unless he could find a wealthy bride.

About the middle of the sixteenth century the nature of the family began to change among the upper social orders. More significance was attached to the nuclear core (parents and children), and affection between spouses apparently became more important as a determinant of family relationships. The decline of kinship dominance is manifested in both decreasing hospitality and the diminishing sense of kin responsibility for individual acts. As states expanded their control of justice, protection, and the preservation of property, the responsibility for social control shifted from kin to the state. Simultaneously, Protestantism increased the significance of the nuclear family by stressing marital affection and by treating the family as a miniature parish with distinct religious responsibilities in instruction and worship.

In contrast to the modern nuclear family, patriarchal authority was reinforced. The Renaissance state supported the domination of the husband-father on the grounds that his authority was analogous to that of a sovereign over his subjects. The decline of kinship could increase the wife's subordination to her husband by leaving her more exposed to exploitation in the nuclear family. Capitalizing on this, the state relied on husbands to keep their wives law-abiding. Yet the development of the nuclear family could also facilitate better relations between spouses by providing them with more time to be alone, away from the prying eyes of relatives, retainers, and servants.

When marriages did go awry, no divorce in the modern sense was possible in medieval Europe. If the existence of an impediment or bar to a marriage could be demonstrated, the marriage could be annulled, but any children resulting from the union were thereby made illegitimate. Annulments were granted in such cases as marriage to relatives or in-laws, impotence, or forced marriage. The only other alternative, separation, did not bastardize the children, but neither did it leave the spouses free to remarry. In cases of wife-beating, church and state courts in Spain and France permitted legal separation.

The Reformation reduced the grounds for annulment but established divorce in the modern sense in some areas, including the Lutheran states, Zürich, Geneva, and Basel. Catholic states retained the medieval canon law, with its absolute prohibition of divorce. Among the poor, unhappy spouses often ran away, while others committed bigamy.

THE STATUS OF WOMEN

Although many women might have been powers within their families, their role in general was highly subordinate. They inhabited a male-dominated world, and their chief claim to status was as breeders of sons. Women were less valued from birth virtually everywhere. Females were subject first to their fathers and brothers, then to their husbands and to their husbands' male relatives.

In late medieval Europe, aristocratic women were regarded largely as bearers of children, sexual companions, and comrades in social functions. Few administered family estates or raised their own children, a task that was left to nurses and tutors. Nurturing of an infant was turned over to a wet nurse, typically a peasant woman hired for the occasion and often blamed for subsequent medical or psychological problems. Wet-nursing apparently doubled the infant mortality rate in cities and contributed to death rates as high as 75 percent in some French provinces in the eighteenth century. Among the factors responsible for such high mortality rates were the indigestibility of a wet nurse's milk and the often insufficient amount of it, inasmuch as a wet nurse typically fed her own or other infants at the same time. Wet-nursing freed the mother from the inconvenience of nighttime feeding, did not interrupt her social engagements, and served the father's sexual appetites; nursing mothers tended to shun intercourse, mostly because of their fear that breast-feeding would starve an embryo. However, wet-nursing declined sharply in the 1700s.

Aristocratic women had relatively little to occupy their time apart from such leisurely pursuits as reading, social visits, card playing, and theater-going, especially since many had stewards to run their households as well as nurses and tutors to care for their children. Women of the landed gentry, however, often played a major role in the household economy and managed the family estates when their husbands were away. Because of her social status, a gentlewoman or a merchant's wife had little choice of occupation, for manual labor was incompatible with her position and the professions were closed to women. Some became ladies-in-waiting to aristocratic women, some governesses of children, and a few, such as the English dramatist Aphra Behn, authors. Catholics, of course, had the option of joining a convent or a teaching order.

Near the lower levels of society the wives of artisans and peasants had to labor with their husbands to survive, for most Europeans lived at or near the subsistence level. Peasant women engaged in virtually every aspect of farming and additionally handled the household chores, provided food, and cared for any poultry or dairy animals. In both urban and rural areas many wives supplemented the family income by weaving or other side employments and occasionally by prostitution.

Late medieval craft guilds allowed masters' wives to share in their work, and wives often carried on the business when their husbands died. Although women had been admitted to the guilds, the new forms of business organization were almost exclusively male, and there was mounting hostility to women in the trades because they worked for lower pay. Apart from the cloth industry, women were being pushed out of many trades, such as brewing, which at one time was largely a female preserve. In England, men even moved into the occupation of midwife. Women could practice folk medicine and compete with barber-surgeons, but they were generally excluded from the profession of physician as well as those of attorney and minister. Although women found it increasingly difficult to compete for jobs in most trades, they found employment in the cottage industry concerned with cloth manufacturing, but the pay was poor and the hours were long. Women also found employment making gloves; in the late eighteenth century, nearly two-thirds of Grenoble's more than 6,000 glovers were women. Life was difficult for single women. Some worked in the coal and iron mines, where they typically received lower wages than their male peers. Most single women earned their living by spinning yarn, a practice that gave rise to the term *spinster* for an unmarried woman.

In certain respects the legal position of European women declined in the late medieval period. French women could no longer participate in public affairs, testify before various courts, or act in place of an absentee or insane husband. The laws of Saxony and England prohibited women from undertaking legal actions. Bavarian law prohibited a woman from selling anything without her husband's consent, though beginning in 1616 an exception was made for goods specified for her personal use. In England a husband enjoyed absolute control over his wife's personal property and could profit by leasing her real estate to others.

In the seventeenth century, however, marriage contracts guaranteed the wife "pin money" for her personal expenses, and the courts increasingly recognized the existence of her "separate estate," a handy device if her husband was sued for bankruptcy. French courts began to demonstrate greater concern for a wife's rights, including control over her dowry. A French wife whose husband mismanaged her property could win a legal separation, the most she could expect in a society without divorce. By the eighteenth century, Russian noblewomen and wives of artisans and merchants became the heads of their households when their husbands died, although only in urban areas. Legally, then, women's rights reached their nadir in Europe in the 1500s and then began to improve slowly in the seventeenth and eighteenth centuries.

SEXUAL CUSTOMS

The teachings of the church generally determined European attitudes toward sex, although these were often merely a veneer imposed on centuries of folk custom and were often ignored. For the masses, sex appears to have been largely oriented toward procreation and usually confined officially to marriage or engagement. In the eyes of the medieval Christian church, sexual relations were acceptable only within marriage and were intended primarily for procreation. Little attention was attached to love in a sexual context, and lust was condemned. During the Reformation, Protestants began to treat love and procreation as related and to regard sexual pleasure in marriage as a legitimate expression of the conjugal relationship.

Among the propertied orders, sexual relations before marriage were regarded with disapproval, largely because of the importance of bearing a legitimate heir. Because a woman was regarded as the sexual property of a man, her value diminished if she had been "used" by another male. Despite the church's official disapproval, males of the propertied elite frequently engaged in extramarital sex, normally with women from professional or merchant backgrounds whose families had fallen on hard times. The same freedom did not extend to women of their rank. A woman's honor was based on her reputation for chastity, a man's on his word. A wife who committed adultery insulted not only her husband's virility but his ability to govern her, which resulted in dishonor. In this respect the elite embraced a double standard that enhanced male dominance.

Among the lower orders in Europe, pressure for premarital sex was created by the late ages at which people wed—typically in their upper twenties. Late marriage helped to hold down population growth; figures for illegitimacy indicate relatively little sexual activity apart from engaged and married couples, probably owing to religious and socioeconomic pressure. Infanticide may also have contributed to low bastardy levels. The bastardy rate was 3 percent in rural England in the 1590s and 2 percent at Frankfurt in the early 1700s. Sexual activity was common among engaged couples. Approximately 21 percent of English brides were pregnant at their weddings in the late sixteenth century; the rate in the German town of Oldenburg was the same in the seventeenth century, although the French town of Lyon (10%) and the Spanish province of Galicia (7.5%) had lower figures.

Because Catholics considered the purpose of the sexual act to be primarily procreative, they regarded most attempts at contraception as mortal sin. By the sixteenth century, however, many Catholics accepted *coitus reservatus*—withdrawal before ejaculation—as a permissible technique for the economically destitute. *Coitus interruptus*—ejaculation outside the vagina—was condemned as an unnatural act on biblical grounds, although it became increasingly widespread in the 1700s.

In Protestant lands, religious leaders discouraged birth control methods, believing that they were contrary to the biblical command to multiply. Instead, they argued, children should be accepted as blessings from God, a means to maintain the commonwealth and church, and the means for women to recover the honor lost to their sex when Eve disobeyed. Medical manuals provided information on how to induce an abortion, typically through the ingestion of vegetal or mineral poisons, all of which were dangerous to the mother. Desperate women attempted to kill fetuses with sharp objects. Interest in the use of birth control methods was undoubtedly strong among women who wanted relief from the repeated cycle of pregnancies that often brought death. In the sixteenth and seventeenth centuries, perhaps one of every ten pregnancies ended in the mother's death, while 30 to 50 percent of all children died before the age of five.

Because abortion could be as dangerous to the mother as to the fetus, infanticide was a common alternative, particularly since it could be disguised as accidental "overlaying" or suffocation. Infanticide figures for Renaissance Florence indicate that more girls than boys died, presumably reflecting the greater value placed on males, though in eighteenth-century Paris there was no significant discrepancy between female and male victims.

Many parents, already victims of poverty, abandoned their children in the streets. More foundling hospitals were built to deal with the problem, but the availability of such places seems to have encouraged more parents to abandon their infants. In the 1770s and 1780s the number of children abandoned in Paris reached 4,500 per year, more than double the number at the beginning of the century. Conditions were so bad in foundling homes that at times no more than 5 percent of the infants admitted to them in Paris survived to adulthood. Children from other French towns were routinely shipped to Paris, sometimes by provincial hospitals that refused to care for them.

Catholic and Protestant leaders alike denounced homosexuality. In England the Tudor Parliaments of the sixteenth century made it a capital offense, though the statutes seem not to have been enforced. The magistrates were more concerned with heterosexual intercourse outside marriage because it could lead to illegitimate children and thus pose a financial burden to the community. Homosexuality appears to have been common in secondary schools, where boys often shared beds, and in universities. It was probably also common among servants and in tiny rural communities where access to persons of the opposite sex was severely restricted.

By the 1600s, organized prostitution was common in European cities, often with the tacit acceptance of authorities. In Seville, brothel keepers and prostitutes were licensed by the city, which even leased houses for this purpose. Church officials tried to close down the brothels, but the city fathers would do no more than require the prostitutes to attend church on Sundays and holy days. Many of the women who were drawn into a life of prostitution were economically destitute, including unwed mothers and cast-off mistresses; others chose it in preference to a 14- to 16-hour day as a seamstress. Some domestics were forced out of service and into prostitution when their employers got them pregnant. Other prostitutes were wives whose families were economically destitute or young girls introduced to this life by their mothers, themselves often former prostitutes. Prostitution was frequently a criminal offense for which women were typically pilloried, flogged, imprisoned, or sometimes expelled from a city, though usually to little effect. Nor were punitive measures effective against operators of houses of prostitution.

The late ages at marriage as well as the proximity of family members in small houses tempted some Europeans to commit incest. Among the peasants on the

1620- Mayflower

Continent, family members and servants alike shared communal beds, some as much as nine feet wide, a practice that encouraged illicit sex. Apprenticing male children and placing girls in other homes as servants were safety valves, but incest was still sufficiently common to trouble church authorities. People who were caught in the act were usually punished by shaming, as in the case of other sexual offenses. Usually confined to the lower orders, shaming typically required the offender to appear in church clad only in a white sheet or to ride through town in a cart with a sign proclaiming the offense; "carting" was usually accompanied by flogging.

Parents of bastards were treated more harshly because their misdeed was a potential burden on the community's funds; such people were regularly stripped to the waist, whipped, and placed in the stocks. In keeping with the double standard of the age, mothers of bastards were often subjected to punishment while the fathers escaped, although there were growing efforts to hold the latter accountable. Whether suffering from the double standard or undergoing frequent pregnancies, sexual experience for the early modern woman was fraught with hazard and anxiety and was potentially life-threatening as well.

LITERACY, THE PRINTED WORD, AND EDUCATION

The effects of printing in Europe were widespread, especially as universities and other schools enlarged their enrollments to educate the children of merchants and artisans. The demand for texts could now be met. Furthermore, the process was self-reinforcing: the more books there were, the more people learned to read. Thus the impact of printing was not merely to facilitate the circulation of ideas among educated people but also to make available on a popular level a vast range of material to which access had formerly been difficult, such as almanacs, herbals, and prophesies.

The new technology was employed in conducting political, religious, and scholarly debate. Among the first masters of the medium was Martin Luther, who published tracts on church reform and a German translation of the Bible that became a cornerstone of the Reformation. The reformers introduced printed pamphlets, hymns, religious texts, and sacred pictures to much of northern Europe, calling not only for religious changes but for social ones as well.

Between the Reformation and the French Revolution, mass literacy began to develop in Europe and spread through European colonizers elsewhere in the world. The first battleground for printed texts had been a sacred one, but pamphlets could now be distributed and books published to advocate or galvanize social and political change, and the spread of popular literature had an enormous impact on the English, American, and French revolutions. Not only did pamphleteers advance specific causes or claim individual wrongs; they also served to make accessible at a popular level ideas that had hitherto been debated largely by intellectuals.

The pamphleteers of the French civil wars at the end of the sixteenth century and the English Revolution in the mid-seventeenth century argued fundamental religious and political ideas, and their works, often cheaply printed, attracted wide circulation. The seventeenth century saw the first newspapers established in Augsburg, Strasbourg, London, and Paris. The role of print expanded in the eighteenth century, making it possible for growing numbers of people to keep abreast of public events and political issues. Not until the advent of the "penny press" in the eighteenth century did newspapers become fully accessible to the masses. Such exposure required not only literacy and the availability of an extra penny to spend for a paper, but also a desire to use the money to acquire the news rather than other goods.

The growth of knowledge and its relatively easy transmission were fundamental to the sudden surge of scientific development in the West. In the eyes of thinkers such as Francis Bacon and Rene Descartes, it was pointless to continue to depend on ancient writers and their books; new research was needed, and fresh ideas had to be circulated. In medicine and astronomy, chemistry and physics, the basis of modern scientific practice was laid in books published in the sixteenth and seventeenth centuries.

Popular literacy was also responsible for instruction and pleasure. From the beginning, many of the most popular books were horoscopes and prophecies, cookbooks, collections of tales, and reports of extraordinary events. New literary forms such as the novel and the short story met popular demand for fiction and expressed new social values and aspirations.

The Expansion of Education

The early modern period saw a notable increase in the number of schools and in the continued development of the universities. In keeping with their broad range of intellectual and cultural interests, Renaissance humanists founded new schools and reformed the traditional curriculum by challenging its heavy reliance on Aristotle. The success of Protestant reformers rested on their ability to educate younger generations in their religious principles; in turn, the Catholics relied heavily on education to thwart Protestant expansion and to provide the foundation for their missionary work.

Protestants and Catholics alike looked to the universities to provide them with vigorous intellectual leadership. The Protestant stress on Bible-reading, especially with the availability of new vernacular translations, was a powerful incentive to education. The Scientific Revolution, with its rapid communication of ideas, was also dependent on learning, and the rapid growth of state bureaucracies increased the demand for skilled officials, particularly those with legal training.

Many educational developments were closely linked to religion. Catholic orders such as the Jesuits and the Ursulines are famous for their educational work, but other groups were active too. The Oratory of Jesus, a society of priests, established colleges and seminaries throughout France, mostly for children of the French nobility; their schools rejected physical punishment as an educational tool. Several Catholic organizations were established in France in the late 1600s to teach the children of the poor; among them were the Brothers of the Christian Schools. Although Protestants had no teaching orders, they, too, actively founded schools, including "charity schools" for children of the poor.

Protestants and Catholics alike founded a host of new universities in the sixteenth and seventeenth centuries, in large measure because they did not want their young people studying at schools run by their opponents. Among the more noted were Würzburg (1582), which was supervised by the Jesuits, and Leiden (1575), founded as a Protestant alternative to Louvain (1425) and Douai (1562). One of the most successful Protestant institutions was the University of Halle in Germany, founded in 1694 by evangelical Pietists. By its emphasis on independent thinking, the faculty at Halle helped to pioneer the development of modern academic freedom.

The Jewish communities of Eastern Europe and Spain were keenly interested in education. At the elementary level, education was mandatory for boys, and some girls were taught to read, especially after the appearance of printed vernacular literature. Gifted male students studied medicine and religion, the latter a specialty of rabbinical academies. Because of the importance of rabbinical law in the ghettos, legal studies as well as religion were an important part of the curriculum. Nonreligious subjects often had to be learned from private tutors.

Progress in the founding of schools and the increase of literacy was pronounced in early modern Europe. Between 1580 and 1650, more than 800 schools were endowed in England and Wales. By the late seventeenth century the number of parishes with schools was near 90 percent in the diocese of Paris and the lowland counties of Scotland, though the figure was only 42 percent in the diocese of Verdun and even less in some areas.

Universal education effectively began when Prussia made attendance at elementary school mandatory in 1717. The founding of new schools was accompanied by substantial increases in literacy. By 1800 the literacy rate for males approached 90 percent in Scotland and 67 percent in France, whereas in 1600 only one male in six had been able to read. Among women, whose educational opportunities were more restricted, literacy rates generally rose more slowly. In Amsterdam, where literacy greatly enhanced employment opportunities, the rates were 57 percent for men and 32 percent for women in 1630. Because the Swedes required literacy for confirmation and marriage, by the 1690s at least one Swedish diocese had achieved a rate approaching 100 percent, though for many people this may have represented little more than the ability to sign one's name.

POVERTY, CRIME, AND SOCIAL CONTROL

Authorities in France and England in the late 1600s probably exaggerated in estimating that over half of *50%* their people lived at or below the subsistence level, but the number was high. The large number of the poor seriously strained the ability of religious and civic authorities to provide assistance. In the plague year of 1580, more than half the population of Genoa was on poor relief. For the poor the greatest problem was often the uncertainty of the food supply, which was frequently threatened by inflationary pressures as well as natural disasters. The bulk of the population still lived in rural areas, often in mud huts with thatched roofs. Living quarters were severely cramped, so an entire family often lived in a single room. In towns the poor were victims of polluted water and filthy living conditions. In general, the lot of the rural poor was marginally better than that of their urban counterparts, since many of the former were able to raise some of their own food. This was not usually true of landless day laborers, who made up as much as half the population of some districts in

Spain and Switzerland. As the general population increased, it was imperative to find means to relieve the destitute.

Various factors contributed to the severity of poverty in the early modern period. As the population grew, landlords improved the efficiency of their farms to provide additional food, but industry did not expand rapidly enough to absorb the surplus labor displaced as landowners switched from raising crops to grazing sheep. Inflation took a heavy toll as rents and prices rose faster than wages, leaving urban workers particularly vulnerable. Short-term increases in poverty were caused by extreme fluctuations in the cloth industry, which was adversely affected by such things as plague, war, and bad harvests. Whereas rural textile workers might weather a slump by finding temporary farm work, urban laborers were typically reduced to poor relief or begging.

When harvests failed, the plight of the poor often became desperate. Food was so scarce in France in the early 1660s that the poor ate the rotting flesh of dead animals they found in the fields or lapped up the blood spilled in urban slaughterhouses and devoured the guts of the animals slain to feed the rich. In England from the late fifteenth century to the early seventeenth century, harvests failed on an average of every four years. When the harvests were bad several years in a row, the problem was more acute, and food riots were common. Finally, as the size of European armies expanded in the early modern period, the number of demobilized and often unemployable soldiers increased, adding further burdens to relief rolls.

Various attempts were made to deal with the poor. In the late 1400s, local authorities ordered beggars to leave their districts, although exceptions were sometimes made for local beggars who were handicapped, ill, or elderly. In Brabant, France, and Venice, vagabonds rowed the galleys; in England a 1495 law ordered that the idle be whipped, placed in the stocks for three days, and then returned to their parishes of origin. Intended to keep the destitute from flooding into the towns, virtually all early measures to deal with the poor relied on some form of coercion but failed to provide organized means to relieve the needy.

The widespread social unrest sparked throughout Europe by the harvest failures of the 1520s brought major changes in social policy. Between 1531 and 1541 the Netherlands, England, and France prohibited begging and insisted that the able-bodied poor work. Funds for those who were unable to work were raised through taxes or donations, but the emphasis shifted from private charity to public welfare. The English Poor Law of

In early modern Europe, many indigent people took to the highways in search of employment, but in so doing they risked severe punishment as vagabonds. This 1520 engraving is by Lucas van Leyden. [Staatliche Museen Preussischer Kulturbesitz, Kupferstichkabinett, Berlin/Jörg P. Anders]

1601, for example, prohibited begging, required the able-bodied poor to work on local projects, centralized poor relief, and provided for the education of paupers' children. Where there was industry to employ the able-bodied at low wages, as in Flanders, France, and England, the new system achieved some success. Scotland and Spain, which had little need for the labor of unskilled paupers, licensed beggars in an attempt to keep them under control. Since licenses could easily be forged, this system was ineffective.

Because employment could not always be found for the able-bodied poor, many cities established workhouses to discipline the poor as well as to provide job training and moral instruction. Although these institutions could not accommodate all the able-bodied poor, officials hoped to coerce the remainder into finding employment. Some workhouses became little more than places of punishment, while others were sources of cheap labor for private employers. French workhouses at first were used to benefit private business, but after 1640 they were primarily utilized to control rebellious peasants and workers. The inmates of these institutions rarely benefited from their enforced stays.

Crime and Poverty

As the living standards of European workers and peasants deteriorated, criminal activity increased, especially beginning in the mid-1500s. In rural areas a clear connection existed between crime and destitution. Most rural felons were common laborers who did not repeat their criminal activity after their initial arrest. Records for the Spanish province of Toledo show that nearly all defendants in larceny cases came from the lower ranks of society. Theft was often the most common crime. Yet in some Spanish regions, violence was more common than theft, partly because firearms were widely possessed. Urban growth, with its attendant problems of unemployment, inadequate housing, and food shortages, spawned crime. At Madrid in the period 1665–1700, approximately half of all reported crimes involved violence. These were followed by sex offenses and marital feuding; theft was less frequent than any of these.

In the early modern period, some changes occurred in the type of larceny. During the medieval period, mostly subsistence items—food, clothing, and tools—were stolen, but later there was a growing tendency to steal luxury goods, which were readily sold in the expanding towns. Whereas the poor had hitherto stolen mostly from each other, they now increasingly robbed the rich. A major exception to this pattern of crime occurred during the unsettled times of fourteenth- and fifteenth-century Europe when bands of lawless nobles and gentry engaged in robbery and extortion. Not even the wealthy were immune, for they provided tempting targets for kidnapping and extortion. Known as "fur-collar criminals" because of the fur worn on nobles' collars, these aristocratic culprits thrived until governments were strong enough to stamp most of them out in the 1500s.

Banditry did not cease with the decline of fur-collar crime, but henceforth nearly all bandits were from the lower social orders and included many men who were unable to find employment. In Granada some of the bandit groups were led by women. As major roads were more effectively patrolled by the seventeenth century, most of these bandits were forced into remote areas. Russia, however, experienced considerable turmoil throughout the 1600s because of large roving bands. Russian bandits were commonly viewed as heroes and defenders of the common people, particularly since most victims were bureaucrats, tax collectors, and wealthy merchants. Some Spanish bandits made a distinct effort to convey an image of piety and justice, sharing their booty with the poor.

Early modern towns were increasingly troubled by business fraud and swindlers. Another facet of urban crime was the growth of neighborhoods in the larger European cities where a genuine underworld existed. In Paris the criminal sector was so extensive that officials dared not enter it until it was subdued by an army detachment in 1667. Curtailing crime in the cities was particularly difficult because the poor were packed into grossly overcrowded slums where shanties filled even the narrow alleys and where criminals could easily hide.

Controlling Crime

European states responded to the rise in crime by reorganizing the personnel and procedure necessary to control it. In the medieval period, criminal control was based on the existence of small populations in compact, mostly isolated areas. As the population expanded and interregional contacts increased, it became imperative to develop more effective government controls beyond the local level. In France this need was met by expanding the powers of the royal *procureur,* who handled the prosecution in criminal proceedings. In England the Tudors, who had no police force, enlarged the role of the justices of the peace, who, as unpaid agents of the crown, had the authority to arrest, indict, and grant bail. They also enforced labor codes and social laws that governed such things as alehouses and unlawful games. By the late sixteenth century, justices of the peace were responsible for enforcement of the poor law.

Revised criminal procedures were instituted that had the effect of depersonalizing the judicial process and treating criminal activity as an offense against society rather than the individual. Punishment became more severe. In contrast to the less severe medieval system, in which justice was intended to settle disputes between individuals, the new criminal proceedings punished the guilty but ignored compensation for the victim. Corporal punishment became more widespread, although a status distinction was generally made in meting out justice; the rich were often fined, the poor imprisoned, flogged, or mutilated. The increased severity of punishments was intended to discipline the lower orders and curb the rise in crimes by the poor against the rich. Public punishment thus had a twofold purpose: to deter crime and to demonstrate the authority of the state to regulate the behavior and command the obedience of its citizens. When the punishment was unduly harsh for the crime, however, onlookers were sometimes outraged. The frequency with which brutal punishments were publicly imposed also had the unintended effect of desensitizing observers. Harsh public punishments were apparently not effective deterrents to crime in early modern Europe.

Criminals were tried and laws and punishments enforced by civil courts run by the state and presided over by magistrates, rulers or their representatives, community elders, or learned men. Sometimes there was no prior assumption of guilt or innocence; in such cases, judgment was made and sentences were arrived at on the basis of evidence, including the testimony of witnesses. Torture was sometimes used to complete testimony, although confession was not essential for a conviction. European law and the system of official justice was designed to awe all who appeared before its majesty. Plaintiffs, defendants, and witnesses knelt before the magistrate or judge and could be whipped if they were not suitably reverential—another expression of a strongly hierarchical, authoritarian society.

Punishment for major crimes of violence was almost invariably death, commonly by beheading or strangulation. Death could also be imposed for many minor crimes; theft was a capital crime in England, although the sentence was often commuted to banishment. For especially dreadful crimes, such as treason, convicted persons were briefly hanged, cut down while still alive, and then dismembered ("drawn and quartered").

The treatment of criminals varied considerably from place to place. Although the Russians imposed capital punishment only for treason, other penalties could be extraordinarily brutal; there were instruments to break arms and legs, slit the nostrils, and brand the flesh. The Germans generally led the way in treating prisoners more or less humanely, providing reasonably clean cells, heating in winter in some cases, and constructive employment. Yet even German jailers were still using instruments of torture as late as the eighteenth century. Public shaming was commonly used as an official punishment in Europe. Criminals were publicly exhibited and were often paraded through the streets carrying placards indicating their offenses. Punishments were seen as deterrents to would-be criminals; the heads of executed criminals were exhibited on poles until they rotted. For lesser offenses, criminals were displayed in painfully small cages or mutilated. Prisons were often

dreadful places where inmates might starve if they were not fed by relatives.

In early modern Europe a double standard of justice continued to exist that was much harder on the poor than on their social betters. Laws were made and administered by elite groups, whose interests in the preservation of their privileged status and property were at least as great as their devotion to justice.

THE FOOD OF COURT AND COUNTRY

Malnutrition was the plight of both rich and poor throughout much of early modern Europe—the rich because they overindulged in eating meats and animal fats, the poor because they often had insufficient food to consume. Not until the eighteenth century did agricultural productivity increase sufficiently to have a dramatic impact on life expectancy, which rose from age 25 in 1700 to 35 in 1800. During the sixteenth century, when the population began to increase dramatically, European farmers could not keep pace with the demand for food, and even larger numbers of people lived at the subsistence level and periodically faced starvation. Inflation, famine, and war directly affected the diet of the masses, whereas the wealthy enjoyed a luxurious range of foods. Inadequate diet may have adversely affected both the amount of labor that workers could perform and their ability to withstand major illnesses.

The diet of the poor was simple and usually devoid of meat. The more fortunate peasants might occasionally have a little mutton or pork, but the poor usually had to survive on a diet consisting of dark bread, peas, beans, and soup. Bread was a valuable source of carbohydrates, vitamins, proteins, and minerals. Not surprisingly, substantial increases in grain prices could easily incite massive social unrest.

Many peasants kept stock simmering in a pot, adding to it whatever foods were available each day. These might include hard yellow radishes, carrots, turnips, dried beans and peas, herbs, perhaps leeks, and, for the fortunate, salted pork fat. Peasants who lived near rivers or the sea might have fish soup. Whatever the type, the soup was typically poured over a piece of hard bread. Some peasants were fortunate enough to have hard cheese, curds, butter, cabbage, wild greens, and, in some regions, sweet chestnuts that could be boiled or mashed. Continental peasants made heavy buckwheat pancakes.

Meat was rarely part of the peasant diet, although people of modest means might enjoy salted pork on occasion, or, if they were willing to poach, wild rabbits. Fish was more plentiful for those who lived near the water, although access to streams and lakes was sometimes restricted, and in some areas fish was available only at the risk of poaching. On religious holidays or other special occasions the poor might have meat, especially in the sixteenth century, when some aristocrats continued to provide hospitality on a lavish scale at weddings and funerals. On holidays, servants and day laborers were usually treated to the leftovers and bones from their employers' lavish meals.

Festivals were normally the only time many peasants tasted wine, apart from those in the wine-producing regions of Italy, France, the Rhineland, and Greece. Ale was not available in all regions. Some peasants concocted fermented beverages by pouring water over grape stalks and skins or by using berries and leaves; others made cider. Milk was shunned by some as unhealthy, and rightly, since much of it was undoubtedly contaminated with unhealthy bacteria. Some authorities recommended that children, invalids, and the elderly drink milk; wet nurses were sometimes sought for such people. For most peasants and urban workers the normal beverage was water, often polluted by everything from feces to linseed oil (a by-product of flax processing) and therefore a frequent cause of disease and of the deaths of the newly born.

The aristocracy was addicted to meat. Members of the English nobility typically consumed more than eight pounds apiece each week. Modest amounts of fruits and vegetables appeared on menus of the wealthy, especially in the summer. The French created a distinctive style of cooking that marked the beginning of modern French cuisine, as in the use of the bouquet garni, butter bases, fat- rather than vinegar-based sauces, and more subtle spices.

The wealthy could indulge themselves with beverages to their liking, of which good wine was commonly preferred. The Roman bourgeoisie sought costly wines that were high in alcohol and sugar, while the English aristocracy had a liking for French wines and white wine from the Rhineland. English tastes altered somewhat as a result of a trade war with the Dutch between 1651 and 1653 and closer ties to Portugal; sweet wines such as port and Madeira became popular. The Dutch and the Irish were fond of spirits; the English acquired a taste for

Dutch gin when they fought in the Netherlands in the late 1580s and 1590s, but they were also attracted to Irish whiskey and French brandy.

Coffee, which apparently originated in Ethiopia, spread throughout the Middle East before it appeared in Constantinople in the mid-sixteenth century and possibly Italy in 1580. It did not become popular in Europe until the mid-seventeenth century, when coffeehouses appeared; the first in the New World opened in Boston in 1670. Such establishments quickly became fashionable for social gatherings and as meeting places to discuss politics and literature.

Tea, so popular in China and Japan, appeared in Europe in the early seventeenth century, apparently first in the Netherlands and Portugal. Initially very costly, tea increased in popularity, especially in England, as its price fell. Coffeehouses sold tea and the more expensive drinking chocolate; imported from the New World by the Spaniards, chocolate was popular in Spain, Italy, Flanders, and France.

In addition to chocolate the New World provided Europeans with other new foods such as maize (corn), which soon became a staple in northern Spain, Italy, and Portugal. Tomatoes, lima beans, red and green peppers, peanuts, tapioca, pineapple, and turkey were among the other discoveries. More important than any of these was the potato, first introduced to Spain. In some regions, such as Italy, the southern Netherlands, and Ireland, the potato was welcomed, not least because an acre planted in potatoes could feed five times as many people as the same land devoted to wheat. Potatoes provided nutritious food for the poor at a time when grain production could not keep pace with demographic growth. Potatoes were not universally welcomed, however, in part because many people, as in most of France, preferred bread. The Burgundians banned potatoes in 1619 in the mistaken belief that they caused leprosy. The English adopted them in the late eighteenth century only after observing how they fattened cattle and when bad harvests caused the price of grain to soar.

Dietary patterns thus changed significantly in the early modern era. In part this entailed a growing divergence between the diet of the well-to-do, with their meat- and fish-laden tables, and that of the masses, who were dependent on heavy bread and, by the eighteenth century, maize and potatoes. Dietary patterns altered as well because of the introduction of new foods and beverages brought to Europe as part of the greatly expanded trading routes that took merchants to Asia and the Americas.

MEDICAL CARE

Medicine changed rapidly in early modern Europe, particularly as medical practitioners sought to define themselves professionally and as scientists vigorously debated physiology and proper treatment for physical and mental ailments. The exchanges were often bitter, and the rivalries among competing practitioners intense. The quality of medical care therefore varied enormously. Just as the diet of many peasants was undoubtedly healthier than that of the wealthy, so the general inability of the poor to afford most medical care may in many instances have been to their advantage, given the state of medical knowledge.

Doctors, Nurses, and Charlatans

People who sought medical treatment could get it from a variety of persons, the most educated and socially respected of whom were normally the physicians. As far back as the medieval period, European states had begun to require would-be physicians to pass examinations, and they alone in the medical world typically had university training. Yet their position was undermined to some degree by the publication and distribution of vernacular texts, which made medical knowledge more readily accessible to a wider audience. Attempts to educate, license, and regulate physicians were never very effective in this period.

Surgeons had less prestige than physicians, primarily because they received their training like apprentices in other trades and were sometimes organized into guilds. They were, moreover, associated with barbers in England by an act of Parliament in 1520. Some surgeons benefited from anatomy lectures and surgical demonstrations, usually under the auspices of a guild rather than a university. Traditionally, the physicians tried to supervise the surgeons, although beginning in the sixteenth century the latter increasingly sought their independence and, in the minds of some modern authorities, surpassed physicians in their medical skills.

Medical treatment of a different sort could be obtained from apothecaries, who functioned not only as pharmacists, filling prescriptions for physicians, but virtually as doctors who dispensed their own elaborate concoctions, especially laxatives. Some were gardeners and botanists who grew their own herbs, including some newly imported from the Americas. In England they were members of the grocers' guild, since grocers them-

A surgeon uses a saw to amputate a patient's leg. [The Mansell Collection]

selves could freely sell drugs, until 1617; at that point, the apothecaries won their independence. Because they normally charged only for the drugs they dispensed, apothecaries tended to be popular among the masses, serving them as general practitioners. Like surgeons, apothecaries received their training through a traditional guild apprenticeship.

An assortment of other people purported to offer medical care, especially in rural areas where trained personnel were rare. Midwives played an essential role and were common everywhere, as were quacks of all sorts, with their worthless nostrums and miraculous cures. Faith healers, who practiced the laying on of hands and pretended to cast out demons, enjoyed some success in aiding the mentally disturbed. People with broken bones could have recourse to bonesetters as well as surgeons, while bone benders functioned as primitive chiropractors. Legitimate physicians examined urine for the presence of blood, bile, or sediment, but uroscopy was also a specialty of urine casters, who claimed, among other things, the ability to determine the sex of an unborn child by studying the mother's urine.

Women were involved in nearly every area of medicine, especially nursing and midwifery. Many worked as apothecaries or specialized in female disorders and children's ailments; others were in demand to treat the poor in workhouses or other municipal institutions. Other women offered their services as bonesetters, surgeons, and faith healers. This is not to suggest that women enjoyed equal treatment as medical practitioners. Although some women apparently studied at Salerno, universities were generally male bastions. In 1517 the English Parliament authorized women barber-surgeons to practice, but this only diminished the status of all barber-surgeons in the eyes of physicians. For the most part, women were relegated to medical tasks that were shunned by men or to practice among the poor or in the countryside.

Treating the Sick

Accurate diagnosis is the essential prerequisite to the proper treatment of any illness, but diagnosis itself is conducted in the context of a theoretical framework about disease processes. As long as grossly inaccurate views of the human body and the operation of disease prevailed, accurate diagnosis and proper treatment were more a matter of chance than of medical knowledge. Under these circumstances, commonsense care prescribed by a layperson familiar with successful "home" remedies was often likely to prove more beneficial than the mysterious concoctions of apothecaries or the methods of physicians. Such successes as the medical community enjoyed were often due to nothing more than the human body's general ability to heal, not to their prescribed care.

Most doctors still subscribed to the classical Greek theory that attributed illness to an imbalance in the body's four qualities (hot, dry, cold, wet) and four humors (blood, yellow bile, black bile, phlegm). Treatment of a disease of the yellow bile (associated with the liver), which was "hot" and "dry," therefore entailed the use of "cold" and "wet" remedies. Physicians who embraced this view oriented their diagnosis to a determination of whether the patient was hot, cold, dry, or moist, a conclusion that was typically reached after scrutinizing a urine sample, "excrements" (e.g., nasal discharge, coughs, or phlegm), the pulse, and astrological data. This view was challenged in the sixteenth century by the Swiss-born German physician Paracelsus (1493–1541), who attributed illness to an imbalance in the basic chemicals that compose the human body, namely, mer-

cury, sulfur, and salt. Each disease, he believed, has a chemical cure, and it was therefore essential to study the effects of specific chemicals on each illness. Paracelsus' views were bitterly controversial in his own day, and historians are still not agreed in assessing his importance, but he raised crucial questions and provoked needed discussion on the causes and treatment of illness.

Medical care commonly entailed the administration of prescribed drugs, purging, and bleeding. Purgatives were used to treat stomach and intestinal disorders, common enough given the contaminated water supply, the frequency with which food spoiled, and the general lack of sanitation. Enemas made of saltwater, oil, or milk were used to treat constipation and other ailments as well as to reduce sexual desire. Purgatives were intended either to draw out the disease, which was viewed as a foreign element, or to expel the corrupt humors. Bloodletting was a way of treating a host of ailments, ranging from fevers and liver problems to toothaches and depression. This was usually undertaken by surgeons, who made incisions to draw blood, monitoring the patient's pulse in the process. The use of leeches was common, although they sometimes completely burrowed into a patient's body and had to be purged with a saltwater enema. Bleeding supposedly removed impure blood and restored the balance of humors, although some physicians warned that bloodletting and laxatives were debilitating. Bleeding remained common as a course of treatment in some parts of Europe well into the twentieth century.

Surgeons had fewer diagnostic problems than physicians. Wounds inflicted by gunshot, swords, and other weapons or compound fractures and gangrenous limbs were obvious, and the methods of treatment were severely restricted. Most operations were traumatic in the absence of effective anesthesia. Surgeons sometimes administered ointment, alcohol (to the point of inebriety), or opium, but the latter was ineffective unless used in dangerously large amounts. Patients with a compound fracture or a gangrenous limb had the affected arm or leg amputated with a saw and the exposed wound cauterized with fire. Probably half of those operated on died from shock or infection. Traditional medical theory mandated that wounds be left open to fester, but the French surgeon Ambroise Paré (1510–1590) revived the ancient practice of closing wounds with a ligature. The English surgeon John Woodall made numerous amputations without losing a patient by cutting through dead tissue very near the point where it adjoined healthy tissue; this technique reduced bleeding and the pain of extensive cauterization. As anatomical knowledge advanced, especially through a practice of dissecting corpses, which the Fleming Andreas Vesalius (1514–1564) popularized, surgery too become more sophisticated.

From Hospices to Hospitals

Most medieval hospitals were hospices, places that offered hospitality to the elderly, the disabled, the homeless, and sometimes the sick. They were, in other words, places of charity rather than medical institutions. Some were run by monasteries, others by bishops or guilds. Three developments played a major role in transforming hospices into medical institutions. The first was the influence of the medical hospitals founded in Palestine under the auspices of the crusaders in the twelfth century. Important too was the need to provide shelter and care for pilgrims, especially those who were sick, to Europe's famous shrines. Finally, the catastrophic impact of the Black Death made it necessary to use hospices to house the afflicted. Although medieval Europe had hundreds of lazar houses were lepers lived, these were more like isolated communities than hospitals. Well into the early modern period, hospitals of all sorts continued to thrive, although their financial support was increasingly derived from state and municipal governments and voluntary groups.

Conditions in the medical hospitals varied, though in general they were overcrowded, unsanitary, understaffed, and foul-smelling. Since there was no real understanding of communicable disease, people with infectious ailments were not isolated from other patients. With several people sometimes sharing one bed, diseases could spread quickly. However unpleasant they were, by the latter half of the early modern period the better European hospitals were making a contribution to improved health care, not least by providing the best medical minds with opportunities to study a variety of cases and thereby advance the frontiers of knowledge.

The outlook was considerably bleaker for the mentally ill, whose confinement was tantamount to imprisonment with little or no treatment provided. Institutions often confined their patients in cells and restrained them with leg irons or other devices, sometimes on the assumption that the insane had no feeling. Bloodletting, purging, blistering, and cold water passed for treatment. The primary purpose of such hospitals was not to cure the sick but to provide for their minimum physical needs while protecting the public.

The beginnings of a new policy finally appeared in the 1790s. The English Quaker Samuel Tuke persuaded the Society of Friends in York to found an asylum where patients would be treated humanely. In Paris, Philippe Pinel removed the chains from his patients, some of whom had been fettered for as long as 40 years. As part of his treatment, Pinel adapted the Dutch practice of assigning patients constructive duties in the asylum. The reforming endeavors launched by Tuke and Pinel were but the first steps in the slow evolution of effective treatment for the mentally ill.

SUMMARY

In the late eighteenth century some of Europe's leading thinkers focused on the theme of progress to explain the past and chart the future. The record of the previous four centuries contained much to substantiate this view: the population of Europe had recovered from the demographic disaster of the Black Death and had begun to increase sharply, especially after 1750; the voyages of exploration and the subsequent expansion of trade routes around the world brought important new foods to European tables; efforts were underway to reform prison conditions and treatment for the mentally ill; medical care in general was beginning to improve because of advances in science, more effective medical training, and better hospitals; and literacy and schools were increasing, thanks in part to the rapidly expanding availability of printed materials. In other respects, however, the period from 1400 to 1800 left a sobering, inhumane legacy. The gulf between rich and poor widened, violent crime increased, women were still denied social equality, and serfdom was revived in eastern Europe. All of these trends continued into the twentieth century. By 1800 the foundations of modern society were firmly in place, for better or for worse.

Suggestions for Further Reading

Cartwright, F. F. *A Social History of Medicine*. London: Longman, 1977.

Granshaw, L., and Porter, R. *Hospitals in History*. London: Routledge, 1989.

Greaves, R. L. *Society and Religion in Elizabethan England*. Minneapolis: University of Minnesota Press, 1981.

Kamen, H. *European Society 1500–1700*. London: Hutchinson, 1984.

Ladurie, E. L. *The French Peasantry, 1450–1660.* Berkeley: University of California Press, 1986.

Laslett, P. *The World We Have Lost Further Explored,* 3rd ed. London: Methuen, 1983.

Maynes, M. J. *Schooling in Western Europe: A Social History.* New York: State University of New York Press, 1985.

Mennell, S. *All Manners of Food: Eating and Taste in England and France from the Middle Ages to the Present.* Oxford: Blackwell, 1985.

Ozment, S. *When Fathers Ruled: Family Life in Reformation Europe.* Cambridge, Mass.: Harvard University Press, 1983.

Schalk, E. *From Valor to Pedigree: Ideas of Nobility in France in the Sixteenth and Seventeenth Centuries.* Princeton, N.J.: Princeton University Press, 1986.

Shorter, E. *The Making of the Modern Family.* New York: Basic Books, 1977.

Stone, L. *The Family, Sex and Marriage in England 1500–1800.* New York: Harper & Row, 1977.

Stone, L., and Stone, J. C. F. *An Open Elite? England, 1540–1880.* New York: Oxford University Press, 1984.

Traer, J. F. *Marriage and the Family in Eighteenth-Century France.* Ithaca, N.Y.: Cornell University Press, 1980.

Wiesner, M. E. *Working Women in Renaissance Germany.* New Brunswick, N.J.: Rutgers University Press, 1986.

15

THE AGE OF ABSOLUTISM

The sixteenth century had witnessed the emergence of centralized states in western Europe. The seventeenth and eighteenth centuries saw their consolidation. By the end of the Thirty Years' War it was clear that the future lay with the powers that were capable of mobilizing their resources most effectively for both war and peace. From the middle of the seventeenth century to the end of the eighteenth the major states of Europe embarked on a variety of programs designed to increase centralized political and economic control. On the political level, this process generally took the form of absolutism, which concentrated power in the hands of monarchs; on the economic level it took the form of mercantilism, which tied merchants and entrepreneurs to state controls.

Each of the major states took a somewhat different path to these ends. What proved workable in the France of Louis XIV required a different approach in England or in the Russia of Peter the Great. But by the mid-eighteenth century, every major power had succeeded in its program of centralization or had paid the price of failure.

This process was not accomplished without difficulty. Merchants generally welcomed the economic initiatives of the state and in some cases actively sought them. The landed aristocracy, fearful of losing its privileges and jealous of its traditional authority, often opposed centralization. Workers demanded wage and price controls, a dependable supply of bread, and restrictions on cheap imported labor. Peasants sought relief from the onerous burdens of taxes and traditional obligations. Thus the state's quest for political unity and economic control raised a host of demands from competing constituencies. It sharpened the differences between the estates and led eventually to the demand for political representation. By the eighteenth century some European rulers frankly regarded themselves as arbiters between the competing interest groups in their countries. But the centralizing states were not always able to control the forces they had unleashed. By the late eighteenth century, absolutism had created the conditions that would lead to its own demise and its replacement by the modern state.

FRANCE UNDER LOUIS XIV

Of all the absolute monarchs, none stamped his age as decisively as Louis XIV (1643–1715) of France. No other western European ruler exerted greater or more uncontested control of a country during the 1,000-year period between the reign of Charlemagne and the French Revolution of 1789. Yet even Louis faced daunting obstacles and resistance in his efforts to bend the people and institutions of France to his will, and even he was forced to acknowledge the limitations of his power.

Provincial Autonomy and Central Control

The France of Louis XIV was a patchwork of widely varying provincial customs and powers. In many re-

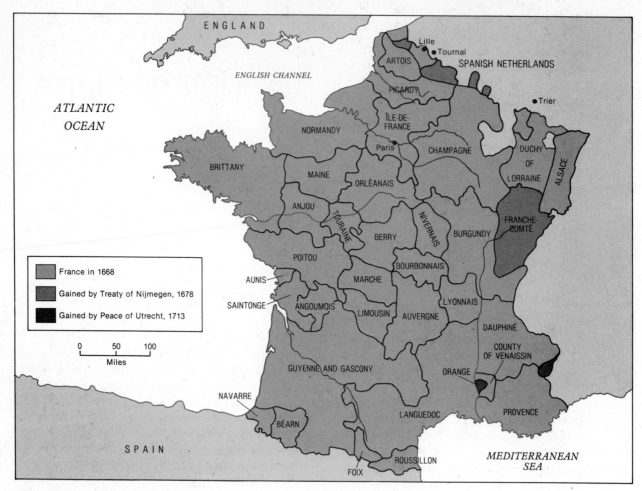

15.1 France Under Louis XIV

spects the crown's relations with the larger and older provinces, called *pays d'état* because they had their own representative assemblies or estates, resembled treaties with quasi-sovereign powers. These provinces set their own tax rates and passed laws independent of the central government. Many of the towns not only enjoyed their own councils and magistrates but also levied their own customs duties and raised their own militias. A good number of them were wholly exempt from the basic property tax of the realm, the *taille*. So were whole classes of the population, notably the clergy and, in at least some of the forms in which it was levied, the nobility. The hated excise tax on salt, the *gabelle*, was applied so unequally that the price of this vital commodity was as much as 25 times higher in one province than in another. The only constant in the system was that it bore most heavily everywhere on the poor, particularly

the peasantry. Thus it combined both the greatest inequity and the greatest inefficiency.

The basis for a policy of effective centralization was clear: standardization of laws and taxes, reduction of internal tariffs, promotion of key industries, and the neutralization of seigneurial courts and provincial legislatures. The foundations for this policy had been laid in the previous two reigns. Henry IV had curbed the power of the provincial estates and established government monopolies over mining and the production of gunpowder and salt. Louis XIII's minister, Cardinal Richelieu, had dispatched special agents, the *intendants,* to oversee provincial administration. Both Henry IV and Louis XIII had studiously ignored the national representative assembly, the Estates General, which met only twice during their combined reigns. The revolt of the Fronde (see Chapter 13), in which the nobility had made its last

The personification of divine right monarchy, a mature Louis XIV is posed in the full pomp and regalia of his office in this portrait by Hyacinthe Rigaud. [Cliché des Musées Nationaux, Paris]

serious attempt to assert power on a national level, had ended in failure.

Divine Right Monarchy

It was Louis XIV, however, who most successfully exploited the powers of personal monarchy to create a centralized state. For Louis, increasing the power of the state was not merely a matter of policy. It was a natural consequence of his authority as a divine right king. Whether or not Louis actually made the famous statement attributed to him, "I am the state," he clearly lived by the thought. Louis identified himself wholly with the French state. Even his private life was lived in public, among a throng of courtiers; for him there was no distinction between the man and the monarch. Fortunately, Louis had the ideal temperament for a king. He was highly conscious of his dignity; it was said that even as a child he seldom laughed. But Louis did not experience the cares of state as a burden. "The calling of a king is great, noble, and delightful," he said. Louis took his pleasures and his responsibilities with the same equa-

nimity. In 54 years of active rule, he never lost his zest for governing.

For Louis the aim of the state was *gloire*—glory. *Gloire* was both an attribute of a person—the dignity of a noble, the majesty of a king—and the collective aspiration of a nation. The glory of France was in its wealth and productivity, the splendor of its arts, and above all its military power. France was already the richest and most powerful state in Europe at the accession of Louis XIV. For Louis that was only the measure of its potential for further achievement and greater *gloire*.

JEAN-BAPTISTE COLBERT, MINISTER OF FINANCE

The king assembled around him a small group of ministers recruited not from the nobility but from the bourgeoisie. Chief among these was Jean-Baptiste Colbert. The son of a wealthy merchant banker, Colbert shared his master's vision of glory. From 1661 until his death in 1683 he was the most important man in the kingdom after Louis himself.

Colbert had entered government service when not yet 20, and his talents and capacity for hard work soon commended him to the secretary of state for war, who made Colbert his private secretary. By 1649, at the age of only 30, Colbert had become himself a councillor of state, and two years later he entered the service of Cardinal Mazarin, who had succeeded Richelieu as the dominant figure in French politics. Mazarin at first treated the upstart young bourgeois with reserve, if not disdain, but he soon found Colbert's services indispensable. In the late 1650s, Colbert was charged with suppressing a major revolt of the nobility, and at Mazarin's death in 1661 he became comptroller-general of finance.

Colbert was the embodiment of the mercantilist state. He took the whole of French economic life for his province, including trade and commerce, the merchant marine and the navy, the colonies, and internal security. His first task was to reform the king's finances. While decreasing the taille, Colbert doubled the tax yield within six years by curbing the abuses of collectors, exploiting the royal demesne more efficiently, and compelling the *pays d'état* to increase their share of taxes. He presided over a council of prominent merchants that charted a *intendents - King appointed to govern provinces.*

course for France's commercial and industrial supremacy. He established hundreds of new workshops and factories under direct royal control or licensed as monopolies. His agents scoured Europe to recruit the most skilled technicians—dyers, glassblowers, gun founders. At home, meanwhile, he tried to organize all French artisans into guilds, subject to minute regulations and supervised by an army of state inspectors.

The purpose of new industry was to provide material for commerce; the purpose of commerce was to amass wealth; and the purpose of wealth was power. Economic activity was thus for Colbert, as for Louis, both a preparation for war and a kind of warfare in itself. "If your Majesty could constrain all your subjects into these four kinds of profession," Colbert wrote the king, "agriculture, trade, war by land or by sea, it would be possible for you to become the master of the world."[1]

Colbert was particularly active on behalf of maritime trade and warfare. He built canals, modernized ports, and chartered trading companies for the West and East Indies. He was the real founder of the French navy, and he searched the prisons and poorhouses of France to man his new ships. In some cases he commuted death sentences to procure sailors, but in many others he arbitrarily lengthened prison terms, compelled judges to sentence convicts to the galleys, and forcibly impressed beggars and vagrants. Such actions showed the darker side of a man obsessed with the goals of power. Assiduous in cultivating his superiors, he seemed a tyrant to many when at last he had no superior but the king. When he died in 1683, his body was buried secretly lest his tomb be desecrated by his enemies. Yet Colbert was France's greatest economic statesman and perhaps its greatest cultural patron as well.

Louis XIV and the Bureaucracy

Ironically, the chief obstacle to the king's dreams appeared to be his own bureaucracy. According to one contemporary estimate, the number of government offices in France had increased by 50,000 during the first half of the seventeenth century. The reason for this explosion of bureaucrats lay in the nature of officeholding itself. Each occupant of a venal office bought and owned it. In return for his investment, he acquired a blue-chip property that yielded a handsome income in fees and whose resale value was very likely to appreciate. There was status value too, since even minor offices often entitled the holder or his heir to ennoblement.

The entire system constituted a form of indirect taxation. Purchasers advanced a lump sum to the crown and recouped their outlay by charging the public for their "services." For the financially pressed monarchy the lure of ready cash was irresistible. Administratively, however, the system was a nightmare. The number of offices created bore no relation to function or need. In return for short-term financial relief, the crown had traded long-term political paralysis.

In contrast to this bloated bureaucracy, Louis XIV gathered around him a tiny nucleus of advisers. Besides Colbert the only important ministers were Lionne for foreign affairs and Le Tellier for war. By streamlining his government at the top, Louis was able to act swiftly and in secret and to keep all major threads of policy in his own hands. If there was chaos at the extremities of the state, the king was determined to counteract it by command at the center.

The key to the royal strategy was the revived use of intendants. At first, as under Richelieu, they were sent out on specific assignments to the provinces. Later, however, they took up permanent residence. Their commissions were all-embracing, and their powers superseded those of all other officials, including the provincial governor. Not since Roman times had central authority exerted such continuous and effective control at the local level.

By such means, Louis was able to cut through his own bureaucracy and impose his will on France. To be sure, he often met stubborn resistance. Local noblemen, jealous of their independence, made common cause with local officials to frustrate his intentions. In the last analysis, however, there could be no disputing the command of a divinely anointed king. He was God's representative on earth, so his will was supreme. Bishop Bossuet (1627–1704), Louis' chief spiritual adviser, went so far as to declare that the king was God himself.

Versailles: The Sun King Enthroned

For the king's power to be felt, it had to be visible. Louis had his architects and decorators turn the royal hunting lodge at Versailles, ten miles from Paris, into the most splendid palace in the Western world. Surrounded by formal gardens and artificial lakes, it stretched in a great semicircle for more than a quarter of a mile. Fountains and statues adorned it on all sides. Inside, a hall of mirrors lit by thousands of candelabras led to the main apartments. Louis himself was portrayed in triumph everywhere, ruling over Europe, Asia, and the Americas in the frescoes that lined the halls of state or garbed as a Roman emperor surrounded by classical gods and goddesses. The king had taken the sun as his personal emblem early in his reign, and every aspect of Versailles, from the smallest decorative details to the long, tree-lined avenues that spread out from the palace like the rays of a great orb, reflected the solar theme. An army of workers and engineers the size of a city—36,000 were counted on the site at one time—toiled to construct this ultimate monument to *gloire,* digging trenches and canals, erecting temples, stocking the game parks, and trimming the gardens to create a perfect world where nature as well as humanity obeyed an absolute ruler.

This artificial paradise enclosed one of the most artificial societies ever created. The most distinguished noblemen of France vied for the honor of living in the cramped and squalid conditions of an overcrowded court. Proximity to the king determined one's status. Personal attendance on him was the most coveted honor of all. Great dukes fought for the right to serve as his footmen, adjusting his livery or holding his candlestick. Louis lived in Versailles not as a man but as an idol, displaying himself to the privileged few who were permitted to worship him in person. In this way he tamed his great nobility. Absorbed in etiquette, obsessed with their own vanity, they neglected the most important aspect of status: power.

As Voltaire remarked, "Louis liked the ladies, and it was reciprocal." The prominence of women in the court life of Versailles reflected the general softening of manners that had come to the French court with its increasing refinement and sophistication of taste. The king himself was finally tamed by a remarkable woman, Madame de Maintenon (1635–1719). Born Françoise d'Aubigné, she was taken to the Caribbean island of Martinique as a child and left penniless at her father's death. She struggled back to France with her mother and married to escape penury. After her husband's death a chance connection brought her the estate of Maintenon and a position at court, where she eventually became the king's confidante. When Queen Marie-Thérèse died in 1683, Louis secretly married the woman who was now called Madame de Maintenon. Although the wedding was never acknowledged, she was the dominant presence at Versailles until his death.

Under Maintenon's influence, the court, still brilliant, took on a more pious and sober tone. Remembering the hardships of her own life, Maintenon had begun to educate poor children as early as 1674, and in 1686 she opened St. Cyr, a school for the daughters of impover-ished nobility, which proved a milestone in the history of women's education. Maintenon was buried in the school's chapel, beside her beloved children. St. Cyr itself was closed during the French Revolution, and in 1794 some workmen, engaged in demolishing the chapel, discovered her grave, pulled out her preserved body, dragged and kicked it about the grounds, and threw it into a pit.

THE WARS OF LOUIS XIV

Louis' first military adventure, an attack on the Spanish territories of Flanders and the Franche-Comté, was a prelude to war with the Dutch. For Louis the Dutch were both commercial rivals and religious heretics. More important, they alone stood between Louis and his long-range goal to dominate the Low Countries and Germany and even—as a book published under royal sponsorship in 1667 declared—to revive the empire of Charlemagne in the West.

Louis struck in the spring of 1672. The French occupied three of the seven Dutch provinces, and Amsterdam was saved only by opening the dikes and flooding the province of Holland. The Dutch offered concessions, but Louis demanded a virtual surrender of sovereignty: major territorial concessions within the seven provinces themselves, French commercial and religious penetration, an indemnity of 24 million livres, and, most insulting of all, an annual embassy to present a medal in tribute to Louis, like a Roman satellite acknowledging its emperor.

These humiliating demands may have been the worst mistake of Louis' career. The Dutch dug in, determined to resist to the end. The republic that had governed the Netherlands since 1650 was overthrown; its leader, Jan de Witt, was torn to pieces by an angry mob, and the 22-year-old Prince William of Orange was summoned as stadholder and captain general of the army. Louis thus raised up his own worst enemy, for the dour but capable William was to be the heart and soul of European resistance to Bourbon France for the next 30 years. The war was soon stalemated, and by 1674 the French had withdrawn from Dutch soil. The Treaty of Nijmegen (1678) not only affirmed Dutch independence but forced the French to lower their own tariffs against Dutch goods. Louis had lost the war.

Aggression Without War: Louis Against Germany

Despite this check, the French had the most powerful army in the world. The Dutch were exhausted, the Spanish in decline, and the Austrians preoccupied by a new Turkish advance along the Danube that brought Ottoman armies to the gates of Vienna in 1683. Only a relief army commanded by the king of Poland, John Sobieski, saved the imperial capital. Louis, meanwhile, annexed large parts of Flanders, Luxembourg, Alsace, and the Saarland after 1680, certifying his legal claim to each territory in special courts set up for that purpose, the Chambers of Reunion. As his courts and armies pushed farther and farther into the heartland of Germany, the princes of the Holy Roman Empire became alarmed. Alarm turned to panic when, in 1685, Louis revoked the Edict of Nantes, which had guaranteed freedom of worship to French Protestants. Under Habsburg leadership the German princes hastily formed a defensive alliance, the League of Augsburg (1686).

The War of Five Continents

[handwritten: English: King William's war"; Continent: of War of Augsburg"]

When Louis climaxed his campaign of aggression by invading the Rhenish Palatinate in September 1688, he began a war that was to outlast all the protagonists but himself. Ranging over five continents and lasting 25 years, it was the first truly global war in history. No war of comparable scale was to be seen again until the twentieth century. For the first time the quarrels of Europe became the affair of the world.

The conflict had two distinct phases. The Nine Years' War (1688–1697) was fought largely along the disputed frontiers of Flanders and Germany, though it reached as far afield as North America. Louis was chiefly opposed by an Anglo-Dutch alliance forged when William of Orange, responding to a secret invitation from a coalition of English lay and religious leaders, sailed to England in November 1688 and deposed James II. William became king of England (as William III), reigning jointly with his wife Mary (1689–1694), James' elder daughter, while continuing to govern the Netherlands. With such a base, William soon brought Spain, Austria, and Savoy to-

The 1683 siege of Vienna, here depicted in a composite view, marked the last great Muslim advance in Europe, although the Turks remained a presence on the continent until the early twentieth century. [Austrian National Library, Vienna, Picture Archives]

Anne male heir:
age 13 - Duke of Gloucester

gether in a grand anti-French alliance. By the end of the war, virtually all of Europe east of the Elbe was ranged against Louis, and a famine at home had claimed 2 million lives, a disaster comparable in its effects on France only to World War I.

The Treaty of Ryswick (1697) compelled Louis to restore almost all the territories he had occupied since 1678 and to acknowledge his archenemy William III as king of England. But a new round of warfare was in the offing, for even higher stakes. For a third of a century the dynastic politics of Europe had swirled about the fate of the Spanish throne, whose occupant was the feeble and childless Charles II. When Charles died at last in 1700, his government was so impoverished that it could not pay for masses for the repose of his soul. Yet Spain still held much of the southern Netherlands and most of Italy, as well as its great empire in the Americas. In the hands of a competent ruler it might still regain its former glory; in the hands of a foreign one it was an incomparable asset.

So thought both Louis XIV and his Habsburg rival, the Austrian emperor Leopold I (1658–1705), both of whom claimed the throne for their own dynastic candidates. Since neither was willing to concede control of the whole Spanish patrimony, they had begun to negotiate for Spain's division as early as 1668. As Charles II's death at last became imminent, they sought to find a compromise candidate for the throne. This failed, however, and when Charles died, he unexpectedly willed his throne and all his dominions to the Bourbon claimant, Philip of Anjou, Louis' grandson, who became Philip V of Spain (1700–1746).

Britain and France: The Contest for Empire

Continent: "War of the Spanish Succession"
England: "Queen Anne's war"

The result was the second phase of the great war of France against Europe, the War of the Spanish Succession (1701–1713). Louis moved quickly to consolidate his hold on Spain and its possessions. It was a foregone conclusion that Austria would resist. England and the Netherlands were even more directly menaced. With the occupation of the Spanish Netherlands the last buffer between French and Dutch territory had been stripped away. The English found their access to the Mediterranean cut off and their empire in the New World threatened.

William III swiftly organized a new Grand Alliance against Louis. It was his last accomplishment. He died in March 1702, to be succeeded in England by James II's younger daughter, Anne (1702–1714). The Anglo-Dutch alliance held, though England was now decidedly the senior partner. The English general John Churchill, duke of Marlborough (1650–1722), repelled French armies in Germany and Flanders, while Prince Eugene of Savoy (1663–1736) drove them out of Italy and the Anglo-Dutch fleet kept France at bay in the New World and Africa. By 1709, Louis' position was desperate. Allied armies were poised on the borders of France itself, the treasury was empty, and famine ravaged the land. A bitter parody of the Lord's Prayer circulated at court: "Our father who art at Versailles, whose name is no longer hallowed, whose kingdom is no longer large, give us our daily bread. . . ."

Louis held out, stiffened by demands not only that he surrender all the conquests of his reign but that he help drive his grandson from the Spanish throne as well. At Malplaquet, the bloodiest battle on European soil up to that time, he blunted the allied advance. Thereafter, the Grand Alliance dissolved, and the war wound down. The cluster of treaties known as the Peace of Utrecht (1713) left Spain and its overseas dominions to Philip V, though on condition that his throne never be united with that of France. Spain's possessions in the Netherlands and Italy were given to Austria, partly to compensate it for the lost Spanish throne and partly as a buffer against French expansion. England's prizes reflected its preoccupation with empire. Gibraltar and Minorca gave it control of the Mediterranean, Nova Scotia and Newfoundland entrenched it on the North American coast, and trading concessions offered a foothold in the lucrative slave trade of Spanish America.

Asiento - Monopoly of the Atlantic slave Trade - 30 years - 4,800 per year

The wars of 1688–1713 were fought to contain the territorial ambitions of the French in Europe. In retrospect, however, they marked the first stage in the great contest of empire between England and France that, resumed in the war cycles of 1740–1763 and 1792–1815, would end only with Wellington's defeat of Napoleon at the Battle of Waterloo. They also marked the final eclipse of Spain as a great power. The Austrians gained the most territory in Europe itself, but their greatly distended borders were to prove more of a burden than an asset in the long run.

Louis XIV and the Climax of Absolutism

Despite its defeat, France was still the greatest power on the European continent. When Louis XIV died on Sep-

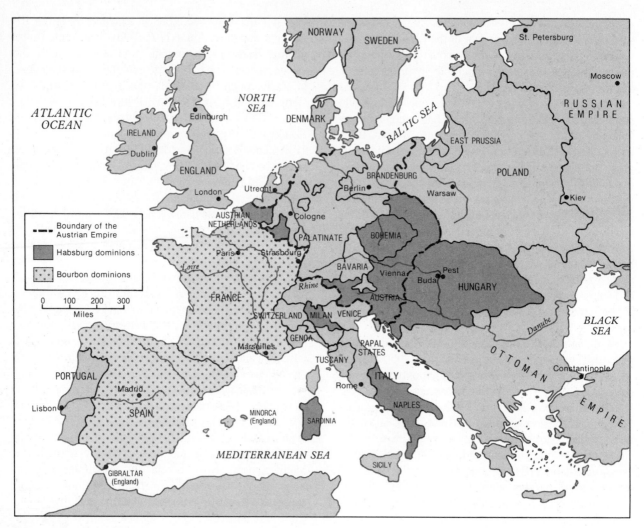

15.2 Europe in 1714

tember 1, 1715, he had reigned longer than anyone else in the history of the world and had dominated his time more completely than anyone since Charlemagne. If he had failed ultimately to impose his will on Europe, it had taken the united strength of his adversaries to contain him. Yet if he showed what could be accomplished by a determined royal absolutism, he showed the limitation of such a system as well. It was left to his archrivals, the English, to develop on a large scale what the Dutch polity had already suggested: that a politically stable oligarchy with a moderate representative base could be a far more effective instrument of government than an absolute monarchy dependent on the will and energy of a single man.

PETER THE GREAT AND THE EMERGENCE OF RUSSIA

As forceful as Louis XIV and far more despotic, Peter I (1682–1725), called "the Great," consolidated autocracy in Russia and brought his country into the European state system. From its modest beginnings in the fourteenth-century duchy of Muscovy, Russia had become the largest state in the world by Peter's time. Three times the size of Europe, it spanned the Eurasian landmass from the Polish steppe to the Pacific Ocean, embracing some 5.7 million square miles.

15.3 Russia in the Age of Peter the Great, 1689–1725

The Tsarist State

This vast land had a population of only 14 million, giving it only one-fortieth the density of France or Italy. Grain yields were comparable only to those of pre-Carolingian agriculture in the West, compelling almost the entire population to farm; only 2 percent lived in towns. The tsarist state and its nobility had undertaken to control this scarce labor supply since the late fifteenth century by enserfing the peasantry. The *Ulozhenie* (law code) of 1649, which served as the basis of Russian society for the next 200 years, formalized its rigid, castelike divisions. Each person's status was fixed by law down to the last detail. Townsmen as well as peasants were bound to their dwellings and occupations. The nobility had become a civil service class, since only people who performed state service were permitted to own land. Few societies have ever been more tightly controlled.

Peter became a dentist to improve the look of the people

Peter and the West

This was the throne that passed to Peter the Great. Nearly 7 feet tall and with strength and appetites to match, he was no less ambitious than the ruler of Versailles but far less prudent. All but one of his 36 years of active rule were spent at war. Military expenditures consumed more than 80 percent of his revenue. Even church bells were melted down into cannon. The Russian state was turned into a gigantic battering ram, and it was aimed west.

At the same time, Peter was deeply impressed by the advanced technology of the West. He studied tactics and fortifications and built a standing army of 300,000 men, conscripted for life. In 1697–1698 he became the first Russian prince to visit the West, where he and his entourage made a sensation. A bemused William III was his host in Holland and England, where he ignored protocol by touring and even working in foundries and dockyards. The ruler of the world's largest landmass was fascinated by the sea and proudly flourished a certificate declaring him a master shipwright. William invited him to attend a session of England's Parliament. Peter was impressed by the sight of subjects speaking openly to their sovereign, but constitutional monarchy was not one of the Western innovations he brought home.

Peter built a new capital in the north, St. Petersburg, whose royal residence, the Winter Palace, rivaled Versailles in its splendor. From here he waged war on Sweden for control of the Baltic, a struggle known as the Great Northern War (1700–1721). Sweden's warlike king Charles XII (1697–1718), not yet out of his teens, humiliated Peter at Narva (1700), crushing an army five times the size of his own. Peter persisted, however, and slowly won back the ground he had lost. Not content with fighting a major war, he was simultaneously building his new capital and attempting to join the two major rivers of his country, the Don and the Volga, by canal.

Peter turned back a new invasion by Charles at Poltava (1709) and overran the Baltic littoral, seizing the coveted ports of Revel and Riga. His gains were confirmed by the Treaty of Nystad (1721), which established Russia as the major power in northern Europe. Peter celebrated by assuming the titles of father of his country and emperor and accepted formally the appellation of "the Great." "By our deeds in war," he exulted, "we have emerged from darkness into the light of the world."

The Reforms of Peter

Peter reorganized his government on the latest Western models. He replaced the old boyar *duma* (council of nobles) with a nine-member senate, in effect a supreme council of state, and reduced the 40-odd ministries to 12, each headed by a "college" of senior officials reporting to the senate. The countryside was also divided into new provinces and districts. The purpose of the whole, as Peter straightforwardly told the senate, was "to collect money, as much as possible." In this it was successful; tax revenues tripled over the course of the reign.

Foreigners were at first brought in to staff and coordinate the new system. But Peter had always intended that his boyars be bound, as before, to state service. To make them learn Western ways, he compelled them to adopt Western food and dress and to shave their beards, personally shearing off any he saw in his presence. He capped his reforms in 1722 with the Table of Ranks, which created a new hierarchy of 14 military and civil service grades. It permitted commoners as well as nobles to enter state service, ennobling them upon either receiving an officer's commission or attaining the civilian rank of collegiate assessor. In this way, Peter broadened the base of the landowning class and gave room to talent from below, though the most privileged positions were still reserved for the old nobility. This system remained essentially intact down to 1917.

The church was also thoroughly restructured. The office of patriarch, assumed by the metropolitan of Moscow in 1589, had at times rivaled the power of the tsar. In 1700, Peter permitted it to lapse, and in 1721 he replaced it with the Holy Synod, a body closely tied to the state. Tireless in his efforts to modernize Russia, he reformed the calendar and redesigned the alphabet, ordered translations of the Greek and Roman classics, and hired a German troupe to perform French comedies in the Kremlin Square. In 1703 he introduced the first newspaper into Russia, which he edited himself. He built the first Russian greenhouses and laboratories and in 1724 established the Russian Academy of Sciences, though its first members were all Germans.

Peter died in February 1725, leaving an unsettled succession and an exhausted realm. In many ways his life had been a struggle to tame himself as well as Russia. The young tsar who loved to trick his courtiers by signing decrees with pseudonyms became the statesman who introduced orderly, bureaucratic government into his realm. The man who corresponded on politics with the great philosopher Leibniz had ungovernable fits of rage, beat his ministers, and put his son Alexis to death. As a foreign visitor observed, "He is a prince at once very good and very bad; his character is exactly that of his country." In his passionate contradictions,

Peter mirrored the conflicts of a Russia torn between the isolation of its past and the world presence of its future.

AUSTRIA: THE DYNASTIC STATE

After the division of the Habsburg crown in 1555 between its Spanish and Austrian branches, the Austrian monarchy consisted of three major units: the hereditary provinces of Austria itself; the so-called crown of St. Wenceslas, comprising Bohemia, Moravia, and Silesia; and the crown of St. Stephen, including Hungary, Transylvania, and Croatia. Only the persistent threat of the Ottoman Turks could have united so disparate a group of peoples—Germans, Czechs, Magyars, Croats, Slovaks, Slovenes, Italians, Romanians, Ruthenians—under a single head.

Austria in the seventeenth century might thus be described as a power but not a state. The imperial title was recognized only in the Austrian provinces proper; the Habsburg emperor was separately king of Bohemia and Hungary. The chief unifying factor in this strange polity, whose ruler lacked a single title and whose lands lacked a common name, was the person of the monarch himself. His government was actually a series of ongoing negotiations with the provinces of his realm, whose noble estates possessed extensive powers, including the right to veto imperial taxes and, in Hungary, even to rebel.

After the failure of Ferdinand II's attempt to reassert his power as Holy Roman Emperor in the Thirty Years' War, his successors, Ferdinand III (1637–1657) and Leopold I, concentrated on achieving internal consolidation. The Counter-Reformation in Austria was, in its political dimension, a struggle against the Protestant nobility that was dominant in Bohemia and Hungary. Bohemian Protestantism had been ruthlessly suppressed after 1620, and the native nobility was replaced by Catholic loyalists. A similar policy was applied in Hungary after 1671 following an abortive rebellion. Thus for the Habsburgs the effort to impose religious uniformity went hand in hand with the effort to assert centralized control. Such persecution fell most heavily on the Jews, who were expelled from all of Lower Austria by Leopold I despite the fact that his principal financier, Samuel Oppenheimer, was and remained a Jew.

Religious orthodoxy was linked to what the Habs-burgs saw as their special mission: the defense of Christian Europe against the Turkish menace. After a period of quiescence the Turks crossed the Danube in 1683 with an army of 200,000 men. Its repulse at the gates of Vienna by the international army led by John III Sobieski of Poland (1673–1696) was a historic moment, for it marked the last great thrust of Muslim power that had threatened Europe for nearly 1,000 years. In the war that ensued, climaxed by Prince Eugene of Savoy's great victory at Zenta (1697), the Turks were driven permanently from the Danube basin and back upon the Balkans. They might have been expelled completely from Europe had France heeded the appeal of Pope Innocent XI to join the Habsburg alliance. But the rivalry between the Bourbon and Habsburg dynasties prevented any such union, leaving a Turkish presence on the continent for more than two centuries.

The Treaty of Karlowitz (1699) gave the Habsburgs possession of virtually all of Hungary, Transylvania, and Croatia. Hungary's crown of St. Stephen was declared hereditary in the Habsburg family (1687). The Magyar nobility was not purged, as in Bohemia, and was permitted to retain its provincial assemblies and national diet. But its power was curbed, and non-Magyar nobles were settled in the new lands, as well as German and Slavic peasants. The result was a Maygar rising under Prince Ferenc Rákóczy, which lasted from 1703 to 1711. The defiant Magyars, with their proud sense of isolation among the surrounding Slavic populations, remained the most refractory of the Habsburg empire's many peoples.

Despite its unwieldiness, however, the Habsburg monarchy continued to expand. Its victories against the Turks had doubled its effective size during the reign of Leopold I. The Treaty of Rastadt (1714) brought it the Spanish Netherlands and most of Italy. Another brief war with Turkey (1716–1718) pushed its borders into the Balkans. A swollen empire now stretched from the Carpathian Mountains to the North Sea. The Habsburgs had multiplied their subject populations but had devised no strategy for integrating them.

PRUSSIA: THE GARRISON STATE

A very different course was pursued by Prussia, which emerged from the rubble of post-Westphalian Germany to become a major European power and the ultimate

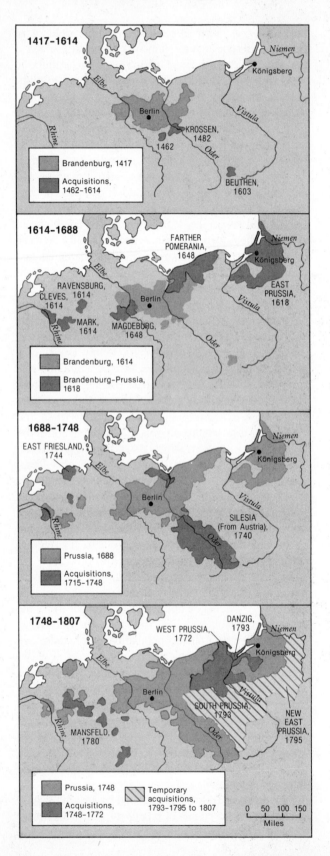

unifier of Germany as a whole. Prussia had its origin in the electoral mark of Brandenburg, a flat, sandy terrain south of the Baltic coast that passed in 1417 to the princely house of Hohenzollern. In 1618 the elector of Brandenburg acquired the duchy of Prussia, then a fief of Poland, giving the dynasty its first access to the sea. At about the same time (1614) he fell heir to Cleves, a small duchy on the Rhine. These three entities were widely separated on the map. Their populations, half German and half Pole, half Lutheran and half Catholic, half serf and half free, had nothing in common but their ruler. During the Thirty Years' War, all three territories were overrun by foreign armies, and many towns were destroyed completely.

Under these circumstances the 20-year-old Frederick William (1640–1688), later known to history as the Great Elector, succeeded to the Hohenzollern legacy. Though he lacked a royal title, he considered himself as much a divine right ruler as Louis XIV. Frederick William found the key to state-building in the maintenance of a standing army, which made him a force in northern Germany. The army was both his excuse for raising taxes and his means of compelling payment. His soldiers collected taxes directly and exercised police powers as well. Thus, from the first, the Great Elector broke down the distinction between civilian and military functions. Like Peter the Great, he required the service of the nobility, particularly in the army, thereby integrating them into his absolutist state.

The elector Frederick III (1688–1713) was recognized as King Frederick I of Prussia in 1701 in return for his participation in the War of the Spanish Succession against Louis XIV, though Prussia contributed little. The task of state-building was resumed by his eccentric but capable successor, Frederick William I (1713–1740). The Great Elector had seen the army as an instrument of state power; under his grandson and namesake, the army to all intents and purposes became the state. With the establishment in 1723 of the General Directory, which combined the functions of the war and finance councils, the entire governing apparatus down to the lowliest tax collector or quartermaster in the provinces revolved around the army's needs. In addition to the regular career army, every Prussian male was subject to three months of military service a year. Thus Frederick William was able to maintain a standing army of 80,000

15.4 The Rise of Brandenburg-Prussia, 1417– 1807

men on a population base of only 1.5 million. Not since ancient Sparta had a society lived so completely by the military ideal.

Under Frederick II (1740–1786), called "the Great," Prussia reached the status of a great power. Frederick was the most impressive monarch of the eighteenth century. He was a son of the Enlightenment who flirted with atheism and entertained the philosopher Voltaire, and a soldier-king whose armies, like those of Louis XIV, held off half of Europe during the Seven Years' War. In his social policies, however, he adhered closely to the practice of his father. Each class was assigned its duties from above. The higher ranks in the army and the state bureaucracy were reserved for the nobility. Merchants and townsfolk were obliged to accept a subordinate position. Frederick had kind words for the peasantry, which, he declared, deserved the greatest respect because it carried the heaviest burdens. He did little to relieve those burdens, however, even in East Prussia, where peasants were enserfed and in many respects little better than enslaved by the local nobility, known as Junkers.

ENGLAND: THE TRIUMPH OF PARLIAMENTARY GOVERNMENT

Far different from the autocracies of eastern Europe was England. The Stuart monarchy has been restored in 1660 under a formula that defined the government as consisting of king, lords, and commons. But it was not clear where the balance of authority lay among these three elements. A newly constituted Convention Parliament, composed chiefly of nobles and other great landowners, compelled the king, Charles II (1660–1685), to accept its terms. The crown could no longer create special courts outside the jurisdiction of the common law, nor could it collect taxes not authorized by Parliament. Charles agreed to exchange his traditional feudal revenues for a permanent grant of customs and excise taxes, thus freeing the magnates from all restrictions on the ownership of their estates and shifting the tax burden from the landed classes toward the towns.

Charles was not even able to reward those who had supported him. Royalists whose estates had been confiscated during the revolution were permitted to sue for their recovery, but those who had sold them, even under duress, received no compensation. This too confirmed the rebel gentry in their gains and accelerated the tendency toward concentration of land ownership. Charles' promise of religious toleration was swept away by his first elected parliament. This "Cavalier" Parliament, as it was nicknamed for its initially reactionary tone, restored the supremacy of the Anglican church and placed severe restrictions on all other forms of worship. Some 1,200 ministers were ejected from their parishes for refusing to accept a revised prayer book and to take an oath of conformity, creating a schism within English Protestantism that persists today.

Charles' most persistent problem was money. The grant of taxes he had received in 1660 proved insufficient, leaving him financially and therefore politically dependent on Parliament. The king sought to escape this dependence by obtaining a French subsidy in return for supporting Louis XIV's war against the Netherlands and by agreeing secretly to reimpose Catholicism on the country (Treaty of Dover, 1670). The rumor of this agreement poisoned the remainder of his reign. After three successive parliaments attempted to ram through an act excluding Charles' Catholic brother and heir, James, from the throne, the country seemed again on the verge of civil war. But the opposition party, called the Whigs, was divided in its aims, some members favoring alternative candidates to the throne and some the establishment of a republic. The king was able to rally his own supporters, the Tories, behind the principles of direct hereditary succession and divine right. The leading Whigs were banished or executed, and, on his deathbed, Charles was finally received into the Catholic church.

The Glorious Revolution and the Revolutionary Settlement

James II (1685–1688) succeeded to the throne peacefully. He promised to preserve the constitution and the supremacy of the Church of England. He was already 51 and without a male heir. The country hoped that his brief Catholic reign would pass without serious incident. But James soon revealed his true intentions. He placed Catholics in key civil and military positions. This violated a parliamentary statute, but James claimed that he was not bound by the acts of a previous reign. When he announced the birth of a son and heir in June 1688, thus opening the possibility of a Catholic dynasty, Whigs and Tories called on William of Orange to free the country.

Landing on the coast of Devon in the southwest on November 5, William was hailed as a liberator. Most of James' army deserted him, and James was forced to flee into exile.

William summoned a parliament, which declared him jointly sovereign with his wife, Mary, James' eldest daughter. Over the next dozen years they built a new constitutional order that, much modified by time and circumstance, has remained both the basis of English government itself and the primary model of representative government the world over. The Bill of Rights (1689) declared the supremacy of all law passed by Parliament. Henceforth, no king could levy taxes, maintain an army, or create new organs of government without Parliament's consent. No English subject could be arrested without legal warrant, detained by excessive bail, or subjected to "cruel and unusual punishments"—a formula that was incorporated directly into the U.S. Bill of Rights a century later. Though they lacked the phrase for it, the framers of this new order—which came to be known as the Revolutionary Settlement—worked to contain executive authority by a separation of powers.

The new system worked awkwardly at first. With the threat of James removed, Whigs and Tories fell out with each other over the spoils of power. There were genuine differences between them as well, however. Though both derived from the landed gentry, the Whigs tended to embrace the great London merchants who believed in commercial and colonial expansion and eagerly supported parliamentary supremacy. The Tories, by contrast, were reluctant revolutionaries, rural and isolationist, who regarded 1688 as a tragic necessity rather than a brilliant opportunity. William naturally tended to rely on the Whigs, and with their support he chartered the Bank of England (1694) to help finance his war against Louis XIV. By borrowing rather than taxing, William was able to tap an almost limitless source of funds. Thus was born the idea of a permanent national debt and with it the power of modern government.

By 1713 the public debt stood at £54 million, nearly 100 times more than in 1688. This was the money that defeated Louis XIV. Some feared that without the need to rely on Parliament for taxation the monarchy would soon become independent of any control. But the Whig magnates who funded William through the bank were the same men who supported him in Parliament. The struggle between crown and Parliament had ended in the discovery of common interests: war, empire, and profit.

The only thing that threatened this new partnership was the fragility of the Stuart line in England, represented by Queen Mary. At William III's death he was succeeded by Mary's sister Anne (1702–1714), none of whose 16 children had survived. Parliament settled the succession on the electoral house of Hanover in Germany, distantly related to the Stuarts through the daughter of James I. At the same time it declared that no Catholic could ever sit on the throne of England, thus barring James II and his son, James Edward. As a further precaution, the Whigs united Scotland with England in 1707, thereby creating the modern Great Britain. When Anne died, some Tory leaders, unwilling to relinquish divine right, rashly backed an invasion attempt by James Edward. The Whigs, who staunchly supported the new dynasty, were more firmly entrenched than ever and remained the dominant political force in the country until 1760.

LATE STUART AND HANOVERIAN LONDON

If Paris was the cultural capital of Europe and Amsterdam was its financial center, London's time was fast approaching in the late seventeenth century. With a population of 500,000 to 600,000 by 1700, it was one of the largest cities in the world. Whereas only one of every 40 or 50 Frenchmen was a Parisian, one of every ten Englishmen lived in London, fully half the urban population of the country.

The magnet of London was trade. People engaged in commerce and manufacturing averaged four times the income of those who farmed. The wealth and produce of the entire country flowed daily into the city; London "sucks the vitals of trade in this island to itself," wrote Daniel Defoe. Daily, 3,500 boats and barges plied London's river, the Thames, and by 1700, fully 77 percent of England's foreign trade and nearly 60 percent of its shipping passed through the city.

By the late seventeenth century a lively business culture had grown up around a new London institution, the coffeehouse. Over 500 of them flourished in the reign of Queen Anne. Merchants wrote maritime insurance at Lloyd's, and brokers traded stocks and securities at Jonathan's and Garraway's in Exchange Alley. (A formal stock exchange was finally licensed by the government in 1697; the first crash followed in 1720.) Noblemen and men of fashion, artists and scholars had their favorite houses too. Here men exchanged news and gossip; read the daily newspapers, which, beginning with *The Daily Courant,* had reached a circulation of 67,000 by 1714; and

Gin Lane, **William Hogarth's devastating portrayal of the poverty and degradation that lay at the heart of Britain's imperial capital and their fatal consequences. A besotted, pox-ridden mother is oblivious as her infant falls over a wooden rail; an emaciated drunk is on the brink of death by starvation, while another hangs himself in an exposed tenement; the very walls of the city begin to topple as an indifferent magistrate stands by. *Gin Lane* was one of the earliest examples of the power of social propaganda; a year after it was published, the consumption of cheap gin was sharply curtailed by law. Little was done, however, about the underlying squalor and despair of which gin drinking was only a symptom. [The Metropolitan Museum of Art, Harris Brisbane Dick Fund, 1932 (32.35 (124)]**

avidly consumed political pamphlets and the popular periodicals, *The Tatler* and *The Spectator.* But the new climate of business so evident after 1688 predominated. As Defoe, who was himself the editor of an influential journal, *The Review,* put it simply, "the main affair of life" appeared to be "getting money."

The face of London also changed in this period. The Great Fire of September 1666 burned down 13,000 of the city's old timbered houses. Most were rebuilt with brick and mortar, many in the classical style popularized by Sir Christopher Wren (1632–1723), England's greatest architect. The new West End suburbs of Bloomsbury, Piccadilly, and St. James' were marked by splendid squares and esplanades down which the rich and fashionable paraded. But the vast majority of the population lived quite differently, in one-room tenement apartments without water or sanitation on streets so crowded and obstructed by carts, overhangs, basements, and open sewers that movement was next to impossible. The working poor of the city—porters, coal heavers, dockworkers, scavengers, domestics—lived hand to mouth in squalor and filth. An underworld of thieves and cutthroats preyed on this population, their activities all but uncontrolled in a world where life was cheap, riot common, and policing virtually nonexistent. The introduction of cheap gin in the second quarter of the eighteenth century sent the death rate soaring, particularly among the destitute. The London magistrate and reformer Henry Fielding observed that gin was "the principal sustenance . . . of more than a hundred thousand people in this metropolis." A person who was too poor to eat could get drunk for a penny. Even after an act of Parliament regulated the consumption of gin, 1,000 people a year starved to death in the richest city of the world.

SUMMARY

The state system of Europe in the second half of the seventeenth century and the first half of the eighteenth was characterized by the tension between monarchies that attempted to extend and centralize their authority, often by appeal to divine right, and landed aristocracies that generally resisted them, seeking to reassert traditional privileges. In most cases the monarchies prevailed to a greater or lesser extent. In France, the leading power on the Continent throughout the period, this process was clearly visible in the policies of Louis XIV, who placed men of bourgeois origin in the most important offices of state and kept his nobility in opulent idleness at Versailles. In England, by contrast, the landed and mercantile elites united to create through revolution a uniquely successful partnership between limited monarchy and a broad governing class. In Russia the absence of constitutional tradition enabled Peter the Great to subordinate his nobility and to replace Sweden as the major power in the north, while the retreat of Turkish power left Habsburg Austria, despite its diffuse political structure, dominant in southeastern Europe. The most extraordinary example of state-building was in Prussia, where a series of able and determined rulers welded a scattered and unpromising patrimony into a formidable military machine. These new patterns of power produced a Europe that was more politically complex, competitive, and interdependent than ever before.

Notes

1. G. Treasure, *Seventeenth Century France* (New York: Barnes & Noble, 1966), p. 334.

Suggestions for Further Reading

Anderson, P. *Lineages of the Absolutist State*. London: N.L.B., 1974.

Baxter, S. B. *William III and the Defense of European Liberty, 1650–1702*. New York: Harcourt, Brace & World, 1966.

Blum, J. *Lord and Peasant in Russia from the Ninth to the Nineteenth Century*. Princeton, N.J.: Princeton University Press, 1961.

Carsten, F. L. *The Origins of Prussia*. Westport, CT: Greenwood Press, 1981.

Clark, G. N. *The Later Stuarts, 1660–1714*. 2d ed. Oxford: Clarendon Press, 1958.

Evans, R. J. W. *The Making of the Habsburg Monarchy, 1550–1700*. New York: Oxford University Press, 1979.

Goubert, P. *Louis XIV and Twenty Million Frenchmen*. New York: Pantheon, 1972.

Hatton, R. M., ed. *Louis XIV and Absolutism*. Columbus: Ohio State University Press, 1977.

Kenyon, J. P. *Revolution Principles: The Politics of Party, 1689–1720*. Cambridge: Cambridge University Press, 1977.

Massie, R. K. *Peter the Great*. New York: Knopf, 1980.

Plumb, J. H. *The Growth of Political Stability in England, 1675–1725*. London: Macmillan, 1967.

Rosenberg, H. *Bureaucracy, Aristocracy, and Autocracy: The Prussian Experience, 1660–1815*. Boston: Harvard University Press, 1958.

Rudé, G. *Paris and London in the Eighteenth Century*. New York: Viking Press, 1971.

Sumner, B. H. *Peter the Great and the Emergence of Russia*. New York: Macmillan, 1951.

Wolf, J. B. *Louis XIV*. New York: Norton, 1968.

16

EUROPE'S CENTURY
OF GENIUS

Science is the systematic attempt to understand the physical world and to adapt it to human uses. As such, it is as old as culture itself. The establishment of the first major civilizations was concurrent with the Neolithic revolution that occurred about 8000 B.C. The advances made in China between the third and thirteenth centuries A.D. may be considered a second scientific revolution. But the development of modern science that began in Europe in the sixteenth and seventeenth centuries has transformed not only our relation to the environment but the environment itself. It thus stands as one of the most momentous changes in human history.

FROM ANCIENT SCIENCE TO THE COPERNICAN REVOLUTION

Classical and Oriental antiquity had bequeathed a rich scientific heritage to Western civilization. Mathematics, astronomy, biology, and medicine were all highly developed. Much about the physical world was accurately known, and many modern theories had their origin in Greek science. Pythagoras had deduced that the earth was a sphere in the sixth century B.C., and Anaximander offered the first theory of the earth's evolution. A century later, Leucippus and Democritus put forward the first atomic theory of matter. These theories were not univer-

sally accepted, however; Aristotle supported the rival theory of Empedocles that matter consisted not of complex structures of atoms but of compounds of the four primary elements of earth, air, fire, and water. Similarly, the third-century B.C. speculation of the astronomer Aristarchus that the sun rather than the earth was the center of the universe was rejected in favor of the geocentric view that was sponsored by Aristotle and given its classical expression in the work of Ptolemy of Alexandria (second century A.D.).

The Romans made little contribution to scientific theory, although their technological achievements—dams, irrigation, road building, engineering, plumbing, and heating—were unequaled in the West until the Renaissance. After the fall of Rome the legacy of Greek science was developed in the Islamic world. Arabic science improved on Greek measurements and astronomical calculations and built the world's first observatories in the ninth century. It culminated in the career of Ibn Sina, or Avicenna (c. 980–1037), whose breadth of interest and learning in philosophy, medicine, natural history, physics, chemistry, astronomy, mathematics, and music rivaled that of Aristotle. (See Chapter 3.)

The Medieval World Picture

By the thirteenth century, western Europe had begun to recover the classic texts of ancient science. Reassimilating the pagan heritage meant reconciling it with Christian doctrine. Fortunately, Ptolemy's geocentric model of the universe proved readily compatible with Christian notions about humanity's central position in the divine order. The cosmos was held to consist of an arrangement of ten concentric spheres rotating around a fixed, motionless earth and carrying the sun, the moon, the five known planets, and the stars. Beyond the tenth sphere, whose distance from the earth was estimated by Campanus of Novara (c. 1205–1296) to be 73 million miles, was the throne of God, surrounded by his angels and the souls of the righteous. In keeping with the perfection of the heavens, the celestial bodies were composed of a pure, unchangeable substance, the *quintessence.*

This view of the heavens was deeply satisfying. It combined a credible explanation of the natural world with a religious view of the cosmos as the theater of human redemption. It was true that certain details refused to fit in. Some physical bodies, such as projectiles, failed to behave as the Aristotelian theory of motion said they should. Some of the planets and fixed stars appeared to be wayward in their orbits. But these problems did not seem to be enough to shake an edifice built up over the centuries, hallowed by tradition, and deeply entwined with the belief and value systems of Christianity.

New currents were running beneath this placid surface, however. The fourteenth and fifteenth centuries saw serious challenges to the authority of the church. The views of such figures as the French philosopher and bishop Nicholas of Oresme (c. 1323–1382) and the German theologian Nicholas of Cusa (1401–1464) contradicted official doctrine on such questions as the rotation of the earth and the possibility of bodies beyond the fixed stars, undermining belief in the congruity between faith and reason. With the Reformation there was no longer a single authority to interpret Christian doctrine. By the early seventeenth century the Jesuit cardinal Robert Bellarmine (1542–1621) felt obliged to concede that in cases in which reason and the Bible differed about the natural world, reason must be accepted. For the first time in 1500 years, faith was no longer the final arbiter of knowledge.

The Hermetic Challenge

At the same time the authority of Aristotle was being questioned as well. The Greek scholars who fled after the fall of Byzantium in 1453 brought with them texts not previously known in the West. Prominent among these were the writings of Hermes Trismegistus ("thrice-great"), reputedly a contemporary of Moses but in fact a fiction of third-century A.D. Neoplatonists whose texts were circulated in his name. The so-called Hermetic doctrine viewed the material world as an emanation of divine spirit. Humans, the highest compound of matter and spirit, were destined to command the forces of the natural world by learning to read the book of nature and to decipher its hidden codes.

The Hermetic doctrine greatly stimulated interest in astronomy, since celestial bodies were believed to be the agency by which the divine spirit was transmitted. The sun, as the most important of these, was held to be at the center of the universe rather than the earth. Hermeticism thus revived the heliocentric theory of Aristarchus, although on a mystical rather than a mathematical or mechanical basis. But mathematics was crucially important for the Hermeticists too. They believed that the universe was ultimately constructed in terms of mathematical proportions and harmonies that expressed the Divine Mind. Mathematics was therefore the key to understanding both the physical world and the God who manifested himself in it.

The Neoplatonic revival was only one element that contributed to the crisis of knowledge and belief in the sixteenth century. The Reformation had deeply unsettled people's assurance about the nature of grace and salvation and undermined their faith in the authorities who had interpreted spiritual knowledge. The discovery of the New World shattered their faith in the adequacy of their knowledge of the physical world as well. The scientific revolution was a product of this upheaval and shared in its difficult birth the tensions and contradictions of the age.

THE NEW ORDER OF KNOWLEDGE

The most important convert to the Hermetic doctrine was the Polish astronomer and mathematician Nicholas Copernicus (1473–1543). Born in Toruń on the Polish-German frontier, he imbibed Hermeticism in the course of a ten-year sojourn in Italy. Copernicus was convinced that the majesty of the cosmos demanded that the sun be at its center rather than the earth.

Copernicus devoted the rest of his life to proving not only that the heliocentric theory of the Hermeticists was preferable to the geocentric theory of Ptolemy on aes-

Nicholas Copernicus as a young man. Although Copernicus enjoyed a church living and the encouragement of the pope in his research, he did not publish his findings until he lay on his deathbed. The result overthrew 1500 years of scientific orthodoxy and led to a crisis not only of knowledge but also of faith. [Erich Lessing/Art Resource, New York]

thetic and religious grounds but also that it offered a better account where Ptolemy's theory was weakest, in explaining celestial motion. This claim was reflected in the title of his treatise, *On the Revolution of the Heavenly Spheres,* whose publication he authorized only on his deathbed in 1543. Copernicus assumed that only the earth and the five planets actually moved. The sun was motionless at the center of the universe as the fixed stars were at the periphery, their apparent motion being accounted for by the rotation of the earth. This was a great theoretical simplification, although the mathematics necessary to calculate the actual position of the stars relative to a moving earth were highly complex.

The Copernican theory offered a credible but not compelling alternative to the Ptolemaic system. Martin Luther's reaction was typical. "That is how things go nowadays," the great German reformer said. "Anyone who wants to be clever must not be satisfied with what others do. He must produce his own theory as this man does, who wishes to turn the whole of astronomy upside down."[1] No other astronomer accepted Copernicus, and his theory was kept alive only in Hermetic circles. One such convert, the Italian philosopher Giordano Bruno (1548–1600), argued that the sun around which the earth revolved was only one of innumerable suns in an infinite universe, each of which might harbor planets and species like our own. Bruno fell into the hands of the Inquisition and, refusing to recant his beliefs, was burned at the stake.

But the Copernican theory did not die. The appearance of a bright new star in the sky in the 1570s, followed by a brilliant comet, reminded people that there were phenomena not explained by Ptolemy's static system. The German astronomer Johannes Kepler (1571–1630), who had come to Copernicus through his own Hermetic beliefs, made the crucial discovery that the orbits of the planets were not circular, as both Ptolemy and Copernicus had assumed, but elliptical. This enabled him to simplify Copernicus' calculations, giving his theory a decisive advantage over Ptolemy's for the first time. But the man whose work fatally undermined the Ptolemaic theory was the Italian Galileo Galilei.

Galileo and the Copernican Triumph

Galileo (1564–1642) was a native of Pisa. After completing studies in mathematics and natural philosophy, he joined the faculty of the University of Padua, where Copernicus had studied a century before. Galileo was the first important figure to accept Copernicus outside the Hermetic circle. His own inspiration was the ancient Greek mathematician Archimedes (287–212 B.C.), whose works had been republished in 1543. Archimedes, like Pythagoras, had attempted to describe the world in purely mathematical terms. Unlike Pythagoras, however, he attributed no mystical significance to the mathematical proportions he found in nature, and unlike the Neoplatonists, he posited no spiritual basis in matter. For Archimedes and for his latter-day disciple Galileo, the world was best thought of as a gigantic machine operating by simple principles expressible in geometric ratios.

In such a world there was no room either for Aristotle's mythical quintessence or for the medieval angels who were thought to move the stars. Galileo's own most important work was his discovery of the principle of accelerated motion, in which he brilliantly connected velocity and distance to the variable of time. But he caused a sensation when, in 1609, he turned a newly invented instrument, the telescope, on the heavens. Galileo discovered four moons in orbit around the planet Jupiter and so many hundreds of previously undetected stars that he declared them to be innumerable. This seemed to suggest a startling confirmation of Bruno's belief in an infinite universe. Galileo also demonstrated that the surface of the moon was rough and eroded, thereby demolishing the theory of a perfect and unchanging heaven.

Copernicus had disclosed his findings only with great caution during his lifetime, but Galileo, armed with his new observations, rushed boldly into print. He claimed that the truth of the Copernican theory had now been established, and when confronted with the familiar scriptural story of Joshua making the sun stand still, he retorted that the Bible might be adequate for ignorant laypeople but could hardly qualify as a scientific treatise. This was too much for the Catholic church. When Galileo defiantly published a further defense of Copernicus in his *Dialogue Concerning the Two Chief World Systems* (1632), he was arrested by the Inquisition, threatened with torture, and obliged to recant his belief in the heliocentric system. But though Galileo might be silenced, his challenge to received authority could not. What he represented was not the familiar problem of the heretic who challenged Christian doctrine on its own terms but a rival system of truth that bypassed it as irrelevant to the description and understanding of the physical world. For Galileo, observation was the guide, experiment the test, and mathematics the language of physical reality. No other form of understanding was required, no other authority acceptable.

Other Scientific Advances

If the common language of mathematics made astronomy and physics the cutting edge of the scientific revolution, chemistry, medicine, anatomy, and biology all advanced as well. As in the case of astronomy, the impetus for development often came from Hermetic and Neoplatonic doctrine. The Swiss-born German physician Theophrastus Bombastus von Hohenheim (1493–1541), called Paracelsus, launched a one-man crusade against the influence of Aristotle and Galen in medicine. Paracelsus was imbued with the spirit of medieval and Renaissance magic. He believed that occult forces were at work everywhere in nature and that demons could even divert the courses of the stars. It would be hard to imagine a mind further removed from the cool, rational skepticism of Galileo. Yet Paracelsus' very belief in the omnipresence of magical forces led him away from the

traditional textbooks and back to nature. This meant constant search and experimentation. "A man cannot learn the theory of medicine out of his own head," Paracelsus declared, "but only from that which his eyes see and his fingers touch. . . . Theory and practice should together form one, and should remain undivided."[2]

The emphasis on direct observation of nature produced the first great textbook of anatomy, the *De Fabrica* (1543) of the Fleming Andreas Vesalius (1514–1564), and the discovery of the circulation of the blood (1628) by the Englishman William Harvey (1578–1657). The results of these discoveries, as in the case of astronomy, proved contrary to the theories that had originally inspired them. Vesalius believed that the structure of the human head, as the temple of reason, was necessarily different from that of animals, and Harvey saw the heart as the source of spiritual as well as physical life. What they showed instead was that the anatomies of humans and animals were similar in structure and function. Harvey became an enthusiastic disciple of comparative anatomy, remarking tartly that had the anatomists paid as much attention to animals as to humans, the mysteries of the body would have been solved long before. Indeed, the last element in the circulation of the blood that was unsolved by Harvey himself, the transfer of blood from veins to arteries by capillary action, was discovered in 1661 by the Italian Marcello Malpighi (1628–1694), who examined a frog's lungs with the aid of another optical instrument, the microscope.

New Technology

New inventions and techniques were stimulated not merely by the requirements of scientific curiosity but also by those of practical activity. The great voyages of trade and discovery that began in the late fifteenth century are a case in point. When ships sailed out into open and uncharted seas, they required navigation, or reckoning by the sun and the stars. For this purpose, seamen adapted instruments that had previously been used by astronomers, the quadrant and the astrolabe. The problem of plotting straight-line courses on two-dimensional maps representing a three-dimensional earth was solved by the Fleming Gerhard Kremer, called Mercator, whose map was first published in 1569 and is still used in modified form today. In 1484, King John II of Portugal appointed a commission of mathematicians to work out tables of latitude, and when Gresham College was founded in England in 1597, one of its three scientific chairs was reserved for an astronomer whose duties included the teaching of navigation. Sixteenth-century interest in theories of the cosmos thus had a very practical basis. In similar fashion the development of the cannon took ballistics, the science of calculating the trajectory of missiles, out of the realm of academic theory and onto the battlefield, while the extraction of gold and silver from the Indies stimulated the development of chemical separation processes and mining technology such as subsurface ventilation and hydraulic pumps.

SCIENCE AT THE CROSSROADS

The concern of many religious authorities about the new science and the esoteric doctrines that swirled about it was not unfounded. The confidence of educated laypeople in the traditional picture of the world had already been eroded by the late sixteenth century. "The more I think, the more I doubt," the Jesuit Francisco Suárez confessed in 1581, and 30 years later the English poet and minister John Donne summarized the anxieties many people felt about humanity's loss of its privileged place in the cosmos in "An Anatomy of the World" (1611):

> And new philosophy calls all in doubt;
> The element of fire is quite put out,
> The sun is lost, and the earth, and no man's wit
> Can well direct him where to look for it . . .
> 'Tis all in pieces, all coherence gone;
> All just supply and all relation.

Donne's poem is remarkable in demonstrating the speed with which scientific ideas were circulating, since Galileo had announced his discovery of new celestial bodies only a year before. His familiarity with the dispute about "the element of fire" (challenged by Paracelsus and his followers) and with the revival of interest in Democritus' theory of atoms can also be glimpsed in his lines.

Doubt and Faith: Descartes and Pascal

More extreme reactions to the new science can be seen in the Frenchmen René Descartes (1596–1650) and Blaise Pascal (1623–1662). As Descartes himself related his experience, he was assailed one night by a sudden, paralyzing doubt about the possibility of knowledge.

The senses, he felt, deceived us, faith was undermined by doubt, and the authorities were only people like ourselves. How could one be sure of the existence of the world, of God, or even of oneself? Descartes' famous reply—"I think; therefore, I am"—was the starting point of his attempt to reconstruct all knowledge from the ground up on the basis of such intuitive propositions.

Pascal, a brilliant mathematician and a man of great religious sensitivity, felt the vast new spaces of the Copernican universe as a terrible silence in which humans were alone with their frailty and doubt and God had become a remote conjecture. He was one of the first of his time to realize that the traditional conception of God no longer fit the world revealed by science. But he argued, in his famous "wager" with skeptics, that it was better to affirm the existence of a just and merciful God in whom one might no longer fully believe than to deny him, since there was everything to gain if he did exist and nothing to lose if he did not.

Conflicting Roads to Truth

Science itself had arrived at a crossroads by the mid-seventeenth century. The scientific enterprise was a Babel of languages from which no common grammar had yet emerged. Although important discoveries had been made by scientists working from both Hermetic and mechanistic assumptions, in the last analysis they were incompatible as ways of seeing the world. The cosmos could be a living organism or an enormous machine but not both. A similar division existed regarding scientific method. The English philosopher and jurist Sir Francis Bacon (1561–1626) argued for the inductive or empirical method, by which knowledge was gained through systematic observation of the world and tested by experiment. The deductive method was championed by Descartes, who, as we have seen, rejected the senses as a basis for knowledge and argued that reality could be known only by reasoning from axiomatic principles. Descartes took a step that was decisive in the intellectual history of the West. He divided reality into two distinct entities: spirit, which was characterized by the power of thought but was without physical properties, and matter, which was substance extended in space and the capacity that that implied, motion. In doing so, he completely separated matter and spirit, rejecting the Hermetic vision of the world as a fusion of the two. He was thereby able to treat the material world in completely mechanical terms while reserving an independent realm for spirit. Spirit meant in effect intelligence for Descartes, and the greatest intelligence was that of God, who had created the physical universe of matter in motion and designed the laws by which it operated. By studying and understanding those laws, humankind could understand God. Thus Cartesianism, as Descartes' philosophy came to be called, made science into a religious quest, but one that proceeded in terms not of theology but of mechanical engineering and mathematical reasoning.

The immediate importance of Descartes' work was that it gave impetus to the mechanistic conception of the world, in which the most fruitful line of scientific advance lay, while avoiding the charge of black magic on the one hand and of atheism on the other. Cartesian science itself had serious drawbacks. It relegated observation and experiment to matters of secondary detail at best, thus failing to provide an independent standard of proof for anyone who did not accept the premises of the system. Brilliant strategically as a means of breaking the impasse between Hermeticism and mechanism, it was still inadequate as a general model for science itself.

The Newtonian Synthesis

Sir Isaac Newton (1642–1727) finally carried out the task that Descartes had set: to provide a clear and comprehensive explanation of the physical universe in mathematical terms, a universe created by the will of God but fully subject to the laws of nature. Newton's work was a synthesis of all the elements of the scientific tradition. His solution to the problem of gravity is illustrative. In Aristotelian physics, gravity was the inherent tendency of physical bodies to fall toward the earth as the center of the universe. The Englishman William Gilbert (1540–1603) had discovered that the earth itself acted as a magnet, drawing bodies to itself. But this left a serious problem in a Copernican universe where the sun was the center of the cosmos or (as both Descartes and Newton assumed) there was no center at all. Even granting the principle of inertia—that bodies set in motion would continue along the same path—how could it be explained that heavenly bodies did not simply drift randomly through space but described regular orbits about one another? Descartes rejected the idea of gravity as attraction at a distance because it seemed to him too close to the Hermetic idea of a force inherent in matter emanating from a divine source. Newton, however, had no trouble accepting such a notion, provided that it could be given an adequate mathematical basis—that is, provided that it could be shown to describe the actual orbits and positions of heavenly bodies. He thereupon invented a new mathematics, called calculus, which demonstrated these relations.

Using the assumption of gravity as a universal constant, Newton was able to reduce the movement of all bodies in heaven or on earth to three basic laws. When he published his findings in his *Mathematical Principles of Natural Philosophy* (1687), he completed the work begun by Copernicus a century and a half earlier in replacing the Ptolemaic system. But Newton's model was even farther from that of Copernicus than the latter's had been from Ptolemy's. Copernicus had still assumed that the universe had a definite center and a final boundary. Newton's cosmos was infinite and centerless. The speculation for which Bruno had been burned at the beginning of the seventeenth century had become scientific orthodoxy by its end.

The great success of Newton's synthesis was to reconcile not only the conflicting traditions of the new science but its competing methodologies as well. The conceptual simplicity of his system was a triumph of inductive logic, yet it was fully supported by the most up-to-date astronomical observations. Not only was the Newtonian model mathematically convincing as Descartes' was not, but for the next 200 years every empirical observation and experiment confirmed it in detail. After Newton, scientific method was a matter not of theory or observation but of both. By his death in 1727 his prestige was so great that the poet Alexander Pope could write:

> Nature and nature's laws lay hid in night;
> God said, Let Newton be! and all was light.

The Scientific Method

The most impressive aspect of the scientific revolution was less an increase in knowledge about the world than the creation of a new method for understanding it. It was a method that offered both something less and something more than faith or reason. It was something less because science could not claim, even with Newton, to have arrived at a final truth about the world. It was something more because it amounted to a redefinition of truth itself. Henceforth, truth was not something to be revealed at once and in its entirety, whether by the sacred word or by direct intuition. Rather, truth was to be discovered and refined piecemeal, with each new stage in understanding serving as a step toward the next one. Through individual trial and error, collective truth was to be won.

For this reason, science became more and more a collaborative effort after the mid-seventeenth century. The first scientists had worked alone. Gradually, however, they became linked through chains of correspondence, quasi-public meetings, and finally formal societies. Among the first of these was the Royal Society of London for Improving Natural Knowledge, founded in 1662, of which Newton was an early member and later president. Four years later, Colbert founded the French Academy of Sciences, and similar societies were soon established in Berlin, Uppsala, Stockholm, Copenhagen, and St. Petersburg. By the last decades of the seventeenth century we can speak of a scientific world, international in scope and cosmopolitan in character, in which knowledge could be systematically communicated, new theories debated, and new talent recognized.

PHILOSOPHY: THE AGE OF REASON

In the seventeenth century no strict distinction was made between philosophy—inquiry into the limits of human knowledge as such—and science, the branch of knowledge that addressed itself to the natural world. In that sense, the attack on Aristotle, Ptolemy, and Galen that characterized the scientific revolution was part of a wider movement in European thought that questioned traditional authority in general. But there can be no doubt that the success of science in dethroning medieval cosmology gave impetus and urgency to the development of critical philosophy as a whole.

The two traditions of philosophy that were most influential in the seventeenth and eighteenth centuries, the English and the French, adhered to the norms set down by Bacon and Descartes, respectively. The English tended to begin from concrete observation of the world, the French from à priori assumptions about it. The English, preoccupied with the revolutions of 1640 and 1688, concentrated on the problem of people's relation to the civic orders of state and society, whereas the French, inheriting the skepticism of Descartes, focused on humanity's relation to the cosmos.

Thomas Hobbes and the Natural Man

The Englishman Thomas Hobbes (1588–1679) produced in *Leviathan* (1651) the most important work of Western political philosophy since Machiavelli's *The Prince*. Hobbes argued that human beings are social by neces-

The famous frontispiece of Hobbes' book *Leviathan* shows his absolute sovereign as a giant who incorporates the entire body politic. The Latin quotation at the top, from the Book of Job, reads: "There is not his like upon earth." [The Granger Collection, New York]

sity rather than by nature, as Aristotle had thought. He started from the mechanistic assumption that humans, like all other entities, could be described in terms of matter and motion and that their thoughts, feelings, and desires could be explained as responses to external stimuli, differing in degree but not in kind from those of animals. Even reason, the glory of the mind, was only a complex form of calculation, and the will, which attested to human freedom, was defined simply as the last appetite before choice. Hobbes professed to believe in God, the soul, and the workings of Providence, but, like

Descartes, he separated the realms of matter and spirit so sharply that his view of society appeared to be purely secular.

In Hobbes' view, human beings strive to maximize pleasure and minimize pain. This brings them into conflict with others who, acting on the same principle, compete for scarce goods. The result, Hobbes declared, was a "war of all against all," a condition in which the life of humans was, in his pithy phrase, "solitary, poor, nasty, brutish and short." To avoid this, people gave up their natural freedom and entered society, as rational animals might enter a zoo. Hobbes' zookeeper was the sovereign, who had absolute power to order all social arrangements, allotting each person a share of goods and duties. Only in this way, he believed, could order be guaranteed and the anarchy of the natural human condition avoided. Society was in effect a contract in which freedom was exchanged for security, or at least the hope of security, since the subject, in surrendering all natural rights, had also surrendered the means to enforce the bargain. To critics who complained that this created a license for tyranny, Hobbes replied that it was better to be subject to the arbitrary will of a single individual than to the potential violence of all.

Hobbes' theory scandalized everyone. Liberals rejected it because it left no place for political dissent. Conservatives liked it no better because, although Hobbes condemned rebellion as the greatest of political evils, he accepted all changes of government in a spirit of pure pragmatism. The only test of a regime was its ability to provide security. A government that could not do so forfeited all claim to loyalty, while any government that could possessed a sufficient title to be obeyed.

John Locke and the State of Nature

Writing 40 years later, John Locke (1632–1704) took a very different view of human society. Locke started from the premise that human beings in their natural condition—what had come to be called *the state of nature*—were not competitive but cooperative. People entered society to gain the benefits of communal organization. Their natural rights were not surrendered but rather enhanced in society. Government, in this view, was merely an instrument of common social purpose, and the ruler was entrusted with such powers as were necessary to provide for the general welfare but no more. A ruler who abused this trust might be replaced or deposed without doing violence to the constitution and certainly without dissolving society as Hobbes had thought.

Locke's view of politics derived from his assumptions about human psychology, expressed in the *Essay Concerning Human Understanding* (1690). Taking a radically empirical stance, he argued that the mind at birth was a *tabula rasa* (blank slate), on which experience inscribed itself. It followed from this that careful education could develop the mind in almost any desired direction. Thus, although reason in the state of nature suggested the desirability of human cooperation, people could easily be trained to obey the far more complex rules of society.

French Skepticism

In France a vein of skepticism ran through philosophy from the essayist Michel de Montaigne (1533–1592) to Descartes to Pierre Bayle (1647–1706). Descartes dealt with his own crisis of belief by asserting the power of reason to validate the world, including the existence of God. The idea of an infinite being, he argued, is spontaneously present in the human mind; yet since it would never have occurred of itself to a finite, limited consciousness, it could only have been placed there by God. But Descartes insisted on excluding God from any direct responsibility for the material universe, remarking that his readers could substitute "the mathematical order of nature" for "God" wherever he used the latter term.

For Pascal the absence of God from the material universe was the very source of human despair. Descartes' cool, rational conception of a God who made himself known as an idea but could not be reached as a person had no interest for Pascal. The thrust of his argument was that Descartes, by exalting the powers of the mind, had excluded God, reducing him to a meaningless abstraction. Only by admitting one's frailty and need was it possible to reach the Christian God who had extended himself to humankind by his own suffering.

The skeptical tradition nonetheless continued to gain ground in France. In his *Critical History of the New Testament* (1678) the Oratorian priest Richard Simon subjected the Bible to exhaustive textual scrutiny, seeking to purge it of errors and discrepancies. No such redeeming purpose could be attributed to Pierre Bayle, who satirized biblical and pagan figures side by side in his *Historical and Critical Dictionary* (1697). For Bayle, whose book profoundly influenced such eighteenth-century skeptics as Voltaire, reason and religion were mortal enemies fighting "for possession of men's souls."

THE LENS GRINDER OF AMSTERDAM, BARUCH SPINOZA

The philosophical and religious issues of the seventeenth century were perhaps nowhere better epitomized than in the life of Baruch Spinoza. Spinoza was born in Amsterdam in 1632, the son of a prosperous Jewish merchant whose family had emigrated from Portugal at the end of the sixteenth century. The Amsterdam of his youth was the most cosmopolitan city in Europe. The Jewish community mixed freely with the general population, adopting its manners and dress, intermarrying, and imbibing liberal social and religious ideas. This freedom created great tension within the Jewish community itself, which conservative members feared would soon lose its identity. The brilliant young Spinoza was a case in point. While the elders of the community supported the politi-

The great Jewish philosopher Baruch Spinoza saw God and nature as indivisible. Contemporaries found his ideas "frightening," but he was a hero to later generations. [Collection Haags Gemeentemuseum, The Hague]

cal establishment, Spinoza backed the republican revolution of 1650 and advocated the dissolution of the trading companies and the abolition of their privileges. Above all, he rejected his Jewish heritage, abjuring the synagogue and denying that the Jews were a chosen people. The Amsterdam synagogue responded by excommunicating him in 1656. He was formally cursed, and Jews were forbidden all contact with him. Spinoza renounced the career in commerce he had begun and earned his living by grinding and polishing lenses, a job of deliberately low status but symbolically appropriate for a man determined to see the world by no light but his own.

In his major work, the *Ethics,* Spinoza proposed a radical solution to the central seventeenth-century question of the relation between God and nature. Traditional philosophy had distinguished between substance, the stuff of the universe, and cause, the external agency that acts on it. Spinoza rejected this distinction as false, contending that there could be no separation between God as cause and nature as substance. It followed that God *was* the world, which was contained in him, though he was not confined by it. It is hard to imagine an idea better calculated to give offense. Religious thinkers had speculated that the human soul might be regarded as a spark of divinity within humankind. Spinoza denied the existence of the soul, since there could be no distinction between matter and spirit; on the other hand, he asserted that God was present not only in humans but in the lowest and most degraded phenomena of the world as well. To accept God was to accept everything, and once that was done, false categories such as sin and salvation, which separated humankind from God, lost all meaning.

Spinoza's political ideas were equally radical. Like Hobbes, he argued that sovereignty was absolute and indivisible, and he denounced clerical influence in the state; unlike Hobbes, he demanded complete freedom of thought and considered freedom itself the indispensable human value. When Spinoza died from a long-standing tubercular condition in 1677, his work fell into obscurity until Goethe rediscovered it in the eighteenth century and the Romantics made him a hero in the nineteenth. Since then he has found his place among the great Western philosophers and the champions of freedom—honored at last, but still alone.

LITERATURE: THE TRIUMPH OF THE VERNACULAR

Latin was still the language of educated Europe in the early modern period. But the sixteenth century saw the beginning of a sustained tradition of vernacular literature, that is, literature in the popular spoken tongue. It began in Italy with the immensely popular chivalric poems of Ludovico Ariosto (1474–1533) and Torquato Tasso (1544–1595), in France with the prose epics of François Rabelais (1494–1553), and in Germany with Luther's translation of the Bible. But the development of vernacular literature was particularly associated with the stage, the most popular of all art forms. The late sixteenth and seventeenth centuries were a golden age of theater in England, France, Spain, and the Netherlands, unrivaled from the time of ancient Greece and unequaled since.

The first of these national theaters was the English, where licensed companies of actors appeared from 1574. Large enclosed theaters were built in the 1590s, of which the most famous were the Swan (1596) and the Globe (1599), which boasted seating capacities of 3,000. The audience represented every element of English urban society, and what it saw was the reflection of its own world, from cobblers to kings: Thomas Dekker's *Shoemaker's Holiday* (1599) depicted an upwardly mobile craftsman who becomes Lord Mayor of London; Thomas Middleton's *A Chaste Maid in Cheapside* (1613), a goldsmith; Ben Jonson's *Bartholomew Fair* (1614), Puritans and pickpockets. Well might the greatest of these playwrights, William Shakespeare (1564–1616), whose imaginative world was perhaps larger than that of any person who ever lived, boastfully declare:

> *All the world's a stage,*
> *And all the men and women merely players.*
> *They have their exits and their entrances,*
> *And one man in his time plays many parts.*[3]

Civic theater also flourished in the Netherlands, where it produced a major figure in Joost van den Vondel (1587–1679), a committed republican who protested against the rigidities of Dutch Calvinism. The playwrights of the Spanish school—Lope de Vega (1562–1635), Tirso de Molina (1571–1648), and Pedro Calderón de la Barca (1600–1681)—were immensely prolific; Lope claimed to have written over 1,500 plays, and the titles of nearly 1,000 survive. Performances were held outdoors in the public square, with seats arranged around the stage and rooms rented in private houses to provide the equivalent of boxes for noblemen and ladies. Male and female spectators were strictly segregated, and though the monarchy was often the subject of the Spanish theater, it was considered improper for the king and

queen to attend. The French theater of Pierre Corneille (1606–1684) and Jean Racine (1639–1699), in contrast, was court-sponsored and reflected its patronage in its choice of classical themes, its emphasis on honor and the renunciation of the passions, and its formal, chiseled verse line. But the French produced their comic genius, too, in Jean-Baptiste Poquelin, called Molière (1622–1673), who mocked the social pretensions of his own bourgeois class, although he carefully stopped short of satirizing his aristocratic audiences.

The seventeenth century saw the entry of women into literature for the first time, particularly in France. Women writers of note, such as Christine de Pisan, Marguerite of Navarre, and the English mystic Juliana of Norwich, had occasionally emerged before, but not until the accession of the Bourbon dynasty in France did women begin to occupy an important place in literary life. Madeleine de Scudéry (1607–1701) created a new genre with her historical romance, *Grand Cyrus* (1649–1653), while Marie de Sévigné (1626–1696), whose correspondence touched on all facets of French society, established letter writing as a literary art. No less important as a cultural vehicle was the literary salon, pioneered by the elegant Catherine de Rambouillet (1588–1665), at whose private gatherings aspiring writers came to establish their reputations. Even so, however, literature was not yet a respectable pursuit for women; Scudéry's *Grand Cyrus,* certainly the most popular and influential French novel of its time, was published under the name of her brother Georges, a mediocre playwright.

One of the most remarkable writers of the seventeenth century was Sor (Sister) Juana Inés de La Cruz (c. 1648–1695), the first major Spanish writer of the New World. Born in a small village in New Spain (Mexico), she was raised in Mexico City. Unwilling to marry, she entered the convent of San Jeronimo in 1669 as the only respectable alternative for a woman without means.

Sor Juana's more than 200 surviving poems, including nearly 50 love lyrics, represent some of the finest achievements of Spanish baroque literature, and her plays were steadily in demand at the viceregal court. In 1690, however, she was attacked in a letter by the Bishop of Puebla, who rebuked her sternly: "Literary learning that engenders pride God does not wish in a woman." After a spirited defense she was obliged to give up her writing and study. Her cell, which had contained a library of perhaps 2,000 . . . 3,000 books and a rare collection of scientific and musical instruments, was stripped, and she was left with three devotional books for meditation. Not long afterward, on April 17, 1695, she died of the plague, which she had contracted while caring for other sisters in the convent.

The last of the great epic poets was the Englishman John Milton (1608–1674), whose *Paradise Lost* (1667) looked back to the model of Dante in its account of the fall of Adam and Eve, although its powerful portrayal of the character of Satan anticipates the rebellious Romantic hero of nineteenth century literature. A new medium for narrative had begun to emerge, one that would dominate the literature of the West: the novel. The rambling adventure tales of Rabelais had anticipated the form in the sixteenth century, but the first true example is Miguel de Cervantes' (1547–1616) *Don Quixote* (1605). Cervantes intended to satirize the chivalric tales that were still popular in his native Spain, but he accomplished much more. His two wandering heroes, the idealistic nobleman Don Quixote and his worldly but faithful servant, Sancho Panza, are not mere stock figures on which a tale of adventures can be strung but individualized characters of vividly contrasting temperaments. Another century was to pass, however, before prose fiction became the dominant art form of the West. It was only with Daniel Defoe's enormously popular *Robinson Crusoe* (1719), a story not for the old world of chivalry but for the new one of capital formation and commercial enterprise, that the age of the novel had begun.

THE AGE OF THE BAROQUE

The term *baroque* has come to define the very distinctive art of the seventeenth century, though originally, like the adjective *Gothic,* it was a term of derision. Certainly, to those whose ideal was the serene beauty of a Raphael or the monumentality of a Michelangelo, the dramatic, swirling lines of baroque architecture and the darkened palette of baroque painting could not but seem strained, distorted, and profoundly disturbing. Yet the baroque, like every major art style, had subtle affinities to the wider culture of the age. In its restless, probing, and essentially theatrical nature it reflected a period of conflict, exploration, and doubt, while in its bold redefinition of space it suggests a response to the vision of Copernicus, Bruno, and Galileo.

The baroque originated as a style in Italy. Its first patrons were the Jesuits, and Il Gesù, the church of the order in Rome, is commonly accepted as the first full-fledged example of baroque architecture. But the new

style soon stepped across national and religious frontiers. The spiritual and the sensual, moreover, often blended into one another, as the famous *St. Theresa in Ecstasy* of Gianlorenzo Bernini (1598–1680) vividly illustrates, or settled down happily side by side, as in the fleshily exuberant biblical scenes of the Flemish painter Peter Paul Rubens (1577–1640).

Dutch painters carried the new chiaroscuro style of the Italian Michelangelo Merisi, called Caravaggio (1573–1610), back from Rome. Caravaggio's work, with its dramatic interior lighting, often from no visible source, was soon reflected in the work of artists all over Europe, including Diego Velázquez (1599–1660) in Spain and Georges de La Tour (1593–1652) in France, but it found its apotheosis in the Dutch Mennonite artist Rembrandt van Rijn (1606–1669). Rembrandt was the greatest of a remarkable series of painters who captured the variety and vitality of seventeenth-century Dutch society, leaving an unmatched record of the everyday life of their time. Rembrandt's own work reveals this same curiosity about the unusual and even (by classical standards) the bizarre, as in his *Anatomy Lesson of Dr. Tulp* (1632), in which an anatomist dissects the cadaver of an executed criminal before the Surgeons' Guild of Amsterdam. But it is in his portraits that Rembrandt's unique genius is most fully realized, including the self-portraits that he painted from youth to old age. In these extraordinary images, something of what Spinoza may have meant by the "soul that lives in all things" is visible, for no other artist has ever revealed so much of our common humanity.

The music of the baroque, like its art and architecture, tended toward the dramatic. Sung texts and spoken words had largely existed apart before Claudio Monteverdi (1567–1643), who fused them into a new theatrical form, the opera. Much of seventeenth-century music remained dominated by Italian models, particularly in the secular forms of the oratorio, the cantata, and the concerto. In Germany the tradition of church music introduced by the hymns of Martin Luther produced a series of important composers, including Heinrich Schütz (1585–1672). Later baroque music developed in the direction of elaborate ornamentation and contrapuntal complexity, reaching its climax in the work of Johann Sebastian Bach (1685–1750), in which the Lutheran tradition achieved a universality that, like the art of Rembrandt, reaches across all ages and cultures.

The state gradually superseded the Catholic church as the chief patron of baroque art. It was Louis XIV, characteristically, who saw most clearly the possibilities of bringing art to the service of power. In Versailles the dramatic, heaven-storming qualities of baroque art (suitably refined by French taste) and the pomp of divine right monarchy came together in an image of absolute secular authority. Other rulers rushed to follow Louis' example—Leopold I in Austria, Charles XII in Sweden, Peter the Great in Russia, Frederick the Great in Prussia, Augustus the Strong in Saxony, and a host of lesser princelings, neither great nor strong, who felt that no reign could be complete without a palace to attest to its *gloire*.

ROME: THE REBIRTH OF A CAPITAL

Rome, for most of the population of Europe still the center of Christendom, recovered slowly from the sack of 1527 and the subsequent Spanish occupation. With the new energies of the Counter-Reformation, however, the city began to revive. Work on St. Peter's, still without a facade or dome, was the first order of priority. Pope Sixtus V, working men around the clock for 22 months, finished Michelangelo's dome in 1590. The architect Carlo Maderna (1556–1629) designed the new facade, and Bernini spent nearly a decade (1657–1666) completing the great colonnaded square in front. Bernini's undulating columns in the nave and his daringly open square—the first such space in any European city— completed with baroque exuberance and novelty the great edifice that had been begun in the High Renaissance. In no other building is the contrast between the aims and aspirations of the two epochs more strikingly visible.

With St. Peter's in progress, Popes Paul V (1605–1621) and Urban VIII (1623–1644) undertook the reconstruction and beautification of Rome, giving it the squares and fountains—many designed by the ubiquitous Bernini—that still distinguish it today. With these came new churches as well, notably Bernini's San Andrea al Quirinale (1658–1670) and Francesco Borromini's San Carlo alle Quattro Fontane (1638–1641), whose interior represents the first completely undulating wall space since the reign of the Roman emperor Hadrian. In the work of Borromini (1599–1667), the greatest Italian architect of the century, the flowing space of the baroque—like the post-Copernican universe, itself never defined by any single perspective—achieved its most characteristic form.

By the early eighteenth century the rebuilt city had become a major tourist attraction for Protestants and Catholics alike. One such traveler, the French magistrate Charles de Brosses, declared that Rome was "the most beautiful city in the world" and St. Peter's "the finest thing in the universe." Like a jewel, its facets were endlessly fascinating: "You might come to it every day without being bored. . . . It is more amazing the oftener you see it." Most impressive of all, he thought, were the fountains and firework displays that played constantly and gave the city an air of perpetual festivity. This impression was not far from wrong, as Rome celebrated no fewer than 150 holidays a year, not to mention occasional pageants, local processions and fairs, and weekly summer festivals that included water jousts and mock sea battles in the flooded Piazza Navona.

Rome's population grew steadily during this period, from approximately 80,000 in 1563 to 150,000 by 1709, including some 8,000 members of religious orders. The papacy dominated the political and economic life of Rome just as the dome and square of St. Peter's did its skyline. The papacy governed the city directly and was its chief employer. What the papacy did not provide for directly, it did indirectly in the services that were needed for the hordes of pilgrims, estimated at 100,000 per year in 1700, that formed the bulk of the tourist trade. The result was that Rome's was almost entirely a service economy, living on papal wealth and foreign income. Life was casual if not indolent; even at the Vatican, washing was hung out to dry from the windows. At the bottom of the social scale, Rome's easygoing ways trailed off into squalor, and its poor, favored at least by the climate, spent as little time as possible in their wretched hovels. The very openness of life acted as a safety valve for discontent; there was always distraction in the street, and, in a city full of wealthy strangers, opportunity as well.

The Jewish community, too, was noted in the papacy's ubiquitous accounts, and when Paul V planned his new fountains for Rome, one was duly provided for the city's synagogue. A more curious and less benevolent example of Rome's uneasy relationship with its Jews was in the ceremony that opened the Roman Carnival, the eight-day pre-Lenten celebration that was the most elaborate and tumultuous holiday of the year. The Jews were taxed the cost of the prize money for the horse races and, assembled as a group, were thanked for their "gift" to the city by a pretended kick in the small of the chief rabbi's back.

SUMMARY

The seventeenth century has rightly been called the century of genius. Shakespeare, Milton, Cervantes, Rembrandt—these men shaped the image of humankind in the West and still stand at the forefront of its cultural heritage. Bacon, Hobbes, Descartes, Pascal, and Spinoza shaped the modern quest for knowledge, and the questions they posed, about humankind and the cosmos, about freedom and government, are still alive today. Copernicus, Kepler, Galileo, Newton, and many others created the scientific revolution and with it transformed humankind's capacity to know, to create, and to destroy.

The effects of the changed intellectual climate were visible by the end of the century. The triumph of the mechanistic vision of nature over Aristotelian physics and cosmology and the rival tradition of Hermetic natural magic had a decisive influence on popular superstition as well as educated thought. The beginning of the century had seen the last upsurge in witchcraft persecution, affecting some 100,000 people between 1580 and 1650. By the end of the century, belief in witchcraft itself was largely extinct, and faith in astrology and magic healing had declined sharply.

The cultural shock that greeted humanity's dethronement from its position at the center of the universe gradually gave way to a new pride in the power of human knowledge. The new science came to symbolize faith in the improvement of the human condition, a faith that for some in the eighteenth century took on the quality of religious conviction itself. At the same time the mathematized God of Newton and Descartes was gradually detached from science. For them, God had still been the ultimate guarantor of the truth of their universe. A century later, asked why he had omitted God from his system, the French astronomer Laplace (1749–1827) would answer coolly, "I have no need of that hypothesis."

Notes

1. H. F. Kearney, *Science and Change, 1500–1700* (New York: McGraw-Hill, 1971), p. 101.
2. A. R. Hall, *The Scientific Revolution, 1500–1800* (Boston: Beacon Press, 1956), p. 132.
3. *As You Like It,* Act II, Scene 7.

Suggestions for Further Reading

Cohen, I. B. *The Birth of a New Physics.* New York: Norton, 1985.

Feuer, L. S. *Spinoza and the Rise of Liberalism.* Boston: Beacon Press, 1966.

Gillespie, C. C. *The Edge of Objectivity: An Essay in the History of Scientific Ideas.* Princeton, N.J.: Princeton University Press, 1960.

Hall, A. R. *The Scientific Revolution, 1500–1800.* Boston: Beacon Press, 1956.

Jacob, M. C. *The Cultural Meaning of the Scientific Revolution.* New York: Knopf, 1988.

Kearney, H. F. *Science and Change, 1500–1700.* New York: McGraw-Hill, 1971.

Koyré, A. *From the Closed World to the Infinite Universe.* Baltimore: Johns Hopkins University Press, 1957.

Krautheimer, R. *The Rome of Alexander VII, 1655–1667.* Princeton, N.J.: Princeton University Press, 1985.

Kuhn, T. S. *The Structure of Scientific Revolutions.* Chicago: University of Chicago Press, 1970.

MacPherson, C. B. *The Political Theory of Possessive Individualism: Hobbes to Locke.* New York: Oxford University Press, 1964.

Mesnard, J. *Pascal: His Life and Works.* New York: Philosophical Library, 1952.

Nash, J. M. *The Age of Rembrandt and Vermeer: Dutch Painting in the Seventeenth Century.* New York: Holt, Rinehart and Winston, 1972.

Santillana, G. de. *The Crime of Galileo.* London: Heinemann, 1958.

Warnke, F. J. *Versions of Baroque: European Literature in the Seventeenth Century.* New Haven, Conn.: Yale University Press, 1972.

Westfall, R. S. *Never at Rest: A Biography of Isaac Newton.* Cambridge: Cambridge University Press, 1980.

Wilson, M. D. *Descartes.* Boston: Routledge & Kegan Paul, 1978.

17

EUROPE AND THE AMERICAS

By the eighteenth century the economy of western Europe had become worldwide in scope. Large regional economies, integrated by trade patterns and dominated by strong states, had existed since ancient times. China had long been the center of such an economy in East Asia. The Indian Ocean and Red Sea area constituted another large system. In Europe itself the Mediterranean had provided a natural focus of economic integration under the successive dominion of Egyptians, Phoenicians, Greeks, Romans, Arabs, Venetians, and, most recently, Spaniards.

But Spain had begun to decline in the seventeenth century, and by the early eighteenth century the Mediterranean was dominated for the first time by a power not based geographically in the region: Britain. At the same time the center of European gravity had shifted to the Atlantic states. Britain, France, and the Dutch Netherlands were not merely the dominant economic powers of Europe, but their overseas possessions became the focus of intense rivalry in the eighteenth century. The burgeoning slave trade, too, linked four continents—Europe, Africa, and North and South America—in a complex and highly coordinated relationship. As the importance of the world market grew, Britain and France fought for control of it. After three major cycles of warfare spread across 125 years, the British emerged victorious, though shorn of what had been their largest New World colony, the newly independent United States of America.

THE OLD COLONIAL SYSTEM

The new global economy was based on the establishment of colonies, used both as forward bases for trade, exploration, or further conquest and as passive markets and sources of raw materials. The medieval crusader colonies in Palestine, Cyprus, and Greece were prototypes of the later and much larger Spanish, Portuguese, Dutch, and English colonies in the New World, Africa, and Asia. A second type of colony, developed by the Genoese in the fourteenth century, was based on control by a private trading company operating under a government charter. The English and Dutch East India companies, founded in 1600 and 1602, respectively, administered large territories under such arrangements, as did the Virginia and Massachusetts Bay companies on the Atlantic seaboard of North America. Yet a third type of colony was based on an agreement between individuals for the settlement of a territory; the Mayflower Compact was an example.

The nature of a given colonial enterprise depended on the territory to be settled and the general approach of the colonizing center, or *metropolis*. In the New World and Africa, tiny bands of adventurers were able to conquer large areas through tactical and technological superiority. The Portuguese established their influence in Africa along the Congo and Zambesi rivers in the early sixteenth century, but the unattractiveness of the climate for Europeans deterred large-scale settlement except at the Cape of Good Hope on the southern tip of the continent, where Dutch colonists arrived in the seventeenth century. For the most part, Europeans were content to barter for slaves, gold dust, and ivory with African middlemen, and apart from establishing coastal bases for commerce, they made little attempt to explore the continent.

In Asia, where Europeans possessed no significant technical or military advantage except in ship design, conquest and hence colonization were out of the question. Here the Portuguese and the Dutch competed with Asian and Arab merchants for a share of the lucrative spice trade, often financed by piracy. At the beginning of the eighteenth century, however, the European presence in Asia was still marginal.

GOLD AND THE EXPANSION OF THE EUROPEAN ECONOMY

The importation of massive quantities of precious metals from the Spanish colonies of the New World, ferried home by an annual treasure fleet, had a profound effect on the European economy. The Mediterranean region, whose weak bullion base had been further eroded by the decline of imports from its previous supplier, the Sudan, suddenly burgeoned. From Seville to Antwerp the ports of western Europe teemed with new shipping and trade, presaging the great shift of power to the Atlantic economies that occurred within the next two centuries. Transatlantic trade multiplied eightfold between 1510 and 1550 and tripled again between 1550 and 1610. Through trade and smuggling, a considerable quantity of the new bullion found its way to Asia and the Levant. Gold and silver from the New World created a network of worldwide commerce on a scale and of a complexity never seen before.

The gradual exhaustion of the mines of Mexico and Peru brought this first, precocious global economy to an end. Asia had no interest in Western goods comparable to the European demand for silks and spices, which had to be paid for almost entirely in bullion. As new supplies tapered off, the Asian trade dwindled. At about the same time the European economy, so powerfully stimulated by the influx of precious metals, began to contract. European states blamed the prolonged depression that set in between 1619 and 1622 on their shrinking bullion

reserves, although this was only one factor in a complex process. The anxiety of states to protect their bullion supplies led to import restrictions, thus hindering trade and deepening the slump. This in turn heightened the tensions surrounding the Thirty Years' War, which itself produced ruin in much of Europe.

MERCHANT CAPITALISM AND THE GROWTH OF THE STATE

Nonetheless, the great sixteenth-century boom had permanent effects. The sharp rise in profits and prices enriched the merchant bourgeoisie, whose new political importance was clearly manifested in Britain, France, and the Netherlands. The value of estates and rents tended to fall, thus putting pressure on the landed nobility. In eastern Europe the demand for foodstuffs and raw materials to stoke the expanding Atlantic economies stimulated the enserfment of scarce peasant labor, an apparently "backward" step that was, like the regimentation of Indian labor in the Americas, in significant part a response to growth in the core economies of the West. The results of this were profound. The peasant population was immobilized, stunting urban growth and confirming the power of the landed nobility at a time when it was under challenge in the West. From the sixteenth century onward, the development of eastern and western Europe increasingly diverged; their present economic divisions are a consequence.

The growth of the economy was linked to that of the state. The expansion of the latter was most visible in palace-building and the development of a court-based culture, which reached their climax in the Versailles of Louis XIV. These self-conscious displays of power were accompanied by a proliferation of state offices and the gradual transformation of royal attendants into bureaucratic functionaries. At the same time the state fostered economic development, which provided it with a larger tax base. The fiscal demands of the state stimulated the growth of banking and credit, and these expanded the state's capacities further.

The development of merchant capitalism and of centralized political authority were thus reciprocal. Centralized authority was essential to peaceful commerce at home and the protection of colonial ventures abroad. Often the state allied itself directly with business interests, and the entire process of exploration and colonization in the sixteenth century may be considered a partnership between the state and private entrepreneurs in which the state provided venture capital in return for a fixed share of the profits. War itself took on a more overtly commercial tone, as states fought over trade routes, commercial privileges, and control of profitable territories.

This did not mean that the interests of rulers and merchants were necessarily harmonious. Their partnership was always an uneasy one, and by the eighteenth century some merchants felt that the state had become unduly restrictive. On balance, however, the state and merchant capitalism were mutually supportive during the first stages of global economic growth in the West. If the merchant bourgeoisie had developed to the point at which state intervention was perceived as a handicap, it was only because state power had nurtured it to the point of self-generating growth.

THE SETTLEMENT OF NORTH AMERICA

North America, with neither precious metals nor, except in southern coastal areas, a climate suitable for plantation crops such as sugar, tobacco, cocoa, and cotton, was developed far more slowly than were the vast reaches of the Spanish Americas. Farther up the coast and along the rivers of the interior, notably the Mississippi and the St. Lawrence, British, French, and Dutch settler societies developed in the absence of readily exploitable labor or natural resources. The most populous of these settlements were the British colonies along the Atlantic seaboard, although the most far-flung geographically was the long arc of French trading stations and fortifications that extended from the Gulf of Mexico to Hudson's Bay. The principal Dutch base on the North American mainland was New Amsterdam, at the mouth of the Hudson River. From here the Dutch conducted a lucrative fur trade and an even more profitable smuggling operation until the settlement was conquered in 1664 by the British, who renamed it New York.

British settlement in North America at first proceeded slowly. After several false starts, a small colony was established at Jamestown on the Potomac River in 1607. By 1733 the number had grown to 13 colonies along the coast and the adjacent river valleys from New England to Georgia. The northernmost of these colonies, particu-

larly Massachusetts, Rhode Island, and Connecticut, were essentially subsistence economies of slight value to the mother country. They served, together with the Quaker colony of Pennsylvania, primarily as a dumping ground for religious and political dissidents, some 20,000 of whom migrated to New England between 1629 and 1642. In the Middle Atlantic and southern plantation colonies, indigents and convicts joined religious exiles as settlers, together, of course, with imported slave labor.

Since Britain's mainland colonies were at first perceived largely as a safety valve for excess population or unwanted social groups, the crown exerted relatively little control over them. The French, in contrast, never thought of allowing their colonies to be peopled by paupers, felons, and dissidents. Great efforts were made to procure suitable migrants, down to the provision of tools, seed, and stock and even free passage for women who were willing to marry settlers. The crown first subsidized and controlled the companies that were formed to plant settlements and finally, under Colbert, assumed direct control. Nonetheless, the combined French and British presence in the New World in the seventeenth century was only a fraction of Spain's in size, population, and wealth—and that in spite of the loss in Spanish America of most of its preconquest population, chiefly to epidemic disease. It was not, however, the vast expanses of the North American continent that were to make the New World profitable for Britain and France in the late seventeenth and early eighteenth centuries but the small sugar-producing islands of the Caribbean that came under their control.

SUGAR AND SLAVERY

Sugar had been grown in the New World almost from the beginning of European colonization. As early as the 1510s, sugar cultivation had been introduced into the Caribbean islands, where it was harvested by black slaves imported from Africa to replace an Amerindian population that had already been decimated by white settlers. The Portuguese were the first to introduce sugar on a relatively large scale in Brazil, where some 60 mills were in operation by 1580. Most of the export trade was carried on by Dutch merchants, one of whose spokesman, Willem de Usselincx, farsightedly pointed out that plantation crops had a far greater long-range profit potential than bullion. The Dutch themselves were

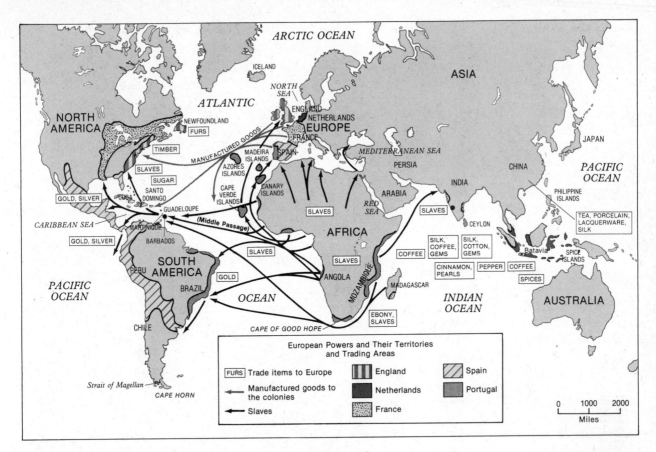

17.1 Overseas Trade in the Seventeenth and Eighteenth Centuries

driven out of Brazil by 1654, but their role in spreading the sugar trade in the West Indies, refining the product, and supplying African slaves, was crucial.

The ouster of Dutch middlemen marked the coming of age of the British and French imperial systems. The British moved swiftly to consolidate control of their colonial trade. The Navigation Acts of 1651 and 1660 provided that colonies could trade certain products only with the mother country or other British colonies and only on British ships. In return they were to accept manufactured goods from Britain. This closed system of trade exemplified the economic theory of mercantilism, which sought to enhance the wealth of the mother country by acquiring a captive source of supply for its commodity needs and a compulsory outlet for its manufactures. The French were never able to develop a system as fully integrated as that of the British, but as commodity suppliers alone, their major West Indian possessions—Guadeloupe and Martin-

ique, settled in 1635, and Santo Domingo, acquired from Spain in 1697—had an increasing impact on the metropolitan economy.

Of all British and French colonial products, sugar was by far the most important. Its cultivation required not only suitable colonies but also a heavy investment in land and labor. Wealthy royalist exiles from the English civil wars provided this in the 1640s and 1650s, driving out poorer white settlers and consolidating their land into large plantations. By 1673, sugar production on tiny Barbados was one-quarter that of Brazil's, and by 1700 the economic value of the West Indian islands exceeded that of all the mainland colonies combined. Jamaica, acquired by Britain in 1655, did not develop into a major supplier until the early eighteenth century, but by 1770 it was producing half of all British sugar and was incontestably the single most valuable colonial territory in the New World.

The Slave System

The labor required for sugar cultivation on this scale could have come only from slaves. Seen in this perspective, the "settlement" of the New World in the seventeenth, eighteenth, and much of the nineteenth century was overwhelmingly by African blacks. A million blacks had been imported into the Americas by 1700, and 6 million more arrived in the course of the eighteenth century, a number nearly equaling both the partially recovered remnant of the native Amerindian population and the white settler population combined. Half of this number was funneled into the West Indies alone, where the permanent British and French population was less than 100,000. Yet despite the 3 million black men, women, and children who entered the Caribbean during this period, the net population increase was only 700,000. The vast majority of slaves perished within ten years of arrival. In part this may be accounted for by disease, the major factor in the destruction of the native population in the sixteenth century. But the primary reason was exploitation. Blacks were systematically worked to death.

At first glance this appears difficult to explain. Slaves were an expensive investment; they accounted for 90 percent of the capital value of Jamaican plantations in the eighteenth century, exclusive of land. Nonetheless, in the calculus of profit, they were expendable. It was cheaper to replace than to maintain them, which meant supporting those too young and too old to work.

The Slave Trade

The mechanism of replacement, the great wheel that turned all of eighteenth-century colonial commerce, was the slave trade. Slaving was a textbook example of what mercantilist economists called the "triangular trade." Ships from Liverpool or Nantes exchanged cheap textiles, gunpowder, or gin for slaves provided by native traders at stations on the West African coast. As new cargo, the slaves were transported to the West Indies. Allowing for a 15 to 20 percent mortality rate en route, the survivors would sell for approximately five times their original purchase price. The ships would then fill up with sugar and return home.

The transatlantic voyage, known euphemistically as the "middle passage," took two months. The slaves were segregated by sex and packed together below decks in chains, helpless amid vermin and rats. In fair weather they were exercised on deck, under the lash; when seas were rough, they were kept below with the portholes shut. The tensions of the voyage provoked insane acts of cruelty. The captain of one ship allegedly flogged a 10-month-old child with a cat-o'-nine-tails for refusing to eat, then plunged the child into scalding water, tied it to a log, flogged it again, this time to death, and forced its mother to throw it into the sea.

Once ashore, the slaves in Britain's Caribbean colonies possessed neither legal nor moral rights. A planter who flogged a 14-year-old girl to death was actually tried

This depiction of the interior of a slave ship seized off the coast of West Africa in 1846 was drawn by Godfrey Meynell, a British naval officer on antislavery patrol. [National Maritime Museum, London]

for murder in Jamaica but was acquitted on the ground that "it was impossible [that] a master could destroy his own property." The Spaniards had tried to justify their conquest of the Americas by the necessity to convert the heathen, but eighteenth-century missionaries were forbidden to proselytize among blacks, and one slave caught going to church in Grenada was given 24 lashes.

In assessing the mutual dependence of sugar and the slave trade and its overall economic impact, it would be a mistake to focus too narrowly on the calculations of the plantation owner, crucial though they were. Only by bringing profitable cargo into the New World on a large scale and a regular basis could the European sugar market be developed, since merchant fleets would not risk the journey across the Atlantic with empty hulls, and the sugar islands were hardly major consumers of manufactured products. Thus slaves were vital not only to the production of the tropical economy but also to its marketing process. If black mortality in the New World had not exceeded reproduction, a saturation level would have been reached, and the slave trade would have died. From this perspective the sugar market could have been sustained only by the continual reduction of the slave population from overwork and disease.

The economic significance of the slave trade was in its business and profit-generating capacity as a whole. The existence of the trade meant a steady demand for shipping; the feeding and clothing of millions of slaves was a major stimulus to textiles and agriculture. The capital spinoff into the European economy was therefore of considerable importance; and it was with the mechanization of the textile industry, financed in part by the slave trade, that the Industrial Revolution began.

Liverpool was the chief port of terminus for the sugar and slave trades, and it prospered accordingly. The corner of Tithebarn Street is shown, with the back of the Town Hall at right. Behind the hall, space is being cleared for the erection of a new commercial exchange, in which the man with the wheelbarrow is presumably employed. [Herdman Collection, Liverpool Public Library]

LIVERPOOL IN THE AGE OF SLAVERY

Even before industrialization the influx of slave-generated wealth was very evident. Liverpool, an English coastal town on the Irish Sea with a population of barely 500 in the sixteenth century, became the chief slave port of Europe, carrying at its height almost two-thirds of the British and nearly half of the total European slave trade. The town's rise to success was in part the result of the bankrupting of the London slave merchants in the South Sea Bubble of 1720. Enterprising Liverpudlians soon took over from them, taking advantage of the port's westerly location. The profitable War of the Austrian Succession in the 1740s also enabled trade, in the words of a local merchant, "to spread her golden wings." By 1750 a flotilla of nearly 200 ships directly served the slave trade, and four years later a splendid new exchange opened on Castle Street—as if to emphasize the alliance of commerce and government, it also housed the town hall. It was serviced by fourteen banks; these operated their own insurance companies, collected the excise, and guaranteed municipal finances.

From Liverpool the prosperity produced by the slave and sugar trade spread visibly across the English landscape in the form of great country houses and the merchant mansions of London and Bath. As early as 1729 the pamphleteer Joshua Gee noted that "all the great increase in our treasure proceeds chiefly from the labor of negroes in the plantations." But conspicuous consumption by the rich was not the principal result of the commerce in human lives. The new wealth was to lay the ground for Britain's rise to world power.

THE FIRST AGE OF GLOBAL WAR

The wars of the early modern period, particularly in what has sometimes been called the era of the second Hundred Years' War (1689–1815), had been fought for a variety of reasons, including religion, dynastic rivalry, and positional advantage on the European continent. Increasingly, however, the major wars of Europe involved conflict in four overseas areas as well—North America, the West Indies, Africa, and India. By the time of the Seven Years' War (1756–1763) these external theaters had become more important than the European struggle itself.

The wars of Europe were, then, in part the effect of expansion; but they were a cause of it as well. The use of firearms and cannon in European warfare became decisive between 1460 and 1540, and during that time, iron production rose by as much as 500 percent and copper by even more. The mechanization of war made it the monopoly of the state. As heavy field pieces replaced horses, armor, and crossbows as the major capital investment in warfare, private noblemen could no longer afford the personal armies that had been the hallmark (and often the bane) of the late medieval period. A modern arsenal containing furnaces, forges, foundries, gunpowder mills, and saltpeter shops might employ, as did the French arsenal at St. Étienne in the early seventeenth century, 700 or more workers. The building of warships, which carried two or three banks of cannon and often exceeded 1,000 tons, was an even more complex activity, requiring specialized skills and materials that might come from halfway around the world. The state alone possessed the resources for such investment, and this in turn spurred its own growth. The increasing scale of warfare, the expanding role of the state, and the widening arc of commerce were all part of the dynamic that made Europe's wars, as well as its economic activity, worldwide.

The New Balance of Power

The wars of Louis XIV marked a turning point in the attempt to achieve a balance of power in Europe. France remained, as it would for the next century and a half, the dominant land power on the Continent. Its main rival, however, was no longer Spain, its great antagonist in the Thirty Years' War, or Austria, the chief barrier to its expansion in Germany, Italy, and the Low Countries, but Britain. Britain owed its new international prominence to its naval supremacy, its commercial wealth, and, perhaps most important, its access to that wealth through the working partnership of the landed elite, the financial community, and the organs of government.

Walpole, Britain's First Prime Minister

The stability of the new British system was epitomized by the man who made it function for two decades, Sir

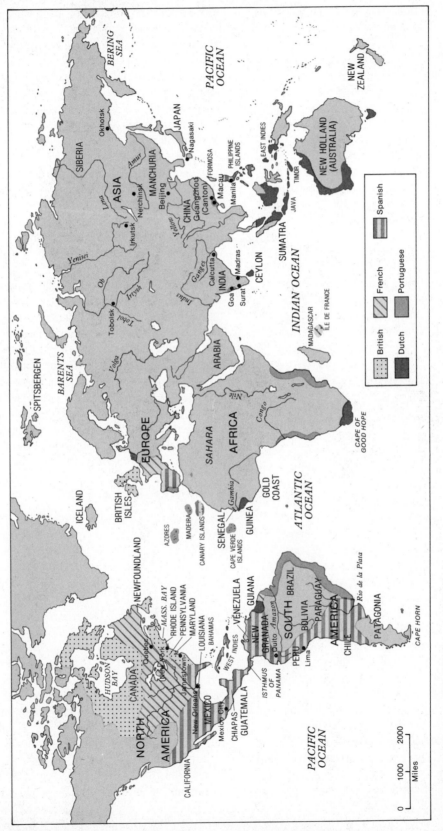

17.2 The Expansion of Europe, 1715

Robert Walpole (1676–1745). The son of a prosperous Norfolk squire, Walpole sat in Parliament for 40 years, held high office for 30, and for some 20—from 1722 to 1742—was the effective ruler of the country, the first prime minister of Britain in fact if not in name.

Walpole grasped the fact that the Glorious Revolution of 1688 had settled the basic issues of seventeenth-century British politics, creating a limited monarchy firmly subject to the wishes of the landed gentry. What remained, with rising prosperity and a stable dynasty on the throne, was to organize the division of spoils. Walpole's command of the system was based on his control of its three major components: the crown, Parliament, and patronage. The support of the first two Hanoverian kings, George I (1714–1727) and George II (1727–1760), was his anchor. He consulted their wishes, cultivated their prejudices, and flattered their mistresses; through them he consolidated and controlled all honors, offices, and contracts, rewarding his friends and punishing his enemies. This monopoly of favor enabled him in turn to ensure a comfortable majority in Parliament.

The Triumph of the Elite

The real stability of the British system, however, was in the unchallenged dominance of the landed elite, particularly its uppermost stratum. The government of eighteenth-century Britain rested securely with some 400 families who controlled one-quarter of the arable land in the country. This concentration of ownership was the result of several interrelated factors. Large estates were protected from partition by laws that required that they be passed on to a single heir, who was prohibited from selling off parcels except under strict conditions. The value of land had been enhanced by increased productivity, the result in part of agricultural improvements, in part of laws that encouraged grain export. This spurred the process known as *enclosure,* by which common grazing land and individual farm plots were fenced in by wealthy landowners armed with sheriffs' writs or private acts of Parliament. By 1840, 6 million acres had been enclosed in this fashion, bringing another quarter of Britain's farmland under elite control. The small independent farmer or yeoman, once the backbone of English agriculture, became virtually extinct in the nineteenth century, disappearing into the mass of wage laborers and tenant farmers who worked the great estates of the few.

Such a process might have been expected to produce unrest and even rebellion, yet Britain's countryside was for most of the eighteenth century among the most peaceful in Europe. This was partly due to the unique nature of its aristocracy. Only about 200 families in England held formal titles of nobility (in contrast to half a million each in France and Spain), and the only distinct advantage that such titles conveyed was the right to sit in the House of Lords. It entailed no other significant legal privileges such as marked off Continental elites from the mass of the population, particularly exemption from taxation. Indeed, the difference between Britain and the other European monarchies might be summarized by saying that whereas on the Continent the landed elite tolerated royal control of taxation on the condition that it fall chiefly on others, in Britain the landed elite accepted the burden of taxation in return for the right to control it through Parliament.

The absence of a status system based primarily on titles and legal privileges meant that wealth itself was the basic criterion for membership in the British elite. This encouraged entrepreneurship and investment, and the ever-expanding wealth of this elite provided the sinews of empire. At the same time it was a true governing class that controlled the instruments of social order from the pay of the local justice of the peace to the provision of the Royal Navy. Few aristocracies in history had exercised so clear and thorough a dominion over their societies as that of eighteenth-century Britain.

France Under Louis XV

The situation of France was quite different. Louis XIV had devoted much of his energy to reducing the nobility to political impotence. He had worked all his life to create a system of government dependent on the will and capacity of the sovereign, only to leave his throne to a 5-year-old boy, Louis XV. Power devolved upon his elder cousin, Philip, duke of Orléans, as regent. With a nobleman heading the government the aristocracy reasserted its claims to power, with disastrous results for central authority. By 1723, Louis XV had proclaimed his majority; but in a real sense he never attained it. Though served by some able ministers, he lacked the discipline and the character to impose his will on the government, and so faint was his impress on the history of his long reign (1715–1774) that the age is better remembered for a shrewd and vivacious royal mistress, Madame de Pompadour, than for its titular ruler. Without forceful leadership the bureaucracy became slack and unresponsive, the intendants pursued policies at variance with those of the government, and the parlements openly defied the crown, supporting opposition groups and successfully resisting all efforts to raise taxes or to bring their collection under effective control. While the British crown had access to virtually unlimited credit through the Bank of England at low interest, tax farmers continued to siphon off one-third of royal revenues in France. An attempt to create a central bank on the British model early in Louis' reign failed, in part through the collapse of its stock and in part from the opposition of the farmers. Thus, although France had three times the population and gross national product of England, its government was far less fiscally stable and efficient.

The Wars of Midcentury

Europe enjoyed a generation of relative calm after the Peace of Utrecht, but a contested dynastic succession brought war again in 1740 when Maria Theresa (1740–1780), the first female sovereign in the history of the Habsburg dynasty, became empress of Austria and queen of Hungary. Her father, Charles VI (1711–1740), had spent the better part of his reign trying to get the princes of Europe to recognize her right to succeed him through a document known as the Pragmatic Sanction. Their promises were worthless. Charles Albert, the elector of Bavaria, immediately claimed the Austrian throne. Bavaria, in turn, was considered a mere stalking-horse for Austria's archrival, France. At the same time, Frederick II of Prussia sought to take advantage of Austria's disarray by seizing the rich province of Silesia. This was the signal for a general conflict, the War of the Austrian Succession (1740–1748).

The war soon turned into another chapter in the great imperial war of the century between Britain and France. Britain entered it on the side of Austria, while France supported Prussia and Bavaria. The Anglo-French conflict once again extended to North America, where fighting ranged from Canada to the isthmus of Panama. In the end, France's success on land was checked by Britain's supremacy at sea. The Treaty of Aix-la-Chapelle (1748) restored Britain and France to their original positions, as the British surrendered Fort Louisburg in Canada in return for their trading station at Madras on the east coast of India. The only belligerent to come out ahead was Frederick of Prussia, who, having realized his objective in the conquest of Silesia, had dropped out of the war six years before.

The Seven Years' War

The absence of a clear winner ensured an early resumption of the conflict. The Seven Years' War (1756–1763) marked the decisive triumph of the British Empire over that of France on all fronts, in North America, Africa, and India. It also marked the end of the rivalry between the Habsburg and Bourbon dynasties that had been the polestar of European politics for the previous 250 years, when Count Kaunitz, the Austrian foreign minister, daringly proposed to cede the Austrian Netherlands to France in return for help in recapturing Silesia from Prussia. Kaunitz completed the diplomatic isolation of Prussia by entering into an alliance with Russia, which thus joined the European concert of powers for the first time. For five years, Frederick fought a war of survival against apparently hopeless odds, earning the appellation "the Great." The toll, however, was immense. The Prussian army was reduced from 150,000 in its first campaign to 90,000 in its last. Frederick himself despaired of the final outcome. "To tell the truth," he wrote a minister, "I believe all is lost. I will not survive the ruin of my country."

For Britain, too, the war went badly at first. In North America the French built a line of forts to block British expansion in the Ohio valley and repelled expeditionary forces sent against them under General Edward Braddock and the young colonial colonel, George Washington. After a series of further reverses culminating in the loss of the Mediterranean island of Minorca, the inept ministry of the duke of Newcastle was replaced in June 1757 with one headed by William Pitt (1708–1778).

Pitt, the son of a great merchant in the Indian trade, was a leader born for crisis. Magnificent in debate, possessed by his vision of Britain's imperial destiny, he had been for 20 years the dominant personality in the House of Commons. Yet power had eluded him. Harsh and uncompromising, often ill, and frequently unstable, he had none of Walpole's managerial skills, and George II despised him. In the crisis of 1757, however, no one else would do. For the next four years he ruled with almost dictatorial powers and brought Britain victory.

Pitt's strategy was to keep Frederick the Great in the field against the French and the Austrians while he applied Britain's naval superiority against France's North American empire and plundered its trade. In effect, while the French refought the Hundred Years' War in Flanders, Britain would fight for everything else.

The French fleet was neutralized, and the sheer weight of numbers in the North American campaign—the 13 colonies now had a combined population of 2.5 million against only 70,000 permanent French settlers—told at last. The French forts on the Great Lakes and the St. Lawrence River fell, and the Ohio valley was evacuated. Quebec was captured after a daring campaign in 1759, and with the fall of Montreal in 1760 the last French army in North America surrendered. French aggression also backfired in India, where the British found themselves after their victory at Plassey in 1757 in possession not only of the rich Carnatic coast but also of the entire hinterland of Bengal.

Pitt resigned in 1761 when his cabinet balked at his plans to conquer the whole of the French West Indies. The Peace of Paris (1763) reflected the view of more cautious men that Britain could not hold onto all it had conquered and that any attempt to do so would shortly provoke another war. The French were restored to the sugar island of Guadeloupe and permitted again to trade in India and to fish off Newfoundland. Havana and Manila, taken from Spain, were returned in exchange for Florida. From his back bench seat, Pitt denounced the treaty as a betrayal of Britain's blood and treasure. Nonetheless, victory over France was complete and decisive. Britain had gained all of Canada, doubling the size of its American territories. France would never, it seemed, pose a threat to Britain's hegemony in the New World again. The significance of the unexpected British victory in India would prove even greater, as India's wealth provided much of the capital for the Industrial Revolution a generation later. If Britain had not achieved all that Pitt desired, it had accomplished more than anyone but Pitt would have thought possible.

With the hope of winning Flanders gone, the French deserted their Austrian allies. Russia too pulled out in 1762. With no hope of accomplishing alone what it had failed to do with two powerful allies, Austria reluctantly made peace with Prussia (1763). Frederick the Great retained Silesia, although it had cost him the near-destruction of his country to do so, and the remainder of his reign was spent largely in rebuilding it. The transfer of this single province from the Habsburg to the Hohenzollern crown was the only territorial result of two great wars in Europe. Those wars were the last to be fought over questions of dynastic succession and among the first to be fought for the high stakes of overseas empire.

THE BIRTH OF THE AMERICAN REPUBLIC

The British prepared to exploit and extend their new conquests in North America, but they failed to take into account the existing colonies, whose inhabitants, themselves largely of English and Scots-Irish stock, had reached a point of economic and political maturity at which they were no longer prepared to subordinate their interests to those of the mother country. The result was rebellion and the creation of the first independent nation in the New World, the United States of America.

The American Colonies and Britain

By 1763 the 13 colonies of the Atlantic seaboard had become an important market for British manufactures, and if they could not yet compete with the West Indian sugar islands in sheer profitability, their size and the potential for expansion opened up by the conquest of Canada ensured that they would eventually dominate Britain's American empire. Yet within 13 years those colonies would begin the first successful rebellion in the New World, within 13 more they would have established the first indigenous non-European republic in history, and little more than three decades later, with their example and in part with their support, the whole of the Western Hemisphere south of Canada would have thrown off the European yoke brought in with the Spanish conquest.

It might be said with justice that the cause of the 13 colonies' rebellion was Britain's attempt actually to govern them. Until 1763 they had enjoyed an extraordinary degree of independence. Though theoretically subject to the British Parliament, they were exempt from British taxation and had their own assemblies, legal systems, and finances. Instead of serving the home economy as envisioned by mercantile theory, the colonists competed with British ships in the Newfoundland fisheries, built their own vessels in competition with British shipyards, and carried on a lively smuggling trade with the West Indies. They considered themselves not a subject people but Britons with the same rights and entitlements as anyone living in Britain itself.

The crown viewed matters differently. It regarded the colonies as a dominion or possession, united to it like Ireland but distinct from the realm of Britain itself, which after 1707 had consisted of England, Wales, and Scotland. Ireland too had its own lawmaking assembly, the Irish Parliament, but its subservience to the acts of the British Parliament had been spelled out in the Declaratory Act of 1719. Whereas Ireland was a plantation economy in which an Anglo-Scottish minority ruled a subject population of Catholic tenantry, most colonists were independent freeholders or wage earners. And while Ireland was geographically in Britain's shadow, the American colonies were 3,000 miles away.

America's distance from Britain made it difficult not only to control but also to defend. Even after the defeat of the French, the western frontiers were insecure, as the general rising of Indian tribes under Pontiac in May 1763 made clear. The British government was anxious to prevent uncontrolled settlement beyond the Appalachian Mountains, which was certain to provoke more such attacks. Accordingly, it placed the trans-Appalachian west under direct royal control, although several of the colonies had already claimed the Mississippi River as their border. At the same time it proposed to maintain a permanent army of 10,000 to guard the frontier and levied new taxes, notably on all stamped or licensed paper, to help pay for it.

Protest and Rebellion

The British were quite unprepared for the explosion of protest that greeted these acts. Rioters burned the official stamps and formed resistance groups called the Sons of Liberty, merchants boycotted British wares, the colonial assemblies passed resolutions denouncing taxation without representation in Parliament, and nine colonies sent representatives to a Stamp Act Congress in New York. The British reacted uncertainly. On the one hand, they affirmed parliamentary control of the colonies, arguing that the colonists were "virtually" represented in Parliament in the same way as Britons at home who lived in boroughs that lacked a parliamentary franchise. On the other hand, they repealed the Stamp Act and reduced the much hated customs levy on sugar to a token penny per gallon.

This did not resolve matters. The American colonies were importing almost £2 million more in British goods by 1770 than they were shipping back across the Atlantic. If they could not recoup that sum in trade with the West Indies, legally or illegally, their economy, particularly that of the mercantile northeast, could not survive. Concern for prosperity merged with concern for legal rights. The closing of the western frontier and the policing of the Caribbean menaced two freedoms that Americans valued highly indeed: freedom of movement and freedom of trade.

A clash between British soldiers and a mob in Boston that left five colonists dead sobered both sides momentarily. The British prime minister, Lord North, withdrew all British imposts except that on tea and announced that no further taxes would be levied. When colonists dumped unwanted East India Company tea in Boston harbor in 1773, however, North responded by imposing martial law on Massachusetts. At the same time, Parliament passed the Quebec Act, extending the Canadian frontier southward to the Ohio River. Unrelated in British eyes, these actions signaled a new campaign of repression to the colonials.

Events now moved swiftly. An assembly of all the colonies calling itself the Continental Congress met in Philadelphia in September 1774. Although it still acknowledged the authority of the crown, its very meeting was regarded as an act of rebellion in Britain. Sporadic fighting broke out in Massachusetts in the spring of 1775, and in May the Continental Congress voted to raise an army in defense of the colonies. Many in Britain opposed the drift to war, but North, pressured by King George III (1760–1820) to bring the colonies to heel, found himself without a politically acceptable way to back down.

The Revolutionary War

On July 4, 1776, the Continental Congress declared the independence of the 13 colonies in a document, drafted largely by Thomas Jefferson of Virginia, whose tone was more of sorrow than of anger. The colonials had little choice but resistance or surrender. Strong forces had already landed from Canada, with reinforcements from Britain. Inferior in numbers and training, with British troops in possession of Boston, New York, and Philadelphia, the colonial army fought at first merely to survive. But in October 1777 a British army blundered into a trap in the wilderness near Saratoga, New York, and was forced to surrender.

This defeat changed the character of the war. France entered on the colonial side in 1778, and Spain a year later. America's war for independence had become an international struggle in which Britain found itself rapidly isolated. Control of not only the Atlantic seaboard but also the West Indies, the Mediterranean, and even India was at stake. Gibraltar withstood a three-year siege

John's Trumbull's famous portrait of the signing of the Declaration of Independence. The drum, trumpets, and crossed flags on the wall symbolize resolve for the war of independence yet to be fought. [Copyright Yale University Art Gallery]

(1779–1782) that was, militarily, the largest operation of the war, and a French thrust at Jamaica was repelled in 1782. But the French fleet, temporarily gaining control of the waters off Virginia, forced the surrender of another large British army at Yorktown in October 1781.

With their empire threatened on all fronts, the British could no longer continue the draining struggle in America. The independence of the colonies was recognized in the Treaty of Paris (1783); Minorca and East Florida were returned to Spain, and the French recovered some West Indian islands and their former strongholds in Senegal. A shattered Britain was left to redirect its imperial energies toward India and East Asia, and in 1788 it began to colonize Australia.

Forming a Nation

Having won their independence, the 13 colonies set about the task of forming themselves into a nation. The Declaration of Independence had boldly asserted that "all men are created equal"—a revolutionary sentiment in a world ruled by monarchy and nobles, although America had never had a hereditary aristocracy—yet the new nation was clearly dominated by a landed and mercantile elite, and one-fifth of its total population consisted of black slaves. But the revolution liberalized

white American society to a significant degree. Primogeniture and entail, which protected large estates from division, were swept away; Anglican and Congregationalist churches lost their privileged positions, paving the way for the complete separation of church and state that would be one of the most radical features of the U.S. Constitution; and the electoral franchise was widened in a number of states. These represented concessions won by workers, farmers, frontiersmen, and religious dissidents in return for support of the rebellion.

Though America was far from having achieved true egalitarianism and though the cloud of slavery hung over its future, it was incontestably the most democratic state in the world and the first since the short-lived English Commonwealth of the 1650s to proclaim the sovereignty of the people, or at least of those who were free and male. As such, it was a potent inspiration for reformers in Britain and elsewhere in the Old World, a unique experiment that embodied much of the advanced political thought of the century.

From Confederation to Commonwealth

At first the 13 states were individually sovereign entities that associated themselves loosely under the so-called Articles of Confederation. Each state had its own constitution, civil laws, militia, and currency. The Continental Congress continued as a national organ, but it lacked the power to tax or to raise an army and could order nothing without the approval of all 13 states. There were no central courts to resolve disputes between the states, most of which had rival territorial claims, and no agency existed to provide for common trade policy, diplomacy, and defense. As John Adams of Boston remarked, trying to provide for any collective interest was like trying to get 13 clocks to chime at once. In addition, the elites feared that continued popular pressure on weak state governments for political and economic reform would lead to anarchy.

The result was a convention that met in Philadelphia in the summer of 1787 with the approval of the Continental Congress to amend the Articles of Confederation. The leading members of the convention, including George Washington (1732–1799), the revolutionary war commander who chaired it, and James Madison of Virginia (1751–1836), scrapped the articles completely and devised an entirely new constitution. This created a new federal entity, the United States of America, with a bicameral legislature composed of a House of Representatives and a Senate empowered to levy taxes, raise an army, regulate commerce, fix a uniform national currency, and, in a sweeping grant of authority, "make all laws necessary and proper for carrying into execution" these powers. A strong executive was also provided, consisting of a president and vice-president, as well as the foundation of a national court system.

Historians of the American Revolution have been divided ever since the publication of Charles A. Beard's *Economic Interpretation of the Constitution* in 1913 over whether the U.S. Constitution was a betrayal of the democratic promise of the new republic by a cabal of rich men anxious to protect their property through a strong government. Unquestionably, the new system reflected suspicion of, if not hostility toward, popular democracy. It was warmly welcomed by the elites and viewed with skepticism by wage earners and small farmers. But Madison, the constitution's most articulate defender, argued that no lesser degree of centralized authority would suffice to govern a state larger than any in Europe except Russia and larger than any republic in history. After turbulent debate, the constitution was ratified by the states, and the new republic was inaugurated in 1789 with George Washington as its first president.

American and Canadian Expansion

The new nation was expansionist from the start. As early as 1787, plans were laid in the Northwest Ordinance for the development of new states in the territory west of the Alleghenies, and new land was systematically acquired by purchase (Louisiana, Florida, Alaska), annexation (Texas), settlement and negotiation (Oregon), and conquest (New Mexico, California). By the midnineteenth century, Americans had fulfilled what they called their "manifest destiny" of becoming a transcontinental power with a larger territorial mass than that of any other nation save Russia and China.

The chief obstacle to the expansion of the United States was the native Amerindian population. Although less sophisticated than the Mayans, Aztecs, and Incas of pre-Columbian America, the Indians of North America were far from primitive. They farmed as well as hunted, formed complex political and commercial networks, and often lived in towns. The Shawnee chieftain Tecumseh (1768–1813), who allied himself with the British during the Anglo-American war of 1812, dreamed of a united Indian nation strong enough to drive whites off the continent altogether, but the withdrawal of the British ended all practicable hopes of resistance. The Amerindians were largely decimated by war, forced migration, disease, and starvation, and by 1890, only a million Amerindians were left in the territorial United States.

Visiting the United States in the 1830s, the French observer Alexis de Tocqueville ventured the bold prediction that the United States would have a population of 100 million within 100 years and would be, with Russia, the great power of the twentieth century. America, Tocqueville asserted, represented the triumph of equality and of the democratic revolution that he believed was destined to sweep the globe. But sectional antagonisms between the urban north and the plantation society of the south, particularly over the issue of the westward expansion of slavery, were destined to divide the new nation, which by 1861 had collapsed in civil war.

Many former Loyalists—supporters of the British cause in the American Revolution—had fled to Canada after independence. The British, attempting to deal with a still preponderantly French population, divided Canada into two jurisdictions in 1791. English-speaking Upper Canada, the future province of Ontario, retained English laws and institutions, while French-speaking Lower Canada, now Quebec, kept French law, seigneurial land tenures, and an officially recognized Catholic church. After 1839, Britain reunited Upper and Lower Canada over the latter's opposition, and the British North America Act of 1867 created the Dominion of Canada, a fully self-governing entity within the British Empire. This voluntary granting of independence, called "devolution," was to be applied later to the other former colonies that remain associated in what is today the British Commonwealth of Nations.

THE ABOLITION OF THE SLAVE TRADE AND THE EMANCIPATION OF SPANISH AMERICA

The last quarter of the eighteenth century witnessed a revulsion against the Atlantic slave trade. At the same time the profitability of the slave trade declined sharply with the collapse of sugar prices in the 1790s. The framers of the U.S. Constitution agreed to abolish the slave trade after 1807, and Britain also outlawed it in that year, soon to be followed by most other European states. Slavery itself, however, remained legal in the British Empire until 1833, in the United States until 1863, and in Brazil and Cuba until 1886 and 1888, respectively. The slave trade continued to flourish illegally for most of the nineteenth century, and a British commission reported in 1844 that more slaves were being transported than at any time in the previous century.

What doomed the slave trade—at least in the West Indies, where the advanced economies of Britain and France predominated—was the obsolescence of the old colonial system itself. As the Scottish economist Adam Smith argued persuasively in *The Wealth of Nations* (1776), free trade was far more profitable to a state such as Britain than a rigid protectionism that tied down capital, engendered pointless wars, and leaked away profits in smuggling. With the loss of the 13 colonies by Britain and of Haiti (whose slaves had rebelled under Toussaint L'Ouverture in 1791) by France, the futility of a closed labor and commercial system became apparent.

The economy of Spanish America had gradually been reorganized in response to pressures from the more advanced imperial powers, but politically it was as tightly ruled from Madrid as before. Despite earlier rebellions in Peru and Colombia and the spread of republican ideas among some of the Creole (American-born) class, disaffection was not widespread until Spain was occupied by Napoleon in 1808. For the next six years the American colonies refused to recognize the French-installed ruler, Joseph Bonaparte, and were left to fend for themselves. When the Bourbon ruler Ferdinand VII was restored in 1814, most of the colonies swore renewed allegiance to him. In the six years of Ferdinand's absence, however, they had come of age politically. When Ferdinand, blind to the new situation, attempted to reimpose royal government and commercial monopoly in its old form, there was widespread resentment.

SIMÓN BOLÍVAR, THE LIBERATOR

Disillusionment with Ferdinand was exploited by republican nationalists, who had staged several abortive revolts during the interregnum of 1808–1814, notably in Mexico, Venezuela, and Argentina. Though formally professing loyalty to Spain, the Argentines refused to readmit the old royal officials and declared independence under their leader José de San Martín (1778–1850) in 1816. By 1821, San Martín had occupied Lima and declared Peru liberated. Royalist forces soon retook it, however, and the real work of revolution was left to another Creole leader, Simón Bolívar.

Bolívar was born in Caracas, Venezuela, in 1783, the fourth child of one of the oldest and wealthiest noble families in the city. Orphaned at an early age, Bolívar was fired as a young man by the republican ideals of the American and French revolutions. Like most Creole aristocrats, he completed his studies in Europe and was present in Paris when Napoleon was crowned emperor.

Bolívar began his revolutionary career in an abortive uprising at Caracas in 1810, in which he played a leading role. After toying with the idea of accepting a commission in the British army in Spain, he raised a new rebel army, declaring war to the death against the Spanish empire. By January 1814 he had returned to Caracas, declaring Venezuela a republic with himself as its head. Rather than choosing a more conventional name as head of state, he adopted the title of "liberator," symbolizing his commitment to the freeing of all of New Granada. Driven out by the Spaniards six months later, he fled to Jamaica but returned to Venezuela in 1817 and, raising an army of native forces and British soldiers of fortune, staged a daring invasion of Colombia. By August 1819 the entire province was in his hands, and three months later he proclaimed a constitution for the United States of Colombia, including Venezuela, where the last pro-Spanish resistance was extinguished in 1821. Ecuador fell in 1822, and Peru was conquered in 1824.

Bolívar hoped to unite this entire area—virtually all

17.3 Latin American Independence

of South America apart from Brazil, Argentina, and Chile—into a single great republic. But his brutal methods of conquest, the indiscipline of his armies, and his undoubted dictatorial tendencies ultimately defeated what remained a noble if tarnished dream. By his death in 1830 the provinces of what he called "Gran Colombia" had splintered again into their old imperial configurations. "He who serves a revolution," he wrote in one of his final letters, "ploughs the sea."

The End of Empire

Backward Brazil, a slave society with few cities worthy of the name, had an even more passive revolution. The regent John came to it in exile after Napoleon's conquest of Portugal, and when he attempted to recall his son Pedro home again in 1822, the Brazilians refused to let him go, raising him to the position of emperor and driving Portuguese troops out of the country. In the viceroyalty of New Spain a rebellion that had broken out in Mexico in 1810 under the leadership of a Creole priest, Father Hidalgo, was brought to completion in 1821 by a renegade royalist, Augustín de Iturbide, who proclaimed himself emperor. The remaining provinces of New Spain—Honduras, Nicaragua, San Salvador, and Costa Rica—all became independent at the same time, rejecting union with Mexico or each other.

Within ten years, Spain had been divested of an empire it had ruled with remarkable equanimity for three centuries, retaining only Cuba and Puerto Rico of its former possessions in the New World. Unlike the newly fledged United States, Spain's colonies were ill prepared for independence. The new states of Central and South America, where a 20 percent white minority continued to perpetuate oligarchic rule over a majority population of native and mixed (*mestizo*) blood, subsided into a period of political oppression, governmental instability, and economic exploitation from which they began to emerge only in the twentieth century.

SUMMARY

The colonies of the New World became a critical element in the advanced European economies of the eighteenth century, and the character of European warfare was gradually reshaped by the struggle for possession of them. By the end of the first quarter of the nineteenth century most of those colonies had gained their independence, and what remained in European hands—Canada and most of the West Indies—had become relatively insignificant in economic terms. Nevertheless, the wealth derived from them was a crucial factor in the development of the new global economy and of capitalist enterprise, particularly in Britain. The transportation of millions of blacks across the Atlantic constituted the largest involuntary migration in human history up to this time, and their settlement throughout North and South America profoundly altered the demographic and social structure of the New World.

Suggestions for Further Reading

Brown, P. D. *William Pitt, Earl of Chatham: The Great Commoner.* London: Allen & Unwin, 1978.

Davis, D. B. *The Problem of Slavery in the Age of Revolution.* Ithaca, N.Y.: Cornell University Press, 1966.

de Vries, J. *The Economy of Europe in an Age of Crisis, 1600–1750.* Cambridge: Cambridge University Press, 1976.

Dorn, W. D. *Competition for Empire, 1740–1763.* New York: Harper, 1940.

Fieldhouse, D. K. *The Colonial Empires: A Comparative Survey from the Eighteenth Century.* New York: Delacorte Press, 1967.

Fox-Genovese, E., and Genovese, E. D. *Fruits of Merchant Capital: Slavery and Bourgeois Property in the Rise and Expansion of Capitalism.* New York: Oxford University Press, 1983.

Heckscher, E. *Mercantilism.* New York: Macmillan, 1955.

Lynch, J. *The Spanish American Revolutions, 1808–1826.* London: Weidenfeld & Nicolson, 1973.

McDonald, F. *We the People: The Economic Origins of the Constitution.* Chicago: University of Chicago Press, 1958.

Mintz, S. W. *Sweetness and Power: The Place of Sugar in Modern History.* New York: Viking, 1985.

Morgan, E. S. *Birth of the Republic, 1763–1789.* Chicago: University of Chicago Press, 1977.

Nef, J. U. *War and Human Progress.* New York: Russell & Russell, 1968.

Parry, J. H. *Trade and Dominion: European Overseas Empires in the Eighteenth Century.* New York: Praeger, 1971.

Wallerstein, I. *The Modern World System.* New York: Academic Press, 1974, 1980.

Wood, G. S. *The Radicalism of the American Revolution.* New York: Alfred A. Knopf, 1992.

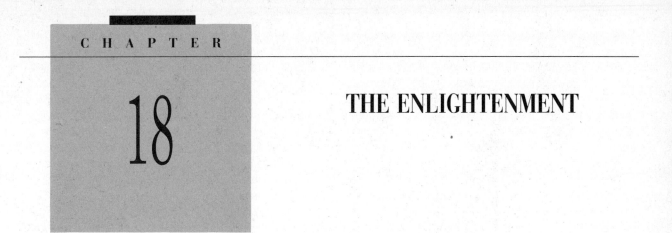

THE ENLIGHTENMENT

The eighteenth century was characterized by a wide-ranging critique of the social and intellectual bases of European culture to which contemporaries gave the name of the Enlightenment. Unlike other movements of renewal and reform in the West since the advent of Christianity, the Enlightenment did not take the form of a religious revival. It grew instead out of the new methods of inquiry bequeathed by the scientific revolution and the questions that its view of the cosmos posed to traditional religion. The thought of the Enlightenment was frankly secular and rationalist, and this, in a society in which all art, science, morality, and political authority had acknowledged the primacy of religious truth for 1,500 years, posed a revolutionary challenge to the social order. At the same time the Enlightenment was a response to economic and political changes at work in European society. Some of the most influential thinkers of the Enlightenment were men of bourgeois origin. Unattached to church or court, they heralded the coming of a new secular society, and their demands for freedom and toleration, their conception of a worldwide human community, and their contempt for inherited privilege echoed the interests of free trade, unfettered enterprise, and an expanding global economy.

The rulers of the eighteenth century could heed or censor their Enlightenment critics, but they could not ignore them. Some monarchs attempted to incorporate Enlightenment principles into an essentially traditional style of governance, with varying results. Other critics, troubled by the divorce of reason from emotional and spiritual values in much of Enlightenment thinking,

urged a new emphasis on feeling and intuition, and a popular religious revival breathed new life into Christian worship. The call to accommodate both intellectual clarity and emotional depth was perhaps best answered in music, whose eighteenth-century masters achieved a balance of feeling and design that has never been surpassed.

THE ROOTS OF
THE ENLIGHTENMENT

The scientific revolution gravely undermined a set of closely interlocked assumptions on which the traditional social order rested. According to the traditional view, all created things had their place on the universal ladder of existence that ultimately led to God. The angels were subordinate to God as humankind was to the angels, beasts to people, and inanimate matter to living organisms, in a descending scale of natural value. Each order of being had its own internal hierarchy as well. There were superior and subordinate angels, higher and lower animals, and nobler and baser persons. The human order was part of the harmony ordained by God for the universe, and anyone who attempted to disturb it was defying God as well as humankind. The historian Arthur O. Lovejoy has named this complex of ideas the "great chain of being."

In social terms, the great chain of being entailed a general principle of subordination by which women and children were subject to the authority of men, commoners to nobles, and all subjects to their rulers. This notion culminated in the idea of the divine right of kings, according to which monarchs received their authority directly from God as a means of enforcing his will on earth.

In practice, the absolute power of monarchs was often subject to challenge. The church of the Counter-Reformation insisted that heretical rulers might be deposed or even killed. The English in 1649 had tried and executed Charles I, and even Louis XIV had known rebellion in the early years of his reign. Beneath the surface of eighteenth-century life, moreover, the Old Regime was not only being reshaped by the stresses of imperial competition and the emerging global economy but also being undermined by the intellectual consequences of the scientific revolution.

The most immediate of these consequences was a weakening of faith in the traditional Christian God of salvation, at least among the more educated classes. It was true that nothing in the new science directly contradicted the tenets of Christianity. But it was difficult to reconcile the biblical God of signs and wonders with the Newtonian universe of self-regulating mechanical motion. Such a God seemed not so much incompatible with this universe as irrelevant to it.

The God of Reason

As scientists began to turn their attention to the natural history of the earth, it was soon apparent that a far longer span was necessary to account for the evolution of its features than the less than 6,000 years that could be calculated from biblical genealogies. The God who had already been exiled to the outer edges of a vast and perhaps boundless universe now seemed to recede as well from the intimate scale of human history to that of a remote, geologic time. Such a God might be conceived of as a creator, but in what sense was he still a father? Yet if the idea of a paternal God had begun to lose its credibility, what would become of the divine right monarchs who ruled in the name of that God? In pulling the linchpin of a traditional Christian God from the great chain of being, the new mechanical universe had called into question the entire justification for the social order that rested on that chain.

For some thinkers, such as Pascal, the erosion of faith in a personal God of salvation was profoundly disturb-

ing. But for many others in the late seventeenth and eighteenth centuries the biblical God died a natural death with the view of nature and the cosmos of which he had been part, to be replaced by a deity more in keeping with the rational world of the new physics. Thus was born what was called "natural religion," or Deism. The rational universe revealed by science, the Deists contended, could never have organized itself by accident and was thus necessarily the product of a rational, divine mind. It followed that the proper way to worship such a God was to study the world itself.

Deists such as John Locke conceded that Christian ethics reflected divine reason. What Christianity could not claim to possess was an exclusive revelation of truth. All religions reflected the "natural religion," which recognized and worshiped the divine intelligence in the world. This was the valid core of each faith, underneath the impurities of dogma and superstition. For this reason, as Locke argued in *An Essay on Toleration* (1689), all religions were worthy of respect but none of priority. Toleration thus emerged as a positive virtue, not merely a truce in a war to the death between rival systems of belief.

The argument that each religion should be sifted for the truth it possessed was akin to the method of science in testing different theories by experiment. Common to both was the assumption that truth was not discovered all at once through external revelation but rather acquired slowly by applying reason to the facts of experience. The scientific revolution itself was the most triumphant demonstration of this process. If the truth about the physical cosmos, obscured even to the greatest minds of antiquity, had been disclosed at last by this method, what mystery could not be made to yield to it? Reason, perfected by the method of science, seemed poised to unlock the final secrets of heaven and earth.

The Idea of Progress

The upshot of these developments was the idea of progress, a notion that changed an entire civilization's conception of itself. For more than 2,000 years the West had thought of its world as the shrunken remnant of a glorious past. The Greeks had looked back to a mythical world of gods and heroes, the Romans of the empire to the virtue of the republic, the Middle Ages to the sanctity of the apostles. Most important of all was the Judeo-Christian account of humankind's fall from grace in the Garden of Eden, a fall that could be redeemed only by divine forgiveness.

The notion of secular progress, the improvement of the human condition through human effort alone, thus required a radical transformation in Western thinking. The scientific revolution, and the Deist faith to which it gave rise, provided the basis of this transformation. The success of the scientific method in explaining the cosmos generated great confidence in its ability to resolve social, political, and even moral problems as well. If humankind could unlock the secrets of the natural world, why should it be unable to master its own human one? At the same time the God of Deism freed humankind from the Christian preoccupation with sin, and it became possible to think of human nature positively.

If, as the idea of progress implied, each historical period could build on the advances of its predecessors, each individual represented a new and untested set of possibilities. The traditional Christian view had assumed that the individual was born in a state of sin and that the primary task of education was to control a natural inclination to evil. In the view suggested by Deism, however, humankind was morally neutral if not instinctively good, and the proper function of education was to maximize society's potential for progress by developing each individual talent to the fullest. John Locke provided the most popular account of this new psychology. In *An Essay Concerning Human Understanding* (1690) he argued that the mind at birth was a blank slate that registered the experience of the senses passively. These sensations were organized by simple categories and processed by reflection. The result was a product called knowledge or understanding. Locke viewed the mind of the child as fluid and malleable. Bombarded by sense impressions and relatively unorganized, it was, he said, "as easily turned this way or that, as water itself." This meant that education was critical in determining human development. Properly guided, the mind could realize its full powers, for both its own benefit and that of society. Deprived of such guidance, or purposely misled, it was prey to superstition, intolerance, and tyranny.

Locke and Liberty

John Locke (1632–1704) was a member of the Whig opposition to Charles II and James II and for a time went into exile under an assumed name. After the Glorious Revolution he published *Two Treatises of Government* (1690), intended to defend the deposition of James II and to refute the theories of Thomas Hobbes.

Hobbes had argued that people contract with a sovereign whose unchallengeable authority erects a society that protects them from one another. Although Hobbes, like Locke, explained human psychology from a materialistic standpoint, his view of the antagonism between individuals reflected traditional Christian pessimism about the depravity of human nature. Locke, by contrast, reflecting the new Deism, argued that humans were innately peaceful, rational, and gregarious in the state of nature, enjoying their natural rights to life, liberty, and the fruit of their own labors. They entered society not from fear but from the desire to increase their wealth and happiness by cooperation with their fellows. The social contract thus involved not a surrender of natural rights but the protection and enhancement of them. Society itself was the voluntary association of free, equal, and separate individuals into the free, equal, and united members of a group.

The first task of society was to establish a rule-making authority or government. Locke rejected Hobbes' assertion that sovereignty must reside in a single person or institution. As each individual had been sovereign over himself or herself in the state of nature, so all were now jointly sovereign over the society they had created together. It followed that government was first and foremost an instrument of the people's will. If the particular government they had chosen proved tyrannical or otherwise defective, the people might amend it or cast if off. Thus the right of rebellion was implicit in the formation of society itself.

Locke's *Treatises* provided what remains the classic foundation of the liberal state, with its emphasis on associative community, representative government, and natural rights. His view of society as an act of collective decision making by free and unconstrained individuals reflected both the Deist vision of humans as rational beings and the values of an emerging secular society with its emphasis on choice and satisfaction. His influence on the American Revolution, with its claim to a people's right to rebel on behalf of their inalienable rights, was obvious, and the convention of the founders who drafted a constitution for the 13 former colonies might almost have stepped from the pages of the second *Treatise* as an illustration of society in the making.

Locke's views remained open to objection, however. His picture of the human mind as a bundle of sensations acted on by reflection did not explain how the capacity to reflect could arise. By locating political sovereignty in the people as a whole, he begged the question of how power is actually exercised in society. In asserting that natural rights disclosed themselves intuitively, he assumed that everyone would agree what these rights were. The English revolutionary Gerrard Winstanley had already rejected one of Locke's rights, the right of property, as incompatible with true liberty, and the abuse of property was to be denounced by Jean-Jacques Rousseau and others in the eighteenth century as well.

PHILOSOPHY IN ACTION

The Enlightenment was a broadly based intellectual movement whose avowed goal was to apply reason to society for the purpose of human betterment. It was led by the *philosophes,* a loose coalition of thinkers and critics who were not philosophers in the traditional sense but social activists for whom knowledge was something to be converted into reform. Many of the leading philosophes were French, but they came from virtually every country in Europe, and their ideas were carried everywhere. The philosophes saw themselves not as subjects of a particular country but as citizens of the world, or, in Peter Gay's phrase, as "the party of humanity." They claimed to speak on behalf of all oppressed by tyranny or blighted by ignorance, and their goal was nothing less than a world where reason alone was sovereign.

The philosophes prided themselves on their political and intellectual independence. The bible of their movement, Denis Diderot's *Encyclopedia,* defined the philosophe as one who, "trampling on prejudice, tradition, universal consent, authority, in a word all that enslaves most minds, dares to think for [himself and] . . . to admit nothing except on the testimony of his experience and his reason." The philosophes did not seek specific political reform so much as fundamental changes in values and attitudes that would bring reform about. Their motto, coined by the German philosopher Immanuel Kant, was "Dare to know," and their object, Diderot boasted, was to make "a revolution in men's minds."

Voltaire

The most famous and influential of the philosophes was François Marie Arouet (1694–1778), known to history as Voltaire. Born in Paris, Voltaire was the son of a notary. He began his career as a satiric playwright but ran afoul of the authorities and was twice imprisoned. Forced into exile, he spent three years in England. This experience was the turning point of his career. Voltaire was deeply impressed by the relative freedom he found in England, and his *Philosophical Letters on the English* (1734)

A lively conversation among the philosophes, dominated as usual by Voltaire, whose arm is raised. International celebrities, the philosophes are each identified by number. Diderot, the editor of the *Encyclopedia*, is seated at Voltaire's left. [The Mansell Collection]

praised that nation's institutions. He was influenced as well by Lockean psychology and Newtonian physics, and his *Elements of the Philosophy of Newton* (1738) is one of the most direct links between the scientific revolution and the thought of the Enlightenment.

Unable to publish freely in France, Voltaire accepted an invitation from Frederick the Great of Prussia, at whose court he spent two years (1749–1751). He then retired with his niece and mistress, Madame Denis, to an estate at Ferney, just over the French border in Switzerland, where he spent the last third of his life. There he functioned as a one-man republic, entertaining a steady stream of visitors, firing off as many as 30 letters a day, and carrying on a tireless series of campaigns for justice. The most famous of these was to clear the name of Jean Calas, a French Protestant put to death on the trumped-up charge of having murdered his son to prevent his conversion to Catholicism. As a Deist, Voltaire had no more use for one form of Christianity than another; his interest was in exposing the consequences of bigotry. *"Écrasez l'infame!"*—crush the foul thing!—he cried, and no one did more, by anger or ridicule, to expose intolerance and to undermine the authority of established religion in Europe. The compliment was returned: his last major work, the *Philosophical Dictionary* (1764), was burned in Paris, Geneva, and Rome, and Voltaire observed wryly that the authorities would gladly have burned the author as well.

Satire remained Voltaire's special forte, and his wit was turned against his friends as well as his enemies. His novel *Candide* (1759), the most popular and enduring of all his works, was a satire on the faith of his contemporaries in automatic or unlimited progress. His influential *Essay on Custom* (1756), the first genuine survey of the history of world civilization, sought to show by examining the diversity of the world's cultures that none had a monopoly on beauty or value, just as no religion had a monopoly on truth. In his last years he was able to return to Paris in triumph. He described himself as bowed down with every infirmity of old age; but nothing, he added, "can deprive me of hope."

THE ENLIGHTENMENT AND SOCIETY

When the philosophes put their own society under the lens of reason, they found it seriously wanting. Supersti-

tion abounded; free thought was stifled; education was in the hands of the established churches. Idleness had been elevated to a way of life by the aristocracy, while the efforts of the most productive class, the bourgeoisie, were for the most part scorned. At the same time the idea that the structure of society reflected the hierarchical order of the universe was under attack. "No society can exist without justice," Voltaire had written; yet could a God of reason have created a society in which justice was so perverted? Some of the more radical philosophes had already gone beyond Deism. For such openly avowed atheists as Julien de La Mettrie (1707–1747), Denis Diderot (1713–1784), and Baron d'Holbach (1723–1789) the idea of God itself was the last superstition. Humankind, they declared, was alone in the universe, and society, its own creation, should respond to its needs. If it did not, the answer to the problem had to be sought in humankind itself, for the only law to which humanity was subject was that of its own nature.

Rousseau and the Social Contract

These questions led the philosophes to investigate the origins of society. The most radical analysis was offered by Jean-Jacques Rousseau (1712–1778). Born in Geneva, Rousseau was, unlike most of the philosophes, poor and ill-educated. He ran away from home at the age of 16 and remained a misfit all his life, betraying friends and even abandoning his own children. Rousseau's personal discontents were reflected in his view of society. "Man is born free," he declared, "yet everywhere we find him in chains." Society had not fulfilled human nature but perverted it. In his *Discourse on the Origin of Inequality* (1755) he found the origin of injustice in the institution of property on which civil society was founded. Rousseau depicted the state of nature as an idyllic primitive communism, corrupted by the sin of possession. This in turn led to greed, the source of all oppression. The love of gain made sons wish for the death of their fathers and helped speculators to profit from plague, famine, and war. Far from being the absolute natural right Locke had thought it, property, when perverted by greed, was the evil that usurped and destroyed all other rights.

The solution, Rousseau argued in *The Social Contract* (1762), was to create a society in which private interest was subordinated to the common good. This, he asserted, could be accomplished only if each individual agreed to give up the final determination of his interest to the collective whole. Rousseau saw in this not loss but a gain of freedom. Since each person, while giving up his or her own rights, received at the same time the surrender of everyone else's, the original rights were actually returned many times over. Yet since everyone had made the same exchange, all persons remained exactly equal to one another. This, in Rousseau's view, was the true meaning of the social contract. In Hobbes' version of it, all persons were equal in their subordination to an absolute ruler, but none were free. In Locke's version, all persons were free to pursue their private interests, which led inevitably to inequity, oppression, and the loss of freedom. Only by guaranteeing both freedom and equality, Rousseau believed, could the conditions for a just society be met.

Rousseau called the collective entity in which all individual rights were vested the *general will.* He took the general will (as contrasted to the will of any segment, including a majority) to mean both the permanent interest of the entire community and the course of action that represented its best interest at any given moment. Ideally, the general will would be enacted by the unanimous consent of the entire community. In practice, however, all citizens could not be expected to transcend their private interests, and to wait for unanimity on every question would, Rousseau admitted, reduce the social contract to an empty formula. It would therefore be necessary at some point to oblige dissenters to comply with the general will, for their own good as well as the community's. In the last analysis, Rousseau declared, citizens who could not recognize where their real freedom lay must "be forced to be free."

State and Utopia

Rousseau's insistence that freedom and equality were inseparable was echoed in the famous assertion of the American Declaration of Independence that all men were created free and equal. But Rousseau never clearly explained how the general will was to be recognized. The American founders therefore turned instead to the ideas of another philosophe, the Baron de Montesquieu (1689–1755), who argued in *The Spirit of the Laws* (1748) that liberty was best secured by a separation of the powers of government. Montesquieu's influential notion found its way not only into the checks and balances of the constitution of the United States but also into the French constitution of 1791, the Prussian Code of 1792, the Spanish constitution of 1812, and the short-lived revolutionary constitutions of 1848.

If Montesquieu had the more practical effect on political reform, Rousseau expressed the more funda-

mental tension that lay at the heart of Enlightenment thought. If human beings were created equal in rights but remained unequal in wealth and power, how was society to achieve justice and promote the common welfare? For the Abbé Morelly, author of the *Code of Nature* (1755), the only answer was to abolish all property and commerce and to establish a rigidly egalitarian society in which each individual was allotted a specific quota of production and consumption. The late Enlightenment figure Simon Henri Linguet predicted a widening gap between rich and poor that would lead to general revolution; never, he wrote, "has Europe been nearer to a complete upheaval."

The majority view, expressed by Bernard Mandeville (1670–1733) and Adam Smith (1723–1790), remained optimistic. In his *Fable of the Bees* (1714), Mandeville argued that just as bees building a hive contributed to the greater good without being aware of it, so even vices such as vanity, envy, and pride were useful because they promoted commerce and industry and gave employment. Adam Smith, expounding a similar view more systematically in *The Wealth of Nations* (1776), asserted that public wealth (and thereby private benefit) was maximized by allowing each individual to pursue his or her own selfish interest. Just as the Newtonian universe produced balance and harmony by obeying its own laws without the need of special divine intervention, so the market was a self-regulating mechanism that functioned best when left alone. As Alexander Pope expressed it in verse, "God and Nature link'd the gen'ral frame, / and bade Self-love and Social be the same."

The Philosophes and Their Public

The philosophes reflected many of the aspirations of the commercial classes. But their ideas were also disseminated in the salons of the liberal aristocracy. The salons undermined the social dominance that the French court had enjoyed in the days of Louis XIV and thus some of its power as well. They gave the leading figures of the Enlightenment an entrée into circles of the highest influence, a point acknowledged by a conservative opponent who commented that "an opinion launched in Paris was like a battering ram launched by thirty million men."

Literacy and Censorship

Beyond the salons the philosophes were able to appeal to a new reading public created by the rapid expansion of literacy. For the first time in the West, literature had not merely a circulation but a market, and this market created a new profession, that of the independent writer. Newspapers and periodicals flourished, among them the remarkable *Journal des dames* ("Ladies' Journal"), whose feminist tone was ringingly set by its first female editor, Madame de Beaumer: "Be silent, all critics, and know that this is a *woman* addressing you!"

The appetite for serious discussion was indicated by the emergence of provincial literary academies that sponsored essay competitions; Rousseau himself first gained recognition through a competition offered by the Dijon Academy. Lower down on the social scale were less formally organized reading clubs and social groups such as the Freemasons, a social brotherhood dedicated to celebrating human dignity whose members included figures as diverse as Mozart and Benjamin Franklin.

The governments of the Old Regime tried vainly to stem the spread of new and seditious ideas through the licensing of printers and booksellers, censorship, and confiscation. In Austria under Maria Theresa, even foreign ambassadors had their luggage searched for forbidden books, and Prussia under Frederick William I exiled its foremost philosopher, Christian Wolff. In addi-

tion, the Catholic church maintained its *Index of Prohibited Books,* and such bodies as law courts and universities could also order the suppression of printed works.

The philosophes used great ingenuity in getting around censorship. Some of them used the device of the fictional reporter, as Montesquieu did in his *Persian Letters,* or fantasy, as the satirist Jonathan Swift (1667–1745) did in *Gulliver's Travels.* A large underground book trade also flourished, fed by presses in Switzerland and the Low Countries that supplemented their business in serious social criticism with scandal, gossip, blasphemy, and pornography. One enterprising Spanish editor even established a journal called *El Censor.*

The Encyclopedia

The most important and embattled publishing project of the Enlightenment was the great *Encyclopedia,* conceived and edited by Denis Diderot (1713–1784). The son of a provincial artisan and himself a prolific author, Diderot commissioned a veritable Who's Who of the Enlightenment, including Voltaire, Rousseau, and Montesquieu, to contribute articles on every aspect of human

In addition to its often provocative articles, Diderot's *Encyclopedia* offered hundreds of unique illustrations of the industrial and mechanical arts of the eighteenth century, such as the brass foundry pictured here, whose workers seem dwarfed by the giant machines and implements they ply. The horse turns wheels that crush crude zinc. The workman at the left cranks a barrel that mixes the zinc with copper to make the brass alloy. The brass is then stamped in a mold and cut by giant shears. [The Granger Collection, New York]

knowledge. The result was the largest publishing venture up to that time in Western history. The first volume, containing controversial articles on atheism and the human soul, appeared in 1751. It was pounced on by the censors, who first suspended and later revoked the publisher's license. The attorney general of France denounced the *Encyclopedia* as a conspiracy against public morals, and the pope declared anyone buying or reading it to be excommunicated. Often carrying on alone, Diderot nonetheless managed to bring out 28 volumes by 1772. By 1789 an astonishing 20,000 full sets had been sold, and many more circulated in abridgments, extracts, and pirated editions. Modern public opinion—the reaction of an audience too large and too independent to be controlled by any institution of church or state—was born in the eighteenth century. No single book did more to create and mold it than Diderot's *Encyclopedia*.

THE ENLIGHTENED DESPOTS

One of the most remarkable aspects of the Enlightenment was the adoption of many of its ideas and principles by some Old Regime rulers themselves, a phenomenon known as *enlightened despotism*. This was less surprising than it might seem. The Enlightenment was a general movement that penetrated the most entrenched bastions of tradition and privilege; even rulers were not immune to new ideas. Moreover, some monarchs saw the philosophes as potential allies in their struggles with the nobility, which almost everywhere resisted the centralizing tendencies of royal governments.

For their part, the philosophes welcomed enlightened despotism as the most efficient means of realizing their objectives. Although Locke and Rousseau had championed popular sovereignty, neither was a democrat; Rousseau, despite his humble origins, scorned the masses. Most philosophes were ready enough to welcome a despot, provided that he or she was willing to use royal power in the service of reason and reform.

Catherine the Great

Russia seemed a particularly unlikely setting for enlightened despotism. In the 37 years following the death of Peter the Great, it had six rulers, including a boy of 12, an infant, and a half-wit. Some observers believed that it was headed toward the kind of aristocratic anarchy that

had befallen Poland, whose king was a mere figurehead. The Russian nobility had largely emancipated itself from the code of state service that Peter imposed on it, and the status of the peasantry had deteriorated even further. The criminal code of 1754 listed serfs only under the heading of property; they had lost even the legal status of human beings.

Strong rule returned to Russia in 1762 when Catherine the Great (1762–1796), the German-born wife of Tsar Peter III, organized his assassination and seized the throne for herself. In the early years of her rule, Catherine oriented herself almost wholly toward the West. She founded new schools and stimulated the nascent publishing industry. While neighboring states were banning the philosophes, she read Voltaire openly and admiringly, and she subsidized the publication of the *Encyclopedia*. In 1767 she summoned a legislative commission, half of whose members were commoners, to revamp the Russian legal code. Catherine herself drafted an elaborate "Instruction," including long passages cribbed from her favorite philosophes, expressing her commitment to reform.

The Instruction was a remarkable document in many ways, although some of its more liberal provisions were cut out of the final draft. Catherine declared that all persons should be equal before the law. Reflecting her reading of the Marquis of Beccaria's seminal treatise, *Of Crimes and Punishments* (1764), she called for the abolition of torture and the reduction of capital punishment. The Instruction was translated into the major languages of Europe; in France it was banned as subversive.

Despite this fanfare, the legislative commission was a disappointment if not a fiasco. The delegates, most of them inexperienced in public affairs, were bewildered as to what was expected of them, since Catherine's proposals would have stood much of Russian society on its head. The commission divided bitterly over the issue of serfdom, with the peasants and a few of the liberal nobility opposed stoutly by the landed interest, and produced only minor reforms in provincial administration. It was adjourned at the outbreak of war with Turkey in 1768 and never reconvened.

The Russo-Turkish war of 1768–1774 marked a turning point in Catherine's reign. Her dalliance with reform was now over, and she devoted herself instead to the more familiar business of power politics. In this and a subsequent war with Turkey (1787–1792), Catherine annexed the north shore of the Black Sea, although her goal of conquering Constantinople itself remained unfulfilled. The false hopes of reform Catherine raised were also largely responsible for the great rebellion in 1773–

1774 of Emilian Pugachev, a Cossack chieftain who declared himself to be the murdered Tsar Peter, set up a court with the "true" Catherine, and promised an end to serfdom, taxation, and conscription, as well as the abolition of the landed aristocracy. For a time, much of southern Russia was aflame, but Pugachev was defeated at last, brought to Moscow in a cage, and quartered in the Kremlin Square.

Pugachev's Rebellion confirmed the mutual dependence of Catherine and her nobility. As the nobility needed the strength of absolute despotism to protect their privileges, so they alone stood between the empress and peasant anarchy. Their common interest was sealed in the Charter of the Nobility (1785). The charter completely freed the nobility from imperial service, giving it instead sole responsibility for provincial administration. In this way the nobles, in looking after their own interests as landowners, exercised direct political control of the countryside on behalf of the state. Content with their powers, they ceased to meddle in palace affairs, while the imperial government no longer concerned itself with serfdom, human and political rights, and other unpalatable subjects. In the end, Catherine banned even her old friend Voltaire.

Frederick the Great

A far more sophisticated example of enlightened despotism was Frederick the Great of Prussia. Frederick was the most admired monarch of the eighteenth century. Not only did he speak the rhetoric of the Enlightenment, but he was a philosophe of sorts himself. He scorned divine right kingship, declaring that his power rested on his service to the people; a ruler, he said in a famous phrase, was only "the first servant of the state." In effect, Frederick replaced the divine right notion of a mystical relationship between the ruler and God with an equally mystical relationship between the ruler and his people. He identified the king with what Rousseau was to call the general will, for the monarch alone, he argued, standing above all parties and interests, could legislate for the common good.

Frederick himself seemed the perfect illustration of such a ruler. He built a palace at Potsdam in imitation of Versailles but found little time to enjoy it. No breath of scandal ever touched him; he had no private vices and, it almost seemed, no private life. His energies, apart from philosophy, literature, and music, were wholly absorbed in Prussia. He drained its swamps, encouraged its indus-

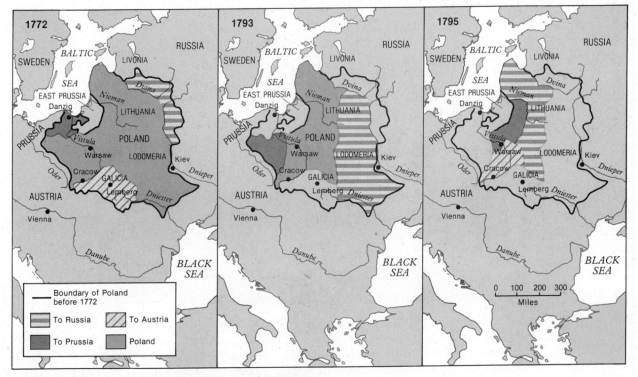

18.1 The Partitioning of Poland, 1772–1795

try, and expanded its agriculture. Within the country he promoted education, welcomed religious refugees of every stripe, and undertook a codification of the laws. "My chief obligation," he wrote, "is . . . to make [my people] as happy as human beings can be, or as happy as the means at my disposal permit."

The people Frederick wished to serve were not the free and equal citizens of Rousseau's commonwealth, however, but the hierarchically divided subjects of an Old Regime society. Prussians were not free; although Frederick, like Catherine, was opposed to serfdom in theory, he did little to alleviate it. Nor were Prussians equal. Frederick favored the nobility even more than his father had, reserving the officer corps of the army and the upper levels of the civil service exclusively for them. At Frederick's death, Prussia was the most aristocratically controlled society in Europe.

If Frederick believed in service to inferiors, he had few behavioral scruples toward his fellow monarchs. Even Louis XIV had attempted to rationalize his aggressions by legal claims, but when Frederick attacked Silesia in 1740, he blandly justified it on the grounds that it was in the nature of states to expand up to the limit of their ability. In 1772, Frederick joined Catherine and

Maria Theresa of Austria in carving up a helpless Poland to "adjust" the balance of power in eastern Europe in the wake of Catherine's gains against Turkey. Poland lost a third of its territory and half its population in this so-called Partition Treaty. Despite desperate attempts to strengthen itself by constitutional reform, it was wholly swallowed up by the subsequent partitions of 1793 and 1795 and ceased to exist as an independent nation. Enlightened despotism might sometimes aim at making states more rational and efficient; it did not make them more peaceful.

Joseph II: The Revolutionary Emperor

In contrast to Catherine and Frederick, the Austrian emperor Joseph II (1780–1790) seriously embraced Enlightenment principles and unreservedly attempted to put them into effect. The eldest of Maria Theresa's 16 children, he became Holy Roman emperor and coregent of Austria in 1765, but his desire for reform was frustrated by his mother's conservatism. When he succeeded her at last, he had a 15-year backlog of frustrated projects and ambitions.

Joseph II and Catherine the Great, two of the Enlightened Despots and rivals in power politics as well as reform, met in 1787. By this time, Catherine had long abandoned her liberal pose, while Joseph's attempt to remodel the Austrian Empire had driven many of its provinces to the verge of revolt. [Historisches Museum der Stadt Wien]

The empire that Joseph inherited was a crazy quilt of territories and populations whose loyalty to the Habsburg throne had been purchased only by conceding a large measure of self-rule, especially in Hungary and Bohemia. Joseph set out to compress this explosive mixture into a single political and social order and to transform some of the most backward regions of Europe into instant models of progress and enlightenment.

In her quiet way, Maria Theresa had done much to put the Austrian empire on the path to modernization. Administration had been centralized in Austria proper and in Bohemia, creating a model for the whole empire. Guild monopolies and tariff barriers had been overthrown, establishing the largest free trade zone in Europe. Church land had been expropriated, and despite Maria Theresa's hostility to secularism, the church's grip on education had been broken. For Joseph, however, the work of reform had barely begun with these steps. In ten years of ceaseless activity he issued 6,000 edicts covering every aspect of life in the empire. Serfdom was abolished, censorship lifted, and freedom of religion instituted. Jews were given civil rights and were permitted to intermarry with Christians. Marriage itself was declared a civil contract, to the horror of conservatives and the outrage of the church. Apostasy and witchcraft were stricken from the legal code. Capital punishment was limited, and judicial torture was abolished. Equality before the law was not only proclaimed but enforced; Vienna was shocked by the sight of a young nobleman sweeping the streets in a chain gang.

There can be no doubt of the sincerity of Joseph's intentions. Although many of the changes he introduced were similar to those of other centralizing eighteenth-century monarchies, he regarded the task of reform as an almost holy calling. "The service of God is inseparable from that of the state," he declared, and he wrote to one of his ministers, "Hasten everything that brings me nearer to the accomplishment of my plans for the happiness of my people." Joseph brushed privilege, tradition, and special interests aside in the spate of his reform, boasting that he had made philosophy alone the legislator of his empire. The result was to unite the nobility, the church, and the provincial estates against him. Faced with general opposition, Joseph redoubled his efforts. He reimposed censorship in an effort to dampen criticism, suspended due process, and set an army of spies on the population. Rebellion flared in Hungary, the Tirol, and Flanders, and by the end of Joseph's reign, large parts of the empire were held only by force. He died a broken man at the age of 48, and within a few years the edifice of his reforms collapsed. Serfdom was restored, to

survive in parts of the empire as late as 1867, and the nobility and clergy resumed their sway.

Enlightened Despotism in Perspective

The creed of enlightened despotism was best summed up in the motto of another reforming monarch, Charles III of Spain (1759–1788): "Everything for the people, nothing by the people." The enlightened despots represented a stage in the transformation of the personal monarchy of the old dynastic states to the impersonal rule of modern bureaucracies. Their very success in consolidating the power of the central state proved to be their undoing. It was true that the nobility and the church had frequently stood in the way of their ambitions. But in the long run, absolute monarchy depended on these institutions as much as they did on it. Together, the church, the aristocracy, and the crown had made up the hierarchical order of authority whose ultimate expression was the divine right of kings. In undermining the foundations of that order, the enlightened despots eroded the ground on which they themselves stood.

THE COUNTER-ENLIGHTENMENT

Reason was not triumphant everywhere in the eighteenth century, nor were its claims accepted uncritically. In his enormously popular novels, *The New Heloïse* (1761) and *Émile* (1762), Rousseau argued that feeling was as important as intellect in the development of moral sentiments. He praised nature not merely as a clever mathematical arrangement but also as a source of beauty and wonder whose effect on human emotions was as crucial as the operation of its laws on reason. *The New Heloïse* went through 70 editions by 1789 and became the bible of people who saw in unspoiled nature a haven from the corruptions of society and a model for the pure and simple life. *Émile,* by stressing the importance of developing each child's individual character and ability and the role of the teacher as a sympathetic guide rather than as a taskmaster, inspired a new movement of educational reform.

The middle and upper classes sought relief from the rationalism of the Enlightenment in a cult of sentiment fed by popular novels. But the official culture left deeper needs unmet. Established religion, buffeted by attacks on the tenets of its faith no less than on its wealth and privilege, was everywhere on the defensive. The Jesuits were so fiercely assailed that their order was temporarily dissolved in 1773, while Protestant theologians in England tried to anchor morality in reason and prudence rather than revelation.

The Revival of Religion

Such ideas were cold comfort to Europe's laboring millions, who sought in religion the promise of consolation and salvation. Grass-roots religion—a phenomenon previously associated with periods of upheaval such as the Reformation and the English revolution—spread out from late-seventeenth-century Germany across Protestant Europe and even to the New World. As Pietism in Germany, Methodism in England, and the Great Awakening in America, it had the same general goal: to revitalize religion by encouraging personal piety, good works, and a communal, often highly emotional experience of worship.

The roots of Pietism lay in the German mystical tradition, revived in the early seventeenth century by Jakob Böhme (1575–1624) and popularized by the evangelist Philip Jakob Spener (1635–1705). Spener's preaching was attacked by the clerical establishment, but by the end of his life, Pietism had become the dominant spiritual movement in Protestant Germany. It was a Pietist who counseled the spiritually troubled young English clergyman John Wesley (1703–1791), who, with his brother, Charles, and a charismatic preacher, George Whitefield, took the evangelical message to the mine pits and the open fields when the churches closed their doors to him. Galvanizing the spiritually starved working classes of England, Wesley created the mass movement known as Methodism, which eventually became a separate church.

Catholicism produced reform movements of its own that stressed personal faith, emancipation from dogma, and the right of individual conscience, notably Quietism in Spain and Jansenism in France, Flanders, and Italy. Because of the greater organizational unity of the Roman church, these movements, unlike the various forms of Pietism, were of elite rather than popular origin, although in some areas they spread more widely among the population; in spite (or perhaps because) of papal and royal opposition, two-thirds of Paris was Jansenist in 1730.

Skepticism and Idealism

Reason itself was subjected to criticism by the Anglo-Irish philosopher George Berkeley (1685–1753) and the Scotsman David Hume (1711–1776). Both stressed that ideas developed in the mind on the basis of sense impressions did not necessarily correspond to the world as it actually existed. Immanuel Kant (1724–1804) went even further. Kant argued that the mind imposed its own structure on experience, creating a picture with which it then lived. This picture could be tested and refined—for example, by science—but the mind could never go beyond it to know what the world was really like in itself. Kant's *idealism,* as his philosophy came to be called, was devastating to the claims of both science and religion; neither faith nor reason, he suggested, could lead to a knowledge of reality in itself.

Both skeptical philosophy and popular religion stressed the subjective experience of the individual, and both laid the ground for the new Romantic sensibility that began to develop in the eighteenth century. We must not think of the Enlightenment in terms of rationalism and the reaction against it, however. Rather it must be seen as a great current whose very strength created countercurrents that are inseparably linked to it. In this respect, its most characteristic figure is perhaps Rousseau, who dreamed of an ideal community yet found himself always an outsider and who insisted on the submission of the individual to the general will while exalting the rights of personal feeling and a liberated human nature.

THE EMANCIPATION OF THE JEWS

There were perhaps a million Jews in eighteenth-century Europe. The overwhelming majority were the Ashkenazim, who lived mainly in the small towns and villages of eastern Poland and Lithuania and spoke the mixed German-Polish dialect called Yiddish. Confined in ghettos, shunned and subjected to periodic outbreaks of looting and massacre known as pogroms, and for the most part desperately poor, they lived in almost complete isolation from surrounding Christian communities.

By contrast the Sephardim, mostly the descendants of Jews expelled from Spain and Portugal in the sixteenth century who settled largely in such urban centers as Amsterdam, Venice, London, Frankfurt, and Bordeaux, were more prosperous and cosmopolitan. But Jews everywhere, still commonly blamed for Jesus' death and disliked for their distinctive practices, were limited by restrictions and prohibitions of every kind, subjected to extortionate taxation, and periodically expelled from their places of residence.

The Sephardic Jews in the west were spared the more horrific experiences of their eastern brethren, such as the pogrom at Uman near Kiev in 1762, in which 20,000 Poles and Jews were massacred by peasants and Cossack tribesmen. But all Jewish communities lived in perpetual fear and anxiety. When in 1665 a charismatic Jew of Syrian origin, Sabbatai Zevi (1626–1676), proclaimed himself the messiah, a wave of millennial fervor swept over European Jewry. Tens of thousands of Jews sold their belongings and prepared to march east. Their hopes were tragically disappointed. The Turkish sultan, alarmed at the commotion Zevi's activities had aroused in his dominions, forced him to convert publicly to Islam on pain of death, and his movement collapsed.

Traditional anti-Semitism was at first reinforced by the Enlightenment. Many of the philosophes were unsympathetic toward the Jews, taking up Spinoza's attack on their adherence to the Mosaic law as an enslavement to a dead past. But others, such as Locke and Montesquieu, promoted their cause as victims of the church. Jewish emancipation was thus a special case of the more general extension of religious toleration in eighteenth-century Europe. After a long crusade, French Protestants regained in 1787 the civil rights and freedom of worship they had lost by the revocation of the Edict of Nantes in 1685, while in England the first legal Roman Catholic chapel since the mid-sixteenth century opened in Westminster in 1792. The Prussian Law Code of 1794 summed up the fruits of a century of agitation by declaring that "every inhabitant of the state must be granted complete freedom of conscience and religion."

But toleration was a two-edged sword for the Jews. Some, such as the philosopher Moses Mendelssohn (1729–1786), embraced it fully. Mendelssohn founded the Haskalah movement, which attempted to reconcile Enlightenment thought with Jewish tradition. Conservatives, however, viewed such overtures with horror. They feared that what centuries of persecution had failed to do, toleration would at last achieve instead: the destruction of the Jewish community and its assimilation into the dominant Christian culture. The fear of losing Jewish identity also stimulated the growth of Hasidism, a popular religious movement akin to Pietism that emphasized the *aliyah,* or return to Israel. But neither tradition and nostalgia nor the revival of Judaism's most ancient dream could prevent the incursion of the new secularism into even the most closed quarter of European society. After centuries the Jews were being forced out of their isolation into a future of uncertain promise.

THE ABOLITIONIST MOVEMENT

The contradiction between the ideals of freedom and equality expressed by the Enlightenment and the reality of eighteenth-century practice was most glaringly evident in the case of slavery. This contradiction was explained away by the assumption of black inferiority. Blacks, it was held, were less developed than whites both biologically and intellectually; therefore they felt physical and mental hardships far less keenly. Perpetual children, they were incapable of taking independent responsibility for their lives and hence of genuine liberty.

The myth of the happy slave ran aground on the fact of black rebellion in Jamaica, Haiti, and elsewhere. But it was not until nearly the end of the century that a movement to abolish slavery and the slave trade gathered force. Significantly, it was led not by the philosophes but by dissenting English Protestant groups such as Quakers and Baptists as well as the Clapham sect, a group of Anglicans seeking to revitalize their church. Not to be outdone, the republican leaders of France's National Convention declared slavery abolished outright and all former slaves citizens in 1794, although this edict was never put into effect, and Napoleon later reestablished slavery in the colonies. British abolitionism proved a longer-lasting cause. It gave religious dissenters their first major social cause in 100 years and a chance to show that Christianity too could take its place in the vanguard of progress. If the actual achievement of abolition owed more to the decline of slavery's profitability than anything else, the abolitionist role in forging the political consensus necessary to act was a crucial one.

THE RIGHTS OF WOMEN

The debate on the rights and status of women already had a long history by the eighteenth century. As early as 1589, a woman suitably named (or calling herself) Jane Anger had written a spirited defense of women. During the English Revolution some women had preached from the pulpits of Independent congregations, and the colonist Anne Hutchinson (1591–1643) was expelled from Massachusetts Bay for demanding religious freedom. By the end of the seventeenth century a number of women had begun to earn independent livings as writers. Catharine Macaulay (1731–1791) wrote an eight-volume *History of England* as well as pamphlets denouncing the British monarchy and defending the French Revolution, and the educational reformer and abolitionist Hannah More (1745–1833) earned more than £30,000 by her writings. These, however, were exceptions to the norm among the respectable classes.

As we have noted, some women played important roles as hostesses of salons during the Enlightenment, and writers such as Locke, Montesquieu, and Voltaire occasionally commented on the legal disabilities of women. Significant changes were also taking place in the most important institution that touched on women, the family. The emphasis on romantic love and companionship first advanced by writers such as the poet John Milton had become general by the late eighteenth century, and with it, women's expectations in marriage had begun to rise. At the same time the attack on divine right hierarchy shook traditional notions of male dominance in the family. The entry for "Women" in the *Encyclopedia* pointed out that marriage was a legal contract with mutual rights and responsibilities. The extension of the idea of a contract to marriage and the family had profound social implications. Its consequences are still unfolding today.

John Opie's portrait of the great English feminist Mary Wollstonecraft shows a powerful, mature woman in her mid-thirties whose introspective expression is tinged with sadness and disillusion. Mary may have been pregnant when this portrait was painted. [National Portrait Gallery, London]

MARY WOLLSTONECRAFT, FEMINIST

Mary Wollstonecraft was the daughter of a tradesman who squandered an inheritance and abused his wife. From an early age she showed signs of rebellion against the conventions of dress and behavior expected of respectable girls. She was also precociously aware of the ill treatment of servants, widows, and the poor generally. Leaving home, first as a lady's companion and then as a schoolmistress, she struck up a passionate friendship with a girl two years her senior, Fanny Blood. It was the first of her many attempts to find the affection and understanding that had been so painfully absent in her family.

In London, Wollstonecraft met the Unitarian minister and political radical Richard Price, who encouraged her attempts at writing. Her first essay, *Thoughts on the Education of Daughters,* was largely conventional in tone but contained a bitter complaint against the lack of occupations open to women. This was followed by an

autobiograhical novel that she called simply *Mary.* In it the author advocates both social reform and sexual liberation, and in an uncompleted second novel, *Maria, or the Wrongs of Women,* Wollstonecraft makes the latter point even more strongly: "When novelists and moralists praise as a virtue a woman's coldness of constitution and want of passion, I am disgusted."

Like many other British radicals, Wollstonecraft placed great hopes in the French Revolution. In *A Vindication of the Rights of Man,* written in answer to Edmund Burke's attack on the revolution, she called for the breakup of large estates as a means of relieving urban poverty and denounced Burke's notion of liberty as a cloak for the defense of property interests. Her most famous and most important work, however, was *A Vindication of the Rights of Woman,* published in 1792 and now regarded as the true beginning of the modern women's movement. The *Vindication* is a work of passionate indignation; Wollstonecraft declares that women have been as brutalized as black slaves and degraded almost beneath the status of reasonable beings:

> The *divine right* of husbands, like the divine right of kings, may, it is to be hoped, in this enlightened age, be contested without danger. . . . I love man as my fellow, but his sceptre, real or usurped, extends not to me, unless the reason of an individual demands my homage; and even then the submission is to reason, and not to man.

It was time, she asserted, not to make place for "a small number of distinguished women" in society but to demand liberation for all.

Wollstonecraft won support in radical circles, but Horace Walpole's denunciation of her as "a hyena in petticoats" was typical of conservative reaction. Her personal life also shocked respectable opinion. She bore a daughter out of wedlock in 1794 and lived openly with the anarchist William Godwin (1756–1836). She died of complications from the birth of a second daughter, Mary. The scandal of Wollstonecraft's personal life led nineteenth-century feminists such as Harriet Martineau to shun her as an unsafe example for the women's movement. It was not until 1889, when Susan B. Anthony and Elizabeth Cady Stanton published the first volume of their *History of Woman Suffrage*, that her name was redeemed; she was given first place among the pioneers to whom the book was dedicated.

THE ARTS: FROM ROCOCO TO NEOCLASSICAL

The dramatic style of the baroque gave way in the eighteenth century to the smaller-scaled and more refined rococo. With its often elaborate ornamentation, rococo was most effective in intimate, interior forms, and it is for the elegance of its aristocratic drawing rooms, furniture, and porcelain that the period is best remembered. The leading French painters of the day, Antoine Watteau (1684–1721), François Boucher (1703–1770), and Jean-Honoré Fragonard (1732–1806) have left us a

The ornate, elegant Hall of Mirrors of the Amalienberg, a summer house on the grounds of the Nymphenburg Palace in Munich, is a fine example of the intimate yet airy style of the rococo, which originated in France and spread to Germany in the 1730s. [Michael Holford]

pictorial record of the privileged classes at play; in their paintings, aristocratic lords and ladies disport themselves against a pastoral background from which all hint of those by whose labor they existed has been removed.

The chief rival to French culture was that of Britain. The brilliant satirist of London life, William Hogarth (1697–1764), showed the world of urban poverty that the French court painters had so carefully eliminated, although Britain's aristocracy too had its chroniclers in Thomas Gainsborough (1727–1788) and Sir Joshua Reynolds (1723–1792). Defoe's *Robinson Crusoe* was translated into French, German, and Swedish, and the novels of Samuel Richardson (1689–1761), Henry Fielding (1707–1754), Laurence Sterne (1713–1768), and Tobias Smollett (1721–1771) had great success. Italy was still regarded as the ultimate finishing school for the cultured European, and a fresh revival of interest in antiquity led to the first excavations of Herculaneum and Pompeii and the beginnings of modern archaeology. European taste was increasingly shaped by connoisseurs and critics, perhaps the most famous of whom was Samuel Johnson (1709–1784), who reigned for more than two decades as the literary dictator of London.

One of the by-products of expanded European contacts with the rest of the world was a vogue for all things Chinese, particularly fine silks and porcelain, that went by the name of *chinoiserie*. The European conception of China, based on reports by earlier Jesuit missionaries, was hardly an accurate one; Confucius, who was translated and widely admired, was read as a kind of philosophe. Nonetheless, the fascination with China marked a stage in Europe's growing consciousness of the outside world. A global culture, as well as a global economy, was taking its first uncertain steps.

VIENNA AND THE GOLDEN AGE OF WESTERN MUSIC

Of all the forms of art, the only one that produced names to rank with the greatest figures of the seventeenth century was music. The baroque forms that had culminated in Bach and George Frederick Handel (1685–1759) gave way to a more linear, less ornamental style, the classical, which was based on the elaboration of an old seventeenth-century form, the sonata. As applied in the orchestral forms of the symphony and the concerto, it produced a music that combined wit, elegance, and formal symmetry in a manner that reflected the balance of intellectual thrust and emotional restraint that was characteristic of much of eighteenth-century culture. Yet it was capable, too, in the hands of its greatest masters, the Austrians Franz Joseph Haydn (1732–1809) and Wolfgang Amadeus Mozart (1756–1791), of achieving extraordinary poignancy and depth, much of it in the setting of religious texts such as the Mass, for which there remained a continuous and steady demand.

For both Haydn and Mozart the Viennese public was the ultimate test of success. The growth of the bourgeoisie in the later reign of Maria Theresa and that of Joseph II had stimulated the development not only of music halls and theaters but also of a very lively salon culture. What verbal display and wit were to the salons of Paris, music was to those of Vienna. There were thousands of amateur musicians and singers in the city, and a British traveler remarked on provincial schools full of young children learning to read, play, and write music. The young Ludwig van Beethoven (1770–1827) came to Vienna at the age of 16, returned to stay permanently at 21, and dominated Viennese musical life for 30 years. His death and that of France Schubert (1797–1828), the only native Viennese among these composers, marked the end of the golden age of Vienna's music. For Beethoven, who burst the bounds of classical tradition to forge the new Romantic style and who commanded an audience throughout Europe, Vienna was merely a stage; but Schubert, who lived his short life in the shadow of his great elder contemporary, was nurtured by the salon culture and the small circle of friends and admirers for whom he wrote his songs, sonatas, and chamber works.

SUMMARY

The Enlightenment had a profound and lasting effect on Western culture. It called into question the basic institutions of European society, subjecting them to the test of reason and condemning whatever fell short by its measure. On the surface it seemed the work of a small, self-appointed band of critics, the philosophes, who for the most part lacked status and position and were frequently hounded, censored, and even imprisoned. Yet the philosophes themselves represented only the cutting edge of the great transformation of Western thought that had begun with the Reformation, the commercial expansion of Europe, and above all the scientific revolution. If they succeeded despite such apparent odds, it was largely because their conservative opponents had capitulated to their values and ambitions or found it imprudent to resist. This was most evident in the phenomenon of enlightened despotism. If the seventeenth century had marked the triumph of a new order of the universe, the eighteenth produced a new vision of humanity to complement it. To many, this vision was troubling. But even those who continued to seek comfort in a traditional Christianity were forced to redefine it in terms of achieving secular progress on earth.

Suggestions for Further Reading

Beales, D. *Joseph II,* Vol. 1. Cambridge: Cambridge University Press, 1987.

Besterman, T. *Voltaire.* New York: Harcourt, Brace & World, 1969.

Cassirer, E. *The Philosophy of the Enlightenment.* Boston: Beacon Press, 1951.

Darnton, R. *The Literary Underground of the Old Regime.* Cambridge, Mass.: Harvard University Press, 1982.

Ferguson, M., ed. *First Feminists: British Women Writers, 1578–1799.* Bloomington: Indiana University Press, 1984.

Gay, P. *The Enlightenment: An Interpretation.* New York: Knopf, 1966, 1969.

Gough, J. W. *The Social Contract,* 2d ed. Oxford: Clarendon Press, 1957.

Lough, J. *The Encyclopedia.* New York: McKay, 1971.

Madariaga, I. de. *Russia in the Age of Catherine the Great.* London: Weidenfeld & Nicolson, 1981.

Rendall, J. *The Origins of Modern Feminism: Women in Britain, France and the United States, 1780–1860.* New York: Macmillan, 1984.

Ritter, G. *Frederick the Great: A Historical Profile.* Berkeley: University of California Press, 1968.

Scott, H. M. *Enlightenment Absolutism.* Ann Arbor: University of Michigan Press, 1990.

Shklar, J. *Men and Citizens: A Study of Rousseau's Social Theory.* London: Cambridge University Press, 1969.

Tomalin, C. *The Life and Death of Mary Wollstonecraft.* New York: New American Library, 1974.

Wade, I. O. *The Intellectual Origins of the French Enlightenment.* Princeton, N.J.: Princeton University Press, 1957.

The West and the World

The Enlightenment

As the sixteenth-century age of discovery passed into one of settlement, colonization, and trade, Europeans attempted not only to assimilate the strange peoples and cultures they had encountered into their own but also to construct an image of the world based on the fact of its diversity. At the same time they increasingly defined themselves in terms of their own difference from and superiority to others.

The subtle shift in Western attitudes toward the outer world was reflected in its art and iconography. At first, non-Western culture and topography appeared chiefly in the form of trophies or ornaments. Tropical parrots, for example, appeared in otherwise conventional portraits or religious scenes, and represen-

tations of the Garden of Eden or Noah's Ark were updated to include such exotic beasts as elephants, tigers, and rhinoceroses. At the coronation of Henry II of France in 1547, the Brazilian rain forest was recreated along the banks of the Seine, with 300 nude Amerindians—of whom 50 were authentic, the rest being French sailors made up to play the part—acting out tableaux of native life.

The exoticism of these first representations gradually gave way to imagery that incorporated elements of the New World into an imperial theme. America took its place among the four known continents, which were often shown as allegorical figures offering tribute to European sovereigns or princes of the church. Thus four "ambassadors" representing the

Amerindians figured prominently in European spectacles and pageants, as in this seventeenth-century ballet titled *Tobacco*.

continents paid homage to the Jesuits' founder Ignatius Loyola during his canonization at Lisbon in 1623, and one of the triumphal arches commemorating the restoration of Charles II of England in 1661 bore figures of the four continents. The connection between the four continents and European empire was particularly popular in France, where it persisted down to the mid-nineteenth century.

The notion of Europe's hegemony among the four continents was based on the tacit assumption of the West's superiority to other cultures. Eighteenth-century Europeans divided the world into four races, each corresponding to its particular continent. The Swedish botanist Linnaeus, for example, distinguished between Europeans, who were governed by "laws," and native Americans, Asians, and Africans, who were governed, respectively, by "customs," "opinions," and "caprice." The Scottish philosopher David Hume declared:

I am apt to suspect the negroes and in general all the other species of men (for there are four or five different kinds) to be naturally inferior to the whites. There never was a civilized nation of any other complexion than white, nor even any individual eminent either in action or speculation.[1]

Hume's view rested on cultural arrogance, buttressed by the assumption that the lack of achievement by other races was the result of mental inferiority. Africans and native Americans, it was asserted, lacked the capacity for abstract thought. Thomas Jefferson thought the idea of a black or Amerindian philosopher absurd.

Enlightenment attitudes toward black Africans were particularly disparaging. Ironically, Europeans' relations with black Africans were far older and better established than with any other non-Western people. Egyptians, Greeks, Romans, and early Christians had accepted blacks among them, represented them frequently in their art and coinage, and enshrined them in their religions. Ethiopians, whom the historian Herodotus praised as the handsomest of all races, were derived in Greek mythology from one of the

Black Africans being lured, captured, and taken away on a slave ship. From a contemporary print.

most ancient Hellenic deities, Kronos, and blacks figured in the Bible from Moses' Kushite wife to the magi who attended the Christ child. Black merchants, soldiers, and priests were common throughout the Mediterranean world, and the Ethiopian king Ergamenes was a student of Greek philosophy.

The commercial relations between the black kingdoms of Ethiopia and Nubia and the West in ancient times were continued during the Middle Ages with the kingdom of Mali, which provided the West's chief supply of gold. Blacks were still represented as equals in Renaissance art, but their enslavement by Europeans during the early modern period inevitably changed their image. To be sure, black slaves had existed in ancient times. But they were typically war captives, and since whites were also enslaved under the same circumstances, their subjection was not taken to be a mark of personal or racial inferiority. In contrast, early modern slavery involved the systematic recruitment of labor by barter, sale, or direct seizure. The victims were not honorably defeated opponents but articles of commerce or the objects of organized hunts. Under these circumstances their status could only be degraded until they were regarded as inferior beings, if human at all.

The principles of the Enlightenment facilitated such a conclusion. The philosophes defined humans as innately rational and possessed of equal natural rights. To treat blacks unequally—indeed, to deny them the exercise of natural rights, altogether—could be justified only by an assumption of their natural inferiority. Thus the first American edition of the *Encyclopaedia Britannica* defined blacks as subject to vice, devoid of conscience, and incapable of moral reasoning. It was a short step to conclude that such a race was suitable only for enslavement. The ethnologist Edward Long went further, declaring that "none but the blind" could doubt that black and white were separate species.

Once a single race had been postulated as inferior to whites, others soon followed. For Count Buffon the question was not whether other races were inferior but why. All races, he speculated, had once been white, but owing to unfavorable conditions of climate, diet, and culture, they had degenerated in color, physique, and intellectual capacity. This could be remedied, he thought, by French cuisine, European education, and removal to a temperate location. Buffon declared that the "genuine color" of humankind was to be found among peoples living between the fortieth and fiftieth degrees of latitude across a belt from Britain to the Caucasus Mountains of Russia. Neighboring peoples to the south of this zone—in southern Germany and France, Switzerland, northern Spain, Italy, Hungary, Turkey, the Ukraine, Russian Georgia, and Circassia—were also "civilized," though less perfect. The farther from these fortunate latitudes a people was, the more corrupt it would be.

The Jews of Europe were a special case for Enlightenment theorists. Exposed to Western climate and culture, they continued to exhibit what was deemed physical and intellectual inferiority to the native races of Europe. This, according to Voltaire, was because they stubbornly refused to give up their ancient customs and superstitions of diet, dress, and doctrine. The startling appearance of a Jewish philosophe, the German Moses Mendelssohn (1729–1786), gave point to this argument and reinforced the claim that the Jews could be integrated into European society only by being emancipated from their ghettos.

Not all participants in the Enlightenment debate shared the assumption that nonwhite races were inferior. The Abbé Grégoire (1750–1831) pointed to Jewish and black writers, scientists, and men of learning as proof that the races were equal. It was significant that Grégoire was a churchman. Like Bartolomé de Las Casas, the sixteenth-century "apostle to the Indians," Grégoire derived the races of humankind from Adam, concluding that their common paternity ensured their mutual equality. Much effort had been expended in attempting to trace the genealogies of the Amerindian peoples, some suggesting that they were descendants of the ten lost tribes of Israel. However fanciful such speculation may seem today, the attempt to trace all humans back to a common ancestor was a strong argument in favor of their equality.

In contrast, the philosophes felt no need to square their ideas with the biblical account of Genesis. As archaeological and fossil data accumulated in the eighteenth century, it became apparent that the traditional date of creation, 4004 B.C., was seriously in error. If the world was older than Adam, it was possible that some races had pre-Adamite ancestors. This could account not only for the evident physical diversity of the races but for their presumed moral and intellectual differences as well.

Science could thus be invoked to justify theories of racial inequality.

Despite the West's growing ethnocentrism, the older image of the noble savage still had appeal. Jean-Jacques Rousseau, the most influential writer of the eighteenth century, did much to refurbish it. His *Discourse on the Origin of Human Inequality* (1755) argued that the root of social injustice was private property, an institution unknown among the Indians of North America, who regarded land as a common patrimony and freely shared their goods with tribes in distress. It did not seem to be a coincidence that Indian society was highly democratic (among males) and that status was awarded only for achievement. This, together with an idealized view of the free and healthy woodland life of the Indians, made a provocative contrast with the decadent customs of Europe, its artificial social distinctions, its extremes of wealth and poverty, and its concentration of power and privilege. Certainly, the allure of the North American wilderness had a formative influence on the Romantic conception of nature, already illustrated in Rousseau's novel *Émile* (1762), while the valor of the Indian brave, acknowledged by all who encountered him, shamed the effete European courtier with his powdered wig and parade sword.

The discovery of Tahiti and its neighboring Pacific islands in 1767 revealed an even more idyllic society, that of the South Seas. The voyages of the French explorer Bougainville popularized the idea of Tahiti as a sensual paradise. It was, wrote a member of his expedition,

> perhaps the only [society] on earth inhabited by men without vices, without prejudices, without wants, without dissensions. Born beneath the fairest sky, nourished by the fruits of an earth that is fertile without cultivation, [it is] ruled by fathers rather than by kings.[2]

Here too the Europeans found a harmonious society without private possessions, including sexual property. Tahitians, they reported, enjoyed perfect sexual freedom without shame or jealousy, holding wives and daughters in common. The philosophe Diderot speculated that free love was the basis of the Tahitians' social order, since the repression of the erotic instinct led invariably to misery and conflict. Although Captain Cook, another eyewitness observer of Tahiti, derided the view that the

The Noble Savage. This portrait of Paracoussi, a South American chieftain, combines a lofty expression with savage attire. [Library of Congress]

Tahitians lacked a property system or lived without labor, Bougainville's description proved the more popular. As Diderot remarked of the process of civilization, "There was once a natural man, then an artificial man was created inside him." In Tahiti, "natural man" seemed to have been rediscovered, alive and well and living in peace and harmony with his fellows.

Just as North American Indians and South Sea islanders provided Europeans with images of primitive innocence, so China offered the example of an ancient civilization where refinement had not decayed into vice nor wisdom into doctrine. In an age when dogmatic Christianity was under attack in Europe, Confucius was hailed as the first philosophe, a man without passion, prejudice, or superstition. The general image of the Chinese sage as a man of reason, presented in Leibniz' *Novissima Sinica,* enjoyed great popularity. Leibniz gained most of his knowledge of China through correspondence with the Jesuits, but he remarked that it would have been more appropriate for the Chinese to send missionaries to civilize Europe than the other way around.

Thus both the primitive and the sage offered the West unfavorable comparisons with its own defects and vices and undercut its assumptions of racial superiority. Unfortunately, both were based on stereotypes that, having served the immediate purposes of the philosophes, were soon to be discarded.

A broader view was taken by Voltaire in his famous *Essay on Customs* (1756). Although reserving pride of place for the age of Louis XIV, he lavished praise on both Chinese and Islamic culture, arguing that there could be no single standard of civilization by which all others could be measured and to which all others should be expected to conform. This view was to be largely ignored during the nineteenth century.

1. David Hume, "Of National Characters," in *The Philosophical Works,* ed. T. H. Green and T. H. Grose (London, 1882), p. 252n.
2. G. S. Rousseau and R. Porter, eds., *Exoticism and the Enlightenment* (Manchester: Manchester University Press, 1990), p. 119.

19

THE FRENCH REVOLUTION AND NAPOLEON

Great economic, religious, and intellectual changes had taken place in Western society between the beginning of the sixteenth century and the end of the eighteenth. Yet the political order of Europe had remained relatively static. The nations of Europe were still governed by monarchs and princes. The nobility was still predominant, its privileges seemingly more entrenched than ever.

The French Revolution challenged all that. Within a matter of weeks in the summer of 1789 a social and political edifice that had stood for 1,000 years was torn down, and for a generation all of Europe was caught up in the convulsive changes that ensued. From the very beginning, the revolution was recognized as the most important event of the age. In its turmoil and agony the shape of the modern world first became visible.

THE CRISIS OF THE OLD ORDER IN FRANCE

The revolution began with an uprising by the French aristocracy. It was only to be expected that the nobility would react against the autocratic rule of Louis XIV and seek to reassert its power. The long reign of Louis XV (1715–1774) provided them with an opportunity to do so. Thus while in most other places the privileges of the nobility were being reshaped and in many cases cur-

tailed by enlightened despots, in France the nobles remained unchecked. The intendants whom Louis XIV had sent to break the nobles' control of the provinces had been neutralized. The parlements, the chief courts of the realm, had regained much of their old power to challenge and obstruct royal edicts, claiming broad powers of judicial review and even jailing provincial governors and military commanders who attempted to execute royal orders that they held to be illegal. At the same time, the nobility remained exempt from many forms of taxation and tenaciously resisted any attempt to impose even token new levies without consent, a position echoed by the bourgeoisie. This obliged the state to rely on the poorest and most depressed sectors of the economy for support.

Reform and Reaction

Stung by the open defiance of his authority, Louis XV at last attempted to act. Guided by a reforming minister, René Charles de Maupeou (1714–1792), he took the daring step of abolishing the parlements outright and exiled their former judges to remote parts of the country. In their place he created new courts whose members would no longer have life tenure in office but could be removed at pleasure. At the same time he undertook reforms to reduce the public debt to manageable proportions and to put the state's finances in order. These steps came too late. The king's death in 1774 brought his 20-year-old grandson, Louis XVI (1774–1792), to the throne. Louis was an affable, pious young man, fond of hunting and gardening and eager to please. He was soon persuaded to abandon his father's reforms and to restore the old parlements.

The Fiscal Crisis

The new king was ably served by his chief ministers, the philosophe Turgot (1774–1776) and the banker Necker (1776–1781). Both had connections to the Physiocrats, a circle of economic reformers who advocated liberal trade and fiscal policies. The two ministers sought to relieve the chronic indebtedness of the crown by easing trade restrictions and internal tariff barriers, abolishing guild monopolies, and raising new taxes. Their efforts were stymied, however. The revived parlements rejected their proposals out of hand, and factional intrigue undermined their position at court. Each in turn was forced from office, having accomplished nothing of substance.

The crown's plight was worsened by its participation in the American War for Independence, which added considerably to the debt burden. By 1786, interest payment on the existing debt amounted to half the royal budget, and the treasury was borrowing to meet that. The king's comptroller, Charles de Calonne, informed his master that the state was bankrupt.

A new tax seemed the only possible solution. To circumvent the inevitable opposition of the parlements and to appeal directly to the more liberal nobility, Calonne proposed that Louis call a handpicked Assembly of Notables. This body convened in February 1787 but, suspicious of Calonne's motives and unwilling to bypass the parlements, it refused to support his program. Louis dismissed Calonne and dissolved the assembly.

The Constitutional Crisis

The financial crisis now became a constitutional one. The parlements insisted that new taxes could be granted only by the representative assembly of the whole realm, the Estates General. This ancient feudal body had not met since 1614, but the judges made it into a symbol of popular liberty. Adopting the language of the Enlightenment, they insisted that law was the expression of reason, the general will, and the rights of man. It could no longer be accepted as the will of a single individual.

The crown found itself isolated, the natural focus of all discontent. The nobility feared it as the usurper of its privileges. The peasantry, ground under by taxes, re-

sented it as the expropriator of its labor. The bourgeoisie saw it as a barrier to wealth and status. Whereas the pomp of Versailles under Louis XIV had reflected the glory of France, it now symbolized the decadence of personal monarchy.

Louis finally attempted to suppress the parlements as his father had done and set up new courts in their place. But the tide of reform could no longer be stopped by a show of force. Rioting and near-rebellion broke out in the provinces, and committees of correspondence were formed on the model of the American Revolution. The clergy threatened to reduce their annual "gift" to the treasury, and the king's own courtiers opposed him. Louis backed down. In July 1788 he recalled the parlements and agreed to summon the Estates General. The revolt of the nobility had triumphed.

The Parlement of Paris promptly ruled that the new Estates General must have the same form as the old, with three separate chambers representing the clergy, the nobility, and the commoners of the realm. Because each chamber voted as a separate unit, the two privileged orders could always outvote the Third Estate of the commons, which in fact was made up of merchants, financiers, petty officials, and members of the professions, the group loosely referred to as the bourgeoisie. Except in theory, none of these groups represented the actual majority of peasants and workers who made up four-fifths of the population.

The Bourgeoisie and the Third Estate

The situation now boiled down to a complex struggle among the king, the nobility, and the bourgeoisie. The resentment of this last group was of long standing. The bourgeoisie, whose members as we have seen included merchants, entrepreneurs, bankers, professionals, and officials, regarded themselves as the most productive element in society. They chafed at economic restrictions, which they saw as largely designed to protect the interests of the nobility and the crown and, though some of them had acquired fortunes as great as any nobleman's, they were bitter at their exclusion from the highest echelons of status and power. As the political debate widened, they also came to see themselves as speaking, through the Third Estate, for the nation as a whole. Some of the more liberal clergy and nobility had come to sympathize with their demands for broader political participation. Their position was summarized in a pamphlet circulated early in 1789 by a clergyman, the Abbé Sieyès (1748–1836), which asked pointedly:

What is the Third Estate? Everything.
What has it been thus far in the political order? Nothing.
What does it demand? To be something.[1]

The Third Estate's discontent was the king's opportunity. If he could exploit it properly, he could outflank the opposition to tax reform and break the back of the nobles' revolt. Urged on by Necker, who had been restored to power, Louis decreed that the Estates General be popularly elected: nobles by nobles, clergy by clergy, and the Third Estate by all other males over 25 whose names appeared on the tax rolls. With a stroke of the pen the king had enfranchised millions of Frenchmen for the first time.

In deference to this greatly expanded electorate, Louis agreed to "double the Third," that is, to permit twice as many representatives to be chosen for the Third Estate as for the other two orders. But this did not affect the voting balance of the three estates. Each order would still vote as a separate unit. In terms of actual power, therefore, the Third Estate's position remained that of a minority.

Election fever swept over France. In 40,000 electoral districts all over the country, lists of grievances were compiled to be sent along with the delegates; the lists revealed widespread dissatisfaction with the social system. The same demands were repeated insistently: popular representation, legislative control of taxation, a limitation of the monarchy, a reduction of church tithes, and the elimination of noble privileges, including the traditional payment by the peasant to his lord of from a tenth to a third of his crop. The lists of the Third Estate were virtually unanimous in demanding full civil equality for all Frenchmen.

In these grievances and demands lay the seeds of a social revolution. The nobility had wanted to protect its privileges, the bourgeoisie to share them. What arose from the countryside was a cry of protest at the exploitation that the peasantry had suffered at the hands of both. Throughout the eighteenth century, noble and bourgeois landholding increased as the peasants were squeezed onto smaller and smaller plots and sometimes entirely off them. Many peasants who still owned land had to supplement their income by wage labor. This meant that more French people were vulnerable to a subsistence crisis—crop failure compounded by price rises and hoarding—than ever before.

As it happened, the harvests of 1788 were the worst in nearly a century. Starving peasants fled to the towns, swelling the urban unemployment rate to as high as 50 percent. Even people who had work found up to 80 percent of their earnings consumed by the cost of bread. By the spring of 1789 there were violent uprisings against grain prices and shortages, and wandering bands roved the countryside, attacking the castles of the nobility.

THE REVOLUTION OF 1789

France had known periods of disorder before, but the circumstances that now converged on it—a constitutional crisis that was a thinly veiled struggle for power among contending political and economic groups, a monarchy enfeebled not only by an incompetent ruler but also by attacks on its fundamental legitimacy, a widespread sense of social injustice and an assumption that radical change was inevitable—all combined to bring about the collapse of the government, the destruction of the manorial order, and the replacement of a society based on the division of estates and orders into one predicated, at least in theory, on the legal and political equality of all citizens. This was the revolution of 1789.

From the Estates General to the National Assembly

The 1,165 delegates to the Estates General were the focus of all hopes as they convened at Versailles on May 5, 1789. The First Estate of the clergy consisted of 291 delegates, of whom 46 were bishops; the majority were hardworking and underpaid parish priests, close to the peasantry they served and sympathetic to reform. The 270 nobles of the Second Estate also included a vociferous reform group. Among its number was the marquis de Lafayette (1757–1834), already celebrated as a hero of the American Revolution. Of the 578 commoners who comprised the Third Estate,* well over half were lawyers, most of whom also held government jobs, and another quarter were merchants, businessmen, and rentiers, persons who lived off the profits of government bonds, propertied investments, and feudal dues. Despite the wide franchise, not a single worker or peasant had been elected. The result was that the full Third Estate was represented only by its narrowest elite, though an elite that was angry and embittered at its rebuff by the nobility.

---

*The remaining 26 delegates were unclassified.

Had the crown been able to assert itself at this point, a compromise might still have been found. But Louis and Necker had no program to present, no solution to offer. The king spoke of caution, his minister of deficits. Leaderless, the Estates General fell to wrangling over the question of voting by orders, the Third Estate insisting that the three orders merge into a single body. As this not only would have given the Third Estate a numeric voting majority but also would have abolished the principle of separate orders on which the privileges of the clergy and the nobility rested, it was stoutly resisted. On June 17, after weeks of deadlock, the Third Estate took the decisive step toward revolution: it declared itself an independent body, the National Assembly, with the right to legislate alone in the public interest. Three days later, the members of the Third Estate found themselves locked out of their chamber. They gathered in a nearby indoor tennis court, where in great passion and excitement they took a vow, the so-called Tennis Court Oath, not to disband until they had given France a constitution.

Louis now acted. He told the Estates General that he would give it a permanent place in the state, with wide though unspecific rights over the administration and the budget. In this he seemed to accept the principle of a limited monarchy that had been demanded on all sides. But he also declared the self-created National Assembly (whose numbers had now been swollen by dissident clergy and nobility) null and void and ordered the Estates to return to their separate chambers. The nobles were elated, but the Third Estate remained defiant. Louis once more backed down. On June 27 the first two Estates united with the Third. The National Assembly was now a fact.

The Popular Revolution

The revolution now moved into the streets. The workers and tradespeople of Paris, fearing both rural mobs and military repression, broke into the civic arsenals and armed themselves. On July 14 they stormed the ancient fortress of the Bastille and seized its weapons after a pitched battle. This event, still celebrated annually in France, was of enormous symbolic significance. It gave the revolution its baptism of blood and resulted in the final collapse of the king's authority. Riots broke out and arsenals were pillaged in other major cities. In many places the intendants and municipal officials simply fled, leaving the local population to organize citizen militias

Symbolically an attack on the monarchy itself, the fall of the ancient fortress called the Bastille soon led to a general revolt against seigneurial privilege throughout France. [Cliché des Musées Nationaux, Paris]

and revolutionary committees, or *communes,* on the model already established in Paris.

Disorder broke out simultaneously in the countryside, often triggered by a wave of rumor and hysteria, the so-called Great Fear, which centered on reports of advancing royalist or bandit armies. This soon became a pretext for looting, and by late July a full-scale agrarian insurrection was in progress. Peasants broke into the manor houses of the nobility, systematically destroying the legal records of debts and feudal dues. What went up in flames was more than paper. In the high summer of 1789 the Old Regime itself was dying in a thousand bonfires throughout France.

The Abolition of Privilege and the Declaration of the Rights of Man

The National Assembly quickly moved to ratify what it was powerless to prevent. On the night of August 4, two liberal noblemen, coached by leaders of the Third Estate, moved to abolish all compulsory labor service, such as road maintenance, and to offer redemption for all other dues and obligations. What can only be described as a psychological stampede ensued. Member after member arose to volunteer renunciation of his own privileges and those of cities, corporations, and provincial estates. Hoarse and exhausted, the delegates adjourned at 2 A.M. with the declaration "Feudalism is abolished." By morning many had repented their enthusiasm and tried to reinstate various qualifications and exemptions. It was too late. The people of France took them at their most generous word and simply ceased to pay all former dues.

The assembly's next step was to issue a constitutional blueprint, the Declaration of the Rights of Man and the Citizen (August 26). Its 17 brief articles summarized the political principles of the Enlightenment. All men, it stated, "are born and remain free and equal in rights." Those rights were defined as "liberty, property, security, and resistance to oppression," which it was the duty of every state to preserve. Sovereign power was declared to be vested in the nation as a whole, and law was to be the expression of the general will.

The declaration was to remain the basic document of the revolution, however far subsequent regimes departed from its principles in practice. At one stroke it eliminated the archaic, cumbersome divisions of French society. It replaced the system of orders by one based on formal civil equality and cleared the ground for the modern political and economic development of France. It also made devastating propaganda. Translated into every major European language, it shook the established order and galvanized demands for reform across the Continent.

The king alone remained passive and aloof in the face of these developments. This led to the last of the revolutionary tremors of 1789. On October 5 a contingent of Parisian housewives, angered by continuing shortages and high prices, marched to Versailles and demanded that Louis return to the capital. They were soon backed up by the arrival of the newly formed National Guard under Lafayette, 20,000 strong. Virtually defenseless, the royal family was forced to accompany this motley procession back to Paris, where they took up residence in the Palace of the Tuileries. The National Assembly followed a few days later, and Louis gave his unhappy consent to the August 4 decrees and the Declaration of the Rights of Man.

THE NEW ORDER, 1789–1791

The poet Chateaubriand was later to remark that the nobility had begun the revolution and the people had finished it. But despite the slogan that now epitomized the goals of the Revolution—"Liberty, equality, fraternity"—there was no single "people" of France, only groups with divided and often bitterly contending interests. At one extreme were the aristocratic emigrés who had left the country and rejected the revolution; at the other were the impoverished *sans-culottes** or working class of the towns, whose claims had not yet been satisfied. In between were the great mass of the peasants, who wished chiefly to consolidate the fruits of their rebellion in July: the destruction of the manorial regime and the freeing of their title to the lands they farmed.

The Bourgeoisie in Power

Actual power was in the hands of none of these groups, however, but rather those of the bourgeoisie, the chief political beneficiaries of the collapse of royal authority and the abolition of the noble order. The bourgeoisie was itself composed of varying elements, but it comprised in general the urban-dwelling possessors of capital,

---

*Literally, "without breeches." For practical reasons, working men wore long pants instead of the silk or muslin stockings and breeches of the nobility and the bourgeoisie.

whether in the form of property, stocks, or securities. Augmented by former members of the nobility and by clergymen like Sieyès, it dominated the National Assembly, or, as this body was called from October 1789, the Constituent Assembly. The assembly had two crucial tasks: to write a new constitution for France and to govern the nation while doing so.

The assembly's essential caution was reflected in the constitution of 1791. Contrary to Article 6 of the Declaration of the Rights of Man, the constitution distinguished between "active" and "passive" citizens. Both groups enjoyed full civil rights, but only the actives, those meeting a minimum property qualification, had the right to vote for some 50,000 electors, who in turn chose the 500 representatives of the Legislative Assembly. This costly and cumbersome process ensured that the representatives would necessarily be men of means and leisure—in short, men of the bourgeoisie.

The Reorganization of Church and State

The most pressing issue before the Constituent Assembly was the unresolved crisis of the public debt. The simplest recourse was to repudiate it as a legacy of the discredited Old Regime. As a substantial portion of the debt was owed to members of the bourgeoisie, however, there was no question of doing that. Instead, the assembly decided to pay the debt off by selling the lands of the church, which it declared to be confiscated in the name of the nation. A special bond, the *assignats,* was issued to facilitate the purchase of these lands.

This massive transaction destroyed the financial independence of the church and made it a ward of the state. Clergymen became salaried officials, chosen from a qualified slate by popular election like other state functionaries. Archbishoprics were abolished, and the number of bishops was reduced from 135 to 83. Monasteries and convents were dissolved, and the taking of religious vows was prohibited. The pope was to be informed as a matter of courtesy when a bishop was installed, but his authority was in no other way recognized.

These changes were embodied in the Civil Constitution of the Clergy (1790). To sweeten their impact, it was proposed to double the personal income of the lower clergy. The problem, however, was ratification. The church wanted to adopt the Civil Constitution on its own authority, thereby affirming its continued identity as a corporate body. To the assembly, this would have been tantamount to recognizing the existence of a First Estate

again, when all estates and orders had been abolished. The assembly therefore promulgated the new constitution alone and backed it up with an oath of allegiance that all clergymen were required to swear.

Half of the lower clergy and all but seven of the bishops refused to take the new oath. The "refractory" or "nonjuring" clergy, as they were called, emigrated or went underground, where, protected by loyal parishioners, they formed a natural focus of resistance to the revolution. Far from becoming an obedient servant of the state, the church would henceforth be its bitterest enemy.

Equally far-reaching was the assembly's reorganization of administration and government. All former courts and jurisdictions were abolished. A uniform code of administration was instituted for the 44,000 rural and urban districts of the country. The 26 old provinces, many of them rich with history (and memories of previous rebellions), were replaced by 83 "departments," all newly named and democratically equal in size. An independent judiciary was established, with elected judges and juries for criminal trials. Yet, although the administration was thus radically standardized, it was actually less centrally controlled than under the Old Regime. Anxious to avoid the charge of despotism leveled at the Old Regime, the Constituent Assembly left the implementation of its decrees in the hands of officials over whom it had little effective control. Counterrevolutionary disturbances broke out in the region of the Midi in the spring of 1790, precursors of full-scale rebellion to come.

The status of the king posed a difficult question. Louis was the only remaining link between the old France and the new and the only valid symbol of authority for millions of French citizens. At the same time, despite his grudging approval of the Declaration of the Rights of Man and the Civil Constitution of the Clergy, his hostility to the revolution was plain. His powers were therefore restricted to a three-year suspensive veto over the Legislative Assembly.

But Louis refused to play the role assigned him. On June 20, 1791, he attempted to flee the country with the royal family. Captured by peasants at the border town of Varennes, they were forced to return to Paris in a humiliating procession. The assembly accepted the fiction that the king had been "kidnapped." It was clear to all, however, that even before its formal adoption the new constitution had been repudiated by the man intended to serve as its head of state.

In the long run, the work of the Constituent Assembly was of great importance. It dissolved and replaced the institutions of the Old Regime and laid the foundations of the modern French state. But it failed to solve almost all of the immediate problems before it. It passed out of existence on September 30, 1791, leaving behind a sharply polarized nation, mounting political and economic chaos, and a constitution that, satisfying no one, survived it by barely ten months.

THE REVOLUTION AND EUROPE

At first many people outside France greeted the revolution with enthusiasm and even rapture. "How much the greatest event that has happened in the world, and how

Jacques-Louis David's remarkable portrait of a woman of Paris' working class shows the anxiety and suffering but also the dignity and determination of those who struggled in the French Revolution, not merely for survival but also for justice. [Musée des Beaux-Arts de Lyon]

much the best!" exulted the British politician Charles James Fox. In Hamburg the bourgeoisie turned out to celebrate the first anniversary of the fall of the Bastille. An uprising in the Austrian Netherlands drove the imperial army out of Brussels in December 1789, while in the Rhineland, peasants refused to pay seigneurial dues to their lords.

Not all reaction was favorable, however. In his *Reflections on the Revolution in France* (1790) the British statesman Edmund Burke argued forcefully against the assumption that all men possessed identical natural rights. Not men, he contended, but nations were the basic units of history. Each nation was a unique cultural entity shaped by its distinctive historic experience. Reforms that respected the time-tested institutions of the nation were right and proper. But for a single generation to destroy those institutions on behalf of an abstract conception of justice, he declared, was an act of folly and arrogance, a "fond election of evil" that could bring only ruin.

Despite general concern about the "French plague," it was not until August 1791 that the two largest Continental powers agreed on a joint statement of policy toward France. The Declaration of Pillnitz, issued by Prussia and Austria, stated as its goal the restoration of the French monarchy. A declaration of war without an actual call to arms, it served only to strengthen republicans in France, who argued that the revolution would never be complete or secure as long as Louis remained king.

PARIS AND THE FALL OF THE MONARCHY

Paris was the nerve center of the revolution, the seat of national government and the home of the volatile sansculottes, who comprised half its population of 600,000. The city had enjoyed its own revolution in July 1789 when it overthrew its royal administration and improvised, almost on the spot, a new governing authority, the Commune, which remained the heart of the city's political activity. This activity included numerous popular clubs and societies, of which the most famous, the Jacobins,* had more than 400 provincial affiliates by

---

*So named from their original meeting place in the former convent of the Jacobin order.

1791 and debated before audiences of up to 2,000. To such groups were added the *fédérés* ("federations"), spontaneously formed unions of the provincial councils and militias that converged on Paris on the first anniversary of the fall of the Bastille to affirm their loyalty to the revolution. When not gathered in the large crowds and assemblies that were so characteristic of the revolution, Parisians themselves avidly consumed the scores of newspapers, pamphlets, and petitions that poured forth daily from the press.

By the summer of 1792 the revolution had reached a new flashpoint. Swept on by a combination of ideological fervor and traditional anti-Habsburg sentiment, the new Legislative Assembly had declared war on Austria in April. The war went badly, while inflation ravaged the economy, peasants hoarded crops, and rumors of counterrevolutionary plots and betrayals abounded. The Jacobin republicans blamed the failure of their crusade on Louis. How, they demanded, could a war against all monarchs be led by a king?

By the end of July, 47 of the 48 voting districts of Paris had declared against the monarchy. The Jacobin leadership, alarmed by the prospect of a new popular insurrection, now backtracked and offered Louis support. But a more radical faction, led by Maximilien Robespierre, threw its lot in with the crowd. On August 10, Louis and his entourage were driven from the Tuileries by an armed mob, with heavy loss of life. It was an event as crucial as the fall of the Bastille. A new revolutionary council, composed largely of sans-culottes and lesser bourgeois, seized control of Paris. The constitution was suspended, the Legislative Assembly was dispersed, and a new National Convention was summoned to create a republic.

THE RADICAL REVOLUTION,
1792–1794

The National Convention, elected by unrestricted male suffrage, met on September 20 in an atmosphere of near anarchy. Earlier in the month, angry mobs had rampaged through the prisons of Paris in search of "counterrevolutionaries," killing between 1,100 and 1,400 inmates, including 37 women. A Prussian army had penetrated deep into northern France and was stopped only at Valmy, on the road to Paris, on the very day of the convention's first meeting.

Reform and Regicide

Nevertheless, the convention set to work undaunted. It abolished not only the monarchy but also the calendar, declaring September 22 the first day of Year I of the republic and subsequently renaming and reordering the months of the year. The convention's faith in the future was soon repaid. French armies, fired by patriotic ardor and reorganized under officers promoted from the ranks, drove the Austro-Prussian invaders out and swept across the border, occupying Frankfurt and Brussels. In two months they conquered more territory than Louis XIV had in 50 years. The convention decreed feudal dues and services abolished in all areas occupied by French forces and offered "liberation" to any people wishing it. On February 1, 1793, war was declared on Britain, Spain, and the Dutch Netherlands.

The king remained to be dealt with. Placed on trial for treason, he was condemned to death by a majority of one vote in the convention. On January 21, 1793, he went to the guillotine. Ten months later, his Austrian queen, Marie Antoinette, followed him.

The revolution now entered its climactic phase. The center of its activity was the National Convention, whose members were still recruited almost entirely from the merchant and professional classes. Politically, it was divided between what had emerged as the two warring factions of the Jacobin club, with the great mass of delegates in the middle. The Girondins, so called because many of their leaders came from the southwest department of the Gironde, had been the war party of the Legislative Assembly, but in the eyes of their opponents they had been compromised by an attempt to deal with the king the previous summer. The more radical faction was the Montagnards (the "mountain men"), so called because they sat in the upper tiers of the convention, whose base of support was among the sans-culottes of Paris. Their leaders were Maximilien Robespierre, a provincial lawyer, the popular journalist Jean Paul Marat (1743–1793), and the worldly politician Georges Danton (1759–1794).

The two parties were separated by no great issues or principles. Both accepted the republic, both had shed the king's blood, and both believed in the mission of the revolution to liberate Europe. But the Montagnards proved more adept at riding the tiger of mass politics that the second revolution of August 1792 had unleashed. On June 2, after a spring of military reverses, renewed inflation, and a major royalist uprising in the western region of the Vendée, Robespierre led a purge of Girondist leaders by the sans-culottes.

The condemned queen, Marie Antoinette, dressed in a prisoner's smock and ironically crowned with a liberty cap, was sketched by David on her way to execution. [Bulloz]

The Montagnards were now in power, though largely at the sufferance of their working-class allies, who came daily to the convention to harangue them. The sans-culottes demanded, and for the first time got, price controls on bread, flour, and other commodities, as well as a general increase in wages. Their wider demands for social justice, however, continued to go unmet.

Robespierre and the Terror

Maximilien Robespierre now emerged as the most conspicuous figure of the revolution. Robespierre was born in 1758 in the coastal town of Arras, the son of a lawyer and a brewer's daughter. Abandoned by his father at the age of 8, he was raised by aunts and educated in the school of the Oratorian order. He grew up a reserved and serious young man, followed his father's profession, and became a judge in the local episcopal court. He remained unmarried, and his sister Charlotte kept house for him. Elected to the Estates General in 1789, he caught the eye of Count Mirabeau, who remarked cynically, "He will go far; he believes everything he says." Above all, Robespierre believed in himself. "You have no idea," he said, "of the power of truth or the energy of innocence when sustained by an imperturbable courage."

Robespierre's ability to formulate and even personify the ideals of the revolution brought him to prominence. By the summer of 1793 he stood at the forefront of events. The convention, setting aside a newly drafted and radically democratic constitution, continued to govern the country on an emergency basis through its councils and committees. To one of these, a body with vague but extensive supervisory functions called the Committee of Public Safety, Robespierre was elected on July 27. Galvanized by his presence, it soon became the focal point of the revolution.

Steps were now rapidly taken to put down the revolts in the Vendée and elsewhere. So-called representatives on mission, armed with almost unlimited authority, struck terror into the provinces. At the same time, a *levée en masse,* or general conscription of all able-bodied males, was decreed. Of all the acts of the convention, this was perhaps the most significant. War was no longer to be the sport of kings and nobles but the sacred cause of the nation, a mass mobilization of all human and material resources. Young men who could not fight were to make weapons, munitions, clothing, and banners; women were to serve as nurses; elderly men were to make patriotic speeches.

Out of this fevered atmosphere was born the Terror, a systematic attempt to root out and destroy all enemies of the revolution. To catch these enemies, special tribunals were set up, spies encouraged, and new categories of counterrevolutionary offense established that were so broad as to include almost anything. Robespierre defended the Terror as inflexible justice applied to the enemies of the people and so "an emanation of virtue." As his young colleague Saint-Just put it more succinctly, "Between the people and its enemies there is only the sword." In the ten months between September 1793 and July 1794, perhaps 300,000 people were arrested and 40,000 executed.

The Terror had another aim: to centralize all authority in the revolutionary government and to eliminate all opposition and dissent. By the law of 14 Frimaire (December 4, 1793), all subordinate authorities were placed under the direct control of the Committee of Public Safety, to which they were ordered to report every ten days. All local officials became "national agents," subject to immediate removal by Paris. Committees of surveillance—that is, teams of spies—were placed over government functionaries at every level. The law of 14 Frimaire became the real constitution of France.

The Republic of Virtue

The revolution produced not only a new political apparatus but a new culture as well, the "Republic of Virtue." Dress and decorative objects became means of displaying political commitment, and the popular symbols of the revolution—the red, white, and blue ribbons or "cockades" worn on the hat, the liberty trees planted in the tens of thousands all over France—became enduring badges of republican affiliation that long outlived the revolution itself. The government soon began to channel spontaneous activities such as dances and celebrations into organized festivals. These revolved at first around mass loyalty oaths but soon became replacements for the old religious festivals on which the regime now frowned. As patriotic outlets, as propaganda forums, and as a means of surveillance, the festivals were no less important than the guillotine in maintaining political discipline.

By the spring of 1794, order had been restored and the armies of the *levée en masse,* 850,000 strong, poured victoriously again into the Low Countries. Yet the Terror, like a mindless machine, ground on. Danton went to the guillotine for suggesting that too much blood had been shed, the ultra-left Enragés and their leader, Hébert, for complaining that there had been too little. The Enragés were to get their wish. The law of 22 Prairial (June 10) declared spreading rumors and defaming patriots to be capital crimes and limited the Revolutionary Tribunal to two verdicts: acquittal or death. In the next six weeks more people were guillotined in Paris than in the entire preceding year. Even the members of the all-powerful Committee on Public Safety walked in fear of one another, especially of Robespierre. A group of them conspired to denounce him before the convention on 9 Thermidor (July 27). Robespierre attempted to defend himself but was shouted down and arrested. The next day he and Saint-Just were executed.

His enemies called Robespierre a tyrant who sought absolute power for himself. When he participated in the Festival of the Supreme Being, an attempt to set up a Deist God of Reason as a revolutionary religion, many were convinced that he aimed to be not merely the dictator of the revolution but its high priest. Yet he never held any title but delegate to the convention, and his estate at his death came to barely 100 livres. Among the corrupt and disillusioned, and even at last the horrified, he retained absolute faith in the justness of the revolution.

MADAME ROLAND: A WOMAN IN THE REVOLUTION

Few women not of royal blood came closer to the center of political power in the eighteenth century than Marie Jeanne Phlipon (1754–1793), better known by her married name, Madame Roland. The daughter of a Parisian engraver, Manon—as family and friends called her—exhibited her gifts early and was taught to read before the age of 4. Profoundly influenced by Rousseau, she found a kindred feminine spirit as well in the writings of Madame de Sévigné. The American Revolution fired her enthusiasm as a war against kings, and she followed its progress eagerly. At about the same time she composed an essay deploring the gulf between the rich and the poor in France, the absence of representative government, and the monarchy's use of force to stifle dissent. In revolution alone did the 20-year-old Manon see any hope for her country's future.

In 1780, Manon married Jean Marie Roland de la Platière, the inspector of manufactures for the province of Picardy, 20 years her senior. With characteristic frankness the young bride described her wedding night as "surprising and disagreeable," but a daughter, Eudora, soon resulted from the union. Madame Roland threw herself into her husband's career, collaborating on his technical studies and polishing his awkward literary style. When her husband was transferred to Lyons, Madame Roland was appalled at the condition of the local peasantry and tended so assiduously to the sick among them that Roland feared for her health.

From the moment the revolution began in 1789, Madame Roland lived for little else. She chafed at her provincial isolation, wrote to warn her friends in Paris of the reactionary tendencies of the smaller cities, and urged from the beginning the abolition of the monarchy. The Rolands returned to Paris in 1791, where Manon created a salon that attracted such figures as Robespierre and Tom Paine. In June 1792, Roland delivered a letter to the king, actually written by Manon, demanding that the king revoke his veto of the legislation against nonjuring priests. Louis responded by dismissing Roland from his post as minister of the interior, and the entire Girondist ministry soon fell. This triggered an attack on the royal palace and, following a summer of heated intrigue in which Madame Roland took an active part, the fall of the monarchy and the summoning of the National Convention. When it was moved in the convention that Roland be invited to resume his ministry, Georges Danton, a political opponent, suggested that the invitation be extended to Madame Roland as well. The convention, knowing her influence, burst into laughter. But Roland's star was already on the wane, while Manon, appalled by the September massacres and now deeply distrustful of Robespierre, began to waver for the first time in her belief in the revolution. She so triumphantly acquitted herself of charges of conspiring with royalist emigrés that she received a standing ovation from the convention, but six months later she was arrested in the coup of June 1793. Imprisoned for five months, she hastily composed her memoirs, knowing that she would be permitted no other defense. Condemned and executed on the same day, November 8, she showed great courage and composure on the scaffold and uttered before the guillotine fell what have come down as the most famous words of the French Revolution: "O Liberty, what crimes are committed in thy name!" Roland, who had gone into hiding, committed suicide at the news of her execution.

CONQUEST AND REACTION, 1795–1799

The fall of Robespierre was followed by a sharp swing to the right, known as the Thermidorian reaction. People were tired of terror and virtue alike. Political opportunists, money men, and speculators abounded. Aristocratic styles and even sentiments returned to fashion among the *jeunesse dorée* ("gilded youth") of the bourgeoisie. Ex-Robespierrists in the provinces were purged by a semiofficial White Terror that rapidly degenerated into a brutal settling of scores with radicals in general. The democratic Constitution of the Year I was shelved for good, and with surviving Girondists readmitted to the convention, a new constitution was devised in 1795 that

reinstated the old system of electors, with a property qualification so high that only 20,000 men in France met the test. The electors chose all department officials and a new Legislative Assembly, which in turn chose a five-member executive, the Directory, from which the new regime was to take its name.

These events spelled final defeat for the sans-culottes. The convention removed economic controls, prices skyrocketed, and the bread ration was cut to 2 ounces a day. In May 1795 the sans-culottes stormed the convention, crying, "Bread or death!" It was less a demand than a statement. But loyal units of the National Guard dispersed them, and, leaderless, they were spent as a political force.

Despite this, however, the Directory was inherently unstable. It had neither the ideological attraction of Jacobinism nor the traditional appeal of monarchy. When elections in April 1797 produced startling gains for the right, the results were annulled, and the Directory declared that anyone advocating either the monarchy or the democratic constitution of 1793 would be shot on sight. With this, it shed its last pretense to legitimacy. What remained was simply a cabal in search of a strongman.

Despite its difficulties at home, the revolution went militarily from success to success abroad. Its conquering armies annexed the Austrian Netherlands, the left bank of the Rhine, and the principalities of Nice and Savoy to France outright and turned the proud Dutch republic into a satellite state. A daring foray by Napoleon Bonaparte in 1796 produced a string of new satellite republics in Italy. The Swiss cantons were also herded into a so-called Helvetic Republic. Austria was compelled to recognize these conquests by the Treaty of Campo Formio (October 1797). As a sop, the Austrians received Venice, thus extinguishing the independence of Europe's oldest republic.

Propped up by this success, the Directory drifted on for two more years. But the outbreak of war again in 1799 made a strong government imperative. A group led by the Abbé Sieyès put forward Napoleon Bonaparte, whose rapid rise to military prominence seemed to make him an ideal front man for a reorganized executive. A coup in November 1799 ousted the Directory and dispersed the Legislative Assembly. It was the eighth major change of power in the revolution. Napoleon rapidly dispensed with his civilian allies and assumed complete power. For the next 15 years he governed France alone as first consul, then consul for life, and finally emperor of the French. The revolution was over.

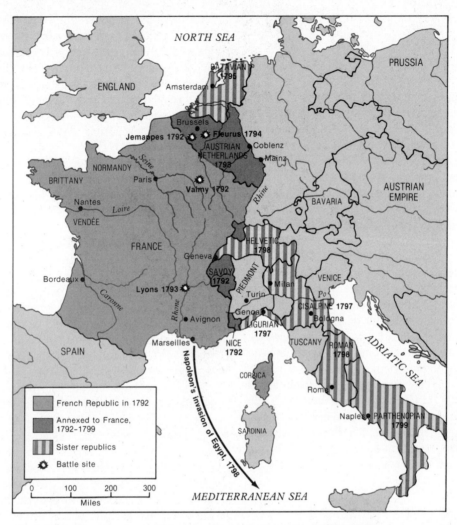

19.1 The Expansion of Revolutionary France, 1792–1799

WOMEN AND THE FRENCH REVOLUTION

The group least satisfied by the revolution was women, particularly those of the urban working class. Although women bore the brunt of the revolution's hardships at all times and, at least at one point, in the march on Versailles in October 1789, played a critical role in events, their interests were not addressed by any of the dominant factions of the revolution. The actress Olympe de Gouges demanded civil equality for women in a tract pointedly titled *Declaration of the Rights of Women and Citizenesses* but met only ridicule. Very few women were in the position of Madame Roland, whose salon was a center of revolutionary intrigue; most spent their days on ration lines, often to receive spoiled or unpalatable goods or nothing at all. Women and children were the first to succumb to starvation or malnutrition, as local records show, and one can only imagine the desperation of the mothers of Masannay who in May 1794 demanded the elimination of all people over 60 so that the young might be fed enough to survive. When the women of Paris tried to organize their own clubs, they were shut down by the procurator of the Commune, who observed that sansculottes had a right to expect their wives to keep house while they attended political meetings.

THE LEGACY
OF THE REVOLUTION

The revolution has remained a focus of intense research and debate from its own time to the present. Some conclusions, however, seem unlikely to be seriously modified. The revolution destroyed the localism of Old Regime France, welding it into a single political and economic unit and opening it to the forces of market capitalism. It produced the first citizen army of modern times and showed for the first time what an entire society mobilized for war and driven by ideology could achieve. It introduced modern mass politics and made the sovereignty of the people, already proclaimed in America, the fundamental legitimating principle of Western governments. It also introduced in the name of the people the suspension of recognized legal rights and forms and the condemnation of dissenters, a practice that began with the Jacobins but was equally characteristic of the Directory and has since become an increasingly casual weapon of modern regimes. In that respect the revolution may be said to have opened up the Pandora's box of modern politics in which, as the Russian novelist Feodor Dostoevsky remarked, "everything is permitted." But it also, like Pandora, gave the great mass of the human race what it had never had before except from religion: hope.

THE NAPOLEONIC ERA

It was not immediately clear that Napoleon's coup d'état would be very different from the previous changes of government of the past ten years, let alone that it would usher in a new era both for France and for Europe. As Napoleon slowly but firmly drew the reins of power into his own hands, however, and as his campaigns of conquest brought more and more of the continent under French sway, it became apparent that France had a master and Europe a ruler such as neither had known before.

From Republic to Empire

Born in 1769 into a family of impoverished minor nobility on the island of Corsica, Napoleon was barely 30 when he attained power. Italian by descent (Napoleon dropped the *u* in the family name Buonaparte when he invaded Italy in 1796), he was French only by virtue of Corsica's annexation to France in 1768, and his first adventure was fighting for his island's independence in 1789. Soon swept up in the revolution on the mainland, he gained notice in the taking of the port of Toulon in 1793, and after putting down a royalist uprising in October 1795, he became a central figure in the Directory. His brilliant campaign in Italy made him the man of the hour, and despite the failure of a campaign against the British in Egypt in 1798, his reputation was undimmed.

Napoleon promulgated a new constitution, which created a token legislature and centralized executive authority in the hands of three "consuls." Napoleon took the title of first consul, with full authority to appoint all officials and magistrates, conduct diplomacy, declare and wage war, and protect the public safety. Napoleon had vowed to keep the republic, but the powers he gave himself made him an uncrowned king. In a masterful stroke of public relations he submitted the constitution to a popular referendum, although he had already proclaimed it to be in effect. The result was predictably lopsided, with 3,011,007 votes counted for and 1,562 against. Napoleon could now claim his "mandate" from the people. In 1802 he extended the term of his consulship from ten years to life, and in 1804, after making peace with the church, he assumed the title of emperor. Both acts were ratified by popular referendum, but for his coronation Napoleon summoned Pope Pius VII to Paris, and in a gesture deliberately reminiscent of Charlemagne's at his coronation as Holy Roman emperor 1,000 years before, he took the crown from the pontiff's hands and placed it on his own head. Shortly afterward, he created an aristocracy, mostly from the upper bourgeoisie. The revolution against monarchs, priests, and nobles had come full circle.

Napoleon ruled through propaganda, press censorship, a highly efficient secret police, and, on occasion, acts of political terrorism. Yet his popularity was genuine, and he enjoyed the support of all classes almost to the end. Only diehard royalists and republicans refused to accept him. Simply stated, Napoleon gave the rich what they wanted, the poor what they would accept, and, through an unprecedented career of conquest, a measure of glory to everyone such as Louis XIV had only dreamed of.

Napoleon promoted new industry, built an extensive network of roads and canals, and chartered a Bank of France to free the government from reliance on private credit. He capped his reforms with the Civil Code of 1804, known, with later additions and modifications, as the Napoleonic Code. The code was the culmination of efforts to produce a digest of French legal and administrative principles dating back to the sixteenth century, and it became the most influential code of secular law outside the Anglo-Saxon tradition since Roman times. The main principles of the early revolution—civil and legal equality, religious toleration, and the abolition of feudal obligations and legally privileged orders—were confirmed. Beneath the veneer of formal equality, however, the code envisioned a hierarchical society based on subordination to wealth and gender. The emphasis, as in the Old Regime, was on the flow of authority downward from the state to the patriarchal family. Women were enjoined to obey their husbands and prevented from acquiring property without written consent and from administering joint property. Children might be imprisoned for up to six months on the mere word of their father and had to gain his consent to marry up to the age of 30. A similar hierarchy was established in the workplace; for example, the word of an employer automatically prevailed over that of a worker in court. The code was extremely detailed in its guarantees of property rights and its provisions for contracts and debts, but as for labor, denied as before the right of association, it was merely "free"—free to survive or perish as market conditions might dictate.

Napoleon's other major settlement was with the church. By the Concordat of 1801 the Vatican recognized the confiscation of its lands and tithes as permanent, thereby accepting the role of the clergy as salaried employees of the state. In return for his concessions the pope was recognized as head of the church, and Catholicism was declared to be the religion "of the majority of Frenchmen." By this careful formulation, Napoleon stopped short of making Catholicism the official state church, thus preserving the principle of religious toleration; yet it served that function in effect. With the Concordat, the empire, and the code, his structure of authority was complete.

France Against Europe

France's military victories had been unprecedented, but Europe could not tolerate indefinitely a French frontier than ran from the North Sea to the Ionian. Backed by British money and Russian troops, a new coalition drove the French back on a broad front in 1799. If the original revolutionary impetus of the French army was ex-

hausted, however, it was now replaced by an equally powerful force: Napoleon's own dream of world empire. Napoleon smashed the Austrians at Hohenlinden and Marengo, forcing them to sue for peace (Treaty of Lunéville, 1801) on even worse terms than those at Campo Formio; and with the fall of the 18-year ministry of William Pitt the Younger, the son of the hero of the Seven Years' War, the British made a reluctant peace at Amiens in 1802.

Full-scale war resumed in 1805 with Britain, again under the leadership of Pitt, subsidizing Russian troops to the tune of £1,250,000 for each 100,000 recruits. But at Ulm on October 15 an Austrian army, completely outgeneraled, surrendered without firing a shot, and six weeks later, Napoleon won the greatest of all his battles over a combined Austro-Russian force at Austerlitz. Prussia, neutral since 1795, blundered into war alone in 1806, only to have its reputedly invincible army destroyed in the simultaneous battles of Jena and Auerstadt. The French now pursued Russia along the Baltic shore into East Prussia, where, after bloody battles at Eylau and Friedland, Tsar Alexander I (1801–1825) too offered peace. Napoleon was unsuccessful only at sea, where his plan for invading Britain was dashed by the fleet under Lord Horatio Nelson at Cape Trafalgar off the coast of Spain. Nelson sank or captured 18 French ships without the loss of a vessel. Although he himself was slain in the battle, Nelson had assured British control of the seas.

The Grand Empire

After the defeat of the so-called Third Coalition in 1805, Napoleon began to construct his Grand Empire. The debris of petty German principalities was swept away, to be replaced by the Confederation of the Rhine, whose 38 members acknowledged Napoleon as their protector and agreed to furnish troops for his army. The 1,000-year-old Holy Roman Empire was summarily abolished in 1806. Only Prussia retained its nominal independence, but shorn of half its territory and with its army reduced to a mere 42,000 men. Prussian Poland was reconstituted as the Grand Duchy of Warsaw, another satellite. Napoleon created a kingdom of Italy for his stepson Eugène, later annexing some of it to France and imprisoning Pius VII when he objected to the occupation of the Papal States. Similarly, a kingdom of Holland was created for Napoleon's brother Louis but was absorbed outright four years later. Using his siblings essentially as prefects, Napoleon made his brother Jérome king of the German

Horace Vernet's portrait of Napoleon in battle at Jena catches the intensity and concentration that made him a great field commander but also the arrogance that presaged his ultimate downfall. [Cliché des Musées Nationaux, Paris]

satellite of Westphalia in 1807 and his brother Joseph king of Spain in 1808, deposing the reigning Bourbon dynasty.

By the time this structure of satellite kingdoms was complete, however, Napoleon considered it obsolete. National entities, even ruled by members of the emperor's own family, were still too insubordinate, too conscious of their separate historical identities. As the Constituent Assembly had abolished the old provinces of France, so Napoleon decided to abolish the nations of Europe, replacing them with a single imperial administration. But events overtook him, and this last design was never carried out.

The Napoleonic Code was used as the basis of administration in the Grand Empire, whence its influence spread throughout Europe and beyond, reaching places as distant as Bolivia, Egypt, and Japan. By abolishing serfdom, dissolving the Old Regime system of orders, and introducing public education, the code opened careers in commerce, industry, and government to men of talent. If the code represented the revolution at its least liberal, it was startlingly new and progressive elsewhere in Europe, and its importance as a solvent of feudal structures and as a model of modern society can scarcely be exaggerated.

Despite the code, however, Napoleonic rule provoked

universal opposition. The chief common grievance was the Continental System, an attempt by Napoleon to close the ports of the empire to British commerce. This exposed such ports to reprisals by the British, and had a crippling effect on European commerce. The deeper cause for resentment, however, was the suppression of national culture in the subject territories and the exploitation of the wealth and resources of a continent for the benefit of a single nation and ultimately a single family. By far the most serious resistance came from Spain. Spaniards of all classes rose up spontaneously against the French occupation and waged a fierce guerrilla war for six years whose atrocities were recorded for all time by the painter Francisco Goya. Napoleon thought that 20,000 men could hold the country; ten times that many failed. The British joined the battle under Arthur Wellesley, later duke of Wellington, in what came to be known as the Peninsular War. By early 1814, southern France itself was under attack. The war ended with the British in Toulouse.

A more lasting effect of the Napoleonic occupation was the stimulation of national feeling, particularly in Italy and Germany. Passed from hand to hand since the sixteenth century, Italy had been parceled out in bits and pieces to in-laws and even cabinet ministers by Napoleon. But despite heavy taxes and a general distaste for

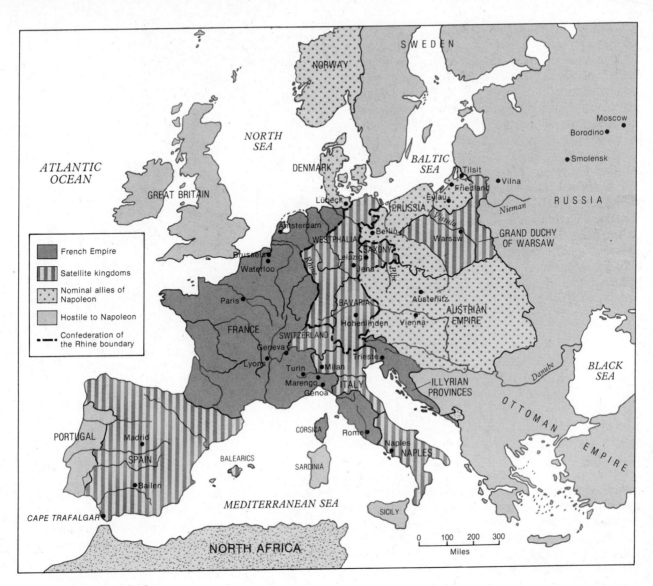

19.2 Europe in 1810

the French presence, Italian commerce and industry benefited from the abolition of tariff barriers, the building of new roads, and the introduction of uniform weights and measures. It is significant that many of the future leaders of the movement for Italian unification were descended from families that became rich under Napoleon.

National consciousness had been promoted in eighteenth-century Germany by the philosopher Johann Gottfried von Herder (1744–1803), who argued that each people had a separate and unique historical destiny shaped by its *Volksgeist* ("native spirit"). But most

German intellectuals of the Enlightenment prided themselves on a lofty cosmopolitanism instead. They despised Prussian militarism, and many initially welcomed the Napoleonic invasion; on the eve of the Battle of Jena the philosopher Hegel, himself a Prussian, wrote, "As I [did] formerly, now everybody wishes success to the French army."

The collapse and dismemberment of the Prussian state changed all that. Defeat brought Prussia what victory never had: a sense of nationhood. As French troops paraded through the streets of Berlin, the philosopher and publicist Johann Gottlieb Fichte (1762–1814)

"And They Are Like Wild Beasts." Spanish women, virtually unarmed, give battle to Napoleon's troops in this print from Goya's series of etchings *Disasters of War*. No other artist has ever captured so directly the naked ferocity of war. [The Metropolitan Museum of Art, Rogers Fund, 1922 (22.60.25(5))]

delivered a series of "addresses to the German nation" in which he called for a movement of national liberation to drive out the French oppressor and to protect the German Volksgeist from contamination by outside cultures. Under the lead of Baron Stein and Prince Hardenburg, meanwhile, the Prussian monarchy initiated significant land reforms, including the abolition of serfdom, liberalization of land tenures, and the reform of the bureaucracy.

For the moment, however, liberation seemed far away. From the Atlantic to the Polish steppe, from the Baltic to the Mediterranean, Napoleon ruled or dominated the whole of Europe. A swollen France itself stretched from the north German port of Lübeck to south of Rome. When Austria rose in 1809 and called on the former states of the Holy Roman Empire to assist it, not a single one responded. The Habsburg army was crushed at Wagram, and it was now Vienna's turn to entertain a triumphal parade of French troops.

Yet Napoleon's empire was inherently unstable. As the flush of idealism and reform it had borrowed from the revolution wore away, the cynical and exploitive nature of its administration was increasingly apparent.

It preached human equality but demanded permanent subjection. It violated the entire history and tradition of the European state system. It was not even in the interest of France, whose distended borders resembled a jaw open on the whole continent.

Napoleon himself was now obsessed with founding a dynasty. When his first wife, Joséphine de Beauharnais, failed to provide him with an heir, he divorced her in favor of Princess Marie Louise of Austria. In 1811 she bore Napoleon a son, whom he grandly called the king of Rome. But nothing could obscure the fact that Napoleon, who had so often humiliated Austria, felt compelled to buy legitimacy by mixing his blood with that of the Habsburgs.

The Collapse of the Napoleonic Order

By the Treaty of Tilsit (1807), France and Russia had formally become allies, on terms advantageous to the French. An uneasy truce prevailed for the next five years as each side probed for the other's weaknesses. Alexander attempted to gain control of the Grand Duchy of Warsaw, which under Napoleonic rule was a dagger pointed at Russia itself. Napoleon in turn sought influence in Istanbul, which he regarded as the "center of world empire," an empire presumably to be controlled by himself.

When Russia reopened trade with Britain and erected tariffs against French goods, Napoleon resolved on war. In June 1812 he crossed into Russia with over 600,000 men, the largest army ever assembled for a single campaign. Napoleon envisaged a quick victory. But the Russians gave ground instead of fighting, leaving behind only scorched earth. They surrendered Moscow after an indecisive but bloody battle at Borodino, and Napoleon entered it on September 14. What had been a city of 300,000 was all but deserted. Without food or shelter, Napoleon could not winter in the devastated city. On October 19 he began a retreat. Mired in snow and mud, dogged by Russian snipers, his army laid a 1,000-mile track of corpses along its way. More than half a million men died, deserted, or disappeared.

Abandoning his army to its fate, Napoleon raced back to Paris. He raised new forces to face a revived coalition led by Britain, but he was defeated outside Leipzig in the so-called Battle of the Nations (October 1813) and thrown back upon France. The Austrian foreign minister, Count Klemens von Metternich, alarmed at Prussia's new nationalism and eager to have the Russians out of Europe, offered to guarantee the French borders of 1792, including the former Austrian Netherlands and the left bank of the Rhine. Napoleon refused. For the emperor of the French, the only stakes were all or nothing. Allied armies now poured into France from the north, the west, and the south. Napoleon fought brilliantly, but the result was foregone. On April 4, 1814, he abdicated as emperor in favor of his 3-year-old son, a day after his Senate had deposed him.

The Bourbon Restoration

The victorious allies, aided by Napoleon's turncoat foreign minister, Talleyrand, restored the Bourbon dynasty in the person of Louis XVIII,* count of Provence, who signed the Treaty of Paris on May 30 that ended France's 22-year war with Europe. Wishing to support the new monarch, the allies demanded no indemnities or reparations. France was simply required to return to its prewar

---

*The son of Louis XVI, who died in prison at the age of 10 without ever reigning, was recognized as Louis XVII.

boundaries. Napoleon was exiled to the island of Elba off the west coast of Italy but permitted to retain the title of emperor and granted a pension of 2 million francs a year.

Louis XVIII was in theory an absolute king, but he confirmed the revolutionary land settlement and the Napoleonic Code and issued a Constitutional Charter that provided for a bicameral assembly chosen by a restricted suffrage of large landowners. The thousands of vengeful emigrés who returned with him, however, would be satisfied by nothing less than a complete restoration of the Old Regime. The activities of these Ultraroyalists, or Ultras, as they were popularly called, together with a severe postwar depression, cost the Bourbon regime whatever credibility it had. Napoleon, sensing his opportunity, returned to France and with 1,000 veterans marched unopposed on Paris. The Bourbons fled, and the emperor declared himself restored "by the unanimous wish of a great nation."

The allies, gathered in Vienna, promptly declared Napoleon a public outlaw. Napoleon himself, courting support at home, made conciliatory gestures both to the right and to the left. But only a trial by battle could reestablish him. Raising an army he crossed into Belgium, where on June 18, 1815, he was defeated at Waterloo by a force under the duke of Wellington and the Prussian general Gebhard von Blücher. Returning to Paris, he was met with a stony demand for abdication. His second reign had lasted exactly 100 days.

Napoleon was now exiled to St. Helena, a bleak, tiny island in the south Atlantic, 4,000 miles from Europe, where in 1821 he died, reportedly of stomach cancer. His legend lived on in France, where a veritable cult grew up around him that was climaxed by the return and reentombment of his body in 1840.

SUMMARY

Napoleon himself said that the man of genius is a meteor who illuminates his time but does not transform it. Yet he did leave a permanent legacy. His code became the basis of modern French society. His conquests stimulated both anti-French nationalism and aspirations for a liberal society on the French model. His suppression of the Holy Roman Empire was the first step toward the unification of Germany. If the ideas he spread were those of the revolution rather than his own, they might never have traveled as far as they did without him. Napoleon failed to make Europe a province of France, but he did much to make the French Revolution European.

Notes

1. J. H. Stewart, *A Documentary Survey of the French Revolution* (New York: Macmillan, 1951), p. 42 (modified slightly).

Suggestions for Further Reading

Applewhite, H. B., and Levy, D. G., eds. *Women and Politics in the Age of the Democratic Revolution.* Ann Arbor: University of Michigan Press, 1990.

Bergeron, L. *France Under Napoleon.* Princeton, N.J.: Princeton University Press, 1981.

Cobb, R. C. *The People's War.* New Haven, Conn.: Yale University Press, 1987.

Cobban, A. *The Social Interpretation of the French Revolution.* Cambridge: Cambridge University Press, 1964.

Doyle, W. *Origins of the French Revolution.* Oxford: Oxford University Press, 1980.

Furet, F. *Interpreting the French Revolution.* New York: Cambridge University Press, 1981.

Godechot, J., Hyslop, B., and Dowd, D. *The Napoleonic Era in Europe.* New York: Holt, Rinehart and Winston, 1971.

Hunt, L. *Politics, Culture and Class in the French Revolution.* Berkeley: University of California Press, 1984.

Jones, P. M. *The Peasantry in the French Revolution.* Cambridge: Cambridge University Press, 1988.

Jordan, D. *The Revolutionary Career of Maximilien Robespierre.* New York: Free Press, 1985.

Lefebvre, G. *The French Revolution.* New York: Columbia University Press, 1962, 1964.

Palmer, R. R. *The Age of the Democratic Revolutions.* Princeton, N.J.: Princeton University Press, 1959, 1964.

Soboul, A. *The Sans-Culottes and the French Revolution.* Princeton, N.J.: Princeton University Press, 1980.

Thompson, J. M. *Napoleon Bonaparte: His Rise and Fall.* New York: Oxford University Press, 1969.

Venturi, F. *The End of the Old Regime in Europe, 1776–1789.* Princeton, N.J.: Princeton University Press, 1991.

THE INDUSTRIAL REVOLUTION

From the beginning of history to the nineteenth century, all physical labor was accomplished by human or animal muscle or by implements using such muscle. This power was reinforced by levers, pulleys, and weights and supplemented by running water, moving air, or fire. Since then, work has been performed increasingly by machines powered by steam, electricity, combustible gases, and the exploding atom. The enormous consequent increase in productive capacity has transformed work, society, and the face of the planet itself more than any single development since the introduction of agriculture. This process is still known by the name given to it by the nineteenth-century British historian Arnold Toynbee: the Industrial Revolution.

THE BACKGROUND: POPULATION, ENERGY, AND TECHNOLOGY

The Industrial Revolution began in western Europe, particularly in Great Britain. Europe had achieved an aggregate growth of population, commerce, and energy between the fifteenth and eighteenth centuries. Such growth, at an even faster relative rate, had been experienced between the eleventh and thirteenth centuries, only to be succeeded by the demographic catastrophe of the fourteenth. Some observers, such as the Englishman Thomas Robert Malthus (1766–1834), feared at the end of the eighteenth century that Europe was on the brink of such a catastrophe again. In his *Essay on Population* (1798), Malthus noted with alarm a new surge in Europe's population and calculated that Europeans would soon outstrip their resources. The result would be scarcity, famine, and war.

Had the Industrial Revolution not transformed Europe's productive capacity, Malthus' dire prophecy might have come true. By the end of the eighteenth century, Europe's once abundant forests had been seriously depleted by industrial demand and agricultural clearance. At existing rates of consumption the exhaustion of the continent's major energy source and chief industrial material seemed inevitable.

The solution was the replacement of wood by coal. Coal had been an important fuel source in certain industrial processes since the sixteenth century, but its more general use was restricted by the difficulty and danger of mining it, the lack of overland transportation to distribute it, and the foul-smelling sulfur released in burning it.

One of the chief hazards of coal mining was subsurface water. At the beginning of the eighteenth century, Thomas Savery and Thomas Newcomen developed a steam-powered pump that Savery called "the Miner's Friend." The efficiency of this pump was increased fourfold when the Scotsman James Watt (1736–1819) introduced a condenser that kept the steam from being dissipated. By 1782 he had converted the pump into a double-action rotary engine capable of turning heavy

Coal mining operations such as the one depicted above in the county of Northumberland, belching their black smoke for miles around, transformed much of the British landscape in the early nineteenth century. [Trustees of the Science Museum, London]

machinery. By 1800, some 500 such engines were in use in Great Britain.

Just as industrial progress was limited by the use of wood as its primary source of energy, so too was it limited by its dependence on wood and stone as its chief construction materials. Running a poor third to these was iron. The smelting of iron, which involved separating it from its ore, was a complex, labor-intensive process requiring heavy machinery and great amounts of fuel. The product itself, like coal, was difficult to transport, and most iron for domestic use was produced in small quantities on the village level.

Smelting was accomplished by the use of charcoal, which required that all large ironworks be located near forests. The search for an alternative fuel as the forests dwindled led to coke, a waste product obtained from coal essentially as charcoal is from wood. Its high sulfur content resulted in an unacceptably brittle product, however, until Abraham Darby was able to produce a coke-smelted iron suitable for heavy utensils and military ordnance in 1709. The demand for munitions during the Seven Years' War led to a considerable expansion of coke-fed blast furnaces in Great Britain. But it was not until 1784, when Henry Cort introduced the puddling process for converting crudely cast pig iron into lighter and more tensile wrought iron, that the iron industry was freed from its dependence on wood.

The result of these technical innovations was that by the 1780s Europe stood on the verge of a great breakthrough in its industrial capacity. The use of steam facilitated the extraction of coal; the use of coal made possible the increased production of iron; and iron (with other metals) was first to supplement and then to replace wood and stone as the prime industrial material. At the same time, transportation was improved by new highways called turnpikes that could bear far heavier loads and by canals that turned Britain's waterways into an integrated transport system. The first phase of the Industrial Revolution culminated in the 1820s in the locomotive, which, made of iron and powered by steam and coal, was to provide industry with an incomparably cheap and efficient method of transportation.

These neatly interlocking developments suggest that the Industrial Revolution was a more or less straightforward consequence of certain technical improvements in mining and metallurgy prompted by a threatened scarcity of traditional resources. But such an explanation by itself would be misleading. Other societies, including previous European ones, had faced scarcity without finding a key to increased productivity. Other societies, notably China, had achieved technical levels comparable to and even in advance of those of eighteenth-century Europe without an industrial breakthrough. The industrial transformation of eighteenth-century Europe should therefore be seen not as the beginning but as the end product of a complex process of social change. That process had at least three distinguishable components: commercial, agricultural, and scientific.

COMMERCE AND THE FORMATION OF CAPITALIST SOCIETY

Before the Industrial Revolution was known by that name, the nineteenth-century social critics Karl Marx (1818–1883) and Friedrich Engels (1820–1895) had identified the banking and commercial classes of Europe—the bourgeoisie—as critical in the development of the new industrial society. Marx and Engels saw the bourgeoisie as a group unique to modern Western society, differing from merchant elites in all previous societies in its ability to grasp, organize, and exploit the basic elements of production: capital, land, and labor. Exaggerated though this view may be, it is certainly true that the development of business and commerce had become critical to the prosperity and expansion of Europe.

Commerce becomes a specialized economic function when consumers no longer obtain their goods directly from producers. In commercial economies, producers and consumers typically consummate their exchange through a person appropriately called a *middleman,* or merchant. By extending the links in this chain—by adding more intermediaries—goods can be shipped around the world, joining producers and consumers who share no common language or currency or even knowledge of one another's concrete existence.

What expands the number of links, and hence the economy itself, is capital. Capital can be defined in stocks of goods or resources, in warehousing and shipping facilities, in command or control of a labor supply. But its simplest form is money, since money can freely be interchanged with all the other elements. The term *capital* in this sense was first used in the West in the twelfth and thirteenth centuries. A *capitalist,* as the term emerged by about the mid-seventeenth century, was someone who possessed a large stock of money, whether or not he or she chose to invest it. Although the term *capitalism* was used as early as 1753, it emerged as a descriptive term for an entire economic system only in the early twentieth century. Marx himself never used the term.

Capitalist society—the distinctive form of the modern West—may then be understood as one in which economic relations are integrated by those who possess, as personal or corporate property, the means of production, through which they command both the labor force and the range of consumer choice. In this sense, capitalism as a fully developed system cannot be said to have existed before the transformation of European society by the Industrial Revolution in the nineteenth century. Yet if the Industrial Revolution made capitalism possible as a distinctive economic system, the capitalist element in the preindustrial economy—the activity of the bourgeois or merchant class—was the most dynamic element in that economy, the activity that enabled it to grow.

Preindustrial capitalism was, in short, commercial capitalism, a capitalism not of producers but of distributors. The two states of eighteenth-century Europe where this capitalism was most advanced were Great Britain and the Netherlands. Dutch prosperity, the envy of Europe in the previous century, was chiefly the result of commercial activity; at its height, Dutch shipping carried half of the world's trade, exclusive of China.

The culture of early modern capitalism was nowhere better displayed than in the Netherlands. Dutch harbors were crammed with the treasures of the Americas and the Indies—sugar, silks, spices, cocoa, tobacco; their shipyards launched 2,000 new seagoing vessels each year. Cloth manufacture and finishing remained the staple industry, as it had been since the Middle Ages; but there were hundreds of other industries and specialized trades such as diamond cutting, lens grinding, and bookmaking. Business was serviced by a host of bankers, factors, jobbers, and commodity and discount brokers. The great commercial families, the so-called regent class, ruled with all the aplomb of the traditional European aristocracies.

The Dutch had had a miniature Industrial Revolution of their own in the sixteenth and seventeenth centuries. The introduction of a movable cap and a drive shaft crank to the windmill, traditionally an important power source in the Netherlands, enabled the Dutch to hew the giant Baltic timbers they used in shipbuilding with far greater precision and efficiency. By adapting the crank to other kinds of implements—hammers, rams, paddles—they were able to convert the windmill to a host of industrial uses: hulling, oilseed crushing, fulling, boring, and paper and dye preparation, among many others. Even more significant was the development of the water-pumping mill, which enabled the Dutch to drain lakes and marshes and thus to add significantly to their land-poor country. Such large-scale reclamation projects were financed by groups of wealthy merchants, particularly Amsterdammers; thus once again commercial capital, industrial innovation, and economic development went in tandem.

The British were slower to develop as a commercial power, but during the eighteenth century their growing naval and imperial supremacy, their control of the lucrative slave trade, and the systematic creation of capital and credit through the expansion of the national debt enabled them to outstrip the Dutch. At first much of this expansion was financed by the Dutch themselves, who as late as 1776 held 43 percent of the British debt, but this share rapidly declined thereafter. By 1815 it was held almost entirely by the British upper classes themselves: nobility, gentry, and well-to-do merchants. This oligarchy not only determined the expenditure of the debt through their control of the government but also reaped a direct return through the payment of interest on it, estimated in 1815 at nearly a tenth of the government's revenue. In effect, the British state itself had been converted into a giant corporation paying dividends to its wealthy shareholders. This great capital, the spoil of commercial profit, war, and empire, was a fuel that stoked the engines of the Industrial Revolution no less than coal and steam.

THE AGRICULTURAL REVOLUTION

The backbone of European society was the traditional peasant village, typically structured around open fields divided into narrow, unfenced strips. These strips were worked by individual peasants, but since they comprised a single large field, the strips were all plowed, sown, and harvested as one. These rhythms enforced the communal cooperation and solidarity that characterized peasant

society. The peasants' life was the life of their villages: traditional, conservative, immemorial as the soil and the seasons, and highly resistant to change. But that life was soon not only to be altered but within a few generations actually to disappear.

The two necessities of the peasant's life were to feed the family and to pay dues and taxes—to the lord, the church, and the state. These two necessities constituted the task of subsistence—survival—since peasants who could not meet their obligations to the lord would lose the use of the land. Subsistence was difficult in the best of times, and only the wealthiest of peasants could think of producing for the market. The majority dared not experiment with new crops or techniques that promised greater productivity. Their existence held no margin for error.

But changes in both demography and the structure of land ownership undermined these traditional patterns. The general surge in population in the sixteenth century had put great pressure on the food supply, driving up land and food prices. This made life harder for the average peasant, whose increased cost for seed was not compensated by higher food prices, since peasants did not produce for the market and indeed were often purchasers of food themselves. But it opened great opportunities for those who were able to speculate in land and sell grain. In England this class of substantial landowners, the gentry, had already been enriched by the purchase of church lands at the time of the Reformation. In the seventeenth and eighteenth centuries the gentry set out to maximize its profits, partly through land acquisition and enclosure (expropriation of communal grazing land) and partly through the importation of new techniques developed by the Dutch and the Flemish.

Most enclosure in England before the seventeenth century was for the purpose of pasturing sheep, which the gentry raised for market. Thereafter, enclosure was increasingly justified as a means of raising agricultural productivity to feed a growing population through the introduction of crops and fertilizers on land that peasants lacked either the means or the desire to "improve." But when the increase in population temporarily leveled off, as it did in the late seventeenth century, the lure of profit did not. Agrarian capitalism—the replacement of small-scale farming for subsistence by large-scale farming for the market—had begun to transform the traditional village; it would end by destroying it.

The improvement of enclosed land involved a variety of new techniques. As in the Low Countries, where the scarcity of land for enclosure stimulated more intensive methods of cultivation, marshland was extensively drained and filled in. Marl and clay were mixed in sandy soils to make them more productive. Jethro Tull (1674–1741) introduced the planting of seeds in straight, even rows in place of the wasteful old method of sowing them at random (broadcast), while Lord Charles Townshend —"Turnip" Townshend, as he came to be nicknamed— demonstrated that yields could be significantly improved by rotating crops and planting with turnips and clover fields that had previously lain fallow. Both plants replenished the soil and provided winter fodder to sustain animals that would otherwise have been slaughtered for lack of feed. Not only did this substantially increase the size of herds, but thanks to the tireless experiments of the Leicestershire breeder Robert Bakewell, the animals became larger and heavier as well. By the mid-eighteenth century a veritable craze for agricultural improvement had swept the country. Even King George III contributed to an agricultural journal under the pen name "Farmer George."

Spurred by personal competition and the quest for profits, improving landlords hastened to acquire and enclose more and more land. The unquestioned control of Parliament by the gentry facilitated a policy of legalized confiscations. Between 1760 and 1815 some 3,600 acts of Parliament enclosed 6 million acres of land, or roughly a quarter of the arable land in England. By 1840 the communally farmed open field had ceased to exist.

What emerged in its place was a system of great estates worked by tenant farmers and hired laborers— no longer a peasantry but an agricultural work force. This system, with its vastly greater productivity and efficiency, enabled Britain to feed a population that had begun to grow at an unprecedented rate. In 1700 the population of England was about 5.5 million; by 1801 it had increased to 9 million, and by 1851 it was 18 million. This growing population provided both the work force and the primary market for the products of the Industrial Revolution.

Despite the growth in national wealth, many English men and women, reduced from a real if precarious independence as propertied cultivators to the status of mere laborers, felt dispossessed from their own country. The poet Oliver Goldsmith caught the popular sense of alienation and bitterness in "The Deserted Village" (1770):

Ill fares the land, to hastening ills a prey
Where wealth accumulates and men decay.
Princes and lords may flourish, or may fade
A breath can make them, as a breath has made
But a bold peasantry, their country's pride
When once destroyed, can never be supplied.

Even Arthur Young, the foremost propagandist of the new agriculture, came at last to deplore its human cost. "I had rather," he wrote at the end of the eighteenth century, "that all the commons were sunk in the sea than that the poor should in future be treated as they have generally been hitherto."

Apart from Britain, the Low Countries, and Denmark (where Dutch methods were also introduced), the agricultural revolution was slow to spread. Enthusiasm for agricultural improvement ran high in France, particularly among the group of reformers called the Physiocrats, led by François Quesnay (1694–1774). Louis XV wore a potato flower in his lapel in an attempt to popularize the plant. But the French aristocracy was not eager to disturb the system of seigneurial dues that constituted its chief profit from the peasantry, and the revolution of 1789, in abolishing the manorial regime, left France a nation of small proprietors and delayed the introduction of large-scale capitalist agriculture for a century.

The agricultural revolution was a revolution in soil management and animal husbandry rather than mechanization. The scythe gradually replaced the sickle in the eighteenth century, but it was not until the nineteenth that threshers and reapers were introduced, and their use spread slowly. The abundance of cheap labor—and the necessity to absorb a rapidly growing population— made the introduction of laborsaving machinery in agriculture not only less necessary but also politically dangerous. No similar inhibitions were at work in industry, where machine technology created more work than it destroyed. But if the agricultural revolution was not in this sense a part of the Industrial Revolution, at least until the introduction of combine harvesters in the 1880s, it was an indispensable precondition of it.

SCIENCE, TECHNOLOGY, AND THE STATE

The last major element in the Industrial Revolution was the development of machine technology itself. As will now be clear, the new technology was not a cause but rather an effect of conditions that favored and to some degree compelled an attempt to expand productive capacity—the extension of a market economy and the pressure of a growing population.

Bodies such as the Royal Society and the Society of Arts in England as well as informal working groups of scientists and manufacturers coordinated efforts to find solutions for specific industrial problems and sponsored prize competitions. These efforts were addressed particularly to the textile industry, England's largest. England had traditionally specialized in woolens, but the leading edge of the industry was in cotton, stimulated by the popularity of fine calicoes from India and by the supply of raw cotton provided by slave labor in the colonial plantations. Raw materials were thus available, and a market was waiting, but productive capacity lagged. The first breakthrough occurred in 1733 when a Lancashire clockmaker, John Kay, invented the flying shuttle. This device enabled weavers to drive the shuttle across their looms by pulling strings attached to hammers, doubling the capacity of the loom. Yet the weavers could produce their cloth no faster than spinners could provide them with thread. The Royal Society offered a prize for a spinning machine, but not until James Hargreaves devised a set of spindles driven by a single wheel, the "spinning jenny," could the supply of thread keep up with the capacity of Kay's loom. A former barber, Richard Arkwright, attached the jenny to the water frame, a system of rollers that drew the thread taut before it was spun. The supply of thread now exceeded loom capacity until the clergyman Edmund Cartwright invented a power loom that could be operated by water or steam. Arkwright made a fortune and was rewarded with a knighthood in 1786, the first ever given to an industrialist, while Cartwright was voted £10,000 by a grateful House of Commons.

The official recognition given these men of humble status indicated the importance the state attached to commercially viable inventions. Yet the British government was far less directly involved in promoting industrial development than mercantilist France, with its state-sponsored factories, or the Prussia of Frederick the Great. The British concentrated instead on seeking raw materials, opening markets, and securing naval supremacy. From the age of the Navigation Acts (1651, 1660), designed to ensure control of the colonial trade, the government pursued a consistent policy of commercial advantage. Britain fought not for *gloire* but for trading posts and privileges; what it sought above all from the wars against Louis XIV was penetration of the rich market of Spanish America, and when, 70 years later, it obtained logging rights along 300 leagues of wooded Mexican coastline, a British diplomat noted sagely, "If we manage this area wisely, there ought to be enough wood for eternity." If free enterprise and laissez-faire, the gospel so compellingly preached by Adam Smith in *The*

Wealth of Nations, were to prove the formula for industrial expansion at home, it was within the framework of unfettered access to world markets and vital resources opened up by a century and a quarter of conscious imperial policy.

THE TRANSFORMATION OF BRITAIN

Between about 1780 and 1830, Great Britain was transformed more profoundly than any nation in recorded history. This transformation affected the size of the population and the distribution and living conditions of the vast majority. It altered the nature and in some respects the very notion of family life, work, and leisure. It profoundly affected the bonds of social organization and even the physical face of the land itself. From Britain the effects of this transformation rippled outward, first to the rest of Europe and then, through the mechanism of imperialism, to the farthest corners of the globe.

During this period, the eyes of all Europe were fixed not on Britain but on the revolutionary upheavals in France. Yet economically and even socially, France in 1830 was still in many respects the France of 1780, a nation of peasant proprietors tilling the soil much as their ancestors had done for hundreds of years. The events in France were significant, certainly, and indeed they were broadly related to the great transformation in Britain. But if we can in the last analysis see the same fundamental change at work in both countries—the triumph of the capitalist mode of production and its integration with the powers of the state—the method of this change was very different in each. In France the drama was played out as a contest for control of the state, while in Britain, where the interests of the commercial classes and the state had been already harmonized, a social transformation of unprecedented magnitude was achieved with relatively little political disturbance.

The magnitude of economic change in Britain can best be suggested by statistics. In 1700, Britain produced 2.5 million tons of coal; in 1815, 16 million. Pig iron production rose from 17,000 tons in 1740 to 125,000 in 1796 and then doubled again to 256,000 tons in 1806. Much of this production went to service the booming cotton industry, whose output rose from 21 million yards of cloth in 1796 to 347 million by 1830. During this period, cotton cloth rose from ninth to first place in the value of British manufactures, accounting for almost half of all exports. Even after 1830, textiles in general and cotton in particular constituted the essential product of the Industrial Revolution.

The Organization of Labor

The enormous increase in production attested by these figures entailed not only new energy sources and new machines but also new methods of commercial and industrial organization. Thus arose the two distinctive institutions of the Industrial Revolution: the bank and the factory. The function of banks was to concentrate capital; of factories, to concentrate labor. There were still only 12 banks in Great Britain outside London in 1750; by 1793 there were nearly 400, and by 1815 about 900. The intimate connection between banking and industrialization was demonstrated by the fact that some of the leading inventor-industrialists of the period—Richard Arkwright and James Watt among them—formed banks of their own as their businesses expanded.

The modern factory was the result of the machine. Previously, production had been carried on by four more or less distinct means of organization: the small workshop; the "cottage" or "domestic" system of home labor; the urban "manufactory," which concentrated large numbers of workers under the same roof; and the preindustrial factory, or "arsenal," which assembled workers on an open-air site such as a mine, dockyard, or foundry.

Of these four, the first two were by far the most important. The small workshop, consisting typically of a master artisan, two or three journeymen, and a like number of apprentices, had been characteristic of the medieval city. The workshops were organized on the basis of craft or trade into guild associations, which set general conditions of work and wages and standards of production. The guild system was in decay in the eighteenth century and in Britain had been legally abolished, although the workshop itself, with its distinction among master, journeyman, and apprentice, still remained. The result was that journeymen increasingly tended to organize in defense of their working conditions and wages, a phenomenon noted with deep disapproval by the German Imperial Diet in 1731.

The cottage or domestic system was particularly widespread in the clothing trade, although it was common as well in metalworking and other pursuits. Under this arrangement the clothier provided the yarn and the looms to spinners and weavers who worked at home and

whose product the clothier then collected and marketed, thus combining the function of capitalist and merchant in one. Cloth-producing centers on the Continent were similarly organized. At its most developed, the domestic system converted rural hamlets into integrated productive units in which the workers were separated only by walls.

The urban manufactory was typical of more specialized textile production such as hat, lace, and tapestry making; the Gobelins tapestry works established by Colbert was perhaps the most famous example. The manufactory concentrated as many as 500 workers under a single roof, thus making possible a greater division of labor and a closer supervision of the production process—both typical of the nineteenth-century factory. The manufactory differed from a modern factory chiefly in that machinery was still directly hand-operated and hand-powered; human muscle still supplied the energy.

The eighteenth century reserved the term *factory* itself for industrial or mining operations in which human energy was supplemented by wind, running water, or fire. Iron foundries, arsenals, and shipyards were typical examples, and large-scale water-powered mining was well established in central Europe by the sixteenth century. What converted such concentrations of labor into modern units of production was, again, the development of iron machinery powered by coal and steam and the expanding market economy prepared by commercial capitalism.

The factory system of the Industrial Revolution was thus essentially an adaptation of the urban manufactory to the new machines. These machines doomed the domestic system. The engines that powered them required buildings of unprecedented size and complexity of design. The factory at Stockport, England, for example, consisted of a main body 300 feet long, 50 feet wide, and 7 stories high with two lateral wings 58 feet long; the whole was supported by a huge masonry pier whose largest stone was nearly 5 tons in weight. The first floor was occupied by twin 80-horsepower steam engines that powered the entire complex. The coordination of human and mechanical power meant that the factory was not merely a gigantic enclosure for heavy machinery but an integrated system of production. As the Scottish industrialist Andrew Ure defined it: "The term *Factory System* . . . designates the combined operation of many workpeople, adult and young, in tending with assiduous skill a series of productive machines continuously impelled by a central power."[1]

Industrial Discipline

Ure's words reflected a profound transformation in attitudes toward work itself. The work patterns of an agrarian society had been dictated by the rhythms of nature. People satisfied with subsistence quit when they had achieved it. But production for the market was open-ended, and long before the advent of the modern factory, entrepreneurs such as the Scotsman John Law had deplored the fact that many agricultural laborers were "idle one half their time." From this equation of leisure time with idleness it was only a short step to regarding typical workers as lazy and unwilling to work—especially for their employer's profit—except when goaded by necessity. Daniel Defoe was irked when "strolling fellows" refused his offer of day labor, replying that they could earn more money by begging. This did not suggest to prospective employers the desirability of offering better wages; rather, most agreed with Samuel Johnson that "raising the wages of day laborers is wrong for it does not make them live better, but only makes them idler."

In fact, few workers could afford "idleness" in the market-oriented British economy of the eighteenth century, in which most of the rural population could make ends meet only by entering the cottage system. But the productivity of workers in their own homes could be imperfectly supervised at best; only in factories could a genuine work discipline be enforced. Long before such discipline came to Britain, Colbert had applied it to his state manufactories in France. No swearing or idleness was permitted; only hymns might be sung; and workers whose output was chronically defective were put in irons.

The mechanized factory carried this process to its logical conclusion. Instead of assigning one class of worker, the overseer, the task of imposing discipline on the rest of the work force, such discipline was now imposed by the rhythm of the machine itself. No longer did the laborer work a machine; rather, the machine worked the laborer. The penalties for slackness were savage. "Idlers"—often women and children, who comprised the majority of the work force in the textile mills—were flogged, tortured, and hung with weights; had vises screwed to their ears; or were tied three or four at a time "on a crossbeam above the machinery, hanging by our hands," as a witness told an investigating commission in 1835. Sixteen-hour workdays were not uncommon, and many workers toppled from weariness into their machinery. Some commentators compared the treatment of factory workers unfavorably to that of West Indian slaves, and conditions were even worse in the mines.

Family Life: A Tale of Two Cultures

The early Industrial Revolution had a devastating effect on traditional patterns of childrearing and family life among the rural poor. Child labor among the poor had been common in preindustrial Europe, but parents maintained direct supervision of their children in the field or, in the cottage system, at the wheel or loom. Once families were brought under the discipline of the factory, however, it was no longer the father but the overseer who determined the nature, duration, and rhythm of work. Adult males were indeed a minority in the typical textile

WOMAN DRAGING COAL   OLD WOMEN AT WORK   CHILDREN PICKING UP

These horrific images of work in a British coal mine of the 1840s, recorded by a French visitor, speak for themselves. Women and children were preferred for work in the coal galleries because of their smaller stature and greater docility. Notice that the woman in the left frame is chained to her cart so that she can drag it forward on all fours. The height of the galleries was approximately that of the holds on slaving vessels. [The Mansell Collection] mill. Employers preferred women and children, the younger the better; Andrew Ure confessed that it was "near impossible to convert persons past the age of puberty . . . into useful factory hands." Children entered the factory at the age of 5 or 6, as they enter school today; in some mills, children as young as 3 were employed, and in one recorded case a child of 2. The child mortality rate among Britain's working poor in the mid-nineteenth century was two to three times that of the suburban middle class, and children who emerged from what the poet William Blake (1757–1827) called the "dark Satanic mills" of early industrialism were so puny and stunted that they seemed to many observers to belong to another species.

Many young women went into domestic service in middle- and upper-class households; by the middle of the nineteenth century, female servants made up the second largest occupational category in Britain, after farmworkers. Such women were often sexually exploited by their employers; others went into prostitution in the new factory towns. Under these circumstances the male-dominated family unit that had been characteristic of early modern Europe at all social levels was gravely undermined among the new working class. Many of what we regard as typical family problems of the modern poor—single-parent, female-headed households, high rates of illegitimacy and child delinquency, participation in the underground economies of prostitution and theft—were already in evidence in early industrial Britain. The British Poor Law of 1834 herded paupers into workhouses, where husbands were separated from wives, as if in jail, and parents from children. Those who died there were denied church burial. Poverty itself was thus made a crime in both this world and the next.

In contrast to the working-class family, the bourgeois household was becoming more closely knit. It was also more child-centered than ever before. "The child," declared the poet Wordsworth, "is father to the man," and the bourgeois household was gradually redefined as a kind of factory whose product the child was, an attitude still reflected in our language today when we speak of children as "products" of either good or broken homes.

While thus internalizing the values of industry within the home itself, the bourgeois household was also viewed as a refuge from the competitive pressures of society, "a tent pitch'd in a world not right," in the picturesque phrase of the poet Coventry Patmore. The influential Victorian critic John Ruskin called it "the place of peace; the shelter, not only from all injury, but from all terror, doubt, and division." This idealized vision of "home, sweet home" implied a domestic division of labor be-

tween a male breadwinner and a woman whose function as wife and mother was to maintain a secure and idyllic refuge. This reinforced patriarchal dominance in the bourgeois household just when it was being shattered in the working-class one.

The bourgeois wife and mother was expected to subordinate herself totally to her husband and to have no thought or interest beyond his welfare and comfort. Such subordination began in the bedroom. The Victorian woman was taught not merely to put her husband's pleasure before her own but to experience no pleasure at all. As one physician wrote, "A modest women seldom desires any sexual gratification for herself. She submits to her husband, but only to please him; and, but for the desire of maternity, would far rather be relieved of his attentions."

In every respect, then, working-class and bourgeois family experiences were sharply contrasted. In the bourgeois home the husband was the master and sole provider; in the working-class one the wife might well be the breadwinner. The bourgeois family exalted the child as the "product" for which the good home existed, while the children of the working class, sent to labor as early as possible, were typically treated as expendable units in the dredging of coal or the making of textiles.

Capital, Labor, and the Rights of Man

Writing in the 1830s, the French novelist Honoré de Balzac (1799–1850) remarked that the three orders of Old Regime society "have been replaced by what we nowadays call classes. We have lettered [professional] classes, industrial classes, upper classes, middle classes, etc." Balzac's "etc." would include the growing army of industrial laborers, which Marx would call the proletariat and others, more simply, the working class.

The novelty in a social division between classes instead of orders was that it no longer assumed a harmony but rather a conflict of interests between the various groupings, particularly between the two broad categories known as capital and labor. The traditional medieval distinction among those who worked, those who fought, and those who prayed—the peasantry, the aristocracy, and the clergy—was based on the idea that each order had a distinctive function that was essential to the good of the whole. But Adam Smith sounded the modern attitude of a liberal, capitalist society when he declared that the public interest was not something that could be determined in advance as a common goal but rather the result of each person pursuing his or her private interest in an arena of competitive equality. Taking this a step further, Smith's successors, notably David Ricardo (1772–1823), argued that capital and labor were governed by natural laws as fixed and immutable as the laws of physics. Those laws enshrined the clash of interests at the heart of society. Competition, not cooperation, was the law of social life.

The doctrine that the market was best served by being left to its own devices was called, in a phrase borrowed from the French, *laissez-faire* (roughly, "leave it alone"). It followed that the chief economic role of the state was to ensure that competition was free and unrestrained, thus enabling the market to maximize productive efficiency and hence general prosperity. The British government did indeed act, prohibiting workers from uniting for any purpose whatever in the Combination Acts (1799, 1800). However, it did nothing about industrial lobbies such as the General Chamber of Manufacturers, organized by Matthew Boulton and Josiah Wedgwood to promote the interests of capital. Nor did most advocates of laissez-faire seem to regard the thousands of enclosure acts passed by Parliament on behalf of private interests to be unwarranted state intervention.

Long before proletarians began to perceive their employers as class antagonists, the spokesmen of the new industrial order had portrayed the proletariat as enemies of progress. The only desire of the working class, according to writers such as William Temple, was to be as idle as possible. "Great wages and certainty of employment render the inhabitants of cities insolent and debauched," Temple declared. He concluded that "the only way to make [the poor] temperate and industrious is to lay them under a necessity of laboring all the time they can spare from meals and sleep, in order to procure the common necessities of life." Ironically, both Adam Smith and David Ricardo regarded labor as the source of all economic value, an idea that was to be crucial to the thought of Karl Marx. But Smith and Ricardo failed to relate the abstract value of labor to the actual toil of the laborer. In effect, labor was seen as something to be extracted from the recalcitrant body of the worker as coal was hacked out of the side of a hill.

At first, workers' resistance to the new industrial order was directed chiefly at the introduction of new machinery or the importation of foreign labor or products. The most sustained violence occurred between 1811 and 1817, a period marked not only by an intensive mechanization of textile production that threw tens of thousands of traditional weavers out of work but also by general economic depression. The rioters were called Luddites after a legendary figure, Ned Ludd, who may have destroyed stocking frames in Yorkshire in the 1780s. *Luddism* has gone into the dictionary as a synonym for mindless opposition to change. In fact, the Luddites were chiefly artisans and skilled workers who put forward a platform of political grievances and demands, including the right to organize.

As the catastrophic efforts of industrialization on the working class became apparent, however, widespread demand arose for government regulation of the conditions of child and female labor. "A feeling very generally exists," the conservative Thomas Carlyle remarked, "that the condition and disposition of the Working Classes is a rather ominous matter at present; that something ought to be said, something ought to be done, in regard to it." The result was a series of Factory Acts, of which the most significant included the Factory Act of 1833 and the Mines and Collieries Act of 1842, which prohibited the employment of children under the age of 9 in textile mills and children under 10 and women underground in mines, and the Factory Act of 1847, which established a ten-hour day for women and children. Slowly, the pulverizing conditions of industrial labor were relaxed, and its devastating impact on the working-class family was mitigated.

ROBERT OWEN, INDUSTRIAL REFORMER

The most sustained opposition to laissez-faire economics came from Robert Owen (1771–1858), industrialist, philanthropist, and founder of British socialism. Owen rejected the claim of laissez-faire economics to scientific status. Far from being an objective conformity to the immutable laws of economics, he contended, it was only one means among many for ordering society, in fact a "low" and "inferior" one that created not wealth and harmony but misery and conflict.

Owen was born in a small Welsh town, the son of a saddler and ironmonger and a local farmer's daughter. At the age of 15 he migrated to Manchester. Here he shared rooms at one point with Robert Fulton, the inventor of the steamboat, whom he lent £100 out of his first savings. Shy and diffident, Owen was nonetheless manager of a cotton mill employing 500 people by the age of 19. In 1794 he became a partner in the Chorlton Twist Company, one of Manchester's principal textile firms, and five years later he persuaded his fellow partners to purchase the New Lanark spinning mills near Glasgow from the industrialist David Dale.

Thus far Owen's career resembled that of many other self-made industrialists of the era. But he was already a member of the Manchester Board of Health and keenly interested in reform. Determined to make New Lanark a model for industrial development, he rebuilt the workers' houses, cleaned and paved their streets, provided cheap coal for heating, and opened a company store that sold goods at cost.

As Owen's views grew more radical, his business partners became restive. In 1813 he bought them out and formed a new company whose partners, including the philosopher Jeremy Bentham, agreed to limit themselves to a 5 percent return. This enabled Owen to carry out the educational theories he had gradually developed, which he first spelled out in *A New View of Society* (1813). Owen argued that people were wholly the products of their environment and education. He built a large educational complex at New Lanark, characteristically named the Institute for the Formation of Character, the heart of which was the first nursery school in Great Britain. His school, which anticipated much of progressive education, was run on the principle of play; no child was forced to do anything against his or her wishes, and no

punishment was imposed. New Lanark became a mecca for reformers of every stripe and a major tourist attraction as well: between 1816 and 1826, nearly 20,000 visitors streamed through its gates.

Owen himself had meanwhile turned his interests to reform on a national level. His agitation was largely responsible for the passage of the early (though ineffective) Factory Act of 1819. By now he had become convinced of the radical injustice of contemporary society. Always a religious skeptic, he openly denounced the clergy from 1817, thus parting company with mainstream reformers who sought to mitigate the evils of the Industrial Revolution by an appeal to Christian ethics. Owen shocked a meeting of his fellow magnates by declaring that it would be better for the cotton industry to perish altogether than to be carried on under conditions that destroyed the health of its workers.

Between 1817 and 1820, Owen put forward a sweeping plan to reorganize society on the basis of small, cooperative communities. Each community would contain 500 to 2,000 members and would be both agriculturally and industrially self-sufficient. The major buildings, suitably spaced and landscaped, would be contained in a large rectangle, giving everyone access to light and air. Production for profit was prohibited; goods

A view of the New Lanark mills and village in Scotland in 1818, about the time of Robert Owen's social experiments. Including a school and a community center, the community attracted many important visitors from overseas. [Reproduced by kind permission of New Lanark Conservation Trust]

were to be distributed on the basis of labor performed, an anticipation of Marx's formula, "From each according to his abilities, to each according to his needs." Each community was to be completely self-governing. Owen envisioned such communities as establishing regional and national federations and, ultimately, a worldwide one. It was, he feverently believed, the social, economic, and political form of the future.

Owen traveled widely over the next several years in Ireland and on the Continent to promote his plan, and in 1825 he set up the model community of New Harmony on a 20,000-acre site in Indiana. Despite initial enthusiasm, it collapsed after three years, having cost Owen the bulk of his fortune. He returned to England in 1829 to find that he had become a hero to the nascent British labor movement, which, after the repeal of the Combination Acts in 1824, had adopted his call for worker self-governance. In October 1833 he launched what was to become the Grand National Consolidated Trades Union, the first nationwide confederation of labor in history. Local unions and associations rushed to join, and the Grand Union claimed no fewer than 500,000 members by the spring of 1834.

Thoroughly alarmed, employers initiated lockouts of workers who joined the Union, and the government cracked down as well. What doomed the Grand Union, however, was the very speed at which it had grown, outstripping both its organizational resources and its agreed-on goals. Owen himself was disillusioned as the Union, far from evolving peacefully toward communal living, appeared to be bent on a bloody confrontation with capital. By late 1834 it had ceased to exist in all but name, and embittered labor militants turned their backs on socialism in Britain for the next 50 years.

Owen contributed to promote his ideal communities, seven more of which were founded in Britain between 1825 and 1847. An exchange founded by the flannel weavers of Rochdale in 1844 became the basis of the modern cooperative movement, which still flourishes in the midwestern United States. Owen himself continued to see America as the best hope for the realization of his principles. All four of his sons became U.S. citizens; the eldest, Robert Dale Owen, served in Congress and had a distinguished career as an advocate of educational reform and women's rights. Active to the end, Owen addressed public meetings into his eighty-eighth year. Carried home to die in his native town, he spent the last day of his life planning the reform of education in the parish.

THE POPULATION EXPLOSION

An observer visiting our planet about 250 years ago and returning today would probably be struck by two things: first, by how many more human beings are inhabiting it, and second, by how densely concentrated they are in specific areas. The first of these phenomena goes popularly by the name of *the population explosion;* the second is called *urbanization*. Both of them are related to the Industrial Revolution, though they are by no means simply its result.

The human population of the earth was probably well under 10 million at the time of the Neolithic revolution 10,000 years ago. Agriculture and animal husbandry made historical civilization possible, and civilization was characterized by city-dwelling. Thus a continuous rise in population and a propensity to urbanization have been characteristic of civilization from the beginning. What has been unprecedented is the surge and concentration of population since about the mid-eighteenth century. In 1750 the world population was under 800 million. It reached 1 billion by about 1830, 2 billion in 1930, 3 billion in 1960, 4 billion in 1975, and 5 billion in 1986. At the same time the number of persons engaged in agriculture has been steadily diminishing. In most places, at least 80 percent of the population was engaged in agriculture in 1750; in most industrialized nations today, the figure is less than 5 percent.

These numbers suggest some obvious conclusions. The population explosion began before the advent of the Industrial Revolution, and it was well underway as a worldwide phenomenon long before the effects of industrialization reached beyond Europe. However, its continued rate of increase has unquestionably been sustained by the Industrial Revolution, including the continuous transformation in the productive capacity of agriculture known today as the "green revolution." Despite the fears of many demographers, overall food supply has kept pace with population growth; indeed, most of the industrially developed nations suffer at present from excess productive capacity. It remains true that world nutritional levels are declining as a whole and that serious famines have broken out in parts of Africa, but this is the result of local climatic patterns, unequal economic development and wealth, and political breakdown rather than of inadequate world productive capacity as a whole.

There is much debate about the causes of the population explosion, but it appears to have been triggered in Europe by a rise in fertility coupled with a striking long-term decrease in rates of mortality. The difference may be summarized by a single statistical comparison. In 1700, only 475 of every 1,000 persons born live would reach the age of 20; by the mid-twentieth century, 960 would do so. The sharp decline in the death rate was essentially the result of a reduction in mortality from infectious diseases and (after the introduction of modern contraceptive devices) infanticide. At the same time, increases in agricultural capacity enabled more developed nations to sustain population growth. Emigration and the settling of new lands also relieved population pressure; some 60 million Europeans left the Continent between 1846 and 1924, mostly for the Western Hemisphere, the Siberian hinterland of Russia, and Australasia. Not all of this resulted in net population gain. White settlers in Australia completely exterminated the native population of the large island of Tasmania, while warfare, deprivation, and disease had destroyed four-fifths of the Maori population of New Zealand and three-fourths of the Amerindian population of the United States by the 1870s.

The first great surge in population was to a large extent a European phenomenon. In the absence of reliable data (only Sweden kept mortality statistics before 1800) we can only speculate that a cyclic remission in the incidence of microbial diseases combined with the increase in agricultural productivity in northern Europe generated sufficient thrust to trigger growth. Given the enormously high level of mortality, even a marginal increase in the survival rate could have had a significant impact on population.

Not until after 1850 was control of infectious diseases made possible by the introduction of hygiene and sanitation, particularly in the purification of water supplies and the disposal of waste. These two measures did more to reduce mortality rates than any others, including the development of vaccines and so-called wonder drugs (the sulfa family in 1935 and antibiotics, most notably penicillin, in the 1940s). The concern for sanitation was at first provoked by the appallingly high mortality rates among workers in early industrial towns and soldiers at war, but it was extended systematically only after the scientific connection between dirt and disease had been established by the research of Louis Pasteur in France, Joseph Lister in Scotland, and Robert Koch in Germany in the 1860s and 1870s. The results were dramatic. Typhoid deaths fell by more than 85 percent in England over a 35-year period, and malaria by nearly as much in

Italy over 20 years. It was not the ability to cure infectious disease but the simple reduction of exposure to it that accounted for this progress.

The population of Europe (including Russia) roughly quadrupled between 1650 and 1900, from about 100 to some 430 million, exclusive of emigration. From less than a fifth of the world's population in the mid-seventeenth century, Caucasians had become a quarter of it by the dawn of the twentieth century. This was the high-water mark of European demographic advance. The introduction of Western standards of sanitation to other areas of the globe—essential to preserve the health of European colonizers in the heyday of imperialism—ignited a similar population explosion in Asia and Africa. By the 1980s, non-Western peoples again accounted for approximately four-fifths of the world's population.

Perhaps the most significant and far-reaching effect of the Industrial Revolution was the urbanization of Western society. The city had occupied a distinctive place in the West since the Middle Ages. With its walls and towers it stood off boldly from the surrounding countryside. No less important were the charters and privileges that gave it a unique degree of self-government and political importance. The late medieval city-states of Italy and the free imperial cities of Germany were the finest flowering of this proudly independent civic culture, and neither the Renaissance nor the Reformation would have been conceivable without them.

The great eighteenth-century cities of London, Paris, and Amsterdam, with their worldwide commercial and financial connections, were prototypes of a new kind of city, the global metropolis. But such cities were still exceptional. Although urbanization had reached 50 percent or more in some highly commercialized regions of the Low Countries, in Britain still less than a third, and in France less than a quarter of the population lived in towns.

The Industrial Revolution changed all that. Factory towns sprang up overnight near the coalfields and iron mines of Britain's industrial heartland. The pulse of manufacture turned regional marketing centers into points on a nationwide distribution grid and old coastal towns into international seaports. These in turn were now linked by a new mode of transportation ideally designed for hauling large quantities of goods, the steam locomotive.

It was to the city that the rapidly growing British population now came—to London above all; from under a million inhabitants in 1800 it swelled to 2.5 million by

Raw industrial waste was dumped directly into Manchester's river, the Irwell, whose still and blackened waters are captured in James Mudd's 1854 photograph. [Manchester Public Libraries]

midcentury and 4.5 million by the early 1900s. Half again as many people lived in its suburbs. No city of its size had ever been seen before in the world. No other British city approached it, but many others achieved rates of growth that were proportionally no less impressive. By 1851, half the population lived in urban areas, and that number would grow to three-quarters by 1900. The percentage of farm laborers declined correspondingly. As the British commentator Robert Vaughan wrote as early as 1843, "If any nation is to be lost or saved by the character of its great cities, our own is that nation."[2]

MANCHESTER: FACTORY TOWN

If any city might have served as a test case for Vaughan's assertion, it was industrial Manchester. Situated in Lancashire, west of the Pennine Mountains and connected to the port of Liverpool by the river Mersey, Manchester had long been a modestly prosperous regional marketing center whose population on the eve of the Industrial Revolution was about 17,000. The cotton industry transformed it in the 1770s and 1780s, and the grim, grime-blackened factories with their surrounding slums, which seemed to mushroom overnight, made it the prototype of the new industrial city. By the 1780s its population had grown to 40,000, by 1801 to 70,000, and by 1831 to 142,000: an eightfold increase in 80 years. Visitors commented on the new appearance of what had once been described as the "fairest" town in the region. A Prussian visitor in 1814 noted the pall that hung over Manchester: "The cloud of coal vapor may be observed from afar. The houses are blackened by it. The river . . . is so filled with waste dye-stuffs that it resembles a dyer's vat." Another visitor proclaimed it "abominably filthy" and its polluted river "as black as ink." The Frenchman Alexis de Tocqueville summed up contemporary opinion in 1835 when he wrote of Manchester, "Civilization works its miracles, and civilized man is turned back almost into a savage."

The result was protest, and the response, repression. In 1817 a band of local destitute weavers set out for London to agitate for higher wages, only to be turned back by force. Two years later, in August 1819, troops fired point-blank into a mass rally at St. Peter's Field in the city, killing 11 persons and wounding some 400, including 113 women and children. It was the first battle of modern labor history, and the "Peterloo Massacre," as it was called in mocking comparison to the Battle of Waterloo, symbolized the threat of class war.

In the 1830s and 1840s, Manchester often seemed on the verge of anarchy. Popular unrest exploded again with the economic slumps of 1829 and 1836. These were compounded by devastating outbreaks of typhoid and cholera, which were added to the normal toll of respiratory and intestinal diseases taken by air and water pollution and by the lack of sanitation. Moreover, despite its phenomenal growth, Manchester was still being governed as if it were a village. There was no regular police force, no provision for social services, and no attempt to regulate growth. Not until 1853, when the population, now in excess of 300,000, had begun to sprawl over into suburbs as chaotic as the center itself, was Manchester formally incorporated as a city.

As the historian Asa Briggs explained:

All roads led to Manchester in the 1840s. It was the shock city of the age, and it was just as difficult to be neutral about it as it was to be neutral about Chicago in the 1890s or Los Angeles in the 1930s.[3]

Reformers focused on it, and novelists such as Elizabeth Gaskell in *Mary Barton* and Charles Dickens in *Hard Times* depicted it, as Gaskell said, to "give utterance to the agony" of the poor. Manchester's mill owners, protesting the unflattering portraits of themselves in such social novels, complained that their services to the nation in creating new wealth and new opportunity were unfairly disparaged. But whichever side one took in the great class debate, all agreed that Manchester was the crucible of an unprecedented phenomenon, as prodigal of energy and power as it was of misery and despair: the industrial city.

Ironically, Manchester itself had already passed the peak of its industrial importance. Its factories were obsolescent in comparison to newer models elsewhere, and its prosperity rested increasingly on its importance as a trading center. The Manchester Exchange, first opened to the public in 1809 and greatly expanded in 1838, was the largest brokerage facility in Europe. With economic maturity came at least the beginnings of civic responsibility. A local sanitary code, one of the first in the country, was drafted in 1845. The next year, Manchester got its first public parks and a bequest to found what became the greatest of the early civic universities. In 1857 it held an exposition that drew more than 1.3 million visitors and led to the founding of an orchestra. By late Victorian times the city that had been described as "the entrance to hell" by the commander sent to quell its disturbances in 1839 had become respectable and almost staid.

THE SPREAD OF THE INDUSTRIAL REVOLUTION

The rest of Europe was not economically idle while Britain was undergoing its great revolution. Population and production, both agricultural and industrial, were rising on the Continent between 1780 and 1830, and cities were growing as well. In France, new methods of iron and steel production were developed, and Joseph-Marie Jacquard invented a silk loom. In Germany the world's first sugar beet refinery began operation. Swiss and Dutch banking were highly developed, and the eighteenth century saw major improvements in roads, bridges, and harbors and extensive canal-building projects in northern France and Prussia. An observer looking for the likeliest place for the Industrial Revolution to begin would probably have suggested the Netherlands in 1700 or France in 1750.

Exploitation and Resistance

Nonetheless, it was in Britain that the spark caught fire. In France a largely parasitic aristocracy drained off capital investment, a top-heavy governmental bureaucracy often crushed the initiative it was trying to promote, and the absence of a central banking system hampered the flow of credit. Germany suffered from its division into hundreds of tiny principalities and the chaos of internal customs barriers and road and river tolls that this engendered. The Dutch republic, the great commercial success of the seventeenth century, had exhausted itself in struggles with Louis XIV. In eastern Europe, including Prussia, Austria, and Russia, the persistence of serfdom hamstrung the movement of labor so critical to industrial development.

Thus it was not until about 1830 that industrialization per se—the use of power-driven machinery and the organization of labor and production in factories—came to the Continent. It appeared first along a belt that included the Low Countries, northeastern France and western Germany, and northern Italy, where the concentration of a skilled and urbanized work force, plentiful deposits of coal and iron, good road and river communications, and access to seaports were most favorable. Its spread, however, was notably uneven. It advanced most rapidly in Belgium, which profited not only from its commercial connections with the Netherlands but also from its rich deposits of coal, which the Dutch lacked.

France, despite its partial development, remained primarily a nation of small farmers throughout the nineteenth century; in 1881 its population was still two-thirds rural. French capital, long sheltered behind government subsidies and high tariffs, was far more timid and less entrepreneurial than its British counterpart, and large-scale financing was still a novelty. French industry, which specialized in luxury items—silks, carpets, tapestries, porcelain, fashions, vintage wines, and brandies—was craft-oriented and not easily adaptable to mass production. A British visitor at a French industrial exhibit in 1802 remarked that there was not a single item of ordinary consumption on display.

As in Britain, industrial expansion in France was at first largely confined to textile manufacture; cotton production doubled between 1830 and 1846. A railway-

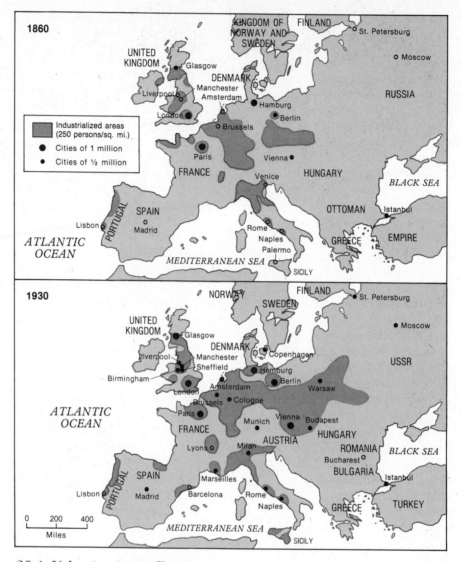

20.1 Urbanization in Europe.

building boom in the 1840s brought increased demand for iron and steel as well. In the two decades after 1848 the French economy entered the industrial era, although many small-scale enterprises continued to flourish. The value of industrial production doubled, foreign trade trebled, internal commerce quadrupled, and railway mileage and total industrial horsepower quintupled.

As in Britain, industrialization was accompanied by ruthless exploitation of the work force, including women and children. Conditions in France had never been idyllic; in 1776 the bookbinders of Paris had struck to *win* a 14-hour day. But the regime of the factory intensi-fied the worst abuses of the preindustrial workshop. An observer in the department of Nord described working conditions in 1826:

> The greed of the manufacturers knows no limits; they sacrifice their workers to enrich themselves. They are not content with reducing these poor creatures to slavery by making them work in unhealthy workshops from which fresh air is excluded, from 5 A.M. to 8 P.M. (and sometimes 10 P.M.) in the summer, and from 6 A.M. to 9 P.M. in the winter; they force them to work a part of Sunday as well. From bed to work and from work to bed—that sums up the life of their victims. . . . They never have a moment for their private affairs; they always breathe a polluted atmosphere; for them the sun never shines.[4]

France, too, had its outbreaks of machine breaking, and the industrial riots in Lyons in 1831 and 1834 paralleled those in Manchester. In Charles Fourier (1772–1837) it had its own utopian reformer as well. Fourier proposed a network of small, self-contained communities called phalansteries that were similar to Owen's experiments at New Lanark and New Harmony; like Owen's, attempts to found such communities were short-lived. More modest goals of reform lagged behind the British example. Despite official concern about the high rate of physical rejection among French army conscripts, the only industrial legislation passed in the first half of the nineteenth century was the Factory Law of 1841, which prohibited the employment of children under the age of 8 in factories.

The German Giant

The Napoleonic wars had been a watershed in German economic development. They had caused serious dislocation, but German industry, sheltering behind Napoleon's trade barriers, had benefited from a respite from competition with British products. The wars had also radically simplified Germany's political geography, reducing its hundreds of principalities to 39 states, of which an enlarged Prussia, now in control of the coalfields of the Ruhr and the Saar, the main river systems of the north, and the prosperous cities of the Rhineland and Westphalia, was the most important. The most critical single item on the economic agenda was the removal of internal tolls and tariff barriers. Under Prussian leadership a free trade zone, the *Zollverein* ("customs union"), had been established by 1834, embracing some 34 million people. This formed the basis for a sustained industrial expansion whose rate of growth was unsurpassed on the Continent.

Textiles and metallurgy flourished, and new mining techniques opened up the coal deposits of the Ruhr. Railways were introduced in 1835, eight years after the French had built their first line; by 1850 there were twice as many miles of track in Germany as in France. Major capital construction was financed by joint-stock ventures underwritten in part by government funds. By virtually every measure—population, production, urbanization—Germany was the most economically powerful nation on the Continent by 1850, and within a generation it would be challenging the lead of Britain itself.

Industrial Development After 1850

The wealth and productivity of the West increased exponentially after 1850. In part this increase was stimulated by the same factor that had stimulated the economic boom of the sixteenth century: the discovery of gold in the New World. The California gold strike of 1848 (and the sizable deposits later found in Australia) added as much gold to the world's stocks in the next 20 years as in the preceding 350. Another source of capital, particularly for Britain and, to a lesser extent, France, was the profits of trade and empire. The traffic of European commerce had constituted 75 percent of the world's trade by 1800. The volume of that trade now skyrocketed, increasing at least 1,200 percent between the 1840s and 1914.

Much of this trade was with the United States, which, already a major economic force by 1860, had become the world's leading industrial power by 1900. Numerous factors created an ideal climate for expansion: vast deposits of iron, coal, and petroleum, which, with a plenitude of gold and silver, provided an unsurpassed source of both raw materials and specie; a domestic labor and consumer market continually fed by immigration; and a political system firmly controlled by northern banking and industrial interests after the civil war. By 1890, U.S. iron and steel production had surpassed that of Britain; by 1900 the United States was making more steel than Britain and Germany combined; by 1910 its rail network was carrying a billion tons of freight per year.

The Harnessing of Science

At the same time, technological developments greatly extended the scope of the Industrial Revolution. A new age of steel resulted from the refining processes that permitted both much higher temperatures in blast furnaces and the use of lower grades of ore. In the last three decades of the nineteenth century, world steel production increased fiftyfold, as steel, both lighter and more tensile than iron, began to replace it everywhere in rail, ship, and building construction.

For the first time as well, applied science and engineering began to feed directly and systematically into technological development, creating new products, processes, and sources of energy. The age of the amateur inventor was rapidly drawing to a close; the American Thomas Alva Edison (1847–1931) was the last of the type. Large firms began to employ their own scientists

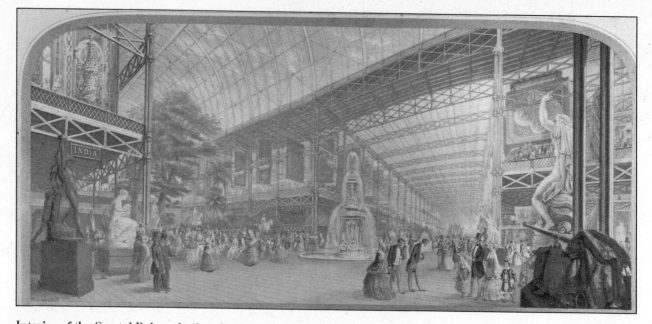

Interior of the Crystal Palace, built to house the world's first international industrial exhibition in London in 1851. Constructed of iron and glass, the palace was a triumph of advanced technology, symbolizing Britain's leadership in the first phase of the Industrial Revolution.

and engineers, working directly on product development and production improvement. At the same time the lag time between basic scientific discovery and its technological application was sharply diminished.

Electricity was as crucial to the nineteenth century as steam had been to the eighteenth. Following the conversion of mechanical motion into electric current by Michael Faraday in 1831, the American Samuel F. B. Morse produced the first practical telegraph in the 1840s. The telegraph was the beginning of a revolution in communications that paralleled that of the steam locomotive in transportation. The telephone followed in 1879, and in 1896 the Italian Guglielmo Marconi adapted radio waves, which had been discovered by Heinrich Hertz a decade before, to a new mass communications device.

The development of electromagnets, the electrolytic process, and the modern dynamo paved the way for the use of electricity in public places such as railways, docks, theaters, and markets, as well as in some factories. The incandescent light bulb, invented independently by Edison in America and Sir Joseph Swan in Britain, brought electrical illumination into the home and the office in the 1880s. In the same decade the steam turbine began to replace the old reciprocal-action engine. It was soon adapted to coal and then to petroleum, the

fuel source that would power the twentieth century. The combustion engine followed in 1886, the airplane in 1903. By the early 1900s, European and American cities were lit electrically by huge generating systems, and their streets were crowded with trams and, increasingly, automobiles. At the same time, organic chemistry (the chemistry of carbon compounds), developed especially in Germany, produced a whole range of synthetic dyes, textiles, paints, and other products. No longer were humans confined to working, blending, crushing, and refining the given raw materials of nature; by manipulating the basic organic components of these materials, new, artificial products could be created.

Despite overall growth, industrial development remained unevenly distributed geographically, and industrial wealth was even more unequally shared socially. Moreover, the disparity between worker and owner in Europe and the United States was greater still between colonizer and colonized as capital penetration and imperial expansion brought the mines, factories, technical processes, and industrial discipline of the West to the far corners of the globe. As this process intensified during the last decades of the nineteenth century, social and political dislocation, and in some cases devastation, occurred on a scale that dwarfed the changes that had taken place in Britain and on the Continent. Only a few places outside Europe achieved industrialization on their own before 1900, most notably the United States and Japan. As the twentieth century dawned, European economic and political hegemony in the world was at its zenith.

Notes

1. A. Ure, *Philosophy of Manufactures* (New York: Kelley, 1967), p. 13. Originally printed in 1861.
2. A. Briggs, *Victorian Cities* (London: Odhams Books, 1965), p. 55.
3. Ibid., pp. 92–93.
4. W. O. Henderson, *The Industrial Revolution in Europe, 1815–1914* (Chicago: Quadrangle Books, 1961), p. 107.

SUMMARY

The Industrial Revolution and the population explosion that accompanied it began in the middle of the eighteenth century, and both continue unabated the processes of change and upheaval that have transformed the globe. Population pressure spurred agricultural and industrial development, at first in Britain and then elsewhere, and success in sustaining an ever-expanding population generated the market and product demand that fed technological growth. When in 1851 Britain celebrated its role as the "workshop of the world" with a great international industrial exhibition at the Crystal Palace in London, the most important technological advance in humanity's recorded history was already an accomplished fact. At the same time, the nature of work and of the social organization that revolved around it was no less radically transformed. The family circle, the primary preindustrial work unit the world over, began to give way to an impersonal industrial discipline that reshaped and often shattered traditional relationships and modes of living at the most basic level. Inexorably, these changes radiated outward from their European origins to embrace the entire world and to create not merely a new global economy but a new global culture as well.

Suggestions for Further Reading

Ashton, T. S. *The Industrial Revolution, 1760–1830.* London: Oxford University Press, 1961.

Braudel, F. *Civilization and Capitalism.* London: Collins, 1979–1985.

Briggs, A. *Victorian Cities.* London: Odhams Books, 1965.

Chambers, J. D., and Mingay, G. E. *The Agricultural Revolution, 1750–1850.* New York: Schocken Books, 1966.

Cipolla, C. M., ed. *The Industrial Revolution, 1700–1914.* London: Penguin Books, 1973.

Cole, M. *Robert Owen of New Lanark.* New York: Oxford University Press, 1953.

Crafts, N. F. R. *British Economic Growth During the Industrial Revolution.* New York: Oxford University Press, 1986.

Dennis, R. *English Industrial Cities of the Nineteenth Century.* Cambridge: Cambridge University Press, 1984.

Henderson, W. O. *The Industrial Revolution in Europe, 1815–1914.* Chicago: Quadrangle Books, 1961.

Hobsbawm, E. J. *Industry and Empire.* London: Penguin Books, 1970.

Landes, D. *The Unbound Prometheus: Technological Change and Industrial Development in Western Europe from the Seventeenth Century to the Present.* London: Cambridge University Press, 1969.

Perkin, H. *The Origin of Modern English Society, 1780–1860.* London: Routledge & Kegan Paul, 1969.

Thompson, E. P. *The Making of the English Working Class.* Harmondsworth, England: Penguin Books, 1964.

Tilly, L. A. and Scott, J. W. *Women, Work and Family.* New York: Routledge, 1987.

Wrigley, E. A., and Schofield, R. S. *The Population History of England, 1541–1871: A Reconstruction.* New York: Cambridge University Press, 1989.

THE AGE OF IDEOLOGY

In the wake of the French Revolution and the Napoleonic conquests, Europe experienced some of its most turbulent and troubled decades. The statesmen of the victorious allies, meeting at Vienna, sought to restore the Old Regime and to find an antidote to revolution. Their attempts foundered on the continuing demands for representative government, free competition, and social justice, often expressed through a fervent desire for national independence or unity. This was in turn linked to the wider cultural movement of Romanticism, which, in its emphasis on the free expressive powers of the individual, questioned traditional values and authority. By 1830 the fragile détente between the old noble elites and the increasingly powerful bourgeoisie had broken down, and a new wave of revolutionary disturbances swept Europe. This was the precursor of the far more widespread and violent revolutions of 1848, in which discontented artisans and workers, fired by the doctrines of socialism, played a leading role for the first time. These revolutions ended largely in apparent failure, but they confirmed the ascendancy of the bourgeoisie as the principal barrier to radical demands for a new social order.

THE LEGACY OF REVOLUTION

The American Revolution, in declaring that all men were created equal and endowed with liberty, and the French Revolution, in asserting liberty, equality, and fraternity to be the goals of a just society, had propounded new political values to the Western world. Freedom or liberty, as the Old Regime understood these terms, meant not general rights applicable to all but franchises or exemptions enjoyed by particular individuals or corporate groups. The foundation of Old Regime society was not equality but hierarchy and subordination; its members were not citizens but subjects.

Even more foreign to the old order was the new revolutionary ideal of fraternity, the solidarity of all citizens with one another. In America these principles had inspired the first nation ever created on the basis of citizen equality, though it still excluded women and blacks. The founding of the United States had in turn been a powerful inspiration to the French revolutionaries of 1789. But whereas the United States was an ocean away, the armies of the French republic, crossing the Alps and the Rhine, had brought their revolution by force to much of Europe.

The champions of the old order had fought and finally defeated the armies of France. Despite this and despite the retreat from representative government and social egalitarianism under the Directory and Napoleon, these ideals remained alive. No longer could the rulers of Europe rely on obedience to authority based on the unquestioned subordination of subject populations to their natural masters, and political agitation everywhere now took the form of demands for basic rights and representation. Of no less importance were the values of freedom and equality in dissolving custom and privilege, the traditional barriers to state centralization. Liberties extended to all and tyranny exerted over all lay uncomfortably close together, as the regime of Robespierre had shown.

The demand for liberty and equality was often linked to another pervasive political sentiment that gained impetus from the French Revolution and the Napoleonic conquests: nationalism. In its simplest terms, nationalism was a sense of cultural and political identity among a given people. Cultural identity was manifested in shared traditions and the possession of a common language; political identity was expressed in the association with a particular region or territory. The ultimate expression of a people's identity was the possession of a state.

Nationalism was expressed with particular vigor in Germany by the philosopher Herder, who argued in the 1770s and 1780s that each people had its own organic development and must pursue its own individual destiny. He urged his compatriots to look to their own heritage for meaning and direction rather than to an imported French model that could be valid only for the French, not the Germans.

Herder's work stimulated a cultural nationalism that was displayed in patriotic literature; research into German philology, folklore, and legend; and attempts to define the "German soul." The Napoleonic conquests spurred nationalism on a political level as well. Johann Gottlieb Fichte called on the people of Prussia to regenerate the lost honor of their fatherland, while his fellow Prussian, the philosopher Georg Wilhelm Friedrich Hegel, claimed that the historical dichotomy between the individual and the community was overcome in the unity of the modern nation-state. The highest manifestation of this unity was not, as Fichte expressed it, in the securing of particular benefits such as life, liberty, and personal well-being, but in a noble patriotism and love of country.

This almost mystical sense of the subordination of the individual to the nation suggests that nationalism was not an essentially liberal cause, even though liberals often expressed their aspirations through it and used it as a vehicle of rebellion against the established order. In Russia, nationalism would be invoked in the 1840s both by liberal Westernizers who wished to see Russia adopt western European values and institutions and by conservative Slavophils who believed that Russia could fulfill its destiny only by remaining true to its traditions. In short, nationalism appealed across the entire political spectrum from economic rationalists, who saw the nation-state as an efficient market mechanism, to messianic enthusiasts who saw it as the vehicle of progress and even of salvation.

These conflicting ideologies and aspirations set the background for the victorious allied powers as they set about to restore, as far as they could, the world they had known. Their attempts to do so, against not only the countervailing forces unleashed by the French and American revolutions but the as yet unreckoned ones of the Industrial Revolution, determined the course of European politics to the middle of the nineteenth century and beyond.

THE CONGRESS OF VIENNA

The major European powers met in Vienna in September 1814 to try to untangle 20 years of war and revolution. Every state on the Continent sent representatives, including defunct members of the old Holy Roman Empire seeking reinstatement. But only five parties really counted—Austria, Britain, Prussia, Russia, and France, represented, respectively, by Prince Metternich, Viscount Castlereagh, Baron Hardenberg, Tsar Alexander I (the only sovereign taking direct part in the proceedings), and Baron Talleyrand, who after serving Napoleon had brokered the return of the Bourbon dynasty to France.

Collective Security

What the allies wanted at Vienna, broadly speaking, was to restore the old order of kingship and aristocracy, to prevent the domination of Europe by any single state, and to contain the virus of revolution wherever it might spread. To accomplish this, they created a structure of collective security that was essentially a classical balance-of-power system tinctured by the agreement to suppress all forms of radical activity. This meant that collective security would be brought to bear not only against states that threatened the stability of the system by external action but also against those whose internal stability was threatened by domestic discontent.

The framework for this system was already in place in the wartime coalition that had defeated Napoleon. Formalized as the Quadruple Alliance in 1815 and extended, after a suitable period of probation, to include France in 1818, it formed the basis of the so-called Concert of Europe, which kept the peace of the Continent, or at any rate took the credit for doing so, down to 1914. The novelty of the system was the recognition that war, because it had the potential to unleash revolution, could no longer be afforded. Alexander I conceived it as a spiritual compact and managed to bully most of his fellow sovereigns into signing a "Holy Alliance" against war and for Christian concord. On a more mundane level, Prince Metternich saw the Concert as a sanction to intervene in the affairs of any state threatened by revolution.

The Diplomatic Settlement

The differences among the allies at Vienna came into the open over the Polish-Saxon question, which nearly torpedoed the congress. Napoleon had taken away almost all the territory gained by Austria and Prussia in the partitioning of Poland to create a satellite entity, the Grand Duchy of Warsaw. Its collapse with the defeat of his empire again left a power vacuum in eastern Europe. Alexander I insisted on restoring the original prepartition Poland, with himself as king. To win Prussia's support, he offered to cede it Saxony. Metternich, appalled, sought out Castlereagh and Talleyrand, who agreed to resist the Russian plan, by force if necessary.

The Polish-Saxon question was finally settled by compromise. Alexander received a reduced "congress" Poland that was roughly equivalent to Napoleon's Grand Duchy, and Prussia was compensated with two-fifths of Saxony. But the whole episode pointed up the inherent contradiction of the congress system, which presupposed lasting cooperation between historical rivals whose interests were fundamentally opposed.

The Congress of Vienna did, however, decide a wide range of issues, which set the diplomatic framework of the nineteenth century. Uppermost in the minds of the allies was the creation of buffer zones, primarily against France but more subtly against Russia as well, whose steady westward encroachment had become a major concern over the preceding 100 years. A new Belgo-Dutch kingdom of the Netherlands was erected as a barrier on France's northern frontier, and Prussia was given a bloc of territory along the Rhine to perform a similar function. With the acquisition of the Rhineland, Prussia now overarched all of northern Germany, facing France to the west and Russia to the east. Austria was reinstalled in northern Italy and expanded along the Dalmatian coast, where, from a southern vantage, it could serve as a check against Russian designs on Turkey and French ones on Italy. The British, following traditional policy, sought no territory on the Continent but added several key islands and stations in the West Indies and the Far East to their unrivaled sea empire.

The thorniest single issue facing the powers was the settlement of Germany. Beset by the rival demands of nationalists who dreamed of a unified German state and the claimants of liquidated states who wanted a return to the Holy Roman Empire, the congress chose to preserve the states carved from the empire by Napoleon, loosely linked in a federation whose main function was to keep the smaller states from gravitating toward France. It was a pragmatic solution that postponed for 50 years the final confrontation between Prussia and Austria for control of Germany.

The dramatic return of Napoleon from Elba and the ensuing Hundred Days compelled the allies to impose harsher sanctions against France, which had been treated leniently at first. The Congress took away some snippets of French territory, imposed an indemnity of 700 million francs, and posted an army of occupation in France for three years. Nevertheless, France's treatment was extremely mild. Events bore out the wisdom of the allies' moderation; the age of French aggression and French preponderance in Europe was over.

By their lights, the diplomats at Vienna accomplished a good deal. They cleared away the debris of a generation of war and converted a wartime coalition into a permanent instrument for maintaining order. The instrument was flawed, and the values it sought to defend—monarchy, aristocracy, and hereditary privilege—were already in eclipse, but the goal of regulating interstate conflict was a first step toward the recognition of the historical obsolescence of war.

What the men at Vienna were unwilling to recognize was the change of their own time. Formed under the Old Regime, their conception of society was still patriarchal; in the words of the Holy Alliance, the sovereigns of Europe were "as fathers of families towards their subjects and armies." In redrawing the map of the Continent they acted in the high-handed manner of old, parceling out peoples and territories solely according to the abstract scales of power. It would never have occurred to them to ask the Belgians whether they wanted to be under the Dutch, the Venetians under the Austrians, or the Poles under Russia. They rightly calculated that nationalism, the new sentiment that a land belonged to its people and not to its ruler, was incompatible with the preservation of the existing order; they wrongly concluded that they could contain it with treaties, armies, and spies.

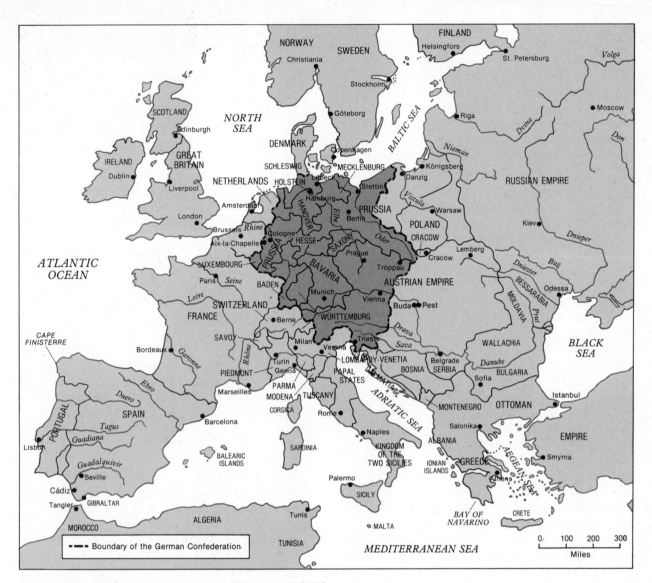

21.1 Europe After the Congress of Vienna (1815)

REACTION AND REVOLUTION

The notion of collective security against revolution—what came to be known as the Congress System—was the brainchild of Prince Klemens von Metternich (1773–1859), who as foreign minister of Austria from 1809 to 1848 put his stamp on the diplomacy of the age. Metternich envisioned the system operating through periodic meetings of the great powers that by monitoring developments in each state could scotch any activity that threatened either internal or external stability. As the Troppau Protocol of 1820 put it,

> States which have undergone a change of government due to revolution, the results of which threaten other states, *ipso facto* cease to be members of the European alliance. . . . If owing to such alterations immediate danger threatens other states, the powers bind themselves, by peaceful means, or if need be by arms to bring back the guilty state into the bosom of the Great Alliance.

The opportunity soon arose to test the system. The restored regimes in Spain and the Kingdom of the Two

Sicilies, both of which had proved highly reactionary, were unpopular. In Spain, Ferdinand VII dismissed an elected assembly, the Cortes, restored confiscated clerical and noble estates, and proclaimed a return to divine right absolutism. Rebellion broke out in early 1820, and the king was compelled to summon the Cortes and to reinstate constitutional rule. In Naples, where King Ferdinand I, like his nephew Ferdinand VII in Spain, had abrogated reforms and alienated both the army and the bourgeoisie, an insurrection broke out at the same time, and revolts and disturbances erupted elsewhere on the Italian peninsula against Spanish, Austrian, and papal rule.

In 1821 a rebellion broke out in Greece as well, which soon became a revolution against three and a half centuries of Ottoman rule. Thus, within the space of a year, insurrection had sparked across the entire Mediterranean coast from Cape Finisterre to the eastern Aegean. Metternich called for action but met a divided response. The British dissented from the Troppau Protocol, and the French, unwilling to serve as the agent of Austrian interests in Italy, sat idle. Metternich was more successful with Prussia and Russia, with whose assent an Austrian army descended on Italy and speedily crushed the rebellions in Naples and Sardinia. France agreed to act in Spain, where it was anxious to restore its influence, and in 1823 sent troops across the Pyrenees to restore Ferdinand VII. Despite promises of clemency, Ferdinand carried out a bloody purge, and his autocratic rule left a bitter legacy.

The case of Greece was more complicated. The Ottoman Empire, battered by the southward expansion of Russia in the eighteenth century, faced revolt among the subject peoples within its own borders. The Serbians had risen in 1804 in the beginnings of a struggle for nationhood that was to have profound consequences for all of Europe. Their rebellion aroused little interest, but when the Greeks, whose merchants dominated the trade of the eastern Mediterranean, rebelled in 1821 with the support of Tsar Alexander I (whose horror of revolutions stopped short at those that advanced Russian interests), the Continent took notice.

The powers forced Alexander to back off and waited for the Greek insurrection to burn itself out. But they failed to take into account both the resolve of the Greeks and a new force that the very idea of collective security had helped to create—public opinion. A new classical revival, spurred chiefly by German scholars and archaeologists in the eighteenth century, combined with the nascent Romantic movement to produce a fascination with things Greek. Committees to support the Greek cause sprang up spontaneously all over western Europe and the United States. In the face of this, the calculated indifference of the powers could not be kept up. After failing to impose an armistice on Turkey in 1827, an allied squadron destroyed the Turkish fleet at Navarino in the Peloponnesus. The Turks were compelled to recognize Greek independence by the London Protocol of 1830.

The Troubled 1820s

The revolt of the Greeks was the political cause célèbre of the 1820s. It gave heart to nationalist movements everywhere, although it showed too that such movements could not hope to succeed merely on the basis of elite elements but required mass support. It left the Congress System in ruins as well. The spectacle of an allied fleet playing midwife to a revolutionary state demonstrated that Metternich's dream of a perpetual status quo could not withstand a united demand for change and that in a crisis each power would consult its own interest first and its treaty obligations second. What emerged was a looser, more informal understanding, the Concert of Europe, by which the great powers would attempt to resolve their major differences and to avoid general war.

While only Russia among the major powers underwent an actual rebellion within its borders between 1815 and 1830—the Decembrist revolt of 1825—all experienced significant unrest. We have touched on the Luddite attacks and urban agitation in Britain. In the wake of the Peterloo Massacre, a package of repressive legislation was passed, the Six Acts, which suppressed public meetings, curbed the press, and speeded up procedures for prosecuting offenders against the public order. It was not until the late 1820s that a less hysterical atmosphere began to prevail.

In France, Louis XVIII (1814–1824) sought a middle ground between the reactionary Ultraroyalist party, which wanted to turn the clock back literally to 1789, and the ex-Bonapartists and republicans, whom Louis knew he would have to conciliate to stabilize his regime. He offered a charter that in essence preserved the structure of the Napoleonic Code and set up a bicameral assembly that could veto royal legislation. However, the assassination in 1820 of the duke of Berry, the heir to the throne, set off a new wave of reaction. Under the intransigent Charles X (1824–1830) the political program of the Ultras was enacted. The Law of Indemnity (1825) compensated nobles who had lost their estates during the revolution by devaluing government bonds held by the bourgeoisie, and the Law of Sacrilege, passed in the same year, imposed the death penalty for the theft of sacred objects and other vaguely defined offenses against the church.

Despite its strengthened geopolitical situation, Prussia was content to allow Metternich to play ideological policeman to the rest of Germany, a role he assumed with relish. By the Carlsbad Decrees of 1819 he suppressed the nationalist student societies that had succeeded the quasi-military gymnastic clubs founded during the Napoleonic wars, whose members, wearing gray-shirted uniforms and imbued with a hatred of "foreign" (including Jewish) influence, strikingly foreshadowed elements of Nazi ideology and practice. Student groups that gathered at Wartburg Castle near Eisenach to

commemorate the tricentennial of Luther's Ninety-five Theses in 1817 toasted unity and freedom but also burned conservative and antinationalist books after a torchlight procession, a rather dubious way to protest censorship.

In Austria itself, Metternich's chief concern was to suppress nationalist stirrings among the many minority groups that comprised the Habsburg empire. The very name *Austria* had been adopted only in 1804 to describe the patrimonial lands of the emperor, and whereas the yearning for national identity might encourage a sense of unity in such regions as Germany and Italy and strengthen it in states already established on the basis of a common language and heritage, it could only foster division and separatism in the Habsburg realm. By

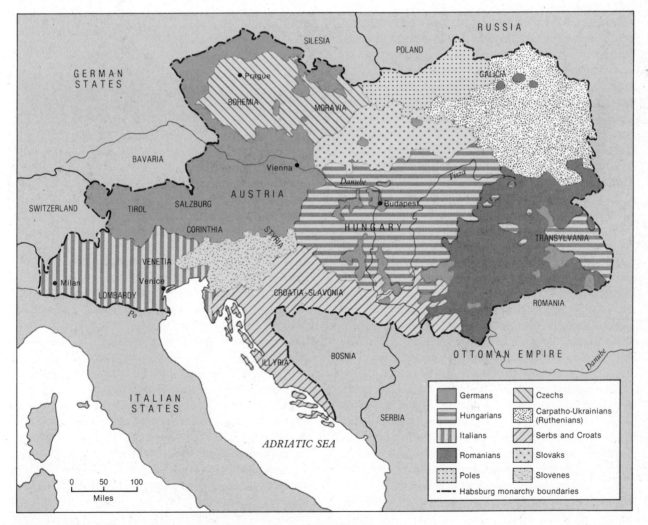

21.2 Ethnic Composition of the Austro-Hungarian Empire

skillfully playing rival minorities off against one another, Metternich delayed his day of reckoning for more than 30 years; by failing to provide a genuine accommodation for nationalist aspirations within the framework of the empire, he ensured that that day would come.

Russia was still by far the most autocratic of all European states. Like Catherine the Great, the eccentric Alexander I (1801–1825) began his reign with a flourish of reform. Men of all classes were legally entitled to hold land for the first time, and masters were encouraged to free their serfs. New schools were founded, and new ideas entered the country, particularly through the medium of the Freemasons and other secret fraternities. The reforming Count Speransky even drafted plans for a system of representative bodies culminating in a national assembly, though without real legislative power. But after the Napoleonic invasions a chastened Alexander, regarding his country's disaster as a providential judgment, lapsed into a reactionary mysticism that made him Metternich's most zealous if not always most reliable ally in the war against reform.

Frustrated liberal aspirations among the officer corps in conjunction with a succession crisis in December 1825 provoked Russia's first attempt at revolution. Alexander's heir, the Grand Duke Constantine, had secretly resigned his claim to the throne in favor of his brother Nicholas, but when the tsar died suddenly, each brother proclaimed the other. In the resulting chaos, some of the disaffected officers raised the standard of "Constantine and constitution," which some of the soldiers apparently thought referred to the tsar and his wife.

Whatever the comic overtones of the Decembrist uprising, it was ruthlessly suppressed. Hundreds of people were imprisoned or exiled, and five officers were executed; these officers' courageous bearing made them symbols of resistance under the despotic reign of Nicholas I (1825–1855). The latent genius of the Russian people flowered in an extraordinary literary generation that included the poets Alexander Pushkin (1799–1837) and Mikhail Lermontov (1814–1841) and the novelists Nikolai Gogol (1809–1852) and Ivan Turgenev (1818–1883). Gogol in particular caught the spirit of Nicholas' Russia in his comic novel *Dead Souls* and his play *The Inspector General*, while the young Feodor Dostoevsky (1821–1881), later one of the century's greatest novelists, began his career by facing a mock firing squad in Siberia for allegedly "socialist" activities. Others, like the journalist Alexander Herzen (1812–1870), sought haven abroad, thus initiating the long tradition of the Russian exile.

Liberalism

The term most frequently used to describe the varied forms of opposition to the Restoration regimes was liberalism, a word that continues to bear different and sometimes contradictory meanings. The origins of liberalism go back to the British philosopher and political theorist John Locke (see Chapter 16), who argued for the supremacy of society over the state or, in practical terms, the control of the Stuart monarchy by the propertied classes. Adam Smith drew out the implications of Locke's argument for the freedom of trade from state interference as well. By the early nineteenth century, liberalism had come to stand broadly for free trade in a laissez-faire marketplace, the limitation of state authority by written constitutions, secular education, and national self-determination. In a general sense, nineteenth-century liberalism may be said to have represented the interests of capitalist enterprise and the aspirations of the commercial bourgeoisie. This was how Karl Marx took it; for him liberalism was simply the ideology of the bourgeoisie. But it was merged as well with a post-Enlightenment skepticism about the role of government and with a profound change in cultural sensibility, Romanticism, to form a complex and potent mixture whose appeal extended far beyond narrow economic interests.

ROMANTICISM AND THE QUEST FOR IDENTITY

Romanticism may be viewed in many ways. The term *Romantic* is often contrasted with the term *classical* to express a mood or movement of art, thought, and cultural sensibility in which feeling and imagination shape form instead of the other way around and in which the expression of individual personality is valued above conformity to established norms of taste and style.

Historically, the Romantic movement that began in the mid-eighteenth century represented an emancipation from the authority of ancient Greece and Rome that had shaped Western culture. Many things contributed to this development. The Renaissance emphasis on the value of the individual and the Reformation idea of personal responsibility for one's own salvation (and one's ethical conduct in the world) laid the basis for a revolt against tradition. The scientific revolution, with its repudiation of ancient and medieval cosmogony and its challenge to the traditional Christianity that rested on it, was a second important step. The Enlightenment doctrine of progress, with its assumption of the inferiority of the past and of the capacity of reason to improve if not perfect the species, had created the utopian hopes that had marked the French Revolution.

The result of all this was a new view of human possibility. At the same time, however, the prospect of an uncharted future provoked anxiety. The past was no longer the model for the present but merely a record of progress to date; culture was not to be inherited but to be created. For the first time the West took on the burden of originality, of the new and avant-garde, that has characterized its culture ever since. Each generation, each decade, was to be reckoned in terms of its difference from its predecessors. The demand for progress and the measure of progress (whether in art, science, politics, or fashion) by originality speeded up the experience of time no less than the factory whistle, the locomotive, or the newspaper.

The Romantic Hero

The dethronement of tradition and the quest for the new put extraordinary emphasis on the role of the individual. A single person, properly placed, could change the destiny of a nation; a single idea could create a new product or industry or a new artistic form. Yet the possibility of failure was implicit in the solitary hero too. The great political figure, like Napoleon, might suffer ignominy and exile; the inventor might fail; the starving artist might die in obscurity. Emancipated from tradition, society was now dependent on genius; and genius, wayward and unpredictable, was to be found only in the individual.

What emerged was a confidence in the collective destiny of Western culture—whether in the form of nation building, utopian experiment, missionary zeal, or imperial expansion—that rested paradoxically on the talent and initiative of the isolated individual. The cultural expression of this paradox was Romanticism. The Romantic hero was typically a sensitive, misunderstood young man (much less often a woman) in revolt against his surroundings or a man of destiny boldly seeking knowledge and power. In the former type, Romanticism portrayed the sense of anxiety and vulnerability that beset the individual in a time of change; in the latter, the vaunting self-confidence of a society that had laid claim to the secrets of nature and would soon take the dominion of the earth.

GOETHE AND THE ROMANTIC SPIRIT

Both kinds of heroes were represented in the work of the great German poet and dramatist Johann Wolfgang von Goethe (1749–1832), whose career spanned the last decades of the Enlightenment and the first ones of Romanticism. Goethe was the son of a town councillor of Frankfurt. He studied and briefly practiced law before turning to a literary career, which by 1775 was prominent enough to secure him an invitation from the young duke of Weimar, Karl August, who had chosen him to be the star of what he hoped to make the most brilliant court in Europe. Arriving with little thought except to gain a temporary sinecure that would free him for writing, Goethe was to remain at Weimar for the rest of his life.

Goethe was not merely the founding figure of modern German literature but also an artist and natural scientist of distinction. Like Rousseau, he was a keen student of botany, and he put forward an elaborate theory of color in opposition to Newton's. Goethe's scientific pursuits were closely tied to his conception of nature as a unity composed of innumerable individual elements. From this sprang Goethe's profoundly Romantic idea of the cosmos itself as the ultimate living organism, a notion that nationalist thinkers would find easy to apply to the relationship between the individual citizen and the nation.

But it was as an author that Goethe exerted his greatest influence. His early novel, *The Sorrows of Young Werther* (1774) brilliantly captured the mood of the early Romantic movement in Germany and portrayed its quintessential hero in the student Werther, who commits suicide out of frustrated love and metaphysical despair. Goethe himself was very much the rebellious young man he wrote about in his early years, tempestuous in his love affairs and radical in his politics. It was only much later, as the venerable Sage of Weimar, that he acquired the image of Olympian wisdom and detachment that has been historically associated with his name. The work that gave continuity to his long career as well as matchless definition to the Romantic movement itself was his dramatic poem *Faust*. The Faust legend originated in a sixteenth-century German physician, astrologer, and magician who called himself Faustus and had reputedly made a pact with the Devil.

This depiction of the great Goethe with his wife and children is more than a fancy-dress family portrait. By his placement in a pastoral setting typical of eighteenth-century aristocratic portraits, Goethe symbolizes the emergent power of his own bourgeois class and its appropriation of the political and material source of aristocratic power: the land. At the same time the towering ruin symbolizes Romantic aspiration and hence Goethe's personal claim to status as an artist. [Freies Deutsches Hochstift, Frankfurt am Main. Photo: Ursula Edelmann.]

Goethe made this figure the very symbol of the Romantic quest for forbidden knowledge and experience. Equally important, his literary Devil, Mephistopheles, is not merely an evil tempter but a tormented being who is a larger symbol of Faust himself. Goethe's difficulty in finishing the poem stemmed from his rejection of the legend of Faust's ultimate damnation; like his fellow Romantics, he believed that the search for knowledge was the essence of the human quest and that good and

evil could not be disentangled from it. In the end his Faust finds salvation rather than punishment, though not before coming to understand the limitations of all knowledge and the abiding mystery of existence.

In his later years, Goethe was the cultur arbiter of Europe, whose favor and blessing were sought by the great and near-great; Napoleon, who met him at Erfurt in 1808, confessed to having read *Werther* seven times. No other poet since Shakespeare had so profound an influence on his fellow artists; the Romantic composers Beethoven, Schubert, Berlioz, Liszt, Mendelssohn, Schumann, and Wagner were only some of the musicians who found inspiration in his work, particularly *Faust*. Goethe himself had a sympathetic interest in younger artists, and he memorialized the English poet Lord Byron (1788–1824), who had died while fighting for Greek independence, in the second part of *Faust*. But his most abiding influence was on his fellow German poets and dramatists.

The Spread of Romanticism

The generation that came to maturity with Goethe included the playwrights Gotthold Ephraim Lessing (1729–1781) and Friedrich von Schiller (1759–1805), in whom the link between Romantic individualism and Romantic nationalism can be seen clearly. In his *Laocoön,* Lessing called for the creation of a national, heroic literature and the rejection of classical models, which were likened (as in the ancient statue from which he drew his title) to a giant serpent strangling human creativity. Schiller responded to that call in plays such as *William Tell* and *The Maid of Orleans* that described charismatically led movements of national liberation.

The last decade of the eighteenth century also saw the advent of Romanticism in Britain, with the poetry of William Wordsworth (1770–1850) and Samuel Taylor Coleridge (1772–1834) and the immensely popular novels of Sir Walter Scott (1771–1832). Coleridge's still widely read *Rime of the Ancient Mariner* (1798) combined Christian symbolism with Romantic quest and atonement, while Wordsworth's epic verse autobiography, *The Prelude* (1807), offered the artist himself as hero. These poets' successors, the tragically short-lived John Keats (1795–1821), Percy Bysshe Shelley (1792–1822), and Byron, brought English Romantic poetry to its finest flowering.

It is arguable that France produced the first truly Romantic figure in Jean-Jacques Rousseau, whose call for a return to nature as a refuge from the evils of a corrupt civilization and whose candid autobiography, the *Confessions,* were the earliest models of Romantic quest literature. However, the neoclassicism that dominated the arts through most of the eighteenth century retained its hold longer in France than elsewhere. The French Revolution harked back to Rome and Greece for its symbols of republican virtue and patriotism, and Napoleon adapted them for this own purposes. Not until after 1815, when defeat had turned France's mood inward, did it produce its first Romantic generation. The crucial transitional figures were the novelist Benjamin Constant (1767–1830), the poet and historian François Auguste René de Chateaubriand (1768–1848), and Madame de Staël (1766–1817), who popularized German Romantic philosophy in France. Chateaubriand in particular was the herald of a Catholic revival in France that rejected the Deism of the Enlightenment and the revolution and signaled a renewal of interest in medieval piety, soon reflected in a neo-Gothic movement in architecture. Madame de Staël caught this new mood as well: "I do not know exactly what we must believe," she declared, "but I believe that we must believe! The eighteenth century did nothing but deny. The human spirit lives by its beliefs." This new, if rather vague, religiosity blended well with Romantic self-absorption, but it clashed with liberalism. The result was that the Romantics tended to sort out politically either on the extreme right or on the extreme left, with very few in the middle.

The post-1815 generation in France included the novelist Stendhal (Marie Henri Beyle, 1783–1842), whose great novel *The Red and the Black* gave the French their own Werther in the character of Julien Sorel; the painter Eugène Delacroix (1798–1863), whose depiction of a Turkish atrocity during the war of Greek independence, *The Massacre at Chios,* profoundly influenced European opinion; and the composer Hector Berlioz (1803–1869), whose *Symphonie Fantastique* (1830), with its lavish orchestral coloration and fevered literary program, was the prototypical Romantic symphony.

Romantic music reached its unquestioned apogee in Germany and Austria, where in the period between 1770 and 1830, four of the greatest geniuses in musical history appeared: Franz Joseph Haydn (1732–1809), Wolfgang Amadeus Mozart (1756–1791), Ludwig van Beethoven (1770–1827), and Franz Schubert (1797–1828). Haydn and Mozart were the supreme masters of the classical style that reigned for most of the latter half of the eighteenth century, with its emphasis on clarity of structure and texture, but their work exhibited elements of the nascent Romantic sensibility as well. Beethoven

Ludwig van Beethoven bridged not only the classic and Romantic periods in music but also, as the first musician to support himself primarily by the sale of his own work, the era of aristocratic patronage and that of the artist-entrepreneur. [The Mansell Collection]

bridged the classic and Romantic eras, particularly in the nine symphonies that remain to this day the most admired synthesis of personal expression and formal control in music. Beethoven was a transitional figure in another respect as well. Whereas Haydn had worn the livery of his aristocratic employers for most of his life and Mozart too had been at the mercy of his patrons, Beethoven was the first composer to make an independent living by the sale of his music. The artist, too, no longer sheltered (and subordinated) by clerical or noble patrons, had entered the marketplace.

Romanticism Beyond the Arts

Romanticism touched not only the arts but philosophy, history, religious thought, and the natural sciences as well. Even as the Enlightenment proclaimed the sovereignty of reason, the German philosopher Immanuel Kant undercut its claims by arguing that the human mind was no mere passive sorter and recorder of experience, as Locke and other empiricists had believed, but a complex mechanism that gave form and shape to phenomena according to its own internal laws. Accordingly, the world could not be experienced or described as it was "in itself" but only as filtered through the processes of intellect and emotion and therefore subjectively.

Kant's philosophy was called idealism, after his distinction between the "ideas" we form of reality through the interaction of world and mind and the world as it exists independently of our perception of it. The implications of Kantian idealism were extended by the Prussian philosopher Georg Wilhelm Friedrich Hegel (1770–1831). Hegel argued that all of human history was a great unconscious drama that tended toward the realization of human freedom, which he called the spirit of reason. The agents of this drama were great individuals such as Caesar and Napoleon, through whose personal passions and ambitions this spirit acted; thus Caesar had created the first world empire, and Napoleon had stimulated the sense of national self-identity that Hegel saw as the final phase of the development of freedom.

Hegel's emphasis on the role of great men in history dovetailed neatly with Romantic individualism, while his identification of nationalism with the progress of freedom had immense appeal to liberals in Germany and elsewhere, despite his personal praise of the conservative Prussian state. No other thinker of the period made so comprehensive an effort to reconcile the two opposite poles of Romantic thought: the attempt to define oneself in opposition to society, whether as explorer, entrepreneur, or artist, and the desire for patriotic identity within the national group.

Romanticism and the Image of Women

The beginnings of modern feminism coincided with those of Romanticism and may be seen as part of the same process of social transformation. Before this time the few women who by sheer force of personality had been able to distinguish themselves were regarded as oddities or freaks. But with the nineteenth century, women began to appear for the first time on a plane of equality with men, particularly as literary artists. At least four Englishwomen stand in the front rank of nineteenth-century literature: Jane Austen (1775–1817), whose social novels reveal a psychological penetration equaled among her contemporaries only by Goethe; the Brontë sisters, Charlotte and Emily; and Mary Ann Evans (1819–1880), known by the pen name George

Eliot, whose novel *Middlemarch,* is rivaled only by the major works of Charles Dickens. At the same time the reclusive New Englander Emily Dickinson (1830–1886) was writing some of the finest lyric poetry since Sappho. In France, Aurore Dupin, who took the name of George Sand (1804–1876), was as celebrated for her scandalous private life—which included a highly publicized liaison with the Polish composer-pianist Frédéric Chopin—as for her voluminous output of novels.

Nevertheless, the disabilities faced by women attempting to compete in what was still a man's world were obvious. The popular English novelist Elizabeth Gaskell was never known by her own forename but simply as "Mrs. Gaskell"; Dupin and Evans both adopted masculine pen names in an effort to gain more serious attention for their work; and Emily Dickinson's poems were never published in her lifetime. If, moreover, a place in literature and to a lesser extent in the other arts was reluctantly conceded to women, it served only to confirm age-old prejudices against them in the fields

George Sand in masculine costume, by Eugéne Delacroix. [Giraudon/Art Resource, New York]

Delacroix's *Liberty on the Barricades*. In this famous depiction of the French Revolution of 1830—perhaps the most celebrated of all images of revolution—an idealized woman of the people leads a charge of workers whose ranks include a single bourgeois. [Cliché des Musées Nationaux, Paris]

of philosophy, politics, and the professions. If women excelled in literature, it only confirmed the prevailing stereotype of them as creatures in whom the imagination prevailed at the expense of the intellect.

The rejection of traditional marriage by women such as Mary Wollstonecraft and George Sand and their demand for free sexual companionship reinforced the widespread male belief that women should be confined as tightly within the bounds of piety and domesticity as possible. Yet the image of woman had come to stand allegorically for revolution itself. In Eugene Delacroix's famous painting of the revolution of 1830, *Liberty on the Barricades,* a female figure leads a charge over the bodies of fallen sans-culottes, a top-hatted bourgeois at her side. Her bared breast recalls the classical image of the Amazon warrior, but the realistic touches—the stained undergarments, the hair under the arms—proclaim her as well to be a woman of the people. Delacroix's striking figure conveys the conflicting impulses behind the early Romantic image of woman: the idealized warrior-goddess and the available woman of the street, the symbol of liberation who remains chained

in her petticoats, leading a battle that will be fought by the sans-culottes but won by the bourgeoisie.

THE JULY REVOLUTION IN FRANCE

By the late 1820s, dissatisfaction with the Bourbon dynasty in France and the slow pace of reform in Britain had reached the flashpoint of revolution. A crisis erupted in France in March 1830 when the Chamber of Deputies voted no confidence in the government of Charles X and its policies of censorship, suffrage restriction, and clerical control of education. Charles dissolved the assembly, but new elections, though limited to an electorate of 100,000, produced a decisive opposition majority. The king, urged by Metternich among others, responded on July 26 by dissolving the Chamber before it could meet, imposing new press censorship, reducing the electorate to a hard core of 25,000 aristocrats, and announcing fresh elections on this basis.

The target of these edicts was the regime's bourgeois opposition, but the reaction came from the working-class sections of Paris. The very next day, barricades appeared spontaneously in the streets, and the army, called out to clear them, refused to do so. Faced with anarchy, Charles abdicated two days later in favor of his grandson and fled into exile. France was left without a government.

The sudden vacuum of power revealed the political division of France. The bourgeois opposition—bankers, industrialists, and merchants—wanted not the overthrow of the Bourbon monarchy but greater favor within it for themselves. The Parisian workers, students, and radical intellectuals who had taken to the barricades and made the revolution wanted a republic, headed by the venerable marquis de Lafayette as president. A compromise was hastily brokered behind the scenes. The duke of Orléans, a collateral relative of the Bourbons but a republican soldier in the army of 1792, was put forward as a constitutional monarch by a coalition consisting of Talleyrand, the liberal journalist Adolphe Thiers, and Jacques Lafitte, the duke's personal banker. When Lafayette publicly endorsed him, the republican opposition melted away. Louis Philippe, as the new king was called, promised to abide by the charter of 1814. With his paunch and umbrella he was indistinguishable from the bourgeoisie that had brought him to power and whose interests he faithfully served.

REVOLUTION EAST AND WEST

The three-day revolution in France was the signal for major uprisings in Belgium and Poland. Catholic Belgium, united with the Netherlands by the Congress of Vienna, chafed under the domination of a Protestant Dutch king, William I. Heartened by the French example, Belgians rose in August 1830 and, after fruitless efforts at conciliation, proclaimed independence under a liberal monarchy of their own. A hastily arranged big power conference in London recognized the new government to forestall French intervention.

The Polish rebellion was triggered by the news that Tsar Nicholas I, who was also king of Poland, was planning to send Russian troops through that country on its way to help suppress the Belgians. Russian rule was

desperately unpopular, however, and almost any pretext might have served. The Polish Diet declared Nicholas deposed, but the tsar's army speedily crushed the revolt. Poland was absorbed directly into the Russian empire and ruled under a state of military emergency that lasted technically from 1833 until the First World War. Thousands of Poles were executed, imprisoned, or banished to Siberia, and many more fled to the West.

Lesser disturbances also shook Germany, Italy, Switzerland, Spain, and Portugal, though for the most part without significant result. Yet liberals could, with the tragic exception of Poland, count 1830 as a year of victory. The bourgeoisie had finally cut a king to their own measure in France. The powers had been forced to acquiesce in an independent Belgium whose constitution acknowledged the sovereignty of the people and provided the widest electoral franchise in Europe. The autocratic William I was forced to embrace reform in the Netherlands, and liberal gains were made in Switzerland. Above all, 1830 marked the year when history seemed to move again in Europe. The liberal triumph was far from complete, but its outlines at last seemed visible.

BRITAIN: REVOLUTION AVERTED

Britain accomplished revolutionary change without revolution. The settlement of 1689 had confirmed the supremacy of Parliament over the king. But neither the size of the electorate—less than 4 percent of the population—nor the distribution of seats had changed in nearly a century and a half, and both were now profoundly unrepresentative of the urban, industrialized society that Britain had become. The long and almost unbroken Conservative domination of British politics from 1760 to 1830 had hardened the nation's rulers in the conviction of their own wisdom.

In fact, reform was already underway. Tariff duties and colonial trade restrictions, some in effect since the seventeenth century, were relaxed, and the Test Act, which had barred Catholics and Dissenters from public life since 1673, was at last repealed (1829). A gesture was even made toward the lower orders; unions were recognized, and the number of offenses punishable by death was cut by 100. But the one issue that had become symbolic of the liberal cause as a whole—parliamentary reform—remained unaddressed.

The reformers' moment came in 1830, when the duke

of Wellington's government fell and a Whig ministry under Lord Grey came to power. Grey steered a parliamentary reform bill through both houses in 1832, although the Lords acquiesced only when faced with the king's threat to create enough Whig peers to override them. It was just in time; riots had broken out all over the country, a tax strike was being organized, and radicals urged a run on the Bank of England to bring the propertied classes to their knees.

The Reform Bill was as important for the revolution it averted as for the rather modest alterations it produced. Some 143 seats in the House of Commons, about a quarter of the total, were redistributed. Slightly fewer than half of these went to new industrial towns that had previously lacked representation of any kind. Some "rotten boroughs"—decayed constituencies that continued to return members to Parliament with a largely phantom electorate—were eliminated. The franchise was extended from slightly under 500,000 to just over 800,000 voters, still little more than 5 percent of the population. The propertied classes in town and country had adjusted their mutual relations in a manner that more adequately represented the influence of the former. Both agreed that the reins of government would continue to rest with them to the exclusion of the vast majority.

The experience of the 1830s and 1840s taught at least the more advanced elements of the working class that their interests could not be encompassed by those of the bourgeoisie. By the end of the 1830s the first sustained workers' movement had emerged in Britain, the Chartists. It began in 1836 when a small shopkeeper, William Lovett, founded the London Workingmen's Association. In 1838 this group devised the first People's Charter. Rejecting the piecemeal reform of Parliament, it demanded a secret ballot, equal electoral districts, annually elected Parliaments on the basis of universal manhood suffrage, the removal of property qualifications for office, and payment for all members of Parliament. The effect of this would have been fully to democratize the political system (at least for men) and to enable workers themselves to sit in Parliament. A petition drive produced a million signatures, but the House of Commons rejected the charter. Despite this, Chartism remained a powerful political force through the 1840s.

A similar rethinking of worker interests was going forward in France, where the government of Louis Philippe set its face against further reform. In 1839 the journalist Louis Blanc (1811–1882) argued in a widely read book, *The Organization of Labor,* that the state should socialize all major economic services, including banking, transportation, and insurance, and establish

"social workshops," cooperative factories operated by and for workers. Like his predecessors, the Count de Saint-Simon (1760–1825), who had advocated control of public services and enterprises by a technocratic elite of scientists and engineers, and Charles Fourier (1772–1837), who like Owen in England urged the formation of self-contained communities, Blanc failed to address the practical problem of power. The state, whether controlled by aristocrats, the bourgeoisie, or, as in much of western Europe by an uneasy combination of both, was highly unlikely to cede authority to either workers or engineers.

FROM REFORM TO REVOLUTION

Such was the conclusion drawn by revolutionaries such as Louis Auguste Blanqui (1805–1881) and Pierre Joseph Proudhon (1809–1865). Proudhon envisioned the abolition of the state in favor of a system of cooperative enterprises that would produce and exchange goods noncompetitively on the basis of social needs. For Blanqui such an arrangement, however desirable in principle, begged the fundamental question of power: How was such a peaceful system to be established against the resistance of the propertied classes and the state machinery they controlled? Blanqui's answer was armed revolution aimed at establishing a "dictatorship of the proletariat," a phrase he coined.

The Socialist Critique

The thinkers and activists that we have just considered subscribed to a common critique of the capitalist system. They accepted Adam Smith's definition of labor as the source of all productive value and believed (as Smith did not) that the wealth produced by this labor should be owned socially or collectively: hence the name *socialism* that is applied to their ideas and demands. The socialists' beliefs were clear-cut: private ownership was the appropriation by force of an excess share of the common social wealth (in the pithy formulation associated with Proudhon, "property is theft"), and unregulated capitalism was the equivalent of unrelieved exploitation. But they disagreed about the remedy. Owen, Fourier, and Proudhon put their faith in small, collectively owned enterprises linked voluntarily into cooperative associations; Saint-Simon and Blanc believed that only state power could break up existing concentrations of private capital and ownership; and Blanqui added that only revolution from below could give the proletariat access to that power. What they all lacked was a theory of social action or, more simply, a credible plan for overthrowing the existing order.

Karl Marx

Karl Marx supplied the theoretical basis for socialism. Marx was the first socialist thinker to challenge the fundamental claims of liberal economists such as Smith

The founder of modern communism, Karl Marx, in bourgeois dress and a Romantic pose. [Globe Photos]

and David Ricardo, who argued that private enterprise—economic competition for individual profit—maximized the production of wealth and hence the aggregate social good. In his major work, *Capital,* Marx advanced a countertheory to demonstrate that capitalism was not merely prone to abrupt contractions in the business cycle and unequal distributions of wealth—points conceded by liberals themselves—but that it was inherently self-destructive.

Marx was born in 1818 in Trier, in the rapidly industrializing Rhineland. He was descended on both sides from a long line of rabbis, but his father, like many other Jews of the time, had submitted to Christian baptism to gain entry into the legal profession. Marx studied philosophy at Bonn and Berlin and became part of a circle of young radicals who were attempting to extend Hegelian thought in a leftward direction. As correspondent for the *Rheinische Zeitung,* he exposed the wretched poverty of the winegrowers of the Trier region in an article that helped lead to the suppression of the newspaper. Quitting Germany in disgust, he settled in Paris, where on the eve of the revolutions of 1848 he hailed the coming of a new socialist order in *The Communist Manifesto,* written with his lifelong friend and collaborator, Friedrich Engels. After 1848, Marx took refuge in London with his large and needy family. He lived there for the remainder of his life, in part supported by Engels, who owned a factory in Manchester.

Marx described history as a social struggle for control of the technical means of production and therefore of subsistence—land, labor, and machinery. Thus ancient society had been founded on slavery, the medieval West on feudalism, and capitalism on wage labor, which Marx saw as a modern form of slavery. Since, like other socialists, Marx regarded labor as the only source of productive value (capital itself, he argued, was only the result of previous labor), all profit extracted from labor by means of the wage system was "surplus" or appropriated value.

Marx praised the bourgeoisie for having greatly expanded the material base of civilization by industrialization and urbanization, even as it forced the great mass of the population to live in conditions of unparalleled exploitation and misery. The contradiction between the prosperity of the few and the poverty of the many could not, however, ultimately be ignored. At the same time the inherent tendency of capitalist competition to contract and profit margins to shrink would lead to ever shorter and severer contractions of the business cycle until the conditions for socialist revolution were ripe.

But revolution could be neither prepared nor accomplished without active class struggle. Marx continually stressed the cooperative nature of the proletarian struggle across all borders, rejecting nationalism as a bourgeois phenomenon that reflected the divisive, competitive nature of capitalism itself. In 1864 he was instrumental in founding the International Workingman's Association, later known as the First International, to promote the proletarian cause throughout Europe and America. At his death in 1883 he was clearly the foremost figure of European socialism, as both a thinker and an activist.

Marx never managed to put his mature ideas into finished, comprehensive form. Half his manuscripts lay unpublished at his death, many to remain unknown for decades; even his masterpiece, *Capital,* the first part of which was published in 1867, was only a torso. In part this reflected his own refusal to settle into any mold, even his own; as he once wittily remarked, "I am not a Marxist." Yet his work helped to shape modern society, and in the universality of his influence he may be regarded as among the few nonreligious thinkers of world significance. Before Marx, no theory of societal development in the West had advanced much beyond Plato and Aristotle 2,000 years before. There was no theory of historical change that dealt adequately with the concrete problems of subsistence, organization, or technological innovation. Yet although Marx emphasized the primacy of economics in determining social forms, his ultimate concern was for the creation of a just society in which men and women would be liberated from the iron compulsion of labor and free to realize their human potential. The challenge he posed to make such a world possible is still with us.

THE REVOLUTIONS OF 1848

When in late 1847 Marx and Engels warned of the imminence of revolution in *The Communist Manifesto,* they may have been the only ones in Europe to expect it. Yet within the first four months of 1848 the Continent was rocked by almost 50 separate revolutions in France, Prussia, Austria, and almost all the lesser German and Italian states. Surveying the wreckage of monarchies, Tsar Nicholas I wrote to Queen Victoria that Russia and Britain seemed to be the last two states standing in Europe. His exaggeration was only slight.

The Causes of the Revolutions

Although the circumstances of revolution differed from place to place, some general causes can be discerned. The Industrial Revolution, which had begun in earnest on the Continent after 1830, had shaken social and demographic patterns and profoundly altered political ones. Nationalist aspirations were a primary impetus in Germany, Italy, and eastern Europe. These tensions and grievances were also exacerbated, as before 1789 and 1830, by hard times. Harvests were poor in the three years preceding 1848; in Ireland, famine and emigration reduced the population from 8.5 million to 6.5 million.

The single most pervasive element in the revolutions of 1848, however, was a general questioning of the existing political order. The monarchs of the Old Regime had based their authority on appeals to divine right and a traditional social order, but the bourgeois or quasi-bourgeois regimes established by the events of 1830–1832 were based on popular sovereignty, and the appeal to tradition had little force in a society in which the most basic relations of property, production, and authority were being transformed and a new financial, commercial, and industrial elite was busily accumulating power. Moreover, the promises of reform by which the new bourgeois regimes had legitimated themselves had not been met; in France, for example, the Legislative Assembly, after two revolutions and 60 years, was a far less representative body than the Estates General of Louis XVI had been.

The Collapse of the Old Order

The revolutions began in Italy, where on January 12 the people of Sicily rose against Ferdinand II. By the end of the month, Milan and Venice had proclaimed their independence and called on King Charles Albert of Piedmont and Pope Pius IX to help unify the entire peninsula. The French were not far behind. When the authorities abruptly banned a political rally in Paris in late February, the events of 1830 swiftly repeated themselves. Riots broke out, barricades went up, and the National Guard, called out to quell the disturbances, joined in instead. Breaking into the Chamber of Deputies, Parisian workers forced the proclamation of a republic, and Louis Philippe fled into exile.

The news from Paris galvanized dissidents in Germany and Austria. In Berlin, Frederick William IV (1840–1861) found himself a virtual prisoner of nationalists who demanded that Prussia take the lead in unifying Germany under a liberal constitution. Student rebels and workers joined in Vienna to extract a promise of reform from the emperor, Ferdinand I, and the aged Metternich fled the city in disguise to join Louis Philippe in exile. In Prague, Bohemian nationalists rose against Habsburg rule, while Hungarians demanded virtual independence from Austria, with a separate army, government, and system of finance. By the end of March the Austrian empire was prostrate, while in Germany in May, existing governments could only stand by as a spontaneously elected all-German parliament convened in Frankfurt to pave the way for unification.

Counterrevolution in Central Europe

The ease with which the revolutions had been accomplished masked the fact that the revolutionaries were in many cases as divided from one another in their aims and purposes as they had been from the kings who served as the common focus of their discontent. Some of the first revolutions to unravel were in the Austrian empire. In Italy, Piedmont had no sooner assumed leadership of the anti-Habsburg coalition when it began to collapse; a counterrevolution restored Ferdinand II in Sicily, while the Venetians rejected any merger with the Piedmontese. In July, Austria badly defeated Piedmont at the battle of Custozza, and a last attempt to resuscitate the cause was crushed at Novara in March 1849. The Italian conflagration was not quite over; in February 1849 a republic was proclaimed in Rome under Giuseppe Mazzini (1805–1872) which declared itself the nucleus of a united Italy. But it fell to a French army in July, and with the surrender of Venice a month later the collapse of the revolutionary cause was complete.

In Hungary the Magyar majority under Louis Kossuth (1802–1894) alienated the minorities under its control by proclaiming what amounted to racial hegemony: it abolished local assemblies in non-Magyar provinces and prescribed that Hungarian be the exclusive language of all higher education as well as of the Diet. This stimulated Slavic nationalism, which culminated in a pan-Slav congress that convened in Prague in June, only to be suppressed by troops still loyal to the Habsburgs. Emboldened by this, the court party retook of Vienna in October after a bombardment and executed or exiled its radical leaders. Two months later, the feebleminded Ferdinand I was induced to step down in favor of his 18-year-old nephew, Franz Joseph I (1848–1916), who completed the process of restoration the following summer by crushing the Hungarian revolt with the aid of 140,000 Russian troops.

In Germany, meanwhile, the Frankfurt Assembly set to its task of providing the country with a national government and a constitution. The fundamental anomaly of its position, however, was soon apparent. Almost all the delegates were members of the upper bourgeoisie, whose vision was of a world made safe for free trade, untrammeled growth, an end to the political monopoly of the aristocracy, and a liberal, constitutional regime. But the masses, whose rebellion had cleared the ground for them, cared little for these things. They were peasants clamoring for land, artisans demanding protection for their trades, and workers who wanted higher wages and industrial regulation. Free enterprise only meant new chains to them, and free speech was less important than bread they could afford to eat.

While the Frankfurt delegates attempted to thrash out their own differences—whether the new Germany should be a federation or a unitary state, a monarchy, an empire, or a republic and above all whether it should seek to incorporate all German-speaking areas within its borders—the existing governments of the German Confederation, supposedly awaiting final extinction but still in control of their armies, recovered their authority. By the time the Assembly had finished drafting a constitution, both Prussia and Austria had become strong enough to reject it out of hand, and when Frederick William IV was approached to become "emperor of the Germans," he replied that he would not pick up a crown from the gutter. At that the Frankfurt Assembly began to collapse. The more moderate delegations, unwilling to contemplate a republic, went home, and the radical remnant was dispersed by force in June 1849. The revolution in Germany was over.

France: From Revolution to Empire

In France the course of events was quite different. Here alone (apart from Mazzini's short-lived Roman republic), the monarch of an independent state had actually been deposed and a new provisional government established. A hasty compromise among revolutionary factions, it consisted of seven moderate and three radical (socialist) republicans. Among the latter was Louis Blanc, who urged immediate relief for the unemployed through a Ministry of Progress that would establish his workshop system. Behind Blanc was the specter of Blanqui, who showed his power by mounting a demonstration of 100,000 workers in Paris in March 1848. When Blanc failed to win the concessions they demanded, one of the marchers denounced him as a traitor. The revolution had already been split.

Most of the wealthier bourgeoisie and nobility had

already fled Paris, and the Unites States was the only foreign power to recognize the French republic. The moderates in the government placed their hopes in speedy elections, which they expected to produce a conservative majority that would isolate the radicals. A Constituent Assembly, elected by universal manhood suffrage, convened on May 4 and immediately replaced the provisional government with a five-man executive of its own that contained no socialists. On June 22, following an abortive coup led by Blanqui, the government announced the dissolution of the workshop program, which had been set up as a sop to Blanc but had provided only ill-paid road work. The reaction was immediate. The workers took up arms, the government proclaimed martial law, and the class war heralded only six months before by Marx in *The Communist Manifesto* became a reality in the streets of Paris. Ten thousand people were killed or wounded in a struggle without quarter (June 24–26) before troops under General Louis Cavaignac regained control of the city.

The so-called June Days sent a shudder of terror throughout bourgeois Europe; one woman likened the strife in Paris to the siege of Rome by the barbarians. The feeling was reciprocated, and not by French workers alone. "Every proletarian," wrote the editor of *Red Revolution* in London, "who does not see and feel that he belongs to an enslaved and degraded class is a *fool*." The ideological breach between the classes was complete, and that division was to remain the formal posture of western European politics for well over a century.

SUMMARY

Looking back on the revolutions of 1848, Karl Marx observed wryly that history repeats itself: the first time as tragedy, the second as farce. There was more than a touch of farce about many of these revolutions, and much tragedy too, but perhaps the dominant emotion was frustration. For a moment, liberals had dreamed of constitutions, nationalists of unification, and radicals of a classless society in which the workers of every land could embrace as comrades. These dreams were not yet to be.

The European elite of the mid-nineteenth century— an amalgam of the upper bourgeoisie and the traditional landed aristocracy—was still powerful enough to maintain itself, while its opponents were too diffuse in their aims, too divided among themselves, and too little rooted in the political and social realities of the population they claimed to represent. Yet the demands they made— political equality, national consolidation, and social justice—reflected deeply felt ideological contradictions within European society. Inherited privilege, the basis of political dominance in Europe for centuries, was no longer self-justifying, while acquired privilege—the accumulation of wealth and capital by the bourgeoisie— was equally suspect as a mandate to rule. If the revolutionaries of 1848 had failed to topple the existing order, they had exposed the essential hollowness and vulnerability of any authority not based on popular consent.

Suggestions for Further Reading

Chevalier, L. *Laboring Classes and Dangerous Classes in Paris During the First Half of the Nineteenth Century.* New York: Fertig, 1973.

Clark, K. *The Romantic Rebellion.* New York: Harper & Row, 1973.

Dakin, D. *The Greek Struggle for Independence.* Berkeley: University of California Press, 1973.

De Ruggiero, G. *The History of European Liberalism,* trans. R. G. Collingwood. Boston: Beacon Press, 1959.

Droz, J. *Europe Between Revolutions, 1815–1848.* New York: Harper & Row, 1967.

Friedenthal, R. *Goethe: His Life and Times.* Cleveland: World, 1965.

Hobsbawm, E. J. *The Age of Revolution: Europe, 1789 to 1848.* New York: New American Library, 1962.

Kohn, H. *The Idea of Nationalism.* New York: Collier Books, 1967.

Krieger, L. *The German Idea of Freedom.* Boston: Beacon Press, 1957.

Lichtheim, G. *A Short History of Socialism.* New York: Praeger, 1970.

McLellan, D. *Karl Marx: His Life and Thought.* New York: Harper & Row, 1973.

Nicolson, H. *The Congress of Vienna.* London: Constable, 1946.

Sheehan, J. J. *Germany, 1770–1866.* New York: Oxford University Press, 1990.

Stearns, P. N. *1848: The Revolutionary Tide in Europe.* New York: Norton, 1974.

Taylor, A. J. P. *The Habsburg Monarchy, 1809–1918.* New York: Harper & Row, 1965.

22

THE TRIUMPH OF NATIONALISM

The revolutions of 1848–1849 left urgent questions unresolved. Divided, Germany and Italy could not hope to compete in the long run with unified states that could shelter their growing industries behind tariffs, conquer foreign markets, and control domestic labor. The building of an industrial infrastructure of transport and communication also appeared to depend on powers and resources that only the nation-state could fully command. At the same time the impressive power of industrial capitalism to create wealth (see Chapter 23) only exacerbated the inequity of its distribution. For many the state was seen as the only arbiter in the growing conflict between capital and labor. Thus, national unification seemed the most promising road both to economic growth and to social reconciliation.

The roots of nationalism were complex. Early nineteenth-century Romanticism, reacting against the rationality of the Enlightenment, had emphasized the unique character both of individuals and of national groups. The nation-state offered a new collective identity for populations harshly divided by social class. Thus its appeal cut across the political spectrum. Only socialists and anarchists insisted that the attainment of a just society required the abolition of the state.

The revolutions of 1848–1849 had completed the ruin of Metternich's Congress System. That system had been based on keeping the European balance of power by preventing the rise of new states. Since states could be created under those circumstances only by defying the existing order, the system forced nationalism into the channel of revolution. After 1850, however, the movements for national unification in Italy and Germany were led by statesmen who sought to uncouple nationalism from revolution and achieved unification by a mixture of force and diplomacy. At the same time, conservative leaders in Britain and France offered such concessions as wider suffrage and legal equality to placate the middle and working classes.

In eastern Europe, Austria and Russia both attempted to implement change from the top. Both countries abolished serfdom, though a free peasantry was slow to emerge, and both began to move toward economic modernization. Both were also increasingly preoccupied by the rapid disintegration of the Ottoman Empire and the zone of instability and political competition that it created between them. Half a world away, meanwhile, the United States experienced its own crisis of identity, purging itself of the institution of slavery only by civil war.

Among the settled peoples of Europe only one, the Jews, laid claim to no territorial homeland on the continent. Many Jewish intellectuals were attracted to socialism, with its commitment to class solidarity across national frontiers, while others, inspired by European nationalism but troubled by the rising incidence of anti-Semitism, called for a return to the Jews' ancestral home in Palestine.

THE POLITICS OF GRANDEUR: NAPOLEON III IN FRANCE

One of the most remarkable careers of midcentury Europe was that of Napoleon III. Combining an appeal to national pride and imperial nostalgia with the skillful manipulation of opinion, he maneuvered for 20 years between class conflict at home and insurgent nationalism abroad, only to be swept away at last by the forces he had so long attempted to contain.

From Republic to Empire

Of all the countries struck by revolution in 1848, France seemed to face the most uncertain future. In the aftermath of the June Days most of the leaders of the insurrection were slain or deported. By the year's end, not a single one of the reform initiatives of the winter and spring—the National Workshops, workers' cooperatives, the guarantee of employment, the ten-hour day—remained. The liberal observer Alexis de Tocqueville summed up the atmosphere: "I saw society split in two: those who possessed nothing united in a common greed; those who possessed something in a common fear."

Yet the work of the Constituent Assembly ground on. In November it presented the new constitution, which provided for a unicameral Legislative Assembly and a president, both to be elected by universal manhood suffrage. Elections followed the next month. General Cavaignac, the acting executive, confidently put himself forward for the presidency; his opponents included two former members of the Provisional Government. The election was won, however, by an obscure ex-revolutionary who had nothing to recommend him but his name: Louis Napoleon.

Louis Napoleon, born in 1808, had been named for his father Louis Bonaparte, King of Holland, and his uncle, Napoleon I, Emperor of the French. When Napoleon's own son died in 1832, Louis Napoleon became the heir apparent to the Bonaparte legacy. Raised in Bavaria by a tutor whose father had been a colleague of Robespierre's, he dabbled in revolutionary politics in the 1830s, twice vainly tried to raise the Bonapartist standard, and finally spent six years in prison. When he appeared on the scene in 1848, few people took note of him. His first speech in the Constituent Assembly was a fiasco, and a colleague dismissed him as a "cretin." How, then, did he

secure election as president only months later, winning nearly three-fourths of the 7.5 million votes cast?

In part, Louis Napoleon was the beneficiary of the Bonapartist revival that had swept over France in the 1840s. Disillusioned by the corruption of the July Monarchy, people turned nostalgically to the great days of empire. To this were added the traumatic events of 1848. The great mass of conservative peasantry yearned for stability and order. The bourgeoisie recalled the social and political favor they had enjoyed at the emperor's court. Even republicans could take heart from Louis Napoleon's revolutionary past. In short, Louis Napoleon was all things to all the French. Yet all were to be surprised by this unprepossessing heir to a great dynasty. As president of the Second Republic and as ruler of a restored empire, Louis Napoleon was to leave his own stamp on a France that he governed for 22 years, far longer than his illustrious uncle.

The election of Louis Napoleon revealed little about the real political temper of France, but the Legislative Assembly returned in May 1849 reflected its underlying divisions. Monarchists and other conservatives occupied some 500 of its 750 seats, while socialist republicans won a surprising 180 and an even higher share of the popular vote. Only 70 seats went to moderate republicans; thus, fewer than 10 percent of the representatives were supporters of the new constitution. It was a very poor start for the Republic.

Emboldened by their success, the socialists attempted to overthrow the government at once but were easily suppressed. New controls over the press and public meetings were imposed, and French troops were sent to put down a republican insurrection in Rome, where they remained to protect the pope. In 1850, the Assembly ensured the elimination of the socialists by cutting the poorest third of the electorate from the voting rolls. At the same time the Falloux law put education at all levels back under the control of the Catholic clergy.

Louis Napoleon distanced himself from the Assembly's actions without opposing them and built up his own popularity by touring the country. A showdown became inevitable when the Assembly refused to alter the constitution to permit him to seek a second four-year term and rejected a request for payment of his debts. On December 2, 1851, the anniversary of Napoleon I's coronation, he seized power, dissolved the Assembly, and staged a plebiscite to expand his authority as president for a new ten-year term. The end of the Republic now merely awaited the recurrence of the family anniversary. On December 2, 1852, Louis Napoleon proclaimed the Second Empire. Remembering Napoleon's son, he called himself Napoleon III.

The Second Empire: Foundation and Development

Napoleon III was neither statesman nor orator, administrator nor diplomat, and his military judgment was fatally flawed. But he possessed a shrewd political instinct, a sense of personal destiny, and a belief that he had found the key to successful modern government. Popular sovereignty, he felt, had been mistakenly identified with parliamentary assemblies. These fostered only party interest and social division. The mass of the people yearned for order and progress. As long as that was provided, they were quite indifferent to the details and personalities of administration. They asked only to be consulted on symbolic occasions and to have a leader with whom they could identify themselves and the nation.

The new emperor provided a brilliant court and took as his bride a Spanish countess, Eugénie de Montijo. He held frequent public festivals and military reviews and in 1855 presented a great exhibition in Paris. The city itself was extensively redesigned by Baron Haussmann, a gifted urban planner, who modernized its water and sanitation systems and laid out broad, tree-lined avenues commanded by wide vistas and monumental public buildings, spacious parks and squares, and new railway terminals. Among the most characteristic projects were a new roofed market, made of glass and metal, and an ornate opera house. Commerce, spectacle, and pleasure: this was the ruling idiom of the Second Empire.

Napoleon III benefited from the boom times that followed the discovery of gold in California in 1848. The

Paris remodeled: pedestrian and horse-drawn traffic along the Champs-Élysées after the renovations by Baron Haussmann. In addition to beautifying and modernizing the city, Haussmann's purpose was also to inhibit the erection of barricades. [© Collection Viollet]

increase in the money supply provided capital not only for grandiose building projects but also for an expansion of the French railway system, which tripled in size between 1851 and 1859 and by 1870 was nearly as extensive as those of Great Britain and Germany. This in turn stimulated the development of the country's coal and iron resources and hence its industrial capacity. Between 1851 and 1870 the energy output of French industry increased fivefold; coal consumption nearly tripled, while at the same time the price of steel was halved.

Most of Napoleon III's initiatives were based on the ideas of Count Claude Henri de Saint-Simon (1760–1825) and his followers, who emphasized the importance of developing the infrastructure of France and encouraging its "productive" classes—builders, developers, scientists, and engineers. Equally important was the expansion of credit. A French company led by Ferdinand de Lesseps built the Suez Canal between 1859 and 1869; such a capital venture would have been unthinkable under the July Monarchy.

By the 1860s, mature industrial capitalism was well underway in France. Large corporations and banking houses, shielded by new limited liability laws that protected investors against financial liability beyond the face value of their stock, had begun to dominate the economy. The first department stores and chain groceries made their appearance, and industrial suburbs sprang up around the larger cities.

The new prosperity was very unevenly distributed, however. While employers' profits increased fourfold between 1850 and 1870, real wages rose by only 28%. Behind the facade of spacious boulevards were the grim and airless tenements that housed the workers, many of which still lacked water and plumbing. Industrial discipline was tighter than ever; unions were prohibited, and each laborer was obliged to carry his *livret*, a certificate that recorded his or her work history. A docile and regimented work force was the counterpart of the entrepreneurial and technocratic elite favored by Saint-Simonian doctrine.

The Liberal Empire

After 1860, Napoleon III faced increasing disaffection. The exiled poet and novelist Victor Hugo (1802–1885) scorned him as "Napoleon the Little," while the poet Charles Baudelaire's (1821–1867) *Flowers of Evil* (1857) celebrated a defiant subculture of drugs and sexual debauchery. The emperor's foreign policy also produced a crop of embarrassments. The French clerical party bitterly criticized him for permitting the occupation of papal territory and for the unification of Italy in general. More tragic was the adventure in Mexico, where Napoleon III attempted to set up a satellite state with the Austrian archduke Maximilian as its puppet ruler. Faced with stubborn resistance and the threat of U.S. intervention, he hastily withdrew, but Maximilian was captured and shot. Finally, Napoleon III was outwitted by Prussia, which tricked him into a war that proved to be his downfall.

Napoleon attempted to placate his critics by reform. He relaxed press censorship, conceded the right to strike, and for the first time permitted his ministers to be questioned in the regime's feeble legislature. The educational curriculum was modestly reformed, and the first stirrings of a genuine feminist movement appeared in the person of Maria Deraismes, who founded the Association for the Rights of Women and agitated for equality, access to the professions, and a liberalized divorce law. In 1870, following a legislative election in which opposition candidates polled 45% of the vote, the emperor called upon a moderate republican, Émile Ollivier, to form a government and introduced a new constitution that moved in the direction of parliamentary rule. This last incarnation of the Second Empire proved to be stillborn, however; within months of its adoption, France was an occupied country, and Napoleon III had fled into exile.

THE UNIFICATION OF ITALY

The first modern state to achieve unification by an appeal to nationalism was Italy, where dynastic ambition, revolutionary fervor, and power politics combined to produce a result that had been directly desired by few and was only partially satisfying to most. A culture without a state, Italy was to become a state in search of a nation.

The Risorgimento

The Italian peninsula is one of the most geographically distinct features of the European continent, with its 4,100 miles of coastline and the barrier of the Alps that cap its northern frontier. Its people looked back on a glorious imperial past; they possessed one of the oldest continu-

22.1 The Unification of Italy, 1859–1870

ous religious traditions in Europe, a common language and culture, and an unrivaled artistic heritage. Yet for 1,300 years, Italy had known no political unity, and in the early nineteenth century it was still the pawn of other powers.

The name given to the nationalist movement that emerged in Italy was the *Risorgimento* ("resurgence"). Its roots can be traced back to the eighteenth century in such figures as Vittorio Alfieri (1749–1803), who called for a free and united Italy. But the first major impetus to unification was given by the Napoleonic occupation of Italy between 1796 and 1814. The peninsula had become an economic backwater after the Franco-Spanish wars that ravaged it in the sixteenth century. Napoleon's regime brought efficient, centralized administration and

a streamlined code of laws that were particularly suited to promoting commerce. Customs barriers and restrictions on the free transfer of land by inheritance were struck down, improved roads and markets built, and uniform weights and measures introduced.

Napoleon also dissolved, at least temporarily, the Papal States, which stretched across the center of Italy, separating north and south. The energies of the Counter-Reformation had long been spent, but the church could still dominate a divided Italy, and it stood solidly with the conservative landowning elite. Its return alienated the merchants and entrepreneurs who had prospered under Napoleon and who embraced nationalism as the only hope for change.

Britain and Austria had both promised Italians independence and liberty in return for their support against Napoleon. But at the Congress of Vienna, Italy was partitioned into seven states and two smaller territories, all under absolute rulers and largely under Austrian influence. Apart from the restored Papal States, only Piedmont, which included the island of Sardinia and the former republic of Genoa, had a native dynasty, the house of Savoy. Italians had neither the vote nor any direct share in the government of their state. Personal liberties were few and were subject to police restraint.

Despite this, many Italians were happy enough to welcome back their old masters. French taxes and conscription had lain heavily on them. In Modena, Duke Francis IV was so enthusiastically received that the people unhitched his coach and carried it themselves to his palace. This state of affairs did not last, however. A number of secret societies dedicated to independence and reform sprang up, of which the most important was the Carbonari ("charcoal-burners"), whose numbers may have reached 300,000, many of them ex-soldiers, artisans, and civil servants of Napoleon's day. They briefly forced a constitution on Ferdinand VII of Naples in 1820 and staged rebellions throughout central Italy in 1830–1831. Both uprisings were put down by Austria, which was clearly determined to keep Italy an extended province of its empire indefinitely.

The rebellions of the Carbonari were local in character, but they stimulated a more general nationalist sentiment that found expression in the plays of Silvio Pellico, the poetry of Giacomo Leopardi, the operas of the young Giuseppe Verdi, and the novels of Alessandro Manzoni. But it was Giuseppe Mazzini (1805–1872) who gave Italian nationalism its most impassioned voice. A doctor's son, he joined the Carbonari, was imprisoned and exiled for his participation in the rebellions of 1830–1831, and founded a group of his own, Young Italy. For Mazzini the sentiment of nationalism was divinely implanted, and the work of unification was therefore a holy calling. The destiny of Italy, however, was special. The Rome of the Caesars had given Europe political unity, and that of the popes, faith. Now a third Rome, capital of a united Italy, would usher in a new era of progress and brotherhood.

With a fellow revolutionary, Giuseppe Garibaldi (1807–1882), Mazzini fomented a series of conspiracies and insurrections in the 1830s and 1840s. But the key to unification rested with the one independent state on the peninsula, Piedmont. When revolution broke out in 1848 in Vienna and Milan, Piedmont moved cautiously, less perhaps to lead a war of independence than to contain it.

Giuseppe Mazzini, the father of Italian nationalism. [The Granger Collection, New York]

Defeated by a regrouped Austrian army at Custozza in July and again at Novara the following March, its king, Charles Albert, was forced to abdicate in favor of his son, Victor Emmanuel II (1849–1878).

The cause of unification now appeared bleak. Mazzinian republicans and monarchists who had hoped to see Charles Albert as king of a united Italy blamed each other for the debacle of 1848–1849. Pope Pius IX (1846–1878), who had toyed with the idea of presiding over a federation of Italian states, repudiated nationalism altogether. The Austrians brutally reimposed their control, executing nearly 1,000 activists.

Cavour and the Crisis of Unification

At this moment a statesman of genius appeared in the person of Count Camillo di Cavour (1810–1861). A former journalist, engineer, and agricultural entrepreneur, he was 40 years old before he entered politics. Within two years he had become prime minister of Piedmont under the constitution adopted in 1848, a position he retained, with brief intervals, until his death.

As a liberal journalist, Cavour had called upon

Charles Albert to lead the crusade to unify Italy in 1848. In office his goal was the more modest one of freeing Italy from Austrian control, with an expanded Piedmont embracing the northern and possibly central portions of the peninsula. To prepare it for this task, he set about to promote trade and industry and to modernize transportation and credit. To repair Piedmont's standing among the powers of Europe, he joined Britain and France in the Crimean War against Russia. The Italian contingent saw only one day of battle at a cost of 28 killed, but it earned Piedmont a seat at the peace conference in Paris and the confidence of an important ally, Napoleon III.

France was the key to Cavour's design. He set about to convince Napoleon III that the liberation of Italy was both a noble cause and a practical advantage to France. The emperor proved receptive. He was a believer in the so-called doctrine of nationalities, which held that the consolidation of nations was historically progressive, and saw France as the natural heir of Habsburg influence in the peninsula. At a secret meeting with Cavour at Plombières in July 1858, he agreed that if Piedmont could provoke a war with Austria, France would come to its "rescue."

The Austrians entered the trap, declaring war in April 1859 after Piedmont had rejected an ultimatum to demobilize its troops. Napoleon III landed personally in Genoa to command his armies, which won decisive victories over Austria at Magenta and Solferino. Tuscany and several smaller Italian states thereupon applied for annexation to Piedmont. The emperor realized that a state of such size would no longer be amenable to French control. When Prussia mobilized troops along the French frontier in protest, Napoleon abruptly pulled out of the war. The Austrian army, battered but intact, remained on Italian soil.

Napoleon III's venture had been a fiasco. He had deserted an ally, betrayed a cause, attacked a fellow sovereign, and shed French blood, all without gaining a single objective. Cavour offered him a face-saving alternative: in return for the border provinces of Savoy and Nice, the emperor would agree to uniting the central Italian states with Piedmont. A series of plebiscites ratified the deal. Cavour had occupied most of the north except for the province of Venetia, which was still in Austrian hands but was now geographically isolated from the rest of the peninsula.

The Final Phase

Mazzini and Garibaldi pronounced the job of unification only half done. When Garibaldi landed in Sicily with a guerilla force in May 1860, the island greeted him as a deliverer, and his so-called Army of a Thousand, dressed like their leader in bold red shirts, swept into Palermo, crossed the straits of Messina to the mainland, entered Naples unopposed, and prepared to march on Rome. To forestall this, Piedmont occupied the Papal States, carefully skirting Rome itself, and Victor Emmanuel rode south to intercept Garibaldi. The latter, with Piedmont's forces in front of him and the still-active Neapolitan army at his rear, reluctantly surrendered command. Further plebiscites united the newly conquered territories to Piedmont. In March 1861 the kingdom of Italy was proclaimed, with Victor Emmanuel II as its ruler.* Three months later, Cavour died, with the words "Italy is made. All is safe" upon his lips.

Italia Irredenta: Problems and Prospects for the New Italy

All, perhaps, was safe; but all had not been made. Venetia was annexed in 1866 after Austria's defeat in its war with Prussia, but Rome remained a sticking point. Pius IX refused to surrender his claim to the city, stating flatly, "This corner of the earth is mine. Christ has given it to me. I will give it up to him alone." To emphasize the point, he issued his *Syllabus of Errors* in 1864, which condemned among other propositions the suggestion that "the Roman pontiff can and should reconcile himself to progress, liberalism, and modern civilization." Taking advantage of Napoleon III's defeat by Prussia, Victor Emmanuel took possession of Rome, occupying all but the Vatican itself, where a defiant Pius sequestered himself, and the Pope's summer residence of Castel Sant'Angelo. The papacy's temporal power—the oldest sovereignty in Europe—was thus extinguished.

Like other nationalist movements, the Risorgimento had been associated with political liberalization, economic modernization, and the replacement of a landed aristocracy by a professional and merchant elite, often in alliance with a new middle class of landed gentry. Cavour had been the very prototype of this new elite, and even Garibaldi's Thousand had consisted largely of students, artisans, and itinerant urban professionals. Few men of great wealth or established position supported the nationalist movement, though they soon made themselves at home in it, and few peasants did either, though they welcomed the chance to revolt against

---

*The king kept the regnal number of II, although properly he should have been Victor Emmanuel I of Italy.

feudal regimes. The bourgeoisie had made the Risorgimento, and, in a real sense, the Risorgimento made them.

The new regime faced a host of problems, and for many disillusionment was swift. "I thought to call up the soul of Italy," said the aged Mazzini, "and I see only its corpse." The mass of its 22 million people were impoverished and illiterate. The government was virtually an oligarchy, since it made no effort to extend suffrage to newly annexed territories, and barely 2 percent of the population had the right to vote. Communication was difficult; the Apennine Mountains divided the country geographically into east and west as historic separation and uneven development separated it culturally into north and south. In all of the former kingdom of Naples there were only 100 miles of railway, and nine out of ten villages had no roads at all. "Italy is made," said Count Azeglio, reflecting on Cavour's last words. "We have still to make the Italians."

The country had few resources to deal with these problems. It lacked both the capital and the natural resources to develop an industrial infrastructure. Despite higher taxes, the government was chronically in debt. Its free-trade policies were devastating to the protected industries of the south, and the removal of export curbs on grain drove up bread prices for the poor. Many in the south felt more exploited by their fellow Italians than they had by their Austrian predecessors, and the gulf between these two Italies, far from being bridged by unification, steadily widened.

The government also faced a war with the church. Pope Pius IX and his successors spurned any accommodation with the new regime, and it was not until 1929 that the Vatican recognized the government of Italy. Good Catholics were enjoined to abstain from any participation in the political process, and Pius' successor, Leo XIII (1878–1903), even threatened to remove the papacy to Avignon as in the days of the fourteenth-century Babylonian Captivity of the church. In retaliation the state abolished tithe payments to the church, took control of its charitable foundations, and secularized education. This confrontation was damaging to both parties; it was particularly costly, however, to a new government seeking to establish itself in the face of rejection by the oldest authority in the land.

Finally, there was pressure to recover *Italia irredenta* ("unredeemed Italy"), those territories that, like Nice and Savoy, had been surrendered to France as the price of support for the war of liberation and those, including Trentino (south Tyrol) in the north and Venezia Giulia on the Dalmatian coast, that had not been incorporated into the new state. Trentino in particular was resented as

an Austrian encampment on Italian soil, and Italians watched in helpless rage as the Habsburgs aggressively Germanized the province.

BLOOD AND IRON: THE FORGING OF THE GERMAN EMPIRE

Italy's unification was rapidly followed by that of Germany. Whereas Italian unification had been a triumph of daring and guile over intrinsic weakness, however, Germany's was the assertion of an economic strength that had already made it one of the preeminent industrial powers of Europe.

Germany After 1848

Like Italy, Germany had been long divided. Napoleon I had reduced its 396 principalities to 39, but apart from the *Zollverein* ("customs union") introduced by Prussia, no significant step to unite the country had been taken after 1815. After the debacle of 1848 the prospects for unification seemed more remote than ever.

Yet the forces promoting a united Germany remained strong. Lacking the spur of foreign domination, the Germans had not produced a Risorgimento. But economic development and cultural nationalism pointed to the logic of a single German state. Both were summed up in the figure of the economist Friedrich List (1789–1846), the chief architect of the Zollverein. List was incensed at the shortsighted policies of the separate German states. He looked to a future colossus that would embrace not only the existing 39 states but would absorb the Netherlands and Denmark as well, thus laying the basis for a maritime empire. In this, List went beyond mere ethnic cohesion to the idea of the nation-state as inherently imperialistic. It was, he wrote,

a society which, united by a thousand ties of mind and of interest, combines itself into one independent whole . . . and in its united character is still opposed to other societies of a similar kind in their national liberty, and consequently can only under the existing conditions of the world maintain self-existence and independence by its own power and resources.[1]

List's legacy, the Zollverein, united 34 million Germans in the largest free-trade zone on the European continent. Cultural nationalism was uniting Germany too. The composers Carl Maria von Weber (1786–1826) and Richard Wagner (1813–1883) glorified German history in their operas, while the brothers Jacob and Wilhelm Grimm documented the German cultural heritage in their famous collections of fairy tales. As in the case of Italy, however, the political catalyst to unification was as yet lacking.

The German revolutions of 1848 had settled some matters at least. Liberalism, thoroughly discredited by the failure of the Frankfurt Assembly, would not unify Germany. Nor would the Habsburg dynasty, the hope of some nationalists who favored a greater Germany federated with Austria. The Habsburg had reasserted their traditional hegemony in Germany after 1815, and Austria had assumed the presidency of the German Confederation, the common assembly of the 39 states. But Austria's chief interest, in Germany as well as in Italy, was to prevent unification at all costs. Beset by its own national minorities, it could neither lead a new German state nor countenance any rival.

Throughout the 1850s, Prussia kept a low profile in European affairs; alone among the major powers, it remained neutral during the Crimean War. Internally, however, it shared the explosive economic and demographic growth that marked Germany after 1850 and that bound it ever more closely to its neighbors. By 1853 the Zollverein embraced virtually every state in the German Confederation except Austria. Though the Habsburgs might still dominate Germany's present, they had refused to join its future.

Bismarck and the Achievement of Prussian Hegemony

In 1861 the ineffectual Frederick William IV was succeeded by his brother, William I (1861–1888). William was determined to reassert Prussia's leadership within Germany and its military credibility in Europe. He undertook to raise the size of the army from 150,000 to 220,000 men, to extend the term of compulsory service from two to three years, and to reduce dependence on the civilian militia. These plans ran into opposition in the *Landtag,* the lower house of the Prussian assembly created in 1850. The Landtag was dominated by the Rhenish industrialists who had come to prominence during the boom of the 1850s and who resented the pervasive influence of the military. They refused to grant William the necessary taxes. For the first time in Prussian history, civilians had challenged the primacy of the army in the affairs of the nation.

Bismarck, who forged the modern German state, is shown in 1871, the year the new empire was proclaimed. [Culver Pictures]

In this crisis, William turned to a veteran diplomat, Count Otto von Bismarck (1815–1898). Bismarck was a Junker, as members of the East Prussian aristocracy were called, with estates in Brandenburg. Like his fellow Junkers, he was deeply conservative and contemptuous of liberal ideals and institutions. Unlike them, he was adroit and sophisticated, and as ambassador to St. Petersburg and Paris he had taken the measure of the leading statesmen and sovereigns of his time. They held no terrors for him, nor did a mere electoral body. Appointed minister-president, or head of government, in September 1862, he at once announced his intention to ignore all contrary votes in the Landtag: "The great questions of our time," he stated defiantly, "will not be decided by speeches and majorities . . . but by blood and iron." The phrase stuck, and under the title of the office he later held, Bismarck would be known to history as the Iron Chancellor.

For four years, Bismarck continued to collect taxes in defiance of the Landtag as William ignored calls for his impeachment. Bismarck relished taunting public opinion with such remarks as "It is the destiny of the weak to be devoured by the strong" and "If I have an enemy in my power, I must destroy him." Later, he would describe his philosophy of government as *Realpolitik* ("the politics of reality"), but he never meant much more than the pursuit of the material interests of power by any means necessary. For abstract goals such as peace or justice he had only scorn. "If I had to go through life with principles," he said, "I would feel I had to walk a narrow path in the woods . . . [with] a long pole in my mouth."[2]

Bismarck was determined to subdue what he regarded as Prussia's two enemies: liberalism and Austria. The need to strengthen Prussia militarily against its Habsburg rival had provided an occasion for confrontation with domestic liberals; now war with Austria would both confirm Prussian dominance in Germany and complete the subjugation of the Landtag.

The time was ripe. Austria's defeat by Napoleon III in Italy had diminished Habsburg prestige while raising fears of French aggression. Liberal nationalists throughout Germany once again appealed to Prussia to take the initiative in uniting and defending the fatherland, despite their bitter distaste for Bismarck personally.

Bismarck's original goal was not national unification but the limited expansion of his own state. As Cavour had envisioned a greater Piedmont without wishing to tie it to the problems of the backward south, so Bismarck saw a greater Prussia that would dominate southern Germany without having to integrate its Catholic population into Prussia's Lutheran one.

An ideal pretext for war arose over the disputed duchies of Schleswig and Holstein. These territories were affiliated with the kingdom of Denmark, but their population was substantially German. When Denmark attempted to absorb Schleswig outright, the diet of the German Confederation called for intervention. Austria and Prussia responded, and after driving Danish troops out of both territories in 1864, the Prussians occupied Schleswig and the Austrians Holstein. In June 1866, after clashes between the occupying armies provoked by Bismarck himself, Prussia invaded Holstein.

The resulting Seven Weeks' War established Prussia as the major power not only in Germany but in all of central Europe. Austria was swept from the field at Sadowa, and the states of the German Confederation that were luckless enough to have heeded its call for support were quickly subdued. Prussia annexed Schleswig and Holstein, the kingdom of Hanover, the duchies of Nassau and Hesse-Cassel, and the free city of Frankfurt, thus giving it for the first time land bridges across northern

and central Germany to its territories on the Rhine and adding 5 million subjects. These were incorporated in 1867 into the Prussian-sponsored North German Confederation, which contained all of Germany north of the river Main.

Bismarck's horizons, like Cavour's, expanded with success. The remaining independent states of south Germany—Bavaria, Baden, Württemberg, and Hesse-Darmstadt—were unorganized and would inevitably fall prey to Prussia, Austria, or France. Union with Austria, which was both Catholic and German, was a logical preference, but Austria's defeat had crippled it. Prussia was the only alternative to French domination.

Bismarck worked to make the idea of Prussian annexation more palatable. The North German Confederation was organized as a showcase of Prussia's intentions for a fully unified Germany. It was presided over by the king of Prussia, with a bicameral legislature consisting of the Bundesrat, an upper house consisting of representatives from each member state, and the Reichstag, a lower chamber elected by universal suffrage and secret ballot.

There was something for everyone in this package. The Prussian monarchy dominated the executive, but majority rule prevailed in the Reichstag, while the Bundesrat, whose approval was required for all laws, protected the interests of the smaller states, at least in theory. To legalize his former actions, Bismarck asked the Prussian Landtag to vote a bill of indemnity, approving the budgets of the previous five years. Liberals, viewing this as an acknowledgment of the Landtag's constitutional powers as well as a promise of future good behavior, joined conservatives to pass the bill overwhelmingly. Even socialists, mollified by Bismarck's constitutional concessions, agreed to recognize the new union.

The last ingredient in what Bismarck called his "national omelette" was France. For 200 years, French dominance on the continent had rested on the absence of any strong, unified state between Paris and Vienna. Now, in the space of a decade, two such states had arisen on the borders of France, and they had already made common cause. Napoleon III's doctrine of nationalities had come home to roost. Not merely French dominance but French security appeared to be at risk.

The contrast between Napoleon III and Bismarck was visible at home as well. Whereas Bismarck had built up his army over the protests of the liberals and only conciliated them afterward from a position of strength, Napoleon attempted to pacify his domestic opposition in the 1860s at the expense of military preparedness. Bismarck had liberalized Prussia in the wake of victory and on his own terms; Napoleon was liberalizing France on the eve of defeat.

The Franco-Prussian War

War between France and Prussia was not long in coming. In 1868 a revolution in Spain had deposed the unpopular Queen Isabella II (1833–1868); a successor was sought on the basis of constitutional monarchy and universal manhood suffrage. Bismarck discreetly spread bribes, and the Spanish offered Prince Leopold of Hohenzollern, King William's cousin, the crown. Napoleon III could no more permit a Prussian ruler in Spain than Louis XIV could an Austrian one in 1700, and once again a crisis on the Spanish throne seemed likely to plunge Europe into war.

Under intense French pressure, Leopold refused the Spanish offer. The French ambassador intercepted William at the resort of Ems, insisting that he renounce the Spanish throne for any Prussian candidate. William indignantly declined and cabled an account of the incident to Bismarck with the suggestion that it be published. Bismarck seized the opportunity, paraphrasing the king's statement to suggest that the French had delivered an ultimatum. Angry words followed on both sides, and trapped by his own rhetoric, Napoleon III did precisely as Bismarck had intended him to do. On July 19, 1870, he declared war on Prussia.

Prussia's victory was again stunningly swift. On September 2 the main French army was encircled and defeated at Sedan, northeast of Paris; Napoleon III himself, caught in the city, surrendered with it. The war was won, but it was not over. Two days later, liberal French ministers proclaimed a republic and vowed to fight on. Paris was besieged, while the new government conscripted an army of 600,000 men. Finally, in January 1871 the French accepted an armistice and, at Bismarck's insistence, elected a constituent assembly by universal manhood suffrage empowered to make peace and form a legitimate government. The spectacle of a Prussian aristocrat imposing democratic elections on France was as startling as it was, for the French, humiliating.

Meanwhile, on January 18 the rulers of Germany assembled at Versailles, where so many of their ancestors had been summoned to pay homage to Louis XIV, and proclaimed the German Empire. In form, the new empire closely resembled the recent North German Confederation. It was a federation of 25 nominally sovereign states, presided over by the king of Prussia with the title of German emperor (*Kaiser*). Each state retained its

separate government and issued its own passport. All sent delegates to the upper house of the imperial legislature and elected representatives to the lower one by universal manhood suffrage. As in the North German Confederation, however, the emperor appointed the imperial chancellor (the first occupant of this post was, of course, Bismarck) and controlled the imperial bureaucracy and the army. The divorce of the executive from the legislature prompted the socialist leader William Liebknecht to denounce the new constitution as a mere "fig-leaf of absolutism."[3] Many others had misgivings as well, including William, who was reluctant in the end to merge the proud lineage of Prussia into a mere federal entity. But Bismarck prevailed. Germany was his creation. Forty million strong, with an army that had easily defeated the ranking powers of Europe and an industrial capacity that was rapidly overtaking Britain's, it was at the moment of its birth the most powerful state on the Continent.

BERLIN: A NEW CAPITAL

If all eyes were turned on the new Germany in 1871, the natural focus of attention was the imperial capital of Berlin. The city had grown from a pair of fishing villages that amalgamated in 1307. Over the next century it grew and prospered, trading with the cities of the Hanseatic League. In 1442 the counts of Hohenzollern took advantage of a dispute between Berlin's craft guilds and the patrician elite to assert their own control and built a castle to dominate the city. The burghers rebelled and were subdued only by a force of 600 knights. As a symbol of their subjection, the bear on the city's coat of arms was dropped on all fours and given a chain collar, and the Hohenzollern eagle was fastened to its back. Three hundred years later, in the time of Frederick the Great, Goethe remarked on the independence of Berliners, and when the Hohenzollern dynasty collapsed at the end of World War I, the city removed the eagle from its flag and freed the bear.

Like much of Germany, Berlin had been devastated by the Thirty Years' War and in 1648 had only 7,500 inhabitants. That number had tripled by the time it became a royal capital in 1701; it multiplied tenfold by 1815 to nearly 200,000 and tenfold again to 2.1 million by 1910, with nearly as many more in its sprawling suburbs. Long eclipsed by Vienna, it had drawn abreast of it

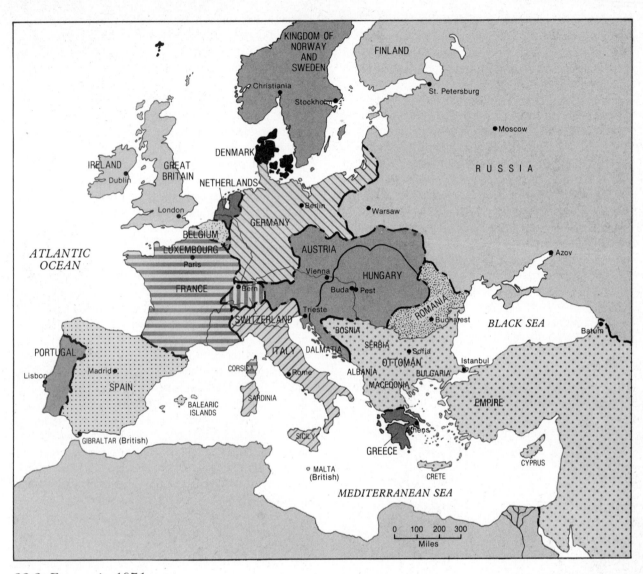

22.2 Europe in 1871

in population by the mid-nineteenth century, and at the moment of German unification, Berlin was the largest German-speaking city in the world.

Despite its relative geographical isolation, Berlin's population was cosmopolitan. Frederick William, the Great Elector, invited Huguenot refugees to settle there after the revocation of the Edict of Nantes in 1685, and within three years, 20 percent of the population was French. Substantial minorities of Belgians, Italians, and Slavs arrived later. The Jews had been driven from Berlin "for all eternity" in 1573, but Frederick William readmitted them a century later, and by the 1870s their

numbers had reached 45,000—nearly as many as in all of France.

King Frederick William I made a garrison town of Berlin in the early eighteenth century, billeting troops in its citizens' homes and widening its streets to accommodate parades, and a century later the poet Heinrich Heine remarked on the number of medals and decorations to be seen even on people wearing civilian dress. But the city was growing more sophisticated as well. Wilhelm von Humboldt established the University of Berlin in 1810, and in the next generation the city attracted many of the major figures of German Romanticism, including the writer E. T. A. Hoffmann, the philosopher Hegel, and the composer Felix Mendelssohn. Berlin began as well to acquire some of its most distinctive features, including the 65-foot-high Brandenburg Gate and the fashionable boulevard of Unter den Linden.

Frederick the Great promoted Berlin's manufactures, but the industrialization of the city began only in the 1830s and 1840s. The first rail track was laid between Berlin and Potsdam in 1838, and by 1846, links had been added to Frankfurt and Hamburg. The city soon acquired a sizable and impoverished proletariat as well. Many of the new workers were migrants from depressed Silesia, whose inhabitants rebelled in 1844. On March 18, 1848, Berlin raised its own revolt, demanding constitutional government and the unification of Germany. When Bismarck unified the country on his own terms in 1871, a victory statue was erected above a 200-foot column in the city's main park, the Tiergarten, flanked with the barrels of captured French cannon; later, a helmeted statue of the chancellor himself was added, facing it. Berlin, like Germany itself, had begun a new imperial career.

EASTERN EUROPE IN TRANSITION

If Austria and Russia did not experience the political upheaval that characterized Western Europe in the decades after 1848, they nonetheless underwent profound changes. Serfdom died out in Austria and was abolished by edict in Russia, although the lot of the peasantry did not notably improve in either country. Austria suffered severe defeats in Italy and Germany, where unification meant the end of long-standing Habsburg influence, and it was forced to grant internal autonomy to Hungary. In Russia, defeat by the Western powers in the Crimean War prompted efforts at modernization, although the framework of tsarist autocracy remained unchanged.

Austria-Hungary: The Formation of the Dual Monarchy

Of all the states of Europe, none had come closer to dissolution in 1848 than the Austrian empire, and for none was the problem of nationalism more perilous.

Austria alone, of all the states of Europe, lacked a single ethnic group that identified with it fully. Germans predominated in the territories of Austria and Bohemia, while Magyars—the descendants of the central Asian invaders of the ninth century—were dominant in Hungary. Both of these groups ruled over indigenous Slavic populations: Czechs and Slovaks in Bohemia; Yugoslavs ("southern Slavs") along the Dalmatian coast and in Hungary and Transylvania, including Serbs, Croats, and Slovenes; Ruthenians and Romanians in Moldavia and Wallachia; and Poles in Galicia. These Slavic groups, which together made up more than half the inhabitants of the empire, had national aspirations of their own. In Italy meanwhile, the Austrians still ruled the province of Lombardy-Venetia.

Austria was saved in 1848 only by the steadiness of its army, Russian aid, and the nerve of the Archduchess Sophia, who had rallied conservative forces behind her eighteen-year-old son, Franz Joseph (1848–1916), who succeeded the Emperor Ferdinand I. The constitution that had been granted under duress in 1849 was abrogated, and the imperial ministry reasserted control, unchecked by a representative assembly or any recognition of civil liberties. The empire was divided into districts administered by German-speaking officials appointed in Vienna, and all organs of self-government were dissolved in Hungary. As in France, education was again placed under the control of the Roman Catholic Church. The objective was to create a powerful, centralized bureaucracy that would modernize the nation's economy without liberalizing its institutions.

The end of Austrian power in Italy prompted the monarchy to offer new concessions at home. The provincial diets were reinstated, and in 1861 a new imperial legislature, the *Reichsrat,* was created. This new body was largely a symbolic entity. Its consent was not required to raise armies or levy taxes, the imperial ministry was not accountable to it, and the emperor was free to make laws on his own authority when it was not in session. Despite minor subsequent reforms, the Habsburg empire was to remain essentially an autocratic state.

Austria's defeat by Prussia in 1866, which eliminated it as a power in both Germany and Italy, forced the monarchy to reach agreement with the Magyars. The *Ausgleich,* or Compromise of 1867, created in effect two separate nations united under one crown, the so-called Dual Monarchy. Franz Joseph was recognized as sovereign in both states, which shared joint ministries for foreign affairs, defense, and finance. The new federal entity was to be known as Austria-Hungary, reflecting the parity of the two partners.

Parliamentary government, Austrian style. Such demonstrations between Czech nationalists and Austrians had virtually paralyzed the legislature by the late nineteenth century. [Austrian National Library, Vienna, Picture Archives]

The Ausgleich gave the Habsburg monarchy another 50 years of life but at the cost of perpetuating not only autocratic but also minority rule, by Germans in Austria and by Magyars in Hungary. The cynicism with which the two official elites regarded their Slavic populations was summed up in a remark by the Austrian prime minister, Count Beust, to his Hungarian counterparts: "You look after your barbarians and we'll look after ours." But the Ausgleich only stimulated Slavic nationalism, particularly among the Czechs, who demanded autonomy for their ancestral homeland of Bohemia. The Magyars vetoed the idea, fearing to encourage their own Slavs, but the Czechs continued to agitate. To make the point forcefully, Czech representatives disrupted debates in the Reichsrat by playing musical instruments, and by the end of the century, electoral politics in Austria had been brought to a virtual standstill.

Czech nationalism was buttressed by a developed economy and an active middle class, but in Hungary, where semifeudal conditions still prevailed, the Slavic minorities made less headway. Here the Magyar aristoc-

racy ruled from estates the size of small nations; in contrast, many peasants farmed only a handful of acres, and others, entirely landless, formed an agrarian proletariat that was removed only in principle from serfdom. The majority, unable now to look to Austria as a countervailing force, turned increasingly to the Slavic states that emerged from the crumbling Ottoman Empire, particularly after 1878, and to the only true Slavic power in Europe, tsarist Russia.

Russia: Reaction and Reform

Russia alone among the major continental powers had experienced no revolutionary disturbance in 1848; on the contrary, Tsar Nicholas I (1825–1855) had crushed rebellion in Hungary on behalf of Austria and in Moldavia and Wallachia on behalf of the Ottoman Empire. Nicholas had faced an officer's revolt at his accession in 1825, the so-called Decembrist uprising, and a far more serious rebellion by his Polish subjects in 1830. His response was to create a police state so pervasive that, as a French

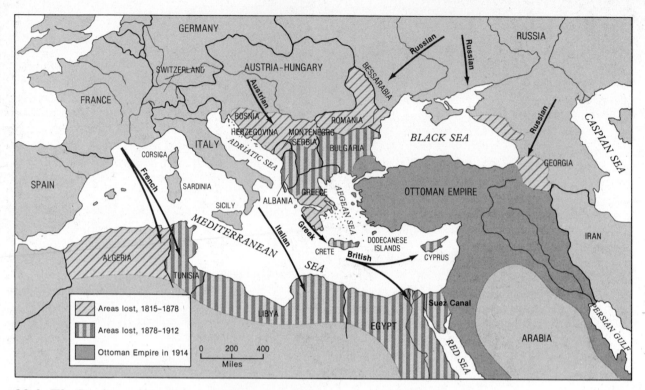

22.3 The Decline of the Ottoman Empire to 1914

visitor remarked in 1839, one did not even dare to die without authorization.

Nonetheless, Russia was not immune from the intellectual currents that stirred its European neighbors. The influential critic and publicist Vissarion Belinsky (1811–1848) argued that Russia's only hope lay in adopting the liberal values of the West. Belinsky's followers were called Westernizers; they were opposed by the Slavophils, who maintained that Russia must seek a path based on its own experience and particularly on the values of Orthodox Christianity. In essence, the contest of Westernizers and Slavophils was a debate between the values of the Enlightenment, with its ideal of a unified human community, and those of Romantic nationalism.

Tsarist autocracy was absolute at home, but its weakness abroad was revealed in the disastrous Crimean War (1853–1856), which had its roots in a rivalry for control of the decaying Ottoman empire. The war was notable as the first to be covered by newspaper correspondents and the first in which women served on the battlefield as nurses. It was also the first in 200 years in which Britain and France, both opposed to Russia, had fought on the same side.

The principal campaign of the war was the siege of Sevastopol, a naval base on the Black Sea, whose fall in August 1855 signaled Russia's defeat. Both sides suffered heavy losses, but the incompetence of the Russian command, the inadequacy of its supply system, and the corruption of its administration were revealed for all to see. Simply put, half a million troops had been lost while failing to repel an invasion force of 100,000 men. At the Peace of Paris (1856), Russia was forced to accept the so-called Pontus clause, which forbade it to maintain a fleet on the Black Sea, even to defend its own shores or shipping. This was tantamount to excluding it from all interest in the Mediterranean or the Middle East.

Nicholas' son, Alexander II (1855–1881), moved swiftly to institute reforms and announced his intention to abolish serfdom. Affecting as it would some 40 percent of the population, it was the most sweeping social decision in Russian's history. It was also a decision that was clearly overdue. Sunk in hopelessness and ignorance, serfs made poor farmers and, as the war had shown, worse soldiers. If, moreover, Russia was to compete with the industrial West, it would need a free labor market. Only an emancipated peasantry could provide this.

To placate the nobility, however, newly freed peasants were required to buy the land they had formerly tiled, an average of nine acres (but in some cases as little as two) being allotted to each peasant. Since the peasants lacked the purchase price, the government advanced it in the form of interest-bearing bonds to the nobility. The peasants were held collectively responsible for repaying the bonds as well as the annual interest. To provide for this, the ancient institution of the peasant commune, or *mir,* was revived. The mir was traditionally a self-governing village community; under the terms of emancipation it was, in effect, a taxing agency responsible for collecting and paying the allotment for its district. Peasants in most parts of Russia were bound to the mir as they had formerly been to the lord's estate, and those defaulting on their share of the communal payment might be required to perform forced labor.

These terms were embodied in the Act of Emancipation (1861). With the supplementary Act of 1866, which affected state-owned peasants, it gave personal independence and legal recognition to 52 million human beings, who were now free, at least in theory, to own property, engage in business, marry at will, and go to court. In fact, if anyone had been truly emancipated, at least in an economic sense, it was the landed gentry. A tiny minority, the gentry continued to own half the arable land of the country while receiving what amounted to government-backed rent on most of the remainder. Members of the gentry were no longer responsible for the maintenance of their former serfs and no longer liable to provide for them in famine, sickness, or old age. These were now the problems of the mir, that is to say, of the peasants themselves.

The Act of Emancipation, so eagerly awaited, thus proved to be for many a crushing disillusionment. The literate elite, or *intelligentsia,* from whom Alexander had hoped to win support for his reform program, was more alienated than ever, and some began to engage in to what a new generation of activists called "propaganda of the deed"—terrorism. In an economic sense, too, emancipation was in many respects a failure. Agricultural productivity remained low, and the mir system precluded the development of a genuine pool of free labor.

The abolition of serfdom brought long-overdue changes to the legal system. A new system of district and provincial councils, called *zemstvos,* was established to oversee public welfare and to keep the peace. Trials were made public, and the worst corporal punishments, such as lashing and branding, were prohibited. For the most part, however, the judicial system remained under the control of the gentry and the nobility, particularly at the local level, where magistrates and justices often judged their former serfs in court.

Alexander also moved to reform the army and the educational system. Press censorship and travel restrictions were relaxed (though by no means removed); by the end of his reign there were more than 500 periodicals and journals in Russia. The universities received charters of self-government, although all deans had to be confirmed by the minister of education, and the rector or senior administrator by the tsar himself. Reform in Russia, however wide-ranging, continued to begin and end at the top.

In 1866 an attempt to assassinate Alexander was made. The attempts continued, by bullet, bomb, and dynamite, until he was blown up in his carriage in March 1881. The pace of reform had long since slowed, and much of the latter part of his reign had been devoted to extending Russian dominion in Eastern Europe, Central Asia, and the Far East. With the tsar's death and the accession of his son, Alexander III (1881–1894), reform was succeeded by reaction.

THE UNITED STATES: THE CRISIS OF UNION

The United States had remained on the periphery of the Western world for the first 40 years of its history. Its rapid expansion and economic growth in the middle years of the nineteenth century had made it an emerging power, but internal division threatened its union; and only a bloody civil war would determine its future direction.

One Nation, Two Cultures

When Alexis de Tocqueville visited the United States in 1830–1831, he found a nation that had made what seemed to him a new beginning. Unencumbered by entrenched class divisions, its future seemed limitless to the French traveler. Tocqueville predicted that the two great continental nations, the United States and Russia, would be the dominant powers of the next century.

The American future did not seem so assured to all observers. Many doubted that a single state could govern so vast an area and expected that, like Europe and South America, it would fragment into several independent powers. But the union proved remarkably adaptable. With the purchase of Louisiana from France in 1803 and of Florida from Spain in 1819, the original size of the country was doubled. The west was added to it in the 1840s by the acquisition of Texas and the Oregon territory and the conquest of the vast provinces of California and New Mexico from Mexico. Meanwhile, millions of new immigrants accommodated themselves to the American way of life, assimilating its values of self-government, self-reliance, and free enterprise. What brought the union to crisis was what contemporaries called the "peculiar institution": slavery.

The Slave Question

Slavery had been the most divisive issue in the country from the beginning. It had been originally confined to the plantation south, but the so-called Missouri Compromise of 1820 provided that each new free state admitted to the union would be matched by the admission of a slave state. This extended slavery into areas where it would compete with free labor, a situation that created bitter antagonism. The territorial acquisitions of the 1840s made the question acute.

The gulf between free and slave labor had created two opposed economies and, in many respects, two opposed societies as well. The South became primarily the furnisher of a single raw material, cotton, while the North diversified into a variety of industrial manufactures. The planter aristocracy of the South, with its quasi-feudal emphasis on valor, honor, and tradition, was mountingly at odds with a North that it saw as ruled by the gods of commerce. The North, for its part, resented the South's assumption of cultural superiority, and the fiery abolitionist William Lloyd Garrison denounced slavery as a covenant with hell. At the same time the success of westward expansion in the 1840s inspired belief in the "manifest destiny" of the United States to rule the continent from sea to sea and to spread the blessings of liberty abroad. Liberty and union thus became entwined in northern thinking, while the South was identified with slavery and sectionalism.

The union slid rapidly toward dissolution in the 1850s. Southerners repudiated the Missouri Compromise, setting off a border war in the Kansas Territory, while in the Dred Scott decision (1857) a southern-dominated Supreme Court declared that Negroes could not be considered citizens. When Abraham Lincoln

Abraham Lincoln with his generals at the battlefield of Antietam. [Brown Brothers]

(1809–1865) was elected president in 1860 as the candidate of the anti-slavery Republican Party, the ten southern states seceded from the union, forming the Confederate States of America.

The Civil War

Lincoln denied the legality of the secession and ordered troops to defend federal territory and property. The civil war that followed (1861–1865) was the bloodiest conflict in the Western world between 1815 and 1914. Six hundred thousand men were killed, and much of the South was devastated. The war and its aftermath remained the dominant political issue in American life for the remainder of the century, and, at least in the South, the war between the states remains embedded in popular memory.

The North's advantages in the war were overwhelming and, in the end, irresistible. The Union states had a combined population of 21 million compared to the 9 million of the Confederacy, of whom 3.5 million were slaves. Since the slaves were not trusted to bear arms, the actual numerical superiority of the North was nearly four to one. Its manufacturing capability was seven times that of the South, and its control of the navy and merchant marine enabled it to blockade the coasts of the Confederacy.

Superior generalship gave the South an advantage early in the war, but with the simultaneous defeat of General Robert E. Lee's army at Gettysburg and the capture of the strategic port of Vicksburg (July 4, 1863), the Confederacy was thrown on the defensive and ground down in a war of attrition. On January 1, 1863, all slaves in the Confederacy were declared free, and in 1866 the Fourteenth Amendment to the Constitution conferred state and federal citizenship on every person born or naturalized within the United States. In the United States, as in Italy and Germany, the nation-state had triumphed over sectional interest and unified by force those who would not be united by agreement.

The postwar era of reconstruction (1865–1877), which began in tragedy with the assassination of Lincoln, sowed new bitterness. The ruined South was exploited by unscrupulous northern entrepreneurs, often screening themselves behind African-American freedmen elected to state office. African-Americans found themselves the victims of a backlash of racial prejudice both in the North and in the South, and with the eventual departure of their northern patrons they were subjected to a regime of coercion, peonage, and legalized discrimination in the South that differed little in most practical respects from their former condition. Not for another century were they to enjoy the legal entitlements of the Fourteenth Amendment, which was chiefly used in the decades after the war to protect not personal rights but the power of corporations. By that time many African-Americans had become a ghettoized underclass in the large cities of the North.

The Civil War marked the triumph not only of the democratic ethos in the United States but also of industrial capitalism. A transcontinental railroad was built with public subsidies. Tariffs—long opposed by the South—were imposed to protect domestic industries, and new banks were chartered with federal assistance. Liberal immigration policies provided the necessary labor. In 1860, despite a tenfold increase in the value of manufactures over the preceding 50 years, the United States was still primarily an agricultural country. By 1900 it was the leading industrial power in the world.

THE JEWS IN THE NINETEENTH-CENTURY WORLD

Nationalism posed a special challenge to the Jews of Europe, who were torn between their desire to maintain a cultural and religious identity and their wish to be accepted as citizens and patriots. Shocked by rejection and persecution, many Jews turned to Zionism, with its goal of a specifically Jewish homeland in Palestine.

A People Without a State

The national heritage of the Jews was older than that of any other people of Europe. Throughout 18 centuries of exile they had never ceased to wait for the messiah who would lead them back to Israel. Several candidates had proclaimed themselves, including Sabbatai Zevi, who in 1666 had led thousands of Jews in a futile attempt to recover the Holy Land.

With the Enlightenment some well-to-do Jews began to leave their Orthodox communities and to venture forth into the Gentile world for the first time since the end of antiquity. Many underwent baptism as a means of facilitating their acceptance by the outside world. At the same time, laws were passed granting Jews civic and political equality in most Western nations between 1780 and 1830.

Because of laws that had prohibited Jews from owning land or practicing trades other than commerce and moneylending, they had become perhaps the most highly urbanized group in Europe. With civil restrictions lifted, they flocked to the larger cities and rapidly became prominent in banking, manufacturing, the arts, and the liberal professions. The great Rothschild banking clan symbolized the emergence of the Jews in European society; one family member was decorated by the pope himself.

As the secular Enlightenment gave way to Romantic nationalism, however, and the concept of a single human community was superseded by that of distinct groups, the Jews were once again looked upon as an alien presence. In Count Gobineau's (1816–1882) *Essay on the Inequality of the Human Races* (1853–1854) the modern doctrine of racism made its first appearance. Gobineau claimed that the so-called Aryan race of Europe had been contaminated by mingling with lesser breeds, including Jews. Historians, anthropologists, and others used the pseudoscientific terms *race* and *people* interchangeably in the late nineteenth century, as if each nationality represented not merely a distinctive cultural group but a separate bloodline or genetic type. From all such groups the Jews, people without a homeland, were necessarily excluded.

Critics of assimilation also came from within the Jewish community. This was naturally to be expected from defenders of Orthodoxy, but the most scathing criticism came from the Jewish left. Karl Marx's "On the Jewish Question" accused Jews of forming a business and financial elite and thus of being among the chief exploiters of the proletariat. A similar disillusionment led Moses Hess (1812–1875) to espouse a new, secular Jewish nationalism in his *Rome and Jerusalem* (1862). Declaring emancipation to be a failure and assimilation a mirage, he called upon Jews to found a modern, socialist commonwealth of their own in Palestine.

THEODOR HERZL
AND THE BIRTH OF MODERN ZIONISM

Hess' call went unheeded for 20 years. The outbreak in 1881 of officially sanctioned pogroms—widespread loot-

ings and massacres in the Jewish communities of southern Russia—led Jewish leaders to reappraise their situation. One consequence was massive emigration; some 3 million Jews left Russia between 1882 and 1914, mostly for the Western hemisphere. But the idea that the Jews could find both security and identity only in their historic homeland awaited the last charismatic figure of nineteenth-century nationalism, Theodor Herzl (1860–1904).

Herzl was born in Budapest of well-to-do parents. He received a law degree from the University of Vienna in 1884 but took up a literary career instead. After marrying Julie Naschauer, he moved to Paris in 1891 as correspondent for the *New Free Press,* Vienna's leading newspaper. Herzl had been inured to the deep-seated anti-Semitism of Austria and Hungary, but he was shocked to find it equally pervasive in the capital of the French Revolution. He read Moses Hess, but his thinking was galvanized by the Dreyfus affair, a scandal involving the purported sale of military secrets to Germany by a Jewish army officer (see Chapter 23). Hard on the heels of this came the election of Karl Lueger as mayor of Vienna on an openly anti-Semitic platform.

In 1896, Herzl published *The Jewish State,* which argued that European anti-Semitism was intractable and called for the establishment of a national homeland in Palestine. The timing of its publication and the campaign he launched to realize his goal made it a sensation. Undaunted by failure to win financial backing from Jewish magnates, he appealed directly for support to the Turkish sultan, the pope, and Emperor William II of Germany. Presenting himself as the self-appointed ambassador of European Jewry, he bluffed his way into the courts of power and created a personal following through sheer boldness, presumption, and zeal. In 1897 he convened in Basel the First Zionist Congress, a name derived from the biblical citadel of Zion in Jerusalem. Its 200 delegates set up a permanent organization, declaring as its objectives the creation of a "publicly guaranteed homeland for the Jewish people in the land of Israel." In his diary, Herzl boasted, "At Basel I founded the Jewish state."

Herzl spent the remainder of his short life nursing his infant organization. Like Hess, he envisioned the new Israel as a socialist community of producer cooperatives in which Jews could shake off the mercantile occupations that centuries of persecution had forced on them and reclaim both their own identity and the soil of their homeland by the labor of their hands.

SUMMARY

The tide of nationalism that surged over the Western world in the mid-nineteenth century was both a response to industrialization and a further stimulus to it. It created two new states in the heart of Europe, Italy and Germany, thus permanently altering the balance of power, while in North America the triumph of the Union paved the way for the rapid emergence of the United States as a world power. It swept away agriculturally based systems of serfdom and slavery in Eastern Europe and the United States that impeded industrial growth, although the residual power of the aristocracy, particularly in Hungary and Russia, kept much of labor in a semiservile condition.

Economic modernization and national unification were accompanied by the demand for liberal institutions, as the systems of control that had served peasant-based societies slowly yielded to the needs of an urban, industrial world. However, neither in the new states of Italy and Germany nor in the older ones of Eastern Europe did representative government take firm root, and Russia remained autocratic. In the United States, democracy was vindicated in battle, while in France, ironically, a republic was imposed in the wake of military defeat.

Nationalism did not always unify. In Italy and Austria-Hungary it exacerbated regional tensions; elsewhere, class antagonisms remained high. The new European powers sought a place in the sun, while peoples who had not yet achieved a territorial state, particularly in the Balkans, demanded self-determination. Finally, national consciousness was accompanied by the growth of racism, which rationalized the subjugation of colonies abroad and of minorities at home. This was an important spur to the last of the nineteenth-century nationalist movements, Zionism.

In all, European nationalism was a complex and powerful phenomenon. It created the nation-state, the basic unit of territorial sovereignty in modern times, redrew the map of the West, and redefined the nature of citizenship. It can be described by, but not reduced to, the emergence of new elites and the requirements of an emerging industrial society. Carried abroad by imperialism, nationalism would transcend the time and circumstances that gave it birth and become one of the shaping forces of the modern world.

Notes

1. Louis L. Snyder, *Roots of German Nationalism* (Bloomington: Indiana University Press, 1978), p. 15.
2. John L. Snell, ed., *The Democratic Movement in Germany, 1789–1914* (Chapel Hill: The University of North Carolina Press, 1976), p. 158.
3. Donald S. Detweiler, *Germany: A Short History* (Carbondale: Southern Illinois University Press, 1976), p. 132.

Suggestions for Further Reading

Avineri, S. *The Making of Modern Zionism: The Intellectual Origins of the Jewish State.* New York: Basic Books, 1981.

Beales, D. *The Risorgimento and the Unification of Italy.* London: Longmans, 1982.

Emmons, T. *The Russian Landed Gentry and the Peasant Emancipation of 1861.* Cambridge: Cambridge University Press, 1968.

Gall, L. *Bismarck: The White Revolutionary.* Boston: Allen & Urwin, 1986.

Hamerow, T. S. *The Social Foundations of German Unification, 1815–1871.* Princeton, N.J.: Princeton University Press, 1969, 1972.

Kaelble, H. *Industrialization and Social Inequality in Nineteenth-Century Europe.* New York: St. Martin's Press, 1986.

Kann, R. A. *The Multinational Empire: Nationalism and National Reform in the Habsburg Monarchy, 1848–1918.* New York: Columbia University Press, 1950.

Kohn, H. *The Idea of Nationalism.* New York: Macmillan, 1944.

Lichtheim, G. *Marxism: A Historical and Critical Study.* New York: Praeger, 1965.

McPherson, J. M. *Battle Cry of Freedom: The Civil War Era.* New York: Oxford University Press, 1988.

Merriman, J. M. *The Agony of the Republic: The Repression of the Left in Revolutionary France, 1848–1851.* New Haven, Conn.: Yale University Press, 1978.

Mosse, W. E. *Alexander II and the Modernization of Russia.* London: English Universities Press, 1958.

Plessis, A. *The Rise and Fall of the Second Empire, 1852–1871.* Cambridge: Cambridge University Press, 1985.

Venturi, F. *Roots of Revolution: A History of the Populist and Socialist Movements in Nineteenth-Century Russia.* Chicago: University of Chicago Press, 1960.

Wright, D. G. *Popular Radicalism: The Working-Class Experience, 1780–1880.* London: Longman, 1988.

23

INDUSTRIAL SOCIETY AND THE LIBERAL ORDER

The second half of the nineteenth century saw the maturation of an industrial society based upon new technology, organized by capitalist enterprise, and dominated by the goals and imperatives of production for profit. Its material output far surpassed that of any previous society, and it created, for the first time on a large scale, a predominantly urban civilization. This meant that the two social groups central to all previous civilizations, those who worked the land and those who owned it, became progressively less significant and ultimately less numerous. Peasants had comprised some 80 percent of the population of preindustrial Europe and comparable proportions in other societies. By the end of the nineteenth century they were less than half the population of the advanced industrial nations, and their numbers fell even more precipitously in the twentieth century.

As urbanization advanced, lord and peasant were replaced as the dominant social categories by capitalist and worker. Although the urban merchant, the urban artisan, and the casual laborer were as old as civilization itself, the capitalist and worker of nineteenth century society were products of the Industrial Revolution. Under the factory system, capitalists controlled the means and provided the arena of production, and workers, owning only their labor, sold it for the wage upon which their subsistence depended. Seldom before had one nominally free class of individuals been so dependent on another for the conditions of its material existence.

This new system was described by a word that came into fashion in the 1860s: *capitalism*. The term *capitalist* did not apply simply to factory owners but also to businessmen, financiers, legal specialists, and corporate shareholders who collectively controlled the means of production and the distribution of socially produced wealth. In the same way, *workers* must be distinguished by skill and trade: there was a great deal of difference between artisans whose specializations were in relatively high demand, workers in small shops, and factory laborers subject to the commands of overseers. In addition, there was an intermediate urban population of shopkeepers, artisans, jobbers, cabmen, and clerks that lived on the fringes of the so-called middle class and was sometimes called the *petty bourgeoisie*. Nonetheless, the existence of two broadly defined strata, "labor" and "capital," was widely recognized. It was generally assumed that the relations between them were antagonistic and could be maintained to the advantage of capital only through vigilant discipline and, where necessary, by force.

With increasing economic organization the lone entrepreneur or family business was more and more replaced by the large corporation, which sought to dominate markets and to control or "integrate" the industrial process from the acquisition of raw materials to the distribution of the finished product. This in turn required the assistance of the liberal state, in theory a neutral arbiter whose function was to maintain a free market but in practice readily responsive to the needs of the business elite. Yet with the expansion of the franchise, labor and socialist parties began to challenge the bourgeois monopoly of political power, subjecting the state to new pressures and demands. As the century drew to a close, socialists debated whether the achievement of their goals lay in peaceful succession through the ballot box or in the violent overthrow of the capitalist order.

The transformation of society also redefined the roles of women. The feminist revolt against the constraints of bourgeois culture and its demands for political rights and representation posed for the first time the issue of gender equality. At the same time the naturalistic novel mirrored the conflicts and aspirations of nineteenth-century society for a wide public, offering it both a vehicle for self-examination and a forum for debate.

THE SECOND INDUSTRIAL REVOLUTION

The first phase of the Industrial Revolution, lasting roughly to 1850, had been primarily concerned with the development of a pivotal industry, textiles; the replacement of wood as a fuel and as a material by coal and iron; the extension of transport and communications by railway and telegraph; and the introduction of the factory system. It had been largely accomplished by the application of existing knowledge to the problems of technology, engineering, and management. The second phase involved the coordination of science and industry in the development of new alloys and metals such as steel and aluminum; new products such as plastics, fabrics, and dyes; and new energy sources, including gas and petroleum. Industrial organization too became more complex as business elites strove to exert unified control over production, distribution, and labor.

Monopoly Capitalism and the Rise of Big Business

Until well into the nineteenth century most industrial enterprises were small in scale. The majority were owned by a single individual or a small group of partners, who ran the enterprise by and for themselves, and employed at most a few dozens or hundreds of workers. Most capital came from the owners themselves, from the profits of business, or through borrowing from family, friends, acquaintances, or, for short-term purposes, banks. Major plant expansion was, for most, out of reach.

Building utilities such as rail and telegraph lines or gas and water supplies required much larger capital outlays. These were provided in part by government funds and in part by investment banking, which involved the sale of stock and bonds by lending institutions as a means to accumulate capital. Such capital was then available for large-scale financing and long-term loans.

An alternative to banks was the joint-stock company, which could raise capital by selling profit shares, or stock. Investors demanded security and liquidity for purchasing such shares. These demands were met by external auditing, by limited liability, which provided that the investor could not be held responsible for losses beyond the face value of the stock, and by the formation of stock exchanges on which securities were bought and sold. Such exchanges grew rapidly after 1840.

The rise of businesses financed by outside investors transformed industrial enterprises from small family partnerships into public *corporations,* legal entities enjoying limited liability and access to stock exchanges. Joint-stock companies had long been chartered by governments, but what had been essentially personal compacts between monarchs and entrepreneurs now became routine, standardized acts of licensing. As governments themselves became more bureaucratic, so corporations too, whose "ownership" shifted with each day's transactions on the stock market, reflected the depersonalization of a society increasingly defined by the common denominator of mobile capital.

As corporate ownership became more diffuse, actual management devolved, as in government bureaucracies, upon a new elite: the executives. Executives might well be shareholders themselves, but their power derived from their operational control of the corporation. The structures of governments and corporations under industrial capitalism thus came to resemble one another, with an inner core of decisionmakers theoretically responsible to the "voters," whether the shareholders of the corporation or the citizens of a nation, but in practice largely removed from scrutiny. As time progressed, this structural resemblance revealed a convergence of interest as well. Big business and big government grew together, their senior personnel ultimately becoming interchangeable, as in the "revolving-door" relationships between regulated industries and their government agencies or military contractors and their purchasers.

The advent of the corporation stimulated the growth of large-scale enterprises. In the United States the average capital value of each manufacturing plant in the 13 leading industries multiplied 39-fold between 1850 and 1910. By 1914, nearly half the industrial production of

This painting by Otto Bollhagen depicts the interior of the great Krupp steelworks at Essen, Germany. Krupp was one of the largest firms in Germany's dynamic industrial sector. [Courtesy Fried. Krupp GmbH]

the country came from businesses with an annual output of more than $1 million; by 1929 it was more than two-thirds.

The Age of Trusts

The consolidation of capital in large firms—a few often dominating an industry—replicated the process seen earlier in British agriculture when small farms were squeezed out by big estates. Consolidation fostered combination, as large firms not only absorbed smaller ones but also combined with each other through mergers, trade agreements, or holding companies. The phenomenon of industrial combination created industrywide monopolies—called "trusts" in the United States, "amalgamations" in Britain, and "cartels" in Germany—that had become the dominant factor in economic life by the early twentieth century.

Such trusts achieved what was called *horizontal integration,* or control of an entire market. They also frequently sought *vertical integration,* or control of the entire productive process from the acquisition of raw materials to the final distribution point; thus, steel manufacturers bought up coal and iron mines and chemical plants, and oil companies built their own refineries. The greatest empires, however, were built through control not of individual industries but of the

finance capital that was the lifeblood of every industry. In 1933 the investment house of J. S. Morgan (London) held 167 directorships among 38 industrial corporations, 15 banks and trust companies, 12 holding companies (including 5 public utilities), 10 railroads, 6 insurance companies, and several miscellaneous enterprises.

The most obvious effects of monopolies were the fixing of prices and wages and the elimination of competition. In theory the role of the liberal state was to prevent this and to keep markets free. Antitrust legislation had little impact, however. The great corporations and their lawyers could outlast litigators and find or buy sympathetic judges and legislators to legitimate their practices. The cozy relationship between big business and government in the United States was epitomized by President Calvin Coolidge (1925–1929), who declared, "The business of America is business."

Not all states regarded it as their business to regulate corporations. In Germany, where cartels were legal, their number rose from 400 in 1906 to 2,400 by 1932. In no other country was monopoly capital so clearly dominant, and nowhere else were banking and industry so closely integrated. As a result, German business was able to coordinate efforts to capture foreign markets as well as to control domestic ones. To be sure, some of the largest enterprises in Germany were still family concerns, such as the famous Krupp armament works in

Essen; similarly, the Rockefellers controlled the Standard Oil trust in the United States. But family connections only linked the great industrial magnates more strongly; like Renaissance princes, they dealt with each other above the heads of governments, creating a new world order that was safe for profits. Their admirers called them captains of industry; their detractors, the robber barons.

The Integration of Labor

The role of labor changed too with advances in mechanization. Even unskilled workers now needed at least basic literacy to understand written instructions on the job, while larger firms required a growing number of administrative personnel—clerks, typists, and supervisors—who were recruited from the working class. The result was the development of public education systems, which taught both fundamental literacy skills and the discipline necessary to sustain the tedium of factory and office labor. By 1900, 99.95% of adult Germans were literate.

As the size of firms and the scale of their output increased, productivity became critical to industrial profits. Time-and-motion studies were conducted to break down and reorder work activities for maximum efficiency. In this way the last bit of autonomy on the production line, the rhythm of labor itself, was to be removed, and workers were to be made as far as possible indistinguishable from their tools. This system was brought to perfection on the assembly line. Henry Ford (1863–1947), the American automobile manufacturer who introduced the assembly line, had no scruple about its dehumanizing effects; rather, he considered it a blessing for his workers, whom he believed craved nothing more than mindless tasks that relieved them of the burden of thought and judgment.

The greatest threat to management control of labor was unionization. Unions gained legal status in most industrialized countries in the 1870s and 1880s, but business was unremittingly hostile, often making pledges not to join unions a condition of employment, engaging in lockouts to dry up strike funds, and resorting to violence when other methods failed. Confrontational tactics proved unsuccessful in the long run, however, and by 1919, nearly 40 million workers in Europe and the United States had been organized. Some businesses offered shorter hours, higher pay, and other benefits to ward off unions; others organized so-called company unions, nominal bargaining units dominated by employers.

THE NEW SOCIAL ORDER

The sweeping changes in industrial organization and the relationship between labor, industry, and the state created new social relations that affected people at every level and occupation. The ruling elite became more homogeneous as landed capital flowed into business enterprise, while the proletariat absorbed more and more peasants and independent artisans into itself. These changes finally left no one unaffected, whether in town or country or in greater or less industrialized nations.

Bourgeoisie and Aristocracy: A Merging Elite

The abolition of recognized orders by the French Revolution of 1789 had not, as some republican enthusiasts hoped, created a society of equals; but it did mark the end of unchallenged aristocratic predominance. The success of citizen armies in the French Revolution had destroyed the myth of aristocratic command, and the Industrial Revolution had shifted the locus of wealth from the land to the factory, the countinghouse, and the quay. Nonetheless, the European aristocracy was by no means spent as a social or political force. In Britain the titular aristocracy retained its prestige, while the landed gentry invested in capital ventures. In France, where land held much of its former value until late in the nineteenth century, the aristocracy maintained its social position through republican and Napoleonic times alike. In Germany and Austria-Hungary the Junker and Magyar aristocracies ruled their estates much as of old, and the Russian nobility retained its economic and political power down to 1917.

It would thus be a great mistake to regard the aristocracy as having been "replaced" by the bourgeoisie. Rather, we should think in terms of a merging elite, in which the aristocracy availed itself of new investment opportunities and the bourgeoisie bought respectability by acquiring aristocratic business partners. This interaction between landed and commercial wealth was far from new, of course, but with the growth of cities and the decline of the peasantry the bourgeoisie became the dominant partners in the relationship. It was they who ran the municipal councils in the towns and cities where the majority of the population now lived in western Europe, and they whose interests and votes had begun to prevail in representative assemblies.

The Industrial Bourgeoisie

The bourgeoisie, who comprised roughly 15 percent of the population of the industrial West, ranged in wealth and status from "captains" of industry to the professional class of lawyers, doctors, clerics, and artists, and finally the "petty" bourgeoisie of small shopowners and artisans. What unified these groups was not so much the amount of their income but its source. Bourgeois income was derived from the earnings of capital through profit, interest, and rent; and the bourgeoisie as a whole may be defined most simply as the possessors of capital. Never before, indeed, had capital—defined mostly broadly by Karl Marx as the means of production—been so nearly monopolized by a single social group in the West. In contrast, a growing segment of the population possessed no capital resources of any kind. Peasants, at least the more fortunate of them, had owned their own lands, cottages, and livestock; artisans had possessed their own tools. The new urban working classes owned, beyond a few personal possessions, nothing but their own labor.

The Urban Middle Classes

As the activities of the corporations became increasingly varied and complex, so too they became physically distinct from the actual worksite. With the development of industrial discipline as well as communicative tools such as the telephone and the typewriter, the manager's presence was no longer required at the point of production. The center of the modern industrial city became increasingly dominated by a skyline of great office buildings, retail outlets, and banks, while the warehouse and the factory receded into an urban limbo bounded by rail, trolley, and other transport networks. In short, the city was more and more a place of work and commerce rather than of residence, at least for the business classes. The fashionable rich had often lived in proximity to the poor, but the development of commuter rail lines spawned new suburban rings to house the bourgeoisie, safe from the crowding, violence, and industrial pollution that plagued much of the "inner" city.

Thus it was that the spheres of work and home, once separated by no more than a wall, became physically and psychologically distinct. "Going to work," for the business executive, became an important and time-consuming part of the day; it was also a ritual journey that took him from the security of hearth and home to the harshly competitive demands of the workplace. This led to the cult of domesticity that characterized late nine-teenth-century bourgeois living. Carpets and curtains softened the step and screened out the world, deep chairs offered relaxation, and ornate furnishings provided a sense of permanence and solidity. Servants, often with their own quarters, kept this miniature world functioning smoothly. Its triumph, however, was the bourgeois woman, who as wife and mother was the living symbol of successful accumulation.

Workers and Peasants

The nineteenth-century working class may be defined as those persons who performed nonagricultural manual or clerical labor for wage hire. The pervasive experiences of this vast labor army were rootlessness and insecurity. Most of the great modern cities were both built and populated by people who had not been born in them. The cultural shock of migration—whether from farm to city, country to country, or continent to continent—only compounded the insecurity of the laborer's position. Often paid on an hourly or piece goods basis, many workers did not know at the beginning of a week how much money they would earn or whether they would still be employed at the end of it. In their forties if unskilled or perhaps their fifties if skilled, they would no longer be able to do a full day's work or compete with younger laborers. Without a pension or social security and with few if any savings, they faced penury and dependence. Should they fall ill or become disabled, there was no compensation or insurance. Poor relief meant in most cases the workhouse, charity was haphazard, and community had vanished with the rural village.

Even while employed, approximately half the nine-teenth-century work force lived in poverty, and almost all workers could expect to end their days as paupers. After 1850, general prosperity brought a gradual improvement in health and living standards, although the disparity between bourgeois and working-class incomes continued to increase. By the end of the century, at least the most skilled workers might expect to retire to the modest comfort of a cottage and garden. This was the dream of "respectability" cherished by many a worker's wife; but genuine access to middle-class life was, for most, an illusion. In dress, manner, appearance, gait, and speech, in their worlds of recreation, socialization, and religion no less than of work, and even in their physical size (children of the rich in England were five inches taller than those of the poor on average, largely because of superior nutrition), the classes remained divided by a generally impassable gulf.

The only avenue of upward mobility for the working class was into the new white-collar world of office and laboratory workers, salespeople, teachers, and other service personnel created by the growth of large industry. Such people, who became a substantial proportion of the urban population by the late nineteenth century and formed a majority by the late twentieth, were anxious to distance themselves from mere manual laborers, although, like them, they worked long hours, experienced frequent turnover, and, in comparison with skilled factory labor, often earned less money.

The peasantry was a dwindling but still important part of the social order. The railroad and the threshing machine had brought important changes to peasant life, the former opening up distant markets and the latter speeding up the harvest and relieving millions from the toil of sorting wheat. Small family farms were still common in France, Germany, and Austria-Hungary, while in Spain, Italy, and East Prussia the majority of peasants were landless, working as day laborers on great estates. Often, small farming enclaves survived on the outskirts of large cities, where peasants brought their produce directly to market and mingled with the lower classes, with whom they often still shared a common dialect and outlook. In more isolated hamlets, particularly in southern Europe, peasants continued to insist on their traditional identities. Rural Greeks and Italians referred to fellow peasants from other regions as "Christians" but lumped town-dwellers as well as people from other countries together as "foreigners." When student radicals fanned out into the Russian countryside in the 1870s to proselytize among the *narod* ("people"), the peasants frequently stoned them and turned them over to the police. On the other hand, the landless agricultural proletariat of western Europe was often susceptible to radical ideas.

Whereas the first industrial workers had often been forcibly recruited by enclosure, opportunity now beckoned the rural populations of Europe toward the city, thus hastening the breakup of traditional peasant society. Even unskilled workers could hope to earn twice the income of most peasants, and a steady stream of young adults left the countryside. When there were too few young men for farmwork and too few young women to provide wives for them, villages died. Where agriculture could still be made profitable, outside interests bought and worked the land using migrant labor. Only in eastern Europe did peasant society survive in more or less traditional forms until the imposition of Communist regimes in the late 1940s.

The Urban Setting

By 1900 much of the countryside of the advanced industrial nations had been emptied out, and city life was now the norm. By rail, as once by cart and wagon, the produce of the country was shipped to great urban markets. Paved streets and sidewalks, water and sewage mains, and gas, electric, and telephone lines facilitated transport, communication, and commerce; improved housing; and raised health standards. This new infrastructure, which by the early twentieth century covered thoroughfares with a network of iron trolley rails and residential streets with a forest of telephone poles, gave the city itself the look of a technological prodigy, a work of machine art.

At the same time the city accentuated class differences. The 85 miles of new streets that Baron Haussmann had given Paris were lined with the spacious homes and fashionable shops of the rich, whose mansions also bordered the newly designed Central Park in New York and the great circular avenue of the Ringstrasse in Vienna. These splendid arteries were filled out with grand public buildings and monuments, department stores, and cultural venues. Reinforced concrete and steel and other advances in construction made possible soaring monuments such as the New York skyscrapers and the Eiffel Tower in Paris, which dwarfed the medieval cathedrals of older cities.

The laboring poor, on the other hand, found themselves squeezed into progressively smaller space as their numbers increased and the value of urban real estate rose. On New York's Lower East Side, population density reached the beehive level of 520 people per acre. Much working-class housing was hastily thrown together in the form of tenements—rent barracks as they were called in Germany—or put up by small contractors. In one district of Vienna, only four persons in 100 had rooms of their own in 1910. Casual or transient laborers were frequently lodged in dormitory-style "flophouses," while more settled single workers often resided in boardinghouses with seven or eight occupants each. Perhaps no other generation of Europeans was more uprooted and lonely than the mass of those who lived between 1870 and 1914. Millions endured solitary lives, and even the worker who had a room in the home of a working-class family was treated as an outsider and forced to find his meals and companionship elsewhere.

These conditions and their attendant ills—crimes of battery and theft, alcoholism, prostitution, child abandonment, and general alienation—produced a variety of responses. Social crusaders such as the American Jacob Riis (1849–1914) sought to publicize the miseries of slum life, and temperance societies, church organizations, and private philanthropies tried to inculcate middle-class virtues among the poor. With the coming of public education, public health regulation, and the beginnings of social insurance the management of poverty, or at least its effects, became a task of the state.

The size, congestion, and squalor of the modern city prompted first suburban flight and then reform. The Englishman Ebenezer Howard (1850–1928) decried the bourgeois separation of home and work, proposing instead the creation of self-contained communities surrounded by green belts. For others the new possibilities afforded by lighter, more tensile building materials and advances in structural design stimulated utopian visions of the city as the new natural habitat of humankind. Inevitably, proposals for new kinds of cities were also blueprints for social engineering. The influential French architect Le Corbusier (Charles Édouard Jeanneret, 1887–1965) proposed giant vertical apartment complexes, raised on stilts, in which one could live an entirely self-contained life, including shopping, working, and recreational areas, without ever descending to the street. Le Corbusier spoke enthusiastically of the "supreme pleasure of working for the collective," and his beehive concept of the city clearly lent itself to statist if not totalitarian visions of social organization.

No one more clearly or boldly grasped the implications of industrial society for the future of the city—and the city itself as the supreme expression of that society—than the Scots environmentalist Patrick Geddes (1854–1932). Geddes maintained that the capitalist economic regime, with its fixation on production, consumption, and profit as ends in themselves regardless of social need or environmental cost, reflected preindustrial conditions of scarcity rather than modern realities and that the huge cities it had spawned, for which he coined the term "megalopolis," were themselves crazed machines that devoured their inhabitants and despoiled the earth. Unlike his fellow urbanologists, however, Geddes offered no futuristic blueprints or grandiose schemes of social reconstruction. Instead, he pleaded for planning based on awareness of history and tradition, social cooperation, and respect for the earth.

BARCELONA AND THE MODERN TEMPER

One of the most successful examples of late nineteenth-century urban renewal and modernist experimentation was Barcelona, a city of over 500,000 people in the Catalan region of northeast Spain. Barcelona's bourgeois

The highly original talent of the Barcelona architect Antonio Gaudí is seen here in a photograph of the Casa Milá, an apartment house completed in 1910. [Vanni/Art Resource, New York]

elite, proud of both the city's modern prosperity and its heritage as the historic capital of Catalonia, was determined to make it a European showcase. A master plan adopted in 1859—one of the first to govern a modern city—proposed to expand it along a grid pattern, bisected by diagonal avenues and broken up with extensive parks and gardens. In 1888 the city held its first international fair, which stimulated the development of a new building style, the *modernista*. Modernista blended the varied historical traditions of Barcelona with the highly ornamented Art Nouveau style of the 1890s to produce some of the most challenging urban architecture in Europe. Much of it was an exuberant celebration of the material progress of the nineteenth century, but the movement's greatest figure, Antonio Gaudí (1852–1926), evoked the intense religiosity still embedded in Iberian culture, most notably in his still-unfinished Church of the Holy Family.

Modernista was not limited to architecture, and Barcelona at the turn of the century was home to a remarkable flowering of the fine and decorative arts. The three greatest Spanish painters of the twentieth century, Pablo Picasso (1881–1973), Joan Miró (1893–1983)), and Salvador Dalí (1904–1989), all began their careers in Barcelona. No less brilliant was the city's musical life, centered on the pianist-composers Isaac Albéniz (1860–1909) and Enrique Granados (1867–1916) and the great cellist Pablo Casals (1876–1973). The revival of the Catalan language produced a literary and theatrical renaissance, and new schools were founded to promote it.

As so often happens, artistic excellence was linked to political ferment. The demands of Barcelona's new proletariat, combined with a trade depression following the Spanish-American War of 1898, led to a wave of strikes and protests, culminating in violent anticolonial demonstrations in 1909 that left 116 dead. Despite attempts at repression, the labor movement, with its deep roots in the city's tradition of craft guilds and fraternities, continued to grow, becoming the most radical and militant in Europe.

WOMEN AND SOCIETY

In the West as elsewhere, women had hitherto been defined largely by their reproductive function and particularly by their ability to reproduce males. High birth rates were generally offset by high mortality, and where substantial gains in population accrued there were eventual subsistence crises, as in early fourteenth-century Europe and mid-nineteenth-century China. Thomas Malthus had predicted another such crisis in Europe at the end of the eighteenth century. But the fourfold rise in European population between 1750 and 1900 had been actually sustained in spite of a decline in the agricultural work force.

This had two profound consequences. It meant that population maintenance could be achieved with a far lower birth rate (since decreased mortality largely accounted for the demographic surge); it meant, too, that urban women, freed from the necessity of frequent childbearing, were no longer tied to the home. City life offered other inducements to lower birth rates as well. The introduction of child labor laws and of compulsory education meant that children had to be nurtured longer and at greater expense; a large family meant, for all but the very wealthy, a lower standard of living. After 1875, birth rates steadily declined throughout the Western world. The phenomenon coincided with the attempt to redefine the social role of women and the rise of the mass movement for gender equality known as feminism.

The Bourgeois Ideal

Class differences sharply affected the consequences of industrialization, urbanization, and declining child mortality rates for women. For the poor, such differences often meant regimented labor in factories and sweatshops or, at best, domestic service in the homes of others. Among the well-to-do bourgeoisie they meant just the reverse: lives of boredom, frustration, and triviality. The bourgeois woman of preindustrial times had worked beside her husband in shop or business and often managed it in his absence, illness, or death. The separation of home and business brought about by the new industrial organization of factory and office left her as the largely ornamental mistress of a household run by servants. At the lower level of the clerical and professional classes, too, the ideal of the "housewife" was born, whose function was to provide a comfortable environment for her breadwinner. At both upper and lower levels of the bourgeoisie (the latter now broadly referred to as "the middle classes," though often distinguished from the proletariat only by the performance of white-collar rather than manual labor) the feminine ideal was one of providing comfort. Women were seen, and were encouraged to see themselves, as too delicate and sensitive for the brutal world of work outside the home.

Fashion played its role as well, for respectable dress meant confinement in whalebone stays, corsets, and bustles that restricted movement and made physical exertion impossible.

The social control of bourgeois women was anchored in marriage and the cult of domesticity that accompanied it. The bourgeois woman was raised for marriage, since no independent station was available to her. The desperate status of the spinster was exemplified by the annual arrival of boatloads of unwed Englishwomen in British India; those who failed to find husbands were shipped back home as "returned empties." At the same time that women were taught to regard marriage as their destiny, however, they were taught to experience no sexual pleasure from their husbands. One physician wrote confidently that women embrace their husbands "without a particle of sex desire." It would be rash to assume that such a statement described most actual behavior. But it encouraged a double standard that enjoined fidelity on women while men sought satisfaction of their "natural" needs with prostitutes recruited from the lower orders. Sex, like work, was increasingly divorced from the bourgeois household.

Working Women

If the condition of the bourgeois woman was one of inhibition, that of her working-class counterpart was one of exploitation. Women of the lower orders were fully expected to work, at least until marriage, and they filled the greater part of the work force in the clothing, textile, and food processing industries. Many were also employed in domestic service, although with the shrinking size of the bourgeois household the serving class contracted too. Others became nurses, telephone operators, and office workers; by World War I, one-third of all clerks were women. The spread of elementary education opened up teaching as an occupation that, since it could be looked upon as an extension of the household care of children, was respectable enough to employ women of the "middle classes." Women's work was uniformly ill-paid, and at marriage women were conscripted into the unpaid labor force of housekeeping, although many working-class wives continued to make money through such domestically related occupations as laundering and taking in boarders.

For working-class women, marriage was a matter of economic necessity. Few if any jobs paid women a living wage; it was assumed that males would support them. The notion of an economically independent woman seemed dangerous if not absurd, and lacking not only citizen rights but until late in the nineteenth century most property rights as well, women were neither legally nor politically in a position to emancipate themselves. Quite literally for most the only "independent" occupation for a woman was prostitution, and it was thus no coincidence that the first demands for female economic independence were identified with immorality. Working-class women were spared the double standard of bourgeois sexual mores, though they paid its price in brothels and behind domestic stairwells. If they remained nearly as ignorant of their bodies as their bourgeois sisters, they were considerably more experienced; premarital sex was common, and with the sharp decline in churchgoing in the late nineteenth century there was, in the words of a contemporary observer, "seldom a trace of consciousness that it can be looked upon as sin."

The Rise of Feminism

The movement for women's rights had grown slowly through the middle decades of the nineteenth century. One of the first legal victories won by organized feminism was in the United States, with the passage of a Married Woman's Property Bill by the New York State Legislature in 1848. That same year, a Women's Rights Convention was held at Seneca, New York, which issued a Declaration of Sentiments that stated, "We hold these truths to be self-evident, that all men *and women* are created equal." Subsequent conventions led by Elizabeth Cady Stanton (1815–1902) and Susan B. Anthony (1820–1906) agitated for the right of women to collect their own wages, to sue in courts, to retain custody of their children, and to inherit their husbands' property.

The demands of these pioneer feminists were met with stiff resistance. In 1871 *The Saturday Review* denounced the demand for women's votes as subversive of all moral and family values. The American historian Francis Parkman, conjuring up the image of bloodthirsty female mobs in the French Revolution, contemplated with horror the idea of "the most impulsive and excitable half of humanity" having "an equal voice in the making of laws."

By the 1870s, however, the "woman question" was occupying a prominent place on the social agenda. With Gustave Flaubert's (1821–1880) *Madame Bovary* (1857) and Leo Tolstoy's (1828–1910) *Anna Karenina* (1877), novels whose heroines are driven to adultery and suicide by loveless marriages, fiction took up the plight of the bourgeois woman; these works, however, still implied that the wage of sin was death. The great Norwegian dramatist Henrik Ibsen (1828–1906) shocked audiences with *A Doll's House* (1879), whose heroine, Nora Helmer, walks out on both husband and children to find her own identity.

Despite entrenched patriarchal attitudes, the economic realities of late nineteenth-century Western society encouraged emancipation. With fewer children, fewer servants, and husbands away at work, bourgeois women gained control of the family purse, thus becoming the objects of advertising. At the same time the maintenance of unwed daughters was an increasing financial strain on the less affluent bourgeoisie, while the surge of new jobs for women in the service sector provided respectable employment. Working and shopping made it possible for women to appear in public unchaperoned, and motorized transportation enabled them to escape the prying eyes of neighbors and relatives. A new emphasis on sport, recreation, and leisure opened up opportunities for young men and women to meet; the turn of the century vogue for hiking, cycling, and mountaineering, no less than for mixed bathing and ballroom dancing, reflected this.

Feminists found allies among some socialists, who welcomed them as comrades and provided them with a wider frame of reference; many were influenced by Friedrich Engels' *The Origin of the Family, Private Property and the State* (1884), which argued that monogamy was based on the sexual ownership of females necessary to establish male lineage. Seen in this fashion, the family was not the fulfillment of a woman's purpose but of her enslavement to men, and monogamy was an institution of oppression. Women, whose unique labor function was reproduction, were therefore the first exploited workers, and their liberation was bound up with that of the proletariat as a whole.

The feminist crusade advanced along many fronts in the late nineteenth century—for legal majority and property rights, divorce, birth limitation, access to higher education and the professions, as well as moral reform and child welfare—but the touchstone issue of the women's movement after 1860 was the right to vote. A National Society for Women's Suffrage was established in Britain in 1867, and a similar organization was founded in the United States the following year. The struggle was protracted; although women won the right to vote in national elections in New Zealand in 1893 and in Australia in 1902, only Finland (1907) and Norway (1913) followed suit before World War I.

European feminists became increasingly militant in the early twentieth century. In Britain, Emmeline Pankhurst (1858–1928) led mass marches and disrupted political meetings; when arrested, she and her followers rejected bail and went on hunger strikes. Many feminists refused to pay taxes and, from 1911, began systematic campaigns against public property, smashing windows, burning railway carriages, and digging up golf courses. Violence spread to the Unites States, where militants set "watch fires" outside the White House and burned President Woodrow Wilson in effigy. Women demonstrators were killed, and an Englishwoman, Emily Davison, threw herself under the king's horse at Epsom Derby in 1913.

Women did have the support of male feminists such as John Stuart Mill (1806–1873), author of *The Subjection of Women* (1869). But many found that even their spouses and socialist colleagues gave only lip service to their cause. As Emmeline Pankhurst noted, "Most of us who were married found that 'Votes for Women' were of less interest to our husbands than their own dinners. They simply could not understand why we made such a fuss about it."[1]

THE LIBERAL ORDER IN POLITICS

Liberalism was the demand that the eighteenth- and nineteenth-century bourgeoisie made on the social order. It encompassed a wide range of political and philosophic objectives, from the securing of individual rights and civil equality to free trade and parliamentary government. Between 1830 and 1870 it established itself ideologically everywhere in Europe with the exception of the Ottoman Empire and Russia.

In its earliest form, liberalism was the ideology of the preindustrial bourgeoisie. Derived from the thought of John Locke and Adam Smith, it contended that natural economic laws governed the marketplace, much as physical ones did the material world. In contrast to the prevailing doctrine of mercantilism, which emphasized government regulation of the economy, its counsel to the state was "laissez faire" ("let it be"). The state's only legitimate economic function, it held, was to maintain the integrity of the market against hoarders and monopolists who upset its natural, self-regulating balance. A free economy would foster growth by permitting capital to seek profit opportunities and respond to market demands with maximum flexibility. In a sense, economic liberalism was hostile to the very idea of the state; at best it was a necessary evil, and at worst it was a drain upon capital and a barrier to enterprise.

In practice, early or "classical" liberalism tolerated and even welcomed intrusion by the state, provided that it maximized the advantages of capital. But the coming of industrialization required a far more active and interventionist state. Only the state could undertake the global economic tasks necessary for modern capital accumulation: to expropriate socially idle capital; to consolidate inefficient productive units and ensure a mobile labor supply; to provide the education required by a modern labor force; to facilitate and protect capital transfers by commercial law codes; to provide large-scale transport and communications systems; to help widen markets and provide access to natural resources and cheap labor through imperial conquest, and finally—since for all these reasons the Western economy was increasingly organized on the basis of nation-states—to maintain national competitive advantage through protective tariffs, a patent system, and, where necessary, war. Without ceasing to pay homage to the virtues of the free market, mature liberal doctrine accommodated itself to these realities of industrial capitalism.

Liberal political ideology exhibited a similar flexibility. In theory, liberalism demanded popular sovereignty and civil equality, positing, in the words of the British philosopher Jeremy Bentham (1748–1832), "the greatest good for the greatest number"; in fact, liberal regimes extended the franchise and accepted social legislation only under duress. The dangers inherent in a liberalism that lived up to its premises were clear enough. The working classes were a numerical majority in advanced industrial societies; for bourgeois elites to permit them to become an electoral majority was to run the risk of dispossession. The French Revolution avowed the principle of universal manhood suffrage but at once retreated from it in practice. The British Parliament had expanded the electorate from 4 to 6 percent of the population only under severe duress in 1832, and not until 1884 were most working-class men enfranchised. Nineteenth-century liberals seemed to fear nothing so much as democracy, and it was left, ironically, to the antiliberal Bismarck to introduce permanent universal manhood suffrage to Europe.

In a famous remark, Marx described the state as the executive committee of the bourgeoisie. Although it was clear that liberal regimes served the bourgeoisie, however, the interests of capital and the state were not wholly identical. Ideally, capital knew no political boundaries and no law but profit. National barriers meant restrictions on markets and trade, inefficiency and duplication, and the ultimate business inconvenience, war. Capitalism, in short, was inherently transnational in character, a point made in the modern world by the growth of the multinational corporation.

The state had the further dilemma of legitimacy. It was obliged not only to govern all its citizens, including economically redundant ones but to do so with their at least theoretical consent. The state was also taxed with responsibility for dealing with the social and environmental consequences of capitalism, including exacerbated poverty, crime, disease, pollution, and unemployment. This led it to a variety of interventions, including factory and child labor legislation, public health measures, and public assistance. As the electorate expanded, moreover, it was compelled to respond to new and ever-widening constituencies. The regimes of virtually every Western state exhibited the pressure of these circumstances in the late nineteenth century.

Victorian Britain

The long reign of Queen Victoria (1837–1901) marked the climax of the first Industrial Revolution and the high-water mark of the British Empire, the largest in history. While Britain dominated much of the world, however, the rule of its elite was challenged at home. The Reform Bill of 1832, despite the agitation that surrounded it, was in large part a symbolic contest between the aristocracy and the bourgeoisie. In its wake, however, came the Owenite labor agitation of 1833–1834 (see Chapter 20) and, in the decade after 1838, Chartism. The People's Charter was a six-point program adopted by the London Workingmen's Association, including universal male suffrage, electoral districts apportioned by population, annual general elections, the secret ballot, the removal of the property qualification for members of Parliament, and payment of wages while they served. The Chartists impressively organized a series of open-air meetings and petitions; the third and last, which claimed 6 million signatures and probably contained at least half that many, took several cabs to carry. It represented 20–25 percent of the entire adult population and four to five times the size of the franchise that had elected the House of Commons, but the Commons rejected it in 1848 by a vote of 287–49. There was fear of insurrection, and a sizable military force was assembled under the aged duke of Wellington to protect order. But the threat soon receded, and the movement with it. As one commander remarked, "We have the physical force, not they. . . . Poor men! How little they know of physical force."

The failure of the Chartists contrasted with the efforts of a smaller but far more potent lobby, the Anti–Corn

Queen Victoria (1837–1901) of Great Britain. Dressed modestly in black, she exemplified bourgeois ideals of virtue—a fitting symbol for the liberal order that found its fullest expression in nineteenth-century Britain. [Courtesy of the Board of Trustees of the Victoria & Albert Museum]

Law League. Led by the publicists Richard Cobden and John Bright, it aimed at the removal of traditional tariffs, which, originally meant to keep grain from being exported in time of dearth, now supported high prices by keeping out cheaper imports. The campaign against the Corn Laws pitted manufacturing interests against the gentry who owned most of Britain's land. Cobden shrewdly proposed to use the Chartists "to frighten the Aristocracy" while weaning the Chartists from their "rascally leaders" by the promise of lower prices. Aided by a serious famine in Ireland, the League gained repeal of the Corn Laws in 1846.

The League's victory was the beginning of the primacy of industrial over landed wealth in Britain. It would be misleading, however, to see in this the triumph of the bourgeoisie over the landed gentry. Parliament voted to repeal the Corn Laws not because it had yielded to bourgeois interests, but because its members perceived that there was greater fortune to be made by exporting the products of industry than by propping up agriculture. The gentry, whose capital had been flowing into commerce and industry for generations, gradually merged with the bourgeoisie, remaining distinguished

from it only by the social prestige that still attached to landholding and rural blood sports. Most new titles of nobility in Britain went to businessmen and professionals, while the gentry were drawn to the money markets of London, the financial capital of the world. This contrasted with the experience of France and Germany, where the nobility continued to disdain bourgeois values and liberal institutions.

As the old rural economy passed out of existence and Britain created the first Western society without a peasantry, bourgeois artists and intellectuals looked back on it nostalgically, and the critics John Ruskin (1819–1900) and Matthew Arnold (1822–1888) inveighed against the acquisitiveness of industrial society. The hero of George Gissing's novel *The Private Papers of Henry Ryecroft* (1903) summed up this mood of pastoral regret in a phrase: "The last thought of my brain as I lie dying will be that of sunshine upon an English meadow."

This idealization of gentry values admirably served elite interests. It softened the image of confrontation between the classes and reinforced the habit of deference, the respect automatically accorded one's superiors in a hierarchical society. In return for deference the elite was prepared to make concessions in the name of conscience to the working classes. This was mediated by the rise of Evangelicalism, a broad-based reform movement among Anglican reformers and the dissenting churches. Evangelicalism taught social responsibility and moral reform to its bourgeois adherents and godliness, sobriety, and docility to its humbler ones.

The great political champion of reform was William Ewart Gladstone (1809–1898), who served four times as Prime Minister between 1868 and 1894. Raised in the Church of England, Gladstone had considered becoming a clergyman before entering Parliament in 1833, and he carried a tone of moral uplift throughout his six decades in politics that many found overbearing but that won him a broad constituency among the reform-minded middle classes and among the working classes enfranchised by his Reform Bill in 1884. Gladstone's Liberal ministries saw the passage of legislation for a secret ballot, for educational and civil service reform, and for employers' liability in industrial accidents, but those of his Conservative rival, Benjamin Disraeli (1804–1881), were marked as well by an important franchise bill and laws on public health, urban housing, and the reform of conditions in the merchant marine. In short, the late nineteenth century saw a broad elite consensus to mitigate the effects of industrialism while preserving existing social and property relations.

The plight of the Irish attracted increasing attention. Ireland had been formally annexed to Britain in 1801, and its peasantry, thinned by famine and migration and exploited by British landlords, was among the poorest in Europe. Gladstone introduced a Home Rule bill to grant Ireland autonomy in 1886, only to split his own party. The issue would not fade, however, and a new era of confrontational politics lay ahead.

Many attributed the stability of Victorian Britain to the balance of its political system and saw its history as the triumph of its constitution. Above all, however, Britain was symbolized by Victoria herself, who, ascending the throne as a young woman of 18, had matured through marriage to Prince Albert of Saxe-Coburg-Gotha, and after a long period of seclusion following his death in 1861, had emerged, supported by her large family, to form a picture of virtuous and constant widowhood. In a century when so many values were in question, Victoria personified the bourgeois ideal of domestic bliss secured through feminine submission.

The Third Republic in France

The Third Republic was born amid foreign conquest and social revolution. Proclaimed in Paris by Napoleon III's political opposition after his capture at Sedan, it was forced by the Treaty of Frankfurt (1871) to cede the border provinces of Alsace and Lorraine to the new German empire and to pay an indemnity of 5 billion francs. The treaty was signed by a new National Assembly that was elected for the purpose at the insistence of Bismarck, and led by the veteran Orleanist politician Adolphe Thiers (1797–1877).

Rebelling against the treaty and the conservative makeup of the Assembly, two-thirds of whose members were monarchists, angry Parisians seized control of the city government on March 18. They renamed it the Commune in honor of the municipal government of 1792 and called for new elections based on a France of decentralized, self-governing communities like their own.

For the next ten weeks, Paris conducted an unprecedented experiment in social democracy while withstanding military siege. The Commune abolished the police and the army in favor of a civilian militia with elected officers. It made all public offices elective and limited them to workers' wages. Unions and workers' councils took over factories abandoned by their owners, running them as cooperatives. Clerical property was expropriated, and the city's churches were converted into free schools and social forums. Demanding sexual equality as a prelude to social revolution, the Union of Women for the Defense of Paris called for "the abolition of all competition between men and women workers, since their interests are absolutely identical and their solidarity is essential to the final and universal strike of Labor against Capital."

This rhetoric was not exceptional; as one manifesto declared, "We believe that workers have the right today to take possession of the tools of production, just as in 1789 the peasants took possession of the land." As 1848 had been the year of bourgeois revolution, socialists throughout Europe believed that their hour had now struck; only Marx himself hung back, believing the insurrection doomed. Thiers' troops broke through on May 21, and the city fell after a week of savage fighting, leaving 25,000 dead.

The violent suppression of the Commune hovered for many years over the political life of France and the Continent. In the short term, however, it was greeted with approval by the French electorate, which had already expressed its preference for a return to monarchy. The Republic survived only because that preference was evenly divided between supporters of the Legitimist (Bourbon) and Orleanist candidates; when the two sides failed to compromise, Thiers simply continued to rule. Not until 1875 was a resolution passed that legalized the de facto rule of the Assembly, adding an upper chamber, a premier and cabinet responsible to the legislature, and a ceremonial president. Born in defeat, scarred by violence, the Republic crept in by stealth. Yet despite its lack of support and the chronic instability of its parliamentary system—there were 60 governments between 1870 and 1914—it lasted longer than any other postrevolutionary French regime.

The reason for the Republic's durability was largely the relative stability of French society itself. France remained, apart from the mines and factory towns of the northeast, largely a nation of small peasant proprietors. French industry was similarly small-scaled for the most part, and the bourgeoisie remained more interested in the unadventurous returns of finance and banking than in the risks of production. The proletariat too, except in Paris and a few other cities, was relatively weak and politically undeveloped. The civil service of the Republic, inherited from the Second Empire and essentially undisturbed since the time of Napoleon I, provided further continuity.

The Republic weathered severe crises in the last two decades of the century. A charismatic general, Georges Boulanger (1837–1891), rose to prominence in the mid-

Members of the Paris Commune stand before a toppled statue of Napoleon I at the Place Vendôme. [Gernsheim Collection, Harry Ransom Humanities Research Center, The University of Texas at Austin]

1880s and was urged by his supporters to seize power, but he hung back at the critical moment, was forced to flee the country, and died in disgrace.

Far more traumatic was the Dreyfus affair. In 1894 a Jewish staff officer, Captain Alfred Dreyfus (1859–1935), was convicted of trying to sell military secrets to Germany, although the only evidence produced was an unsigned letter whose handwriting did not match that of Dreyfus. An army court nonetheless found him guilty after a campaign of anti-Semitic vilification. Dreyfus was publicly degraded and sentenced to life imprisonment on Devil's Island, the notorious penal colony off French Guiana.

Slowly, evidence of Dreyfus' innocence emerged. In January 1898 the novelist Émile Zola (1840–1902) published an open letter under the headline *"J'accuse"* ("I accuse"), charging the army with a coverup. Zola himself was tried and convicted of slander, but the army was at last compelled to give Dreyfus a new trial in August 1899. To save face, it found him guilty again, but with extenuating circumstances, and the president of the Republic promptly pardoned him. A civilian court exonerated him in 1906, and he was restored to rank.

The Dreyfus affair divided but also energized French public life. It gave republicans a dramatic cause and brought socialists for the first time in 50 years into a coalition government. At the same time it gave fresh impetus to the right, led by Charles Maurras (1868–1952). Maurras, whose long career would end in his disgrace as a Nazi collaborator in World War II, appealed for unity and order through the army, the church, and the monarchy. If for liberals the core of the Dreyfus affair was that justice must be done at all costs, for the new French right it was the reverse: that the fundamental institutions of state and society must be protected, even at the sacrifice of individuals. This was particularly the case, as one of Maurras' associates remarked, when the individual was a Jew.

The Dreyfus affair also brought to a climax the anticlericalism that had been a part of the republican tradition since the Revolution of 1789. The government had moved in the early 1880s to break up the Catholic monopoly on education, to reduce the influence of its orders, and to legalize divorce. Hostilities were renewed over Dreyfus, and by 1905 the religious orders were dissolved, all ties between church and state were abolished, and title to all church property was transferred to the state. In protest, Catholics worshiped in the streets, while in country parishes some of the faithful defended their churches with shotguns, set wolf traps for government officials, and in one case even chained a wild bear to the church door. Gradually, however, separation was accepted as a fact, and the church, emancipated from its century-long status as a dependency of the state, began to define a new role for itself in French life.

Germany Under Bismarck

"The German nation is sick of principles and doctrines," wrote the educator Julius Froebel in 1859: "What it wants is Power, Power, Power!" Twelve years later, the new German empire brought into being by Otto von Bismarck was the strongest state on the Continent, and for the next three-quarters of a century the containment of German power would be the overriding political issue in Europe.

Bismarck presided over the empire during its first two decades. Each of its 25 constituent states retained its own government, whose rulers were represented in a federal council, the Bundesrat. William I, who remained king of Prussia, was German emperor by virtue of his permanent presidency of the council. The approval of the Bundesrat was required for all laws, and it thus served as the upper chamber of the national legislature, whose lower house, the Reichstag, was elected by universal manhood suffrage.

The votes in the Bundesrat as well as in the Reichstag were counted in proportion to population, ensuring Prussian dominance. As chancellor, Bismarck was appointed by the emperor and was responsible only to him; in addition, he was head of the state bureaucracy. Thus the constitution represented a tradeoff between imperial authority at the national level and princely prerogative among the states; in both cases, popular control was minimized.

Bismarck applied strong-arm tactics to crush domestic opposition. In 1871 he launched a so-called *Kulturkampf* ("battle for civilization") against the Catholic church, which, as in France, served as a focus of discontent with the new regime. Although his direct authority was limited to Prussia, Bismarck succeeded in imposing limits on Catholic worship and education and the political activities of Catholic clergy throughout most of the empire. The Jesuits were expelled, most other orders dissolved, and many bishops arrested or forced into exile. By 1878, Bismarck detected a new menace to civilization in the rise of the Social Democratic Party (SPD), founded in 1875 and already demonstrating widespread appeal among the working classes. Abruptly

abandoning the Kulturkampf and enlisting many of his erstwhile foes, Bismarck outlawed the Social Democrats and banned all socialist meetings and newspapers. At the same time he sought to win over workers by introducing the first comprehensive social welfare program in Europe in the 1880s. Workers were insured against illness, accident, and disability, and pensions were provided for widows, orphans, and the aged. The workers were not, however, cured of social democracy by this, and when the SPD was again legalized in 1890, its representation rose steadily until by 1912 it was the largest party in the Reichstag.

Bismarck's power was anchored in the confidence he enjoyed from William I. But he soon ran afoul of the impetuous William II (1888–1918), who was anxious to exercise power directly. In March 1890 the Iron Chancellor was compelled to resign.

Bismarck had molded the German nation and with it the destiny of modern Europe. His success rested on a dazzling and unscrupulous ability to manipulate antagonistic interests. Over and over, he pitted his enemies against each other rather than himself. He conceded to his foes far more than they could have won for themselves—universal manhood suffrage to the liberals, social insurance to the workers—but only the more firmly to entrench his own power. By thwarting the institutions of responsible self-government he retarded the development of a genuine political culture in Germany, leaving it vulnerable to the adventurism of William II, and worse to come.

Italy and Spain: Crises of the State

Italy, a constitutional monarchy with a parliamentary system, experienced the difficulties that beset other liberal regimes but with greater force. Fewer than 2 percent of the population enjoyed the vote when the country was unified in the 1860s, and as late as 1912, fewer than 6 percent. The north and south were deeply split along cultural and political lines, a division compounded by unequal economic development, and only mass emigration served to relieve social discontent. The church refused to recognize the new state, and the papal decree *Non Expedit* (1871) forbade Catholics to vote or take part in national affairs.

The resulting system was marked by corruption and violence. King Umberto I (1878–1900) was killed by an anarchist workman, and when his successor, Victor Emmanuel III (1900–1946), attempted to conciliate the left, he set off a wave of violent strikes. The failed promises of liberalism were rejected not only by workers and peasants but also by intellectuals such as Vilfredo Pareto (1848–1923) and Gaetano Mosca (1858–1941), who developed theories of the inevitable dominance of political elites. Fifty years after the birth of modern Italy, democracy had few takers.

In Spain the course of midcentury politics was set when King Ferdinand VII (1808–1833) excluded his brother, Don Carlos, from the succession in favor of his infant daughter Isabella. Supporters of the pretender, known as Carlists, waged a long civil war against the regime, which resumed when Isabella was deposed in 1868. Relative stability returned with the reign of Alfonso XII (1874–1885), and northern Spain, led by Barcelona, began to industrialize. Liberal and conservative politicians agreed tacitly to alternate in power; this was not affected by the introduction of universal manhood suffrage in 1890, since electoral fraud and intimidation were widespread.

The country was jolted from its lethargy by the loss of most of its remaining empire in the Spanish-American war of 1898. A new group of bourgeois intellectuals, the so-called Generation of 1898, urged national regeneration, but as in Italy many of them, including Miguel de Unamuno (1864–1936) and José Ortega y Gasset (1883–1955), despaired of democratic self-government.

Northern Europe

The smaller states of northern Europe experienced social, economic, and political developments similar to those of their larger neighbors. In Belgium, where divisions along linguistic and cultural as well as political lines provoked repeated crises, rapid industrialization nonetheless brought prosperity and liberal constitutionalism. In the Netherlands, prosperity was buttressed by the profits from a still-substantial empire and by agricultural modernization that, as in Denmark, enabled Dutch farmers to hold their own against competition from abroad. Norway and Sweden had been united under the Swedish crown in 1815, though each country retained its own parliament. Depressed agricultural prices caused large-scale emigration from both countries, but the Swedes gradually developed a formidable industrial base, and the Norwegians built the world's third largest merchant fleet. The two countries separated peacefully in 1905.

The United States

With the defeat of the Southern Confederacy in the civil war, the United States embarked on an explosive period of industrial and commercial growth. The federal government promoted settlement and investment through land grants and other incentives, herding the Indian populations of the high plains onto reservations, where they lived as indigent wards of the state. Interests less powerful than railroads, cattle barons, mining interests, and trusts found the government less accommodating. Falling agricultural prices after 1873 led to a grass-roots farm movement known as Populism, which sought cheap credit, an enhanced money supply including silver currency, regulation of railroad rates, and producers' cooperatives. Following a sharp slump in 1893, unemployed workers marched on Washington demanding federal assistance, only to be beaten back by club-wielding policemen, and in 1896, business interests secured the election of a Republican president, William McKinley, over the pro-silver Democratic candidate, William Jennings Bryan, in a bitterly contested campaign. The few gestures toward control of big business, such as the Interstate Commerce Act (1887) and the Sherman Antitrust Act (1890), were largely negated by the courts.

THE SOCIALIST CHALLENGE

If the ideology of the liberal bourgeoisie was individualism, the response of class-conscious workers was solidarity, the affirmation of the common interest of the proletariat against the empire of capital. This solidarity was based on the historical example of guilds, with their ideal of craft fraternity and independence, and was reinforced by the experience of the factory. The development of socialist thought raised the sights of labor beyond mere resistance, suggesting the eventual overthrow of the bourgeoisie by class struggle.

Varieties of Socialism

The ideal of a society based on communal ownership goes back to Plato's *Republic,* which was inspired in part by the practice of ancient Sparta. It was kept alive in the Christian orders and fraternities of the Middle Ages and among such groups as the Family of Love in the sixteenth-century Netherlands and the Diggers of seventeenth-century England.

Marxism was the dominant vision of nineteenth-century socialism, and most of the great revolutions of the twentieth century were to be made in its name; but it was not without rivals, chief among them anarchism. Anarchism was founded by Pierre Joseph Proudhon (1809–1865), a French printer, whose dictum was that "property is theft" and that the state was the instrument of its protection. Proudhon and his successors, the Russians Mikhail Bakunin (1814–1876) and Peter Kropotkin (1842–1921), contended that the abolition of the state was not the fruit but the precondition of revolution. Bakunin sharply rejected the concept of a transitional "dictatorship of the proletariat" between capitalism and socialism put forward by Friedrich Engels, as well as Marx's emphasis on the necessity for organization, which, he argued, could only inhibit spontaneous action. Anarchism took firm root among many workers in Italy and Spain and among radical intellectuals in Russia. Because of its emphasis on revolutionary activism, many of its adherents supported assassination and other forms of political violence.

The Trade Union Movement

The most immediate form that worker solidarity took was the trade union. The first unions were formed by artisans such as printers and carpenters, who, fearful of being absorbed into the factory regimen, organized to protect their wage levels and job autonomy. Unions spread in the late nineteenth century to mining, shipping, and railroads, and more slowly to factories, where labor was easier to supervise, to discipline, and usually to replace. Often, a large strike was the occasion for organizing an industry. Transport industries were particularly vulnerable to strikes, and a stoppage in any major sector could bring much of the economy to a halt. This suggested the idea of a general strike to paralyze the economy, or even a complete standdown as a prelude to revolution. The Chartists had experimented with a general strike as a means of attaining political goals in 1842, and widespread strikes were common by the early twentieth century. Repression was often sharp, but unions gained legal recognition in every Western country by 1906, organizing more than 20 percent of the industrial labor force in Britain and Germany. In addition to seeking economic and political goals, they set up pension and disability funds, established training schools, and sponsored holiday excursions. They thus offered sustenance both on and off the job, replacing many of the social functions of churches and contributing to a distinctively working-class culture.

Both unions and individual workers were integrated into the first successful mass labor movement, the General German Workers' Association founded in 1863 by Ferdinand Lassalle (1825–1864). The following year, Marx and other socialists founded the International Workingman's Association, later known as the First International, and in 1875 Marxists and Lassalleans merged to form the German Social Democratic Party (SPD). Workers' parties were thereupon rapidly founded elsewhere. A Second International was formed in 1889, and in 1891 the SPD adopted the Erfurt Program, calling for a mass uprising by the proletariat and the liquidation of private property. Other workers' parties followed suit. The Marxist vision of revolution thus became the official program of European socialism.

Despite this rhetoric, the revolutionary goal appeared to be receding. Marx's prediction of an impoverished proletariat had not been borne out; the general living standard was rising, however unequally, and by the early 1900s most industrial states had begun to put in place a social safety net. In his *Evolutionary Socialism* (1898), Eduard Bernstein (1850–1932), a member of the SPD, challenged Marx's belief in the inevitable failure of capitalism and the consequent necessity of revolution. He suggested that socialism could evolve gradually from capitalism by incremental reform and the gradual acceptance of public ownership. Bernstein's ideas were officially repudiated by the SPD, but they had already been adopted by most socialist parties in practice.

ROSA LUXEMBURG: APOSTLE OF REVOLUTION

No one rejected Bernstein's views more forcefully than Rosa Luxemburg. Born in Poland to Jewish parents in 1870, she was involved in revolutionary activity from her schooldays and fled to Switzerland to avoid arrest at the age of 18. There, with her lover Leo Jogiches and other emigrés, she helped to found the Polish Social Democratic Party in 1893, soon becoming its most eloquent spokesperson. Needing a larger forum, she migrated to Germany in 1898, joining the SPD just as the Bernstein controversy was unfolding. In a series of articles she attacked Bernstein's position as a surrender of socialist principles to liberalism, resting as it did on the premise that capitalism could stabilize itself and that the bourgeoisie would yield or share power without a

The Polish-born socialist Rosa Luxemburg (1870–1919). [The Granger Collection, New York]

of the famous Roman slave rebellion. Imprisoned in Germany once more, she continued to write, appealing for worker solidarity and calling for a Third International. The Bolshevik Revolution of 1917 again raised her hopes. She was soon disillusioned with Lenin, with whose tactics she had long quarreled, and in a scathing critique of his regime she warned that without general elections and freedom of press and assembly, dictatorship would result. Freed from prison in November 1918, she returned to Berlin and formed the German Communist Party with Karl Liebknecht. On January 15, 1919, she was arrested; her head was smashed in by a rifle butt, and she was finished off by a bullet at point-blank range. Liebknecht met a similar fate. Luxemburg's body was thrown into a canal, not to be retrieved until May.

A small, frail woman who walked with a limp, Luxemburg was the most extraordinary of many women who were prominent in the socialist movement, including Emma Goldman and Luxemburg's close friend Clara Zetkin. Lenin called her "the eagle of the Revolution" (and tried to suppress her works), and György Lukács, himself an important Marxist theoretician, wrote that she was the only scholar who had advanced Marx's thought. Enemies called her "Red Rosa" and reviled her even in death; to this day she remains controversial. In her last article she wrote that the revolution would return again and again to proclaim: "I was, I am, I shall be!" Twenty-four hours later, she was dead; the words became her epitaph.

struggle. Her own views were subsequently developed in a major study, *The Accumulation of Capital* (1913). Luxemburg pointed out that, though organized by competitive nationalisms, capitalism was global in scope, as illustrated by the phenomenon of imperialism. For the working class to become enmeshed in the politics of parliamentary regimes was therefore to trap itself on the level of national interests, whereas the class struggle, like capitalism itself, was international in scope.

True to her convictions, Luxemburg returned to Warsaw during the Russian Revolution of 1905 to agitate for a general strike. Arrested with Jogiches, she was confined for several months but escaped to Finland and joined the Russian Social Democratic Party. The moment of truth for international socialism came in 1914 with the outbreak of World War I. The SPD and most of the other socialist parties of Europe supported the war, and the Second International collapsed.

Luxemburg denounced the war and, with a few like-minded colleagues, formed a new group, subsequently known as the Spartacus League after the leader

SUMMARY

The late nineteenth century saw the expansion of the Industrial Revolution, the rise of big business, and the consolidation of the liberal order in politics. Material prosperity and public health measures sustained a rapid growth in population and urbanization. At the same time, wealth and power were concentrated in the hands of the male propertied classes, provoking a feminist revolt among the women of the bourgeoisie and the rise of trade union socialism among the working classes. As the crisis of the liberal order approached, the demands of these groups became increasingly imperative.

Note

1. Sheila Rowbotham, *Hidden From History: Rediscovering Women in History from the 17th Century to the Present.* (New York: Pantheon Books, 1974), p. 81.

Suggestions for Further Reading

Blum, J. *The End of the Old Order in Rural Europe.* Princeton, N.J.: Princeton University Press, 1978.

Delamont, S., and Duffin, L. *The Nineteenth-Century Woman: Her Cultural and Physical World.* New York: Barnes & Noble, 1978.

de Ruggiero, G. *The History of European Liberalism.* Boston: Beacon Press, 1959.

Elon, A. *Herzl.* New York: Holt, Rinehart and Winston, 1975.

Evans, R. J. *The Feminists: Women's Emancipation Movements in Europe, America, and Australasia, 1840–1920.* New York: Barnes & Noble, 1979.

Gay, P. *The Bourgeois Experience.* New York: Oxford University Press, 1984, 1986.

Hobsbawm, E. J. *The Age of Capital, 1848–1875.* New York: Scribner, 1975.

Merriman, J. M., ed. *Consciousness and Class Experience in Nineteenth-Century Europe.* New York: Holmes & Meier, 1979.

Milward, A. S., and Saul, S. B. *The Development of the Economies of Continental Europe, 1850–1914.* Cambridge, Mass.: Harvard University Press, 1977.

Mitchell, H. *Workers and Protest: The European Labor Movement, the Working Classes, and the Origins of Social Democracy, 1890–1914.* Itasca, Ill.: Peacock, 1971.

Moraze, C. *The Triumph of the Middle Classes: A Study of European Values in the Nineteenth Century.* Cleveland, Ohio: World, 1967.

Nettl, J. P. *Rosa Luxemburg.* New York: Schocken Books, 1989.

Porter, G. *The Rise of Big Business, 1860–1910.* Arlington Heights, Ill.: AHM, 1973.

Weber, E. *Peasants into Frenchmen: The Modernization of Rural France, 1870–1914.* Palo Alto, Calif.: Stanford University Press, 1976.

Williamson, J. G. *Coping with City Growth During the British Industrial Revolution.* Cambridge: Cambridge University Press, 1990.

24

THE AGE OF DOMINATION

Empires have been associated with the development of civilizations from earliest times. Through them, widely different human cultures have come into contact, exchanging language, custom, religion, art, and technology. Whether as a creative or a destructive force, and sometimes as both, empires have been a moving force in world history.

Modern European imperialism began with the conquest of the New World in the sixteenth century. Its first phase ended with the liberation of the Western hemisphere between 1775 and 1825, though it left behind there more or less Europeanized cultures, and intensive European migration continued for another century.

The second phase of European empire involved the exploitation of Africa between 1650 and 1800 and the penetration of western and central Asia, most notably in the British conquest of India. Most of this activity was stimulated by commercial rivalry, which triggered a series of major European wars from the mid-seventeenth century. By the beginning of the eighteenth century a global world market had begun to emerge.

The third phase began shortly after the end of the Napoleonic wars and culminated in the extension of European power over most of the world. No corner of the globe was untouched by Western influence by the end of the nineteenth century, and no nation, with the exception of Japan, escaped the direct or indirect control of Western cultures. Never before had a single civilization been so dominant in the world.

THE NEW IMPERIALISM

By the nineteenth century the leading European powers had become capable of controlling civilized populations that, like India's, were far larger than their own. Where the capacity existed, domination soon followed. The new imperialism systematically extended the flags of Europe and the United States to every continent. Although the primary motive remained profit, national pride created empires whose economic return was marginal if not negative. Not only were large markets and rich orefields scooped up, but desert wastes and remote islands. In its final phase, beginning about 1870, the process of empire acquired a seemingly irresistible momentum. Imperialism became an end in itself.

What made domination possible on the most basic level was the clear military and naval superiority of the West. With the coming of iron-hulled ships, telegraphic communications, and heavy artillery, the West's advantage became insuperable. A mere show of force—"gunboat diplomacy"—would often suffice to gain Western objectives.

Conflicting Interpretations of Empire

Military capacity alone could not provide a sufficient incentive for domination. By the end of the nineteenth century, various theories were being put forward by

Westerners themselves to account for imperialism. The debate over the nature and meaning of the imperial phenomenon continues to the present day.

The Englishman John A. Hobson (1858–1940) argued in his book *Imperialism* (1902) that his country's imperial ventures had resulted from an inequitable distribution of income in the British economy. Because the propertied class received more income than it could profitably invest while the laboring majority received less than it needed to sustain demand for existing products, the economy was trapped between "oversaving"—the tendency of the rich to accumulate surplus capital—and "underconsumption"—the constriction of the market caused by inadequate purchasing power. Hence capital interests were driven to find new markets abroad.

In Hobson's view the problem was not capitalism itself, but monopoly. Like Adam Smith, he wished to restore a fully competitive economy, using electoral power to break up the interests that restrained free trade and pauperized the domestic market. Imperialism, the symptom, would disappear when monopoly, the cause, had been cured.

Marxist commentators accepted Hobson's description of imperialism but rejected his hopeful diagnosis, contending that trusts that had destroyed free competition and dictated economic policy would continue to seek cheap labor and captive markets abroad. The early Marxist critique was summed up by Vladimir Ilyich Lenin's *Imperialism, the Highest Stage of Capitalism* (1916). In Lenin's view, imperialism was the coordinated effort between monopoly capital and the state to sustain the level of profit on which the capitalist system depended. Competing states, however, would inevitably clash over control of colonial territories, and these wars, together with the revolt of the colonized themselves, would bring about the collapse of the capitalist order.

Not all Marxists shared Lenin's faith in capitalism's pending demise. The German Social Democrat Karl Kautsky suggested that international cartels might find a way to divide the world market without conflict. Nor did all commentators share the assumption common to both Hobson and the Marxists that imperialism was essentially an economic phenomenon. Tracing imperialism back to its historic roots, Joseph Schumpeter (1883–1950) argued that it was essentially the pastime of the warrior elites that dominated aristocratic societies, whether ancient or modern. Schumpeter's views were close to those of the German sociologist Max Weber (1864–1920), who pointed out that imperial conquest enhanced the domestic power of elites, although he noted its connection with monopoly capital as well. Later theorists have attempted to emphasize the interrelationship of social, economic, and political factors in promoting imperialism, as well as the interaction between colonizers and colonists.

Probably no single theory can account for all instances of imperialism. It is, however, possible to offer at least some generalizations about the imperialism of late nineteenth-century European states. These states shared not only a clear-cut military superiority over non-Western states and regions, but a dynamic economic system that, having embraced much of the world in a network of production and trade, now universalized it as a potential market that could absorb the products of the industrial machine. Such states, driven as well by competitive nationalism, were further motivated to acquire colonies for purposes of prestige and to preempt rivals. With no serious impediment to their expansion, they required only the pretext of a noble cause. This was readily supplied by politicians, missionaries, anthropologists, and believers in the historical mission of the white race.

THE SCRAMBLE FOR AFRICA

The continent of Africa is eight miles from Europe at the Straits of Gibraltar. Nonetheless, there was virtually no European presence in Africa as late as 1815 except for the Dutch settlement at the Cape of Good Hope (acquired by Britain in that year) and a string of Portuguese, Spanish, French, and British trading posts along the coasts. Even in 1870, less than a tenth of Africa was in European hands. That situation changed rapidly in the next 30 years. By 1900 the only area that remained substantially independent was the kingdom of Abyssinia (now Ethiopia). Europe has swallowed the world's second largest continent whole.

Africa Before 1870

The peoples and cultures of Africa have been linked to those of the West since Egyptian times, although most contact with populations south of the equator was cut off by the Sahara Desert and the lack of anchorage along Africa's coastlines, and the true dimensions of the continent were unknown until the fifteenth century. Christianity took root early in North Africa, but the major cultural influence after the seventh century A.D. was Islam, which spread first to the kingdoms of the Sudan and later to those of western Africa. At least two-thirds of the gold supply of later medieval Europe came from the rich and powerful kingdom of Mali (c. 1250–c. 1460), and Europeans continued to seek precious metals in Africa in the centuries thereafter.

Slavery was widely practiced in both Africa and the Middle East, and European traders found a well-established market when they began to ship black Africans to the New World in large numbers after 1650. There was thus no incentive for them to acquire more than the coastal ports that served them for barter and transshipment. As late as the mid-nineteenth century, Lord Palmerston declined the suggestion that Britain take possession of Abyssinia with the remark, "All we want is trade and land is not necessary for trade; we can carry on commerce on ground belonging to other people."

Explorers and Missionaries

This situation changed in the later nineteenth century, when products such as rubber that required cultivation came into demand. The forerunners of merchants and politicians were explorers and missionaries. The interior of Africa was almost unknown to Europeans, and until it had been mapped, neither trade nor colonization would be practicable. The British Foreign Office sent a team of explorers into central Africa in 1849, and results were prompt: British exports to sub-Saharan Africa more than tripled by 1871, and doubled again in the next decade. The key to both discovery and exploitation was control of the great rivers of the continent—the Niger, the Nile, the Congo, the Zambesi—which both steamers and gunboats plied freely by the 1870s.

Explorers were followed when not accompanied by missionaries, and often the two were combined, as in the case of David Livingstone (1813–1873), a medical missionary who traveled in Africa for 30 years, explored the Congo and Zambesi rivers, and became the object of a famous publicity stunt when the New York *Herald* sent a journalist, Henry M. Stanley, to "rescue" him. One of the prime objectives of African missionaries was to eradicate the slave trade, which had been formally abolished but was still flourishing in the 1840s and 1850s. The British government supported these efforts, convinced, as were the missionaries themselves, that slaving was now a hindrance to economic development. Nor was any incompatibility felt between the purposes of conversion and commerce, although few perhaps would have gone as far as one businessmen, who declared that "Jesus Christ is Free Trade and Free Trade is Jesus Christ."

Dividing the Spoils: Conquest and Accommodation

By 1870, African was ripe for political partition. Europe had developed an increasing trade in the continent's exports—cotton, sisal, palm oil, ivory, rubber, cocoa, coffee, hides. At the same time there was already substantial capital investment to protect. The arrival of two new potential competitors on the European scene, Germany and Italy, increased the pressure on Britain and France to stake out the richest areas for themselves. Palmerston's dictum that land was not essential to trade was no longer true. Britain's Colonial Secretary, Joseph Chamberlain, now declared that control of Africa's possessions and markets was "a matter of life and death."

Pride as well as profit was a factor in the scramble for Africa. The Frenchman Léon Gambetta spoke for a general sentiment when he said that "to remain a great nation or to become one, you must colonize." Schoolchildren grew up with maps colored to show their country's possessions in the world and imbibed stories of imperial martyrs such as the British General Charles Gordon, killed by Sudanese rebels. Colonizers regarded it as their duty to impose their own cultural values on those they ruled; the British called this "the white man's burden," the French their *mission civilisatrice,* and the Germans *Kultur.* Expansion thus became a duty, and any nation that failed to maximize its imperial holdings might be regarded as holding back the material progress of the world, and therefore as morally derelict.

With unification, the new powers of Germany and Italy sought to make up for lost time in staking their imperial claims. In Germany, colonial societies were formed to promote expansion. Bismarck proceeded cautiously at first, but after 1884, Germany laid claim to Togoland, the Cameroons, and what is now Tanzania and Namibia, eventually building an African empire of a million square miles. Italy, though equally determined to share the spoils, was less successful. It occupied part of the Eritrean coast in 1883 and three years later gained a foothold in Somalia, but was defeated in an attempt to wrest Abyssinia from the emperor Menelik (1889–1913) at the Battle of Adowa in 1896. The smaller European powers could not realistically hope to compete with the giants, and some, like Denmark, gave up bases they had held earlier; but the venturesome King Leopold II of Belgium created an empire of his own in central Africa and gained recognition for his Congo Free State, an area of some 900,000 square miles, as a private fiefdom.

The Congo Free State brought the question of jurisdiction in Africa to a head. In effect, the competing claims and frontier disputes that had brought war to Europe repeatedly before 1815 had been transferred to Africa. To defuse the potential for conflict, Bismarck convened an international conference at Berlin in 1884–1885 that laid down ground rules for further imperial claims. To register such claims, formal notice was to be served to the other powers, backed by effective control of the territory concerned.

There were several gradations of imperial control. A *colony* was understood to be a territory governed by the imperial authority, backed by an army directly under its control. A *protectorate* was a territory governed by a native ruler but effectively controlled by imperial advisers. *Spheres of influence*—a term first introduced at the Berlin conference—were territories that were nominally independent but subject to exclusive concessions granted to an imperial power, such as the use of ports, the exploitation of mineral resources, and the right of jurisdiction over its own nationals. These categories, of course, applied outside Africa as well.

The Berlin conference accelerated the final partition of Africa. The British negotiated a series of bilateral agreements that recognized their claims to Zanzibar, Kenya, Uganda, Northern Rhodesia (now Zambia), Bechuanaland, and Nigeria; in return, they acknowledged French interests in western Africa and the island of Madagascar, as well as German and Portuguese frontiers. Britain had obtained a protectorate over Egypt in 1882 after its ruler, the Khedive (sultan) Ismail, had defaulted on loans to European bankers, and in 1898 it reconquered the Sudan, which had broken away from Egypt in the 1880s. The French, who had taken control of Algeria in the 1830s, extended protectorates over Tunisia and Morocco, consolidating their control of the region of North Africa known as the Maghreb.

These claims were by no means established without incident. The Germans repeatedly challenged French hegemony in Morocco, and French and British armies faced off at Fashoda in the Sudan in 1898, bringing their countries close to war until the French withdrew. The potential for imperial conflict remained strong in Africa.

The Impact of Colonial Rule

Once the glamour of conquest had been replaced by the realities of administration, there was a marked decline in public interest in Africa. Few Europeans were willing to

settle in a tropical climate where there was little prospect of immediate profit, and most of the migrants to Africa were traders and artisans from India. Only in Algeria and later in southern Africa did a significant colonial population develop.

If the impact of Africa on Europe was limited, however, that of Europe on Africa was profound and often devastating. European rule cut across regional and tribal boundaries all over Africa, destroying long-established patterns of settlement, migration, and land tenure. Colonial administrators favored tribes that were willing to cooperate with them, offering them lands and goods confiscated from rival groups. This created deep bitterness between tribes and was the source of bloody postcolonial conflict, as in Uganda. Often there was fierce and protracted resistance to colonial rule, as in Algeria and the Sudan and among warrior peoples such as the Masai of Kenya and the Zulus of southern Africa. Such resistance served as a pretext for further dispossession, as rebel tribes were herded onto reservations, much as was done to the Indians of North America. A worse fate befell the Herero of southwestern Africa, two-thirds of whom were exterminated in the wake of a rebellion against German rule.

Europeans prided themselves on eliminating African slavery, only to substitute equally brutal forms of forced labor. With a booming mineral and rubber market, Leopold II leased much of the Congo Free State to private developers who conscripted native press-gangs to work mines and plantations and build roads and railways. Tens of thousands died before the Belgian government stepped in to assume control of the country in 1908. The French also granted concessions to developers in Equatorial Africa, which encouraged similar abuses: 20,000 workers alone died constructing a railway between Pointe Noire and Brazzaville as late as 1921–1934.

Such exploitation both reflected and fostered attitudes of racial and cultural superiority. Imperialists argued that the value of a people or the quality of its civilization was measured by its contribution to the world's wealth; those who failed to develop the productive capacities of their countries forfeited the right to self-rule. From there it was a short step to open racial contempt, embedded in any case from centuries of exploiting black slaves. As the Nile explorer Sir Samuel Baker wrote in his diary,

> I wish the black sympathizers in England could see Africa's inmost heart as I do[;] much of their sympathy would subside. Human nature viewed in its crude state as pictured amongst African savages is quite on a level with that of the brute, and not to be compared with the noble character of the dog.[1]

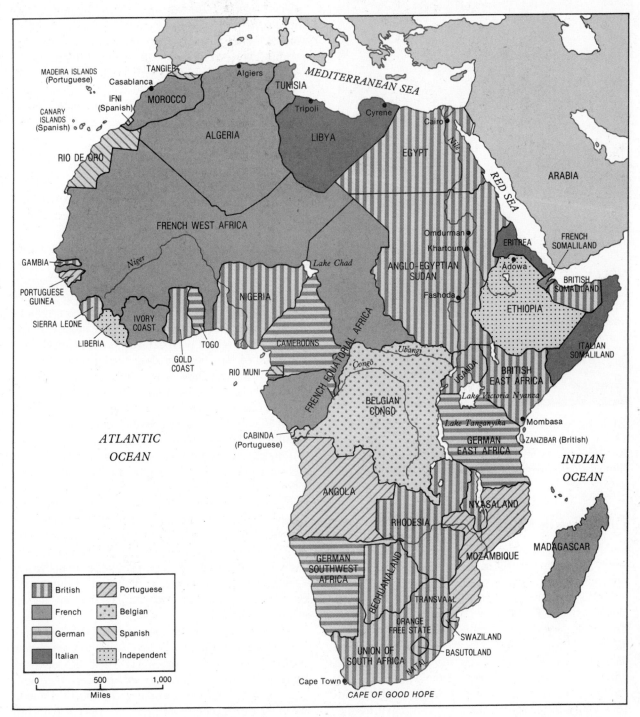

24.1 Africa on the Eve of World War I

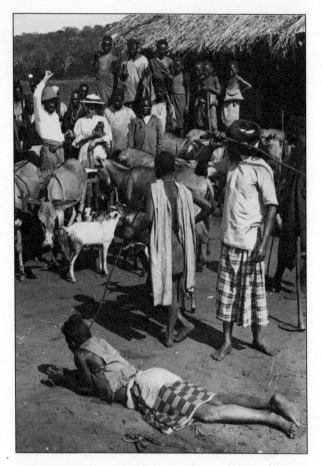

Labor discipline: a German overseer on an East African rubber plantation counts strokes as a native is flogged. [Keystone-Mast Collection, California Museum of Photography, University of California, Riverside]

The Boers in South Africa

South Africa exhibited a unique colonial pattern. Here Dutch settlers, popularly called Boers after the Dutch word for "farmer," had arrived in 1652 to help secure control of the Cape of Good Hope for the Dutch East India Company. The Boers, who called themselves Afrikaners, developed apart from other European settlements in Africa. Clinging to their Dutch Calvinist roots, they saw themselves, much like the New England Pilgrims, as an elect nation planting the wilderness. The arrival of the British, who seized the Cape Colony in 1806, ended their long isolation. With contempt for the Anglican missionaries who sought to convert the black population and horror at the plan to give legal rights to former slaves, the Boers migrated into the interior and established two independent states, the South African

Republic in the region known as the Transvaal and, to the south, the Orange Free State.

The Boer republics were based from the first on the principle of white supremacy. With the discovery of the world's richest diamond and gold deposits in Boer territory, however, British capital and black labor flooded into the republics. The Boers beat back British attempts to recolonize them, and the Transvaal, under the aggressive presidency of Paul Kruger (1883–1902), sought to become the dominant force in South Africa.

CECIL RHODES AND THE IMPERIAL VISION

Kruger was opposed by Cecil Rhodes (1853–1902), a man who dreamed on a far broader scale. The son of a British vicar, Rhodes migrated to South Africa in 1870. Despite frail health, he amassed an immense fortune in diamond and gold mining, and by 1890 he had both cornered the world diamond market and become prime minister of the Cape Colony. Neither personal wealth nor political position satisfied him, however. Negotiating privately with local African chieftains in the 1880s, he established control of a large territory watered by the Zambesi River between the Boer republics and the Congo, which he called Rhodesia and administered through a chartered venture, the British South Africa Company.

Rhodes saw his private colony as the crucial wedge in a north-south axis that, linked by railways and development, could unite Africa from Cairo to the Cape. This empire would of course be British but not controlled by Britain. Rhodes despised the politicians at Whitehall; he believed that only people who had settled in Africa could realize the continent's potential. Many in Britain agreed, and with enthusiasm for empire at its height, his yearly appearances in London were in the nature of state visits. Cabbies and porters greeted him, and Victoria herself entertained him.

The key to Rhodes' schemes remained the Transvaal, whose mines, worked by British developers, were now providing one-third of the world's gold. Rhodes was particularly vexed with Kruger, whose Boers were now, with the influx of foreign workers and traders, a minority in their own country. In December 1895 he launched an attack on the Transvaal with troops led by a company administrator, Leander Starr Jameson. The Jameson Raid became an international incident. The invaders were taken prisoner within days, and when Rhodes

Cecil Rhodes, prime minister of the Cape Colony and founder of Rhodesia. [Library of Congress]

forces had been defeated. The British prevailed only by imprisoning much of the civilian population in compounds behind barbed wire, the first large-scale use of concentration camps. European opinion, led by William II, was outraged, and much of British opinion turned as well. For this reason the Boers were treated leniently at the war's end. Though forced into a federation with the British—the Union of South Africa—they retained considerable autonomy, including the right to exclude blacks from citizenship. This became significant when the Afrikaners became the majority white population, enabling them to impose a radical system of racial segregation, known as apartheid, on a population that was ultimately four-fifths black.

THE WEST IN ASIA

The European presence in Asia was a familiar one by the early nineteenth century. By far the largest Asian territory, however, was Russia's. The Russian Orient stretched from the Caspian Sea to the Bering Strait, bordering Persia, Turkestan, and China. Its frontiers pressed on a number of points sensitive to British interest, particularly India. The stakes of commerce were far higher than in Africa, and the potential for conflict was acute.

Conflict in Central Asia

The Russian Empire expanded on virtually all frontiers in the nineteenth century. It had annexed the small principalities of the Caucasus by 1864, thus situating itself directly on the borders of the Ottoman Empire and Persia (now Iran). To the east, it occupied the vast, sparsely inhabited Kazakh steppe, and about 1860 it began its push into Turkestan, which abutted the whole of Persia's northern frontier as well as those of Afghanistan and western Tibet. By 1895, Russia had reached to within 20 miles of British India; fortunately for both sides, those 20 miles were 20,000 feet above sea level, in the Himalayas.

Tension nonetheless remained high throughout this region. The British regarded India as the heart of their empire, and Queen Victoria assumed the title of Empress of India in 1876 to emphasize the strength of Britain's commitment. Russo-British rivalry in the Mediterranean

refused to disavow them, he was forced to resign as prime minister of the Cape Colony. A lesson had been learned; imperial politics were too sensitive to be left to amateurs. The age of the private freebooter was over.

Rhodes' final years were spent trying to promote his idea of a Cape-to-Cairo railway. Conscious of his now-failing health, he spent much time on his estate at Groote Schuur, sitting for monumental portraits and sculptures and dreaming of an impossible glory: "I would annex the planets if I could," he said. When he died in March 1902, he had recovered much of his popularity and even his influence; but the public's view of him was tinged by nostalgia. The dreamer who had, for a moment, embodied Britain's imperial ideal, was now a man of the past.

Britain set out to annex the Transvaal where Rhodes had failed, provoking the Anglo-Boer War (1899–1902). What had been conceived as a brief campaign, however, turned into a large-scale war of attrition, with guerillas from both republics fighting on after the main Boer

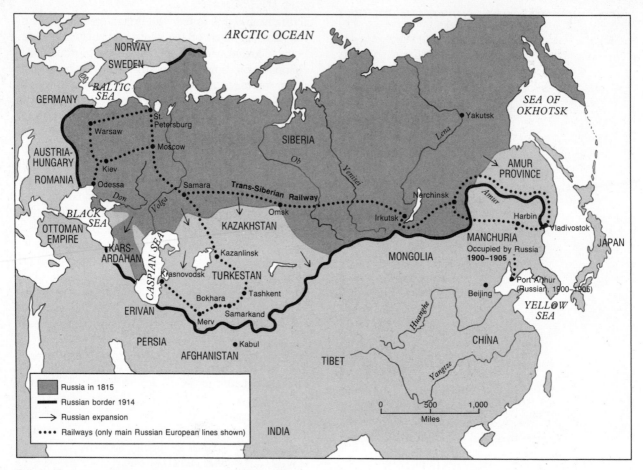

24.2 Russian Expansion in Asia, 1815–1914

had led to the Crimean War, and led later both to Britain's occupation of the island of Cyprus and to its assertion of a protectorate over Egypt. The stakes were no less great in the inhospitable wastes of Central Asia.

The British moved first. In 1838 they attacked Afghanistan, occupying its capital, Kabul. They were unable to pacify the country, however, despite repeated attempts. Border friction continued, and there were two major war scares in the last years of the century, but a settlement was finally reached in 1907. Afghanistan was recognized as a British sphere of influence in return for the neutralization of Tibet, from which the British withdrew their military mission. Persia was divided into a Russian and a British sphere, with a neutral zone in between.

Imperial India

The Indian subcontinent is the home of both the world's oldest continuous civilization and its oldest religion, Hinduism, but it has seldom known political unity. Invaders have swept through it from earliest times, many leaving their mark or monument but all merging in the great stream of its culture. From the mid-tenth century a series of Turco-Afghan invasions established an Islamic presence in northern India, culminating in the establishment of the Mughal dynasty in 1526. Mughal rule had degenerated by the late seventeenth century, and the intolerant rule of the emperor Aurangzeb (1658–1707) provoked widespread rebellion among the Hindu princes. By the early eighteenth century, central control of India had largely broken down.

At the margins of this unfolding drama were the small Western trading posts established along the coasts of the subcontinent in the sixteenth and seventeenth centuries. The English first arrived in 1608 and in 1618 were granted a concession at Surat after a show of force. After vainly attempting to penetrate the Dutch stronghold in Bengal, they set up a small base in 1639 at what was to become Madras. Portugal ceded them Bombay in 1661, and in 1690 they built a fort near the mouth of the Hooghly River on a site soon to be known as Calcutta. The three greatest cities of modern India thus began as tiny colonial settlements.

With the collapse of Mughal authority the British East India Company found itself a de facto government in the areas around its major bases and was even permitted to collect tax revenues for the enfeebled Mughals. Its position was challenged in the 1740s by Joseph Dupleix, chief agent for the French East India Company, but he and his native allies were defeated in 1750 by a young British company clerk, Robert Clive (1725–1774).

With the outbreak of the Seven Years War in 1756,

Clive moved swiftly to drive the French from their bases in Bengal. Anticipating his arrival, the nawab (king) of Bengal, a French client, seized Calcutta and locked some 60 British prisoners overnight in an airless dungeon; all but 20 were dead by morning. The incident, which became infamous as the "Black Hole of Calcutta," gave Clive the excuse not only to retake Calcutta but, by defeating the nawab at the Battle of Plassey (June 1757), to become master of all Bengal. Supported by the British navy, he blockaded the remaining French ports.

The British now faced a turning point. Should they expand further into India? How should they administer what they already possessed? The answer came in a series of parliamentary acts and government commissions that by 1784 had created a dual system of control. The Crown undertook the basic political functions of government (defense, justice, legislation, and the like) while leaving the details of administration and the conduct of trade to the British East India Company. It was a compromise that reflected the practical difficulties of administering a distant colony.

The British postponed the question of further expan-

Tea being loaded for shipment to England at a plantation in India. [E. T. Archive]

sion while they consolidated their base in Bengal. War with Napoleon compelled them to act; they dared not leave room for a French diversion in India. By 1818 they had brought the rest of the country under their control, either by direct administration through the new India Civil Service or by puppet rulers living under the "protection" of British military missions. The last Mughal emperors were left to sit on the throne for another 40 years while the British extended their northwest frontiers by annexing Sind and the Punjab and establishing protectorates in Kashmir and Baluchistan. Ceylon (now Sri Lanka) was occupied by 1815, and by midcentury many of the surviving principalities of Maharashtra and Rajput were incorporated directly into the British dominion, or *Raj,* as was the kingdom of Oudh. By 1886 the piecemeal annexation of Burma had rounded out the frontiers of imperial India.

At the height of empire a mere 40,000 British residents controlled some 150,000,000 Indians. Clearly, this could not have been accomplished without the acquiescence of the population. Most Indians saw the British as the only force capable of averting renewed civil war and brigandage. It must be borne in mind as well that India was as regionally and linguistically diverse as Europe itself, and rule by outsiders, provided that they respected basic customs, was the historic norm. Moreover, the very rarity of Britons themselves meant that most practical contacts with the new imperial government were through fellow Indians, as agents, overseers, and low-level bureaucrats. British rule, though firm, was for the most part indirect.

Britain's attitude toward India revealed a fundamental ambivalence of purpose. The India Act of 1784 declared all "schemes of conquest and extension of dominion in India" to be "repugnant to the wish, the honour and [the] policy of this nation." While this statement should hardly be taken at face value, it does indicate that Britain saw the subcontinent primarily as a source of commercial profit, to be managed with the least possible commitment of public resources. Only when its patchwork of administered territories, protectorates, and alliances on the subcontinent began to add up to actual sovereignty did the British begin to see India in terms of dominion, and only when it began to visualize the whole of its dependent territories around the globe as parts of a single empire did India become its center. Interestingly, this perception came from some of the territories themselves as early as it did from the mother country; about 1830, Nova Scotians were urging the British to recognize "a vast confederacy of kingdoms, islands and provinces

. . . [and] to endeavor to comprehend the whole dominions of Great Britain as one society."[2]

The growth of this sentiment produced both pride in Britain's might and a sense of responsibility for the welfare of the people it ruled. Many Britons, notably Evangelicals, came to feel that it was their duty to bring the blessings of Christianity and material prosperity—in a word, progress—to less favored regions of the globe. This involved an assumption of British cultural superiority that easily acquired racist overtones. Whereas the British had once freely associated and intermarried with Indians, adopted their customs, and admired their proud and ancient civilization, many Britons now saw savagery and heathenism, if not subhumanity. Such attitudes provided justification for the permanent subordination of India, just as similar ones did for that of Africa. The more "liberal" view supposed that Indians were capable of improvement and that their cultural backwardness derived from unenlightened customs rather than natural inferiority. Thus the liberal historian Thomas Babington Macaulay looked forward to raising "a great people sunk in the lowest depths of slavery and superstition" to responsible self-government; such an achievement, he said, would be "the proudest day in English history."[3]

The Revolt of 1857

The Indians proved less than grateful for their instruction. At first the British had provided the stability necessary for Indian commerce and agriculture to revive from the anarchy of the early eighteenth century. As India's economy was subordinated to that of Britain, however, cottage textile production—the country's chief industry—was destroyed by cheap imports from Lancashire. At the same time, Indian peasants were diverted from rice cultivation to produce indigo dye for British cloth, thus assisting the ruin of their own cotton manufacture. More important than economic grievances, however, was the displacement of native elites by imperial officials who had little understanding of, and less sympathy for, the web of traditional customs and caste relationships that bound the countryside. The British were not necessarily more exploitive than such elites, but they were a foreign presence, speaking a strange tongue, practicing an alien religion, and disturbing ancient folkways.

This was the setting for a major revolt in 1857, which began among the native recruits, known as sepoys, who comprised five-sixths of the British army in India, many of them high-caste Hindus. Matters came to a head when the government attempted to supply greased cartridges for its new breech-loading rifles, the tips of which had to be bitten off before insertion. Rumor spread that the grease was a compound of pig and cow fat, forbidden to the devout, and that by forcing them to taste it the British hoped to defile the sepoys, destroy their caste status, and forcibly convert them to Christianity. Marching on Delhi, they proclaimed a restoration of the Mughal dynasty and called on the population to join them in a holy war of liberation.

The revolt thus begun became a full-scale war, raging for more than a year across India's central provinces, engaging the largest British expeditionary force of the century, and costing tens of thousands of lives. No quarter was given, and there were acts of great savagery on both sides. The octogenarian Mughal emperor, Bahadur Shah II, was exiled to Burma, and his sons were summarily executed, thus extinguishing the last dynasty in Indian history.

The revolt of 1857 was a turning point in the history of British India. Macaulay's dream of a grateful people bred up to British standards of civility was exploded, literally, in the bodies of rebel soldiers strapped to cannons and blown apart. Thereafter, the British ruled frankly as masters. The Crown assumed imperial authority under the Government of India Act (1858), ending its long condominium with the East India Company and placing residents in the remaining princely states to ensure their loyalty. The proportion of British officers and troops in the army was increased, and elite regiments were formed. A viceroy was appointed with responsibility for India as a whole. Nonetheless, British India continued to be ruled by very small numbers of Britons: never more than 12,000 in all branches of government, including district officers, judges, and police, or less than 1 percent of the civil service.

For Indians, too, 1857 was a watershed. Despite their overwhelming numbers, they had been unable to cast off British rule. The leaders of the great revolt had offered the country only a revival of the long-faded Mughal dynasty. As Jawaharlal Nehru remarked, the revolt was the last convulsion of the old India rather than the birth of a new nation able to compete among the powers of the modern world. To create such a national consciousness would be the task of succeeding generations, culminating in the mass movement led by Mohandas K. Gandhi that resulted in independence 90 years later.

NEW DELHI: IMPERIAL CAPITAL

The British had political as well as strategic reasons for locating the capital of their Raj in Delhi. Situated at the head of the Ganges valley, it controlled routes from both the east and the south to the heart of India. As the old Mughal capital, it was the symbol of Britain's dynastic succession. The British did not, however, occupy Delhi but built a new planned city, New Delhi, adjacent to it in the early 1900s. A 340-room palace with surrounding gardens, larger than Louis XIV's residence at Versailles, was built for the viceroy on an artificial hill, and, flanked by monumental public buildings, it dominated the city. From it radiated broad boulevards along which the elite of the Indian Civil Service lived in splendor and the Indian princes maintained residences of their own like embassies in a foreign country. Unlike the Victorian architecture that marked the British presence in Calcutta and Bombay, New Delhi was built in a style that tried to harmonize both Western and Indian traditions, using the local red sandstone that the Mughal emperors had quarried for their own palaces.

Nonetheless, New Delhi was an imperial compound, deliberately cut off from the multitudes it ruled. This was even more the case at Simla, the colonial community's summer retreat in the Himalayan foothills north of Delhi, where, diverting itself with cricket, golf, picnics, and parties, it governed in splendid isolation. Most Britons never encountered the native population except as subordinates and menials, and the sign that appeared in all the hotels of India in the 1860s—"Gentleman are earnestly requested not to strike the servants"—speaks volumes on the relationship between ruler and ruled. In 1907, while Britain was offering dominion status to white settler colonies, a liberal government declared as its aim the eventual establishment of an independent India. It took no steps to accomplish this, however. British social policy in India was intensely conservative after 1857. A landlord class was cultivated, and tenancy rose as poorer peasants were dispossessed by the commercialization of agriculture. India continued to be a dumping ground for British goods, and native entrepreneurs were discouraged. Living standards fell as economic growth failed to match rising population except

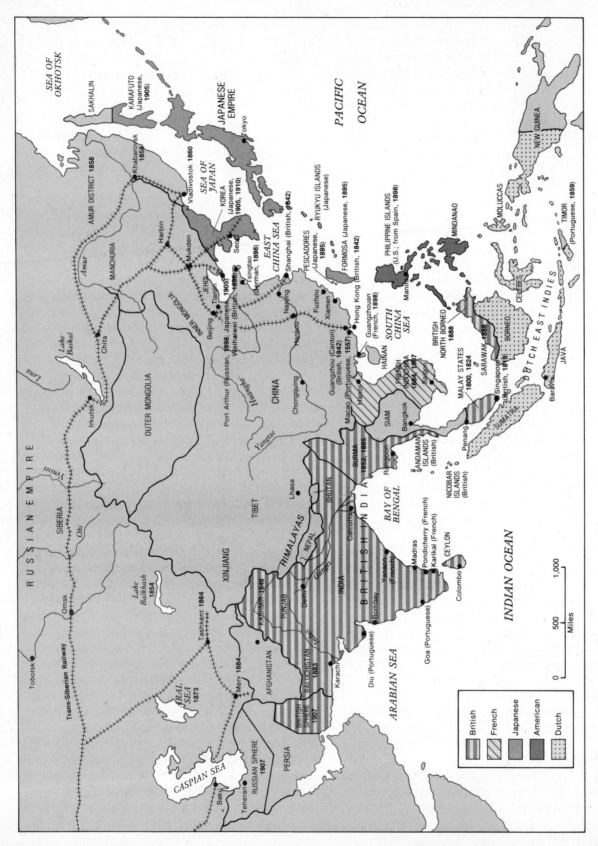

SEA OF
OKHOTSK

SAKHALIN

KARAFUTO
(Japanese,
1905)

JAPANESE
EMPIRE

PACIFIC

OCEAN

Khabarovsk 1858

AMUR DISTRICT **1858**

Vladivostok **1860**

SEA OF
JAPAN

KOREA
(Japanese,
1905, 1910)

Tokyo

RYUKYU ISLANDS
(Japanese)

MOLUCCAS

NEW GUINEA

RUSSIAN EMPIRE

Harbin

MANCHURIA

Mukden

Amur

JEHOL

EAST
CHINA SEA

Shanghai (British, **1898**)

PESCADORES
(Japanese,
1895)

FORMOSA (Japanese, **1895**)

PHILIPPINE
ISLANDS
(U.S.: from Spain, **1898**)

MINDANAO

TIMOR
(Portuguese, **1859**)

Lake
Baikal

Chita

INNER MONGOLIA

Beijing

Tianjin

Port Arthur (Russian, **1905**)

Weihaiwei (British, **1898**)

Tsingtao
(German, **1898**)

Nanjing

Fuzhou

Xiamen

Hong Kong (British, **1842**)

Guangzhou
(French, **1898**)

SOUTH
CHINA
SEA

BRITISH
NORTH BORNEO
1888

BORNEO

CELEBES

DUTCH EAST INDIES

Irkutsk

OUTER MONGOLIA

Huanghe

CHINA

Chongqing

Yangtze

Hankou

Guangzhou (Canton)
(British, **1842**)

Macao (Portuguese, **1557**)

HAINAN

FRENCH
INDOCHINA
1854, 1897

Hanoi

Saigon

SARAWAK **1888**

MALAY STATES
1800, 1824

Singapore
(British, **1819**)

SUMATRA

JAVA

Batavia

Lena

Yenisei

SIBERIA

Obi

TIBET

Lhasa

XINJIANG

HIMALAYAS

NEPAL

BHUTAN

BURMA
1852, 1885

SIAM

Bangkok

Rangoon

ANDAMAN
ISLANDS
(British)

NICOBAR
ISLANDS
(British)

Penang

Lake
Balkhash
1854

KASHMIR **1846**

PUNJAB

Delhi

Indus

Ganges

BRITISH INDIA

INDIA

BAY OF
BENGAL

Calcutta

Madras

Pondicherry (French)

Karikal (French)

CEYLON

Colombo

INDIAN OCEAN

Omsk

Tashkent **1864**

ARAL
SEA
1873

AFGHANISTAN

BALUCHISTAN
1883

Karachi

Bombay

Diu (Portuguese)

Yanaon
(French)

Goa (Portuguese)

ARABIAN SEA

Tobolsk

Trans-Siberian Railway

Merv **1884**

BRITISH
SPHERE
1907

PERSIA

RUSSIAN SPHERE
1907

CASPIAN SEA

Teheran

Baku

1,000

500

Miles

0

	British
	French
	Japanese
	American
	Dutch

24.3 *Colonial Empires in Asia*

for the favored few, and regional famines remained common and often severe.

The British did move rapidly to suppress two Indian practices, thagi and sati. *Thagi,* or sacred murder (the English word "thug" is derived from it), involved the ritual assassination of travelers by roving bands who believed that they were carrying out the commands of their goddess to maintain the balance of population. Each member had a quota of 1,000 kills to achieve salvation, and one captured "thug" claimed to have reached 719. *Sati,* or widow-burning, was the custom of women being immolated on their husbands' funeral pyres. Many Hindus believed that such a sacrifice was an act of high spiritual merit, and the British were at first cautious, merely requiring that no woman be burned without a government certificate. The burnings were finally proscribed in Bengal, Madras, and Bombay in 1829–1830, but they continued in the princely states and, though banned throughout modern India, are practiced surreptitiously to this day.

The Conquest of Southeast Asia

The Dutch had colonized widely in the seventeenth century, planting settlements from Manhattan Island and Pernambuco in the New World to the Cape of Good Hope in Africa to Java in the East Indies (now Indonesia), where after 1815 they established control over the entire 3,000-mile archipelago. Their rule was structurally similar to that of the British, though considerably more exploitive and harsh; the profits of the East Indies played a major role in sustaining Dutch prosperity.

The British and the French were the other major imperial powers in Southeast Asia. The British gradually incorporated Burma into their Indian empire, as we have seen, and in search of a trading base in the South China Sea, they acquired Singapore in 1819. The growing importance of that trade, as well as the need to secure new tin mines and, later, rubber plantations, led Britain to establish a protectorate in Malaya after 1873. Siam (now Thailand) remained nominally independent, though under British influence. Britain's naval and commercial domination of the region was complete.

Using a familiar pretext, the protection of missionaries, the French established themselves in the Chinese tributary state of Vietnam after 1858. Competition with Britain for control of the remainder of the region, known collectively as Indochina, resulted in the annexation of neighboring Cambodia and Laos and in 1885 of Annam

(northern Vietnam) as well. The resolution of a trade syndicate urging this latter step expressed the goals of French imperial policy with admirable clarity:

> The conquest of a new group of near to fifty million consumers which will open to our commerce markets where our manufactures will be easily exchanged for raw materials is a matter assuredly worth the trouble it entails.[4]

China Besieged

The great prize of Asia was China itself, whose population of some 400 million was larger than all of Europe's combined. When a British representative, Lord Macartney, came seeking a commercial treaty in 1793, the Emperor Ch'ien Lung dismissed him with a lofty remark: "Our Celestial Empire possesses all things in abundance. We have no need of barbarian products." Subsequent Western missions fared no better.

Until the eighteenth century, China had been the world's most prosperous and in many respects its most technologically advanced society. Ch'ien Lung was only stating the fact when he said that the West had nothing to offer Asia; European traders had found a similar indifference to their wares in India and had had to pay for their purchases almost entirely in scarce gold.

The situation began to change in the late eighteenth century when opium addiction spread in China. The government declared the use or sale of opium a capital offense, but it was smuggled in from India, where the British East India Company grew opium poppies in huge quantities for the Chinese market. The result—apart from the social devastation wrought by the addiction itself—was a reversal in China's once highly favorable balance of trade in silks, tea, jade, lacquer, and porcelain. By 1828, annual British profits from the opium trade reached $6 million in bullion.

The imperial government was understandably determined to take the matter in hand, but the British, chafing at continued trade restrictions, were no less dissatisfied. When a Chinese commissioner burned drug stocks and fired on British vessels carrying them, the so-called Opium War (1839–1842) broke out. The British easily asserted their naval and military superiority, as they had in India, and by the Treaty of Nanjing (Nanking), China paid an indemnity of $21 million, opened up five new "treaty" ports to trade, and ceded the port of Hong Kong directly to Britain. Most important, it provided that China could not impose a tariff of more than 5 percent on imported goods, thus opening up the entire Chinese market. These concessions were extended to France and the United States in 1844, and after a second Anglo-Chinese war from 1856 to 1860, 12 new ports were opened to Western commerce, as well as the Yangtze River. The Chinese agreed to receive permanent embassies at Beijing (Peking) and to permit foreigners, including missionaries, to travel throughout the country. To enforce these terms, Anglo-French forces occupied the imperial capital itself. The Russians had meanwhile occupied northern Manchuria, cutting China off from the Sea of Japan.

While Western pressure intensified, China was all but paralyzed by the largest and most devastating civil war in history. The Taiping Rebellion (1850–1864) was essentially the product of China's growing inability to feed its soaring population, but the impotence of the ruling Manchu (Qing; Ch'ing) dynasty in the face of Western penetration was a factor as well. Perhaps 40 million people perished in disturbances that lasted until 1873, and a subsequent famine in northern China killed another 12 or 13 million people.

The situation apparently resembled that of eighteenth-century India, with an enfeebled dynasty crumbling amidst anarchy and violence. Unlike India, however, China was too large to be mastered by any single power. As in the case of the Ottoman Empire, therefore, the Western powers chose to preserve a weak throne upon which they could impose conditions while avoiding serious conflict among themselves. But Japan's swift and decisive victory over the Manchus in the war of 1894–1895 touched off a scramble reminiscent of that for Africa. By 1898 it seemed that China might actually be dismembered, though the United States called for an "Open Door" policy that would avoid territorial annexations. China's major ports were controlled by foreign states. Foreign nationals were exempt from Chinese law, a principle known as extraterritoriality. Foreign gunboats patrolled China's rivers, enforcing the will of half a dozen governments. Much of China's northwest and most of its offshore territories had been detached; its tribute states had fallen away. Banditry was endemic, hunger widespread, and the throne despised.

The upshot was a general uprising against foreigners in 1899–1900, led by a patriotic society calling itself "the fists of righteous harmony" and promptly dubbed the Boxers. After slaughtering missionaries and converts, the Boxers besieged the foreign legations in Beijing until an international army relieved them. Heavy reprisals were taken, and the Manchus, who had covertly encouraged the rebels, were saddled with a further indemnity of $330 million.

The so-called Boxer Rebellion was only one of a series

Western troops entering the imperial palace at Beijing in 1900, two months after the Boxer Rebellion had been subdued. [Keystone View Company]

of upheavals that shook China from 1895 and marked the final phase of the Manchu dynasty. When the aged dowager empress Cixi (Tzu Hsi) died and was succeeded by a two-year-old child, the government collapsed, and a republic was proclaimed in 1911 under Sun Yat-sen (1866–1925). With foreign powers still claiming their concessions and warlords contesting the civilian administration, however, there was little chance of establishing an effective government. Under the impact of Western imperialism, China had abandoned the system that had served it for more than 2,000 years and embarked on an uncertain future.

Japan: Challenge and Response

Japan's destiny was in part dictated by its geography. An island chain, Japan had long boasted a vigorous merchant class and a thriving overseas trade. At the same time its rugged terrain made the development of central authority difficult. The Japanese acknowledged an emperor, but real power was exercised by warrior dynasties known as *shogunates,* which ruled over subordinate warlords (*daimyos*) and their retainers (*samurai*) in the manner of the feudal kingdoms of medieval Europe.

After a period of turmoil in the sixteenth century a new shogunate was established by Tokugawa Ieyasu (1542–1616). The Tokugawa shogunate gave Japan civil peace but suppressed the merchant class, expelled all foreigners, and virtually isolated the country from the rest of the world. The Tokugawa scuttled all ships that were capable of overseas commerce and forbade their subjects to travel abroad. Only a single Dutch ship was permitted to land in Nagasaki harbor each year to bring news of the outside world.

Despite their diminished status and restricted trade, however, the merchants soon prospered again. As in Europe, their daughters married into the aristocracy, blurring rigid class distinctions. At the same time the shogunate had begun to outgrow its feudal origins and to take on some of the attributes of a bureaucracy. Japan was ripe for change when American Commodore Matthew Perry sailed his squadron into Tokyo Bay in 1853 and demanded that Japan open itself to the modern world after two and a half centuries.

Humiliated by its inability to withstand Western pressure for trade concessions, the shogunate surrendered its authority to the boy emperor Meiji and his advisers by 1868. The so-called Meiji Restoration marked the beginning of modern Japan. Because the imperial system, unlike that of China, existed in name only, the Japanese were able to adapt it freely to the circumstances that now faced them. Western technology was imported, and a conservative constitutional monarchy based on that of Germany was proclaimed in 1889. With unerring discrimination and astonishing cultural flexibility, the Japanese adopted industrial, political, and legal models from the West without losing their own cultural identity. This was due in part to ingrained habits of discipline and obedience, which enabled the government to mobilize the population rapidly in pursuit of new goals, and in part to the absence of any strongly conflicting traditions or values. Nonetheless, the modernization of Meiji Japan was surely the most remarkable transformation ever achieved by any people in a comparable period of time. Whereas China, with its vastly greater human and material resources, spent itself vainly in trying to expel "foreign devils," Japan, by embracing the West, not only retained its independence but became a world power in its own right.

One of the earliest lessons Japan learned was imperialism itself. The Sino-Japanese War of 1894–1895 was the climax of two decades of encroachment by Japan against Chinese interests, particularly in Korea. The Japanese emerged from it as a recognized imperial power with treaty ports of their own, the right of navigation up the Yangtze River, and the right to set up factories in China. By 1902 the British had entered into an alliance with Japan, which they saw as an effective makeweight against Russia. Although of little practical consequence, the agreement was a landmark in East-West relations. After a century of what Asians bitterly called "the unequal treaties"—encroachments on their sovereignty dictated by the West—a European state had negotiated with an Asian one on terms of parity.

In 1904–1905, Japan defeated another imperial rival of far greater size, Russia. This war marked Japan's emergence as the dominant force in modern Asia as well as the beginning of its rivalry with the United States in the Pacific basin. The Japanese inherited the Russian position in Manchuria and in 1910 annexed Korea outright to their growing empire. Nominally an Allied partner in World War I, Japan took advantage of the conflict to extend its influence in China. In 1915 it forced upon the Chinese government a list of concessions, the Twenty-One Demands, that established Japan's economic control of north China. By 1931, when they attacked Manchuria and set up a puppet state, the Japanese were the principal holders of China's debt. Their designs soon extended over the whole of Southeast Asia, placing them on a collision course with the other rising naval power of the Pacific, the United States.

America Enters the Pacific

The United States had acquired treaty port rights in China as early as 1844, and within 50 years was China's third largest trading partner. In 1867 it acquired Alaska, placing it within reach of mainland Asia across the Bering Strait, and in 1875 it set up a protectorate over the Hawaiian Islands. Until 1898, however, its principal focus of attention had been the Western Hemisphere, over which it had proclaimed a protectoral responsibility since 1823 in the Monroe Doctrine.

It was the United States' hemispheric interest that projected it into the Pacific basin as a major power. U.S. policymakers had long had an interest in the island of Cuba, which rebelled against Spain in 1895. When an American battleship, the *Maine*, blew up in Havana harbor in February 1898, Congress swiftly recognized Cuban independence and set up a protective blockade. Spain reluctantly declared war, knowing defeat to be inevitable. The Spanish-American War brought the United States not only the Caribbean islands of Cuba (which, after three years' occupation, it retained as a protectorate) and Puerto Rico but also the Philippine

Islands and the island of Guam. At the same time it annexed the Hawaiian Islands and seized the strategic coaling station of Wake Island, thus linking its new Pacific territories in a single chain. By 1899 the United States controlled virtually all of the Pacific west of the International Date Line. It fought as well the first of its Asian wars against Filipino guerillas, a bitter struggle that cost 600,000 lives.

The United States thus committed itself to empire in the Pacific. In 1899 it enunciated the "Open Door" principle of equal access to China for all Western nations, thereby asserting its own parity with other major powers. In 1903 it began a canal that would link the Atlantic and Pacific oceans across the isthmus of Panama. The Panama Canal opened in 1914, shortening the route to America's Pacific possessions giving its eastern seaboard direct access to the markets of Asia, and symbolizing its emergence as a full-fledged imperial power.

AUSTRALIA AND THE PACIFIC ISLANDS

The last inhabited region of the globe to be opened to Western imperialism was Oceania, which embraced Australia and the island groups north and east of it. Altogether, this region extended across a quarter of the earth's surface, although it occupied less than one-fifteenth of its landmass, most of it concentrated in Australia.

The motivations of the imperial powers in Oceania were partly exotic, partly economic, and partly political. The depiction of the South Seas in the writings of Herman Melville (1819–1891) and Robert Louis Stevenson (1850–1894) and the paintings of the Paul Gauguin (1848–1903) had piqued the curiosity of a public jaded by material civilization and in search of new models for the Noble Savage, while the seemingly idyllic life of its natives enticed missionaries and anthropologists. Plantation products such as copra, coconut oil, coffee, cocoa, sugar, and cotton could be grown by using native labor that could be virtually enslaved far from prying philanthropists and government agencies; workers were often recruited by simple kidnapping, a practice known as "blackbirding." Oceania was also a dumping ground for social undesirables and political prisoners, a purpose for which the British had originally used Australia.

Australia and New Zealand: Convicts, Wool, and Gold

The great explorer James Cook (1728–1779), who mapped much of the Pacific, claimed Australia for Britain in 1770, although only in 1801 was it realized that this vast territory was not an archipelago but a true continent. Captain Arthur Philip arrived to colonize it with 700 convicts at Botany Bay, the site of modern Sydney, in 1788. By the mid-nineteenth century the convict population numbered some 160,000, many of whom were assigned to work off their sentences as indentured laborers to the free colonists, many of them retired soldiers.

Wool became the continent's staple product after 1820, and by 1886, with a sheep population of 100 million, Australia was by far the world's largest provider of wool, shipping over 400 million pounds annually to Britain alone. In 1851, gold was discovered in Victoria territory, the continent's southernmost province, which for a brief time provided one-third of the world's supply. The resulting immigration was devastating to the native, or Aborigine, population, a Stone Age people whose numbers fell from 300,000 to 80,000 and who were exterminated on the island of Tasmania.

By the end of the nineteenth century the wool trade assured Australia of stable prosperity; indeed, Australia's rate of growth and standard of living surpassed those of Britain itself. The six territories that covered the continent were federated as the Commonwealth of Australia in 1901; as in the United States, the central government possessed only limited authority, and a genuine national sentiment began to emerge only with World War I.

The two large islands that comprise New Zealand, approximately 1,200 miles southeast of Australia, were also claimed for Britain by Captain Cook, although they were not formally annexed until 1840. At that time the settler population was only 2,000. The native Maori population, numbering some 250,000 and already proselytized by missionaries, was guaranteed its lands and fisheries by treaty; as in the case of similar agreements with American Indians, these were disregarded by settlers and laxly enforced by the colonial government. The Maori took up settler weapons and began a revolt that took 10,000 British troops to put down. Far more devastating in the long run were the white man's diseases, which had reduced the Maori population to a mere 40,000 by the late nineteenth century.

New Zealand's development closely paralleled that of

Australia, with which it was briefly federated. Wool comprised half of the country's exports in 1880, but with refrigerated transport, meat and dairy products soon equaled wool in value. Gold discoveries lured migrants, and by 1914 the European population exceeded 1 million. Parliamentary government evolved from the first colonial legislature, and in 1893, New Zealand became the first country in the world to grant full suffrage to women.

Islands of the Pacific

The smaller island groups that had chiefly attracted itinerant whalers and missionaries earlier in the nineteenth century were ripe for partition with the development of plantation agriculture by the 1880s. The conquest of Oceania was a microcosm of the imperial pattern played out on the larger stages of Africa and continental Asia. Explorers, adventurers, and missionaries came first, staking out the territory; capital interests followed, setting up mines and plantations, subjugating labor, and attracting settlers; finally, governments arrived to protect colonial interests, repel squatters, and police the natives. The disproportion between the might of the imperial powers and the tiny island populations whose worlds they destroyed only made the spectacle more striking than elsewhere. Perhaps the ultimate imperial act occurred in 1946, when the United States evicted the inhabitants of Bikini in the Marshall Islands group in order to test its new atomic weapons by obliterating their homeland from the face of the earth.

THE IMPACT OF EMPIRE

The imperialism of the late nineteenth century completed the creation of a global economy that had begun with the conquest of the New World 350 years earlier. Historians continue to debate the economic and political imperatives that drove the West outward. What is not in question is the scope of Western conquest and its impact on the world's peoples. By 1930, five-sixths of the globe was under direct or indirect Western control, and scarcely any inhabited portion of it had been unaffected by Western culture, capital, and technology.

The effect of Western domination varied widely with the type and degree of control exerted, the size and nature of the subject population, and the goals and interests of the colonial power. In Australia and New Zealand the native population was catastrophically reduced, chiefly by disease but in isolated cases by genocide as well. At the same time the population of India, a developed country, doubled in the first century of British rule, largely owing to a falling death rate, while that of Java increased from 5 million in 1815 to 48 million by 1942. As in the West itself, this was due chiefly to sanitation, inoculation, and, later, the use of sulfa drugs; however, the rise in population often resulted in depressed overall living standards.

Western influence permeated virtually every aspect of life in the non-Western world. Western language and to a lesser extent religion brushed aside native speech and worship, especially among the educated classes; English became the common language of India, and English and French those of Africa, while Christianity had considerable success in Africa and Oceania, though less elsewhere. The slaughter of Christian converts in seventeenth-century Japan and in China during the Boxer Rebellion showed the depth of anger toward those who had betrayed native custom and religion to adopt the white man's faith. Less voluntary were the changes in labor, domicile, and living conditions enforced by Western standards of what was right, just, and profitable. Regnal, tribal, and parental authority was often undermined to the point of social collapse, forcing the imperial powers to assume control whether they wished to or not; likewise, land tenure systems, trade and industrial patterns, and established boundaries were swept aside, leaving subject populations at the mercy of their new rulers. In some cases the destruction of native custom was deliberate and systematic, but in others it was unwitting, as when the introduction of rail travel in India forced different caste groups into forbidden contact. Above all, the immense transformative power of capitalism itself, forcibly integrating self-contained regional economies into the new global one, created permanent change. Western imperialism would recede; its effects remained.

Elites and the Exploited

Imperialism could not have succeeded without the collaboration of comprador (collaborationist native) elites; the case of India, where more than 99 percent of the administration and police was composed of Indians themselves, is only the most striking example. Where direct control by the metropolis was not exerted, traditional elites were left in place and often encouraged in their rapacity. The children of comprador elites were often sent to the metropolis for education and acculturation; Gandhi, as a young man, wrote a guidebook to London for his fellow Indians. As the market economy became more pervasive, elites were bound to their imperial masters by their dependence on rents, commercial and speculative profits, and corruption. At the same time the indispensable role they played often gave them considerable bargaining power. Comprador relationships often survived the dissolution of formal imperial ties in the mid-twentieth century, a phenomenon known as *neocolonialism*.

The burden of both the colonial and comprador elites fell upon the mass of the population. The role of this majority was to supply cheap labor, to serve as a passive market for the products of the metropolis, and to support the machinery of exploitation by the taxes it paid. Any benefits it derived from imperial rule—improved transport and sanitation facilities, a gradual increase in literacy—were largely incidental. While some colonizers and missionaries showed genuine concern for the welfare of the majority—Livingstone in Africa was one such—the colonies were judged by the amount of return they produced for the metropolis, whether in terms of economic profit, strategic value, or national prestige.

Seeds of Revolt

From the beginning, imperialism was resisted not only by subject populations but by at least some Westerners on moral, political, and sometimes economic grounds, and its more farsighted supporters recognized that perpetual dominion was neither possible nor even desirable. Almost all the imperial powers paid lip service at least to preparing their colonies for eventual self-government, although their timetables were vague and the practical steps they took were few and halting. Effective pressure for independence came for the most part from the comprador middle class of tradesmen, artisans, petty officials, and professionals who saw their own aspirations for profit or advancement stymied by imperial controls. Both Mao Zedong (Mao Tse-tung) and Mohandas Gandhi came from this class. Both, too, acknowledged their debt to Western critics of imperialism, Mao to Marx and Lenin, Gandhi to John Ruskin and Leo Tolstoy. Even in revolt, the colonial movements for independence would be shaped in their formative stages by the Western imagination. The ubiquity of the imperial impact could have had no greater testimony.

SUMMARY

The new imperialism of the late nineteenth century was the culminating phase of the long process that created a global economy based on the commercial and industrial system of the West and was carried to the remotest shores of the earth by Western capital, arms, and technology. The reasons for this expansion are complex and in part still controversial, but however explained, its effects were incontrovertible. Everywhere, traditional cultures were challenged and transformed by the Western presence, and colonial populations were subjected to the discipline of the market. Imperialism was the primary means by which the Industrial Revolution was diffused throughout the world, the most rapid and far-reaching technology transfer in history. These changes brought with them profound social, political, and environmental consequences whose effects are still unfolding today.

Notes

1. R. Hyam, *Britain's Imperial Century 1815–1914: A Study of Empire and Expansion* (New York: Barnes & Noble, 1976), p. 82.
2. Ibid., p. 32.
3. P. Spear, *India: A Modern History* (Ann Arbor: University of Michigan Press, 1961), p. 257.
4. D. K. Fieldhouse, *Economics and Empire, 1830–1914* (Ithaca, N.Y.: Cornell University Press, 1973), p. 397.

Suggestions for Further Reading

Baumgart, W. *Imperialism: The Idea of British and French Colonial Expansion, 1880–1914.* New York: Oxford University Press, 1982.

Fieldhouse, D. K. *Economics and Empire, 1830–1914.* Ithaca, N.Y.: Cornell University Press, 1973.

Franke, W. *China and the West.* Oxford: Blackwell, 1967.

Gifford, P., and Louis, W. R., eds. *France and Britain in Africa: Imperial Rivalry and Colonial Rule.* New Haven, Conn.: Yale University Press, 1971.

Hobsbawm, E. J. *The Age of Empire, 1875–1914.* New York: Pantheon, 1987.

Hyam, R. *Britain's Imperial Century, 1815–1914: A Study of Empire and Expansion.* New York: Barnes & Noble, 1976.

Lewis, D. L. *The Race to Fashoda: European Colonialism and African Resistance in the Scramble for Africa.* London: Weidenfeld & Nicolson, 1988.

Lichtheim, G. *Imperialism.* New York: Praeger, 1974.

Liska, G. *Career of Empire: America and Imperial Expansion over Land and Sea.* Baltimore: Johns Hopkins University Press, 1978.

Mommsen, W. J. *Theories of Imperialism.* New York: Random House, 1980.

Moon, P. *The British Conquest and Domination of India.* Bloomington: University of Indiana Press, 1989.

Rotberg, R. I. *The Founder: Cecil B. Rhodes and the Pursuit of Power.* New York: Oxford University Press, 1988.

Spence, J. *The Gate of Heavenly Peace: The Chinese and Their Revolution, 1850–1980.* New York: Penguin, 1982.

Storry, R. *A History of Modern Japan,* rev. ed. New York: Penguin, 1982.

Thornton, A. *Doctrines of Imperialism.* New York: Wiley, 1965.

The West and the World

The Age of Empire

Throughout the early modern period, Western attitudes toward other peoples and cultures had been varied and complex. Europe's reaction to the New World was ambivalent: Amerindians were idealized as primitive innocents, but they were also exploited and enslaved. In the Islamic lands and the Far East, by contrast, Europeans were generally obliged to adapt themselves to their host cultures, which they often came to admire. Racist attitudes toward nonwhites in the eighteenth century were at least partly offset by a growing appreciation of cultural diversity and the relativity of custom. Above all, the West's attitude was conditioned by its still modest position among the world's civilizations. Its military and especially naval superiority had not yet been translated into conquest except where resistance was feeble, and neither its trade nor its technology was thought particularly desirable.

These circumstances changed rapidly in the nineteenth century. The simultaneous weakening of the world's major non-Western states and empires—Ottoman Turkey, Mughal India, and Manchu China—together with the

A satirical view of Lord Macartney's reception at the Chinese imperial court in 1792. [Reproduced by Courtesy of the Trustees of the British Museum]

457

This painting glorifies the exploits of Captain Charles Stanley Gough during the British conquest of India. [Courtesy of the Director, National Army Museum, London]

enormously increased wealth and productivity brought about by the Industrial Revolution, enabled the West to extend its influence throughout the world, and a variety of circumstances—commercial profit and expansion, imperial rivalry, and a renewed missionary impulse—caused it to do so. By the end of the century it directly or indirectly controlled more than four-fifths of the world's population.

The West interpreted its success not as the result of temporary technological advantage but as proof of its general superiority to all other cultures. The Chinese sage gave way before the opium entrepreneur, the Noble Savage before the homesteader. Whereas Westerners had once been respectfully curious of older cultures, their attitude was now a mixture of condescension and contempt. Whereas Asian styles and products—so-called *chinoiserie*—had been a mark of cultivation in eighteenth-century Europe, the West now stamped its architecture on the cities of the East, just as it stamped rail and telegraph lines on its countryside.

The West's cultural arrogance grew gradually. Europe was preoccupied with its own wars and revolutions early in the nineteenth century, and the loss of colonial empires in the New World by Britain and Spain was a shock to both countries. Accordingly, some of the more positive attitudes of the Enlightenment persisted into the new century. Philologists studied the connections among the Indo-European languages, and the classics of Asian literature were translated. The movement against colonial slavery that had gathered force in the late eighteenth century resulted in its gradual abolition, though it was replaced in many cases by peonage and forced labor.

The antislavery movement had been led by the Evangelical churches in Britain. The Protestant churches, unlike the Catholic one, had been generally indifferent to proselytizing among the heathen until the late eighteenth century and hence to addressing the question of their human entitlement. When they ultimately did so, however, it was with a vigor that had long since faded from Jesuit and other Catholic missions.

The Evangelical opposition to slavery, combining as it did missionary zeal with an Enlightenment belief in equal human rights, was the product of a uniquely propitious historical moment. Previous missionaries, with individual exceptions, had accepted slavery as a fact of life within which they had to operate; secular reformers, often dubious about the innate capacities of savage populations, limited their demands for equal rights to Caucasians. The Evangelicals united egalitarianism with a passionate commitment to human individualism; slavery, which rejected the first goal and mocked the second, therefore seemed to them an absolute evil. Had the Evangelicals appeared before equal rights became the overriding political issue in Europe, they might well have adopted the attitude of earlier missionaries toward slavery; had they appeared after the triumph of racist theories in the nineteenth century, they might have despaired of emancipation as a responsible option for "inferior" races. Certainly there were other reasons for the decline of slavery, and certainly there were other groups opposed to it, but the Evangelicals alone were able to see it as a transcendent moral issue, and their successors continue to work toward its complete eradication today.

The revival of missionary zeal may be seen as part of the larger thrust of European expansion that began in the late eighteenth century. It gained practical impetus from Europe's advance into the South Pacific and the Indian subcontinent. British rule in India meant that for the first time the West had gained dominion over a population substantially larger than its own and a civilization of equal sophistication and antiquity. The impact of this on the West was to shape its attitudes toward the rest of the world well into the twentieth century.

The image of India in Europe had been largely favorable. The Brahmins, India's priestly caste, were often equated with Chinese sages, and their language, Sanskrit, was widely studied and admired. Goethe, Schiller, Herder, and other figures of the German Enlightenment praised Indian culture, and the Romantic philosopher Arthur Schopenhauer declared Indian Buddhism to be "the most excellent [religion] on earth," both older and nobler than Christianity. The British Orientalist Sir William Jones agreed. "I am no Hindu," he stated, "but I hold the doctrines of the Hindus concerning a future state to be incomparably more rational, more pious, and more likely to deter men from vice than the horrid opinions inculcated by Christians on punishments without end."[1] The classical religious and literary texts of India, including the *Bhagavad Gita* (1785), *Shakuntala* (1787), and the *Upanishads* (1801), were translated into the major European languages, and a chair in Sanskrit linguistics was

established at the University of Bonn in 1816.

These attitudes could not survive the imposition of British rule. The British at first claimed that their presence in India was to rescue the Hindu masses from the oppression of the Muslim Mughal dynasty. This pretense was soon abandoned. "Europeans lord it over the conquered natives with a high hand," reported an observer; "every outrage may be committed almost with impunity."[2] Some of this behavior was attributed to the brutality of East India Company adventurers, but increasingly it reflected the settled prejudice of conquerors. As the British subjected India's economy to their own, they bent Indian society, politics, law, education, and religion with it. This was justified by stigmatizing India as backward and Indians themselves as inferior. The Evangelical reformer William Wilberforce characterized the Hindu deities as "absolute monsters of lust, injustice, wickedness and cruelty," and James Mill, in his *History of British India* (1818), depicted all of Indian history as dismal and sordid. The reversal of attitudes was climaxed by Thomas Macaulay's "Minute" on education in India (1835), which called for the replacement of native languages by English. Macaulay dismissed Hindu culture as "absurd history, absurd metaphysics, absurd physics, [and] absurd theology," arguing that it was Britain's duty as well as its advantage to create a class of Anglicized Indians that could gradually impose civilized norms on the population. The reformer Charles Trevelyan professed his desire to dedicate himself to "the moral and intellectual regeneration of the people of India." The cultural arrogance and paternalism enshrined in Rudyard Kipling's poem "The White Man's Burden" was well established in the first decades of British rule in India.

The greatest of all prizes, to imperialist and evangelist alike, was China. A Prussian cleric enthused:

Millions of Bibles and tracts will be needed to supply the wants of the people. God, who in his mercy has thrown down the wall of national separation, will carry on the work. We look up to the ever blessed redeemer, to whom China with all its millions is given; in the faithfulness of his promise we anticipate the glorious day of a general conversion, and we are willing to do out utmost in order to promote the great work.[3]

Many missionaries devoted themselves self-lessly to the material as well as the moral welfare of their charges and came to oppose the opium traffic as their predecessors had the slave trade. But the great William Wilberforce argued that Christianity and commerce were complementary; it was not only in order to transmit the truths of religion that providence had entrusted Europe with the command of Asia, he said, but to offer as well "the blessings of well-regulated society" and "the improvements and comforts of active industry."[4]

Few nineteenth-century Europeans contested the superiority of their civilization or its duty to instruct inferior races. The question that remained was how far capable those races were of assimilating Western techniques and values. Benthamite and Saint-Simonian reformers in Britain and France looked forward to rapid progress early in the century, but that vision was not fulfilled, and as the Frenchman Gustave Le Bon told the International Colonial Congress of 1889:

> Neither by education, institutions, religious beliefs, nor by any means at their disposal will Europeans be able to exercise a civilizing action on the Orientals, and even less so on peoples who are completely inferior. The social institutions of these peoples are the consequences of a mental make-up which is the work of centuries and which centuries alone can transform.[5]

In short, the late-nineteenth-century West blamed its inability to coax, persuade, or force its values and institutions on the non-Western world on the latter's inferiority. This was in turn most readily explained by theories of race. Linnaeus and Buffon had developed racial classifications in the eighteenth century, and their work was eagerly taken up by an assortment of pseudoscientists who correlated mental and moral attributes with skull shape and facial proportion. A further spur to racial typing was the increasing popularity of polygenesis, the idea that humans had developed not from a single common ancestor but from several separate ones. By 1850 the Scottish anatomist Robert Knox could declare, "With me, race or hereditary descent is everything; it stamps the man." A landmark was the publication of Count de Gobineau's treatise *The Inequality of the Races* (1853–1854), which identified the "Nordic-Aryan" race as

superior to all others and warned against the degenerative effects of race mixing.

Charles Darwin's *On the Origin of Species* (1859) altered the racial argument but ultimately strengthened it. Darwin refuted the idea that any species, including the human one, could have sprung from a single mature ancestor; rather, he contended, all species had evolved from lower forms. In later writings he suggested that among humans, savage or "primitive" races might be regarded as lower evolutionary forms intermediate between civilized humanity and other primates. This led to a spate of studies attempting to define the differences between civilized and primitive humans, as well as to a new discipline, physical anthropology, which purported to measure and describe such differences scientifically. At the same time, racial typologies became more and more elaborate. Gobineau had spoken of only three races, but one anthropological study divided the Irish into seven separate racial categories. People had long since spoken of ethnic groups as if they corresponded to racial entities, referring, for example, to the "French race" or the "German race," but now it appeared as if there were more races than nations.

Racial theory, the idea that humans formed biologically distinct groups, led inevitably to racism, the belief that such groups could be ranked as superior or inferior. This in turn both explained and justified imperialism as the predestined rule of the "master" white race over all others. The existence of distinctive racial characteristics was assumed by virtually everyone; the French critic Hippolyte Taine contended that race was the decisive criterion in explaining all human culture and behavior. Racial stereotyping was the norm: "Orientals," for example, were depicted as clever, crafty, and cruel; Hindus as lazy and apathetic; Arabs as sensual and untrustworthy; blacks as wanton and superstitious. Occasionally, the image of the tropical native still served as a foil to the overbred culture of Europe, as in the Tahitian paintings of Paul Gauguin, but for the most part the West did not doubt that its mission was to civilize the lesser breeds while avoiding racial contamination by them.

The racist attitudes formed by the West in the nineteenth century persisted well into the twentieth. The decline of Western imperialism and the racial nightmare of the Third Reich finally compelled scholars and scientists to rethink their assumptions. Since World War II

Chinese and Europeans going to the horse races in Shanghai, 1879. [The Mansell Collection]

they have attempted to understand human diversity in terms of genetic adaptation rather than overt characteristics such as physical size, shape, and color, and with a few controversial exceptions, race has tended to disappear as a scientific category. It nonetheless remains firmly embedded in popular discourse, and it may be that generations must yet pass before we fully recover the wisdom and humanity expressed by the fourth-century Christian writer Lactantius:

> All men are begotten alike, with a capacity and ability of reasoning and feeling, without preference of age, sex, or dignity. . . . God, who produces and gives breath to men, willed that all should be equal. . . . In his sight no one is a slave, no one a master; for all have the same Father, [and] by an equal right we are all children.[6]

1. C. K. Pullapilly and E. J. Van Kley, eds., *Asia and the West: Encounters and Exchanges from the Age of Exploration* (Notre Dame, Ind.: Cross Roads Books, 1986), p. 152; P. Mudford, *Birds of a Different Plumage* (London: Collins, 1974), p. 90.

2. V. G. Kiernan, *The Lords of Human Kind: European Attitudes Towards the Outside World in the Imperial Age* (London: Weidenfeld & Nicolson, 1969), p. 34.

3. George Woodcock, *The British in the Far East* (New York: Atheneum, 1969), p. 103.

4. J. H. Parry, *Trade and Dominion: The European Overseas Empires in the Eighteenth Century* (New York: Praeger, 1971), p. 317.

5. Raymond F. Betts, *The False Dawn: European Imperialism in the Nineteenth Century* (Minneapolis: University of Minnesota Press, 1975), p. 175.

6. Nancy Stepan, *The Idea of Race in Science: Great Britain, 1800–1960* (Hamden, Conn.: Archon, 1982), pp. 1–2.

25

CULTURE AND CRISIS

European civilization seemed triumphant in the last decades of the nineteenth century and the first years of the twentieth. It had successfully negotiated the most far-reaching technological change in recorded history, the Industrial Revolution, and with it gained dominion over the human and material resources of virtually the entire planet. It had attained unparalleled material prosperity: its steel-girded cities pulsed with electricity; its ports were crammed with the spoils and produce of the world; the air and the oceans teemed with its message and commands. Its populations were better housed, better fed, better educated, and longer-lived than any other in history. If toil and poverty were still the lot of many, there was confidence that the bounty of the machine would ultimately raise everyone above want.

Outwardly, Western society reflected this confidence. Its skyscrapers and railway stations, its temples of sport and culture, its monuments and statuary, even its clinics and hospitals, exuded the sense of a world planted on sure foundations. If the eighteenth century had promised progress, the nineteenth century appeared to have made good on it. The twentieth was eagerly anticipated. "We stand on the last promontory of the centuries," declared the Italian Filippo Marinetti. "Why should we look back[?] . . . The past is necessarily inferior to the future."[1]

Yet beneath the surface of official optimism, currents of doubt and even despair ran deep in Western culture. To its critics the machine civilization dwarfed humanity, and philosophers, psychologists, and artists began to describe the individual not as a free, rational being but as the prisoner both of social conditioning and of unfath-

omed inner drives. At the same time, science too was reexamining its own premises, a process that led to revision of the most basic concepts of time, space, and matter. By 1914 there was a widespread sense in elite cultural circles that Western society had passed its zenith, that decline was already perceptible, and catastrophe perhaps imminent.

SCIENCE AND SOCIETY

To a large extent the intellectual foundations of the nineteenth century rested on the Newtonian synthesis of the seventeenth century. In the Newtonian view, the world and its properties could be reduced to the action of mechanical forces operating on matter. Such action, reduced to the language of mathematics, could provide a theoretically complete description of all physical events. The material world, then, was fully knowable; and what was known could be controlled.

If humanity could master nature by understanding its laws, then by extension it could master itself by understanding the laws of social interaction. This had been the task of the Enlightenment and of the nineteenth-century school of thought known as positivism associated with the Frenchman Auguste Comte (1798–1857). Comte traced the evolution of human thought from animism, the worship of primitive natural forces, to theology, which transferred this worship of a supreme being, to positivism, which revealed the laws of nature and society. The new disciplines that developed in positivism's wake—history, politics, economics, sociology, and anthropology—aimed accordingly to deduce universal laws from the data of social experience, thereby putting the science of society on a footing with natural science and completing the task of human understanding.

For many, science itself had become a surrogate for religion, supplying a comprehensive view of the world and giving answers to the riddles of existence. Yet while nineteenth-century science appeared to be advancing from strength to strength, cracks had begun to appear in its fundamental postulates. The first of these was opened up by the British naturalist Charles Darwin (1809–1882), whose theory of evolution suggested a disturbing randomness in the development of life.

The Darwinian Revolution

The idea of evolution was not new when Darwin published *The Origin of Species* in 1859. For more than a century, since the Italian Giambattista Vico (1668–1744) had put forward a developmental account of language and society, evolution had been a structural model for both the human and natural sciences. Evolutionary theory had entered biology with Jean-Baptiste Lamarck (1744–1829) and astronomy with Laplace, and had been part of a major debate in geology on the origin and antiquity of the earth's topography.

At the same time, however, evolution clashed with the dominant mechanical model of the physical sciences. The Newtonian universe had been created perfect and ruled from its inception by immutable laws; its history was the story of quantifiable motion, not qualitative change. Evolution, however, like the idea of progress that was so closely related to it, suggested a gradual development from lower to higher, or at any rate from less to more complex. The two models—developmental and static—had clashed in a famous debate over the origin of life at the Paris Academy of Sciences in 1830, and the evolutionary concept had won out.

Evolution was thus a well-established idea when Darwin published his work. What made it so influential was his account of plant and animal origins and the general theory of biological development that supported it. Darwin noted that most species reproduced far more of their kind than could possibly mature. From this he concluded that life was a struggle for existence within an environment in which, as the popular formulation had it, only the fittest could survive. Survival, he observed, was

Charles Darwin. His theory of evolution transformed Western society's vision of itself. [National Portrait Gallery, London]

enhanced by randomly occurring mutations—a stronger beak, a sleeker wing—that helped certain species members to adapt to their environment. Darwin called this process *natural selection* and held it to account for the prevalence of certain individuals or species over others.

Darwin's theory was immediately hailed by his scientific colleagues, but it created passionate controversy among the general public. It directly challenged the traditional idea, now called creationism, that God had made each species perfect by a single act of genesis and had created humanity to rule over the earth. Darwin did not discuss human evolution, but his omission of the subject only made his vision all the more fearful. A world without humans was obviously not a world made for humanity, and if the human species had subsequently evolved, it had done so on the same terms as the tiger or the reptile, by force or cunning. Darwin, his critics charged, had reduced human beings to brutes and God to a fiction.

In a later work, *The Descent of Man* (1871), Darwin suggested that humans had most likely sprung from a common ancestor of the anthropoid age. Theologians were scandalized, but defenders of Darwin declared that it made the human achievement of scientific understanding and moral consciousness all the more remarkable. When in a celebrated debate the Bishop of Oxford sneeringly asked the Darwinian Thomas Henry Huxley (1825–1895) on which side of his family he claimed descent from a monkey, Huxley replied that he would not be ashamed to have descended from a brute but only to ignore the truth of his origins.

The shock that Darwinian thought gave to respectable opinion was less fundamentally the derivation of humanity from lower orders than the picture it painted of a world whose sole commandment was survival. If Newton's world had been a machine, Darwin's was a jungle. Struggle was its sole activity, and strength its only good. The Newtonian order invited admiration for the wise Creator who had shaped its harmonies, but Darwin's vision made the most innocent meadow a battlefield where life and death were continually wagered and nothing was to be won but the next day's strife. What did moral consciousness mean in such a world except the awareness of a struggle without purpose or end?

Yet the Darwinian vision was compelling precisely because it fit the facts of not only the physical but also the human world that Victorians knew. In that world, individuals competed without quarter in the daily struggle for bread, as capital fought labor and nation fought nation. Darwin himself refrained from addressing political questions. But his work put a stamp of scientific prestige on what many already believed about society and culture and justified, at least implicitly, what was already practiced.

After Darwin the evolutionary model was so pervasive that no one who wished to be taken seriously on any social question could afford to ignore it, and few would fail to claim it in support of their case. Scholars as well as partisans were eager to appropriate it and pressed it into the study of human history and behavior. This phenomenon was known as Social Darwinism.

Social Darwinism

The most aggressive popularizer of Darwin was Herbert Spencer (1820–1903). Society, he asserted, was nothing other than an adaptive response by humans to their vulnerability as individuals. Ultimately, the artificial environment it created would replace that of the external world, freeing humans from the tyranny of nature.

Spencer's utopia was the liberal state sketched out in John Stuart Mill's influential *On Liberty* (1859), in which each person would pursue his or her own ends, subject only to respect for the freedom of others to pursue theirs. It followed from this that the state could not compel the fit to care for the unfit. Darwin had noted that human society was the only kind that protected the weak and the infirm. This, said Spencer, was wrong on two counts. It violated the principle of natural selection, which could only jeopardize social progress, and it negated the principle of individual freedom. Compulsory charity was bad biology, bad ethics, and bad social planning.

Although some argued that human solidarity strengthened society, for the most part the Spencerian view prevailed. It fit in handily with the bourgeois conception of wealth as the product of strength and merit and poverty as the result of moral inferiority. On the political level, too, the struggles of Italy and Germany for unification and of the United States for national self-preservation seemed to illustrate vividly the ideas of evolutionary struggle and survival of the fittest. As the American sociologist William Graham Sumner (1840–1910) expressed it, war was the natural condition of nations: "It is the competition of life that makes war, and that is why war has always existed and always will."[2]

Such attitudes merged easily with a "scientific" racism. In Germany, social theorists portrayed human history as an unending struggle between races, classes, and nations, while one French writer found in racial division "the great explanation of the history of civilization." The triumphs of Western imperialism made this seem obvious. "What is Empire," asked the British statesman Lord Rosebery, "but the predominance of Race?" Although Darwin himself had insisted that all humans sprang from a common ancestor, the idea that the races had a separate or at least unequal biological development persisted. Racist attitudes in the name of Darwin were particularly blunt in the United States, where segregation had replaced slavery in the post–civil war period. "If the Negro stands in the way of progress," asserted one southern spokesman, "he will have to get off the earth."[3]

The subordinate status of women was assumed by most Social Darwinists, although August Bebel, while granting the inferiority of blacks, defended the equality of women. Most Darwinian discussion of women centered on the dangers of miscegenation, or racial mixing. Spencer endorsed mixing between European stocks but thought that marriage with blacks and orientals should be "positively forbidden." Darwin's cousin, Francis Galton, proposed to create a new race of supermen by requiring the physically and mentally superior to breed and the unfit to practice birth control or be sterilized. One of the few women invited to address the scientific academies where these weighty questions were discussed was Clemence Royer, Darwin's French translator; when she pointed out to her male colleagues that the oppression of women made them less eager to be mothers, they struck her remarks from their published proceedings.

Reformers and socialists were unwilling to concede that Darwinism favored conservatives. The American Lester Frank Ward (1841–1913), who coined the term Social Darwinism, deplored its abuse to justify existing social inequities, while an Italian criminologist called it an excuse for "cannibalism." Such critics claimed that Darwin had been willfully misread. They contended that, properly understood, evolution demonstrated a progressive development from brute struggle to social cooperation. This view was the basis of the anarchist Prince Kropotkin's *Mutual Aid* (1902). Drawing upon a wealth of biological and anthropological data, Kropotkin argued that those species had adapted best that had repressed conflict in favor of cooperation. Mutual aid, he asserted, must be considered as much the law of life as mutual contest and in the long run the superior principle.

In the end, "Darwin" became simply a name for the pervasive influence of the evolutionary model throughout the cultural life of the late nineteenth-century West. The novels of Émile Zola (1840–1902) and the Americans Frank Norris (1870–1902) and Theodore Dreiser (1871–1945) depicted peasants and workers crushed in the struggle for existence under capitalism, while the immensely popular stories of Jack London (1876–1916) portrayed isolated heroes fighting for survival in a hostile Arctic wilderness. Both the natural and social worlds had become, in the popular imagination, more threatening places; and just as the West's control of the material environment had become greater than ever, so the individual had become less and less secure within it.

The Breakdown of the Scientific Order

The emergence of the evolutionary model in the biological and earth sciences had as yet no effect on the remainder of science. This was particularly true in physics, in which the Newtonian model continued to prevail. It was now generally accepted that the universe was as old as 500 million years. This was not significant to the Newtonian system, however, because if the laws of

physics were fixed and unvarying, then their operation had been the same from the beginning of time and would remain so to the end of it. Local systems might have their patterns of evolution and decay, but the structure of the universe remained constant.

The Newtonian cosmos was composed of matter, which consisted of chemical elements occurring singly or in combination and made up of atoms. Matter was disposed in space, which was not mere emptiness but a continuum filled with an invisible substance, the ether, which made motion possible by conducting gravitational and electromagnetic forces. The ether was a transparent medium without properties of its own, but its existence was crucial, since matter itself was held to be solid and impermeable. The universe could then be conceived as a kind of soup with chunks of matter suspended in it that, when stirred by cosmic forces, produced the effects of light and motion. All action implied a corresponding reaction; all cause had its appropriate effect, and all effect its antecedent cause.

This view was actually full of difficulties. It was not clear why matter should be ultimately indivisible, nor what cosmic forces were, whether a kind of moving matter or an impulsion, like a wave through water. Moreover, although science based itself on empirical demonstration, the Newtonian model depended upon presupposing a medium that, though all-pervasive, was invisible, undetectable, and immeasurable. From a philosophical standpoint the Newtonian model was at this point hopelessly lacking in rigor or even logical consistency. Like its Ptolemaic precursor, however, it was the basis of a great many other beliefs. From Adam Smith's model of a free market that functioned according to the laws of supply and demand to the concept of character as a bundle of discrete moral qualities, the Newtonian model structured the way in which men and women thought about their everyday world. The premise of the model was that the behavior of all objects, whether inanimate or animate, was ultimately uniform, intelligible, and predictable and that whatever in nature or culture seemed otherwise was merely misunderstood.

The first crack in this foundation was Darwin's idea of mutation, or random variation in organisms. Whether mutations would thrive or fail depended on natural selection, but whether they would occur seemed to depend entirely on chance, for which there was no place in a Newtonian world. The second crack was made by the recently discovered laws of thermodynamics, or heat transfer. Because it was assumed that matter, being irreducible, could be neither created nor destroyed, it followed that the sum of matter and energy in the universe was constant. Energy, however, tended to distribute itself uniformly throughout the universe by heat dissipation, thus leading to a condition called *entropy*, in which energy was so dispersed that it could perform no useful work. The result would be a dark and deadened universe, incapable of sustaining life.

If entropy was the fate of the universe, progress was mocked, and civilization itself, with its unbridled dissipation of the earth's finite energy sources, might be hastening the end of planetary life. This was the conclusion drawn by the American historian Brooks Adams (1848–1927), who, citing evidence from paleobotany and paleozoology, argued that humanity had arrived only when the physical decadence of the earth—the decline of its capacity to support life—had already begun. Humanity was thus not the highest but the last term in the evolutionary process, a dysfunctional animal in a degraded environment. Like patients searching anxiously for signs of terminal illness, Europeans of the 1890s examined themselves for the telltale symptoms of decay. Mortality statistics revealed a rise in deaths from heart disease and cancer, and police records an alarming increase in crime, madness, and suicide. The most popular tract of the decade, Max Nordau's *Degeneration* (1893), portrayed the West as a civilization in both moral and physical decline.

The Newtonian order had thus already ceased to be comforting even before its scientific props were kicked away. That occurred in the last two decades of the nineteenth century. A young German physicist, Heinrich Hertz (1857–1894), discovered radio waves, and Wilhelm Roentgen stumbled on the X-ray in 1895. Almost simultaneously, researchers in Paris discovered the radioactive properties of uranium. Suddenly, the world appeared to be full of mysterious cosmic rays that could pass through the supposedly impenetrable barriers of matter, and matter itself appeared to be emitting high-energy particles. The idea of the stable atom could not hold.

The final blow to Newtonian physics was administered by two Americans, Albert A. Michelson (1852–1931) and Edward W. Morley (1838–1923), who devised an ingenious experiment in 1887 to test the existence of the ether. Using a broken beam of light, they attempted to measure the passage of the earth through the ether, which, if material at all, had to offer some resistance. None was discovered. An attempt was made to rescue the concept of the ether by suggesting that motion itself might alter the shape of an object, thus distorting the results of the Michelson-Morley experiment. This only

brought the far more disturbing implication that the perceptions of time and space on which all scientific experiment was based might be conditional.

At this moment a young German physicist, Albert Einstein (1879–1955), published a paper on the special theory of relativity (1905), which, together with the general theory that followed it (1916), simultaneously demolished the Newtonian model and completed the revolution that Newton himself had begun in Western thought. Newton had refuted Aristotle's assumption that bodies were naturally at rest, suggesting instead that, once moved, they could theoretically continue in motion indefinitely. But the physics of his day did not enable (or require) him to speculate about the nature of bodies themselves; for his purposes they could be considered solid objects, internally immobile and quantifiable as mass. What Einstein gave up was the absolute character of matter and the clear distinction classical physics had made between matter as the stuff of the universe and energy as the external force that acted on it. Matter and energy were not different things but different states, freely convertible into each other by the celebrated formula $E = mc^2$. Matter could in this sense be considered stored energy, and since the energy contained in a given object was, according to the formula, enormous relative to its mass, a small object was capable of releasing tremendous quantities of energy. The atomic bomb was to result from this discovery.

In Einstein's world, not matter but motion was the only constant, expressed in terms of the ultimate velocity, that of light (186,282 miles per second). Einstein noted that objects would shrink as they approached the speed of light and, upon reaching it, would lose their three-dimensional character altogether. This meant that space had no absolute character but would expand or contract with motion.

The idea of time fared no better. As space had been used in classical physics to situate objects, so time had been used to track their movements. Accordingly, it made no sense to think of them as independent coordinates; rather, said Einstein, they were part of a four-dimensional field that could be mapped only on the surface of a non-Euclidean geometry.

If Newtonian physics had forced the educated public to abandon the idea of a cosmic up and down, Einstein's model compelled them to give up their notions of here and there or before and after, at least in any absolute sense. With these went the notion of cause and effect that had depended on the idea of serial progression. In Einsteinian physics, space and form were plastic, and events were discontinuous. The German Max Planck (1858–1947) had shown that energy was emitted not in a wave or a stream but in short bursts (*quanta*) that were now here, now there, without any apparent triggering mechanism or even any traversal of space. A further complication was the uncertainty (or indeterminacy) principle, introduced by Werner Heisenberg (1901–1976) in 1927. Heisenberg noted that it was impossible to measure both the position and the velocity of an electron because observations of one distorted observations of the other. Heisenberg concluded that the behavior of subatomic particles could not be predicted, but only estimated as probabilities.

The Newtonian universe, though strange and unsettling in its day, could still be reconciled with customary perception. Things existed in a certain time and place, and events occurred in a determinate sequence. Rules applied; those rules, whether laws of motion or laws of conduct, were uniformly valid. Moral as well as physical responsibility thus rested upon the stable universe. As the mechanical lever produced motion and work, the moral one produced good and evil.

The Darwinian world had introduced a single element of chance, mutation, into what was still an otherwise deterministic system. More disturbingly, it suggested not only that the physical world lacked a moral basis, but that traditional morality might be a handicap to survival. The Social Darwinists had argued the consequences of this, and ethnologists and anthropologists, in recording the cultural variations among different peoples, had anticipated something like the Einsteinian principle that systems are relative to those experiencing them. Nonetheless, the new world of physics offered a radically different conception of material reality. In place of matter, it left flux; in place of causation probability; in place of necessity indeterminacy.

Einstein's discoveries were not unaided; he built upon the work of many gifted physicists and mathematicians. As in other cases of what the philosopher Thomas S. Kuhn has called a paradigm shift—a change in the basic model by which people comprehend reality—there was no single road to revelation. A change in the way in which space, time, perspective, and motion were perceived was apparent in philosophy, the arts, and the human sciences in the generation preceding Einstein's theory. If that theory gave immediate impetus to developments in these fields, it was not because painters, poets, and musicians were reading obscure physics journals but because Einstein's formulations chimed intuitively with what they already apprehended.

THE CRISIS OF WESTERN CULTURE

As science chipped away at the established image of reality and art, too, began to offer new and unfamiliar pictures of it, the world the West had so recently conquered began to seem at least philosophically insecure in its grasp. For the first time the very idea of a moral order was called into question. For centuries, reason and faith had defined that order, sometimes in collaboration, sometimes in competition, but always in dialogue. When traditional faith began its slow decline in the seventeenth century, elite culture exalted reason in its place, a process that culminated in the philosopher Hegel's identification of reality itself with reason. If faith had placed God in the center of the universe, then reason put humanity there, whence the search for God could always be renewed. But Darwin's revolution had dethroned humanity from that center, while Einstein's had destroyed the notion of a center or even a stable core as such. By the end of the century the newly proclaimed science of psychoanalysis would probe the last sanctuary of value, the mind itself, revealing there the same struggle of blind forces that seemed to rule the natural, social, and political world.

Religion in an Age of Science

At the beginning of the nineteenth century the climate for religion seemed more hospitable than at any time in the previous 150 years. Romanticism had brought the Middle Ages back into fashion, with its presumed spirituality; even pilgrimages to the Holy Land were again in vogue. The German Friedrich Schleiermacher (1768–1834) summed up the new spirituality in his *Speeches on Religion to Its Cultured Despisers* (1799). Schleiermacher, like most of the Romantics, dismissed dogma in favor of the religious instinct, whose fundamental characteristic was the feeling of absolute dependence that preceded knowledge of the divine. The "despisers" of religion, he contended, missed the point in ridiculing outmoded doctrine, for the instinct that led humanity to God was a fact of experience that nothing could refute.

The revival of religion had a political dimension as well. When Pope Pius VII returned to Rome in 1814 at the fall of Napoleon's rule, his restoration symbolized the return of the old order to Europe more vividly than any other event. Gone, at least temporarily, were the acrimonious disputes between throne and altar that had marked the Old Regime; in France, Italy, Spain, Portugal, Germany, and the Netherlands the Catholic church allied itself firmly with the restored monarchies. The Jesuit order was revived, and scores of new orders and pious societies were founded, many of which had active political connections and aggressively combated liberal tendencies. Popular devotions such as the Sacred Heart also sprang up, and there were frequent reports of miracles, the most famous of which were the purported healings at Lourdes in southern France in 1858.

The papacy itself reaffirmed its sovereign powers and sought to extend their scope, a policy known to critics as *ultramontanism*. Under Pope Pius IX (1846–1878) the doctrine of papal infallibility was formally proclaimed (1870), by which the pope was declared to be incapable of error when he pronounced on matters of faith and morals. Church liberals had already suffered a crushing defeat in Pius' *Syllabus of Errors* (1864), which denounced the view that "the Roman Pontiff can and ought to reconcile himself and come to terms with progress, liberalism, and modern civilization." With this pronouncement, Pius IX threw down the gauntlet to the modern world, initiating a period of bitter struggle between church and state in Italy, France, Germany, and Spain. His successor, Leo XIII (1878–1903), alarmed at the growing isolation of the church, attempted to recapture alienated Catholic workers in his encyclical *De Rerum Novarum* (1891). At the same time he affirmed the sanctity of contracts and denounced socialism and all violence against property. The solution to the class struggle was for employers to pay a "fair wage" to "a frugal and well-behaved wage-earner" under the benevolent eye of the church.

The battle between church and state affected Protestant denominations too. Frederick William III of Prussia aroused angry resistance when he tried forcibly to unite the Lutheran and Calvinist churches in 1817. Clashes with the authorities occurred in Scotland, Switzerland, Norway, and the Netherlands, often complicated by nationalist stirrings and conflicts between ordained clergy and evangelicals. In Britain the Oxford Movement attempted to reinvigorate the Anglican Church; it was compromised, however, by the defection of its leading figure, John Henry Newman (1801–1890), who converted to Catholicism and ended his days as a cardinal.

These controversies were irrelevant to much of the urban proletariat. Few churches had been built in the new industrial towns; in England, two-thirds of the urban population was unpastored, while the churches of Berlin could accommodate only 25,000 of the city's 800,000 people in 1880. While a few organizations such as George Williams' Young Men's Christian Association (YMCA, founded 1844) attempted to address the problems of workers, only William Booth's Salvation Army (1878) went directly into the slums to aid the destitute. On the whole, the response of the organized churches to the needs of the emerging urban majority was uninformed and desperately inadequate.

There were many reasons for this failure. The churches had lost much of their traditional function of charity to the state, and they were no longer effective instruments of social control. Engels may have exaggerated when he found an almost total indifference to religion among the English working classes, but there was a great decline in religious practice. When churches were finally built in the cities, workers frequently excused themselves on the grounds that they lacked proper clothes to attend. Churchgoing was now viewed by many as a middle-class activity, as distant from working-class culture as opera was.

Social irrelevance and the shortage of pulpits were important in marginalizing the nineteenth-century churches, but these could be overcome; the decline of belief was a more difficult problem. The Romantic enthusiasm for the beyond was short-lived, and advances in geology and biology had once again called into question the biblical account of creation. The skepticism that was common among the elite in the eighteenth century gradually penetrated all classes. Militant atheists, called freethinkers, vied with revivalists for the attention of crowds; in 1844, Emma Martin preached *against* religion before 5,000 people in the factory town of Leicester.

The questioning of Christianity inevitably led to its founder. The nineteenth century produced a host of biographies of Jesus that treated him as a purely historical figure. Many of them did so to rescue the core of his ethical teaching from what they regarded as the dogma and superstition that surrounded it, but the effect was nonetheless shocking. Once so liberated, Jesus could be claimed for progressive and even radical causes. Thus the German Wilhelm Weitling could declare that Jesus was the first Communist, and the Frenchman Étienne Cabet that no one could be called a Christian who was not a Communist. This was not as incongruous as it seemed; many earlier reformers, notably the sixteenth-century Anabaptists, had identified Christianity with community of property, and during the French Revolution, Jesus had been called a sans-culotte. Nonetheless, a merely ethical Jesus was at best a symbol of human hopes, and a secular religion was simply another political cause.

The crisis of Christianity was one for Judaism as well. Emancipated Jews converted to Christianity in large numbers or simply abandoned their religion. Many converts were merely in search of social acceptance, although some became prominent in their new faiths. Nonetheless, Christian extremists blamed Jews for the decline of faith and, more generally, for the evils of secularism and social alienation. Anti-Semitism thus became a way for some Christians to rationalize their own doubts about the modern world. Many Jews embraced new liturgical forms designed to make their worship more "modern" and, perhaps, less offensive to their Christian neighbors. But anti-Semitism was also a stimulus to Zionism, with its affirmation of the historic destiny of Jews and the imminence of their return to Palestine.

The hunger for religious truth gave rise to various millennial movements in the United States, while spiritualists and mediums claimed contact with a spirit world or with the souls of the deceased. The great Irish poet William Butler Yeats (1865–1939) was only one of a large number who took such manifestations seriously. At the same time there was a growth of interest in Asian religions, which has continued to the present day. The variety of religious experiment amid the general climate of disbelief led the English writer G. K. Chesterton (1874–1936) to remark, "When people cease to believe in God, they don't believe in nothing, but—what's far worse—in anything."[4]

Standing apart from almost every religious tendency of the nineteenth century was the Danish theologian Søren Kierkegaard (1813–1855). Kierkegaard took doubt and disbelief for granted as the precondition for religious knowledge. God, he contended, was necessarily veiled by human sin and could be found only at the limits of despair by each individual alone. Kierkegaard's bleak doctrine was ignored by his contemporaries, but in the twentieth century it became the basis for a revived Protestant theology and the postwar philosophy of existentialism.

FRIEDRICH NIETZSCHE AND THE QUEST FOR VALUE

If the nineteenth century was not prepared to take up Kierkegaard's solitary quest for God, it was far more receptive to the suggestion that humans create the values they need for themselves. This was the message of Friedrich Nietzsche, a prophetic figure and the most influential social thinker of the generation before 1914.

Nietzsche was born in Saxony in 1844, the son of a Lutheran minister. He studied theology and classical philology at the University of Bonn and in 1869 was appointed to a chair in philology at the University of Basel, where he met the composer Richard Wagner (1813–1883). Wagner was a profound influence; Nietzsche later confessed that "All things considered, I could not have endured my youth without Wagner's music." The two men grew apart, however, and Nietzsche broke violently with Wagner, denouncing him as a racist, chauvinist, and anti-Semite.

Ill health forced Nietzsche to resign his chair in 1879, but a private income enabled him to spend much of the next decade traveling. During this period he composed his major philosophical works, including his masterpiece, *Thus Spake Zarathustra* (1883–1885). These were written in a highly original and provocative style, combining aphorisms and short meditations with parables

Friedrich Nietzsche. His challenge to traditional philosophy and morality made him a herald of the modern world. [The Granger Collection, New York]

and stretches of prose poetry that Nietzsche called "dithyrambs." Nietzsche broke with classical philosophy in refusing to write formal treatises or to expound any system. His thought came in bursts of insight that ranged over the entire cultural tradition of the West, from the origins of Greek tragedy to the politics of his own day. The intensity of his intellectual and emotional life told on his frail health, and in January 1889 he lapsed into a madness from which he never recovered. Ignored by all but a few friends and supporters during his active lifetime, his writings achieved renown in the decade that preceded his death in 1900. Living under the care of his sister, he enjoyed occasional lucid intervals but could never bear mention of the works that had made him one of the most famous figures in Europe.

Nietzsche was the first major philosopher to take culture rather than nature as his province. Whereas his predecessor Arthur Schopenhauer (1788–1860) had decried the will as an enslavement to desire, Nietzsche exalted it as the prime faculty of creation. The power to create in free individuals, he insisted, was the source of all value, and anything that restrained it, whether religious commandments or so-called natural laws, was the enemy of life.

Frankly embracing atheism—"God is dead" was his most famous aphorism—Nietzsche traced the root of modernity's ills to the ethical residue of Christianity, with its stifling conventionality and suppression of instinct. He called for a heroic individual, the superman, who would spurn the herd morality of the masses and realize what Nietzsche called the transvaluation of all values. He did not specify what such a transformation would entail. He saw his role as prophetic, not instrumental. Indeed, it was precisely his rejection of all proposed solutions, radical and conservative, that seemed liberating, a clearing of accounts that called on people to confront the culture crisis as a matter of personal responsibility. Thus, while lacking any specific program, Nietzsche's critique remained a call for engagement rather than a pretext for despair or withdrawal.

Realism and Naturalism

Nietzsche's call to break with old forms and values in philosophy struck a sympathetic chord in the arts. Much of mid-nineteenth-century art was representational, an attempt to portray reality in familiar, conventional, and reassuring terms. This art was an outgrowth of positivism, which regarded the world as governed by immutable laws that needed only to be faithfully represented. The same assumptions held for the preeminent literary form of the period, the novel. Novels were composed of characters who acted in predictable ways, seeking their fortunes if male and protecting their virtue if female, in much the same way that atoms moved along their destined paths. Just as atoms and chemicals combined to form the visible texture of the world, so characters by their interactions created the texture of society. Artists, like scientists or for that matter historians, had only to depict an objective reality, injecting as little of themselves into the picture as possible.

The style that resulted from these positivist assumptions was called realism. The great realists, Charles Dickens (1812–1870) in Britain, Honoré de Balzac (1799–1850) in France, and Leo Tolstoy (1828–1910) in Russia, tried to pack as much of human experience as possible into the vast canvas of their novels, Dickens depicting the teeming life of the industrial city, Balzac the emerging world of finance capital, and Tolstoy the drama of the Napoleonic wars. The novel was ideally suited to such representation, with its ability to accommodate a multitude of characters and branching plots, and the Romantic symphonies and tone poems of Hector Berlioz (1803–1869) and Franz Liszt (1811–1886), with their boldly individual themes, shifting colors and harmonies, and intricate transformations, soon captured the same expansive structure in music. The physical limitations of painting and sculpture made them, paradoxically, the least successful of the representational arts. Nonetheless, they exhibited the same assumptions as realist art in other forms: that nature and society were plainly revealed to the observing eye and needed only to be recorded, not interpreted.

This is not to say that realism refrained from judgments; no reader of a Dickens novel could fail to see with which characters his sympathies lay. But what Dickens appealed to were the moral pieties he shared with his middle-class audience, in which hard work, thrift, and virtue were rewarded and greed, hypocrisy, and chicanery were punished. The devices of realism did not permit as a rule much psychological penetration, nor much social criticism beyond pointing out abuses to be rectified. As they believed that the laws of nature were sufficient to account for social and natural phenomena, so they assumed that the liberal state was adequate to remedy what was amiss in the body politic. Only a conservative and deeply religious writer of genius, Feodor Dostoevsky (1821–1881), was able to question the drift of a society in which, since humans had mastered nature and dispensed with sin, objective moral standards no longer existed. In novels such as *Crime and Punishment* (1866) and *The Brothers Karamazov* (1880) he probed the roots of violence and pondered the dilemma of a culture whose most privileged children had turned against it.

Realism was also a style that appealed to the mass market that now purchased and consumed books, artworks, and music like any other commodity. This market was served by critics, salons, and public museums that wielded considerable power in fashioning (and sometimes legitimating) popular taste. No late-nineteenth-century bourgeois home was complete without its piano and its glass cabinet of books. The art market had already begun its spectacular rise; Jean-François Millet's *Angelus,* with its depiction of pious rural toil, was sold for $320,000 in 1881. Authors such as Dickens and Dostoevsky were paid by the word for their serialized works, and on Dickens' reading tours he performed to sold-out houses.

Commercial success was a double-edged sword for the arts, however. Freed from dependence on aristocratic patrons, artists found themselves at the more amorphous but often equally capricious mercy of public taste. The artist's new function as the servant of that taste conflicted with his Romantic role as a sovereign creator. These problems were compounded by the development of the mass media and particularly by the new processes of photography and mechanical reproduction. The writer's imaginative skill was at a discount when the daily newspaper brought tales of the fabulous and the bizarre with every breakfast, as was the painter's technique when photography offered images of reality more precise than those of any brush. If art was defined as the representation of reality as it appeared to ordinary perception, then the artist no less than the artisan was in danger of being displaced by advancing technology.

One response to these limitations was naturalism. Naturalism differed from realism by its attention to the gritty underside of late-nineteenth-century life. Naturalism sought to be hyperobjective, making of literature a branch of science; Émile Zola, who followed the fortunes of a peasant family in a series of novels, likened his art to the work of a clinical pathologist. The protagonists of naturalist literature were not heroes but victims, the prisoners of poverty, environment, and heredity.

The subject matter of naturalist literature was harrowing and often deliberately provocative. The scenes of animal copulation and of scarcely less brutal human sexuality in Zola's novels were obviously meant to shock, as was the scandalous *Olympia* exhibited by the painter Édouard Manet (1832–1883) in 1866, which portrayed an ordinary nude model of the working classes in

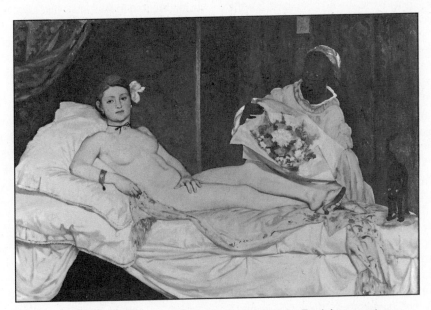

Édouard Manet, *Olympia*. Manet's great portrait of a Parisian courtesan, exhibited in 1865, was shocking not for its nudity but for its sexual frankness. The black servant—fashionable in bourgeois circles since the eighteenth century—bears a bouquet from an admirer. [Cliché des Musées Nationaux, Paris]

the pose of Titian's famous *Venus*. Even more direct was Gustave Courbet's (1819–1877) *Venus,* a canvas that consisted simply of an enlarged and anatomically precise female sex organ. Such affronts to bourgeois sensibility went hand in hand with radical politics; Courbet was a Communard of 1871 who ended his days in exile. If naturalism reflected the Darwinian view of life as a struggle for survival, its sympathies were at least with the weak rather than with the strong.

The Revolt Against the Academy: Symbolism, Decadence, and the Rise of the Avant-Garde

For the artist the prime focus of rebellion was the academy. Louis XIV had established an Academy of Fine Arts to promote French painting and to glorify his reign. Britain followed with the Royal Academy in 1768, and similar institutions were soon established elsewhere.

The art sponsored by the academy was decorative, conventional, and edifying. Pastoral landscapes, historical tableaus, and genre scenes were favored; the rich were shown at play, and poverty was depicted as rustic and charming. With the nineteenth century the bourgeoisie made their appearance, sitting for their portraits. Biblical scenes became popular with the revival of religion and exoticism with the spread of empire, but the nature of academic art remained the same: to turn out a standard product at a high level of technical competence that was gratifying (or discreetly titillating) to public taste, and morally uplifting.

Not all artists accepted these terms. Some, like William Hogarth (1697–1764), depicted urban life and social mores candidly, and some, like William Blake (1757–1827), pursued their own private visions. But it was not until the second half of the nineteenth century that artists successfully rebelled against the academy.

This was made possible in part by the expansion of the market. The art public was larger and wealthier, and the number of artists increased as well. Many were of humble birth, crowding into the poorer quarters of the great cities in hopes of attracting purchasers and patrons. When Henri Murger published his *Scenes from Bohemian Life* (1851), describing the lifestyle of the Latin Quarter in Paris, there were 10,000 to 20,000 artists in the city. They were far too numerous to attend the licensed academies and for the most part too poor as well.

The poverty of the artist's life was compensated by its freedom; the word "bohemian" was a French term for gypsy. Manet's *Picnic on the Grass* (1863), with its image

of a nude model sitting between two artists, typified the sexual availability associated with bohemian lifestyles, and the revolutions of 1830, 1848, and 1871 had confirmed its radical politics.

Bohemia was not confined to Paris, of course, nor to the plastic arts. The composer-performers Niccolò Paganini (1782–1840), Frédéric Chopin (1810–1849), and Franz Liszt were celebrated for their love affairs as well as their music, and Victor Hugo, author of *Les Miserables,* carried on a one-man war against the repressive regime of Napoleon III. Hugo gave the artist moral authority and the abiding image of a rebel. Romanticism gave him an even more valuable function as a diviner of sacred truths hidden to others. These images fused in the person of the German composer Richard Wagner. Wagner's gigantic operatic cycle, *The Ring of the Nibelungen,* was a vast meditation on cultural origins, romantic love, and artistic creation, with Wagner serving as both object and high priest of his own cult. The international audience that attended the annual performances of the cycle at Bayreuth in Bavaria came more as worshippers at a shrine than as mere music lovers, and it was not surprising that Wagner's final work, the opera *Parsifal* (1883), should have had an explicitly religious theme.

Wagner was the most influential cultural figure of the late nineteenth century. He gave to artists the kind of prestige that had been enjoyed by the philosophes of the Enlightenment. As rulers had once courted Voltaire and Rousseau, so the late-nineteenth-century public now looked to the artist for special revelation. If not every artist could have a Bayreuth, then at least every major city would have its massive public library, museum, concert hall, and opera house—the temples of a secular religion.

The revolt against established norms of reality was summed up in the slogan "Art for art's sake." Not to reflect an existing world but to create an individual one, often through drugs and what the French poet Arthur Rimbaud (1854–1891) called the "systematic derangement of the senses," became the goal of "advanced," or avant-garde art. The literary school that emerged from this was known as Symbolism. Led by the French poet Stéphane Mallarmé (1842–1898), the Symbolists investigated language for the play of sound and association it could evoke rather than for its conventional meanings. Like Wagner's music, Symbolist poetry was meant to appeal directly to the senses and emotions rather than the intellect. Mallarmé abandoned rhyme, regular syntax, and punctuation in his later poems, often leaving isolated words on the page to focus the reader's attention on their sound qualities. Under his influence,

Symbolism became the dominant literary movement of the 1890s, while on the stage the dramas of Maurice Maeterlinck (1862–1949) and August Strindberg (1849–1912) ranged freely across time and space, treating such subjects as sexual pathology and the transmigration of souls.

Symbolism was closely allied with Aestheticism and Decadence. Aestheticism, chiefly identified with the British critic Walter Pater (1839–1894), involved the search for increasingly refined sensation, whether in art or life. The Decadents, on the other hand, indulged in anything that could excite, intoxicate, or shock. In an age preoccupied with social and racial decadence, they proudly wore the label attached to them.

All of these movements were embraced under the rubric of the avant-garde. The avant-garde was not itself a movement but an aesthetic attitude, best summed up by the dictum of the American poet Ezra Pound (1885–1972) to "make it new." Rejecting inherited taste and tradition, it put a premium on originality, or at least novelty. Above all, it was a response to the conditions of art in bourgeois society. In an age of standardized commodity production it insisted on the uniqueness of the work of art; in a world of material values it presented the artist as a prophetic figure. At the same time, the avant-garde was ultimately a bourgeois phenomenon itself, dependent upon the society it provoked for its existence. At its most frivolous it degenerated into mere fashion-mongering, but at its best it sought to offer an ideal of social renewal through cultural challenge.

The New Order of the Arts

Among the forces to which the avant-garde responded was the new world being shaped by science in the late nineteenth century, a world that it intuited in some cases ahead of scientific discoverers themselves. In all of the arts the familiar outlines of reality began to blur and dissolve, especially in the visual ones, where in a few short decades they disappeared altogether.

In the fine arts this process began with Impressionism. Impressionism was given its name by its greatest figure, Claude Monet (1840–1926), who declared that his object was to paint not things but time itself, as reflected in the ever-changing play of light. Monet painted certain objects—haystacks in a field, the cathedral at Rouen—over and over again, recording the gradations of light on their surfaces not only from painting to painting but within each painting so that each canvas was the depiction not of an object but of its duration in time. His

Edvard Munch, *The Scream.* **Munch's image of a twisted, sticklike figure whose cry engulfs the world expressed the underlying alienation of prewar bourgeois society. [©Nasjonalgalleriet, Oslo]**

great contemporary, Paul Cézanne (1839–1906), painted the view around his home in Aix-en-Provence for 30 years, probing less for the effects of light than for the geometry of forms. Both artists, by different approaches, made ordinary objects uncanny and strange, one dissolving the facade of a famous cathedral in shimmering patterns of color, the other breaking up a familiar landscape into rough, shifting planes.

Impressionism has become one of the most popular styles in Western art, but the first Impressionist exhibit in 1874 was shocking; one critic warned pregnant women to avoid it lest they miscarry. Far more startling transformations of reality lay ahead. Noting that solid objects were actually a composite of color impressions on the retina, Georges Seurat (1859–1891) aimed to represent this process by building up his canvases from a myriad of dots that blended to produce recognizable images and scenes—a quiet seaport, a Sunday promenade. Seurat's style, called pointillism, enabled one to see objects in their solid and atomized state simultaneously, thus calling attention to the synthetic nature of perception. The Belgian Vincent van Gogh (1853–1890) took an entirely different approach, applying brilliant colors in thick, clotted swirls to suggest the surging, volcanic movement of the natural world that underlay the seeming placidity of landscape. Van Gogh's style, called Expressionism, was taken in a different direction by the Norwegian Edvard Munch (1863–1944) in *The Scream* (1893). The visual and dramatic center of Munch's painting is a distorted, wide-eyed figure uttering a cry that seems to resound through the entire canvas, bending the shapes of sea, land, and sky with it.

Expressionism, as defined by Munch and others, was the attempt to express the artist's emotion directly in paint. The object portrayed, whether an individual or a landscape, was merely the inspiration or the vehicle for this emotion. The most obvious Expressionist subject was the artist himself, and both van Gogh and Munch have left us haunting self-portraits. In principle, however, anything could embody the artist's feeling; van Gogh was able to invest even a handful of sunflowers or a yellow wicker chair with his own agitation.

Since the conveying of emotion rather than the realistic representation of objects was the primary goal of the artist, it followed that expressive distortions of line and color were fully justified. Such distortions seemed shocking and even deranged to a public still wedded to the assumption that the artist's task was to portray a stable and objective reality. Emotion in art, it was felt, should be confined to arousing edifying sentiments in the beholder, for example, love of country through a patriotic scene or piety through a religious one. Religious images were in fact common in Expressionist painting, but they served a highly unorthodox and provocative function. Munch's *Madonna* (1895) offered a nude temptress with flowing black hair, while James Ensor's *The Entry of Christ into Brussels* (1888) portrayed Jesus at the head of a grotesque carnival. The Expressionists were drawn particularly to Jesus as a symbol of universal suffering and protest. They saw in him their own image of the modern artist as one who bore creative witness to the misery and injustice of life and to the spiritual void left by a mechanistic civilization. To the pious this seemed the ultimate sacrilege, but for the Expressionists themselves the projection of the suffering self upon nature was a means of expressing the sense of void left by the withdrawal of God. Their fascination with Jesus thus linked up with that of the earlier Romantics, both as an expression of religious despair and as a rejection of a purely material civilization and a mechanistic universe.

The two major movements of late-nineteenth-century art, Impressionism and Expressionism, led by different though related paths to a startling dénouement—the abandonment of the image in the first years of the twentieth century. In the first case this was realized by a new movement, Cubism; in the second, by what came to be called Abstract Expressionism.

Cubism was an outgrowth of Impressionism's use of light to penetrate the flux of reality. What Monet and others had shown was that objects could not be represented as stable entities but had to be seen as successive states that varied with the passage of time and the perspective of the observer. Time and space, in short, could not be absolutely located on the picture plane any more than they could in Einstein's equations. Cubism took this one step further. Instead of portraying successive images of a subject on separate canvases, it offered multiple images on the same canvas.

Cubism was developed from 1907 by two young artists living in Paris, the Spaniard Pablo Picasso (1881–1973) and the Frenchman Georges Braque (1882–1963). The broke up simple objects—a pitcher, a pipe, a guitar—into a host of abstract planes and shapes, suspending these in a solid, two-dimensional field of color. Soon both men were painting pictures whose subject matter could be inferred only from the titles on the canvases, for nothing recognizable could be seen. By reducing objects to primary geometrical forms and by eliminating perspective, the distinction between one object and another and between objects and their space was abolished.

Shortly afterward, the Russian Vasily Kandinsky (1866–1944) pressed forward to complete abstraction. Kandinsky believed that the artist's emotions were the proper subject of painting and that they could be rendered through line and color without any reference to external objects. By 1913 he was painting nonobjective watercolors that consisted of strips, patches, and loops of color threaded by black calligraphy. Kandinsky disdained the label of Abstract Expressionism that was applied to his work. He insisted that his paintings were not at all abstract but were highly concrete expressions of his inner experience. Nonetheless, they represented a clear break with the entire pictorial tradition of the West. Viewers searched Cubist canvases for signs of the objects "concealed" in them, but the drifting, dreamlike shapes of Kandinsky's works resisted any effort at categorization. They represented nothing but simply presented themselves.

Sculpture took a similar path. The Frenchman Auguste Rodin (1840–1917) had broken with the academic tradition, little changed since the Renaissance, of idealized nudes and realistic animal portraiture. Working his bronze into tormented, strongly kneaded shapes, he exploited the play of light on surface textures to create figures of great power and expressiveness. Like Monet and Cézanne, he repeatedly visited the same subject from different perspectives, particularly in his epic portrait series of Balzac. Early in the twentieth century the Expressionist painter Henri Matisse (1869–1954) carved a series of relief panels that verged on abstraction, and a few years later, Rodin's student Constantin Brancusi (1876–1957) produced the first fully nonobjective sculpture. Because of its freedom in space and the almost endless variety of its materials—wood, stone, metal, glass, and synthetics—the vocabulary of sculpture has undergone greater expansion than that of any other twentieth-century art form, ranging from tiny boxes and pulverized auto parts to earthworks spanning hundreds of miles.

Literature and Music

Analogous developments took place in literature and music. The late-nineteenth-century novel, already large, grew gargantuan in the works of Henry James (1843–1916), Marcel Proust (1871–1922), Thomas Mann (1875–1955), and Robert Musil (1880–1942). Plot receded before character, and character dissolved in an endless regression of meaning and motive. A crack in a glass bowl served James as the basis of a novel, and the tinkling of a bell was the summons for Proust's multivolume *Remembrance of the Things Past*. Influenced by the philosopher Henri Bergson (1859–1941), who contended that all knowledge is grounded in the sense of passing time, Proust retraced the continuity of his life along the byways of memory. In one scene he lovingly evokes the village church of his childhood, whose worn and hollowed stone appears to him the material repository not only of his own experience but of generations past so that it seems truly to exist, as he says in words that anticipate Einstein's, across "four dimensions of space—the name of the fourth being Time." Despite this, however, he finds that the past is fundamentally ungraspable and that "remembrance of a particular form is but regret for a particular moment."

This perception did not inhibit others from exploring memory and seeking to freeze the passing moment, in art if nothing else. James Joyce's (1882–1941) massive *Ulysses* (1922) takes place in a single day that seeks to encompass the whole of Irish history as well as the mind of its central figure. Plot in the usual sense is wholly forgone here; instead, there is merely a succession of events, themselves reflected through the sensations of those who experience them. Joyce carried this technique

still further in *Finnegans Wake* (1939), breaking up not only syntax but also words themselves in the attempt to get at a deeper core of consciousness.

As the traditional devices of literature—character, plot, and narrative—began to break down after 1880, so tonality, the basis of classical music for 300 years, gave way too. Tonality organized musical composition by sounding all the notes of the chromatic scale in relation to a single one designated as the tonal center or key. Dissonant passages would be resolved by returning at intervals to chords based upon the key. In the search for expressive new harmonies and freer musical forms, Romantic composers had stretched the limits of dissonance, slowly redefining tonality as well. At the same time, melody had become more flexible, and "development," the manipulation and fragmentation of melodic material, more fluid. This process had reached a climax in Wagner, whose music stretched the tonal system to its limits. In addition, Wagner made duration itself an explicit part of his musical and dramatic strategy. His libretti dealt with the ritual passages of time—birth, maturity, death, and resurrection—and the music that conveyed the drama was woven around recurrent themes or motifs that expressed these passages.

In the generation after Wagner, composers such as Gustav Mahler (1860–1911), Claude Debussy (1862–1918), and Richard Strauss (1864–1949) gradually abandoned the idea of a fixed tonal center, while Igor Stravinsky (1882–1971) broke up conventional rhythms in his ballet *The Rite of Spring*. Arnold Schoenberg (1874–1951) at last broke decisively with tonality, and in the song cycle *Pierrot Lunaire* (1912) he began to evolve a new system of composition that took final form a decade later as serialism. In serialism, all notes of the chromatic scale were regarded as equal, and each was to be sounded in a pattern called a tone row before any might be repeated. Schoenberg's system eliminated the distinction between consonance and dissonance; many listeners, unaccustomed to the removal of all familiar auditory guideposts, heard only noise.

The Fine Arts and Public Taste

The revolution in the arts that took place between 1880 and 1920 paralleled that of contemporary physics. In both, ordering concepts of time and space were eclipsed by theories that created shifts in the Western understanding of the human and material worlds. It is impossible to assign clear priority for these developments or to trace precise lines of influence. It cannot be said that Cubism was a response to relativity any more than Heisenberg's uncertainty principle can be called an application of Munch's Expressionism; both developed out of a common cultural milieu in which there was little direct connection but a great deal of informal cross-fertilization. If science required a shift in the arts, it can be said equally that the arts required one in the sciences.

For the lay population these changes were bewildering and often incomprehensible. The sexuality and neurosis portrayed in avant-garde art scandalized many; Nordau in *Degeneration* attacked Nietzsche, Wagner, Ibsen, and others as moral criminals bent on corrupting civilization. A group of French Expressionists was dubbed the "Fauves" (wild beasts) by critics and the public, and the first performance of Stravinsky's *The Rite of Spring* ended in a riot.

The development of avant-garde art coincided with the emergence of a mass culture and the beginnings of an entertainment industry. Taverns, music and dance halls, cafe concerts, cabaret theaters, vaudeville, circuses, travel tours, and spectator sports proliferated, competing for the leisure income of the middle and working classes. Popular songs and pulp fiction that embodied the yearnings and aspirations of these groups were made widely accessible through the phonograph, the nickelodeon, the mass-circulation newspaper, and the cheap edition. The first commercial films were produced in the 1890s and had an overnight impact; by 1914, 50 million Americans were attending the movies each week. Much of this culture continued to base itself on materialist and positivist assumptions that had been discarded at elite levels, thus widening the gap between the fine and popular arts.

Sigmund Freud, the founder of psychoanalysis, reshaped the West's conceptions of consciousness, sexuality, and civilization. [National Library of Medicine]

Psychoanalysis and the Science of the Irrational

The revolt against positivism brought with it an emphasis on subjective experience and instinctual behavior that stimulated a general interest in mental processes. At the same time, advances in neurophysiology brought medical researchers back to the old Cartesian problem of the relationship between body and mind. The result of this was a new theory of human psychology that was to shape, no less profoundly than had evolution or relativity, the way in which Western culture thought about itself.

Psychoanalysis, as both the theory and the therapeutic practice based on it were called, was the work of a Viennese physician, Sigmund Freud (1856–1939). Freud's basic insight was that "abnormal" psychological states were the key to understanding normal mental functioning, a point he underlined with the title of one of his books, *The Psychopathology of Everyday Life* (1901). In one sense, this was little more than the medical maxim that one studies sickness to understand health. There was intense resistance, however, to acknowledging Freud's contention that psychic life was governed by patterns formed in earliest childhood and infancy and inaccessible to rational control. It was one thing to exalt the primacy of instinct and emotion but quite another to accept that the mind was, as Freud described it, a mechanism for releasing drives toward pleasure and avoiding experiences of pain. This seemed to undermine the basis of morality in what had become for many its last bastion, the human intellect.

Freud's theory posited that the greater part of the mind consisted of what he called the unconscious, which served as a connecting vessel between the body and its consciousness. The unconscious was the repository of memory as well as the conductor of instinctual drives, whose totality he called the *id* (Latin for "it"). *Libido,* or energy from the id drove the body toward satisfaction of its needs, but it was subject to a censoring mechanism, the ego, which suppressed libido when its expression would endanger the organism. Cultural adaptation added another censor, the superego, which restrained libido on the basis of learned patterns of behavior, or, in ethical terms, right and wrong. Thus the ego would warn a hungry person not to take food from someone stronger, but the superego would prevent the person from taking it from someone weaker.

Libidinal energy deflected by the ego or superego would return to the body, causing physical and emotional stress. Where possible, the ego would find alternative outlets for this energy, a process called sublimation; where these outlets were inadequate, neurosis resulted. The commonest substitutes were dreams and fantasies, in which the mind enacted (though in censored form) the fulfillments of its wishes. Dream analysis, as described in Freud's *The Interpretation of Dreams* (1900), thus became a crucial element in therapy, whose purpose was to bring to conscious scrutiny the desires repressed by the ego and superego.

Libido was often used as a synonym for sexual energy because sexual drives were associated with the earliest experiences of infantile dependence and anxiety, and because their satisfaction was hemmed in by social restrictions. Freud did not call for greater sexual freedom, however, as did other contemporaries who emphasized the importance of sexuality. In his view, civilization required at least a partial sublimation of the sexual drive, which was the only form of libidinal energy that could be turned to socially productive purposes. In addition, the frustration caused by early sexual attachments to either parent, called the Oedipus complex in boys and the Electra complex in girls, left a residue of unsatisfied desire in the psyche that was only partly compensated by mature sexual liaisons. These problems were inherent in all human culture, but the higher the civilization, the more sexual sacrifice it demanded. Thus the most sensitive, cultivated, and culturally valuable people in a society were characteristically the most neurotically unhappy.

Freud's work was greeted with shock and protest, but he gathered a band of younger disciples around him, notably Alfred Adler (1870–1937) and Carl Jung (1875–1961), and after World War I his influence was pervasive not only in the field of psychology but across the entire cultural spectrum. More recent critics have pointed out the residual positivism in Freud's thought, particularly in his conception of the mind as a mechanism powered by libido; others have found his account of the mind-body relationship unconvincing and his view of female sexuality inadequate or even demeaning. Nonetheless, the power, suggestiveness, and explanatory range of Freudian theory made it by far the most comprehensive account of the human mind ever developed to that point, and nothing of equal scope has succeeded it.

FIN-DE-SIÈCLE VIENNA

Freud was only one of Vienna's famous citizens in the generation before 1914, a time when the city concentrated perhaps as much native genius as any in European history. Prewar Vienna was at the cutting edge of Western thought and culture. The Vienna Secession led by Gustav Klimt (1862–1918) stood at the forefront of Expressionist art and modernist architecture, while the members of the Vienna Circle, notably Ludwig Wittgenstein (1889–1951), were redefining language, logic, and philosophy. Vienna was the home of Mahler, a great symphonist in his own right who had made the city's opera the most renowned in the world, as well as Arnold Schoenberg. It was the acknowledged medical capital of the world and one of the centers of theoretical physics. Yet this same city, many of whose intellectual luminaries were Jewish, was the most openly anti-Semitic capital in Europe, the home of a reactionary court and aristocracy, a bourgeoisie that reveled in good times and bad taste, and a disaffected proletariat. In its deep divisions as well as the brilliance of its high culture, it mirrored the contradictions of Europe on the eve of the Great War.

Vienna was still an imperial capital in the late nineteenth century. The Habsburg throne was occupied throughout the period by Franz Joseph, who signified his rejection of modern life by retaining oil lamps in the Hofburg Palace long after the city had been electrified. The aristocracy, which continued to control the government despite the imposing parliament building on the new circular thoroughfare of the Ringstrasse, took its cue from the emperor. City politics, on the other hand, were dominated in the late nineteenth century by Karl Lueger, who became mayor in 1895. Lueger was a populist demagogue who appealed to the petty bourgeoisie from which he sprang, and together with progressive welfare and public service reform he made anti-Semitism an electoral issue; one of his most admiring constituents was the young Adolf Hitler.

The political losers in Vienna were the liberal bourgeoisie, whose hopes for constitutional government were dashed by the reactionary cast of the court and the increasing fragmentation of the empire. Disillusioned, they threw their energies into business and intellectual pursuits, and it was from their ranks that the leading figures of Viennese culture emerged. This cultural elite was a remarkably close-knit group that crossed easily between the arts and sciences; Mahler was a patient of Freud's and a frequent guest at the mansion of the Wittgensteins, while Schoenberg was closely associated with the Vienna Secession as well as with Expressionist circles in poetry and modernist architects.

The fate of Vienna's liberal intelligentsia is summed up in the career of Ludwig Wittgenstein. Born into a converted Jewish family of fortune and talent, he saw three of his elder brothers commit suicide and a fourth, a concert pianist, lose an arm in World War I. Deeply ascetic, he struggled throughout his life to master a sense of worthlessness and lived his last years as a recluse. His fame as the greatest philosopher of the twentieth century rested on a single 75-page treatise, the *Tractatus Logico-Philosophicus* (1921), which succinctly demolished the claims of science and logic to provide an ultimate description of reality. The *Tractatus* was the final blow to nineteenth-century positivism, and to the hope, implicit in all of Western culture since the seventeenth century, that science could provide answers to the questions of meaning and value it had forced dogma to abandon.

The Sense of an Ending

Not only in Vienna but throughout Europe the sense of an impending collapse pervaded the years before World War I, dreaded by some, welcomed by others. Nietzsche had predicted an era of "monstrous wars" in the 1880s, and his prophecy was echoed in such Expressionist titles as *Twilight of Mankind, Day of Judgment,* and *World's End.* The "apocalyptic landscapes" painted by the German Ludwig Meidner (1884–1966) in 1912 and 1913 offered an uncanny anticipation of the aerial bombardments, shattered bodies, and burning cities that would shortly be a reality.

SUMMARY

The last half of the nineteenth century witnessed a crisis in Western culture at the moment of its greatest material and political success. The theories of Darwin and Einstein undermined the prevailing positivism of the age and replaced the Newtonian model that had buttressed Western thought for 200 years. At the same time, the most sensitive artists and thinkers of the period began to probe the borders of perception and imagination and to question the nature of value in a godless world. At the century's end, Freudian psychoanalysis offered a picture of the unconscious mind as a vortex that collapsed time and space no less surely than the new physics and deprived humans even of the sanctuary of reason. Some saw violence as the law of life, and as the twentieth century dawned, some saw it on the horizon.

Notes

1. S. Kern, *The Culture of Time and Space, 1880–1918* (Cambridge, Mass.: Harvard University Press, 1983), p. 98; E. J. Hobsbawm, *The Age of Empire, 1875–1914* (New York: Pantheon, 1987), p. 219.
2. R. C. Bannister, *Social Darwinism: Science and Myth in Anglo-American Thought* (Philadelphia: Temple University Press, 1979), p. 109.
3. Ibid., p. 194.
4. E. Weber, *Europe Since 1715: A Modern History* (New York: Norton, 1972), p. 611.

Suggestions for Further Reading

Altholz, J. L. *The Churches in the Nineteenth Century.* Indianapolis: Bobbs-Merrill, 1967.

Bowler, P. J. *Evolution: The History of an Idea,* rev. ed. Berkeley: University of California Press, 1989.

Burrow, J. W. *Evolution and Society: A Study in Victorian Social Thought.* Cambridge: Cambridge University Press, 1968.

Calder, N. *Einstein's Universe.* New York: Penguin Books, 1980.

Chadwick, O. *The Secularization of the European Mind in the Nineteenth Century.* Cambridge: Cambridge University Press, 1977.

Dale, P. A. *In Pursuit of a Scientific Culture: Science, Art, and Society in the Victorian Age.* Madison: University of Wisconsin Press, 1990.

Gay, P. *Freud: A Life for Our Times.* New York: Norton, 1988.

Herbert, R. L. *Impressionism: Art, Leisure, and Parisian Society.* New Haven, Conn.: Yale University Press, 1988.

Hughes, H. S. *Consciousness and Society: The Reorientation of European Social Thought, 1890–1930.* New York: Vintage Books, 1981.

Hughes, R. *The Shock of the New: Art and the Century of Change.* New York: Knopf, 1981.

Kaufmann, W. *Nietzsche: Philosopher, Psychologist, Antichrist.* Princeton, N.J.: Princeton University Press, 1968.

Kern, S. *The Culture of Time and Space, 1880–1918.* Cambridge, Mass.: Harvard University Press, 1983.

Rose, P. L. *Revolutionary Antisemitism in Germany from Kant to Wagner.* Princeton, N.J.: Princeton University Press, 1990.

Schorske, C. E. *Fin-de-Siècle Vienna: Politics and Culture.* New York: Vintage Books, 1981.

Tannenbaum, E. *1900: The Generation Before the Great War.* Garden City, N.Y.: Anchor/Doubleday, 1976.

26

THE GREAT WAR

THE ROAD TO WAR

The origins of the war have long been entangled in the question of its blame. The victorious Allies—Britain, France, Italy, and the United States—affirmed the guilt of Germany and tried to bring the deposed German emperor to trial. Most Allied historians of the 1920s upheld this verdict, while German scholars vigorously rebutted it, publishing masses of diplomatic material from the imperial archives to support their case. Reacting against the search for a single villain, some historians located the causes of the war in a breakdown of

The world before 1914 is cut off from modern memory by the event that contemporaries called simply the Great War and that we now more commonly refer to as World War I. The unparalleled scope and devastation of the conflict and the apparent helplessness of statesmen and generals in the face of it made it seem monstrous, a thing beyond human comprehension or control. It transfigured both war and politics, and from it emerged the modern authoritarian state. It marked as well the end of European hegemony in the world, a process that was completed by World War II. Never had a society achieved such world domination as had Europe in the nineteenth century. Never was one to fall more quickly from the heights of power.

international order characterized by the growth of imperialism and militarism. The debate came full circle in 1961 when a German historian, Fritz Fischer, argued that Germany's aggression had been the principal cause of both world wars. Most recent historiography has tended to make Germany more culpable for the Great War, although it is still seen primarily as the outcome of interstate rivalry and competition.

The traditional European balance of power had depended on a politically weak Germany that could serve as a buffer between France and the Austrian Empire. The unification of Germany and to a lesser extent of Italy had created a new center of gravity on the continent, leaving France isolated and vulnerable. The diplomacy of the late nineteenth century was preoccupied with this, and it may be said that the central political issue of Europe between 1870 and 1945 was the containment of Germany. That issue had three interlocking dimensions: imperial competition and conflict, the new alliance system, and the growing arms race.

Imperial Competition and Conflict

The colonial scramble transferred the old territorial struggles of Europe to a global stage. National security no longer meant simply the protection of one's own frontiers but also of those of colonies, dependencies, and client states half a world away.

The most serious imperial conflict was far closer to home, in the crumbling borderlands of the Ottoman

Empire. At the beginning of the nineteenth century the Ottomans had still occupied nearly 250,000 square miles of territory in southeastern Europe, but their power had steadily eroded. Greece had been the first of their domains to win independence in the 1820s; Serbia had won autonomy at the same time after a protracted struggle, and Romania achieved similar status in 1859. Russian designs on Ottoman territory had provoked the Crimean War in the 1850s, and another major confrontation occurred in 1877 when Russia came to the aid of rebellions in the Turkish provinces of Bosnia and Herzegovina. The crisis was settled at an international conference in Berlin called by Bismarck. The Turks could only watch helplessly as the powers rearranged their frontiers. Romania gained full sovereignty, and Serbia and the small Adriatic district of Montenegro likewise became independent, but Bosnia and Herzegovina, which Serbia coveted, were placed under Austrian control to balance Russian gains. Bulgaria, its borders reduced, was granted autonomy rather than independence. Turkey was left with about half of its former European territory, less from any general objection to completing the partition than from a desire to restrain Russian influence in the region.

The Congress of Berlin did not so much avoid a war as postpone one. Russia felt cheated of its gains on the battlefield, and Serbia, Romania, Bulgaria, and Greece were frustrated in their own territorial ambitions. From the standpoint of the great powers, the goal of the Congress was to adjust their rival claims in the east; the aims and sensitivities of the new Balkan states, which had come into existence by their sufferance, were of secondary consequence. Bismarck and his colleagues, for all the fashionable talk about the doctrine of nationalities, still behaved as their predecessors had at the Congress of Vienna, disposing of the lives of others as their own interests dictated. The result was that the Balkans remained at a boil, throwing up repeated crises and brush wars. The last of these crises triggered World War I.

Despite Bismarck's claim to be a neutral arbiter, German colonialists were eager to expand their country's interests into the Balkans and beyond. They talked of the *Drang nach Osten* ("drive to the east") and of building a Berlin-to-Baghdad railway that would rival the Cape-to-Cairo line envisioned by Cecil Rhodes in Africa. These aims were loudly proclaimed after 1890, much to the alarm of the British. At the same time, Germany challenged French hegemony in North Africa. In March 1905, Emperor William II (1888–1918) made a provocative speech in Tangier on behalf of Morocco's independence,

only to be rebuffed a year later when an international conference at Algeciras affirmed its status as a French sphere of influence. This first Moroccan crisis was followed by a second one in 1911 when a German gunboat appeared off the port of Agadir; it withdrew after concessions by the French in the Congo, but not without again antagonizing European opinion. This imperial aggressiveness appeared boastful and menacing. "Let us have yet another three to four years of peaceful development," the industrialist Hugo Stinnes declared, "and Germany will be undisputed master of Europe."[1]

Imperial instability was not, of course, produced by Germany alone. The British and the Russians remained prime rivals in central and eastern Asia until they reached settlement in 1907, and Britain and France had come close to war at Fashoda in the Sudan in 1898. Such incidents, added to the friction of territorial disputes in Eastern Europe, had produced a series of war scares from 1875. But the very complexity of imperial conflicts tended to keep political alignments in flux. The politics of Europe in the prewar period were thus characterized both by increasing anarchy and by increasing rigidity. The alliance system that developed from the 1870s promoted rigidity, tending to divide the continent into armed, hostile camps; but imperial rivalry separated allies as well as antagonists, creating mutual suspicion and the fear of betrayal. The whipsaw effect of these forces—the dependence on allies whom one could never trust—created the climate of instability that slowly sucked Europe toward war.

The Alliance System

The alliance system was, like so much else, the legacy of Bismarck. Bismarck's goals after 1871 were twofold: to protect Germany, whose borders were exposed on both the east and the west, and to isolate France. The chancellor's analysis was supported by Karl Marx, ever a shrewd observer of the international scene, who predicted that France would seek to recover its lost provinces of Alsace and Lorraine in alliance with Russia.

To forestall this, Bismarck entered into a pact with Austria-Hungary in 1879. This alliance represented an act of reconciliation between the two German-speaking powers of Europe and a means of advancing their interests in the Balkans. The inclusion of Italy in 1882 transformed the Austro-German pact into a Triple Alliance, thus creating the bloc known as the Central Powers. From this strong position, Bismarck bullied Russia in 1887 into signing a secret agreement, the

Reinsurance Treaty, that guaranteed Russia neutrality in the event of a war with France. This completed his diplomatic design.

France, alarmed, attempted to draw closer to Russia by investing heavily in its industrial program. This bore fruit in 1894 when, after Germany had permitted the Reinsurance Treaty to lapse, France and Russia entered a military alliance that called on either to assist the other in case of attack by Germany or Austria-Hungary. By the mid-1890s, therefore, the system of opposed alliances was in place, and the German military had begun to draw up contingency plans for a two-front war.

The one major European power that remained outside the alliance system was Britain. The British had long refused to enter into any peacetime alliances, a policy they called "splendid isolation." This now seemed untenable to many. Britain's far-flung empire was vulnerable, and Europe's hostile reaction to the Boer War brought British opinion up short. It was no longer safe to play a lone hand.

Britain's first, tentative approach was to Germany. There was considerable Anglophile feeling in Germany; Queen Victoria was William II's grandmother, and the two countries felt a strong ethnic kinship. These sentimental advantages were offset, however, by Germany's imperial aggressiveness and by its decision in 1897 to build a battle fleet. If, as William had announced, Germany's future was on the sea, then that future was inevitably in conflict with Britain's. The British turned to France instead and in 1904 reached a general agreement to collaborate in international affairs, the Entente Cordiale. In 1907, Britain and France concluded a similar agreement with Russia, thereby forming the so-called Triple Entente. With this, the rival alliances were essentially locked in place. Within each alliance, joint military plans were mapped that presupposed the other alliance as the enemy. The freedom of maneuver that had enabled diplomats to talk their way out of crises was sharply reduced, and the influence of military elites was correspondingly enhanced. The emphasis was no longer on avoiding war but on preparing for it.

The Arms Race

After 1870 every major power maintained a standing army, and spending on weapons bulked larger and larger in each nation's account. Military expenditure doubled in France between 1875 and 1914 and trebled in Britain and Germany; in 1914 it accounted for one-third of the Russian budget. By the time Europe went to war, there were 19 million men on active duty or in reserve.

Almost insensibly, military thinking and military values had begun to pervade European society.

Militarism was especially pervasive in Germany. Prussia had been built around its army, and the Prussian army had created the German empire. The military was scarcely less important in Austria-Hungary, where it provided one of the few unifying elements in a multiethnic state. In France the Dreyfus affair had damaged the army's prestige, but by 1912 a new chief of staff, Marshal Joffre, would boast that "We shall have a war, I will make it, I will win it"—hardly a testimony to strong civilian control. The navy was paramount in Britain, but as the British contemplated involvement in a land war on the Continent, they began to pay serious attention to building the army too.

Technology also spurred the arms race. The French introduced the machine gun to European warfare in the 1860s, and new industrial processes made possible the development of far larger and more accurate artillery; by 1914 the Germans had a fieldpiece that could fire a shell 75 miles. Iron bottoms revolutionized naval warfare, and by the early 1900s a new vessel of unprecedented size and firepower, the battleship, was being built in large numbers. The destructive potential of the airplane was swiftly realized, and chemical weapons were being fashioned in secret laboratories.

Military planners quickly absorbed these new weapons into their arsenals, but were slower to realize their strategic significance. The Franco-Prussian War had been decided by rapid mobilization and troop movement. The general staffs of the major powers all believed that the next war would be decided in similar fashion. The larger the armies and the greater their firepower, the swifter the result would be. Germany's Schlieffen Plan was typical in this respect. It contemplated victory over France in six weeks.

These calculations permitted no delay in time of crisis. The army that struck first would have an overwhelming advantage. Each military alert put Europe on tenterhooks and left its generals more certain that the next crisis would be the last. Under the circumstances some of them pleaded for a preemptive strike, as the German general staff did in 1904. The alliance system, with its joint military planning, complicated matters further. No nation was now master of its own destiny; the security of each was hostage to its friends as well as to its foes.

The tide of militarism was resisted by virtually all socialist parties, and the nations themselves recognized the threat posed by the arms race and pondered ways to control it at the Hague conferences of 1899 and 1907. Among the difficulties they encountered was what later came to be called the military-industrial complex. The British Admiralty pointed out that any attempt to scale back naval construction would massively affect the economy, rendering Britain commercially as well as militarily weaker. Admiral Tirpitz, the architect of the German naval program, said the same thing in Berlin. Arms control was too dangerous to risk.

The Failure of Diplomacy

The immediate cause of the Great War lay in the disintegrating political situation of Eastern Europe. In 1908–1909 a revolution by junior army officers, the Young Turks, deposed the corrupt and despotic sultan Abdul Hamid II (1876–1909). The Young Turks announced their intention to rejuvenate the Ottoman state and moved to reassert control over its nominal possessions in southeastern Europe. Neither the great powers nor the Balkan principalities were prepared to accept this. Bulgaria at once proclaimed its independence, and Austria annexed the provinces of Bosnia and Herzegovina, which it had occupied since 1878. Italy, sensing its own opportunity, seized Tripoli (now Libya) in North Africa and the Dodecanese islands from Turkey in the first Balkan war (1911–1912). This was in turn the signal for a second Balkan war (1912–1913), in which Bulgaria, Serbia, and Greece drove Turkey from all but the narrow corner of eastern Thrace surrounding Constantinople. Four and a half centuries after the fall of Byzantium, Turkey had ceased to be a European power.

Austria-Hungary and Russia were now pitted in an open struggle for control of the region. The Balkan states themselves fell to squabbling over the spoils of their Turkish war, precipitating another conflict (1913) in which Serbia, Greece, and Romania, aided by Turkey, stripped Bulgaria of much of its former gains in Macedonia and Thrace.

The Balkan wars set the stage for the final crisis. Serbia, nominally a Russian client, harbored ambitions of its own to create a greater South Slav state, including the Croatian and Slovenian provinces of Austria-Hungary itself. Many Serbian nationalists believed that Austria-Hungary was ready to collapse just as Turkey had. The Austrians, for their part, were determined to crush Serbia as a means of containing the mounting pan-Slavic agitation within their own borders.

On June 28, 1914, a young Bosnian Serb, Gavrilo Princip, assassinated the heir to the Austrian throne, the archduke Franz Ferdinand, in the Bosnian capital of Sarajevo. The death of Franz Ferdinand left no competent successor to the 84-year-old Franz Joseph. Over the next five weeks, the crisis precipitated by this event brought Europe to war.

The archduke's assassin was armed by the Black Hand, a terrorist group with links to the Serbian government. After receiving unqualified assurances of German support, the Austrians issued an ultimatum to Serbia, accusing it of complicity in the assassination and demanding the arrest of certain officers, the purging of anti-Habsburg officials, and the right of Austrian representatives to pursue their own investigation on Serbian soil.

The Austrians had grounds for their suspicion; the assassination had in fact been planned directly by the head of Serbian army intelligence. On the other hand, the Serbs could hardly accede to the Austrian ultimatum without ceasing to exist as an independent state. Rejecting the demand for an on-site investigation, they appealed to Russia for support.

Events now moved swiftly. The Germans, far from restraining their ally, urged the Austrians to liquidate Serbia. Russia responded by mobilizing troops on the Austrian frontier, an act that took the matter out of diplomatic hands. Germany now mobilized and, after demanding that Russia pull back its troops, declared war on Russia on August 1 and on France two days later. Britain joined its allies on August 4 after German troops invaded neutral Belgium.

Probably no event in Western history has been more exhaustively studied than the crisis that produced World War I. The major blunders, in retrospect, appear to have been two: the "blank check," as it has been called, that Germany offered Austria-Hungary in its dealings with Serbia after the assassination in Sarajevo and the mobilization ordered by Russia. Neither act was intended to produce a general war. Once the guns had begun to sound, however—the first shots were actually fired on July 29, when Austria bombarded Serbia—they could no longer be stopped.

The most striking aspect of Europe's mood in 1914 was its fatalism. Everyone, even those for whom war was "unthinkable," regarded it as inevitable. The French, for whom *revanche* ("revenge") had been the watchword of diplomacy for four decades, could not hope to regain their lost provinces without war. The Russians had concluded that only war would open the Straits to them, a goal of tsarist policy for 200 years. The German and Austrian military looked forward to a showdown with Slavic nationalism that would establish Teutonic supremacy in Eastern Europe. Except for Britain, each of the major powers had concluded that its long-term policy goals could not be achieved without war.

French troops on their way to the front, 1914. This remarkable photograph suggests the festive, almost joyful mood in which Europe went to war. [Larousse–Moreau]

More broadly, the idea of violence had become culturally acceptable. Marxists, Social Darwinists, and racists all posited struggle as historically necessary. *Jingoism,* or bellicose nationalism, had become the approved standard of patriotic expression everywhere. At the outbreak of war there was a rush to the colors. Pacifists and socialists picked up their rifles with the rest. Europe went to war as if it were taking a holiday.

STRUGGLE AND STALEMATE

Six million men immediately went to war. Their generals had promised to have them home in six weeks; more than four years later, they were still killing one another, and 10 million had died.

All the major combatants launched offensives to begin the war. The Germans, obliged to fight on two fronts, swept through Belgium and into northern France while conducting a holding operation against Russia in the east. They made rapid initial gains, but two Russian armies pushed into East Prussia, compelling the German commander, Moltke, to strip his western army for reinforcements. This slowed the German momentum, and the French, in a week-long battle along the Marne River, forced the Germans back from Paris. The Russian advance had been halted, but a quick victory had eluded the Germans. They had battered their foes but had failed to crush them.

By November the battle lines had stabilized in the west. They were hardly to budge for nearly four years. From the North Sea to the Swiss border the Allied and German armies were dug into fortified trenches. Both sides had already sustained over a million casualties. Here, along a perimeter 1,000 miles long but never more

26.1 World War I, 1914–1918

Map legend:
- Major battles
- Central Powers
- Land occupied by Central Powers at their height
- Allied Powers

than a few miles wide, millions more were to perish in what came to be called No Man's Land.

Attrition: The Strategy of Slaughter

When the armies dug in on the western front, they froze the battle line, since the logistics of trench warfare overwhelmingly favored defense. Each side maintained multiple lines of trenches, protected by dense meshes of barbed wire, machine gun nests, and mortar batteries. Farther back was a support line and, behind this, heavy artillery. Sometimes the front lines were so close that enemy soldiers could converse. Enormous firepower was concentrated on a field that was too short for maneuver.

Because a static situation was unacceptable, general offensives were launched periodically by both sides. Typically, these were preceded by protracted artillery barrages designed to flatten enemy defenses and weaken morale, although the deafening noise (and uncertain aim) had a shattering impact on both sides—"shell shock," as it came to be called. Attacks were frequently accompanied by the release of deadly chlorine gas, though the wind might blow it back on the attacking troops. These moved forward in waves toward the enemy trenches, under fire and over terrain so pitted by bombardment that it was often impassable. During all of 1915 the French gained no more than 3 miles at any point, at a cost of nearly 1.5 million casualties.

The Germans, determined to break French morale, launched a massive attack in February 1916 on the embattled fortress of Verdun. The battle turned into a test of will, since the fortress had no strategic value. After six months and 360,000 French casualties, Verdun stood, but parts of the French army were on the verge of mutiny. In July the British launched a diversionary attack on the Somme River. By October the combatants had suffered 1.1 million casualties; the front line was unchanged.

The only battle plan left at this point was slaughter. The generals pretended to fight for strategic objectives, but their real goal was to amass body counts. The military stalemate was complete.

As the war of attrition ground on, both sides looked for advantage elsewhere. The battle lines in the east were far more fluid than those in the west, and territory changed hands freely. The Germans had the better of the Russians, who were so poorly equipped that some soldiers were able to arm themselves only by picking up the weapons of those who fell in front of them. Despite appalling losses, however, the Russians held on through sheer weight of numbers. To shore up the eastern front, the Allies persuaded Italy, which had remained neutral despite its treaty commitments, to join them in 1915 by promises of territorial gain. Germany induced Turkey to fight for the Central Powers, thus spreading the war into the Middle East, where in 1917 the British general Allenby entered Jerusalem.

The one option that was not seriously explored was peace. This was in part the consequence of inflated or unrealistic goals among the combatants. The Germans, for example, had a huge wish list that included annexations in Europe and Africa and an indemnity so crippling as to make the revival of France, in the words of the German chancellor, "impossible for all time."

These fantastic visions, which Hitler resurrected a generation later, were pure illusion in the Europe of 1915. They were not the fruit of any victory the Germans might hope to win, but a substitute for that victory. The same was more or less true elsewhere. The war had begun over what now seemed the unimaginably trivial issue of Serbia's sovereignty. The combatants made up reasons for fighting as they went along. Those reasons then imprisoned them. If they did not achieve victory, then what could justify the enormous sacrifice of blood? If "victory" were defined in terms of ever-escalating goals, then which side could possibly win, and which side could afford to lose?

Mobilizing the Home Front

None of the combatants had anticipated a long war, and none was prepared for one. The French army had less than a month's supply of shells in September 1914, with much of France's industrial plant already in German hands. The Germans calculated that their stock of essential raw materials would last less than a year; with the British naval blockade, clamped down from the beginning of the war, it would not be replenished. The German government thereupon impounded existing stocks, curtailed luxury production, launched a crash program to develop synthetic substitutes, and began to loot occupied territories. All belligerents took similar steps to mobilize their economic and labor resources. War production received priority over everything else, and rationing was universal. Strikes were prohibited, and labor disputes were referred to binding arbitration boards.

Minds as well as bodies were regimented. Censorship was imposed on all communication, and suspected subversive or enemy sympathizers were interned. In Britain the Defense of the Realm Act authorized the government to search homes without warrants, to prohibit public meetings, and to imprison or deport persons held guilty of unpatriotic utterances or the possession of suspicious literature. Bertrand Russell, the country's most eminent philosopher and an outspoken pacifist, was among those imprisoned.

Censorship was the prelude to propaganda, which replaced unpalatable truths with official lies. In a war in which civilian morale was as crucial as that of the military, the will to fight on could not be allowed to flag on the home front any more than in the trenches. At times, civilian needs even took precedence; Verdun was defended as a patriotic symbol, not a military necessity. As the conflict dragged on, the rhetoric grew increasingly shrill. The war was represented not as a defense of national interests but as a struggle for civilization itself. The hatred thus engendered was to poison the peace no less than the war.

THE RUSSIAN REVOLUTIONS

At the beginning of the twentieth century the Russian empire was the largest but also the least developed of the major European powers. Its population, probably 170 million in 1914, was greater than that of Germany, Britain, and France combined. Four out of five of its inhabitants were still peasants, most of them illiterate. On the farm and in the cities most Russians continued to live at or near subsistence level. Although Russia's industry had made impressive strides since the 1890s, its output was barely comparable to that of France and only a fraction of Germany's. Its subjects had, in 1900, no constitution, no nationally representative institutions, and no recognized political rights. For the most part, Russia was closer to a preindustrial state of the Old Regime than to a modern power. In the first two decades of the twentieth century, it was shaken by a series of revolutions that reached to the deepest roots of its culture. Few events had so powerful an impact on the history of the twentieth century.

The Revolution of 1905

The revolution of 1905, like its successors, was triggered by war. In February 1904, Japan attacked the Russian naval base at Port Arthur, climaxing a period of intensifying rivalry between the two powers over control of Korea and Manchuria. Tsar Nicholas II (1894–1917) and his ministers were confident of victory and not displeased by the opportunity to deflect attention from economic unrest and pent-up demands for reform.

Japan's victory was quick and astonishing. Russia's army was defeated at Mukden in Manchuria, Port Arthur fell, and the Russian imperial fleet, after sailing halfway around the world, was sunk in the Tsushima Straits. The call-up of reserves disrupted the harvest, causing food shortages and factory layoffs and heightening political tension.

Amid fresh demands for constitutional reform, strikes broke out in St. Petersburg in January 1905. On January 9 a great crowd gathered in front of the tsar's Winter Palace. The marchers were peaceful; they carried petitions demanding better working conditions and the convening of a constituent assembly, but also icons and portraits of Nicholas. As they approached, they sang a traditional hymn, "God Save the Tsar." The government panicked. Troops opened fire, killing and wounding hundreds of men, women, and children.

This 1905 cartoon of government repression in Moscow suggests the ferocity of the political struggle in the declining Russian Empire. [Tretyakov Gallery, Moscow]

Bloody Sunday, as the massacre was called, led to general strikes in St. Petersburg, Moscow, and other large cities, while in the countryside, peasants attacked noble estates. As agitation mounted, the government wavered between concession and repression. At last, after a general strike carried out by a new revolutionary organ, the Soviet (Council) of Workers' Deputies, Nicholas issued the October Manifesto, which decreed constitutional government by an elected legislature, the Duma; granted freedom of conscience, speech, assembly, and association; and reorganized the imperial council with a Western-style prime minister at its helm. Religious toleration had already been granted, and a further decree ended redemption payments by the peasantry. These gestures conciliated the majority, although sporadic violence continued well into the following year.

The Duma was crippled and discredited before it could meet, however, by a series of decrees that restricted its functions and reaffirmed the tsar's "supreme autocratic power." The leading groups on the left, the Social Revolutionaries (SR) and the Social Democrats (SD), largely boycotted it, as did the far right, which, blaming the Jews for socialist agitation, called for a restoration of autocracy in the state and the church.

When the Duma convened in April 1906, it was no longer the genuine representative assembly that had been sought for so long but a rump body despised by much of public opinion.

The Twilight of Imperial Russia

In retrospect the 1905 revolution was a missed opportunity. With the October Manifesto, Nicholas had seized the middle ground and opened the way toward the evolution of a constitutional monarchy that would have left him with considerable authority. But Nicholas had yielded only under duress, and he retreated as quickly as possible. Disillusioned intellectuals gravitated toward the left or drifted into despair or indifference. On the right, meanwhile, acts of violence carried out by vigilante gangs known as the Black Hundreds intensified.

All hope was not lost, however, at least for a time. Strides were made toward industrializing the country and modernizing the army. The Christian dissenters known as the Old Believers had been granted toleration after centuries of persecution, and some cultural if not political autonomy was given to minority nationalities. Under the moderate prime minister Peter Stolypin (1863–1911), agricultural entrepreneurs knows as *kulaks* were encouraged to produce for the new urban market. Attacked by the left as an exploiter of the poor and by the right as a dangerous liberal, Stolypin was assassinated by a double agent who was simultaneously in the pay of the Social Revolutionaries and the police. Once again, the center had failed to hold in Russia.

By 1914, Russia seemed once again on the verge of political crisis. With no minister able to gain a credible mandate, the imperial court was a hotbed of reactionary intrigue. The tsar was increasingly ruled by his wife, the tsarina Alexandra, who in turn had come under the sway of a disreputable monk, Grigori Rasputin (1871–1916). In July a massive strike in St. Petersburg brought 140,000 workers into the streets. Barricades were raised, and a bloody suppression followed. The events of 1905 seemed ready to repeat themselves. It was at this moment that the Serbian crisis erupted, plunging Russia into a war for which it was neither politically nor militarily prepared.

Russia suffered cruelly from the Great War. By the end of 1916 its armies had sustained 7 million casualties. Many of the new recruits were peasant breadwinners, previously exempt from service, who bitterly resented being forced to abandon their families. It did not help matters when the tsar decided to assume personal command of the army at the front. In his absence, Alexandra served as a virtual regent, with Rasputin as an unofficial chief minister. The assassination of Rasputin in December 1916 brought universal rejoicing but also further weakened the government. The Duma, recalled shortly before, began a sustained attack on the tsarina, who was not only deeply unpopular but also suspect for her German ancestry.

The situation on the home front was meanwhile increasingly desperate. Almost a tenth of the country's population had been displaced by the war; St. Petersburg and Moscow teemed with refugees. The loss of the industrialized western provinces to the Germans and the breakdown of transport had reduced production below prewar levels. Inflation had increased fourfold; food and fuel were in short supply, even for factories; corruption and speculation were rife. What effective government remained was largely provided by the provincial zemstvos, or assemblies, which undertook to coordinate the war effort in the absence of any effective leadership by the tsarist regime. Imperial Russia existed in name only.

The February Revolution

Russia's second revolution, like its first, began in St. Petersburg, which had been renamed Petrograd in 1914. Crowds poured into the streets on March 8, 1917,* this time singing not "God Save the Tsar" but "La Marseillaise." Soldiers from the Petrograd garrison joined them, and after four days of unchecked demonstrations the city was in their hands. The Duma, after appealing to the tsar for a new government, appointed a ministry on its own authority. At the same time, workers and soldiers formed a new soviet, which began to issue orders as well. Hoping to save the throne, the tsar abdicated on March 15 in favor of his brother, Grand Duke Michael. When Michael learned that neither the Duma nor the army would support him, he declined. The Romanov dynasty, the last divine right monarchy in the world, was no more.

PETROGRAD BETWEEN WAR AND REVOLUTION

The cabinet of ministers appointed by the Duma, mostly composed of moderates, now emerged as the provisional

---

*February 23 according to the old, unreformed Julian calendar, still in use in Russia; hence the term "February Revolution" that is traditionally applied to these events.

government. As its title implied, the provisional government's task was to rule until a constituent assembly could be elected that would decide the nation's constitutional future.

It was by no means clear that this mission could be carried out. The revolutionary events in Petrograd intensified the chaos that already gripped the country. The provisional government was in competition with the Petrograd Soviet, which reproduced itself quickly in other cities. The new soviets were led largely by socialists whose program included land reform, worker democracy, and a speedy end to the war against Germany. Here, in effect, was a parallel government. The next eight months were to see a struggle between the provisional government and the soviets for control of the apparatus of the state and by the parties of the left for control of the soviets themselves.

Crucial to this struggle would be control of Petrograd itself. The last of the great European capitals to be founded, it was built as St. Petersburg on the marshes of the Neva River by Peter the Great (see Chapter 15). Peter had intended it to be his "window on the West" and, determined to distinguish it from all other Russian cities, commissioned Italian architects to design it. A late-eighteenth-century visitor enthused:

> The united magnificence of all the cities of Europe could but equal Petersburg. There is nothing little or mean to offend the eye: all is grand, extensive, large, and open. The streets, which are wide and straight, seem to consist entirely of palaces.[2]

Long after Peter's death, his image continued to dominate the city in the form of a huge equestrian statue that inspired both Pushkin's famous poem "The Bronze Horseman" and Andrei Biely's *Petersburg* (1913), the last great novel of prerevolutionary Russia. Biely (1880–1934), like Pushkin, imagined the statue springing to life, with Peter's great horse neighing across the city like a locomotive's whistle. The industrial image was appropriate, for St. Petersburg had become the chief manufacturing center of Russia by the late nineteenth century, its perimeter ringed with metal-processing plants, foundries, and textile mills. These brought with them vast new slums to house the proletariat that now made up a third of the city's population.

Most of St. Petersburg's workers were peasants recruited through a ruthless land tax designed to force them into the city. The life they found was a hard one. A married worker required an annual income of at least 400 rubles, but four out of five workers earned less. The women and children who made up the majority of the work force in the textile mills were particularly exploited, often working for wages below subsistence level. The population had reached 2.1 million by 1914, and the average density of individuals in some districts was nearly five to a room. Many were simply on the street, without work or papers, dodging the authorities, who deported as many as 200,000 people from the city in a year.

To tsarist officials this new proletariat did not exist. Count Witte, the architect of Russian industrialization, believed that the centuries-old subordination of the peasant to lord would be transferred intact to the factory. Employers were given virtually complete control of their labor force and the conditions under which they worked. Strikes were illegal; the very term for strike, *stachka*, was derived from a word meaning criminal conspiracy.

Under such circumstances an explosion was inevitable. The concentration of a frustrated and increasingly violent proletariat in the nation's capital made Petrograd a political tinderbox. Petrograd was thus as essential to the Russian Revolution as Paris had been to the French Revolution. It was there that the throne had first tottered in 1905, and there that it had finally been toppled. It was even clearer in the spring of 1917 that whoever controlled Petrograd would control the nation.

Lenin and the Struggle for Control

Among those anxiously watching developments in Russia was Vladimir Ilyich Lenin, the leader of the Bolshevik ("majority") faction of the Marxist Social Democrats, who had been living in exile since 1903. Born Vladimir Ilyich Ulianov, the son of a provincial school director and a landowner's daughter, he became a revolutionary after his elder brother was hanged for participating in a conspiracy to assassinate the tsar. He read Marx with the fervor of an apostle and scorned those who tried to soften his teachings or hedge his insistence that capitalism must be overthrown by violent insurrection. In 1912 he had formed the Bolsheviks into a separate party, directing their activities from Switzerland.

After the outbreak of the war, remnants of the international socialist movement adopted a pacifist platform, urging a peace without victory. Lenin argued instead that the war would exhaust capitalism and present the proletariat with its historical opportunity for revolution. Few agreed with him. When the February revolution broke out, there were only 20,000 Bolsheviks in Russia, a tiny minority even on the left.

Among those who took Lenin seriously was the German high command. In April 1917 it transported him among a group of prominent exiles to Petrograd, hoping to foment chaos. Lenin at once took command of the Bolsheviks. He argued that the provisional government was the class enemy and must be overthrown as surely as tsardom. All land, he declared, must be given to the peasants and all power to the soviets.

Lenin's views were, as usual, in the minority. Not only did rival socialists reject them, but many Bolsheviks as well. The soviets had entered an uneasy alliance with the provisional government to prosecute the war. Lenin insisted that the government be liquidated as quickly as possible; those who did not consider him a fool or a lunatic denounced him as a German agent.

It was no longer clear, however, what Russia's war aims might be. The provisional government fought, it said, to honor its treaty commitments. Lenin's simple formula—peace, land, bread—had broad appeal to major groups in the country. But the shape of the future remained unclear, while the existing situation—militarily, economically, and politically—continued to slide toward disaster.

The regime suffered its first crisis in July. A cabinet reshuffle brought Alexander Kerensky (1881–1970), a Social Democrat, to the fore as prime minister and minister of war. Kerensky, under intense Allied pressure, ordered an offensive. His exhausted and demoralized troops were routed, and the army at last collapsed; some 700,000 men had deserted by October. Many joined the mounting agitation in the cities.

The Bolshevik Revolution

By October, Lenin was ready to act. In September the Bolsheviks had won a formal majority in the Petrograd and Moscow soviets as well as in those of several provincial capitals. They were victorious in a number of district council elections as well. Since the latter elections were open to all citizens of voting age, the broad appeal of the Bolsheviks among peasants as well as workers was obvious. Indeed, many peasants had begun implementing Lenin's promise of land distribution on their own, occupying large estates and state property.

Lenin was particularly anxious to seize power before a nationwide Congress of Soviets, scheduled to meet in Petrograd on November 7, could assemble. He could then appeal for unity and support to save the revolution from its enemies. Overriding the objections of more cautious colleagues, he carried the majority of the Bolshevik Central Committee with him.

Control of operations fell to Leon Trotsky (Lev Bronstein, 1879–1940). A political independent, he had joined the Bolsheviks only after the February revolution, but his remarkable skills as an organizer and his legendary prestige as the leader of the first Petrograd Soviet in 1905 ensured his rise. By October he was both a member of the Bolshevik Central Committee and a force in the Revolutionary Military Committee (RMC), the action arm of the Petrograd Soviet.

Prodded by Trotsky, the RMC moved to assert control over the Petrograd garrison and the estimated 200,000 deserters who roamed the city. Kerensky, roused at last, tried to arrest the Bolshevik leaders and the members of the RMC but found only a handful of troops willing to support him. In the early morning of November 7, forces of the RMC, supported by regular army units, seized the city's power stations and transport links and surrounded the Winter Palace, seat of the provisional government. Kerensky fled, his fellow ministers were arrested, and when some members of the city council arrived at the Winter Palace to protest, a sailor threatened to spank them. Thus, with minimal casualties and disturbance, Petrograd fell into Bolshevik hands. Even the city opera went on with its scheduled performance.

That evening, Lenin and Trotsky appeared at the Congress of Soviets to announce the coup. The Bolsheviks were just shy of a majority in the Congress, which their rivals the Mensheviks (the old minority faction of the Social Democrats) promptly gave them by walking out in protest. This was a fatal mistake; as a Menshevik delegate later commented, "By quitting the congress, we . . . gave the Bolsheviks a monopoly of the Soviet, of the masses, and of the revolution."[3] The remaining delegates approved the formation of an all-Bolshevik government with Lenin at its head and Trotsky as commissar (minister) for foreign affairs. They also passed two decrees laid before them by Lenin, one calling for immediate land redistribution and the other for a peace without annexations or indemnities.

Within a month the Bolsheviks had gained control of most of Russia's cities. The peasants were conciliated by the confiscation of great estates, and workers' committees took control of factories; the latter, however, were soon superseded by a Supreme Economic Council, which oversaw all production. After some hesitation, Lenin permitted elections for the Constituent Assembly to proceed. The Bolsheviks had justified their coup as an attempt to save the revolution, and the assembly was its symbol. Some 36 million voters went to the polls in late November. The non-Marxist Social Revolutionary party, which enjoyed wide support among the peasantry, won a clear majority with 21 million votes. The Bolsheviks, strongest in the cities, received 9 million, the Center parties and the Mensheviks sharing the remainder. Lenin was neither surprised nor disturbed by this result. With control of the cities, the army, and the government apparatus, the Bolsheviks could ignore their rivals' mandate. When the assembly met on January 18, 1918, some brave souls rose to denounce Lenin's dictatorship, and after a tumultuous debate the assembly refused to ratify the Bolshevik program. The next day, the assembly was dispersed by armed force.

The Constituent Assembly was the least of the Bolsheviks' problems. Poland had already broken away from the Russian empire, and the Baltic provinces of Finland, Lithuania, Latvia, and Estonia followed suit. When peace was concluded with Germany in March 1918, a total of 1.3 million square miles of western Russia, containing more than a third of the country's population, had been lost. So exposed was Petrograd that the capital was hastily moved to Moscow. For the moment, however, the Bolsheviks had consolidated their grip on power and launched their new program.

THE END OF THE WAR

The effect of the events in Russia on the Allied war effort was not immediately apparent. What was clear, however, was the increasing weariness on both sides. U.S. President Woodrow Wilson had called from the beginning of the war for a "peace without victory." Peace feelers began to circulate in 1916, and a negotiated end to the war was openly debated in the German Reichstag in December. Nothing came of these efforts, though Lord Landsdowne warned the British House of Lords that the fabric of civilization was being rent by the unending slaughter. All observers agreed that the year 1917 would be decisive for the war. It was.

American Intervention

Woodrow Wilson (1856–1924) had proclaimed his nation's neutrality at the outbreak of hostilities, and he campaigned for reelection in 1916 on the slogan "He kept us out of war." American neutrality had, however, a pronounced tilt. Trade between the United States and the Allies had increased fourfold between 1914 and 1916, two-thirds of it in war materials. In addition,

loans and credits extended to the Allies by American bankers amounted to $2.2 billion. At the same time the United States acquiesced in the blockade that prevented it from trading with the Central Powers, although not without protest. In theory the United States continued to insist on "freedom of the seas," that is, the right of neutrals to trade with all belligerents; in practice it limited its trade to the belligerent with the largest navy.

The Germans' surface fleet could not challenge Britain directly on the high seas, but in the submarine they had a weapon that could ravage Allied shipping. Declaring a war zone around the British Isles, Germany warned neutrals that it would sink any vessel inside the zone without warning. In May 1915 a German submarine torpedoed a passenger liner, the *Lusitania*, causing 1,198 fatalities. More than 100 of these were U.S. citizens, and American outrage at the incident forced the Germans to curtail their policy.

As the stalemate on the ground continued, the German general staff pushed for a resumption of unrestricted submarine warfare as the only means to victory. The admiralty calculated that an all-out campaign could sink 600,000 tons of shipping a month, bringing Britain to its knees. The German command knew full well that this would bring the United States into the war on the Allied side. Their confident gamble was that the Allies would crumble before the Americans could arrive. "I give Your Majesty my word as an officer," the naval chief of staff assured the emperor, "that not one American will land on the continent."[4]

On January 31, 1917, the Germans informed Wilson that unrestricted submarine warfare would commence the next day. At the same time they proposed an anti-American alliance to Mexico, causing renewed outrage in the United States. When American cargo ships were sunk soon after, the die was cast. Wilson called for a crusade to make "the world safe for democracy." On April 6, Congress voted a declaration of war against the Central Powers.

American help was, however, a year away. Meanwhile, the Allied cause was bleak. A costly spring offensive finally broke French morale. Troops mutinied, waving red flags and singing "The Internationale," the socialist anthem. The Russian and Italian fronts collapsed amid similar demonstrations, forcing the British into another bloody and futile offensive in Flanders. At the same time the submarine campaign took a terrible toll of Allied shipping. At one point, British food reserves were down to six weeks. Only with the introduction of a convoy system did Britain succeed in containing its losses and preserving its nautical life-line.

The German Collapse

The Bolshevik revolution gave the Germans a last hope. The Treaty of Brest-Litovsk, signed with Russia on March 3, 1918, freed 52 divisions for an all-out assault on the western front, which began 18 days later. For the first time since 1914 the Germans advanced into open terrain, driving a wedge between the British and French lines. The Allies at last agreed to a joint command under French Marshal Ferdinand Foch (1851–1929) and, with U.S. troops in combat for the first time, halted the Germans almost within sight of Paris. By mid-July the German commander, Erich Ludendorff (1865–1937), had broken off the offensive.

The Germans had now failed at sea and on land. The western offensive had cost 1 million casualties, numbers that could no longer be made up with new recruits. Fuel and supplies were short, and desertions mounted. By September the Germans were in general retreat. They still had 2.5 million men in the field and a chance for a stand in Belgium. But though they could prolong the war, they could not win it. At best the generals could buy time for the diplomats to negotiate a compromise peace. They were unwilling to wage war on these terms.

On September 29, Ludendorff suddenly demanded that the foreign office obtain an armistice. The politicians counseled delay, but Ludendorff hysterically insisted that if the war was not halted within 24 hours, the army might be lost. This was manifestly exaggerated, but faced with an army in retreat, a commander who had given up, and allies who had deserted, the imperial cabinet had little choice but to negotiate a cessation of arms.

In late October the German fleet mutinied at Kiel. Workers and soldiers joined the uprising, immediately forming revolutionary councils similar to the soviets in Russia. The insurrection spread rapidly across the country, overthrowing the princely federal states and proclaiming republics based on universal suffrage. On November 7 the socialist Kurt Eisner proclaimed an independent Bavarian People's Republic. Two days later, a general strike erupted in Berlin, forcing William II to abdicate. On November 11 the German armistice delegation, now representing a republic, signed an agreement with the Allied powers in a railway dining car near Compiègne. The Germans renounced the Treaty of Brest-Litovsk, agreed to surrender their fleet, and withdrew their army beyond the Rhine. The guns fell silent. The Great War was over.

WILFRED OWEN AND THE LOST GENERATION

"No one will come out of this war who has not become a different person," wrote a German volunteer from the trenches of World War I.[5] To some, like the writer Ernst Junger, its survivors were a new elite, destined to remake the world. For most the war was an ordeal that gradually became devoid of purpose, value, and hope and could end only in maiming or death. It was for these, the lost generation of 1914, that Wilfred Owen spoke.

Owen, the eldest of four children, was born into a middle-class British family in 1893. His father was a poorly paid railway clerk, and though Owen matriculated at London University in 1911, he was unable to attend for lack of money. He found work as an English tutor in Bordeaux, where he was living at the outbreak of the war. Returning to England in September 1915, he enlisted for service and in June 1916 was commissioned as an officer. By January he was on the front lines during some of the bitterest fighting of the war.

At first, Owen shared the excitement of many young men for whom going to war was still an adventure. The full horror of the trenches was soon borne in on him. He and his men were trapped in a dugout for 50 hours, standing in two feet of water, until they could crawl to safety under fire from their own guns.

In March, Owen suffered a concussion that left him with severe headaches, and in April he was blown bodily from his foxhole by a shell that landed six feet away and buried a fellow officer alive. The next month, Owen was furloughed to a war hospital in Edinburgh. He had survived five months of trench warfare; the life expectancy of an officer was two.

While recuperating, Owen met the poet Siegfried Sassoon. Under Sassoon's influence, Owen's own literary ambitions jelled, and in a burst of creativity he produced some of the finest war poetry in the English language. Upon his release he was placed in charge of training officers. Unwilling to send men to a fate he could not share, he returned to the front in August 1918.

Owen had by now become a pacifist, but he could not, he felt, bear moral witness simply as an observer. In October he was awarded the Military Cross for bravery. On November 4, while helping his men to bridge a canal, he was killed by machine gun fire.

"The Poetry," said Owen, "is in the pity." In the poems that he never lived to see published, he spoke for all the dead of the Great War:

What passing-bells for those who die as cattle?
Only the monstrous anger of the guns.
Only the stuttering rifles' rapid rattle
Can patter out their hasty orisons.
No mockeries now for them; no prayers nor bells,
Nor any voice of mourning save the choirs,—
The shrill, demented choirs of wailing shells;
And bugles calling for them from sad shires.[6]

The Peace of the Victors: Versailles and After

Twenty-seven nations assembled in Paris in January 1919 to make the peace. The significant decisions were made, however, by three men: Woodrow Wilson, British Prime Minister David Lloyd George (1863–1945), and French Premier Georges Clemenceau (1841–1929). Russia was unrepresented; Allied forces had invaded it in March 1918, ostensibly to keep vital supplies and war materials from falling into German hands but more importantly to help to overthrow the Bolshevik regime. Germany had observer status only; its representatives had no power to negotiate terms.

Wilson's aims, set out a year before in his Fourteen Points, were well known. They included free trade and freedom of the seas, the self-determination of peoples, an end to secret treaties, a reduction of armaments, and the formation of an international body to resolve conflicts and keep the peace. Two of these principles had already been compromised. The United States had permitted Britain to continue its blockade of Germany, and it had reluctantly agreed to respect the secret pacts made between the Allies during the war, notably the Treaty of London (1915) with Italy and the Sykes-Picot agreement (1916), which envisioned the division of the Middle East into British and French spheres of influence under nominal Arab rule.

The victors at Versailles. From left to right, David Lloyd George of Britain, Vittorio Orlando of Italy, Georges Clemenceau of France, and Woodrow Wilson of the United States. [Brown Brothers]

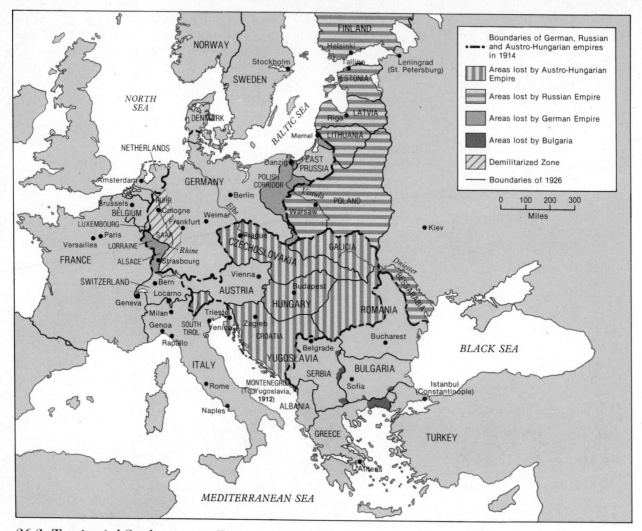

26.2 Territorial Settlements in Europe, 1919–1926

These compromises reflected the profound differences between Wilson's approach to the peace and that of his allied partners. The United States, already the world's greatest industrial power before 1914, had expanded its capacity enormously during the war. With only a few months of serious fighting, it had won the chief place at the victors' table. Its main interest was in protecting its advantages by guaranteeing free trade. The British and the French were in far different circumstances. Drained and exhausted, they were primarily concerned with rebuilding their shattered economies, reasserting their imperial supremacy, and weakening their former adversaries.

These goals were clearly reflected in the Treaty of Versailles with Germany. Alsace and Lorraine were returned to France. An Allied army was to occupy the German Rhineland for 15 years, and the French obtained a 15-year lease on the coal mines of Germany's Saar basin, after which a plebiscite would be held to determine the region's future. Parts of Silesia and the bulk of West Prussia were ceded to the newly recognized state of Poland, and the German port of Danzig (now Gdansk) was declared a Free City. These losses deprived Germany of about 15 percent of its productive capacity and cut off East Prussia from the remainder of the country. Germany was also stripped of its colonies and forbidden to possess submarines, military aircraft, and heavy artillery. Its army was reduced to 100,000 men. Its navy scuttled itself rather than surrender. Finally, Germany was made to acknowledge its sole responsibility for the war and to pay an unspecified reparation for war damages.

The Allies freely redrew the map of Eastern Europe. Austria-Hungary collapsed with the end of the war, as the new nations of Czechoslovakia and Yugoslavia emerged from its former territory with Wilson's blessing, and Austria and Hungary, both radically diminished, remained as separate states. The nations carved from Russia by the Treaty of Brest-Litovsk—Finland,* Lithuania, Latvia, Estonia, and Poland—were recognized at Versailles; Poland, in addition to obtaining West Prussia and Silesia from Germany and Galicia from Austria, attacked Russia in hopes of securing part of the Ukraine as well. The dismantling of the Ottoman Empire was completed on the basis of the Sykes-Picot agreement, leaving a Turkish republic occupying only Constantinople and Asia Minor.

In all, nine new nations had emerged in Eastern Europe, and no frontier had been left untouched. It was by no means clear that the results were an improvement. Notwithstanding the principle of ethnic self-determination, each new state contained disaffected minorities. The Poles ruled Germans, Russians, and Ukrainians; the Romanians all these and Bulgarians as well; the Czechs, Germans and Hungarians; the Italians, Germans and Slavs. The Yugoslavs, who comprised three contending Slavic groups—Serbs, Croats, and Slovenes—as well as Hungarians and Bulgarians, were the most divided of all. In place of three multiethnic empires there was now a series of multinational states, for the most part poor, undeveloped, and ill-equipped for the democratic regimes suddenly thrust upon them.

The largest failure of Allied diplomacy in the east, however, was the vain attempt to exclude German and Russian power from the region. Determined to thwart future German ambitions and to halt the spread of Bolshevism but without a buffer against either, the Allies merely created a vacuum of power that the Nazi-Soviet pact would later exploit.

The treaty with Germany was presented in May. No German could be found to sign it, and only the threat of renewed war compelled acceptance of what the Germans called the *Diktat*—the dictated peace. Germany's foes put in their claims for reparations; Belgium asked for more than its own entire net worth. The final bill amounted to $33 billion, a sum whose collection could

*Finland's independence had been recognized voluntarily by the Bolsheviks earlier.

only bankrupt Germany—and did. The only hopeful result of the conference was the establishment of an international body, the League of Nations, to resolve conflict. Neither Germany nor Russia was admitted, and Britain and France, cynically exploiting it, took up their new African and Middle Eastern empires under the guise of League "mandates" granted them to prepare their territories for self-government. The most fateful of these was Palestine, in which the British had promised to support a national homeland for the Jews of Europe.

Woodrow Wilson, who had sacrificed much of the substance of the Fourteen Points to gain approval for the League, went home to win ratification of its covenant. While campaigning to rouse support, he suffered a disabling stroke. Isolationist opinion prevailed, and the Senate rejected all the peace agreements, negotiating separate treaties with its former enemies in 1922. The United States never joined the League of Nations.

THE GREAT WAR
IN PERSPECTIVE

The scale of the Great War is best appreciated by considering its toll. Some 38 nations mobilized 74 million men, of whom 10 million died in battle. Ten million more were captured, and a million of these died. Thirty million were wounded, a quarter of them crippled for life. Millions of civilian casualties were also caused directly or indirectly by the war—from shelling and bombing, from privation and disease, from civil war, and, in Eastern Europe and Armenia, from massacre. At the end of the war a great influenza epidemic struck the ravaged populations of Europe and killed 20 million more.

The war cost Germany and France a sixth of their male populations, including a third of those between the ages of 20 and 32. It consumed roughly a quarter of their national wealth. Britain spent a sum nearly equivalent to its capital value; Italy exhausted virtually its entire gold reserve. There were theaters of battle in Africa, the Middle East, and the Far East; both Canada and Australia, which came to the aid of Britain, suffered losses proportionally as severe as those of the European combatants themselves. The Japanese, nominally allying themselves to the Allied Powers, took advantage of the war to enhance their imperial position in Asia, laying the ground for war with China and confrontation with the United States a generation later.

The Class of 1914–1918. Millions of war survivors were maimed or crippled.
[Imperial War Museum, London]

The Politics of Total War

The problems of sustaining so vast a conflict required an unprecedented degree of control over all social resources, human and material. This could be accomplished only by governments, and the state expanded its scope and function everywhere during the Great War. Production, consumption, and investment were all subordinated to the needs of the war effort; vital materials were rationed; necessary skills and labor were requisitioned.

War had once been waged by military castes and mercenaries. The masses had not been expected to fight in them, nor the intellectual elite to support them. All of that had changed with the passing of the Old Regime. The nineteenth-century commentator Karl von Clausewitz recognized that war had become a total activity involving the whole of society. Like imperialism and monopoly capital, total war was inimical to such liberal values as freedom, personal autonomy, and voluntary community. It blurred the line between soldier and civilian, combatant and noncombatant, and thus broke down the rules that had tacitly contained it as a social activity. Thus, while on the surface the war swept away the imperial regimes of Germany, Austria-Hungary, and tsarist Russia and nominal republics were installed in

the new states of Eastern Europe, its deeper impact was to undermine democratic values. The war had not made the world safe for democracy, in Woodrow Wilson's phrase, but much more precarious.

The beginning of the war had seen a general outburst of patriotic fervor. But war profiteering soon became a scandal in most countries, and many analysts traced the prolongation of the war, if not its actual cause, to the greed of arms merchants. Strikes resumed, desertions mounted, and class antagonism returned to crisis levels. No defeated government survived the war, and even victor states, such as Italy, soon succumbed to authoritarian regimes.

Women and the War

The Great War had arrived just at the crest of feminist agitation for suffrage. It provided an opportunity for social reaction against women just as it did against working-class men, emphasizing the passive roles of wife and mother (soon joined by that of widow). But women soon had to take their husbands' and brothers' places in fields, offices, and factories. In some war industries, women constituted as much as 60 percent of the work force. With so many women now breadwinners, the gap in pay between the sexes narrowed, and a minimum wage was introduced.

After the war, women returned largely to their traditional roles. The labor market contracted rapidly, and returning veterans took women's places. In Britain, women were rewarded for their work with the vote in 1918, but a similar bill was thrown out by the French Senate. In France, long obsessed with its demographic stagnation, the loss of a third of its male youth led to draconian postwar legislation against birth control and abortion. A renewed emphasis on motherhood was essential, it was felt, if the nation were to remain a world power. At the same time that women were being discouraged from remaining in the work force, however, many war widows were subsisting on pensions that did not meet basic necessities.

Women did not forget their wartime experience of freedom and mobility. Fashion accentuated the trend toward greater ease of movement as hemlines rose above the ankle, bathing bloomers disappeared, and page boy cuts replaced long hair. These changes, though striking, were nonetheless superficial. For the most part, women were forced back into their former roles and occupations. The war had given them a taste of liberty, but the battle for gender equality remained to be won.

The End of European Hegemony

The Great War had only one real winner, the United States. With a net transfer of $14 billion in foreign wealth, it had become the world's largest creditor nation. Both the vast sums owed it by the other belligerents and their continuing postwar needs made the United States the arbiter of Europe's financial destiny. The extent of American influence was masked by political isolationism, but Europe's economic viability and hence its political stability were increasingly dependent on the United States. The effects of the U.S. stock market crash in 1929 made this glaringly evident. The United States was now the world's leading power.

The productive capacity of the United States had also been greatly enhanced by the war; twice the size of Germany's in 1914, it now exceeded that of all the powers of Europe combined. The war had stimulated the economies of Latin America, India, Japan, and Australasia as well; these would now claim an increasing share of the world's wealth. Even after recovery, Europe would never enjoy the dominant economic role that it had played in the prewar decades.

This massive shift in wealth was soon reflected on the political level. From the Pan-African Congress to the revolutionary Wafdist Party in Egypt to the movement of national regeneration led by Kemal Ataturk (1881–1938) in Turkey, Africa and the Middle East were stirring toward independence. The year 1919 saw the beginning of Mohandas Gandhi's revolution against British rule in India and the nationalist May Fourth movement in China. Bolshevik Russia, newly refurbished as the Union of Soviet Socialist Republics (USSR), would soon be assisting anticolonial uprisings around the world, while Japan challenged Western hegemony in East Asia. The end of European empire was not yet at hand, but its days were numbered.

SUMMARY

The Great War was a turning point in Western history. The assurance of progress that had sustained the liberal faith in Europe was shattered by a conflict whose scope could neither be imagined in advance nor comprehended in retrospect. Kings had been swept from their thrones, empires uprooted, and the world's largest country engulfed by revolution. An entire civilization had faced the abyss.

The survivors could only resolve, as many did, that this had been "the war to end all wars" and that a new international order must henceforth guarantee the peace. This was the dream of Wilson's League of Nations. Not all believed it. "This isn't peace," Marshal Foch said of the treaties that had ended the war. "It is an armistice for twenty years." He was precisely correct.

Notes

1. J. Joll, *The Origins of the First World War* (London: Longman, 1985), pp. 155–156.
2. A. Kennett and V. Kennett, *The Palaces of Leningrad* (New York: Putnam, 1973), p. 23.
3. J. M. Thompson, *Revolutionary Russia* (New York: Scribner, 1981), p. 153.
4. G. A. Craig, *Europe Since 1815* (New York: Holt, Rinehart and Winston, 1966), p. 524.
5. E. J. Leed, *No Man's Land: Combat and Identity in World War I* (Cambridge, England: Cambridge University Press, 1979), p. 1.
6. C. Day Lewis, ed., *The Collected Poems of Wilfred Owen* (New York: New Directions, 1964), p. 44.

Suggestions for Further Reading

Ascher, A. *The Revolution of 1905: Russia in Disarray.* Stanford, Calif.: Stanford University Press, 1988.

Calleo, D. *The German Problem Reconsidered: Germany and the World Order, 1870 to the Present.* Cambridge: Cambridge University Press, 1978.

Chamberlin, W. H. *The Russian Revolution, 1917–1921.* New York: Macmillan, 1965.

Clark, R. *Lenin: A Biography.* New York: Harper & Row, 1988.

Evans, R. J. W., and von Strandmann, H. P., eds. *The Coming of the First World War.* New York: Oxford University Press, 1989.

Ferro, M. *October 1917: A Social History of the Russian Revolution.* Englewood Cliffs, N.J.: Prentice-Hall, 1972.

Fussell, P. *The Great War and Modern Memory.* Oxford: Oxford University Press, 1975.

Hale, O. J. *The Great Illusion, 1900–1914.* New York: Harper & Row, 1971.

Hardach, G. *The First World War, 1914–1918.* Berkeley: University of California Press, 1977.

Marwick, A., ed. *Total War and Social Change.* New York: St. Martin's Press, 1988.

Mayer, A. J. *The Politics and Diplomacy of Peacemaking.* New York: Knopf, 1968.

Mosse, G. L. *Fallen Soldiers: Reshaping the Memory of Modern Wars.* New York: Oxford University Press, 1990.

Schmitt, B. E., and Vedeler, H. *The World in the Crucible, 1914–1919.* New York: Harper & Row, 1984.

Wall, R., and Winter, J. *The Upheaval of War: Family, Work and Welfare in Europe, 1914–18.* New York: Harper & Row, 1984.

Wohl, R. *The Generation of 1914.* Cambridge, Mass.: Harvard University Press, 1979.

27

THE WEST AND THE AUTHORITARIAN CHALLENGE

The Paris peace settlement that ended the Great War resolved some of the national and imperialistic rivalries that had figured so prominently among its causes and provided, through the League of Nations, the framework to mediate others. Yet the war had exacerbated other problems by dislocating economies, creating new but unstable states, and imposing a ruinous peace on Germany. International tensions were further heightened by the emergence in Russia of a Bolshevik regime that was initially committed to exporting social revolution. Thus the 1920s provided the setting for an increasingly bitter struggle between liberal democratic and emerging authoritarian forms of government throughout much of Europe.

In the wake of the Great War came not only the authoritarian challenge to liberal states and institutions but also a striking period of cultural and intellectual activity as artists, musicians, and writers reexamined traditional values. Whereas most Europeans reflected the postwar crisis of values, many Americans turned inward as they searched for "normalcy" and enjoyed the material prosperity of the "Roaring Twenties." Theirs was the Jazz Age, a generally ebullient time though marred by the "red scare" of the 1920s. Some Europeans shared the Americans' optimism, but despite the glittering social life of bourgeois Paris and Berlin, much of European art reflected disillusionment and anger. Yet Paris and Berlin were impressive as the setting for artistic and intellectual experimentation. The 1920s were at once an age of hope, anxiety, and searching—for peace, order, prosperity, and new values.

THE AUTHORITARIAN PHENOMENON: THE CHALLENGE TO DEMOCRATIC LIBERALISM

In the century between the Congress of Vienna and the outbreak of the Great War, liberalism had made impressive gains. Universal manhood suffrage had been established throughout most of western Europe by 1918. Norway and Denmark instituted women's suffrage in 1913 and 1915, respectively, but not until after the war were similar advances made in Britain, Germany, the United States, and Sweden. Before the war, parliamentary governments were thriving in Britain, France, Italy, and some of the smaller western states, and even the empires of Germany, Austria-Hungary, and Russia had parliamentary institutions, albeit anemic ones. Important strides had been made to improve the rights of workers, as reflected by the legalization of trade unions in Britain, France, and Germany and the growth of unions in the United States.

Much remained to be done: women were still treated as inferior both legally and socially; poverty, despite a rising standard of living, was still widespread; and the effectiveness of most parliamentary institutions was impeded by a multiplicity of parties or authoritarian traditions that curtailed their power. Moreover, the trend toward democracy posed new problems for international relations by increasing the pressure of the masses on decisions of war and peace. Ironically, democracy helped to create the climate in which authoritarian governments could emerge by encouraging political leaders to appeal to the masses. In the hands of demagogues, militant nationalism, imperialism, and racism were potent tools to transform democracy into authoritarian rule.

The liberal democratic governments of the early twentieth century had demonstrated their ability to wage war on a scale hitherto unparalleled in history and to survive with their parliamentary institutions intact. Such was their influence that even the defeated nations experimented with liberal governments after the war. So great was the economic cost of the war, however, that in its aftermath each state was primarily concerned with its own economic recovery. France was also preoccupied with its security from further German aggression, and few people in the United States were willing to endorse major international commitments, as reflected in part by America's withdrawal from mutual security agreements intended to protect France. Scant attention was paid to the problems of the small states of central and eastern Europe, and such staggering economic burdens were imposed on Germany that democracy had little chance to succeed.

Authoritarian governments were imposed in several major states—in the Soviet Union, in Nazi Germany, and at least to a degree in Italy. An authoritarian state is an extreme form of dictatorship in which the government not only eliminates all individual rights and liberties but also subordinates institutions to a single party and its leader. Authoritarian states have no independent political parties or institutions.

The authoritarian state claims the prerogative to control every aspect of life through a single-party system. Authoritarian regimes rely on propaganda and terror, including such devices as censorship, clandestine surveillance, torture, and the incarceration or execution of dissidents. Such regimes use the mass media to indoctrinate their subjects; before the advent of modern communications, authoritarian rule on a large scale would have been impossible. Authoritarian governments did not succeed in subordinating every aspect of society to their ideology, and their demand for unconditional submission provoked resistance.

Authoritarian leaders depict themselves as the saviors of their people, with the right to unchallenged obedience. Lenin unwillingly set the stage for Joseph Stalin by typically proclaiming the superiority of the party's will to all laws, traditions, and institutions, and Hitler brazenly linked his mission to divine providence. By identifying the state with the party and the people

with the leader, authoritarianism made the leader an extension of the people. By identifying himself with the people, both as their savior and as the embodiment of their being, the authoritarian leader becomes more than a dictator. In authoritarian imagery, those who defy the leader defy themselves. The only necessary virtues are loyalty and obedience. No sacrifice is too great for the state, no principle of conscience so sacred that the government cannot abrogate it.

Although authoritarian states shared many characteristics, important differences existed. In Russia the Bolsheviks toppled an aristocratic government, whereas in Germany the Nazis overthrew a democratic state. Unlike the Nazis, the Bolsheviks at least professed democratic ideals. Moreover, the Nazis seized control of a leading industrial nation and for some years enjoyed peaceful relations with the major European states, whereas the Russian economy was backward, and the major powers soon intervened in the Russian civil war in an attempt to overthrow the Bolsheviks. Finally, in World War II the Soviet Union was an ally of the democratic states against Germany.

THE BOLSHEVIK CONSOLIDATION

Born in the midst of military defeat, the Bolshevik revolution soon faced a bitter civil war in which its opponents enjoyed the support of powerful foreign enemies. The infant regime was locked in a life-and-death struggle that forced it to temper its ideology to survive. By doing so, it preserved Bolshevik power but at the cost of failing to establish the classless, egalitarian society in whose name it claimed authority.

Allied Intervention and Civil War

Throughout 1918, former tsarist military leaders recruited volunteers to oppose the Bolshevik regime. The Whites, as they were known, received modest support from foreign powers, particularly the British, the French, and the Japanese. The Western allies were primarily interested in toppling the Soviet regime, whereas the Japanese sought territorial gains. Altogether, well over 100,000 foreign troops representing 22 countries, including the United States, were eventually involved in the Russian civil war but never with sufficient determina-

27.1 Russia in War and Revolution, 1917–1921

tion, consistency, or organization to tip the scales to the side of the Whites. On the contrary, foreign intervention enabled the Bolsheviks to depict themselves as defenders of Russia from alien predators.

Initially, the Bolsheviks had no disciplined military force with which to confront the Whites, but in April 1918, Leon Trotsky persuaded his colleagues to recruit ex-tsarist officers and conscript troops. Former officers who refused to serve faced imprisonment for themselves

and detention for their families; nearly 50,000 agreed to fight in the Red army, which by year's end numbered 800,000 men.

At one point the Reds controlled only the region around Moscow and Petrograd, but by November 1920 they had prevailed, thanks in large measure to Trotsky's organizational skills and his effective use of propaganda. The Reds had the advantage of internal supply lines and communications, whereas their opponents were too widely separated and divided in aim to operate as a cohesive force. The Reds also proved more successful at winning popular support, primarily because the peasants knew that a White victory would jeopardize the revolutionary land settlement. White Russian leaders, moreover, were handicapped by having to recruit in areas dominated by ethnic minorities that were cool to Russian interests.

War Communism: The Imposition of Controls

The civil war provided Lenin with the rationale and the opportunity to impose authoritarian rule in Russia. In theory the country was run by the Congress of Soviets, which derived its authority from provincial congresses of soviets and ultimately from local soviets of peasants and workers, but real power rested in the hands of the Communist Party, as it became known in 1918. Lenin chaired both the Council of People's Commissars, a cabinet appointed by the Congress of Soviets, and the party's Central Committee; the membership of the two groups was essentially identical. Theoretically, power flowed from the soviets up; under Lenin's system of "democratic centralism," each echelon of the party elected the one above it, but in practice, real authority moved from the top down in the party. The party in turn governed the state. At first, rival reformist parties were tolerated, but in 1922, Lenin and his cohorts imprisoned or expelled leading Social Revolutionaries and Mensheviks and had a dozen of the most prominent Social Revolutionaries executed.

The economic counterpart to political centralization was war communism, the intent of which was to prevent resistance to the party. The government nationalized all land and most industry and mining without compensation, claimed the exclusive right to distribute foodstuffs, closed private banks and appropriated their holdings, and terminated private trade, whether domestic or foreign. The Supreme Council of National Economy oversaw industrial production through some 90 trusts, each of which comprised a segment of nationalized industry. The state expropriated all royal and ecclesiastical properties as well as such private possessions as art collections and jewelry and abolished the right of inheritance. Henceforth the government had the power to compel any citizen to undertake necessary work; the first labor battalions were organized in 1920.

When these measures provoked widespread hostility, Lenin responded with the Red Terror. The primary agency responsible for carrying out his campaign against dissidents was the Extraordinary Committee for the Suppression of the Counterrevolution, or Cheka. Prisons and forced labor camps were packed, while firing squads executed striking workers, peasants who hoarded food, and political enemies, including Tsar Nicholas II and his family. Sailors who mutinied at the Kronstadt naval base in March 1921 were executed as well. By the beginning of that year, approximately 1.5 million people, most well-to-do, had fled Russia.

Although the Bolsheviks survived the civil war, the economy was a shambles, popular resentment was high, and many of Russia's brightest and most productive citizens had been executed, imprisoned, or forced into exile. Moreover, the tsar's civil servants had refused to serve the Bolshevik regime and instead supported the Whites, leaving Lenin with largely unskilled people to run the state. War, starvation, and executions killed approximately 7 million people in Russia between 1918 and 1920. In Lenin's mind, such measures were the necessary product of a war by "revolutionary Marxism" against its enemies.

Lenin and the New Economic Policy

Whether the Bolsheviks could have survived the civil war and foreign intervention without implementing war communism is debatable, but by early 1921 the economy was in a state of near collapse. Since 1913 the real wages of workers had declined 67 percent and the productivity of heavy industry by 80 percent. More than a third of the population of the larger cities had fled to the countryside in a desperate effort to feed themselves, while tens of thousands of veterans roamed the country in search of food and employment. This misery was compounded in 1921 by a drought-induced famine in which 3 million people perished. In the absence of stable currency or manufactured goods for which to exchange their produce, the fortunate peasants who had surplus crops refused to bring them to market. Had the country not been exhausted by war and famine, the Bolshevik regime might have collapsed.

To save the revolution, Lenin charted a bold new course in March 1921 when he replaced war communism with the New Economic Policy (NEP). The core of the NEP was the restoration of private incentive to agriculture, commerce, and petty manufacturing. The state allowed peasants to lease land and, after paying a modest tax, to sell their surplus crops as they saw fit. Beginning in 1922, the peasants enjoyed secure land tenure, with the right to lease or sell their land and to employ farmhands to work it. Although heavy industry, banking, foreign trade, and transport remained under government control, small enterprises and merchants who traded within Russia were free. To help bring inflation under control, the Bolsheviks established a new state bank and issued new currency.

It took a while for the mixed economy to work. Unemployment soared to 2 million, or more than 25 percent of the urban work force. After 1926, however, most industries reached prewar production levels, and both private parties and cooperatives experienced increased volumes of trade. Dissatisfied with the pace of industrialization, the government decided in 1926 to increase investment in heavy industry by reducing the prices it paid for agricultural produce, especially grain. Understandably, the peasants began switching to other crops and using more of their grain to feed livestock or distill vodka (which could also be made from potatoes). The amount of grain available to the government for export and to feed soldiers and workers declined by 30 percent between 1927 and 1928. The NEP, despite its success in stabilizing the economy, would be sacrificed to expedite the growth of heavy industry.

Stalin and Trotsky: The Struggle for Succession

Lenin did not live to see the success of his NEP. In December 1922, after Lenin suffered a stroke, he and his wife, Nadezhda Krupskaya, pondered possible successors, including Trotsky and Joseph Stalin (1879–1953), a shoemaker's son who had proven his loyalty to the party as a prisoner of the tsar, a Siberian exile, and the editor of the newspaper *Pravda*. In the early years of the Bolshevik regime, Stalin proved to be an adept administrator and party functionary. Lenin had a clear-cut choice between Trotsky, founder of the Red Army, revolutionary hero, skilled orator, and proponent of world revolution, and Stalin, who would later advocate "socialism in one country," the policy of focusing scarce resources on the development of communism in the Soviet Union. Two other men were considered: Grigori Zinoviev, head of the Third, or Communist, International (Comintern), established in 1919, which was responsible for supporting revolutionary movements in other countries, and Nikolai Bukharin, editor of *Pravda* ("Truth"), the official party newspaper.

Stalin's rivals underestimated the strength of his party contacts and erroneously assumed that they would

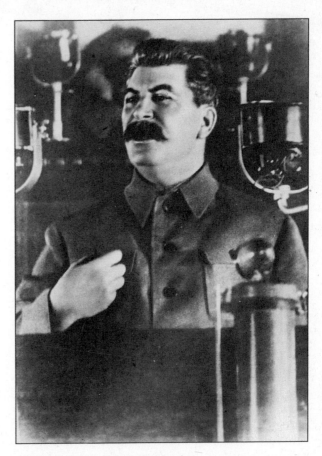

Joseph Stalin in 1936. [Sovfoto]

share in running the party and the country through the five-man Politburo, or executive council. Their expectations were shattered as Stalin isolated and then destroyed his competitors, beginning with Trotsky, who was forced to resign as head of the armed forces in 1925. Within a year, Stalin ousted the leaders of the party's left from the Politburo. Stalin exiled Trotsky and finally, in 1940, had him assassinated in Mexico. Beginning in 1929, Stalin turned against his former allies on the party's right, emerging peerless.

THE FASCIST REVOLUTION IN ITALY

Although Italy had been among the victors in World War I, the unsatisfactory peace terms it received and the critical postwar economic problems it suffered created massive unrest. Territorial ambitions, which had led Italy to join the Allied cause, were only partially satisfied at the Paris Peace Conference: the Italians extended their northern border and annexed the Istrian peninsula, including the port of Trieste, but they were denied Dalmatia and the port of Fiume. Extreme nationalists led by Gabriele d'Annunzio (1863–1938) seized Fiume in September 1919, but in December 1920 the Italian army expelled the adventurers. D'Annunzio's actions, including his use of torch-lit rallies and the ancient Roman salute, were keenly observed by the leader of Italy's Fascist party, Benito Mussolini (1883–1945).

Contrary to government promises, military victory did not inaugurate an age of prosperity and political equality but economic misery in Italy. To pay the costs of war, the government had not only borrowed but also printed exorbitant amounts of paper currency, thereby fueling postwar inflation. By 1920 the lira had declined more than 80 percent from its prewar level, and the balance of trade reflected a mounting deficit. Unemployment surpassed 2 million, strikes increased in number, and in 1920, desperate workers temporarily seized control of factories in the north. Conditions were equally deplorable in the countryside, where most peasants had no land at all. Hopes for land redistribution raised by wartime promises were dashed when the liberal-led governments of the postwar era failed to initiate meaningful reforms that went against the interests of large landowners. Taxes rose, with the burden distributed inequitably; the position of the middle class declined; and food shortages contributed to the misery.

The Fascist Movement

As the political crisis escalated, Mussolini bluffed his way to power. Before the outbreak of World War I, Mussolini had led the Socialists' opposition to the 1911 Libyan war and served as editor of the Socialist newspaper *Avanti!* Initially opposed to the war, he soon became convinced that participating on the side of Britain and France would provide the opportunity for political and social revolution. Forced to resign as editor of *Avanti!* and expelled from the Socialist party, he enlisted in the army and was wounded. At Milan in March 1919 Mussolini organized "combat groups" (*fasci di combattimento*), whose name derived from a symbol of authority used in classical Rome, the *fasces,* a bundle of rods tied around an axe shaft. The early recruits to these black-shirted terrorist squads were mostly students, disillusioned veterans, militant Socialists, and extreme nationalists. Financial backing came from landlords and industrialists worried about the growing disorder and the Bolshevik threat. The government's expulsion of d'Annunzio from Fiume was a boon to Mussolini's recruiting. In November 1921 he founded a regular political organization, the National Fascist Party, with a membership in excess of 250,000.

The Fascists made a calculated appeal to conservatives who feared Communist ideology and Socialist plans for extensive socioeconomic reforms. In the countryside, Fascist paramilitary squads prevented farm workers from unionizing, and in the cities they broke up Socialist rallies, protected strikebreakers, and wrecked trade union and Socialist offices. Unsympathetic public officials likewise experienced Fascist wrath. But such tactics offered no reasonable prospects of an electoral victory that would enable Mussolini to govern constitutionally. In the 1921 election, 35 Fascists won seats in the Chamber of Deputies, but in a body of 535 they constituted an inauspicious group compared to the 123 Socialists and 107 Christian Democrats (as the Catholic party was now called).

The March on Rome

While shaky coalitions attempted to govern Italy, Mussolini vacillated between monarchical and republican sentiments and for a time considered an alliance with the Communists. When the Socialists called a general strike in August 1922 to protest Fascist violence, Mussolini's thugs, urged on by d'Annunzio, ousted the Socialist government in Milan. Other city governments met similar fates. In September, Mussolini made a further bid for conservative backing by announcing his support for the monarchy. Ironically, King Victor Emmanuel III, who commanded the loyalty of the Senate and the army, might have stopped Fascist violence had he not feared that Mussolini would overthrow him.

In October 1922, against a background of recurring cabinet crises, Mussolini negotiated with traditional political leaders to form a new government that would include the Fascists. Before these discussions were concluded, hotter heads in the party apparently pressured him to order tens of thousands of his Blackshirts to march on Rome. Despite being poorly armed and ill-prepared to occupy the capital, Fascist contingents were underway on October 27.

Victor Emmanuel authorized the cabinet to impose martial law if necessary, but the military refused to act without written orders. Having lost his nerve, the king refused to sign a decree and instead invited Antonio Salandra, a political ally of the Fascists, to form a new government of the right. Mussolini declined to cooperate with Salandra, gambling that the king would invite him to form a cabinet and permit the march on Rome to continue unchallenged. Mussolini was right on both counts: accepting the king's invitation to form a cabinet, he arrived in Rome on October 30. Although the transfer of power technically took place within the framework of the Italian constitution, the spirit of that document was violated not only by Fascist intimidation but also by the political and moral cowardice of hitherto respected political leaders.

Mussolini and the Corporative State

Against a background of civil unrest, Mussolini persuaded Parliament to give him extraordinary powers to govern for 12 months. He also began restaffing local police and government agencies with Fascists and replacing the national militia with Fascist squads. Cutting inheritance taxes 50 percent, suspending land reform, and terminating state assistance to Socialist cooperatives won him the support of conservatives, and the Catholic church applauded his attack on "red atheism." In 1923, Mussolini persuaded Parliament to pass the Acerbo law, guaranteeing that two-thirds of the seats in the Chamber of Deputies would go to the party or coalition that had a minimum plurality of 25 percent.

In the 1925 election, characterized by more Fascist violence, Mussolini's right-wing coalition polled 63 percent of the vote. The election was shadowed by the assassination of a prominent Socialist, Giacomo Matteotti, who had dared to condemn Fascist violence. Despite Mussolini's admission of responsibility, the king did nothing, preferring a Fascist government to the Socialist alternative. When the opposition deputies protested by walking out of the Chamber of Deputies, Mussolini barred their return and outlawed opposition parties.

Beginning in December 1925, Mussolini rammed laws through Parliament that gave him dictatorial powers, including the right to issue decrees that had the force of law without parliamentary approval. Three years later, the king lost his right to choose the prime minister when that power was vested in Mussolini and the Fascist Grand Council, over which Mussolini, as *Duce* ("leader"), presided. A 1928 electoral law empowered the council to approve candidates for Parliament. Like Lenin, Mussolini meshed the party and the state, ensuring that all political decisions were the province of the party.

A number of traditional institutions, including the monarchy, the judiciary, the Catholic church, and the military, generally retained their functions under the Fascists. Victor Emmanuel, however, had no real power, no contact with the leftists who opposed the Fascist regime, and minimal ties with the church. Aided by the complaisance of Pope Pius XI, Mussolini neutralized the church. Pius signed the Lateran Treaty in 1929, recognizing the Kingdom of Italy in return for Italian acceptance of an independent Vatican City. The accompanying Concordat declared Catholicism the state religion of Italy, confirmed the church's liberty in theological matters, exempted ecclesiastical bodies from taxes, extended Catholic teaching from elementary to secondary schools, and required church marriages. The state received the right to block ecclesiastical appointments and promotions. Thus the Catholic church, which since 1870 had refused to recognize the legitimate government of the Italian nation, sanctioned a dictatorial regime.

Mussolini opted to work with rather than refashion the judiciary and the military. Judges retained their independence, and traditional courts continued to function, although a special Fascist tribunal tried political cases. Apart from cosmetic changes, such as the introduction of the goose step and the Fascist salute, the primary impact of fascism on the army was a decline in morale stemming from the promotion of inferior officers and a decline in effectiveness resulting from the inundation of Mussolini's Blackshirts.

Mussolini introduced major economic changes as a result of the great depression that deprived 1 million Italians of their jobs after 1929. Private ownership of property was not challenged, but the government exerted a much greater role in controlling the economy through a "corporative" system. The economy was reorganized into 22 corporations, each of which comprised employers and employees and was supervised by the National Council of Corporations. In theory the corporative system was intended to end class conflict, but in practice its purpose was to control labor and eliminate independent unions, thus reflecting the interests of the bourgeoisie and the landowners who provided the backbone of fascism's support in Italy. The culmination of the corporative system came in 1939 when the Chamber of Fasces and Corporations replaced Parliament.

The Fascists subjected more and more Italian life to government control, but with ineffective results. The so-called Battle for Grain doubled domestic production by 1939 and reduced imports by switching marginal land from the raising of cattle, fruit, or olives, but at a cost of sharply increasing prices. Mussolini's Battle for Births aimed to increase the population by a third (to 60 million) by 1960, thereby providing more men for the army and more people to found overseas colonies and to keep wages low. In most careers, being single was an impediment. The state encouraged women to remain at home to raise children and barred them from government service. The Battle for Births failed: 1932 was the first year since 1876 when there were fewer than 1 million live births.

The regime founded a Fascist Academy to coordinate work in the arts and sciences, and Mussolini himself appointed its 60 members. The stress on orthodoxy worked against scientific advances, leaving Italian scientists unprepared to contribute to the war effort in the 1940s. Italian Fascists never developed a systematic education policy; emphasis was placed on teaching children the virtues of war, a goal that was accomplished partly by enrolling them in quasi-military units beginning at age 4.

Italian fascism was less an ideology than a dynamic, eclectic movement. Mussolini borrowed and discarded ideas as his mood and political circumstances dictated. Fascists rejected the notion that they were responsible to any external system of morality; the Fascist state created its own ethics, at the core of which was the conviction that war is ennobling. Mussolini placed a high value on imperialism, borrowing political symbols from classical Rome. Marble relief maps of the Roman Empire were prominently displayed in the capital, and part of the city was razed to build a monumental Imperial Way. Propaganda was a key tool of government; the regime plastered its slogans throughout the country, and the Ministry of Popular Culture controlled the media and cultural life. At root, Italian fascism was the quest of the landed and industrial elite for power through order and for glory through conquest.

THE TRIAL OF DEMOCRACY

With the extension of parliamentary government through virtually the whole of Europe, liberal democratic regimes had an excellent opportunity to implement their programs in the 1920s. Their contributions included an extension of political and legal rights and improvements in the living and working conditions of the masses. They also built a foundation for lasting peace through international cooperation and constructive foreign policies that eschewed purely nationalistic gains in favor of benefits shared by the community of nations. The primary threat

to these goals came from chauvinistic nationalism, imperialism, extremist political groups, and the propertied classes' determination to resist major social reform. Only in the area of legal and political rights did some of the liberal states achieve any significant success. For the most part the 1920s were a decade of lost opportunity.

The Search for Collective Security

Diplomacy in the period from the Congress of Vienna to the end of World War I had been conducted primarily in secret. In the popular mind, this system had given birth to the tangled alliances of the prewar period and to the Great War itself. Consequently, in the aftermath of the war the liberal governments tried to conduct diplomacy in the open, particularly through international conferences. But this method was susceptible to political posturing for the benefit of the electorate and generated unrealistic hopes and claims of success.

As the principal instrument for the maintenance of collective security, the League of Nations was seriously flawed. Three of the four permanent members of its Council were European states: Britain and France, whose foreign policy goals in the 1920s were often at odds, and Italy, whose Fascist government beginning in 1922 focused its concerns on narrowly nationalist issues. The fourth permanent member, Japan, displayed little interest in League affairs. In the League's early years, two major states, Germany and the Soviet Union, were excluded from membership; Germany joined in 1926 and received a permanent seat on the Council, and the Soviet Union became a member only in 1934. Despite Woodrow Wilson's support for the League, the United States opted not to join. In practice the League's focus was Eurocentric. The League was further weakened by a provision in its covenant that required a unanimous vote in the Assembly to apply sanctions against an aggressor state. Despite these shortcomings, the League provided a forum in which most nations could express their concerns, seek the resolution of disagreements, and foster international cooperation.

France revealed its lack of faith in the League by allying itself with the Little Entente—Romania, Czechoslovakia, and Yugoslavia—and Poland, which collectively replaced Russia as France's partner in eastern Europe and theoretically served as a counterweight to German expansion. Germany in turn sought security through an alliance formalized with the Soviet Union in the 1922 Treaty of Rapallo, which pledged the two countries to military and economic cooperation.

Friction between Germany and France reached the flashpoint in 1923 when the former defaulted on its reparations payments. When French and Belgian troops occupied the Ruhr valley in retaliation, German miners, encouraged by their government, refused to work and engaged in sabotage. The French were unable to keep the mines and railroads operating, but passive resistance in the Ruhr threw hundreds of thousands of Germans out of work and increased inflation. The crisis ended in September 1923 when the Germans terminated their resistance. The French soon reopened reparations talks, which culminated in the 1924 Dawes Plan, negotiated under the auspices of the American Charles G. Dawes. Under its terms, German reparations were reduced to $250 million a year, with a provision for steadily rising payments over the ensuing five years. To help stabilize the German economy, most of the initial $250 million was loaned to Germany, much of it by American financiers. Henceforth, Germany's ability to meet its reparations obligation depended heavily on funds from the United States.

The newfound spirit of cooperation between France and Germany, the work especially of the French foreign minister Aristide Briand and Germany's Gustav Stresemann, led to the signing of the Locarno agreements in 1925. Germany accepted its borders with France and Belgium as defined in the Versailles Treaty, including the loss of Alsace and Lorraine and the demilitarization of the Rhine, though Germany's eastern borders were not dealt with. The agreements were the prelude to Germany's admission to the League of Nations. Briand later worked closely with U.S. Secretary of State Frank Kellogg to draft the so-called Kellogg-Briand Pact (1928), which denounced war as an instrument of national policy. Although 65 nations signed the agreement, it made no provisions for punishing an aggressor and thus constituted no more than a noble ideal. Nor did disarmament negotiations in the 1920s measurably increase collective security. The leading states renounced the idea of war but not the instruments with which to wage it.

Britain: From Gandhi to the General Strike

Britain was preoccupied throughout the 1920s with independence movements in India and Ireland. Many Indians had supported Britain in the Great War in the hope that they would be rewarded with self-government, a hope fostered by the British as long as the fighting continued. Britain's failure to honor its promise expedi-

tiously prompted Mohandas K. Gandhi (1869–1948) and his Congress party to protest on behalf of independence. Tens of thousands of people flocked to Gandhi's cause, leading to violence on both sides despite his advocacy of passive resistance. The British Parliament eventually passed the 1935 Government of India Act, placing provincial rule in Indian hands in preparation for independence. The outbreak of another world war in 1939 delayed India's independence until 1947.

Parliament had passed a home rule bill for Ireland in 1914, but the threat of violence by Ulster Protestants was so pronounced that the Liberal government used the outbreak of war as an excuse to delay the bill's implementation. Impatient Irish voters returned more than 70 members of the independence party, Sinn Fein ("We Ourselves"), to Parliament in 1918. Defying Westminster, they convened in Dublin in January 1919, recognized themselves as Ireland's legitimate Parliament, and declared their island independent. Instead of using the regular army to restore obedience, the British government reinforced the Irish constabulary with undisciplined volunteers known as the "Black and Tans." Finally, in 1921, David Lloyd George, the British prime minister, negotiated a settlement that made Ireland self-governing. Ulster alone, with its Protestant majority, opted not to be part of the Irish Free State and received autonomy within the United Kingdom, a solution that left a dissatisfied Catholic minority within its borders and has spawned sectarian violence to the present day.

British domestic politics in the 1920s reflected growing polarization along class lines, thanks to the emergence of the Labour party as the primary alternative to the Conservatives. Lloyd George, a Liberal, led the postwar coalition government but only with the sufferance of the numerically dominant Conservatives. The first Labour prime minister, the Scotsman Ramsay MacDonald (1866–1937), lacked a parliamentary majority and had little opportunity to govern effectively. Nevertheless, his foreign policy was innovative: Britain gave diplomatic recognition to the Soviet Union and embarked on a policy of conciliation with the Germans. MacDonald's government, after ruling a mere ten months, fell when the Conservatives played up a Red scare.

MacDonald's successor, the Tory Stanley Baldwin (1867–1947), failed to deal decisively with Britain's economic problems, notably unemployment and depressed regions. Although the Conservatives had passed legislation to provide pensions for the elderly, widows, and orphans, their general outlook favored the propertied classes. This was especially apparent in 1926, when the trade unions called a general strike in support of coal miners. Baldwin broke the strike by mobilizing nonunion volunteers from the propertied classes, thereby intensifying class animosity. The Conservatives capped their victory in 1927 with the Trade Disputes Act, which curtailed union power.

France and the Question of Germany

France's status as a great power had been eroded in 1870, but neither its leaders not its people had fully accepted that fact. Nor, in the aftermath of the Great War, were they able to think much beyond the perceived need to contain Germany. France more than any other nation was determined to squeeze maximum reparations from the Germans and emasculate their power through territorial acquisition and military alliances. France's display of enmity against Germany was grist for the mill of militant German nationalists. The French were almost as hostile toward the Soviet Union, which had expropriated foreign property within its borders and repudiated all tsarist debts, much of them owed to France. Thus French diplomacy unwittingly drove the Soviets and the Germans into each other's arms in the 1922 Treaty of Rapallo. Thereafter, the Soviets allowed the Germans to conduct secret aviation and army exercises—prohibited by the Treaty of Versailles—in Russia.

After the failed occupation of the Ruhr basin enabled the French to see the limits of military force, Briand improved relations with Germany. Nevertheless, the French failed to appreciate the devastating impact of reparations on Germany and the extent to which France had tied its own economic health to those payments. Underlying suspicion of the Germans remained strong and continued to shape French foreign policy. Encirclement of Germany through ties with the Little Entente was not sufficient to provide a sense of security; in 1929 the French began constructing the Maginot Line, a massive row of fortifications along their northeastern border.

Part of France's problem stemmed from the weak leadership that was endemic to recurring coalition governments. The 1919 election produced a right-wing coalition notable for its punitive attitude toward Germany and the Ruhr fiasco. In 1924 the country turned to the Radicals, a party committed to laissez-faire principles that could govern only with the support of the Socialists, to whom laissez-faire policy was anathema. This center-left coalition proved unable to cope with the country's economic problems, including inflation and the costs of reconstruction. A national union cabinet headed by Raymond Poincaré (1860–1934) took over in 1926 and succeeded in stabilizing the economy on the eve of the Great Depression.

PARIS, CAPITAL OF THE TWENTIES

The rivalry between Paris and Berlin, so brutally manifested in the Great War, continued in the 1920s, this time constructively as the two capitals battled for cultural leadership. Berlin—modern, industrial, and less bound by cultural tradition—distinguished itself by its iconoclastic spirit and novelty of expression, as reflected in the works of dramatist Bertolt Brecht (1898–1956) and the painter George Grosz (1893–1959). But Paris retained its cultural supremacy and its reputation as the *Ville lumière* ("City of Light"). Paris in the 1920s was a magnet that attracted trend-setting artists and writers from the United States, Russia, Italy, and Spain. Some, such as the American writer Ernest Hemingway (1899–1961), had come during the war; others, such as the Spanish painter Joan Miró (1893–1983), came only after guns had fallen silent.

The community of artists that Miró joined in Paris included such great pioneers of the Cubist style as Pablo Picasso (1881–1973) and Georges Braque (1882–1963) and the Surrealist Max Ernst (1891–1976). Even as Picasso continued his Cubist idiom in such works as *The Three Musicians,* he developed a neoclassical style that focused on female nudes and maternal figures, and then, after 1925, he turned to a more Expressionistic style characterized by dislocated heads and bodies. By that point, Picasso was questioning the values and traditions of civilization; so too, in a very different way, were the Dada ("hobby horse") painters such as Marcel Duchamp (1887–1968), who attacked everything traditional and elevated the nonsensical and absurd. A protest movement, Dada quickly became caught up in surrealism, defined by its practitioners as a style that "sets out to express, verbally, in writing or in any other manner, the real functioning of thought without any control by reason or an aesthetic or moral preoccupation." Painters such as Miró, Paul Klee (1879–1940), and later Salvador Dalí explored the subconscious realm and, in the process, appealed to Parisians fascinated by Sigmund Freud's dream symbolism.

The artistic ferment that characterized Paris in the 1920s was reflected in music as well. Igor Stravinsky (1882–1971), whose *Rite of Spring* was performed in

Paris in 1913, settled there after the war and continued his musical innovation. A fellow Russian composer, Sergei Prokofiev (1891–1953), also lived in Paris but, unlike Stravinsky, returned to his homeland in 1932. Leading French musicians took up residence in Paris as well; among them were Darius Milhaud (1892–1974), whose dissonant compositions included ballet scores and operas, and Francis Poulenc (1899–1963), whose more traditional harmonies and lyricism provided a link with eighteenth-century French music.

The American author Gertrude Stein (1874–1946) was the heart of the expatriate Parisian cultural scene. A collector of Impressionist, Fauvist, and Cubist art, she was a friend of Picasso's but disdainful of the Dada rebels. Stein was also the hub around which many of the period's leading writers revolved, among them the novelists Ernest Hemingway and Ford Madox Ford (1873–1939). The Irish writer James Joyce (1882–1941) went to Paris in 1920, and there his revolutionary novel *Ulysses* was published in 1922. Banned for years in the United States and Britain, the novel employed a "stream of consciousness" technique that explored reality through complex symbolism and by establishing associations through the juxtaposition of ideas and events.

Paris, the backdrop of this glittering cultural scene, was itself changing. Banks and office buildings multiplied, especially in the Latin Quarter, the traditional haunt of students. Among the city's leading fashion designers was Gabrielle (Coco) Chanel, whose austere but graceful styles were created for both career women and the wealthy and whose perfume became immensely popular. Gone from the city's streets were horse-drawn cabs; automobiles had come to stay. Music and dance halls, cinemas, theaters, and the ballet offered entertainment to satisfy any taste.

JOSEPHINE BAKER AND THE JAZZ AGE

Among the most remarkable figures of this brilliant cabaret life was Josephine Baker. Born in St. Louis in 1906 to a black mother and a father reputedly of Spanish descent, Baker left school at the age of 8 to help support her family. She starred in basement musicals as a child and ran away with a vaudeville troupe at the age of 13. Four years later, she appeared at Radio City Music Hall in New York in a musical. In 1925 she went to Paris with

a show called *La revue nègre*, which capitalized on the vogue for jazz and for "exotic" black entertainers. The show failed, but Baker caught on with the Folies Bergère, a club famous for its lavish sets and its scantily dressed performers. She created a sensation in her debut, in which she appeared clad only in a tutu made of rhinestone-studded bananas and three bracelets.

Baker's talents as a singer and dancer soon made her an international celebrity. Billed only as Josephine, the former slum child earned and spent enormous sums of money; mimicking her own exotic image, she strolled down the streets of Paris with a pet leopard. After a successful world tour, she appeared in films and light opera.

In 1937, Baker married a wealthy industrialist, Jean Lyon, converted to Judaism, and became a French citizen. At the outbreak of World War II she joined the Red Cross and was later recruited into the French Resistance, gathering intelligence and also entertaining Free French forces. At the end of the war she received France's highest decorations. Baker's wide travel and her experience of poverty and discrimination led her in 1947 to found what she called a World Village at Les Milandes, her estate in southwestern France. Here, she and her second husband, Jo Bouillon, adopted a "rainbow family" of 12 children of all races and religions. In the 1950s, Baker began a crusade against segregation in her native country and succeeded in integrating theaters and nightclubs from Las Vegas to Miami. In 1963 she stood with Dr. Martin Luther King, Jr., at the climax of his march on Washington, D.C., and delivered an impassioned speech.

Bankrupted finally by her debts at Les Milandes, Baker received a villa for herself and her children from Princess Grace of Monaco. In 1973 she triumphed at Carnegie Hall in a comeback tour, and despite failing health, she repeated her success in Paris on April 10, 1975. Two days later, she died of a stroke. On or off the stage, Josephine Baker was for half a century a uniquely vivid symbol of glamour, compassion, and commitment to the struggle for human equality. Few women of the twentieth century have combined careers and interests so daringly, served the human cause so passionately, and triumphed so indomitably.

The Weimar Republic in Germany

Like France, Weimar Germany—so named because the republic's constituent assembly met in the city of Weimar—suffered from the political instability inherent in a parliamentary government with a multiplicity of parties. Before the rise of the Nazis, Germany had six major parties: the Communists and Social Democrats on the left, the Democratic party and the Catholic Center party in the middle, and the right-wing People's party and the Nationalists. Throughout the 1920s, no party commanded a parliamentary majority, leaving Germany to be governed either by minority coalitions made possible only with the sufferance of the majority or by broad-based coalitions that combined republicans and monarchists. Frequent changes of government—20 in 13 years—undermined respect for parliamentary government. Between 1919 and 1923 alone, ten cabinets came and went.

The republic's early years were characterized in large measure by the efforts of extremists to impose their will on the nation. The first challenge, mounted even before the constitution had been completed, came from the left. In January 1919 a group of Spartacists, soon to become the Communist Party of Germany, launched a revolution in Berlin; their leaders were Rosa Luxemburg and Karl Liebknecht. To suppress it, the government of Chancellor Friedrich Ebert relied on volunteer forces known as the Free Corps, whose ranks included frustrated veterans, patriots, drifters, and restless university students. Nearly 1,500 leftist insurgents died. The Communists mounted revolutions in other German cities and briefly established a "Soviet Republic" in Bavaria. Although all these efforts failed, repeated Communist agitation cut into worker support that would otherwise have been monopolized by the Social Democrats, the country's largest party.

Extreme right-wing nationalists, led by Wolfgang Kapp, challenged the republic in March 1920 following the government's attempt to disband two Free Corps brigades. Rank-and-file troops in the army, which had helped to repress the Spartacists, refused to act, since the rebels were former comrades-in-arms. The revolt collapsed in the face of a general strike, but the army's commitment to parliamentary government and the constitution was now in question. Ebert might have purged the officer corps of its right-wing dissidents, but a Communist uprising in the Ruhr basin the same month forced him to rely on the army once again. Right-wing fanatics further threatened the republic in November 1923 when Adolf Hitler and his fledgling Nazi party launched an abortive coup in Munich.

The republic also survived the occupation of the Ruhr valley in 1923 and the resulting increase in inflation that saw the mark fall from 65 to the U.S. dollar in the spring of 1921 to 9 million to the dollar in September 1923 and

4.2 trillion two months later. For much of the middle class and those living on fixed incomes, this caused financial ruin. The Dawes Plan, which stabilized German reparations payments for five years, helped to set the stage for economic recovery and continued rule by the moderate parties, but confidence in the Weimar government was less easily restored, and in the 1925 presidential election the country turned to Field Marshal Paul von Hindenburg, a symbol of Germany's imperial past.

The Successor States and Their Neighbors in Central and Eastern Europe

With the exception of Czechoslovakia, democratic regimes were no more successful in the other countries of central and eastern Europe than in Germany during the interwar period. The four successor states—Czechoslovakia, Poland, Romania and Yugoslavia—were so called because their lands, in whole or in part, had been acquired in the process of dismantling the Habsburg empire. Unlike Austria, Hungary, and Bulgaria, which had fought on Germany's side, the successor states were numbered among the victors. Moreover, they were regarded by the French and the British as counterweights to Germany and as a line of defense against Bolshevism. Ostensibly, therefore, their postwar parliamentary governments had a chance to put down stable roots.

Economically and socially, the successor states as well as their vanquished neighbors lagged behind the advanced states of western Europe, which historically had used this region as a source of raw materials and agricultural produce and as a market for manufactured products. Any serious downturn in the western European economy had a strong negative impact on this region. These countries, moreover, were deficient in technology, investment capital, and modern transportation and communication networks. Only Czechoslovakia, Austria, and Poland had a bourgeoisie prepared to oversee major industrial development if resources were available. In general, these were heavily peasant societies with widespread illiteracy, inadequate health care, and low standards of living. Thus they were not yet fertile ground for the growth of democratic institutions.

Some of these states faced additional problems stemming from competing ethnic and religious groups. The most serious instances of this occurred in Poland, the home of Germans and Slavs, and in Yugoslavia, where Serbs, Croats, and Slovenes considered themselves distinct nationalities and where religion further divided the

Greek Orthodox Serbs from the mostly Roman Catholic Slovenes and Croats. Only in Czechoslovakia, which was similarly composed of various national groups—Czechs, Slovaks, Germans, and Ruthenians—did these groups generally cooperate with one other.

Apart from Czechoslovakia, the parliamentary governments of these states fell during the interwar period. The first to go was in Hungary, where the harshness of the peace terms doomed the postwar government, which was replaced in March 1919 by a Communist republic. This in turn collapsed five months later when reactionary landowners established control. A military coup overthrew the democratic government in Bulgaria in 1923; 12 years later, King Boris ran the country as a dictator. When the Poles split sharply between landowners and the bourgeoisie on the one hand and workers and peasants on the other, the military hero Józef Piłsudski mounted a coup in 1926 that ended Polish democracy. Two years later, ethnic violence in Yugoslavia provided an excuse for the establishment of a military dictatorship. King Carol of Romania took advantage of parliamentary infighting in the early 1930s to assert dictatorial control, and at about the same time, democratic government in Austria was pressured by both economic problems and the Nazis. The Czechs alone preserved democratic rule as the result of the moderate leadership of President Tomás Masaryk (1850–1937), responsible land reform, a balanced and diversified economy, and a general willingness to resolve tensions through political compromises worked out in a constitutional framework.

America Turns Inward: The Quest for Normalcy

Although U.S. intervention was decisive in ending the Great War, the United States played only a backstage role in sustaining the postwar world that President Woodrow Wilson had done so much to shape. Senator Warren G. Harding, who would succeed Wilson as president in 1921, had expressed popular sentiment the previous year when he called for normalcy, serenity, and "triumphant nationality." The country was ready to trade the progressive ideology and internationalism of Wilson for prosperity at home and a general retreat from foreign engagement, or what has often been termed *isolationism.* In reality the Republican administrations of Harding (1921–1923) and Calvin Coolidge (1923–1929) pursued a foreign policy oriented toward conciliation, disarmament, and dollar diplomacy. U.S. troops remained in Haiti (1915–1934), the Dominican Republic

(1916–1924), and Nicaragua (periodically, 1910–1933). The United States would not, however, guarantee European political security.

Viewed through the lens of World War II, the diplomatic achievements of the 1920s have generally been denigrated, but in fairness they were hardly in place before they were subjected to extreme pressures by the Great Depression. Both the 1924 Dawes Plan and the 1929 Young Plan were constructive, if imperfect, attempts to deal with German reparations, and the Washington Conference in 1921–1922 made two substantive contributions toward disarmament. In the first of these the United States, Japan, Britain, Italy, and France signed the Five Power Naval Treaty to stop the construction of large warships for a decade and to cap the total size of such ships of each nation. The same conference produced the Nine Power Treaty, in which the imperial states endorsed Chinese sovereignty and agreed to observe the Open Door principle by renouncing special trading privileges in China. As already noted, the United States and France took the lead in persuading 65 nations to sign the 1928 Kellogg-Briand Pact outlawing war. Although these agreements failed to prevent another global conflict, they provided valuable lessons for the future, including the need to incorporate enforcement provisions in such pacts.

At home the Roaring Twenties were a decade of prosperity: the real income of the average American increased 40 percent in this period, high tariffs protected domestic jobs, the national debt was reduced, and corporate and personal income taxes fell. Women's suffrage was achieved with the ratification of the Nineteenth Amendment in 1920. The decade was memorable in many ways: Charles Lindbergh and Amelia Earhart flew the Atlantic; the Harlem Renaissance and jazz reflected the pride and creativity of African-Americans; George Gershwin and the Ziegfeld Follies entertained enthusiastic audiences; and Americans were introduced to airmail postal service, frozen food, and the first motel. This was a period of mass mobility via automobiles; mass communication by means of telephones, radios, and motion pictures; and mass consumption of electrical appliances.

But American life had a distinctly darker side in the 1920s. Its political tone was set by the corruption of the Harding years and the Teapot Dome scandal, involving illegal leases on oil lands in Wyoming and California. Bigotry flared in the form of anti-Semitism and overt racism, particularly in the revival of the Ku Klux Klan and in racial violence that became common in northern cities as African-Americans fled there to escape chronic poverty and oppression in the south. Congress implemented a quota system designed to prohibit Asian immigrants. The decade was also marked by a conservative religious revival: in 1925, William Jennings Bryan attacked the concept of evolution in the trial of the science teacher Thomas Scopes, and assorted religious groups, with the support of the Republican party and some Democrats, kept up their crusade against vice, which had already given the nation Prohibition in 1919.

Thus America in the 1920s was preoccupied with the largely domestic issues of financial prosperity, material pleasures, nativism, racism, and religious fundamentalism. Most Americans knew little and cared less about problems in Europe and Asia, although U.S. power was increasingly active in these areas.

THE GREAT DEPRESSION AND THE CRISIS OF CAPITALISM

The optimism that generally pervaded the West before 1914 slowly revived in the 1920s, making the unprecedented economic crisis that befell capitalism beginning in 1929 all the more shattering. Downturns in the economy were not new; since the late nineteenth century, cyclical crises had become the normal pattern, and by the 1920s most people were reasonably accustomed to the fluctuations inherent in the free market system. But never in the history of capitalism had the world confronted a financial crisis of the kind that occurred between 1929 and 1933, the ramifications of which contributed to the onset of a second global war in 1939.

The Credit Economy and the American Crash

Three factors were responsible for the economic crisis. First, the Great War severely disrupted the economy as belligerents shifted production to meet military needs and depended increasingly on neutral nations for many nonmilitary goods. As neutral countries expanded their production to satisfy this demand, they acquired a disproportionate share of gold and "hard" currency, such as British pounds and Swiss francs. After the war, nations that were capital-poor, such as Germany and the successor states, depended on capital-rich countries, especially the United States, for loans, investments, and purchases. A crisis in the U.S. economy would therefore have serious repercussions in Europe.

Second, the growth of tariff barriers in the 1920s restricted international trade and promoted the return to the idea of national self-sufficiency. Such protectionism contributed to the short-term prosperity enjoyed by the United States in the 1920s, but it inhibited the growth of strong European trading partners, which was essential to the health of the global economy.

Third, productivity increased more rapidly than consumption, primarily because wages lagged behind production and because agricultural prices fell as a result of overproduction and inadequate facilities for distribution. These developments made it difficult for primarily rural states to import sufficient quantities of manufactured goods. Demand for industrial goods decreased, and unemployment rose.

As consumer spending declined, retail inventories grew, and factory output dropped, the United States slipped into a recession in mid-1929, well before the stock market crashed in October. An orgy of speculative stock buying had been made possible by trading on margin—purchasing shares with a small down payment in the expectation of paying the balance with profits made after the stock rose in value. Once professionals lost confidence in the market and began selling, investors panicked.

After the crash, American financiers no longer infused capital into the European economy. U.S. foreign investments plummeted 67 percent by 1932. Germany, which had used short-term American loans for long-term investments and relied on foreign loans to help meet reparations payments, was hit hard. More important, the sharp decline in international trade had a serious impact on Germany, whose economy depended on exports. By 1931 the gold reserves in the Reichsbank had plunged 90 percent, and alarmed depositors started a run on the banks. In May, Austria's main bank, the Kreditanstalt, declared insolvency, and other central European institutions followed suit. The United States compounded the crisis by raising tariffs in 1930, thereby cutting imports by nearly 50 percent. As industries reduced production and laid off workers, unemployment mounted.

Coping with Crisis: The Governments Respond

At first, governments reacted to the crisis by implementing deflationary policies based on balanced budgets and reduced spending. This course only increased unemployment by further reducing demand. The figures were staggering: 3 million people (nearly 25 percent of the labor force) were unemployed in Britain in 1931; 16 million in the United States in 1932; 6 million in Germany in 1933, where 40 percent of union workers lost their jobs and another 20 percent had only part-time work. At the depth of the depression, in 1932, some 30 million people—22 percent of the West's labor force—were out of work. In France a more balanced economy held unemployment to 850,000, while in Italy and the agricultural states of eastern Europe the jobless rate was also lower, although falling prices further depressed the peasants' standard of living and reduced many to partial employment.

Some government measures, such as increased tariffs and stiff currency controls, encouraged economic nationalism and thus heightened international tensions. Such policies not only further reduced global trade and aggravated the crisis but also undercut the spirit of international cooperation that had been nurtured in the 1920s. By 1933, world trade had declined by a third from its predepression level, and industrial production in Europe had dropped at a similar rate. Widespread economic suffering forced political leaders to focus on measures designed to help their own people. Exploring solutions on an international basis was made virtually impossible by the growth of extremist groups, such as the fascists, who blamed foreign powers for the disaster. The British and the French pursued a course of economic nationalism through the 1930s, leaving neither country financially strong enough to repulse the fascist threat.

Eventually, some governments realized that the most effective means to counteract the depression was to put people to work again. In general, there were two ways to do this: massive public works projects and extensive military production. In the short term the latter course, as practiced, for example, by Nazi Germany, achieved impressive results, although over a long period a high degree of militarization is economically debilitating.

Beginning with modest initiatives by President Herbert Hoover (1929–1933), including the appropriation of funds for the Boulder and Grand Coulee dams and the provision of loans to endangered businesses through the Reconstruction Finance Corporation, the United States fought the depression through federal initiatives. President Franklin D. Roosevelt's New Deal went further by blending economic recovery with an attempt to alleviate suffering. Among the programs of the New Deal was the Federal Deposit Insurance Corporation, which insured bank deposits; the Public Works Administration, which provided funds for roads, sewers, and public buildings; the Tennessee Valley Authority, a seven-state project designed to generate inexpensive electricity and control

flooding; the Works Progress Administration, which put millions of unemployed people to work; and the Social Security Act, which provided old-age pensions and unemployment insurance. The New Deal reshaped American society and helped to provide the economic foundation that prepared the United States to reenter the arena of global conflict in 1941. Only rearmament finally ended the depression in the United States, as it did in Nazi Germany.

THE NAZI SEIZURE OF POWER

Germany, the state most vulnerable to the economic crisis, was the first to experience political upheaval. A moderate coalition led by the Centrist Heinrich Brüning (1885–1970) favored a deflationary policy, including budget retrenchment and a reduction in unemployment benefits. When the Reichstag refused to support his measures, he ruled by emergency decree, a constitutional measure authorized by President Hindenburg. Brüning and his backers in the military and business community hoped to bolster their position in the September 1930 election, but the voters, worried about the economy and attracted by Hitler's charisma, made the Nazis the second largest party in the Reichstag. The Nazis won 107 seats, a dramatic increase from their previous total of 12, and were second only to the Social Democrats, who had 143 seats, still a minority. In a mere two years, Hitler's electoral support in the country had rocketed from 809,000 to 6.4 million votes cast. Most of this support was from the lower middle class, farmers, and young people.

Hitler and the Origins of National Socialism

A purveyor of hatred, racism, and militarism, Adolf Hitler was born in Austria in 1889, the son of a petty bureaucrat. As a young man in Vienna he imbibed the theories of Aryan supremacy, anti-Semitism, anti-Marxism, and pan-German unity. He learned to hate the Slavs as well. Serving with the German infantry in World War I, he twice received the Iron Cross but never rose above the rank of corporal.

After the war, Hitler joined the tiny German Workers' Party, renamed in 1920 the National Socialist German Workers' Party, commonly known as the Nazis. The

German soldiers wait for Adolf Hitler to speak at a Nazi party rally in Nuremberg. [The Bettmann Archive]

term *socialist* was not intended in a Marxist sense but as a reflection of the experience of soldiers in the trenches who had purportedly shared a sense of solidarity rather than class consciousness. As *Führer* ("leader"), Hitler imposed rigid discipline on the party and founded its paramilitary group, the storm troopers (*Sturmabteilung,* or SA), who were responsible for protecting Nazi orators and were subsequently used to attack party enemies. The SS, or *Schutzstaffel,* was added later as an elite bodyguard for the Nazi leaders. The first SA recruits were mostly veterans and members of the Free Corps, but in the early 1930s their ranks were swollen by the unemployed.

For his role in the Munich coup in 1923, Hitler spent nearly nine months in prison, during which time he wrote *Mein Kampf* ("My Struggle"). In it he exalted the strong, the masculine, and the militant. The world, he insisted, must have "a peace supported not by the palm branches of tearful pacifistic female mourners but founded by the victorious sword of a master race which places the world in the service of a higher culture." The master race—the Aryans—were the foes of the Bolsheviks and the Jews, whom he blamed for Germany's plight. Anti-semitism was central to his thinking, and he

assigned most of the blame for European cultural and moral decline to the Jews, who, he claimed, headed an international conspiracy grounded in socialism and capitalism directed against the Aryan race. Hitler extolled propaganda as the means to rally the masses and shamelessly advocated the use of the "big lie"; the people, he declared cynically, "will not even believe that others are capable of the enormous insolence of the vilest distortions." Driven by ideology, Hitler had contempt for both intellectuals and the masses as well as aristocrats and humanitarians.

In Hitler's judgment, Germany had to adopt an aggressive foreign policy to achieve its historical destiny, a point on which he elaborated in 1928 when he insisted that the German army had to be rebuilt to conquer essential "living space" (*lebensraum*) in eastern Europe. Although France would remain Germany's implacable enemy, Britain and Italy, he opined, would not go to war to prevent this expansion. These core elements in Hitler's thinking provided the basis of future Nazi policies.

Hitler Comes to Power

Despite the September 1930 election results, Brüning continued as chancellor with Hindenburg's support, aided by the fact that the Social Democrats were unwilling to risk additional Nazi gains by bringing down the government. Brüning proved unable to halt rising unemployment, in part because he pressed ahead with his austerity program. He was successful, however, in persuading the Allies to impose a moratorium on reparations payments. As the economic crisis deepened, Hitler challenged Hindenburg for the presidency in March 1932. The Social Democrats reluctantly supported the old soldier, enabling him to defeat Hitler.

Two months later, Hindenburg, angered by Brüning's proposed land reform, replaced the chancellor with Franz von Papen, a nominal Centrist and stand-in for the reactionary general Kurt von Schleicher, now the dominant figure behind the scenes. Schleicher had fallen out with Brüning over the chancellor's attempt to ban the SA and SS. Although not a Nazi himself, Schleicher was sympathetic to the party's militarism and nationalism, and both he and Papen hoped the Nazis would support the new government. Hitler, fresh from an electoral triumph in July 1932 that left the Nazis with 230 of 611 seats, unsuccessfully demanded the chancellorship.

In the fall, Hitler used his Reichstag delegation to force Papen's resignation, but in the ensuing election the Nazis suffered their first major electoral reversal, losing 34 Reichstag seats. Although they were still the strongest party numerically, the election endangered the Nazis' momentum. The Nazi phenomenon, it seemed, was waning, while the Communists, whose representation had risen to 100 seats, continued to expand their electoral base.

As Schleicher, now the chancellor, tried to govern by forging a political alliance between labor and the military, worried Rhineland industrialists offered the Nazis funds in return for Hitler's promise to leave German industry alone if he gained power. When Schleicher could not persuade Hindenburg to ban the Nazis and the Communists, he resigned, unable to govern. Hindenburg offered Hitler the chancellorship in a coalition cabinet containing only 3 Nazis among its 11 seats.

Hitler moved quickly to consolidate power, demanding that new elections be held in March 1933. After the Reichstag building burned down on February 27 as the result of arson, Hitler blamed the Communists. By noon the following day, 4,000 Communists had been arrested, and Hindenburg had signed an emergency decree suspending individual liberties for the duration of the emergency. Nazi thugs terrorized the party's opponents, setting the stage for a Nazi electoral triumph. Having cowed many voters, the party won 288 seats compared to the Social Democrats' 120 and the Communists' 81; with his allies in the Nationalist party, Hitler had a majority in the Reichstag. Less than three weeks later, that body, with the Communists absent and only the Social Democrats in opposition, approved the Enabling Act, authorizing the government to rule by decree for four years. Hitler had achieved dictatorial power through parliamentary means, but only, like Mussolini, by perverting the process through intimidation and violence. At no time through 1933 did a majority of the German electorate vote for the Nazis, though Hitler had won the support of many industrialists, bankers, bureaucrats, and military men.

The Face of the Third Reich

The tentacles of Nazi power spread through every area of German life. Beginning with the Communists, Hitler eliminated opposition parties until only the Nazis remained. Party officials who took their orders from Berlin directed the affairs of the once semiautonomous federal states, and new tribunals, concerned especially with political offenses, took their place alongside the traditional courts. Two factors made Nazi influence especially pervasive: the work of the secret police, or Gestapo, who were later incorporated into the SS, and the willingness of many bureaucrats and state officials to join the party to advance their careers. As in Italy and the Soviet Union, government institutions became agencies of the ruling party. A massive propaganda campaign headed by Joseph Goebbels used radio, films, art, music, and printed material to inculcate Nazi ideals in the people.

The traditional institution that was most likely to give Hitler trouble was the army, whose leaders had little respect for the Führer and contempt for the SA. Despite the SA's contribution to his rise to power, Hitler sided with the generals, whose support for his ambitious foreign policy would be crucial. Hitler was swayed as well by the fact that the SA leader, Ernst Röhm, threatened the Führer's plans for Germany by demanding further revolutionary action to strip traditional elites of their wealth and power. Hitler ordered the SS to assassinate the SA leaders on June 30, 1934, the "night of the long knives." At the same time he used the occasion to rid himself of several political enemies, including Schleicher, who was murdered. When Hindenburg died five weeks later, Hitler combined the offices of chancellor and president, an act that was overwhelmingly approved in a subsequent plebiscite.

Effective opposition to the Nazis might also have come from the Christian churches, although Hitler's electoral triumphs had been made possible in part by bourgeois Protestant voters. Once in power, Hitler attempted to unify all German Protestants in a Reich church. Although most Protestant clergymen remained politically neutral, a brave minority organized the Confessional church and denounced authoritarianism and racism. Because of their criticism, more than 800 Confessional ministers were interned in concentration camps.

Hitler achieved a diplomatic coup in 1933 when he signed a concordat with the Vatican. Pope Pius XI agreed to the pact in return for Hitler's recognition of the traditional liberties of the Catholic church in Germany. Because the pact undermined the ability of the Center party to oppose the government, disillusioned Centrist leaders dissolved their own organization. Hitler's assurances to the papacy proved to be worthless when he attacked Catholic schools and youth groups, which competed with the Hitler Youth organization. By the time Pius XI condemned racism and authoritarianism in 1937, Nazism had become firmly entrenched. Many Catholic priests later died in concentration camps.

Nazi racism manifested itself in 1933 when the government expelled most Jews from state administrative positions. Two years later, the Nuremberg Laws denied German citizenship to individuals who had two or more Jewish grandparents and prohibited marriage and sexual intercourse between Jews and Germans. Henceforth some German towns began refusing entry to Jews, and

German businesses were pressured to dismiss non-Aryan employees. By 1938 more than 100,000 Jews had fled the country after being forced to surrender their property to the state. On November 9–10, 1938, Nazi terrorists and fellow travelers subjected Jews to the so-called *Kristallnacht,* the "night of broken glass." Scores of Jews were killed and thousands beaten, and more than 25,000 were subsequently incarcerated in concentration camps. In addition, nearly 200 synagogues were razed and more than 7,000 Jewish businesses were destroyed. These early attacks on the Jews continued a pattern of anti-Semitism in Europe that stretched back to the Middle Ages. What made the Nazi program revolutionary was the later attempt to annihilate European Jewry through methodical genocide.

Because of his massive programs of public works and rearmament, Hitler faced no serious opposition from workers or industrialists. By 1938, unemployment had been virtually eliminated, and most German workers tolerated a government that provided job security, adequate though rigidly controlled working conditions, and an organization called Strength Through Joy that arranged vacations and subsidized travel. In return the workers saw their trade unions replaced by the Nazi-run Labor Front. Industrialists and big businessmen were satisfied with a regime that preferred to deal with large firms. Industrialists enjoyed prestigious party positions, and Nazi chieftains often acquired substantial business holdings, usually by confiscating Jewish property. Hitler could not sustain this prosperity without aggressive territorial expansion; the economic well-being that won him widespread support was an illusion.

Before the late 1930s the Nazis did not want women to participate in the industrial work force, as a third of them had done in the mid-1920s. Instead, Nazi ideology stressed that women's place was in the home, where they could fulfill their "natural" responsibility to bear and raise children, thereby strengthening the Aryan race. Given the fact that most jobs for women in the Weimar Republic had been poorly paid and regarded as little more than an interim stage between schooling and marriage, German women did not find the Nazi elevation of the housewife's importance objectionable. When Hitler prepared for war in the late 1930s, however, women were needed in the factories and the service sector. As in the Weimar period, they were paid approximately a third less than their male counterparts. Most German women, like German men, looked upon Hitler with great favor and even adulation, blaming his underlings for the regime's crimes. In the words of Hitler's chief of women's affairs: "It is our duty to produce this

The cover of this Nazi women's magazine illustrates the way in which all aspects of German life were subordinated to the goals of the Nazi state. [Staatsbibliothek Preussischer Kulturbesitz, Berlin]

new Führer personality . . . to create and mold people who are ready to devote themselves totally to Germany."[1]

SUMMARY

The 1920s were for the most part a decade of lost opportunity. The Western democracies gave up any chance to maintain constructive relations with the Soviet Union by intervening in the Russian civil war and then shunning relations with Russia. The United States, moreover, turned its back on the League of Nations, thereby undermining that organization's ability to resolve international crises. Despite these developments, important steps were made in the 1920s toward constructive international relations, including the first major disarmament treaty of the twentieth century. Further progress was impeded by the Great Depression and the resulting popularity of economic nationalism. The depression signaled the end of the ebullience that was so characteristic of much of society in the 1920s, especially in the United States. If Josephine Baker symbolized the Jazz Age, the hobo wandering from city to city in search of work and food represented the Great Depression. In his shadow came the Nazi storm trooper.

Although the foundation for authoritarian regimes had been laid in the Soviet Union and partly in Italy well before the depression, that catastrophe made possible the triumph of Nazism in Germany, which in turn reinforced the existing Fascist state in Italy. Ultimately, the Fascist and Communist governments were rooted in the experience of World War I and the flawed peace settlement that marked its conclusion as well as in the profound economic crisis that stemmed primarily from the economic dislocation of that war. Authoritarian government, the heart of which is terror and the essence of which is the state's attempt to dominate and integrate all elements of civil society, was born in the brutality of conflict and the greed of financial exploitation, which together mark the nadir of human experience.

Notes

1. C. Koonz, *Mothers in the Fatherland: Women, the Family, and Nazi Politics* (New York: St. Martin's, 1987), p. 249.

Suggestions for Further Reading

Arendt, H. *The Origins of Totalitarianism,* 2nd ed. Cleveland, Ohio: World Publishing, 1958.

Berghahn, V. R. *Modern Germany: Society, Economy and Politics in the Twentieth Century,* 2nd ed. Cambridge: Cambridge University Press, 1987.

Carr, E. H. *The Russian Revolution: From Lenin to Stalin.* New York: Free Press, 1979.

Carsten, F. L. *The Rise of Fascism,* 2nd ed. Berkeley: University of California Press, 1980.

Fest, J. C. *Hitler,* trans. A. Winston and C. Winston. New York: Harcourt Brace Jovanovich, 1974.

Galbraith, J. K. *The Great Crash.* New York: Avon, 1980.

Garraty, J. A. *The Great Depression.* New York: Harcourt Brace Jovanovich, 1986.

Gellately, R. *The Gestapo and German Society.* New York: Oxford University Press, 1990.

Jones, L. E. *German Liberalism and the Dissolution of the Weimar Party System, 1918–1933.* Chapel Hill: University of North Carolina Press, 1988.

Kindleberger, C. P. *The World in Depression, 1929–1939.* Berkeley: University of California Press, 1973.

Lyttelton, A. *The Seizure of Power: Fascism in Italy, 1919–1929.* London: Weidenfeld & Nicolson, 1973.

Mack Smith, D. *Mussolini.* London: Weidenfeld & Nicolson, 1981.

Seton-Watson, H. *Eastern Europe Between the Wars, 1918–1941.* Cambridge: Cambridge University Press, 1962.

Shannon, D. A. *Between the Wars: America, 1919–1941,* 2nd ed. Boston: Houghton Mifflin, 1979.

Turner, H. A. *German Big Business and the Rise of Hitler.* New York: Oxford University Press, 1985.

28

WORLD WAR II AND THE PARTITION OF EUROPE

Twice in a quarter of a century, European states plunged the world into war. In the two decades that separated the conflicts, statesmen tried to ensure peace through international cooperation, including the League of Nations, disarmament negotiations, and the repudiation of war as an instrument of policy. There was nothing inherently wrong with any of these measures apart from the absence of effective means to curb aggressor states. The great failure of the first postwar decade was not diplomatic or military but economic: statesmen failed to recognize that peace is ultimately dependent on a stable, reasonably equitable economic order. The heavily punitive measures imposed on Germany and the political restructuring of central and eastern Europe without sufficient attention to economic factors were destabilizing.

The collapse of the American economy beginning in 1929 forced Europe and the world into depression. The strain was more than many liberal states could bear, and the ideologies of the traditional parties seemed inadequate to deal with the crisis. States such as France and Britain rejected extremist groups in favor of broad coalition governments. Historians have often judged these governments harshly because of their ineptitude in dealing with the fascist threat, but they preserved liberal institutions and values. Other states supported proponents of extreme solutions. No state was immune from the economic nationalism that exacerbated the international crisis and helped to fuel the aggressive chauvinism of dictators such as Hitler and Mussolini. From the Great Depression ultimately came the renewal of a global conflict that lasted from 1939 to 1945 and sowed the seeds for the Cold War.

A NEW ROAD TO WAR: AGGRESSION AND APPEASEMENT

Many historians agree that Hitler's aggression could have been stopped short of all-out war as late as 1936. His early successes—rearming Germany and sending his army into the Rhineland—defied the Treaty of Versailles; both moves were calculated gambles intended to test the resolve of the former Allies. Successful beyond expectation, Hitler then laid plans in 1937 to move against Austria and Czechoslovakia.

The Divided Democracies

The weaknesses of multiparty coalitions in Europe during the 1930s help to explain why the western democracies were unable to stop Hitler. In Britain, Ramsay MacDonald had led the Labour party to victory in 1929, in part because of growing unemployment, which he proposed to relieve by expanding public assistance. When American investors began pulling their funds out of Britain after the stock market crash, unemployment soared. By mid-1931 the government's precarious financial position forced MacDonald to endorse a proposal to reduce unemployment benefits. He sacrificed the unity of his party to serve in a so-called National Government, most of whose supporters were Conservatives. The Labour party expelled MacDonald and the few Labourites who supported him, but in 1931 the country overwhelmingly endorsed the ruling coalition.

The National Government took the country off the gold standard to spur exports. Labourites were angered by a reduction in unemployment benefits, and the Liberals withdrew from the coalition when the government raised tariffs. Unemployment was still 20 percent above its 1929 level when Neville Chamberlain (1869–1940) succeeded Stanley Baldwin as prime minister in 1937. Throughout the 1930s these men pursued a conservative economic policy highlighted by a balanced budget, relatively low taxes on industry, and protective tariffs. Within the parameters of this policy there was room neither for major rearmament nor for a foreign policy that might require military intervention.

The political situation in France differed from that in Britain in several key respects. Because of heavy war losses, the French population decreased in the interwar period. Simultaneously, heavy industry expanded, creating new jobs and significantly enlarging the proletariat, the traditional constituency of the leftist parties. The French economy was relatively self-sufficient and well-balanced, with industry employing 45 percent of the labor force in 1931. The depression hit France later than any other major western country and caused less severe unemployment, which stood at nearly 500,000 in 1935.

As the country slipped into the depression, a majority of French voters supported center and left-wing parties in 1932. The most important of these, the laissez-faire Radicals and the Marxist-leaning Socialists, disagreed strongly on economic issues. The tenure of prime ministers was measured in months—five ministries in two years. Conservative-oriented national governments then muddled along until 1936, when voters entrusted power to a Popular Front comprised of left-wing parties, among them the Socialists and the Communists. For the first time the Communists had established themselves as a primary force in French politics. Participation in popular front governments represented a new policy of Communist collaboration with liberal parties born out of a growing nervousness about fascist success.

The new prime minister, Léon Blum (1872–1950), a Jewish Socialist and a pacifist, faced opposition on two fronts: the business community, which despised his economic views as well as his religion, and the Communists, who refused to serve in his cabinet because of their political rivalry with the Socialists. Blum nationalized the armaments industry, placed the Bank of France under state control, and launched public works programs. The cost of such measures incited fears of inflation, and the extent of government intervention in the economy infuriated conservatives, as reflected by their slogan, "Better Hitler Than Blum." In 1938 the right regained control of the government under the leadership of Édouard Daladier (1884–1970). Bitterly riven by its domestic problems, France had neither the stomach for a military confrontation with Nazi Germany nor a serious commitment to its allies in eastern Europe.

Stalin and the Great Purges

The Russians learned a basic economic lesson from their participation in the Great War: without major industrialization and central planning, they could not compete successfully on the battlefield against opponents with modern armies. Convinced that the threat of another imperialist war was genuine, they resolved in 1927 to restructure the Soviet economy. Their goal was both to modernize their military and to resume building a socialist society after the temporary halt imposed by the semicapitalist New Economic Policy. To help raise the funds for industrialization, the government reduced the money it paid the peasants for their crops. When the peasants retaliated by withholding their commodities, food shortages plagued the cities, and foodstuffs for export, which the Soviets traded for machinery, dwindled.

Seizing on the crisis as a means to consolidate his power, Stalin imposed a "revolution from above," beginning with a five-year plan to increase the production of coal, iron, electricity, and machinery. The plan was tantamount to running the economy on a wartime basis. As the effects of the depression took hold in western Europe and the United States, however, agricultural prices dropped, forcing the Soviets to export ever larger quantities of food, even at the expense of starving many of their own people.

The second aspect of Stalin's revolution involved a program to "collectivize" agriculture by confiscating the land, livestock, and tools of the peasants. With this property the state established some 200,000 collective farms. Kulaks—well-to-do peasants, who were the country's best farmers as well as critics of the Soviet regime—were banned from the new collectives and imprisoned, banished, or executed. Peasants killed perhaps half their livestock rather than allow the collectives to appropriate the animals. Collectivization contributed to massive food shortages and the deaths of 6 to 7 million people.

Prepared to pay any human cost, Stalin pronounced the first five-year plan an economic success. Between 1928 and 1932 the production of oil, iron, and steel doubled, and that of electricity tripled, although the standard of living in the cities dropped sharply. A second five-year plan followed, and by the end of the decade the Soviet Union had become the world's third industrial power and had made important strides in education and medical care.

Stalin's programs had a major impact on Soviet women. During the decade following the 1917 revolution the Soviets had made important strides toward sexual equality, including the recognition that women and men were legally equal in political and economic life. Among the leaders of the feminist movement were Inessa Armand, head of the party's Women's Department, and Alexandra Kollontai, who challenged traditional sexual mores and served her country as an ambassador. Under Stalin the rhetoric of liberation continued, but emphasis once again focused on traditional family values and women's procreative role. Women worked equally with men on the new collectives, but it was an equality of servitude, not opportunity.

The five-year plans created substantial demand for women in the factories and on large construction projects. In 1930 some 3 million women worked in industry; by 1937 that number had more than tripled, at which point 34 percent of the labor force was female. The number continued to grow until by 1945, under wartime conditions, 56 percent of the workers were women. As real wages fell in the Stalinist era, many of these women were forced into the workplace to help their families survive. The growing demand for female laborers also stemmed from the five-year plans and from the devastating impact of collectivization, the Stalinist purges, and ultimately the staggering Soviet military losses in World War II.

The number of Soviet citizens who died of starvation, execution, neglect, and maltreatment in forced-labor camps in the quarter century of Stalin's rule may have been as high as 40 million. Moderates such as Sergei Kirov voiced opposition in 1933 to Stalin's ruthlessness. Kirov's murder in December 1934, almost certainly ordered by Stalin, was the pretext for a purge of alleged counterrevolutionaries. The secret police operated without legal restraints against all suspected political opponents, ranging from intellectuals and party officials to diplomats, military officers, and ordinary citizens.

Ultimately, Stalin struck down most of the "Old Bolsheviks," the men who had led the Communist movement in the preceding two decades. Between 1936 and 1938 the government staged three major show trials in which the accused, after being tortured, confessed to crimes against the state. Millions of citizens were incarcerated in concentration camps or executed; among the victims were half of the officers in the military, including the army's commander-in-chief. Thus Stalin unwittingly played into Hitler's hands by weakening the Soviet army.

Hitler and Mussolini: The Brutal Friendship

Like Stalin, Mussolini underestimated Hitler. When Hitler wrote *Mein Kampf,* he had admired the "strong man south of the Alps," and he later obtained subsidies from the *Duce* as well as facilities in Italy to train young Nazis before he came to power. In the early 1930s, Mussolini saw himself less as an ally of Hitler than as a power broker between the Germans on the one hand and the British and French on the other. Concerned about a Nazi behemoth on his northern frontier, Mussolini supported the Austrian dictator Engelbert Dollfuss. When Austrian Nazis assassinated Dollfuss in 1934, Mussolini dispatched troops to the frontier in a show of force intended to prevent German annexation of Austria.

Undeterred by the rift with Mussolini, Hitler announced in March 1935 that Germany would not respect the military limitations imposed on it by the Treaty of Versailles. Mussolini joined the British and the French in the so-called Stresa Front, which condemned Hitler's actions, leaving Germany virtually isolated; Hitler had ended German military cooperation with the Soviet Union in late 1933, and his only nominal ally at this point was Poland.

Mussolini's consuming interest was now Ethiopia, a tempting addition to Italy's meager African holdings and the object of revenge for its defeat of the Italians in 1896. Prominent politicians in the French and British governments had no serious objection to Mussolini's plans, but British popular opinion was outraged. Undaunted, Mussolini ordered his forces to invade Ethiopia in October 1935. The League of Nations condemned the aggression and banned the export of strategic materials (except oil) to Italy by member states and their import of Italian products. An army of 650,000 men, aided by mustard gas, finally vanquished the Ethiopians in May 1936. The Ethiopian invasion contributed to the shattering of the

Stresa Front (as did an Anglo-German naval treaty in 1935), demonstrated the impotence of Anglo-French diplomacy, embarrassed the League, and drove Mussolini and Hitler into each other's arms.

Hitler, who alone among the major western leaders did not condemn the Ethiopian invasion, took advantage of it to defy the Versailles treaty again by sending German troops into the Rhineland in March 1936. The Germans justified their action by pointing to the Franco-Soviet pact, obviously directed against them, and proclaiming the right to defend their frontiers. Committing only 22,000 troops and 14,000 policemen, Hitler was prepared to withdraw if France took military action. But the French chief of staff, erroneously believing that the Germans had 265,000 men in the Rhineland, was unwilling to risk general mobilization. For their part, the British were complacent. Without firing a shot, Hitler secured the Ruhr basin from French attack and bolstered German defenses against a possible French invasion. Seven months later, in October 1936, Germany and Italy closed ranks diplomatically in what Mussolini called the Rome-Berlin Axis.

The Spanish Civil War

The Spanish civil war provided an opportunity for both fascist dictators to test their military forces in a common cause. Spain had moved into the fascist orbit in the mid-1920s when its military strongman, Miguel Primo de Rivera, allied his country with Italy. King Alfonso XIII ousted the unpopular dictator in January 1930, and 15 months later, voters in Spanish cities recorded a clear preference for republican candidates. Despite strong support in rural areas, Alfonso fled the country; his opponents proclaimed a republic in April 1931.

The young republic instigated moderate reforms, including autonomy for Catalonia and the Basque provinces. The government began needed land reform, which angered landowners but proceeded too slowly to satisfy peasants. In 1933, unhappy Spaniards gave conservatives a majority in the Cortes, but the parties of the left and center, including Communists and anarchists, banded together in a popular front and narrowly defeated the right in 1936. Emboldened by their victory and impatient of constitutional reform, leftist groups began seizing land, attacking conservative churchmen, and destroying ecclesiastical property.

Civil war erupted in July when military units under the command of General Francisco Franco (1892–1975) revolted in Spanish Morocco, sparking uprisings in Spain. The Nationalists, as they called themselves, included monarchists, Falangists (Spanish fascists), most of the army, the large landowners, and conservative Catholics. The Republican supporters, who ranged from moderate democrats to Socialists, Communists, and anarchists, drew many of their adherents from the major cities and the Basque provinces. Left alone to pursue their struggle, the two sides, roughly equal in strength, might have permanently divided Spain into an authoritarian south and a republican north.

Outside powers saw in the Spanish civil war an opportunity to champion their own ideological causes, thereby turning the conflict into an international struggle. Mussolini, intent on establishing Italian hegemony in the Mediterranean, dispatched troops and military equipment to the Nationalists. Hitler used the war to test his new tank units and his air force, which subjected the Basque city of Guernica to merciless bombing. Although the Popular Front in France was sympathetic to the Republican cause, the Blum government was hamstrung because popular opinion was divided in its support for the two sides and because Britain, also riven by the conflict, had adopted a neutral stance. Nevertheless, volunteers from the Western democracies fought for the Republicans; among them was Ernest Hemingway, whose 1940 novel *For Whom the Bell Tolls* captures the spirit of the war. These volunteers fought in international brigades organized by the Soviet Union, which supplied war materials, skilled personnel, and political commissars.

As Communist influence quickened, fighting broke out within Republican ranks, thereby weakening their cause. With little prospect of victory, no assistance from the United States or Britain, and only secret arms shipments from France, Stalin terminated Soviet aid in mid-1938. The Republicans fell to Franco's forces in March 1939. Some 600,000 people had died during the war, and Franco incarcerated a million Republicans after it ended.

The Czech Crisis

Mussolini's absorption with the Spanish civil war played into Hitler's hands by distracting attention from southern and eastern Europe, the real target of Nazi expansionism. The first objective was to incorporate Austria into a Greater Germany, a goal not shared by Austria's dictatorial chancellor, Kurt von Schuschnigg. When Schuschnigg called for a plebiscite to endorse his position, Hitler massed troops on the frontier. Schuschnigg resigned, and his Nazi successor "invited" the German forces into Austria, but only after the invasion had already begun. *Anschluss* ("union") was accomplished in 1938, and Hitler had once again broken the Versailles treaty with impunity.

The incorporation into the Third Reich of 8 million Austrians, many of whom welcomed the Nazis, set the stage for Hitler's plan to acquire *lebensraum* ("living space"). In November 1937 he had obtained an assurance that Britain had no objection to the peaceful solution of the issue of self-determination for the Germans in Austria and the Sudeten region of Czechoslovakia. British foreign policy at this point was motivated by the policy of appeasement: acquiescing to the demands of dictators in the assumption that their aims were limited and not without some justification; once the demands were met, the appeasers believed, the aggressors would behave responsibly, and war would be averted. Many thought that the Germans were justified in complaining of the terms of the Versailles settlement, particularly the loss of territory to Poland and the prohibition of union with Austria. But appeasement failed in 1938 and 1939 because the fascist dictators were neither governed by traditional morality and diplomatic principles nor limited in their territorial aims. Western democratic leaders, whose populations were averse to confrontation or warfare, were reluctant to grasp this fact. They were also aware that many of their citizens were more or less sympathetic to fascism, partly because of its seemingly more efficient government, partly out of the conviction that the Versailles settlement had been unjust, and partly because of its hostility to communism. More significantly, Britain and France did not have the United States as an ally in the event of renewed war, and Britain, unlike France, was unwilling to join forces with the Soviet Union.

Fresh from his annexation of Austria, Hitler turned to the Sudetenland, whose more than 3 million German-speaking inhabitants he incited to demand first autonomy within Czechoslovakia and then union with their "fatherland." Czechoslovakia posed a more serious diplomatic challenge than Austria because of its alliances with France and the Soviet Union. A German invasion could touch off war not only with those states but also with Britain because of its treaty obligations to France. Chamberlain therefore met with Hitler in September 1938. The Czechs were willing to grant virtual autonomy to the Sudeten Germans, but Hitler, having already ordered his generals to prepare for war, demanded the annexation of those parts of Czechoslovakia where Germans made up more than 50 percent of the population.

After the British and the French pressured the Czechs to accept Hitler's new demand, Chamberlain returned to Germany, only to be told that the territories in question had to be ceded on October 1, not in stages. Dismayed, the allies prepared for war. Mussolini seized the opportunity to posture as Europe's mediator in a conference at Munich on September 29 between Britain, France, Germany, and Italy; Czechoslovakia and the Soviet Union were excluded. Chamberlain was anxious to avoid fighting for a "far-off place inhabited by people of whom we know little." Left to themselves and distrustful of the Soviets, the French were unwilling to go to war over Czechoslovakia. Chamberlain and Daladier capitulated to Hitler's demands, coming away only with an agreement that the Sudetenland would be occupied in stages. The Czechs, betrayed by their allies, could only acquiesce.

WORLD WAR II

Hitler's plans for conquest in the east involved the isolation of the Soviet Union. In November 1936 he signed the Anti-Comintern Pact with Japan; Italy joined a year later. In quest of an Asian empire the Japanese had already conquered Manchuria in 1931–1932. In 1937 they invaded China, seizing Beijing (Peking), Shanghai, and Nanjing (Nanking), but mountain ranges, overextended supply lines, and Communist guerrillas prevented them from taking western China.

While the fighting raged in China, Hitler bullied the Czech government, virtually defenseless after the loss of the mountainous Sudetenland, making Bohemia and Moravia German protectorates in March 1939 and leaving Slovakia as a puppet state. The specter of Nazi troops occupying Prague finally roused British popular opinion against Hitler. Even Chamberlain, appalled at Hitler's duplicity in reneging on his Munich pledge to leave Czechoslovakia alone, abandoned appeasement. Daladier agreed, and both Britain and France pledged military aid to Poland in the event of a German attack and began negotiations for a military pact with the Soviet Union.

The heart of Hitler's quarrel with Poland was the autonomous city of Danzig and access to it through the Polish Corridor. As early as November 1938 the German army had begun preparing to seize Danzig, and in April 1939, Hitler ordered contingency plans to destroy the Polish military if it resisted. He was unwilling to act

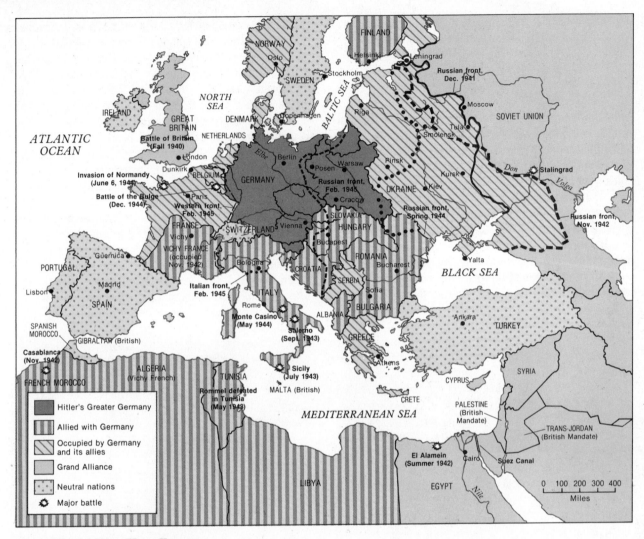

28.1 World War II in Europe

before he knew the intentions of the Soviet Union. While he sought the answer to this question, Europe moved closer to war. The Italians invaded Albania in April and signed a formal military alliance, known as the Pact of Steel, with Germany the following month. Hitler told Mussolini nothing about his plans to seize Danzig. There would be no war, Hitler promised, until 1943, so the general staffs of the two countries made no military plans. Not until August 1939 did Hitler inform the Italians of his imminent attack on Poland.

In the meantime, French and British diplomats failed to negotiate a military alliance with the Soviets, in part because Stalin had territorial ambitions in Finland, the Baltic states, and eastern Poland. Nor were the British and French governments anxious to reach agreement

with Stalin. To defend Poland, moreover, the Soviets needed permission to send their troops through that country to attack the Germans; the Poles, who had suffered at Russian hands in the past, refused. Although Stalin had signed mutual defense treaties with France and Czechoslovakia in 1935, his offer to participate in the Munich conference had been rebuffed. By 1939 he was suspicious that the British and the French were prepared to accede to Hitler's demand for lebensraum in the east to protect their own interests. Stalin therefore met with the German foreign minister, who offered to partition Poland with the Soviets and to give them a free hand in Finland, the Baltic states, and Bessarabia. The nonaggression pact to which the Nazis and the Soviets agreed on August 23 enabled Hitler to attack Poland on September

1 without fear of Russian reprisal. By this point, Hitler would settle for nothing less than the partition of Poland.

The Nazi Conquest of Europe

Although the British and French responded to Hitler's invasion of Poland with declarations of war, they could do nothing to save the Poles. Introducing the tactics of *blitzkrieg* ("lightning war"), the Germans crushed the Poles with a coordinated assault involving 1.75 million men, bombing raids against the cities, and rapidly deployed tank columns that cut Polish supply lines. Soviet forces invaded Poland on September 17, and by month's end the Nazi-Soviet victory was complete. Germany annexed Danzig, the Corridor, and western Poland, while the Soviets seized the eastern part of the country; central Poland became a German protectorate.

The British and French demonstrated a lack of will to do battle. In the west they had 76 divisions to Hitler's 32 as well as the capability to bomb German factories in the Ruhr. Aware of this, Hitler decided on September 27 to launch an offensive in the west in mid-November. The offensive had to be delayed until the spring of 1940 because of supply problems and bad weather, but the British and French failed to exploit this opportunity to strike directly at Germany, nor did they act expeditiously to aid Finland when Soviet troops invaded in November 1939. Hitler demonstrated little interest in Scandinavia until the British and French prepared to mine Norwegian harbors to prevent their use by German U-boats. The Nazis invaded Denmark and Norway in April 1940.

The fall of Norway and the German invasion of the neutral countries of the Netherlands and Belgium on May 10 finally drove Chamberlain to resign, opening the

German troops pass the Arc de Triomphe as they march through occupied Paris in June of 1940. [Roger Schall, Paris]

way for Winston Churchill (1874–1965), First Lord of the Admiralty, to become prime minister. Dutch resistance lasted a mere four days, but the Belgians, aided by the French and the British, fought until May 27. Shortages of fuel and tactical errors by the Germans enabled the British to evacuate 338,000 Allied soldiers from Dunkirk. Meanwhile, the German army, skirting the Maginot Line, broke through the French defenses on May 12. The French sued for an armistice on June 17, three days after the Germans occupied Paris. The Nazis allowed the French, under the nominal direction of Marshal Henri Philippe Pétain, to govern southeastern France and North Africa under the so-called Vichy regime. The Free French movement, organized by Charles de Gaulle (1890–1970), continued to oppose the Nazis, both by acts of resistance in France and by fighting abroad.

Mussolini, who had refused to commit his unprepared country to the war in 1939, decided in May 1940 that it was time to fight. To remain neutral not only deprived Italy of the opportunity for territorial gain but also risked Hitler's wrath. Italy declared war on France on June 10, in time only for an inconsequential Alpine campaign before the French sought an armistice with Germany. Mussolini would have to search elsewhere for glory. He selected Greece, which he anticipated would capitulate quickly. The Italians invaded on October 28, only to be repulsed by the Greeks; in the spring of 1941, Mussolini's embarrassed forces, cowering in the Albanian mountains, had to be rescued by the Germans, who quickly defeated Greece.

The Battle for Britain and the Invasion of the Soviet Union

Hitler had expected the British to sue for peace in the aftermath of the French defeat, thereby enabling him to concentrate on the east. When this did not happen, he resolved to crush the Soviet Union as the best means of destroying British hopes and of checking the United States by giving the Japanese a free hand in East Asia. Hitler wanted to launch the Russian campaign in May 1941. In the interim he intended to inflict a death blow on Britain, thereby avoiding a two-front war. He ordered a massive air assault on Britain in August, after which the German army would mount a cross-Channel invasion—Operation Sea Lion—in September. The German air force, under the command of Hermann Göring, could neither overpower the Royal Air Force, which had the benefit of newly discovered radar, nor break British morale. Officially, Operation Sea Lion was postponed

until the spring of 1941; with the invasion of Russia, Hitler then had to face a two-front war.

Hitler's invasion of the Soviet Union was further frustrated when he dispatched German troops to the Balkans in the spring of 1941, in part to rescue the Italians and in part to repress Yugoslavia after it repudiated its alliance with Germany. By late spring, all of the Balkans were under German control, but this campaign had delayed the attack on Russia. Hitler was so confident of Germany's ability to inflict a swift defeat on the Soviet Union that he dissuaded Japan from joining him, whereupon the Japanese and the Soviets signed a neutrality pact in April 1941.

Operation Barbarossa, as the Germans called the Russian invasion, got underway on June 22 when Hitler launched 145 divisions into Soviet territory. The early gains were stunning, for Soviet forces had only partially mobilized despite the fact that intelligence agents had informed Stalin of Hitler's plans as early as November 1940. German generals believed that Nazi troops could take Moscow in August, but Hitler was unwilling to extend his lines that far without first destroying Soviet armies in Leningrad and the Ukraine. Although the German campaign in the Ukraine was a success, Leningrad resisted, giving Stalin time to bolster the forces guarding Moscow. Not until December 2 did the Germans, dressed in their summer uniforms and lacking antifreeze for their vehicles, reach Moscow's suburbs. Within days the weary, half-frozen German troops were repulsed by fresh Soviet forces from Siberia. Overruling his generals, who favored a strategic retreat until the weather improved, Hitler demanded that his army stand firm against the Soviets along a 1,000-mile front. The Soviets had already sustained 4.5 million casualties, and Hitler sensed victory.

Pearl Harbor and After: A World at War

Germany's invasion of the Soviet Union enabled Japan to expand the war in Asia without risking Soviet retaliation. In July 1940 the Japanese invaded Indochina, prompting the United States and Britain to impose economic sanctions; Roosevelt also froze Japanese assets in the United States and closed the Panama Canal to Japanese shipping. The Japanese offered to withdraw from Indochina if the United States canceled the sanctions and agreed to Japan's annexation of part of China. Roosevelt's refusal infuriated Japanese extremists, whose leader, General Tojo Hideki, became premier in

The "date which will live in infamy": Pearl Harbor, December 7, 1941.
[AP/Wide World]

October. While the Japanese continued to negotiate, they were convinced that war with the United States was inevitable and therefore ordered their fleet to sail toward Hawaii on November 25. Although American intelligence operatives had cracked the Japanese secret code and knew that an attack was imminent, commanders at Pearl Harbor in Hawaii, headquarters of the U.S. Pacific fleet, did not have their forces on alert when the Japanese struck on December 7. By day's end, the Japanese had sunk or seriously damaged 18 large warships, destroyed approximately 180 aircraft, and killed more than 2,000 Americans. Had the aircraft carriers not been at sea, America's ability to challenge Japan in the critical months that followed would have been nil.

The United States declared war on Japan on December 8; Germany and Italy declared war on the United States three days later. Hitler apparently assumed that the Americans would direct their forces against Japan, leaving him free to destroy the Soviet Union. Thanks to the 1940 Selective Service and Training Act, the United States already had 1.6 million men under arms. Its navy, however, had been badly crippled at Pearl Harbor, and only 1,100 of its 9,000 planes were ready for battle. Under Roosevelt's leadership the country manifested a remarkable resolve; before the war ended in 1945 more than 15 million people had been trained for the military, the air force flew 72,000 planes, and the navy floated

4,500 ships. All of this cost approximately $320 billion, causing the national debt to soar from $49 billion to $259 billion. The government kept inflation within tolerable limits by fixing prices and raising taxes.

As 1942 dawned, the fighting extended around the globe. The British were on the verge of driving the Italians out of Africa when Hitler came to Mussolini's rescue by dispatching General Erwin Rommel with two divisions in the spring of 1941. British soldiers battled Arab and Vichy French forces in the Middle East as well to keep that region from falling under Axis control. Japanese forces struck quickly in the aftermath of Pearl Harbor to seize the Philippines, Malaya, Indonesia, and Burma, extending their mastery over most of southeastern Asia.

Although more than 90 percent of Americans had opposed involvement in the European conflict as late as the spring of 1941, Roosevelt had been doing what he could to aid the British, including the exchange in 1940 of 50 American destroyers for 99-year leases on bases in Newfoundland and the Caribbean. In March 1941 he persuaded Congress to pass the Lend-Lease Act, authorizing the president to provide military equipment to friendly countries. After Hitler invaded the Soviet Union, the Soviets received lend-lease assistance. That summer, Roosevelt and Churchill issued a statement regarding the world's future; known as the Atlantic Charter, it recognized that all peoples should have the right of self-determination and that no nation should benefit territorially by the war. The Atlantic Charter was not, however, a military alliance. Once the United States had entered the war, the United States, Britain, and the Soviet Union formed the Grand Alliance and made the defeat of Germany its first priority.

The Final Solution and the Holocaust

Hitler determined to cause a "New Order" on Europe, a task that would cause suffering and death on a scale that had hitherto been inconceivable. Nazi leaders such as SS Chief Heinrich Himmler pushed lebensraum to its logical conclusion: the removal—by annihilation if necessary—of 30 million "subhuman" Slavs. Concentrating at first on captured communists and Jews, as Hitler had directed, Himmler authorized special SS "action units" to slaughter at will in the Soviet Union. These units typically forced their victims, the majority of whom were Jews, to dig mass graves and then line up to be shot. The executioners sent many wounded victims toppling into the pits still alive, there to be smothered by the bodies of others. Through its actions the German army also shared the responsibility for the deaths of 3.7 million Soviet prisoners of war.

Even lower than the Slavs in Nazi racial doctrine were the Jews, and Hitler was determined to eradicate the 11 million who lived in Europe. Soon after the outbreak of the war, Jews in Poland were herded into ghettos. It was from the ghettos that many Jews were sent for final liquidation, but the death rate within the ghettos was already 20 percent per year by 1942. At first the ghettos were a temporary expedient to isolate Jews while their ultimate fate was determined. In July 1941, Göring, at Hitler's command, issued the fateful order for the mass murder of the Jews: "a total solution of the Jewish question in the German sphere of influence in Europe." The following January, Nazi leaders mapped out plans to deport the Jews to camps that were specially equipped to exterminate large numbers efficiently. Execution by machine guns was deemed too slow and costly; the preferred method was the gas chamber, after which gold dental fillings and hair could be removed, the corpses burned in crematoria, and the bones and ashes utilized to make fertilizer. The most notorious of these camps was at Auschwitz in Poland, a model of German efficiency that was capable of killing up to 12,000 people a day. By war's end, its devilish masters had murdered 2.5 million people in gas chambers and slain 500,000 more by barbaric treatment.

The Nazi scheme to exterminate "inferior" peoples extended as well to gypsies, homosexuals, the incurably diseased, and the mentally ill. Jehovah's Witnesses and communists died for their anti-Nazi beliefs. Between 1938 and 1941 the Nazis perfected their gassing technique on 70,000 mentally ill Germans. At its most "efficient," gassing took between 15 and 20 agonizing minutes to kill most victims in chambers designed to look like shower rooms. The government called on the medical profession to help develop the techniques of mass slaughter even as it bestowed rights to concentration-camp labor on such German industrial firms as I.G. Farben, Telefunken, and Siemens.

Altogether the Nazis slaughtered 5.1 million Jews, half of them from Poland, more than a million from the Soviet Union, nearly as many from eastern Europe, 250,000 from Germany, and lesser numbers from the occupied west. A quarter of those killed were children. At first Allied and even Jewish leaders were incredulous at reports of the genocide, but even when these were confirmed, no effort was made to bomb the camps or the rail lines leading to them. Although underground church groups assisted the Jews, Pope Pius XII (1939–1958) never directly condemned the atrocities, even when Jews were herded into cattle cars in Rome for deportation to the death camps. There was scant sympathy for the Jews in Poland, especially among the anti-Semitic clergy. However, the Danish, Hungarian, and Bulgarian governments (unlike that of Vichy France) resisted Nazi demands to turn over their Jewish subjects, and many Dutch and Italians did what they could to help the Jews. Efforts to blame the slaughter on a mere handful of deranged Nazi leaders are indefensible: approximately 50,000 people were directly involved in Hitler's "Final Solution." Few of them were ever held accountable for their crimes.

THE CITY AS INFERNO: LIFE IN THE WARSAW GHETTO

World War II subjected some of the world's cities to widespread destruction; among the most heavily damaged were Hiroshima and Nagasaki, both targets of atomic bombs; heavily bombed capitals such as Chungking, London, and Berlin and industrial centers such as Rotterdam and Hamburg; and Dresden, where up to 135,000 people were killed and much of the city was destroyed by firebombs, purportedly to pressure Hitler to surrender and to expedite the Soviet advance. The Polish city of Warsaw was not only extensively damaged during nearly four weeks of fighting in September 1939 but also subjected to Nazi occupation in which its Jewish population was horribly decimated. Deliverance came only in January 1945, when Soviet troops liberated the ruined city.

On the eve of the war, 375,000 of Warsaw's population of nearly 1.3 million people were Jewish. The Jewish section of the city was the most heavily bombed in September 1939. Thereafter, the Nazi occupation forces conscripted thousands of Warsaw Jews into labor battalions and interned many more in concentration camps. Jewish schools were closed, Jewish children excluded from public schools, and Jewish-owned businesses and factories seized by the state. The Jews received minimal food rations and had to wear special armbands and register their property.

In the spring of 1940 the Nazis began relocating many of the Jews in ghettos, the largest of which were in Warsaw and Łódź, and which eventually served as holding areas for Jews deported from other eastern territories. These ghettos were turned into labor camps, cut off from the rest of the city by barbed wire and administered by the SS through community "elders." The density of population in the Warsaw ghetto was 20 times that of the surrounding city, and the inmates' rations fed them no more than one-half to two-thirds the nutrition necessary to sustain human life, leading to mass starvation and epidemics.

In late 1941 the Nazis began deporting Jews to concentration camps. By late 1942 the population of the Warsaw ghetto had declined from nearly 500,000 to a mere 40,000, spared only because they worked in German factories. On April 19, 1943, the desperate Jews of the ghetto and thousands of others who joined them attacked Jewish police and German troops sent into the ghetto to complete the deportation. For four weeks the Jews fought, providing time at least for the Polish underground to smuggle some of them out of the ghetto. The Germans destroyed the area, bombing and burning the buildings, and ultimately constructed a concentration camp on its site. In suppressing the rebellion the Germans killed more than 12,000 Jews and transported most of the others to death camps.

The city faced one more major ordeal. As Soviet forces moved toward Warsaw on August 1, 1944, the inhabitants rebelled against their Nazi overlords. For two months the Poles battled the Germans in the streets, while Stalin, hoping to see the Polish resistance de-

stroyed, kept his army encamped. Not until approximately 100,000 Poles had died did the rebellion collapse. The Nazis deported tens of thousands of people to concentration camps and barred many others from the city. Then they turned much of it into a wasteland, destroying palaces, the old castle, churches, libraries, museums, and apartments in a flaming inferno.

THE WITNESS OF SIMONE WEIL

Resistance groups such as that which aided the Warsaw Jews existed throughout fascist-dominated Europe and often worked closely with the Allies. Some, such as de Gaulle's Free French, maintained offices in exile and troops in the field. The contribution of such groups to the war effort was substantial, and the number of lives they saved is incalculable. The resistance drew its support from all ranks of society and all religious beliefs. One of the most powerful minds and literary spirits of the resistance was that of Simone Weil, a Frenchwoman of Jewish ancestry.

Born in Paris on February 3, 1909, she learned about war as the family accompanied her father, a physician, when he was posted to various hospitals to treat the wounded during World War I. As a child she relinquished her sugar ration for soldiers at the front and corresponded with them, yet she was angered by the humiliating treatment of Germany at Versailles. Superbly educated, she taught philosophy at various French academies in the 1930s, wrote pacifist articles, and labored in an automobile plant for a year to study—and, despite her physical frailty, to share—the impact of heavy industry on workers. Troubled by the inhumanity she saw, Weil turned to religion—not to the Judaism that was her heritage but to Catholicism; however, she never formally joined the Catholic church.

When the Spanish Civil War erupted, Weil joined a Republican unit, seeing in that conflict a manifestation of the revolutionary spirit that had moved the French in 1789 and 1871 and the Russians in 1917. Her wartime experience, which lasted only a matter of days, ended when she accidentally burned herself. However brief, her days on the battlefield left their mark on her: threatened by an enemy bomb, she set aside her pacifism.

Although Weil remained opposed to war, Hitler's aggressive policies caused her increasing anxiety. As late as 1939 she hoped that Nazism would collapse without a war, but she soon recognized an obligation to work for Hitler's overthrow. In her essay "The Great Beast" she compared Hitler's expansionism with that of ancient Rome; both, in her view, opposed the classical Greek spirit of virtue that she saw as fundamental to the ideals of Western civilization.

Weil's fertile mind turned to resistance. When students in Prague revolted against the Nazis, she proposed that an armed volunteer force—including herself—be dropped into the city by parachute, but no one listened. She then advocated the formation of an elite corps of nurses who would go into battle with soldiers and tend their wounds instantaneously; trained in first aid, she wanted to serve in such a unit. Again the idea fell on deaf ears. Forced to flee Paris by advancing German troops, Weil and her family sought refuge in Marseilles, where she joined the French resistance, wrote for and helped to distribute one of its newspapers, and worked tirelessly on behalf of prisoners and detainees in concentration camps. As she had done as a child, she shared food from her own meager ration with prisoners. Arrested several times, she refused to break under interrogation.

In 1942, Weil accompanied her family to New York, where she continued to write and pursue her spiritual odyssey. Restless, she left for London in November and there rejoined the French resistance. Despite deteriorating health, caused primarily by her determination to eat no better than her resistance compatriots in France, she pleaded unsuccessfully to be dropped by parachute into her occupied homeland. Fatally ill with malnutrition and pulmonary tuberculosis, she died in England on August 24, 1943, too early to see the downfall of the fascism she had opposed with such courage and self-sacrifice.

Profoundly spiritual, Weil devoted her life to a search for absolute goodness and truth in a time of evil. For her, truth was reality, not the product of mere intellectual speculation. The pursuit of philosophy changes the soul, for truth, she argued, is a manifestation of goodness. Weil's concerns were at once mystical and ethical; the search for God helped her to find a basis for action in life, and that action, she believed, must be rooted in love. From this followed her impassioned opposition to fascism.

The Grand Alliance and the Defeat of Germany

The first crucial strategic decision of the Grand Alliance dealt with the question of how best to defeat Germany.

As the Soviets, with their superior knowledge of winter combat, pushed back the Nazi forces, Stalin pressed his allies to mount a cross-Channel invasion of France to reduce the pressure on his own troops. With their imperial interests, the British, however, were committed to theaters of operation as far afield as Asia, North Africa, and the Middle East, while their American allies, preoccupied as well with Japanese aggression in the Pacific, were hardly prepared for a direct attack on Hitler's Fortress Europe in their first year of fighting. Churchill and Roosevelt therefore focused on North Africa, where Rommel appeared on the verge of overrunning Egypt in the spring of 1942. Simultaneously, the German forces in Russia, having withstood the Soviet counteroffensive, were ready to launch a new campaign to force Stalin to capitulate. The year 1942 proved pivotal in the war against Germany and Italy.

Hitler adopted a new strategy to defeat the Soviets: his forces would strike from the Ukraine to Stalingrad and ultimately to the Caspian Sea, leaving Russia's vast oil supplies in his hands and severing the south from the rest of the country. To succeed, the Nazis had to capture Stalingrad, the epic battle for which commenced on August 23. The Soviet defenders held out long enough for Stalin to mount a surprise attack that threatened to encircle a German army of 250,000 men. Against all advice, Hitler refused to order his troops to retreat before the trap closed. By the time their general defied the Führer and surrendered on February 2, 1943, all but 80,000 Germans had perished. Henceforth, Stalin had Hitler on the defensive (except for a final German thrust against Kursk that summer), but it would take 27 months for the Russians to traverse the road from Stalingrad to Berlin.

To drive the Axis powers out of North Africa, the Americans and the British launched a pincers movement. Beginning in October 1942 at El Alamein, near Alexandria, British forces under General Bernard Montgomery pushed Rommel's troops westward, while American and Free French units led by General Dwight Eisenhower (1890–1969) attacked across Morocco and Algeria. In May 1943 the two armies met and overwhelmed the Axis forces in Tunisia.

The way was now clear to invade Sicily, a decision that Roosevelt and Churchill had made in January over Stalin's objection, since it again delayed the cross-Channel assault. In July the Allies landed 160,000 men in Sicily, where they met stiff German resistance before prevailing. Motivated by the Sicilian invasion, dissident Fascists and monarchists persuaded King Victor Emmanuel to arrest Mussolini on July 25 and replace him with Marshal Pietro Badoglio. When the new premier refused Allied demands for unconditional surrender, British troops invaded southern Italy on September 2, followed a week later by the Americans. Badoglio's government agreed to an armistice. German forces thereupon seized Rome, forcing Victor Emmanuel and his premier to flee south. Two days later, on September 11, Nazi paratroopers rescued Mussolini, who subsequently presided over a puppet state in northern Italy. The following month, Victor Emmanuel's government declared war on Germany.

Roosevelt and Churchill held their first summit conference with Stalin in the Iranian capital of Tehran from November 28 to December 1. The three reaffirmed the decision reached by Roosevelt and Churchill at Casablanca the previous January that Germany must surrender unconditionally. It would then be divided into occupation zones, demilitarized, subjected to reparations, and denazified. Churchill and Roosevelt acquiesced to Stalin's demand that the Soviet Union be allowed to extend its western frontiers and that Poland be compensated for the loss of its eastern territory with German land. Churchill argued unsuccessfully for the British and Americans to concentrate on the Balkans, thereby holding down the casualties that a cross-Channel invasion would entail and keeping the Soviets out of the region. Roosevelt accepted Stalin's plea to strike directly at France in return for a Soviet pledge to enter the war against Japan as soon as Germany was defeated. Without Soviet assistance, American military advisers feared a protracted struggle to defeat Japan.

During the early months of 1944, Eisenhower readied a mammoth invasion force in England while Allied troops fought their way up the Italian peninsula, entering Rome unopposed on June 4. Two days later—D Day—Eisenhower's troops invaded Fortress Europe along a 60-mile stretch of the Normandy coast. Convinced that this was a feint, Rommel held back his armored units, giving the Allies time to secure their position. By the end of the first week, Eisenhower had more than 300,000 men in France, although not until late July did they break out of the beachheads. Eisenhower allowed the French resistance to liberate Paris on August 25, and by mid-September, Allied units had reached the German border.

The war might have been over by this point had the conspiracy to assassinate Hitler in July succeeded. The plot involved generals such as Rommel, diplomats, clergymen, union leaders, and civil servants. Their bomb injured Hitler, perhaps reinforcing his fanatical determi-

The war in Europe ended with Soviet troops occupying most of eastern Europe, which gave Stalin considerable leverage at Yalta and Potsdam. Here Soviet soldiers raise their flag over the ruins of the Reichstag after conquering Berlin in May 1945. [Bildarchiv Preussischer Kulturbesitz, Berlin]

nation to fight to the end. In the aftermath of the plot, nearly 5,000 people were executed, including aristocrats and military officers, and thousands of others were sent to concentration camps.

In mid-December the Germans mounted one last, desperate offensive, the intent of which was to break through Allied lines in the Ardennes forest and capture the Allied supply base at Antwerp, Belgium. For a time, German units repulsed the Allies, but the Battle of the Bulge was over by late January. In the meantime, Soviet forces continued their push through Poland and deep into Germany.

American, British, and French forces crossed into Germany early in the spring, and on April 11, American units were at the Elbe River 60 miles from Berlin. The

Soviets were already at the Oder River, 40 miles on the other side of the city. Eisenhower opted not to take Berlin, primarily because he wanted to use the Elbe to separate his troops from the Soviets and because he was concerned by reports that the Nazis intended to make their final stand in the Alps. Churchill was convinced that Eisenhower's decision was wrong; Roosevelt might have agreed and ordered U.S. forces to take Berlin, but he died on April 12, one day after American soldiers reached the Elbe. Four days later the Soviets attacked Berlin; as Russian soldiers overran his capital, Hitler committed suicide on April 30. Germany surrendered unconditionally on May 7, 1945.

The Atomic Bomb and the Defeat of Japan

The tide in the Asian war turned in mid-1942 when American naval forces defeated the Japanese in the Coral Sea and near Midway Island. They followed with "island-hopping" amphibious warfare and naval battles fought by aircraft carrier–based planes. General Douglas MacArthur retook the Philippines in 1944. After fierce battles for the islands of Iwo Jima and Okinawa in March and May 1945, respectively, the Americans were poised to invade Japan itself. Submarines cut Japan's supply lines, and long-range aircraft bombed the Japanese cities; raids on Tokyo in the spring of 1945 killed nearly 100,000 people.

American intelligence experts wrongly assumed that the Japanese would surrender only after an invasion of their home islands, which, it was thought, would cost a million Allied casualties. In fact, some Japanese were ready to surrender in the spring and made this known to the Soviet Union, which had not yet declared war on Japan. Stalin was determined to expand Soviet influence in eastern Asia and did not forward the peace feeler to Washington or London. In mid-July, however, U.S. intelligence sources learned of Japan's interest in ending the war.

By that time, President Harry Truman (1945–1953) had the atomic bomb at his disposal. The secret Manhattan Project had been working on it since 1942 and successfully tested it in July 1945, after Germany had surrendered. Some scientists and other advisers wanted Truman to drop the atomic bomb on Japan, either as a demonstration in a place where it would not kill many people directly or on a military target. Although it appeared that the "conventional" firebombing, the sub-

marine blockade, and attrition had doomed Japan, Truman ordered that the atomic bomb be dropped on Hiroshima, a major city, on August 6. It killed some 78,000 of its 327,000 residents and military personnel and injured tens of thousands more. Two days later, the Soviet Union declared war against Japan and sent its army into Manchuria and then into Korea. On August 9 the Americans dropped an atomic bomb on Nagasaki, killing approximately 40,000 people. Insisting that his people must "endure the unendurable," Emperor Hirohito urged surrender, and the Japanese cabinet accepted Allied terms on August 14. Hostilities officially ended on September 2, 1945.

War statistics are still being revised, but the death toll has been estimated to have been between 50 million and 70 million. Estimates of deaths vary widely, ranging from 14 million to 27 million for the Soviet Union, 12 million to 20 million for China, 3.5 million to 7.5 million for Germany, and 1.7 million to 3.5 million for Japan. Poland (including its Jewish population) may have suffered 6 million and Yugoslavia over 1.6 million deaths. By comparison the estimate for the United States ranges from 319,000 to 485,000. In addition, tens of millions of refugees, freed prisoners of war, and concentration camp survivors had to rebuild shattered lives.

THE UNITED NATIONS AND THE QUEST FOR PEACE

Western democratic leaders were convinced that the world had returned to war in 1939 in large measure because of financial tensions rooted in aggressive nationalism. Peace, they believed, required not only open political dialogue but also financial stability and reasonably free trade. In Roosevelt's judgment the United States shared the blame for the failure of the League of Nations to keep the peace, and he resolved in early 1942 to help create a new international organization to maintain peace and security.

Roosevelt's vision was fulfilled when the United Nations Conference on International Organization convened at San Francisco in April 1945. The charter endorsed by the 50 original members pledged "to save succeeding generations from the scourge of war," to reaffirm faith in human rights, to establish justice and respect for international law, and to promote social progress. The charter established six organs in the United Nations (UN): the General Assembly, in which each member state had one vote and where international issues could be debated; the Security Council, which decided important issues and was comprised of five permanent members (the United States, the Soviet Union, Britain, France, and China) and six elected members; the Economic and Social Council; the Trusteeship Council to supervise states responsible for administering trust territories (regions, such as the Marshall Islands, deemed not ready for self-government); the International Court of Justice; and the Secretariat, headed by the secretary general.

In some respects—the General Assembly, the Security Council, the dominance of the major powers, and the provision for trusteeship—the United Nations resembled its predecessor, the League of Nations. But whereas the League had had a predominantly European focus, the inclusion of the United States and the Soviet Union as founding members gave the UN a more global orientation. So too did the subsequent addition of new states, most of them in Asia and Africa.

The United Nations was established to further cooperation between nations, not to replace them with a world government. The sovereignty of individual states was recognized in various ways, including the crucial provision that requires unanimity on the part of the five permanent members before the Security Council can act, thus giving a powerful veto to each of those five states. The integrity of individual states has also been recognized in the work of the International Court of Justice. United Nations membership had more than tripled by 1990, although admittedly the UN has been more successful in dealing with social and economic issues than in preserving peace.

Roosevelt was also concerned to stabilize economic relations between nations, at least in part to benefit the American economy. The result was the International Monetary Fund (IMF). Launched in March 1946, the IMF was designed to stabilize international exchange rates. Each member state had to deposit a specific amount of its currency into the IMF's reserve fund, which was used to provide loans to countries with balance-of-payments problems. These loans provided states with an alternative to imposing stiff tariffs or other economic measures that could set off trade wars. Member states were entitled to use their own monies to purchase gold or foreign currencies according to fixed rates of exchange. Many chose to buy U.S. dollars, which could then be redeemed through the IMF for gold at $35 an ounce. So

great was the subsequent drain on U.S. gold that its export was prohibited in 1971, and the price of gold was allowed to fluctuate according to market conditions. Nevertheless, the IMF played a major role in saving threatened currencies during financial crises. The IMF has served as a forum for negotiations to resolve international monetary disputes, but it has also acted to influence Third World economies and protect U.S. banking interests by imposing austerity measures on countries that overborrowed.

THE ONSET
OF THE COLD WAR

The Cold War pitted former members of the Grand Alliance against each other in a struggle that was at once ideological and nationalistic. Both sides had been deeply affected by their wartime experiences: the United States and its western allies were determined to prevent the revival of fascism by encouraging democratic governments sympathetic to their own political values and, in so doing, protect their national interests; the Soviet Union, having suffered staggering human losses, was committed both to dominating the states on its western frontier for security reasons and to extending its territorial boundaries to recover the lands lost in World War I. The ideological and nationalistic rivalry was especially keen in eastern and central Europe and in Korea.

Yalta, Potsdam, and the Reshaping of Europe

The crucial decisions about the shape of postwar Europe were made by the leaders of the United States, the Soviet Union, and Britain in conferences at Yalta and Potsdam. The tone for these meetings had been set in a conference between Churchill and Stalin in October 1944 after Soviet troops had liberated eastern Poland, Romania, and Bulgaria and had helped Marshal Tito (born Josip Broz, 1892–1980) and his partisans to oust the Nazis from Yugoslavia. Unwilling to wait another month until Roosevelt completed his campaign for a fourth presidential term, Churchill feared that all of the Balkans might soon fall under Soviet domination. In practical terms, Churchill conceded the Soviet presence in Romania and Bulgaria in the hope of keeping the Russians out of

Greece. Interest in Yugoslavia and Hungary would be split evenly. Hungary still lay within the Nazi orbit, and the future of Yugoslavia, which had a pro-Western government in exile but was largely in the hands of Tito, a Communist, had yet to be settled. Poland and Czechoslovakia were not included in this offer, but Stalin readily accepted the division of the Balkans. At Teheran the previous year, Churchill's hopes of attacking Germany through the Balkans rather than across the English Channel had been dashed; now he acted to save what he could of Western influence in the region.

Roosevelt, Churchill, and Stalin met at Yalta on the Black Sea in February 1945 to confer on the postwar settlement. In contrast to their previous meeting at Tehran, which had concerned primarily military matters, the sessions at Yalta concentrated on political issues. It was agreed that Germany and Austria would each be divided into four occupation zones (American, British, Soviet, and French) and that the capitals of Berlin and Vienna would be jointly occupied by the four powers. Roosevelt and Churchill postponed a resolution of Stalin's demand for $20 billion in reparations from Germany.

Because of its strategic location and disputed frontiers, Poland presented special problems. Stalin insisted on keeping the Polish territory that he had received in his 1939 pact with Hitler, in return for which he proposed compensating the Poles by moving their frontier westward to the Oder and Neisse rivers; Germany would therefore lose Silesia, eastern Prussia, and part of Pomerania. Roosevelt and Churchill, though willing to permit the Soviets to retain the Polish territory annexed in 1939, objected to Poland's proposed western boundary because of the large number of Germans in the region. A decision on the western boundary was therefore postponed. No less unsettled was the issue of Poland's future government, especially since two competing ones already existed—a democratic one in London and a Communist rival in Lublin. Stalin agreed to include "democratic leaders" in the Lublin government, a promise that he honored only in token fashion, and to hold free elections, a pledge he later ignored.

Stalin promised to declare war against Japan within three months after Germany's surrender in return for the southern Sakhalin Islands (seized by Japan in the 1904–1905 war), the Kuril Islands, territorial concessions in northern China, and restoration of the "special rights" that imperial Russia had enjoyed in Manchuria.

The Yalta agreement was in accord with that reached by Churchill and Stalin in 1944. Poland was already occupied by Soviet troops, and the promise of free elections was enforceable only at the risk of renewed war. In February 1945, Stalin needed nothing from the Western democracies, but with the availability of the atomic bomb still uncertain, Roosevelt believed that he would require Soviet help to shorten the war against Japan. Given this assumption, the Asian concessions seemed a small price to pay. By mediating between Churchill and Stalin, Roosevelt preserved the unity of the Grand Alliance and secured Soviet support for the establishment of the United Nations. Roosevelt erred not in the terms to which he agreed but in his assessment of Stalin's flexibility on postwar arrangements.

At Potsdam, outside Berlin, Stalin, Truman, and the new British prime minister, Clement Attlee,* met in July 1945 to tidy up Yalta's loose ends. Truman and Attlee, both inexperienced, agreed to permit Poland to administer the contested western region to the Oder-Neisse line, in effect accepting the border proposed by Stalin. The Soviet dictator also won the right to collect $10 billion in reparations from Germany, but Truman and Attlee rejected his demands for joint rule over the Ruhr basin, naval bases in Greece, a UN mandate for Libya, and Soviet participation in the administration of Lebanon, Syria, and Tangier. Stalin in turn repudiated Truman's demand that free elections be held in eastern Europe. The spirit of the Potsdam discussions was more confrontational than cooperative. While the meeting was underway, Truman learned that the test of the atomic bomb at Alamogordo, New Mexico, had been successful. The new tone set the stage for future Soviet-American relations.

Soviet Hegemony in the East

In the aftermath of the war the states of eastern Europe were subject in varying degrees to Communist influence. Stalin apparently had no master plan to ensure that all of them had pro-Soviet governments, although well before the war ended he had organized "national liberation" or "patriotic" fronts in Moscow that could serve as provisional governments once their nations were liberated. The key leaders in these fronts were Communists. Many in the liberated states themselves wished for revolutionary change. In addition to the long-standing need for land reform and industrialization, most people wanted a thorough purge of fascists and collaborationists. Be-

---

*Churchill briefly participated at Potsdam before his party was defeated in the British general election in July.

cause of their racial views, the Nazis had treated most of the eastern European peoples more harshly than those in the west, thereby creating a heritage of bitterness, especially against the propertied classes that had so often collaborated in the east.

Under these circumstances the Soviet-imposed "people's democracies"—leftist coalitions akin to the popular fronts of the prewar era—received substantial support. The coalitions embraced communist, socialist, and peasant parties and sometimes moderates as well. Typically, they included representatives of the "official" London-based exile governments from the war period. Stalin ensured that the ministries of defense and internal security in these coalitions were in Communist hands. Left alone, most of the eastern European states might have evolved stable left-leaning parliamentary democracies of the kind that governed Sweden and developed in postwar Finland. Apart from Poland, however, these states became victims of the emerging Cold War.

Poland, because of its contested borders and strategic position, was a special case. From the beginning, Stalin was determined to impose a puppet regime and prevent free elections; Poland's fate was decided before the Cold War began. Stalin installed a pro-Moscow coalition at Lublin, although to placate the British and Americans, he added members of the Peasant party. That party challenged the pro-Soviet bloc in the 1947 elections but won only 20 percent of the vote. After the Workers' party and the Socialist party merged in December 1948 to form the United Workers' (Communist) party, Poland was virtually a one-party state.

Yugoslavia too was a special case. By war's end the Communist partisans under Tito's leadership controlled the country and dominated the provisional government. Elections for a constituent assembly in November 1945 resulted in victory for the People's Front, but the assembly did the bidding of the Communist party. A republic made up of six autonomous republics replaced the monarchy. Having liberated Yugoslavia with virtually no Soviet assistance, Tito was determined to maintain national independence against both the Soviets and the Western powers, which he feared would intervene to restore monarchical government. He refused to subordinate his country to a Soviet master plan for the economies of eastern Europe and further angered Stalin by proposing to establish a South Slav federation with the Bulgarians. For its deviation, Yugoslavia was expelled from Cominform, the revived Third International, in 1948. This provided Albania, a Communist state with a pronounced dislike for its Yugoslav neighbor, with the opportunity to throw off Tito's hegemony by declaring

its fealty to Moscow. Tito's defiance of Stalin won his country valuable support in the West.

Stalin was more successful in his dealings with the Bulgarians and Romanians. The Communists were prominent in Bulgaria's coalition government, the Fatherland Front, established in September 1944, but not until October 1946 did a Communist become premier after rigged elections. Leading critics of the regime were later imprisoned or executed. Romania had switched sides in the war after a coup supported by King Michael II; Communists played a major role in the ensuing coalition governments. Because of Romania's strategic position in the last stages of the war, Stalin decided in early 1945 that its premier must be pro-Communist. Michael had little choice but to acquiesce. Following the government bloc's victory in the rigged November 1946 elections, leading opponents were arrested, and the National Peasant party, which most Romanians favored, was declared illegal. Communist domination was assured after Michael abdicated under pressure in December 1947.

In Hungary and Czechoslovakia the "people's democracies" were at first legitimate popular front coalitions. Free elections in Hungary in November 1945 gave the peasant Smallholders party 60 percent of the votes compared to the Communists' 17 percent, but the commander of the Soviet occupation forces insisted on the continuation of the prewar Independence Front. After a coalition of Communists and Socialists won the 1947 election with 37 percent of the vote, the Communists continued to expand their influence with Soviet support, until in 1949, voters were given only a single list of candidates to elect, most of them Communist.

In free elections in November 1945, Czech voters gave the Communists a plurality. The country's venerable president, Edvard Beneš, therefore appointed a Communist as premier. The government operated democratically until February 1948, when Beneš agreed to a cabinet devoid of anti-Communists. The following month, Czechoslovakia officially became a one-party state.

From the Truman Doctrine to the NATO Alliance

In March 1946, Churchill uttered the phrase that would define the West's description of Soviet policy: "From Stettin in the Baltic to Trieste in the Adriatic, an iron curtain has descended across the Continent." That characterization was premature, although the Soviet sphere of influence would be complete within two years. During this time, America's attitude toward the Soviet Union began to shift. Truman's suspicion of Soviet behavior was given substance in February 1946 by George F. Kennan, minister-counselor at the U.S. Embassy in Moscow. Hitherto, experts on Soviet foreign policy had assumed that it was shaped primarily in response to the great powers' treatment of Russia. Rejecting this thesis, Kennan argued that since the late Middle Ages, when the Russians had thrown off their Mongol overlords, they had been expansionistic and distrustful of all peoples on their borders. The appropriate policy for the Western powers to adopt in dealing with the Soviets was therefore one of containment.

Truman implemented the policy of containment in March 1947 in connection with the withdrawal of aid by the British to Greece and Turkey. The Soviets had already coerced the Turks into ceding land adjacent to the Caucasus in 1945, and the following year, Greek Communists launched a civil war against the pro-Western government in Athens. Moreover, the Communists fared well in postwar elections in Italy and France. With Communism seemingly menacing more and more of Europe, Truman outlined the containment policy, later known as the Truman Doctrine:

> Totalitarian regimes imposed on free peoples, by direct or indirect aggression, undermine the foundations of international peace and hence the security of the United States. . . . It must be the policy of the United States to support free peoples who are resisting attempted subjugation by armed minorities or by outside pressures.[1]

The president requested and received $400 million for economic and military aid to Turkey and Greece.

The positive aspect of the containment policy was framed primarily in the European Recovery Program, commonly called the Marshall Plan. The brainchild of Secretary of State George C. Marshall, the plan was implemented in June 1947 to counter Stalin's reputed determination to prevent European economic recovery; without aid, Stalin reportedly believed, Europe would turn to the Communists. In lieu of stopgap economic measures, Marshall invited European nations to formulate a long-range program for economic rebuilding, to be funded by the United States. Seventeen countries, including Britain, France, and Italy, prepared a joint proposal with a budget of $22 billion, of which $12 billion was spent between 1948 and 1952. The Soviet Union refused to participate, since the United States demanded access to its budget and quotas for the purchase of American goods; the Soviets also prevented Czechoslovakia and

Poland from participating. So successful was the plan that in 1952, productivity in western Europe was double that of 1938. Equally impressive was the coordination achieved by the participating countries through the Organization of European Economic Cooperation, a predecessor of the Common Market.

Shortly before Marshall proposed his rebuilding program, Britain and the United States merged their German occupation zones into a single economic unit to spur recovery. This was the first step toward the establishment of a new German state, known as West Germany. A second followed in the spring of 1948 when the three western powers introduced a new German currency in their zones. A unified Federal Republic of Germany, including the western occupation zones in Berlin, would be founded, they determined, in 1949. Concerned about an imperialist bloc of Western countries that included West Germany, Stalin attempted to prevent the emergence of the new state by blockading West Berlin in June 1948. Road, rail, and canal traffic was halted, thereby cutting off the 2.5 million inhabitants of the western zones of the city from fuel and food; even electric power was terminated. American and British transport planes rendered the blockade ineffectual, and Stalin lifted it in May 1949. Three months earlier, he had dropped his opposition to the creation of a West German government, but in turn he established the German Democratic Republic in the Soviet zone. Germany thereafter existed as the separate states of West and East Germany until reunification in October 1990.

Deteriorating relations between the Soviet Union and the Western democracies raised fresh concerns about defense. Five Western nations—Britain, France, the Netherlands, Belgium, and Luxembourg—signed a mutual defense agreement known as the Brussels Pact in March 1948. By themselves these states were militarily incapable of stopping Soviet aggression, and they appealed to the United States for assistance. Truman persuaded Congress to endorse a new direction in U.S. foreign policy by joining a military alliance in peacetime. The result was the formation of the North Atlantic Treaty Organization (NATO) in April 1949, consisting of the United States, Canada, Iceland, the Brussels Pact nations, and four other western European states. The key provision of the treaty specified that an armed attack on one would be treated as an armed attack on all. The Soviets did not formally establish their own defensive alliance, the Warsaw Pact, until 1955. The year 1949 also marked the first successful test of an atomic bomb by the Soviet Union, which had already begun work on a vastly more powerful hydrogen bomb. Henceforth the

United States and the Soviet Union engaged in a feverish race to ensure that each had sufficient nuclear weapons to deter aggression by the other.

SUMMARY

No two decades in history have been more violent and economically volatile than the period between 1929 and 1949. In those years much of the world was plunged into a severe economic depression. Authoritarian governments emerged in many states and totalitarian ones in the Soviet Union and Germany. The most extensive global war in history was fought; atomic bombs devastated two Japanese cities; the Nazis exterminated 6 million Jews in history's most appalling crime; and within four years after the war's conclusion, former allies were arrayed against each other in new military alliances that reflected the antagonisms of the Cold War.

Amid the ashes and gloom of these decades a few rays of hope emerged: the founding of the United Nations recognized the necessity of providing a forum, however imperfect, to resolve international disputes and work jointly for social and economic progress, and the establishment of the International Monetary Fund was testimony to the realization that economic stability and reasonably free trade were essential for the maintenance of world peace. From global war the nations of the world had begun to realize the importance of international cooperation. Simultaneously, the onset of the Cold War threatened to plunge the world into a new abyss.

Notes

1. *New York Times,* March 13, 1947.

Suggestions for Further Reading

Bell, P. M. H. *The Origins of the Second World War in Europe.* London: Longman, 1986.

Bridenthal, R., Grossmann, A., and Kaplan, M., eds. *When Biology Becomes Destiny: Women in Weimar and Nazi Germany.* New York: Monthly Review Press, 1984.

Browne, H. *Spain's Civil War.* London: Longman, 1983.

Conquest, R. *The Great Terror: A Reassessment.* New York: Oxford University Press, 1990.

Fiori, G. *Simone Weil: An Intellectual Biography.* Athens: University of Georgia Press, 1989.

Gallicchio, M. S. *The Cold War Begins in Asia: American East Asian Policy and the Fall of the Japanese Empire.* New York: Columbia University Press, 1988.

Herken, G. *The Winning Weapon: The Atomic Bomb in the Cold War, 1945–1950.* Princeton, N.J.: Princeton University Press, 1988.

Hogan, M. J. *The Marshall Plan: America, Britain, and the Reconstruction of Western Europe, 1947–1952.* New York: Cambridge University Press, 1987.

Knox, M. *Mussolini Unleashed, 1939–1941: Politics and Strategy in Fascist Italy's Last War.* Cambridge: Cambridge University Press, 1982.

Lapidus, G. W. *Women in Soviet Society: Equality, Development, and Social Change.* Berkeley: University of California Press, 1978.

Lee, L. E. *The War Years: A Global History of the Second World War.* London: Unwin Hyman, 1989.

Mastny, V. *Russia's Road to the Cold War.* New York: Columbia University Press, 1979.

McNeal, R. H. *Stalin: Man and Ruler.* New York: Columbia University Press, 1988.

Parker, R. A. C. *Struggle for Survival: The History of the Second World War.* New York: Oxford University Press, 1990.

Yahil, L. *The Holocaust: The Fate of European Jewry, 1932–1945.* New York: Oxford University Press, 1990.

COLD WAR AND IMPERIAL SUNSET

The first two postwar decades were a time of questioning, rebuilding, and reshaping international relations. Shaken by the wartime experience, philosophers and theologians explored fresh ways to explain human nature and society. Simultaneously, the work of reconstructing destroyed cities and returning economies to their peacetime functions went forward against a background of tension between the Soviet Union and the Western democracies. This period was the most confrontational period of the Cold War, during which nuclear weapons were amassed by the two superpowers, the United States and the Soviet Union. The world changed, partly because European powers divested themselves of their empires and partly because the superpowers extended their rivalry to more and more regions of the globe. The Middle East in particular was altered as Jewish refugees founded and defended an essentially Western state in Palestine despite militant Arab nationalism.

NEW DIRECTIONS

Authoritarianism and the outrages to which it led in World War II drove philosophers and theologians to probe anew the questions of human existence and responsibility. The pervasiveness of death and the desperate straits to which many people had been driven during the war to survive challenged commonplace assumptions about the role of divine providence and the simplicity of ethical choices. The war had forced people to make life-and-death decisions in the context of competing claims to obedience espoused by state, church, and conscience. Nor did the coming of peace end the feeling of despair experienced by the homeless, by bereaved survivors, and by all sensitive to the Holocaust and the bombing of Hiroshima and Nagasaki.

Existentialism and Neoorthodoxy

Founded in the 1920s by the German writers Martin Heidegger and Karl Jaspers, existentialism was less a school of philosophy than a fresh manifestation of the revolt against reason launched in the nineteenth century by Søren Kierkegaard and Friedrich Nietzsche. In lieu of rational analysis the existentialists urged people to give meaning to life by establishing their values through specific deeds. By choosing one course of action instead of another, they asserted, people certify their worth and accept responsibility for their conduct. Existential atheists denied that an individual could find a reliable guide for action in organized religion, nor did they find comfort in science. Existentialists insisted that people become what they are by the choices they make, not by a "human nature" that they inherit at birth.

The leading existentialist of the war and postwar years was the Frenchman Jean-Paul Sartre (1905–1980), whose major works—the treatise *Being and Nothingness*

A Soviet political cartoon from the Cold War era shows the White House trying to encircle the Soviet Union by grabbing (counterclockwise, from top left to right) Korea, Iran, Turkey, Taiwan, and Vietnam. [John Freeman]

(1943), novels such as *The Reprieve* (1947), and plays such as *No Exit* (1944)—reflect the political events of the late 1930s and the war. Acting on his conviction that each person is responsible for advancing the freedom of others, he fought in the French resistance during the war and later promoted leftist political causes. Existentialists were not associated exclusively with the political left; Heidegger, for instance, collaborated with the Nazis.

Sartre's colleague, the Algerian-born Frenchman Albert Camus (1913–1960), is often linked to the existentialists, primarily because he shared their quest for meaning through action as well as the atheism of many of their leading figures. Like Sartre, Camus served in the French resistance, an experience reflected in his allegorical novel *The Plague* (1948). He condemned not only the terror of the Nazis but also that of Stalin's regime. Camus defended responsibility in the face of the emptiness of existence that he characterized as the Absurd.

Postwar existentialism was graphically represented by the Theater of the Absurd. Taking its cue from the French actor and playwright Antonin Artaud (1896–1948), the Theater of the Absurd depicted a world bereft of meaning, whose characters found themselves isolated in rooms without doors, in spaces piled high with useless clutter, or in hallucinatory landscapes. Sartre and Camus contributed to this theater; in the former's *No Exit* the characters, each of whom hides a guilty past, discover that "Hell is other people," while in the latter's *Caligula* the Roman emperor is portrayed as a man driven to acts of desperate cruelty by his rejection of the terms of life. The most important postwar playwright was the Irish-

man Samuel Beckett (1906–1989). His masterpiece, *Waiting for Godot,* depicts a pair of tramps who alternate between hope and despair as they wander a desolate landscape in quest of a meaning that forever eludes them. Beckett's tramps became the symbol of the postwar human condition, his barren stage the image of a world whose spiritual poverty anticipated the final extinction of nuclear apocalypse.

The Theater of the Absurd was particularly associated with France, where Beckett made his home. Elsewhere, the postwar theatrical revival took other forms. In the United States, Arthur Miller (b. 1915) portrayed the broken promises of American capitalism in *Death of a Salesman* and attacked McCarthyism in *The Crucible.* Britain's Harold Pinter (born 1930) combined Absurdist techniques with a sense of the pervasive violence of modern life in *The Homecoming.*

The Holocaust and the specter of nuclear war hung over the postwar world. The matter-of-fact descriptions by Tadeusz Borowski (1922–1951) in *This Way to the Gas Chamber, Ladies and Gentlemen* conveyed the horror of the death camps through understatement. Borowski was a Holocaust survivor who, haunted by his experience, eventually took his own life. Sweden's Ingmar Bergman reached back to the Black Plague of the fourteenth century to depict a world menaced by death in *The Seventh Seal* (1956). On a more popular level the 1950s saw a spate of films about mutant monsters that reflected public anxiety about nuclear testing. The target imagery of the American painter Jasper Johns derived from the same source, while the violent arabesques of

Jackson Pollock suggested the unleashing of unrestrained primordial forces. If World War I had seemed a war to end all wars, World War II produced the bitter knowledge that civilization was at permanent risk.

Christian and Jewish theologians also had to rethink traditional views in the context of global war. Many of them found inspiration in the works of Kierkegaard and the early existentialists. In Protestant circles, the teachings of the Swiss professor Karl Barth (1886–1968) established a theological movement known as Neoorthodoxy, a reaction against nineteenth-century liberalism. Like Kierkegaard, who had discovered religious peace only after rejecting ritual and dogmatic formulas in favor of a personal quest for God, Barth urged the survivors of his generation to seek God not through reason but by a leap of faith. Barth's Reformed Protestant view of a depraved human nature reflected the nightmarish experience of the world wars. Unlike existentialists such as Sartre, Barth offered hope to fallen humanity by reasserting the gift of divine grace.

Catholic theologians too were influenced by existential themes. The most prominent of these thinkers was the Frenchman Gabriel Marcel (1889–1973), son of a Jewish mother and an atheist father. Marcel joined the Catholic church in 1929 after he became convinced that it offered hope and assurance. In *Homo Viator* (1945) he rejected atheistic existentialism and argued instead for the importance of loving others and encouraging their freedom in an unselfish way as the means to find God-centered being. Like Barth, Marcel's gospel of trust, love, and commitment made Christianity relevant to the postwar period of recovery.

The war had a profound impact on Jewish thought. Before the war the leading Jewish existentialist philosopher, Martin Buber (1878–1965), had stressed the idea of a dialogue between the individual and God. One could talk *to* God, he argued, but not *about* God. The practical effect was to make God more accessible and familiar to the common people. This simple trust in God was badly shaken by the Holocaust, the horrors of which drove Buber to speak of the "eclipse of God." Was life with God still possible after Auschwitz, he wondered? "The estrangement has become too cruel, the hiddenness too deep," he wrote in despair. Buber found his answer in the biblical book of Job, which reaffirmed God's presence after a torturous period of evil and darkness. Both the Holocaust and war, Buber concluded, were human problems, to which the proper response was a renewed effort to heal the alienation between God and humanity—to encourage dialogue and to restore trust.

The Ecumenical Movement

Much of the Christian community was influenced by the rejuvenated spirit of internationalism and unity that manifested itself after the war. The ecumenical movement had roots in the great age of missionary activity in the nineteenth century, out of which came the first World Missionary Conference in 1910. Not until 1948, however, did most Protestant churches form the World Council of Churches, which committed itself to furthering Christian unity and church renewal. Several Orthodox churches joined in 1961, but the Catholics, though participating in some aspects of the Council's work, and many conservative Protestant groups have declined to become members.

Roman Catholics initiated sweeping changes in their church in the ecumenical council known as Vatican II (1962–1965), summoned by Pope John XXIII (1958–1963) and continued by Paul VI (1963–1978). Protestant and Orthodox churches sent observers and participated in some of the discussions. Among the achievements of Vatican II were freedom to celebrate the mass in the vernacular, an expansion of the authority and responsibility of bishops, and a statement praising the ecumenical movement and acknowledging that salvation is possible outside the Catholic church. The Council did not, however, permit priests to marry, open the priesthood to women, or accept the use of contraceptive devices for birth control. Vatican II's denunciation of anti-Semitism and its recognition of positive elements in the world's other major religions helped to lay the foundation for better relations among all peoples.

THE SOVIET UNION: THE LEGACY OF STALIN AND KHRUSHCHEV

No nation had more firsthand experience of death and despair than the Soviet Union, much of which lay devastated in 1945. The war had postponed the day when Stalin's emphasis on heavy industry at the expense of consumer goods could end. Although the Soviet people had endured appalling hardships, the postwar period brought no relief from Stalin's oppressive authoritarianism. He was exalted in an expanding cult of personality, and the state renewed its persecution of critics. Stalin had been dead only three years when Soviet premier Nikita Khrushchev denounced "his intolerance, his brutality and his abuse of power." By the time Khrushchev was forced to resign in 1964, the worst features of Stalinism had been mitigated, although the Soviet people still faced shortages of food and consumer goods, and a new era of conformity replaced a brief period of relative freedom.

Rebuilding the Soviet Union

In addition to the 20 million Soviets who had died in the war, 1,700 cities and towns and 70,000 villages lay in ruins. The damage was most extensive in the west, which before the war had been the most advanced region of the country. The termination of lend-lease at war's end and America's subsequent refusal to aid the Soviet Union without exacting political concessions rendered the Soviet condition more difficult. Wherever possible the Soviets extracted reparations in the form of industrial equipment from Germany and Manchuria, though the Western governments soon halted this in their occupation zones.

Stalin was determined not only to rebuild the western part of the Soviet Union but also to develop industries and modern transportation systems along the Volga and the Urals and in Siberia. To do this, he maintained rigid economic controls. Faced with an inadequate labor supply and insufficient housing, he organized a vast network of forced-labor camps. Agriculture too was affected. Desperate to increase productivity during the war years, the government had allowed private agriculture to exist in an arc that extended from the Baltic states through Byelorussia to the Ukraine. After the war, peasants were again forced into collectives, where most of the exploited workers were women.

As in the West, the social position of women changed during and after the war. Especially in the Soviet Union, where the death toll was so high, women were pressed into service in industry as well as agriculture, and many of them temporarily attained positions of responsibility. But the heavy human losses also prompted Stalin to place a high priority on marital stability. The 1944 Family Edict restricted divorce, terminated unregistered marriages, banned paternity suits, and offered material rewards and honorary titles to mothers. Women alone bore the legal responsibility for extramarital relationships. The postwar emphasis on motherhood coupled with the return of men to resume their traditional places of leadership in industry and on farms had a negative impact on the role of women. Although women made up 47 percent of the work force in 1959, they held only 13 percent of the managerial positions.

Stalin attempted to stamp out all traces of opposition to his rule after the relative freedom of the war years. Hundreds of thousands of Soviet troops, believed to have been ideologically tainted by their contact with Western troops, as well as minority groups from the Caucasus and the Crimea who had allegedly collaborated with the Nazis were interned in forced-labor camps in Siberia. American and British authorities contributed to this persecution by forcibly repatriating approximately 1 million Soviet citizens, including prisoners of war, exiles, and labor camp workers. Stalin shipped most of them to labor camps.

Stalin's associate, Andrei Zhdanov, purged scientific and literary groups of anyone suspected of "degenerate" (pro-Western) attitudes. Zhdanov and his associates denounced the poet Anna Akhmatova as "not exactly a nun, not exactly a whore, but half nun and half whore" and the composers Dmitri Shostakovich and Sergei Prokofiev for introducing bourgeois "formalism" (modern rhythm and harmony) into their music. People who were suspected of conspiring against Stalin were arrested and summarily executed by the secret police. At the root of this new repression was Stalin's conviction that he had won the battle against fascism and was embarking on a war to eradicate capitalism.

The status of Soviet Jews worsened in Stalin's later years. Although the Soviet Union had supported the establishment of a Jewish state in Palestine, the Soviet attitude toward its own Jews changed once the Stalinists perceived Zionism as a tool of U.S. foreign policy. In 1952, Stalin cynically proposed that all Jews in Moscow and Leningrad be resettled "in a safe place." Brutal camps for Jews were therefore established near the Chinese border. Most victims of the alleged physicians' plot against Stalin, Zhdanov, and the generals in 1952 and 1953 were Jews, some of whom had allegedly schemed to poison the dictator. Had Stalin not died in 1953, Soviet anti-Semitism might have intensified; his successors, however, moderated it.

Aggression in Asia: The Korean War

Stalin played only a minor role in the defeat of Chiang Kai-shek (1887–1975) by the Communist rebels of Mao Zedong (Mao Tse-tung, 1893–1976) in the Chinese civil war (1946–1949). However, he was more directly involved in the outbreak of the Korean War. Following Japan's surrender, Soviet forces occupied Korea north of the 38th parallel while American troops held the south. The Soviets and the Americans turned their zones into heavily armed client states before withdrawing their forces. In late 1949, Kim Il-Sung, head of the Democratic People's Republic (North Korea), apparently obtained the approval of Stalin and Mao to invade South Korea.

Trained by Soviet advisers and armed with Soviet equipment, the North Koreans attacked on June 25, 1950. Aided by secret intelligence reports, Truman, who knew the invasion was imminent, had prepared a resolution for the UN Security Council that branded the North Koreans as aggressors and authorized the defense of the south. The Soviets, who were boycotting the UN because it had refused to recognize Mao's government, were caught off guard and unable to veto the resolution. Truman ordered the American air force into action on June 26 and U.S. ground forces four days later. By September, however, the invaders had overrun most of the south, wedging U.S. forces into a narrow perimeter around Pusan.

Under the command of General Douglas MacArthur the Americans and their Korean allies recovered and by October, with UN approval, invaded the north. As they approached the Yalu River—the border between Korea and Manchuria—Mao's government warned them to stop. Determined to drive the Communists out of Korea, MacArthur wanted to bomb North Korean sanctuaries on Chinese soil. Mao sent his military to North Korea's defense; it took them only two weeks to repulse the Americans, and for the duration of the fighting the front remained in the region of the 38th parallel. When MacArthur urged the use of nuclear weapons against China to break the deadlock, Truman relieved him of duty in April 1951. Truman's successor, Dwight Eisenhower, agreed to an armistice in July 1953 that ended the fighting but left Korea divided at the 38th parallel.

The Khrushchev Era

After Stalin died in March 1953, five Politburo members shared power, the most prominent of whom, Georgi Malenkov, became premier. Malenkov moderated Stalinist policies by curbing the powers of the secret police, reducing the emphasis on heavy industry, increasing the production of consumer goods and housing, reducing economic demands on the satellite states, allowing artists and writers a measure of freedom, and improving conditions in the forced-labor camps. Reactionaries in the party and the military forced his resignation in February 1955.

The principal architect of Malenkov's fall, the Party Secretary Nikita Khrushchev (1894–1971), soon became the unchallenged leader of the country. In February 1956, in a speech before the Party Congress, he denounced Stalin's crimes, including the suppression of legitimate disagreement, the use of torture to extract confessions, and a policy of terror. The attack on Stalin signaled the beginning of a policy of de-Stalinization, which entailed dropping the idea that war with the capitalist states was inevitable; improving relations with other countries; accepting the principle that the Soviet path was not the only road to communism; increasing the production of consumer goods; and ousting hard-line Stalinists.

Khrushchev's attack on Stalin encouraged moderate Communists in Poland to force the resignation of Stalinist leaders, whom the party secretary himself had branded Soviet puppets. Khrushchev became alarmed when an outspoken reformer, Władysław Gomułka (1905–1982), was about to be elected secretary of the Polish Communist Party in October 1956. Concerned to prevent the rise of another Tito, Khrushchev flew to Warsaw to pressure the Poles and simultaneously ordered Soviet troops to advance toward Warsaw. The crisis was resolved when Gomułka persuaded Khrushchev of his fidelity to communism and pledged to continue Poland's membership in the Warsaw Pact. Gomułka offered modest reform by recognizing workers' councils in the factories and seeking better relations with the Catholic church and the peasants.

The unrest in Poland, coupled with Khrushchev's denunciation of Stalin, inspired protests in Budapest the same month (October, 1956) against the Stalinist regime in Hungary. Police fired on the demonstrators, inciting open rebellion. As hard-line political leaders retreated, Imre Nagy (1896–1958) became premier. Driven by popular pressure, he called for political freedom, the withdrawal of Soviet troops, and the end of Hungary's membership in the Warsaw Pact. Hungary, he proclaimed, would become a neutral nation.

Unwilling to permit Hungary to set such an example for the other Soviet satellites, Khrushchev ordered Soviet armored divisions to attack on November 4. The Hungarians were no match for Soviet tanks and troops. The Soviets deposed and later executed Nagy. Approximately 200,000 Hungarians fled into exile, and thousands more died. Eight days before Soviet troops invaded, the U.S. Secretary of State, John Foster Dulles, had praised the Hungarian patriots and offered them aid to restructure their economy. Confronted with Soviet military intervention and with its British and French allies preoccupied with the Suez crisis, the United States limited itself to procuring resolutions condemning the Soviets in the UN General Assembly.

Hungarian rebels futilely tried to oust the Soviets in 1956. [Erich Lessing/Magnum]

toward communism. Khrushchev continued to encourage high birth rates, and family law was not reformed while he ran the country. Nevertheless, he claimed to appreciate the contribution of women to the Soviet economy and supported boarding schools as a means for the state to help women raise their children.

Simultaneously, Khrushchev introduced changes in Soviet higher education that discriminated against women. During the war, with so many men at the front, 77 percent of the students in institutions of higher education were female; by 1955 the number had dropped to 52 percent, which corresponded to the proportion of women in Soviet society, but by 1962, Khrushchev's "reforms" had further reduced the number to 42 percent. After his departure the number rose again. Thus Khrushchev, while rhetorically addressing the problem of women's role in Soviet society, did little to alleviate it.

De-Stalinization meant limited freedom for writers and artists. Alexander Solzhenitsyn (born 1918) depicted the dehumanizing life in a Stalinist concentration camp in *One Day in the Life of Ivan Denisovich* (1962). But the regime refused to permit the publication of Boris Pasternak's masterwork in the Soviet Union: in addition to describing Stalinist brutality, Pasternak (1890–1960), in *Doctor Zhivago,* extended his criticism to the 1917 revolution. The novel was published to acclaim in the West and in 1958 garnered its author the Nobel Prize, which Pasternak was not permitted to accept. The poet Yevgeni Yevtushenko (born 1933) wrote a moving memorial to Jewish victims of a Nazi massacre, "Babi Yar," but the text was censored when set to music in Shostakovich's Thirteenth Symphony (1962). Artistic expression thus remained subject to state pressure, periods of relative relaxation alternating with repression.

The problems in Poland and Hungary did not deter Khrushchev from his program of de-Stalinization at home. He resumed Malenkov's policy of deemphasizing heavy industry and military expenditures in favor of consumer goods, although living standards remained well below those of the West. Khrushchev's goal was not to imitate Western consumer society but to establish a welfare state in which the people would enjoy free housing, health care, education, and transportation.

Khrushchev's attack on Stalin signaled a slight improvement in the status of Soviet women, although his own policies were inconsistent. In 1956 he deplored the party's reluctance to place women in positions of authority, but he was not a radical in his social outlook. He took credit for the 1944 Family Edict and repudiated the views of those, such as Alexandra Kollontai, who had predicted the demise of the family as the country moved

From Berlin to Cuba

Unlike Stalin, who was convinced of the necessity of military confrontation to destroy capitalism, Khrushchev believed that capitalist society could evolve into socialism without war. Consequently, he espoused a theory of peaceful coexistence, hoping thereby to persuade the West to scale down its military preparations and thus the risk of nuclear war. Constructive diplomatic steps followed, including the withdrawal of Soviet troops from Finland, the normalization of relations with West Germany, and the dissolution of the Communist Information Bureau (Cominform). In 1955, Khrushchev proposed the first summit conference, which was held in Geneva, and followed it with a visit to the United States four years later.

Simultaneously, Khrushchev, with one eye on hardliners in his own country and the other on the West, strove to expand Soviet power. To win friends in the Middle East, he channeled military aid to Egypt through Czechoslovakia. Under Khrushchev the Soviets bolstered their military capabilities by developing a rocket capable of putting the first satellite (*Sputnik*) into space; using the same technology, the Soviets now threatened the West with rocket-borne nuclear warheads.

Much of Khrushchev's foreign policy was a failure. Relations with China deteriorated after Mao Zedong proclaimed his leadership of the Communist movement and launched a so-called Great Leap Forward in an attempt to make his country the first truly communistic society. Relations were further strained when Mao denounced Moscow's "revisionism" as an abandonment of Marxist-Leninist principles and threatened in 1958 to go to war to acquire Taiwan, the last Chinese territory under the control of Chiang Kai-shek. Khrushchev had promised Mao help in developing a nuclear bomb the previous year, but in 1959 he terminated Soviet assistance.

Khrushchev was no more successful in his policy toward Germany. The prosperity of West Berlin, maintained by Western aid, contrasted sharply with the grimness of life in East Germany. The German problem was to have been a key topic at the stillborn Vienna summit between Khrushchev and President John F. Kennedy in June 1961. Embarrassed by the fact that 3 million people had fled from East Germany into West Berlin between 1949 and 1961, Khrushchev in August ordered the construction of a massive wall to prevent further emigration.

Khrushchev's final foreign policy embarrassment involved Cuba. Fidel Castro (born 1927), who had overthrown the dictator Fulgencio Batista in 1959, confiscated some American property in the course of implementing agrarian reforms. When the Eisenhower administration terminated U.S. aid, Castro sought help from Moscow. Kennedy compounded the problem by authorizing CIA assistance for anti-Castro exiles who invaded Cuba at the Bay of Pigs in 1961 in the hope of fomenting a rebellion. The invasion failed, with many of the attackers killed or captured. The following year, Khrushchev ordered the construction of launching sites for nuclear missiles on the island, in part to retaliate for American bases in Greece and Turkey and to compensate for the fact that the United States had far more nuclear bombs than did the Soviet Union (over 6,000

Kennedy and Khrushchev at the Vienna summit in 1961. [Eastfoto]

compared to 200 in 1960). When American reconnaissance photographs revealed the Soviet scheme, Kennedy demanded the removal of the missiles and ordered the navy to intercept others en route to Cuba on Soviet ships. After a tense standoff, Khrushchev agreed to remove the missiles if the United States pledged not to invade Cuba. Kennedy accepted the offer and later removed U.S. missiles from Turkey. Khrushchev's handling of the crisis contributed to his political problems at home, and in October 1964 his opponents forced him to resign.

THE WESTERN DEMOCRACIES

For the European states the major postwar problem was reconstruction. France had lost half of its industrial capacity, 90 percent of its automobiles and trucks, over 75 percent of its railroad engines, and 500,000 buildings, with another 1.5 million damaged. Although most destruction in Germany had occurred in urban areas, approximately 75 percent of its industrial buildings were still standing. The British and the Italians sustained considerable damage to their industrial centers and ports, and much of the Netherlands was devastated. Thanks largely to funds provided by the United States through the Marshall Plan and the United Nations Relief and Rehabilitation Administration (largely funded by the United States), much of the reconstruction was completed by 1955.

The United States and Canada faced the problem of demobilization and the reorientation of their economies to peacetime. Thanks to the demands of the war, Canada emerged in 1945 as a major industrial state, and its postwar Liberal government concentrated on public works programs, aid to veterans, and price supports for farm products to ease the economic transition. American leaders feared a new depression and massive unemployment as the government trimmed the military from a force of 12.5 million to 2 million and canceled war contracts in plants that had employed 27 million people. Serious unemployment was averted by Marshall Plan aid, domestic expenditure, rearmament, and implementation of the 1944 Servicemen's Readjustment Act ("the G.I. Bill of Rights"), which provided education funds to veterans, financial aid to those who launched new businesses, and a guarantee that veterans could return to their prewar jobs.

Recovery in Western Europe

In July 1945, Britons gave the Labour party and its leader Clement Attlee a parliamentary majority. For the first time in the history of the largest democratic countries, a socialist party had won a parliamentary mandate. Although not ungrateful to Churchill for his wartime service, Britons remembered the Conservative party's bungled handling of prewar unemployment and looked to Labour to lead in the task of rebuilding Britain. Labour nationalized approximately 20 percent of British industry, including coal mining, transportation, gas and electricity, and steel. It also implemented a social insurance program that provided benefits to the unemployed, the sick, the disabled, and the retired as well as to widows, orphans, and needy mothers. The welfare state was capped in 1948 with the introduction of the National Health Service, which provided tax-funded medical and hospital care to all Britons.

When Churchill and the Conservatives regained control of Parliament in 1951, they left the welfare state intact, except for denationalization of the steel industry. Despite an embarrassing foreign policy crisis involving the Suez Canal that forced a prime minister from office in 1957 (discussed later), the Conservatives dominated British politics until 1964.

In France the problem of reconstruction was compounded by an ineffective constitution. None of the three major parties—the Socialists, the Communists, or the Popular Republican Movement (MRP), a party of the center-right with a strong Catholic affiliation—was satisfied with the constitution of the Third Republic and its weak coalition governments. But whereas the leftist parties wanted virtually all power in a unicameral parliament, de Gaulle and the MRP favored a strong executive. The constitution of the Fourth Republic was approved in 1946, but shifting coalitions in the bicameral parliament resulted in cabinets of even shorter duration than those of the Third Republic. Despite the weak governments, the major parties established a welfare state, including a social security program, supplemental pay for needy families, and the nationalization of coal mines, gas and electricity, and the major banks and insurance companies.

The Fourth Republic collapsed when the government attempted to negotiate a settlement to end a revolt for Algerian independence. Angered by the policy of conciliation, French forces in Algeria mutinied, creating a political crisis in France. To resolve it, in June 1958 the National Assembly gave de Gaulle virtually dictatorial power for six months and a mandate to draft a new constitution. Approved overwhelmingly in September 1958, the constitution of the Fifth Republic retained a prime minister, who conducted the routine affairs of government and was accountable to the National Assembly, but added an elective president with the power to appoint and dismiss the prime minister and dissolve the Chamber of Deputies. Under de Gaulle's leadership, France charted a foreign policy that was increasingly independent of the United States, developed its own nuclear weapons, effected a reconciliation with West Germany, and offered diplomatic recognition to the People's Republic of China.

Like France, Italy had three relatively strong political parties in the post-1945 era: the Socialists, the Communists, and the Christian Democrats, a party that was similar in outlook to France's MRP. The Italians abolished the monarchy in 1946 and approved a new constitution the following year. Although the constitution provided for a president, real power was shared by the prime minister and a bicameral parliament. The leader of the Christian Democrats, Alcide De Gasperi (1881–1954), emerged as the country's preeminent politician, thanks in part to a disastrous split among the Socialists. In 1947,

De Gasperi dropped the Communists from his cabinet and charted an economic policy based on free enterprise, backed by American aid. Italians were sufficiently impressed in 1948 to vote the Christian Democrats the first freely elected parliamentary majority since unification.

Although the Christian Democrats lost their parliamentary majority in 1953, they continued in power by forming coalitions with smaller parties. The result was a series of weak governments that were unable to end the country's economic woes. In 1960 the Christian Democrats tried to solve the problem by initiating an "opening to the Right"—an alliance with monarchists and neofascists. Popular violence between fascists and Communists doomed this experiment after only four months. Hitherto, the papacy had opposed a political alliance between the Christian Democrats and leftist parties, but Pope John XXIII changed Vatican policy, facilitating a center-left coalition. Beginning in 1962, the Socialists supported the Christian Democratic government, and the following year they joined the cabinet. The "opening to the left" did not, however, end the problem of frequently rotating ministries.

German democracy reemerged in the western occupation zones, where the Allies permitted the establishment of state governments administered by Germans. Two parties were dominant: the Social Democrats and the Christian Democrats, the latter a revival of the prewar Catholic Center party. In 1949, after the western Allies approved a constitution for the German Federal Republic (West Germany), the Christian Democrats won the elections, and Konrad Adenauer (1876–1967) became chancellor. Committed to rebuilding Germany's relations with its neighbors and opposing communism, he refused to give diplomatic recognition to any nation (except the Soviet Union) that had diplomatic ties with the German Democratic Republic (East Germany).

With Marshall Plan assistance, Adenauer led West Germany's rapid recovery. Convinced that economic nationalism had played a major role in the outbreak of World War II, he supported the establishment of organizations that were intended to foster European economic unity. West Germany joined the European Coal and Steel Community in 1952 and helped to found the European Economic Community two years later (see Chapter 30). Unlike the United States, West Germany, whose remilitarization was staunchly opposed by France in particular, was not burdened with heavy military expenditures and foreign commitments, and hence it could invest more in capital improvements. Industrial production increased 600 percent between 1948 and 1964. Adenauer's government also implemented a social security system and gave workers an opportunity to share in the management of industry. In contrast to their British counterparts, German workers were virtually assured of employment and rarely mounted strikes; unemployment dropped from 8.1 percent in 1950 to 1 percent in 1960 and only 0.5 percent five years later. Between 1950 and 1965, real wages more than doubled.

Throughout the western European democracies, women made important advances in the postwar years. France and Italy joined the ranks of European democracies that gave women the franchise, although Switzerland continued to restrict the vote to men. Women had played a major role in the work force during the war, and some continued their employment in the ensuing years. In 1950, nearly 25 percent of married women in western Europe worked outside the home, and that number rose in subsequent years. A shift was also underway with respect to the occupational distribution of women workers as more of them took positions as clerks and typists. Most women continued to have access only to low-status jobs and minimal wages, but expanding educational opportunities provided a foundation for enhanced career possibilities.

The United States: From the Fair Deal to the New Frontier

While Britain and France were developing their welfare states, American voters reacted coolly to Truman's attempt to expand Roosevelt's social program under the banner of the Fair Deal. Truman's agenda included a national health insurance program, federal aid for education, and civil rights legislation, but he had little success with a Congress dominated by southern Democrats and Republicans. His chief domestic successes were a federal housing act, a higher minimum wage, and the inclusion of the self-employed in the social security system. Truman's successor, Dwight Eisenhower, modestly extended the New Deal program during his two terms (1953–1961), increasing social security benefits and the minimum wage and launching the interstate highway program. He vetoed federal housing and antipollution legislation, partly out of concern for their impact on the federal deficit. Eisenhower's middle-of-the-road program reflected his desire to govern by consensus.

Two major issues—the Red Scare and desegregation—threatened Eisenhower's hope for consensus. The Red Scare had originated during Truman's administration when, in the context of the early stages of the Cold War, the president had instigated a loyalty check of federal officeholders. The Un-American Activities Committee of the House of Representatives heightened suspicion of Communist infiltration when it investigated the movie industry, and Wisconsin Senator Joseph McCarthy claimed in 1950 that he had a list of 205 Communists in the State Department. Although proof was never forthcoming, he launched a crusade against the Democrats for being "soft on Communism." When Republicans won control of the Senate in 1952, McCarthy became chairman of the Subcommittee on Government Operations, a post he used to expand his witch-hunt for alleged Communists. His political demise came when the nation witnessed his bullying tactics during a televised investigation of the army; the Senate finally censured him in 1954.

The second threat to the Eisenhower consensus was the movement to end legal discrimination against African-Americans. Although the Fourteenth Amendment to the Constitution had guaranteed all citizens equal protection under the law, the Supreme Court had accepted the legality of separate but equal facilities in *Plessy* v. *Ferguson* (1896), in effect sustaining racial segregation. The Court repudiated that principle in 1954 in *Brown* v. *Board of Education of Topeka,* which ruled that segregation per se was unequal. The following year, the Court ordered school desegregation "with all deliberate speed," but resistance to the directive was common throughout the south.

Inspired by a successful boycott to end segregation on the buses of Montgomery, Alabama, African-Americans organized the Southern Christian Leadership Conference in 1957 to fight segregation with nonviolent tactics. Its founder, Dr. Martin Luther King, Jr. (1929–1968), led protest demonstrations and sit-ins across the south. Although white extremists resorted to force, King remained faithful to his philosophy of nonviolence. With Congress at last ready to consider major civil rights legislation, King held a massive demonstration in Washington, D.C., in August 1963. There he proclaimed his dream that "one day . . . the sons of former slaves and the sons of former slaveowners will be able to sit together at the table of brotherhood."

The proposed civil rights legislation had the belated support of President John Kennedy. His New Frontier, an extension of the New Deal and Fair Deal programs, called for national health insurance and federal aid for education as well as a federal program to train the unemployed and a Peace Corps, whose volunteer members would help Third World countries to educate their people and develop their resources. Congress gave him only the Peace Corps, although it did appropriate huge sums for a manned space program. Congress was still considering Kennedy's civil rights bill when he was assassinated in Dallas, Texas, on November 22, 1963.

Postwar Canada

The Liberal party that had guided Canada through the wartime years continued in power until 1958, during which time the country grew dramatically. Between 1941 and 1976 the population doubled, to 22 million, nearly 2 million of whom were European immigrants. The war-primed economy grew at a record rate; between 1939 and 1967 the gross national product soared from $6 billion per annum to $62 billion. This prosperity enabled the Liberals to establish a welfare state centered on a strong social security program, including allowances for needy families and unemployment benefits. The federal government coupled this with funds to the provinces to help them provide services. The Liberals and the Progressive-Conservatives who succeeded them in 1958 substantially increased federal support for education.

Relations with the United States continued the wartime spirit of cooperation. The two countries built the St. Lawrence Seaway, which, when opened in 1959, enabled ocean-going vessels to serve ports in the industrial heartland of both countries. Canada and the United States also implemented the North American Air Defense Agreement (NORAD), providing for the joint defense of the continent. Canada was a founding member of both the United Nations and NATO. Canadians served in the UN contingent in the Korean War, but a decade later, Canadian-American amity was strained when the United States tried to pressure Canada into arming its missiles with nuclear warheads. The Liberals, running in part on a pledge to restore Canadian independence, ousted the Progressive-Conservative government in 1963.

Friction also arose on another front. In the late 1950s the French-speaking population of Quebec became increasingly disenchanted with the government in Ottawa. French-speaking interests had been represented in Quebec since the 1930s by the Union Nationale, but by the 1950s it had become complaisant and corrupt. In 1960, Jean Lesage, leader of Quebec's Liberal party, defeated the Union Nationale by attacking corruption and appealing to French Canadians who were angry about the economic domination of Anglo-Americans. Lesage worked toward greater autonomy for Quebec within the Canadian federation, while radical patriots advocated nationhood for the province. The issue was sensitive for other provinces with significant numbers of French

Canadians, notably New Brunswick and Ontario, and reached crisis proportions in the late 1960s (see Chapter 30). In the meantime, Lesage pushed ahead with his "quiet revolution," nationalizing the hydroelectric industry in Quebec and implementing major educational reforms. Dissatisfied with this progress, extremists adopted terrorist tactics. The twin threat of separatism and terrorism clouded Canada's future.

THE END OF EUROPEAN EMPIRES

Nationalism was largely responsible for undermining Western imperialism, both because it sparked ruinous wars between the colonial powers and because native elites, espousing national sentiments in imitation of their rulers, aspired to achieve independence. The myth of Western invincibility disappeared in the face of Japanese victories over the Russians in 1904–1905 and in the early years of World War II and of resistance to Italy by the Ethiopians in 1896 and the Turks in 1911–1912. The British were slowly preparing for Indian independence, which they granted after World War II, and their 1956 defeat in the Suez convinced them to accelerate their withdrawal from Africa. More reluctant to relinquish their empire, the French were forced to withdraw from Indochina in 1954 after their defeat at Dien Bien Phu, and in 1962 their principal African colony, Algeria, won its freedom after a bitter conflict that helped to bring down the Fourth Republic. Belgian and Portuguese imperialism ended amid violence and rancor. The demise of the colonial empires did not mean the termination of Western influence in the non-Western world. On the contrary, the disappearance of imperialism created an opportunity for more constructive relationships between nations. Nevertheless, economic dependence often remained after direct political controls were relinquished, and in some cases the bitter memories of colonial suppression have inspired enmity against the West to the present day.

South Asia

Labour's defeat of Churchill, an avowed imperialist, speeded the way for Britain to grant long-delayed independence to India. Growing hostility between the Hindu-dominated Congress party and the Muslim League of Muhammad Ali Jinnah (1876–1948) delayed Britain's

withdrawal while the British mediated between the two sides. The Congress party leaders, Mohandas Gandhi (1869–1948) and Jawaharlal Nehru (1889–1964), resisted Jinnah's efforts to establish largely autonomous states within a federal structure and opposed any scheme to partition India into Hindu and Muslim states. In the face of escalating violence, Lord Louis Mountbatten (1900–1979), the royal viceroy, finally persuaded the Congress party to permit the creation of the independent state of Pakistan, formed out of northwestern India, the western Punjab, and eastern Bengal. In 1947, the year India and Pakistan became independent, more than 10 million people fled from one region to another to escape the violence that marked the birth of the two nations and has continued to poison relations between them to this day. The most notable victim of this hatred was Gandhi himself, who was assassinated in 1948 by a Hindu angered by Gandhi's tolerance of Muslims.

Once India was independent, the British liberated Ceylon (now Sri Lanka) and Burma in 1948. Like India and Pakistan, Ceylon opted to remain a member of the British Commonwealth of Nations, which had been officially recognized by the 1931 Statute of Westminster. The Commonwealth united autonomous states in a mutual trade and defense association through formal allegiance to the British monarch, described from 1950 as "head of the Commonwealth." In return, Commonwealth members enjoyed special trade privileges. Burma, having had its ties with Britain severed by Japanese occupation during the war, rejected Commonwealth membership. Malaya posed a special problem for the British because of the presence of Communist guerrillas and the intense rivalry between the largely agricultural and Islamic Malays and the Chinese, who controlled much of the urban economy. Upon the suppression of the local Chinese Communists, Malaya became independent in 1957, retaining its membership in the British Commonwealth. Six years later, it united with former British dependencies on the island of Borneo to form the Federation of Malaysia.

Southeast Asia and the Origins of the Vietnam War

The Dutch and the French withdrew from their colonies only after failed attempts to repress native insurrections by military force. During the period of Japanese occupation, Indonesian nationalists had established underground organizations that, after the liberation of the islands, were in a position to challenge the returning

Dutch. Four years of fighting finally convinced the Dutch to liberate Indonesia in 1949. In contrast, the Philippines received their independence from the United States in 1946 by mutual consent, although U.S. influence continued, partly generated by the extensive financial assistance provided by the United States for postwar reconstruction. The American presence was further strengthened by a 1947 pact authorizing the United States to maintain military bases in the Philippines and a 1951 mutual-defense treaty.

Following Japan's surrender, the French agreed in 1946 to recognize the independence of the Democratic Republic of Vietnam, founded by the Moscow-trained Ho Chi Minh (1890–1969), leader of the Vietnamese Communist party, in the north and to hold a referendum in the south to determine whether its residents wanted to unite with the Democratic Republic. Before the referendum could be held, the French viceroy established a separate government in the south. Ho's efforts to persuade the French to honor their agreement were fruitless, and as tension escalated, the French bombarded the northern port of Haiphong in November 1946.

The Vietnam War proved costly to the French. So unpopular in France was the fighting that the government relied on professional troops rather than conscripts. Ho Chi Minh's cause received an important boost after the Communists won their civil war in China in 1949 and began providing Ho with supplies. As the Cold War intensified, the United States stepped up financial aid to the French, until by 1954 the United States was paying 80 percent of France's military expenses. It was to no avail. In May 1954, Ho's forces, the Viet Minh, overran Dien Bien Phu, where the French had determined to make their stand.

The same year an international conference at Geneva partitioned the country at the 17th parallel, leaving the north under the control of the Viet Minh and the south in French hands until elections could be held in 1956 to reunite Vietnam. The American-installed ruler in the south, Ngo Dinh Diem, fearing Communist victory in the elections, canceled them. The United States and its allies thereupon accorded diplomatic recognition to South Vietnam. Diem's authoritarianism and his persecution of Buddhists incited hostility to his rule and led, in 1960, to the formation of the Viet Cong, an alliance of Communists and Vietnamese nationalists. By that time, American military advisers were helping the Diem regime. Kennedy increased their number and dispatched military units to Vietnam.

In response to Communist activity in Korea and southeast Asia, the United States played the major role in organizing the Southeast Asia Treaty Organization (SEATO) in 1954. South Vietnam and the neutral states of Cambodia and Laos were not included in the new defense organization, whose membership comprised Thailand, the Philippines, and Pakistan in addition to France, Britain, the United States, Australia, and New Zealand. Shortly after SEATO was established, Britain took the lead in founding the Baghdad Pact, an anticommunist treaty organization whose members extended from Turkey to Iran. NATO, SEATO, and the Baghdad Pact countries ringed the Soviet Union and the People's Republic of China in an "arc of containment."

The Growth of Arab Nationalism

When World War II ended, Britain was still the paramount power in the Middle East, directly controlling Egypt, Palestine, Transjordan, Iraq, southern Arabia, and the Persian Gulf. In the next decade, however, it withdrew almost completely from the region, leaving a vacuum of power that was filled by Arab nationalism, superpower rivalry, and the emergence of the state of Israel.

Until the late nineteenth century, communal identity among the Arab peoples of the Middle East had little to do with political self-determination or territorial units. Under the Ottoman system, members of each religious faith—Muslim, Christian, and Jewish—lived in an independent community governed according to its own law by its clerical hierarchy. Communal consciousness was therefore awareness of religious values and customs rather than ethnic differentiation. Although religious rivalries often had a territorial dimension, not until the final breakup of the Ottoman Empire and the arrival of Western imperialism were such rivalries identified with control of distinct states. The idea of the nation in its modern meaning was, as in so many other parts of the world, a Western import that cut across religious, cultural, and tribal affiliations.

In 1920, Britain and France divided the Arab provinces of the former Ottoman Empire between them as mandates under the League of Nations; Britain added Palestine, Transjordan, and Mesopotamia (Iraq) to its former protectorate in Egypt, and France gained Syria and Lebanon. Although Abdul-Aziz ibn-Saud united the vast interior of the Arabian peninsula in the 1920s, proclaiming the kingdom of Saudi Arabia in 1932, Britain remained in firm control of most of the coastline. At the same time, American companies began exploiting oil resources in Saudi Arabia and Iraq. World War II

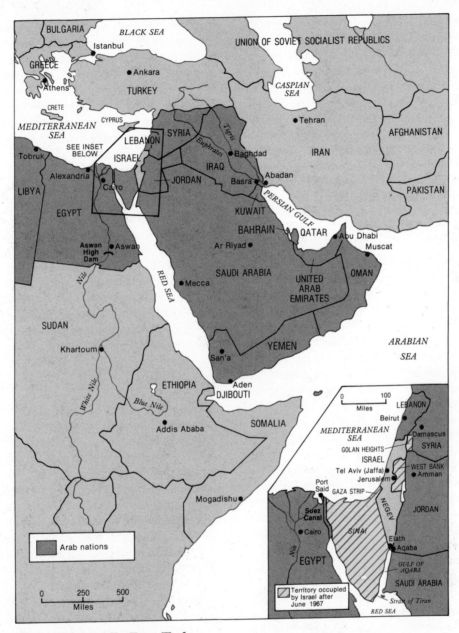

29.1 The Middle East Today

underscored the strategic importance of the Middle East, Germany's failure to gain access to the oil fields being a crucial factor in its defeat.

A slow evolution in the status of some of the Arab trust territories had begun during the interwar period. Iraq was admitted to the League of Nations in 1932, although British influence remained strong. In Transjordan a strongman who ruled with British backing was recognized as king in 1946, but British control was still so transparent that not until 1955 was the Kingdom of Jordan, including the West Bank area seized in the Palestine War, admitted to the United Nations. In Syria and Lebanon, French control lapsed during the Nazi occupation, and in 1946 both became independent. Although more advanced economically than Britain's mandates, both countries faced special challenges. There was no sectarian majority in Lebanon, where Muslim and Christian groups vied for dominance, while Syria was fragmented by religious and tribal divisions among both its majority Muslim and minority Christian populations.

The end of World War II brought rapid changes. In 1945 the League of Arab States was formed under British auspices, consisting originally of Egypt, Syria, Lebanon, Iraq, Transjordan, Saudi Arabia, and Yemen. Although many of these states were as yet in no credible sense independent, they rapidly became so as British influence waned, and the league coordinated the 1948 invasion of Palestine. Defeat produced an upsurge in anti-Western sentiment and a reassessment of the wider problems of Arab development and unity.

Nasser and the Egyptian Revolution

The most significant result of this ferment came in Egypt, where in 1952 the military revolution led by Gamal Abdel Nasser (1918–1970) drove out the corrupt, British-supported King Farouk, ending Britain's role in the Middle East and the last direct Western presence in the region. At first a revolutionary council attempted to govern Egypt through its civilian institutions and bureaucracy. When the latter refused to implement the council's directives on land reform, a military dictatorship was proclaimed. The council's nominal head was a senior general, but Nasser remained its true leader.

Nasser implemented a policy he called "guided democracy." Political parties and parliamentary institutions remained the goal of the regime, he declared, but until the masses had been prepared for active political life by reform and education, these could only serve the interests of the few. The press was brought under government regulation, and political activity was exercised through a single mass party, the Arab Socialist Union. In 1954, Nasser assumed direct control of the revolution as prime minister, and two years later, he unveiled a constitution guaranteeing basic rights, including racial, religious, and sexual equality.

Nasser's revolution was as much a social as a political one. While most of Egypt's 25 million people lived on an annual per capita income of $60, an elite of 12,000 people owned 37 percent of its arable land. Nasser broke up the great estates and distributed them among the peasantry, the smaller lots being subsumed into cooperative farms. The Permanent Council for National Production was established in 1953 to draft first a five-year and then a ten-year plan for integrated industrial and agricultural development. Crucial to the success of these plans was the Aswan Dam, which aimed to increase cultivated land by a third by harnessing the Nile River. When the United States, alarmed at Nasser's rising popularity in the Arab world and irked by his lack of enthusiasm for the Baghdad Pact, announced that it would not help to fund the dam, Nasser retaliated. He nationalized the Suez Canal, with the stated purpose of using its income to build a project that had become symbolic of his revolution as well as Third World hopes for independent development. His action sparked concern in Britain and France, which, with Israel, invaded Egypt to secure the canal in October 1956.

The effects of the episode were profound. Nasser emerged as a hero and became the recognized leader of the Arab world until his death. The government of Sir Anthony Eden was forced from office in Britain, and with the assassination of the Iraqi king Feisal II and his prime minister in 1958, the British were forced from their last bases in the Middle East. The United States entered the breach to forestall Soviet influence, and in 1958 its forces invaded Lebanon in support of pro-Western leadership. With Nasser and other Arab radicals looking to the Soviet Union for aid and the crucial oil resources of the region at stake, the Middle East became an important new area of superpower rivalry.

Israel and the Struggle for Palestine

Britain's first withdrawal from its position in the Middle East was in Palestine, where the conflict between Palestinian Arabs and Jewish settlers, compounded by an influx of refugees and Holocaust survivors, had reached a flashpoint. That conflict, in turn, represented a clash between the traditions of two great religions and the aspirations of two nascent nationalisms.

A small number of Jews had always lived in Palestine, to which the faithful believed their people would someday return to reestablish the ancient nation of Israel and await the coming of the messiah. The serious immigration to the region that commenced in the nineteenth century was spurred, however, not by millennial fervor but by a secular nationalist movement, Zionism. Theodor Herzl's vision of a Jewish homeland and Hitler's persecution had combined to increase the Jewish population of Palestine tenfold between the end of World War I and the end of World War II. From less than a tenth of the total population of the territory in 1917, it had increased to a third by 1947. The Arab majority greeted the Jewish influx first with suspicion and then with alarm. The entry of Western powers into the Middle East after World War I stimulated Arab nationalists, who saw the Jews as a spearhead of Western colonization.

Confronted by bitter and sometimes violent Arab resistance, the British government decided in 1939 to cap Jewish population in Palestine at one-third of the whole and to limit future land purchases. These new controls had broader implications as Britain, the United States, and other powers sought to restrict Jewish emigration from Nazi-held Europe. When the dimensions of the Holocaust were discovered at the end of World War II, there was humanitarian pressure to establish Palestine as a refuge for the remnants of European Jewry. The British Labour Party endorsed Zionist demands for the immediate creation of a Jewish commonwealth and in December 1944 called for the transfer of Palestinian Arabs to neighboring countries. Nothing came of these or more moderate postwar proposals for a federated Jewish-Arab state, which both sides rejected. The British, unwilling to maintain their trusteeship in the face of mounting terrorist attacks and unable to contain the illegal Jewish immigrants who ran their blockade, laid the problem before the United Nations in 1947. The General Assembly adopted a proposal to divide Palestine into three Jewish and three Arab sectors to form a Jewish and an Arab state, with Jerusalem as an international zone. All seven areas were to be linked in an economic union.

The resolution was welcomed by the Jews but rejected throughout the Arab world. The British refused to implement it on the grounds that it had not been accepted by both sides and withdrew their troops without transferring authority to either side. When the last units departed on May 14, 1948, the Jewish communal government proclaimed the State of Israel. A struggle immediately ensued for control of Palestine. Armies from Egypt, Syria, Lebanon, Jordan, and Iraq poured across the frontiers to assist the Palestinian Arabs, but the better-organized Jewish forces more than held their own. When a United Nations armistice halted the fighting in 1949, Israel controlled a third more territory than had been granted the Jews under the partition plan, while nearly 750,000 Palestinian Arabs had taken refuge in Lebanon, Syria, Jordan, and the Egyptian-occupied Gaza strip in southern Palestine.

DAVID BEN-GURION, ISRAEL'S FOUNDER

While still fighting, Israel held its first elections in January 1949. The fiery socialist, David Ben-Gurion (1886–1973), became Israel's first prime minister and its dominant political figure until his retirement in 1970. Born David Gruen in Plonsk, Poland (then a part of the Russian Empire), he was the son of a local Zionist leader.

At the age of 17 he startled the local Jewish community by calling for armed resistance against state-backed pogroms. Three years later, in 1906, he emigrated to Palestine, where he worked as a farmer in Jewish settlements and adopted the Hebrew name of Ben-Gurion ("son of the lion"). At the outbreak of World War I the Turks expelled him for his political activity.

Ben-Gurion responded to the Balfour Declaration by joining the British-sponsored Jewish Legion. Returning to Palestine after its capture from the Turks, he threw himself into political organization and in the next two decades forged the institutions that were to become the nucleus of the Jewish state, including the first agricultural cooperative in Palestine, the kibbutz. In 1920 he founded the Histadrut labor confederation, and ten years later he founded its political arm, the Mapai, or Israeli Workers' Party. Besides leading both organizations, he was elected chairman of the Zionist Executive, the supreme directive body of the Zionist movement, and head of the Jewish Agency, its executive branch.

When Britain, responding to Arab pressure, reneged on its commitment to a Jewish state in 1939, Ben-Gurion urged and later led armed resistance to it. In 1942 he convened an emergency meeting of Zionists in New York to decide on the establishment of a Jewish state as soon as the war in Europe ended. With the proclamation of Israel six years later, he became simultaneously its first prime minister and its minister of defense.

With a brief interval, Ben-Gurion remained Israel's prime minister from 1948 to 1963. During that period he shaped Israel's identity as a modern industrial state and the West's chief ally in the Middle East.

The First Arab-Israeli Wars

The most explosive question in the Middle East is the general nonrecognition of the Israeli state by the other powers in the region apart from Egypt and the insistence of Palestinian Arab nationalists that Palestine be restored to them. Four wars have been fought to date over this question. The Palestine War of 1948–1949 established Israel as a viable state while creating a major refugee problem. The Israelis refused to allow the 750,000 Palestinians who had fled their homes to return without guarantees of security from the neighboring Arab states, a point that became moot as the Arabs' abandoned homes and lands were occupied by the almost equal number of Jewish immigrants, mostly from the other countries of the Middle East, who flocked to the new state in the first two years of its existence. In effect, the massive population transfer envisioned by Zionists had taken place. But the surrounding Arab states were unable and for political reasons unwilling to accept the tide of Palestinian refugees who crowded at their borders. Instead, the Palestinians were interned in squalid camps along the narrow Gaza strip and on the West Bank of the Jordan River, previously part of Palestine but now annexed by Jordan. The Palestinian Arabs thus became a people without a country.

Arab nationalists regarded Israel not only as a usurper in the region but also as an agent of Western interests. These suspicions were confirmed when, in October 1956, Israel joined a Franco-British force in an invasion of Egypt after Nasser nationalized the French- and British-owned Suez Canal Company. For the British in particular, Egypt's control of the Canal threatened important interests in the Far East, while Israel, alarmed at an Egyptian arms buildup, felt that a preemptive strike was essential to its security. The United States, furious at the independent action of its allies, joined the Soviet Union in calling for an immediate cease-fire and withdrawal. Faced with the threat of ruinous economic sanctions, the British and French capitulated. Israel too withdrew, the damaging identification with colonial interests only partially compensated by the opening of the Gulf of Aqaba to Israeli shipping.

In 1964, Israel began to divert water from the Jordan River to irrigate the Negev. Jordan protested, and an Arab summit conference set up a command force to coordinate guerrilla activities against Israel and to serve as a provisional government for the refugees, the Palestine Liberation Organization (PLO). Egypt, Syria, and Jordan announced plans to attack Israel. When Nasser ordered UN peacekeeping forces to leave the Sinai in May 1967 and closed the Gulf of Aqaba, the Israelis struck. In a campaign lasting only six days, Israel swept across the Sinai, seized the West Bank, including Jerusalem, and drove Syria off the strategic Golan Heights. Israel had occupied some 28,000 square miles, three times its own territory, in one of the swiftest, most decisive military victories in modern times. In November the UN Security Council adopted a resolution demanding Israel's withdrawal from the occupied areas but also calling for a settlement that would recognize the nation's right to exist.

North Africa

Nasser's revolution in Egypt was a model for many emerging nations in the postwar period, but its influence was most direct on its North African neighbors. By 1956 the French protectorates of Morocco and Tunisia and the British-occupied Sudan had achieved full self-government, largely under the impetus of Egypt's example, and the former Italian colony of Libya became independent in 1951.

The French refused to consider withdrawal from Algeria, which had the largest population of European settlers in North Africa. A war of national liberation ensued between 1954 and 1962. The French poured troops into Algeria until, in 1958, the domestic strain proved more than the Fourth Republic could bear. In May, rightist elements working with military authorities in Algeria took over the colonial government in Algiers. From there the rebels extended their control to Corsica and were on the verge of sending paratroopers into Paris itself, whereupon the National Assembly, as we have seen, gave de Gaulle virtually dictatorial powers for six months to restore order and draft a new constitution. Once he had established the Fifth Republic, he imposed its rule in Algeria and finally arranged a plebiscite that approved Algerian independence.

The rapid formation of new states in the postwar period failed to give definitive shape or stability to Arab nationalism. Tribal groups that were dispersed over various borders, such as the Kurds of Turkey, Syria, Iran, and Iraq, demanded a homeland of their own. Radical nationalist parties, such as the Ba'ath movement in Syria and Iraq, remained dissatisfied with the conservative, pro-Western regimes left behind in the wake of the imperial powers. Pan-Arabic pressures for political unification between separate states also remained strong. In 1958, Syria and Egypt formed the United Arab Republic, with Nasser as president. Ardent Arab nationalists saw this union as the precursor of a grand Islamic federation but were soon disillusioned when the Egyptians moved to control Syria's government and economy. Following a Syrian army rebellion in 1961, the union was dissolved by mutual consent, but the dream of a single, unitary state remains embedded in Arab nationalism.

Sub-Saharan Africa

The first important stirrings of nationalism in Africa south of the Sahara had begun in the 1910s in West Africa, but not until after World War II did independence movements begin to take hold. Britain began preparations for the independence of its colonies by sharing power with native officials and continuing the substantial financial grants for economic development that had

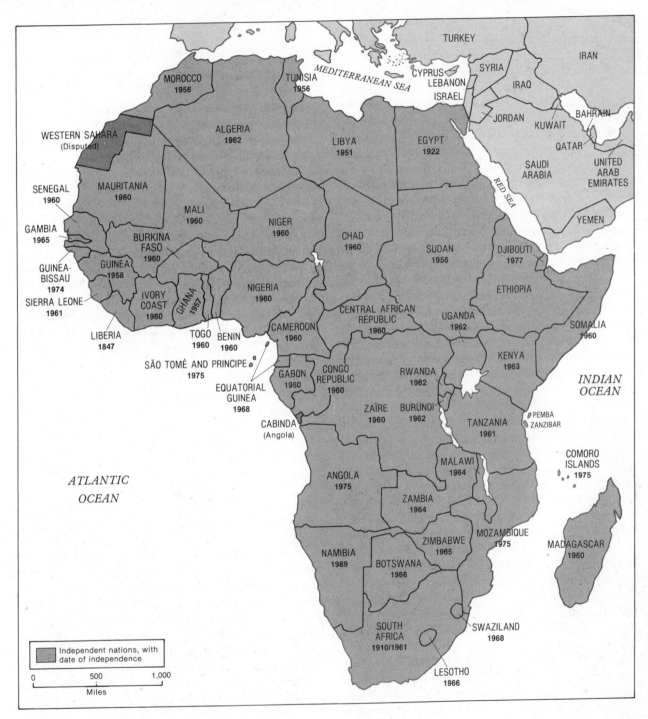

29.2 Africa Today

been initiated in the interwar period. The British also gave priority to educational development and the provision of technical assistance in such areas as medicine and communications. Thus the British did more than other European colonial powers to prepare their colonies for independence. When, for example, the Gold Coast became the independent state of Ghana in 1957, 1,500 Africans already held top positions in the civil service.

Fewer than a dozen Africans held such posts in the Belgian Congo at the time of its independence in 1960.

Although the British peacefully vacated the rest of their West African colonies, including Nigeria (1960), Kenya posed problems. There the European settlers strongly opposed the loss of their privileged status, while African militants known as the Mau Mau used terrorist tactics in an effort to drive the British out. By the time they were crushed in 1956, the Mau Mau had murdered more than 12,000 Africans who refused to join them as well as nearly 100 Europeans and various Asians. In the ensuing years all of the British territories in East Africa became independent with the exception of Southern Rhodesia, which repudiated its ties to Britain in 1965 to maintain a white supremacist regime.

In contrast to its militant imperialism in North Africa, France adopted a more flexible policy toward its colonies in West Africa and Madagascar. In 1956 the French created representative institutions in these territories, and two years later the colonies were allowed to vote for independence or membership in the French Community as autonomous republics. By 1960 all were independent, though they relied on France for economic and technical assistance and their elites remained largely French in culture.

Africans in the Belgian Congo, inspired by what was happening in the French colonies, demanded independence. After riots in 1959 the Belgian government decided to hold parliamentary elections and declared the Congo independent in June 1960. Not only had the Belgians failed to educate and train African leaders, but they also made no effective provision to ensure the peaceful transition of power in a land torn by tribal rivalries. Belgian irresponsibility condemned the Congolese to a decade of civil war when the province of Katanga seceded in July 1960. American support for the authoritarian rule of Joseph Mobutu, who became president in 1965, finally restored order to Zaïre, as the Congo became known.

Apart from the white supremacist states of Rhodesia and the Union of South Africa, only the Portuguese colonies of Angola and Mozambique and small Spanish holdings on the Moroccan coast remained under white domination after the mid-1960s. Another decade would pass before Portugal liberated its African colonies after nearly 15 years of guerrilla warfare. Guerrillas and an international boycott combined in 1979 to win majority rule for Africans in Rhodesia, henceforth known as Zimbabwe.

SUMMARY

The early 1960s were a watershed in the history of the postwar West. For the most part the West, responding reluctantly to the nationalistic aspirations of its colonies, reconciled itself to their loss. Newly emergent nations struggled to establish themselves, often in the context of the global political rivalry of the United States and the Soviet Union. As the sun set on Western imperialism, the United States embarked on a costly and ultimately futile effort to contain the communist advance in Southeast Asia. Half a world away, Israel defended its existence in the Six Day War and, in doing so, made Jerusalem wholly its own. Kennedy and Khrushchev took the world to the brink of nuclear war in the Cuban missile crisis, and the Berlin wall stood as mute testimony not only to the failure of communism in eastern Europe but also to the inability of the great powers to resolve the future of Germany. In Rome the Catholic church undertook its most important reform in modern times.

The years 1963 and 1964 witnessed a host of crucial changes in political leadership in the Western world. Kennedy, whose efforts to revive Roosevelt and Truman administration programs met with only minimal success, was assassinated in 1963; the outpouring of grief and adulation that followed enabled his successor, Lyndon Johnson, to launch the ambitious and costly Great Society. The following year, Kennedy's nemesis, Nikita Khrushchev, was forced to resign as premier of the Soviet Union in favor of a more conservative regime. Conservative governments fell in Canada in 1963 and Britain in 1964, while in Italy the "opening to the left" led to the inclusion of Socialists in the cabinet for the first time in 1963. Adenauer of West Germany and Ben-Gurion of Israel resigned their offices in 1963, the year of Pope John XXIII's death. The years that followed brought new leaders to the helms of their nations; the United States, Canada, Britain, Italy, and West Germany all moved politically to the left; and tension between the superpowers slowly eased. Ahead, however, lay a period of profound social turbulence.

Suggestions for Further Reading

Dockrill, M. L. *The Cold War, 1945–1963.* Atlantic Highlands, N.J.: Humanities Press, 1988.

Donhoff, M. *Foe into Friend: The Makers of the New Germany from Konrad Adenauer to Helmut Schmidt.* London: Weidenfeld & Nicolson, 1982.

al-Fassi, A. *The Independence Movements in Arab North Africa,* trans. H. Z. Nuseibeh. New York: Octagon, 1970.

Fejto, F. *A History of the People's Democracies: Eastern Europe Since Stalin,* trans. D. Weissbort. New York: Praeger, 1971.

Kaufman, B. I. *The Korean War: Challenges in Crisis, Credibility, and Command.* Philadelphia: Temple University Press, 1986.

Kurzman, D. *Ben-Gurion: Prophet of Fire.* New York: Simon & Schuster, 1983.

Louis, W. R. *The British Empire in the Middle East, 1945–1951.* New York: Oxford University Press, 1986.

———, and Owen, R., eds. *Suez 1956: The Crisis and Its Consequences.* New York: Oxford University Press, 1989.

Milward, A. S. *The Reconstruction of Western Europe 1945–51.* Berkeley: University of California Press, 1984.

Nove, A. *Stalinism and After: The Road to Gorbachev,* 3rd ed. London: Unwin Hyman, 1989.

Ovendale, R. *The Origins of the Arab-Israeli Wars.* London: Longman, 1984.

Robbins, K. *The Eclipse of a Great Power: Modern Britain 1870–1975.* London: Longman, 1983.

Tarrow, S. *Democracy and Disorder: Protest and Politics in Italy, 1965–1975.* New York: Oxford University Press, 1989.

Ulam, A. *Expansion and Coexistence: The History of Soviet Foreign Policy, 1917–1967.* New York: Praeger, 1974.

Urwin, D. W. *Western Europe Since 1945.* London: Longman, 1985.

30

OLD CONFLICTS,
NEW BEGINNINGS

In the last decades of the twentieth century the superpowers began to realize the limits of their influence, especially after the American experience in Southeast Asia and the Soviet invasion of Afghanistan. They discovered as well that some areas of the globe, such as Iran and parts of the Middle East, bitterly opposed their involvement. Relations between the superpowers themselves were in considerable flux. The 20-year Cold War eased in the mid-1960s as the era of détente—relaxation of tensions—dawned. The Reagan presidency (1981–1989) brought renewed hostility and diplomatic strain until the initiatives of Soviet leader Mikhail Gorbachev in the late 1980s offered the best hope for improved U.S.-Soviet relations since World War II. The Cold War ended in 1990 when the occupying powers along with East and West Germany signed the Treaty on the Final Settlement with Respect to Germany, paving the way for German reunification in October of that year. The Soviet Union itself disintegrated in 1991 amid economic chaos and competing nationalisms, and Yugoslavia broke up as well.

The post-1965 era was also marked by important strides toward European unity and decreased tensions between eastern and western Europe, especially as the Soviet sway over eastern Europe collapsed. Relations between Western nations and the Middle East, however, were rocked by the rise of Islamic fundamentalism and the continuing Palestinian conflict. Another major source of instability was the assertion of separatist tendencies in numerous areas, including the Catholics in Northern Ireland; the Kurds in Iran, Iraq, and Turkey;

and the Shi'ites in Lebanon. The late 1960s was a time of social upheaval, and the 1970s and 1980s brought renewed demands for the rights of women and minorities.

WESTERN EUROPE

Beginning in the mid-1960s, the western European states entered into a period of creative experimentation designed to find workable solutions to old problems. The Italians embraced the "opening to the left" and pondered the inclusion of the Communists in the government, while the Social Democrats of West Germany made overtures to improve relations with their eastern European neighbors, a policy referred to as *Ostpolitik*. The Greeks, the Spaniards, and the Portuguese introduced democratic governments after periods of dictatorship, and the British in the 1980s reacted sharply to postwar socialism by embracing the Conservatives' program of "privatization." The most ambitious movement was the concerted effort toward European unification; the most dramatic was German reunification.

Bold Initiatives
in the Major Democracies

Alone among the major western European countries, France did not turn to a government of the left in the

30.1 Postwar Europe to 1990

1960s, although the Socialists and Communists increased their strength throughout the decade. Despite angering both the ultranationalists by his program of Algerian independence and the left by his authoritarian style, Charles de Gaulle beat back all opponents, appealing to yearnings for the recovery of France's lost grandeur. After creating a strong, popularly elected presidency, he charted a foreign policy intended to demonstrate French independence of American influence, including the development of a nuclear arsenal. He treated the United Nations with disdain, accorded diplomatic recognition to the People's Republic of China, withdrew French forces from NATO, blocked British entry into the Common Market, ended aid to Israel, and improved relations with the Soviet Union. Distrustful of Soviet aims, however, he sought to forge closer links with West Germany and three of the more restive Soviet satellites, Czechoslovakia, Hungary, and Romania.

De Gaulle's haughty demeanor nearly enabled the Socialists and Communists to overcome his majority in the Assembly in 1967, but the following year the left sustained a setback when university students, angered by overcrowded classes and rigid examinations, scornful of postwar materialism, and inspired by antiwar agitation in the United States, rioted. The students were soon joined by millions of workers who occupied factories. The crisis became the most serious civil disturbance in France in a century. De Gaulle secured the army's support, urged massive right-wing demonstrations, and called for new elections, which his supporters won handily. Within a year, however, he lost a vote of confidence and resigned.

The Gaullist tradition dominated French politics for another five years under Georges Pompidou. He dropped French opposition to British membership in the Common Market, devalued the franc to increase French exports, and adopted a more cooperative attitude toward NATO, all signs that Gaullist stridency was ebbing. The center-right continued in power under Valéry Giscard d'Estaing, whose presidency (1974–1981) was marked by unfulfilled promises of social reform.

Giscard d'Estaing's growing unpopularity, coupled with a rebuilding of the Socialist party in the 1970s, enabled its leader, François Mitterrand, to win the presidency in 1981 while his party gained control of Parliament. Although Mitterrand included Communists in his cabinet, he condemned Soviet policy in Afghanistan and was friendlier to the United States than the Gaullists had been. He nationalized French banks and some industries, but unlike most European leftists, he was not opposed to nuclear deterrence and continued France's nuclear armaments.

Under Mitterrand's leadership, French women made notable gains, including the right to hold any civil service post, parental leave to care for sick children, and government monitoring of employment conditions for women in the private sector. In 1986 a conservative coalition gained control of the National Assembly, forcing Mitterand to appoint the Gaullist Jacques Chirac as prime minister.

Chirac returned some of the nationalized industries to private ownership. The French electorate, however, proved unwilling to move decidedly in either a liberal or a conservative direction, voting Mitterrand a second term as president in 1988 but giving neither the Socialists nor the conservatives a majority in the National Assembly.

In West Germany, following Adenauer's retirement in 1963, the Christian Democrats retained their hold on the chancellorship through the tenure of Ludwig Erhard, the architect of his country's economic recovery. Erhard, like Adenauer in 1957 and 1961, had to govern in a coalition with the centrist Free Democrats. In 1966 the Christian Democrats, weary of being hostage to this small party, formed a coalition with their major rivals, the Social Democrats, who had renounced the vestiges of their Marxism seven years earlier. The new chancellor, Kurt Kiesinger, appointed the Social Democratic leader Willy Brandt as his foreign minister, but their government was stymied by conflict. Brandt's desire to improve relations with West Germany's Communist neighbors, for example, was checked by Kiesinger, who shared Adenauer's dislike of Moscow and its satellites.

After the 1969 elections the Free Democrats threw their support to the Social Democrats, enabling Brandt to become the country's first Socialist chancellor. The hallmark of Brandt's tenure was his policy of *Ostpolitik,* a bold attempt to improve relations with the Communist states of eastern Europe. The results were striking: a treaty with the Soviet Union in which each country renounced the use of force to settle security issues, a treaty with Poland accepting the Oder-Neisse boundary imposed at the Potsdam conference, improved relations with East Germany, and the admission of both German states to the United Nations. Brandt's spirit of reconciliation was no less dramatically manifested when he knelt on the site of the Warsaw ghetto to indicate Germany's remorse for Nazi crimes and when he visited Jerusalem to express sorrow for the Holocaust.

Although Brandt resigned in 1974, the Social Democrats retained control of the government under the leadership of Helmut Schmidt. His chief accomplishment was an extension of the policy of "codetermination," under which workers in all companies employing more than 2,000 people enjoyed equal representation with their employers on supervising boards. Schmidt, a victim of the conservative reaction that swept much of the West in the 1980s, was ousted in 1982 by Helmut Kohl, a Christian Democrat. But the Brandt legacy continued as Kohl sought to heal the wounds of World War II and to improve relations with the Soviet Union, in part by reducing nuclear weapons in Europe.

Thanks in part to financial subsidies from West Germany, Communist East Germany enjoyed the highest standard of living and the strongest industrial base in eastern Europe. Nevertheless, East Germans experienced shortages of consumer goods, massive environmental damage, and a decaying infrastructure. As the spirit of reform swept eastern Europe in 1989, Erich Honecker was ousted with the acquiescence of the Soviet Union. After antigovernment demonstrations in East Germany in the fall of 1989, the Berlin Wall was breached, the border with West Germany was opened, and the resulting influx of East Germans to the West set the stage for negotiations that led to the reunification of Germany in October 1990. The process was speeded when the Soviet Union agreed that the new country could be a member of NATO and that Soviet troops would be withdrawn from East Germany within three to four years. The four powers that had occupied Germany since 1945—the United States, the Soviet Union, Britain, and France—joined with West and East Germany in signing the Treaty on the Final Settlement with Respect to Germany, effectively ending the Cold War. In the treaty, Germany pledged to respect its existing border with Poland and renounced the manufacture or possession of nuclear, biological, and chemical weapons. Despite the costs of integration, including the restructuring of East German industry, the united Germany is one of the world's major economic powers, ranking first in exports in 1990 ($354.1 billion, compared to $321.6 billion for the United States) and second in favorable balance of trade ($73.9 billion, compared to $77.5 billion for Japan and a deficit of $138 billion for the United States). In 1990 Germans held their first free national elections since 1932; with the victory of the Christian Democrats, Helmut Kohl became the first chancellor of a reunited Germany. The cost of unification coupled with growing numbers of immigrants subjected the country to mounting civil unrest, much of it sparked by neo-Nazis.

Like West Germany, Italy experimented with its own version of a grand coalition of the two major political parties, the Christian Democrats and the Communists, but only after Aldo Moro's "opening to the left" proved ineffective and succeeding cabinets were undermined by feuding among Italy's numerous political parties. Italian students and factory workers, inspired by their French counterparts, launched crippling protest movements in 1968 and 1969, and in the latter year, Communist and neofascist extremists resorted to terrorist tactics to publicize their causes. In the face of this threat to social stability, which evoked memories of the early 1920s, the Communist leader Enrico Berlinguer proposed a "historic compromise" in 1973; under its terms his party offered to cooperate with the Christian Democrats in a coalition government. Berlinguer, who insisted that his party was independent of Moscow, pledged to respect constitutional rights and continue Italian membership in NATO. His version of Socialism, increasingly popular in Spain and France as well, was known as Eurocommunism; largely a reaction to Soviet intervention in Hungary and Czechoslovakia, it was built on the principle of cooperation and dialogue with Western democratic governments.

Opposition to the historic compromise by the United States and conservative elements within the Christian Democratic party kept the Communists out of the cabinet, although Aldo Moro consulted with them about affairs of state. The Communists controlled local governments in such cities as Florence and Naples, participated in some of the regional governments, and, commencing in 1976, held key posts in Parliament. Two years later, they formally voted with the parliamentary majority, the first time this had happened since 1947. Although the Communists continued to be excluded from the cabinet, largely at the insistence of the United States, the Christian Democrats yielded the premiership in 1981 to a member of the small Republican party. In 1983 the Christian Democrats supported a coalition government led by the Socialist Bettino Craxi, although by decade's end it too had given way to more cabinets headed by Christian Democrats.

The Christian Democrats' traditional influence was shaken by the passage of reform legislation permitting divorce (1970) and abortion (1978), both of which were opposed by the Catholic church. Legal abortion quickly became widespread in Italy: the approximately 240,000 abortions in 1980 represented more than 800 for every 1,000 live births. The feminist movement, which had pushed hard for the abortion law, achieved other successes in the 1970s, including state support for nursery schools, the founding of women's health clinics offering birth control counseling, and legislation guaranteeing equal pay for equal work.

British voters, signaling their unhappiness with the gradual weakening of welfare programs under the Conservatives, gave Labour a narrow victory in 1964. Under the leadership of Harold Wilson the welfare state was rejuvenated with increased funds for social services and public housing, but deficits inherited from the Conservative governments forced Wilson to devalue the pound, thereby undermining the country's financial prestige, and to relinquish Britain's military commitments east of the Suez. The reduction of overseas responsibilities was not enough to offset the Conservative deficit and expanded domestic programs, forcing Labour to increase taxes by 80 percent between 1964 and 1970.

Calling for reduced taxes and less government, Edward Heath and the Conservatives regained control of the government in 1970. Although he secured British admission to the Common Market, Heath's battle with the unions to hold wages down cost his party the 1974 election and returned Wilson to power. Wilson tried vainly to curb wage demands by the unions through a "social contract," by which the Trades Union Congress agreed to urge its members to be moderate. Inflation, which had risen steadily since 1967, peaked at nearly 25 percent, a record high, in 1975, and the pound plunged an equal amount in value. The following year, Wilson resigned. His heritage included an equal-pay-for-equal-work act (1970) and a sex discrimination law (1975).

Under Wilson's successor, James Callaghan, the economy improved dramatically, thanks in part to North Sea oil production. By 1978, inflation had dropped to approximately 7 percent, but unemployment was growing, and taxes on the wealthy were nearly confiscatory, with rates of 83 percent for salaried income and 98 percent for investment income in the highest tax bracket. During the winter of 1978–1979 the unions spurned the social contract, discrediting Callaghan and setting the stage for the victory of Margaret Thatcher and the Conservatives.

Margaret Thatcher and U.S. Secretary of State Henry Kissinger meet in 1975. [UPI/Bettmann]

MARGARET THATCHER: BRITAIN'S "IRON LADY"

Margaret Thatcher's triumph in 1979 made her the first woman prime minister in the West, an ironic fact given Britain's dismal performance in entrusting high office to women. Thatcher did not owe her victory to the feminist movement, nor did she expand the role of women in British government; apart from the prime minister herself, her first cabinet included only one woman, her second none. Although dismissive of efforts to legislate women's rights, she was convinced of women's ability to govern.

The daughter of a grocer and a dressmaker, Margaret Roberts was born on October 13, 1925, and graduated from Oxford University with a degree in chemistry. Although she failed to win her first two races for a seat in the House of Commons, in 1950 and 1951, she passed the bar examination. By the time she ran again, in 1959, she was married to the businessman Denis Thatcher. As member of Parliament (M.P.) for a London borough she advanced rapidly, serving as joint parliamentary secretary to the Ministry of Pensions and National Insurance in 1961 and then, during the Wilson years, as an opposition spokesperson for transportation and education. For this, Edward Heath rewarded her in 1970 with the ministry of education, a post in which her propensity for strong action and decisive leadership made enemies quickly; Heath soon relieved her of the position. A year after his loss to Wilson in 1974, Heath was ousted by Thatcher from the party leadership. In the 1979 election she led her party to victory on a campaign of lower taxes and war on crime.

Thatcherism, as the conservative programs associated with Thatcher have been labeled, was rooted in a commitment to reduce and redefine the role of government, with an emphasis on private initiative and enterprise. To curb inflation, she cut taxes, reduced social programs, raised interest rates, subjected local government to tight central controls, and made unions responsible for illegal industrial action. The cost in unemployment was high—1 million in the 1980s—evoking memories of the Great Depression. Although Thatcher won general elections in 1983 and 1987, her popularity plummeted in 1989 in the face of major economic problems. A controversial poll (head) tax that replaced property taxes as the principal source of revenue for local governments sparked bitter resentment.

Thatcher's foreign policy was marked by close ties to the United States and West Germany and firm but friendly discussions with the Soviet Union. She took Britain into war against Argentina in 1982 to retain one of the last British colonies, the Falkland Islands off the Argentine coast. Britain's victory in the largest naval engagements since World War II restored a degree of national self-esteem but at the cost of straining British and U.S. relations with Latin America. Thatcher's policy toward Northern Ireland, with its sectarian rivalries, had little effect, although she negotiated a 1985 agreement with the Republic of Ireland granting that country a major advisory role in Northern Irish affairs. British troops have had only mixed success in curbing terrorist violence by the Irish Republican Army, funded in part by private donations from the United States, and the Ulster Freedom Fighters, a group of Protestant extremists.

Courageous, headstrong, and determined to deregulate the economy in the interests of the financial and service sectors, Thatcher elicited strong reactions from supporters and opponents alike. As her unpopularity increased, Thatcher's own party forced her to resign in 1990, but she retained enough influence to ensure the selection of her protégé, John Major, as the new prime minister. Despite a lingering recession, he led his party to victory in the 1992 election.

Fledgling Democracies in the Mediterranean

In the late twentieth century the Mediterranean states of Greece, Portugal, and Spain struggled to establish stable democratic governments. Greek democracy sustained a severe blow in 1967 when army officers seized control of the state to prevent a center-left coalition from governing. Their dictatorial regime collapsed in 1974 when intervention in Cyprus against the minority Turkish population prompted Turkey to invade the island and place a portion of the Greek majority under military rule. In the aftermath of the colonels' disgrace, democracy

was restored under the leadership of Constantine Karamanlis, and the Greeks officially declared themselves a republic in 1975. Unlike Britain and France, which took the conservative road in the 1980s, Greece turned to the left in 1981, electing the Socialist Andreas Papandreou prime minister. In 1989, Greek voters unseated Papandreou's scandal-ridden government, and in 1990 they gave a narrow majority to the conservative New Democratic party.

The Portuguese suffered under the dictatorial rule of Antonio Salazar (1889–1970) and his protégé Marcelo Caetano until insurgent army officers, angered by the costly effort to maintain imperial control over Angola and Mozambique, overthrew the government in 1974. Free elections followed, but no party won a parliamentary majority, leaving the Portuguese with precarious coalition governments.

The sun set on Fascist Spain in 1975 with the death of Francisco Franco, whose regime had been gradually moderated as its leader aged. As Franco had decreed, the Bourbon monarchy was restored, although King Juan Carlos moved quickly to give Spain a liberal constitution. Cooperating effectively in the Cortes (parliament), the major political parties dealt with the country's most explosive problem, the separatist demands of the Basques and the Catalonians, by granting substantial autonomy to the peoples of each region. The Cortes also reduced the special privileges of the Catholic church and encouraged industrial expansion. With the support of women's groups, which were stronger in Spain than in Greece or Portugal, reformers passed a limited divorce law in 1981. Despite relatively high inflation and a growing trade deficit, the Socialist party dominated Spanish politics in the 1980s.

The Search for European Unity

Tentative steps toward political unity in Europe were taken in 1949 with the establishment of the Council of Europe, made up of a consultative assembly, popularly called the European Parliament, and a committee of ministers. Originally designed to create a political and economic union, the council lowered its expectations from unification to international cooperation in the face of opposition by western European states to relinquishing their sovereignty.

The movement for European unity made substantial headway in the economic sphere. The first important step came with the founding in 1951 of the European Coal and Steel Community, whose six members (France,

West Germany, Italy, Belgium, the Netherlands, and Luxembourg) agreed to the joint administration of their coal and steel industries. This was an enlightened solution to the long-standing interest of Germany in the iron ore deposits of Belgium, France, and Luxembourg and of France's desire for Saarland coal. Britain, however, refused to participate in the consortium. Six years later, the six nations signed the Treaty of Rome establishing the European Economic Community (EEC), popularly called the Common Market, the major purpose of which was the gradual elimination of tariff barriers among members. Feeling threatened by the potential economic power of the EEC, Britain and six other nations (the Scandinavian states, Austria, Switzerland, and Portugal) founded the European Free Trade Association in 1959. When the British, tempted by the EEC's dramatic success, belatedly sought admission, the French opposed their membership, primarily because the British insisted on retaining privileged economic ties to their Commonwealth of Nations. Britain, along with Ireland and Denmark, finally gained admission in 1973, and Greece, Portugal, and Spain joined in the following decade.

The European Community made ambitious plans for the further integration of their economies. If implemented, no major barriers to internal trade among the 12 member nations would remain, their citizens would have unrestricted travel rights within the community, and national sales taxes would be "harmonized." The 12 are also considering a common currency and a central bank. The community, with a population of 340 million (including the united Germany), would be larger than the United States (population 248 million) and have a gross national product nearly as large ($4.29 trillion compared to $4.53 trillion in 1987).

THE SOVIET UNION AND EASTERN EUROPE

The decades following Khrushchev's fall gave rise to domestic and foreign policy initiatives that were no less bold than those that occurred in the Western democracies, climaxed by the upheavals in eastern Europe and the Soviet Union that began in 1989. The Brezhnev years (1964–1982), while repressive at home, featured an attempt to reach an accommodation with the West, a policy referred to as détente. More dramatic were the changes initiated by Mikhail Gorbachev in the late 1980s under the rubric of *perestroika* ("restructuring") and *glasnost* ("openness"), both of which signaled major changes in domestic policy and ultimately contributed to the disintegration of the Soviet Union in 1991.

The Brezhnev Era

With Khrushchev forced into retirement, leadership of the Soviet Union was exercised by Leonid Brezhnev (1906–1982), the party secretary, with the assistance of premier Alexei Kosygin. Cautious bureaucrats, both had reacted negatively to Khrushchev's cult of personality, his open denunciation of Stalin's crimes, and the limited freedom he allowed to critics of the regime. Henceforth most dissent was sharply curtailed: Alexander Solzhenitsyn was expelled in 1974, and the government silenced other critics by declaring them insane, imprisoning them, exiling them, or blacklisting them from employment. Soviet Jews who wished to emigrate to Israel found it virtually impossible to obtain exit visas. The resumption of repression prompted intellectuals, including the Nobel Prize–winning physicist Andrei Sakharov and the Jewish activist Anatoli Shcharansky, to protest.

In other respects, Brezhnev's policies were constructive, as in the case of his increased emphasis on consumer production, which still lagged behind that of the West and even some of the satellite states. People who could afford automobiles had to place their names on long waiting lists, although public transport, like rent, was inexpensive. The quality of housing and consumer goods remained shoddy, agriculture lagged, and large but unacknowledged pockets of poverty as well as budget deficits characterized the economy. These problems had reached crisis proportions by the mid-1980s.

Like Khrushchev, Brezhnev urged the appointment of more women to executive positions, and he demonstrated concern as well for the onerous demands made on women who combined industrial and domestic responsibilities. Such obligations contributed to a rising divorce rate (which nearly tripled between 1960 and 1976), increased juvenile delinquency, and family instability. The position of women in Soviet society improved under Brezhnev: the proportion of women in institutions of higher education rose to 50 percent by 1976, the number of women associate and full professors increased, and the percentage of women holding management positions in the economy rose. Despite this effort, the percentage of women serving on the party's central committee was the same in 1976 as it had been in 1961 (3.3) and only one-third that of 1917.

Crises in Czechoslovakia and Poland

While Brezhnev was clamping down on dissent in the Soviet Union, the Communist leader in Czechoslovakia, Alexander Dubček, began to lift restrictions on political expression in 1968, with the encouragement of Romania and Yugoslavia. Dubček intended to give socialism "a human face" by liberalizing his country, at least to the extent of introducing modest economic freedom to spur growth. Mindful of Hungary's experience in 1956, Dubček reiterated Czechoslovakia's loyalty to the Warsaw Pact; simultaneously, however, he responded favorably to West German feelers for closer economic ties. Czech intellectuals published a manifesto entitled *Two Thousand Words* in which they pressed for democratic reforms and urged their government not to back down in the face of Soviet pressure. When the Czech Communists proposed major changes to liberalize their party, Brezhnev, pressured by Soviet generals, lost his patience.

On August 21, 1968, 175,000 troops, mostly Soviet but with Polish, East German, Hungarian, and Bulgarian contingents, invaded Czechoslovakia. At least 300,000 reinforcements followed in the greatest military operation Europe had seen since World War II. The Soviets forced Dubček to overturn his reforms before removing him from office and purging liberal elements. In November 1968, Brezhnev asserted the limited sovereignty of socialist states and the right of their sister regimes to intervene to protect the socialist system.

Notwithstanding the Brezhnev Doctrine (as this position was known), the Soviets refrained from sending troops into Poland, undoubtedly because the Polish government remained loyal to Moscow and, until 1988, did not introduce major reforms. The troubles began when severe economic problems, including food shortages, sparked massive labor unrest in 1970. As a result, Władysław Gomułka resigned under pressure. When labor unrest erupted again in 1980, the Catholic church and Polish intellectuals supported the striking workers. Under the leadership of Lech Wałęsa (born 1943) the workers won recognition for their independent union, Solidarity, and both it and the church gained legal access to the state-run radio and television. The following year, Polish farmers organized their own union, Rural Solidarity. In the face of continuing labor unrest and Soviet

concern, the Polish Politburo put General Wojciech Jaruzelski in charge of the country in 1981. Jaruzelski imposed martial law, arrested more than 6,000 members of Solidarity, and declared the union illegal.

Gorbachev: Perestroika and Glasnost

Following Brezhnev's death in 1982 and the brief tenures of two successors, Yuri Andropov and Konstantin Chernenko, Mikhail Gorbachev (born 1931) became general secretary in 1985. Breaking with the past, he soon called for public debate on national problems, acknowledging that Soviet economy and society were beset with serious difficulties. This call for open discussion—glasnost—was accompanied by an easing of restrictions on dissent and some relaxation of censorship.

Gorbachev's call for democratization. a logical extension of glasnost, led in 1989 to the first open election in Russia since November 1917. The election, in which numerous Communist dignitaries suffered defeat, featured secret ballots and public rallies. In 1990, Gorbachev persuaded the Communist Party's Central Committee to surrender the party's constitutional monopoly on political power, setting the stage for multiparty elections. Simultaneously, he established a strong presidency. The net effect of the changes was a substantial diminution of the party's power. Popular opposition to Gorbachev himself and support for his chief political rival, Boris Yeltsin, were manifested in massive urban demonstrations in 1991.

The most difficult component of Gorbachev's program was perestroika, an ambitious restructuring of the Soviet economy. At the heart of this policy in its early stages was the 1987 Law on State Enterprise, intended to make Soviet factories profitable by requiring them to purchase raw materials from suppliers, sell what they manufactured, and share any profits. The government dropped production quotas for the factories but replaced them with state orders that were substantial enough to monopolize most of their output. The net effect was to introduce some freedom into the industrial sector without sacrificing government planning. In the agricultural realm, perestroika enabled families to obtain long-term inheritable leases on land with the right to earn profits on what they raised. By moving toward a mixed agricultural economy (collectives continued to exist), Gorbachev hoped to reduce the Soviet Union's need to import food, which in the late 1980s required approximately 15 percent of the country's annual budget. At the

Below a statue of Lenin, Mikhail Gorbachev addresses the Congress of People's Deputies in May of 1989. [**Sergei Guneyev/***Time* **Magazine**]

the 1986 party congress had a higher (though still token) proportion of women than any previous one. Gorbachev built on the work of his immediate predecessors; by the time he took office, women comprised 54 percent of university students, 40 percent of the country's scientists and scholars, and 56 percent of its educated specialists. Women also made up 51 percent of the labor force.

The spirit of glasnost and democratization brought long-simmering tensions to the flashpoint among some of the national and ethnic groups in the Soviet Union. Violence erupted in Armenia in 1988 because of the treatment of Christian Armenians in neighboring Azerbaijan, which is predominantly Shi'ite Muslim. A rebellion by Azerbaijanis who were disenchanted with Moscow's rule in 1990 had to be quelled by the Soviet army. Meanwhile, the three Baltic republics—Latvia, Estonia, and Lithuania—began pressing for independence, and in July 1991 the parliament of the Ukraine passed a declaration of sovereignty but did not insist on independence. Ethnic nationalism mushroomed in the southwestern republics of Moldavia and Georgia, while cultural and religious ferment stirred in the Muslim republics of central Asia.

The proposed solution to this problem was a treaty of union that would have transferred considerable authority to the individual republics. On the eve of its signing in August 1991, a group of hard-liners in the KGB (the secret police), the Communist party, and the military demanded that Gorbachev invoke emergency measures and rule by decree to prevent the weakening of the central government and further erosion of the party's control. When Gorbachev refused, the reactionaries attempted to overthrow him, much as Khrushchev had been toppled in 1964. However, the conspirators failed to apprehend Yeltsin, president of the Russian Republic and an outspoken proponent of democratic reform. Inspired by Yeltsin's defiance, hundreds of thousands of Soviet citizens demonstrated against the coup in Moscow and Leningrad, and miners heeded Yeltsin's call to strike. The army itself was wracked by indecision, and its attempt to crack down on the Baltic republics only provoked increased demands for their independence. Western leaders intensified the pressure on the coup's leaders by suspending financial and technical aid to the Soviet Union. The collapse of the coup after a mere 72 hours was an eloquent testimony to the powerful forces that had been unleashed by glasnost and perestroika. In the aftermath of the coup, reformers led by Yeltsin and Gorbachev stripped the Communist party of its monopolistic powers, reorganized the Soviet Union as a loose confederation of largely autonomous republics,

same time he supported major arms reductions and implemented unilateral cuts in Soviet forces to reduce the pressure of military spending on the budget and the economy. Gorbachev also actively courted foreign investors, particularly West Germans and Americans, to pursue joint ventures in the Soviet Union. In 1990 and 1991 the government authorized the transition to a market economy, which led to increased shortages of consumer goods and food, sparking considerable disaffection.

Gorbachev demonstrated substantial interest in social issues and worked for improvements in the position of women even while underscoring the importance of the family. Like Khrushchev and Brezhnev, he called for the appointment of more women to executive positions, and

a. **Russia**		f. **Ukraine**		k. **Uzbekistan**	
Russian:	84%	Ukrainian:	73%	Uzbek:	69%
Ukrainian:	4%	Russian:	21%	Russian:	11%
Other:	12%	Jewish:	1%	Tajiks:	4%
		Other:	5%	Other:	16%
b. **Byelorussia**		g. **Moldavia**		l. **Kazakhstan**	
Byelorussian:	80%	Moldavian:	64%	Kazakh:	40%
Russian:	12%	Ukrainian:	14%	Russian:	40%
Polish:	4%	Russian:	13%	Ukrainian:	6%
Other:	4%	Other:	9%	Other:	14%
c. **Estonia**		h. **Georgia**		m. **Tajikistan**	
Estonian:	66%	Georgian:	69%	Tajiks:	58%
Russian:	28%	Armenian:	9%	Uzbek:	23%
Ukrainian:	3%	Russian:	8%	Russian:	11%
Other:	4%	Other:	14%	Other:	7%
d. **Latvia**		i. **Turkmenistan**		n. **Armenia**	
Latvian:	49%	Turkmen:	69%	Armenians:	90%
Russian:	38%	Russian:	13%	Azeris:	6%
Byelorussian:	5%	Uzbek:	9%	Russian:	3%
Other:	8%	Other:	9%	Other:	1%
e. **Lithuania**		j. **Azerbaijan**		o. **Kirghiz**	
Lithuanian:	80%	Azeris:	78%	Kirghiz:	48%
Russian:	9%	Russian:	8%	Russian:	26%
Polish:	8%	Armenian:	8%	Uzbek:	12%
Other:	3%	Other:	6%	Other:	14%

(Note: Numbers many not total 100 owing to rounding.)

30.2 Ethnic Composition of the Soviet Republics

and recognized the independence of Estonia, Latvia, and Lithuania. In a desperate attempt to preserve his crumbling authority, Gorbachev dissolved the Communist party, but the Soviet Union collapsed, leaving Yeltsin as the leading figure in a loose federation known as the Commonwealth of Independent States.

The swift collapse of the Soviet Union was the result of two principal factors. First, from the beginning it had felt compelled to build a military machine, buttressed by heavy industry, that was capable not only of defending itself but ultimately of extending its influence abroad. To achieve these ends, the Soviet Union imposed rigid economic and social controls, overburdening its people and channeling vast sums to the military and the arms race with the United States. Ultimately, the Soviet economy proved unable to sustain such demands. Gorbachev's efforts to move to a market economy through an orderly transition failed, bringing down the Soviet Union. Second, the Soviet Union succumbed to the

pressures of nationalist rivalries, which, in the end, proved to be stronger than ideological notions of international brotherhood.

MOSCOW, THE "MOTHER CITY"

Much of Russian history has been reflected in the development of Moscow. The soaring golden domes of the fifteenth-century Cathedrals of the Assumption and the Annunciation that rise from behind the imposing walls of the Kremlin testify to a Russian past in which Moscow, the "Mother City," was both the capital of the country and the spiritual center of the Orthodox faith. Although the site has been inhabited since Neolithic times, the origins of the city date to the twelfth century when a Russian prince constructed a wooden citadel, the Kremlin. Two centuries later, the Kremlin received its first stone walls, which enclosed palaces, churches, monasteries, and government buildings. The rulers of Moscow took the lead in driving the Mongols out of Russia and creating a unified state, but in the eighteenth century, Peter the Great, whose eyes were on the West, moved the capital to his new city of St. Petersburg. There it remained until Lenin transferred the center of government back to the Mother City in 1918.

Much of historic Moscow was destroyed during the Napoleonic invasion of 1812, but the city recovered dramatically. From a population of less than 300,000 in 1812 it mushroomed to nearly 2 million a century later, doubled to more than 4 million by 1939, and more than doubled again in the next 50 years to a population of 9 million in 1989. The city has expanded in a series of concentric rings, at the heart of which is the Kremlin and the adjacent Red Square. Like the spokes of a wheel, major roads radiate from the center of Moscow, reaching eventually to the towering white apartment complexes that dominate the outer rings and house much of the population in small flats. The middle and outer rings contain industrial plants, many of them built in the 1960s and in need of major renovation in the 1990s.

Moscow has been called a museum of Russian civilization and is in fact home to more than 60 museums, one of which is housed in the majestic sixteenth-century Cathedral of St. Basil. The Bolshoi Theater, completed in 1780 and twice reconstructed after fires in the nineteenth century, is the home of both opera and one of the world's greatest ballet companies. Lenin once addressed party meetings amid its splendor, but political gatherings now occur in the Palace of Congresses, built within the Kremlin's walls in 1961. Stalin had begun construction of a mammoth Palace of the Soviets shaped like a wedding cake and with a planned height of 1,161 feet, above which a 200-foot chromium-plated statue of Lenin would have stood; the unfinished building was dismantled in 1941 when its materials were needed for defense. "Stalin-Gothic" architecture can be seen in the buildings of Moscow University, constructed after World War II in the hills above the city; its central tower soars to a height of 994 feet. Fittingly, much of the dominant architecture in Moscow conveys the impression of great size.

Eastern Europe in Ferment

Gorbachev's reforms in the Soviet Union and his more open policy toward Eastern Europe made striking changes possible. The pressures for change were fueled by demands for economic reform and political democracy as well as long-standing nationalist resentment against Soviet domination.

In Poland, continuing economic woes prompted Jaruzelski to negotiate with Lech Wałęsa and other Solidarity leaders in 1989. Out of these talks came an agreement for democratic elections in June, but with the proviso that 65 percent of the seats in the lower house (Sejm) of parliament were reserved for Communists. That reservation applied to the 1989 election only. The Poles voted resoundingly for Solidarity candidates, giving them 99 of 100 seats in the newly created Senate. That body has a constitutional right to veto proposed legislation passed in the Sejm. As a result of this democratization, Jaruzelski, who was narrowly elected president, acquired Solidarity's support to implement economic reforms and obtain Western financial aid. To this end he asked Solidarity, with the cooperation of two minority parties, to form a government. The new prime minister, Tadeusz Mazowiecki, assumed primary responsibility for domestic affairs, though responsibility for the military and police remained in Communist hands. Jaruzelski soon stepped down, opening the way for new presidential elections in late 1990. Wałęsa emerged victorious, but the nation faced enormous economic problems, including an inflation rate of 200 percent, as it made the transition to a free economy.

Like Poland, Hungary experienced major economic difficulties in the late 1980s, including double-digit inflation and an $18 billion foreign debt. As political unrest mounted, Károly Grósz replaced János Kádár, who had run the country since the 1956 uprising, in 1988. Under Grósz's leadership, Hungary adopted a multiparty political system and scheduled elections. Grósz sanctioned economic reforms that entailed considerable private enterprise, including a stock market, and opened Hungary's borders, enabling a flood of refugees to enter from East Germany. In 1989 the Communist party reorganized itself as the Hungarian Socialist party.

Ethnic unrest and serious economic problems plagued Yugoslavia after Tito's death in 1980. A postwar federation forged of six republics and two semiautonomous provinces with five languages, two alphabets, and three major religious groups, Yugoslavia experienced turmoil as economic woes fanned national rivalries. In 1988 the inflation rate stood at 250 percent, unemployment at 16 percent, and the foreign debt at $21 billion. The most prominent Yugoslav political leader since Tito, Slobodan Milosevič, aggravated tensions by championing greater power for the Serbs, who comprised the largest ethnic group (36 percent) in the country. The republics of Slovenia and Croatia elected noncommunist governments in 1990, and both voted overwhelmingly the following year to become independent. After Bosnia-Herzegovina followed suit in 1992, Yugoslavia was reduced to little more than Serbia, which overran much of Bosnia in a fierce civil war characterized in part by the revival of concentration camps and the relentless shelling of urban centers.

Reform swept the other states of eastern Europe. In November 1989, nationwide demonstrations forced the resignation of the hard-line Czech government, and crowds cheered the political return of Alexander Dubček. The new president, Václav Havel, a playwright and champion of human rights, embraced a policy of conciliation at home and abroad, negotiated the withdrawal of Soviet troops from his country, and endorsed German reunification. Ethnic rivalries led to the division of Czechoslovakia into two republics. In Bulgaria a coup deposed the Stalinist ruler in November 1989. After renaming themselves Socialists, the Communists won more than half the seats in the Bulgarian parliament in the June 1990 elections; two months later, that body elected a member of the opposition to the presidency.

Romania's Nicolae Ceaușescu was overthrown and summarily tried and executed in December 1989. Ceaușescu, who had fostered a personality cult, had demolished much of the historic district of Bucharest to construct a government complex. Even more destructive was his program to raze approximately 8,000 of Romania's 13,000 villages and replace them with 500 "agro-industrial centers" at enormous cost to traditional rural life and ethnic minorities. In the spring of 1990, Romanians chose Ion Iliescu, a former Communist Party official, as their president; his goal was to remodel the economy along Socialist lines, with the government retaining control of heavy industry and agriculture. Albania, Europe's last Stalinist state, began implementing reforms in 1990.

NORTH AMERICAN NEIGHBORS

In the late twentieth century the United States vascillated between costly social programs and a laissez-faire approach to society and the economy. To the north, Canadians coped with a crisis over the future of Quebec and faced hard questions about the role of government in their society as well as their relations with the United States. Mexico, plagued by poverty and massive foreign debt, symbolized the vast gulf in the Americas between the affluent United States and Canada on the one hand and the countries of Latin America on the other.

The United States: From the Great Society to the Conservative Reaction

The bullets that killed John Kennedy in November 1963 caused an emotional outpouring that set the stage for passage of the New Frontier legislation. Aided by the political expertise of Kennedy's successor, Lyndon Johnson, Congress enacted landmark civil rights legislation in 1964 that prohibited discrimination both in interstate facilities and public services and by major employers and provided for the withdrawal of federal funds from schools that failed to desegregate. Civil liberties were further strengthened by the 1965 Voting Rights Act, which effectively abolished literacy tests in six southern states. The same year, Congress established the Medicare program to ensure medical care for people aged 65 and over. As part of his effort to build a "Great Society," Johnson launched a "war on poverty," the key elements of which were the creation of the Office of Economic Opportunity, which offered grants and loans to local governments; the Head Start program to provide preschool education for children in the slums; and VISTA, a domestic peace corps. Such programs were too costly for an administration that was also determined to

wage war in Southeast Asia and for a Congress that was too ready to fund the fighting by massive borrowing.

In the face of furious opposition to the Vietnam War, Johnson decided not to seek another term in 1968. A nation already rocked by violence was stunned by the assassination of Dr. Martin Luther King, Jr. in April and Robert Kennedy, a presidential candidate and the younger brother of the slain president, in June. Disillusioned by the war and domestic unrest, voters elected Richard Nixon to the presidency. Nixon's election and the strong showing of a third-party candidate, Governor George C. Wallace of Alabama, indicated the emergence of a new conservative majority that appealed to Americans concerned about the seeming decay of "law and order" and the demands of minorities for equal rights and social justice.

The new conservatism involved a major shift in the direction of domestic policy as Nixon blocked appropriations for Great Society programs and vetoed bills for urban development, education, and hospital construction. The deficit soared to record levels as Nixon spent heavily on the Vietnam War and weapons. An attempt to control inflation by federally imposed wage, rent, and price controls ultimately failed, but Nixon's foreign policy diverted the attention of voters. The president and his secretary of state, Henry Kissinger, normalized relations with the People's Republic of China, which was then admitted to the United Nations in place of the Nationalist government on Taiwan. The voters gave Nixon a huge victory in 1972, but within two years, his presidency in ruins and his reputation tarnished, he resigned after an unsuccessful attempt to cover up the responsibility of his reelection committee for burglarizing the offices of the Democratic National Headquarters in the Watergate complex in Washington, D.C. For two years the country stagnated during the caretaker presidency of Gerald Ford, whose extraordinary use of the veto (66 times in two and one-half years) blocked Democratic efforts to pass new social legislation.

Nixon's disgrace enabled Jimmy Carter and the Democrats to recapture the White House in the 1976 election, but Carter reflected conservative ideals in his call for a balanced budget, a streamlined government, and decreased regulation of airlines, banks, and the trucking and oil industries. Sharply rising oil prices sparked inflation that reached 18 percent, a peacetime record; the prime interest rate soared above 20 percent, also a new high. Carter's domestic woes were compounded by his seeming helplessness when Iranian revolutionaries seized 52 hostages at the American embassy in Tehran in 1979. At the polls in 1980 the voters turned to Ronald Reagan, spokesman of the New Right.

Reagan's political ideals were essentially of a piece with those of Margaret Thatcher. The role of government in society and the economy, he believed, should decrease; hence the Reagan years were marked by deregulation and lower taxes for corporations and the wealthy, yet the government deficit rose to record highs, pushed in part by the cost of a huge military buildup. Programs for the poor, education, and the environment sustained extensive cuts. Soaring deficits meant heavy borrowing overseas, turning the United States into a debtor nation for the first time since 1916. Like the administrations of Harding and Nixon, Reagan's was racked by illegalities and corruption, including the Iran-Contra scandal, which involved the unlawful sale of arms to Iran and the channeling of the profits to Nicaraguan rebels. Scores of presidential appointees were fired or forced to resign because of alleged wrongdoing, corruption in the Department of Housing and Urban Development diverted billions of dollars appropriated for the needy into the pockets of corrupt supporters of the administration, and scandals in the savings and loan industry cost the taxpayers at least $500 billion. These episodes failed to stem the conservative momentum, which continued with the election of George Bush in 1988. He continued the agenda of the New Right by opposing expanded federal aid for child care and urging the Supreme Court to overturn the 1973 *Roe* v. *Wade* decision that permitted virtually unrestricted abortion. Influenced by persistent recession and allegations of Bush's involvement in the Iran-Contra controversy, voters refused to reelect him in 1992, turning instead to Arkansas Governor Bill Clinton, a moderate Democrat who promised to revive the American economy, especially its infrastructure, and reform its health-care system.

Many of the social reforms of the 1960s survived the conservative reaction, although some were weakened. The women's movement remained active. As in Europe, employment opportunities for women rose sharply during World War II, and in the postwar years, women demonstrated a growing interest in careers that had hitherto been deemed largely male preserves. Between 1950 and 1984 the percentage of women engineers increased sixfold, that of lawyers and judges fourfold, and that of physicians nearly threefold. In 1964 the Civil Rights Act prohibited sex-based discrimination. The difficulty of implementing this legislation and overturning other barriers to equality led a number of women in the professions and civil service to found the National Organization for Women in 1966. Among its special concerns were government-supported day-care centers, maternity leaves that did not threaten job security, and abortion and contraceptive rights.

The feminist movement influenced the passage of reform legislation in the 1970s and 1980s, including state laws that banned discrimination in employment and affirmative action statutes that increased job opportunities for women. Carter appointed qualified women to his cabinet, the federal judiciary, and administrative departments; Reagan named the first woman, Sandra Day O'Connor, to the Supreme Court and accorded a similar honor to Jeanne Kirkpatrick, America's first woman ambassador to the United Nations. In 1984 the Democrats selected a woman, Geraldine Ferraro, as their vice-presidential nominee. But the feminists suffered setbacks too. Although Congress passed an equal rights amendment to the Constitution with the support of some prominent conservatives, such as Betty Ford, the Republican party refused to endorse it, and the proposal died when it received the support of only 35 of the 38 states needed for passage. The principal wording of the amendment summarized the fundamental belief of both feminists and human rights advocates: "Equality of rights under the law shall not be denied or abridged by the United States or by any State on account of sex."

Canada: An Identity Crisis

While the United States was bitterly divided in the late 1960s over the Vietnam War, Canada experienced an agonizing crisis over Quebec. The separatist cause gained momentum when Charles de Gaulle, visiting Montreal in 1967, called for "*un Ouébec libre*" ("a free Quebec"). The issue had been simmering for years, and the national government had appointed a Royal Commission on Bilingualism and Biculturalism in 1963. Six years later, federal legislation made both French and English the official languages of Canada. Under the Liberal prime minister Pierre Elliot Trudeau, the federal government attempted to implement this act, in part by requiring all civil servants to become bilingual, thus making French Canadians feel at home anywhere in the country. Still uneasy, Quebec began taking steps to make French the sole language of the province.

Militant separatists who belonged to the Front for the Liberation of Quebec (FLQ) embraced terrorist tactics in 1970, including the kidnapping of the British trade commissioner and the murder of Quebec's minister of labor and immigration. The government imposed the War Measures Act, which gave authorities virtually unlimited power to repress the violence. FLQ terrorism backfired as some Canadians lost faith in the separatist cause. Although the Parti Québécois continued to preach separatism, its popularity declined in the 1980s after nearly 60 percent of Quebec's voters rejected secession from Canada in a referendum. Progressive Conservative prime minister Brian Mulroney sought to resolve the future role of Quebec in 1987 by sponsoring a series of constitutional amendments recognizing the province as a "distinct society." Some of Quebec's sister provinces refused to ratify the amendments, leading to fresh demands by some Quebec citizens for independece.

In the 1980s a second critical question was Canada's relationship with the United States. That issue was sharply focused in the 1988 election when Mulroney urged Canadians to accept a free-trade agreement with the United States that would end tariffs on the movement of goods between the two countries; their bilateral trade was already the largest of any two partners in the world. The Liberal party opposed the proposed treaty, approved by the United States in 1988, largely because of fears that it would undermine Canadian sovereignty and weaken the country's extensive social and welfare programs. Unpersuaded, Canadians gave Mulroney a decisive victory. Although much less populous than their southern neighbor (26 million compared to 246 million), Canada was confident of its ability both to retain its distinctive identity and to enjoy closer relations with the United States.

Mexico: Social Tension and Economic Burdens

Like Canada, Mexico stepped up industrialization during World War II, which it entered on the Allied side in 1942. Between 1930 and 1946 the production of steel nearly doubled, and the generation of electricity increased 20 percent. Because of the wealth produced by industrialization, the national income nearly tripled between 1940 and 1945. Although per capita income rose dramatically, the distribution of wealth was grossly uneven, with little of the new money going to the poor. The social and economic changes had a direct impact on politics. Hitherto the dominant figures of the ruling Mexican Revolutionary Party had been agrarian reformers, labor leaders, and intellectuals, but by 1945, business and industrial magnates and economists had taken their place among the party dignitaries. Henceforth it was known as the Institutional Revolutionary Party (PRI).

Until 1958, Mexico's leaders stressed industrialization at the expense of agricultural reform. Some relief for the unemployed was provided through public works projects such as dams, highways, and a new campus for the National University of Mexico. When the PRI shed much of its traditional socialist rhetoric and the government devalued the peso in 1953, American investment increased substantially. The emphasis on industry and commerce and the neglect of rural problems enticed Mexicans to move to the cities. The population as a whole was also on the rise, doubling between 1934 and 1958.

During the presidency of Adolfo López Mateos (1958–1964) the PRI returned to its original commitment to major agrarian reform. Approximately 30 million acres of land were distributed to needy peasants. López Mateos invested government funds in foreign industries operating in Mexico, increased pensions for the elderly, and expanded public health care, leading to reductions in malaria, tuberculosis, and polio. Perhaps most striking was López Mateos' commitment to education, the single largest item in the national budget. All of this was accomplished without neglecting industry and commerce; by 1964, Mexico no longer needed to import oil, iron, or steel. In spirit and emphasis, López Mateos' administration was comparable to that of Lyndon Johnson, which was just getting underway in Washington. More similarities manifested themselves during the term of López Mateos' successor, Gustavo Díaz Ordaz, who, despite his commitment to social and economic programs, faced militant student demonstrations in 1968. The most violent of these occurred in the district of Tlatelolco, where government troops and vigilantes killed between 300 and 400 students.

The legacy of bitterness that resulted from the Tlatelolco massacre combined with an economic crisis to make the 1970s a turbulent decade in Mexico. New reforms, including the lowering of the voting age to 18 and progress on rural electrification and country roads, were insufficient to offset an inflation rate that exceeded 20 percent in 1973 and 1974 and an economy in which economic prosperity benefited the business community while bypassing the majority of the population. A mounting balance-of-payments deficit forced the government to devalue the peso in 1976 for the first time in 22 years, but the effectiveness of this step was mitigated when wealthy Mexicans rushed to invest their funds in the United States. Some relief came as the result of huge petroleum discoveries in southeastern Mexico. Under the prudent supervision of President José López Portillo, foreign earnings from petroleum mushroomed from $500 million in 1976 to $6 billion in 1980.

Although Mexico's estimated oil reserves are 200

billion barrels, that resource alone is insufficient to cope with the country's staggering economic problems. These problems are due in large measure to Mexico's exploding population, which doubled between 1960 and 1990 to more than 75 million, Mexico City's alone increasing fourfold in this period, to approximately 20 million. Unemployment—nearly 25 percent in the late 1970s—is a recurring problem, as is underemployment. Inadequate income keeps many people with jobs and small farms mired in poverty. To escape such hopelessness, hundreds of thousands of Mexicans illegally enter the United States each year. Oil has been a mixed blessing; because it is not a labor-intensive industry, it employs relatively few workers, and volatile oil prices on the world market contribute to Mexico's economic instability. Inflation skyrocketed to approximately 150 percent in 1987, but wage and price controls introduced the following year reduced it to less than 20 percent in 1989. At the end of the 1980s, Mexico's foreign debt, second in Latin America only to that of Brazil ($121 billion), stood at $106 billion; in 1989 $14 billion was required to service it, an amount equal to approximately 70 percent of the country's exports. Latin America's foreign debt exceeded $400 billion in 1989, forcing states to borrow even more to pay the staggering interest, impeding economic growth, lowering the quality of life, and threatening democratic governments by engendering social unrest. In political terms the economic crisis could end the long domination of Mexican politics by the moderate PRI, in which case Mexico could find itself bitterly split between extremists of the right and the left. Perhaps Mexico's best hope was its decision in 1992 to join Canada and the United States in a free-trade agreement.

SUPERPOWER RELATIONS

Dealings between the United States and the Soviet Union operated at essentially two levels: direct relations, ranging from the kind of confrontation that occurred in the 1962 Cuban missile crisis to summit meetings and disarmament negotiations, and indirect challenges, which typically involved the use of one or more surrogate states, as in the wars in Vietnam and Afghanistan. The unacceptable consequences of a nuclear confrontation forced both countries to view much of the world as a giant playing field on which to demonstrate their resolve by defending client states. Gorbachev's bold gamble on perestroika created new opportunities for disarmament and cooperation, and the demise of the Soviet Union in 1991 terminated the superpower rivalry.

From Détente to Disarmament

During the 1952 U.S. presidential campaign the Republicans promised a more aggressive foreign policy to deal with the Soviet Union; instead of merely containing communism, as Truman had attempted, they promised to roll it back. When, therefore, the People's Republic of China, angered by Nationalist China's bombing of its ports, shelled the tiny islands of Matsu and Quemoy, administration officials discussed the possibility of launching a "preventive" war against the People's Republic. After the prospect of nuclear war convinced Beijing to desist, Eisenhower's secretary of state, John Foster Dulles, summed up administration policy by explaining that diplomacy was the art of going to the verge of war without starting a conflict. This policy of "brinkmanship" culminated in the 1962 Cuban missile crisis, a lesson of the risks inherent in such diplomacy.

Both superpowers embraced the less confrontational policy of détente in 1969, but with different motives. Three considerations moved the Soviets to change course: the intensification of the Sino-Soviet split when fighting erupted along the Soviet-Manchuria border in March 1969; the achievement of approximate military parity with the United States, which made it feasible for the Soviet Union to slow future arms buildup; and domestic economic needs that could not be met without some reduction in military expenditures. Popular support for détente in the United States stemmed from a desire to reduce the heavy costs of military competition and, against a background of widespread disillusionment with U.S. intervention in Vietnam, a resolve to reach an accommodation with the Soviet Union as a means to cut back foreign commitments. More important, however, was the diplomatic philosophy of Henry Kissinger, Nixon's secretary of state. Kissinger framed a policy designed to explore areas of mutual concern, deal on the basis of reciprocity, and negotiate with an eye toward reducing tensions. This would be done not by dealing with issues in isolation but by linking them to improve relations on a broad front.

The policy of détente registered several notable gains, not the least of which was the absence of a major confrontation between the superpowers during the decade of its existence. The consequences of such a confrontation could have been catastrophic, given the state of nuclear weaponry in the arsenals of both powers. Technology had developed rapidly after the Soviets detonated their first atomic bomb in 1949. Fusion-based hydrogen bombs, with considerably greater destructive power, were detonated by the United States in 1952 and the Soviet Union the following year. In the ensuing years both countries developed intercontinental ballistic missles (ICBMs) capable of raining destruction on each other. During the 1960s both the Americans and the Soviets launched nuclear-powered submarines armed with nuclear missiles, thus greatly complicating problems of defense. Antiballistic missile systems (ABMs) were devised for protection, but their effectiveness was questionable, especially when confronted with multiple independently targeted missiles, each of which carried several warheads. The destructive impact of the weapons also increased: the Soviets exploded a 50-megaton (million-ton) bomb in 1961; by contrast, the bomb that destroyed Hiroshima had the explosive power of a mere 20,000 tons of TNT. Moreover, atmospheric testing of some of the weapons had spread lethal contamination, especially over parts of the Pacific region, making it essential to restrict nuclear weapons development.

Building on the 1963 Nuclear Test Ban Treaty, which prohibited atmospheric testing of nuclear weapons, Kissinger entered into Strategic Arms Limitation Talks (SALT) with the Soviets in 1969; the resulting SALT I treaty, signed three years later, limited the number of antiballistic missile launchers and installations but did nothing to restrict multiple warheads on missiles. Although the SALT I treaty did not slow the arms race, it provided a foundation for further negotiations. In the 1975 Helsinki Accords the signatory states agreed to observe both the human rights of their citizens and the inviolability of frontiers in Europe unless these were altered through peaceful negotiation. Détente also set the stage for talks on mutual and balanced force reductions in central Europe.

Although the Carter administration remained committed to détente and negotiated a second SALT treaty that limited the number of ICBMs and called for a general reduction in the number of missiles, two developments eroded the progress of arms negotiations. One was America's determination to link such things as improved trade relations to Soviet concessions on Jewish emigration and the observance of human rights; by publicizing demands for progress in these areas, Washington embarrassed Moscow and embittered relations. The second was the Soviet Union's reluctance to embrace Kissinger's principle of linkage, as evidenced by Soviet intervention in Angola, Mozambique, Ethiopia,

and especially Afghanistan. In response to the 1979 Soviet invasion of Afghanistan the United States imposed a grain embargo, and the Senate refused to ratify the SALT II treaty. The Soviets retaliated by deploying SS-20 missiles capable of striking targets in western Europe. The period of détente had thus ended by the time Reagan took office in 1981.

Reagan's dealings with the Soviet Union in his first term essentially revived the policy of containment. The greatest U.S. arms buildup in peacetime was coupled with an announcement of the Strategic Defense Initiative, commonly called the "Star Wars" program, according to which the United States planned to develop satellite weapons to destroy incoming Soviet ballistic missiles in the event of war. This policy marked a departure from previous strategic thinking based on the concept of deterrence, according to which the so-called "mutual assured destruction" that would result from a nuclear exchange rendered nuclear war unthinkable. As part of the military buildup, Reagan, citing alleged Soviet violations, exceeded the SALT II limits in 1986, which both sides had hitherto observed despite the Senate's refusal to ratify the treaty.

The possibility of a breakthrough in superpower relations came as the result of new initiatives for arms reductions proposed by Gorbachev. He set the tone in 1985 by announcing a freeze on Soviet deployment of medium-range missiles in eastern Europe. A series of summits ensued, beginning at Geneva in 1985. The Soviets and the Americans negotiated major reductions in conventional forces and nuclear weapons in Europe, and in 1991 the nations of eastern Europe formally dissolved the military functions of the Warsaw Pact. The Russians and the Americans subsequently agreed on additional major reductions in their nuclear arsenals.

Much of the Western world greeted Gorbachev's initiatives enthusiastically, according him a stature in the West never before achieved by a Soviet leader. Gorbachev also sought to reduce global tensions by visiting Beijing to meet with Chinese leader Deng Xiaoping (Teng Hsiao-ping) in 1989, thus ending three decades of frozen Sino-Soviet relations.

Peripheral Conflicts

Relations between the superpowers were regularly strained because each engaged in military conflicts in peripheral regions. Although the conflict in Vietnam began as part of France's attempt to relinquish its authority to a pro-Western Vietnamese government, America's decision in the 1960s to make a major commitment in South Vietnam rested on John Kennedy's belief that its fall would lead to the collapse of Southeast Asia—the so-called domino theory. Two military actions led to U.S. escalation: an alleged torpedo attack by North Vietnam on American ships in the Gulf of Tonkin in 1964, which resulted in a Congressional resolution giving the president unrestricted authority to respond militarily, and the Viet Cong shelling of a U.S. compound at Pleiku in 1965. The ensuing decision to seek out and destroy the enemy required the deployment of large numbers of troops, which finally peaked at approximately 550,000.

Pressed by antiwar agitation at home, Nixon and Kissinger proposed to reduce the number of American troops through a process that they called Vietnamization, according to which the South Vietnamese would be trained to win their own war. When the North Vietnamese, who enjoyed Soviet backing, stepped up military activity as the Americans gradually withdrew, Nixon ordered the bombing of North Vietnamese supply routes in Laos and Cambodia and then, in 1970, the invasion of Cambodia. To force the North Vietnamese to negotiate, Nixon ordered wide-scale bombing of that country. A peace treaty signed in 1973 allowed the United States to pull out in reasonable security and gave North and South Vietnam an opportunity to negotiate their political differences. Instead, both sides continued the fighting until the North overran Saigon in 1975. America's inability to shore up a corrupt puppet state underscored the limits to which even a superpower was subject.

A tragic consequence of the war was the destabilization of Cambodia, where Communist Khmer Rouge forces under Pol Pot seized power between 1975 and 1978 and carried on a genocidal "resettlement" policy that resulted in an estimated 1 million deaths. A Vietnamese invasion stopped the bloodletting, but with the withdrawal of occupation forces in 1989, civil war resumed.

Angola became enmeshed in superpower rivalry when its liberation forces, after winning independence from Portugal in 1975, continued their internecine fighting. The Marxist-Leninist Popular Movement for the Liberation of Angola (MPLA) received considerable assistance from the Soviet Union, Cuba, and much of eastern Europe; the rival National Front for the Liberation of Angola (FNLA) was backed by the People's Republic of China and Romania; and the National Union for the Total Independence of Angola (UNITA) had the support of the United States and South Africa. The seriousness of the civil war, which had claimed 200,000 lives by 1991, was reflected in the fact that Angola was the tenth-largest importer of arms in the world in the late

1980s. In 1988 the Cubans agreed to withdraw their 50,000 troops by 1991 in return for South Africa's grant of independence to neighboring Namibia. A peace treaty signed in 1991 paved the way for a multiparty democracy.

On the other side of the continent a military revolution that overthrew Emperor Haile Selassie in 1974 plunged Ethiopia into a civil war between moderates and radical socialists. The latter triumphed in 1976, only to face a new crisis when neighboring Somalia invaded the disputed province of Ogaden the following year. The Soviets responded to an Ethiopian request for military and financial aid that soon brought 17,000 Cuban soldiers and substantial Russian supplies and money to Ethiopia. With this assistance the Ethiopians repulsed the Somalis but found it impossible to crush a rebellion by Muslims and Coptic Christians, aided by Arab states, in the northern provinces of Eritrea and Tigre. In 1987 the Ethiopian leader, Mengistu Haile Mariam, proclaimed his country a Communist republic, but Gorbachev subsequently pressured him to reach a settlement with the rebels, in part by withdrawing most Soviet military advisors and reducing Soviet financial assistance. A coalition of resistance groups toppled the Mengistu government in 1991. Two years later Eritrea won its independence from Ethiopia.

Afghanistan was traditionally within the Russian sphere of interest. Both the United States and the Soviet Union had provided financial aid to the Afghans in the postwar period in an attempt to curry influence. The country became a constitutional monarchy in 1964, but in 1973 a revolution led by Muhammad Daoud toppled the king and led to authoritarian rule. As Daoud's regime grew closer to Iran and Pakistan, Soviet concern mounted and was probably responsible for a successful coup in 1978. The new government, comprised of Soviet clients, signed a friendship pact with the Soviet Union and received ever-greater quantities of Russian weapons. Throughout 1979, insurgents opposed to the pro-Soviet government stepped up their activities, finally provoking the Soviets to invade in December.

For more than nine years the Soviets occupied Afghanistan, seldom controlling more than its cities and never safe from the attacks of the *mujahedin,* fierce Islamic rebels who obtained military equipment from the United States and Pakistan. As in Vietnam, the military might of a superpower proved inadequate against guerrillas imbued with a spirit of independence. Much of Afghanistan was ravaged, and approximately 5 million of the country's 16 to 18 million people took refuge in Pakistan and Iran. The last Soviet troops withdrew in

1989, but the puppet government in Kabul held off the mujahedin until 1992.

Soviet assistance proved to be no more effective in Nicaragua, a country ruled from 1936 to 1979 by the corrupt Somoza family as clients of American interests. Realizing the impending collapse of Anastasio Somoza Debayle's regime, President Carter arranged for the dictator to go into exile in 1979, effectively leaving the country in the hands of the Sandinista National Liberation Front. Trained in the Soviet Union and Cuba, the Sandinista leaders established friendly relations with Communist states, welcomed Soviet and Cuban advisers, and accepted shipments of weapons from eastern Europe. Although the United States at first offered assistance to the Sandinista government, the Reagan administration viewed it as a younger version of the Castro regime and sought to overthrow it by political, economic, and other means, including a blockade and military support for counterrevolutionary rebels known as Contras.

The Sandinistas encouraged revolutionary movements in Guatemala and El Salvador, but the Guatemalan rebels were reduced to a token movement in the late 1980s. In El Salvador, by contrast, extremists on the right and the left engaged in a civil war that threatened to obliterate the prospects of a moderate democracy and civil rights. In 1989, El Salvadorans rejected the centrist Christian Democratic party and elected a reactionary as their new president. The prospects for Nicaragua's future brightened when the Sandinistas held free elections in 1990. Unexpectedly, the Sandinistas lost at the polls. Replacing Daniel Ortega as president was Violeta Barrios de Chamorro, who negotiated an end to the decade-long civil war. The possibility of bringing peace to the region was enhanced by Gorbachev's 1988 proposal calling for both superpowers to terminate military support for their respective Central American clients. In the aftermath of the superpower rivalry the best hope for long-suffering peoples in Central America, Angola, and Ethiopia lay in social, economic, and political reforms.

THE WEST AND THE
TURBULENT MIDDLE EAST

Perhaps no area of the world more dramatically demonstrated the limited range of superpower influence than the Middle East and Iran. The United States, while continuing to support Israel, broke new ground in 1988 by agreeing to talk with representatives of the Palestine Liberation Organization. Shortly thereafter, the Soviet Union attempted to improve relations with Iran. Neither superpower, however, was able to end the bitter warfare that destroyed much of Lebanon.

The Arab-Israeli Wars:
The Conflict Continues

Humiliated by the Six Day War, Egypt rearmed with Soviet assistance and planned a new attack with Syria. This time, preparations were secret. Israel was caught napping by the Yom Kippur War of 1973, so called because it began with a surprise attack on the annual Jewish Day of Atonement. Initially repulsed, Israeli forces quickly recovered and, with American tactical assistance, had regained the offensive when fighting was halted after 18 days on October 24. But they had suffered heavy losses on the ground and in the air and brought the superpowers closer to confrontation in the Middle East than ever before.

The Yom Kippur War underlined the dangers posed by continued instability in the Middle East. It brought in its wake a cutoff of oil exports that struck at the very heart of the Western economy. Accordingly, Henry Kissinger undertook arduous "shuttle diplomacy" between the major Arab capitals and Jerusalem in an attempt to find a basis of accommodation. These efforts bore fruit in the 1978 Camp David accords between Egypt and Israel. The two parties agreed to a phased withdrawal of Israeli troops from the Sinai and a vaguely defined autonomy for the West Bank and the Gaza strip. President Anwar Sadat had ended the humiliating occupation of Egyptian territory and gained a major American subsidy for his ailing economy. Prime Minister Menachem Begin had won diplomatic recognition from an Arab state for the first time, secured Israel's western frontier, and divided its two principal antagonists, Egypt and Syria. But Sadat was denounced in the Arab world for having made a separate peace with Israel and for failing to secure Palestinian rights. Egypt lost the position of leadership that it had enjoyed for the previous quarter century, and Sadat was assassinated by Muslim fundamentalists in 1981.

OPEC and the Politics of Oil

The history of the modern Middle East has been to a large extent determined by oil. Nature has endowed the region with 60 percent of the world's proven oil reserves. In 1960 the Saudis and the Venezuelans took the initiative in forming the Organization of Petroleum Exporting Countries (OPEC). Originally composed of Saudi Arabia, Iran, Iraq, Kuwait, and Venezuela, it subsequently expanded to include Algeria, Ecuador, Gabon, Indonesia, Libya, Nigeria, Qatar, and the confederation of small Persian Gulf sheikhdoms known as the United Arab Emirates. At first, OPEC confined its activities chiefly to gaining a larger share of the revenues produced by Western oil companies and greater control over levels of production. The persistence of the Arab-Israeli conflict, however, turned OPEC from a simple cartel into a formidable political force. After the Six Day War the Arab members of OPEC formed a separate, overlapping group (OAPEC) for the purpose of concerting policy and exerting pressure on the West over Israel. Egypt and Syria, negligible oil producers but populous and militarily powerful, joined the latter group to underline its intentions.

The Yom Kippur war of 1973 galvanized Arab opinion. Furious at the emergency resupply effort that had enabled Israel to withstand the Egyptian and Syrian assault, the Arabs imposed an oil embargo against the United States, western Europe, and Japan. This was followed by a more than fourfold increase in the price of oil, causing sudden inflation and economic recession in the noncommunist industrial world and even greater hardship among the underdeveloped nations. At the same time the Saudis acquired operating control of the oil company Aramco, fully nationalizing it in 1980. As other OPEC nations followed suit, the cartel's income soared. For the first time, Third World nations whose resources and labor had long been exploited by the industrial giants had acquired control of a vital commodity, reversing the flow of capital. Some of this income was dispensed in the form of aid to other underdeveloped nations whose economies had been caught between higher prices for oil and the lower prices for their own commodities and raw materials caused by shrinking Western demand. Much of it, however, was reinvested in the West or absorbed in arms purchases that heightened political tensions, particularly in the Middle East. When reduced demand and overproduction produced a glut on the world market in the mid-1980s, oil prices plummeted, and the cartel lost its unity. Producers such as Mexico, Nigeria, and Venezuela whose economies had expanded recklessly were plunged into near-bankruptcy, and even Saudi Arabia felt the pinch. The enormous reserves and relative underpopulation of the leading Middle East producers guaranteed the region its continuing strategic importance, but the politics of oil had proved dangerous for all concerned.

Modernization and Revolution in Iran

Iran, though ethnologically and linguistically distinct from its Arab neighbors in the Middle East, has shared their geographical destiny. Iran's modernization began with its penetration by two conflicting imperial powers, Russia and Great Britain. Concessions were given to build railroads and develop the country's resources. By 1907 the Russians and the British had formally divided Iran into spheres of influence, but a nationalist uprising in 1921 led by Reza Shah Pahlavi produced a modernizing dictatorship that, like Kemal Atatürk's in Turkey, attempted to introduce Western cultural and industrial models and to reduce the power of the clergy by stressing the country's pre-Islamic past. In 1935, Reza Shah changed the country's Hellenistic name, Persia, to Iran, meaning "land of the Aryans."

This name change was meant to reflect Iran's Indo-European roots but had contemporary significance as well. Reza Shah, dictatorial and often terroristic in his methods, was an admirer of Hitler, and when an Allied force occupied Iran in August 1941, he was forced to abdicate in favor of his son, Muhammad Reza Pahlavi. For the next decade the country was once again a battleground of foreign interests, with the United States replacing Britain soon after World War II and the Soviet Union trying to regain its traditional foothold in the north. A new nationalist insurrection brought Muhammad Mossadegh to power as prime minister in 1951. Mossadegh nationalized the British-owned Anglo-Iranian Oil Company, thereby reasserting the country's independence. The West retaliated with a boycott of Iranian oil, and a CIA-led army coup deposed him in 1953.

The shah, who had been briefly forced to flee the country by pro-Mossadegh crowds, returned with U.S. blessings and remained a Western client thereafter. Like his father, he harbored grandiose ambitions. A "White Revolution" was launched in the early 1960s to complete the process of modernization begun under Reza Shah, although the traditional landed elite remained firmly in control of the countryside. Using the massive oil profits of the 1970s, the shah attempted to turn Iran into the major military power of the Middle East. By the end of the decade his regime was under general assault. The land hunger of the peasantry remained unsatisfied despite promised reform, while the middle classes cultivated by the shah were frustrated by their exclusion from real power. Showy industrial projects and exotic weapons could not be operated without foreign advisors and technicians, reinforcing a sense of dependence on the West. Even the aristocracy, which had never accepted the Pahlavi dynasty, offered little support. The shah's most serious opposition came from the Shi'ite clergy, which opposed his promotion of Western values and mores. By raising a culturally sensitive issue that cut across class lines and evoked powerful religious and nationalist sentiment, the clergy brought to focus a general sense of grievance. Their exiled leader, the Ayatollah Ruhollah Khomeini (1900–1989), became the symbol of popular resistance.

The shah responded at first with repression and then, when strikes brought the economy to the verge of bankruptcy, with desperate concessions. In January 1979 he fled into exile, and on February 1, Khomeini returned to Tehran as head of a revolutionary council that proclaimed an Islamic republic. Real authority emanated from Khomeini, who eliminated political competitors and, armed with near-absolute powers, embarked on a program of fundamentalist religious reform.

Khomeini's appeal reached far beyond the Shi'ites of Iran. His call to all Muslims to overthrow corrupt and tyrannical rulers and to return to the purity of Islamic law and ritual was attractive to the migrant workers who maintained the economies of Saudi Arabia, Kuwait, and Bahrain. His seizure of American embassy officials and workers in 1979, which was motivated at least in part by continued U.S. concern for the exiled shah, was the most popular act in the Middle East since the nationalization of the Suez Canal. Depicting the United States as a "great Satan," Khomeini combined Islamic revivalism with appeals to regional nationalism. In 1980, Iraq's Saddam Hussein launched an invasion of Iran that divided the Arab world, with Syria, Libya, and South Yemen backing Khomeini, and Saudi Arabia and Jordan supporting Iraq. The war enabled Khomeini to keep revolutionary fervor high while consolidating a theocratic regime that outlasted him and burnished his image as the leader of Islam's *jihad* ("holy war") against the West. Hostilities were halted by a truce in 1988, and two years later, Iraq agreed to peace terms that were favorable to Iran.

THE MIDDLE EAST TODAY

The hope of Camp David, that the Israeli-Egyptian accords would pave the way to a general settlement in the Middle East, has not been realized. No other Arab nation has recognized Israel, and the Palestinian issue remains unresolved. During the 1970s the PLO was recognized as the legitimate government of the Palestinian people by many Arab, Soviet bloc, and Third World nations, and its leader, Yasir Arafat, addressed the UN as a head of state. His influence declined in the early 1980s as the PLO's more militant factions fell under Syrian influence. In 1987, however, a popular rising, the *intifada,* broke out on the West Bank against the Israeli occupation. Seizing this opportunity to reassert his leadership, Arafat began an intensive diplomatic campaign that climaxed in an address before the United Nations in 1988 and the initiation of direct bilateral talks with the United States. These were suspended in the face of renewed violence, however, and Arafat's standing in the West again fell with his support of Iraq's invasion of Kuwait in 1990.

Legacy of Violence: The Lebanese Civil War and the Gulf War

A tragic by-product of the Arab-Israeli conflict was the civil war in Lebanon. On the surface, Lebanon had been one of the most successful of the states to win independence following World War II. Its thriving commercial economy had given it one of the Middle East's highest standards of living, and the political coexistence of a varied community of Christian, Jewish, and Muslim groups had made it a model of religious pluralism. Lebanon's equilibrium was, however, precarious. Urban prosperity masked rural poverty, a rising Muslim birth rate threatened the traditional Christian hegemony, and the country's semiofficial neutrality in the Arab-Israeli conflict brought it under increasing pressure from Arab nationalists. The sudden influx of some 300,000 Palestinian refugees after the Six Day War, followed by others expelled from Jordan in 1971, exacerbated these tensions. The PLO made Lebanon its principal base of operations, drawing retaliatory fire from Israel. The Lebanese divided sharply over the Palestinian presence, Christian groups tending to regard them as unwelcome intruders and Muslims seeing them not only as victims seeking to regain their homeland but also as patriots fighting in the common Arab cause against Israel. By 1975 the country slid into full-scale civil war. When Syrian troops finally enforced a cease-fire 19 months later, 60,000 lives had been lost and nearly a third of the population had been displaced.

The presence of Syria diminished the bloodshed but

Iraqi troops surrender to Saudi and U.S. forces, February 25, 1991. [AP/ Wide World]

did nothing to restore stability. The PLO intensified its raids and terrorist attacks against Israel, while the Israelis sought to cultivate Christian allies in Lebanon. The Israelis invaded Lebanon, driving the PLO from Beirut and occupying the southern third of the country, but the Israelis, now a target for all forces, soon withdrew after heavy losses. U.S. intervention in 1983 ended disastrously with the death of 241 marines in a terrorist attack. By the late 1980s, Lebanon had vanished as a nation in all but name, a symbol of sectarian anarchy and failed multiethnic community.

Instability in the region increased when Iraq invaded oil-rich Kuwait in August 1990. The annexation of Kuwait gave Iraq, with its own substantial oil fields, control of 20 percent of the Persian Gulf reserves. Concerned that Saddam Hussein would order his army into neighboring Saudi Arabia, the United States, with support from its allies and many Arab states, responded with massive troop deployments along the Saudis' border with Kuwait and Iraq. Cooperation between the United States and the Soviet Union made possible the passage of resolutions in the UN Security Council condemning Iraqi aggression and approving naval and air embargoes of Iraq.

When Saddam Hussein refused to withdraw from Kuwait, a U.S.-led coalition attacked Iraq in January 1991. The myth of Arab unity exploded as numerous Arab states, including Egypt, Syria, and Saudi Arabia, joined in the assault. The Gulf War lasted only six weeks, the climactic land campaign taking a mere 100 hours. Much of Iraq's military, the fourth largest in the world, was destroyed. Most of Iraq's economic infrastructure was in ruins, and the damage to the Kuwaiti oil fields, much of it deliberately inflicted by Iraqi troops, had created the worst human-made ecological disaster in history. Some 500 of Kuwait's oil wells were aflame, huge oil slicks polluted the Persian Gulf, and many Iraqi and Kuwaiti refineries were extensively damaged.

The Gulf crisis was noteworthy in several respects. It marked the first time in the post–Cold War era that the United States and the Soviet Union (which did not participate in the fighting) cooperated diplomatically to condemn aggression. No less important was the fact that Israel, though bombarded by Iraqi missiles, refrained from retaliating in order not to provoke Arab states into leaving the coalition. But Saddam Hussein had focused renewed attention on the Palestinian problem by promising to withdraw his forces from Kuwait if Israel would relinquish the occupied Arab territories in the West Bank, the Golan Heights, and the Gaza strip. Hussein's proposal further split the Arab world, pitting the moderate Arab states against the PLO and Jordan, with its large Palestinian population.

The Threshold of a New Era

In 1945 the world consisted of a few large empires and fifty-odd nation-states. By the early 1990s, decolonization had produced more than 100 new states, mostly in Africa and Asia, and with the breakup of the Soviet Union the last territorial empire disappeared. The nation-state, so often consigned to the dustbin of history by Marxist and non-Marxist utopians alike, had thus not only shown remarkable vitality but had emerged as the paradigm form of world political organization.

At the same time the nation-state was subject to severe pressures and strains that seemed likely to modify if not to transform its nature in the years ahead. Internally, explosive ethnic conflicts contributed to the demise of the Soviet Union and Yugoslavia. Externally, the convergence of regional and global markets produced a movement toward federal associations such as the European Community, whose member states agreed in principle to merge in a larger union such traditional sovereign functions as currency and customs regulation, border control, and national defense.

The revolutionary events that began in 1989 with the collapse of Soviet power in eastern Europe and went on to bring down the Soviet Union ended the Cold War and the age of the superpowers. The remaining Communist states are isolated and vulnerable. Liberal capitalist regimes have replaced one-party political systems and guided economies around the globe, though many countries remain dominated by military and landowning elites. In the final decade of the twentieth century the grand wars of ideology that characterized much of its history have been superseded by localized ethnic and sectarian conflicts and by polarization between the developed and underdeveloped regions of the world over such questions as economic independence, resource and population control, and environmental management.

SUMMARY

Beginning in the mid-1960s, the world began to emerge from the long shadows of World War II and the legacy of imperial domination. The rivalries of the Cold War lingered on for a few more years and were temporarily revived by Ronald Reagan in the early 1980s. But by the end of that decade both superpowers, increasingly cognizant of the financial burdens imposed by their competing militarism and sensitive to the lessons of Vietnam and Afghanistan, began pursuing more constructive, less confrontational courses. The 1970s brought democracy to Spain, Portugal, and Greece, and in 1989 the citizens of Poland and the Soviet Union participated in genuine elections; most of their eastern neighbors followed in 1990. As the influence of the Soviet Union waned sharply in eastern Europe, reform movements swept through every country. Next to the collapse of the Soviet Union and its empire in 1991, the most significant event of this period was the reunification of Germany the previous year.

Elsewhere, Canadians continued their efforts to resolve the Quebec crisis in the hope of preserving their nation and confidently entered into a free-trade agreement with the United States. Simultaneously the 12 members of the European Community hoped to forge a degree of western European unity never before achieved by peaceful means. Throughout the Western world, women won major victories and moved closer to genuine social and political equality.

For all these achievements, this period failed to achieve peace in the Middle East, to deal with the mountainous debts that threatened to destroy democratic governments in countries such as Mexico, or to slow population growth and curb environmental pollution. Nevertheless the West, having recovered from the great world wars, demonstrated a new vitality and commitment to its ancient heritage.

Suggestions for Further Reading

Bark, D. L., and Gress, D. R. *A History of West Germany.* Vol. 2: *Democracy and Its Discontents, 1963–1988.* Oxford: Blackwell, 1989.

Brown, J. F. *Surge to Freedom: The End of Communist Rule in Eastern Europe.* Durham, N.C.: Duke University Press, 1991.

Browning, G. K. *Women and Politics in the USSR: Consciousness Raising and Soviet Women's Groups.* New York: St. Martin's, 1987.

Hahn, W. G. *Democracy in a Communist Party: Poland's Experience Since 1980.* New York: Columbia University Press, 1987.

Harrison, J. P. *The Endless War: Vietnam's Struggle for Independence.* New York: Columbia University Press, 1989.

Hiro, D. *Holy Wars: The Rise of Islamic Fundamentalism.* London: Routledge, 1989.

Kamrava, M. *Revolution in Iran: The Roots of Turmoil.* London: Routledge, 1990.

Kavanagh, D. A. *Thatcherism and British Politics: The End of Consensus?* 2nd ed. New York: Oxford University Press, 1990.

Lewin, M. *The Gorbachev Phenomenon: A Historical Interpretation.* Berkeley: University of California Press, 1988.

Lovenduski, J. *Women and European Politics.* Amherst: University of Massachusetts Press, 1986.

Mowat, R. C. *Creating the European Community.* New York: Barnes & Noble, 1973.

Pastor, R. A. *Condemned to Repetition: The United States and Nicaragua.* Princeton, N.J.: Princeton University Press, 1988.

Raat, W. D., and Beezley, W. H., eds. *Twentieth-Century Mexico.* Lincoln: University of Nebraska Press, 1986.

Ross, G., Hoffmann, S., and Malzacher, S., eds. *The Mitterand Experiment: Continuity and Change.* New York: Oxford University Press, 1987.

Waterbury, J. *The Egypt of Nasser and Sadat.* Princeton, N.J.: Princeton University Press, 1983.

The West and the World

Toward the Twenty-First Century

Western civilization has traditionally been expansionistic. Such were the early civilizations of western Asia, Egypt, Greece, and Rome. Later, expansion into western Asia occurred with the establishment of the medieval crusader states in Syria and Palestine. From the fifteenth century, when Portugal established bases in Africa and the great voyages of discovery got underway, to the early twentieth century, when Western powers competed vigorously for the last unclaimed lands of Africa, Asia, and the Pacific, the West has attempted to impose its domination on the rest of the world. Its peoples became the targets of Western imperialists determined to control their trade, dominate their supplies of raw materials, use their lands as strategic bases to maintain far-flung empires, and convert native populations to their political, social, and religious values. From at least the fifteenth century, Westerners have generally assumed the superiority of their culture to those of non-Western peoples.

The heavy losses sustained by the Western powers in World War II, coupled with the emergence of strong nationalist movements in Africa, Asia, and the Middle East, gradually brought an end to the direct political control of most non-Western peoples by Westerners. By 1990 the principal exceptions involved the continued subjugation of nonwhites in South Africa and various Asian peoples by the Russians. In the context of the Cold War, however, the superpowers used small states, both Western and non-Western, as battlegrounds for limited military conflict (such as the Korean and Vietnam wars) or as client states (Cuba, Afghanistan, the Philippines). The ability of the Russians to maintain their hold over the numerous ethnic minorities in the Soviet Union was imperiled and finally destroyed by the severe weakening of its economy in the late 1980s and early 1990s, and the capacity of the United States to sustain its role as a superpower has been sharply eroded by the massive debt that has made it the largest debtor nation. By the end of the twentieth century, countries such as Japan, Mexico, Canada, and Germany that had once rather tamely followed the American lead in international affairs had become increasingly determined to forge their own policies. Historians of the twenty-first century will probably see the period from 1947 to 1990 primarily in terms of a retreat from empire and the concomitant attempt by the two superpowers to maintain a semblance of imperial authority without the formal vestiges of such a dominion.

Whereas political imperialism has waned, its economic counterpart has not, although its forms have undergone major changes in the late twentieth century. Colonies no longer exist as convenient and controllable sources of raw material and markets for manufactured items, but major Western corporations have established factories in developing countries to take advantage of inexpensive labor and government support. Such multinational enterprises have provided the developing countries with new technology as well as expanded employment opportunities, though the workers have often been forced to perform their duties at salary levels reminiscent of early industrialization in advanced Western states. In the production of automobiles and many electronic products, East Asians established superior technology in the postwar period and then, beginning especially in the late 1980s, began to construct plants in North America that used this technology, thereby sharing some of the employment benefits with Americans and Canadians while simultaneously reducing shipping costs. Developing countries such as Nigeria and Venezuela that are rich in oil or other natural resources that are critical to industrialized nations have the financial means to benefit from expanded productivity, but states such as Bangladesh, India, and Ethiopia, which have undernourished populations and few natural resources, have experienced widespread poverty. In 1989 the industrialized states, with 23 percent of the world's population, controlled 80 percent of its goods and were responsible for most of its pollution. The world's population will double in the twenty-first century, but 90 percent of the growth will occur in the developing countries, especially in Africa, further increasing the gap between the "have" and "have not" nations. More than a third of the people of India are already too impoverished to purchase sufficient food to sustain themselves. Despite references to a "global village" and a "global factory," in reality the superior technology and education of eastern Asia, western Europe, the United States, and Canada have not been universally disseminated, nor has most of the business community in these advanced regions relinquished the notion that the rest of the world is a vast area to be economically exploited.

Economic interdependence was graphically manifested in the early 1980s when Western governments and major financial institutions increased interest rates to combat rising inflation. An international recession followed, making it virtually impossible for debtor countries such as Mexico and Brazil to repay their loans. Major Western banks consequently had to renegotiate the loans or in some cases write them off, in effect transferring the losses to

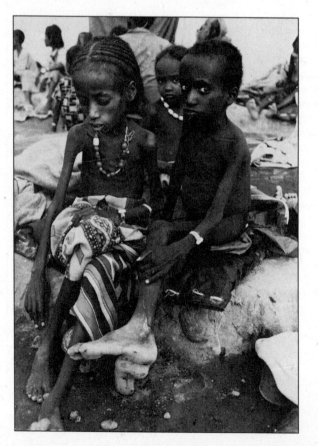

Starving children in Ethiopia, 1985. [Patrick Frilet/Sipa]

their shareholders. The problem was compounded by the misuse of loans by political leaders in the borrowing countries, through either graft or poorly designed investment programs. In such circumstances, economic investment by the leading industrial nations actually impaired standards of living in developing countries. In 1989 the developing nations of the Third World owed $1.2 trillion to the industrialized states; the previous year the former made net payments of $43 billion to the latter.

The failure of the United States to curtail its deficit spending further threatened international economic growth, both by channeling huge sums of money into servicing the debt rather than investment in new technology, factories, and education and by reducing the amount of funds available to assist developing countries. The conservative movements in the United States and Great Britain in the 1980s argued in any case for increased reliance on private enterprise rather than government aid as a means to assist developing nations. In 1988 the Japanese spent $10 billion on foreign aid—outspending the United States, despite the latter's far larger economy. Despite such assistance, 40,000 babies died of starvation each day in Third World countries.

Traditional imperialism may have disappeared, but the advanced societies in the West and East Asia have not relinquished their attempts to influence the ideology and customs as well as the economics and politics of other peoples. Much of this is now being done through the technology of mass communication—radio, film, and television. These media regularly help to shape the perception of Westerners in non-Western lands and vice versa, often by perpetuating stereotypes or by tailoring coverage to create specific impressions. Because of the pervasive coverage of the modern media, their manipulation by political leaders can inflame passions, create animosities, or incite popular action. Instantaneous communications can seriously complicate international relations. In the nineteenth century, reports of hostile action on another continent could take a week or more to reach a concerned government, a delay that provided time for a considered response. With the advent of the telegraph in 1844 and communication satellites in the present day, the pressure for rapid decisions at the expense of deliberate analysis is increased, thereby intensifying the risks of war. Communications

technology in the late twentieth century nevertheless enables citizens with access to television, radios, and newspapers the opportunity to observe and respond to developments in lands far beyond their own.

Despite the advent of the communications revolution, most Westerners maintain the long-held belief in the supremacy of their society and values. That judgment has been increasingly rejected by non-Westerners. Mohandas Gandhi, one of the principal architects of India's independence, was educated in Britain but came to espouse native traditions and values, especially the ancient Hindu idea of *ahimsa,* or reverence for life. Adopting the ways of a traditional saddhu, or holy man, he urged his followers to pursue the simple life, wearing cotton and spinning and weaving for themselves wherever possible. The spinning wheel became the most famous symbol of the nationalist movement in India. Western ways and values were stridently denounced by the Ayatollah Ruhollah Khomeini, leader of the Iranian revolution and spokesman for a militant, fundamentalist Islam. Members of Israel's most conservative sects have also been harshly critical of modern Western materialism. The nineteenth-century assumption that all peoples would readily embrace Western values and institutions upon exposure to them has been proven wrong. In most respects we live in a world of many communities, not a global village, although the escalating problem of environmental pollution, the threat of nuclear contamination (whether by war or by accident), and the vulnerability of global economies to major fluctuations in oil supplies or economic recessions underscores a sense of global unity.

If the twentieth century has witnessed a dramatic decline of empires, it has also experienced a significant change with respect to its understanding of the realms beyond our own planet. At the beginning of the twentieth century the size of the universe was estimated to be no more than 10,000 light-years, and the existence of other galaxies was still an unproven hypothesis. This picture was rapidly transformed by the development of powerful new telescopes, the analysis of light spectra, and the discovery of stars whose variable luminosity enabled astronomers to use them as cosmic yardsticks, like beacons at sea. By 1930, Edwin Hubble had demonstrated not only that other galaxies existed but also that they were

Mohandas Gandhi shown here in front of 10 Downing Street, London, embraced Western political thought but appealed to traditional Indian values as he led his people to independence. [AP/Wide World]

A powerful symbol of twentieth-century technology, the U.S. space shuttle *Discovery* roars off the lauchpad in September of 1988. [NASA]

receding at a velocity proportional to their distance from our own. Hubble's law, as this discovery was called, suggested both that cosmic magnitudes were far greater than had been hitherto supposed and that those magnitudes were indefinitely expanding. Estimates of the present size of the universe have been extended continuously since then. Hubble calculated the edge of the universe to be 500 million light-years away, but by midcentury that estimate had doubled, and with the introduction of radio telescopes after World War II and the consequent discovery of quasars (quasi-stellar discrete radio sources), it was soon revised tenfold upward again. In the farthest reaches of space, stars may be beaming their light toward us while simultaneously receding from us at a speed nearly equal to that of light itself, and it appears certain that light has reached the earth that was propagated before our planet existed.

Exploring these new worlds has required not only extraordinary technological advances but also huge outlays of money. The primary impetus at the outset of the space race was superpower rivalry in the Cold War. The Soviet Union, using rocket technology developed for its nuclear weaponry, put the satellite *Sputnik* into orbit in 1957, and four years later the cosmonaut Yuri Gagarin orbited the earth. The United States achieved a brilliant triumph of its own when it landed three of its astronauts on the moon in 1969 and followed this with four more moon landings in the ensuing three years. While the Soviet Union constructed a space station and kept its cosmonauts in space for long periods of time, the United States developed a reusable space shuttle and devoted billions of dollars to developing the Strategic Defense Initiative, a hypothetical shield to destroy incoming nuclear missiles. Numerous practical discoveries and applications have been made in the course of the space program, not least the deployment of state-of-the-art communications satellites that enable both words and pictures to be transmitted around the globe almost instantaneously. The very process of exploring the realms beyond our own planet has enabled us to better understand the inhabitants of our own world. Late-twentieth-century space exploration, dominated by the United States and the Soviet Union, may best be seen perhaps as the final extension of the West's drive towards worlds beyond its own.

INDEX